CONTAINS 2500 MCQS

50 PRACTICE SETS

REASONING

(Verbal, Non-Verbal & Analytical Reasoning)

HIGHLY USEFUL FOR

SSC (CGL, CPO, 10+2 & Multitasking), IBPS (PO & Clerk), LIC (ADO & AAO), Railway and Other Competitive Exams

ARIHANT PUBLICATIONS (INDIA) LTD

ARIHANT PUBLICATIONS (INDIA) LTD

卐 Administrative & Production Offices

Regd. Office 'Ramchhaya' 4577/15, Agarwal Road, Darya Ganj, New Delhi -110002
Tele: 011- 47630600, 43518550; Fax: 011- 23280316

Head Office Kalindi, TP Nagar, Meerut (UP) - 250002
Tel: 0121-2401479, 2512970, 4004199; Fax: 0121-2401648

卐 Sales & Support Offices

Agra, Ahmedabad, Bengaluru, Bhubaneswar, Bareilly, Chennai, Delhi, Guwahati, Haldwani, Hyderabad, Jaipur, Jhansi, Kolkata, Kota, Lucknow, Meerut, Nagpur & Pune

卐 ISBN 978-93-5094-473-8

卐 Price ₹ 245.00

PO No. : TXT-59-T070384-4-26

Typeset by Arihant DTP Unit at Meerut
Printed & Bound by Arihant Publications (I) Ltd. (Press Unit)

For further information about the products from Arihant,
log on to www.arihantbooks.com or email to info@arihantbooks.com

PREFACE

Reasoning is the most important part of any competitive examination. It basically tests candidates's thinking power and mind applicability skills. The questions that are asked in different examination are not easy to solve without having a good practice. This section covers questions from various topics of Verbal Reasoning, Non-Verbal Reasoning and Analytical Reasoning.

This book 50 Practice Sets on Reasoning is highly useful for all Competitive Examinations viz. SSC (CGL, CPO, 10+2 and Multitasking), Bank (PO and Clerk), LIC (AAO and ADO), Railway and other Competitive Examinations.

This book 50 Practice Sets is a collection 2500 Multiple Choice Questions covering all the concepts and all types of questions according to latest pattern of Examination.

Detailed explanations with answers has been given at the end of each practic set.

As we know *'Practice is the only key to Success'*, after practicing this book you will get higher score and 100% success in the Examination.

Authors

CONTENTS

REASONING : AT A GLANCE

VERBAL REASONING

Verbal reasoning is understanding and reasoning using concepts framed in words.

It aims at evaluating the ability to think correctly and constructively, rather than at simple fluency or vocabulary power. It is also a test of intelligence, provides an assessment of individual's ability to think logically and solve problems in shortest of time. Verbal Reasoning Test use words, letters and numbers and require logical reasoning and a reasonable knowledge of English language words.

Verbal reasoning involves following topics

1. Analogy, 2. Classification, 3. Series, 4. Coding-Decoding,
5. Direction and Distance, 6. Sitting arrangement, 7. Ranking etc.

Analogy

Analogy means 'similar' or 'correspondance'. It can be described as the logical similarity between two or more groups of numbers/letters/ words/ alpha-numerics.

Analogy can be divided into following types :

1. Word Analogy

In this type, candidate has to find the relationship between given words in a pair.

Example 1. 'Smell' is related to 'Flower', in the same way 'Taste' is related to

(a) Tongue (b) Food (c) Water (d) Sweet

Sol. (b) As, 'Smell' comes from 'Flower', in the same way, 'Taste' comes from 'Food'.

2. Letter Analogy

In this type, the candidate has to find out the relationship between the given letters or group of letters in a pair.

Example 2. AFHO : GBDJ : : CHFM : ?

(a) GBIM (b) IDBH (c) GBLD (d) GPLD

Sol. (b)

As,

	1	6	8	15
	A	F	H	O
	+2 ↓	+2 ↓	−2 ↓	−2 ↓
	C	H	F	M
	3	8	6	13

Similarly,

	7	2	4	10
	G	B	D	J
	+2 ↓	+2 ↓	−2 ↓	−2 ↓
	I	D	B	H
	9	4	2	8

3. Number Analogy

In this type, numbers are given in a pair or group and the candidate has to find the relationship between the numbers or group of numbers.

Example 3. 10 : 100 : : ? : 121

(a) 10 (b) 11
(c) 12 (d) 13

Sol. (b) Square of first term is the second term.

As, $10^2 = 100$

so $11^2 = 121$

4. Alpha-Numeric Analogy

In this type, there is a certain relationship between the given group of letters and a number on one side and candidate is asked to find out the correct alternative based on the relationship.

Example 4. NICE : 14935 : : PRICE : ?

(a) 1618935 (b) 1817359
(c) 1618953 (d) 1719539

Sol. (a) As,

	N	I	C	E	
	↓	↓	↓	↓	
	14	9	3	5	Positional values

Similarly,

P	R	I	C	E	
↓	↓	↓	↓	↓	
16	18	9	3	5	Positional values

Classification

Classification means finding an odd term from a given set of terms.

In this chapter, the candidates are required to find out the term which is different from others. It is also known as 'Odd One Out'.

Classification can be divided into following types:

1. Word Classification

In this type, a set of words having a common property is given and the word having different property from the rest is to be identified.

Example 1. Choose the word which is different from others.

(a) Brick (b) Heart (c) Diamond (d) Spade

Sol. (a) Except brick, all others are suits of cards.

2. Letter Classification

In this type, a set of letters (letters' group) having some common property is given and the letter (letters' group) which is different from the rest is to be identified.

Example 2. Choose the group of letters which is different from others.

(a) AC (b) FH
(c) IJ (d) PR

Sol. (c) As,

A C, F H, I J and P R
(A →+2→ C), (F →+2→ H), (I →+1→ J), (P →+2→ R)

So, IJ is odd one out.

3. Number Classification

In this type, a set of numbers having some common property is given. The numbers can be such that all except one are of the same kind, such as odd numbers, prime numbers, squares/cubes, etc. The number which is different from the rest of numbers is to be identified.

Example 3. Choose the number which is different from others.

(a) 124 (b) 235
(c) 789 (d) 510

Sol. (d) All the above numbers have digits in ascending order but in option (d), it is in descending order. So, 510 is odd one.

Series

Series means finding the next term in a given arrangement of letters, numbers or combination of both. The candidate is required to study the given series, identify the pattern followed in the series and then complete the given series with the most suitable alternative or find the wrong term in the series. *Series can be divided into following types*

1. Number Series

In this type, various numbers are arranged in an order by following certain mathematical rules based on +, −, ×, ÷ or a combination of these, square root/cube root, odd/even numbers etc

The questions are asked in two formats :

(a) Find the Missing Term

Example 1. Find the next term for the given series.

23, 24, 26, 29, 33, ?

(a) 34 (b) 37 (c) 38 (d) 39

Sol. (c) The pattern of the series is as follows

23 →+1→ 24 →+2→ 26 →+3→ 29 →+4→ 33 →+5→ (38)

So, the next term is 38.

(b) Find the Wrong Term

Example 2. Find the wrong term in the given series.

7, 9, 16, 25, 41, 68, 107

(a) 107 (b) 16 (c) 41 (d) 68

Sol. (d) As, $7 + 9 = 16$, $9 + 16 = 25$, $16 + 25 = 41$

$25 + 41 = 66 \neq 68$ and $41 + 66 = 107$

So, in the series 68 is wrong as $25 + 41 = 66 \neq 68$.

2. Letter Series

In this type, the letters of the English alphabet are arranged in a certain order by following some rule like their positions in the alphabet, reverse order of letters, skipping of letters etc.

Example 3. Find the next term for the given series.

Y, V, S, P, M, ?

(a) I (b) K
(c) J (d) H

Sol. (c) The pattern of the series is as follows

$$Y \xrightarrow{-3} V \xrightarrow{-3} S \xrightarrow{-3} P \xrightarrow{-3} M \xrightarrow{-3} \text{(J)}$$

So, the next term will be J.

3. Alpha-Numeric Series

In this type, the pattern of series is based on the combination of both numbers and letters.

Example 4. What comes in place of question mark (?) in the series given below?

P3C, R5F, T8I, V12L, ?

(a) Y17O (b) X16M (c) X17O (d) X16O

Sol. (c) The pattern of the series is as follows

$$P \xrightarrow{+2} R \xrightarrow{+2} T \xrightarrow{+2} V \xrightarrow{+2} X$$

$$3 \xrightarrow{+2} 5 \xrightarrow{+3} 8 \xrightarrow{+4} 12 \xrightarrow{+5} 17$$

$$C \xrightarrow{+3} F \xrightarrow{+3} I \xrightarrow{+3} L \xrightarrow{+3} O$$

So, the next term be X17O.

4. Continuous Pattern Series

This type of series consists of a series of capital/small letters that follow a certain pattern like repetition of letters.

Example 5. Which one set of letters when sequentially placed at the gaps in the given letter series shall complete it?

g _ _ g _ _ gh _ g _ i

(a) h i h i i h (b) h h i i h h (c) j k l j k l (d) h i j k l i

Sol. (a) ghi/ghi/ghi/ghi ⇒ h i h i i h

Alphabet and Number Sequence Test

Alphabet and Number Sequence Test are based on arrangement of English letters and numbers in a certain defined pattern. There are two types of questions covered in this chapter as follow:

1. Alphabet Test

In this type, we deal with the questions which are based on finding the place of an English letter to the left or right of another English letter in the alphabetical order, finding the number of English letter(s) between two different English letters, letters in forward/reverse order, etc.

Example 1. In the English alphabet, find the position of S from right.

(a) 8 (b) 5 (c) 4 (d) 9

Sol. (a) Position of S from left = 19

∴ Position of S from right = 27 − 19 = 8

Example 2. How many such letters are there in the word 'CATEGORY' each of which is as far away from the beginning of the word as when they are arranged in alphabetical order?

(a) None (b) One (c) Two (d) Three

Sol. (b) The given word, C A T E G O R [Y]

Alphabetically, A C E G O R T [Y]

We find that, only Y maintains its position when the word is arranged in alphabetical order.

Example 3. If each alphabet in the word 'FRACTION' is arranged in alphabetical order and then each vowel is changed to the next letter in the English alphabetical series and each consonant is changed to previous letter in English alphabetical series, which of the following will be 4th from the right side of the new arrangement thus formed?

(a) M (b) T (c) P (d) E
(e) Q

Sol. (a) Original word, F R A C T I O N

I. Change, A C F I N O R T

II. Change, B B E J (M) P Q S

Clearly, M will be fourth from the right.

2. Letter/Number Sequence Test

In this type, a sequence of letters/numbers in which a series of letters/numbers with or without repetitions is given. The candidates are required to find the total number of a particular letter/number in the series applying certain condition or rules.

Sometimes, the given sequence also includes symbols along with letters/numbers.

Example 4. How many 7's are there in the given series which are immediately preceded by 6 but not immediately followed by 8? 3 4 8 7 6 1 5 6 7 8 4 9 6 7 5

(a) 1 (b) 2 (c) 3 (d) 4

Sol. (a)

3 4 8 ⑦ 6 1 5 6 ⑦ 8 4 9 6 ⑦ 5

✔ = Condition fulfilled
✗ = Condition not fulfilled

∴ Required 7 = 1 time

Directions (Ex. Nos. 6-7) *Study the following arrangement carefully and answer the questions given below.*

F 4 © T 2 E % M P 5 W 9 @ L Q R 6 U H 3 Z 7 * A T B 8 V # G $ Y D

Example 5. What should come in place of question mark (?) in the following series based on the above arrangement?

TEM 59L RU3 ?

(a) 7AB (b) 7AT
(c) *78 (d) ABV
(e) None of these

Sol. (a) F 4 © T 2 E % M P 5 W 9 @ L Q R 6 U H 3 2
7 * A T B 8 V # G $ Y D

So, following the sequence will be 7 AB.

Example 6. In the following letter series, how many times do PQR occur in such a way that Q is the middle of P and R? QMPNPQRROPQNOPPQRPMQROP QRPPRRPQRP

(a) 5 (b) 6
(c) 4 (d) 3

Sol. (c) Q M P N P Q R R O P Q N O P P Q R P M Q R O P Q R P P R R P Q R P

So, in the above arrangement, PQR occur 4 times in such a way that Q is the middle of P and R.

Sequencing and Formation of Words

In sequencing of words, we arrange the words in a chronological order according to the occurrence of words in dictionary or in our surroundings. It is a step-by-step completion of a process that exists in the word. Whereas, formation of words means creating meaningful words from the alphabets of given word.

Example 1. Arrange the following words in a logical and meaningful order.
1. Study 2. Earn 3. Job 4. Examination
5. Apply

(a) 2, 3, 4, 5, 1 (b) 1, 4, 5, 2, 3
(c) 2, 3, 5, 1, 4 (d) 1, 4, 5, 3, 2

Sol. (d) Here, the process of an adult person is given from his study to the mode of his earning. So, it can be arranged as

Study → Examination → Apply → Job → Earn

i.e. 1, 4, 5, 3, 2

Example 2. Arrange the following words as given in dictionary.

1. Horoscope 2. Hockey
3. Heroine 4. Health

(a) 1, 2, 3, 4 (b) 4, 3, 2, 1
(c) 4, 3, 2, 1 (d) 2, 1, 3, 4

Sol. (c) Here, the words are arranged according to dictionary as

Health → Heroine → Hockey → Horoscope
i.e. 4, 3, 2, 1

Example 3. From the given alternatives select the word which cannot be formed using the letters of the given word.

INFLATIONARY

(a) FLAIR (b) FAULTY (c) NATIONAL (d) RATION

Sol. (b) Due to absence of letter U word FAULTY cannot be formed from the word INFLATIONARY.

Example 4. If it is possible to make a meaningful word from the second, sixth, seventh, eighth and tenth letters of the word 'PERFORMANCE' using each letter only once. Middle letter of the word is

(a) C (b) M (c) E (d) R

Sol. (c) In the given word

P	E	R	F	O	R	M	A	N	C	E
↓	↓	↓	↓	↓	↓	↓	↓	↓	↓	↓
1	2	3	4	5	6	7	8	9	10	11
	E				R	M	A		C	
	2nd				6th	7th	8th		10th	

The word formed is CREAM.

C R E A M
Middle letter

So, middle letter of the word CREAM is 'E'.

Coding-Decoding

Coding means to hide the meaning of any message and decoding means to understand the actual meaning of that message.

In this type of questions, a word is coded in a particular way and the candidates are asked to code other word in same way.

Different types of questions asked from this topic such as:

1. Coding based on rearrangement/ replacement of letters
2. Opposite letter coding
3. Number coding/Symbol coding
4. Coding by substitution/word replacement
5. Fictitious language coding
6. Conditional coding
7. Matrix coding

Example 1. In a certain code, ABROAD is written as RBADAO, then how will SACHET be written in that code?

(a) HETSAC (b) TEHCAS (c) STAECH (d) CASTEH

Sol. (d) Here, the coded word has been obtained by interchanging the positions of first and third letters and fourth and sixth letters with each other.

As, A B R O A D
R B A D A O

Similarly, S A C H E T
C A S T E H

So, the code for SACHET will be CASTEH.

Example 2. In a certain coded language, GONE is coded as '5 % 2 #' and MEDAL is written as '4 # 3 $ @'. How is ENAMEL written in that code?

(a) # 2 $ 4 % @ (b) # 2 $ 3 # @
(c) # 2 $ 4 # @ (d) $ 2 # 4 $ @

Sol. (c) Given codes

GONE ↓↓↓↓ 5 % 2 # and MEDAL ↓↓↓↓↓ 4 # 3 $ @

Similarly, from the corresponding symbols of above alphabets, we get

ENAMEL
↓↓↓↓↓↓
2 $ 4 # @

Example 3. If 'water' is known as 'food', 'food' as 'tree', 'tree' as 'sky', 'sky' as 'well' and 'well' as 'pond', then which of the following would yield (produce) fruits?

(a) Sky (b) Food
(c) Well (d) Tree

Sol. (a) As we all know that, tree yields fruits and according to code tree is called sky. So, sky yields fruits.

Example 4. In a certain code language, 'ha sa ka' means 'you are reading', 'na sa pa' means 'they are walking' and 'ka ma pa' means 'reading and walking'. Which word in that language means reading?

(a) ka (b) ha (c) ma (d) na

Sol. (a) Here, the codes can be written as

ha sa ka → you are reading ...(i)
na sa pa → they are walking ...(ii)
ka ma pa → reading and walking ...(iii)

On comparing the Eqs. (i) and (iii), we get

ka ⇒ reading

So, the code for reading is ka.

Example 5. A word is represented by only one set of numbers as given in anyone of the alternatives. The set of numbers given in the alternatives are represented by two classes of alphabets as in the two matrices given below. The columns and rows of Matrix I are from 0 to 4 and that of Matrix II from 5 to 9. A letter can be represented first by its row and next by its column number. e.g. 'C' can be represented by 02, 21 etc. 'T' can be represented by 65, 96 etc. Similarly, you have to identify the correct set for the word given in each question.

Matrix I

	0	1	2	3	4
0	D	V	C	P	M
1	P	M	D	V	C
2	V	C	P	M	D
3	M	D	V	C	P
4	C	P	M	D	V

Matrix II

	5	6	7	8	9
5	S	A	U	T	J
6	T	J	S	A	U
7	A	U	T	J	S
8	J	S	A	U	T
9	U	T	J	S	A

PAST

(a) 10, 56, 41, 58 (b) 22, 68, 55, 66

(c) 34, 75, 67, 58 (d) 41, 99, 98, 88

Sol. (c) According to the matrices,

P - 03, 10, 22, (34), 41

A - 56, 68, (75), 87, 99

S - 55, (67), 79, 86, 98

T - (58), 65, 77, 89, 96

∴ PAST ⇒ 34, 75, 67, 58

Direction and Distance

Direction can be defined as the measurement of an object's or person's position with respect to another object or person and displacement is the measurement of distance between the starting point and final point.

The diagram given below shows the four main directions and the four cardinal (sub-directions) directions.

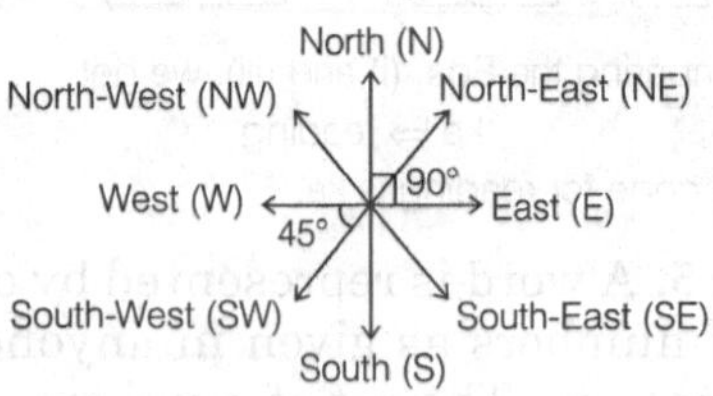

(Main directions–E, W, N, S and cardinal directions – NE, NW, SE, SW)

There are two cyclic directions namely clockwise and anti-clockwise. The direction in which the hands of a clock move is called clockwise direction while its opposite direction is called anti-clockwise direction as shown below.

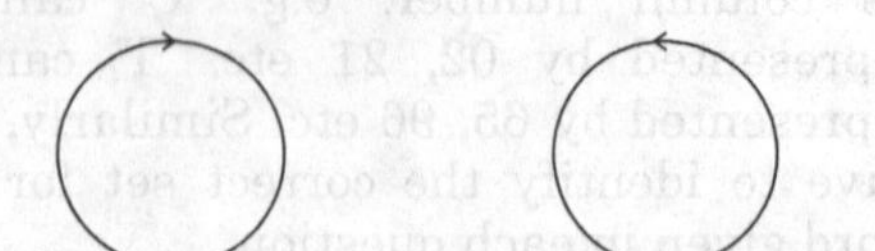

Clockwise direction Anti-clockwise direction

Concept of Shadow

In the morning, when the Sun rises in the East, the shadow of any person or object is in the West direction. Similarly, in the evening, when the Sun sets in the West, the shadow of a person or an object is towards the East.

Shadow at the time of Sun rise

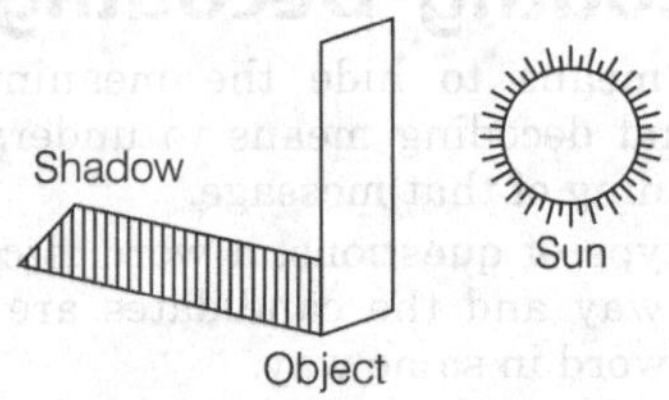

Shadow at the time of Sunset

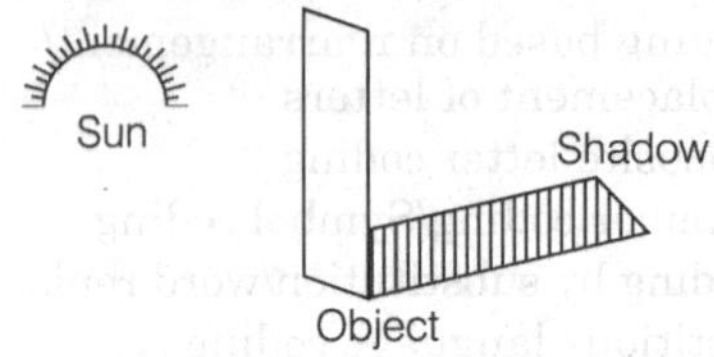

Note At 12:00 noon, there will be no shadow as the rays of the Sun are vertically downwards at that time.

In order to determine the shortest distance between the two given points, the Pythagoras formula,

$$h^2 = b^2 + p^2$$

Here, h = Hypotenuse, b = Base and p = Perpendicular

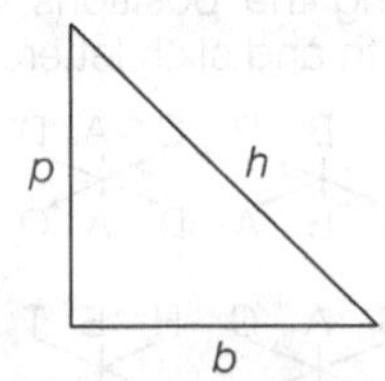

Example 1. Sakshat drives 4 km to the South, then turns left and drives 3 km. Again, he turns left and drives 4 km. In which direction is he from the starting point?

(a) North (b) East (c) South (d) West

Sol. (b) Sakshat drives 4 km to the South.

Now, he takes left turn and drives 3 km. Again, he turns left and drives 4 km.

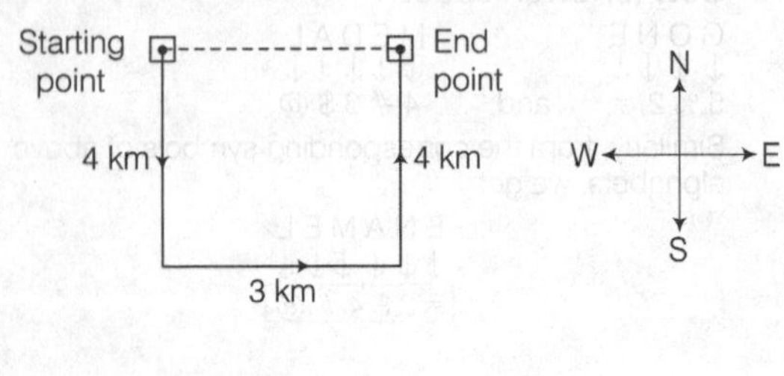

Now, comparing the above direction graph with the standard direction graph, we see that Sakshat is in East direction from his starting point.

Example 2. A girl was going towards West, then she turned left, then turned 90° in clockwise direction. In which direction was she going now?

(a) East (b) West
(c) North (d) South

Sol. (b) The direction of a girl is as follows:

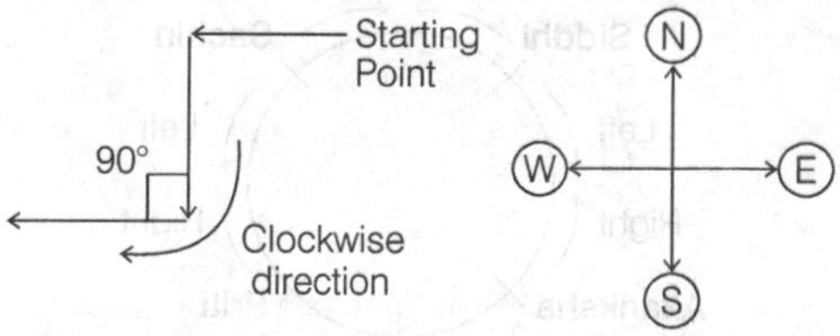

So, the girl was going in West direction.

Example 3. One morning after sunrise, Sita and Gita were standing in a chowk in Mumbai with their back towards each other. Sita's shadow fell exactly towards right hand side. Which direction was Gita facing?

(a) East (b) West (c) North (d) South

Sol. (c) The direction diagram of Sita and Gita is as follows:

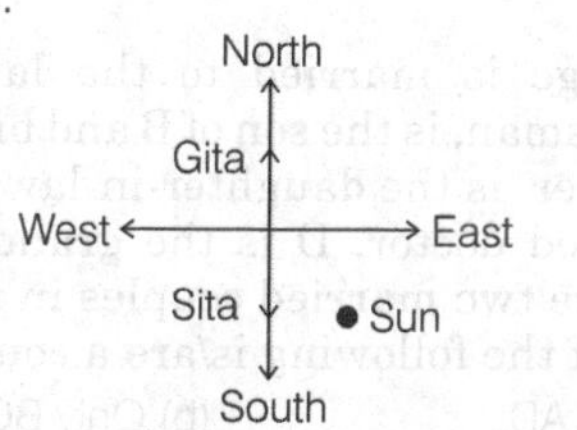

So, Gita was facing in North direction.

Example 4. Ridhan goes 5 km towards North-East and then he goes 4 km towards South. How far is he now from his starting point?

(a) 8 km (b) 2 km (c) 6 km (d) 3 km

Sol. (d) Ridhan goes 5 km towards North-East.

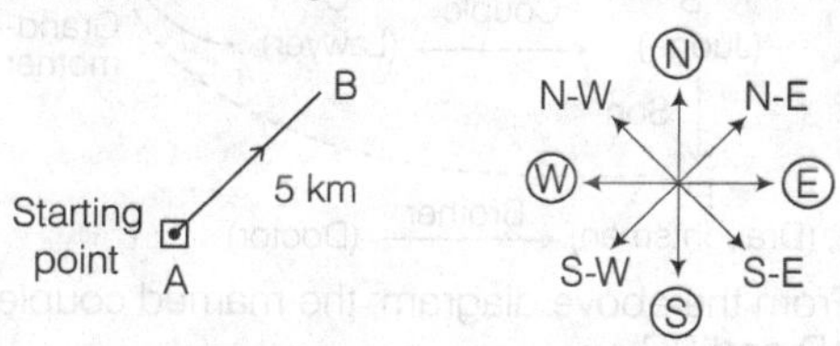

Then, he goes 4 km towards South.

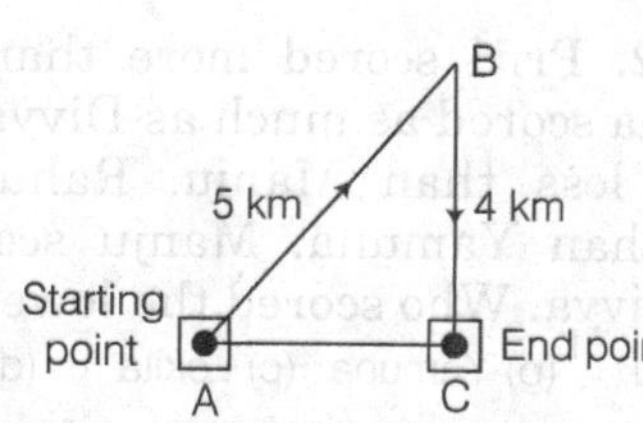

From the above direction graph, total distance from starting point to the ending point = AC

Using Pythagoras theorem, $AB^2 = BC^2 + AC^2$

$\Rightarrow \quad 5^2 = 4^2 + AC^2$

$\Rightarrow \quad 25 - 16 = AC^2$

$\therefore \quad AC = 3\text{ km}$

Ranking

Ranking means arranging a set of objects/persons from top to bottom or bottom to top and from left to right or right to left, as per the given relation between them. In this chapter, the problems are related to the arrangement of the persons/objects in ascending/descending order (based on different parameters like age, salary, height, etc) and determining the position of a person/object in a row/queue.

The Ranking test follows three formulae

(i) Rank of a person/object from lower or right end = (Total number of persons/objects in row) – (Rank of that person/object from upper or left end) + 1

(ii) Rank of person/object from upper or left end = (Total number of persons/objects in row) – (Rank of that person/object from lower or right end) + 1

(iii) Total number of persons/objects in a row or class = (Rank of a person/object from upper or left end) + (Rank of that person/object from lower or right end) – 1

Example 1. In a list, Shikha is 15th from the upper end and 17th from the lower end, then find the total number of people in the list.

(a) 41 (b) 33 (c) 31 (d) 32

Sol. (c) Clearly, using formula,

Total number of people in a row or class = (Rank of a person from upper end) + (Rank of that person from lower end) – 1 Total number of people in the list

$\Rightarrow 15 + 17 - 1 \Rightarrow 32 - 1 \Rightarrow 31$

Example 2. Priti scored more than Rahul. Yamuna scored as much as Divya. Lokita scored less than Manju. Rahul scored more than Yamuna. Manju scored less than Divya. Who scored the lowest?

(a) Manju (b) Yamuna (c) Lokita (d) Rahul

Sol. (c) According to the given information, the arrangement is shown below

Priti	>	Rahul
Yamuna	=	Divya
Manju	>	Lokita
Rahul	>	Yamuna
Divya	>	Manju

So, the final order is as follows

Priti > Rahul > Yamuna = Divya > Manju > Lokita

Hence, Lokita got the lowest scored.

Puzzles

In Puzzles, we deal with the questions, in which the information is given in a confusing manner or regarding arrangement. The candidates are required to proceed systematically by interrelating all the given information in order to arrive at the correct answer. *The questions are based on following types:*

1. Classification Type Questions
2. Seating/Placing Arrangements
3. Conditions, Grouping and Team Formation
4. Sequential Order of Things
5. Family Based Problems

Example 1. Shaan and Kunal are good in cricket and football. Sonu and Shaan are good in cricket and hockey. Abhishek is good in hockey. Who is good in all the three games?

(a) Shaan (b) Kunal (c) Sonu (d) Abhishek

Sol. (a) Information given in the question can be arranged as

	Cricket	Football	Hockey
Shaan	✔	✔	✔
Kunal	✔	✔	
Sonu	✔		✔
Abhishek			✔

It is clear from the above table that, Shaan is good in all the three games.

Example 2. Five persons are sitting facing the centre of a circle. Priti is sitting to the right of Ashwani. Siddhi is sitting between Akanksha and Sachin. Siddhi is to the left of Akanksha and Ashwani is to the right of Akanksha. Who is sitting to the left of Sachin?

(a) Priti (b) Siddhi (c) Akanksha (d) Ashwani

Sol. (a) The given information can be represented as shown below

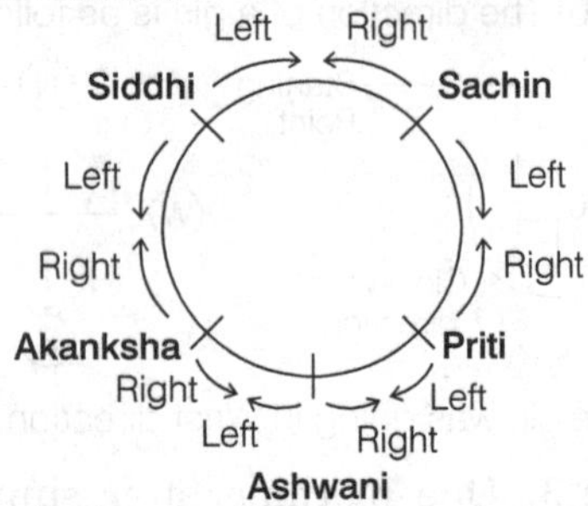

Clearly, Priti is sitting to the left of Sachin.

Example 3. *Read the passage given below and answer the question that follows.*

A, B, C, D, E and F are members of a family. They are engineer, stenographer, doctor, draughtsman, lawyer and judge (not in order). A, the engineer, is married to the lady stenographer.

The judge is married to the lawyer. F, the draughtsman, is the son of B and brother of E. C, the lawyer, is the daughter-in-law of D. E is the unmarried doctor. D is the grandmother of F. There are two married couples in the family. Which of the following is/are a couple/couples?

(a) Only AD (b) Only BC
(c) AD and BC (d) AC and BD

Sol. (c) From the given information, the relation chart can be drawn as

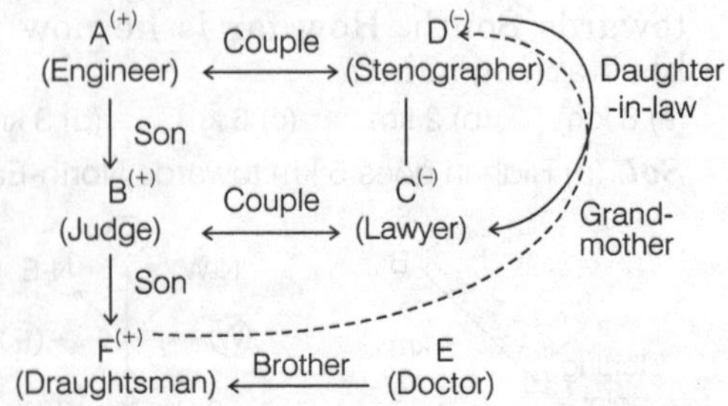

From the above diagram, the married couples are AD and BC.

Inserting the Missing Character

Inserting the missing character is based on diagrammatic arrangement of letters/numbers or combination of both in which a missing term is asked to be calculated.

Direction (Ex. Nos. 1-4) *Select the missing character from the given responses.*

Example 1.

63	7	9
30	5	6
20	4	?

(a) 8 (b) 3 (c) 5 (d) 2

Sol. (c) As, $7 \times 9 = 63$ and $5 \times 6 = 30$

Similarly, $4 \times ? = 20$

$$? = \frac{20}{4} = \boxed{5}$$

Example 2.

	5			21			51	
16	109	2	22	53	19	17	?	48
	6			15			13	

(a) 7 (b) 25 (c) 49 (d) 129

Sol. (b) The pattern is

$$(16 - 6)^2 + (5 - 2)^2 = 10^2 + 3^2 = 109$$

$$(22 - 15)^2 + (21 - 19)^2 = 7^2 + 2^2 = 53$$

So, the missing number $= (17 - 13)^2 + (51 - 48)^2$

$$= 4^2 + 3^2 = 25$$

Example 3.

R	Q	L
S	P	M
T	?	N

(a) O (b) R (c) W (d) V

Sol. (a) According to English alphabet, Moving columnwise

$$R \xrightarrow{+1} S \xrightarrow{+1} T$$

$$Q \xrightarrow{-1} P \xrightarrow{-1} \boxed{O}$$

$$L \xrightarrow{+1} M \xrightarrow{+1} N$$

So, the missing character is O.

Problems Based on Ages

Problems based on ages mainly deals with the concept of relative age, i.e. age of a person at two different times or age of two persons.

Rules Related to Problems Based on Ages

1. If the present age of A is a yr, then *b* yr ago, *A*'s age would be (a − b) yr and after c yr will be (a + c) yr.
2. If the age of a person n yr ago was p yr, then after n yr his age will be (p + n + n) yr.
3. If the age of a person after m yr will be p yr, then his age n yr ago was (p − m − n) yr.

Example 1. The ratio of the present ages of Jai and Ajay is 4 : 5. If Ajay is 6 yr elder than Jai, then what was the ratio of their ages 4 yr ago?

(a) 10 : 13 (b) 8 : 9
(c) 14 : 17 (d) 1 : 2

Sol. (a) Let the age of Jai be x yr.

Then, age of Ajay $= (x + 6)$ yr

According to the question,

$$\frac{x}{x+6} = \frac{4}{5} \Rightarrow 5x = 4(x+6)$$

$$\Rightarrow 5x = 4x + 24 \Rightarrow x = 24$$

$\therefore$ Age of Ajay 4 yr ago $= (24 + 6) - 4 = 26$ yr

and age of Jai 4 yr ago $= 24 - 4 = 20$ yr

Hence, ratio of their ages 4 yr ago

$$= 20 : 26 = 10 : 13$$

Blood Relation

Blood Relations means any relation between two or more persons which is acquired by them by the virtue of their birth.

Blood relationship is defined as the social relationship among the members of the family. The relationship can be divided into two main categories:

1. Maternal
2. Paternal

Relations on the mother's side are called maternal, while the relations on the father's side are called paternal.

The typical relationships that are commonly used in blood relation problems are summarised as follows:

Mother's or Father's father	Grandfather
Mother's or Father's mother	Grandmother
Grandfather's or Grandmother's father	Great grandfather
Grandfather's or Grandmother's mother	Great grandmother
Grandfather's or Grandmother's only daughter-in-law	Mother
Grandfather's or Grandmother's only son	Father
Mother's or Father's brother	Uncle
Mother's or Father's sister	Aunt
Husband's or Wife's father	Father-in-law
Husband's or Wife's mother	Mother-in-law
Husband's or Wife's sister	Sister-in-law
Husband's or Wife's brother	Brother-in-law
Husband of the daughter	Son-in-law
Wife of the son	Daughter-in-law
Wife of the brother	Sister-in-law
Sister's husband	Brother-in-law
Brother's or Sister's son	Nephew
Brother's or Sister's daughter	Niece
Uncle's or Aunt's son or daughter	Cousin
Children of same parents	Siblings
Children's children	Grandchildren

For differentiating a male and a female, we use (+) symbol for 'male' and (–) symbol for 'female'.

Generally two types of questions asked from this chapter such as:

1. Blood relation based on conversation
2. Symbolically coded blood relationship

Example 1. A is B's sister. is B's mother. D is C's father. E is D's mother. Then, how is A related to D?

(a) Daughter (b) Granddaughter
(c) Grandmother (d) Grandfather

Sol. (b)

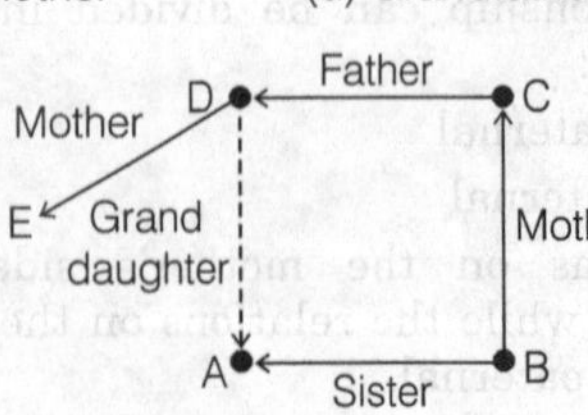

So, A is granddaughter of D.

Example 2. A man said to a woman, "The only son of your brother, is the brother of my wife". How is that woman related to the wife of that man?

(a) Aunt (b) Sister
(c) Mother (d) Grandmother

Sol. (a)

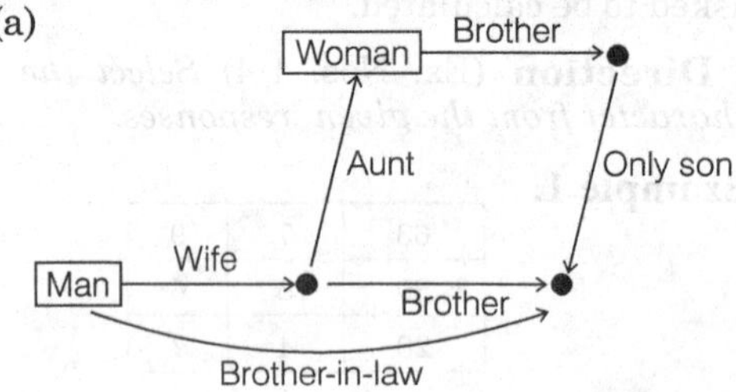

So, that woman is aunt to the wife of that man.

Example 3. Read the following information carefully and answer the questions that follows

(i) 'A+ B' means 'A is the son of B'.
(ii) 'A – B' means 'A is the wife of B'.
(iii) 'A × B' means 'A is the brother of B'.
(iv) 'A ÷ B' means 'A is the mother of B'.
(v) 'A = B' means 'A is the sister of B'.

What does 'P× R÷ Q' mean?

(a) P is the nephew of Q (b) P is the uncle of Q
(c) P is the brother of Q (d) P is the niece of Q

Sol. (b) By decoding the given information using symbols of family diagram, we get

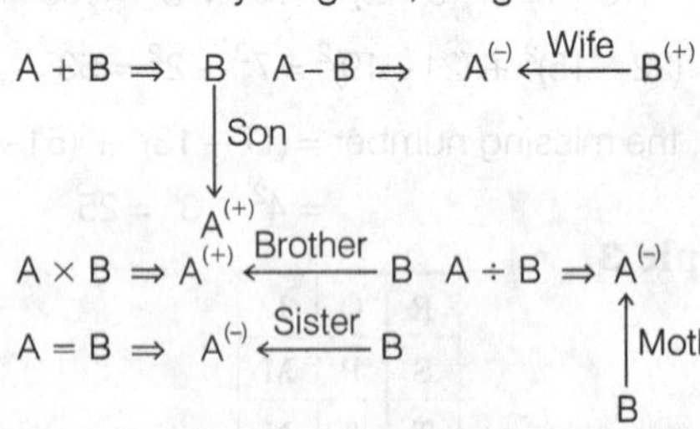

By applying above decoding method for the given equation, we get the following family diagram,

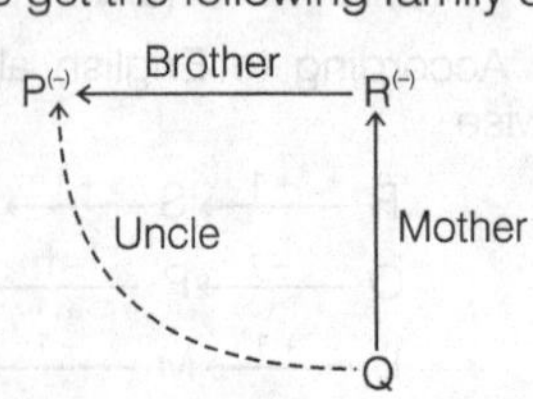

From the above family diagram, we get that P is the uncle of Q, since P is the brother of R.

Mathematical Operations

Mathematical Operations can be defined as the simplification of expression containing numbers and different mathematical signs. Mathematical operations involve basic arithmetic operations such as addition (+), subtraction (–), multiplication (×) and division (÷) but here, the signs are not given as such but in a coded form and the candidates are required to find out the actual meaning of the coded symbols.

There are different types of questions which are asked, such as:

1. Symbol Substitution
2. Balancing the Equation
3. Interchange of Signs/ Numbers
4. Simple/Coded Inequalities

Example 1. If '×' stands for '+', '÷' stands for '–', '–' stands for '×' and '+' stands for '÷', then find the value of following equation.

$$54 \div 16 - 3 \times 6 + 2 = ?$$

(a) 9 (b) 12 (c) 8 (d) 15

Sol. (a) According to the question,

$$? = 54 \div 16 - 3 \times 6 + 2$$
$$ \downarrow \quad \downarrow \quad \downarrow \quad \downarrow$$
$$ - \quad \times \quad + \quad \div$$

$= 54 - 16 \times 3 + 6 \div 2$ (using VBODMAS rule)

$= 54 - 16 \times 3 + 3$

$= 54 - 48 + 3$

$= 6 + 3 = 9$

Example 2. Select the correct combination of mathematical signs to replace '*' signs and to balance the given equation.

24 * 34 * 2 * 5 * 12

(a) + ÷ × = (b) = ÷ + –
(c) = ÷ – + (d) + = ÷ ×

Sol. (c) From option (c),

$24 = 34 \div 2 - 5 + 12 \Rightarrow 24 = 17 - 5 + 12$

$\Rightarrow 24 = 29 - 5 \Rightarrow 24 = 24$

Example 3. In the questions that follow, the symbols are used as follows.

'A © B' means 'A is greater than B'.

'A $\underline{\underline{©}}$ B' means 'A is either greater than or equal to B'.

'A = B' means 'A is equal to B'.

'A @ B' means 'A is smaller than B'.

'A $\underline{\underline{@}}$ B' means 'A is either smaller than or equal to B'.

Now, in the following question, assuming the three statements to be true, state which of the two Conclusions I and II given below is definitely true.

Statements Q @ R, R @ M, M © D

Conclusions I. D © R II. D © Q

(a) Conclusion I is true
(b) Conclusion II is true
(c) Each Conclusion I or II is true
(d) Neither conclusion I nor II is true
(e) Both Conclusions I and II are true

Sol. (d) Given that,

A © B ⇒ A > B i.e. © represents >

A $\underline{\underline{©}}$ B ⇒ A ≥ B i.e. $\underline{\underline{©}}$ represents ≥

A = B ⇒ A = B i.e. = represents =

A @ B ⇒ A < B i.e. @ represents <

A $\underline{\underline{@}}$ B ⇒ A ≤ B i.e. $\underline{\underline{@}}$ represents ≤

(d) According to the question,

Q @ R ⇒ Q < R ...(i)

R @ M ⇒ R < M ...(ii)

M © D ⇒ M > D ...(iii)

On combining the statements (i), (ii) and (iii), we get

Q < R < M > D

Conclusions I. D © R ⇒ D > R (False)

II. D © Q ⇒ D > Q (False)

So, it is clear that neither Conclusion I nor II is true.

Clock, Calendar and Time Sequence Test

A **clock** is an instrument which shows time. The time is divided into hours, minutes and seconds. The dial of a clock numbered from 1 to 12 and each successive number is 5 min spaces ahead of its previous number. A clock has three hands, the larger one is known as minute hand, the smaller one is known as hour hand and the thinner one is known as second hand.

Important Points

- In 60 min (1 h), the minute hand gains 55 min over the hour hand.

- The minute and the hour hands are in the same straight line when they are coincident or opposite to each other.
- The hands of a clock coincide once in every hour but between 11 o'clock and 1 o'clock they coincide only once.
- Both the hands of a clock are opposite to each other when they are 30 min spaces apart, such a situation occurs once in an hour.
- Angle traced by the minute hand in 60 min (1 h) $=360°$
- Angle traced by the hour hand in 12 h $=360°$ i.e. angle traced by the hour hand in 60 min (1 h) $=30°$
- Each minute space on the dial of clock corresponds to an angle of 6°.

Example 1. In 30 min, the hour hand of a clock rotates through an angle of ....

(a) 30° (b) 60° (c) 15° (d) $7\frac{1}{2}°$

Sol. (c) Angle traced by the hour of a clock in 12 h = 360°

∴Angle traced by the hour hand in 1 h (60 min)

$$=\frac{360°}{12}=30°$$

Hence, angle traced by the hour hand in 30 min

$$=\frac{30°}{60}\times 30=15°$$

Example 2. The train for Mumbai leaves every two and a half hours from New Delhi Railway Station. An announcement was made at the station that the train for Mumbai had left 40 min ago and the next train will leave at 6 pm. At what time was the announcement made?

(a) 3 : 30 pm (b) 6 : 30 pm
(c) 5 : 10 pm (d) 4 : 10 pm

Sol. (d) The last train left two and a half hours before 6 pm, i.e. at 3 : 30 pm; and this happened 40 min before the announcement was made. So, the announcement was made at 3 : 30 + 0: 40 = 4 : 10 pm.

Calender mainly deals with finding the day of a week on a particular given date. The process of finding such day depends on the number of odd days.

Important Terms Related to Calendar

- **Odd days** The number of days more than the complete weeks for a given period are called odd days.
- **Ordinary year** A year will be an ordinary year, if it is not divisible by 4.
- In an ordinary year, there are 365 days/52 weeks + 1 day.
- Number of odd days in an ordinary year is one.
- **Leap year** If a year is divisible by 4, then it will be a leap year.
- In a leap year, there are 366 days or 52 weeks + 2 days.
- In a leap year, there are 29 days in February.
- Number of odd days in a leap year is two.
- **Leap century** If a century year is divisible by 400, then it will be leap century.
- Day of the week related to odd days

Number of days	Day
0	Sunday
1	Monday
2	Tuesday
3	Wednesday
4	Thursday
5	Friday
6	Saturday

Example 3. If January 1 is a Friday, then what is the first day of the month of March in a leap year?

(a) Tuesday (b) Wednesday
(c) Thursday (d) Friday

Sol. (a) Total number of days from January 1 to March 1 = 31 + 29 + 1 = 61 days

February in a leap year = 29 days) = 61÷7

= 8 weeks and 5 odd days

So, the fifth day from Friday = Tuesday

Example 4. If the day before yesterday was Wednesday, then when will Sunday be?

(a) Today (b) Tomorrow
(c) Day after tomorrow (d) Two days after tomorrow

Sol. (c) If the day before yesterday was Wednesday, then today will be Friday and the day after tomorrow will be Sunday.

Time Sequence Test

In time sequence test, the candidate is required to find out a particular day/date on the basis of several statements provided to them. The questions asked from this, neither require a special methodology nor any special formulae. The questions are very basic in nature and require common sense.

Example 5. Radha remembers that her father's birthday is after 16th but before 21st of March, while her brother Mahesh remembers that his father's birthday is before 22nd but after 19th of March. On which date is the birthday of their father?

(a) 19th (b) 20th
(c) 21th (d) Cannot be determined

Sol. (b)

According to	Possibility of Date
Radha	17, 18, 19, (20)
Mahesh	(20), 21

Here, 20th is common to both.
So, their father's birthday is on 20th March.

Data Sufficiency

In Data Sufficiency, we deal with the questions which contain a problem followed by two/three statements containing certain information which may be required for solving the given problem.

The candidates are required to determine whether the problem can be solved with the help of the information provided in the given statements.

The candidates are not to assume anything beyond the information given in the question and the following statements. The questions may be asked from ranking, puzzles, coding-decoding, blood relation, ages and so on.

Direction (Ex. Nos. 1-2) *Each of the questions given below consists of a question and two statements numbered* I *and* II. *You have to decide whether the data provided in the statements are sufficient to answer the question.*

Give answer

(a) if the data in Statement I alone is sufficient to answer the question, while the data in Statement II alone is not sufficient to answer the question.

(b) if the data in Statement II alone is sufficient to answer the question, while the data in Statement I alone is not sufficient to answer the question

(c) if the data either in Statement I alone or in Statement II alone is sufficient to answer the question

(d) if the data in both the Statements I and II together are not sufficient to answer the question

(e) if the data in both the Statements I and II together are necessary to answer the question

Example 1. In a code language, 'al ed hop' means 'we play chess'. What is the code for word 'chess'? If

I. 'id nim hop' means 'we are honest'.

II. 'gob ots al' means 'they play cricket'.

Example 2. Who among P, Q, S, T, V and W is the shortest? If

I. S is taller than T, P and W and is not the tallest.

II. T is shorter than Q but is not the shortest.

Sol. 1. (e) From both the statements, we find that

[al] ed (hop) → [we] [play] chess

id nim (hop) → [we] are honest

god ots [al] → they [play] cricket

It is clear that 'ed' is the code for chess.

Sol. 2. (d) The question cannot be solved even using both the statements.

Example 3. This question consists of a question and three statements numbered I, II and III. You have to decide whether the data provided in the statements are sufficient to answer the question.

Point D is in which direction with respect to point B?

I. Point A is to the West of point B. Point C is to the North of point B. Point D is to the South of point C.

II. Point G is to the South of point D. Point G is 4 m from point B. Point D is 9 m from point B.

III. Point A is to the West of point B. Point B is exactly midway between A and E. Point F is to the South of point E. point D is to the West of point F.

(a) if the data in Statements I and II are sufficient to answer the question, while the data in Statement III are not required to answer the question.
(b) if the data in Statements I and III are sufficient to answer the question, while the data in Statement II are not required to answer the question
(c) if the data in Statements II and III are sufficient to answer the question, while the data in Statement I are not required to answer the question
(d) if the data in either Statement I alone or Statement II alone or Statement III alone are sufficient to answer the question
(e) if the data in all the Statements I, II and III together are necessary to answer the question

Sol. (b) The data in Statements I and III are sufficient to answer the question, while the data in Statement II are not required to answer the question.

Input-Output

In Input-Output, the questions are solved by organising the given input line of words or numbers step by step by following a particular rule to arrive at the final step. Thus, in order to solve such questions first of all detect the rule of arrangement of words or numbers in each step. Once you detect the rule of arrangement, the questions based on input become very easy. There is no fixed number of rules involved in these questions. Every set of questions follows a specific rule.

There are mainly four types of questions which are asked from this chapter, such as:

(1) Shifting
(2) Arranging
(3) Arithmetic Operations and
(4) Miscellaneous

Direction (Ex. Nos. 1-2) *A word and number arrangement machine when given an input line of words and numbers rearranges them following a particular rule in each step. The following is an illustration of input and rearrangement.*

Input 'go now 52 38 17 for again 65'
Step I 65 go now 52 38 17 for again
Step II 65 again go now 52 38 17 for
Step III 65 again 52 go now 38 17 for
step IV 65 again 52 for go now 38 17
Step V 65 again 52 for 38 go 17 now
Step VI 65 again 52 for 38 go 17 now

Step VI is the last step of the rearrangement.

As per the rules followed in the above steps, find out in each of the following questions the appropriate step for the given input.

Example 1. Step IV of an input is 58 box 47 dew 15 21 town pot.
Which of the following steps will be the last?

(a) VII (b) VI
(c) VIII (d) IX
(e) None of these

Example 2. Input 'buy win task 52 38 43 door 12'. Which of the following will be Step IV?

(a) 52 buy 43 door 38 task 12 win
(b) 52 buy 43 door 38 task win 12
(c) 52 buy 43 door task win 38 12
(d) There will be no such step
(e) None of the above

Sol. (Ex. Nos. 1-2) In Step I, the largest number goes to the extreme left pushing rest of the line rightward; in the next step the word that comes first in alphabetical order goes to the second position from left pushing rest of the line rightward, thus the numbers and the words get arranged alternately till all the numbers are in descending order and all the words are in alphabetical order.

***Sol.* 1.** (b) **Step IV** 58 box 47 dew 15 21 town pot
Step V 58 box 47 dew 21 15 town pot
Step VI 58 box 47 dew 21 pot 15 town
Clearly, last step = Step VI

***Sol.* 2.** (e) **Input** buy win task 52 38 43 door 12
Step I 52 buy win task 38 43 door 12
Step II 52 by 43 win task 38 door 12
Step III 52 buy 43 door win task 38 12
Step IV 52 buy 43 door 38 win task 12

Logical Venn Diagram

Logical Venn Diagram is a pictorial representation of classes representing items/ things and their common properties. We usually use geometrical shapes (circle, triangle, etc) to draw a Venn diagram.

Generally two types of questions are asked from this topic such as,

(1) Find Out the Diagram

(2) Find Out the Number/Thing

Example 1. Which of the following diagrams indicates the best relation amongst the following?

Lion, Dog and Snake

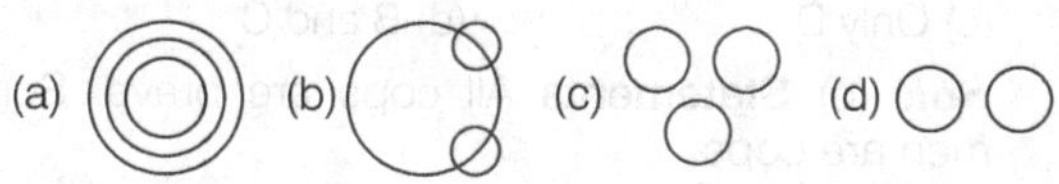

Sol. (c) All three are different from each other.

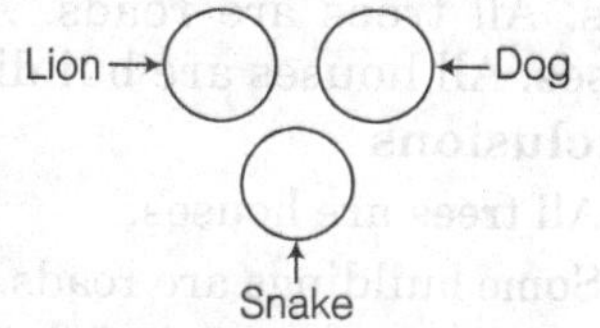

Example 2. Which number is in the square, ellipse and triangle?

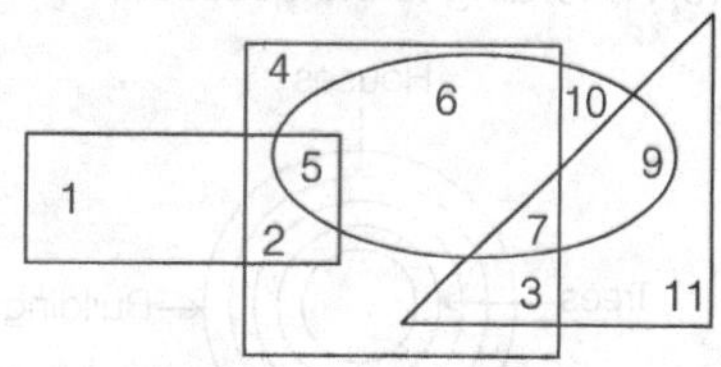

(a) 5 (b) 6 (c) 7 (d) 1

Sol. (c) The number common to the square, ellipse and triangle is 7.

LOGICAL AND ANALYTICAL REASONING

Logical and analytical reasoning can be defined as the process of knowledge involving transition from the known to the unknown. It involves use of reasons, especially to form conclusions, inferences or judgements from the given facts, figures and evidences. Thus, logical reasoning measures your ability to understand, to analyse and to evaluate a given situation.

Generally questions asked from this segment based on syllogism, statements & conclusions, arguments, etc.

Syllogism

A syllogism is a logical argument where a quantified statement of a specific form (the conclusion) is inferred from two other quantified statements (the premises).

Basically, syllogism is deduction of an inference (conclusions) from the given statements. In syllogism, generally three types of questions are asked.

(i) Statement and Conclusion Based questions.

(ii) Correctness of the Statements

(iii) Checking Correctness of a Set of Statements

Direction (Ex. Nos. 1-3) *In each of the questions below is given two/three/four statements followed by two/three/four conclusions, numbered* I, II, III *and* IV. *You have to take the given statements to be true even if they seem to be at variance from commonly known facts. Read all the conclusions and then decide which of the given conclusions logically follows from the given statements disregarding commonly known facts.*

Example 1. Statements Some rats are cats. All cats are bats.

Conclusions I. No rats are cats.

II. Some rats are bats.

(a) Only I follows (b) Only II follows

(c) Either I or II follows (d) Neither I nor II follows

Sol. (b)

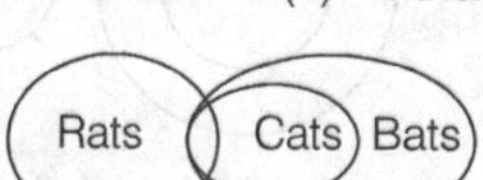

So, only II follows.

Conclusions I. No rats are cats (✗)

II. Some rats are bats. (✓)

Example 2. Statements All jungles are trees. All trees are roads. All roads are houses. All houses are buildings.

Conclusions

I. All trees are houses.

II. Some buildings are roads.

(a) Only I follows (b) Only II follows
(c) I and II follow (d) None follows

Sol. (c) According to the question,

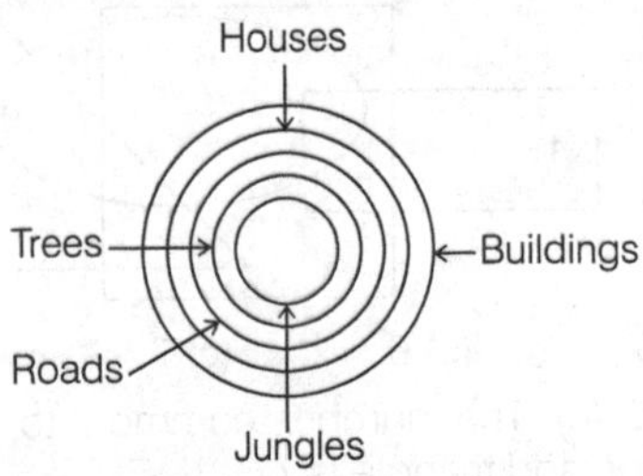

So, both I and II follow.

Conclusions I. All trees are houses. (✓)

II. Some buildings are roads. (✓)

Example 3. Statements All shares are debentures. No debenture is an equity.

Conclusions

I. No equity is a share.

II. Some debentures are shares.

III. No share is an equity.

(a) Only I follows
(b) Only II follows
(c) Only III follows
(d) All follow

Sol. (d) According to the question,

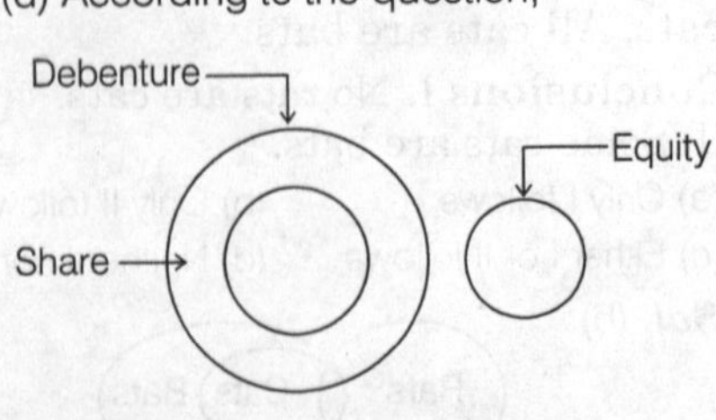

So, all the three conclusions follow.

Conclusions I. No equity is a share. (✓)

II. Some debentures are shares. (✓)

III. No share is an equity. (✓)

Example 4. The following question has four statements of three segments each. Choose the alternative where the third segment in the statement can be deduced using both the preceding two but not just from one of them.

A. Sonia is an actress. Some actresses are pretty. Sonia is pretty.

B. All actors are pretty. Manoj is not an actor. Manoj is not pretty.

C. Some men are cops. Some men are brave. Some brave people are cops.

D. All cops are brave. Some men are cops. Some men are brave.

(a) Only C (b) Only A
(c) Only D (d) B and C

Sol. (c) **Statements** All cops are brave. Some men are cops.

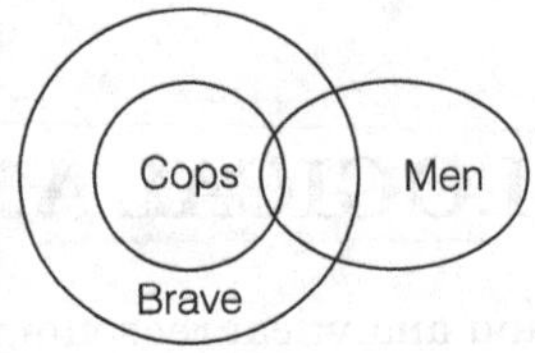

Conclusion Some men are brave. (True)
Hence, only D follows.

Example 5. In the question a set of three statements are given. You have to identify whether the three statements in each of these sets are logically related.

I. No trees are decorations. Some trees are decorated. No decorated are decorations.

II. Some trumps are cards. Some fakes are trumps. Some fakes are cards.

III. All oils are splits. No splits are tanks. No tanks are oils.

(a) Only II (b) I and II
(c) Only III (d) Only I

Sol. (c) **Set A**

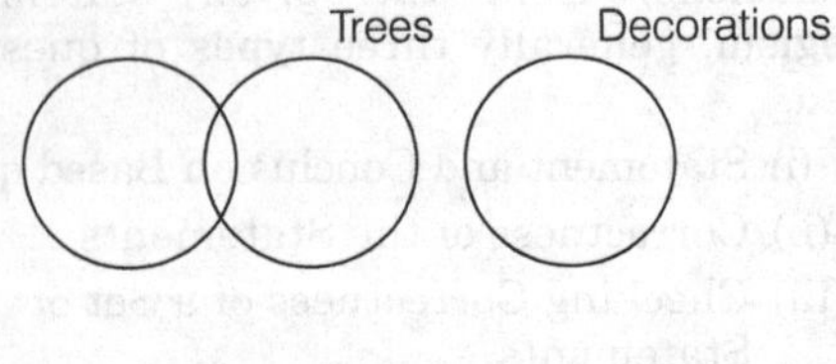

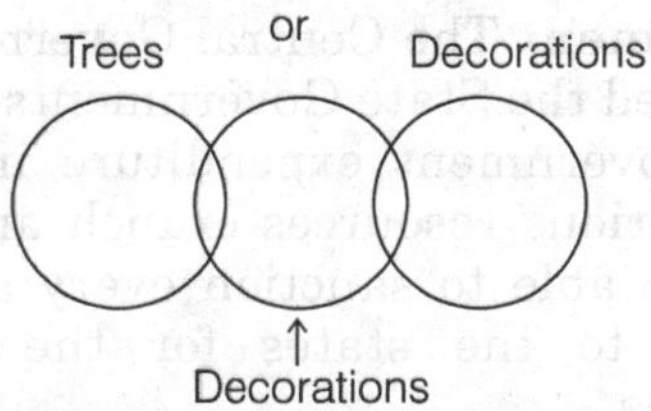

So, there is no certainty of conclusion.

Hence, it is not logically follow.

Set B

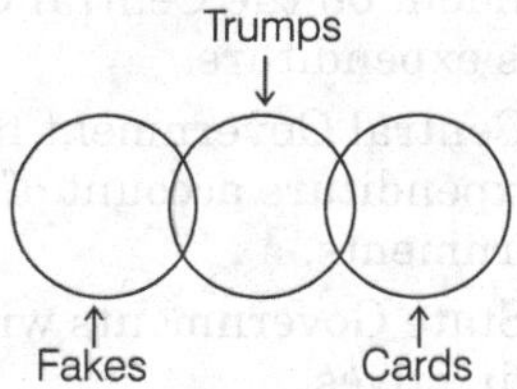

So, it is also logically not in sequence.

Set C

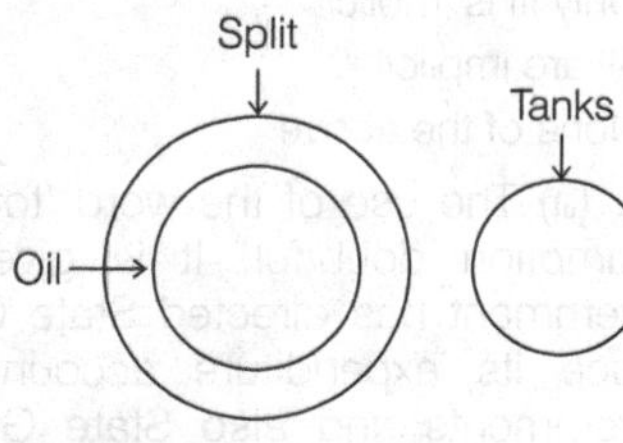

So, it is logically in sequence.

Hence, option (c) is correct.

Statements and Arguments

An argument is a series of statements meant to convince another person about one's point of view. Arguments express different views and most of the time opposes one another. Such a situation creates a puzzling situation and demands a logical analysis of the arguments. After analysing logically, we need to decide the nature of the arguments as which one is strong and which is weak.

Strong Argument

An argument is a strong one, if it is directly related to the given statement and the reason given in the argument addresses all the points put forward in the given statement.

Weak Argument

An argument is a weak one, if it is not directly related to the given statement and it does not address all the points put forward in the given statement.

There are two types of questions are asked:

1. Based on Two Arguments
2. Based on Three/Four Arguments

Example 8. The following statement is followed by two arguments numbered I and II. Decide which of the options is correct about the given arguments.

Statement Should there be a complete ban on strike by government employees in India?

Arguments

I. Yes, this is the only way to teach discipline to the employees.

II. No, this deprives the citizens of their democratic rights.

(a) Only I is strong
(b) Only II is strong
(c) Both I and II are strong
(d) Neither I nor II is strong

Sol. (b) Clearly, strike is not a means of indiscipline but only a practice and tool in which the citizens of any particular country exercise their fundamental rights. So, argument I is not clear and argument II is valid.

Example 9. The following statement is followed by four arguments. Decide which of the options is correct about the given arguments.

Statement Should all the youngsters below 21 years of age be disallowed from going to a beer bar?

Arguments

I. Yes, the entry fee to such pubs should also be hiked.

II. Yes, this will help in preventing youngsters from getting into bad company and imbibing bad habits.

III. No, it is not correct to prevent matured youngsters above 18 years of age, who can vote, from having fun.

IV. No, there is no such curb in Western countries.

(a) Only I is strong (b) I and II are strong
(c) II and III are strong (d) All are strong

Sol. (c) Hiking the entry fees is no way to disallow them. So, argument I is weak. At bars, youngsters may come in contact of bad company and imbibe bad habits. So, argument II is strong. Our constitution considers youngsters above 18 years of age, mature enough to take decisions and judge good or bad for them. So, argument III is strong. Following other countries is not logical. So, argument IV is weak.

Statements and Assumptions

Statement is an information or a fact related to any general subject and Assumption is the hidden or unsaid part of the statement. An assumption is said to be hidden because it is generally assumed, supposed and taken for granted. Here, generally two types of questions are asked:

1. Based on Two Assumptions
2. Based on Three/Four Assumptions.

Example 10. In the question given below, a statement is followed by two assumptions numbered I and II. Consider the statement and decide which of the given assumptions is implicit.

Statement A sentence in the letter to the candidates called for written examination – "You have to bear your expenses on travel etc."

Assumptions

I. If not clarified, all the candidates may claim reimbursement of expenses.

II. Many organisations reimburse expenses on travel to candidates called for written examination.

(a) if only I is implicit
(b) if only II is implicit
(c) if neither I nor II is implicit
(d) if both I and II are implicit

Sol. (d) Specific instruction has been given in writing to prevent chance of claim of reimbursement for travelling expenses. Morever, it is also assumed that instruction has been given, because expenses are paid by other organisations. Hence, both the assumptions are implicit in the statement.

Example 11. In the question given below, a statement is followed by three assumptions numbered I, II and III. Decide which of the given assumptions is implicit in the statement.

Statement The Central Government has directed the State Governments to reduce the government expenditure in view of the serious resources crunch and it may not be able to sanction every additional grant to the states for the next six months.

Assumptions

I. The State Governments are totally dependent on the Central Government for its expenditure.

II. The Central Government has reviewed the expenditure account of the State Governments.

III. The State Governments will abide by the directives.

(a) II and III are implicit
(b) Only III is implicit
(c) All are implicit
(d) None of the above

Sol. (a) The use of the word 'totally' makes the assumption doubtful. It is given that Central Government has directed State Governments to reduce its expenditure account of the State Governments and also State Governments will abide by the directives.

Statements and Conclusions

Statement A statement is a formal account of certain facts, views, problems or situations expressed in words.

Conclusion A conclusion is a belief or an opinion that is the result of reasoning out a given statement. It can also be defined as a proposition in an argument to which other propositions in the argument given support.

Generally, two types of questions are asked

1. Based on Two Conclusions
2. Based on Three/Four conclusions

Example 12. In the question given below, a statement is followed by two conclusions numbered I and II. You have to take the statement to be true and decide which of the conclusion(s) follow.

Statement In the art gallery, paintings of an artist are displayed for the public. The prices of the paintings are too high for a common man.

Conclusions

I. Common man purchases paintings from other places.

II. Costly paintings are generally displayed at the art gallery.

(a) Only I follows
(b) Only II follows
(c) Both I and II follow
(d) None follows

Sol. (d) None of the conclusions definitely follows from the statement as neither it is given in the statement that common man does not purchase paintings from the art gallery nor that costly paintings are generally displayed at the art gallery.

Example 13. Examine the following statements.

I. Only those who have a pair of binoculars can become the members of the birdwatcher's club.

II. Some members of the birdwatcher's club have cameras.

III. Those members who have cameras can take part in photo-contests.

Which of the following conclusions can be drawn from the above statements?

(a) All those who have a pair of binoculars are members of the birdwatcher's club
(b) All members of the birdwatcher's club have a pair of binoculars
(c) All those who take part in photo-contests are members of the birdwatcher's club
(d) No conclusion can be drawn

Sol. (b) Only those who have binoculars can be a part of birdwatcher's club, hence all the members of birdwatcher's club must have binoculars for sure. But all those who have binoculars may not be part of birdwatcher's club.

Statement and Courses of Action

Course of Action is a concept which tests logical reasoning ability, which is essential for taking a quick and effective decision. A course of action is nothing but a decision that is taken in order to solve any problem or improve the situation.

A course of action will be correct, if

(i) it solves or reduces or minimises the problem.

(ii) suggested solution is a practical one. It means, it is succeed or be effective in real circumstances.

Generally, two types of questions are asked

1. Based on Two Courses of Action
2. Based on Three/Four Courses of Action

Example 14. In the question given below, a statement followed by two courses of action. You have to assume everything in the statement to be true, then decide which of the given courses of action is logically follow(s).

Statement Every year, at the beginning or at the end of the monsoon, we have some cases of conjunctivitis, but this year, it seems to be a major epidemic, witnessed after nearly four years.

Courses of Action

I. Precautionary measures should be taken after every four years to check the epidemic.

II. People should be advised to drink boiled water during the monsoon season.

(a) only I follows
(b) only II follows
(c) neither I nor II follows
(d) I and II follow

Sol. (b) It is not necessary that such an epidemic occurs after four years. So, action I is not the right course of action. Secondly, prevention during monsoon season is the right step to face the problem of conjuctivitis. So, action II is the right course of action.

Example 15. In the question below, a statement followed by three courses of action numbered I, II and III. You have to assume everything in the statement to be true, then decide which of the given courses of action in logically follow(s).

Statement Without the active co-operation between the proprietor and the employees of the mill, it cannot remain a profitable concern for long.

Courses of Action

I. The mill should be closed down.

II. The workers should be asked to co-operate with the owners.

III. The owners should be asked to cooperate with the employees.

(a) I and II follow (b) None follows
(c) All follow (d) II and III follow

Sol. (d) It is given in the statement that, cooperation between the proprietor and the employees is required for a profit-making reason. It is therefore required that both employees and proprietor should cooperate each other.

Assertion and Reason

An Assertion is an affirmation, a declaration or a strong statement. According to dictionary, assertion refers to stating something forcefully and that is called Reason which is a fact. Normally, assertions have reasons. Here, we shall deal with the combination of assertion and reason and relate with each other in order to find their correct syntax.

Example 16. **In the question given below, there are two statements labelled as Assertion (A) and Reason (R).**

Assertion (A) Biogas is a good source of energy in rural Rajasthan.

Reason (R) Rajasthan has a large number of domestic animals.

(a) If both A and R are true and R is the correct explanation of A
(b) If both A and R are true but R is not the correct explanation of A
(c) If A is true but R is false
(d) If A is false but R is true

Sol. (a) Rajasthan has a large number of domestic animals that is why it is possible to make biogas. So, A and R are true and R is the correct explanation of A.

Cause and Effect

A strong point behind any reason is known as 'Cause' and the impact of the cause is known as 'Effect'. It is a natural truth that every event happens only when there exists atleast a reason or a cause. These causes are nothing but the conditions under which any event occur and whenever any event occur it leaves an 'Effect' on related matter. Here, it is required to establish the relation between the 'Cause' and 'Effect' if any relation exists.

There are two types of questions asked

1. Based on Two Statements
2. Choosing Logically Related Cause and Effect

Example 17. **In the question below, two statements are given. There may be cause and effect relationship between them. Identify the relation between them, if any.**

I. The local comparative credit society has decided to stop giving loans to farmers with immediate effect.

II. A large number of credit society members have withdrawn major part of their deposits from the credit society.

(a) If statement I is the cause and statement II is its effect
(b) If statement II is the cause and statement I is its effect
(c) If both the statements I and II are independent causes
(d) If both the statements I and II are effects of independent causes

Sol. (b) The local cooperative credit society has decided to stop giving loans to farmers with immediate effect because the deposit of society has decreased as many members have withdrawn their money.

So, statement B is the cause and statement A is its effect.

Example 18. **Government has recently decided to hike the procurement price of paddy for the rabi crops. Which of the following will be a possible effect of the above cause?**

(a) The farmers may be encouraged to cultivate paddy for the rabi season
(b) The farmers may switch over to other cash crops in their paddy fields.
(c) There was a drop in production of paddy during kharif season
(d) Government may not increase the procurement price of paddy during the next kharif season.

Sol. (a) The step of the government will encourage farmers to cultivate paddy for the rabi season.

NON-VERBAL REASONING

Non-verbal reasoning involves the ability to understand and analyse visual information and solve problems unsing visual reasoning.

Non-verbal reasoning involves the following topics.

1. Analogy
2. Classification
3. Series
4. Water/Mirror Image
5. Figure Formation and Analysis
6. Counting of Figures
7. Figure Completion
8. Cube and Dice

Some Basic Facts of Non-Verbal Reasoning

While moving the questions on Non-Verbal reasoning candidate must keep in mind the following points.

(i) First of all detect the main design and other secondary components.

(ii) Have an acute vision on rotation, angular movement, repetition, reverse, linear movement, mirror/water image of the designs.

(iii) Observe addition, deletion etc., of the design.

1. Directions

There are eight directions of which candidate should be aware of

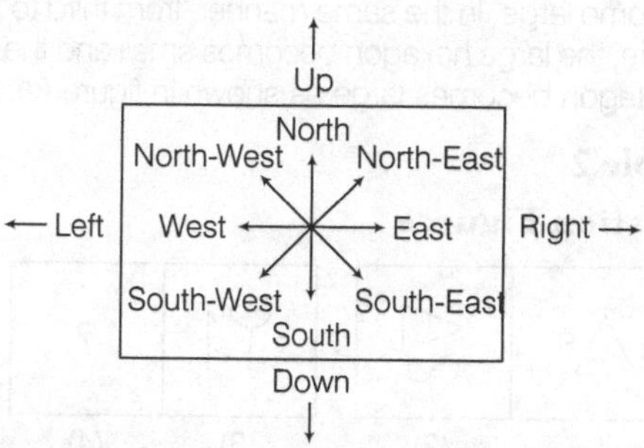

2. Rotational Directions

The rotational directions basically state the clockwise and anti-clockwise directions. In problems of figure series, the sense of rotational direction will play an important role.

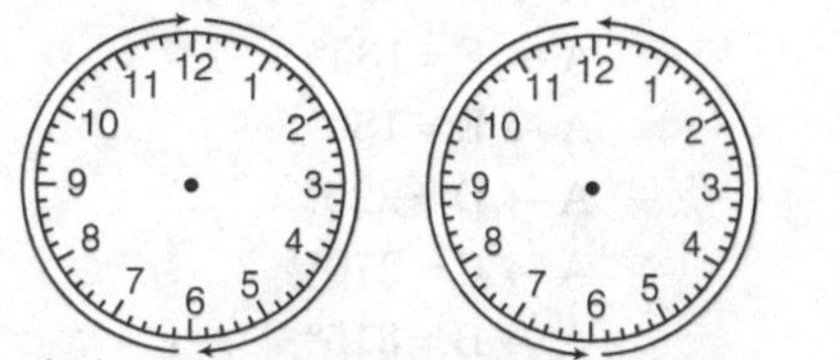

Clockwise movement Anti-clockwise movement

3. Positions of Elements

The candidate should be aware of the positions of the elements to grasp their movement.

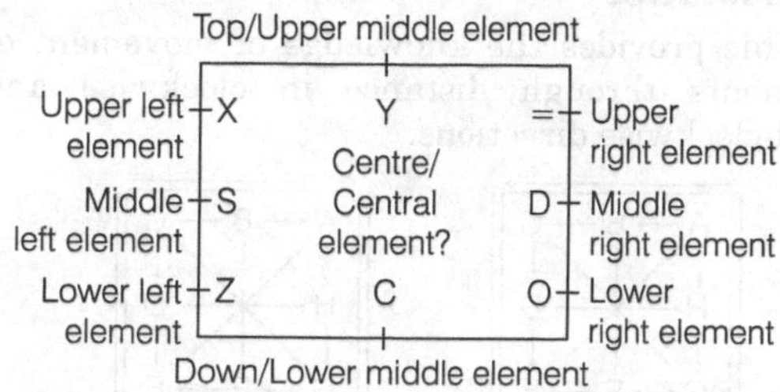

4. Directional Movement of Elements

This provides the knowledge of angular movement of elements in clockwise and anti-clockwise directions.

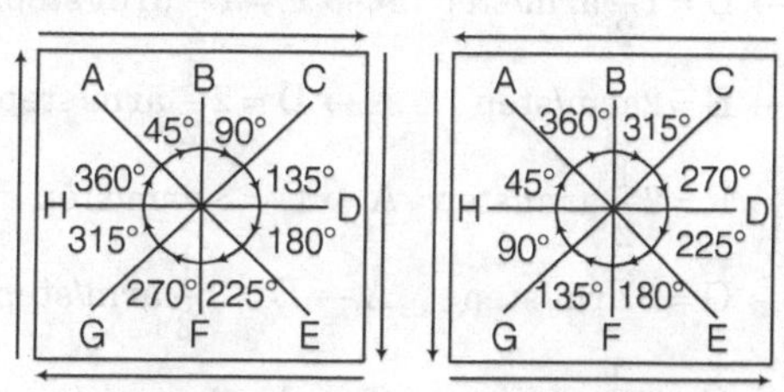

Clockwise movement Anti-clockwise movement

Clockwise Movement

$A \rightarrow B = 45°$

$A \rightarrow C = 90°$

$A \rightarrow D = 135°$

$A \rightarrow E = 180°$

$A \rightarrow F = 225°$

$A \rightarrow G = 270°$

$A \rightarrow H = 315°$

$A \rightarrow A = 360°$

$A \rightarrow A = 0°$

Anti-clockwise Movement

$A \rightarrow H = 45°$

$A \rightarrow G = 90°$

$A \rightarrow F = 135°$

$A \rightarrow E = 180°$

$A \rightarrow D = 225°$

$A \rightarrow C = 270°$

$A \rightarrow B = 315°$

$A \rightarrow A = 360°$

$A \rightarrow A = 0°$

5. Movement of Elements Through Distance

This provides the knowledge of movement of elements through distance in clockwise and anti-clockwise directions.

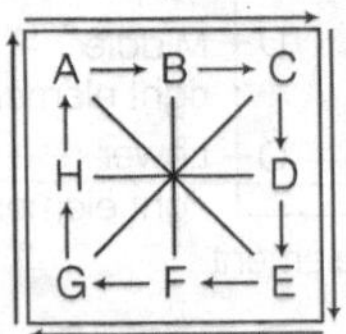

Clockwise movement

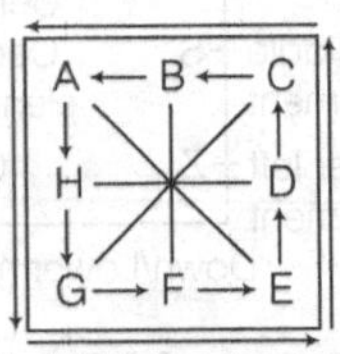

Anti-clockwise movement

$A \rightarrow B = 1/2$ arm/step $A \rightarrow H = 1/2$ arm/step

$A \rightarrow C = 1$ arm/step $A \rightarrow G = 1$ arm/step

$A \rightarrow D = 1\frac{1}{2}$ arm/step $A \rightarrow F = 1\frac{1}{2}$ arm/step

$A \rightarrow E = 2$arm/step $A \rightarrow D = 2\frac{1}{2}$ arm/step

$A \rightarrow F = 2\frac{1}{2}$ arm/step $A \rightarrow C = 3$ arm/step

$A \rightarrow G = 3$ arm/step $A \rightarrow B = 3\frac{1}{2}$ arm/step

$A \rightarrow H = 3\frac{1}{2}$ arm/step $A \rightarrow A = 4$ arm/step

Analogy

Analogy means 'similarity' or 'having' similar feature. If a pair of figures exhibits some kind of relationship on the basis of shape, size, rotation, etc. and another pair of figures exhibits the same kind of relationship between them, then the two pairs are said to be analogous to each other. In this, two pairs of figures are given which are related to each other is some ways. The candidates are required to find out the relationship between the two figures of the first pair and on the basis of similar relationship, find out the second figure of the second pair from amongst the answer figures.

The questions based on analogy are divided into following types such as

1. Based on size/shape of elements
2. Based on number of lines/elements
3. Based on rotation of elements
4. Based on shifting of elements
5. Mixed cases

Example 1. Find the figure from the answer figure that will replace the question mark (?) from the problem figure.

Question Figures

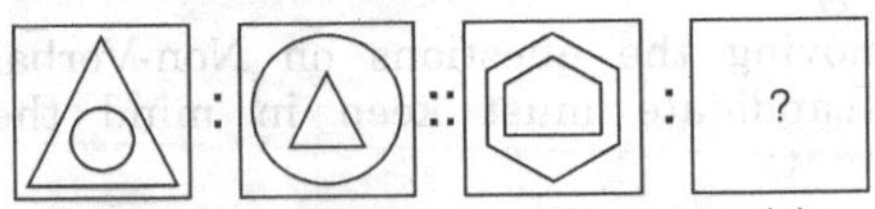

(1) (2) (3) (4)

Answer Figures

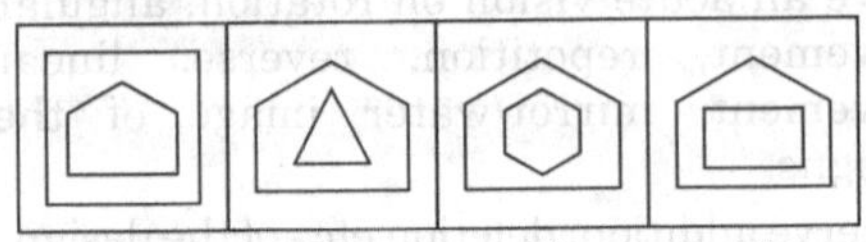
(a) (b) (c) (d)

Sol. (c) By the careful analysis of first part of the problem figure, we find that from first to second figure, the large triangle become small and the small circle become large. In the same manner, from third to fourth figure, the large hexagon becomes small and the small pentagon becomes large as shown in figure (c).

Example 2.

Question Figures

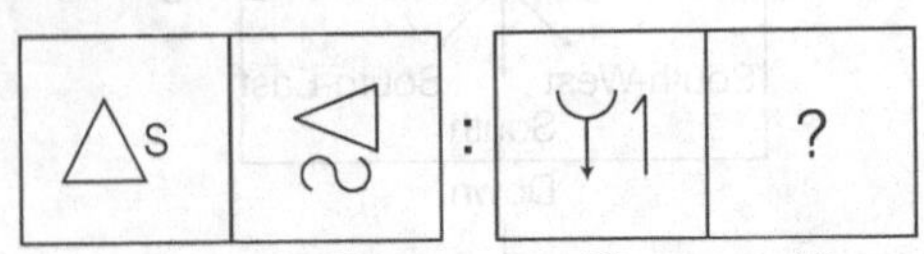

(1) (2) (3) (4)

Answer Figures

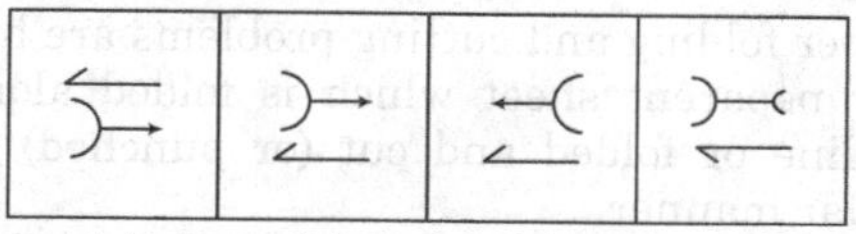

(a) (b) (c) (d)

Sol. (b) The whole figure rotates by 90° anti-clockwise. The LHS element reduces in size and is placed above while the RHS gets enlarged in size and its water image is placed below. Hence, option (b) is correct.

Classification

Classification means to assort the different items of a given group on the basis of certain common quality they posses and spot the odd one out.

In such problems, a set of four figures is given, such that all except one have similar features. The candidates are required to select the figure which differs from all other figures in the given set.

The questions based on classification are divided into following categories such as

1. Based on size/shape of elements
2. Based on number/lines of elements
3. Based on rotation of same figure
4. Based on position of elements

Examples 1. Find the odd one out.

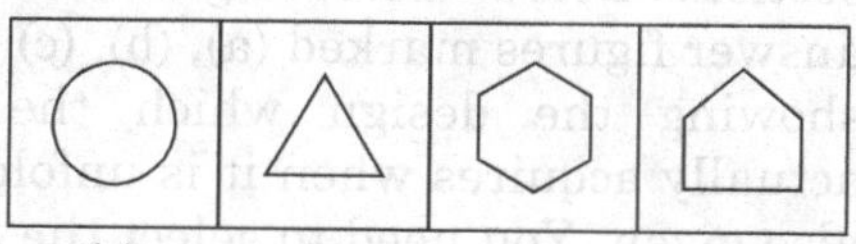

(a) (b) (c) (d)

Sol. (a) Except (a), in all the other figures the designs are made of straight lines while in figure (a) there is a circle which is not made of straight lines.

Example 2.

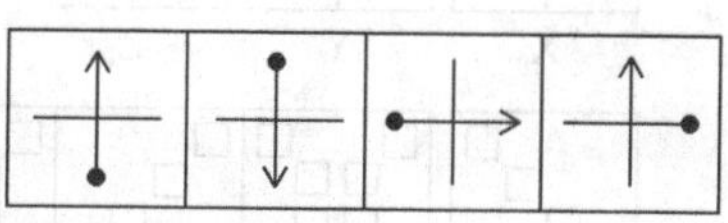

(a) (b) (c) (d)

Sol. (d) Except figure (d), all other figures are same when rotated.

Series

A series is a sequential arrangement and pattern of figures following a certain rule.

The candidates are required to identify the rule of the sequence, i.e. the rule on the basis of which the series continues and determine the answer that follows.

The question based on series are divided into following categories such as

1. Based on number of elements
2. Based on missing figure in a series
3. Based on wrong figure in a series
4. Based on rotation of elements
5. Based on replacement/rearrangement of elements.

Example 1. The next figure of the given series will be

Question Figures

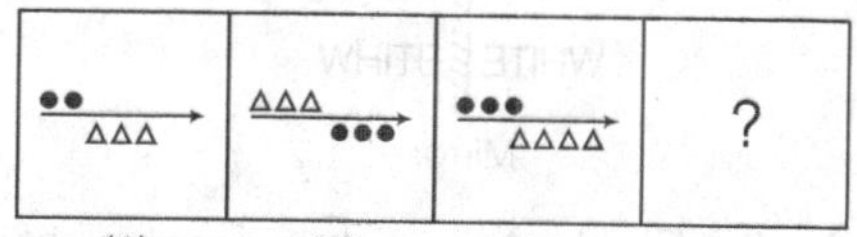

(1) (2) (3) (4)

Answer Figures

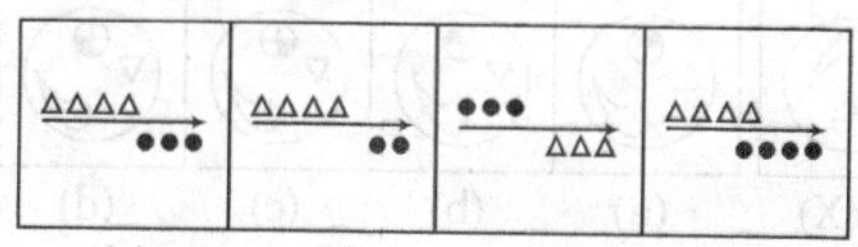

(a) (b) (c) (d)

Sol. (d) In each subsequent figure both types of designs interchange positions and the number of these designs is increased alternately.

Example 2. Find the figure which does not fit in the given series.

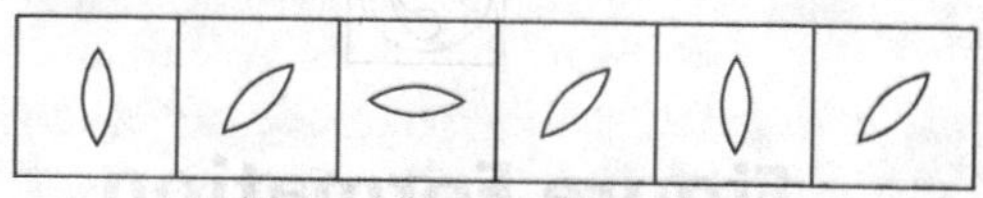

(a) (b) (c) (d)

Sol. (c), Clearly, the leaf rotates 45° clockwise in each step. However, figure (c) does not fit into the series as here the leaf shows an anti-clockwise movement. Hence, option (c) is correct.

Mirror & Water Images

The image of an object as seen in a mirror is called as mirror image while the reflection of an object as seen in water is called as water image.

In mirror image of an object, right side of the object appears at the left side and vice-versa. In water image, the upper part of an object is seen downward and vice-versa.

There are two types of questions, which are generally asked :

1. Based on Letter/Number Images
2. Based on Geometrical Images

Example 1. Which of the following is the mirror image of the given word?

WHITE

(a) ƎLIHW (b) ƎTIHM
(c) ƎTIHW (d) ETIHW

Sol. (c) The mirror image of WHITE is

Example 2. Find the water image of the figure (X).

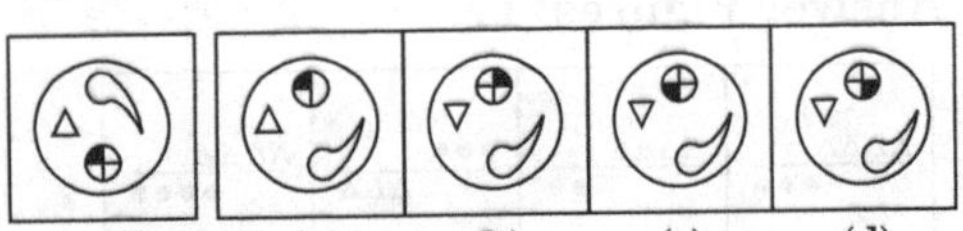

(X) (a) (b) (c) (d)

Sol. (c) The water image of given figure (X) is

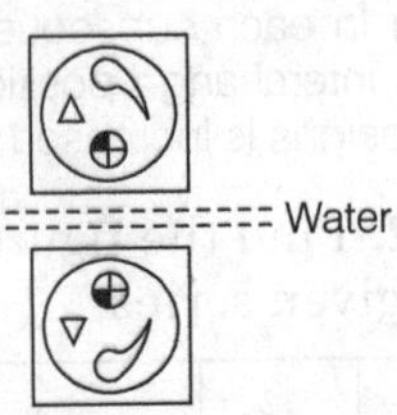

Figure Formation and Analysis

In this chapter, we deal with questions which are based on paper folding/cutting, grouping of identical figures, embedded figures and formation of figures.

1. Paper Folding & Paper Cutting

Paper folding and cutting problems are based on a transparent sheet which is folded along a dotted line or folded and cut (or punched) in a particular manner.

Example 1. In the following problem, a square transparent sheet with a pattern is given. Figure out from amongst the four alternatives as to how the pattern would appear when the transparent sheet is folded at the dotted line.

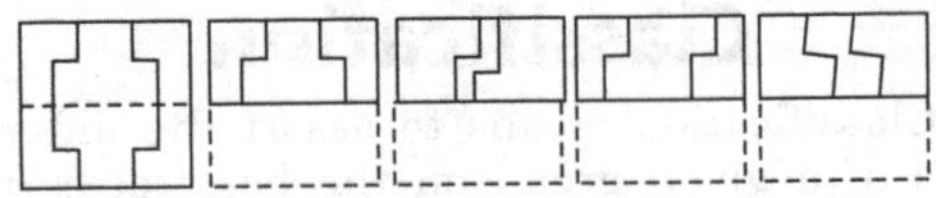

(X) (a) (b) (c) (d)

Sol. (a) The lower half of the transparent sheet is folded along the dotted line and placed on the upper half of the transparent sheet.

The design on both the halves are identical. Hence, option (a) resembles the pattern formed when the transparent sheet is folded along the dotted line.

Example 2. In the following question, a set of three figures (X), (Y) and (Z) have been given, showing a sequence in which paper is folded and finally cut from a particular section. Below these figures a set of answer figures marked (a), (b), (c) and (d) showing the design which the paper actually acquires when it is unfolded are also given. You need to select the answer figure which is closest to the unfolded piece of paper.

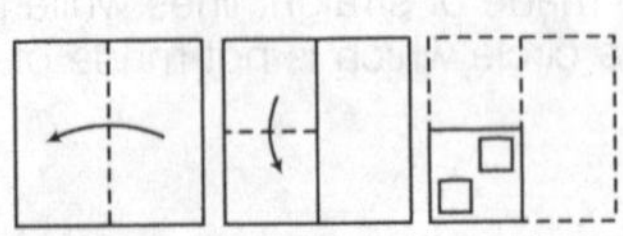

X Y Z

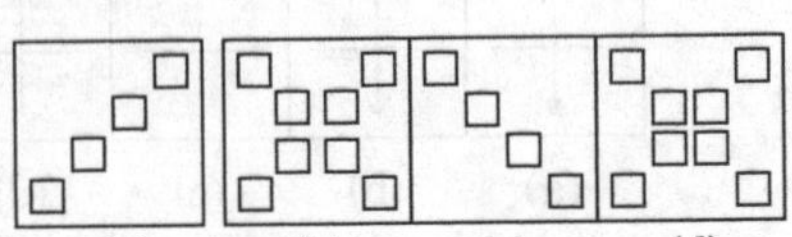

(a) (b) (c) (d)

Sol. (d) In figure (X), the square sheet of paper is being folded along the vertical line of symmetry so that right half of the sheet overlaps the left half. In figure (Y), the sheet is folded further to a quarter. In figure (Z), two squares are punched in the folded sheet. Clearly, the punched squares will be created in each quarter of the paper.

2. Grouping of Identical Figures

In this type, we have a set of few figures which are numbered as 1, 2, 3, 4 and so on. The candidates are required to analyse these figures and classify them into groups consisting of figures having more or less than same properties. The best answer is to be selected from a given set of fairly close alternatives.

Example 3. In the following question, group the given figures into three classes using each figure only once.

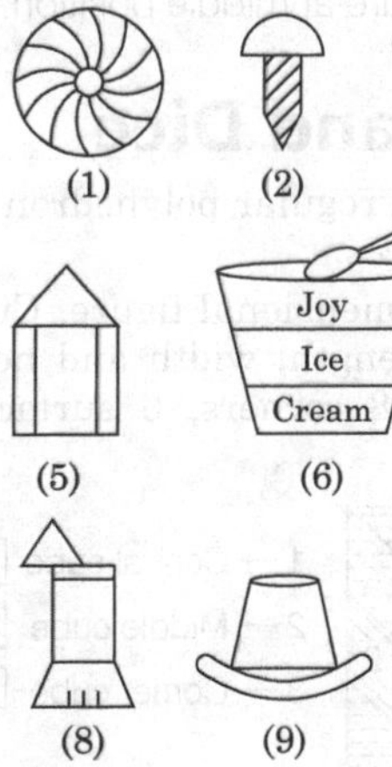

(a) 1, 4, 7
2, 5, 8
3, 6, 9

(b) 1, 3, 6
2, 5, 8
4, 7, 9

(c) 1, 2, 4
3, 5, 8
6, 7, 9

(d) 1, 4, 9
2, 5, 8
3, 6, 7

Sol. (a) Figures which have one small and one big circle = 1, 4, 7

Figures which have one sharp point = 2, 5, 8

Figures which have shapes like bucket = 3, 6, 9

3. Embedded Figures

In this type, we deal with questions in which an original/main figure is embedded/hidden in anyone of the four alternative figures.

The candidate is required to select the figure from the alternatives that clearly shows the embedded/ hidden portion of the original/main figure.

Example 4. Figure (X) is embedded in one of the four alternative figures (a), (b), (c) and (d). Find the alternative which contains figure (X) as its part.

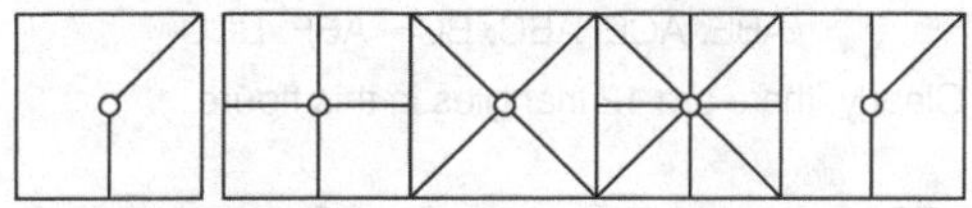

(X) (a) (b) (c) (d)

Sol. (c) On close observation, we find figure (X) is embedded in figure (c) as shown below

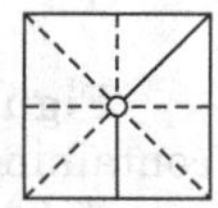

4. Formation of Figures

Formation of figures deal with the problems which are based on fragmentation of a figure into simple parts, choosing the patterns with identical components and rearrangement of pattern.

Example 5. Find out which of the alternatives (a), (b), (c) and (d) will exactly make up the key figure (X).

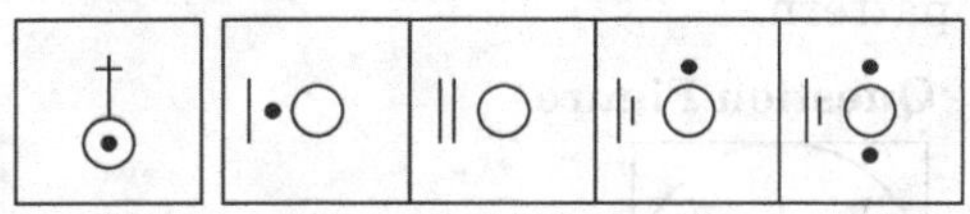

(X) (a) (b) (c) (d)

Sol. (c) The exactly key figure (X) can be made by the figures given in option (c) i.e.

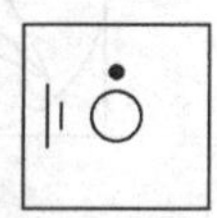

Counting of Figures

Counting of figures involve counting geometrical figures in a given complex figure.

Example 1. How many total triangles are there in the following figure?

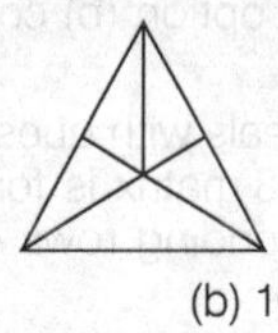

(a) 9
(b) 10
(c) 12
(d) 7

Sol. (c)

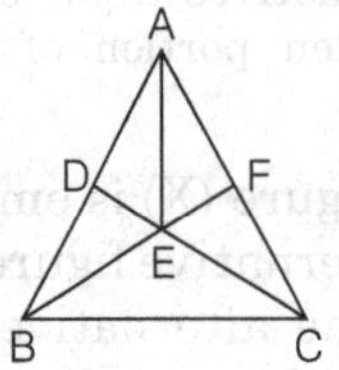

ADE, AEF, BDE, BCE, CEF, ADC,
ABE, ACE, ABC, BCF, ABF, BCD

Clearly, there are 12 triangles in this figure.

Figure Completion and Figure Matrix

Figure completion deals with questions containing figure/matrix. Figure/Matrix contains a set of figures following a particular pattern, in which a part, usually a quarter is left blank. The incomplete figure/matrix is followed by few choices including the missing element, which will complete the given figure.

Example 1. Select a figure from the four alternatives, which when placed in the missing portion of the original figure, as shown by figure (X), would complete the pattern.

Question Figure

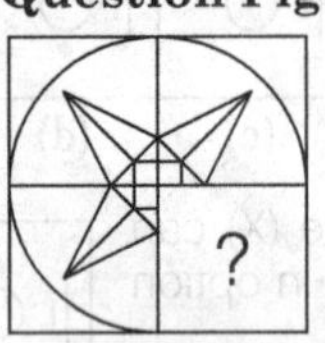

(X)

Answer Figures

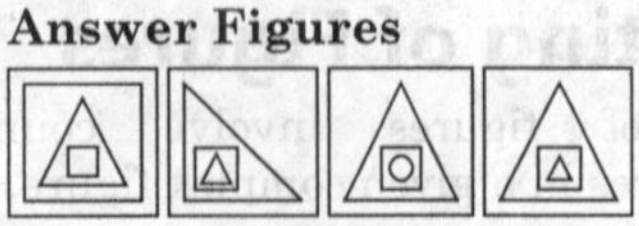

(a) (b) (c) (d)

Sol. (b) Clearly, option (b) completes the original figure.

Figure matrix deals with questions in which either a 2×2 or a 3×3 matrix is formed by a group of figures. Corresponding rows or columns follow a certain pattern.

Example 2. Which figure will replace the question mark?

Question Figure

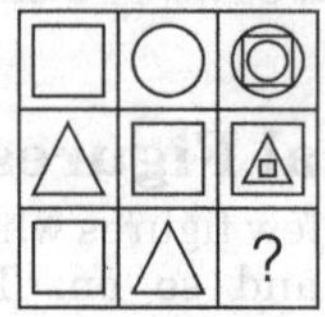

(X)

Answer Figures

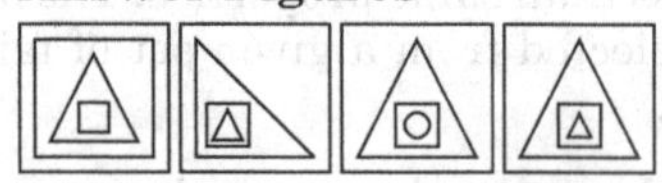

(a) (b) (c) (d)

Sol. (d) Clearly, in each row, the second figure forms the innermost which is also at the outermost position and first figure at middle position.

Cube and Dice

A cube or dice is a regular polyhedron having six identical square faces.

A cube is three-dimensional figure. Cube is a figure which has its length, width and height in equal form and has 8 corners, 6 surfaces and 12 edges.

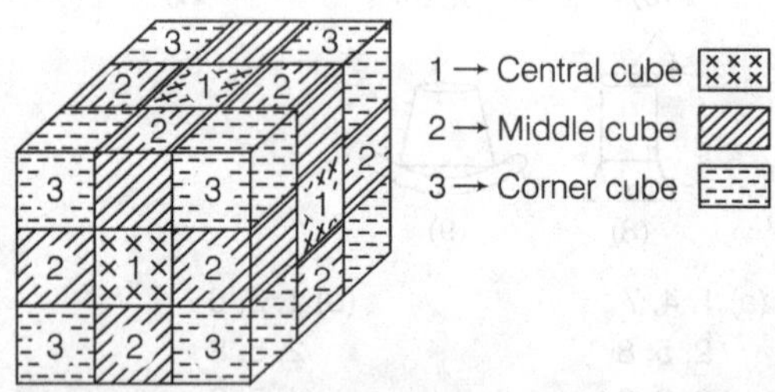

Example 1. A solid cube of 4 inches has been painted red, green and black on pair of opposite faces. It has been cut into one inch cubes. How many cubes have only one face painted?

(a) 4 (b) 8 (c) 16 (d) 24

Sol. (d) $n = \frac{4}{1} = 4$ inches

∴ Number of cubes have only one face painted

$= (n-2)^2 \times 6$

$= (4-2)^2 \times 6 = 24$

Dice are cubical or cuboidal shape objects containing numbers/figures/symbols/embedded on their surfaces.

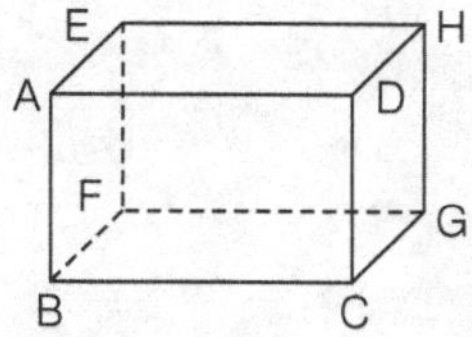

Front surface ⟶ ABCD ┐ Opposite
Back surface ⟶ EFGH ┘
Top surface ⟶ ADHE ┐ Opposite
Bottom surface ⟶ BCGF ┘
Left surface ⟶ ABFE ┐ Opposite
Right surface ⟶ DCGH ┘

1. Ordinary Dice

In ordinary dice, the sum of opposite faces is not 7 but the sum of adjacent sides are 7.

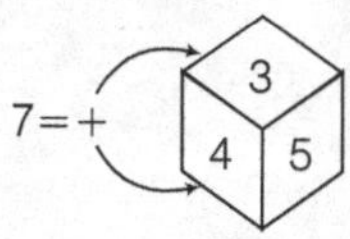

Ordinary dice

2. Standard Dice

In standard dice, the sum of opposite sides is 7. In other words, we can say that a dice which does not has 7 as total of two adjacent sides known as standard dice.

Standard Dice

Here,
Opposite of 1 ↔ 6
Opposite of 4 ↔ 3
Opposite of 5 ↔ 2

Example 2. Two positions of a dice are shown below. Identify the number at the bottom when the top is '3'?

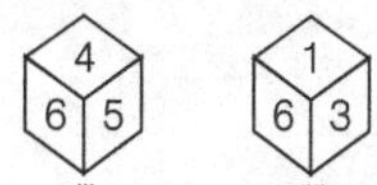

(i) (ii)

(a) 2 (b) 4
(c) 5 (d) 16

Sol. (c) Using both dice, we can say 1, 3, 4 and 5 are adjacent sides of 6. So, 2 is opposite to 6 Here, 4 and 6 are adjacent to 5. So, either 1 or 3 is opposite to 5. But 1 and 3 both are adjacent and when 1 is at top, then 3 is its adjacent side. So, 3 lies opposite of 5. Hence, when the top is 3, then the number at the bottom will be 5.

PRACTICE SET 1

Direction (Q. Nos. 1-3) *In the following questions, select the related word/letters/number from the given alternatives.*

1. DHLPTX : BFJNRV : : CGKOSW : ? **[SSC (CPO) 2015]**

(a) IJKLMN (b) AEIMQU
(c) UMQEIA (d) AIOMUQ

2. Alleviate : Aggravate : : Elastic : ?

(a) Rigid (b) Flexible
(c) Malleable (d) Strong

3. 24 : 126 : 48 : ?

(a) 433 (b) 192 (c) 240 (d) 344

Direction (Q. Nos.4-6) *In each of the following questions, a series has been given with one/two term(s) missing. Choose the correct alternative from the given ones that will complete the series.*

4. 7, 25, 61, 121,? **[BSSC (CGL) 2015]**

(a) 210 (b) 211 (c) 212 (d) 209

5. 17, 36, 74, 150, ?, 606

(a) 250 (b) 303
(c) 300 (d) 302

6. A, P, C, Q, E, R, G, ?, ?

(a) S, I (b) H, I (c) I, S (d) T, J

Direction (Q. Nos. 7-9) *In the following questions, find the odd term from the given alternatives.* **[SSC (10+2) 2015]**

7. (a) Crayon-Chart (b) Pencil-Lead
(c) Pen-Ink (d) Brush-Paint

8. (a) RNMP (b) JFEH
(c) RPOQ (d) HDCF

9. (a) Sand (b) Cement
(c) Building (d) Wood
(e) Bricks

10. From the given alternatives, select the word which cannot be formed using the letters of the given word. **[SSC (10+2) 2013]**

INFLATIONARY

(a) FLAIR (b) FAULTY
(c) NATIONAL (d) RATION

11. How many meaningful English words can be formed with the letters ITRM, using each letter only once in each word?

(a) None (b) One
(c) Two (d) Three
(e) More than three

12. In the given question, which one of the following diagrams represents the correct relationship among

Manager, Labour union and Worker **[SSC (10+2) 2014]**

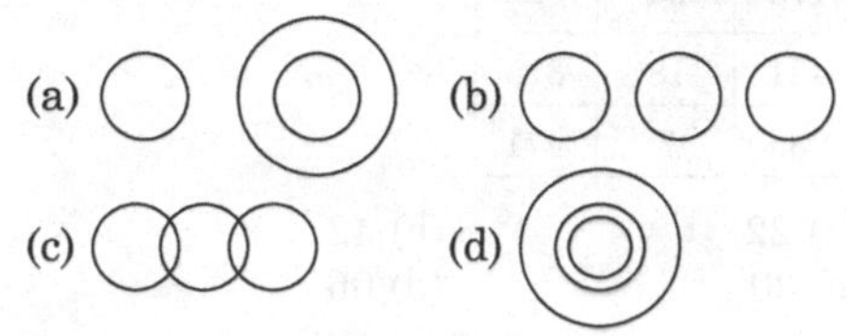

Direction (Q. Nos. 13-15) *Study the given information carefully to answer the given questions.* **[SBI (PO) Pre 2015]**

In a certain code language,

'Cinderella shouted for rescue' is written as 'pr co ly bu'.

'rescue all the bugs' is written as 'ke mt co rx'.

'bugs ate all carrots' is written as 'vg rx ke sh'.

'carrots for pretty Cinderella' is written as 'ly pr vg as'.

(All codes are two-letter codes only)

13. In the given code language, what does the code 'pr' stand for?

(a) Either 'bugs' or 'shouted'
(b) rescue
(c) Either 'Cinderella' or 'for'
(d) for
(e) pretty

14. What will be the code for 'the pretty' in the given code language?

(a) bu rx
(b) ke as
(c) Other than those given as options
(d) mt bu
(e) as mt

15. What is the code for 'bugs' in the given code language?
(a) Other than those given as options
(b) co
(c) sh
(d) Either 'co' or 'vg'
(e) Either 'ke' or 'rx'

16. If '+' means '÷', '−' means '+', '×' means '−' and '÷' means '×', then what will be the value of $8 \div 4 - 6 + 3 \times 4$?
(a) 30 (b) 8
(c) 46 (d) 13

Direction (Q. Nos. 17-18) *In the following questions, select the missing number from the given responses.*

17.

173	24	526
431	18	325
235	?	471

(a) 22 (b) 42
(c) 30 (d) 06

18.

5	9	15
16	29	?
49	89	147

(a) 45 (b) 48
(c) 51 (d) 54

19. Raju wants to go to the planetarium. So, he walked 1.5 km towards East from the place and then turned to right and walked 2.5 km and then turned towards East walked 1 km and turned to South and walked 4 km and reached the place by walking 2.5 km towards West. What distance is he from the starting point?
(a) 6.5 km (b) 9.5 km
(c) 10 km (d) 9 km

20. At what time between 4 and 5 O'clock will the hands of clock be at right angle?
(a) $5\frac{5}{11}, 38\frac{2}{11}$ min past 4
(b) $\frac{60}{11}, \frac{210}{11}$ min past 4
(c) $\frac{70}{11}, \frac{240}{11}$ min past 4
(d) $\frac{80}{11}, \frac{250}{11}$ min past4

Direction (Q. Nos. 21-23) *Study the following information carefully and answer the given questions.* **[LIC (ADO) 2015]**

Twelve people are sitting in two parallel rows containing six people each in such a way that there is equal distance between adjacent persons. In row 1, M, N, O, P, Q and R are seated and all of them are facing North but not necessarily in the same order.

In row 2, U, V, W, X, Y and Z are seated and all of them are facing South but not necessarily in the same order. Therefore, in the given seating arrangement each member seated in a row faces another members of the other row.

N sits second to the right of R. The one who faces N sits to the immediate right of Y. Only two people sit between Y and Z. Only two people sit between N and O. P sits to the immediate left of M. The one who faces M sits second to the left of V. U sits to the immediate right of W.

21. Which of the following statements is true regarding Q?
(a) None of the given statements is true
(b) Only one person sits between Q and M
(c) The one who faces Q sits to the immediate right of U
(d) Only two people sit to the left of Q
(e) Q faces V

22. Who amongst the following is facing V?
(a) N (b) O (c) M (d) Q
(e) R

23. Who amongst the following is facing M?
(a) W (b) Y (c) U (d) X
(e) Other than those given as options

24. Select the choice out of the given choices which gives the given words in the correct alphabetical order. **[FCI (Assistant) Grade III 2015]**

Blue, Bluff, Blurt, Blush

(a) Blurt, Blush, Blue, Bluff
(b) Blue, Bluff, Blurt, Blush
(c) Bluff, Blue, Blurt, Blush
(d) Blush, Blue, Bluff, Blurt

25. While travelling in a train with his friend, Rushil meets another man, whose mother is the wife of Rushil's father's only son. How is the man related to Rushil?
(a) Son (b) Father
(c) Uncle (d) Nephew

26. In the given diagram, circle represents athletes, square represents tall men and triangle represents bank officers. Which region represents bank officers who are athletes?

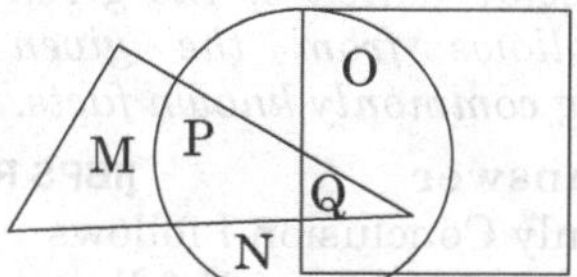

(a) P and M (b) P
(c) Q (d) P and Q

27. The average age of four boys five years ago was 9 yr. On including a new boy, the present average age of all the five becomes 15 yr. The present age of the new boy is **[BSSC (CGL) Pre 2015]**

(a) 14 yr (b) 6 yr
(c) 15 yr (d) 19 yr

28. How many circles are there in the following figure? **[SSC (CGL) 2015]**

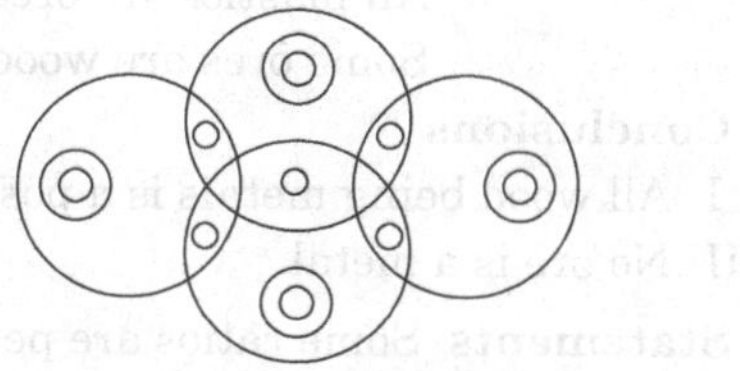

(a) 13 (b) 16
(c) 17 (d) 22

Direction (Q. Nos. 29-30) *In these questions, relationship between different elements is shown in the statements. These statements are followed by two conclusions.*

Give answer

(a) if only Conclusion I follows
(b) if only Conclusion II follows
(c) if either Conclusion I or II follows
(d) if neither Conclusion I nor II follows
(e) if both Conclusions I and II follow

29. Statement $P \geq Q = R > S > T$

Conclusions I. $P \geq T$

II. $T < Q$

30. Statement $L \leq M < N > O \geq P$

Conclusions I. $O < M$

II. $P \leq N$

Direction (Q. Nos. 31-32) *Read the following information carefully and answer the questions that follow.* **[FCI (Assistant) 2015]**

There were six persons U, V, W, X, Y, Z playing a game of cards. U's father, mother and uncle were in the group. There are two ladies in the group. V the mother of U got more points than her husband. X got more points than Y but less than Z. Niece of Y got lowest points. Father of U got more points than Z but could not win the game.

31. Who won the game and who got the lowest points, respectively?

(a) V and U (b) Only U
(c) W and Y (d) X and V

32. Who is the husband of V and what was his position in the game on the basis of points?

(a) Z, 2nd (b) Y, 3rd (c) X, 2nd (d) W, 2nd

Direction (Q. Nos. 33-34) *Read the following information carefully and answer the questions given below.*

Ravish and Kamlesh like hockey and volleyball. Suresh and Ravish likes hockey and badminton. Giri and Kamlesh like chess and volleyball. Suresh, Giri and Mukesh like football and badminton.

33. Who likes chess, hockey and volleyball?

(a) Suresh (b) Kamlesh
(c) Ravish (d) Giri

34. Who likes badminton, chess, football and volleyball?

(a) Suresh (b) Kamlesh
(c) Giri (d) Ravish

35. Select the answer figure in which the question figure is hidden/embedded?

Question Figure

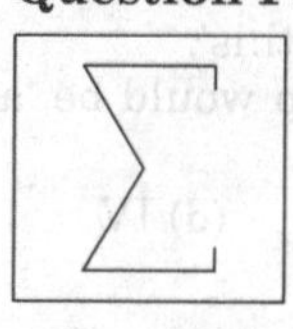

Answer Figures

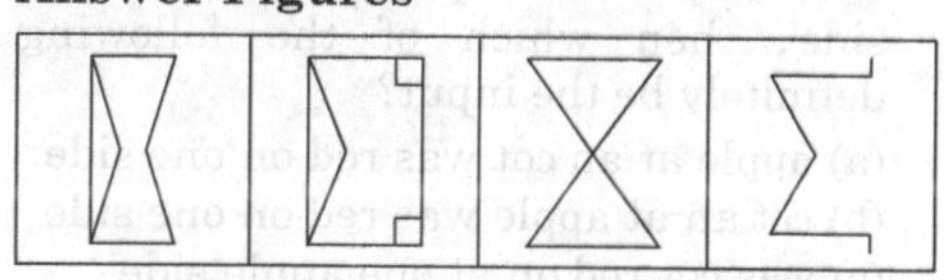

(a) (b) (c) (d)

36. There are five friends—Sachin, Kamal, Mohan, Arun and Ram. Sachin is shorter than Kamal, but taller than Ram. Mohan is the tallest. Arun is a little shorter than Kamal and a little taller than Sachin. Who is the second tallest? **[SSC (CGL) 2014]**

(a) Ram (b) Sachin
(c) Kamal (d) Arun

37. If R stands for '–', A stands for '+', B stands for '÷' and C stands for '×', then what is the value of 25 A 37 C 2 B 4 R1 ? (BODMAS rule will not be applicable)

(a) 32 (b) 35
(c) 30 (d) 27

Direction (Q. Nos. 38-40) *Study the following information to answer the given questions.*

A word arrangement machine, when given an input line of words, rearranges them following a particular rule in each step. The following is an illustration of input and the steps of rearrangement.

Input 'As if it on as zoo figure Of in at.'
***Step* I** as As if it on zoo figure Of in at.
***Step* II** as As at if it on zoo figure Of in.
***Step* III** as As at figure if it on zoo Of in.
***Step* IV** as As at figure if in it on zoo Of.
***Step* V** as As at figure if in it Of on zoo.
(and Step V is the last step for this input).

As per the rule followed in the above steps, find out in the given questions the appropriate step for the given input.

38. Input 'Him and His either or her'.
Which step will be the last step for this input?

(a) I (b) II (c) III (d) V
(e) VII

39. Input 'You are at fault on this'.
Which of the following step would be 'are at fault on you this'?

(a) I (b) II (c) III (d) IV
(e) V

40. If IV step is 'an apple at cot was red on one side', then which of the following will definitely be the input?

(a) apple at an cot was red on one side
(b) cot an at apple was red on one side
(c) was cot red on at one apple side
(d) Cannot be determined
(e) None of the above

Direction (Q. Nos. 41-43) *In each question below are three statements followed by two conclusions numbered* I *and* II. *You have to take the two given statements to be true even if they seem to be at variance from commonly known facts and then decide which of the given conclusions logically follows from the given statements disregarding commonly known facts.*

Give answer **[IBPS RRB (PO) 2015]**

(a) if only Conclusion I follows
(b) if only Conclusion II follows
(c) if either Conclusion I or II follows
(d) if neither Conclusion I nor II follows
(e) if both Conclusions I and II follow

41. Statements Some ratios are per cent.
All per cent are fractions.
No fractions is a sections.

Conclusions
I. No section is a per cent.
II. All ratios being fractions is a possibility.

42. Statements All metals are plastics.
All plastics are ores.
Some ores are wood.

Conclusions
I. All wood being metals is a possibility.
II. No ore is a metal.

43. Statements Some ratios are per cent.
All per cent are fractions.
No fraction is a section.

Conclusions
I. All sections being ratios is a possibility.
II. At least some fractions are ratios.

44. All UAE visa applicants who are not banned get the visa. Aditya has been banned by his employer from entering the UAE. Nevertheless he applies for UAE explaining that the ban is unfair. Will Aditya get the UAE visa?

Decide whether the date provided in the following two statements are sufficient to answer the above question. **[CMAT 2015]**

Statements
I. If immigration department is convinced that the ban is unfair they will revoke ban.
II. Aditya succeeds in convincing the immigration official that the ban is unfair.

(a) Both I and II are required
(b) Both I and II together are not sufficient
(c) Only II alone is sufficient
(d) Only I alone is sufficient

45. A word is represented by only one set of numbers as given in any one of the alternatives. The sets of numbers given in the alternatives are represented by two classes of alphabets as in two matrices given below.

The columns and rows of Matrix I are numbered from 0 to 4 and that of Matrix II are numbered from 5 to 9. A letter from these matrices can be represented first by its row and next by its column, e.g. A can be represented by 01, 20, 42, etc., and H can be represented by 65, 57, 98, etc. Similarly, you have to identify the set for the word.

FAITH

Matrix I

	0	1	2	3	4
0	F	A	N	O	I
1	I	O	F	A	N
2	A	N	O	I	F
3	O	F	I	N	A
4	N	I	A	F	O

Matrix II

	5	6	7	8	9
5	S	E	H	B	T
6	H	S	E	T	B
7	B	T	S	E	H
8	E	H	T	B	S
9	T	S	E	H	B

(a) 24, 31, 10, 59, 57 (b) 12, 20, 40, 68, 65
(c) 31, 34, 23, 76, 79 (d) 43, 42, 41, 78, 89

Direction (Q. Nos. 46-48) *In each of these questions, two Statements* I *and* II *are provided. These may have a cause and effect relationship or may have independent causes or be the effects of independent causes.*

Give answer
(a) if Statement I is the cause and Statement II is its effect
(b) if Statement II is the cause and Statement I is its effect
(c) if both Statements I and II are effects of independent causes
(d) if both Statements I and II are effects of some common cause

46. I. This year the cut-off percentages for admission to junior colleges have increased over the last year.
II. This year's performance of students in Xth final exam was considerably higher than the previous year.

47. I. The conditions of most of the national highways are very bad.
II. Government has now sanctioned a huge amount of money to maintain the national highways.

48. I. Rain and thunder showers lashed the city during the past three days.
II. Many people stayed indoors during the past three days.

49. Find the odd figure from the given alternatives.

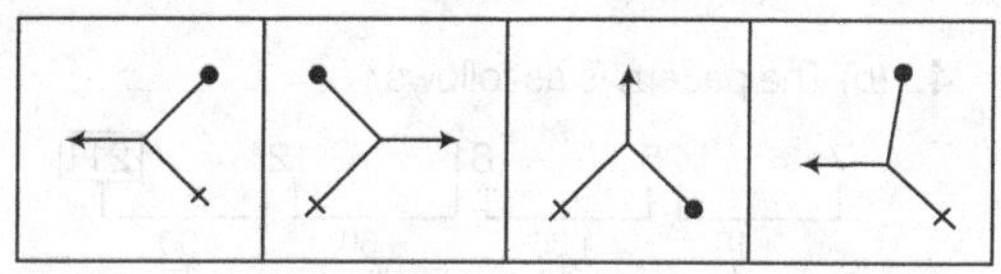

(a) (b) (c) (d)

50. Which one of the answer figures is the correct mirror image of the given figure?

Question Figure

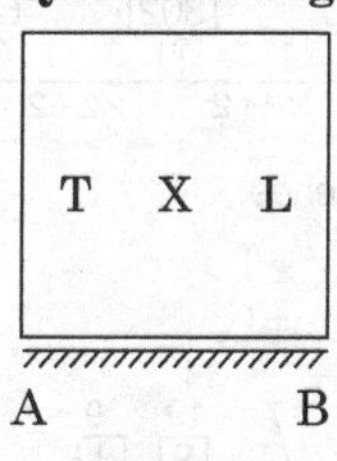

Answer Figures

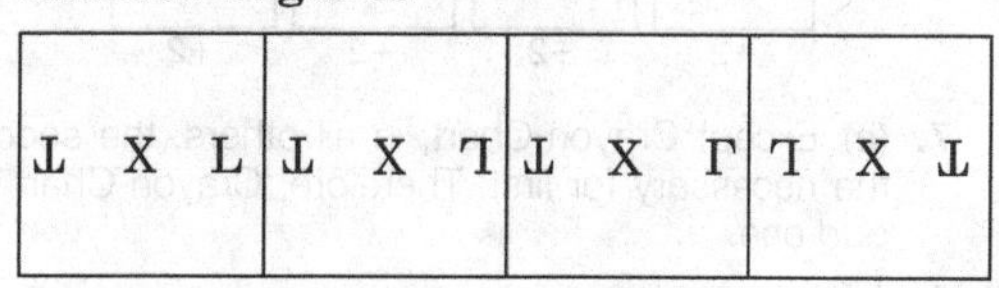

(a) (b) (c) (d)

Hints and Solutions

1. (*b*) As,

D H L P T X
↓−2 ↓−2 ↓−2 ↓−2 ↓−2 ↓−2
B F J N R V

Similarly,

C G K O S W
↓−2 ↓−2 ↓−2 ↓−2 ↓−2 ↓−2
A E I M Q U

2. (*a*) 'Alleviate' means 'to Reduce' and 'Aggravate' means 'to Intensify'. So, it is clearly a opposite words analogy and it is similar to 'Elastic' and 'Rigid' which are mutually opposite.

3. (*d*) As, 24 : 126 ; (5^2-1) (5^3+1) Similarly, 48 : 344 ; (7^2-1) (7^3+1)

4. (*b*) The pattern is as follows

7, 25, 61, 121, 211
+18, +36, +60, +90
18, 24, 30
+6, +6

5. (*d*) The pattern is as follows

17 → 36 → 74 → 150 → 302 → 606
×2+2, ×2+2, ×2+2, ×2+2, ×2+2

6. (*a*) There are two interwoven series.
The pattern is as follows

+1 +1 +1
1 16 3 17 5 18 7 19 9
A P C Q E R G S I
+2 +2 +2 +2

7. (*a*) Except Crayon-Chart, in all others, the second is the necessary for first. Therefore, Crayon-Chart is the odd one.

8. (*c*) As,

18 14 13 16 , 10 6 5 8
R N M P , J F E H
−4 −1 +3 , −4 −1 +3

18 16 15 17 , 8 4 3 6
R P O Q , H D C F
−2 −1 +2 , −4 −1 +3

Clearly, RPOQ follows a different pattern from others.

9. (c) All the others are materials used in a building.

10. (*b*) By using the letters of the given word, we cannot make the word 'FAULTY' because in the given word letter U is not present.

11. (*b*) The only required word = TRIM

12. (*a*) Workers are part of labour union but manager is different.

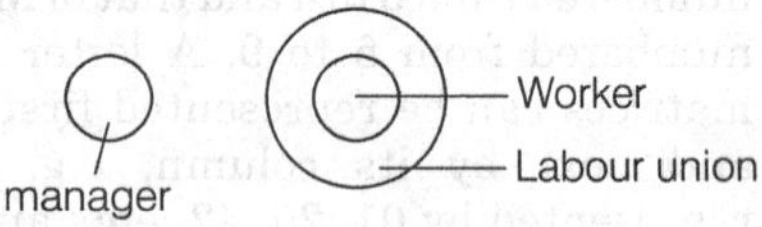

Solution (Q. Nos. 13-15) From the given information, we have to find the possible code for a particular word, such as

Cinderella shouted for rescue → pr co ly bu ...(i)
Rescue all the bugs → ke mt co rx ...(ii)
Bugs ate all carrots → vg rx ke sh ...(iii)
Carrots for pretty Cinderella → ly pr vg as ...(vi)

In Eqs. (i) and (ii), the word 'rescue' is common.
So, rescue → co
In Eqs. (iii) and (iv), the word 'carrot' is common.
So, carrot → vg
In Eqs. (i) and (iv), the words 'Cinderella' and 'for' are common.
So, for/Cinderella → ly/pr
So, it is clear from the Eq. (i),
'shouted' → bu
In Eqs. (ii) and (iii), the words 'all bugs' are common.
So, all/bugs → ke/rx
From Eq. (iii), it is clear that,
'ate' → sh
From Eq. (iv), it is clear that,
'pretty' → as
From Eq. (ii), it is clear that,
'the' → mt

13. (*c*) Either 'Cinderella' or 'for' stands for 'pr'.

14. (*e*) The code for 'the pretty' is 'as mt'.

15. (*e*) The code for 'bugs' is either 'ke' or 'rx'.

16. (*a*) According to operations in coded meaning the simplification becomes

$$8 \times 4 + 6 \div 3 - 4$$

Now, applying BODMAS in order to solve the simplification

$$8 \times 4 + 2 - 4 = 32 + 2 - 4 = 30$$

17. (*a*) As, $1+7+3+5+2+6=24$

$4+3+1+3+2+5=18$

Similarly, $2+5+3+4+7+1=22$

18. (*b*) As, $5\times3+1=16$

$16\times3+1=49$

$9\times3+2=29$

$29\times3+2=89$

Similarly, $15\times3+3=\boxed{48}$

$48\times3+3=147$

19. (*a*) The direction of Raju is as follows

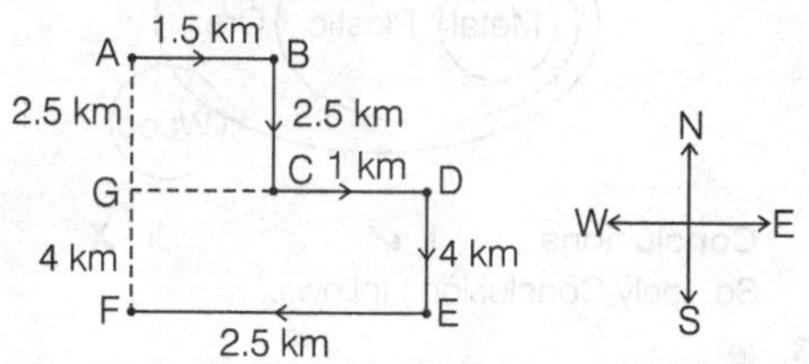

Let A is the starting point of Raju and F is the ending point.

Now, GC = AB = 1.5 km

and GF = DE = 4 km

Now, distance of Raju from his starting point

= AG + GF = 2.5 + 4 = 6.5 km

20. (*a*) At 4O'clock, there is 20 min of space between minute hand and hour hand.

So, angle difference = $20\times6°=120°$

To make it 90°, minute hand must move 30°.

Relative angle = $5\frac{1°}{2}$

$\therefore \frac{30}{5.5}=\frac{300}{55}=\frac{60}{11}=5\frac{5}{11}$ min past 4

Between 4 and 5 O' clock, minute hand makes another 90° with hour hand.

So, total angle to cover = 90° + 120° = 210°

Time to cover this distance = $\frac{210}{5.5}$

$=\frac{210\times10}{55}=\frac{420}{11}=38\frac{2}{11}$ min

Between 4 and 5 O' clock, right angle between hour hand and minute hand is measured twice one at $5\frac{5}{11}$ min past 4and another at $38\frac{2}{11}$min past 4.

Solution (Q. Nos. 21-23) According to given information, the seating arrangement is as follows

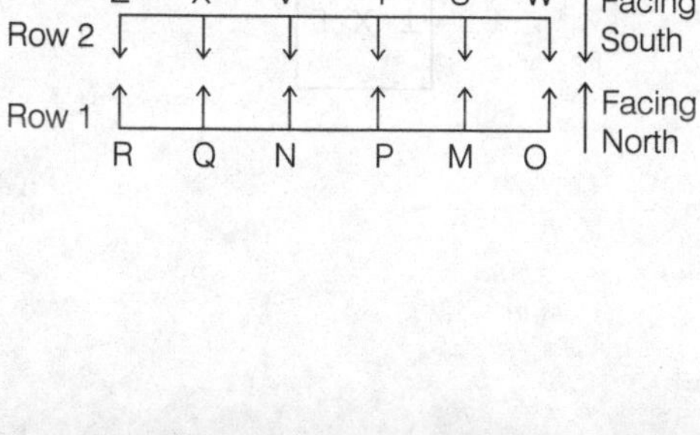

21. (*a*) None of the given statements is true.

22. (*a*) N is facing V.

23. (*c*) U is facing M.

24. (*b*) Alphabetical order of the given words is as below

Blue → Bluff → Blurt → Blush

25. (*a*) According to the question,

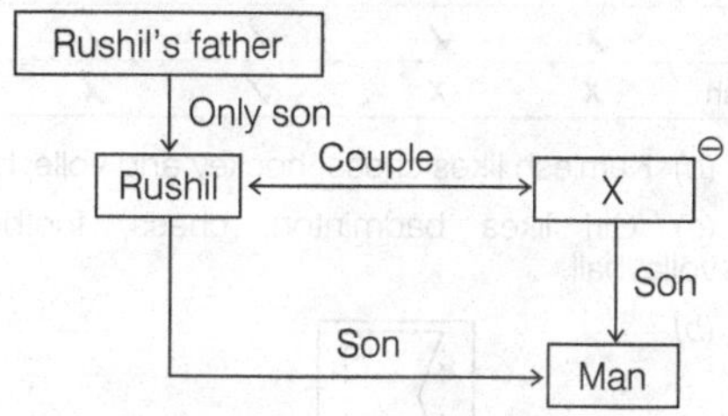

It is clear from the above diagram that *X* is the mother of man and she is also Rushil's wife, therefore man is the son of Rushil.

26. (*d*) The required region should be common to circle and triangle. Such region is marked as P and Q.

27. (*d*) Given, the average age of four boys five years ago = 9 yr

$\therefore$ Total age of four boys five years ago = $9\times4=36$ yr

Their present age = $36+5\times4=56$ yr

and average age of five boys = 15 yr

$\therefore$ Total age of five boys = $15\times5=75$ yr

$\therefore$ Present age of new boy = $75-56=19$ yr

28. (*c*) There are 17 circles.

29. (*b*) **Statement** $P\geq Q=R>S>T$

Conclusions

I. $P\geq T$ (it cannot follow, because $R>T$. If the conclusion was $P\geq R$, then it would be correct)

II. $T<Q$ (it follows)

So, only Conclusion II follows.

30. (*d*) **Statement** $L\leq M<N>O\geq P$

Conclusions

I. $M>O$ (it cannot follow because $M<N>O$)

II. $N\geq P$ (it cannot follow)

So, neither Conclusion I nor II follows.

Solution (Q. Nos. 31-32) According to the given information we can conclude that

$V>W>Z>X>Y>U$

W ↓ (Husband), U ↓ (Niece)

31. (*a*) V won the game and U got the lowest point.

32. (*d*) W is the husband of V and his position in the game on the basis of points is 2nd.

Solution (Q. Nos. 33-34) Given information can be summarised in the following table.

	Hockey	Volleyball	Badminton	Chess	Football
Ravish	✓	✓	✓	✗	✗
Kamlesh	✓	✓	✗	✓	✗
Suresh	✓	✗	✓	✗	✓
Giri	✗	✓	✓	✓	✓
Mukesh	✗	✗	✓	✗	✓

33. (*b*) Kamlesh likes chess, hockey and volleyball.

34. (*c*) Giri likes badminton, chess, football and volleyball.

35. (*b*)

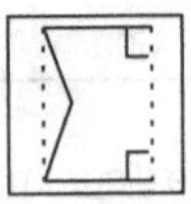

Hence, answer figure (b) is hidden/embeded in the question figure.

36. (c) According to the question,

Mohan > Kamal > Sachin > Ram ...(i)

and Kamal > Arun > Sachin ...(ii)

So, from Eqs. (i) and (ii),

Mohan > Kamal > Arun > Sachin > Ram ...(iii)

It is clear from Eq. (iii) that the second tallest is Kamal.

37. (c) Given equation is 25 A 37 C 2 B 4 R 1

According to the question, after putting signs,

$$25 + 37 \times 2 \div 4 - 1$$
$$= 62 \times 2 \div 4 - 1$$
$$= 124 \div 4 - 1$$
$$= 31 - 1 = 30$$

Solution (Q. Nos. 38-40) Here, each word of the input has been arranged in the alphabetical order giving preference to the word starting with small letter.

38. (c) **Input** Him and His either or her
***Step* I** and Him His either or her
***Step* II** and either Him His or her
***Step* III** and either her Him His or

39. (*d*) **Input** You are at fault on this
***Step* I** are you at fault on this
***Step* II** are at you fault on this
***Step* III** are at fault you on this
***Step* IV** are at fault on you this

40. (*d*) We cannot determine the input for the given step as the position of each word cannot definitely be known in the input.

41. (*e*)

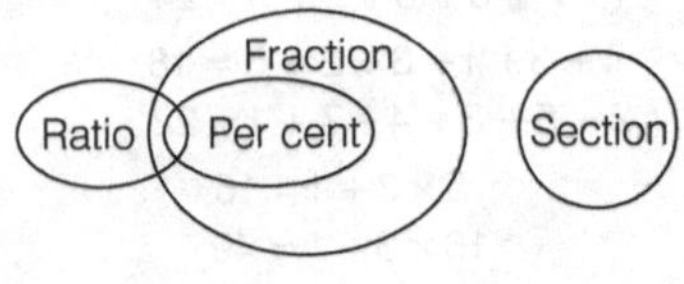

Conclusions I. ✔ II. ✔

So, both Conclusions I and II follow.

42. (a)

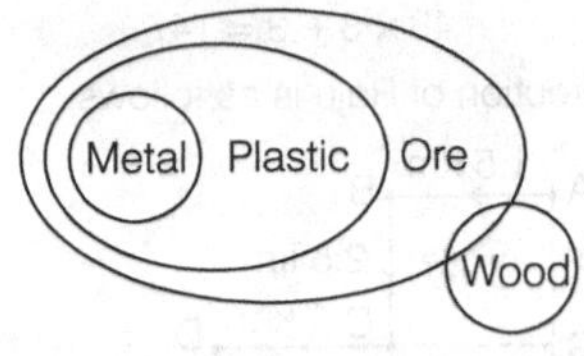

Conclusions I. ✔ II. ✗

So, only Conclusion I follows.

43. (*e*)

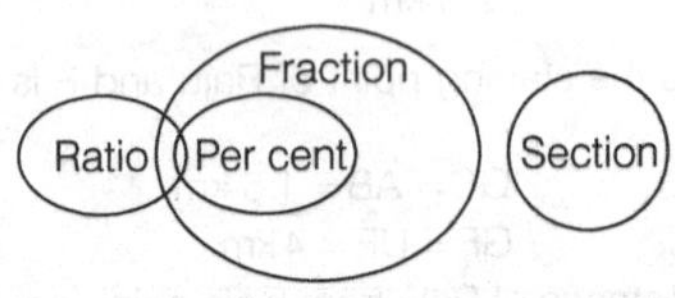

Conclusions I. ✔ II. ✔

So, both Conclusions I and II follow.

44. (*a*) Both Statements I and II are required to answer the question.

45. (c) F = 00, 12, 24, (31), 43
A = 01, 13, 20, (34), 42
I = 04, 10, (23), 32, 41
T = 59, 68, (76), 87, 95
H = 57, 65, (79), 86, 98

∴ FAITH = 31, 34, 23, 76, 79

46. (*b*) Here, Statement II is the cause and Statement I is its effect.

47. (*a*) Here, Statement I is the cause and Statement II is its effect.

48. (*a*) Here, Statement I is the cause and Statement II is its effect.

49. (*b*) If we proceed clockwise pin, head is followed by T-shaped design.
In option (b), head is not followed by T-shape design.

50. (c) The correct vertically inverted mirror image of the question figure is as follows

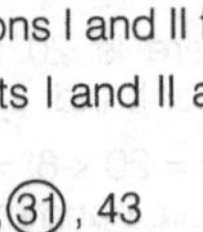

PRACTICE SET 2

1. In a certain code language, the word NUMERICAL is written as LMUIREACN. How will the word PUBLISHED be written in that language? **[FCI (Assistant) Grade III 2015]**

(a) DBUSLIHEP (b) DBUSILEHP
(c) DUBSLIEHP (d) DUBILSEHP

2. If 'DELHI' is coded as '73541' and 'CALCUTTA' as '82589662', then how will 'CALICUT' be coded? **[MAT 2012]**

(a) 5279431 (b) 5978213
(c) 8251896 (d) 8543691

3. Select the related numbers from the given alternatives.

NEWS : 14, 5, 23, 19 : : PAPER : ?

(a) 16, 5, 16, 1, 18
(b) 18, 5, 16, 1, 16
(c) 16, 1, 16, 5, 18
(d) 32, 2, 32, 10, 36

Direction (Q. Nos. 4-5) *In the following questions, select the missing number from the given responses.*

4. **[SSC (10+2) 2015]**

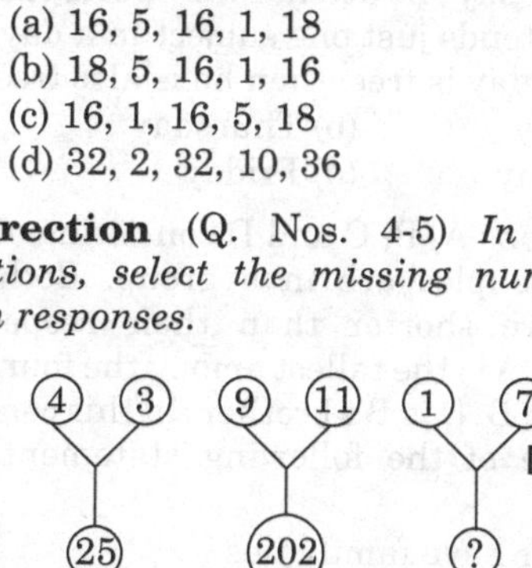

(a) 50 (b) 25
(c) 75 (d) 100

5.

2	7	8
7	5	3
3	8	?
42	280	120

(a) 4 (b) 5
(c) 6 (d) 7

6. Select the correct combination of mathematical signs to replace * signs and to balance the following equation

(8 * 7 * 6) * 5* 10.

(a) × − ÷ = (b) − × ÷ +
(c) + − ÷ × (d) × + = ÷

7. Select the related letters from the given alternatives. **[SSC (10+2) 2015]**

GFEH : RQPS : : LKJM : ?

(a) ONMP (b) VUWX
(c) LKNM (d) IHJG

8. What was the day of the week on 17th June, 1998 ?

(a) Monday (b) Tuesday
(c) Wednesday (d) Thursday

9. 'Umpire' is related to 'Match' in the same way as 'Judge' is related to

(a) Bar council (b) Lawyer
(c) Judgement (d) Lawsuit

Direction (Q. Nos. 10-11) *In the following questions, find the odd numbers/word from the given alternatives.*

10. **[SSC (CGL) Pre 2015]**

(a) Eyes
(b) Nose
(c) Ears
(d) Vestibular

11. (a) 9, 49 (b) 13, 121
(c) 10, 61 (d) 7, 25 **[SSC (CPO) 2013]**

12. How many such pairs of letters are there in the word MEDICAL each of which has as many letters between them in the word as in the English alphabet? **[NICL (Assistant) Cadre III 2015]**

(a) None
(b) One
(c) Two
(d) Three
(e) More the three

13. The positions of the first and the fifth digits of the number 81943275 are interchanged. Similarly, the positions of the second and the sixth digits are interchanged and so on till the fourth and the eighth digits. Which of the following will be the third digit from the right end after the rearrangement?

(a) 1 (b) 9
(c) 2 (d) 4
(e) None of these

14. Which one of the given responses would be a meaningful order of the following words?

(i) Diagnosis (ii) Doctor
(iii) Sick (iv) Treatment
(v) Recovery

(a) (ii), (i), (iii), (iv), (v)
(b) (iv), (v), (i), (iii), (ii)
(c) (i), (ii), (iii), (iv), (v)
(d) (iii), (ii), (i), (iv), (v)

Direction (Q. Nos. 15-17) *Study the following information to answer the given questions.*

Eight people - K, L, M, N, O, P, Q and R are seated in a straight line facing North but not necessarily in the same order. L sits third from the left end of the line. Only three people sit between L and R.

O sits to the immediate left of Q. Only one person sits between M and Q. P sits third to the left of N. L is not an immediate neighbour of K.

15. What is the position of Q with respect to P?

(a) Second to the left
(b) Third to the left
(c) Second to the right
(d) Third to the right
(e) Fifth to the left

16. Which of the following pairs represents persons seated at the two extreme ends of the line?

(a) L, K (b) Q, R
(c) Q, N (d) O, N
(e) O, R

17. How many persons are seated between M and R?

(a) Two (b) Four
(c) One (d) Three
(e) More than four

18. Study the given figure and answer the question given below. How many teachers are neither authors nor singers? **[SSC (CPO) 2013]**

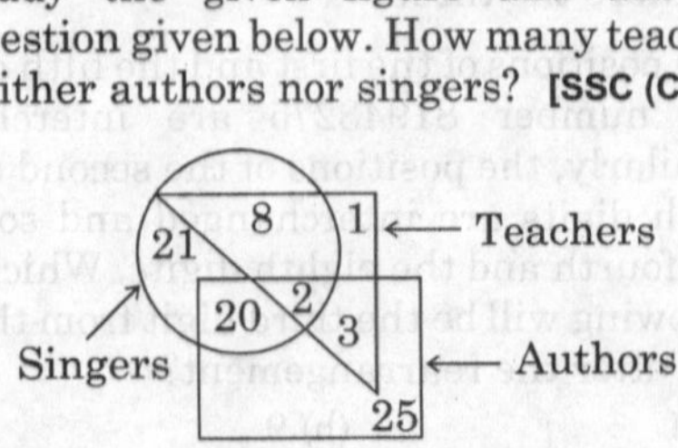

(a) 1 (b) 8
(c) 2 (d) 3

Direction (Q. Nos. 19-20) *In the following questions, a series is given, with one term missing. Choose the correct alternative from the given ones that will complete the series.*

19. SHG, RIF, QJE, PKD,? **[SSC (CGL) Pre 2014]**

(a) NME (b) NLB
(c) OLE (d) OLC

20. 10, 9, 16, 45, 176, ?

(a) 815 (b) 222
(c) 555 (d) 875

21. Examine the following statements:

(i) George attends Music classes on Monday.
(ii) He attends Mathematics classes on Wednesday
(iii) His Literature classes are not on Friday.
(iv) He attends History classes on the day following the day of his Mathematics classes.
(v) On Tuesday , he attends his Sports classes.

If he attends just one subject in a day and his Sunday is free, then he is also free on

(a) Monday (b) Thursday
(c) Saturday (d) Friday

22. Four persons A, B, C and D consisting of two married couples are in a group. Both the women are shorter than their respective husbands. A is the tallest among the four. C is taller than B. D is B's brother. In this context, which one of the following statements is correct?

(a) All four have family ties
(b) B is the shortest among the four
(c) C is taller than D
(d) None of the above

23. In a cricket team, Dhoni is taller than Virat but not as tall as Raina, Rohit is shorter than Dhoni but taller than Shikhar. Who among them is the shortest? **[NIFT (PG) 2014]**

(a) Dhoni (b) Virat
(c) Shikhar (d) Cannot be determined
(e) None of these

Direction (Q. Nos 24-25) *Read the following information carefully and answer the questions given below.*

There are six children playing football, namely P, Q, R, S, T and U. P and T are brothers, U is the sister of T. R is the only son of P's uncle. Q and S are the daughters of the only brother of R's father.

24. How is R related to U?
(a) Cousin (b) Brother
(c) Son (d) Uncle

25. How many male players are there?
(a) One (b) Three
(c) Four (d) Five

26. Find the correct group of signs to solve the equation.

24 * 16 * 8 * 32

(a) ÷ − = (b) − + =
(c) × ÷ = (d) + − =

27. After starting from a point, A walks 3 km towards East, that turning to his left he moves 3 km. After this, he again turns left and moves 3 km. In which direction is A from his starting point? **[NICL (Assistant) 2015]**
(a) North (b) East
(c) West (d) South
(e) None of these

28. Which number is on the face opposite to face having number 1 ?

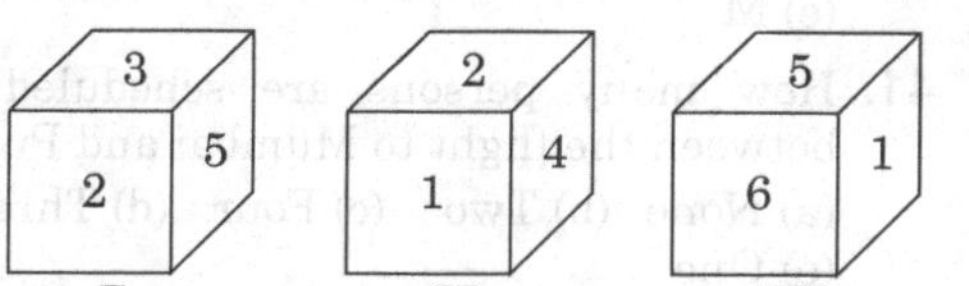

(I) (II) (III)

(a) 2 (b) 3
(c) 4 (d) 5

29. If +, −, |, ϕ, × and i stand respectively for greater than, not less than, less than, not greater than, equal to and not equal to, then x i y + z may give **[UPPSC (RO) 2014]**
(a) x + y i z (b) x × y | z
(c) x i y ϕ z (d) x − y ϕ z

Direction (Q. Nos. 30-31) *In these questions, relationship between different elements is shown in the statements. These statements are followed by two conclusions.*

Give answer
(a) if only Conclusion I follows
(b) if only Conclusion II follows
(c) if either Conclusion I or II follows
(d) if neither Conclusion I nor II follows
(e) if both Conclusions I and II follow

30. Statements $H > J = K$
$K \geq L$,
$L > T$,
$T < V$

Conclusions I. $K > T$
II. $L \leq H$

31. Statements $A \leq B = C$,
$D > C = E$

Conclusions I. $E \geq A$
II. $A < D$

Direction (Q. Nos. 32-33) *Study the following information carefully and answer the given question.*

A word arrangement machine when given an input line of words, rearranges them following a particular rule in each step. The following is the illustration of the input and the steps of arrangement.

Input Vani is the most beautiful girl on earth
***Step* I** beautiful Vani is the most girl on earth
***Step* II** beautiful earth Vani is the most girl on
***Step* III** beautiful earth girl Vani is the most on
***Step* IV** beautiful earth girl is Vani the most on
***Step* V** beautiful earth girl is most Vani the on
***Step* VI** beautiful earth girl is most on Vani the
***Step* VII** beautiful earth girl is most on the Vani

Since, the words are already arranged, the machine stops after this step. Otherwise the machine may carry on its logic until the words get fully arranged.

32. Input 'is you are again famous on this'. Find the Step III.
(a) again are famous is you on this
(b) on this you is famous are again
(c) this on you is famous are again
(d) famous this on you is are again
(e) None of the above

33. Step IV of an input is 'option pen rose Seema tape yolk', what will be the input?
(a) pen option rose tape Seema yolk
(b) yolk Seema tape rose option pen
(c) tape Seema yolk rose option pen
(d) Cannot be determined
(e) None of the above

Direction (Q. Nos. 34-36) *In each question below are three statements followed by two conclusions numbered* I *and* II. *You have to take the two given statements to be true even if they seem to be at variance from commonly known facts and then decide which of the given conclusions logically follows from the given statements disregarding commonly known facts.* **[NICL (AO) 2015]**

Give answer

(a) if only Conclusion I follows
(b) if only Conclusion II follows
(c) if either Conclusion I or II follows
(d) if neither Conclusion I nor II follows
(e) if both Conclusions I and II follow

34. Statements All dogs are monkeys.
No monkeys is a cat.
Conclusions I. No dog is a cat.
II. No cat is a dog.

35. Statements Some phones are watches.
All watches are guns.
Conclusions I. All guns are watches.
II. Some guns are phones.

36. Statements All umbrellas are aeroplanes.
Some aeroplanes are birds.
Conclusions I. Some umbrellas are birds.
II. Some birds are umbrellas.

Direction (Q. Nos 37-41) *Study the following information to answer the given questions.* **[NICL (AO) 2014]**

Seven different people *viz.* J, K, L, M, N, O and P have to fly to different destinations *viz.* Delhi, Ahmedabad, Mumbai, Chennai, Pune, Lucknow and Chandigarh but not necessarily in the same order. Each one of them flies on a different day of a week starting from Monday and ending on Sunday of the same week.

- P flies on Wednesday. The one who flies on Friday flies to Chennai.
- Only one person flies between P and J.
- Only two people flying between M and the one flying to Pune. The one who flies to Pune flies after M. M does not have his flight on Monday.
- Only three people have their flights between the people flying to Pune and Chandigarh.
- O flies immediately after the one flying to Mumbai. J does not fly to Mumbai. O does not fly to Pune.
- Only one person has his flight between O and L.
- The person flying to Delhi flies immediately after the person flying to Lucknow.
- K does not fly to Delhi.

37. Who amongst the following flies to Ahmedabad?
(a) J (b) M (c) K (d) P
(e) O

38. On which of the following days does the one flying to Lucknow have his flight?
(a) Monday (b) Thursday
(c) Tuesday (d) Saturday
(e) Wednesday

39. On which of the following days does N have his flight?
(a) Sunday (b) Thursday
(c) Monday (d) Saturday
(e) Tuesday

40. Who amongst the following has his flight exactly between the days on which O and L have their respective flights?
(a) N (b) J (c) P (d) K
(e) M

41. How many persons are scheduled to fly between the flight to Mumbai and Pune?
(a) None (b) Two (c) Four (d) Three
(e) One

Direction (Q. Nos. 42-43) *Each of the following questions below consists of a question and two statements numbered* I *and* II *given below it. You have to decide whether the data provided in the statements are sufficient to answer the question.*

Give answer

(a) if the data in Statement I alone are sufficient to answer the question, while the data in Statement II alone are not sufficient to answer the question
(b) if the data in Statement II alone are sufficient to answer the question, while the data in Statement I alone are not sufficient to answer the question
(c) if the data either in Statement I alone or Statement II alone are sufficient to answer the question
(d) if the data in both the Statements I and II together are not sufficient to answer the question
(e) if the data in both the Statements I and II are together necessary to answer the question

42. Seventeen people are standing in a straight line facing South. What is Bhavna's position from the left end of the line?

I. Sandeep is standing second to the left of Sheetal. Only five people stand between Sheetal and the one who is standing at the extreme right end of the line. Four people stand between Sandeep and Bhavna.

II. Anita is standing fourth to the left of Sheetal. Less than three people are standing between Bhavna and Anita.

43. How is D related to M?

I. D has two brothers and one sister.

II. Brother of M is married to D's sister.

Direction (Q. Nos. 44-45) *Read the paragraphs carefully and determine the main point the author is trying to make. What conclusion can be drawn from the argument? Each paragraph is followed by four statements. One statement supports the author's argument better than the others do.* **[SNAP 2014]**

44. Now-a-days people are so busy in their work that they do not take care of their health. A lot of diseases like diabetes, arthritis, heart attack, blood pressure are increasing due to unhealthy lifestyle.

People do not find time to exercise. Stress is continuously increasing. The fast food is quick, easy and tastes better but it is not healthy. Habits like smoking and drinking alcohol have many side effects.

Polluted city environment has also negative impact on the health of citizens. To live happy and healthy life, it is important to take care of oneself.

(a) Now-a-days, everybody smokes and drinks.
(b) Diseases are increasing only because of pollution.
(c) People are happy and stress free because their life is too busy.
(d) Current city environment, life style and habits are affecting health of citizens.

45. Diwali is a festival of lights; which signifies that good will always be better than evil. In the present day, many people have developed a lot of negativity in their minds and hearts, which has led to high corruption and higher crime rates.

Value based education is the need of the day to eliminate darkness of cruelty, selfishness and greed and bring the light of wisdom, peace, kindness, truthfulness, right attitude, hard work and cooperation. Mahatma Gandhi also said that we should eradicate sins from hearts not the sinners. If a society has people with good heart, then it will definitely flourish.

(a) Now-a-days, nobody is good.
(b) Now-a-days everybody is corrupt and criminal.
(c) Value based education can save the from crime and corruption.
(d) It is not possible to fight against corruption as everybody is corrupt.

46. Select the missing figure from the given responses.

Question Figures

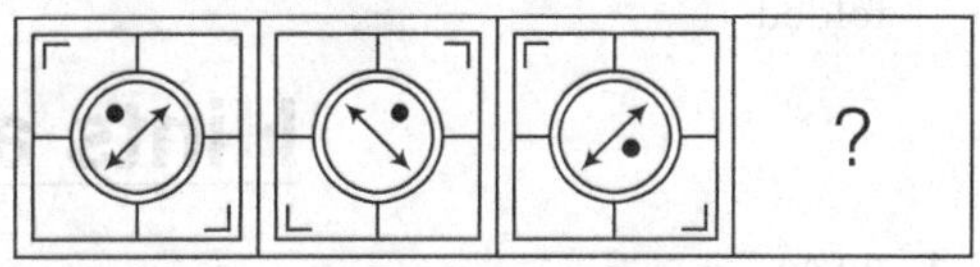

1 2 3

Answer Figures

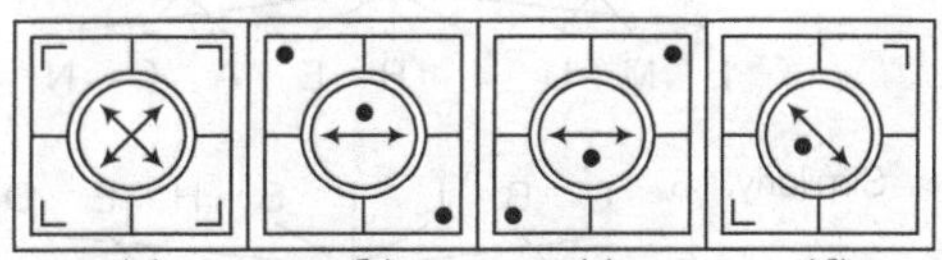

(a) (b) (c) (d)

47. The time in a clock is quarter past twelve. If the hour hand points to the East, then which is the direction opposite to the minute hand?

(a) South-West (b) South
(c) West (d) North

48. Identify the missing part of the question figure and select it from given answer figures.

Question Figure

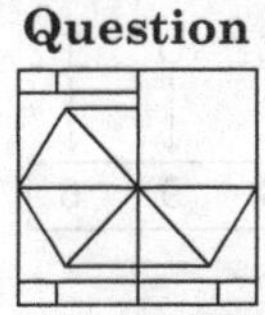

Answer Figures

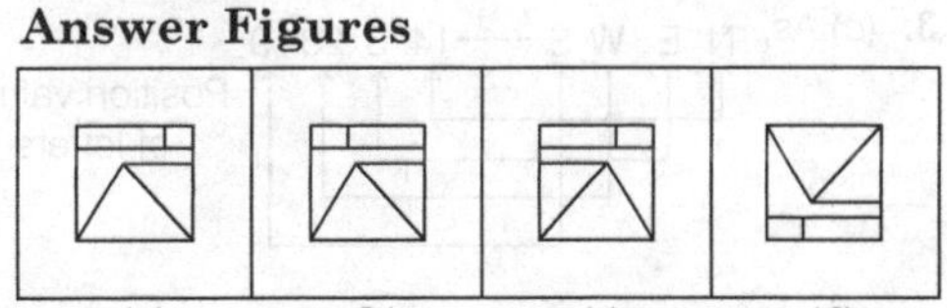

(a) (b) (c) (d)

49. Select the answer figure in which the given question figure is hidden/embedded.

Question Figure

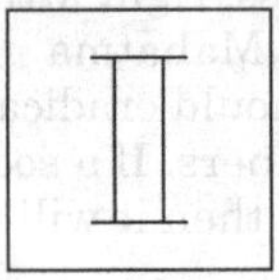

Answer Figures

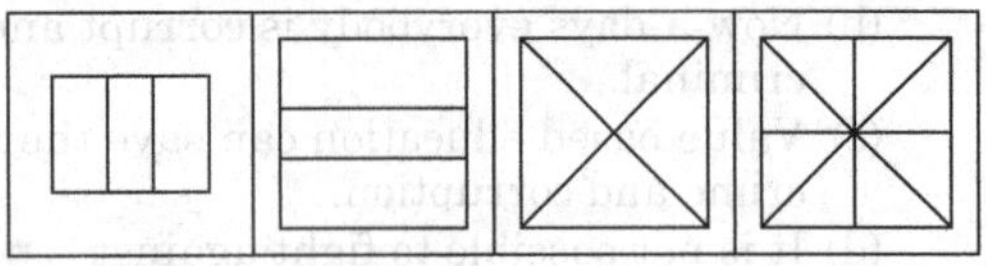

(a) (b) (c) (d)

50. In this question, a piece of paper is folded and then cut as shown below. The dotted lines shown are the portion which have been folded. The curve arrow shows the directions of folding. And the number of scissors beneath the figure show the number of portions cut. From the given responses, indicate how it will appear when opened. The opening is in the same order as folding.

Question Figures

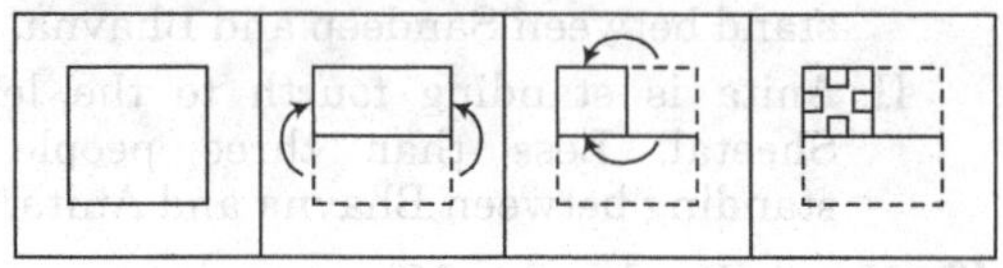

Answer Figures

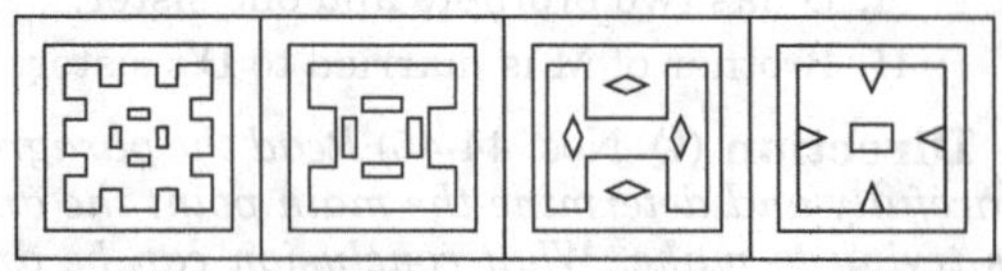

(a) (b) (c) (d)

Hints and Solutions

1. (*b*) As,

N U M E R I C A L

L M U I R E A C N

Similarly, P U B L I S H E D

D B U S I L E H P

So, PUBLISHED will be written as DBUSILEHP.

2. (c) As,

D E L H → 7 3 5 4 and I → 1; C A L C U T T A → 8 2 5 8 9 6 6 2

Similarly, C A L I C U T → 8 2 5 1 8 9 6

∴ CALICUT ⇒ 8251896

3. (*c*) As, N E W S ⟶ 14 5 23 19 Position values of letters

Similarly,

P A P E R ⟶ 16 1 16 5 18 Position values of letters

Second part is the position of the letters written in first part.

4. (*a*) As, in 1st figure,

$$4^2 + 3^2 = 16 + 9 = 25$$

In 2nd figure, $9^2 + 11^2 = 81 + 121 = 202$

In the same way,

In 3rd figure, $1^2 + 7^2 = 1 + 49 = 50$

5. (*b*) 1st column,

$$2 \times 7 \times 3 = 42$$

2nd column, $7 \times 5 \times 8 = 280$

3rd column, $8 \times 3 \times ? = 120$

$$\Rightarrow \quad ? = \frac{120}{24} = 5$$

6. (*a*) Given equation, (8 * 7 * 6) * 5 * 10

Now, replacing * sign with the mathematical sign of option (a).

$$(8 \times 7 - 6) \div 5 = 10$$

$$(56 - 6) \div 5 = 10 \quad \text{[using VBODMAS rule]}$$

$$50 \div 5 = 10$$

$$10 = 10$$

7. (*a*) As,

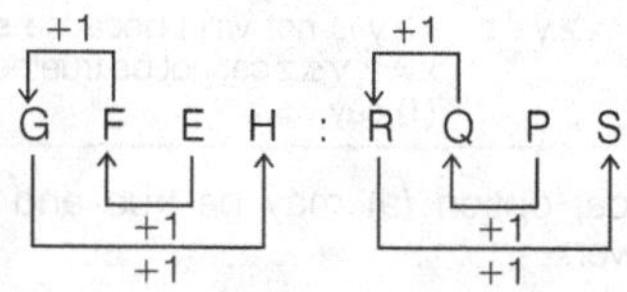

Similarly,

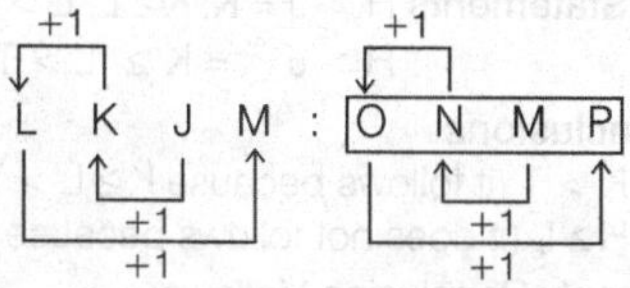

8. (*c*) 17th June, 1998

= (year1997+Period from 01.01.1998 to 17.06.1998)

Odd days in 1600 years = 0 odd day

Odd days in 300 years = $(5 \times 3) = 15 = 1$ odd day

97 years has 24 leap years and 73 ordinary years.

Number of odd days in 97 years = $(24 \times 2 + 73)$

$= 121$

$\Rightarrow \quad \frac{121}{7} = 17\frac{2}{7} = 2$ odd days

Jan Feb March April May June

31 + 28 + 31 + 30 + 31 + 17 = 168 days

∴ 168 days = 24 weeks = 0 odd day

∴ Total number of odd days = (0 + 1 + 2 + 0) = 3

Hence, 17th June, 1998 was Wednesday.

9. (*d*) 'Umpire' is required to give decision in 'Match'. Likewise 'Judge' is required to give decision in a 'Lawsuit'.

10. (*d*) Except vestibular, all others are the sense organs.

11. (*c*) As, $9 - 2 = 7 \rightarrow 7^2 = 49$,

$13 - 2 = 11 \rightarrow 11^2 = 121$,

$10 - 2 = 8 \rightarrow 8^2 = 64 \neq 61$,

$7 - 2 = 5 \rightarrow 5^2 = 25$

Thus, option (c) is odd.

12. (*e*) As,

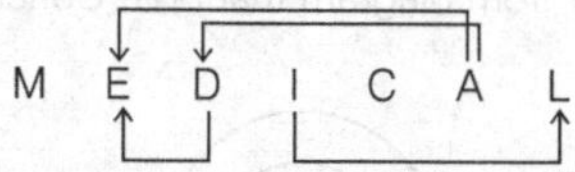

Hence, number of such pairs IL, AD, AE and DE i.e. four pairs.

13. (*a*) Let us see

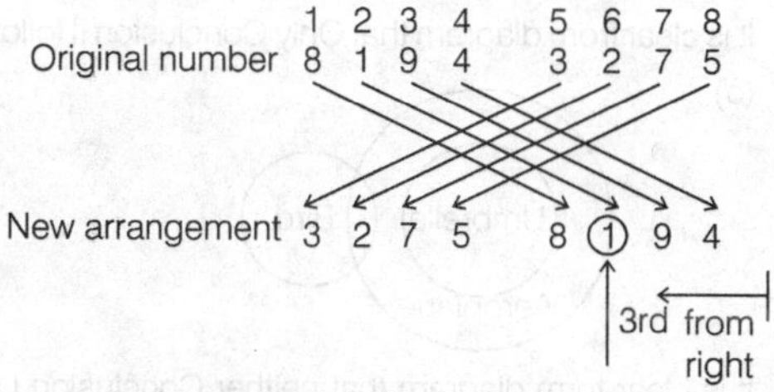

So, the required digit is 1.

14. (*d*) Meaningful order of words.

(iii) Sick

↓

(ii) Doctor

↓

(i) Diagnosis

↓

(iv) Treatment

↓

(v) Recovery

Solution (Q. Nos. 15-17) According to the given information, the arrangement is as following

O Q L M P K R N ↑ Facing North

15. (*b*) The position of Q with respect to P is third to the left.

16. (*d*) Pair (O, N) represents persons seated at the two extreme ends of the line.

17. (*a*) There are two persons seated between M and R.

18. (*a*) The area represented by teachers who are neither authors nor singers is 1.

19. (*d*) The pattern is as follows

$S \xrightarrow{-1} R \xrightarrow{-1} Q \xrightarrow{-1} P \xrightarrow{-1} O$

$H \xrightarrow{+1} I \xrightarrow{+1} J \xrightarrow{+1} K \xrightarrow{+1} L$

$G \xrightarrow{-1} F \xrightarrow{-1} E \xrightarrow{-1} D \xrightarrow{-1} C$

Hence, in the above series, OLC will come in place of question mark.

20. (*d*) The pattern is as follows

10 → 9 → 16 → 45 → 176 → (875)

×1 − 1, ×2 − 2, ×3 − 3, ×4 − 4, ×5 − 5

21. (*d*) From the given information, his week schedule can be concluded as

Days	Classes
Monday	Music
Tuesday	Sports
Wednesday	Mathematics
Thursday	History
Friday	Free
Saturday	Literature
Sunday	Free

Apart from Sunday George is also free on Friday.

22. (*b*) Given, A is the tallest among the four. Hence, A is male, D is also male, as D is the brother of B. Hence, B and C are females; D is the husband of C; D is shorter than A and is taller than his wife C. It is given that C is taller than B. Thus, B is the shortest.

So, only option (b) is correct.

23. (*d*) The data is inadequate because it is not given that who is taller between Virat and Shikhar . Hence, answer cannot be determined.

Solution (Q. Nos. 24-25) Let us draw the family diagram with the help of given information.

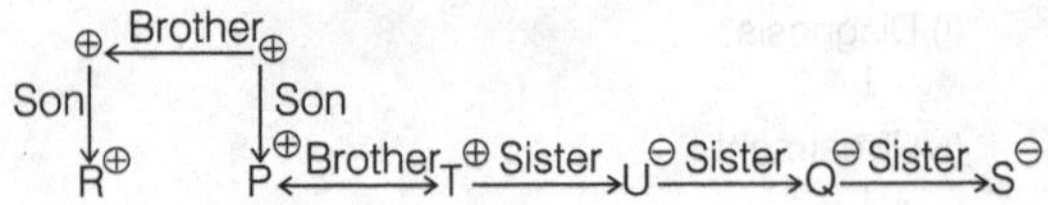

24. (*a*) R is the cousin of U.

25. (*b*) Clearly, there are three male players among them.

26. (*d*) Given equation is 24* 16*8*32

After applying option (d)'s mathematical symbols

$\Rightarrow \quad 24 + 16 - 8 = 32$

$\Rightarrow \quad 40 - 8 = 32$

$\Rightarrow \quad 32 = 32$

27. (a) According to the question,

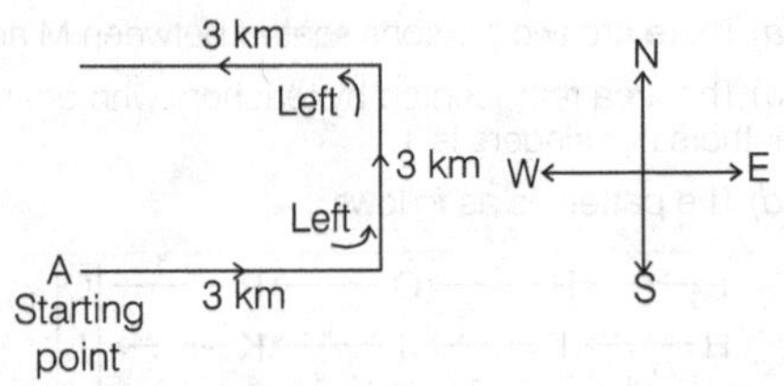

From the above direction diagram, it is clear that A is in North from his starting point.

28. (*b*) In the given figures, we observe that adjacent to face 1 are 2, 4, 5, 6

We know that, adjacent faces are not opposite faces.

Therefore, x remaining face i.e. 3 is the opposite face to the face having number 1.

29. (a) Symbol and given interpretation

$+ \rightarrow$ greater than ($>$)

$- \rightarrow$ not less than ($\geq$)

$| \rightarrow$ less than ($<$)

$\phi \rightarrow$ not greater than ($\leq$)

$\times \rightarrow$ equal to ($=$) and

$i \rightarrow$ not equal ($\neq$)

Hence, statement x i y+ z $\Rightarrow x \neq y > z$ statement (1)

Now, observing the options to check which of the given may be valid

Option (a)	$x > y \neq z$	Here, $x > y$ which is possible because in the given statement (1) $x \neq y$, although x can also be less than y and $y \neq z$ is also followed in $y \neq z$.
Option (b)	$x = y < z$	$x = y$ is not possible because in statement (1) it say $x \neq y$.
Option (c)	$x \neq y \leq z$	$x \neq y$ is followed as in statement (1) but $y \leq z$ is not valid because $y > z$ given in statement (1).
Option (d)	$x \geq y \leq z$	$x \geq y$ is not valid because statement (1) say $x \neq y$, $y \leq z$ cannot be true because statement (1) say $y > z$.

Hence, option (a) may be true and hence it is the answer.

30. (*a*) **Statements** $H > J = K, K \geq L, L > T$ and $T < V$

$\therefore \quad H > J = K \geq L > T < V$

Conclusions

I. $K > T$ (it follows because $K \geq L > T$)

II. $H \geq L$ (it does not follows because $H > J = K \geq L$)

So, only Conclusion I follows.

31. (*e*) **Statements** $A \leq B = C$ and $D > C = E$

$\therefore \quad A \leq B = C = E < D$

Conclusions

I. $E \geq A$ (it follows because $E = C = B \geq A$)

II. $A < D$ (it follows because $D > B \geq A$)

So, both Conclusions I and II follow.

Solution (Q. Nos. 32-33) In this problem, we notice that

(i) it is a forward order alphabetical arrangement.

(ii) arrangement takes place from left side only.

32. (*a*) **Input** 'is you are again famous on this'

***Step* I** again is you are famous on this

***Step* II** again are is you famous on this

***Step* III** again are famous is you on this

Hence, option (a) is the correct answer.

33. (*d*) Option (d) is the correct answer as in the arrangement problem previous steps cannot be determined (see Rule B)

34. (*e*)

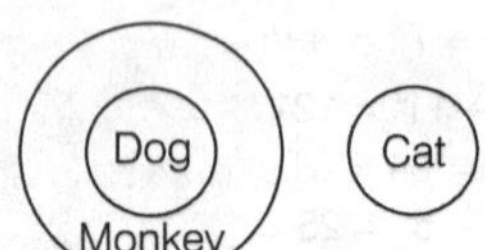

It is clear from diagram that both Conclusions I and II follow.

35. (*b*)

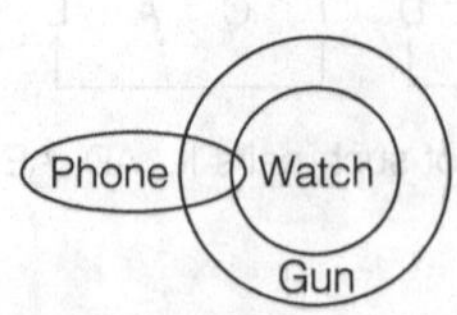

It is clear from diagram that Only Conclusion II follows.

36. (*d*)

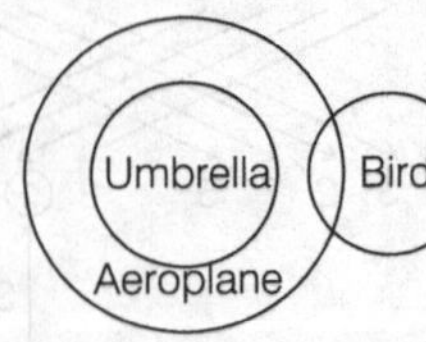

It is clear form diagram that neither Conclusion I nor II follows.

Solution (Q. Nos. 37-41) According to the given information, the arrangement is as shown below.

People	Day	Destination
J	Monday	Lucknow
N	Tuesday	Delhi
P	Wednesday	Chandigarh
M	Thursday	Mumbai
O	Friday	Chennai
K	Saturday	Ahmedabad
L	Sunday	Pune

37. (c) K flies to Ahmedabad.

38. (*a*) The one who flying to Lucknow have his flight on Monday.

39. (*e*) N have his flight on Tuesday.

40. (*d*) K has his flight exactly between the days on which O and L have their respective flights.

41. (*b*) Two persons are scheduled to fly between the flight to Mumbai and Pune.

42. (*e*) From Statements I and II,

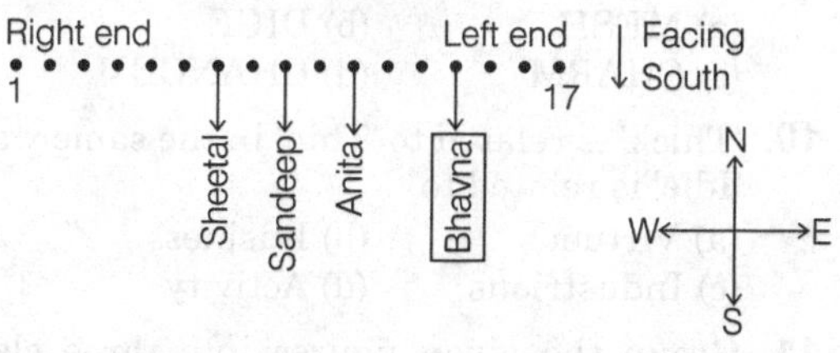

Thus, position of Bhavna can be found out by using both of the statements.

43. (*d*) From Statement I,

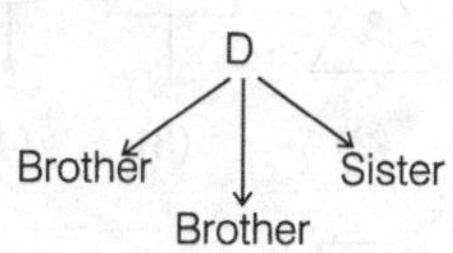

Statement I is insufficient in itself.

From Statement II,

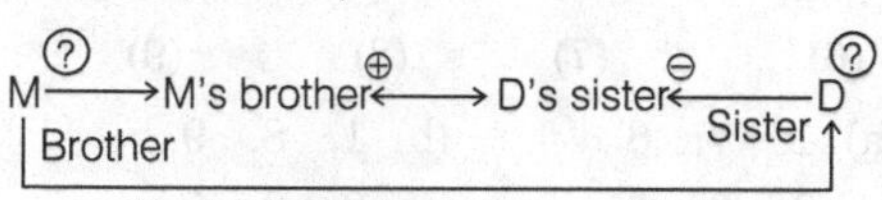

No definite relation is the possible as gender of both M and D are unknown

So, Statement II is also insufficient.

Further, no relation is possible from Statements I and II also.

So, both statements are insufficient to answer the question.

44. (*d*) Argument, current city environment, life style and habits are affecting health of citizens, is better than other.

45. (*c*) Argument, value based education can save the society from crime and corruption, is better than other.

46. (*d*) Clearly, in questions figures (1) to (2) the entire design is rotated through 90° in clockwise direction.

So, option (d) will follow the pattern of question figures.

47. (d) Time quarter past twelve means that the time is 12:15.

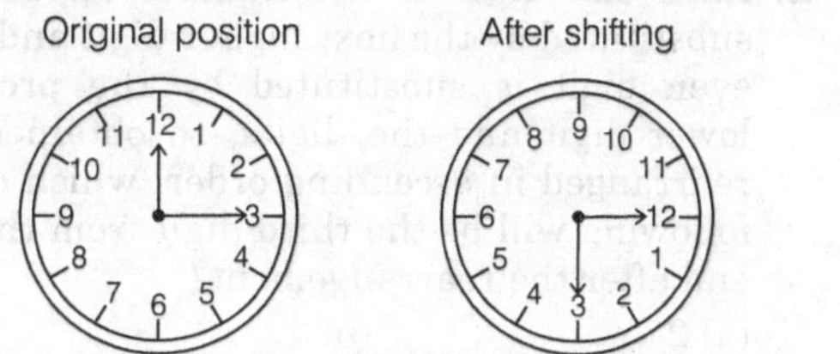

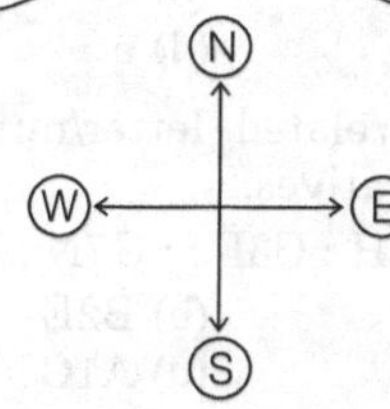

Hence, when hour hand is pointing towards East, then the minute hand is pointing towards South.

So, the direction opposite to minute hand is North.

48. (*c*) Option (c) will complete the given pattern as follow.

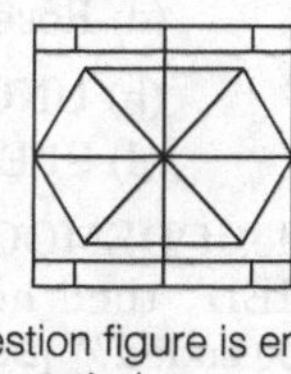

49. (*a*) Clearly, question figure is embedded in answer figure (a) as shown below

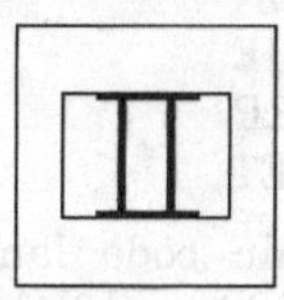

50. (*a*) After folding and cutting the paper, answer figure (a) will appear.

PRACTICE SET 3

1. Select the related word from the given alternatives.

Palaeontology : Fossil : : Phrenology : ? **[SSC (CGL) Pre 2015]**

(a) Pancreas (b) Thyroid
(c) Lungs (d) Skull

2. Each odd digit in the number 5263187 is substituted by the next higher digit and each even digit is substituted by the previous lower digit and the digits, so obtained are rearranged in ascending order, which of the following will be the third digit from the left end after the rearrangement?

(a) 2 (b) 4
(c) 5 (d) 6

3. Select the related letter/number from the given alternatives.

D4H : C3F : : G7N : ?

(a) F6M (b) B2E
(c) I9R (d) A1C

Direction (Q. Nos. 4-5) *In the following questions, find the odd letters / word from the given alternatives.*

4. (a) Marigold (b) Tulip **[SSC (CPO) 2015]**
(c) Lotus (d) Rose

5. (a) RKD (b) UNG
(c) MTF (d) SLE

6. In a certain code, if 'DEMOCRACY' is written as 'YCARCOMED', then how will the word PRESIDENT be coded? **[BSSC (CGL) Pre 2015]**

(a) EIETPRSDN
(b) NDSRPTEIE
(c) TNEDISERP
(d) RSDNPEIET

7. If in a certain code language 'GOAL' is written as '5139' and 'LAME' is written as '9327', then how will 'MOLE' be written in that language?

(a) 2197 (b) 2917
(c) 3197 (d) 2157
(e) None of these

8. From the given four positions of a single dice, find the colour at the face opposite to the face having red colour.

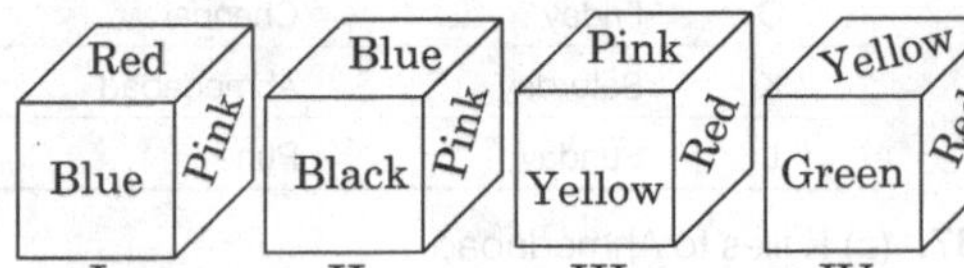

I II III IV

(a) Yellow (b) Pink
(c) Green (d) Black

9. From the given alternative words, select the word which cannot be formed using the letters of the word given below. **[BSSC (CGL) Pre 2015]**

MERCHANDISE

(a) MESH (b) DICE
(c) CHARM (d) CHANCE

10. 'Thick' is related to 'Thin' in the same way as 'Idle' is related to

(a) Virtuous (b) Business
(c) Industrious (d) Activity

11. Group the given figures into three classes using each figure only once.

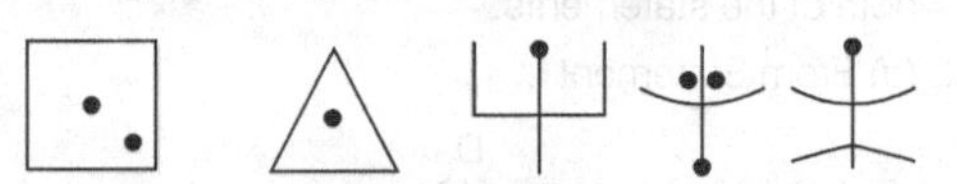

(1) (2) (3) (4) (5)

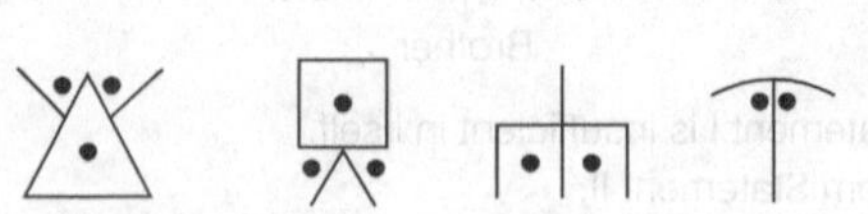

(6) (7) (8) (9)

(a) 1, 7, 8
2, 6, 5
3, 4, 9

(b) 1, 8, 9
2, 3, 5
4, 6, 7

(c) 2, 3, 5
1, 7, 8
4, 6, 9

(d) 2, 6, 7
1, 3, 4
5, 8, 9

Direction (Q. Nos. 12-13) *Read the following information carefully and then answer the questions that follow.*

A group of seven singers, facing the audience, are standing in a line on the stage as follow.

I. D is to the right of C.
II. F is standing beside G.
III. B is to the left of F.
IV. E is to the left of A.
V. C and B have one person between them.
IV. A and D have one person between them.

12. Who is on the extreme right?
(a) D (b) F (c) G (d) E

13. If we start counting from the left, then on which number is C?
(a) 1st (b) 2nd (c) 3rd (d) 5th

14. Some equations are solved on the basis of a certain system. On the same basis, find out the correct answer for the unsolved equation.
4 – 5 – 1 = 514, 3 – 5 – 6 = 563, 0 – 6 – 8 = ?
[SSC (CGL) Pre 2015]
(a) 860 (b) 680 (c) 806 (d) 068

15. If Neena says, "Anita's father Raman is the only son of my father-in-law, Mahipal", then how is Bindu, who is the sister of Anita, related to Mahipal?
(a) Niece (b) Daughter
(c) Wife (d) Granddaughter

16. Select the missing number from the given responses. **[SSC (Steno) 2011]**

36	64	100
6	8	10
12	16	?

(a) 10 (b) 20 (c) 22 (d) 110

17. P, Q, R, S, T and U are 6 members of a family in which there are two married couples. T, a teacher, is married to a doctor who is mother of R and U. Q, the lawyer, is married to P. P has one son and one grandson. Of the two married ladies one is a housewife. There is also one student and one male engineer in the family. Which of the following is true about the granddaughter of the family?
(a) She is a lawyer (b) She is an engineer
(c) She is a student (d) She is a doctor

18. A is the brother of B, B is the daughter of C and D is the father of A. Then, how is C related to D?
(a) Husband (b) Wife
(c) Granddaughter (d) Grandfather

19. Find the missing number from the given alternatives.

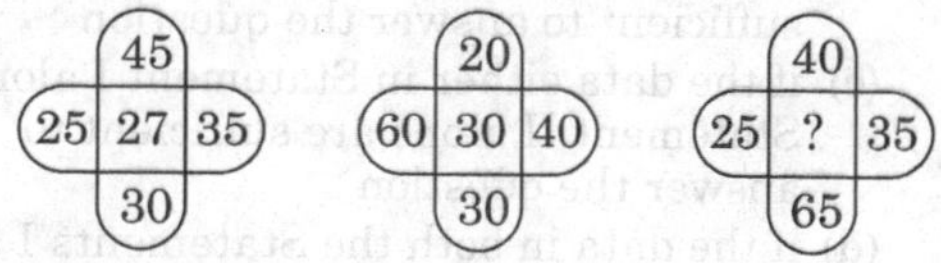

(a) 36 (b) 33
(c) 45 (d) 60

20. Select one alternative, which exactly matches with the mirror image of the given word.
NIRMALA
(a) ALAMRIN (b) AJAMRIИ
(c) NRILAMA (d) INRMALA

21. A clock is set right at 5 am. The clock loses 16 min in 24 h. What will be the correct time when the clock indicates 10 pm on 4th day?
(a) 12 am (b) 6 am
(c) 11 pm (d) 10 pm

22. Which of the following diagrams represents the relationship among Sun, Moon and Star?

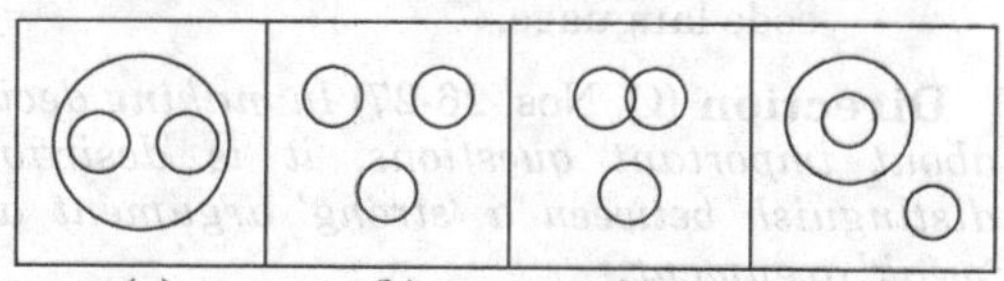

(a) (b) (c) (d)

23. Which one of the given responses would be a meaningful order of the following?
(i) Destination (ii) Booking
(iii) Boarding (iv) Travel
(v) Planning
(a) (iv), (iii), (i), (ii), (v)
(b) (v), (ii), (iii), (iv), (i)
(c) (i), (ii), (iii), (iv), (v)
(d) (iii), (iv), (v), (i), (ii)

Direction (Q. Nos. 24-25) *Each of the following questions below consists of a question and two statements numbered* I *and* II *given below it.*

You have to decide whether the data provided in the statements are sufficient to answer the question.

Give answer

(a) if the data in Statement I alone are sufficient to answer the question, while the data in Statement II alone are not sufficient to answer the question

(b) if the data in Statement II alone are sufficient to answer the question, while the data in Statement I alone are not sufficient to answer the question

(c) if the data either in Statement I alone or Statement II alone are sufficient to answer the question

(d) if the data in both the Statements I and II together are not sufficient to answer the question

(e) if the data in both the Statements I and II are together necessary to answer the question

24. The sum of ages of M, N and O is 50 yr. What is N's age?

I. N is 10 yr older than M.

II. O is 30 yr old.

25. If 'over and above' is written as 'ja na ta' in a code language, then how is 'and' written in that code language?

I. 'come and go' is written as 'ha la ja' in that code language.

II. 'he and you' is written as 'da ja ma' in that code language.

Direction (Q. Nos. 26-27) *In making decisions about important questions, it is desirable to distinguish between a 'strong' argument and a 'weak' argument.*

A 'strong' argument must be both important and directly related to the question. A 'weak' argument may not be directly related to the question and may be of minor importance or may be related to the trivial aspect of the question. Each question below is followed by two arguments numbered I and II. You have to decide which of the arguments is 'strong' and which is 'weak'.

Give answer

(a) if only Argument I is strong

(b) if only Argument II is strong

(c) if either Argument I or II is strong

(d) if neither Argument I nor II is strong

(e) if both Argument I and II are strong

26. Statement Should political parties be banned?

Arguments

I. Yes, it is necessary to teach a lesson to the politicians.

II. No, it will lead to an end of democracy.

27. Statement Should coal engines be replaced by electric engines in trains?

Arguments

I. Yes, coal engines cause a lot of pollution.

II. No, India does not produce enough electricity to fulfil even the domestic needs.

28. In this question below is given a statement followed by two assumptions numbered I and II. An assumption is something supposed or taken for granted.

You have to consider the statement and the following assumptions and decide which of the assumption(s) is/are implicit in the statement.

Statement A good executive has to be task oriented as well as people oriented.

Assumptions

I. Some executives are people oriented.

II. Some executives are not people oriented.

(a) if only Assumption I is implicit

(b) if only Assumption II is implicit

(c) if either Assumption I or II is implicit

(d) if neither Assumption I nor II is implicit

(e) if both Assumptions I and II are implicit

Direction (Q. Nos. 29-30) *Three statements are given followed by two/four conclusions* I, II, III *and* IV. *You have to consider the three statements to be true even if they seem to be at variance from commonly known facts. You have to decide which of the given conclusions, if any, follow from the given statements.* **[SSC (10+2) 2014]**

29. Statements

A. Rabindranath Tagore wrote many poems.

B. Every poet has aesthetic knowledge.

C. Aesthetic is a part of axiological study.

Conclusions

I. Rabindranath Tagore did different axiological study.

II. He followed the base of logic and ethics.

(a) Only Conclusion I

(b) Both Conclusions I and II

(c) Only Conclusion II

(d) None of the above

30. **Statements**

A. All clerks are superintendents.
B. All superintendents are managers.
C. All managers are supervisors.

Conclusions

I. All supervisors are clerks.
II. Some clerks are supervisors.
III. Some managers are clerks.
IV. All superintendents are clerks.

(a) Only Conclusion I
(b) Only Conclusion II
(c) Only Conclusion III
(d) Only Conclusion IV

Direction (Q. Nos. 31-32) *Study the following information carefully and answer the given questions.*

Given an input a coding machine generates pass-codes for six batches everyday as follows.

Input the shopkeeper offered discount to customers.

Pass-code for

Batch I customers the shopkeeper offered discount to

Batch II customers discount the shopkeeper offered to

Batch III customers discount offered the shopkeeper to

and so on until the arrangement is completed.

After the arrangement is completed the next batch gets the same code as that for Batch I.

Duration of each batch is 1 h. There is a break of one hour after the fourth batch. Sixth batch is the last batch.

31. If the pass-code for the second batch is " do lean window out of not", then what will be the pass-code for the fourth batch?

(a) do lean of not out window
(b) do lean of out not window
(c) do lean not out window of
(d) do lean not of window out
(e) None of the above

32. If the input is 'please do not delay the matter', then what will be the pass-code for third batch?

(a) do please not delay the matter
(b) delay do matter please not the
(c) delay do matter not please the
(d) delay do matter not the please
(e) None of the above

33. Find the odd figure from the given alternatives.

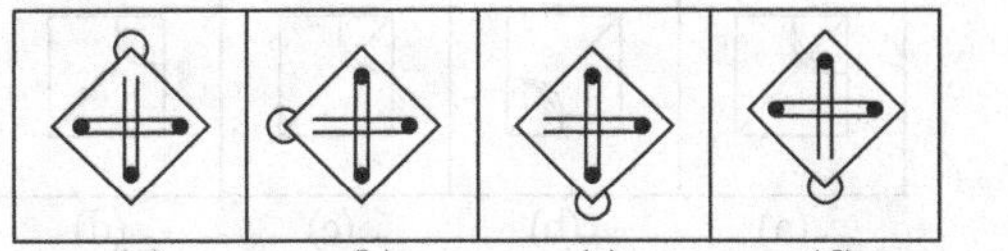

(a) (b) (c) (d)

34. Choose the correct alternative from the given ones that will complete the series.

Question Figures

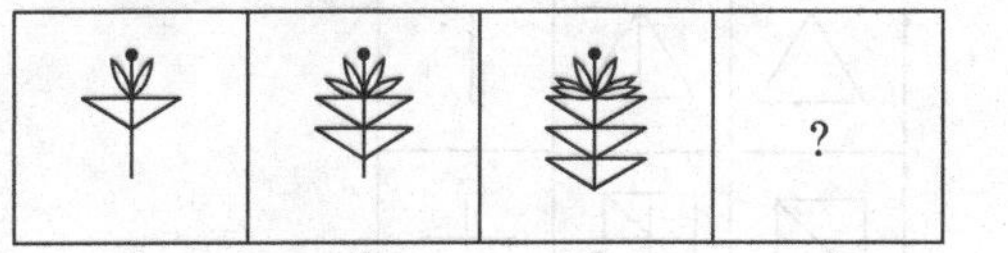

1 2 3 4

Answer Figures

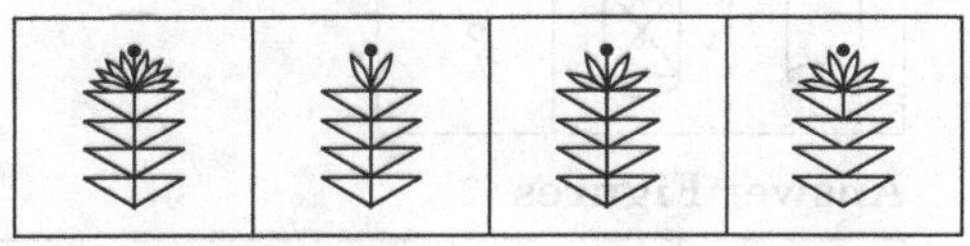

(a) (b) (c) (d)

35. In the question given below are three statements followed by two conclusions numbered I and II. You have to take the three given statements to be true even if they seem to be at variance from commonly known facts and then decide which of the given conclusions logically follows from the three statements disregarding commonly known facts. Then, decide which of the answers (a), (b), (c), (d) or (e) is the correct answer.

Statements Some books are stories.
All stories are fictions.
All fictions are poems

Conclusions I. Some poems are books.
II. All stories are poems.

(a) if only Conclusion I follows
(b) if only Conclusion II follows
(c) if either Conclusion I or II follows
(d) if neither Conclusion I nor II follows
(e) if both Conclusions I and II follow

36. Which answer figure will complete the pattern in the question figure?

Question Figure **[SSC (10 + 2) 2015]**

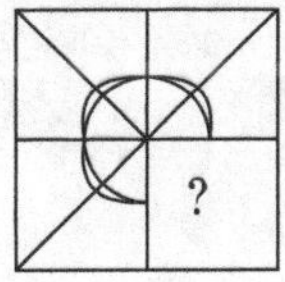

Answer Figures

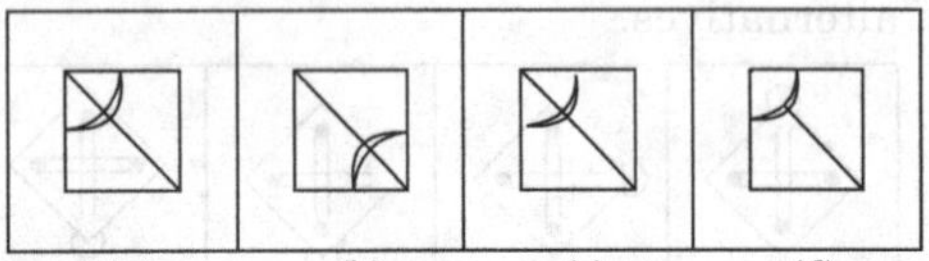

(a) (b) (c) (d)

37. Which of the answer figures (a), (b), (c) or (d) completes the figure matrix?

Question Figures

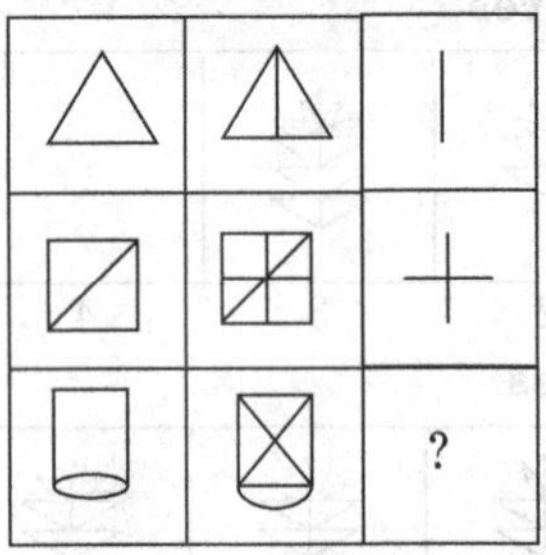

Answer Figures

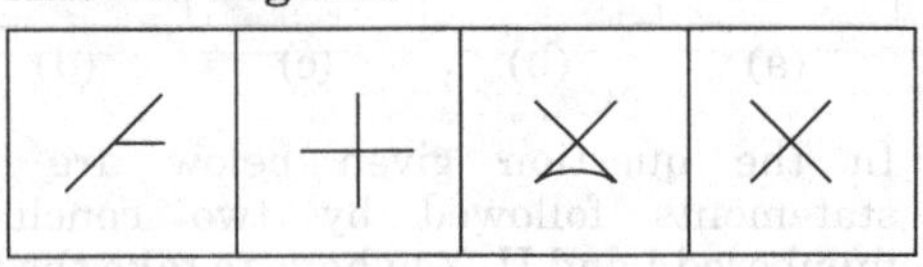

(a) (b) (c) (d)

38. If a mirror is placed on the line MN, then which of the answer figures is the right image of the given figure?

Question Figure

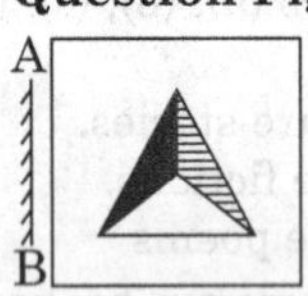

Answer Figures

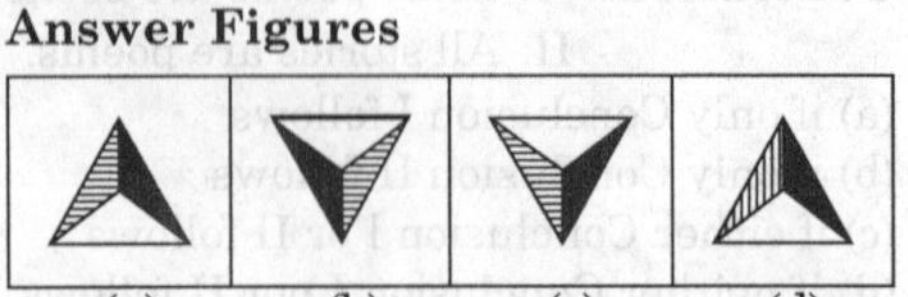

(a) (b) (c) (d)

39. How many triangles are there in the following figure?

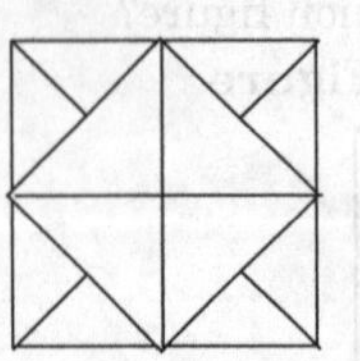

(a) 16 (b) 20 (c) 12 (d) 22

Direction (Q. Nos. 40-41) *In the following questions, a series is given, with one term missing. Choose the correct alternative from the given ones that will complete the series.*

40. 462, 420, 380, ?, 306

(a) 322 (b) 332 (c) 342 (d) 352

41. What comes in place of question mark (?) in the following letter series?

R, O, L, I, F, ?, Z

(a) A (b) C (c) E (d) I

Direction (Q. Nos. 42-44) *Study the given information carefully to answer the given questions.*

M, N, O, P, Q, R, S and T are sitting around a circular table facing the centre with equal distances between each other (but not necessarily in the same order). Each of them also belongs to a different field of work- Author, Designer, Doctor, Engineer, Journalist, Policeman, Singer and Teacher (but not necessarily in the same order).

Q sits second to the left of the Singer. Only two people sit between S and the Singer. Only one person sits between Q and the Designer. N sits second to the left of the Designer, P is neither an immediate neighbour of N nor Q. P is not a singer. T is an immediate neighbour of P.

The Doctor sits second to the right of T. Only three people sit between the Doctor and the Engineer. R sits second to the left of the Engineer, T is not a Journalist. The Journalist is neither an immediate neighbour of S nor T. Q sits to the immediate left of the Journalist. The Teacher sits to immediate right of the Author.

42. Who sits exactly between N and M?

(a) S (b) T
(c) O
(d) Other than those given as options
(e) R

43. Which of the following statements is/are true as per the given arrangement?

(a) Only one person sits between S and O
(b) The Engineer sits second to the left of O
(c) S is a Teacher
(d) All the given options are true
(e) The Author sits to the immediate right of O

44. Who amongst the following is a Designer?
(a) M (b) R (c) S (d) T
(e) P

45. A, B, C and D are playing cards. A and C, B and D are partners. D is to the right of C. The face of C is towards West. Find the direction that D is facing.
(a) West (b) East (c) South (d) North
(e) None of these

46. *In question below a statement is given followed by three assumptions numbered* I, II *and* III. *You have to decide which of the assumptions is implicit.*

Statement "One day token strike was called by the employees in Government organisations to protest against privatisation of profit making Public Sector Undertakings."

Assumptions

I. The Government may favourably consider the views of the employees.
II. Strike is the most popular tool used by people to protest.
III. The strike may bring pressure on the Government, forcing them to reconsider the decision.

(a) Only I is implicit
(b) Only II is implicit
(c) I and III are implicit
(d) All I, II and III are implicit
(e) None of the above

47. In a row of girls, if Madhu, who is tenth from the left, and Veena, who is ninth from the right interchange their places, Madhu becomes fifteenth from the left. How many girls are there in the row?
(a) 16 (b) 18 (c) 23 (d) 22

48. The age of Amit is same as Sumit because they are twins, Richa is younger than Sumit, Richa is younger than Jyotsana but elder than Saurabh, Sumit is younger than Jyotsana. Who is the eldest among them?
(a) Amit (b) Jyotsana
(c) Richa (d) Saurabh

49. A person starts walking from his home towards his friends place. He walks for 25 m towards West. He takes a 90° right turn and walks for 20 m. He again takes a 90° right turn, and walks for 10 m. He then walks for another 10m after taking a 90° left turn. Turning 90° towards his right, he walks for 15 m to reach his friend's place. How far and in which direction is the friend's place from his home? **[SBI (PO) Pre 2015]**
(a) 30 m towards East
(b) 30 m towards North
(c) 40 m towards South
(d) 30 m towards South
(e) 40 m towards North

50. The Independence day in year 1988 was celebrated on Wednesday. On what day was it celebrated in the year 1989?
(a) Monday (b) Tuesday
(c) Friday (d) Thursday

Hints and Solutions

1. (*d*) 'Palaeontology' is the study of 'Fossils' in the same manner 'Phrenology' is the study of 'Skull'.

2. (*b*)

Original number	5	2	6	3	1	8	7
	+1	−1	−1	+1	+1	−1	+1
Step I	6	1	5	4	2	7	8
Step II	1	2	(4)	5	6	7	8

From left → 3rd

So, the required digit is 4.

3. (c) As,

D 4 H

So, D is at 4th position.

D 4 H (×2)

$4 \times 2 = 8$ th position is of alphabet H.

Similarly,

I 9 R

Position of I is 9th.

So, $9 \times 2 = 18 \longrightarrow$ R is at 18th position.

4. (*b*) Except Tulip, all are flowers whereas Tulip is a one kind of plant.

5. (*c*) As,

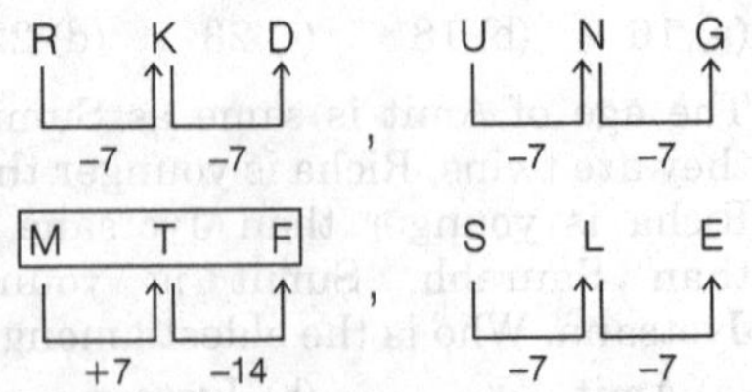

From above, it is clear that MTF is different from all other options.

6. (*c*) As,

Similarly,

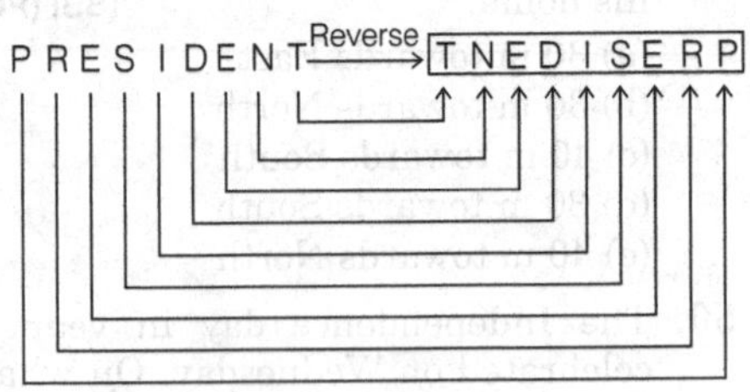

7. (*a*) As,

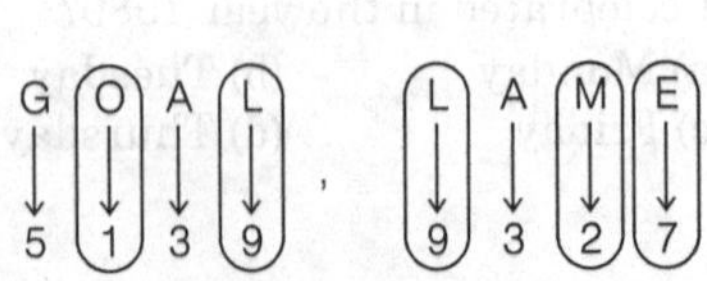

By direct substitution method, we get

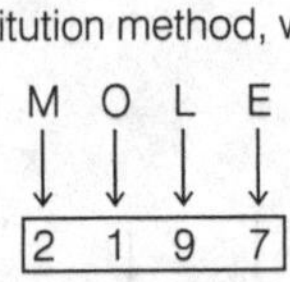

8. (*d*) From the given four positions of a single block, faces adjacent to face having red colour = blue, pink, yellow, green.

Clearly, black is opposite to red.

9. (*d*) 'CHANCE' cannot be formed by using letters of the word MERCHANDISE.

10. (*c*) The given words in each pair are antonyms of each other.

11. (*b*) Figures 2, 3 and 5 are one pointed structure.

Figures 1, 8 and 9 are two pointed structure.

Figures 4, 6 and 7 are three pointed structure.

Solution (Q. Nos. 12-13) On the basis of given information, the arrangement of the singers in a line is as follows

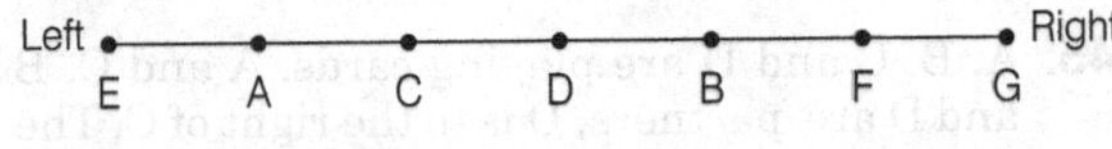

12. (*c*) Clearly, singer G is on the extreme right of the line.

13. (*c*) C is third from the left.

14. (*b*) As,

and

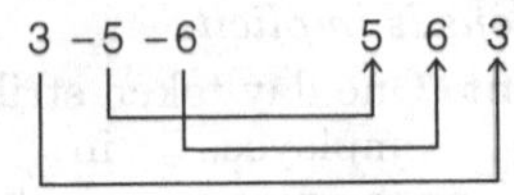

Similarly,

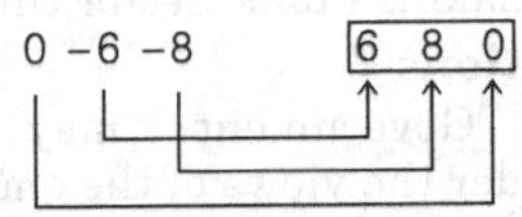

15. (*d*) According to the given information,

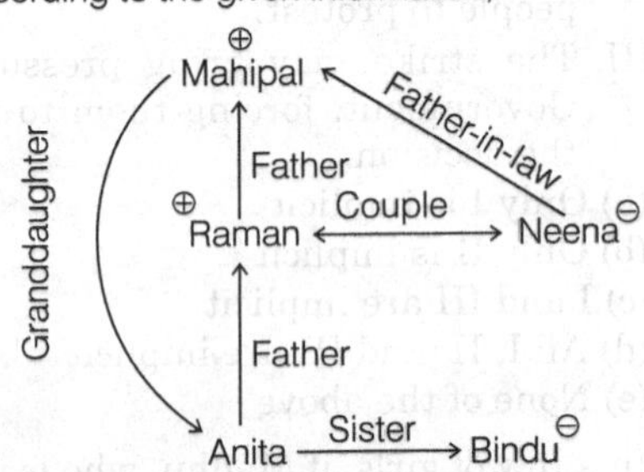

So, Bindu is granddaughter of Mahipal.

16. (*b*) As, 1st column $\sqrt{36} = 6$; $6 \times 2 = 12$

and 2nd column $\sqrt{64} = 8$; $8 \times 2 = 16$

Similarly, 3rd column $\sqrt{100} = 10$; $10 \times 2 = 20$

17. (*c*) According to the information, the arrangement is as follows

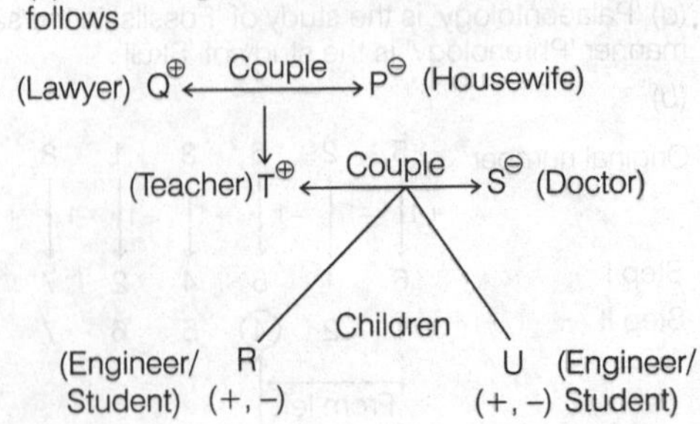

So, she is a student is correct. And either R or U is a student.

18. (*b*) Making the relation diagram from the given information,

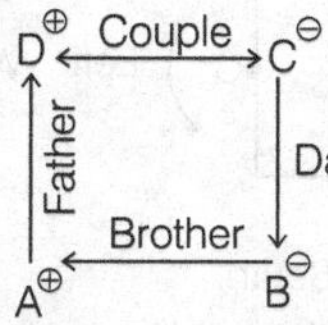

Hence, it is clear from diagram that C is wife of D.

19. (*b*)As, $25 + 45 + 35 + 30 = 135 = \frac{135}{5} = 27$

and $60 + 20 + 40 + 30 = 150 = \frac{150}{5} = 30$

Similarly, $25 + 40 + 35 + 65 = 165$

$\therefore \frac{165}{5} = 33$

Hence, option (b) is correct.

20. (*b*) Option (b) is the correct mirror image of the given word.

21. (*c*) Total time from 5 am on a day to 10 pm on 4th day = 89 h

Now, 23 h 44 min of this clock = 24 h of correct clock

$\frac{356}{15}$ h of this clock = 24 h of correct clock

$\therefore$ 89 h of this clock $= \frac{24 \times 15}{356} \times 89$

= 90h of correct clock

So, the correct time of clock is 11 pm.

22. (*d*) Sun is a Star. Moon is a Satellite.

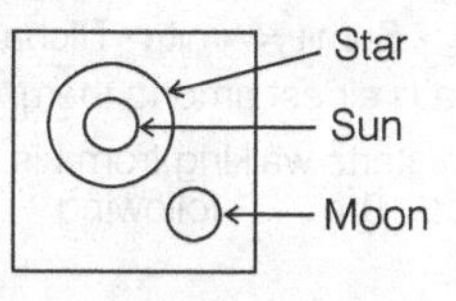

23. (*b*) Meaningful order of words is

(v) Planning, → (ii) Booking, → (iii) Boarding,

→ (iv) Travel, → (i) Destination

24. (*e*) As, given in the question, M + N + O = 50 yr

On combining Statements I and II, we get

N = 15 yr

So, both statements are required to answer the question.

25. (*c*) Given that, over <u>and</u> above = <u>ja</u> na ta ...(A)

From Statement I, come <u>and</u> go = ha la <u>ja</u>

From Statement II, he <u>and</u> you = da <u>ja</u> ma

Clearly, either from Eq. (A) and Statement I or from Eq. (A) and Statement II,

and = ja

So, either Statement I or Statement II is sufficient to answer the question.

26. (*b*) Only Argument II is strong because ban on political parties will definitely lead to an end of democracy.

27. (*e*) Both the arguments are logical and directly related to the statement and hence, are strong arguments.

28. (*d*) The statement advises that an executive should be task oriented as well as people oriented. It is based on the assumptions that some executives are only people oriented and some executives are only task oriented. Hence, none of the assumptions follows.

29. (*a*) From given statements, it is clear that Rabindranath Tagore did different axiological study.

30. (*c*) According to the question,

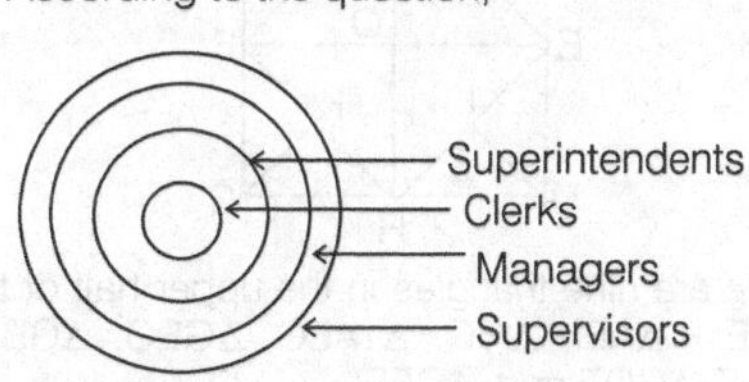

Conclusions I. All supervisors are clerks. (✗)

II. All superintendents are managers. (✗)

III. Some managers are clerks. (✔)

IV. All superintendents are clerks. (✗)

Hence, only Conclusion III follows.

Solution (Q. Nos. 31-32)

The given machine is in alphabetical order of dictionary.

31. (*d*) The pass-code for second batch is given as

Batch II do lean window out of not

Batch III do lean not window out of

Batch IV do lean not of window out

32. (*b*) If input is given, then pass-code for third batch is

Input please do not delay the matter

Batch I delay please do not the matter

Batch II delay do please not the matter

Batch III delay do matter please not the

33. (*c*) The figure (c) is different from the other three figures. The position of semi-circular in figure (c) is different.

34. (*a*) From figure (1) to (2) two leafs and two triangles are added. So, option (a) will follow the same pattern.

35. (*e*)

Conclusions I. Some poems are books. (✔)

II. All staries are poems. (✔)

So, both Conclusions I and II follow.

36. (*a*) It is clear that answer figure (a) will complete the given figure.

37. (*c*) The third figure in each row comprises of parts which are not common in the first two figures.

38. (*a*) The correct laterally inverted mirror image of the question figure is as follows

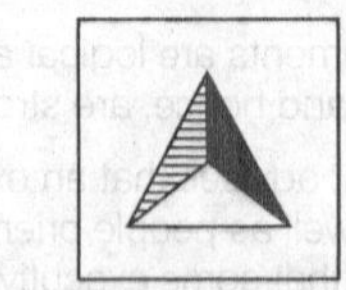

39. (*b*) The figure in the question may be labelled as shown below

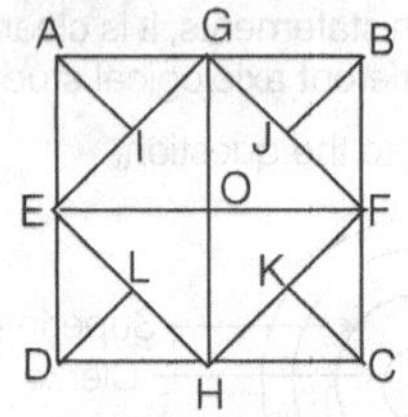

There are nine triangles in the upper half of the figure ABFE = ΔAEI, ΔAIG, Δ AEG, ΔGEO, ΔGBJ, ΔBFJ, ΔGBF, ΔGOF and ΔGEF.

Similarly, there are nine triangles in the lower half figure, i.e. EFCD.

There are two more triangles ΔEGH and ΔFGH.

Hence, there are a total of 20 triangles.

40. (*c*) This pattern is as follows

462 420 380 (342) 306

−42 −40 −38 −36

∴ ? = 342

41. (*b*) The pattern is as follows

R O L I F [C] Z

−3 −3 −3 −3 −3 −3

Solution (Q. Nos. 42-44) According to the given information the arrangement is as follows:

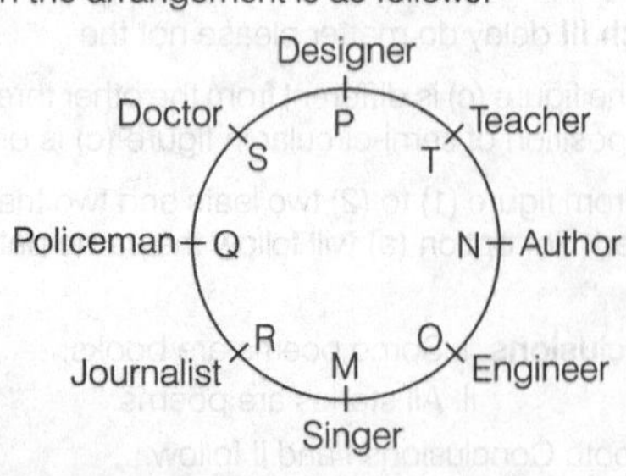

42. (c) O sits exactly between N and M.

43. (e)The author sits to the immediate right of O is true.

44. (e) P is a Designer.

45. (c) According to the question, the arrangement is as follows

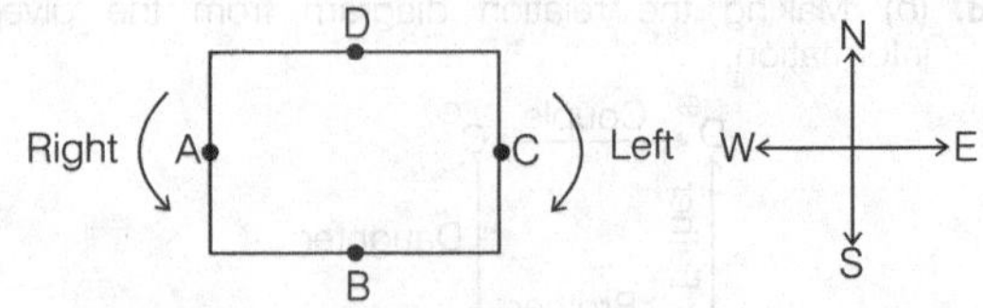

Clearly, D is facing South.

46. (*c*) The thinking of the employees behind the protest must be that the Government may favourably consider their views and it may bring pressure on the Government, forcing them to reconsider the decision.

47. (*c*) Given ranking in the row is as follows

Madhu
Left ⟶ 10th
Veena
9th ⟵ Right

After interchange,

Madhu
Left ⟶ 15th

We see that interchanging the places rank of Madhu changes 5 places than the previous ranks which implies Veena was at 15th position of the row and adding 8 to the rank of Madhu will give the total number of girls in the row which is

$$15 + 8 = 23$$

48. (*b*) Given that, Amit = Sumit, Sumit > Richa

Jyotsana > Richa > Saurabh

Jyotsana > Sumit

On arranging the above data, we get

Jyotsana > Sumit = Amit > Richa > Saurabh

So, Jyotsana is eldest among them.

49. (*b*) A person starts walking from his home towards his friends place. The following figure shows its movement

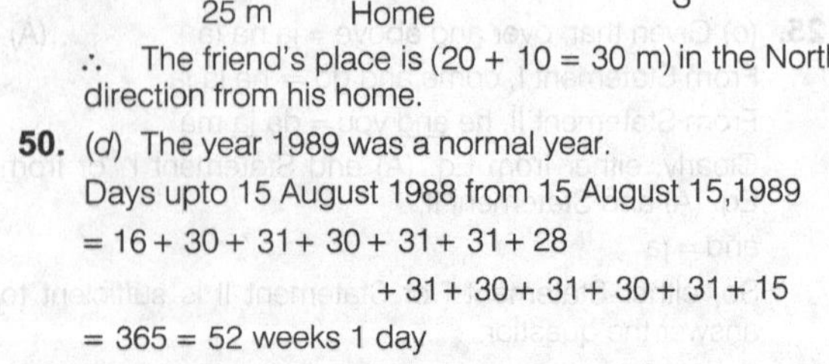

∴ The friend's place is (20 + 10 = 30 m) in the North direction from his home.

50. (*d*) The year 1989 was a normal year.

Days upto 15 August 1988 from 15 August 15,1989

= 16 + 30 + 31 + 30 + 31 + 31 + 28
+ 31 + 30 + 31 + 30 + 31 + 15

= 365 = 52 weeks 1 day

Therefore, Wednesday +1 = Thursda

PRACTICE SET 4

1. In a certain code, 'MODE' is written as '#8%6' and 'DEAF' is written as '%67$'. How FOAM is written in that code? **[NICL (AO) 2015]**

(a) $87# (b) $#7%
(c) #87% (d) $87%
(e) None of these

2. The sum of the ages of father and a son presently is 70 yr. After 10 yr, the son's age is exactly half that of the father.What are their ages now?

(a) 45 yr,25 yr (b) 50 yr,20 yr
(c) 47 yr, 23 yr (d) 50 yr, 25 yr

3. In which answer figure is the question figure embedded?

Question Figure

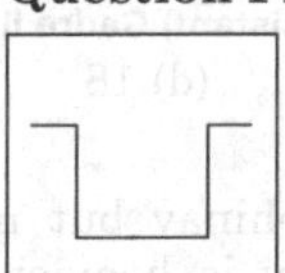

Answer Figures

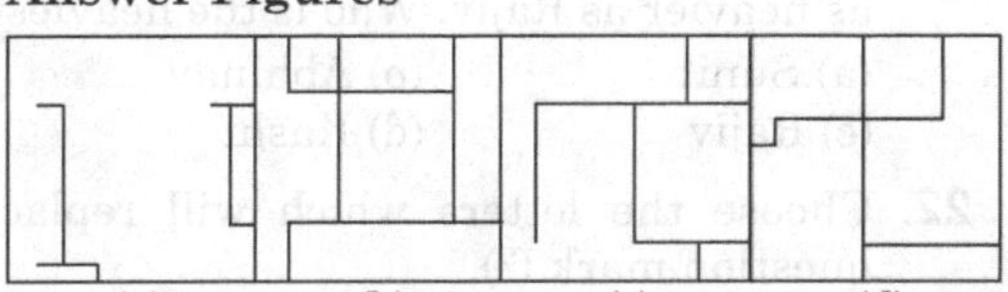

(a) (b) (c) (d)

4. Which one set of letters when sequentially placed at the gaps in the given letter series shall complete it? **[SSC (10 +2) 2014]**

_cb_ca_bacb_ca_bac_d

(a) badddb (b) bbbddd
(c) addddb (d) addbbb

Direction (Q. Nos. 5-6) *In the following questions, a series is given, with one term missing. Choose the correct alternative from the given ones that will complete the series.*

5. 15, 30, 60, 120, 240, ?

(a) 480 (b) 518
(c) 445 (d) 715

6. DF, GJ, KM, NQ, RT ? **[MAT 2013]**

(a) UX (b) UW (c) YZ (d) XZ

7. In a given combination of alphabets and/or numbers followed by four alternatives (a), (b), (c) and (d). Choose the correct water image out of given alternatives.

96FSH52

(a) ∂ɘĿƧHƼƻ (b) ∂9ĿƧHƻƼ
(c) ∂ɘĿƧHƻƼ (d) ∂ɘĿƧHƼ5

8. If '+' means '–', '–' means '×', '×' means '÷' and '÷' means '+', then what is the value of $9-7+85\times17\div15$? **[NICL (AO) 2015]**

(a) 68 (b) 73 (c) 79 (d) 83
(e) 87

9. Select the missing number from the given responses.

6	7	5
7	8	6
8	9	?
62	79	47

(a) 4 (b) 7 (c) 8 (d) 9

10. A solid cube is formed with 27 smaller cubes. One pair of opposite faces of this cube is painted red, another pair is painted yellow and third pair of opposite faces is painted white. How many smaller cubes are painted yellow and white only?

(a) 4 (b) 8 (c) 12 (d) 16

11. Arrange the following words according to the dictionary.

(i) Eagle (ii) Earth
(iii) Eager (iv) Early
(v) Each

(a) (ii), (i), (iv), (iii), (v)
(b) (i), (v), (ii), (iv), (iii)
(c) (ii), (iii), (v), (iv), (i)
(d) (v), (iii), (i), (iv), (ii)

Direction (Q. Nos. 12-13) *In the following questions, the symbols #, %, @, $ and © are used with the following meanings as illustrated below.*

'P # Q' means 'P is not smaller than Q'.
'P % Q' means 'P is not greater than Q'.
'P @ Q' means 'P is neither smaller than nor equal to Q'.

'P \$ Q' means 'P is neither greater than nor equal to Q'

'P © Q' means 'P is neither smaller than nor greater than Q'

In each of the following questions assuming the given statements to be true, find out which of the two Conclusions I and II given below them is/are definitely true.

Give answer

(a) if only Conclusion I is true
(b) if only Conclusion II is true
(c) if either Conclusion I or II is true
(d) if neither Conclusion I nor II is true
(e) if both Conclusions I and II are true

12. Statements H © W, W % R, R @ F
Conclusions I. R © H II. R @ H

13. Statements M \$ T, T @ K, K © D
Conclusions I. D \$ T II. K \$ M

14. Which one of the following diagram that represents the relationship among Squares, Rectangles, Geometric figures?

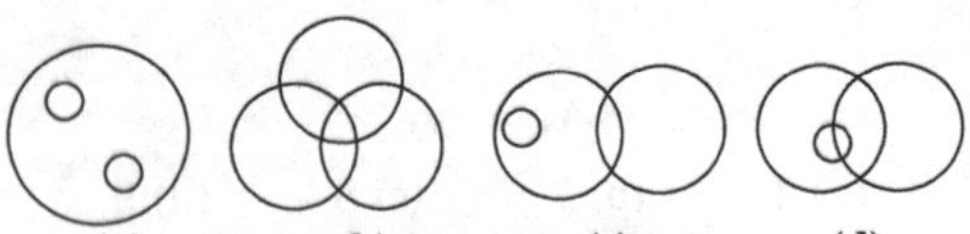

(a) (b) (c) (d)

15. Sonu travelled from a point A straight to B in East direction, a distance of 12 km. He turned right and travelled 8 km and reached point C. From that point took right turn and travelled 6 km and reached point D. How far is he away from the starting point?
(a) 10 km (b) 12 km
(c) 13 km (d) 14 km

16. Its dinner time and Snowwhite is serving soup to the seven dwarfs namely Grumpy, Happy, Bashful, Dopey, Sneezy, Sleepy and Dreamy. The dwarfs are standing in a line where Sneezy is between Bashful and Dopey. Grumpy is just before Happy and Dreamy is just before Sleepy. Bashful is not the last and he is behind Sleepy. Dopey is also not last. Who is standing just before Grumpy?
(a) Sleepy (b) Dreamy
(c) Happy (d) Dopey

Direction (Q. Nos. 17-18) *In the following questions, select the related word/ number from the given alternatives.*

17. Governor : State : : President : ?
[SSC (10+2) 2015]
(a) Country (b) Organisation
(c) Constituency (d) District

18. 123 : 13^2 : : 235 : ?
(a) 23^3 (b) 25^3 (c) 35^2 (d) 25^2

19. 3 persons A, B and C are sitting along the corners of a triangular table. A is to right of B. Who is sitting to right of C?
(a) A
(b) B
(c) C
(d) Cannot be determined
(e) None of the above

20. In a row of letters, a letter is 5th from left end and 12th from the right end. How many letters are there in a row?
[NICL (Assistant) Cadre III 2015]
(a) 15 (b) 16 (c) 17 (d) 18
(e) 19

21. Sunil is heavier than Abhinav but not as heavier as Rajiv. Abhinav is heavier than Jayesh. Kashi is heavier than Sunil but not as heavier as Rajiv. Who is the heaviest?
(a) Sunil (b) Abhinav
(c) Rajiv (d) Kashi

22. Choose the letters which will replace the question mark (?).
DEF : EFD : : FGH : ? **[SSC (10+2) 2014]**
(a) FHG (b) HGF
(c) HFG (d) GHF

23. Find the odd letters from the given alternatives.
(a) DW (b) LO (c) JR (d) HS

24. A child walks 25 ft towards North, turns right and walks 40 ft, turns right again and walks 45 ft. He then turns left and walks 20 ft. He turns left again walks 20 ft. Finally, he turns to his left to walk another 20 ft. In which direction is the child from his starting point?
(a) North (b) South
(c) West (d) East

25. How many triangles are there in the following figure?

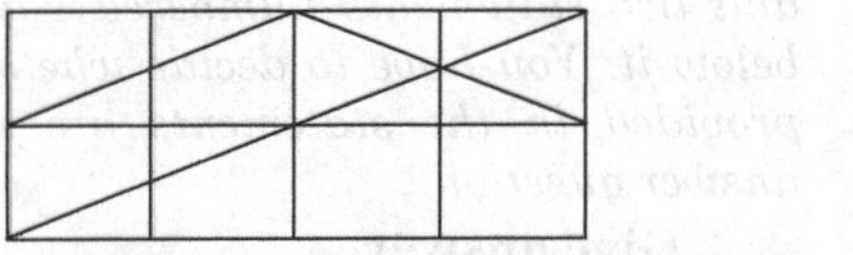

(a) 29 (b) 23 (c) 19 (d) None of these

26. Five persons are sitting facing centre of a circle. Pramod is sitting to the right of Ranjan. Raju is sitting between Brejesh and Naveen. Raju is to the left of Brejesh and Ranjan is to right of Brejesh. Who is sitting to the left of Naveen?

(a) Pramod (b) Raju
(c) Brejesh (d) Rajan

27. From the given alternative words, select the word which cannot be formed using the letters of the given word. **[SSC (CGL) 2014]**

INCARCERATION

(a) RELATION (b) TERRAIN
(c) INACTION (d) CREATION

28. How many such letters are there in the word 'CATEGORY' which remains same in its position, when they are arranged in alphabetical order?

(a) None (b) One
(c) Two (d) Three

29. In the given diagram, police officer represents circle, corrupt represents triangle, poet represents square, married represents rectangle. The area representing unmarried police officers who are not corrupt but are poets is **[SSC (Multitasking) 2013]**

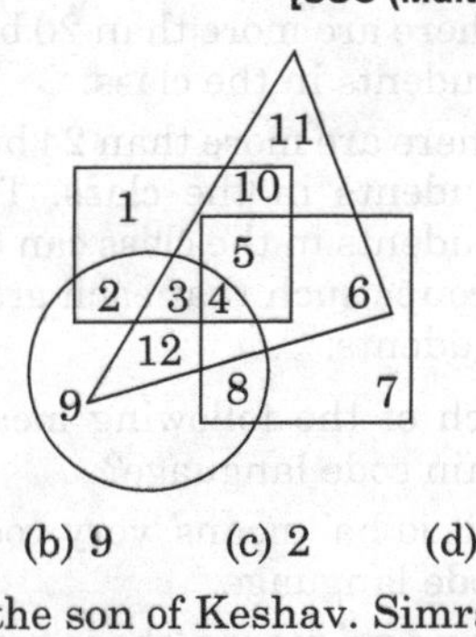

(a) 8 (b) 9 (c) 2 (d) 4

30. Sunil is the son of Keshav. Simran, Keshav's sister, has a son Maruti and daughter Sita. Prem is the maternal uncle of Maruti. How is Sunil related to Maruti?

(a) Cousin (b) Uncle
(c) Brother (d) Nephew

31. Select the related figure from the given alternatives. **[SSC (10+2) 2013]**

Question Figures

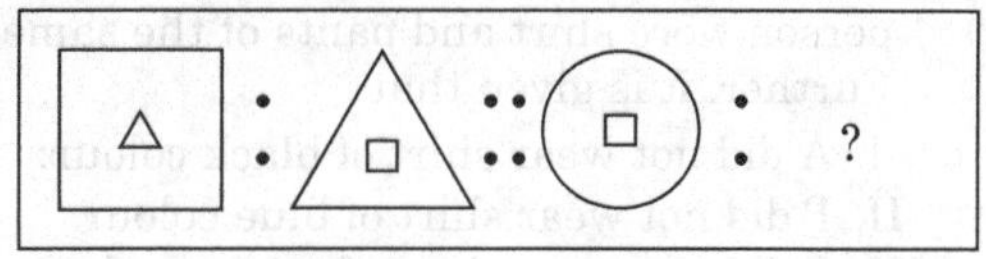

Answer Figures

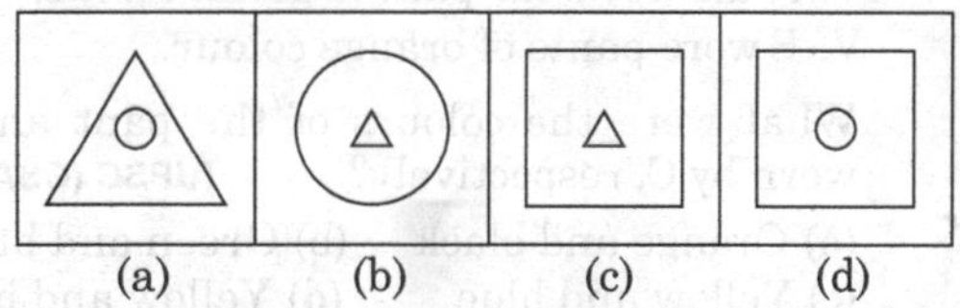

Direction (Q. Nos. 32-33) *Read the following information carefully and answer the questions given below.*

Four young men Anil, Mukesh, Piyush and Yogesh are lovingly called Munna, Babboo, Prince and Pappoo by everyone. They are married to Madhu, Sunanda, Jyoti and Arti.

I. Arti and Madhu are neither married to Piyush or Anil nor their husband is called Babboo.

II. Babboo is not married to Sunanda and his name is not Piyush.

III. Sunanda is not married to Munna.

IV. Mukesh is neither Munna nor Prince and is not married to Madhu.

32. Which of the following pair of husband-wife is not correct?

(a) Munna, Madhu
(b) Babboo, Jyoti
(c) Pappoo, Arti
(d) None of these

33. What is the nick name of Mukesh?

(a) Babboo (b) Pappoo
(c) Munna (d) Prince

34. Reaching a place of appointment on Friday. I found that I was two days earlier than the scheduled day. If I had reached on the following Wednesday, then how many days late would I have been?

(a) One (b) Two
(c) Three (d) Four

35. *Read the following information carefully and answer the question that follows.*

Three persons A, B and C wore shirts of black, blue and orange colours (not necessarily in that order) and pants of green, yellow and orange colours (not necessarily in that order). No person wore shirt and pants of the same colour. Further, it is given that

I. A did not wear shirt of black colour.
II. B did not wear shirt of blue colour.
III. C did not wear shirt of orange colour.
IV. A did not wear pant of green colour.
V. B wore pants of orange colour.

What were the colours of the pant and shirt worn by C, respectively? **[UPSC (CSAT) 2012]**

(a) Orange and black (b) Green and blue
(c) Yellow and blue (d) Yellow and black

36. All good athletes want to win and all athletes who want to win eat a well balanced diet; therefore all athletes who do not eat a well balanced diet are bad athletes.

The best conclusion from this statement is that

(a) No bad athlete wants to win
(b) No athlete who does not eat a well balanced diet is good athlete
(c) Every athlete who eats a well balanced diet is a good athlete
(d) All athletes who want to win are good athletes

37. In this question below is given a statement followed by two assumptions numbered I and II. An assumption is something supposed or taken for granted.

You have to consider the statement and the following assumptions and decide which of the assumption(s) is/are implicit in the statement.

Statement Why don't you invite Anthony for the Christmas party this year?

Assumptions

I. Anthony is not from the same city.
II. Unless invited, Anthony will not attend the party.

(a) if only Assumption I is implicit
(b) if only Assumption II is implicit
(c) if either Assumption I or II is implicit
(d) if neither Assumption I nor II is implicit
(e) if both Assumptions I and II are implicit

Direction (Q. Nos. 38-40) *Each of the following questions below consists of a question and two statements numbered I and II given below it. You have to decide whether the data provided in the statements are sufficient to answer question.*

Give answer

(a) if the data in Statement I alone are sufficient to answer the question, while the data in Statement II alone are not sufficient to answer the question
(b) if the data in Statement II alone are sufficient to answer the question, while the data in Statement I alone are not sufficient to answer the question
(c) if the data either in Statement I alone or Statement II alone are sufficient to answer the question
(d) if the data in both the Statements I and II together are not sufficient to answer the question
(e) if the data in both the Statements I and II are together necessary to answer the question

38. Point X is in which direction with respect to Y?

I. Point Z is at equal distance from both point X and point Y.
II. Walking 5 km to the East of point X and taking two consecutive right turns after walking 5 km before each turn leads to point Y.

39. How many students are there in the class?

I. There are more than 20 but less that 27 students in the class.
II. There are more than 24 but less than 31 students in the class. The number of students in the class can be divided into groups such that each group contains 5 students.

40. Which of the following means 'very' in a certain code language?

I. 'pit jo ha' means 'very good boy' in that code language.
II. 'jo na pa' means 'she is good' in that code language.

41. Find out which of the figures (a), (b), (c) and (d) can be formed from the pieces given in question figures.

Question Figure

Answer Figures

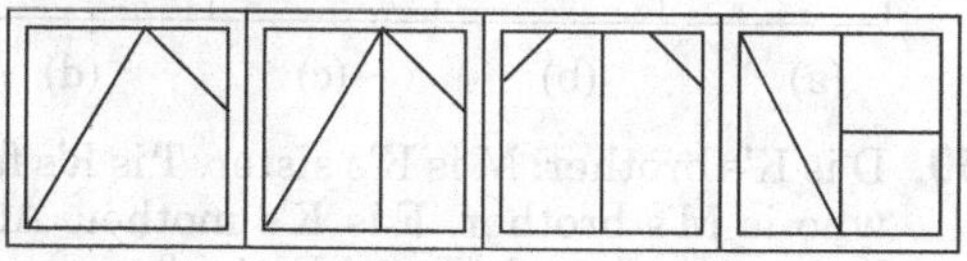

(a) (b) (c) (d)

42. At what time are the hands of clocks together between 6 and 7 ?

(a) $32\frac{8}{11}$ minutes past 6

(b) $34\frac{8}{11}$ minutes past 6

(c) $30\frac{8}{11}$ minutes past 6

(d) $32\frac{5}{7}$ minutes past 6

Direction (Q. Nos. 43-44) *In each of the questions below are given two statements followed by two conclusions numbered I and II. You have to take the two given statements to be true ever if they seem to be at variance from commonly known facts and decide which of the given conclusion(s) logically follow(s) from the two given statements, disregarding commonly known facts.*

Give answer

(a) if only Conclusion I follows
(b) if only Conclusion II follows
(c) if either I or II follows
(d) if neither I nor II follows
(e) if both I and II follow

43. Statements Some dews are drops.
All drops are stones.

Conclusions

I. Atleast some dews are stones.
II. Atleast some stones are drops.

44. Statements Some squares are circles.
No circle is a triangle.
No line is a square.

Conclusions

I. All squares can never be triangles.
II. Some lines are circles.

45. If P = 16 and TAP = 37, then Cup = ?

(a) 40 (b) 38 (c) 36 (d) 39

46. Select the odd figure from the given responses.

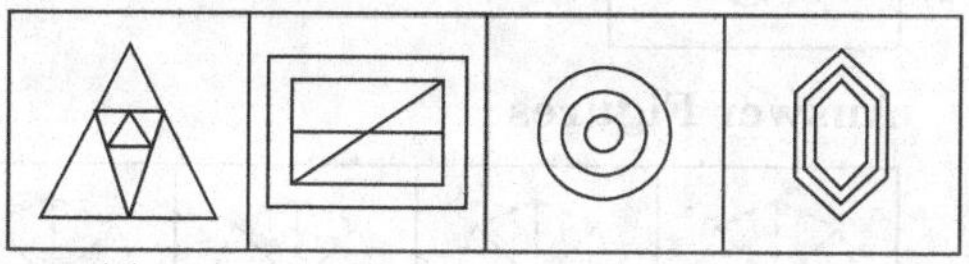

(a) (b) (c) (d)

47. In the question below is given a statement followed by three courses of action number I, II and III. A course of action is a step or administrative decision to be taken for improvement, follow-up or further action in regard to the problem, policy,etc.

On the basis of information given in the statement, you have to assume everything in the statement to be true and then decide which of the three given suggested courses of action logically follows worth pursuing. Then, decide which of the alternatives (a), (b), (c), (d) or (e) is correct

Statement Many school buses have fitted CNG kit without observing the safety guidelines properly. This results into some instances of these buses catching fire due to short circuit and endangering the lives of the school children.

Courses of Action

I. The regional transport authority should immediately carry out checks of all the school buses fitted with CNG kit.
II. The management of all the schools should stop hiring buses fitted with CNG kit.
III. The Government should issue a notification banning school buses for the use of CNG kit.

(a) Only I follows (b) Only II follows
(c) Only III follows (d) Both I and III follow
(e) None of the above

48. An octagonal paper is folded in a particular manner and a punch is made. When unfolded the paper appears as given below. Find the manner in which the paper is folded and punched form the answer figures?

Question Figure

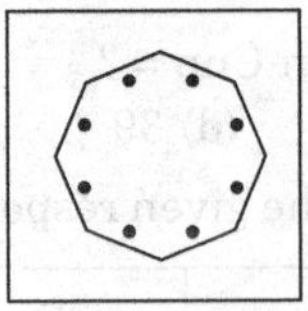

Answer Figures

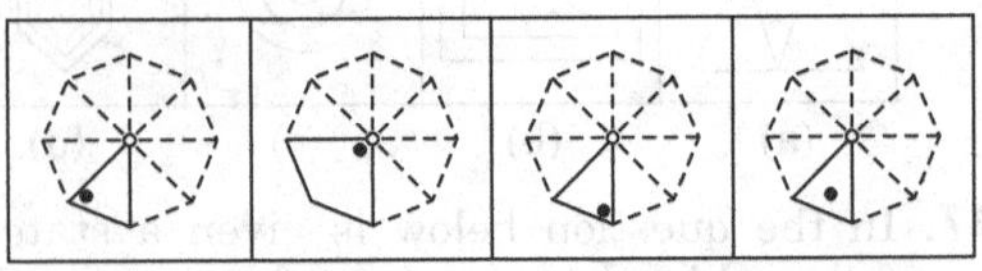

(a) (b) (c) (d)

49. Which answer figure will complete the question figure? **[SSC (10+2) 2014]**

Question Figure

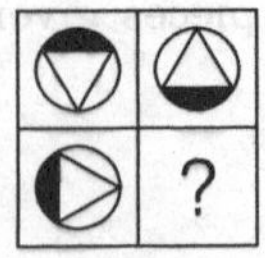

Answer Figures

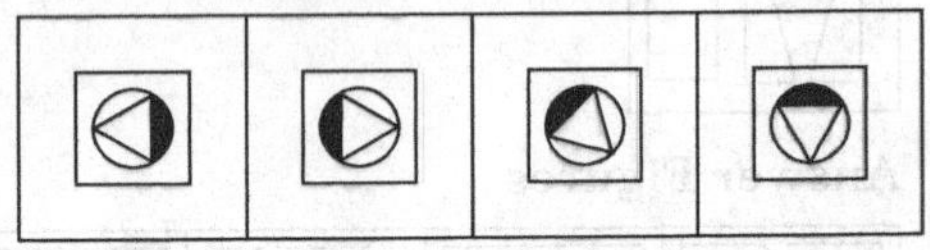

(a) (b) (c) (d)

50. D is K's brother. M is K's sister. T is R's father who is M's brother, F is K's mother. Atleast how many sons do T and F have?

(a) 2 (b) 3
(c) 4 (d) Data inadequate
(e) None of these

Hints and Solutions

1. (*a*) As,

M	O	D	E	and	D	E	A	F
↓	↓	↓	↓		↓	↓	↓	↓
#	8	%	6		%	6	7	$

So, by direct substitution method, we get

F	O	A	M
↓	↓	↓	↓
$	8	7	#

2. (*b*) Suppose, the present age of son = x yr and present age of father = $(70 - x)$ yr

According to the question,

$$2(x + 10) = (70 - x + 10)$$
$$\Rightarrow 2x + 20 = 80 - x$$
$$\Rightarrow 3x = 60$$
$$\Rightarrow x = 20$$

So, son's present age = 20 yr and father's present age = 70 − 20 = 50 yr

3. (*b*) Clearly, question figure is embedded in answer figure (b) as shown below

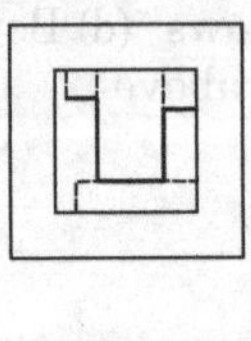

4. (*c*) acb<u>d</u>/cad<u>b</u>/acb<u>d</u>/cad<u>b</u>/acb<u>d</u> ⇒ adddb

5. (*a*) The pattern is as follows

15 →(×2) 30 →(×2) 60 →(×2) 120 →(×2) 240 →(×2) (480)

∴ ? = 480

6. (*a*) The pattern is as follows

DF, GJ, KM, NQ, RT, (UX)

First letters: D +3 G +4 K +3 N +4 R +3 U
Second letters: F +4 J +3 M +4 Q +3 T +4 X

∴ ? = UX

7. (*c*) The water image of the given sequence will be

96FSH52

8. (*b*) Given, 9 − 7 + 85 × 17 ÷ 15

Now, change the signs as per given in the question, we have

$$= 9 \times 7 - 85 \div 17 + 15$$
$$= 63 - 5 + 15 = 63 + 10 = 73$$

9. (*b*) As, $7 \times 8 + 6 = 56 + 6 = 62$

and $8 \times 9 + 7 = 72 + 7 = 79$

Similarly, $6 \times ? + 5 = 47$

$\Rightarrow \quad 6 \times ? = 47 - 5$

$\therefore \quad ? = \frac{42}{6} = 7$

10. (*a*)

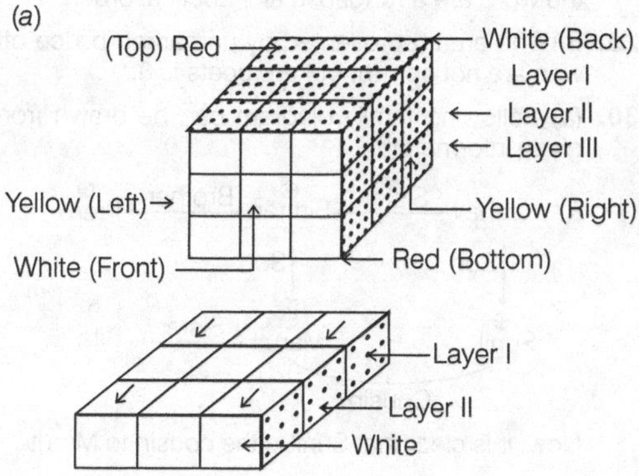

From the given figure , it is very much clear that the four corner cubes in the second layer have one face painted with white and one face painted with yellow.

11. (*d*) Arrangement of words as per dictionary

Each → Eager → Eagle → Early → Earth

(v) (iii) (i) (iv) (ii)

12. (*c*) $H © W \Rightarrow H = W$

$W \% R \Rightarrow W \leq R$

$R @ F \Rightarrow R > F$

Therefore, $H = W \leq R > F$

Conclusions I. $R © H \Rightarrow R = H$ (may be)

II. $R @ H \Rightarrow R > H$ (may be)

R is either greater than or equal to H.

13. (*a*) $M \$ T \Rightarrow M < T$

$T @ K \Rightarrow T > K$

$K © D \Rightarrow K = D$

Therefore, $M < T > K = D$

Conclusions I. $D \$ T \Rightarrow D < T$ (True)

II. $K \$ M \Rightarrow K < M$ (Not True)

So, only Conclusion I is true.

14. (*a*) Squares and rectangles both are geometric figures but different from each other.

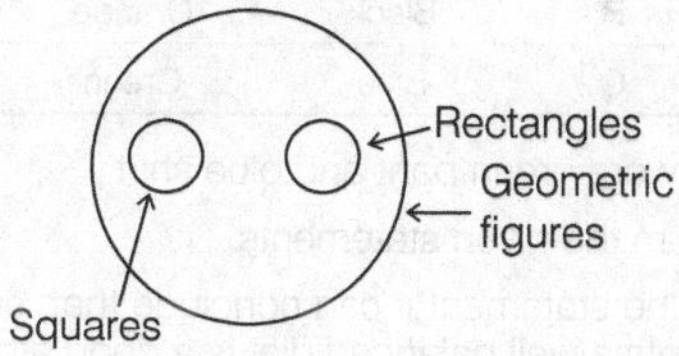

15. (*a*) Route followed by Sonu

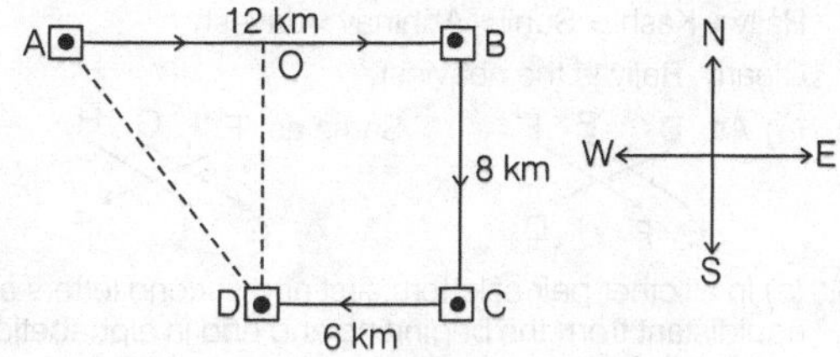

$AD = \sqrt{(AO)^2 + (OD)^2}$

$[AO = AB - CD = 12 - 6 = 6 \text{ km}]$

$= \sqrt{(6)^2 + (8)^2}$

$= \sqrt{36 + 64}$

$= \sqrt{100} = 10 \text{km}$

16. (*d*) Order of their standing position

- Dreamy
- Sleepy
- Bashful
- Sneezy
- Dopey
- Grumpy
- Happy

∴ Dopey is standing just before Grumpy.

17. (*a*) Here, second is the constitutional head of the first.

Governor : State : : President : Country

Therefore, country is the correct answer.

18. (*b*) As,

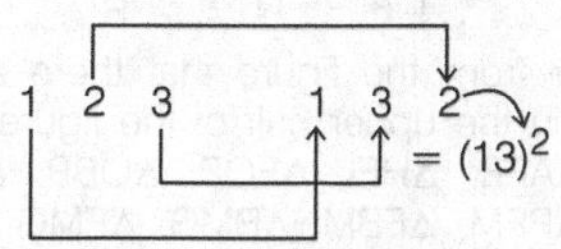

Similarly,

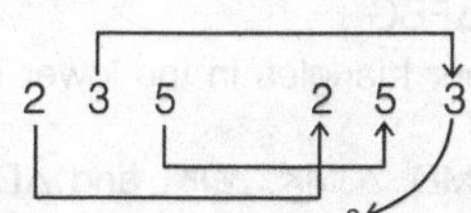

19. (*b*) Arrangment according to the question is as follows

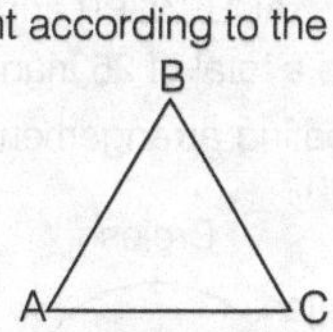

Clearly, B is sitting to the right of C.

20. (*b*) Number of letters in the row

$= 5 + 12 - 1 = 16$

21. (*c*) According to the question,

Rajiv > Sunil > Abhinav

Abhinav > Jayesh

Rajiv > Kashi > Sunil

On arranging the above data, we get
Rajiv > Kashi > Sunil > Abhinav > Jayesh
Clearly, Rajiv is the heaviest.

22. (*d*) As,

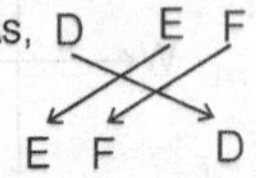

Same as,

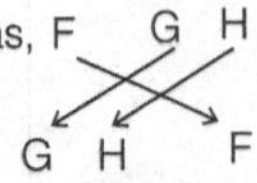

23. (*c*) In all other pair of letters, first and second letters are equidistant from the beginning and end in alphabetical series.

24. (*d*) Route followed by child

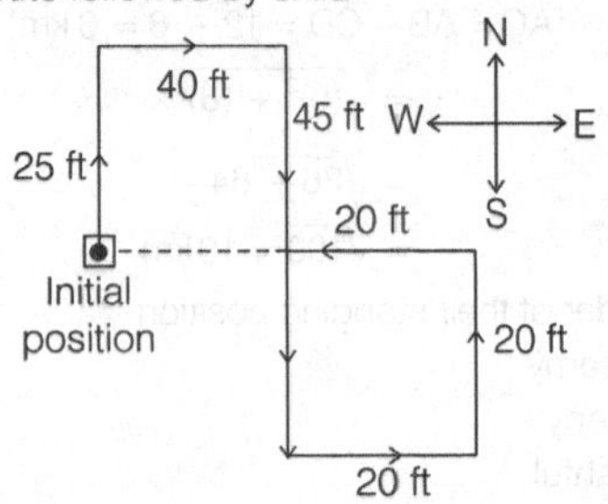

The child is in East direction from the starting point.

25. (*d*) The figure may be labelled as shown in the following figure

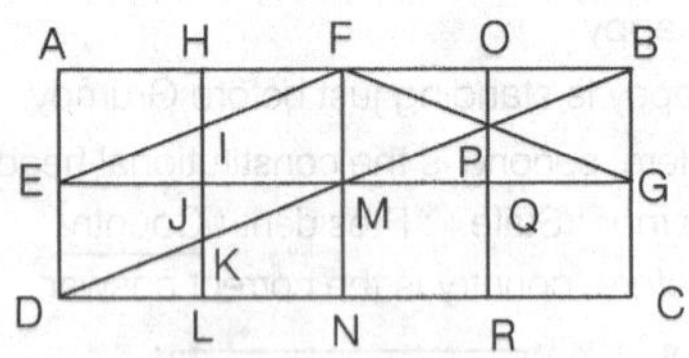

It is clear from the figure that there are seventeen triangles in the upper half of the figure ABGE=ΔEIJ, ΔEFM, ΔAFE, ΔHFI, ΔFOP, ΔOBP, ΔPBG, ΔPGQ ΔPMQ, ΔPFM, ΔFBM, ΔBMG, ΔFMG, ΔFEG, ΔFBP ΔMPG and ΔFBG.

There are four triangles in the lower half of the figure EGCD
= ΔEMD, ΔJMK, ΔDKL and ΔDMN.

There are four triangles in the main figure ABCD
= ΔDBC ,ΔADB, ΔDPR and ΔHBK.

Hence, there are a total of 25 triangles in the figure.

26. (*a*) Following seating arrangement is formed from the given information.

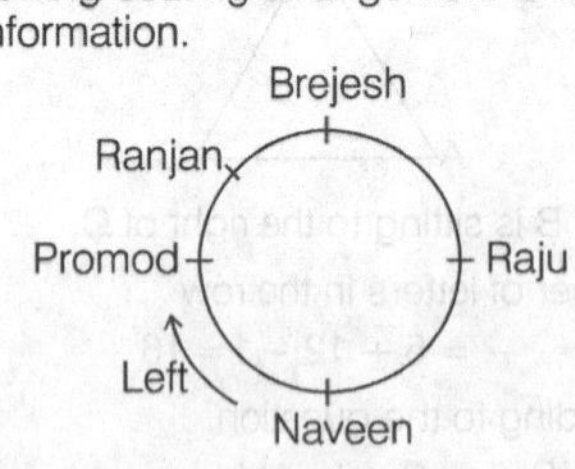

Clearly, Pramod is to the left of Naveen.

27. (*a*) 'Relation' cannot be formed using the letters of the given word due to the absence of letter 'I' in the main word.

28. (*b*) Given word, C A T E G O R |Y|
Alphabetically, A C E G O R T |Y|
Clearly, only Y maintains its position when the letters of the word are arranged in alphabetical order.

29. (*a*) The area represented by unmarried police officers who are not corrupt but are poets is 8.

30. (*a*) Following family diagram can be drawn from the given information,

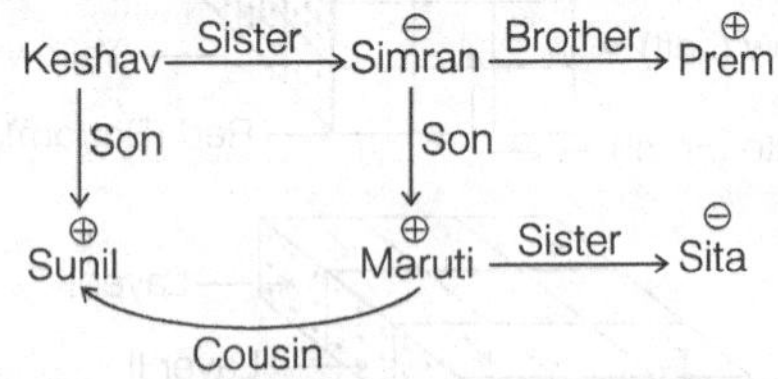

Now, it is clear that Sunil is the cousin to Maruti.

31. (*d*) Clearly, figure 1 to figure 2 the outer figure comes inside, the inner figure comes outside.

Solution (Q. Nos. 32-33) Following table can be drawn from the given information.

	Nickname				Wife			
	Munna	Babboo	Prince	Pappoo	Madhu	Sunanda	Jyoti	Arti
Anil	✗	✔	✗	✗	✗	✗	✔	✗
Mukesh	✗	✗	✗	✔	✗	✗	✗	✔
Piyush	✗	✗	✔	✗	✗	✔	✗	✗
Yogesh	✔	✗	✗	✗	✔	✗	✗	✗

32. (*d*) All the correct.

33. (*b*) The nick name of Mukesh is Pappoo.

34. (c) Friday → 2 days earlier

Therefore. scheduled day = Friday + 2 = Sunday, Sunday + 3 = Wednesday

Therefore, I would have been late by 3 days.

35. (*b*) Following table can be drawn from the given information.

Persons	Shirt	Pants
A	Orange	Yellow
B	Black	Orange
C	Blue	Green

So, C wore green pant and blue shirt.

36. (c) From the given statements.

From the statement it can conclude that, every athlete who eats a well balanced diet is a good athlete.

37. (*b*) We cannot say that Anthony is not from the same city. But it is assumed that unless invited, Anthony will not attend the party as invitation has been emphasised in the statement.

Hence, only Assumption II is implicit.

Solution (Q. Nos. 38-40)

38. (*b*) Statement I is insufficient as no direction is mentioned in it.

From Statement II.

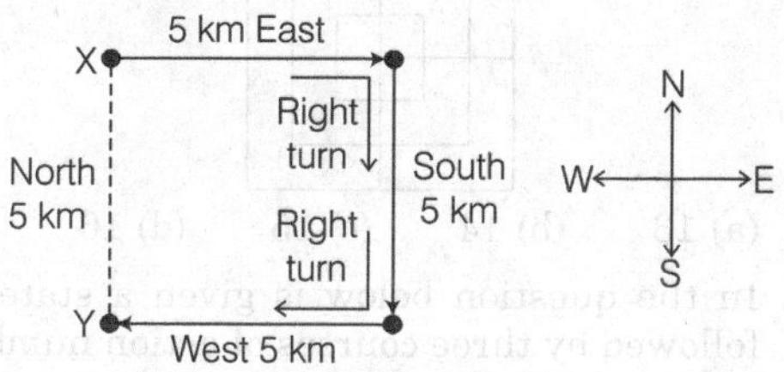

Hence, X is to the North of Y.

So, Statement II alone is sufficient to answer the question.

39. (*e*) From Statement I.

Number of students in class = 21 or 22 or 23 or 24 or 25 or 26

From Statement II,

Number of students in class = 25 or 26 or 27 or 28 or 29 or 30

Since, number of students can be divided into groups of 5 students, therefore number of students must be a multiple of 5.

∴ Number of students in the class = 25 or 30

On combining Statements I and II,

Number of students in the class = 25

Hence, the data in both the Statements I and II together are necessary to answer the question.

40. (*d*) From Statements I and II,

pit (jo) ha = very (good) boy

(jo) na pa = she is (good)

∴ very = pit/ha

So, both the statements are not sufficient to answer the question.

41. (*b*) Optiobn (b) can be formed from the pieces given in problem figures.

42. (*a*)Hands of clock will be together at $32\frac{8}{11}$ minutes past 6.

There are 30 minute spaces between hour and minute hand at 6 O'clock.

The minute hand gains 55 minutes in 60 minutes

∴ It will gain 30 minutes in

$\frac{60}{55} \times 30 = 32\frac{8}{11}$ minutes

Solution (Q. Nos. 43-44)

43. (*e*)

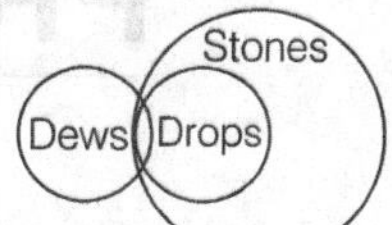

Conclusions I. Atleast some dews are stone. (✔)

II. Atleast some stone are drops. (✔)

44. (*a*)

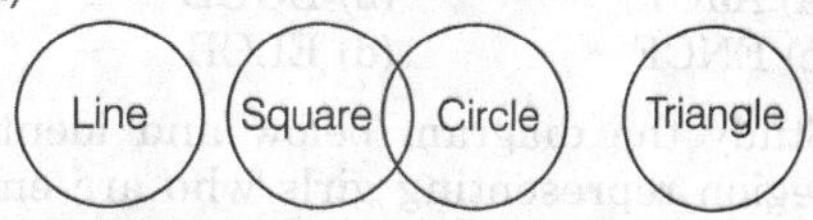

Conclusions

I. All squares can never be triangles. (✔)

II. Some lines are circles. (✗)

45. (*a*) As, P = 16

and 20 1 16 → T A P → 20 + 1 + 16 = 37

Similarly, 3 21 16 → C U P → 3 + 21 + 16 = 40

∴ CUP = 40

46. (*b*) Except in figure (b), in all other figures, there are three similar designs.

47. (*a*) Course of action I is the correct course of action. Courses of action II and III would create a bigger problem, like pollution.

48. (*d*)

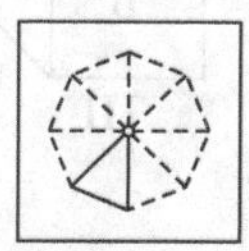

So, option (d) is correct answer.

49. (*a*) As, in first row both figures are opposite to each other.

Similarly, answer figure (a) is opposite to the figure in second row.

50. (*a*) Let us draw the family diagram

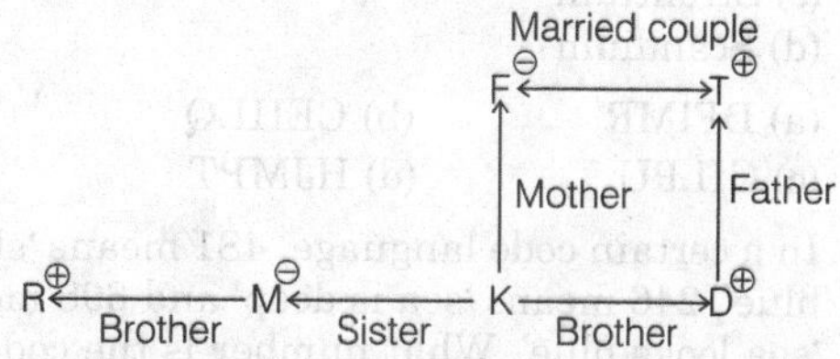

Clearly, R, M, K and D are the children of T and F in which M is a female and gender of K is not known but R and D are the male children of F and T. Hence, T and F have atleast two sons.

PRACTICE SET 5

1. Select the related letters from the given alternatives.

MIKE : OGMC : : CIAD ? **[SSC (CGL) Pre 2015]**

(a) AJCT (b) EGCB
(c) ENCF (d) ELCB

2. Study the diagram below and identify the region representing girls who are employed but unmarried.

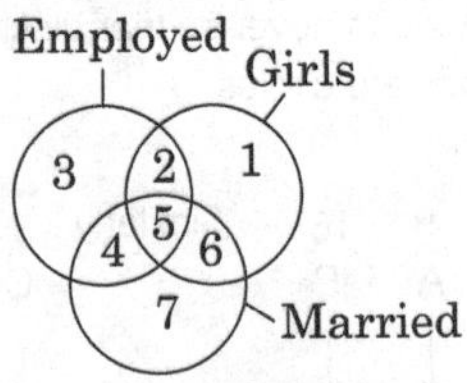

(a) 1 (b) 2
(c) 4 (d) 5

3. Three positions of a dice are given below. Identify the number on the face opposite to 6.

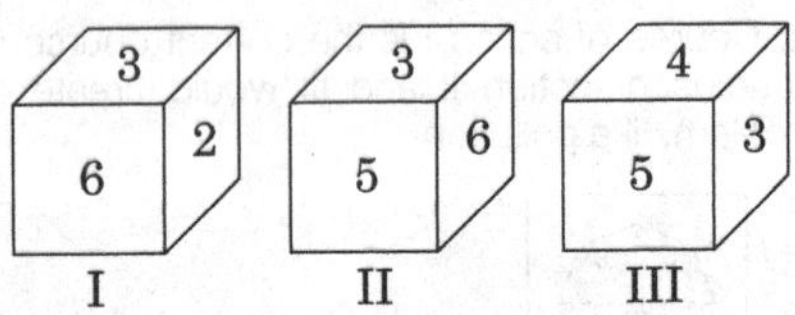

(a) 1 (b) 4
(c) 5 (d) 7

Direction (Q. Nos. 4-5) *In the following questions, find the odd letters/ word from the given alternatives.*

4. (a) Tellurium **[UPPSC (RO) 2014]**
(b) Francium
(c) Strontium
(d) Scandium

5. (a) DFIMR (b) CEHLQ
(c) GILPU (d) HJMPT

6. In a certain code language, 481 means 'sky is blue', 246 means 'sea is deep' and 698 means 'sea looks blue'. What number is the code for 'blue'? **[SSC (CGL) Pre 2015]**

(a) 1 (b) 6
(c) 8 (d) 9

7. How many squares are there in the following figure?

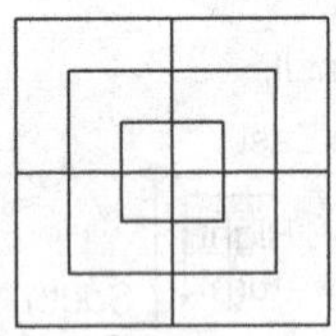

(a) 13 (b) 14 (c) 15 (d) 16

8. In the question below is given a statement followed by three courses of action numbered I, II and III. A course of action is a step or administrative decision to be taken for improvement, follow-up or further action in regard to the problem, policy, etc. On the basis of information given in the statement, you have to assume everything in the statement to be true and then decide which of the three given suggested courses of action logically follows worth pursuing. Then, decide which of the alternatives (a), (b), (c) or (d) is correct.

Statement If the faculty members also join the strike, there is going to be a serious problem.

Courses of Action

I. The faculty members should be persuaded not to go on strike.
II. Those faculty members who join the strike should be suspended.
III. The management should not worry about such small things.

(a) Only I follows
(b) Only II follows
(c) Both II and III follow
(d) None follows

Direction (Q. Nos. 9-10) *Study the following information to answer the given questions.*

There are 3 females A, B and E and 4 males C, D, F and G standing in a straight line. No two females are together. B is to right of C, F and D are not together as A is placed between them. G is not near B or E but E and F are together. D is not to the right of B. **[SNAP 2014]**

9. Who is in the extreme end?
(a) G and B (b) C and F
(c) B and D (d) None of these

10. Who is exactly in the middle?
(a) A (b) F
(c) E (d) None of these

11. Select the one in which the question figure is hidden/ embedded.

Question Figure

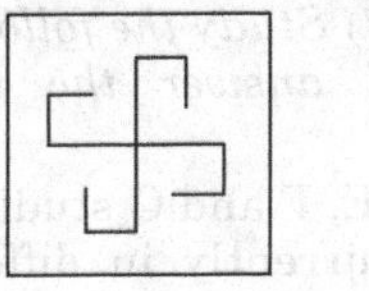

Answer Figures

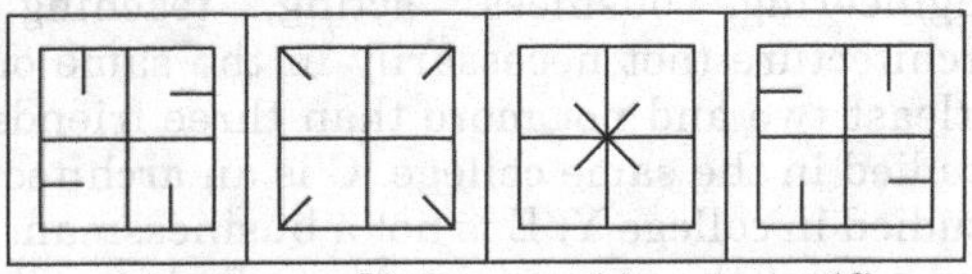

(a) (b) (c) (d)

Direction (Q. Nos. 12-13) *In the following questions, one or two statements is given followed by two conclusions* I *and* II. *You have to consider the statement to be true, even if it seems to be at variance from commonly known facts. You are to decide which of the given conclusions can definitely be drawn from the given statement. Indicate your answer.*

12. Statements I. All poets are daydreamers.
II. All painters are daydreamers.
Conclusions I. All painters are poets.
II. Some daydreamers are not painters.
(a) Only I follows
(b) Only II follows
(c) Neither I nor II follows
(d) Both I and II follow

13. Statements I. Some men are good.
II. Some men are wise.
Conclusions I. Some wise men are good.
II. Some good men are wise.
(a) if I alone can be drawn
(b) if both I and II can be drawn
(c) if II alone can be drawn
(d) if both I and II cannot be drawn

Direction (Q. Nos. 14-15) *In the following questions, a series is given, with one term missing. Choose the correct alternative from the given ones that will complete the series.*

14. 1, 2, 2, 4, 3, 8, 7, 10, ? **[SSC (CGL) Pre 2015]**
(a) 9 (b) 8 (c) 11 (d) 13

15. 2B, 4C, 8E, 14H, ?
(a) 22 L (b) 16 K
(c) 20 L (d) 23 L

16. Find out which of the answer figures (a), (b), (c) and (d) completes the figure matrix?

Question Figure

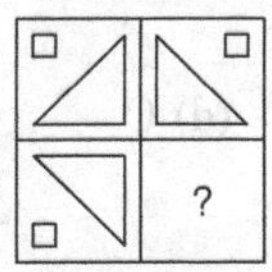

Answer Figures

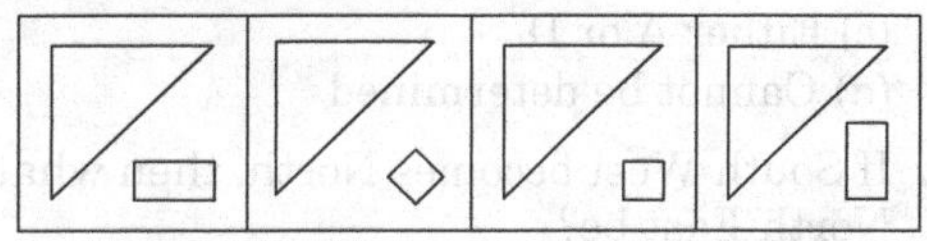

(a) (b) (c) (d)

17. In making decisions about important questions, it is desirable to distinguish between a 'strong' argument and a 'weak' argument. A 'strong' argument must be both important and directly related to the question. A 'weak' argument may not be directly related to the question and may be of minor importance or may be related to the trivial aspect of the question. Each question below is followed by two arguments numbered I and II. You have to decide which of the arguments is 'strong' and which is 'weak'.

Statement Does President's rule in a State improve law and order in the disturbed areas?

Arguments
I. Yes, the Chief Minister does not know how to cope with the deteriorating conditions of law and order.
II. President rule is better than rule by State Government.
(a) if only Argument I is strong
(b) if only Argument II is strong
(c) if either Argument I or II is strong
(d) if neither Argument I nor II is strong

18. If in a certain code language 'FIRE' is written as '# % @ $' and 'DEAL' is written as '© $ ★ ↑', then how will 'FAIL' be written in that language?

(a) # ★ % ↑ (b) # $ % ↑
(c) # ★ @ $ (d) # ★ © ↑

Direction (Q. Nos. 19-20) *Read the following information given below to answer the questions that follow.*

Among A, B, C and D, B is heavier than A and C but C is taller than him. D is not as tall as C while A is the shortest. C is not as heavy as A. D is heavier than B but shorter than him.

19. Who is the heaviest?

(a) B (b) A (c) D (d) C

20. Who is the tallest?

(a) D
(b) C
(c) Either A or D
(d) Cannot be determined

21. If South-West becomes North, then what will North-East be?

(a) North (b) South-East
(c) South (d) East

22. Which of the following figures when placed at the blank space will complete the given pattern?

Question Figure

Answer Figures

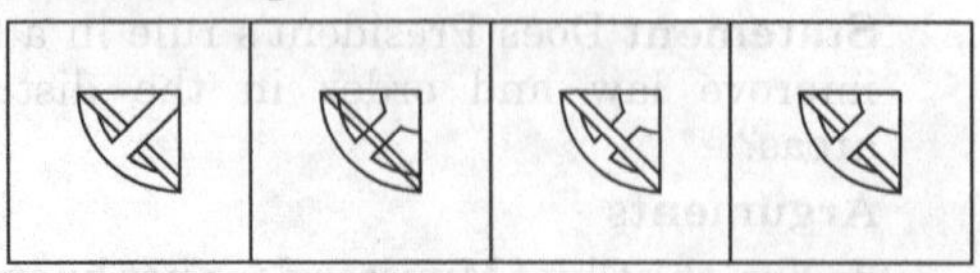

(a) (b) (c) (d)

23. In the given question, unscramble the letters to form a meaningful word. Then, find out the correct numerical position of the letters. **[SSC (10+2) 2015]**

N I T I F E I N
2 4 5 4 3 6 4 2

(a) 3 2 4 3 5 2 4 6 (b) 4 2 3 4 2 4 5 6
(c) 2 4 3 2 4 2 5 6 (d) 3 2 5 3 5 2 4 6

24. If it is possible to form only one three digit number which is a perfect square of a two digit number from the second, the sixth and the seventh digits of the number 76483912 using each digit only once. The second digit of that number is your answer. If no such number can be formed, your answer is '0' and if more than one such number can be formed, your answer is '5'.

(a) 5 (b) 0 (c) 1 (d) 6

Direction (Q. Nos. 25-27) *Study the following information carefully and answer the given questions.*

Seven friends A, B, C, D, E, F and G studied in colleges X, Y and Z are currently in different professions, namely medicines, fashion designing, engineering, business, acting, teaching and architecture (not necessarily in the same order). Atleast two and not more than three friends had studied in the same college. C is an architect and studied in college Y. E is not a businessman. Only G amongst the seven friends studied in college X along with E. F is an engineer and did not study in college Y. B is an actor and did not study in the same college as F. A did not study in college Z. Those who studied in college X are neither fashion designers nor teachers. None of those who studied in college Y is a teacher.

25. Who amongst the following have studied in college Z?

(a) B, A (b) C, F (c) B, D, F (d) A, D
(e) D, F

26. Which of the following groups represents the students of college Y?

(a) C, E, G (b) A, C, D
(c) A, B, C (d) D, B, C
(e) None of these

27. What is the profession of F?

(a) Engineering (b) Business
(c) Medicines (d) Acting
(e) None of these

28. Identify the missing part of the question figure and select it from given answer figures.

Question Figure

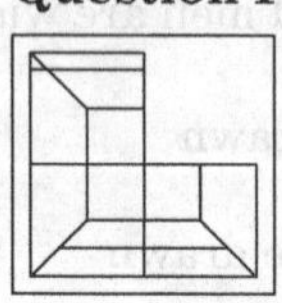

Answer Figures

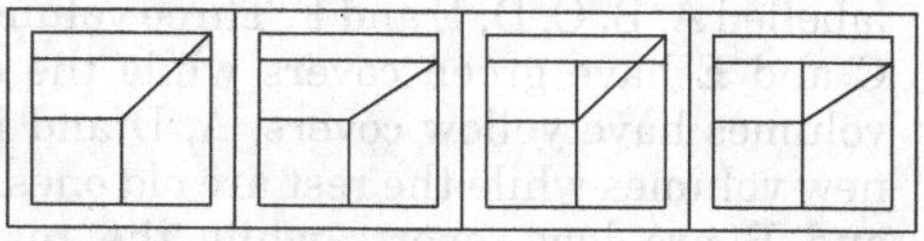

(a) (b) (c) (d)

29. How many rectangles are there in the figure given below?

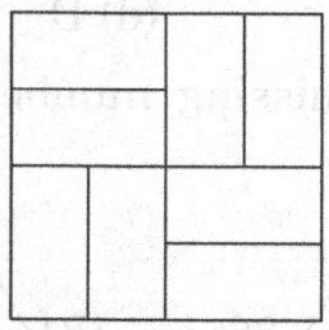

(a) 24 (b) 16 (c) 22 (d) 14

30. Pointing towards A, B said "Your mother is the younger sister of my mother". How is A related to B?

(a) Uncle (b) Cousin (c) Nephew (d) Father

31. Select the missing figure from the given responses.

Question Figure

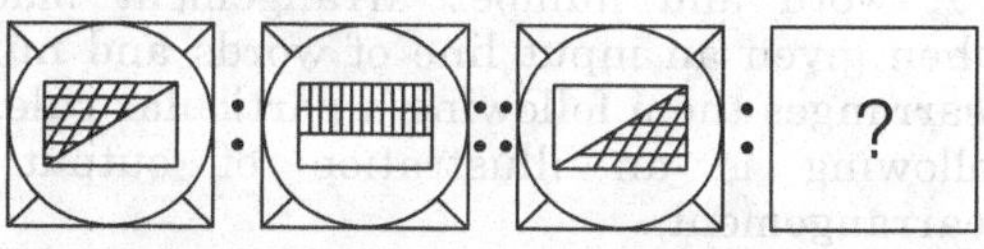

Answer Figures

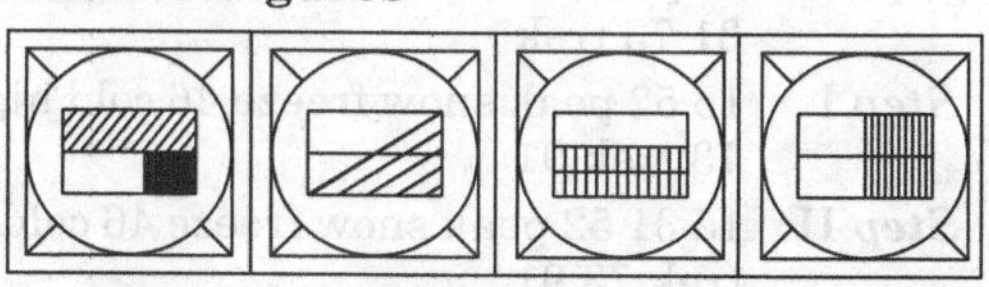

(a) (b) (c) (d)

32. Six persons are sitting in a circle facing the centre of the circle. Parikh is between Babita and Narendra. Asha is between Chitra and Pankaj. Chitra is to the immediate left of Babita. Who is to the immediate right of Babita?

(a) Parikh (b) Pankaj
(c) Narendra (d) Chitra

33. Ravi started walking from his houses towards East direction to bus stop which is 3 km away. Then, he set-off in the bus straight towards his right to the school 4 km away. What is the crow flight distance from his house to the school?

(a) 1 km (b) 5 km
(c) 6 km (d) 12 km

34. A piece of paper is folded and cut as shown below in the question figure. From the given answer figures indicate how it will appear when opened? **[SSC (10+2) 2014]**

Question Figure

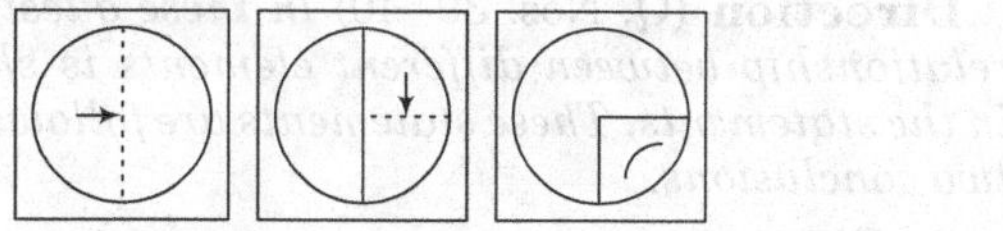

Answer Figures

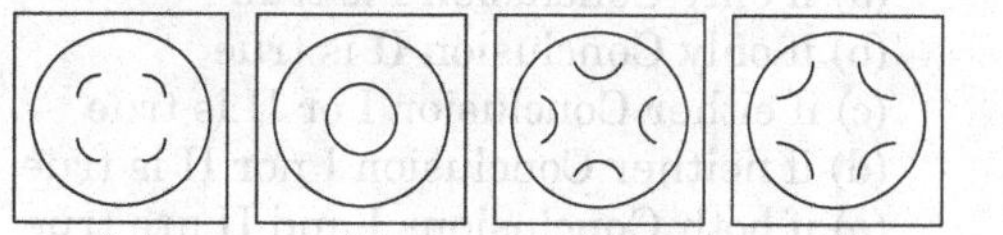

(a) (b) (c) (d)

35. If a mirror is placed on the line AB, then which of the answer figures is the right image of the given figure?

Question Figure

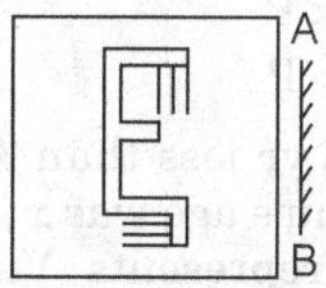

Answer Figures

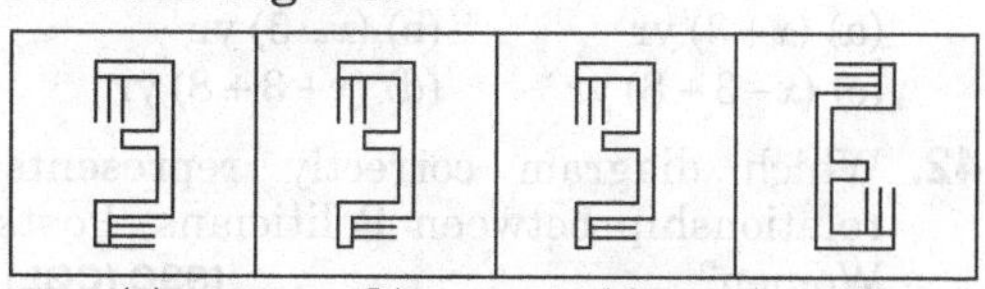

(a) (b) (c) (d)

36. A clock is showing 2:00 pm. If the hour hand is in North-East direction. Then, what will be the direction of hour hand, when the time of clock becomes 9:30 pm?

(a) West (b) South
(c) North (d) East

37. Arrange the following words in a meaningful order.

(i) Reading (ii) Composing
(iii) Writing (iv) Printing

(a) (i), (iii), (iv), (ii)
(b) (ii), (iii), (iv), (i)
(c) (iii), (i), (ii), (iv)
(d) (iii), (ii), (iv), (i)

38. If A is B's sister, C is B's mother, D is C's father and E is D's mother, then how is A related to D?
(a) Granddaughter
(b) Daughter
(c) Aunt
(d) Father

Direction (Q. Nos. 39- 40) *In these questions, relationship between different elements is shown in the statements. These statements are followed by two conclusions.*

Give answer
(a) if only Conclusion I is true
(b) if only Conclusion II is true
(c) if either Conclusion I or II is true
(d) if neither Conclusion I nor II is true
(e) if both Conclusions I and II are true

39. Statement $H \geq I = J > K \leq L$
Conclusions I. $K < H$
II. $L \leq I$

40. Statements $S > C \geq O, P < C$
Conclusions I. $O < P$
II. $S > P$

41. Present age of Vinay is 8 yr less than Anu's present age. If 3 yr ago Anu's age was x, then which of the following represents Vinay's present age?
(a) $(x+3)$ yr (b) $(x-5)$ yr
(c) $(x-3+8)$ yr (d) $(x+3+8)$ yr

42. Which diagram correctly represents the relationship between Politicians, Poets and Women? **[SSC (CGL) 2011]**

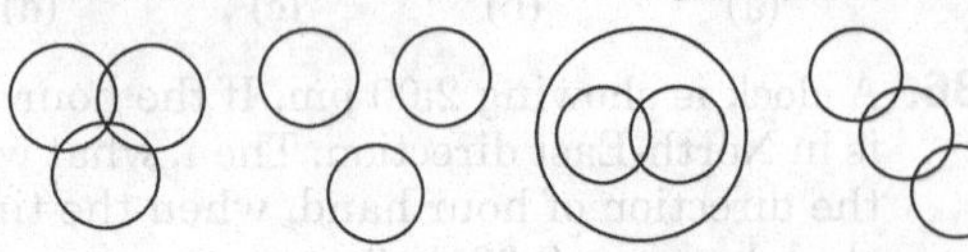

(a) (b) (c) (d)

43. If '+' stands for division, '÷' stands for multiplication and '×' stands for addition, which one of the following equations is correct?
(a) $10 + 5 + 4 = 6$
(b) $10 - 4 + 2 = 6$
(c) $10 + 2 - 5 = 6$
(d) $10 + 2 \times 1 = 6$

44. On a shelf six volumes are placed by side labelled A, B, C, D, E and F. Three volumes B, C and E have green covers while the other volumes have yellow covers. A, D and B are new volumes while the rest are old ones. A, C and B are law reports while the rest are gazetteers. Which of the following volumes is green covered, old and law report?
(a) A (b) B
(c) C (d) D

45. Select the missing number from the given responses. **[SSC (CGL) 2015]**

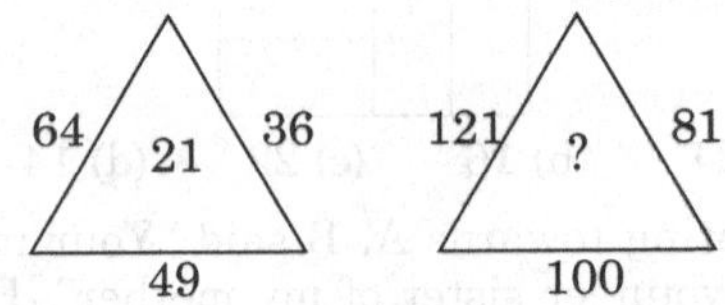

(a) 40 (b) 30
(c) 20 (d) 10

Direction (Q. Nos. 46-49) *Study the following information to answer the given questions.* **[NIACL (AO) 2014]**

A word and number arrangement machine when given an input line of words and number rearranges them following a particular rule. The following is an illustration of output and rearrangement.

Input 52 peak 91 snow freeze 46 cold 15 high 31 73 trek
***Step* I** 15 52 peak snow freeze 46 cold high 31 73 trek 91
***Step* II** 15 31 52 peak snow freeze 46 cold high trek 73 91
***Step* III** 15 31 46 peak snow freeze cold high trek 52 73 91
***Step* IV** 15 31 46 cold peak snow freeze high trek 52 73 91
***Step* V** 15 31 46 cold freeze peak snow high trek 52 73 91
***Step* VI** 15 31 46 cold freeze high peak snow trek 52 73 91

Step VI is the last step of the rearrangement. As per the rules followed in the above steps, find out in each of the following questions the appropriate steps for the given input.

Input 67 hot sun 19 best 83 ice 49 ace 77 cut 37

46. How many steps would be needed to complete the rearrangement?
(a) X (b) VIII (c) IX (d) VII
(e) None of these

47. Which step number would be the following output?
19 37 49 ace best hot sun ice cut 67 77 83
(a) II (b) VI (c) V (d) IV
(e) None of these

48. Which of the following would be the Step I ?
(a) 19 37 49 hot sun best ice ace cut 67 77 83
(b) 83 67 hot sun best ice 49 ace 77 cut 37 19
(c) 19 67 ace best hot sun ice 49 77 cut 37 83
(d) 19 67 hot sun best ice 49 ace 77 cut 37 83
(e) None of the above

49. Which of the following would be the final arrangement?
(a) 67 77 83 ace best cut hot ice sun 19 37 49
(b) 19 37 49 ace best cut hot ice sun 67 77 83
(c) 19 37 49 67 77 83 ace best cut hot ice sun
(d) 19 37 49 ace ice best cut hot sun 67 77 83
(e) None of the above

50. Find the correct water image of the figure given below?

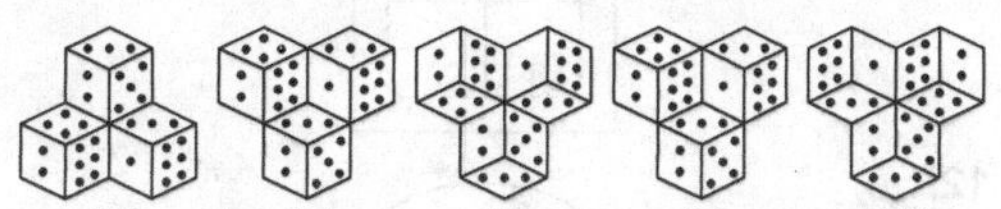

(A) (a) (b) (c) (d)

Hints and Solutions

1. (*b*) As,

M I K E
↓+2 ↓−2 ↓+2 ↓−2
O G M C

Similarly,

C I A D
↓+2 ↓−2 ↓+2 ↓−2
E G C B

2. (*b*) Girls who are employed but unmarried is represented by the common area between the upper two circles (excluding the area common to all the three circles).
Such region is marked '2'.

3. (*b*) From dice II and III, 3 and 5 are two common numbers. Hence, 6 and 4 are opposite to each other.

or

From second method (Dice I and III) (since, 3 is common)

	2	
4	3	6
	5	
	1	

1 is opposite to 3.
2 is opposite to 5.
4 is opposite to 6.

4. (*b*) Francium is metalloid while all others are alkali metals.

5. (*d*) Except 'HJMPT', all three are same and having same difference between the letters in increasing order.

6. (*c*) Given,

④ △8 1 ⟶ sky (is) △blue
② ④ □6 ⟶ □sea (is) deep
□6 9 △8 ⟶ □sea looks △blue

It is clearly shown that, the code for blue is 8.

7. (*c*) The figure in the question may by labelled as shown in the figure below

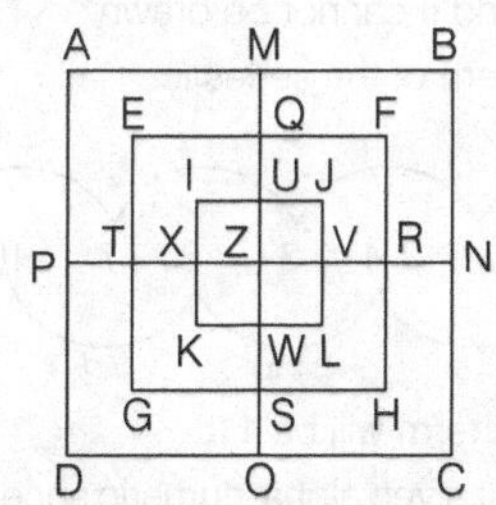

In the inner most square, there are five squares namely □ IXZU, □ UZVJ, □ XKWZ, □ ZWLV and □ IJLK
In the middle square there are five squares namely □ ETZQ, □ QZRF, □ TZSG, □ ZSHR and □ EGHF
In the outer most square there are five squares namely □ APZM, □ MZNB, □ PDOZ, □ ZOCN and □ ABCD
∴ Total number of squares = 5 + 5 + 5 = 15

8. (*a*) The best way to prevent faculty members to go on strike is to persuade them. Hence, Course of action I shows the right course of action.

Solution (Q. Nos. 9-10) Standing arrangement in a straight line is as follows:

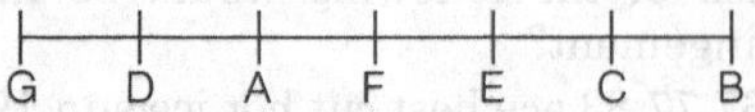

9. (*a*) G and B is in the extreme ends.

10. (*b*) F is exactly in the middle.

11. (*d*) Clearly, question figure is embedded in answer figure (d) as shown below

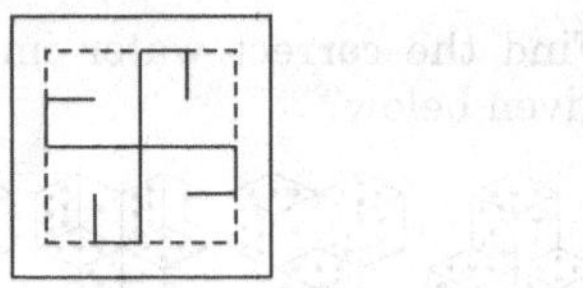

12. (*b*)

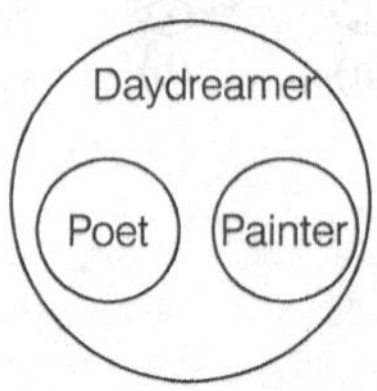

Conclusions I. All painters are poets. (✗)
II. Some daydreamers are not painters. (✓)

So, only II follows.

13. (*d*)

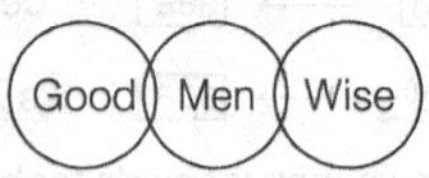

Conclusions I. Some wise men are good. (✗)
II. Some good men are wise. (✗)

So, both I and II cannot be drawn.

14. (*c*) The pattern of the series is

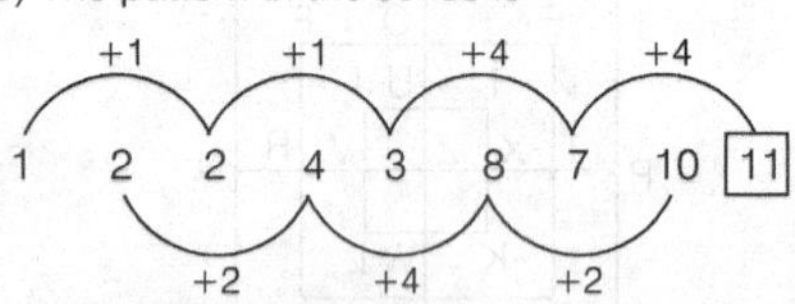

So, the next term will be 11.

15. (*a*) Pattern of given alpha-numeric series is as follows

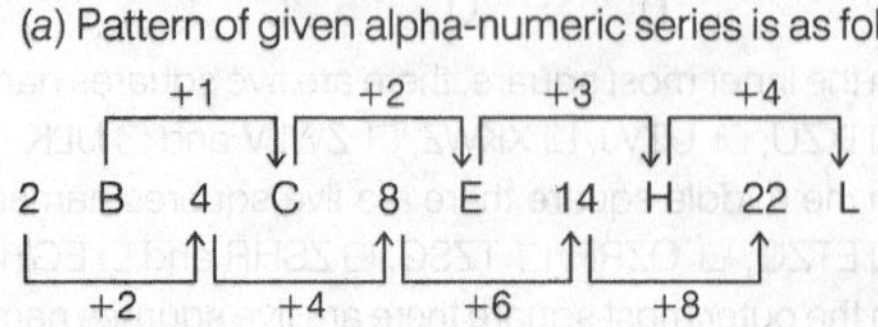

∴ ? = 22 L

16. (*c*) Columnwise, second element is the mirror image of first element.

17. (*d*) Both the arguments are weak. Argument I is weak as it is totally hypothetical. Argument II is irrelevant.

18. (*a*) As,

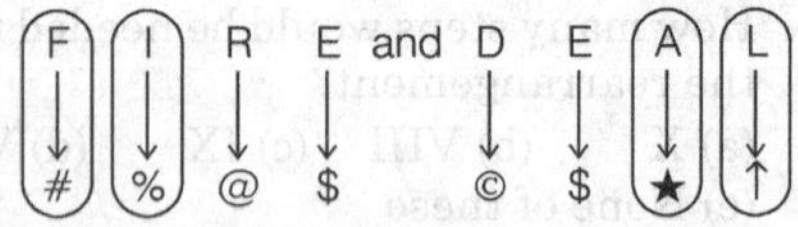

So, by direct substitution method, we get

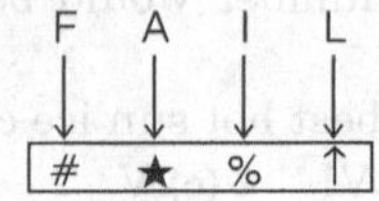

∴ FAIL ⇒ # ★ % ↑

Solution (Q. Nos. 19-20) Here, H and T in the subscript denote heavier and taller.

$B_H > A_H$ and C_H $C_T > B_T$
$A_H > C_H$ $C_T > D_T$, $D_T > A_T$
$D_H > B_H$ $B_T > D_T$

19. (*c*) $D_H > B_H > A_H > C_H$

Here, D is the heaviest.

20. (*b*) $C_T > B_T > D_T > A_T$

Here, C is the tallest.

21. (*c*) The diagrammatic representation of direction is as shown below

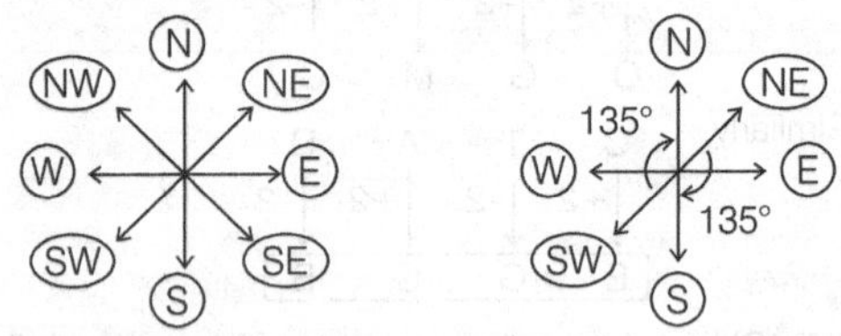

Clearly, directions are moving 135° clockwise. Hence, North-East will become South moving 135° clockwise.

22. (*d*) If the figure, as shown in the option (d) is placed in the missing portion of the original figure, it completes the original figure. Hence, option (d) is the correct option.

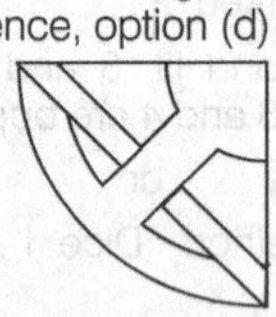

23. (*b*) In the given question,

N	I	T	I	F	E	I	N
2	4	5	4	3	6	4	2

In option (a) 3 2 4 3 5 2 4 6 is coded as F N I F T N I E. It is not a meaningful word.

In option (b) 4 2 3 4 2 4 5 6 is coded as I N F I N I T E. It is a meaningful word so it is true.

24. (*a*) Let us see

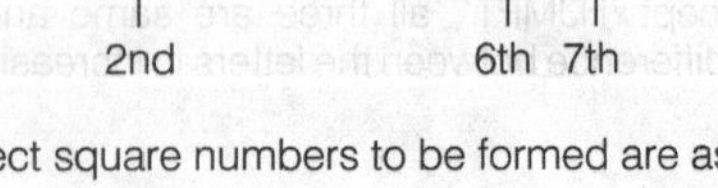

Perfect square numbers to be formed are as follows

(169) (196) (961)
↑ ↑ ↑
$(13)^2$ $(14)^2$ $(31)^2$

∴ Number of perfect square numbers = 3

So, the required answer is '5'.

Solution (Q. Nos. 25-27) Following table can be drawn from the given information

Friend	College	Profession
A	Y	Fashion Desiging
B	Y	Acting
C	Y	Architecture
D	Z	Teaching
E	X	Medicine
F	Z	Engineering
G	X	Business

25. (*e*) D and F studied in College Z.

26. (*c*) A, B and C represent group of students of college Y.

27. (*a*) F is an engineer.

28. (*a*) Option (a) will complete the given pattern as follows

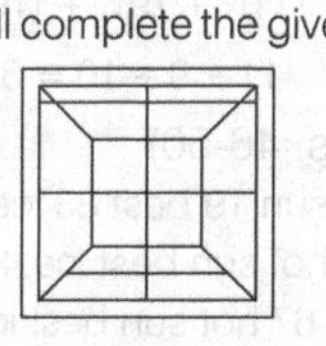

29. (*b*)

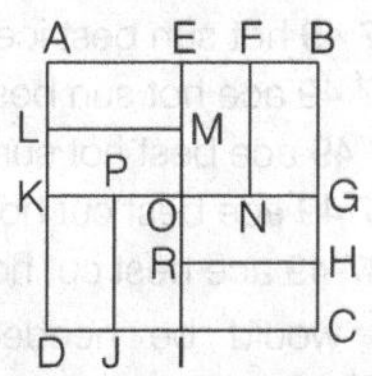

Total 16 rectangles are as follow

▭ AEID, ▭ BEIC, ▭ ABGK,
▭ KGCD, ▭ AEML, ▭ LMOK,
▭ KPJD, ▭ POIJ, ▭ EFNO,
▭ BGNF, ▭ ORHG, ▭ HCIR,
▭ AFNK, ▭ BERH, ▭ PGCJ,
and ▭ LMID

30. (*b*) Following family diagram can be drawn from the given information,

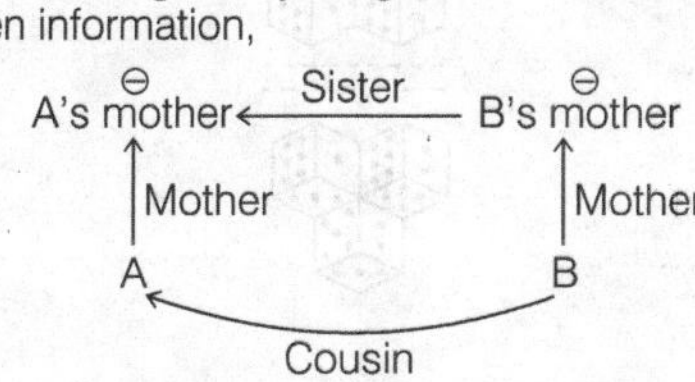

Now, it is clear that A is the cousin of B.

31. (*c*) Clearly, from figure I to figure II the pattern of design is changes and the oblique line becomes horizontal.

32. (*a*) Following seating arrangement is formed from the given information

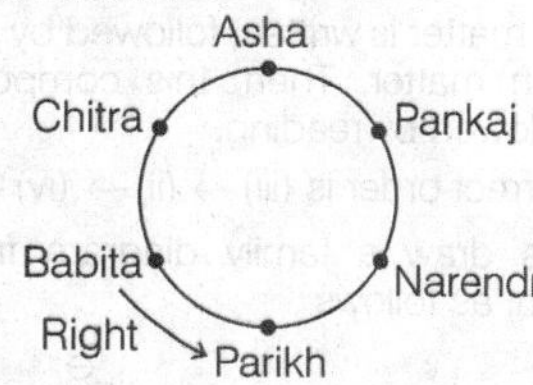

Clearly, Parikh is to the immediate right of Babita.

33. (*b*) Route followed by Ravi,

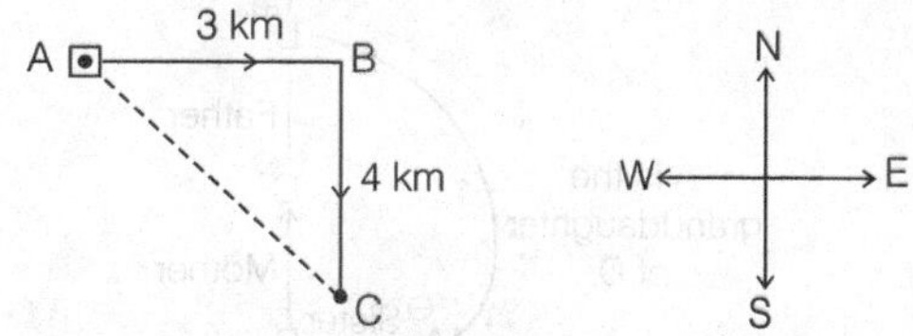

By Pythagoras theorem,

$$AC = \sqrt{(AB)^2 + (BC)^2}$$
$$= \sqrt{(3)^2 + (4)^2}$$
$$= \sqrt{9 + 16} = \sqrt{25} = 5 \text{ km}$$

34. (*d*)

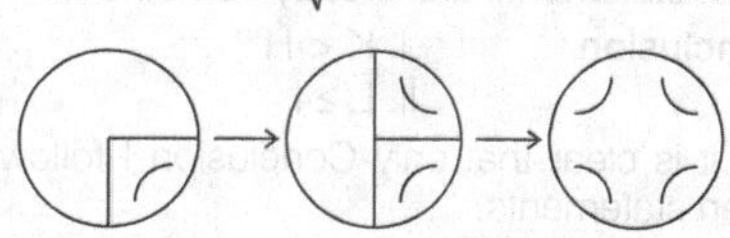

35. (*a*) The correct laterally inverted mirror image of the questions figure is as follows

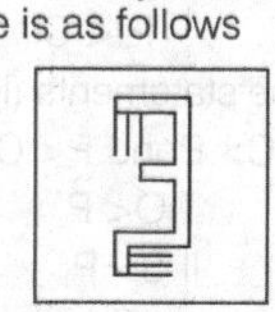

36. (*a*) At 2:00pm, the hour hand points towards the North-East direction.

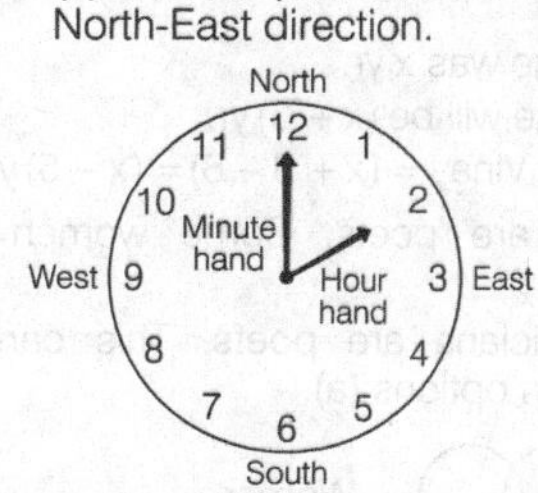

2:00 pm

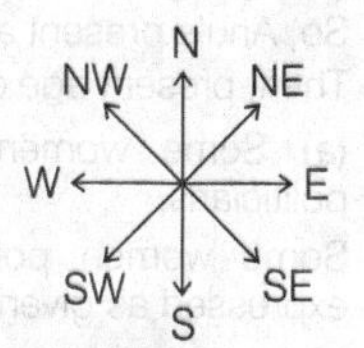

Now, at 9:30 pm

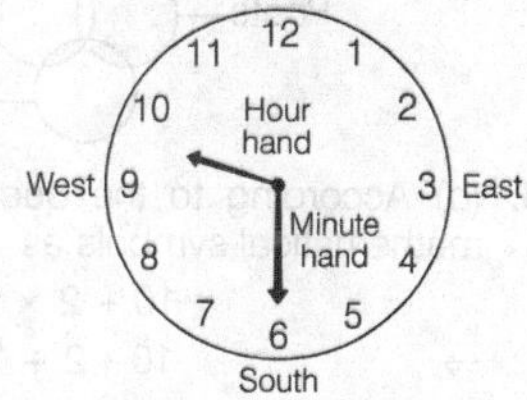

9:30 pm

It is clear that at 9:30 pm, the hour hand points in West direction and the minute hand points in South direction.

37. (*d*) The given words represent the various stages in the process of publishing.
Firstly, the matter is written, followed by composition of that written matter. Then, this composed matter is printed followed by reading.
So, the correct order is (iii) → (ii) → (iv) → (i)

38. (*a*) Let us draw a family diagram from the given information, as follows

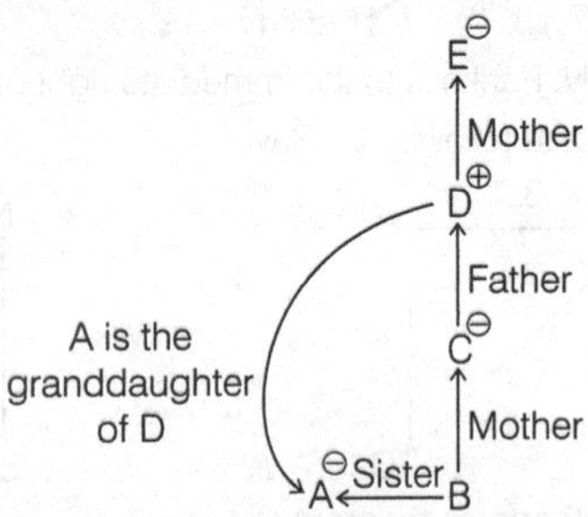

Now, it is clear that A is the granddaughter of D.

Solution (Q. Nos 39-41)

39. (*a*) Given that, H ≥ I = J > K ≤ L
Here, statements are already combined.
Conclusion I. K < H (True)
II. L ≥ I (False)
So, it is clear that only Conclusion I follows from the given statements.

40. (*b*) Given that, S > C ≥ O ...(i)
and P < C ...(ii)
On combining the statements (i) and (ii), we get
S> C> Pand P< C≥ O
Conclusion I.O< P (False)
and II.S> P (True)
So, it is clear that only Conclusion II follows from the given statements.

41. (*b*) 3 yr ago Anu's age was *x* yr.
So, Anu's present age will be $(x+3)$ yr.
Then, present age of Vinay = $(x+3-8)=(x-5)$ yr

42. (*a*) Some women are poets. Some women are politicians.
Some women politicians are poets. This can be expressed as given in options (a).

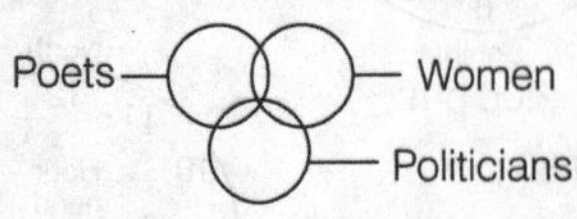

43. (*d*) According to the question, we can arrange the mathematical symbols as
$10 + 2 \times 1 = 6$
⇒ $10 \div 2 + 1 = 6$
⇒ $5 + 1 = 6$

44. (*c*) According to the gives information, the arrangement is as following.

Volumes	Green Cover	Yellow Cover	New	Old	Law Report	Gazetteer
A	✗	✔	✔	✗	✔	✗
B	✔	✗	✔	✗	✔	✗
C	✔	✗	✗	✔	✔	✗
D	✗	✔	✔	✗	✗	✔
E	✔	✗	✗	✔	✗	✔
F	✗	✔	✗	✔	✗	✔

C is the book with green cover, old and law report.

45. (*b*) As, in first figure,
64 36 49
↓ ↓ ↓
$(8)^2 + (6)^2 + (7)^2$
$8 + 6 + 7 = 21$
Similarly, in second figure,
121 81 100
↓ ↓ ↓
$(11)^2 + (9)^2 + (10)^2$
$11 + 9 + 10 = 30$

Solution (Q. Nos. 46-50)

Input 67 hot sun 19 best 83 ice 49 ace 77 cut 37
***Step* I** 19 67 hot sun best ice 49 ace 77 cut 37 83
***Step* II** 19 37 67 hot sun best ice 49 ace cut 77 83
***Step* III** 19 37 49 hot sun best ice ace cut 67 77 83
***Step* IV** 19 37 49 ace hot sun best ice cut 67 77 83
***Step* V** 19 37 49 ace best hot sun ice cut 67 77 83
***Step* VI** 19 37 49 ace best cut hot sun ice 67 77 83
***Step* VII** 19 37 49 ace best cut hot ice sun 67 77 83

46. (*d*) Step VII would be needed to complete the rearrangement.

47. (*c*) Step V would be the output.

48. (*d*) '19 67 hot sun best ice 49 ace 77 cut 37 83' would be the Step I.

49. (*b*) '19 37 49 ace best cut hot ice sun 67 77 83' would be the final arrangement.

50. (*b*) So, option (b) is correct water image.

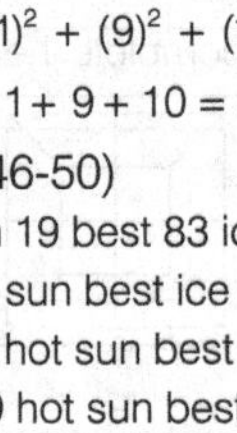

PRACTICE SET 6

1. Select the related word from the given alternatives.

Hive : Bee : : Eyrie : ?

[Delhi Police (CISF) 2015]

(a) Parrot (b) Sparrow
(c) Eagle (d) Pigeon

2. It is 3 O'clock in a watch. If the minute hand points towards the North -East, then the hour hand will point towards the

(a) South (b) South-West
(c) North-West (d) South-East

3. Group the given figures into three classes using each figure only once.

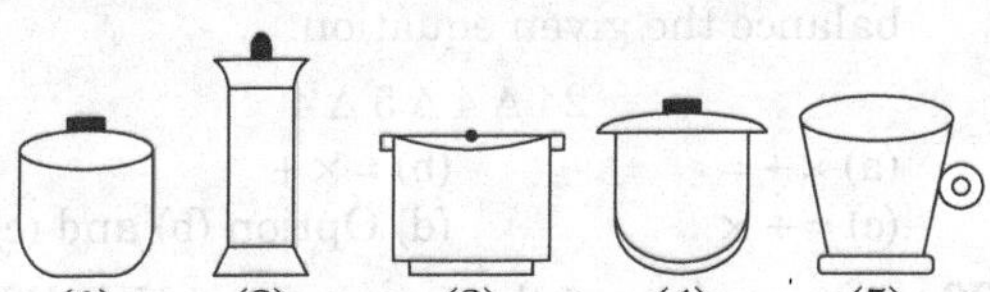

(1) (2) (3) (4) (5)

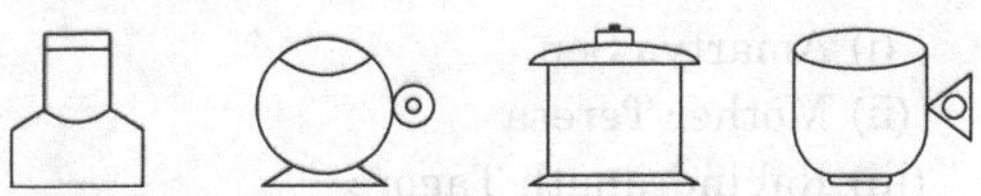

(6) (7) (8) (9)

(a) 1, 4, 6; 2, 3, 8; 5, 7, 9
(b) 2, 3, 8; 4, 5, 7; 1, 6, 9
(c) 5, 7, 9; 3, 4, 8; 2, 9, 1
(d) 1, 4, 6; 2, 3, 5; 6, 7, 8

Direction (Q. Nos. 4-5) *In the following questions, find the odd numbers/word from the given alternatives.*

4. (a) Wood (b) Stone
(c) Tree (d) Engine

5. (a) 1 (b) 9 (c) 48 (d) 16

6. How many three letters meaningful words can be formed from the word TEAR beginning with 'A' and without repeating any letter within that word?

(a) One (b) Three
(c) Five (d) Two

7. In this question, unscramble the letters to form a meaningful word. Then, find out the correct numerical position of the letters.

H N R C A B **[SSC (10 + 2) 2015]**
1 2 3 4 5 6

(a) 6 5 3 4 1 2 (b) 4 1 5 6 2 3
(c) 6 3 5 2 4 1 (d) 3 5 6 4 1 2

Direction (Q. Nos. 8-9) *Study the following information carefully and answer the questions given below.*

Six friends A, B, C, D, E and F are sitting in a row facing towards North. C is sitting between A and E. D is not at the end. B is sitting at immediate right of E. F is not at the right end but D is sitting at third left of E.

8. How many persons are there to the right of D?

(a) One (b) Two
(c) Three (d) Four

9. Which of the following is sitting to the left of D?

(a) F (b) C (c) E (d) A

10. From the given two positions of a single dice, find the digit at the face opposite to the face having digit 4.

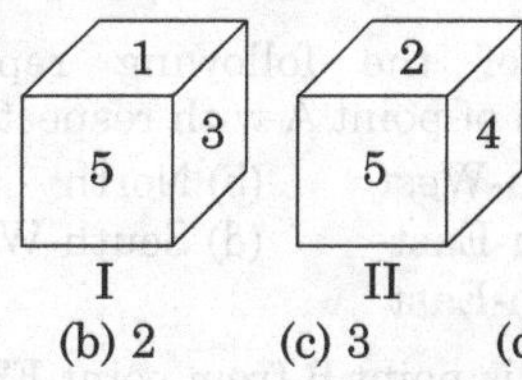

(a) 1 (b) 2 (c) 3 (d) 4

11. Given below are capital letters in the first line and symbols in the second line. Symbols and letters are codes for each other. Choose the correct code for the given letters.

[SSC (CGL) Pre 2014]

<table>
<tr><td>A</td><td>C</td><td>E</td><td>G</td><td>H</td><td>I</td><td>O</td><td>N</td><td>P</td><td>R</td><td>T</td><td>S</td><td>B</td><td>D</td><td>M</td></tr>
<tr><td>+</td><td>−</td><td>÷</td><td>×</td><td>=</td><td>(</td><td>)</td><td>[</td><td>]</td><td>≠</td><td>||</td><td>#</td><td>|</td><td>></td><td><</td></tr>
</table>

BEAST

(a) | ÷ + ≠ || (b) | ÷ × # ||
(c) | ÷ + # || (d) | ÷ + ≠ =

12. If 'blue' is called 'green', 'green' is called 'white', 'white' is called 'red' and 'red' is called 'black', then what is the colour of clear sky?

(a) Blue (b) Green
(c) White (d) Black

13. *Read the following information carefully and answer the questions given below.*

I. Five friends Amar, Kapil , Sarvesh, Rohan and Nagesh put on five shirts of different colours, i.e. Red, Yellow, Blue,White and Green, while they were going to attend a party. These colour are not in order.

II. They have different hobbies as reading , playing, outing, singing and writing.

III. Kapil , who likes singing, does not wear yellow shirt. Sarvesh wears red shirt and he does not like reading or writing . Nagesh likes playing and he does not wear blue or yellow shirt. Amar likes writing and Rohan does not wear yellow or green shirt.

What is the colour of Kapil's shirt?

(a) White (b) Green
(c) Blue (d) Data inadequate

Direction (Q. Nos. 14-15) *Study the following information and answer the given questions.*

Point B is 4 m to the South of point A. Point C is 5 m to the East of point B. Point D is 4 m to the North of point C. Point E is 10 m to the West of point D. Point F is 4 m to the South of point E.

[IBPS RRB (Office Assistant) 2015]

14. Which of the following represents the direction of point A with respect to point C?

(a) North-West (b) North
(c) North-East (d) South-West
(e) South-East

15. How far is point B from point F?

(a) 7 m (b) 5 m
(c) 4 m (d) 10 m
(e) 2 m

16. A father is nine times as old as his son and the mother is eight times as old as the son. The sum of the father's and the mother's age is 51 yr. What is the age of the son?

[UPSC 2015]

(a) 7 yr (b) 5 yr
(c) 4 yr (d) 3 yr

17. Looking at a photograph, a person said, "I have no brother or sister but that man's father is my father's son". At whose photograph was the person looking at?

[SSC (10 + 2) 2011]

(a) His son's (b) His nephew
(c) His father's (d) His own

18. Select the missing number from the given responses.

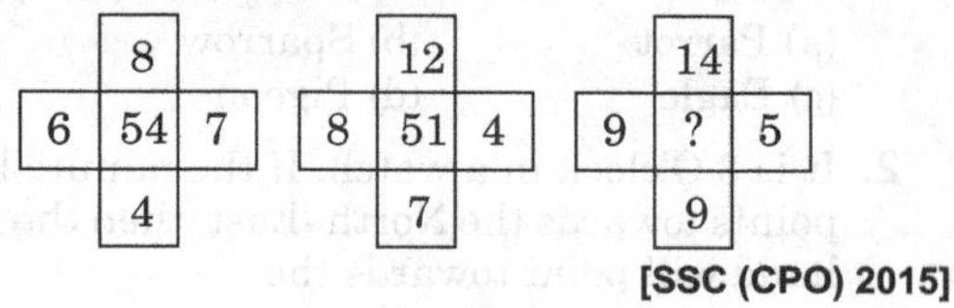

[SSC (CPO) 2015]

(a) 53 (b) 76
(c) 71 (d) 68

19. Select the correct combination of mathematical signs to replace 'Δ' signs and to balance the given equation.

24 Δ 4 Δ 5 Δ 4

(a) × + = (b) = × +
(c) = + × (d) Option (b) and (c)

20. Arrange the following Indian Nobel Prize winners in chronological order.

(i) Amartya Sen
(ii) Mother Teresa
(iii) Rabindranath Tagore
(iv) Venkatraman Ramakrishna
(v) Sir C.V. Raman

[SSC (Assistant) Grade III 2012]

(a) (iii), (v), (ii), (i), (iv)
(b) (iii), (ii), (v), (iv), (i)
(c) (iii), (iv), (i), (ii), (v)
(d) (iii), (v), (ii), (iv), (i)

21. Sati is elder than Renu, Geeta is younger than Renu while Priya is elder than Sati. Who is the eldest ?

(a) Priya (b) Sati
(c) Renu (d) Geeta

Direction (Q. Nos. 22-24) *Study the following information carefully to answer the questions below.*

An electronic device, when fed with the numbers, rearranges them in a particular order following certain rules. The following is step by step process of rearrangements for the given input of numbers.

Input	75	9	312	55	16	61
Step I	312	9	75	55	16	61
Step II	312	75	9	55	16	61
Step III	312	75	61	55	16	9

For the given input Step III is the last step.

22. **Input** '88 172 15 105 412 25'.
Find Step III of this input.
(a) 172 412 15 105 88 25
(b) 412 172 15 105 88 25
(c) 412 172 105 88 15 25
(d) Cannot be determined
(e) None of the above

23. If Step III of an input is '525 175 118 107 112 99 100', then find the input.
(a) 525 118 107 175 112 99 100
(b) 118 525 107 112 175 99 100
(c) 99 100 175 112 107 525 118
(d) Cannot be determined
(e) None of the above

24. Input '173 390 85 188 522 765'
What will be the last step for this input?
(a) IV (b) V (c) VII (d) VI
(e) None of these

25. In a class of students, Sandeep is 25th from top and 32nd from bottom in a class, then total number of students in the class is
(a) 56 (b) 50 (c) 57 (d) 58

Direction (Q. Nos. 26-27) *Each of the following questions below consists of a question and two statements numbered* I *and* II *given below it. You have to decide whether the data provided in the statements are sufficient to answer the question.*

Give answer
(a) if the data in Statement I alone are sufficient to answer the question, while the data in Statement II alone are not sufficient to answer the question
(b) if the data in Statement II alone are sufficient to answer the question, while the data in Statement I alone are not sufficient to answer the question
(c) if the data either in Statement I alone or Statement II alone are sufficient to answer the question
(d) if the data in both the Statements I and II together are not sufficient to answer the question

26. How will 'must' be written in a certain code?
I. In that code language, 'you must see' is written as 'la pa ni' and 'did you see' is written as 'jo ni pa'.
II. In that code language 'you did that' is written as 'pa si jo'.

27. H is in which direction in respect of L?
I. L is to the East of M which is to the North of H.
II. L is to the North of J which is to the East of H.

Direction (Q. Nos. 28-30) *Read the following information carefully to answer these questions.* **[NIFT (UG) 2014]**

A, B, C, D, E, F and G are the names of two rivers, three canals and two valleys. B, G and D are not canals. E and F are not rivers. C is a canal but A is a valley. B, F and G are not valleys.

28. Which are the two rivers?
(a) A and D (b) B and D
(c) B and G (d) A and G
(e) None of these

29. Which are the three canals?
(a) A, C and E (b) C, E and F
(c) A, C and F (d) E, F and G
(e) None of these

30. Which are the two valleys?
(a) A and D (b) D and E
(c) D and G (d) A and B
(e) None of these

Direction (Q. Nos. 31-32) *In the following questions, a series is given with one term missing. Choose the correct alternatives from the given ones that will complete the series.*

31. 12, 12, 24, 72, 288, ?
(a) 1440 (b) 1326
(c) 1456 (d) 1235

32. 3F, 6G, 11I, 18L, ?
(a) 27P (b) 25N (c) 27Q (d) 21O

33. Which of the following figures represents the relationship among dog, cat and pet?

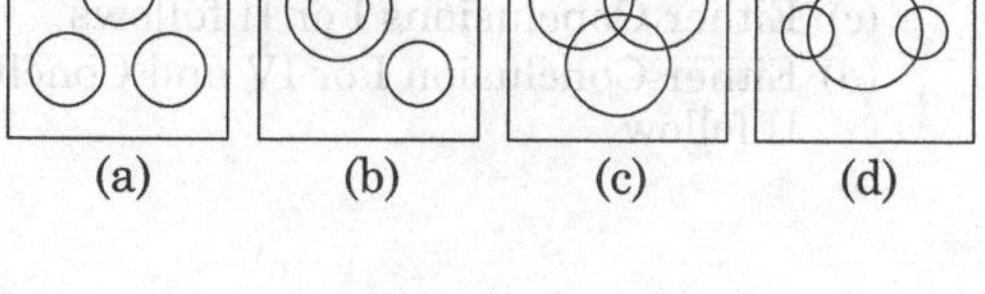

(a) (b) (c) (d)

Direction (Q. Nos. 34-35) *A statement is given followed by several assumptions. An assumption is something assumed or taken for granted. Read the statement carefully and decide which of the assumptions are implicit in the statement.*

Give answer

(a) I and II are implicit
(b) II and III are implicit
(c) I and III are implicit
(d) All are implicit

34. **Statement** "I think that she has gone mad. Last night I saw her barking like a dog."—A tells B about Madhu.

Assumptions I. Madhu is a friend of A.
II. B knows Madhu.
III. Some people do not bark like dogs.

35. **Statement** "The Prime Minister is expected to announce an expansion in his Ministry shortly."—A newspaper report.

Assumptions

I. The newspaper has quoted authentic sources.
II. The newspaper has reliable sources for the news.
III. The Prime Minister has the power to expand his cabinet.

36. Three Statements are given followed by four Conclusions I, II, III and IV. You have to consider the statements to be true even if they seem to be at variance from commonly known facts. You have to decide which of the given conclusion, if any, follow from the given statements. **[SSC (CPO) 2011]**

Statements A. Some books are novels.
B. All novels are magazines.
C. Some magazines are journals.

Conclusions I. Some novels are journals.
II. Some books are magazines.
III. All books are magazines.
IV. No novel is journal.

(a) Only Conclusion II follows
(b) Only Conclusion III follows
(c) Either Conclusions I or II follows
(d) Either Conclusion I or IV and Conclusion II follow

37. Two statements are given followed by four inferences. Select the alternative which is most appropriate. **[SSC (CGL) 2011]**

Statements

India is becoming industrialised.
Pollution is a problem associated with industrialisation.

Inferences

I. All industrial centres are polluted.
II. India is polluted.
III. Polluted nations are industrialised.
IV. India may become polluted.

(a) All are appropriate
(b) None is appropriate
(c) Only IV is appropriate
(d) Only II is appropriate

38. **Cause** A severe cyclonic storm swept away most part of the state during the last two days.

Which of the following cannot be a possible effect of the above cause?

(a) Heavy rainfall was reported in most part of the state during the last two days
(b) Many people were rendered homeless as their houses were flown away
(c) The communication system of the state was severely affected and continues to be out of gear
(d) Government has ordered that all the offices and schools should be kept open
(e) All above are possible effects

39. *Read the following information carefully and answer the questions based on them.*

In the Venn diagram given below, the square represents women, the triangle represents persons who are in Government services, the circle represents educated persons and the rectangle represents persons working in private sector. Each section of the diagram is numbered. Your task is to study the diagram and answer the question that follows.

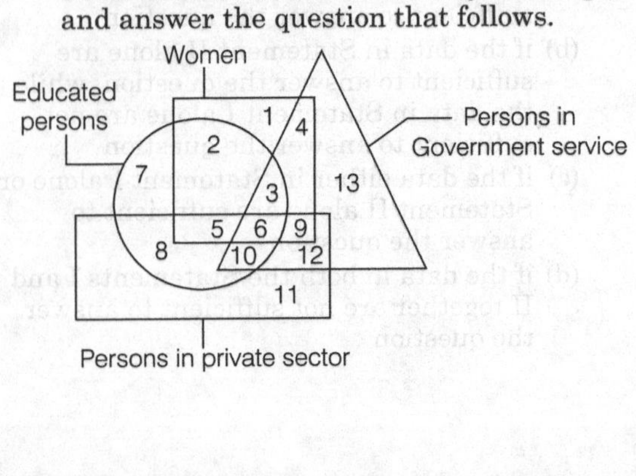

Which number represents educated women, who are in Government jobs?

(a) 2 (b) 3

(c) 6 (d) 4

40. Which one of the following responses is correct?

8*5*27*3*16

(a) ×, =, −, +

(b) −, =, ×, +

(c) ×, =, +, −

(d) +, −, =, ×

Direction (Q. Nos. 41-42) *Read the following information carefully and then answer the questions given below it.*

I. P, Q, R, S, T and U are six members of a family, each of them engaged in a different profession—doctor, lawyer, teacher, engineer, nurse and manager.

II. Each of them remains at home on a different day of the week from Monday to Saturday.

III. The lawyer in the family remains at home on Thursday.

IV. R remains at home on Tuesday.

V. P, a doctor, does not remain at home either on Saturday or Wednesday.

VI. S is neither the doctor nor the teacher and remains at home on Friday.

VII. Q is the engineer and T is the manager.

41. Which of the following combinations is correct?

(a) R-Teacher

(b) Q-Engine

(c) T-Manager

(d) All of these

42. Which of the following combinations is correct?

(a) Lawyer-Tuesday

(b) Teacher-Wednesday

(c) Manager-Friday

(d) Nurse-Friday

43. Find water image from the given responses.

D6Z7F4

Direction (Q. Nos. 44-45) *In the following questions, the symbols @, #, $, ★ and % are used as illustrated below.*

'P @ Q' means 'P is not smaller than Q'.

'P # Q' means 'P is neither greater than nor equal to Q'.

'P $ Q' means 'P is neither smaller than nor greater than Q'.

'P ★ Q' means 'P is not greater than Q'.

'P % Q' means 'P is neither smaller than nor equal to Q'.

Now, in each of the following questions assuming the given statements to be true, find which of the two Conclusions I and II given below them is/are definitely true?

Give answer

(a) if only Conclusion I is true

(b) if only Conclusion II is true

(c) if either Conclusion I or II is true

(d) if neither Conclusion I nor II is true

(e) if both Conclusions I and II are true

44. Statements M $ K, D ★ K, R # K

Conclusions I. D $ M II. M % D

45. Statements F ★ M, M % R, E @ F

Conclusions I. M % E II. R @ E

46. Find mirror image from the given responses.

47. Select the related figure from the given alternatives.

Question Figures

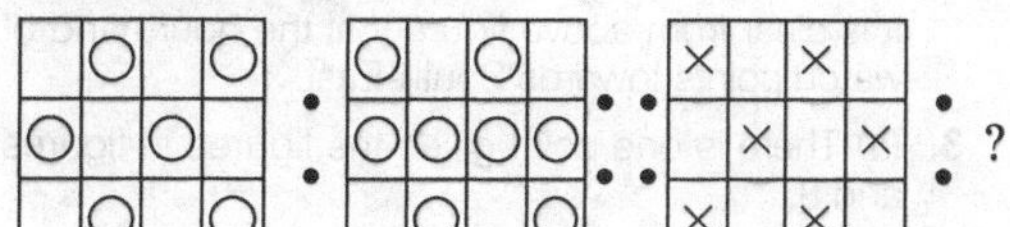

Answer Figures

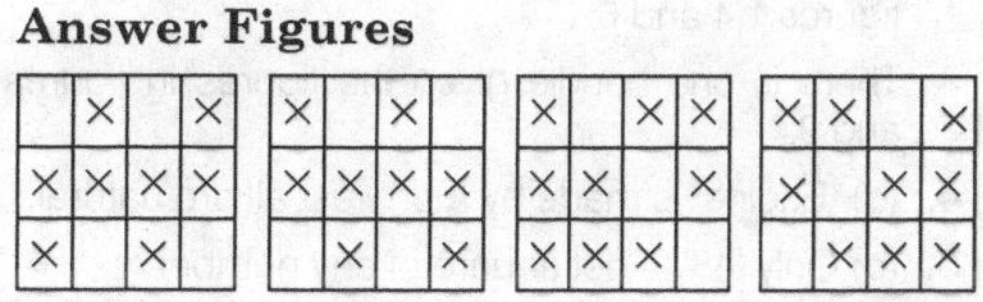

(a) (b) (c) (d)

48. Choose the right water image of the question figure from the given answer figures.

Question Figure

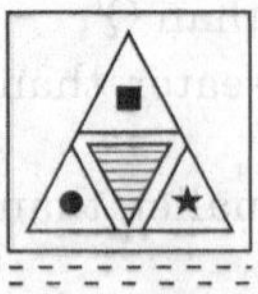

Answer Figures

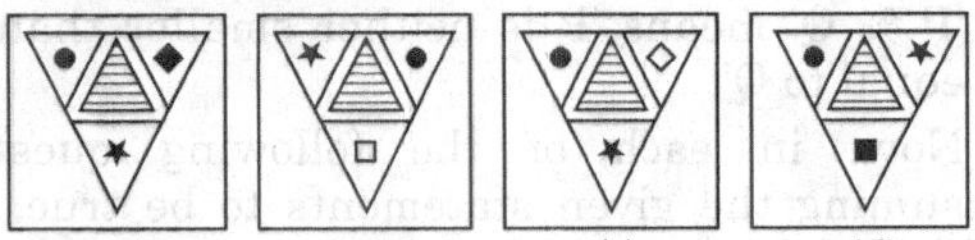

(a) (b) (c) (d)

49. Select the one, which is different from the other three. **[SSC (CGL) 2011]**

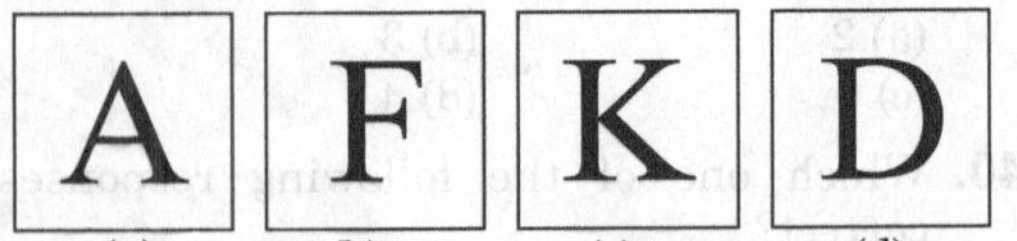

(a) (b) (c) (d)

50. Find the number of triangles in the diagram given below. **[UPPSC (RO) 2014]**

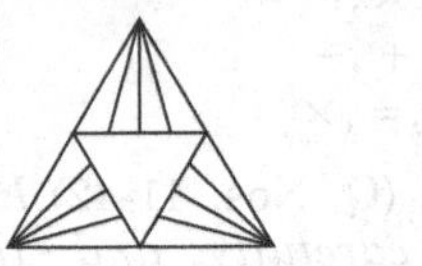

(a) 32 (b) 31 (c) 30 (d) 29

Hints and Solutions

1. (*c*) As, 'hive' is done by 'bee', same as 'eyrie' is made by 'Eagle'.

As, 'bee' residence is called 'hive', in the same way 'eagle' residence is called 'eyrie'.

2. (*d*)

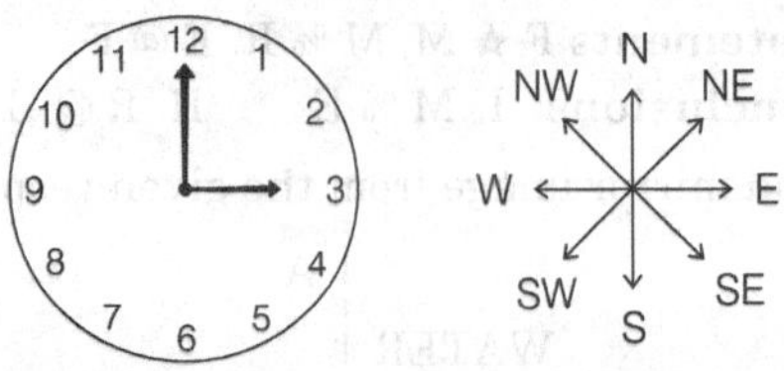

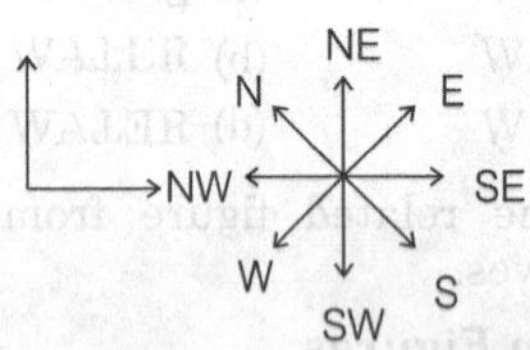

It is clear from above figure that the hour hand of the watch points towards South-East.

3. (*a*) There is one point given the figures in figures 2,3 and 8.

There is one small rectangle given the figures in figures 1,4 and 6.

There is one handle given the figures in figures 5,7 and 9.

4. (*d*) 'Engine' is made by man, rest all are natural.

5. (*c*) Only '48' is not square of any number.

6. (*b*) Required words = ARE, ATE, ART.

7. (*c*) In the given question,

H	N	R	C	A	B
1	2	3	4	5	6

In option (a), 6 5 3 4 1 2 is coded as B A R C H N. It is not a meaningful word.

In option (b), 4 1 5 6 2 3 is coded as C H A B N R. It is not a meaningful word.

In option (c), 6 3 5 2 4 1 is coded as BRANCH. It is a meaningful word.

Solution (Q. Nos. 8-9) The given figure, shows the correct arrangement of six friends.

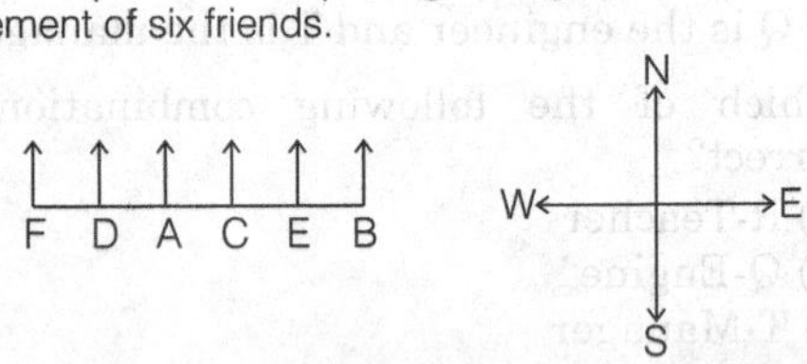

8. (*d*) There are four persons to the right of D i.e. A, C, E and B.

9. (*a*) Clearly, F is sitting to the left of D.

10. (*c*) In both the positions, 5 is at common face (front face). So, digit 3 at the side face in position I will be opposite to the side face having digit 4 in position II.

11. (*c*) By direct substitution method,

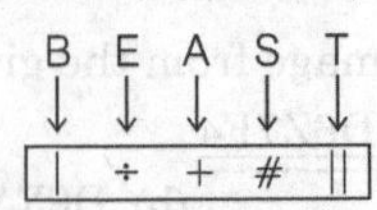

12. (*b*) The colour of clear sky is 'blue' but here 'blue' is called 'green'. Hence, in this case colour of clear sky is 'green'.

13. On the basis of given information, the arrangement can be drawn as shown below

	Hobbies					Colour of shirt				
	Reading	Playing	Outing	Singing	Writing	Red	Yellow	Blue	White	Green
Amar	✗	✗	✗	✗	✓	✗	✓	✗	✗	✗
Kapil	✗	✗	✗	✓	✗	✗	✗			
Sarvesh	✗	✗	✓	✗	✗	✓	✗	✗	✗	✗
Rohan	✓	✗	✗	✗	✗	✗	✗			✗
Nagesh	✗	✓	✗	✗	✗	✗	✗	✗		

(*d*) The colour of Kapil's shirt may be either blue or white or green. Hence, data is inadequate to answer the question.

Solution (Q. Nos. 14-15) The direction can be represented as shown below :

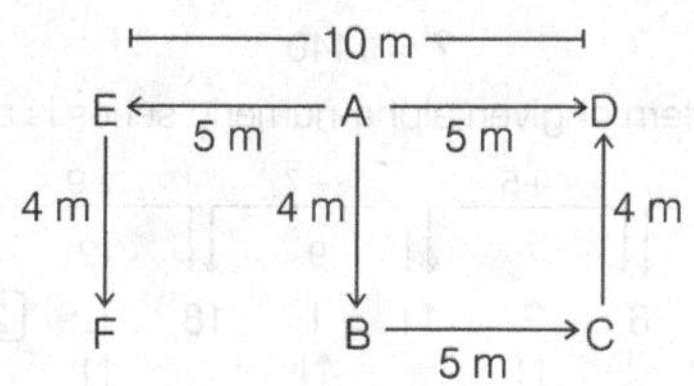

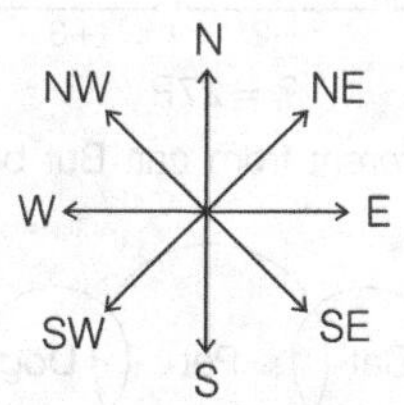

14. (*a*) The direction of point A with respect to point C is North-West.

15. (*b*) Point B is 5 m far from point F.

16. (*d*) Let the age of son = x yr

$\therefore$ Age of father = 9x yr

$\therefore$ Age of mother = 8x yr

According to question, $9x + 8x = 51$

$$17x = 51$$

$$\therefore \quad x = 3$$

So, the age of the son = 3 yr.

17. (*a*) Here, person's father's only son is the person himself and the man in the photograph is the son of that person.

So, the person is looking at his son's photograph.

18. (*d*) As, $6 \times 7 + (8 + 4) = 42 + 12 = 54$

and $8 \times 4 + (12 + 7) = 32 + 19 = 51$

Similarly, $9 \times 5 + (14 + 9) = 45 + 23 = 68$

19. (*d*) Clearly, mathematical symbols in option (b) and (c), are applied for the given equation.

Option (b) $24 = 4 \times 5 + 4$

$\Rightarrow$ $24 = 20 + 4$

Option (c) $24 = 4 + 5 \times 4$

$\Rightarrow$ $24 = 4 + 20$

20. (*a*) The correct order is as follows

(iii) Rabindranath Tagore

↓ (Literature)—1913

(v) Sir C. V. Raman

↓ (Physics)—1930

(ii) Mother Teresa

↓ (Peace)—1979

(i) Amartya Sen

↓ (Economics)—1998

(iv) Venkatraman Ramakrishna

(Chemistry)—2009

21. (*a*) According to the question,

$S > R$ ....(i)

$R > G$ ...(ii)

$P > S.$ ...(iiii)

[S = Sati, R = Renu, G = Geeta, P = Priya]

By combining all equations , we get

$$P > S > R > G$$

So, Priya is the eldest.

Solution (Q. Nos. 22-24) In Step I, the largest number comes at the first place from left interchanging with its replacing number. In Step II, the second largest number comes at the second place from left interchanging with its replacing number. The further steps are obtained in the same manner till all the numbers get arranged in descending order.

22. (*c*) **Input** 88 172 15 105 412 25

***Step* I** 412 172 15 105 88 25

***Step* II** 412 172 105 15 88 25

***Step* III** 412 172 105 88 15 25

23. (*d*) In an arrangement problem, input/previous steps cannot be determined.

24. (*a*) **Input** 173 390 85 188 522 765

***Step* I** 765 390 85 188 522 173

***Step* II** 765 522 85 188 390 173

***Step* III** 765 522 390 188 85 173

***Step* IV** 765 522 390 188 173 85

$\therefore$ Step IV is the last step.

25. (*a*) The information given in the question can be represented as shown below

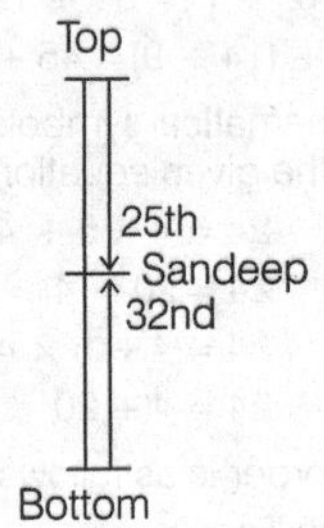

Total students in a class = (Rank of Sandeep from top + Rank of Sandeep from bottom − 1)

= 25 + 32 − 1 = 57 − 1 = 56

26. (*a*) From Statement I,

you must see = la pa ni

did you see = jo ni pa

Clearly, must = la

From Statement II, you did that = pa si so

So, Statement I alone is sufficient to answer the question.

27. (*c*) From Statement I,

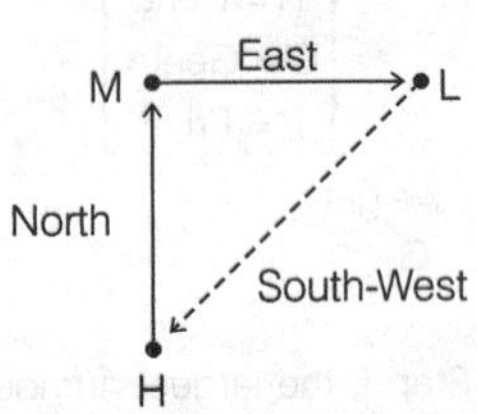

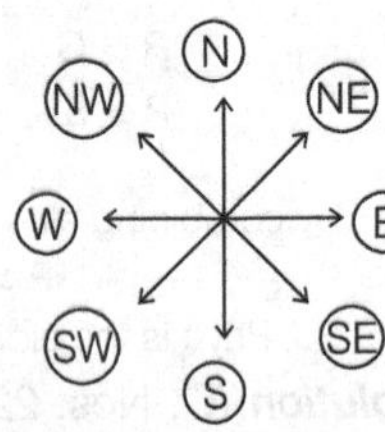

Clearly, H is to the South-West of L.

From Statement II,

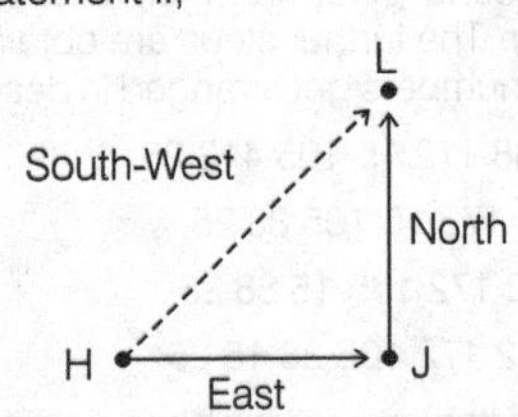

Clearly, H is to the South-West of L.

So, either Statement I or II alone is sufficient to answer the question.

Solution (Q. Nos. 28-30) Given statements

- B, G, D are not canals.
- E, F are not rivers.
- C is a canal.
- A is a valley.
- B, F, G are not valleys.

Conclusions If B is neither a valley nor a canal, then it is a river.

If F is neither a river nor a valley, then it is a canal.

If G is neither canal nor a valley, then it is a river.

Canal	River	Valley
C	B	A
F	G	D
E		

28. (*c*) B and G are two rivers.

29. (*b*) C, E and F are three canals.

30. (*a*) A and D are two valleys.

31. (*a*) The pattern is as follows

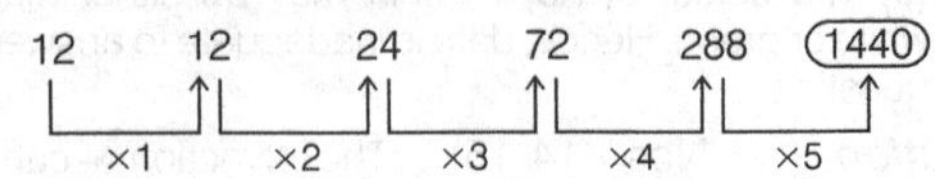

? = 1440

∴ ? = 1440

32. (a) Pattern of given alpha-numeric series is as follows

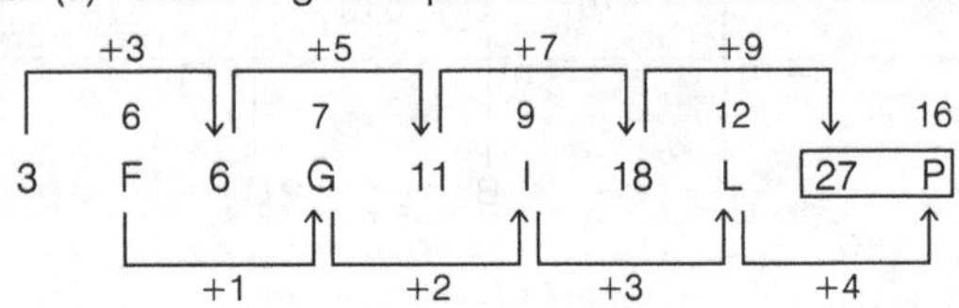

∴ ? = 27P

33. (*d*) Dog is different from cat. But both may be pets or stray.

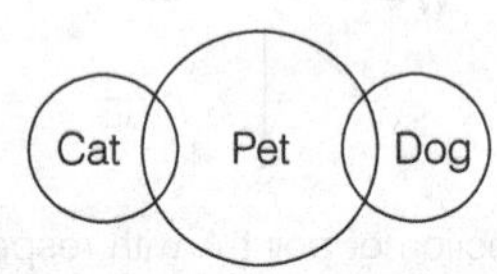

34. (*b*) From statements, it is not clear that Madhu is a friend of A. Because A tells B about Madhu. So, it is clear that B knows Madhu. And of course people do not bark like dogs. Therefore, Statements II and III are implicit.

35. (*b*) The newspaper has not quoted authentic sources, so I is not implicit; but II and III are implicit.

36. (*d*)

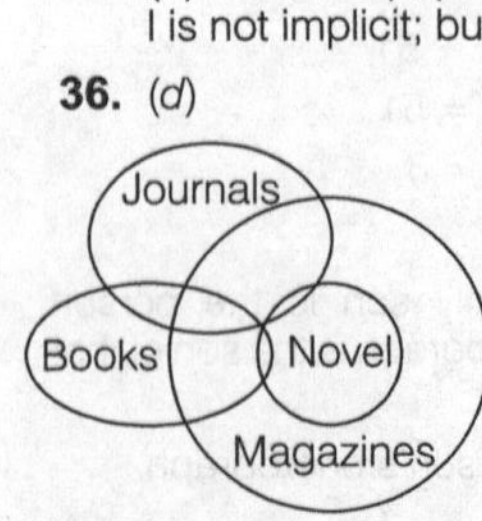

or

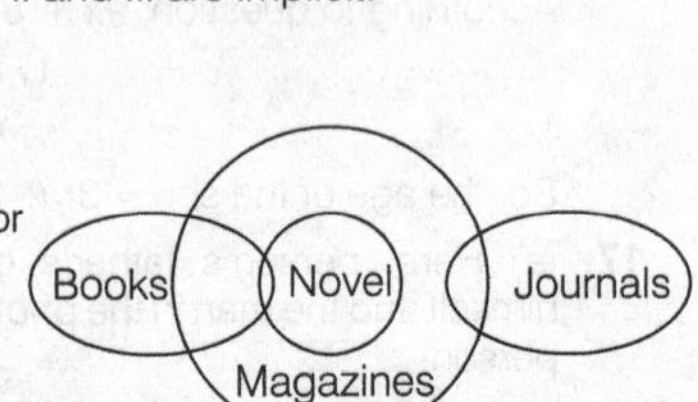

From the above figure, either Conclusion I or IV and Conclusion II follow.

37. (*c*) From a general statement, we cannot derive definite conclusion. Therefore, we cannot definitely say that all industrial centres are polluted and whether India is polluted or not.

We also cannot say that polluted nations are industrialised because there may be many other factors responsible for pollution. As, pollution is problem associated with industrialisation, India may become polluted.

Hence, only inference IV is appropriate.

38. (*d*) In such a cataclysmic scenario, the Government is likely to order the closure of offices and schools.

39. (*b*) Educated women in Government jobs are represented by number 3 as it occupies the space common to circle, square and triangle.

40. (*a*) If we select option (a) and apply the given mathematical symbols then, we get

$$8 \times 5 = 27 - 3 + 16$$
$$40 = 24 + 16$$
$$40 = 40$$

Solution (Q. Nos. 41-42) Following table can be drawn from the given information.

	Professions						Days					
	Doct	Law	Teach	Engg	Nurse	Mag	Mon	Tues	Wed	Thurs	Fri	Sat
P	✔	✗	✗	✗	✗	✗	✔	✗	✗	✗	✗	✗
Q	✗	✗	✗	✔	✗	✗	✗	✗		✗	✗	
R	✗	✗	✔	✗	✗	✗	✗	✔	✗	✗	✗	✗
S	✗	✗	✗	✗	✔	✗	✗	✗	✗	✗	✔	✗
T	✗	✗	✗	✗	✗	✔	✗	✗		✗	✗	
U	✗	✔	✗	✗	✗	✗	✗	✗	✗	✔	✗	✗

From the table, we find that Q, the engineer and T, the manager live at home either on Wednesday or Saturday.

41. (*d*) It is concluded clearly from the above table that all the combinations given are correct.

42. (*d*) From the table, it is clear that S is the nurse and stays at home on Friday.

43. (*c*) Option (c) is correct water image.

Solution. (Q. Nos. 44-45)

@	#	$	★	%
≥	<	=	≤	>

44. (*c*) **Statements**

M $ K ⇒ M = K

D ★ K ⇒ D ≤ K

R # K ⇒ R < K

Therefore,

R < M = K ≥ D

Conclusions

I. D $ M ⇒ D = M (May be)

II. M % D ⇒ M > D (May be)

D is either smaller than or equal to M. Therefore, either Conclusion I or II is true.

45. (*d*) **Statements** F ★ M ⇒ F ≤ M

M % R ⇒ M > R

E @ F ⇒ E ≥ F

Therefore, E ≥ F ≤ M > R

Conclusions

I. M % E ⇒ M > E (Not True)

II. R @ E ⇒ R ≥ E (Not True)

So, neither Conclusion I or II is true.

46. (*c*) The correct laterally inverted mirror image of the question figure is as follows

ЯƎTAW

47. (*b*) Clearly, from figure I to figure II the circles of upper row move one block in anti-clockwise direction and two circles are added in the middle row. But in row three given circle remain in their position. In similar way, the two crosses of lower row move one block in anti-clockwise direction and two crosses are added in the middle row.

48. (*d*) The correct vertically inverted water image of the question figure is as follows

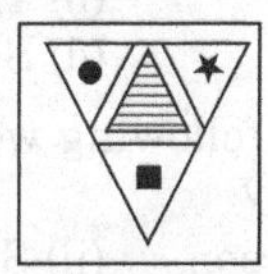

49. (*d*) Except the fourth letter, all other letters have been made up of straight lines only.

Note Some candidates may opt answer figure (a) as the answer, because it is the only vowel in the group. But here the shape of given design is more important.

D has a curvature shape while others have been made up of straight lines.

50. (*a*) In order to count the triangles, we first name the vertices.

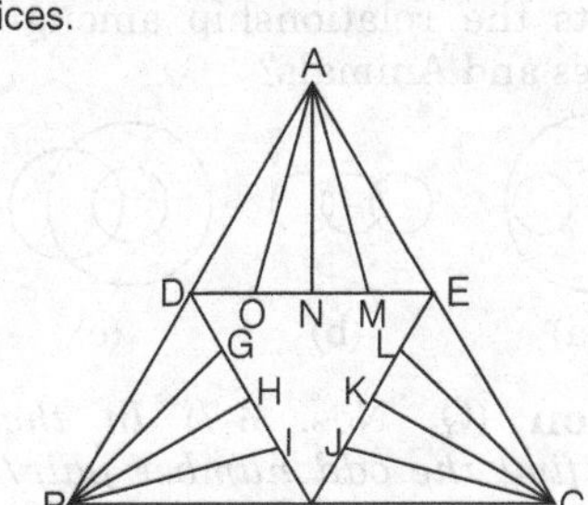

Now, counting can be observed.

In ΔADE, ΔAOD, ΔOAN, ΔNAM, ΔMAE, ΔDAN, ΔOAM, ΔNAE, ΔDAM, ΔOAE, ΔDAE = 10

Similarly, ΔBDF and ΔCEF will have 10 and 10 traingles. ΔDEF and ΔABC will count 2, hence total

$$10 + 10 + 10 + 2 = 32.$$

PRACTICE SET 7

1. Select the related word from the given alternative.

Surgeon : Scalpel **[MAT 2014]**

(a) Musician : Instrument
(b) Carpenter : Cabinet
(c) Sculptor : Chisel
(d) Baker : Oven

2. Find the odd one out from the given alternative.

(a) AbcdE (b) IfghO
(c) ApqrL (d) UlmnE

3. If the day before yesterday was Friday, then what day will two days after the day after tomorrow be?

(a) Saturday (b) Thursday
(c) Friday (d) Sunday

4. Arrange the following words as per order in the dictionary.

(i) Spokesperson (ii) Sportsman
(iii) Spreadsheet (iv) Specification
(v) Sophisticated

(a) (v), (iv), (i), (ii), (iii)
(b) (v), (iv), (i), (iii), (ii)
(c) (iv), (v), (i), (ii), (iii)
(d) (v), (iv), (ii), (i), (iii)

5. Which one of the following diagrams best depicts the relationship among Elephants, Wolves and Animals?

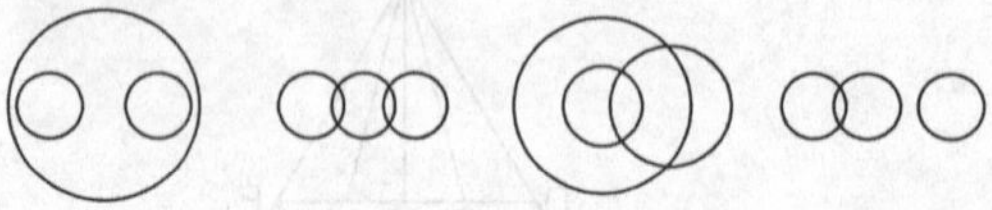

(a) (b) (c) (d)

Direction (Q. Nos. 6-7) *In the following questions, find the odd number pair/word from the given alternatives.*

6. (a) (54, 216) (b) (61, 244)
(c) (24, 96) (d) (27, 135)

[SSC (10+2) 2015]

7. (a) Apple (b) Grapes
(c) Banana (d) Potato

8. A and B are the young ones of C. If C is the mother of B but A is not the daughter of C, then what is the relationship between C and A?

(a) Nephew and aunty
(b) Brother and sister
(c) Mother and son
(d) Niece and aunty

9. A was born 5 yr before B, B is 4 yr older than C and 3 yr younger to D. If A is now 17 yr old,then how old is D?

(a) 19 yr (b) 15 yr
(c) 12 yr (d) 8 yr

10. If in a certain code

'INTELLIGENCE' is written as 'ETNIGILLECNE', then how can 'MATHEMATICAL' be written in the same code? **[SSC (CGL) Pre 2014]**

(a) AMHTMETACILA
(b) TAMMEHITALAC
(c) HTAMTAMELACI
(d) LACITAMEHTAM

11. A person starts from his home and walks 3 km towards North. After that turns right and walks 2 km and then turns right and walk 5 km. After that he turns right and walk 2 km and then again turns right and walk 2 km. In which direction is he from his home?

(a) South (b) North
(c) North-East (d) At the starting point

12. If 'green' is called 'red', 'red' is called 'blue', 'blue is called white', 'white' is called 'yellow' and 'yellow' is called 'violet', then what is the colour of grass?

(a) Blue (b) Yellow
(c) Violet (d) Red

13. How many such pairs of letters are there in the word 'SOUTHERN' each of which has as many letters between them as in the English alphabet?

(a) None (b) One
(c) Two (d) Three

14. If it is possible to make only one meaningful word with the 3rd, the 6th, the 8th and the 11th letters of the word 'COMPUTERISE', using each letter only once in the word, last letter of the word is your answer. If no such word can be formed, your answer is 'X' and if more than one such word can be formed, your answer is 'Z'.

(a) M (b) T (c) R (d) X
(e) Z

15. If 'P' means '+', 'Q' means '×', 'R' means '÷' and 'S' means '–', then 44 Q 9 R 12 S 6 Q 4 P 16 = ? **[SSC (CGL) 2013]**

(a) 36 (b) 124 (c) 25 (d) 112

16. Select the missing number from the given responses.

9	6	?
8	5	6
7	4	3
65	26	39

(a) 10 (b) 8 (c) 7 (d) 9

17. Four positions of a dice are given below:

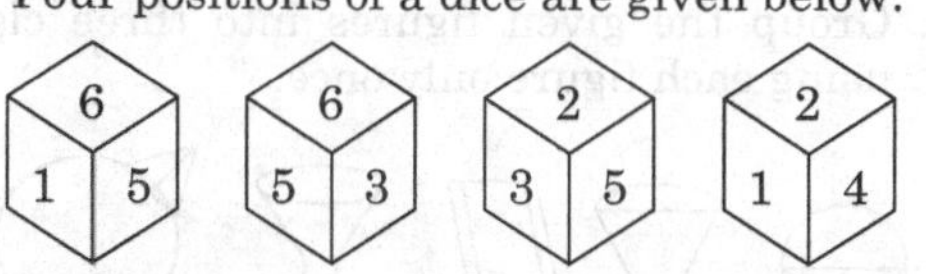

Find the number on the face opposite to the face showing 4. **[SSC (10+2) 2015]**

(a) 5 (b) 1 (c) 6 (d) 3

Direction (Q. Nos. 18-20) *In the following questions, a series is given, with one term missing. Choose the correct alternative, from the given ones that will complete the series.*

18. 36, 28, 24, 22, ?

(a) 18 (b) 19 (c) 21 (d) 22

19. W, T, P, M, I, F, B, ?, ? **[SSC (CPO) 2012]**

(a) Z, V (b) X, U (c) Y, U (d) Y, V

20. C4X, F9U I16R ?

(a) L25P (b) K25P
(c) L27P (d) L25O

Direction (Q. Nos. 21-23) *Study the following information to answer the given questions.* **[SBI (PO) Pre 2015]**

Eight friends G, H, I, J, N, O, P and Q are seated in a straight line, but not necesarily in the same order.

H sits second to right of O. O sits at one of the extreme ends of the line.

Only three people sit between H and N.

I sits third to the left of J. Only two people sit between J and G.

P is not an immediate neighbour of N.

21. Who amongst the following represents the person seated at the extreme right end of the line?

(a) P (b) Q (c) O (d) I
(e) G

22. Who amongst the following sit exactly between J and G?

(a) O, Q (b) H, O (c) O, P (d) N, Q
(e) H, N

23. What is the position of P with respect to N?

(a) Third to the left
(b) Second to the right
(c) Fourth to the right
(d) Third to the right
(e) Second to the left

24. A man drives 10 km straight ahead towards East and 10 km to the right. Then, every time turning to his left he drives 5 km, 15 km and 15 km, respectively. How far is he from the starting point?

(a) 10 km (b) 5 km (c) 20 km (d) 25 km

25. If in a certain code language 'GONE' is written as '5 @ © 9' and 'SEAL' is written as '69 %' ★ then how will 'LOGS' be written in that language?

(a) ★ © 56 (b) ★ 9 © 6
(c) ★ @ 65 (d) ★ @ 56
(e) None of the above

Direction (Q. Nos. 26-27) *In these questions, two/three statements followed by two conclusions numbered* I *and* II *have been given. You have to take the given statement to be true if they seem to be at variance from the commonly known facts and then decide which of the given conclusions logically follows from the even statements disregarding commonly known facts .*

Give answer

(a) Either Conclusion I or II is true
(b) Both Conclusions I and II are true
(c) Neither Conclusion I nor II is true
(d) Only Conclusion II is true
(e) Only Conclusion I is true

26. Statements All bugs are worms.
Some worms are moths.
No moth is a fly.

Conclusions I. No fly is a worm.
II. All moths being bugs is a possibility.

27. Statements Some stars are planets.
No planet is a Moon.

Conclusions I. No star is a Moon.
II. Some stars are Moons.

28. Identify the missing part of the question figure and select it from given answer figures.

Question Figure

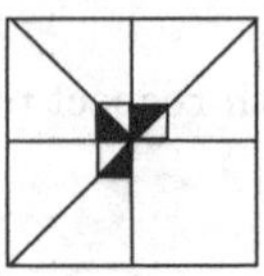

Answer Figures

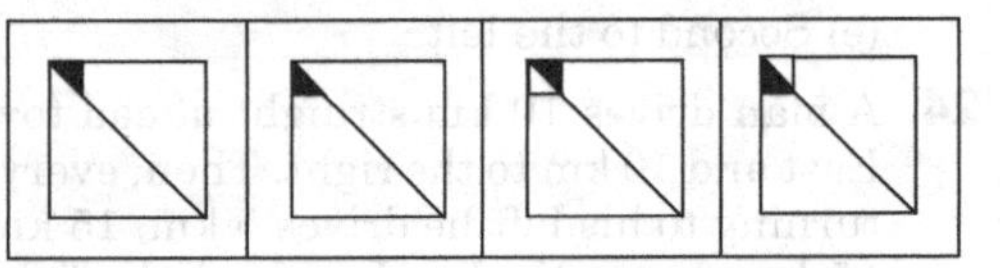

(a) (b) (c) (d)

29. Find out which of the answer figures (a), (b), (c) and (d) completes the figure matrix?

Question Figures

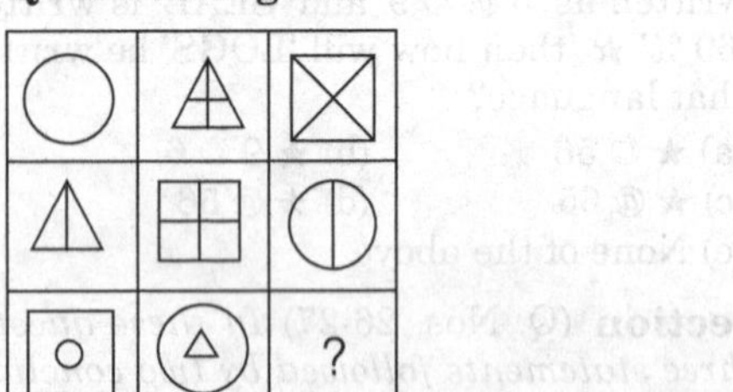

Answer Figures

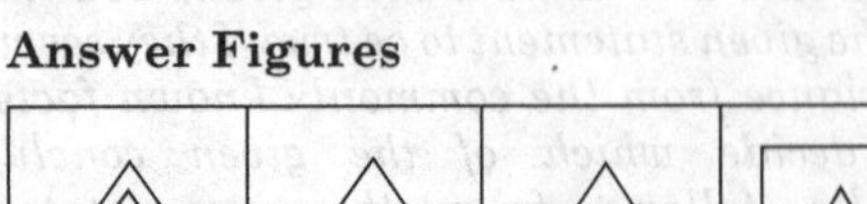

(a) (b) (c) (d)

30. In making decisions about important questions, it is desirable to distinguish between a 'strong' argument and a 'weak' argument. A 'strong' argument must be both important and directly related to the question. A 'weak' argument may not be directly related to the question and may be of minor importance or may be related to the trivial aspect of the question. Each question below is followed by two arguments numbered I and II. You have to decide which of the arguments is 'strong' and which is 'weak'.

Statements Is India going to have elections in near future?

Arguments

I. Yes, some of the political parties are creation a situation that demands elections.

II. No, our Prime Minister is a strong man, has a good support and will complete his term.

(a) if only Argument I is strong
(b) if only Argument II is strong
(c) if either Argument I or II is strong
(d) if neither Argument I nor II is strong
(e) if both Argument I and I are strong

31. Group the given figures into three classes using each figure only once.

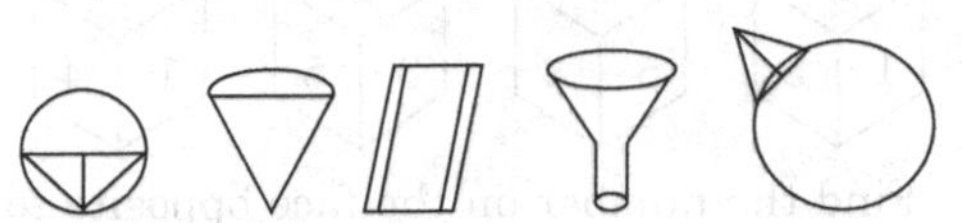

(1) (2) (3) (4) (5)

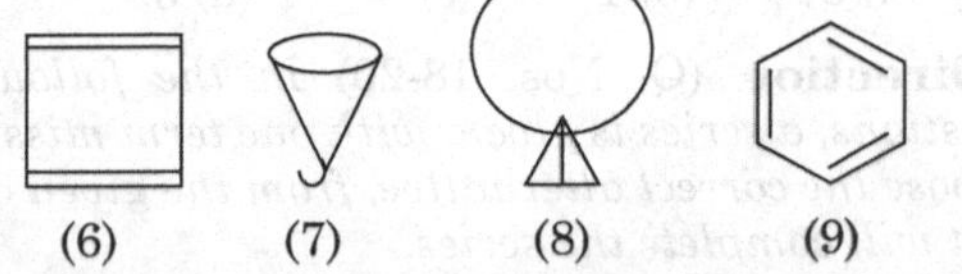

(6) (7) (8) (9)

(a) 1, 5, 8
2, 6, 7
3, 4, 9

(b) 1, 5, 7
2, 6, 8
3, 4, 9

(c) 1, 7, 8
2, 6, 9
3, 4, 5

(d) 1, 5, 8
2, 4, 7
3, 6, 9

32. Arun ranks 17th in a class of 31 students. What is his rank from the last?

(a) 14
(b) 15
(c) 16
(d) 17

33. Five students are sitting in a row. S is on the right of L, P is on the left of L but is on the right of K, S is on the left of Q. The first student in the row from the left is

(a) K (b) L (c) P (e) S

Direction (Q. Nos. 34-36) *Study the following information carefully and then answer the questions based on it.*

I. P, Q, R, S, T and U are six members of a three generation family in which there are two married couples.

II. R, a male member, is neither lightest nor the heaviest in the family but he is the grandfather of this family.

III. T is lighter than R and R is lighter than Q. P, the grandmother in the family, is the lightest.

IV. S is the sister of U. Both S and U are heavier than Q.

V. Q is the mother of S and heavier than T.

34. How many female members are there in the family?

(a) Data inadequate
(b) Two
(c) Four
(d) Three

35. How is T related to U?

(a) Grandfather (b) Sister
(c) Mother (d) Father

36. Which of the following is a pair of married couple?

(a) PS (b) QR
(c) PQ (d) QT

37. *Study the following information carefully and answer the questions given below it.*

There are five friends A, B, C, D and E. Two of them are businessmen while the other three belong to different occupations *viz.* doctor engineer and lawyer.

One businessman and the lawyer stay in the same locality S, while the other three stay in theree different localities P,Q and R. Two of these five persons are Hindus while the remaining three come from three different communities *viz.* Muslim, Christian and Sikh.

The lawyer is the oldest in age while one of the businessmen who runs a factory is the youngest. The other businessman is a cloth merchant and agewise lies between the doctor and the lawyer.D is a cloth merchant and stays in locality S while E is Muslim and stays in locality R. The doctor is a Christian and stays in locality P, B is a Sikh while A is a Hindu and runs a factory.

Who stays in locality Q?

(a) A (b) B (c) C (d) E

38. Pair of opposite faces of a solid cube having sides 3 cm are painted black, blue and yellow, respectively. After the paintings this cube is divided into smaller cubes of side 1 cm. How many smaller cubes have only one face painted?

(a) 4 (b) 6 (c) 9 (d) 12

Direction (Q. Nos. 39-41) *Study the following information to answer the given questions.*

A word and number arrangement machine when given an input line of words and numbers, rearranges them following a particular rule. The following is an illustration of input and rearrangement. (All the numbers are two-digits numbers)

Input 'at 52 93 46 gate join us 19 to 33 dine 27'

***Step* I** 19 at 52 46 gate join us to 33 dine 27 93
***Step* II** 27 19 at 46 gate join us to 33 dine 93 52
***Step* III** 33 27 19 at gate join us to dine 93 52 46
***Step* IV** at 33 27 19 gate join to dine 93 52 46 us
***Step* V** dine at 33 27 19 gate join 93 52 46 us to
***Step* VI** gate dine at 33 27 19 93 52 46 us to join

and Step VI is the last step of the arrangement of the above input as the intended arrangement is obtained.

As per the rules followed in the above steps, find out in each of the following questions the appropriate steps for the given input.

Input '71 14 side wall 97 for hat 65 27 gun 81 bat' (All the numbers given in the arrangement are two-digit members)

39. Which of the following would be the Step III?

(a) for bat 65 27 14 hat gun 97 81 71 wall side
(b) 65 27 14 side wall for hat bat gun 97 81 71
(c) 65 27 14 side wall for hat gun bat 71 81 97
(d) 65 27 14 side wall for hat gun bat 97 81 71
(e) None of the above

40. Which word/number would be at the 7th position from the right in Step V?

(a) hat (b) gun
(c) for (d) side
(e) 14

41. How many steps are required to complete the arrangement?

(a) Four (b) Five (c) Six (d) Seven
(e) Eight

Direction (Q. Nos. 42-43) *Each of the following questions below consists of a question and two statement numbered* I *and* II *given below it. You have to decide whether the data provided in the statements are sufficient to answer question.*

Give answer

(a) if the data in Statement I alone are sufficient to answer the question, while the data in Statement II alone are not sufficient to answer the question
(b) if the data in Statement II alone are sufficient to answer the question, while the data in Statement I alone are not sufficient to answer the question
(c) if the data either in Statement I alone or Statement II alone are sufficient to answer the question
(d) if the data in both the Statements I and II together are not sufficient to answer the question

42. How is A related to B?

I. A is the sister-in-law of C, who is the daughter-in-law of B, who is the wife of D.
II. B is the mother of A's son's only uncle's son.

43. Among five friends—J, K, L, M and N each of a different height, who is the second tallest?

I. N is taller than M and K. K is shorter than M.
II. L is taller than N. J is not the tallest.

Direction (Q. Nos. 44-45) *Two statements are given followed by two Conclusions* I *and* II. *You have to consider the statements to be true even if they seem to be at variance from commonly known facts. You are to decide which of the given conclusions, if any, follow from the given statements. Indicate your answer.*

44. Statements

A. No teacher comes to the school on a bicycle.
B. Anand comes to the school on a bicycle.

[SSC (CPO) 2012]

Conclusions I. Anand is not a teacher.
II. Anand is a student.

(a) Conclusion I alone can be drawn
(b) Conclusion II alone can be drawn
(c) Both conclusions can be drawn
(d) Both conclusions cannot be drawn

45. Statements

A. Most of the 64 number buses go to my office.
B. This is 64 number bus.

Conclusions I. This bus goes to my office.
II. This bus does not go to my office.

(a) Conclusion I and II both can be drawn
(b) Conclusion II alone can be drawn
(c) Conclusion I alone can be drawn
(d) Conclusions I and II both cannot be drawn

46. Choose the correct alternative from the given ones that will complete the series.

Question Figures

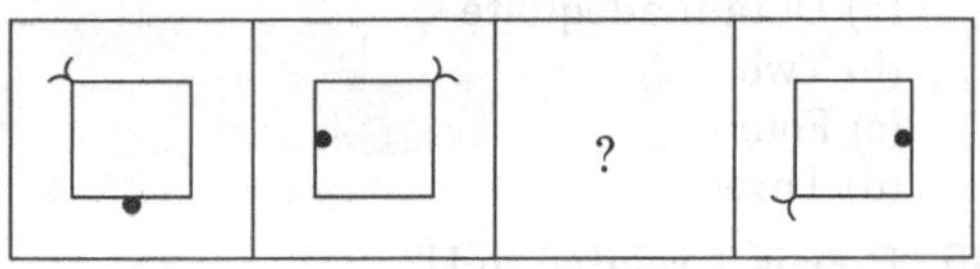

1 2 3 4

Answer Figures

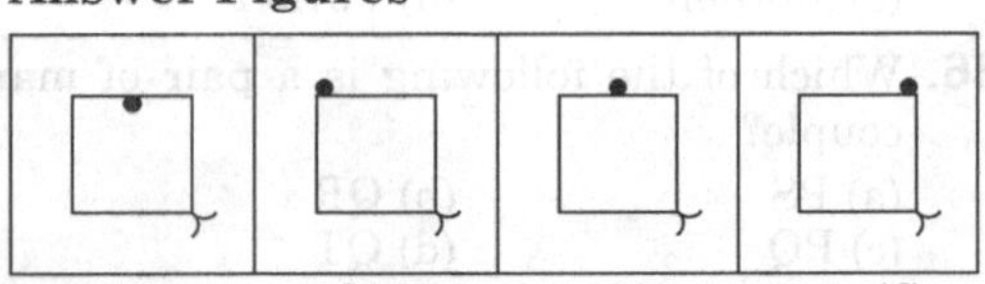

(a) (b) (c) (d)

47. Complete the missing segment by selecting from the given alternatives (a), (b), (c) and (d).

Question Figure

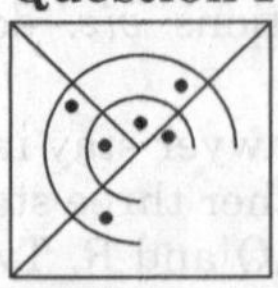

Answer Figures

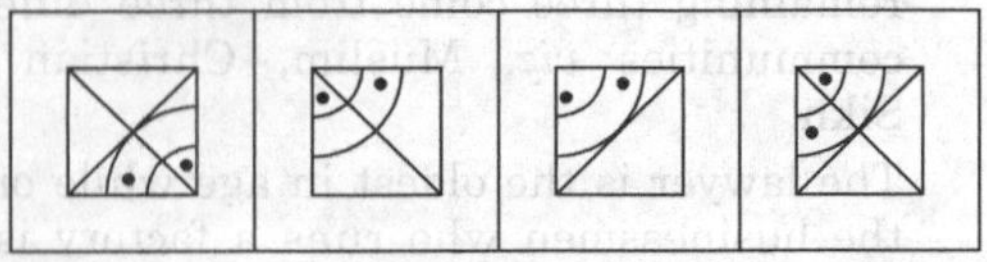

(a) (b) (c) (d)

48. Select the related figure from the given alternatives.

Question Figures

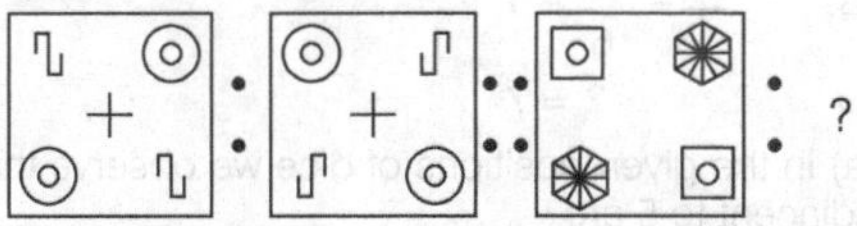

Answer Figures

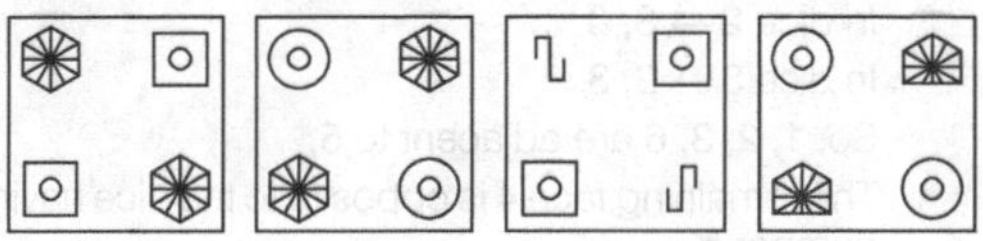

(a) (b) (c) (d)

49. Find the relationship between the letters/numbers from the given alternatives.

RED : 1854 : : LED : ?

(a) 1245 (b) 1154
(c) 1960 (d) 1254

50. How will it look like when a transparent paper with given figure is folded along the dotted line as shown?

Question Figure

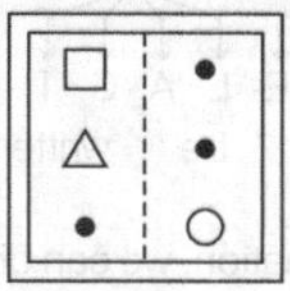

Answer Figures

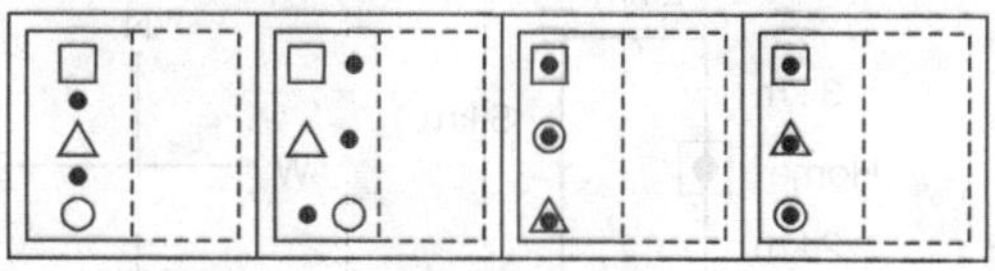

(a) (b) (c) (d)

Hints and Solutions

1. (*c*) 'Scalpel' is a tool which is used by 'Surgeon' in the same way 'Chisel' is the tool which is used by 'Sculptor'.

2. (*c*) Except in A p q r L, in all others the first and the last letters given in capital are vowels.

3. (*b*) Today is Friday + 2 i.e. Sunday

Tommorow will be Monday. The day after tomorrow will be Tuesday and two days after Tuesday will be Thursday.

4. (*a*) Arrangement of words as per order in the dictionary

(v) Sophisticated
↓
(iv) Specification
↓
(i) Spokesperson
↓
(ii) Sportsman
↓
(iii) Spreadsheet

5. (*a*) Wolves and elephants both are animals but are different from each other. This can be expressed as

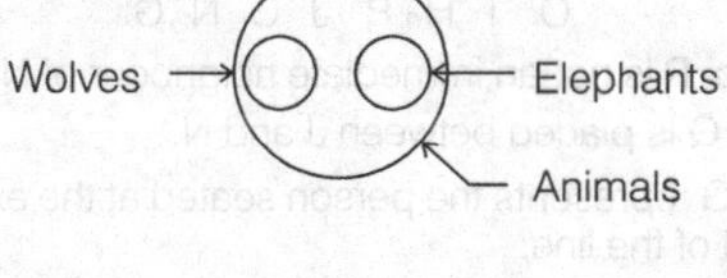

6. (*d*) As,

	(54, 216)	⇒	$54 \times 4 = 216$
	(61, 244)	⇒	$61 \times 4 = 244$
and	(24, 96)	⇒	$24 \times 4 = 96$
But	(27, 135)	⇒	$27 \times 4 = 108 \neq 135$

Therefore, (27, 135) is the odd one.

7. (*d*) Now, when we closely observe the different words we find that all are edibles i.e. consumed as food by human beings. But apple, grapes and banana comes under the category of fruits and potato is a vegetable. So, the odd word from the group is potato.

8. (*c*) Following family diagram can be drawn from the given information.

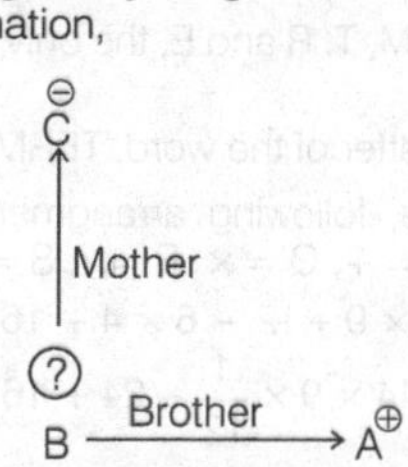

Here, A is not the daughter of C. So, A is the son of C. Now, it is clear that C and A are mother and son.

9. (*b*) A = 17 yr

B = 17 − 5 = 12 yr
C = 12 − 4 = 8 yr
D = 12 + 3 = 15 yr

10. (*c*) As,

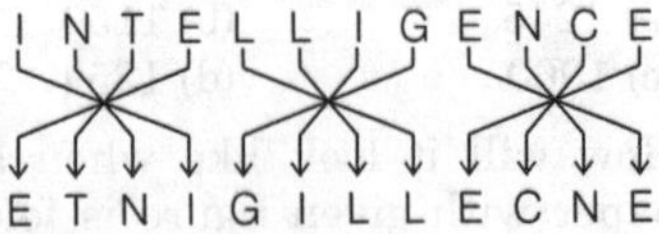

Similarly,

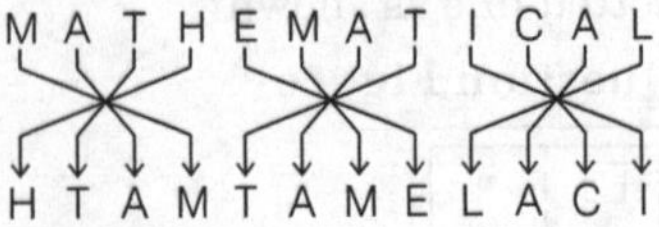

So, MATHEMATICAL can be written as HTAMTAMELACI.

11. (*d*) According to the given information, we can draw the following diagram.

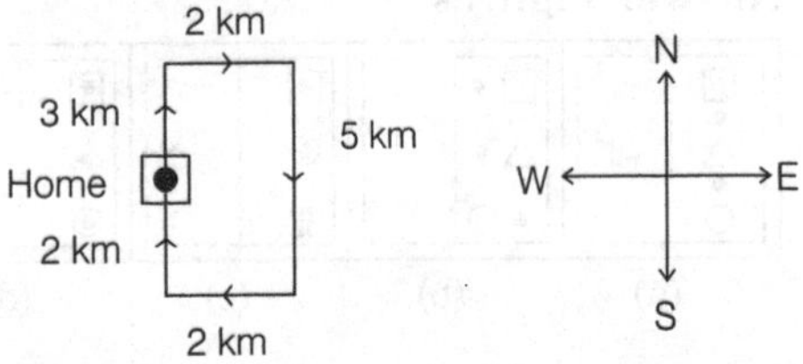

So, the person is at the starting point i.e. home. Hence, the correct answer is (d).

12. (*d*) As, colour of grass is 'green' but here 'green' is called 'red' and hence according to the given information colour of grass must be 'red'.

13. (*c*) Let us see

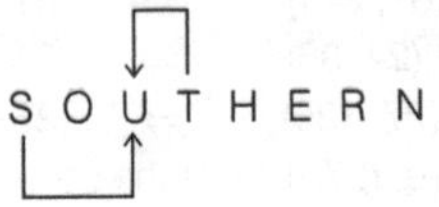

So, letter pairs are SU and TU. Hence, option (c) is the correct answer.

14. (*a*) Let us see

1	2	(3)	4	5	(6)	7	(8)	9	10	(11)
C	O	M	P	U	T	E	R	I	S	E

From letters M, T, R and E, the only word TERM can be formed.

∴ Last letter of the word 'TERM' = M

15. (*c*) We have, following arrangment of mathematical symbols P = +, Q = × R = ÷, S = −

$$44 \times 9 \div 12 - 6 \times 4 + 16 = ?$$

$$\Rightarrow \quad 44 \times 9 \times \frac{1}{12} - 24 + 16 = ?$$

$$\Rightarrow \quad 33 - 24 + 16 = ?$$

$$\Rightarrow \quad 49 - 24 = ?$$

$$\therefore \quad ? = 25$$

16. (*c*) Solving by column,

In first column,

$$9 \times 8 - 7 = 72 - 7 = 65$$

In second column,

$$6 \times 5 - 4 = 30 - 4 = 26$$

In third column,

$$? \times 6 - 3 = 39$$

$$\Rightarrow \quad ? \times 6 = 39 + 3 = 42$$

$$\Rightarrow \quad ? = \frac{42}{6} = 7$$

$$\Rightarrow \quad ? = 7$$

17. (*a*) In the given positions of dice we observe that face adjacent to 5 are

In dice 1 → 1, 6

In dice 2 → 3, 6

In dice 3 → 2, 3

So, 1, 2, 3, 6 are adjacent to 5.

The remaining face 4 is opposite to the dice having face number 5.

18. (*c*) The pattern is as follows

36 →(−8) 28 →(−4) 24 →(−2) 22 →(−1) (21)

? = 21

19. (*c*) The pattern is as follows

W →(−3) T →(−4) P →(−3) M →(−4) I →(−3) F →(−4) B →(−3) [Y] →(−4) [U]

∴ ? = Y, U

20. (*d*) Pattern of given alpha-numeric series is as follows

3 C →(+3) 6 F →(+3) 9 I →(+3) 12 L

4 →(+5) 9 →(+7) 16 →(+9) 25

24 X →(−3) 21 U →(−3) 18 R →(−3) 15 O

∴ ? = L 25 O

Solution (Q. Nos. 21-23) There are total eight friends G, H, I, J, N, O, P and Q seated in a straight line.

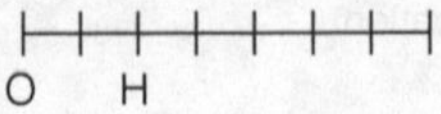

Only three people sits between H and N.

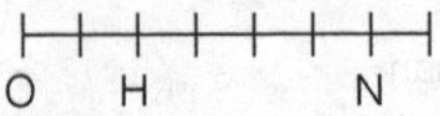

I sits third to the left of J and only two people sits between J and G.

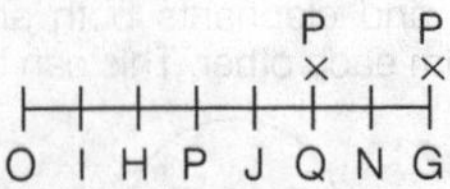

Also, P is not an immediate neighbour of N.

So, Q is placed between J and N.

21. (*e*) G represents the person seated at the extreme right end of the line.

22. (*d*) N, Q sit exactly between J and G.

23. (*a*) P is third to the left of N.

24. (*b*) According to the given information, we can draw the following diagram.

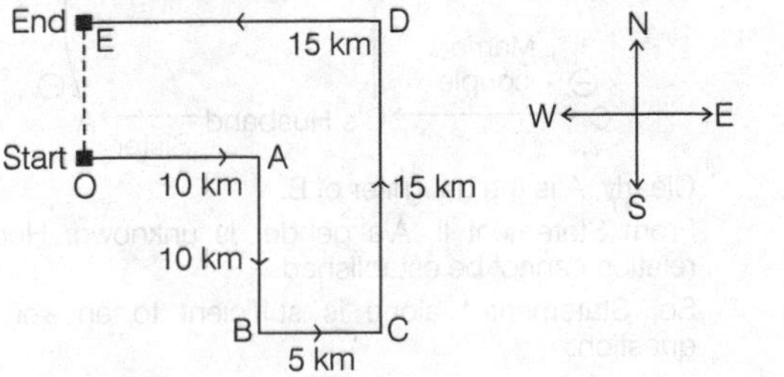

Required distance, OE = CD − AB

= 15 − 10 = 5 km

Hence, the correct answer is (b).

25. (*d*) As,

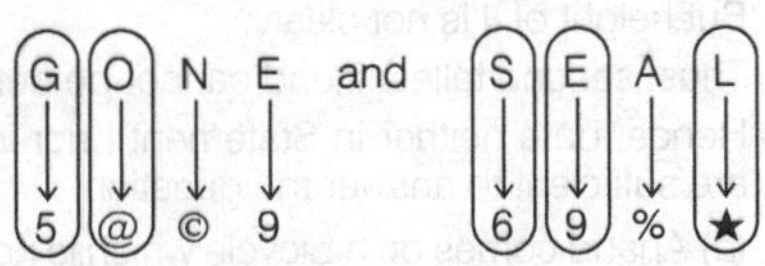

So, by direct substitution method, we get

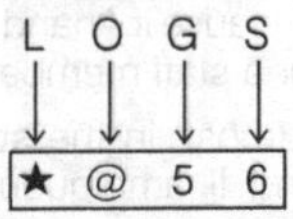

LOGS ⇒ ★@ 56

26. (*d*)

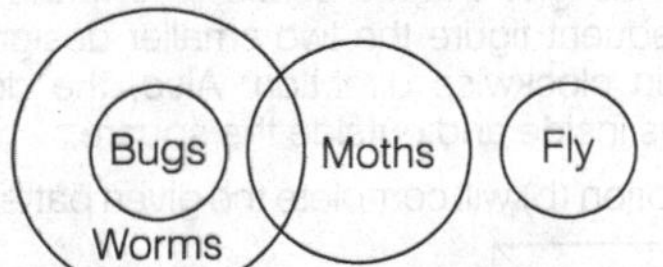

Conclusions I. No fly is a worm. (✗)

II. All moths being bugs is a possibility. (✔)

From above diagram it is clear that moth and fly both are separate. So, only Conclusion II is true.

27. (*a*)

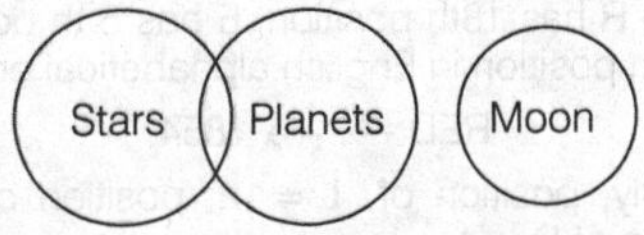

Conclusions I. No star is a moon. (May be)

II. Some stars are moons. (May be)

From above diagram, Conclusion I and II form a complementary pair. So, either Conclusion I or II follows.

28. (c) Option (c) will complete the given pattern as follows.

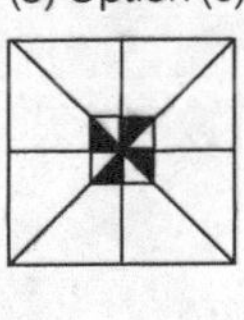

29. (*c*) There is triangle after circle and square after triangle. In the last row, we have to find the figure inside the triangle. In the next segment of circle, there is triangle and a square will be inside the triangle.

30. (*d*) None of the arguments is strong.

31. (*d*) There are three triangles and one circle in figures 1, 5 and 8.

There is one angle in figures 2, 4 and 7.

In figures 3, 6 and 9 consist the half number of inner lines as that of the number of outer lines.

32. (*b*) According to the question, Arun's rank is from the starting is 17th. Then,

Arun's rank from the last

= 31 − 17 + 1 = 15 th

Alternate Method

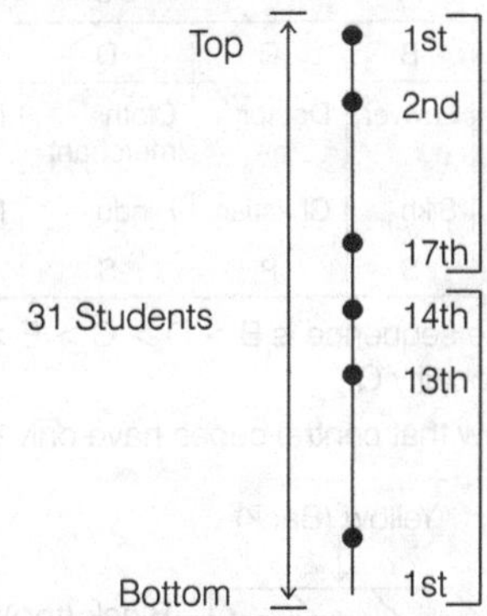

Thus, Arun's rank from the last will be

= 31 − 17 + 1 = 15th

Hence, option (b) is correct.

33. (*a*) According to the question, we have following sitting arrangement

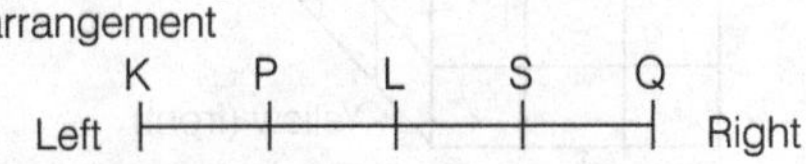

K is the 1st student from the left.

Solution (Q. Nos. 34-38) Let us draw the family diagram

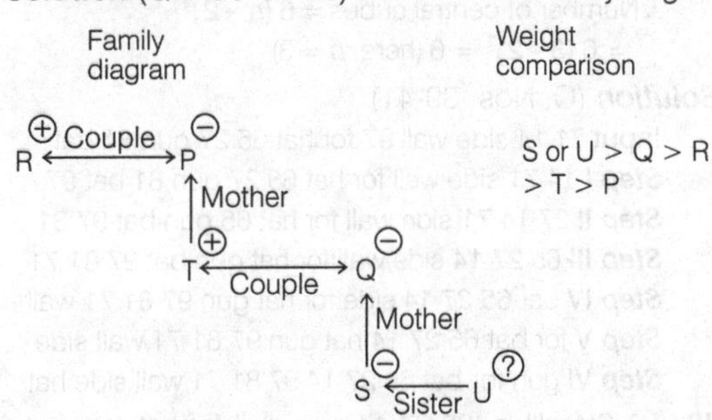

34. (*a*) As gender of U is not known, so the data is inadequate.

35. (*d*) T is the father of U.

36. (*d*) As, QT and PR are two married couples in the family, QT is one of them.

37. (*a*) I. A is a Hindu, B is a Sikh, E is a Muslim. Now, the doctor is a Christian and D is a cloth merchant. So, C is a Christian and D is a Hindu.

II. D stays in locality S. E stays in locality R. Now, one businessman, i.e. D and the lawyer stay in locality S. C is a doctor and A is a factory owner. So,B is the lawyer and stay in locality S. C, the doctor, stays in locality P. Clearly, A stays in locality Q.

III. Clearly, A is a factory owner, B is a lawyer, C is a doctor, D is a cloth merchant and E is an engineer.

IV. B, the lawyer, is oldest. A, the factory owner, is the youngest. D, the cloth merchant lies between doctor and lawyer, i.e. B and C in age.

Person	A	B	C	D	E
Profession	Factory owner	Lawyer	Doctor	Cloth merchant	Engineer
Religion	Hindu	Sikh	Christian	Hindu	Muslim
Locality	Q	S	P	S	R

So, agewise sequence is B > D > C > E > A.
A stays in locality Q.

38. (*b*) As, we know that central cubes have only one face painted.

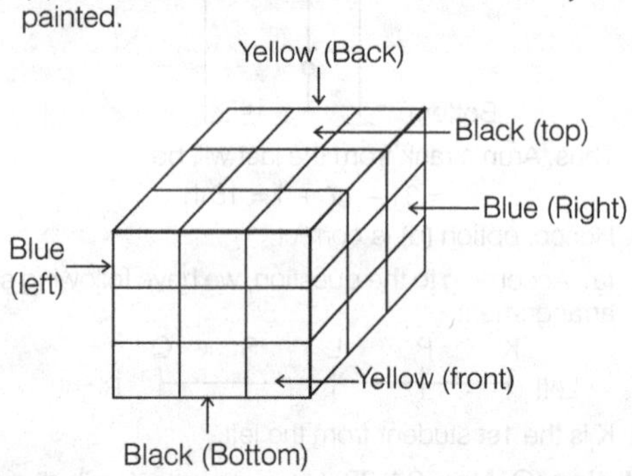

$\therefore$ Number of central cubes $= 6\,(n-2)^2$
$= 6\,(3-2)^2 = 6$ (here, $n = 3$)

Solution (Q. Nos. 39-41)

Input 71 14 side wall 97 for hat 65 27 gun 81 bat
***Step* I** 14 71 side wall for hat 65 27 gun 81 bat 97
***Step* II** 27 14 71 side wall for hat 65 gun bat 97 81
***Step* III** 65 27 14 side wall for hat gun bat 97 81 71
***Step* IV** bat 65 27 14 side for hat gun 97 81 71 wall
***Step* V** for bat 65 27 14 hat gun 97 81 71 wall side
***Step* VI** gun for bat 65 27 14 97 81 71 wall side hat

39. (*d*) Step III is '65 27 14 side wall for hat gun bat 97 81 17'.

40. (*a*) The word 'hat' is at the 7th position from the right is Step V.

41. (c) Step VI are required to complete the arrangement.

42. (*a*) From Statement I,

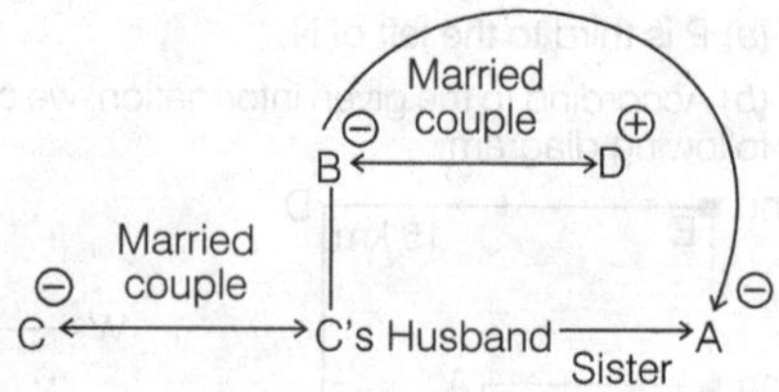

Clearly, A is the daughter of B.

From Statement II, A's gender is unknown. Hence, relation cannot be established.

So, Statement I alone is sufficient to answer the question.

43. (*d*) From Statement I, N > M > K
From Statement II, L > N
From both the statements, L > N > M > K
But height of J is not clear.
Thus, second tallest friend cannot be determined.
Hence, data neither in Statement I nor in Statement II are sufficient to answer the question.

44. (*a*) Anand comes on a bicycle which is not used by any teacher. Hence, Anand cannot be a teacher. Therefore, I is valid. II is not valid because if Anand is not a teacher, he is either a student or a staff member.

45. (*d*) Presence of word 'most' in the statement makes both Conclusions I and II ambiguous. Hence, both I and II cannot be drawn.

46. (*c*) In the given figure series, it is found that in each subsequent figure the two smaller designs move one step in clockwise direction. Also, the dot alternately comes inside and outside the square.

47. (*b*) Option (b) will complete the given pattern as follows

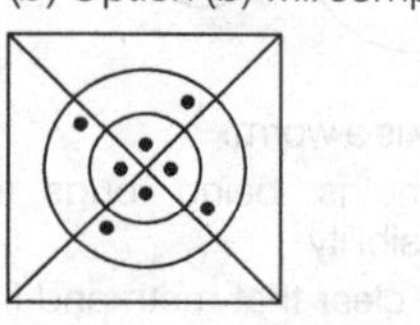

48. (*a*) Clearly, the figure II is the mirror image of figure I.

49. (*d*) As, R has 18th position, E has 5 th position and D has 4th position in English alphabetical order.

RED ⟶ 1854

Similarly, position of L = 12, position of E = 5 and position of D = 4.

LED ⟶ 1254

50. (*d*)

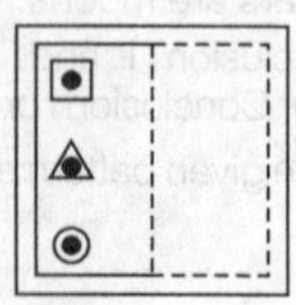

So, option (d) is correct answer.

PRACTICE SET 8

Direction (Q. Nos. 1-2) *In the following questions, find the odd word/number pair from the given alternatives.*

1. (a) 6 : 26 (b) 11 : 46 (c) 9 : 40 (d) 16 : 66

2. (a) Dog (b) Cow (c) Goat (d) Buffalo

3. In a certain code language, 'REFORM' is coded as '426349' and 'FORMULA' is coded as '6349871'. How is 'AMUL' coded in that language?

(a) 1847 (b) 1987 (c) 1784 (d) 1478

4. If John celebrated his victory day on Tuesday, 5th January 1965, then when will he celebrate his next victory day on the same day?

(a) 5th January, 1970 (b) 5th January, 1971
(c) 5th January, 1973 (d) 5th January, 1974

5. From the given two positions of a single dice, find the number of dots at the face opposite to the face having 4 dots.

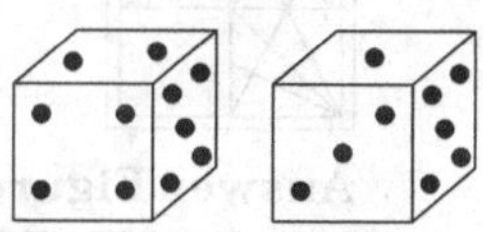

I II

(a) 1 (b) 2 (c) 3 (d) 5

Direction (Q. Nos. 6-8) *In the following questions, select the related word/letters/number pair from the given alternatives.*

6. $\sqrt{AFI} = M : \sqrt{ADD} = L :: \sqrt{ABA} = ?$ **[SSC (CGL) Pre 2015]**

(a) I (b) K (c) N (d) O

7. Taka : Bangladesh : : Lira : ?

(a) Kuwait (b) Italy
(c) Sri Lanka (d) Kenya

8. 5 : 35

(a) 7 : 77 (b) 9 : 45 (c) 11 : 55 (d) 3 : 24

9. How many pairs of letters are there in these words which have as many letters between them as in the English alphabet?

DELIBERATE

(a) One (b) Two
(c) Four (d) Three

10. At sunrise, Amit and Deepak are having a conversation standing in front of each other. The shadow of Deepak is formed towards the right hand of Amit. What direction is Deepak facing?

(a) North-East (b) South
(c) East (d) North

Direction (Q. Nos. 11-13) *Read the given information and answer the questions.*

A word and number arrangement machine when given an input line of words and numbers rearranges them following a particular rule in each step. The following is an illustration of input and rearrangement.

Input 'go now 52 38 17 for again 65'
Step I 65 go now 52 38 17 for again
Step II 65 again go now 52 38 17 for
Step III 65 again 52 go now 38 17 for
Step IV 65 again 52 for go now 38 17
Step V 65 again 52 for 38 go now 17
Step VI 65 again 52 for 38 go 17 now

Step VI is the last step of the rearrangement.

As per the rules followed in the above steps, find out in each of the following questions the appropriate step for the given input.

11. Input 'show 51 36 new far 81 46 goal'

Which of the following steps will be the last but one?

(a) VII (b) VIII
(c) VI (d) V
(e) None of these

12. Input 'home turf 39 24 86 44 roll over'

Which of the following steps will be the last?

(a) X (b) IX
(c) VIII (d) VII
(e) None of these

13. Step II of an input is '76 ask 12 32 begin over join 42'.

How many more steps will be required to complete the rearrangement?

(a) Four (b) Five (c) Six (d) Three
(e) None of these

14. Vikash is more competent than Keshav, Shiv is less competent than Aashu but more competent than Keshav. Vikash is less competent than Shiv. Who is the most competent in the group?

(a) Aashu (b) Keshav (c) Vikash (d) Shiv

15. Rashmi is 14th from the right end in a row of 40 girls. What is her position from the left end?

(a) 25th (b) 27th (c) 21st (d) None of these

16. A word is represented by only one set of numbers as given in any one of the alternatives. The sets of numbers given in the alternatives are represented by two classes of alphabets as in two matrices given below. The columns and row of Matrix I are numbered from 0 to 4 and that of Matrix II are numbered from 5 to 9.

A letter from these matrices can be represented first by its rows and next by its column, e.g., 'A' can be represented by 01, 14 etc, and E can be represented by 55, 66 etc. Similarly, you have to identify the set for the word 'ORGAN'. **[SSC (CGL) 2015]**

Matrix I

	0	1	2	3	4
0	P	A	G	R	Z
1	G	R	Z	P	A
2	Z	P	A	G	R
3	A	G	R	Z	P
4	R	Z	P	A	G

Matrix II

	5	6	7	8	9
5	E	M	L	N	O
6	L	E	O	M	N
7	O	N	E	L	M
8	N	O	M	E	L
9	M	L	N	O	E

(a) 75, 03, 11, 22, 76 (b) 67, 22, 31, 58, 22
(c) 86, 40, 23, 14, 96 (d) 98, 03, 44, 22, 58

Direction (Q. Nos. 17-19) *Study the following information carefully to answer the questions given below.*

P, T, V, R, M, D, K and W are sitting around a circular table facing the centre. V is second to the left of T. T is fourth to the right of M. D and P are not immediate neighbours of T. D is third to the right of P. W is not an immediate neighbour of P. P is to the immediate left of K.

17. Who is second to the left of K?

(a) P (b) R (c) M (d) W
(e) Data inadequate

18. Who is to the immediate left of V?

(a) D (b) M (c) W (d) Data inadequate
(e) None of these

19. Who is the third to the right of V?

(a) T (b) K (c) P (d) M
(e) None of these

20. Find out which of the answer figures (a), (b), (c) and (d) completes the figure matrix?

Question Figure

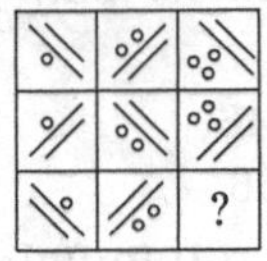

Answer Figures

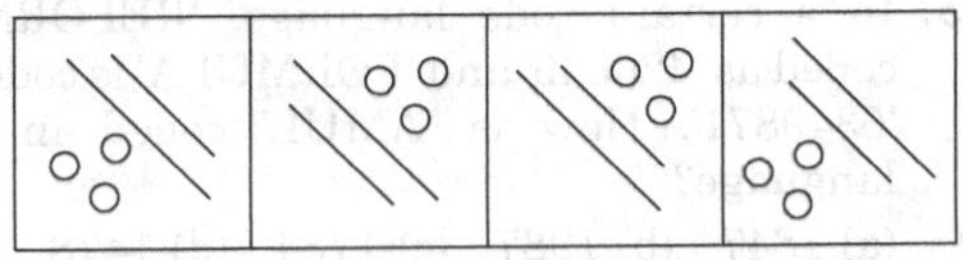

(a) (b) (c) (d)

21. Identify the missing part of the question figure and select it from given answer figures.

Question Figure

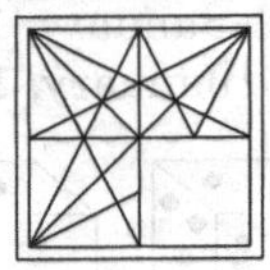

Answer Figures

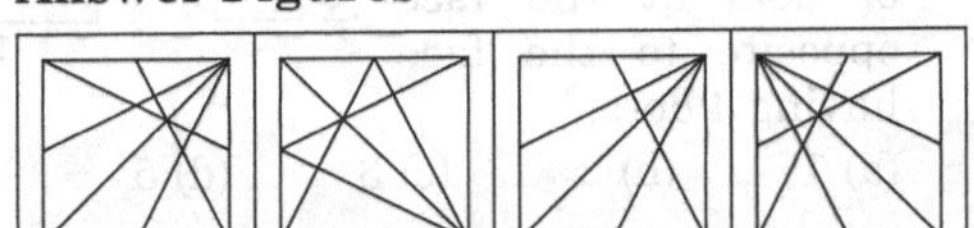

(a) (b) (c) (d)

22. If '>' stands for 'division', '∨' stands for 'multiplication', '–' stands for 'greater than', '×' stands for 'less than', '<' stands for 'addition', '∧' stands for 'subtraction', '+' stands for 'equal to', then which of the following equations is correct? **[SSC (CGL) 2014]**

(a) $10 \wedge 3 < 5 < 4 + 16$ (b) $4 \wedge 6 < 4 < 4 + 16$
(c) $12 \wedge 3 < 5 < 4 + 12$ (d) $11 \wedge 12 < 5 < 4 + 12$

23. Identify the answer figure from which pieces given in the question figure have been cut.

Question Figure

Answer Figures

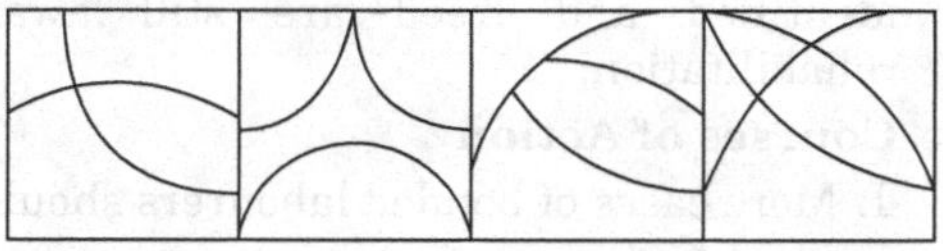

(a) (b) (c) (d)

24. Find the missing character from the given alternatives.

4	5	6
2	3	7
1	8	3
21	98	?

(a) 85 (b) 94 (c) 104 (d) 49

25. Arrange the following words as per order in the dictionary.

(i) Dissident (ii) Dissolve
(iii) Dissent (iv) Dissolute
(v) Dissolution

(a) (iii), (i), (iv), (v), (ii)
(b) (iii), (ii), (i), (iv), (v)
(c) (iii), (i), (iv), (ii), (v)
(d) (iii), (ii), (iv), (v), (i)

26. A result of a survey of 1000 persons with respect to their knowledge of Hindi (H), English (E) and Sanskrit (S) is given below.

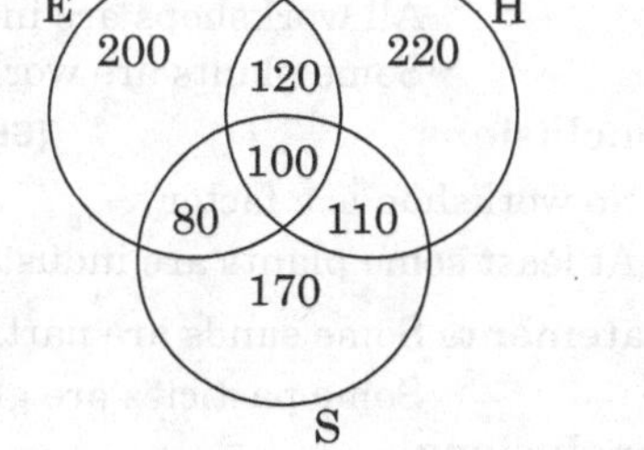

What is the ratio of those who know all the three languages to those who do not know Sanskrit?

(a) $\frac{5}{27}$ (b) $\frac{10}{17}$ (c) $\frac{1}{10}$ (d) $\frac{1}{9}$

27. Which one set of letters when sequentially placed at the gaps in the given letters series shall complete it?

adb_ac_da_cddcb_dbc_cbda

[SSC (CGL) Pre 2015]

(a) bccba (b) cbbaa (c) ccbba (d) bbcad

28. Find out the wrong number.

1, 2, 5, 14, 41, 124

(a) 2 (b) 5 (c) 14 (d) 124

29. Find the missing term.

XWA, VTC, SPF, OKJ, ?

(a) JDN (b) JEO
(c) LPN (d) JDP
(e) None of these

Direction (Q. Nos. 30-31) *Read the following information carefully to answer the questions that follow.*

I. There is a family of six members.
II. Members are A, B, C, D, E and F.
III. A and B are married couple, B being the female member.
IV. B is the daughter-in-law of F.
V. D is the only son of C.
VI. E is the sister D.
VII. F's husband is not alive.
VIII. C is A's brother.

30. How is F related to C?

(a) Sister (b) Mother
(c) Aunt (d) Mother-in-law

31. How is E related to C?

(a) Mother (b) Aunt
(b) Cousin (d) Daughter

Direction (Q. Nos. 32-36) *Study the following information to answer the given questions.*

Eight cars A, B, C, D, W, X, Y and Z are parked around a circular playground (facing the centre of the playground) with equal distances between each other, but not necessarily in the same order. Z is parked to the immediate right of W. Only two cars are parked between W and B. C is parked second to the right of B. A is parked to the immediate right of D. D is not parked immediately near Z. Y is parked second to the left of X.

[LIC (ADO) 2015]

32. Which of the following pairs represents both the cars parked immediately near C?

(a) Y,B (b) W, C
(c) D, X (d) A, Z
(e) X, Y

33. Which car is parked second to the left of A?

(a) Z (b) C
(c) X (d) B
(e) W

34. Which of the following statements is true with respect to the given arrangement?
(a) Z is parked to the immediate left of C
(b) A is parked second to the right of Y
(c) Only three cars are parked between C and Z
(d) Only two cars are parked between Y and B
(e) None of the given options is true

35. If all the cars are parked in alphabetical order in anti-clockwise direction starting from A, the positions of how many cars (excluding A) will remain unchanged?
(a) Three (b) Two (c) One (d) None
(e) More than three

36. Four of the following five are alike in a certain way based on the given arrangement, and so form a group. Which one of the following does not belong to the group?
(a) AX (b) ZD (c) XZ (d) BA
(e) CY

Direction (Q. Nos. 37-38) *In each of the questions below is given a statement followed by three courses of action numbered I, II and III. A course of action is a step or administrative decision to be taken for improvement, follow-up or further at action in regard to the problem, policy, etc. On the basis of information given in the statement, you have to assume everything in the statement to be true and then decide which of the three given suggested courses of action logically follows worth pursuing. Then, decide which of the alternatives (a), (b), (c), (d) or (e) is correct.*

37. Statement Faced with a serious resource crunch and a depressing overall economic scenario, the state 'X' is unlikely to achieve the targeted per cent compound annual growth rate during the 10th plan.

Courses of Action

I. The target growth should be reduced for the next plan.
II. The reasons for the failures should be studied.
III. The state 'X's performance should be compared with that of other states.

(a) Only I follows
(b) Both I and III follow
(c) Both II and III follow
(d) None follows

38. Statement Over 27000 bonded labourers identified and freed are still awaiting rehabilitation.

Courses of Action

I. More cases of bonded labourers should be identified.
II. Till the proper rehabilitation facilities are available, the bonded labourers should not be freed.
III. The impediments in the way of speedy and proper rehabilitation of bonded labourers should be removed.

(a) Only I follows (b) Only II follows
(c) Only III follows (d) Both II and III follow

Direction (Q. Nos. 39-40) *In the following questions, two/ three statements followed by two conclusions numbered I and II have been given. You have to take the given statements to be true even if they seem to be at variance from commonly known facts and then decide which of the given conclusions logically follows from the given statements disregarding commonly known facts.*

Give answer
(a) if only Conclusion I is true
(b) if neither Conclusion I nor II is true
(c) it only Conclusion II is true
(d) if both Conclusions I and II are true
(e) if either Conclusion I or II is true

39. Statements No factory is an industry.
All workshops are industries.
Some plants are workshops.

Conclusions **[SBI (PO) 2015]**

I. No workshop is a factory.
II. At least some plants are industries.

40. Statements Some sands are particles.
Some particles are glasses.

Conclusions

I. Some glasses are definitely not particles.
II. Some glasses being sands is a possibility.

41. In the question below are given four statements followed by two Conclusions I and II. You have to take the given statements to be true even if they seem to be at variance from commonly known facts. Read all the conclusions and then decide which of the given conclusion(s) logically follow(s) from given statements disregarding commonly known facts.

Statements Some scissors are cats.
All tigers are birds.
Some cats are tigers.
No bird is dog.

Conclusions I. Some cats are birds.
II. No dog is bird.

(a) if only Conclusion I follows
(b) if only Conclusion II follows
(c) if either Conclusion I or II follows
(d) if both Conclusions I and II follow
(e) if neither Conclusion I nor II follows

42. Find the water image of the following word from the given alternatives.

CORDIAL

(a) COBDIVL (b) COBDIVT
(c) COBDIVI (d) ꓶAIDꓤOƆ

43. How many triangles are there in the following figure?

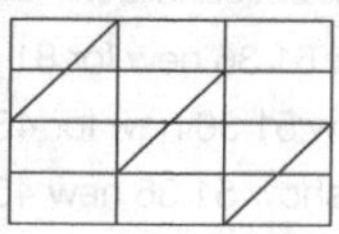

(a) 10 (b) 14 (c) 12 (d) 11

Direction (Q. Nos. 44-46) *In the following questions, the symbols @. ©, $, % and * are used with the following meaning as illustrated below.*

'P © Q' means 'P is not greater than Q'.

'P % Q' means 'P is not smaller than Q'.

'P * Q' means 'P is neither smaller than nor equal to Q'.

'P @ Q' means 'P is neither greater than nor equal to Q'.

'P $ Q' means 'P is neither greater than nor smaller than Q'.

Now, in each of the following questions assuming the given statements to be true, find which of the two Conclusions I and II given below them is/ are definitely true?

Give answer
(a) if only Conclusion I is true
(b) if only Conclusion II is true
(c) if either Conclusion I or II is true
(d) if neither Conclusion I nor II is true
(e) if both Conclusions I and II are true

44. **Statements** K @ V, V © N, N % F
Conclusions I. F @ V II. K @ N

45. **Statements** H © W, W $ M, M @ B
Conclusions I. B * H II. M % H

46. **Statements** D % B, B * T, T $ M
Conclusions I. T © D II. M © D

47. Find the missing figure from the given responses.

Question Figures

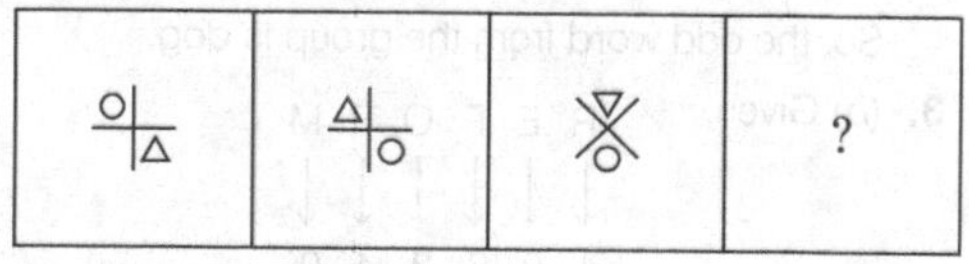

1 2 3 4

Answer Figures

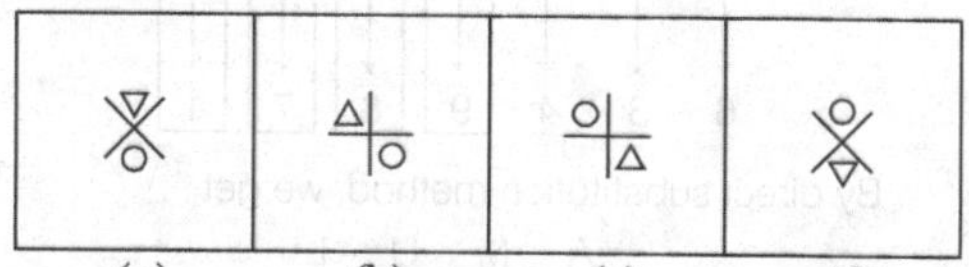

(a) (b) (c) (d)

48. Some equations are solved on the basis of a certain system. Find the correct answer for the unsolved equation on that basis.

5 * 3 = 125; 4 * 3 = 64; 8 * 2 = ?

(a) 28 (b) 16 (c) 32 (d) 64

49. How many even number are there in the following series of numbers, each of which is preceded by an odd number, but not followed by an even number?

5348971653298735

(a) 0 (b) 1 (c) 2 (d) 3

50. If a mirror is placed on the line MN, then which of the answer figures is the right image of the given figure? **[SSC (CPO) 2015]**

Question Figure

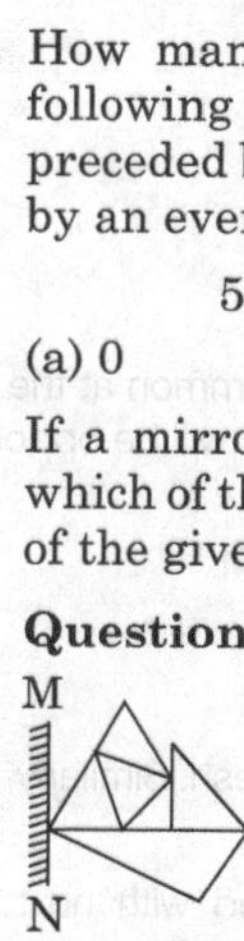

Answer Figures

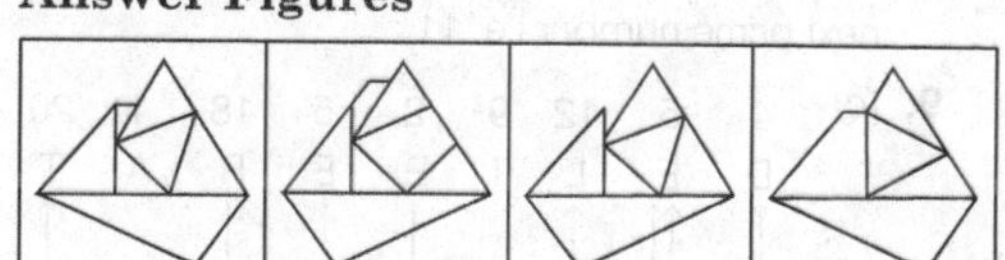

(a) (b) (c) (d)

Hints and Solutions

1. (*c*) In all others, second number is two more than four times the first number.

2. (*a*) All, are pet animals but we have to find the odd amongst them. Except dog, all are herbivorous animals i.e. feed on green grass, whereas dog is an omnivorous animal i.e. feeds on flesh and vegetarian food.

So, the odd word from the group is dog.

3. (*b*) Given,

R	E	F	O	R	M
↓	↓	↓	↓	↓	↓
4	2	6	3	4	9

F	O	R	M	U	L	A
↓	↓	↓	↓	↓	↓	↓
6	3	4	9	8	7	1

By direct substitution method, we get

A	M	U	L
↓	↓	↓	↓
1	9	8	7

Hence, option (b) is correct.

4. (*b*) 5 January, 1965 ⇒ Tuesday
5 January, 1966 ⇒ Wednesday
5 January, 1967 ⇒ Thursday
5 January, 1968 ⇒ Friday
5 January, 1969 ⇒ Sunday
Since, 1968 is a Leap Year.
5 January, 1970 ⇒ Monday
5 January, 1971 ⇒ Tuesday

5. (*c*) In both positions, 5 dots are common at the same (Right) face. So, face having 4 dots will be opposite to face having 3 dots.

6. (*b*) As, $\sqrt{AFI} = \sqrt{169} = 13 = M$

and $\sqrt{ADD} = \sqrt{144} = 12 = L$

Similarly, $\sqrt{ABA} = \sqrt{121} = 11 = K$

7. (*b*) Taka is the currency of Bangladesh. Similarly, Lira is the currency of Italy.

8. (*a*) As, $5 \times 7 = 35$ i.e. 5 multiplied with next prime number i.e. 7. Similarly, $7 \times 11 = 77$ i.e. 7 multiplied with next prime number i.e. 11.

9. (*c*)

4	5	12	9	2	5	18	1	20	5
D	E	L	I	B	E	R	A	T	E

∴ Letters pairs = DE, BE, EL, RT ⇒ Four

10. (*d*) According to the direction, the direction diagram is drawn as

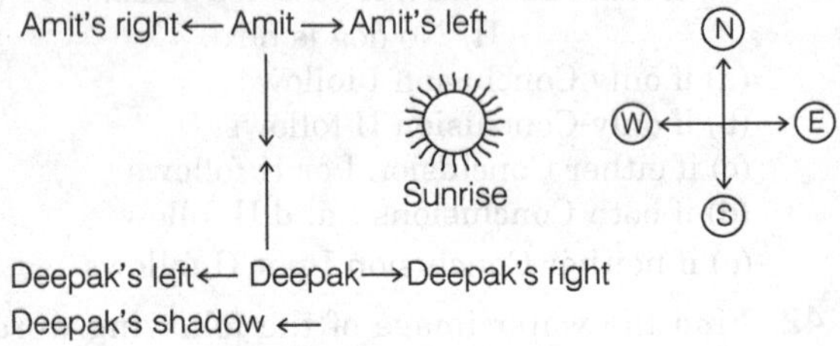

Clearly, Deepak is facing North.

Solution (Q. Nos. 11-13) In Step I, the largest number goes to the extreme left pushing rest of the line rightward; in the next step the word that comes first in alphabetical order goes to the second position from left pushing rest of the line rightward, thus the numbers and the words get arranged alternately till all the numbers are in descending order and all the words are in alphabetical order.

11. (*c*) **Input** show 51 36 new for 81 46 goal
***Step* I** 81 show 51 36 new for 46 goal
***Step* II** 81 for show 51 36 new 46 goal
***Step* III** 81 for 51 show 36 new 46 goal
***Step* IV** 81 for 51 goal show 36 new 46
***Step* V** 81 for 51 goal 46 show 36 new
***Step* VI** 81 for 51 goal 46 new show 36
***Step* VII** 81 for 51 goal 46 new 36 show
∴ Step VI will be last but one.

12. (*e*) **Input** home turf 39 24 86 44 roll over
***Step* I** 86 home turf 39 24 44 roll over
***Step* II** 86 home 44 turf 39 24 roll over
***Step* III** 86 home 44 over turf 39 24 roll
***Step* IV** 86 home 44 over 39 turf 24 roll
***Step* V** 86 home 44 over 39 roll turf 24
***Step* VI** 86 home 44 over 39 roll 24 turf
Clearly, last step = Step VI

13. (*a*) ***Step* II** 76 ask 12 32 begin over join 42
***Step* III** 76 ask 42 12 32 begin over join
***Step* IV** 76 ask 42 begin 12 32 over join
***Step* V** 76 ask 42 begin 32 12 over join
***Step* VI** 76 ask 42 begin 32 join 12 over
Clearly, after Step II, four more steps are required to complete the arrangement.

14. (*a*) According to the question,

Vikash > Keshav

Aashu > Shiv > Keshav

Shiv > Vikash

On arranging the above data, we get

(Aashu) > Shiv > Vikash > Keshav

Clearly, Aashu is the most competent in the group.

15. (*b*) Required Position = 40 + 1 − 14

= 41 − 14 = 27th

16. (*d*) According to the question,

O = 59, 67, 75, 86, (98)

R = (03), 11, 24, 32, 40

G = 02, 10, 23, 31, (44)

A = 01, 14, (22), 30, 43

N = (58), 69, 76, 85, 97

O → 98, R → 03, G → 44, A → 22, N → 58

Solutions (Q. Nos. 17-19) Following sitting arrangement is formed from the given information.

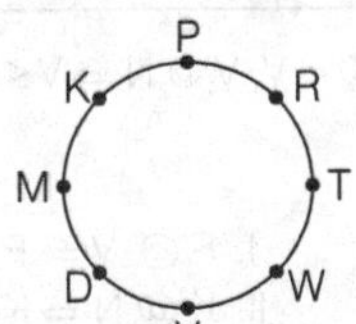

17. (*b*) Clearly, R is second to the left of K.

18. (*a*) Clearly, D is to the immediate left of V.

19. (*e*) Clearly, R is third to the right of V. So, none of the given options is correct.

20. (*a*) The pattern followed is

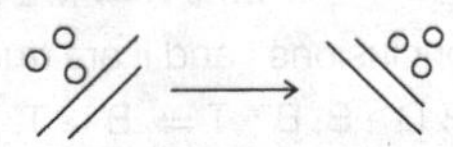

Hence, option (b) is the correct answer

21. (*b*) Option (b) will complete the given pattern as follows.

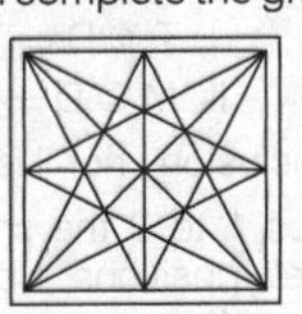

22. (*a*) From option (a), 10^3 < 5 < 4 + 16

After putting signs, we get

⇒ 10 − 3 + 5 + 4 = 16

⇒ 7+5+4=16 ⇒ 16 = 16

23. (*b*) Figure (b) is formed from question figure.

24. (*b*) As, $(4)^2 + (2)^2 + (1)^2 = 21$

$(5)^2 + (3)^2 + (8)^2 = 98$

Similarly, $(6)^2 + (7)^2 + (3)^2 = 94$

Hence, option (b) is the correct answer.

25. (*a*) Arrangement of words as per dictionary

(iii) Dissent, → (i) Dissident, → (iv) Dissolute, → (v) Dissolution, → (ii) Dissolve

26. (*a*) The persons knowing all the three languages are represented by the region which is common to all the three circles. Hence, number of such persons = 100. The persons who do not know Sanskrit are represented by the region outside circle S. So, number of such persons = (200 + 120 + 220) = 540

$\therefore$ Required ratio = $\frac{100}{540} = \frac{5}{27}$

27. (*b*) The pattern of the series is

a d b c / a c b d / a b c d / d c b a / d b c a / c b d a

⇒ c b b a a

28. (*d*) The pattern is as follows

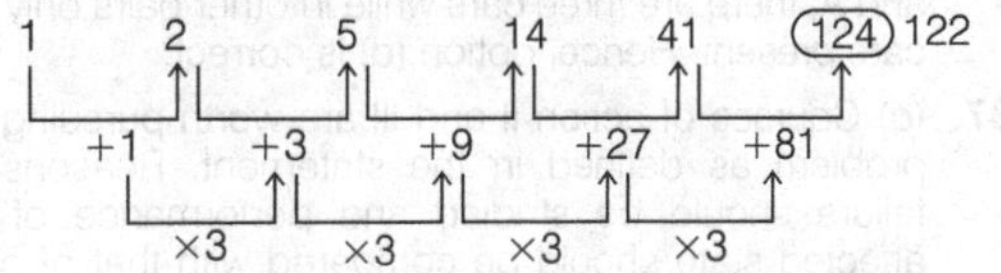

Hence, number 124 is wrong and should be replaced by 122.

29. (*b*) The pattern is as follows

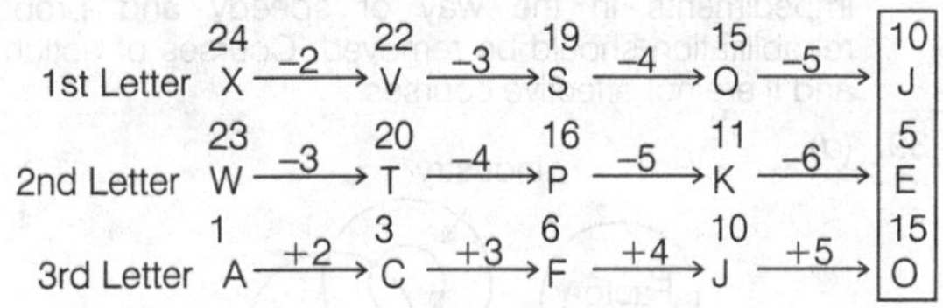

$\therefore$? = JEO

Solution (Q. Nos. 30-31) Let us make the family diagram

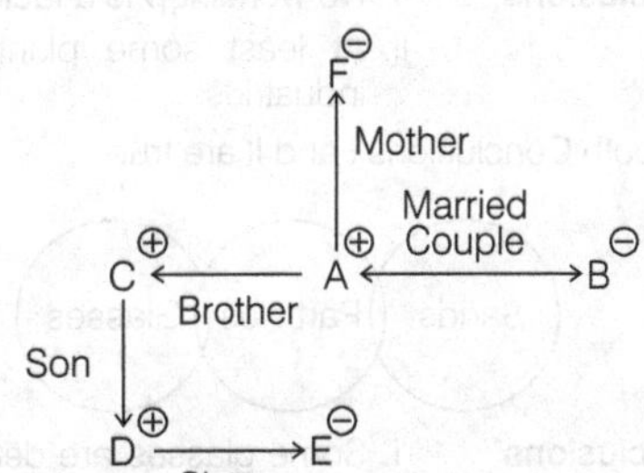

30. (*b*) F is C's mother.

31. (*d*) E is C's daughter.

Solution (Q. Nos. 32-36) According to given information, the parking arrangement of cars is as follows

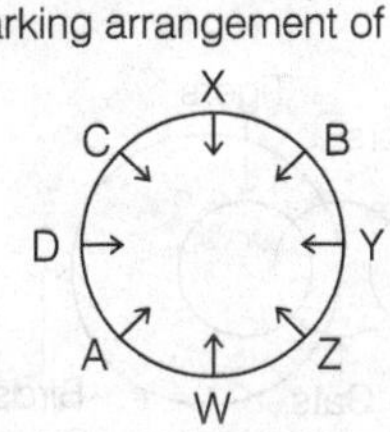

32. (*c*) Cars D and X are parked immediately near C.

33. (*b*) Car C is parked second to the left of A.

34. (*c*) Only three cars are parked between C and Z.

35. (*c*) New arrangement is as follows:

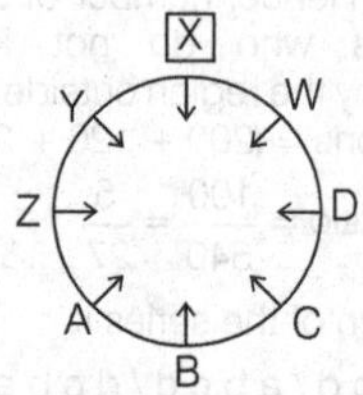

Therefore, the position of car X will remain unchanged.

36. (*d*) Pair BA is different from others because between B and A, there are three cars while in other pairs only two cars present. Hence, option (d) is correct.

37. (*c*) Courses of action II and III are worth pursuing the problem as defined in the statement. Reasons for failure should be studied and performance of the affected state should be compared with that of other states.

38. (*c*) Only Course of action III provides a feasible and effective course to combat the problem, that impediments in the way of speedy and proper rehabilitation should be removed, Courses of action I and II are not effective courses.

39. (*d*)

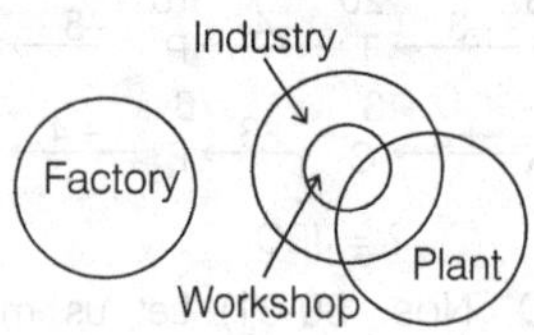

Conclusions I. No workshop is a factory. (✔)
II. At least some plants are industries. (✔)

So, both Conclusions I and II are true.

40. (*c*)

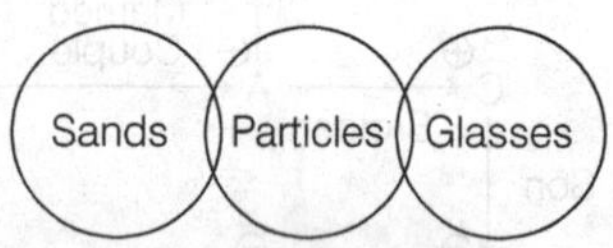

Conclusions I. Some glasses are definitely not particles. (✗)
II. Some glasses being sands is a possibility. (✔)

So, only Conclusion II is true.

41. (*d*)

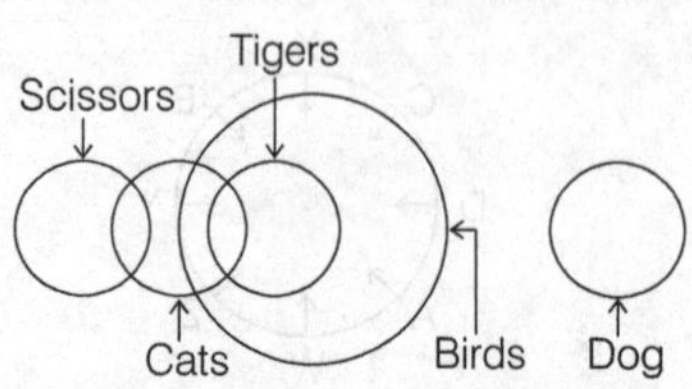

Conclusions I. Some cats are birds. (✔)
II. No dog is birds. (✔)

So, both Conclusions I and II follow.

42. (*b*) Option (b) is correct water image.

43. (*c*) The figure, in question may be labelled as shown in following figure

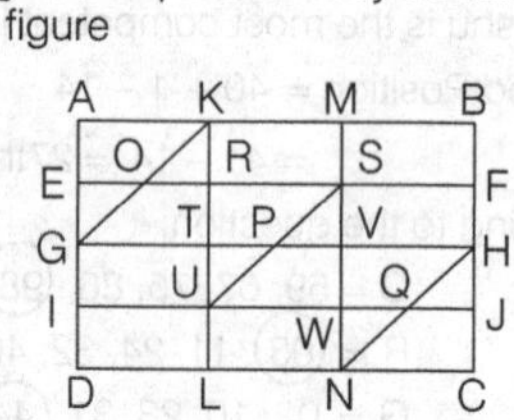

There are 12 triangles in the figure, namely ΔEOG, ΔAGK, ΔKOR, ΔKGT, ΔTUP, ΔRUS, ΔSPV, ΔSUW, ΔWNQ, ΔVNH, ΔHQJ and ΔHNC.

Solution (Q. Nos. 44-46)

© ⇒ ≤	% ⇒ ≥	* ⇒ >	@ ⇒ <	$ ⇒ =

44. (*b*) K @ V ⇒ K < V, V © N ⇒ V≤ N, N % F ⇒ N≥ F

Therefore,

K < V≤ N≥ F

Conclusions I. F @ V ⇒ F < V (Not True)
II. K@ N ⇒ K < N (True)

So, only Conclusion II is true.

45. (*e*) H © W ⇒ H≤ W, W $ M ⇒ W = M, M @ B ⇒ M < B

Therefore,

H≤ W = M < B

Conclusions I. B * H ⇒ B > H (True)
II. M % H ⇒ M≥ H (True)

So, both Conclusions I and II are true.

46. (*d*) D % B ⇒ D≥ B, B * T ⇒ B > T, T $ M ⇒ T = M

Therefore,

D≥ B> T= M

Conclusions I. T © D ⇒ T≤ D (Not True)
II. M © D ⇒ M≤ D (Not True)

So, neither Conclusion I nor II is true.

47. (*d*) From figures 1 to 2 the small circle and triangle interchange their positions. So, option (d) figure will follow the same pattern.

48. (*d*) As, 5 * 3 = 125

⇒ $(5)^3 = 125$

and 4 * 3 = 64

⇒ $(4)^3 = 64$

Same as, 8 * 2 = ?

⇒ $(8)^2 = 64$

∴ ? = 64

49. (*d*) 5 3 4 8 9 7 1 [6] 5 3 [2] 9 [8] 7 3 5

There are three such even numbers 6, 2 and 8 each of which is preceded by an odd number and not followed by and even number.

50. (*c*) Figure (c) is the right image of the given figure.

PRACTICE SET 9

1. Find out the wrong number.

2, 6, 12, 72, 865, 62208

(a) 72 (b) 12
(c) 62208 (d) 865
(e) 6

2. In the question below are given four statements followed by three Conclusions I, II and III. You have to take the given statements to be true even if they seem to be at variance from commonly known facts. Read all the conclusions and then decide which of the given conclusion(s) logically from given statements disregarding commonly known facts.

Statements All lions are tigers.

All tigers are leopards.

Some leopards are wolves.

No wolf is elephant.

Conclusions I. No elephant is lion.

II. Some wolves are lions.

III. Some leopards are lions.

(a) Only I follows (b) Only II follows
(c) Only III follows (d) I and II follow

3. What should come in the place of question mark (?) in the following alpha-numeric series?

1CV, 5FU, 9IT, ?, 17OR

(a) 11LS (b) 14JS
(c) 15JS (d) 13LS

4. Sohan drove 15 km to the West from his house, then he turned left and drove 20 km. He then turned East and drove 25 km and finally turning left covers 20 km. How far he is from his house? **[SSC (CGL) Pre 2015]**

(a) 5 km (b) 10 km
(c) 40 km (d) 80 km

Direction (Q. Nos 5-9) *Study the given information carefully and answer the given questions.* **[IBPS (Office Assistant) 2015]**

Twelve people are sitting in two parallel rows containing six people each, in such a way that there is equal distance between adjacent persons. In row 1, T, U, V, W, X and Y are seated and all of them are facing South. In row 2, B, C, D, E, F and G are seated and all of them are facing North. Therefore, in the given seating arrangement each member seated in a row faces another member of the other row. Only two people sit to the left of E. Only one person sits between E and F. V is an immediate neighbour of the one who faces F. X sits second to the right of V. Only two people sit between X and T. G faces one of the immediate neighbours of X. Y sits second to the right of U. D faces W. B does not face X.

5. What is the position of U with respect to T?

(a) Second to the left
(b) Second to the right
(c) Third to the left
(d) Third to the right
(e) Fourth to the right

6. Four of the following five are alike in a certain way based on the given arrangement and hence form a group. Which of them does not belong to that group?

(a) V (b) E (c) U (d) W
(e) B

7. Who amongst the following is facing V?

(a) B (b) E (c) G (d) F
(e) C

8. Who amongst the following is facing T?

(a) B (b) G (c) E (d) C
(e) F

9. Which of the following statements is true regarding C?

(a) C sits at one of the extreme ends of the row
(b) C is an immediate neighbour of B
(c) C faces U
(d) C faces one of the immediate neighbours of V
(e) None of the given statements is true

10. Select the word which cannot be formed using the letters of the given word. **[SSC (CPO) 2015]**

CHARACTER

(a) TRACER (b) CHARTER
(c) HEARTY (d) CRATE

11. A statement followed by four assumptions numbered I, II, III and IV are given. An assumption is something supposed or taken for granted. You have to consider the statement and the following assumptions and decide which of the assumptions is implicit in the statement, then decide which of the answers (a), (b), (c) or (d) is correct.

Statement The companies that showed relatively high import orientation in India were not the ones that benefited the most from Government interventions during the heydays of import substitution.

Assumptions

I. High import companies do not need Government support.

II. Low import companies received more Government support.

III. Import oriented companies are affected by Government prices.

IV. Exporting of goods get affected by Government.

(a) Only I (b) Only III
(c) Both II and IV (d) All four

12. Each of P, Q, T, A and B has different heights. T is taller than P and B but shorter than A and Q. P is not the shortest, who is the tallest?

(a) A (b) Q (c) P (d) P or B
(e) None of these

Direction (Q. Nos 13-14) *Below are given letters A to Z. Under each capital letter, a small letter is written which is to be used as a code for the capital letter.*

A	B	C	D	E	F	H	G	I	J	K	L	M
l	s	p	k	r	j	c	x	q	g	t	w	z
N	O	P	Q	R	S	T	U	V	W	X	Y	Z
u	m	v	i	a	y	e	d	n	h	b	o	f

In each of the following questions, a group of six capital letters is given and its code equivalent is given below. Select the response containing the correct code.

13. JBEGPV

(a) lkcvmf, pjwiod, gsrxvn, azjcuy
(b) lbvseo, phzgda, gtxcoy, abrwid
(c) afdber, gtmzqp, pyfkol, lasivh
(d) golnrp, lkrunh, pchpwy, aectin

14. CHWCLS

(a) lkcvmf, pjwiod, gsrxvn, azjcuy
(b) lbvseo, phzgda, gtxcoy, abrwid
(c) afdber, gtmzqp, pyfkol, lasivh
(d) golnrp, lkrunh, pchpwy, aectin

15. Identify the missing part of the question figure and select it from given answer figures.

Question Figure

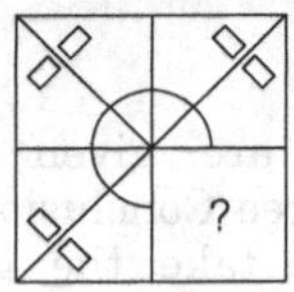

Answer Figures

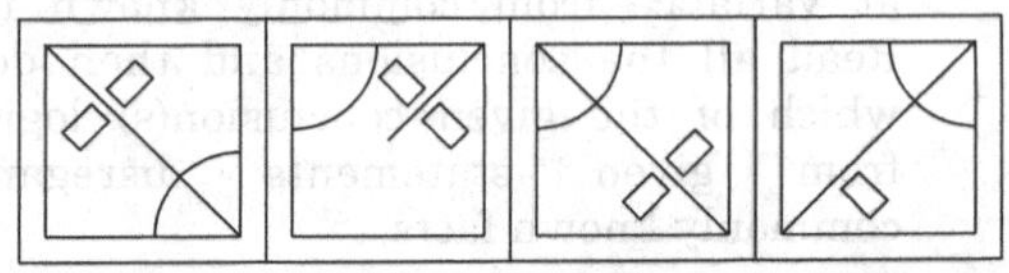

(a) (b) (c) (d)

16. Select the related word from the given alternatives.

Mechanic : Spanner : : Carpenter :?

(a) Tree (b) Wood
(c) Furniture (d) Saw

17. How many rectangles are there in the following figure?

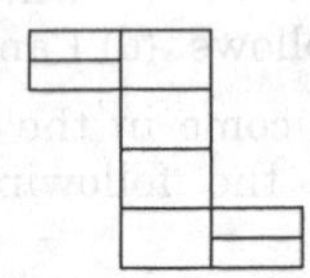

(a) 8 (b) 18 (c) 17 (d) 20

Direction (Q. Nos 18-19) *In the following questions, find the odd letters/words pair from the given alternatives.*

18. (a) Long—Short (b) Black—White
(c) Head—Cap (d) Friend—Foe

19. (a) BADC (b) JILK
(c) NMPO (d) VUWX

20. From the given two positions of a single dice, find the number of dots at the face opposite to the face having 1 dot.

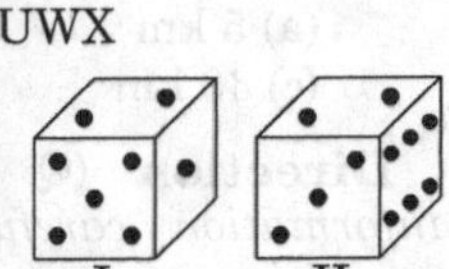

I II

(a) 1 (b) 2
(c) 3 (d) 6

Direction (Q. Nos 21-22) *Read the given information carefully and then answer the questions that follow.*

Six members of a family A, B, C, D, E and F are psychologist, manager, advocate, jeweller, doctor and engineer but not in the same order.

I. Doctor is the grandfather of F who is a psychologist.
II. Manager D is married to A.
III. C, who is a jeweller, is married to advocate.
IV. B is the mother of F and E.
V. There are two married couples in the family.

21. What is the profession of E?
(a) Manager (b) Psychologist
(c) Engineer (d) Doctor

22. How many male members are there in the family?
(a) Two (b) Three
(c) Four (d) Cannot be determined

Direction (Q. Nos 23-24) *Read the given information carefully and answer the questions that follow.*

Seven workmen named Amrita, Bhushan, Ronnie, Deepak, George, Prem and Gunjan are sitting in a circle in a garment fabrication factory. Amrita, Bhushan, Ronnie, Deepak, Prem and Gunjan are sitting at equal distances from each other. Ronnie is sitting third to the left of Prem, who is sitting second to the right of Deepak. Amrita forms an angle of 90° from George and an angle of 120° from Bushan. Bhushan is just opposite Gunjan, who is sitting to the left of George.

23. Who is the only person sitting between Ronnie and Bhushan?
(a) Prem (b) Deepak (c) George (d) Amrita

24. George is not sitting at equal distance from
(a) Deepak and Amrita
(b) Ronnie and Prem
(c) Bhushan and Prem
(d) None of the above

25. A walks around a circular field at the rate of one round per hour while B runs around it at the rate of six rounds per hour. They start in the same direction from the same point at 7:30 am. They will first cross each other at
(a) 8:30 am (b) 8:10 am
(c) 7:48 am (d) 7:42 am

26. Which of the following diagrams represents the relation between Currency, Rupee and Dollar?

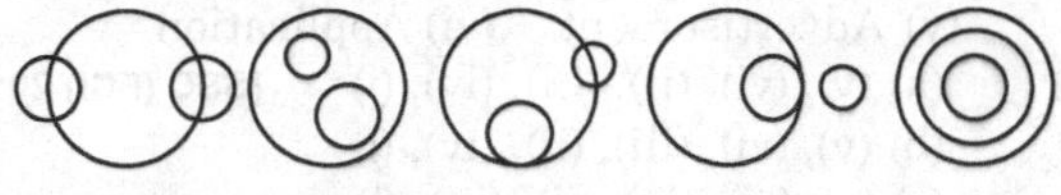

(a) (b) (c) (d) (e)

Direction (Q. Nos 27-28) *Find the missing character from the given alternatives.*

27.

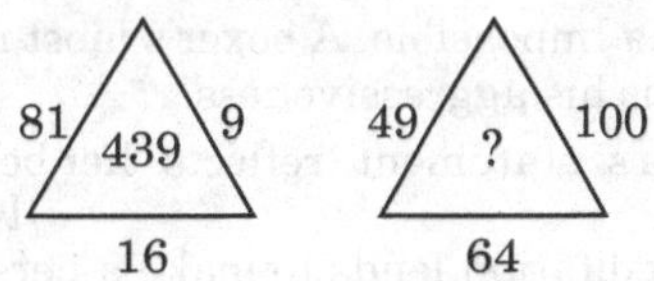

(a) 8710 (b) 1078
(c) 8107 (d) 789

28.

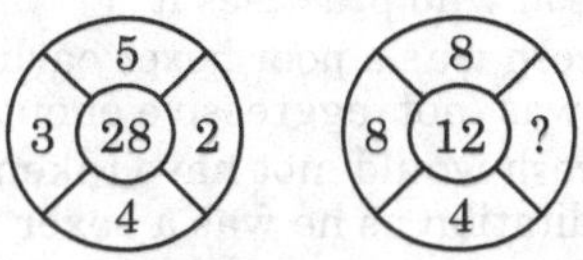

(a) 3 (b) 9 (c) 1 (d) 2

29. Select the odd figure from the given responses.

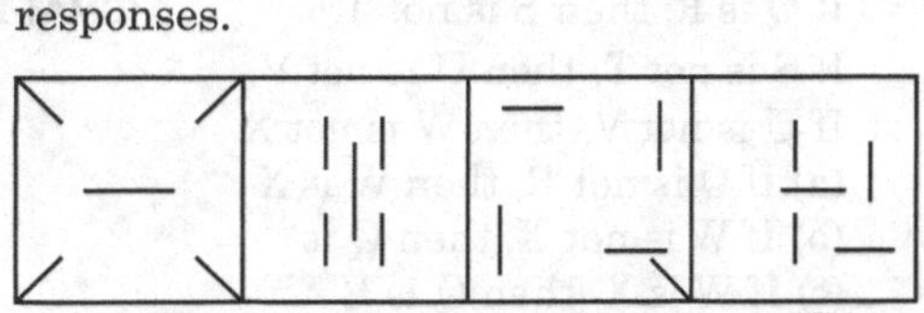

(a) (b) (c) (d)

Direction (Q. Nos. 30-31) *Read the following information carefully to answer the questions that follow.*

'P + Q' means 'P is the father of Q'.
'P − Q' means 'P is the mother of Q'.
'P× Q' means 'P is brother of Q'.
'P÷ Q' means 'P is the sister of Q'

30. Which of the following means 'H is paternal grandfather of T'?
(a) H + J + T (b) T× K + H
(c) H + J × T (d) H − J + T
(e) None of these

31. Which of the following means 'M is maternal uncle of T'?
(a) M ÷ K − T (b) M× K − T
(c) M× K + T (d) M÷ K + T
(e) None of these

32. Arrange the following words in logical order.
(i) Probation (ii) Interview
(iii) Selection (iv) Appointment
(v) Advertisement (vi) Application
(a) (v), (vi), (ii), (iii), (iv), (i) **[SSC (FCI) 2012]**
(b) (v), (vi), (iii), (ii), (iv), (i)
(c) (v), (vi), (iv), (ii), (iii), (i)
(d) (vi), (v), (iv), (ii), (iii), (i)

33. Geeta Naresh has become a better boxer since he started meditation.
Radha Impossible. A boxer's most important asset is his aggressiveness.
Radha's statement reflects her belief that **[CSAT 2015]**
(a) Meditation lends to make a person less aggressive
(b) Meditation has little or no effect on the person who practises it
(c) Naresh was a poor boxer earlier because he was not aggressive enough
(d) Naresh would not have taken to meditation as he was a boxer

34. From among the given alternatives, identify the conclusion of the following arguments : **[CMAT 2015]**
If Q is R, then S is not T.
If S is not T, then U is not V.
If U is not V, then W is not X.
(a) If Q is not R, then W is X
(b) If W is not X, then Q is
(c) If W is X, then Q is R
(d) If Q is R, then W is not X

Direction (Q. Nos. 35-36) *In each of the questions below are given two statements followed by two conclusions numbered I and II. You have to take the two given statements to be true even if they seem to be at variance from commonly known facts and decide which of the given conclusion(s) logically follow(s) from the two given statements, disregarding commonly known facts.*

Give answer
(a) if only Conclusion I follows
(b) if only Conclusion II follows
(c) if either Conclusion I or II follows
(d) if neither Conclusion I nor II follows
(e) if both Conclusion I and II follow

35. Statements All pens are ink.
No ink is an eraser.
Conclusions I. No pen is an eraser.
II. Some erasers are pens.

36. Statements Some gears are wheels.
All wheels are brakes.
Conclusions I. No brake is gear.
II. Atleast some gears are brakes.

37. Find out which of the answer figures (a), (b), (c) and (d) completes the figure matrix?

Question Figure

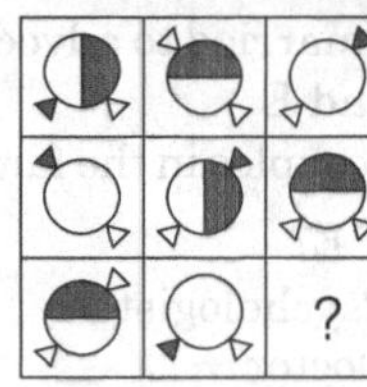

Answer Figures

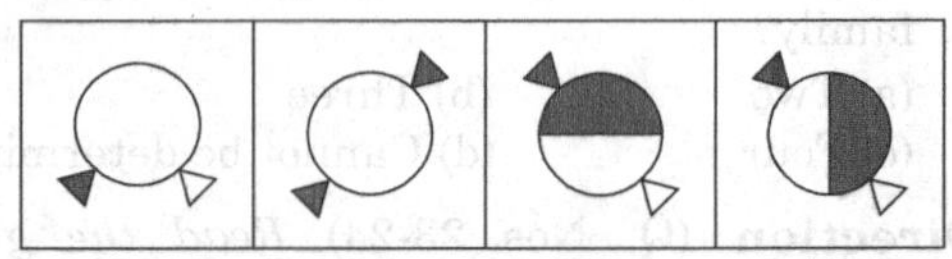

(a) (b) (c) (d)

38. Which of the following expressions will be true, if the given expression $K \geq G > H \leq F$ is definitely true?
(a) $F \geq K$ (b) $H < K$ (c) $F < G$ (d) $K \geq H$
(e) None of the above

Direction (Q. Nos. 39-40) *Read the given information and answer the questions.*

When a word and number arrangement machine is given an input line of words and number it arranges them following a particular rule. The following is an illustration of input and rearrangement. (All the numbers are two-digit numbers) **[IBPS (PO) 2014]**

Input left 46 burn 82 95 part 72 vibe bold 49 mint 59
***Step* I** 95 left 46 burn 82 part 72 vibe 49 mint 59 bold
***Step* II** 82 95 left 46 part 72 vibe 49 mint 59 bold burn
***Step* III** 72 82 95 46 part vibe 49 mint 59 bold burn left
***Step* IV** 59 72 82 95 46 part vibe 49 bold burn left mint
***Step* V** 49 59 72 82 95 46 vibe bold burn left mint part
***Step* VI** 46 49 59 72 82 95 bold burn left mint part vibe

Step VI is the last step of the above arrangement as the intended output of arrangement is obtained.

As per the rules followed in the given steps, find the appropriate steps for the given input.

Input 29 cone 42 pale fear 39 67 fame 32 weld 77 turn

39. Which step number is the following output?
77 29 42 pale fear 39 67 fame 32 weld turn cone
(a) I (b) III (c) VI (d) IV
(e) There is no such step

40. What is the position of 'fame' from the right of '67' in the second last step?
(a) Eighth (b) Third (c) Fifth (d) Ninth
(d) Seventh

Direction (Q. Nos. 41-43) *Each of the questions consists of a question and two statements numbered* I *and* II *given below. You have to decide whether the data provided in the statements are sufficient to answer the question. Read both the statements.* **[IBPS (PO) 2012]**

Give answer

(a) if the data in Statements I alone are sufficient to answer the question, while the data in Statement II alone are not sufficient to answer the question
(b) if the data in Statement II alone are sufficient to answer the question, while the data in Statement I alone are not sufficient to answer the question
(c) if the data either in Statement I alone or in Statement II alone are sufficient to answer the question
(d) if the data given in both the Statements I and II together are not sufficient to answer the question
(e) if the data in both the Statements I and II together are necessary to answer the question

41. Among M, P, T, R and W each being of a different age, who is the youngest?
I. T is younger than only P and W.
II. M is younger than T and older than R.

42. How is 'gone' written in a code language?
I. 'you will be gone' is written as 'ka pa ni sa' in that code language.
II. 'he will be there' is written as 'ja da ka ni' in that code language.

43. On which day of the week (starting from Monday and ending on Sunday of the same week) did Sushant visit Chennai?
I. Sushant visited Chennai two days after his brother visited Chennai.
II. Sushant did not visit Chennai either on Wednesday or on Friday.

44. Among the four answer figures, which one can be formed from the cut out pieces given below in the question figures?

Question Figure

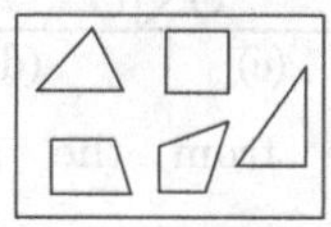

Answer Figures

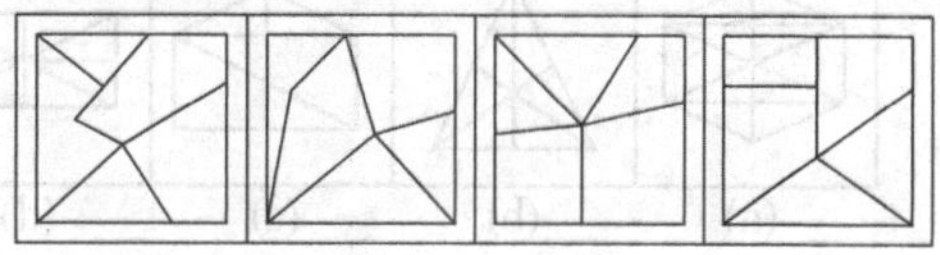

(a) (b) (c) (d)

45. One morning after sunrise. Vikram and Shailesh were standing in a town while their backs towards each other. Vikram's shadow fell exactly towards left hand side. Which direction was Shailesh facing?
(a) East (b) West (c) North (d) South

46. Which of the answer figure is hidden in the question figure? **[SSC (10+2) 2012]**

Question Figure

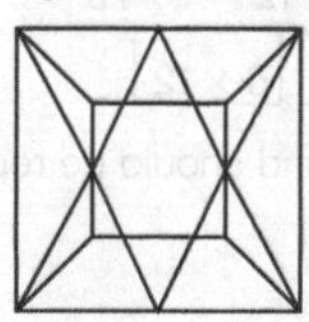

Answer Figures

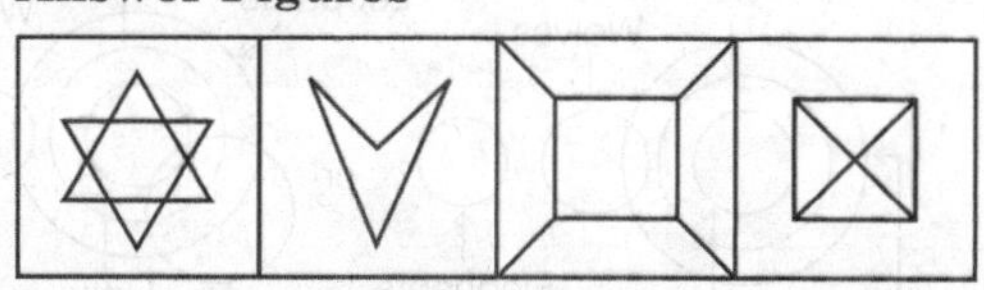

(a) (b) (c) (d)

47. A piece of paper is folded and cut as shown below in the question figures. From the given answer figures, indicates how it will appear when opened.

Question Figures

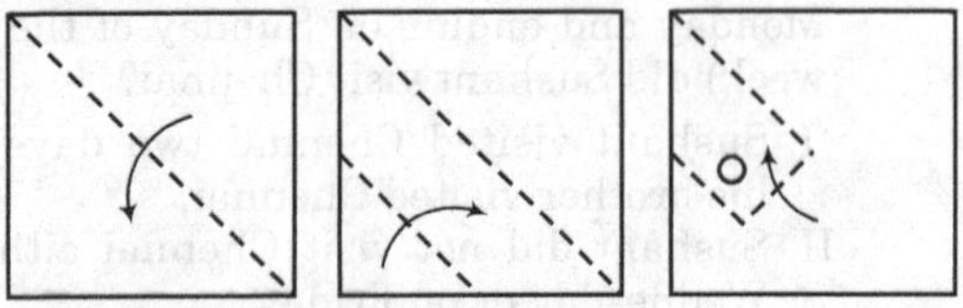

Answer Figures

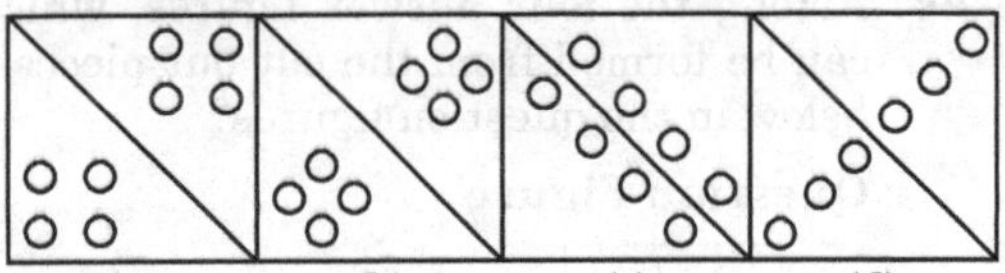

(a) (b) (c) (d)

48. Select the odd figure from the given responses.

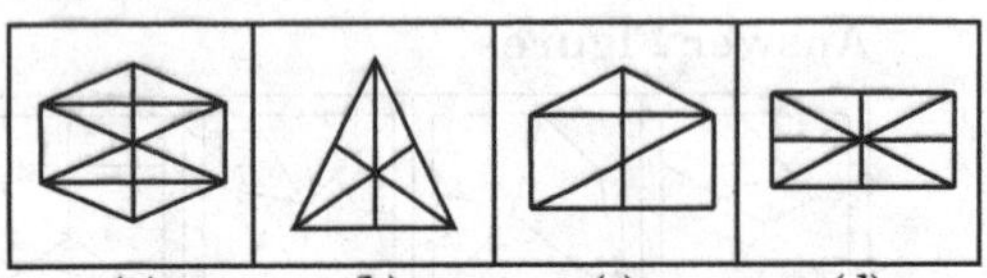

(a) (b) (c) (d)

49. If '÷' means '–', '–' means '×', '×' means '+' and '+' means '÷', then 20 × 60 ÷ 40 – 20 + 10 = ?

(a) 80 (b) 60 (c) 40 (d) 0

50. A square transparent sheet with a pattern is given. Figure out from amongst the four alternatives as to how the pattern would appear when the transparent sheet is folded at the middle line shown.

Question Figure

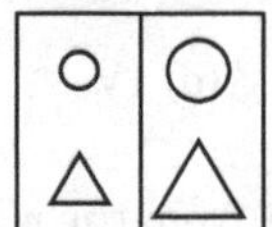

Answer Figures

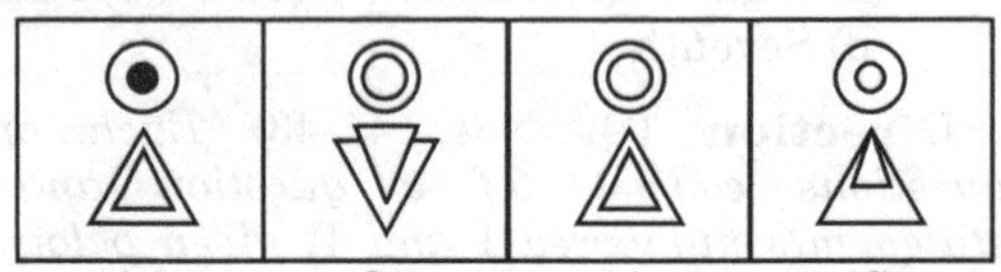

(a) (b) (c) (d)

Hints and Solutions

1. (*d*) The pattern is as follows

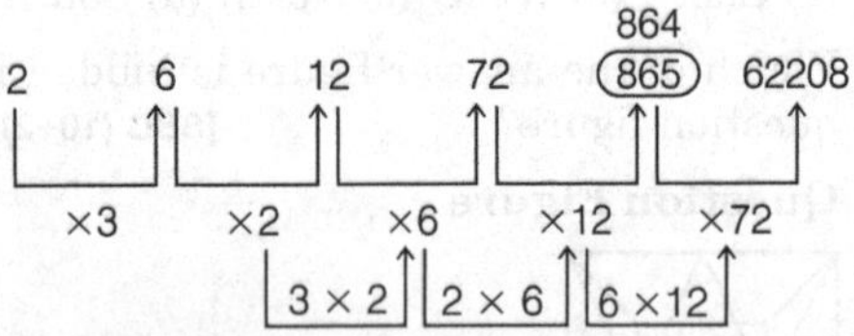

Hence, number 865 is wrong and should be replaced by 864.

2. (*c*)

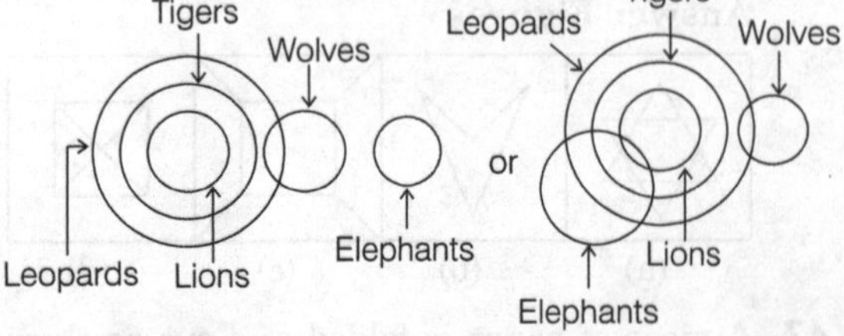

Conclusions I. No elephant is lion. (✗)

II. Some wolves are lions (✗)

III. Some leopards are lions (✔)

So, only III follows.

3. (*d*). The Pattern of given alpha-numeric series is as follows

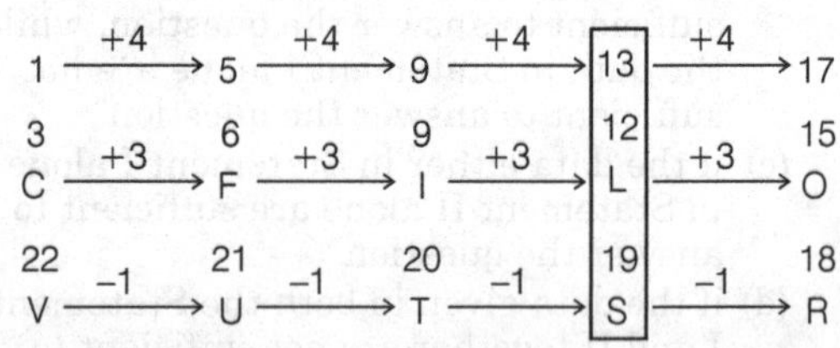

∴ ? = 13LS

4. (*b*) The directions is as follows

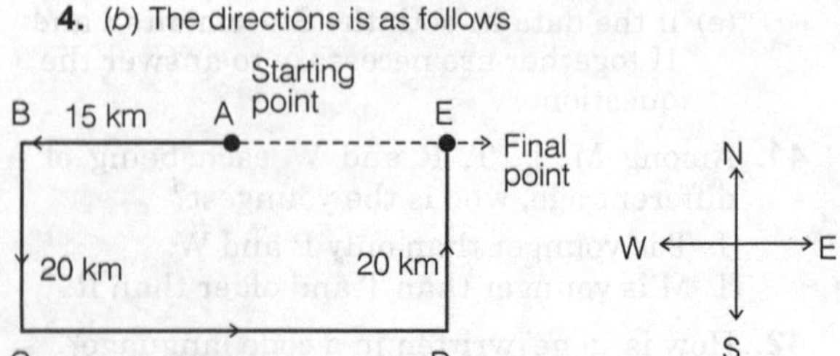

AE = BE – AB ; BE = CD = 25

AE = 25 – 15 = 10 km

Solution (Q. Nos. 5-9) On the basis of given information, the seating arrangement of twelve people in two parallel rows is as follows

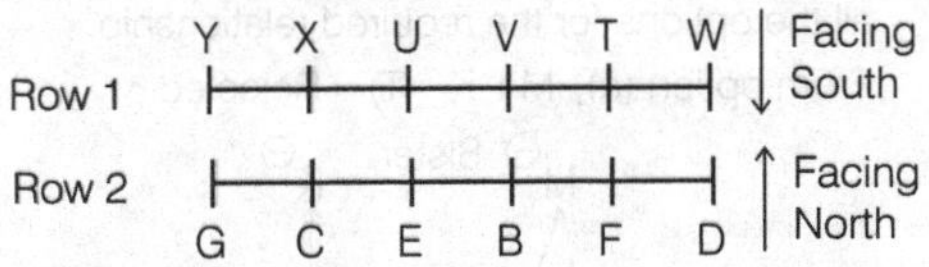

5. (*b*) U is second to the right of T.

6. (*d*) W is sitting at the end of the row.

7. (*a*) B is facing V.

8. (*e*) F is facing T.

9. (*e*) None of the given statements is true.

10. (*c*) By using the letters of given word, HEARTY cannot be formed because in the given word letter Y is absent.

11. (*b*) Only Assumption II is implicit.

12. (*e*) According to the question,

$$A / Q > T > P / B$$

But P is not the shortest

$$A / Q \geq T > P > B$$

So, tallest is either A or Q.

13. (*a*) After using the given coding data, we get

J	B	E	G	P	V
↓	↓	↓	↓	↓	↓
g	s	r	x	v	n

Hence, option (a) is correct.

14. (*d*) After using the given coding data, we get

C	H	W	C	L	S
↓	↓	↓	↓	↓	↓
p	c	h	p	w	y

Hence, option (d) is correct

15. (*c*) Option (c) will complete the given pattern as

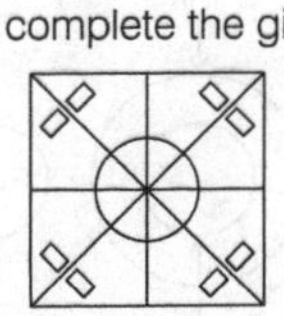

16. (*d*) 'Spanner' is used by mechanic as a tool to loose or tight nut and bolt. In the same way, 'saw' is used by carpenter as a tool to cut wood. Hence, option (d) is correct.

17. (*b*)

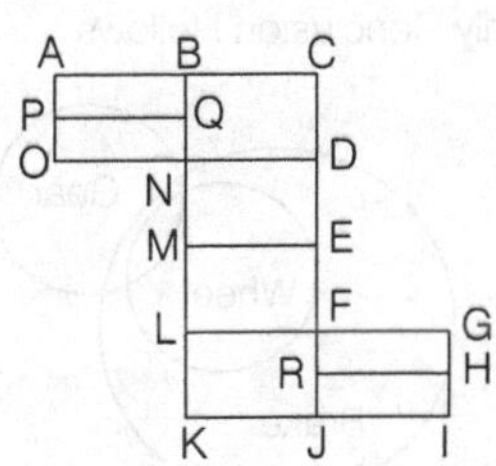

Total 18 rectangles are as follow

ABQP, PQNO, BCDN,
NDEM, MEFL, LFJK,
FGHR, RHIJ, ABNO,
BCEM, NDFL, MEJK,
FGIJ, ACDO, BCFL,
NDJK, LGIK and BCJK

18. (*c*) Except in the pair of word Head—Cap. In all others the two words are antonymous to each other.

19. (*d*) As, $B \xrightarrow{-1} A \xrightarrow{+3} D \xrightarrow{-1} C$

$J \xrightarrow{-1} I \xrightarrow{+3} L \xrightarrow{-1} K$

But, $N \xrightarrow{-1} M \xrightarrow{+3} P \xrightarrow{-1} O$

$V \xrightarrow{-1} U \xrightarrow{+2} W \xrightarrow{+1} X$

Except other (d), all other follow same pattern (– 1, + 3, – 1).

20. (*d*) In both the positions , 2 dots are common at the same (top) face. So, face having 1 dot will be opposite to the face having 6 dots.

Solution (Q. Nos 21-22) Let us draw the family diagram

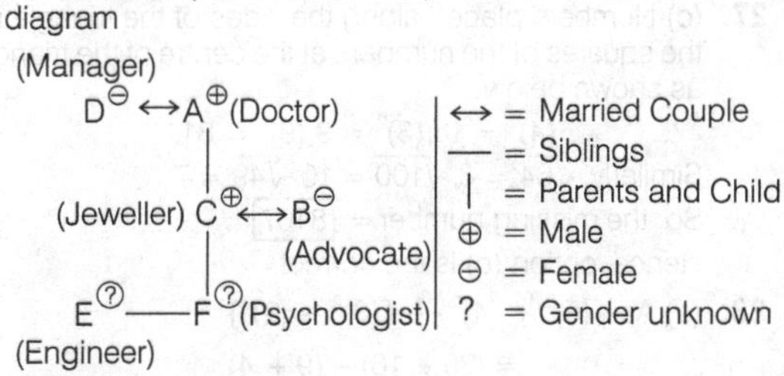

21. (c) E is an engineer.

22. (*d*) Gender of E and F are unknown. So, total number of male members cannot be determined.

Solution (Q.Nos. 23-24) According to the given information, the seating arrangement of seven workmen is as following.

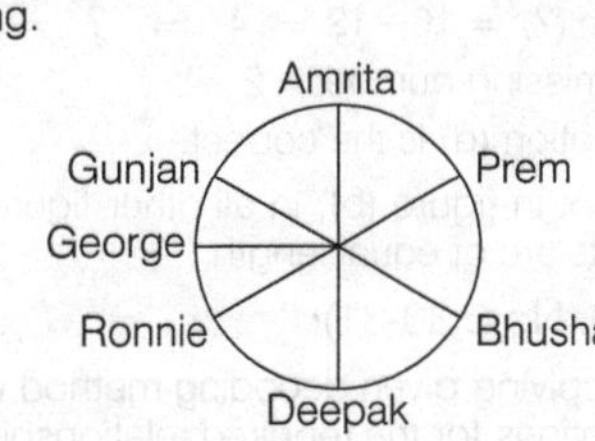

23. (*b*) Deepak is the only person sitting between Ronnie and Bushan.

24. (*b*) George is not sitting at equal distance from Ronnie and Prem.

25. (*d*) As, time taken for 1 round by A = 1 h

$\therefore$ Time taken by B for 1 round = $\frac{1}{6}$ h = 10 min

The angle made by A on centre in 10 min

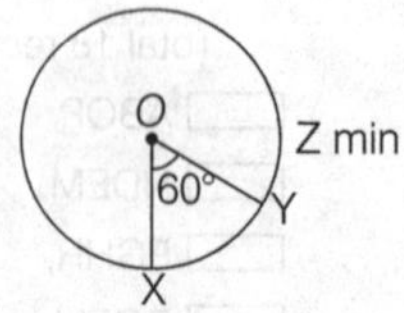

$$= \frac{360° \times 10}{60} = 60°$$

Since, A and B both started walking from the point X.

So, after 10 min A will be on point Y and B on point X.

Suppose that, B will catch A in Z min.

$$\therefore \quad \frac{Z}{10} = Z\left(\frac{1}{60}\right) + \frac{60°}{360°} \Rightarrow \frac{Z}{10} - \frac{Z}{60} = \frac{1}{6}$$

$$\Rightarrow \quad \frac{6Z - Z}{60} = \frac{1}{6} \Rightarrow 5Z = 10 \Rightarrow Z = \frac{10}{5} = 2$$

$\therefore$ B will hold A in 10+2=12 min

Thus, the required time is 7: 42 am.

26. (*b*) Rupee and dollar are entirely different from each other but both come under the category of currency. This can be expressed as given in option (b).

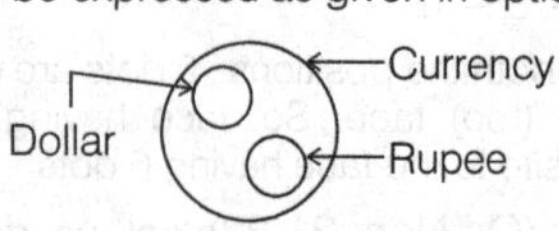

27. (*c*) Numbers placed along the sides of the triangle are the squares of the numbers at the centre of the triangle, as shown below

$$(4)^2 = 16, (3)^2 = 9, (9)^2 = 81$$

Similarly, $\sqrt{64} = 8$, $\sqrt{100} = 10$, $\sqrt{49} = 7$

So, the missing number = $\boxed{8107}$

Hence, option (c) is the correct.

28. (*d*) As, $\{(5)^2 + (4)^2\} - \{(3)^2 + (2)^2\}$

$$= (25 + 16) - (9 + 4)$$
$$= 41 - 13 = 28$$

Similarly, $\{(8)^2 + (4)^2\} - \{(8)^2 + (?)^2\} = 12$

$\Rightarrow \quad (64 + 16) - \{64 + (?)^2\} = 12$

$80 - 64 - (?)^2 = 12$

$\Rightarrow \quad 16 - (?)^2 = 12$

$\Rightarrow \quad (?)^2 = 16 - 12 \Rightarrow 4 \Rightarrow ?^2 = 4$

So, the missing number = 2

Hence option (d) is the correct.

29. (*b*) Except in figure (b), in all other figures, all the five segments are of equal length.

Solution (Q. Nos. 30-31)

30. (*a*) By applying given decoding method we can check all the options for the required relationship from option (a), (H + J + T)

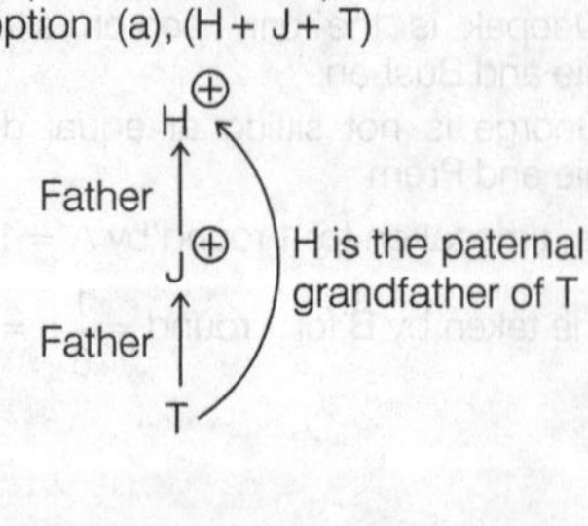

Hence, there is no need to check other options, as we have already obtained the answer.

31. (b) By applying given decoding method, we can check all the options for the required relationship.

From option (a), (M ÷ K − T) = Rejected

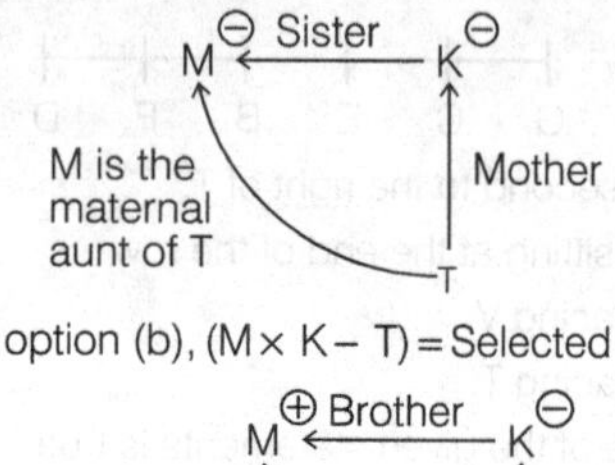

From option (b), (M × K − T) = Selected

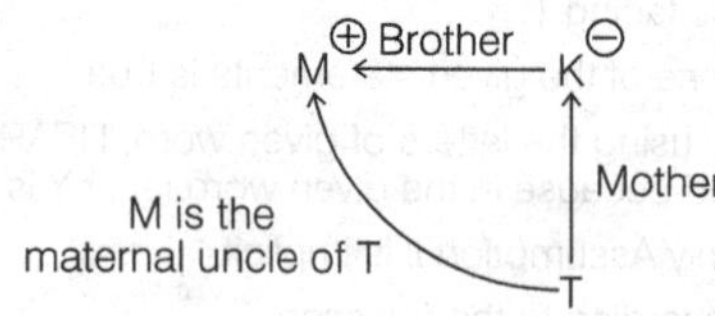

Hence, there is no need to check other options.

32. (*a*) Logical order of words is as follows

(v) Advertisement → (vi) Application → (ii) Interview

(iii) Selection → (iv) Appointment → (i) Probation

33. (*a*) Radha did not accept the argument that a person becomes a better boxer after meditation. The reason for this is that a boxer, according to her, should be aggressive. This indicates that Radha believes that meditation makes a person less aggressive.

34. (*d*) From arguments

if Q = R, then S ≠ T

if S ≠ T, then U ≠ V

if U ≠ V, then W ≠ X

Hence, it is clear that if Q is R, then W is not X.

35. (*a*)

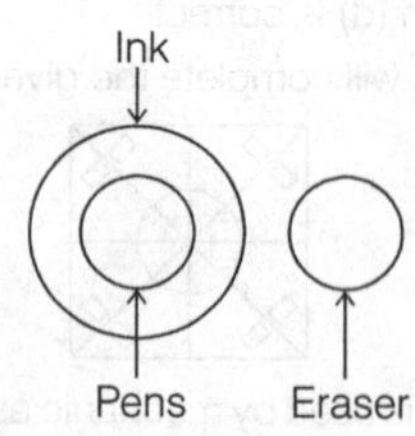

Conclusions I. No pen is an eraser. (✓)

II. Some erasers are pens. (✗)

So, only Conclusion I follows.

36. (*b*)

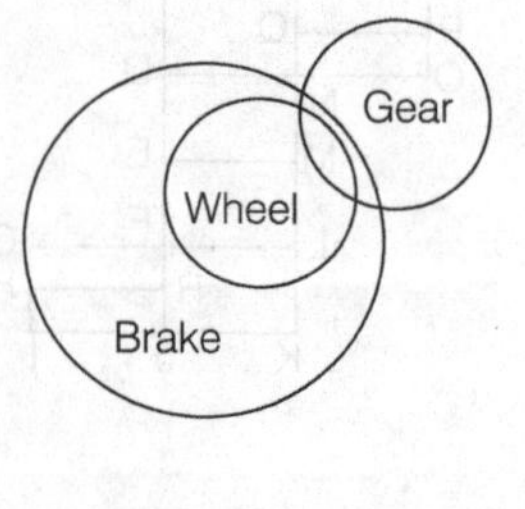

Condusions I. No brake is gear. (✗)
II. Atleast some gears are brakes. (✓)

So, only Conclusion II follows.

37. (*d*) Clearly, there are three types of shadings of circles, one is unshaded. another has its right half shaded and yet another and has its upper half shaded. Also, two of the figures in each row have one triangle shaded.

38. (*b*) Given that, K≥ G> H≤ F

Now, we can check all the options one by one

(a) F≥ K (false) (b) H< K (true)

(c) F< G (false) (d) K≥ H (false)

So, it is clear that option (b) is true.

Solution (Q. Nos. 39-40) In the given machine input

Step I 95 left 46 burn 82 part 72 vibe 49 mint 59 bold

In the above arrangement we observe that, in every step, a number is arranged on the left end and a word on the right end. We begin with the largest number, then the second largest and so on, till all the numbers are arranged in ascending order. Words are arranged in the alphabetical order. Similarly, we can arrange the following input.

Input 29 cone 42 pale fear 39 67 fame 32 weld 77 turn

***Step* I** 77 29 42 pale fear 39 67 fame 32 weld turn cone

***Step* II** 67 77 29 42 pale fear 39 32 weld turn cone fame

***Step* III** 42 67 77 29 pale 39 32 weld turn cone fame fear

***Step* IV** 39 42 67 77 29 32 weld turn cone fame fear pale

***Step* V** 32 39 42 67 77 29 weld cone fame fear pale turn

***Step* VI** 29 32 39 42 67 77 cone fame fear pale turn weld

39. (*a*) The output matches with Step I.

40. (*c*) Step V is second last step

Step V 32 39 42

67 77 29 weld cone fame fear pale tum
1 2 3 4 5

The word 'fame' is at 5th position from the right of 67.

Solution (Q. Nos. 41-43)

41. (e) It is obvious that Statements I or II alone are not sufficient.

From Statements I and II, P / W > T > M > R

Hence, R is the youngest.

So, Statements I and II both are required together to answer the question.

42. (*d*) It is obvious that Statements I or II alone are insufficient.

From Statements I and II,

you will be gone = ka pa ni sa

he will be there = ja da ka ni

Clearly, 'will be' = ka ni

∴ you gone = pa sa

∴ gone = pa or sa

So, both statements are insufficient to answer the question.

43. (*d*) Both the statements are insufficient to answer the question.

44. (c) Option (c) correct answer.

45. (*d*) On sunrise, the shadow of a man forms in the West direction.

According to the question,

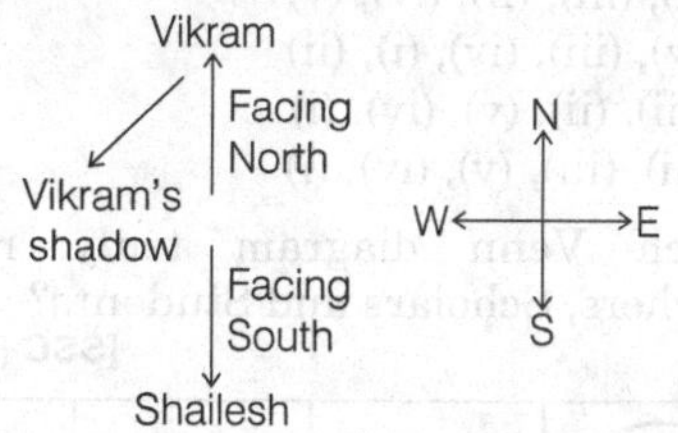

Vikram is facing North direction and they are standing with their backs towards each other. So, Shailesh is facing South direction.

46. (*c*) Clearly, answer figure is embedded in question figure (c) as shown below

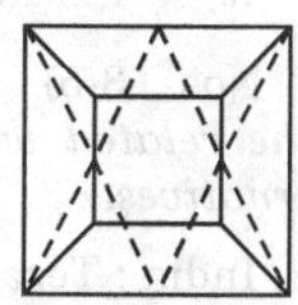

47. (*b*)

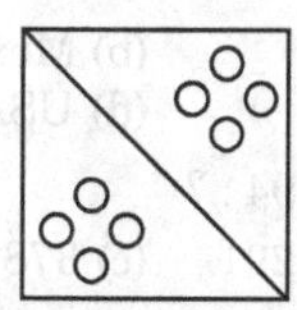

So, option (b) is correct

48. (*c*) Except in figure (c), in other figures, line segments divide the shape into equal parts.

49. (*d*) As, 20 × 60 ÷ 40 − 20 + 10 = ?

? = 20 + 60 − 40 × 20 ÷ 10

= 20 + 60 − 40 × 2

= 80 − 80 = 0

50. (*c*)

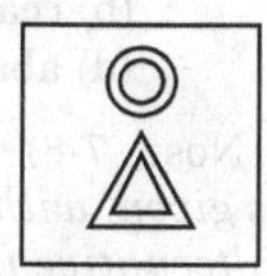

So, option (c) is correct.

PRACTICE SET 10

1. Arrange the given words in a meaningful order.

(i) Rain (ii) Vaporisation
(iii) Water (iv) Condensation
(v) Cloud

(a) (i), (iii), (ii), (iv), (v)
(b) (v), (iii), (iv), (i), (ii)
(c) (iii), (ii), (v), (iv), (i)
(d) (ii), (iii), (v), (iv), (i)

2. Which Venn diagram truly represents Teachers, Scholars and Students? **[SSC (CPO) 2015]**

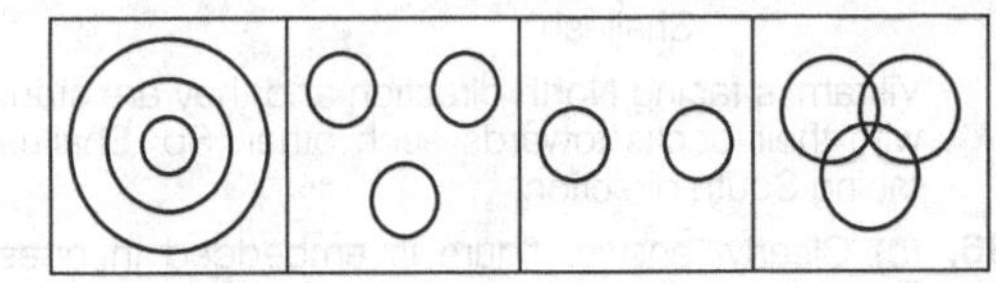

(a) (b) (c) (d)

Direction (Q. Nos. 3-5) *In the following questions, select the related word/number pair from the given alternatives.*

3. Maharashtra : India : Tesax : ? **[SSC (10 + 2) 2014]**

(a) Canada (b) Mexico
(c) Brazil (d) USA

4. 584 : 488 : : 294 : ? **[SSC (CGL) 2013]**

(a) 581 (b) 291 (c) 378 (d) 487

5. (32, 24, 8)

(a) (26, 32, 42) (b) (34, 24, 14)
(c) (24, 16, 8) (d) (42, 34, 16)

6. Which one set of letters when sequentially placed at the gaps in the given letter series shall complete it?

a_baa_aaba_ca_b

(a) bcca (b) ccaa
(c) acaa (d) abac

Direction (Q. Nos. 7-8) *In the following questions, a series is given, with one term missing. Choose the correct alternative from the given ones that will complete the series.*

7. 99, 82, 18, 11, ?

(a) 5 (b) 10 (c) 2 (d) 9

8. Y, X, V, S, O, ?

(a) J (b) M (c) E (d) F

9. If the positions of the letters in the word 'ORGANISE' are rearranged in such way that the position of the 1st and the 2nd letters are interchanged, similarly the position of the 3rd and the 4th letters are interchanged and so on, then which of the following will be the 3rd from the right end after the rearrangement?

(a) N (b) I (c) R (d) A

10. How many words can be formed using letters of the word 'DESIGN' unconditionally?

(a) More than 4 (b) Less than 3
(c) Exactly 4 (d) More than 8

Direction (Q. Nos. 11-13) *Read the following information carefully and then answer the questions that follow.* **[UCO Bank (Clerk) 2011]**

Eight persons P, M, R, T, Q, U, V and W are sitting in front of one another in two rows. Each row has 4 persons P is between U and V and facing North. Q, who is to the immediate left of M is facing W. R is between T and M and W is to the immediate right of V.

11. Who is sitting in front of R?

(a) U (b) Q (c) V (d) P
(e) None of these

12. Who is to the immediate right of R?

(a) M (b) U
(c) M or T (d) Cannot be determined
(e) None of these

13. In which of the following pairs, persons are sitting in front of each other?

(a) MV (b) RV
(c) TV (d) UR
(e) MP

14. In a certain language 'oka peru' means 'fine cloths', 'meta lisa' means 'clear water' and 'dona lisa peru' means 'fine clear weather', which word of that language means 'weather'?

(a) peru (b) oka
(c) meta (d) dona

Direction (Q. Nos. 15-16) *In the following questions, find the odd word/number pair from the given alternatives.*

15. (a) 66-56 (b) 101-90
(c) 41-30 (d) 33-22

16. (a) Confluence (b) Concourse
(c) Radiation (d) Concentration

17. Find the odd figure from the given alternatives. **[SSC (10+2) 2013]**

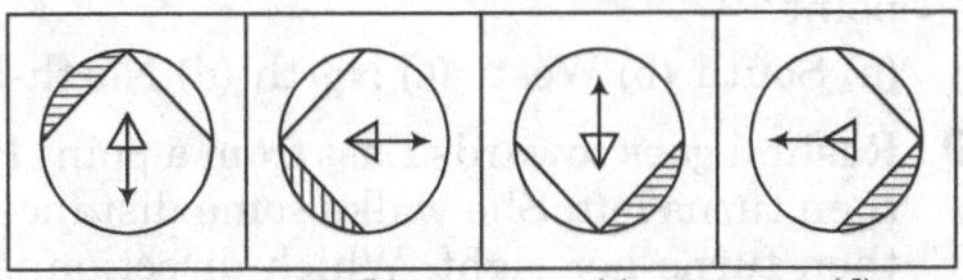

(a) (b) (c) (d)

18. A circular sheet of paper has been folded punched as shown in the following series of figures. How will it appear when opened?

Question Figures

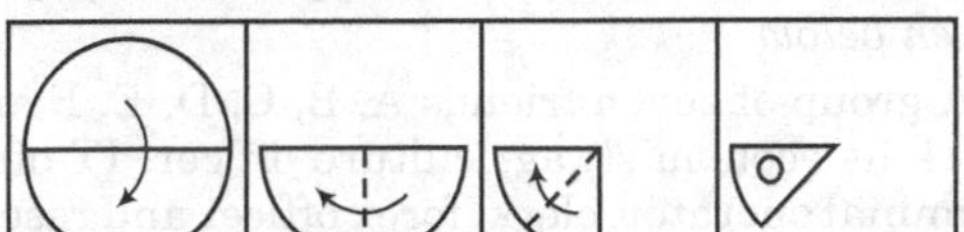

1 2 3 4

Answer Figures

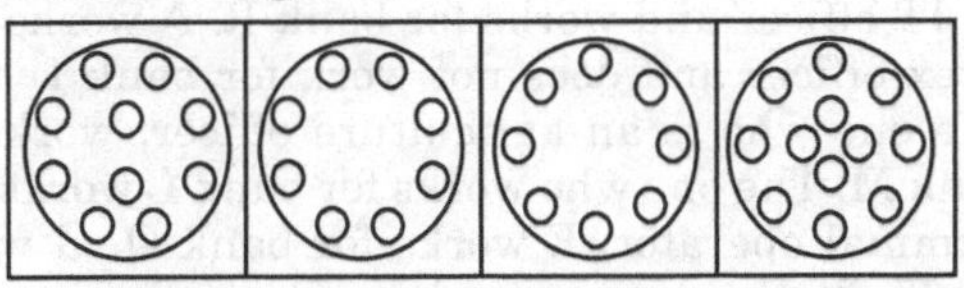

(a) (b) (c) (d)

19. Identify the missing part of the question figure and select it from given answer figures.

Question Figure **[SSC (10 + 2) 2011]**

Answer Figures

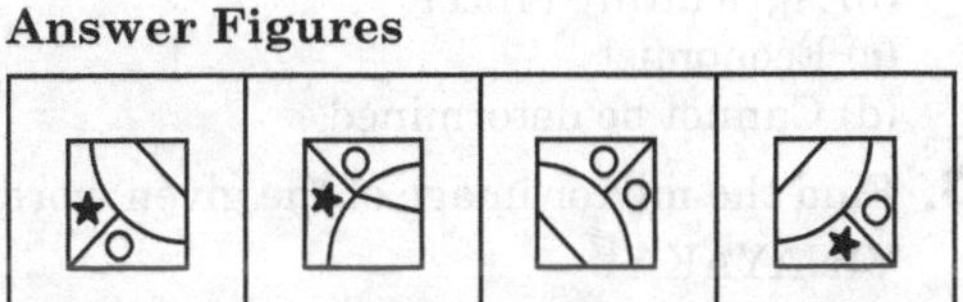

(a) (b) (c) (d)

20. In a certain language, 'ROAD' is written as 'ORDA', how will 'DATE' be written in the same code? **[WBSSC (CGL) Pre 2014]**

(a) ETAD (b) ADET
(c) DTAE (d) EATD

21. Select the alternative in which the specified components of the question figure are found?

Question Figure

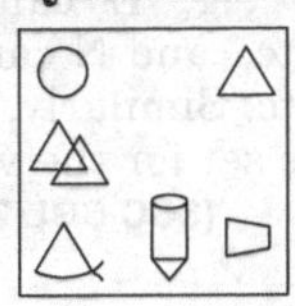

Answer Figures

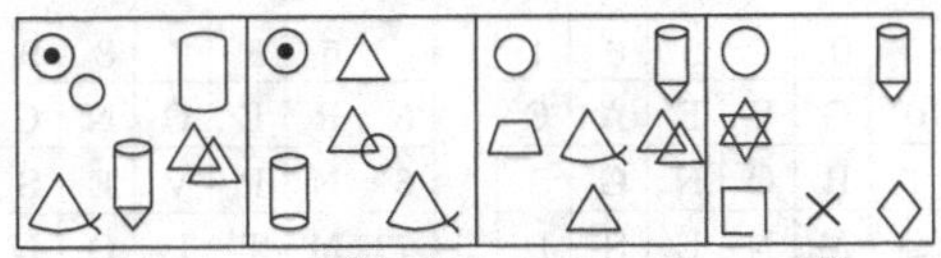

(a) (b) (c) (d)

22. Find the missing figure from the given responses.

Question Figures

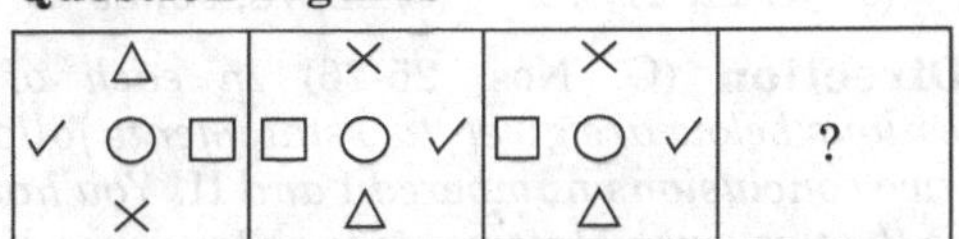

1 2 3 4

Answer Figures

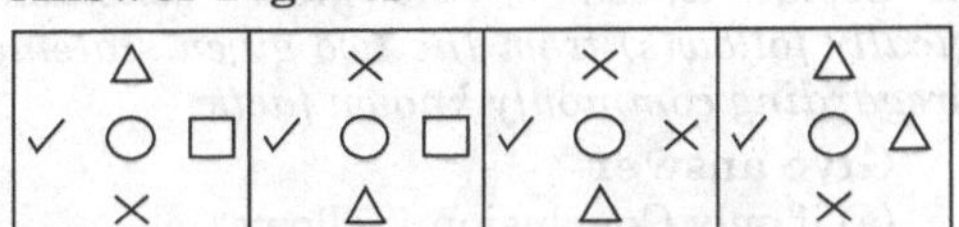

(a) (b) (c) (d)

23. Find the water image.

Question Figure

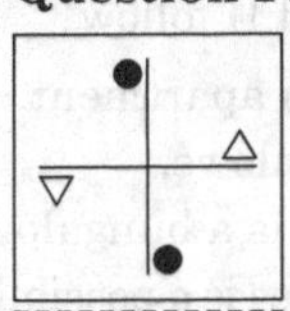

Answer Figures

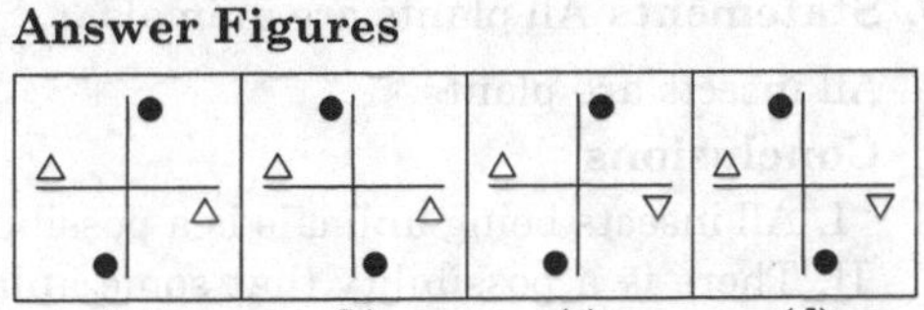

(a) (b) (c) (d)

24. A word is represented by only one set of numbers as given in any one of the alternatives. The sets of numbers given in the alternatives are represented by two classes of alphabets as in two matrices given below. The columns and rows of Matrix I are numbered from 0 to 4 and that of Matrix II are numbered from 5 to 9. A letter from these matrices can be represented first by its row and next by its column, e.g. E can be represented by 02, 43, 68 etc., and N can be represented by 21, 65, 95 etc. Similarly, you have to identify the number set for the word given below : **[SSC CGL 2014]**

COST

Matrix I

	0	1	2	3	4
0	G	V	E	A	C
1	R	O	N	G	S
2	M	N	E	S	I
3	O	T	I	T	A
4	N	S	N	E	P

Matrix II

	5	6	7	8	9
5	R	E	O	N	G
6	N	P	V	E	S
7	M	T	I	O	N
8	E	A	I	C	O
9	N	T	A	R	S

(a) 04, 30, 31, 41 (b) 88, 57, 69, 32
(c) 04, 11, 41, 76 (d) 88, 78, 99, 89

Direction (Q. Nos. 25-26) *In each of the questions below are given two statements followed by two conclusions numbered I and II. You have to take the two given statements to be true even if they seem to be at variance from commonly known facts and decide which of the given conclusion(s) logically follow(s) from the two given statements, disregarding commonly known facts.*

Give answer
(a) if only Conclusion I follows
(b) if only Conclusion II follows
(c) if either Conclusion I or II follows
(d) if neither Conclusion I nor II follows
(e) if both Conclusions I and II follow

25. Statements No house is an apartment.
Some apartments are bungalows.
Conclusions I. No house is a bungalow.
II. All bungalows being houses is a possibility.

26. Statements All plants are animals.
All insects are plants.
Conclusions
I. All insects being animals is a possibility.
II. There is a possibility that some animals are neither insects nor plants.

27. A solid cube is formed with 27 smaller cubes. One pair of opposite faces of this cube is painted red, another pair is painted yellow and the third pair of opposite faces is painted white. How many smaller cubes have two faces painted?
(a) 8 (b) 12
(c) 16 (d) 24

28. If the digit 12 of a clock is pointing towards East, then in which direction will digit 9 point?
(a) South (b) West (c) North (d) North-East

29. Rashmi goes towards East from a point P and then turns left. She walks some distance and then turns her right. Which direction is she facing now?
(a) North (b) East
(c) West (d) South

Direction (Q. Nos. 30-32) *Read the following information carefully and answer the questions given below*

A group of seven friends A, B, C, D, E, F and G work as economist, agriculture officer, IT officer, terminal operator, clerk, forex officer and research analyst, for banks L, M, N, P, Q, R and S but not necessarily in the same order. C works for bank N and is neither a research analyst nor a clerk, E is an IT officer and works for bank R. A works as a forex officer and does not work for bank L or Q. The one who is an agriculture officer, works for bank M. The one who works for bank L works as a terminal operator. F works for bank Q. G works for bank P as a research analyst. D is not an agriculture officer.

30. Who amongst the following works as an agriculture officer?
(a) C (b) B (c) F (d) D

31. For which bank does D work?
(a) Q (b) L (c) N (d) S

32. What is the profession of C?
(a) Terminal operator
(b) Agriculture officer
(c) Economist
(d) Cannot be determined

33. Find the mirror image of the given word.
VINAYAKA
(a) INVAYAKA (b) AKAYANIV
(c) AꓘAYAИIV (d) NIVYAAKA

34. How many triangles are there in the adjacent figure?

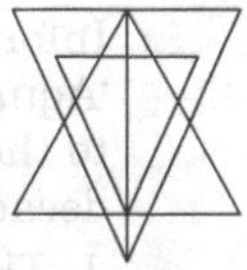

(a) 27 (b) 23
(c) 21 (d) 25

35. At a college party, five girls are sitting in a row. P is to the left of M and to the right of O. R is sitting to the right of N but to the left of O. Who is sitting in the middle?

(a) O (b) R (c) P (c) M

Direction (Q. Nos. 36-37) *Select the missing number from the given responses.* **[SSC (10+2) 2014]**

36.

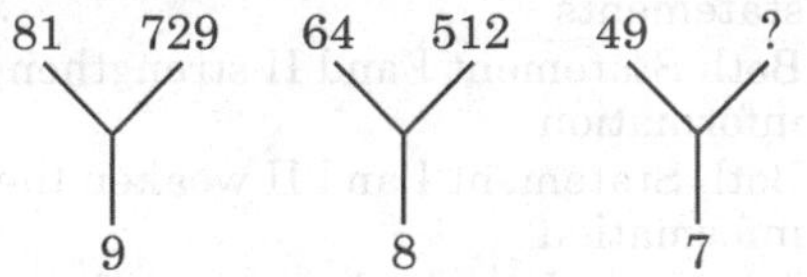

(a) 444 (b) 515 (c) 343 (d) 373

37.

18
9 38 6
17

11
19 32 9
11

6
26 44 3
15

12
9 ? 20
8

(a) 9 (b) 40 (c) 7 (d) 36

38. If '+' means '×', '–' means '÷', '÷' means '+' and '×' means '–', then what will be the value of

$$16 \div 64 - 4 \times 4 + 3 = ?$$

(a) 20 (b) 52
(c) 15 (d) 12

Direction (Q. Nos. 39 - 41) *The symbols @, #, $, % and © are used with different meanings as follows.*

'A @ B' means 'A is smaller than B'.
'A # B' means 'A is not smaller than B'.
'A $ B' means 'A is neither smaller than nor greater than B'.
'A % B' means 'A is greater than B'.
'A © B' means 'A is not greater than B'.

In each of the following questions assuming the given statements to be true, find out which of the two Conclusions I and II given below them is/are definitely true.

Give answer

(a) if only Conclusion I is true
(b) if only Conclusion II is true
(c) if either Conclusion I or II is true
(d) if neither Conclusion I nor II is true
(e) if both Conclusions I and II are true

39. Statements F # H, H % K, K $ R, R © M
Conclusions I. F % R II. F # M

40. Statements L @ D, D © P, P # V, V % G
Conclusions I. P % L II. G @ P

41. Statements E % W, W © Q, Q $ T, T @ H
Conclusions I. H # W II. H # E

Direction (Q. Nos. 42-44) *Study the following information carefully and then answer the question given below it.*

A word arrangement machine when given an input line of words rearranges them following a particular rule in each step. The following is an illustration of the input and rearrangement.

Input Zeal for and yellow bench state goal on
Step I and zeal for yellow bench state goal on
Step II and bench zeal for yellow state goal on
Step III and bench for zeal yellow state goal on
Step IV and bench for goal zeal yellow state on
Step V and bench for goal on zeal yellow state
Step VI and bench for goal on state zeal yellow
Step VII and bench for goal on state yellow zeal
and Step VII is the last step.

As per the rules followed in the above steps, find out in each of the following questions, the appropriate steps for the given input.

42. Input 'ginger year town sour cat bring ink pot'.
Which of the following steps will be the last but one?

(a) VI (b) V (c) VII (d) VIII
(e) None of these

43. Input 'your job is not very important to him'.
Which of the following steps will be the last?

(a) VIII (b) VII (c) VI (d) IX
(e) None of these

44. Step II of an input is 'car down table pen jug water fall sign'.
How many more steps will be required to complete the rearrangement?

(a) Four (b) Five (c) Three (d) Six
(e) None of these

Direction (Q. Nos. 45-46) *Read the following information carefully and answer the questions that follow.*

'P + Q' means 'P is the father of Q'.
'P – Q' means 'P is the wife of Q'.
'P × Q' means 'P is the brother of Q'.
'P ÷ Q' means 'P is the daughter of Q'.

45. If A ÷ C+ D+ B, then which of the following statement is true?
(a) A is the daughter of B
(b) B is the aunt of A
(c) A is the aunt of B
(d) A is the mother of B

46. If A− C+ B, then which of the following statements is true?
(a) A is the daughter of B
(b) B is the aunt of A
(c) A is the mother of B
(d) A is the aunt of B

Direction (Q. Nos. 47-48) *Each of the following questions below consists of a question and two statements numbered* I *and* II *given below it. You have to decide whether the data provided in the statements are sufficient to answer the question.*

Give answer
(a) if the data in Statement I alone are sufficient to answer the question, while the data in Statement II alone are not sufficient to answer the question
(b) if the data in Statement II alone are sufficient to answer the question, while the data in Statement I alone are not sufficient to answer the question
(c) if the data either in Statement I alone or Statement II alone are sufficient to answer the question
(d) if the data in both the Statements I and II together are not sufficient to answer the question
(e) if the data in both the Statements I and II are together necessary to answer the question

47. In which direction is point E, with reference to point S?
I. Point D is to the East of point E and point E is to the South of point F.
II. Point F is to the North-West of point S. Point D is to the North of point S.

48. Who amongst P, Q, R, S and T is the tallest?
I. P is taller than Q. T is not the tallest.
II. R is taller than P. S is not the tallest.

49. This question consists of an information and two statements numbered I and II given below it. You have to decide which of the given statements weaken/s or strengthen/s the information and decide the appropriate answer. **[LIC (AAO) 2014]**

Information according to a report naval ship 'AquaEmp' met with the fatal accident owing to the fact that it was ageing and nearly two decades old.
I. The accident took place when the seaman at the artillery section accidently misfired the missile hitting certain crucial engine machinery.
II. Average age of all ships, battleships or cargo ships, is 30-35 yr, before which these can be operated safely.
(a) Both Statement I and II are neutral statements
(b) Both Statement I and II strengthen the information
(c) Both Statement I and II weaken the information
(d) Statement I strengthens the information, while Statement II weakens the information
(e) Statement I weakens the information while Statement II strengthens the information

50. In the question below is given a statement followed by three courses of action numbered I, II and III. A course of action is a step or administrative decision to be taken for improvement, follow-up or further action in regard to the problem, policy, etc. On the basis of information given in the statement, you have to assume everything in the statement to be true and then decide which of the three given suggested courses of action logically follows worth persuing. Then, decide which of the alternative (a), (b), (c), (d) or (e) is correct.

Statement The army has been alerted in the district following floods triggered by incessant rains.

Courses of Action
I. Relief to flood affected people should be arranged.
II. Supply of flood articles should be arranged.
III. Adequate medical facilities should be arranged.
(a) Only I follows
(b) Only II follows
(c) Both I and III follow
(d) All follow

Hints and Solutions

1. (c) Water is vaporised to form clouds. Clouds are then condensed and rain falls.
(iii) Water, → (ii) Vapourisation, → (v) Cloud,
→ (iv) Condensation, → (i) Rain

2. (*d*) Some students can be teacher as well as scholars.

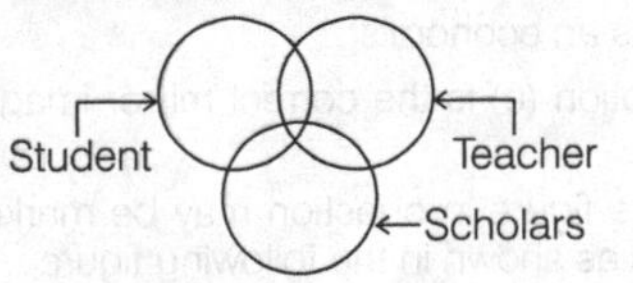

3. (*d*) As, Maharashtra is one of the states in India, in the same way, Tesax is one of the states in the USA.

4. (c) As, sum of digits of 584 = 5 + 8 + 4 = 17
and sum of digits of 488 = 4 + 8 + 8 = 20
Similarly, sum of digits of 294 = 2 + 9 + 4 = 15
∴ Sum of digits of 378 = 3 + 7 + 8 = 18
Here, difference of both are (20 − 17) = (18 − 15) = 3
∴ ? = 378

5. (c) In each set,
2nd number = (1st number − 3rd number)
As, 32 − 8 = 24
Similarly, 24 − 8 = 16

6. (c) The letter series will be
a a b a a c / a a b a a c / a a b ⇒ a c a a
Hence, option (c) is correct.

7. (a) Digits of each term are multiplied and then 1, 2, 3 and 4 are added, respectively to obtain the next elements.

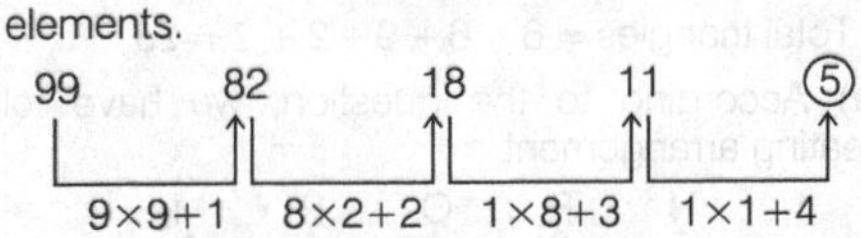

∴ ? = 1 × 1 + 4 = 1 + 4 = 5

8. (a) Every next term is obtained by subtracting 1, 2, 3, 4 and 5 respectively from its corresponding position.

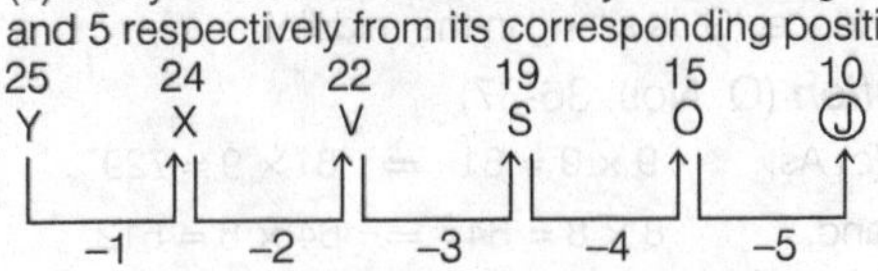

∴ ? = J

9. (a) As,

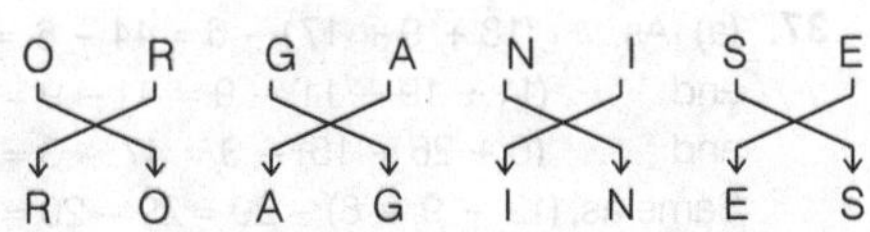

3 rd from right
Hence, N is 3rd from right after rearrangement.

10. (*d*) Required words = DEN, DIG, DING, SIN, SING, SIGN, SIDE, DIE, SEND

Solution (Q. Nos. 11-13) Arrangement according to the question is as follows

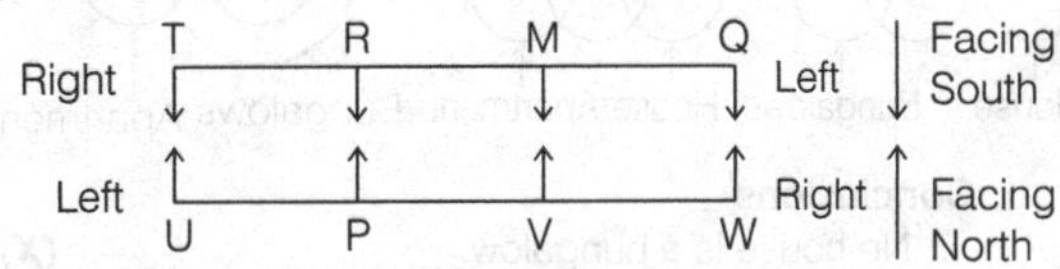

11. (*d*) Clearly, P is sitting in front of R.

12. (*e*) Clearly, T is to the immediate right of R.

13. (*a*) Clearly, M and V are sitting in front of each other.

14. (*d*) Given, oka [peru] ⟶ [fine] cloths ...(i)
meta (lisa) ⟶ (clear) water ...(ii)
dona (lisa) [peru] ⟶ [fine] (clear) weather ...(iii)
From Eqs. (i) and (iii), peru ⟶ fine
From Eqs. (ii) and (iii), lisa ⟶ clear
Hence, weather ⟶ dona

15. (*a*) As, 66 − 56 = 10, 101 − 90 = 11
41 − 30 = 11, 33 − 22 = 11
Hence, option (a) is different from all others. Because, the difference is 10.

16. (c) (a) Confluence → The place where two rivers meet.
(b) Concourse → Open part of a building.
(c) Radiation → Sending out the rays.
(b) Concentration → A lot of something in one place
Thus, we get that radiation is different from other three. All other words show the types of places.

17. (*d*) Except in figure (d), the rotation of triangle is anti-clockwise. In the question, each figure is rotating by 90° in anti-clock wise direction except figure (d). Hence, option (d) is correct.

18. (*b*) Option (b) is correct answer.

19. (*d*) Option (d) will complete the given pattern.

20. (*b*) As, Similarly,

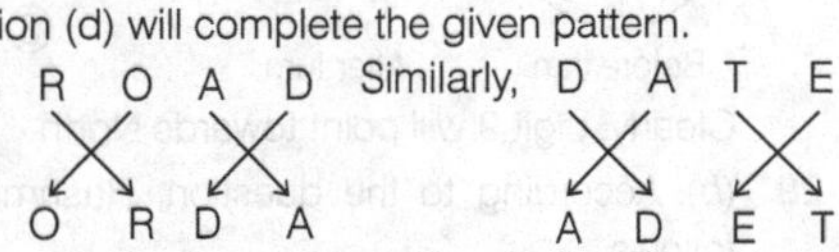

21. (c) Option (c) is correct answer.

22. (*a*) From the given question figures, we see that from question figures (1) to (2), [✓] and [❑] are interchanging their places, [Δ] and [✘] are interchanging their positions.
Similarly, in figure (3) [✘] and [Δ] and in figure (4) [❑] and [✓] will interchange their positions.
Hence, option (a) is correct.

23. (c) Option (c) is the correct water image.

24. (c) C ⟶ (04), 88, O ⟶ (11), 30, 57, 78, 89
S ⟶ (41), 14, 23, 69, 99, T ⟶ (76), 31, 33, 96
∴ COST = 04, 11, 41, 76

25. (*d*)

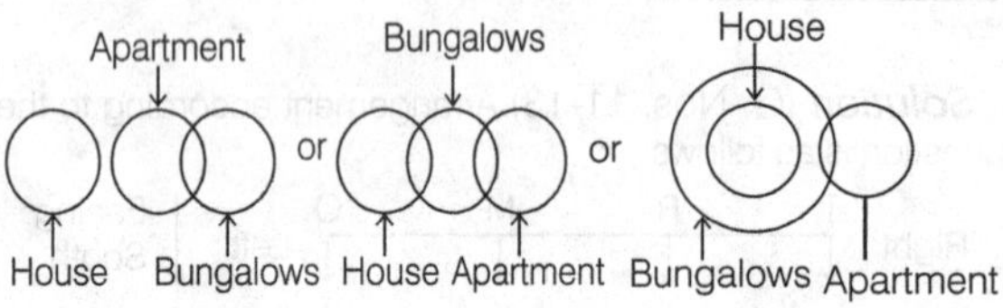

Conclusions

I. No house is a bungalow. (✗)

II. All bungalows being houses is a possibillity. (✗)

So, neither Conclusion I nor II follows.

26. (*e*)

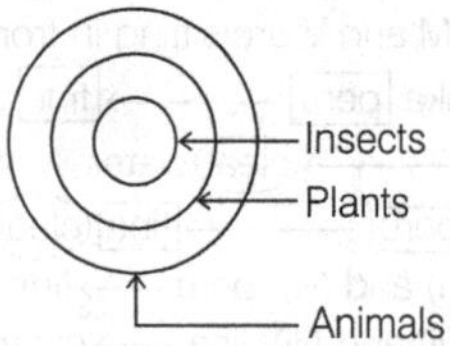

Conlusions

I. All insects being animals is a possibillity. (✓)

II. There is a possibility that some animals are neither insects nor plant. (✓)

So, both Conclusions I and II follow.

27. (*b*) Number of smaller cubes = $(n)^3$

$\Rightarrow \quad 27 = (n)^3 \Rightarrow n = \sqrt[3]{27} = 3$

$\therefore$ Number of smaller cubes having two faces painted

$= 12(n-2) = 12(3-2) = 12$

28. (*c*) According to the question, the diagrams will be as follows

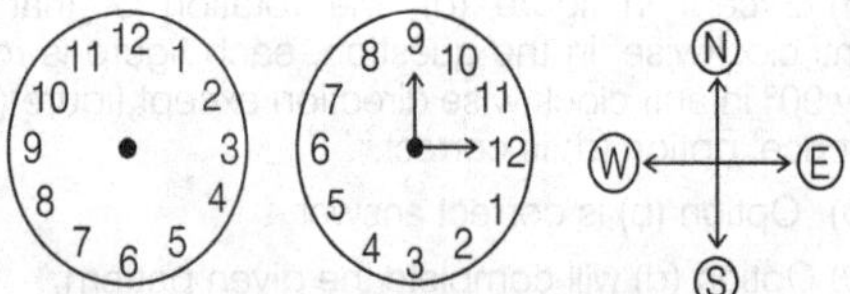

Before turn After turn

Clearly, digit 9 will point towards North.

29. (*b*) According to the question, Rashmi's path is as follows

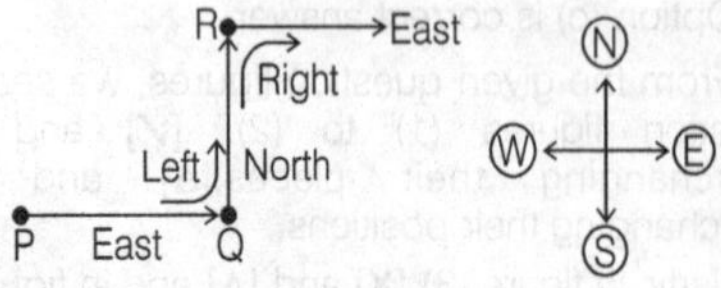

Clearly, Rashmi is facing East.

Solution (Q. Nos. 30-32) Following table can be drawn from the given information

Friend	Profession	Bank
A	Forex officer	S
B	Agriculture officer	M
C	Economist	N
D	Terminal operator	L
E	IT officer	R
F	Clerk	Q
G	Research analyst	P

30. (*b*) B is an agriculture officer.

31. (*b*) D works with bank L.

32. (*c*) C is an economist.

33. (*c*) Option (c) is the correct mirror image of the given word.

34. (*d*) The figure in question may be marked at different points as shown in the following figure

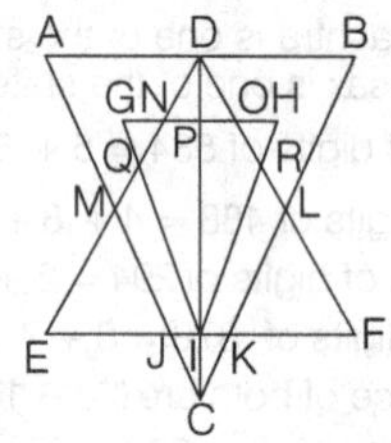

Smallest triangles

= ΔNGQ, ΔOHR, ΔPDO, ΔNDP, ΔJIC, ΔICK = 6

Single triangles

= ΔEMJ, ΔKLF, ΔRIF, ΔEQI, ΔPHI, ΔPGI = 6

Triangle formed with two triangles

= ΔADM, ΔDBL, ΔDNO, ΔDQI, ΔDRI, ΔCJK, ΔGHI, ΔDEI, ΔDIF = 9

Triangles formed with three triangles

= ΔADC, ΔDBC = 2

Largest triangles = ΔABC, ΔEDF = 2

$\therefore$ Total triangles = 6 + 6 + 9 + 2 + 2 = 25

35. (*a*) According to the question, we have following seating arrangement

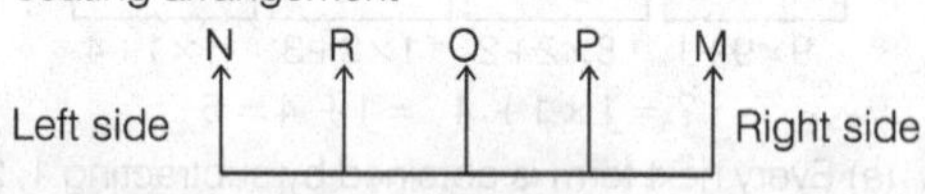

Hence, 'O' is sitting in the middle.

Solution (Q. Nos. 36-37)

36. (*c*) As, $9 \times 9 = 81 \Rightarrow 81 \times 9 = 729$

and, $8 \times 8 = 64 \Rightarrow 64 \times 8 = 512$

Same as, $7 \times 7 = 49 \Rightarrow 49 \times 7 = 343$

37. (*a*) As, $(18 + 9 + 17) - 6 = 44 - 6 = 38$

and $(11 + 19 + 11) - 9 = 41 - 9 = 32$

and $(6 + 26 + 15) - 3 = 47 - 3 = 44$

Same as, $(12 + 9 + 8) - 20 = 29 - 20 = 9$

38. (*a*) According to the question,

$16 \div 64 - 4 \times 4 + 3 = ?$

$\downarrow \quad \downarrow \quad \downarrow \quad \downarrow$

$+ \quad \div \quad - \quad \times$

So, $16 + 64 \div 4 - 4 \times 3 = ?$

$\Rightarrow 16 + 16 - 4 \times 3 = ?$

$\Rightarrow 16 + 16 - 12 = ?$

$\Rightarrow 32 - 12 = ?$

$\therefore ? = 20$

Solution (Q. Nos. 39-41)

@ ⇒ <	# ⇒ ≥	$ ⇒ =
% ⇒ >	© ⇒ ≤	

39. (*a*) F # H ⇒ F ≥ H, H % K ⇒ H > K,
K $ R ⇒ K = R, R © M ⇒ R ≤ M
Therefore, F ≥ H > K = R ≤ M
Conclusions I. F % R ⇒ F > R (True)
II. F # M ⇒ F ≥ M (Not True)
So, only Conclusions I is true.

40. (*e*) L @ D ⇒ L < D, D © P ⇒ D ≤ P
P # V ⇒ P ≥ V, V % G ⇒ V > G
Therefore, L < D ≤ P ≥ V > G
Conclusions I. P % L ⇒ P > L (True)
II. G @ P ⇒ G < P (True)
So, both Conclusions I and II are true.

41. (*d*) E % W ⇒ E > W, W © Q ⇒ W ≤ Q
Q $ T ⇒ Q = T, T @ H ⇒ T < H
Therefore, E > W ≤ Q = T < H
Conclusions I. H # W ⇒ H ≥ W (Not true)
II. H # E ⇒ H ≥ E (Not true)
So, neither Conclusion I nor II is true.

42. (*b*) **Input** ginger year town sour cat bring ink pot.
***Step* I** bring ginger year town sour cat ink pot
***Step* II** bring cat ginger year town sour ink pot
***Step* III** bring cat ginger ink year town sour pot
***Step* IV** bring cat ginger ink pot year town sour
***Step* V** bring cat ginger ink pot sour year town
***Step* VI** bring cat ginger ink pot sour town year
Step VI is the last step, hence Step V will be last but one.

43. (*b*) **Input** your job is not very important to him
***Step* I** him your job is not very important to
***Step* II** him important your job is not very to
***Step* III** him important is your job not very to
***Step* IV** him important is job your not very to
***Step* V** him important is job not your very to
***Step* VI** him important is job not to your very
***Step* VII** him important is job not to very your
Last step = Step VII

44. (*a*) ***Step* II** car down table pen jug water fall sign
***Step* III** car down fall table pen jug water sign
***Step* IV** car down fall jug table pen water sign
***Step* V** car down fall jug pen table water sign
***Step* VI** car down fall jug pen sign table water (final step)
Four more steps are required to reach the final step.

45. (*c*) From the given information, following family diagram can be drawn

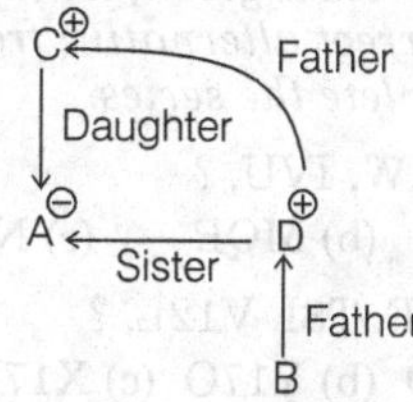

So, it clear that A is the aunt of B.

46. (*c*) From the given information, following family diagram can be drawn

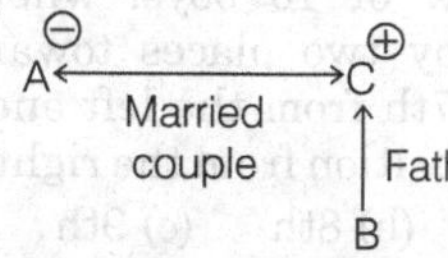

Now, it is clear that A is the mother of B.

47. (*e*) Statement I has no S and Statement II has no E.
Hence, neither of the two statements is sufficient alone.
From Statements I and II.

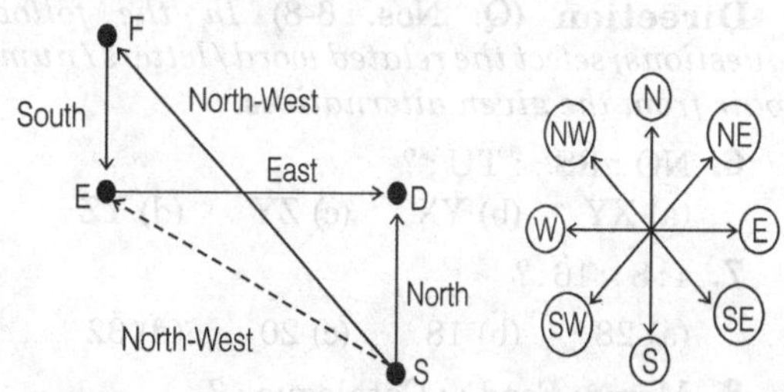

Clearly, E is to the North-West of S.
So, both statements are required to answer the question.

48. (*e*) It is clear that neither of the Statements alone is sufficient.
From statements I and II, R > P > Q and T and S are not the tallest.
Hence, R is the tallest. So, both Statements I and II are required to answer the question.

49. (*d*) Statement I strengthens the information, while Statement II weakens the information.

50. (*d*) All the courses of action are worth pursuing for the problem as defined in the Statement, because flood affected persons need all sort of relief i.e. food, medical facilities, etc.

PRACTICE SET 11

Direction (Q. Nos. 1-3) *In the following questions, a series is given, with one term missing. Choose the correct alternative from the given ones that will complete the series.*

1. AZY, EXW, IVU, ?
(a) MTS (b) MQR (c) NRQ (d) LST

2. P3C, R5F, T8I, V12L, ?
(a) X16O (b) Y17O (c) X17M (d) X17O

3. 16, 22, 34, 58, 106, ?, 394
(a) 178 (b) 175 (c) 288 (d) 202

4. In a row of 16 boys, when Prakash was shifted by two places towards the left, he became 7th from the left end. What was his earlier position from the right end of the row?
(a) 7th (b) 8th (c) 9th (d) 10th

5. Find the angle between the hour hand and the minute hand of a clock when the time is 4 : 10.
(a) 65° (b) 35° (c) 125° (d) 60°

Direction (Q. Nos. 6-8) *In the following questions, select the related word/letters/numbers pair from the given alternatives.*

6. NO : RS : : TU : ?
(a) XY (b) YX (c) ZY (d) YZ

7. 4 : 8 : : 16 : ?
(a) 28 (b) 18 (c) 20 (d) 32

8. Menu : Food : : Catalogue : ?
(a) Rock (b) Newspaper
(c) Library (d) Books

9. Find the missing number.

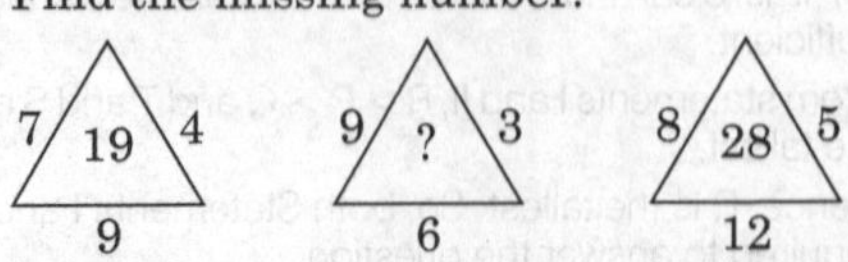

(a) 27 (b) 21 (c) 28 (d) 17

10. If '–' stands for division, '+' for multiplication, '÷' for subtraction and '×' for addition, then which one of the following equations is correct?
(a) $19 + 5 - 4 \times 2 \div 4 = 11$
(b) $19 \times 5 - 4 \div 2 + 4 = 16$
(c) $19 \div 5 + 4 - 2 \times 4 = 13$
(d) $19 \div 5 + 4 - 2 \div 4 = 20$

11. City C is to the South of city B and city A is to the North of city C. In which direction city A is located in respect of city B?
(a) North
(b) South
(c) East
(d) Cannot be determined

Direction (Q. Nos. 12-14) *Study the following information carefully and answer the given questions.*

A word and number arrangement machine when given an input line of words and numbers rearranges them following a particular rule in each step. The following is an illustration of input and rearrangement. (All the numbers given in the arrangement are two digit numbers **[IBPS (SO) 2012]**

Input gone over 35 69 test 72 park 27
***Step* I** 27 gone over 35 69 test 72 park
***Step* II** 27 test gone over 35 69 72 park
***Step* III** 27 test 35 gone over 69 72 park
***Step* IV** 27 test 35 park gone over 69 72
***Step* V** 27 test 35 park 69 gone over 72
***Step* VI** 27 test 35 park 69 over gone 72
***Step* VII** 27 test 35 park 69 over 72 gone

and Step VII is the last step of the rearrangement of the above input as the desired arrangement is obtained.

As per the rules followed in the above steps, find out in each of the following questions the appropriate step for the given input.

12. Input 86 open shut door 31 49 always 45. How many steps will be required to complete the rearrangement?
(a) Five (b) Six (c) Seven (d) Four
(e) None of these

13. Step III of an input is '25 yes 37 enemy joy defeat 52 46'. Which of the following is definitely the input?
(a) enemy 25 joy defeat yes 52 37 46
(b) 37 enemy 25 joy yes defeat 52 46
(c) enemy joy defeat 25 52 yes 46 37
(d) Cannot be determined
(e) None of the above

14. Step II of an input is '18 win 71 34 now if victory 61'. How many more steps will be required to complete the rearrangement?
(a) Three (b) Four (c) Five (d) Six
(e) More than six

15. Ravi travelled 4 km straight toward South. He turned left and travelled 6 km straight, then turned right and travelled 4 km straight. How far is he from the starting point?
(a) 8 km (b) 10 km (c) 12 km (d) 18 km

16. If S means '–', Q means '×', R means '÷' and P means '+', then 1 P 45 R 2 Q 2 S 4 = ?
(a) 40 (b) 42 (c) 36 (d) 46
(e) 38

17. Which one of the given responses would be a meaningful order of the following words in ascending order?
(i) Atomic Age (ii) Metallic Age
(iii) Stone Age (iv) Alloy Age
(a) (i), (iii), (iv), (ii) (b) (iii), (ii), (iv), (i)
(c) (ii), (iii), (i), (iv) (d) (iv), (iii), (ii), (i)

18. In the given figure, the boys who are athletes and disciplined are indicated by which number?

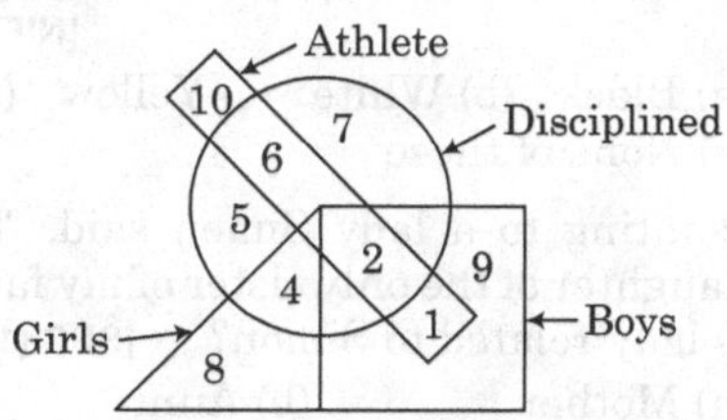

(a) 4 (b) 2 (c) 6 (d) 5

Direction (Q. Nos. 19-20) *In the following questions, find the odd word/letters from the given alternatives.* **[BSSC (CGL) Pre 2015]**

19. (a) Shimla (b) Ooty
(c) Darjeeling (d) Agra

20. (a) RNMP (b) JFEH
(c) RPOQ (d) HDCF

Direction (Q. Nos. 21-23) *Study the information carefully and answer the questions.* **[SBI Associate (PO) 2014]**

A, B, C, D, E, F, G and H are sitting around a circular area of equal distances between each other, but not necessarily in the same order. Some of the people are facing the centre while some face outside (i.e. in the direction opposite to the centre).

D sits second to the left of B. B faces outside. A and F are immediate neighbours of D . H sits second to the right of A. C sits third to the left of H. E sits to the immediate right of G. D sits third to the left of E. D faces the same direction as H. F sits to the immediate right of C. F and G take same directions.

Note Facing the same direction means if one faces the centre, then the other also faces the centre and *vice-versa.* Facing opposite direction means if one person faces centre, then the other faces outside and *vice-versa*

21. Which of the following is true regarding F as per the given sitting arrangement?
(a) Only one person sits between F and B
(b) Only three people sit between F and H
(c) A sits second to the left of F
(d) C sits to the immediate right of F
(e) F faces the centre

22. How many people in the given arrangement face outside?
(a) Four (b) Two
(c) One (d) Three
(e) Five

23. What is C's position with respect to A?
(a) Fourth to the right (b) Third to the left
(c) Second to the left (d) Fifth to the left
(e) Third to the right

24. The ratio between the present ages of A and B is 5 : 3, respectively. The ratio between A's age 4yr ago and B's age 4yr hence is 1 : 1. What is the ratio between A's age 4yr hence and B's age 4yr ago?
(a) 1 : 3 (b) 2 : 1 (c) 3 :1 (d) 4 :1

25. Select the correct combination of mathematical signs to replace* signs and to balance to given equation.

15 * 24 * 3 * 6 * 17

(a) + ÷ – = (b) + × = ÷ (c) – × = + (d) – ÷ + =

26. How many rectangles are there in the question figure? **[SSC (10+2) 2014]**

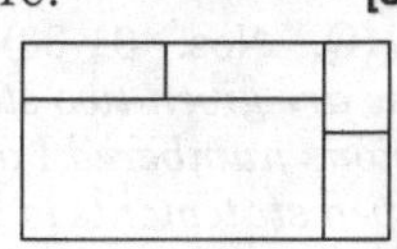

(a) 6 (b) 7 (c) 8 (d) 9

27. Select the one, which is different from the other there responses.

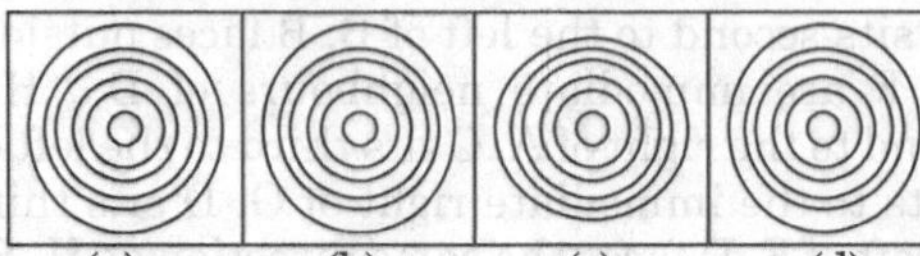

(a) (b) (c) (d)

28. Select the related figure from the given alternatives.

Question Figures

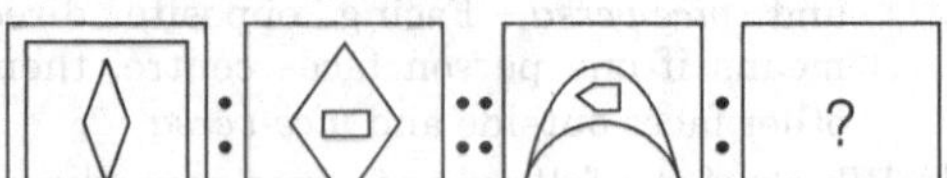

Answer Figures

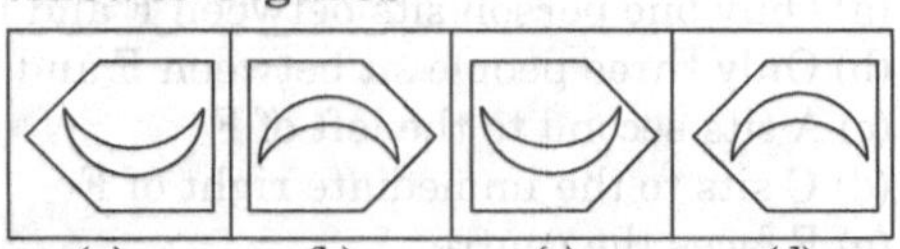

(a) (b) (c) (d)

29. A series is given with one term missing. Choose the correct alternative from the given ones that will complete the series.

Questions Figures

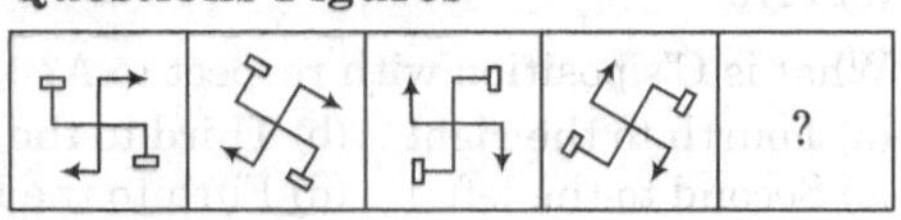

Answer Figures

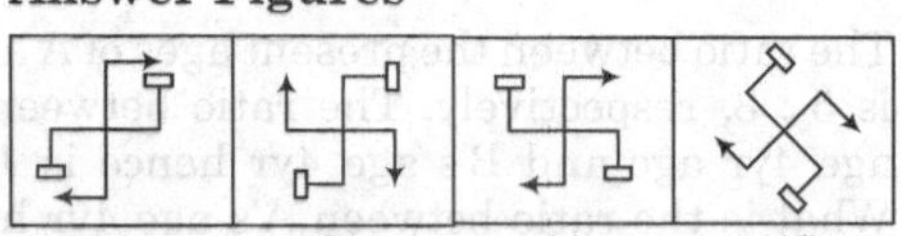

(a) (b) (c) (d)

30. Select the alternative in which the specified components of the question figure are found?

Question Figure **Answer Figures**

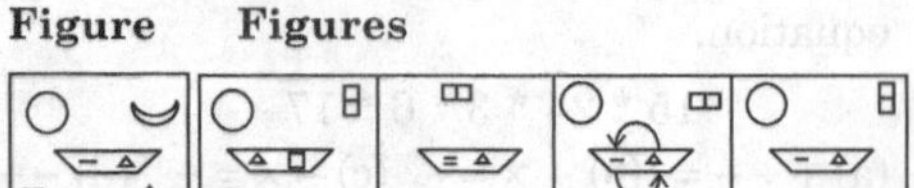

(a) (b) (c) (d)

Direction (Q. Nos. 31-33) *In each of the questions below are given two statements followed by two conclusions numbered* I *and* II. *You have to take the two given statements to be true even if they seem to be at variance from commonly known facts and decide which of the given conclusion(s) logically follow(s) from the two given statements, disregarding commonly known facts.*

Give answer **[SBI (Clerk) 2012]**

(a) if only Conclusion I follows
(b) if only Conclusion II follows
(c) if either Conclusion I or II follows
(d) if neither Conclusion I nor II follows
(e) if both Conclusions I and II follow

31. Statements No colour is a paint.
No paint is a brush.

Conclusions I. No colour is a brush.
II. All brushes are colours.

32. Statements No toffee is coffee.
No sweet is toffee.

Conclusions I. No coffee is sweet.
II. All sweets are coffee.

33. Statements All stars are planets.
All planets are galaxies.

Conclusions I. All galaxies are planets.
II. All stars are galaxies.

34. If 'blue' means 'green', 'green' means 'white', 'white' 'means' 'yellow', 'yellow' means 'black', 'black' means 'red' and 'red' means 'brown', then what is the colour of 'milk'? **[NIFT (UG) 2014]**

(a) Black (b) White (c) Yellow (d) Green
(e) None of these

35. Pointing to a lady Simon said, "She is the daughter of the only sister of my father." How is lady related to Simon? **[SSC (10 + 2) 2013]**

(a) Mother (b) Aunt
(c) Sister (d) Cousin sister

36. In a code language, the following alphabets are coded in a particular way as shown. How are the given letters code in that language?

A	C	N	P	R	M	D	Y	Z	Q
4	9	0	6	2	1	7	8	3	5

Q R C Y N P D

(a) 5298067 (b) 5298061
(c) 5984067 (d) 5298306

37. How many meaningful English words can be made with the letters DLEI, using each letter only once in each word? **[UBI (PO) 2010]**

(a) None (b) One (c) Two (d) Three
(e) More than three

Direction (Q. Nos. 38-40) *Read the following information carefully and answer the questions based on them.*

The staff of a bank are Mr. A, Mr. B, Mrs. C, Miss. D, Mr. E and Miss. F. The positions they occupy are manager, assistant manager, cashier, stenographer, teller and a clerk, though not necessarily in that order. The assistant manager is manager's grandson, cashier is stenographer's son-in-law. Mr. A is bachelor. Miss. D is teller's step sister and Mr. E is manager's neighbour. Mr. B cannot have a grandson or son-in-law as he is only 20 yr old.

38. Who is the manager?
(a) Mr. A (b) Mrs. C
(c) Mr. E (d) None of these

39. Who is the assistant manager?
(a) Mr. A (b) Miss. F (c) Mrs. C (d) Mr. B

40. Who is the teller?
(a) Miss. F (b) Mrs. C (c) Mr. A (d) Miss. D

41. In the given questions, there are two statements labelled as Assertion (A) and Reason (R). Chose the correct alternatives from the given options.

Assertion (A) The steam engine was invented by James Watt.

Reason (R) There was a problem of talking out water from flooded mines.

(a) if both 'A' and 'R' are true and 'R' is the correct explanation of 'A'
(b) if both 'A' and 'R' are true but 'R' is not the correct explanation of 'A'
(c) if 'A' is true but 'R' is false
(d) if 'A' is false but 'R' is true
(e) if both 'A' and 'R' are false

42. Find out which of the answer figures (a), (b), (c) and (d) completes the figure matrix?

Question Figure

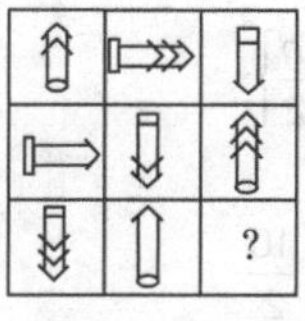

Answer Figures

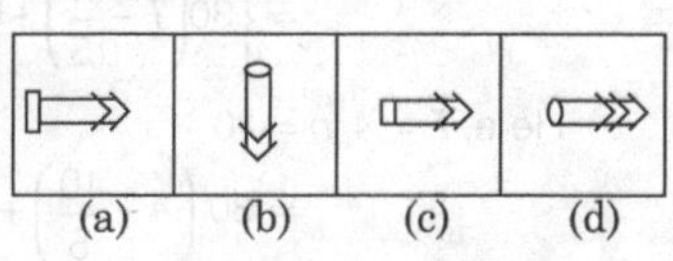

43. In a code language, the following alphabets are coded in a particular way as shown. How are the given letters code in that language?

S	A	C	L	E	D	X	Q	W	J
6	1	0	9	4	7	5	2	8	3

DEXSAJ
(a) 754613 (b) 745163 (c) 746513 (d) 745613

Direction (Q. Nos. 44-45) *In these questions, symbols @, #, %, \$ and © are used with different meanings as follows.*

'A @ B' means 'A is not smaller than B'.
'A # B' means 'A is neither smaller than nor equal to B'.
'A % B' means 'A is not greater than B'.
'A \$ B' means 'A is neither greater than nor equal to B'.
'A © B' means 'A is neither smaller than nor greater than B'.

44. **Statements** J # H, H © T, T \$ R , R % F
Conclusions I. J # S II. R # F
III. J # T
(a) Only I is true (b) Only I and II are true
(c) Only III is true (d) None of the above

45. **Statements** E \$ P, P % H, H @ I, I # K
Conclusions I. P © I II. I % E
III. H % K
(a) Only I is true (b) Only II is true
(c) Only III is true (d) Only I and II are true
(e) None is true

46. Find the digit at the face opposite to the face having digit 2 in the dice given below.

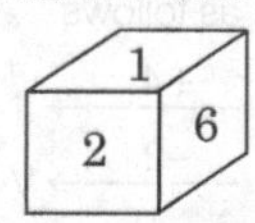

(a) 3/4 (b) 3/5 (c) 4/5 (d) 3/4/5

Direction (Q. Nos. 47-48) *Each of the following questions below consists of a question and two statements numbered I and II given below it. You have to decide whether the data provide in the statements are sufficient to answer the question.*

Give answer
(a) if the data in Statement I alone are sufficient to answer the question, while the data in Statement II alone are not sufficient to answer the question
(b) if the data in Statement II alone are sufficient to answer the question, while the data in Statement I alone are not sufficient to answer the question

(c) if the data either in Statement I alone or Statement II alone are sufficient to answer the question

(d) if the data in both the Statements I and II together are not sufficient to answer the question

(e) if the data in both the Statements I and II are together necessary to answer the question.

47. Among Sanjay, Suresh, Navin, Prakash and Karan, who has secured maximum marks is Mathematics?

I. Karan has secured more marks in Mathematics than Suresh and Navin.

II. Sanjay and Prakash have secured less marks in Mathematics than Navin.

48. How is 'cost' written in the given code language?

I. In the code language 'tell me the cost' is coded a '@ 0 # 9' and 'cost was very high' is coded as '& 6 # 1'.

II. In the code language 'some cost was discount' is code as '187#' and 'some people like discount' is coded a '875%'.

Direction (Q. Nos. 49-50) *Two statements are given followed by two Conclusions I and II. You have to consider the statements to be true even if they seem to be at variance from commonly known facts. You are to decide which of the given conclusions, if any, follow from the given statements. Indicate your answer.*

49. Statements Vitamin B complex is the best for health.

Fruits contain Vitamin B complex.

Conclusions I. We should grow fruits.

II. Fruits are good for health.

(a) Only Conclusion I can be drawn
(b) Only Conclusion II can be drawn
(c) Both Conclusions I and II can be drawn
(d) Neither Conclusion I nor II can be drawn

50. Statements Some Indians are educated.

Educated persons like small families.

Conclusions

I. All small families are educated.

II. Some Indians like small families.

(a) Only I can be concluded
(b) Only II can be concluded
(c) Both I and II can be concluded
(d) Neither I nor II can be concluded

Hints and Solutions

1. (*a*) The pattern is as follows

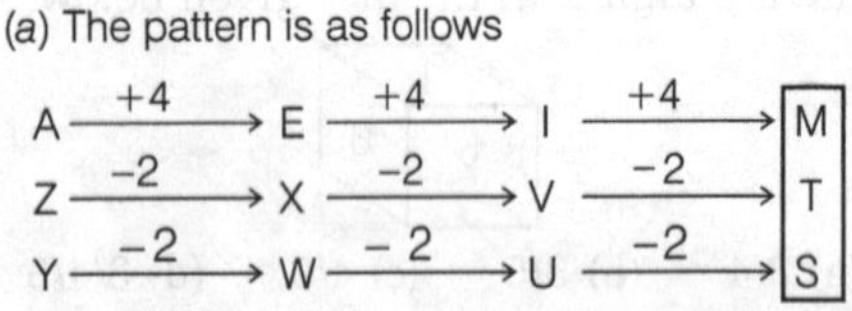

∴ ? = MTS

2. (*d*) Pattern of given alpha-numeric series is as follows

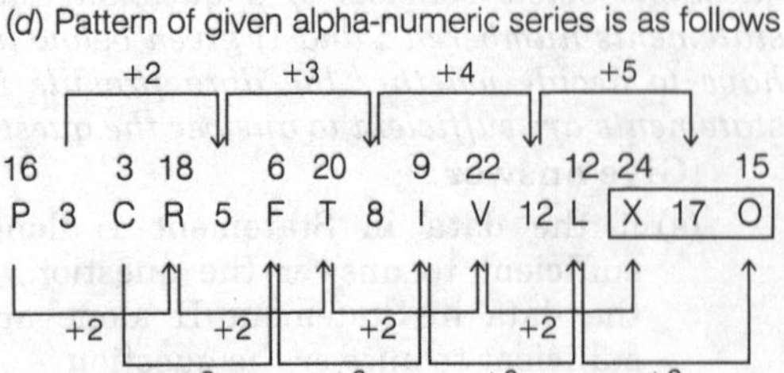

∴ ? = X170

3. (*d*) Here, series moves with the addition of 6, 12, 24, 48, 96 and 192, respectively. Hence, the missing number is 202.

4. (*b*) According to the question, we have original position of Prakash from the left = 9 th

Position from the right end = 16 − 9 + 1
= 8 th

5. (*a*) At 4 : 10, the hour hand is ahead of minute hand.

Now, required angle is given by

$$= \left\{30\left(T - \frac{n}{5}\right) + \frac{n}{2}\right\}^\circ$$

Here, $T = 4$, $n = 10$

$$= 30\left(4 - \frac{10}{5}\right) + \frac{10}{2}$$

$$= 30\,(4 - 2) + 5 = 60 + 5 = 65^\circ$$

6. (*a*) As, 14 N $\xrightarrow{+4}$ R 18, 15 O $\xrightarrow{+4}$ S 19 Similarly, 20 T $\xrightarrow{+4}$ X 24, 21 U $\xrightarrow{+4}$ Y 25

∴ ? = XY

7. (*d*) As, 4 $\xrightarrow{\times 2}$ 8 Similarly, 16 $\xrightarrow{\times 2}$ 32

∴ ? = 32

8. (*d*) 'Menu' lists all the food items in a restaurant and in the same way, a catalogue is a list of all the books in a library.

9. (*b*) As, $7 \times 4 = 28$; $19 + 9 = 28$

and, $8 \times 5 = 40$ $28 + 12 = 40$

Similarly, $9 \times 3 = 27$ $27 - 6 = 21$

10. (c) Given

− ⇒ ÷	+ ⇒ ×
÷ ⇒ −	× ⇒ +

From option (c),

$19 \div 5 + 4 - 2 \times 4 = 13$

$\Rightarrow 19 - 5 \times 4 \div 2 + 4 = 13$

$\Rightarrow 19 - 5 \times 2 + 4 = 13$

$\Rightarrow 19 - 10 + 4 = 13$

$\therefore 13 = 13$

11. (*d*) According to the question, the diagram will be as follows

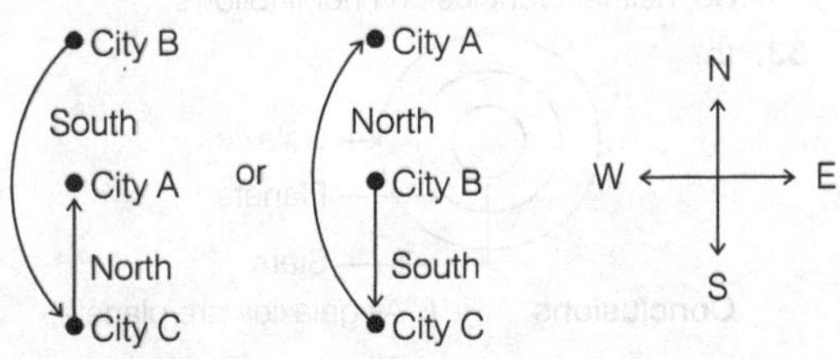

Therefore, the direction of city A in respect of city B cannot be determined.

Solution **(Q. Nos. 12-14)** In Step I, the smallest number comes at the first place from left pushing rest of the line towards right; in Step II, the word coming last alphabetically comes at the second place from left pushing rest of the line towards right, in Step III, second smallest number comes at the third place from left pushing rest of the line towards right; in Step IV, the word coming second last alphabetically comes at the fourth position from left pushing the rest of the line rightward. Thus, numbers and words get arranged alternately till the numbers are in ascending order and the words are in reverse alphabetical order.

12. (*b*) **Input** 86 open shut door 31 49 always 45

***Step* I** 31 86 open shut door 49 always 45

***Step* II** 31 shut 86 open door 49 always 45

***Step* III** 31 shut 45 86 open door 49 always

***Step* IV** 31 shut 45 open 86 door 49 always

***Step* V** 31 shut 45 open 49 86 door always

***Step* VI** 31 shut 45 open 49 door 86 always

∴ Total steps = Six

So, six steps will be required to complete the rearrangement.

13. (*d*) In the arrangement problems, previous steps/Input cannot be determined.

14. (*b*) ***Step* II** 18 win 71 34 now if victory 61

***Step* III** 18 win 34 71 now if victory 61

***Step* IV** 18 win 34 victory 71 now if 61

***Step* V** 18 win 34 victory 61 71 now if

***Step* VI** 18 win 34 victory 61 now 71 if

As, last step = Step VI

So, after Step II four more steps are required.

15. (*b*) According to the questions, the direction diagram will be as follow

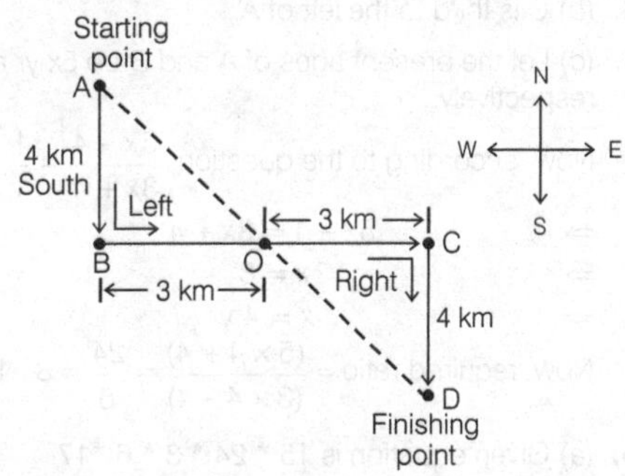

O is the mid-point of BC and AD.

AB = CD = 4 km and BC = 6 km

$OB = OC = \frac{6}{2} = 3$ km AO = OD

$AO = \sqrt{(AB)^2 + (OB)^2} = \sqrt{(4)^2 + (3)^2}$

$= \sqrt{16 + 9} = \sqrt{25} = 5$ km

∴ Required distance,

AD = AO + OD

= AO + AO = 2 × AO

= 2 × 5 = 10 km

(AO = OD as O is the mid-point of AD)

16. (*b*) Given, 1 P45 R 2 Q 2 S 4 = $1 + 45 \div 2 \times 2 - 4$

$= 1 + 22.5 \times 2 - 4$

$= 1 + 45 - 4 = 42$

17. (*b*) Ascending order of words

(iii) Stone Age, → (ii) Metallic Age, → (iv) Alloy Age → (i) Atomic Age

18. (*b*) The required region is the one which is common to the rectangle, circle and square but lies outside the triangle. i.e. 2.

19. (*d*) Except Agra, all others are hill stations.

20. (*c*) As, $R \xrightarrow{-4} N \xrightarrow{-1} M \xrightarrow{+3} P$

$J \xrightarrow{-4} F \xrightarrow{-1} E \xrightarrow{+3} H$

$R \xrightarrow{-2} P \xrightarrow{-1} O \xrightarrow{+2} Q$

$H \xrightarrow{-4} D \xrightarrow{-1} C \xrightarrow{+3} F$

Except option (c), all others follow similar pattern (– 4, – 1, + 3)

Solution (Q. Nos. 21-23) According to the given information, the sitting arrangement is as follows

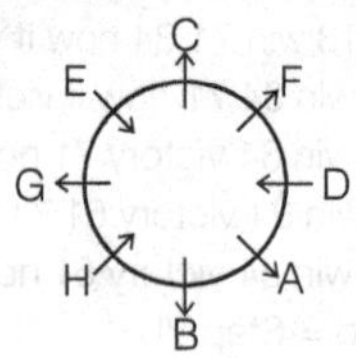

21. (*b*) Only three people sits between F and H.

22. (*e*) Five people in the given arrangement face outside.

23. (*b*) C is third to the left of A.

24. (*c*) Let the present ages of A and B be 5*x* yr and 3 *x* yr, respectively.

Now, according to the question, $\frac{5x-4}{3x+4} = \frac{1}{1}$

$\Rightarrow \quad 5x - 4 = 3x + 4$

$\Rightarrow \quad 2x = 8$

$\Rightarrow \quad x = 4 \text{ yr}$

Now, required ratio $= \frac{(5 \times 4 + 4)}{(3 \times 4 - 4)} = \frac{24}{8} = 3 : 1$

25. (*a*) Given equation is 15 * 24 * 3 * 6 *17

After applying option (a)'s mathematical symbol, we get

$15 + 24 \div 3 - 6 = 17$

$\Rightarrow \quad 15 + \frac{24}{3} - 6 = 17$

$\Rightarrow \quad 15 + 8 - 6 = 17$

$\Rightarrow \quad 23 - 6 = 17$

$\Rightarrow \quad 17 = 17$

26. (*d*) In the given figure, following rectangles are present ABIJ, BCLI, CDEH, HEFG, LGKJ, ACLJ, CDFG, ACGK and ADFK.

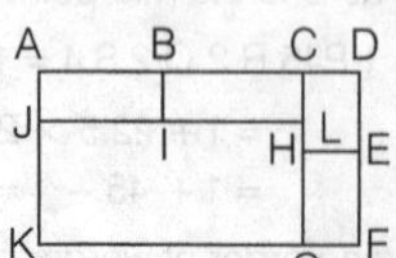

Hence, there are nine rectangles in the given figure.

27. (c) Except in figure (c), in all other figures, the outermost circle almost touches the square.

28. (*d*) Clearly figure I to figure II, both the designs interchange positions.

29. (*c*) In each subsequent figure, the entire design rotates through 45° clockwise direction.

30. (*d*) Option (d) is correct answer.

31. (*d*)

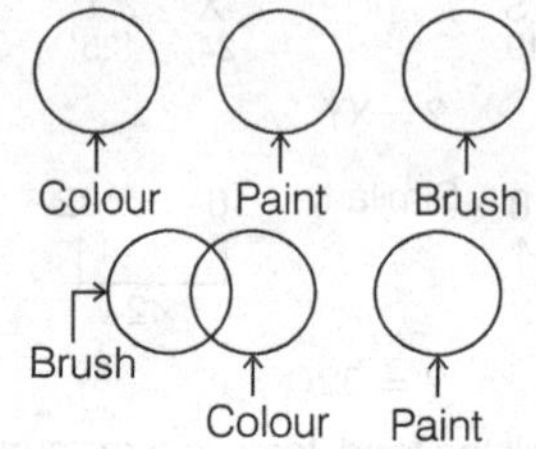

Conclusions I. No colour is a brush. (✗)

II. All brushes are colours. (✗)

So, neither Conclusion I nor II follows.

32. (*d*)

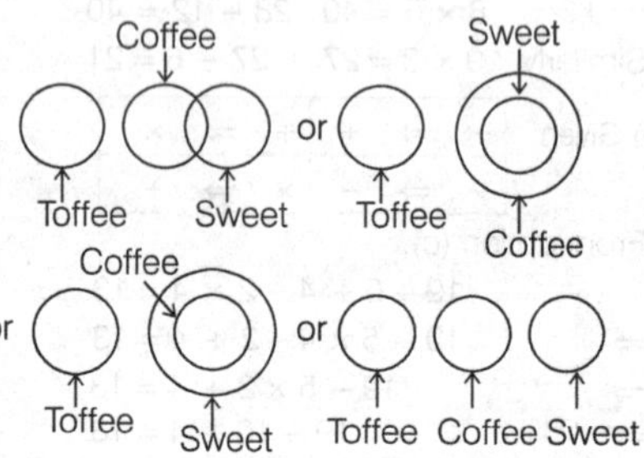

Conclusions I. No coffee is sweet. (✗)

II. All sweets are coffee. (✗)

So, neither Conclusion I nor II follows.

33. (*b*)

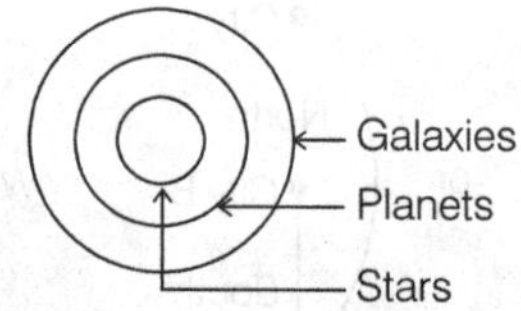

Conclusions I. All galaxies are planets. (✗)

II. All stars are galaxies. (✔)

So, only Conclusion II follows.

34. (c) Colour of 'milk' is 'white' but here 'white' means 'yellow'. Hence, colour of 'milk' is 'yellow'.

35. (*d*) According to the given information,

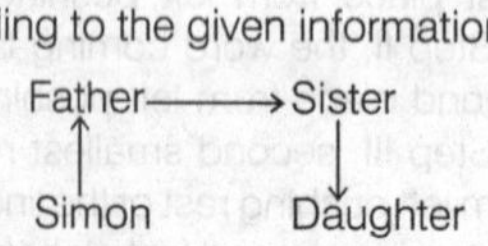

Thus, the lady is cousin sister of Simon.

36. (*a*) According to the question, we have coding for

Q	R	C	Y	N	P	D
5	2	9	8	0	6	7

Hence, option (a) is correct.

37. (*c*) Required words = LIED and IDLE.

Solution (Q. Nos. 38-40) Following table can be drawn from the given information.

	Manager	Asstt. Manager	Cashier	Steno	Clerk	Teller
Mr. A	✗	✔	✗	✗	✗	✗
Mr. B	✗	✗	✔	✗	✗	✗
Mrs. C	✔	✗	✗	✗	✗	✗
Miss. D	✗	✗	✗	✗	✔	✗
Mr. E	✗	✗	✗	✔	✗	✗
Miss. F	✗	✗	✗	✗	✗	✔

Since, the assistant manager is manager's grandson, hence assistant manager is a male and cannot be Mrs. C, Miss. D or Miss. F. Secondly, manager is a married person and hence cannot be Miss. D or Miss. F.

Cashier is stenographer's son-in-law. It means that cashier is a married male and hence cannot be either Mrs. C or Miss. D or Miss. F. Consequently, stenographer is a married person and hence cannot be either Miss. D or Miss. F. Miss. D is teller's step sister, it means that Miss. D cannot be teller and hence Miss. D is a clerk.

Mr. A is a bachelor, therefore he cannot be any one of cashier, stenographer or manager.

Mr. B cannot have a grandson or son-in-law. Therefore, Mr. B can be neither manager nor stenographer.

Mr. E is manager's neighbour. Therefore, Mr. E cannot be the manager. After putting these information in the table, we get the respective professions of Mr. A, Mr. B, Mrs. C, Miss. D, Mr. E and Miss. F as in the table above.

38. (*b*) From the table, we get Mrs. C as the manager.

39. (*a*) Mr. A is the assistant manager.

40. (*a*) Miss. F is the teller.

41. (*a*) Both A and R are true and R is the correct explanation of A. The problem of pumping out water from the flooded mines required the need of a self-working engine which led James Watt to invent the same.

42. (*a*) There are three types of arrows—a single headed arrow, a double headed arrow and a triple headed arrow. There are three positions of arrows upwards, downwards and towards right. The arrows have three types of bases square, rectangular and circular. Each of these features is used once in each row. So, in the missing figure the double headed arrow with rectangular base points towards right.

43. (*d*) After using the question coding data, we get

D	E	X	S	A	J
↓	↓	↓	↓	↓	↓
7	4	5	6	1	3

Hence, option (d) is correct.

Solution (Q. Nos. 44-45)

@ ⇒ ≥	# ⇒ >	% ⇒ ≤	$ ⇒ <	© ⇒ =

44. (*c*) As, J # H ⇒ $J > H$, H © T ⇒ $H = T$, T $ R ⇒ $T < R$

R % F ⇒ $R \leq F$

Therefore, $J > H = T < R \leq F$

Conclusions I. J # R ⇒ $J > R$ (Not True)

II. R # F ⇒ $R > F$ (Not True)

III. J # T ⇒ $J > T$ (True)

So, only III is true.

45. (*e*) As, E $ P ⇒ $E < P$, P % H ⇒ $P \leq H$, H @ I ⇒ $H \geq I$

I # K ⇒ $I > K$

Therefore, $E < P \leq H \geq I > K$

Conclusions I. P © I ⇒ $P = I$ (Not True)

II. I % E ⇒ $I \leq E$ (Not True)

III. H % K ⇒ $H \leq K$ (Not True)

So, none is true.

46. (*d*) According to the question,

$1 + 2 = 3$

$2 + 6 = 8$

$\boxed{6 + 1} = 7$

Clearly, it is not a standard dice.

∴ Digit at the opposite face of 2 = 3 or 4 or 5

47. (*e*) From Statement I, Karan > Suresh/Navin

Clearly, Statement I alone is insufficient.

From Statement II, Navin > Sanjay/Prakash

Clearly, Statements II alone is insufficient.

But from both Statements I and II, it is clear that Karan has secured maximum marks. So, both statements are required to answer the question.

48. (*a*) From Statement I,

tell me the cost → @ 0 # 9

cost was very high → & 6 # 1

cost → #

From Statement II,

some cost was discount → 1 8 7 #

some people like discount → 8 7 5 %

some discount → 8 7

and cost → either 1 or #

Thus, we can get the code of 'cost' from Statement I only. Hence, data in Statement I alone are sufficient to answer the question.

49. (*b*) I does not make any connection with the given statement but II does. Hence, I cannot be drawn but II can be.

Fruits → B Complex → Good for health

50. (*b*) I cannot be concluded because of the presence of word 'all' in it. II is the obvious choice from both the statements.

PRACTICE SET 12

1. Find out the wrong number.

1, 2, 6, 24, 120, 620, 5040

(a) 5040 (b) 620 (c) 120 (d) 24

2. Find out which of the answer figures (a), (b), (c) and (d) completes the figure matrix?

Question Figure **Answer Figures**

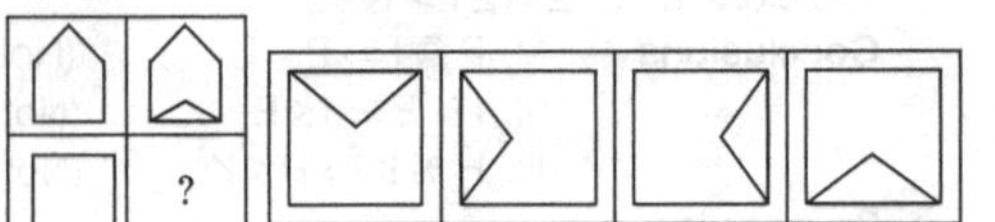

(a) (b) (c) (d)

3. Which one set of letters when sequentially placed at the gaps in the given letter series shall complete it?

_stt_tt_tts_

(a) tsst (b) sstt
(c) ttst (d) tsts

4. Arrange the following words according to dictionary. **[SSC (CPO) 2015]**

(i) Fenestration (ii) Feather
(iii) Feed head (iv) Feature
(v) Feminine

(a) (iv), (ii), (iii), (v), (i)
(b) (ii), (iv), (i), (v), (iii)
(c) (ii), (iv), (iii), (v), (i)
(d) (iv), (ii), (iii), (i), (v)

5. Which of the following diagrams best depicts the relationship between Males, Husbands and Doctors?

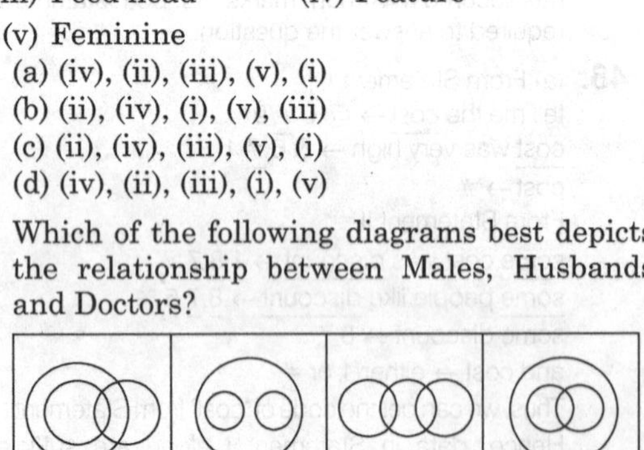

(a) (b) (c) (d)

6. A square sheet of paper has been folded twice and punched and then unfolded. The pattern of holes on the sheet of paper has been shown as in the question figure. Find out the punched hole pattern when the question figure is folded twice.

Question Figure **Answer Figures**

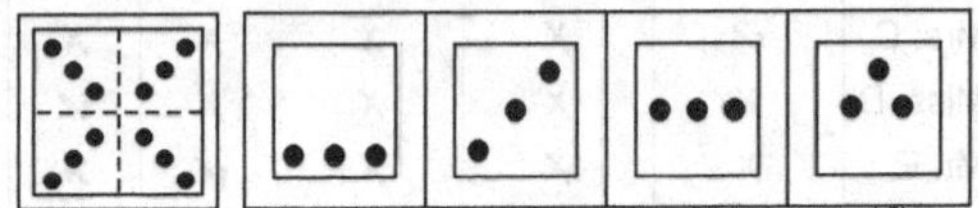

(a) (b) (c) (d)

7. Select the related figure from the given alternatives.

Question Figures

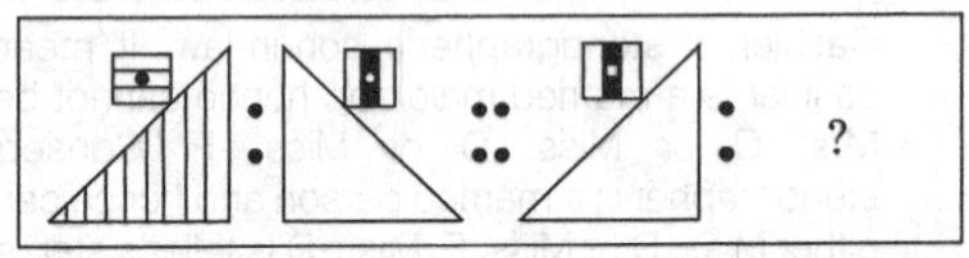

Answer Figures

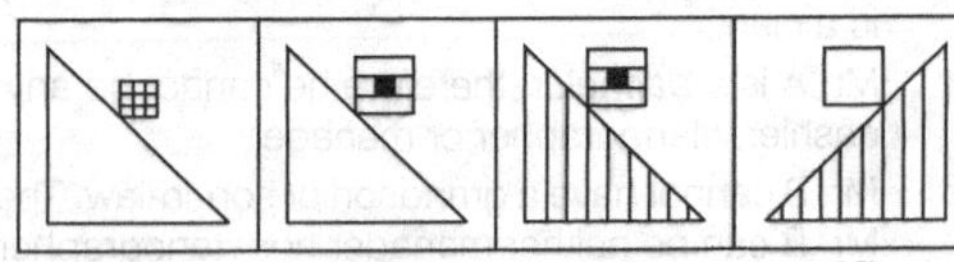

(a) (b) (c) (d)

8. *Read the following information carefully to answer the question that follows.*

'P – Q' means 'Q is father of P'.
'P ★ Q' means 'Q is brother of P'.
'P + Q' means 'Q is wife of P'.
'P ÷ Q' means 'Q is sister of P'.

Which of the following means M is the grandfather of T? **[IIFT 2013]**

(a) – ÷ + ★ M
(b) – ÷ + ★ M
(c) ÷ ★ + –
(d) None of the above

9. Select the word which can be formed using the letters of the given word.

CORRESPONDING

(a) DISCERN (b) RESPONSE
(c) REPENT (d) CORRECT

10. If '@' means '×', '©' means '÷', '%' means '+' and '$' means '–', then 6% 12©3@8 $ 3 = ?

(a) 37 (b) 35
(c) 39 (d) 33

11. Choose the number from the given alternatives which will replace the question mark (?).

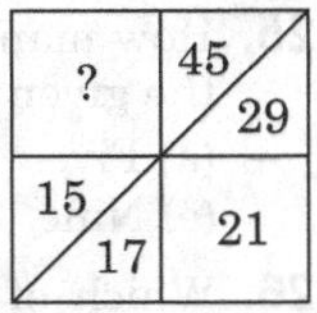

(a) 8 (b) 10
(c) 14 (d) 16

12. In a month of 31 days, third Thursday falls on 16th. What will be the last day of the months ?
(a) 5 th Friday (b) 4 th Saturday
(c) 5 th Wednesday (d) 5 th Thursday
(e) None of these

Direction (Q. Nos. 13-14) *In the following questions, select the related words/number pair from the given alternatives.*

13. Umpire : Game :: ? **[SSC (CGL) 2013]**
(a) Prodigy : Wonder
(b) Chef : Banquet
(c) Legislator : Election
(d) Moderator : Debate

14. 17 : 34 : : ? : 10
(a) 11 (b) 8 (c) 5 (d) 15

15. Group the given figures into three classes using each figure only once.

A M B H W
(1) (2) (3) (4) (5)

D E N U
(6) (7) (8) (9)

(a) 1, 3, 6; 2, 8, 9; 4, 7, 5
(b) 1, 4, 8; 2, 5, 7; 3, 6, 9
(c) 1, 4, 7; 2, 5, 8; 3, 6, 9
(d) 1, 4, 7; 3, 5, 8; 2, 6, 9

Direction (Q. Nos. 16-17) *In each of the questions below are given two statements followed by two conclusions numbered I and II. You have to take the two given statements to be true even if they seem to be at variance from commonly known facts and decide which of the given conclusion(s) logically follow(s) from the two given statements, disregarding commonly known facts.*

Give answer
(a) if only Conclusion I follows
(b) if only Conclusion II follows
(c) if either Conclusion I or II follows
(d) if neither Conclusion I nor II follows
(e) if both Conclusions I and II follow

16. Statements Latha is a beautiful and intelligent girl. She is very good.
Conclusions I. All beautiful girls are intelligent.
II. Beauty and intelligence are the factors of goodness.

17. Statements All cars are balls.
All balls are tables.
Conclusions I. Some tables are balls.
II. Some tables are cars.

18. How many squares are there in the following figure?

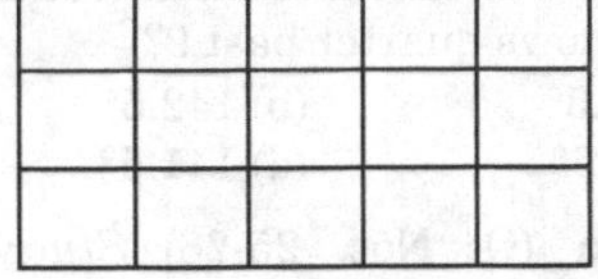

(a) 24 (b) 25 (c) 26 (d) 27

Direction (Q. Nos. 19-20) *In the following questions, find the odd word/letters from the given alternatives.*

19. (a) Mouth Organ (b) Electric Guitar
(c) Keyboard (d) Sonata

20. (a) A B (b) I J (c) D E (d) E F

21. If ' – ', means 'Q is son of P', ' × ' means 'P is brother of Q', ' ÷ ' means 'Q is sister of P', and ' + ' means 'P is mother of Q', then which of the following is definitely true about ' × – ÷ '? **[SNAP 2013]**
(a) K is father of L and M
(b) L is daughter of K and niece of uncle N
(c) K is father of L and M, his son and daughter respectively
(d) M is uncle of K's brother N

Direction (Q. Nos. 22-23) *In each of the questions below, a group of numerals is given followed by four groups of symbol/letter combinations marked as (a), (b), (c) and (d). Numerals are to be coded as per the codes and conditions given below. You have to find out which of the combinations (a), (b), (c) and (d) is correct and indicate your answer accordingly.*

Numerals	3	5	7	4	2	6	8	1	0	9
Letter/Symbol code	★	B	E	A	@	F	K	%	R	M

Following conditions apply

(i) if the first digit as well as the last digits is odd, both are to be coded as 'X'.

(ii) if the first digit as well as the last digit is even, both are to be coded as '$'.

(iii) if the last digit is 'zero', it is to be coded as '#'.

22. 487692

(a) $KEFM@ (b) AKEFM@
(c) AKEFM$ (d) $KEFM$

23. 713540

(a) X%★BA# (b) E%★BA#
(c) E%★BAR (d) X%★BAR

24. A clock is started at 5 pm. Through how many degrees will the hour hand rotate when the clock shows quarter past 9?

(a) 128.5° (b) 142.5°
(c) 127.5° (d) 141.5°

Direction (Q. Nos. 25-26) *Study the given information and answer the following questions.*

When a word and number arrangement machine is given an input line of words and numbers, it arranges them following a particular rule. The following is an illustration of input and rearrangement. (All the numbers are two-digit numbers)

Input 40 made butter 23 37 cookies salt extra 52 86 92 fell now 19

***Step* I** butter 19 40 made 23 37 cookies salt extra 52 86 92 fell now

***Step* II** cookies 23 butter 19 40 made 37 salt extra 52 85 92 fell now

***Step* III** extra 37 cookies 23 butter 19 40 made salt 52 85 92 fell now

***Step* IV** fell 40 extra 37 cookies 23 butter 19 made salt 52 85 92 now

***Step* V** made 52 fell 40 extra 37 cookies 23 butter 19 salt 86 92 now

***Step* VI** now 86 made 52 fell 40 extra 37 cookies 23 butter 19 salt 92

***Step* VII** salt 92 now 86 made 52 fell 40 extra 37 cookies 23 butter 19

Step VII is the last step of the above arrangement as the intended arrangement is obtained.

As per the rules followed in the given steps, find out the appropriate steps for the given input.

Input '32 proud girl beautiful 49 55 97 rich family 61 72 17 nice life'

25. How many steps will be required to complete the given input?

(a) Five (b) Six (c) Seven (d) Eight
(e) Nine

26. Which of the following is the third element from the left end of Step VI?

(a) Beautiful (b) Life (c) 61 (d) Nice
(e) 17

27. The ratio of A's and B's ages is 3 : 2. The product of their ages is 216 yr. Then, the sum of their present ages is

(a) 18 yr (b) 30 yr (c) 36 yr (d) 32 yr

Direction (Q. Nos. 28-29) *Study the following information carefully and answer the given questions.*

Four ladies A, B, C and D and four gentlemen E, F, G and H are sitting in a circle around a table facing each other.

I. No two ladies or two gentlemen are sitting side-by-side.

II. C, who is sitting between G and E, is facing D.

III. F is between D and A and is facing G.

IV. H is to the right of B.

28. Who is sitting to the left of A?

(a) E (b) F (c) G (d) H

29. E is facing whom?

(a) F (b) B (c) G (d) H

30. Average marks obtained by 9 students in one row of a class is 45. One student with 35 marks exchanges his seat with a student securing 48 marks. What is the average marks of these 9 students of this row?

(a) 56.4 (b) 46.4 (c) 47.6 (d) 45.6

31. Amol travels a distance of 10 ft from A to B. Then, he turns to left and travels 5 ft and again turns to left and travels 2 ft. Finally, he turns to left and moves 5 ft. How far is he now from his original position?

(a) 5 ft (b) 8 ft (c) 6 ft (d) 12 ft

Direction (Q. Nos. 32-33) *In these questions, symbols @, $, #, ★ and % are used with different meanings as follows*

'A @ B' means 'A is smaller than B'

'A $ B' means 'A is greater than B'

'A # B' means 'A is either smaller than or equal to B'

'A * B' means 'A is either greater than or equal to B'

'A % B' means 'A is neither smaller than nor greater than B'

In each of the following questions assuming the given statements to be true, find out which of the two Conclusions I and II given below them is/are definitely true.

Give answer

(a) if only Conclusion I is true
(b) if only Conclusion II is true
(c) if either Conclusion I or II is true
(d) if neither Conclusion I nor II is true
(e) if both Conclusions I and II are true

32. Statements H # T, T @ L, L % F
Conclusions I. F $ H
II. H # L

33. Statements V $ I, I * M, M # Q
Conclusions I. I # Q
II. I * Q

34. Identify the missing part of the question figure and select it from given answer figures.

Question Figure

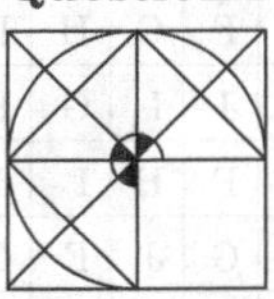

Answer Figures

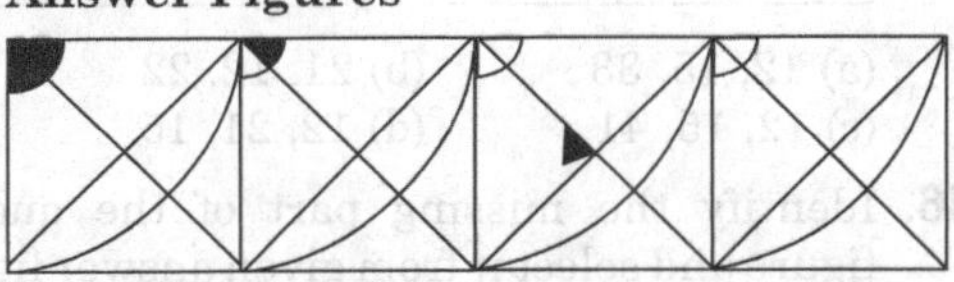

(a) (b) (c) (d)

35. Kavi walks Northward upto 10 m. He turns left and walks 30 m. Finally, he turns left and walks 50 m. At what distance Kavi is now from his starting position?
(a) 50 m (b) 10 m (c) 20 m (d) 90 m

36. In a gathering , seven members are standing in a row. C is sitting left to B but on the right to D. A is sitting right to B. F is sitting right to E but left to D. H is sitting left to E. Find the person sitting in the middle.
[NICL (Assistant) Cadre III 2015]
(a) C (b) D (c) E (d) F
(e) B

Direction (Q. Nos. 37-38) *These questions consists of a question and two statements numbered* I *and* II *given below it. You have to decide whether the data given in the statements are sufficient to the question. Read both the statements.*

Give answer

(a) if the data in Statement I alone are sufficient to answer the question, while the data in Statement II alone are not sufficient to answer the question
(b) if the data either in Statement I alone or Statement II alone are sufficient to answer the question
(c) if the data in Statement II alone are sufficient to answer the question, while the data in Statement I alone are not sufficient to answer the question
(d) if the data in both Statements I and II together are necessary to answer the question
(e) if the data even in both Statements I and II together are not sufficient to answer the question

37. In which month (of the same year) was Ritesh appearing for an exam?
I. Ritesh's brother correctly remembers that he appeared for the exam after April but before November and that the month of his exam had exactly 30 days.
II. Ritesh's sister correctly remembers that he appeared for the exam after June but before December and that the month of his exam did not have 31 days.

38. Five friends P, Q, R, S and T are sitting around a circular table facing the centre. Who sits second to the right of S?
I. Only two people sit between S and T. Only one person sits between T and Q. P is an immediate neighbour of T.
II. R sits second to the left of S. Only one person sits between R and P. Q is not an immediate neighbour of P.

39. If in the word 'CONGREGATION', 1st and 3rd letters are interchanged, 2nd and 4th letters are interchanged, 5th and 7th letters are interchanged and this interchange goes in the same manner, then find the 10th letter from right in the new arrengement.
(a) E (b) C
(c) G (d) P

40. In the given diagram, the triangles represents doctors, the circle represents players and the rectangle represents singers. Which region represents doctors who are singers but not players?

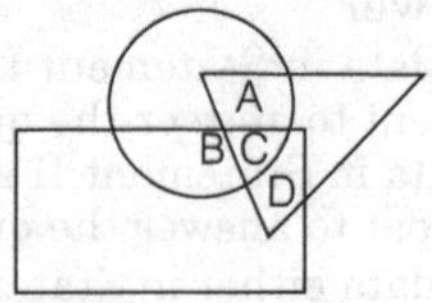

(a) A (b) B (c) C (d) D

41. A cube which is painted red on the outer surface is of 2 inches height, 2 inches wide and 2 inches across. If it is cut into one inch cubes as shown by dotted lines, then indicate the number of cubes which are painted red only on two sides? **[SSC (CGL) 2013]**

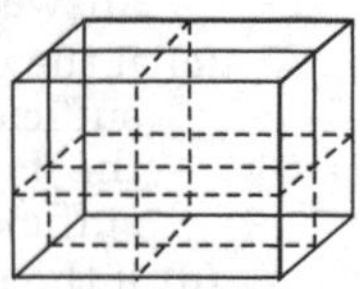

(a) 8 (b) 0 (c) 4 (d) 6

Direction (Q. Nos. 42-44) *Read the following information carefully and then answer the questions given below.*

P, Q, R, S, T, W and Z are seven students studying in three different colleges A, B and C. There are three girls among them studying one each in each of these colleges.

Two of them study mechanical engineering, two study medicine and one each study biotechnology, pharmacy and electrical engineering. R studies with only her best friend P who studies pharmacy in college B.

No girl studies either biotechnology or electrical engineering. T studies mechanical engineering in college A and his brother W studies electrical engineering in college C.

None of the two studying medicines in college B. S studies biotechnology along with T and Z.

42. In which of the colleges do three of them study?

(a) C (b) B
(c) A or C (d) Data inadequate
(e) None of the above

43. Which of the following pairs of students study medicine?

(a) S, Z (b) Z, W (c) Z, Q (d) T, Q
(e) None of these

44. Which of the following is the field of study of Z?

(a) Medicine
(b) Mechanical
(c) Electrical
(d) Data inadequate
(e) None of the above

45. A word is represented by only one set of numbers as given in anyone of the alternatives. The sets of numbers given in the alternatives are represented by two classes of alphabets as in the two matrices given below. The columns and rows of Matrix I are numbered from 1 to 5 and that of Matrix II are numbered from 6 to 10. A letter from these matrices can be represented first by its row and next by its column, e.g., A can be represented by 11, 23 etc. and G can be represented by 67, 78 etc. Similarly, you have to identify the set for the word given below.

BEE **[SSC (10+2) 2014]**

Matrix I

	1	2	3	4	5
1	A	B	C	D	E
2	E	D	A	B	C
3	B	C	D	E	A
4	D	A	E	C	D
5	C	E	B	A	B

Matrix II

	6	7	8	9	10
6	F	G	H	I	J
7	J	I	G	H	F
8	F	H	I	J	G
9	G	J	F	G	I
10	H	E	J	F	E

(a) 12, 15, 33 (b) 21, 12, 22
(c) 12, 15, 41 (d) 12, 21, 15

46. Identify the missing part of the question figure and select it from given answer figures.

Question Figure

Answer Figures

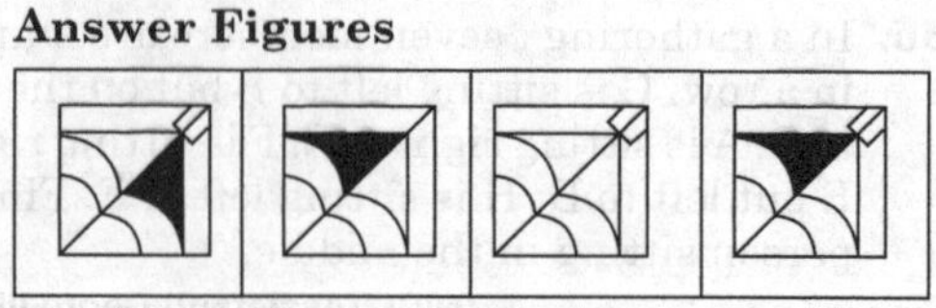

(a) (b) (c) (d)

47. Arun runs faster than Elias, but not as fast as Dinesh. Dinesh runs faster than Chander, but not as fast as Bikram. Who runs fastest?

(a) Arun (b) Bikram
(c) Chander (d) Dinesh

48. The age of Ram is twice the age of Shyam and half the age of Sohan, Shyam is elder than Mohan. Who is the eldest? **[SSC (CGL) 2011]**

(a) Mohan (b) Ram
(c) Sohan (d) Shyam

49. The mangroves can shed tonnes of leaves per acre every year; fungi and bacteria breakdown this leaf litter and consume it, they then are consumed by tiny worms and crustaceans, which in turn feed small fish, which feed larger fish and birds and crocodiles.

Which among the following is the most logical inference of the above statements? **[UPSC CSAT 2015]**

(a) Coastal areas cannot have food chains without mangroves.
(b) Mangroves are an essential component of all marine ecosystems.
(c) Mangroves have a crucial role in some of the coastal food chains.
(d) The composition of marine flora and fauna is largely determined by mangroves.

50. 'By liberty I mean the eager maintenance of that atmosphere in which men have the opportunity to be their best selves.'

Which of the following expresses the view implied in the above statement? **[UPSC CSAT 2015]**

(a) Liberty is the absence of restraint on human action.
(b) Liberty is what law permits people to perform.
(c) Liberty is the ability to do what one desires.
(d) Liberty is the maintenance of conditions for the growth of human personality.

Hints and Solutions

1. (*b*) The pattern is as follows

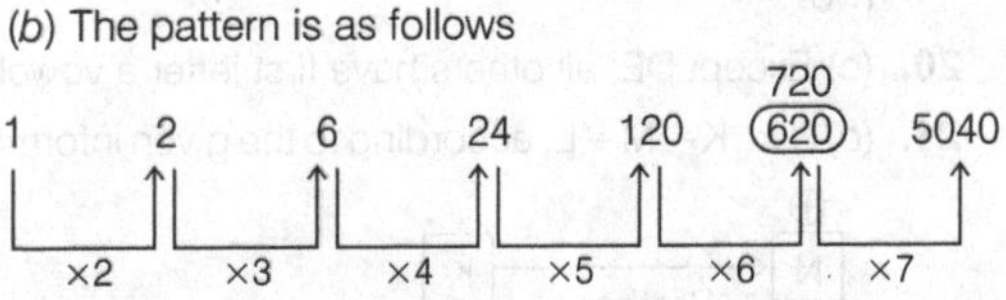

Hence, number 620 is wrong and should be replaced by 720.

2. (*d*) The pattern is as follows

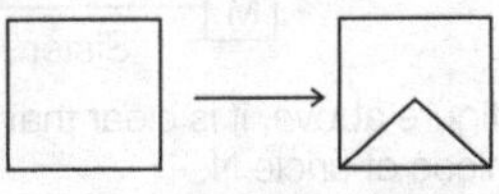

Hence, option (d) is the correct answer.

3. (*a*) The complete letter series will be

t s t/t s t/t s t/t s t ⇒ tsst

4. (*c*) Sequence of given words as per dictionary is as follows

(ii) Feather → (iv) Feature → (iii) Feed head → (v) Feminine → (i) Fenestration

5. (*a*) All husbands are males. Also, some husbands and some males can be doctors. This relationship can be expressed as given in option (a).

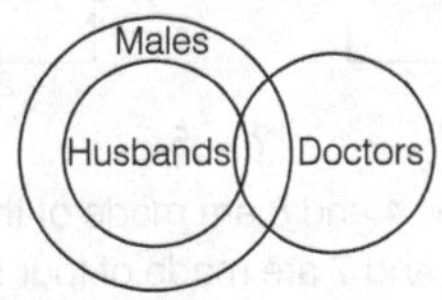

6. (*b*)

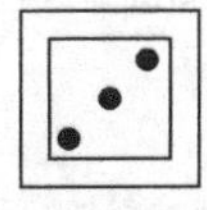

So, option (b) is correct answer.

7. (*c*) Clearly, from figure I to figure II the design is inverted horizontally. The lines of figure I design are deleted. The pattern inside the square rotates through 90° and shaded part becomes white.

8. (*d*) From option (a) T – C ÷ L + N ★ M

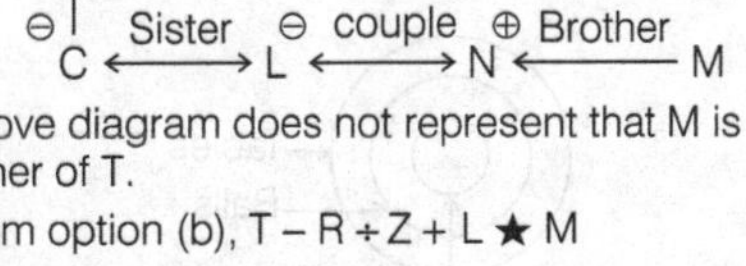

Above diagram does not represent that M is the grand father of T.

From option (b), T – R ÷ Z + L ★ M

$$T \xleftrightarrow{\ominus \text{ Sister}} Z \xleftrightarrow{\oplus \text{ Brother}} L \xleftrightarrow{\ominus \text{ Married couple}} F$$

It is also not a correct diagrams.

Hence, none of the given option shows that M is the grand father of T.

9. (*a*) By using the letters of given word 'CORRESPONDING'. 'DISCERN', is the only word which can be formed.

10. (*b*) Given, 6% 12 © 3 @ 8 $ 3 = ?

$\Rightarrow$ $6 + 12 \div 3 \times 8 - 3 = ?$

$\Rightarrow$ $6 + 4 \times 8 - 3 = ?$

$\Rightarrow$ $6 + 32 - 3 = ?$

$\Rightarrow$ $38 - 3 = ?$ $? = 35$

11. (*c*) As, 14 + 1 = 15; 15 + 2 = 17

17 + 4 = 21; 21 + 8 = 29 29 + 16 = 45

Hence, 14 is the correct answer.

12. (*a*) Since, third Thursday is on 16th. So, for calculation of last day of the month, we should calculate the odd number of days, here total days are 15 till 31.

$\therefore$ Number of odd day $= \frac{15}{7} = 1$ [remainder]

So, day on last date of month will be 5th Friday.

13. (*d*) An umpire decides the course of game in the same way, moderator decides course of debate.

14. (*c*) As, 17 : 34 ($\div 2$) Similarly, 5 : 10 ($\div 2$)

$\therefore$? = 5

15. (*b*) Figures 1, 4 and 8 are made of three lines.

Figures 2, 5 and 7 are made of four sides.

Figures 3, 6 and 9 are circular in shape.

16. (*b*)

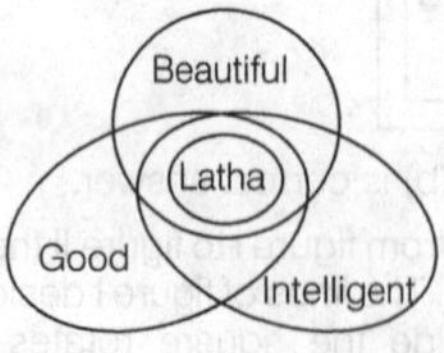

Conclusions

I. All beautiful girls are intelligent. (✗)

II. Beauty and intelligence are the factors of goodness. (✔)

So, only Conclusion II follows.

17. (*e*)

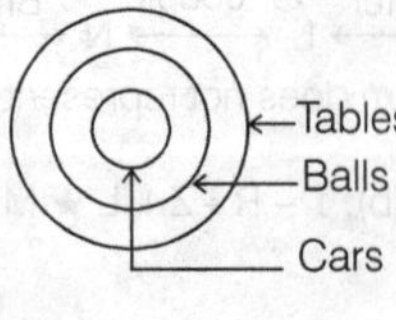

Conclusions I. Some tables are balls. (✔)

II. Some tables are cars. (✔)

So, both Conclusion I and II follow.

18. (*c*)

There are five squares in the upper row of the main figure namely ☐ AEQM, ☐ EGRQ, ☐GISR, ☐IKTS and ☐ KBNT.

Hence, there are fifteen squares, five in each row of the main figure.

Similarly, there are total eight squares — Four in each bigger row formed by combining two rows at a time of the main figure i.e. ☐ AOVG, ☐ EUWI ☐ GVXK ☐ IWPB ☐ MDHR ☐ QFJS ☐ RHLT and SJCN and finally there are three squares ☐ AIJD, ☐ EKLF and ☐ GBCJ from the main figure.

Hence, there are a total of 26 squares in the figure.

Shortcut method

Number of squares

$= (5 \times 3) + (4 \times 2) + (3 \times 1) + (2 \times 0)$

$= 15 + 8 + 3 + 0 = 26$

19. (*d*) Except Sonata, all others are instruments. Sonata is a piece of music composed from one instrument or two.

20. (*c*) Except DE, all others have first letter a vowel.

21. (*b*) N × K – M ÷ L, according to the given information,

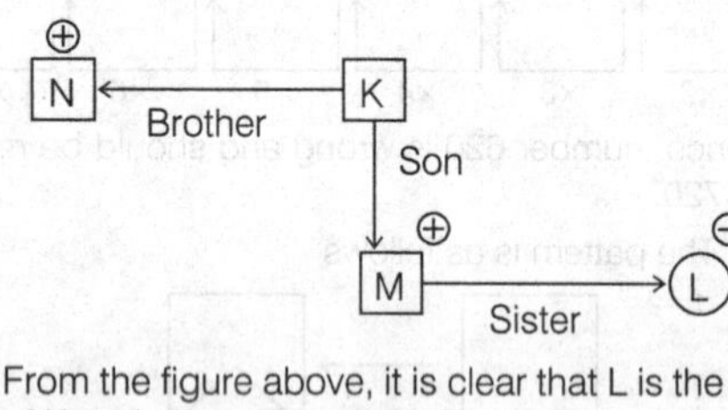

From the figure above, it is clear that L is the daughter of K and niece of uncle N.

Solution (Q. Nos. 22-23)

Numerals	3	5	7	4	2	6	8	1	0	9
Digit/Symbol code	★	B	E	A	@	F	K	%	R	M

Conditions

(i) 1st digit odd, Last digit odd — Both are coded as X

(ii) 1st digit even, Last digit even — Both are coded as $

(iii) Last digit zero – coded as #

22. (*d*)

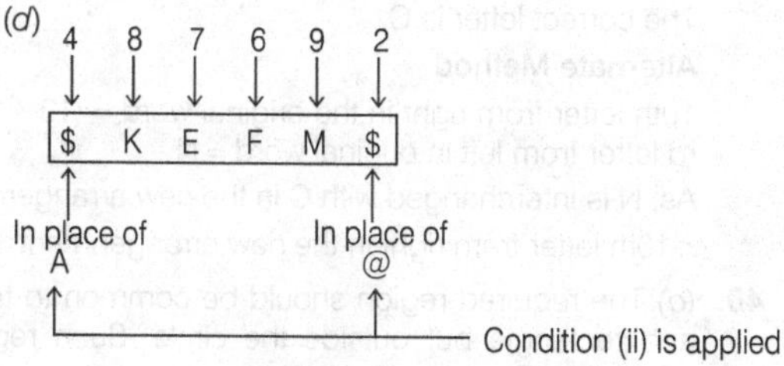

∴ 487692 ⇒ $ KEFM$

23. (*a*)

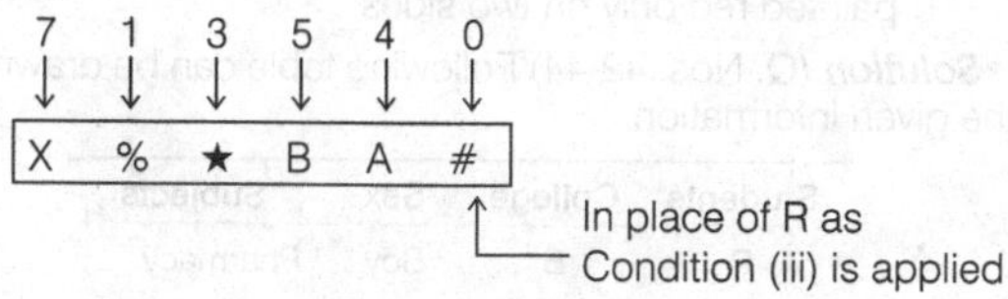

∴ 713540 ⇒ X%★BA

24. (*c*) Angle tracked by hour hand in 12 h = 360°

Angle tracked by hour hand in 4 h 15 min = $\frac{17}{4}$ h

$$=\left(\frac{360}{12}\times\frac{17}{4}\right)^{\circ}=127.5^{\circ}$$

Solution (Q. Nos. 25-26)

Input 32 proud girl beautiful 48 55 97 rich family 61 72 17 nice life

***Step* I** beautiful 17 32 proud girl 48 55 97 rich family 61 72 nice life

***Step* II** family 32 beautiful 17 proud girl 48 55 97 rich 61 72 nice life

***Step* III** girl 48 family 32 beautiful 17 proud 55 97 rich 61 72 nice life

***Step* IV** life 55 girl 48 family 32 beautiful 17 proud 97 rich 61 72 nice

***Step* V** nice 61 life 55 girl 48 family 32 beautiful 17 proud 97 rich 72

***Step* VI** proud 72 nice 61 life 55 girl 48 family 32 beautiful 17 97 rich

***Step* VII** rich 97 proud 72 nice 61 life 55 girl 48 family 32 beautiful 17

25. (*c*) Seven steps are required to complete the given input.

26. (*d*) 'Nice' is the third element from the left end of Step VI.

27. (*b*) Let the present ages of A's and B's be 3x yr and 2x yr, respectively.

Now, according to the question,

⇒ $3x \times 2x = 216$

⇒ $6x^2 = 216$

⇒ $x^2 = \frac{216}{6} = 36$

∴ x = 6yr

So, sum of their present ages = (3x + 2x) = 5x = 5 × 6 = 30yr

Solution (Q. Nos. 28-39) On the basis of given information, the sitting arrangement of the persons will be as follows

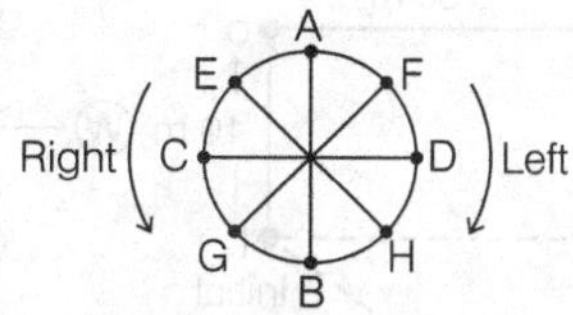

28. (*b*) Clearly, F is sitting to the left of A.

29. (*d*) Clearly, E is facing H.

30. (*b*) Total marks = 9 × 45 = 405

According to question, 405 − 35 + 48 = 418

∴ Average marks $= \frac{418}{9} = 46.4$

31. (*b*) According to the question, the direction diagram is as follows

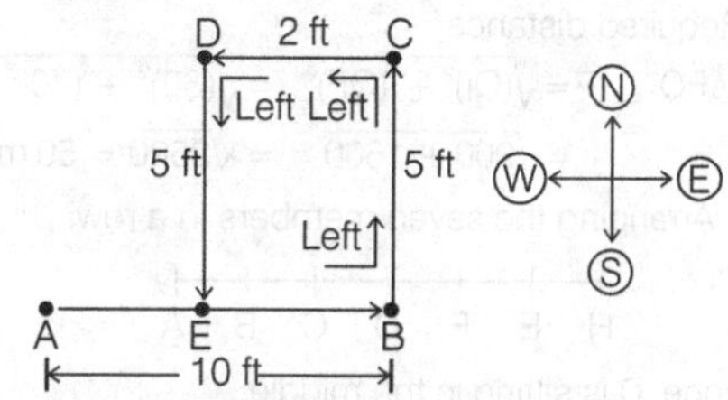

A = Original position, E = Final position

AB = 10 ft, BC = BE = 5 ft

CD = BE = 2 ft

∴ Required distance AE = AB − EB = 10 − 2 = 8 ft

Solution (Q. Nos. 32-33)

@ ⇒ <	$ ⇒ >	# ⇒ ≤	* ⇒ ≥	% ⇒ =

32. (*a*) **Statements** H # T ⇒ H ≤ T, T @ L ⇒ T < L

L % F ⇒ L = F

Therefore, H ≤ T < L = F

Conclusions I. F $ H ⇒ F > H (True)

II. H # L ⇒ H ≤ L (Not True)

So, only Conclusion I is true.

33. (*c*) **Statements** V $ I ⇒ V > I, I * M ⇒ I ≥ M

M # Q ⇒ M ≤ Q

Therefore, V > I ≥ M ≤ Q

Conclusions I. I # Q ⇒ I ≤ Q (Can be True)

II. I * Q ⇒ I ≥ Q (Can be True)

So, either Conclusion I or II is true.

34. (*b*) Option (b) will complete the given pattern as follows

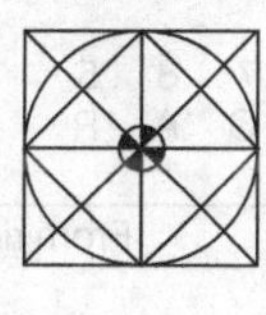

35. (*a*) According to the question, the direction diagram is drawn as shown in given figure

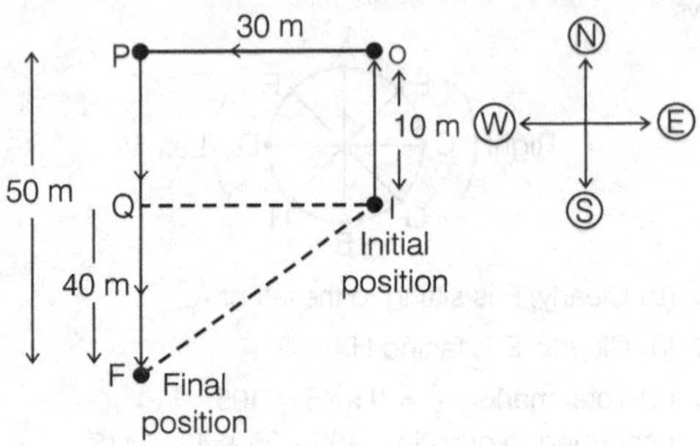

IO = 10m, OP = 30m, PF = 50m

QI = OP = 30m, PQ = IO = 10m

QF = PF − PQ = 50 − 10 = 40m

F represents the final position,

∴ Required distance,

In ΔFQI $IF = \sqrt{(QI)^2 + (QF)^2} = \sqrt{(30)^2 + (40)^2}$

$= \sqrt{900 + 1600} = \sqrt{2500} = 50\text{ m}$

36. (*b*) Arranging the seven members in a row.

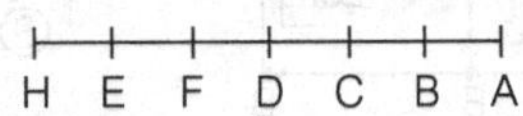

Hence, D is sitting in the middle.

37. (*d*) From Statement I, Ritesh appeared for the exam in June or September.

From Statement II, Ritesh appeared for the exam in September or November.

From both Statement I and II, Ritesh appeared for the exam in September.

Hence, data in both Statements I and II together are necessary to answer the question.

38. (*c*) From Statement I, From Statement II

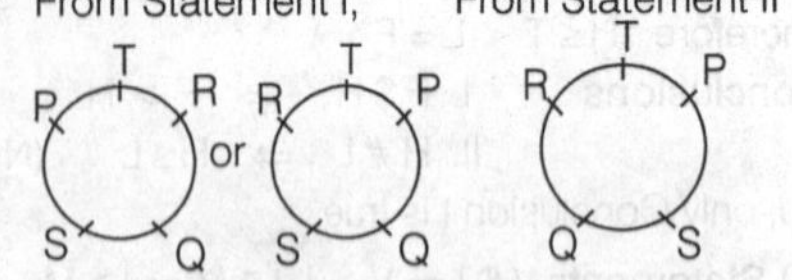

So, Statement II alone is sufficient to answer the question.

39. (*b*)

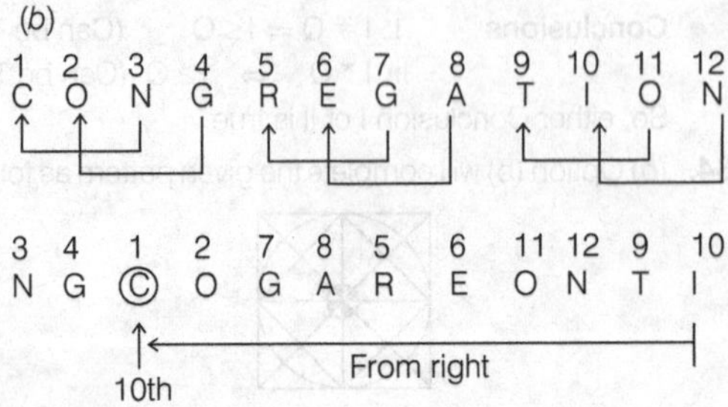

The correct letter is C.

Alternate Method

10th letter from right in the original word = (13 − 10) = 3 rd letter from left in original word = N

As, N is interchanged with C in the new arrangement

∴ 10th letter from right in the new arrangenment = C

40. (*d*) The required region should be common to triangle and rectangle but outside the circle. Such region is marked as D.

41. (*b*) From the figure, there is no such cube which is painted red only on two sides.

Solution (Q. Nos. 42-44) Following table can be drawn from the given information

Students	College	Sex	Subjects
P	B	Boy	Pharmacy
Q	C	Girl	Medicine
R	B	Girl	Mech Engg
S	A	Boy	Biotech
T	A	Boy	Mech Engg
W	C	Boy	Elec Engg
Z	A	Girl	Medicine

42. (*e*) Three of them study in college A.

43. (*c*) Z and Q study medicine.

44. (*a*) Z studies medicine.

45. (*d*) B → (12), 24, 31, 53, 55

E → (15), (21), 34, 43, 52, 107, 1010

∴ BEE → 12, 21 15

46. (*d*) Option (d) will complete the given pattern as follows

47. (*b*) According to the question, we have following arrangement of speed.

Bikram > Dinesh > Chander > Arun > Elias

Thus, Bikram runs fastest.

48. (*c*) Let the age of Shyam = x yr

Then, age of Ram = $2x$ yr

and age of Sohan = $4x$ yr

∵ $4x > 2x > x$

On arranging the above data, we get

∴ Sohan > Ram > Shyam > Mohan

So, Sohan is the eldest.

49. (*c*) Mangroves have a crucial role in some of the coastal food chains.

50. (*c*) Liberty is the ability to do what one desires.

PRACTICE SET 13

1. Find the missing character from the given alternatives.

9	5	6
5	7	?
3	4	5
135	140	150

(a) 4 (b) 5 (c) 8 (d) 10

2. In the given question, one number is wrong in the series. Find out the wrong number.

7.5, 47.5, 87.5, 157.5, 247.5, 357.5, 487.5

(a) 357.5 (b) 87.5 (c) 157.5 (d) 7.5
(e) 47.5

3. If K denotes '×', 'B' denotes '÷', 'T' denotes '–' and 'M' denotes '+', then 40 B 8 T 6 M 3 K 4 = ?

(a) 19 (b) 11 (c) – 31 (d) 23

4. In a family, there are seven persons, comprising two married couples, T is the son of M and the grandson of K. M is a widower. M and R are brothers and W is the daughter-in-law of J, who is the mother of R and the grandmother of D. How is D related to M? **[MAT 2013]**

(a) Son (b) Son-in-law
(c) Nephew or niece (d) Brother

5. Select the related letter pair from the given alternatives.

—:—::—:?

(a) — (b) — (c) — (d) —

6. Find the region that represents those rural students who are not intelligent?

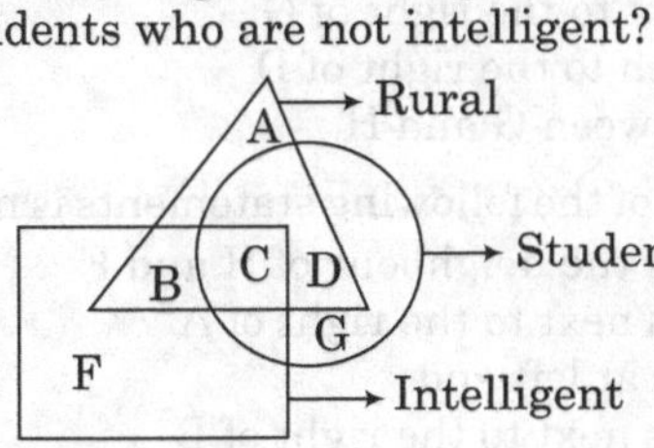

(a) D (b) A (c) B (d) G

Direction (Q. Nos. 7-8) *Each of the following questions below consists of a question and three statements numbered I, II and III given below it. You have to decide whether the data provided in the statements are sufficient to answer the questions.*

7. Who among Girish, Prashant, Kamlesh and Jayesh is the youngest?

I. Kamlesh is younger than Jayesh but older than Girish and Prashant.
II. Jayesh is the oldest.
III. Girish is older than Prashant.

(a) I and II (b) I and III
(c) II and III (d) Only I

8. Which of the following represents 'come' in a code language?

I. 'pit na ja od' means 'you may come here' in that language.
II. 'ja ta ter' means 'come and go' in that code language.
III. 'ha na pit ter' means 'you may go home' in that code language.

(a) I and II or I and III
(b) I and II
(c) All I, II and III
(d) II and III

Direction (Q. Nos. 9-10) *In these questions given a statement followed by two assumptions numbered I and II. An assumption is something supposed or taken for granted. You have to consider the statement and the following assumptions and decide which of those is/are implicit in the person's statement.*

Give answer **[SBI Associate (PO) 2015]**

(a) Only I is implicit
(b) Either I or II is implicit
(c) Only II is implicit
(d) Both I and II are implicit
(e) Neither I nor II is implicit

9. Statement Send employee XYZ for a training in UK to gain more insight into the project which he is handling at present.

Assumptions

I. Some similar training programs are available in the employee's own country as well.

II. With the present skill sets, employee XYZ is incapable of handling the project.

10. Statement Minute traces of nitrate sometimes present in cattle fodder B may be responsible for the poor health of the cattle therefore use fodder G to ensure that your cattle remain healthy.

Assumptions

I. Cattle fodder G does not contain nitrate.

II. Nitrate is toxic to all living beings.

Direction (Q. Nos. 11-12) *In the following questions, select the related figure from the given alternatives.*

11. Question Figures

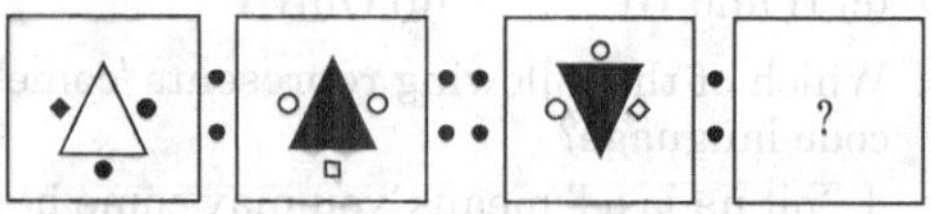

Answer Figures

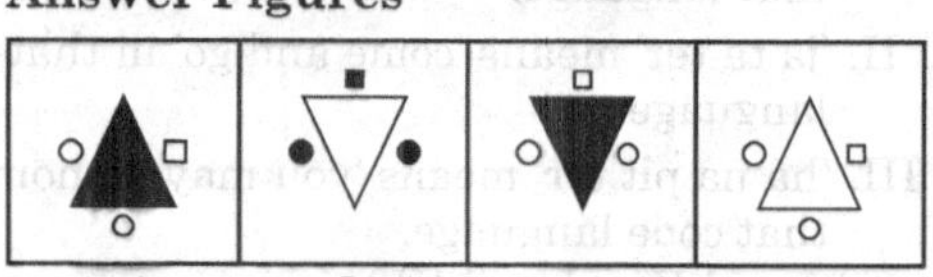

(a) (b) (c) (d)

12. Question Figures

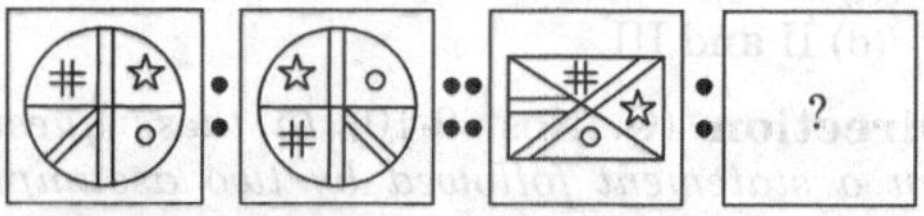

Answer Figures

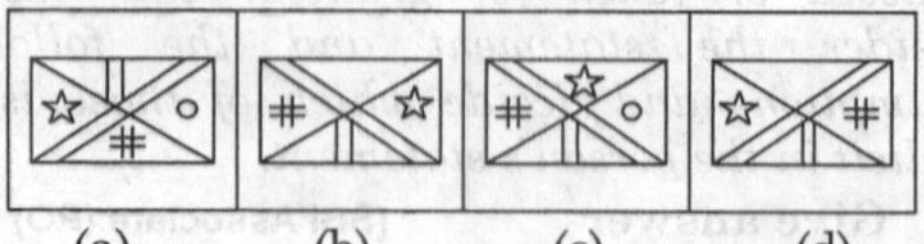

(a) (b) (c) (d)

13. A series is given with one term missing. Choose the correct alternative from the given ones that will complete the series.

Question Figures

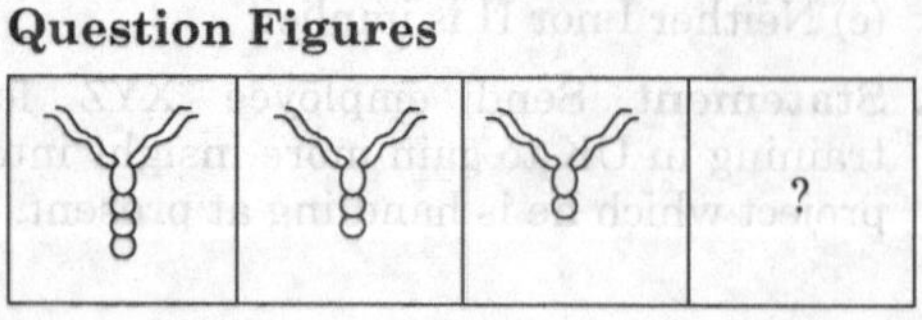

Answer Figures

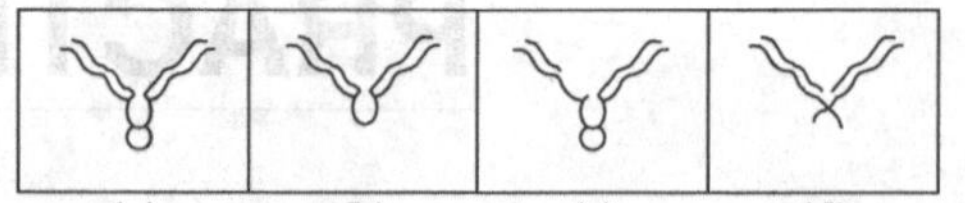

(a) (b) (c) (d)

14. Which of the answer figure is hidden/ embedded in the question figure?

Question Figure

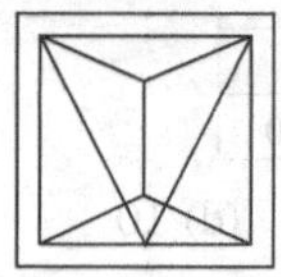

Answer Figures

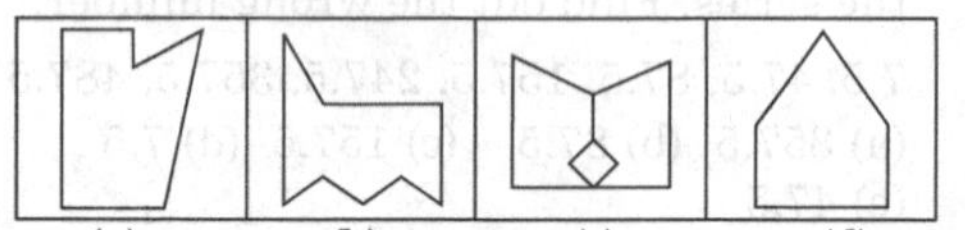

(a) (b) (c) (d)

15. The reflection of a clock in the mirror is 3 h 45 min. What is the actual time shown in the clock?

(a) 8 h 15 min (b) 9 h 30 min
(c) 8 h 45 min (d) 9 h 15 min

Direction (Q. Nos. 16-18) *Read the following information and answer the questions given below*

I. A, B, C, D, E, F, G and H are sitting in a row facing North.

II. A is fourth to the right of E.

III. H is fourth to the left of D.

IV. C and F, who are not at the ends, are neighbours of B and E, respectively.

V. H is next to the left of A and A is the neighbour of B.

16. What is the position of F?

(a) Next to the right of E
(b) Next to the right of G
(c) Sixth to the right of D
(d) Between G and H

17. Which of the following statements is not true?

(a) G is the neighbour of H and F
(b) B is next to the right of A
(c) E is at left end
(d) D is next to the right of B

18. Who is/are the neighbour (s) of D?

(a) F alone (b) C alone
(c) B and C (d) Cannot be determined

19. Mohan correctly remembers that his father's birthday is before 20th January but after 16th January whereas his sister correctly remembers that their father's birthday is after 18th January but before 23rd January. On which date in January is definitely their father's birthday?

(a) 18th (b) 19th
(c) 20th (d) Data inadequate

20. Aman is 16th from the left end in a row of boys and Vivek is 18th from the right end. Gagan is 11th from Aman towards the right and 3rd from Vivek towards the right end. How many boys are there in the row?

(a) 40 (b) 42 (c) 48 (d) 41

21. In the given question, one number is wrong in the series. Find out the wrong number. **[IBPS (PO) 2011]**

7, 12, 40, 222, 1742, 17390, 208608

(a) 7 (b) 12 (c) 40 (d) 1742
(e) 208608

22. Find the missing character from the given alternatives.

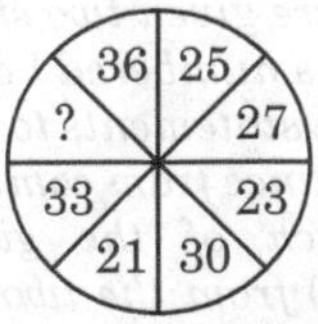

(a) 19 (b) 22 (c) 32 (d) 35

23. Find the missing term in the given sequence.
OTE, PUF, QVG, RWH, ?

(a) SYJ (b) TXI (c) SXJ (d) SXI

Direction (Q. Nos 24-25) *Study the following information carefully and answer the given questions.*

A word and number arrangement machine when given an input line of words and numbers rearranges them following a particular rule in each step. The following is an illustration of input and rearrangement.

Input day 74 night 36 25 68 all for
***Step* I** all day 74 night 36 25 68 for
***Step* II** all 74 day night 36 25 68 for
***Step* III** all 74 day 68 night 36 25 for
***Step* IV** all 74 day 68 for night 36 25
***Step* V** all 74 day 68 for 36 night 25

and Step V is the last step of the rearrangement of the above input.

As per the rules followed in the above steps, find out in each of the following questions the appropriate step for the given input.

24. **Input** war 52 and peace 43 16 now 24

How many steps will be required to complete the rearrangement?

(a) Four (b) Five
(c) Six (d) Seven
(e) None of these

25. Step III of an input is 'bond 86 goal 12 33 like high 46'

Which of the following will be Step VII?

(a) bond 86 goal 46 like 12 33 high
(b) bond 86 goal 46 high like 33 12
(c) bond 86 goal 46 high 33 like 12
(d) There will be no such step
(e) None of the above

26. A word is represented by only one set of numbers as given in any one of the alternatives. The sets of numbers given in the alternatives are represented by two classes of alphabets as in two matrices given below. The columns and rows of Matrix I are numbered from 0 to 4 and that of Matrix II are numbered from 5 to 9. A letter from these matrices can be represented first by its row and next by its column. e.g. A can be represented by 01, 20, 42 etc. and H can be represented by 65, 57, 98 etc. Similarly, you have to identify the set for the word given in the question.

FAITH **[SSC (10+2) 2014]**

Matrix I

	0	1	2	3	4
0	F	A	N	O	I
1	I	O	F	A	N
2	A	N	O	I	F
3	O	F	I	N	A
4	N	I	A	F	O

Matrix II

	5	6	7	8	9
5	S	E	H	B	T
6	H	S	E	T	B
7	B	T	S	E	H
8	E	H	T	B	S
9	T	S	E	H	B

(a) 24, 31, 10, 59, 57
(b) 12, 20, 40, 68, 65
(c) 31, 34, 23, 76, 79
(d) 43, 42, 41, 78, 89

Direction (Q. Nos 27-28) *In the following questions, select the related word/number pair from the given alternatives.*

27. 17 : 102 :: 23 : ? **[SSC (10+2) 2015]**

(a) 216 (b) 413 (c) 112 (d) 138

28. Poetry : Ballad

(a) Reptile : Snake (b) Bulb : Tube light
(c) Snake : Reptile (d) Life : Death

29. Pointing towards a photograph, Ram said, "She is the mother of my brother's son's wife's sister". How is the lady in the photograph related to Ram's brother?

(a) Sister (b) Daughter-in-law
(c) Daughter (d) None of these

Direction (Q. Nos. 30-31) *In the following questions, find the odd numbers/letters from the given alternatives.*

30. (a) D C E B (b) P N Q S T
(c) V K H G M (d) W P Z L H

[SSC (10+2) 2014]

31. (a) 77, 70, 49, 56 (b) 56, 64, 96, 48
(c) 66, 44, 23, 60 (d) 21, 28, 63, 84

Direction (Q. Nos. 32-33) *In the following questions, the symbols δ, ★, %, # and @ are used with the following meaning as illustrated below:*

'P % Q' means 'P is neither greater than nor equal to Q'.

'P δ Q' means 'P is neither smaller than nor equal to Q'.

'P @ Q' means 'P is not greater than Q'.

'P ★ Q' means 'P is not smaller than Q'.

'P # Q' means 'P is neither greater than nor smaller than Q'.

Now, in each of the following questions assuming the given statements to be true, find which of the four Conclusions I, II, III and IV given below them is/are definitely true and give your answer accordingly.

32. Statements H δ J, J # N, N @ R, R δ W

Conclusions

I. W % N II. W % H
III. R # J IV. R δ J

(a) Only I is true (b) Only II is true
(c) Only III is true (d) Only IV is true
(e) Only either III or IV is true

33. Statements B @ D, D δ F, F % M, M ★ N

Conclusions

I. B % F II. M δ D
III. N % F IV. D δ N

(a) None is true (b) Only I is true
(c) Only II is true (d) Only III is true
(e) Only IV is true

34. The ratio of the father's age to the son's age is 4 : 1. The product of their ages is 196. The ratio of their ages after 5 yr will be

(a) 3 : 1 (b) 10 : 3
(c) 11 : 4 (d) 33 : 12

35. Which one of the given responses would be a meaningful order of the following?

(i) Rivulet (ii) Ocean **[Assistant (SI) 2015]**
(iii) Tributary (iv) River
(v) Sea (vi) Rain

(a) (vi), (v), (iii), (i), (ii), (iv)
(b) (v), (vi), (i), (iii), (ii), (iv)
(c) (vi), (i), (iii), (iv), (v), (ii)
(d) (vi), (iv), (i), (iii), (v), (ii)

Direction (Q. Nos. 36-37) *In each of the questions below are given two statements followed by two conclusions numbered I and II. You have to take the two given statements to be true even if they seem to be at variance from commonly known facts and decide which of the given conclusion(s) logically follow(s) from the two given statements, disregarding commonly known facts.*

Give answer

(a) if only Conclusion I follows
(b) if only Conclusion II follows
(c) if either Conclusion I or II follows
(d) if neither Conclusion I nor II follows
(e) if both Conclusions I and II follow

36. Statements Some banks are colleges.
All colleges are schools.

Conclusions

I. Atleast some banks are schools.
II. All schools are colleges.

37. Statements Some exams are tests.
No exam is a question.

Conclusions

I. No question is a test.
II. Some tests are definitely not exams.

38. Find the missing number from the given responses

5	6	12
4	3	4
2	3	?
18	27	96

(a) 4 (b) 5 (c) 3 (d) 6

39. If in a certain code language 'TOMATO' is written as '264126', 'NET' is written as '552', then how will 'TRACTOR' be written in that language?

(a) 2813269 (b) 2913269
(c) 2193269 (d) 2913296

40. Group the given figures into three classes using each figure only once.

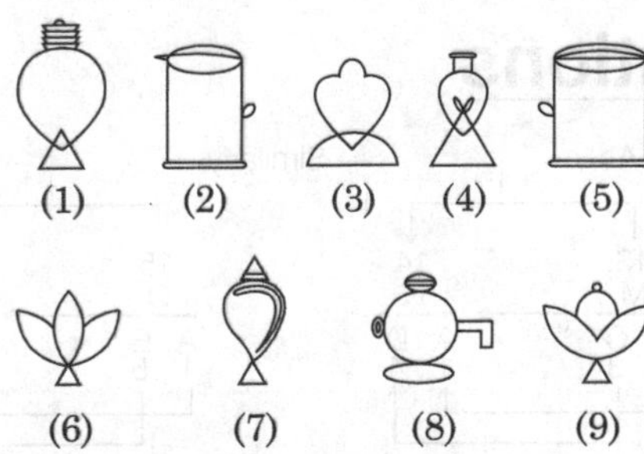

(a) 1, 4, 7
2, 5, 8
3, 6, 9

(b) 1, 4, 5
2, 6, 8
3, 7, 9

(c) 1, 7, 9
3, 6, 8
2, 4, 6

(d) 1, 6, 9
2, 5, 8
3, 4, 7

41. If 'MACHINE' is coded as 19-7-9-14-15-20-11, then how will you code 'DANGER' in the same code?

(a) 11-7-20-16-11-24 (b) 13-7-20-9-11-25
(c) 10-7-20-13-11-24 (d) 13-7-20-10-11-25

42. Name a single letter that can be suffixed to the following words to form new words? **[SSC (CGL) 2015]**

HAT BAR BAT PIN BATH

(a) A (b) E (c) B (d) D

43. Radha, Sheela, Mahima and Seeta are sitting around a rectangular table. Radha is sitting to the right of Sheela. Mahima is sitting to the left of Seeta. Which of the following pair is sitting opposite each other?

(a) Sheela-Seeta
(b) Radha-Seeta
(c) Radha-Sheela
(d) Mahima-Radha

Direction (Q. Nos. 44-46) *Read the information carefully to answer these questions.* **[UPSC (CSAT) 2012]**

Guest lectures on five subjects *viz.* Economics, History, Statistics, English and Mathematics have to be arranged in a week from Monday to Friday. Only one lecture can be arranged on each day. Economics cannot be scheduled on Tuesday. Guest faculty for History is available only on Tuesday. Mathematics lecture has to be scheduled immediately after the day of Economics lecture. English lecture has to be scheduled immediately before the day of Economics lecture.

44. Which lecture is scheduled on Monday?

(a) History (b) Economics
(c) Mathematics (d) Statistics

45. Which lecture is scheduled between Statistics and English?

(a) Economics (b) History
(c) Mathematics (d) No lecture

46. Which lecture is the last one in the week?

(a) History (b) English
(c) Mathematics (d) Economics

Direction (Q. Nos. 47-48) *Study the following information carefully and answer the questions that follow.*

I. A, B, C, D, E, F and G are seven persons wearing a different colour shirt-white, red, black, green, yellow, blue and violet and a different colour trousers blue, red, white, black, cream, yellow and indigo. The persons, colour of the shirt and colour of the trousers above are not necessarily in the same order. No person is wearing shirt and trousers of same colour.

II. B is wearing red colour shirt and is not wearing cream or yellow colour trousers. D is wearing green colour shirt and indigo colour trousers. Colour of A's shirt and F's trousers is same. Colour of E's shirt and C's trousers is same. G is wearing blue trousers. F is not wearing any yellow dress. A is not wearing a white shirt. Red and blue is not the combination of shirt and trousers of any of the persons.

47. Who wears violet colour shirt?
(a) C
(b) F
(c) Either C or F
(d) Data inadequate
(e) None of the above

48. What is the colour of B's trousers?
(a) White (b) Indigo
(c) Red (d) Data inadequate
(e) None of the above

49. There are two statements labelled as Assertion (A) and Reason (R). Read the assertion carefully and decide which of the reason logically follows for pursing.

Assertion (A) We feel calder on mountains than on plains.

Reason (R) Temperature decreases with altitude.
(a) if both 'A' and 'R' are true and 'R' is the correct explanation of 'A'
(b) if both 'A' and 'R' are true but 'R' is not the correct explanation of 'A'
(c) if 'A' is true but 'R' is false
(d) if both 'A' and 'R' are false

50. Anoop starts walking towards South. After walking 15 m he turns towards North. After walking 20 m, he turns towards East and walks 10 m. He, then turns towards South and walks 5 m. How far is he from his original position in which direction?
(a) 10 m, North (b) 10 m, South
(c) 10 m, West (d) 10 m, East

Hints and Solutions

1. (*b*) The pattern is as follows

$$9 \times 5 \times 3 = 135$$
$$5 \times 7 \times 4 = 140$$

Similarly, $6 \times ? \times 5 = 150 \; ? = \frac{150}{30} \Rightarrow ? = 5$

Hence, number 5 will come in place of question mark.

2. (*e*) The pattern is as follows

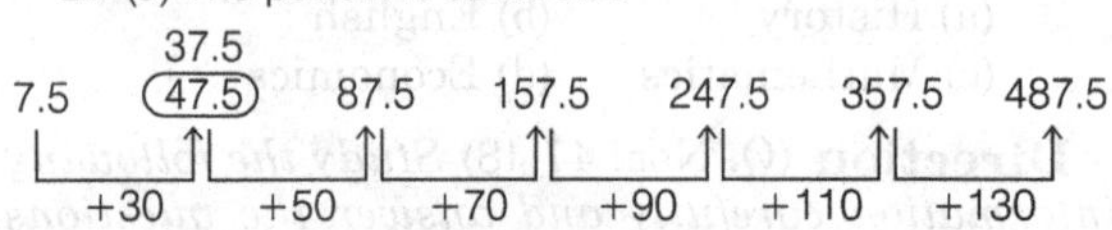

Hence, number 47.5 is wrong and should be replaced by 37.5.

3. (*b*) Given, 40 B 8 T 6 M 3 K 4 = ?

$\Rightarrow \quad 40 \div 8 - 6 + 3 \times 4 = ?$

$\Rightarrow \quad 5 - 6 + 12 = ? \Rightarrow 17 - 6 = ?$

$\therefore \quad ? = 11$

4. (*c*) According to the given information,

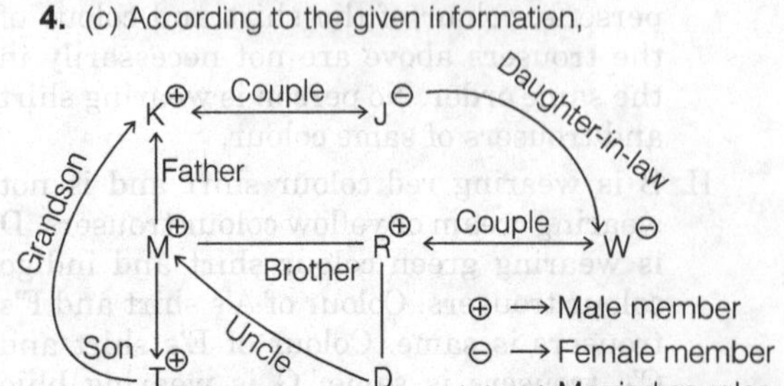

From the above generation diagram, we see that M is uncle of D or D is nephew or niece of M because the gender of D is not clear.

5. (*a*) As, Similarly

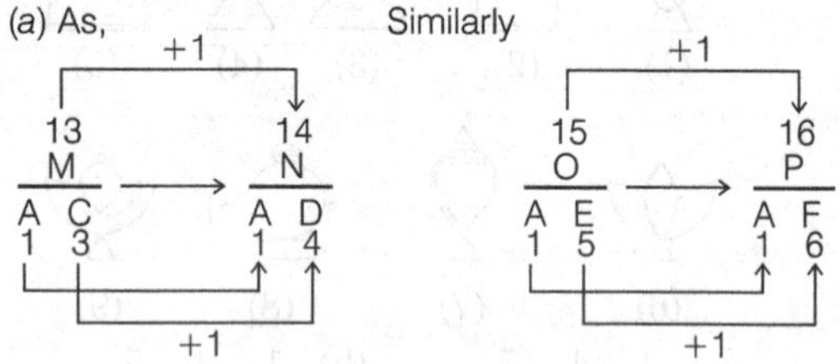

$\therefore \quad ? = \frac{P}{AF}$

6. (*a*) Region D represents rural students who are not intelligent.

7. (*b*) From Statement I, Jayesh > Kamlesh > Girish/ Prashant

Clearly, Statement I alone is insufficient.

From Statement III, Girish > Prashant

Clearly, Statement III alone is insufficient.

From both Statements I and III,

Jayesh > Kamlesh > Girish > Prashant

Clearly, Prashant is the youngest.

So, Statements I and III are required to answer the question.

8. (*b*) From Statements I and II,

pit na ja od = you may come here
ja ta ter = come and go

$\therefore$ come = ja

From Statements II and III,

ja ta ter = come and go
ha na pit ter = you may go home

go = ter

∴ come = ja/ter

From Statements I and III,

pit na ja od = you may come here

ha na pit ter = you may go home

you may = na pit

∴ come = ja/od

Clearly, Statements I and II are sufficient to find the answer.

9. (*d*) From given statement, it is clear that at present skill sets, employee XYZ is feeling uncomfortable of handling the project and similar training programme are available in his own country as well, but it is also possible that this training programme is not related to his present project. So, we can say that in statement both assumptions I and II are implicit.

10. (*c*) From given statement, it is clear that by using fodder G cattle will be remain healthy, but it is not clear that cattle fodder G does not contain nitrate.

It is true that nitrate is toxic to all living beings.

So, only assumption II is implicit.

11. (*b*) Clearly, from figure I to figure II, the shaded designs becomes unshaded and *vice-versa* and other three small designs move in anti-clockwise and the quadrilateral rotates through 45°.

12. (*c*) Clearly, from figure I to figure II, the sectors of given design move in anti-clockwise direction.

13. (*b*) In each subsequent figure, one circle from the lower side is deleted. So, option (b) figure will complete the series.

14. (*c*) Clearly, the answer figure (c) is question figure as shown below

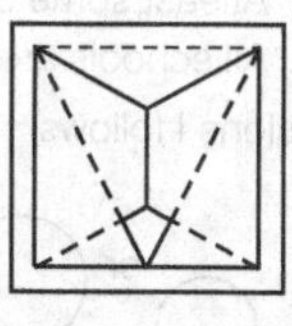

15. (*a*) The actual time shown is 12 : 00-03 : 45 h ≘ 8h 15 min.

Solution (Q. Nos. 16-18) Arrangement according to the question is as follows

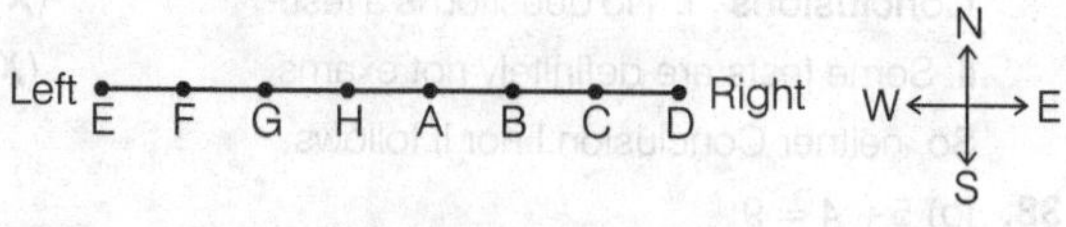

16. (*a*) F is next to the right of E.

17. (*d*) D is next to the right of B is not true. Hence, statement (d) is not true.

18. (*b*) C alone is the neighbour of D.

19. (*b*) Days by Mohan, [17th, 18th or 19th] January.

Days by sister, [19th, 20th, 21st or 22nd] January.

Required day is 19th January as it is common in both the groups.

20. (*d*) Vivek is 18th from the right end and Gagan is third to the right of Vivek. So, Gagan is 15th from the right end. There are 15 boys to the left of Aman, 10 boys between Aman and Gagan and 14 boys to the right of Gagan

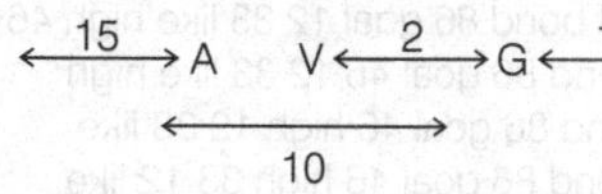

∴ Number of boys in the row

$= 15 + 1 + 10 + 1 + 14 = 41.$

21. (*d*) The pattern is as follows

$$7 \times 2 - (2 \times 1) = 12$$
$$12 \times 4 - (4 \times 2) = 40$$
$$40 \times 6 - (6 \times 3) = 222$$
$$222 \times 8 - (8 \times 4) = 1742 = 1744$$
$$1744 \times 10 - (10 \times 5) = 17390$$
$$17390 \times 12 - (12 \times 6) = 208608$$

Hence, number 1742 is wrong and should be replaced by 1744.

22. (*a*) Starting from 27 and moving clockwise, the number alternate segments form the series, 27, 30, 33, 36, numbers in the remaining segments moving anti-clockwise form the series as shown below.

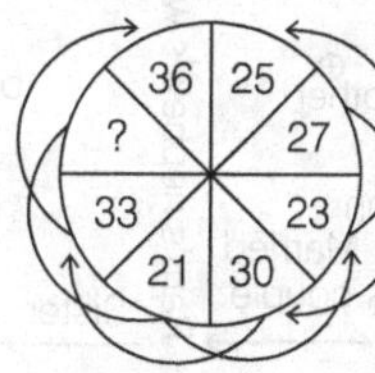

?, 21, 23, 25 or 21, 23, 25, ?

? = 19 or 27.

23. (*d*) The pattern is as follows

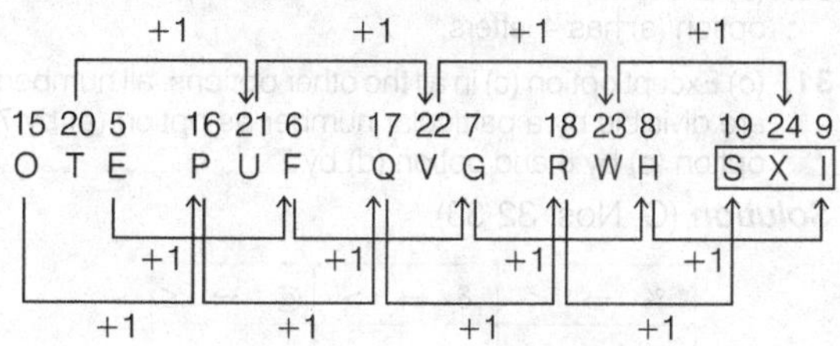

? = SXI

Solution (Q. Nos. 24-25) After careful analysis of the given input and various steps of rearrangement it is evident that in the first step one word is rearranged and in the second step one number is rearranged. These two steps are continued alternately till all the words get arranged in alphabetical order and all the numbers get arranged in descending order.

24. (c) **Input** war 52 and peace 43 16 now 24
Step I and war 52 peace 43 16 now 24
Step II and 52 war peace 43 16 now 24
Step III and 52 now war peace 43 16 24
Step IV and 52 now 43 war peace 16 24
Step V and 52 now 43 peace war 16 24
Step VI and 52 now 43 peace 24 war 16

25. (c) **Step III** bond 86 goal 12 33 like high 46
Step IV bond 86 goal 46 12 33 like high
Step V bond 86 goal 46 high 12 33 like
Step VI bond 86 goal 46 high 33 12 like
Step VII bond 86 goal 46 high 33 like 12

26. (c)
F ⇒ 00, 12, 24, [31], 43
A ⇒ 01, 13, 20, [34], 42
I ⇒ 04, 10, [23], 32, 41
T ⇒ 59, 68, [76], 87, 95
H ⇒ 57, 65, [79], 86, 95
FAITH ⇒ 31, 34, 23, 76, 79

27. (d) As, $17 \times 6 = 102$
Similarly, $23 \times 6 = 138$
So, option (d) is correct answer.

28. (a) 'Ballad' is a type of poem, in the same way as 'Snake' is a type of 'Reptile'.

29. (d) Let us draw the family diagram

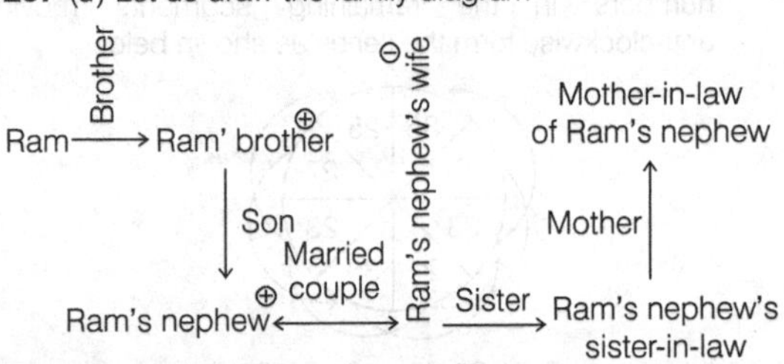

Hence, it is clear that the lady in the photograph is mother-in-law of Ram's brother's son.

30. (a) Except option (a), all other have 5 letters where as option (a) has 4 letters.

31. (c) Except option (c) in all the other options, all numbers are divisible by a particular number as option (a) by 7, option (b) by 8 and option (d) by 7.

Solution (Q. Nos. 32-33)

% ⇒ <	δ ⇒ >	@ ⇒ ≤
★ ⇒ ≥	# ⇒ =	

32. (e) **Statements** $H \delta J \Rightarrow H > J$, $J \# N \Rightarrow J = N$
$N @ R \Rightarrow N \le R$, $R \delta W \Rightarrow R > W$
Therefore, $H > J = N \le R > W$
Conclusions I. $W \% N \Rightarrow W < N$ (Not True)
II. $W \% H \Rightarrow W < H$ (Not True)
III. $R \# J \Rightarrow R = J$ (Can be True)
IV. $R \delta J \Rightarrow R > J$ (Can be True)
R is either greater than or equal to J. Therefore, either III or IV is true.

33. (a) Statements $B @ D \Rightarrow B \le D$, $D \delta F \Rightarrow D > F$
$F \% M \Rightarrow F < M$, M ★ N ⇒ $M \ge N$
Therefore, $B \le D > F < M \ge N$
Conclusions I. $B \% F \Rightarrow B < F$ (Not True)
II. $M \delta D \Rightarrow M > D$ (Not True)
III. $N \% F \Rightarrow N < F$ (Not True)
IV. $D \delta N \Rightarrow D > N$ (Not True)
So, none is true.

34. (c) Let the ages of father and son be 4x yr and x yr, respectively.
Now, $4x \times x = 196$
$4x^2 = 196$
$\Rightarrow x^2 = 49$
$\Rightarrow x = 7$ yr
Now, required ratio $= \frac{(4 \times 7 + 5)}{(7 + 5)} = \frac{33}{12} = \frac{11}{4} = 11 : 4$

35. (c) Logical order of words
Rain → Rivulet → Tributory → River → Sea → Ocean
(vi) (i) (iii) (iv) (v) (ii)

36. (a)

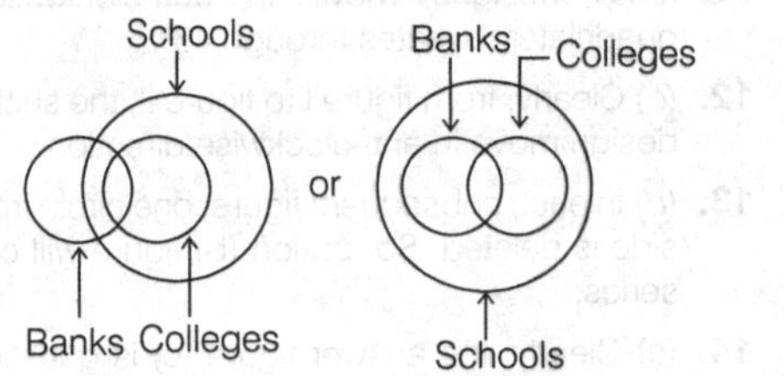

Conclusions I. Atleast some banks are schools. (✔)
II. All schools are colleges. (✗)
So, only Conclusions I follows.

37. (d)

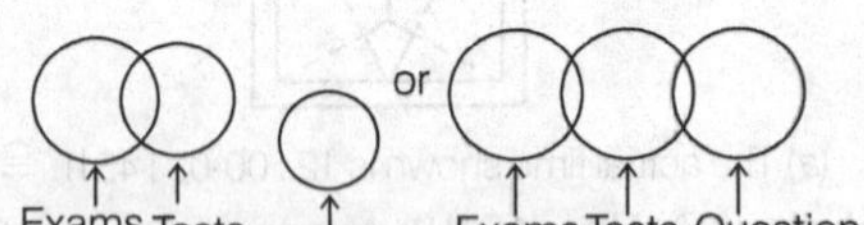

Conclusions I. No question is a test. (✗)
II. Some tests are definitely not exams. (✗)
So, neither Conclusion I nor II follows.

38. (d) $5 + 4 = 9$
and $9 \times 2 = 18$
$6 + 3 = 9$
and $9 \times 3 = 27$
$12 + 4 = 16$
and $? = \frac{96}{16} = 6$

39. (*b*) Each letter is coded with the digits sum of its letter's position in English alphabet. Let us see

As,

T O M A T O ⟶ (2 + 0)(1 + 5)(1 + 3)(0 + 1)(2 + 0)(1 + 5) = 2 6 4 1 2 6

and

N E T ⟶ (1 + 4)(0 + 5)(2 + 0) = 5 5 2

Similarly,

T R A C T O R ⟶ (2 + 0)(1 + 8)(0 + 1)(0 + 3)(2 + 0)(1 + 5)(1 + 8) = 2 9 1 3 2 6 9

∴ TRACTOR ⇒ 2913269

40. (*a*) Figures 1, 4 and 7; 3, 6 and 9; 2, 5 and 8 are similar.

41. (*c*) As,

M (13)	+6 ⟶	19
A (1)	+6 ⟶	7
C (3)	+6 ⟶	9
H (8)	+6 ⟶	14
I (9)	+6 ⟶	15
N (14)	+6 ⟶	20
E (5)	+6 ⟶	11

Similarly,

D (4)	+6 ⟶	10
A (1)	+6 ⟶	7
N (14)	+6 ⟶	20
G (7)	+6 ⟶	13
E (5)	+6 ⟶	11
R (18)	+6 ⟶	24

∴ DANGER ⇒ 10-7-20-13-11-24

42. (*b*) Letter E is suffixed to the following words

HAT + E → HATE, BAR + E → BARE

BAT + E → BATE, PIN + E → PINE

BATH + E → BATHE

43. (*b*) According to the given information, the arrangement is as following :

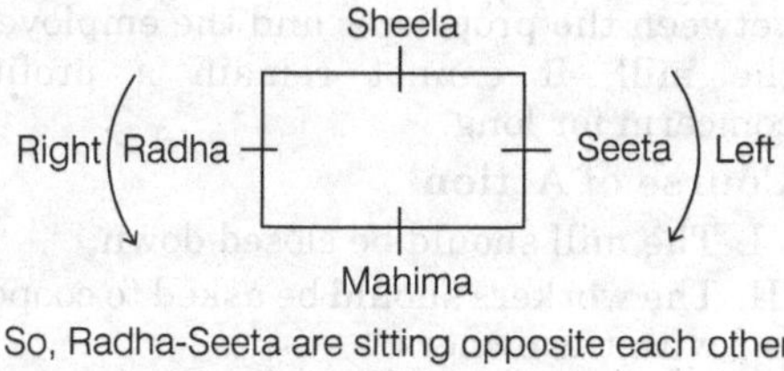

So, Radha-Seeta are sitting opposite each other.

Solution (Q. Nos. 44-46) Information given in the passage can be arranged in the tabular form as shown in below

Days	Monday	Tuesday	Wednesday	Thursday	Friday
Subject	Statistics	History	English	Economics	Mathematics

44. (*d*) Statistics lecture is scheduled on Monday.

45. (*b*) From the table above, History is scheduled between Statistics and English.

46. (*c*) Mathematics lecture is scheduled on the last day of the week .

Solution (Q. Nos. 47-48) On the basis of given information, we get the following table.

Person	A	B	C	D	E	F	G
Colour of Shirt	Black	Red	White/ Violet	Green	Yellow	Violet/ White	Blue
Colour of Trousers	Red	White	Yellow	Indigo	Blue	Black	Cream

47. (c) Either C or F wears Violet colour shirt.

48. (*a*) The colour of B's trousers is White.

49. (*a*) Both A and R are true and R is the correct explantaion of A. Above the sea level, temperature decreases with an increase in altitude which makes mountain peaks colder.

50. (*d*) According to the question, the direction diagram is as follows

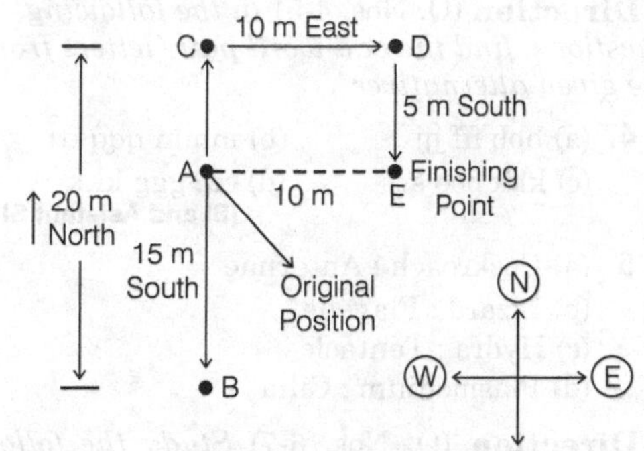

A = Original position, E = Finishing point

BC = 20, AB = 15m,

AC = ED = 5m,

CD = AE = 10m

Clearly, at finishing point E, Anoop is 10 m East from original position A.

PRACTICE SET 14

1. Rama travels a distance of 5 km from a place A towards North, turns left and walks 3 km, again turns right and walks 2 km. Finally he turns right and walks 3 km to reach the place B. What is the distance between A and B?

(a) 7 km (b) 13 km (c) 2 km (d) 10 km

2. Select the related set of numbers from the given alternatives.

(4268, 8426, 8624)

(a) (3567, 7553, 4642)
(b) (6824, 2468, 4862)
(c) (5687, 7691, 2525)
(d) (4523, 5223, 4361)

3. Ayush remembers that Sanjay's birthday is certainly after January 12 but not later than 16th January. If Mehar remembers that Sanjay's birthday is before 17th of Jan but not before 13th Jan. On which of the following day was Sanjay's birthday?

(a) 14 th (b) 15 th
(c) 16 th (d) Either 14 th or 15 th

Direction (Q. Nos. 4-5) *In the following questions, find the odd word pair/letters from the given alternatives.*

4. (a) bbb fff jjj (b) mmm qqq ttt
(c) kkk ooo sss (d) ccc ggg kkk

[SI and Asistant SI 2015]

5. (a) Cockroach : Anternae
(b) Lizard : Flagella
(c) Hydra : Tentacles
(d) Plasmodium : Cilia

Direction (Q. Nos. 6-7) *Study the following information carefully and answer the given questions.*

A word and number arrangement machine when given an input line of words and numbers rearranges them following a particular rule in each step. The following is an illustration of input and rearrangement.

Input 96 gain 63 forest 38 78 deep house
***Step* I** deep 96 gain 63 forest 38 78 house
***Step* II** deep 38 96 gain 63 forest 78 house
***Step* III** deep 38 forest gain 96 63 78 house
***Step* IV** deep 38 forest 63 gain 96 78 house
***Step* V** deep 38 forest 63 gain 78 96 house
***Step* VI** deep 38 forest 63 gain 78 house 96

and Step VI is the last step of the rearrangement of the above input.

As per the rules followed in the above steps, find out in each of the following questions the appropriate step for the given input.

6. Input train 59 47 25 over burden 63 sky
Which of the following steps will be the last but one?

(a) VI (b) V (c) IV (d) VII
(e) III

7. Input service 46 58 96 over there desk 15
Which of the following will be Step VI?

(a) desk 15 over service 46 58 96 there
(b) desk 15 over 46 service there 58 96
(c) desk 15 over 46 service 58 there 96
(d) desk 15 over 46 service 58 96 there
(e) There will be no such step

8. In the question below is given a statement followed by three course of a number I, II and III. A course of action is a step of administrative decision to be taken for improvement, follow-up further action in regard to the problem, policy, etc. On the basis of information given in the statement, you have assume everything in the statement to be true and then decide which of the three given suggested courses of action logically follows worth pursuing. Then, decide which of the alternatives (a), (b), (c), (d) or (e) is correct.

Statement Without the active cooperation between the proprietor and the employees of the mill, it cannot remain a profitable comcerm for long.

Course of Action

I. The mill should be closed down.
II. The workers should be asked to cooperate with the owners.
III. The owner should be asked to cooperate with the employees.

(a) Both I and II follow
(b) None follows
(c) All follow
(d) Both II and III follow

9. Arrange the following words according to the dictionary.

(i) Inventory (ii) Involuntary
(iii) Invisible (iv) Invariable
(v) Investigate

(a) (iv), (ii), (v), (iii), (i)
(b) (iv), (v), (i), (iii), (ii)
(c) (ii), (v), (iv), (i), (iii)
(d) (iv), (i), (v), (iii), (ii)

10. In the given question, a word is represented by only one set of numbers are given in anyone of the alternatives. The sets of numbers given in the alternatives are represented by two classes of alphabets as in the two given matrices. The columns and rows of Matrix I are numbered from 0 to 4 and those of Matrix II from 5 to 9. A letter from these matrices can be represent first by its row and the column number e.g. in the matrices can be represented by 03, 12 etc., M can be represented by 58, 67 etc. Similarly you have to identify the correct set for the word given in each question.

Matrix I

	0	1	2	3	4
0	D	O	B	A	I
1	O	B	A	I	D
2	B	A	I	D	O
3	A	I	D	O	B
4	I	D	O	B	A

Matrix II

	5	6	7	8	9
5	W	N	R	M	L
6	N	R	M	L	W
7	R	M	L	W	N
8	M	L	W	N	R
9	L	W	N	R	M

DOWN

(a) 41, 66, 23, 55 (b) 82, 75, 44, 76
(c) 32, 24, 87, 88 (d) 14, 89, 12, 78

11. In this question, one number is wrong in the series. Find out the wrong number.

1236, 2346, 3456, 4566, 5686

(a) 1236 (b) 3456
(c) 4566 (d) 5686
(e) None of these

12. Find the missing term in the given sequence.

NATURAL, NATURA, ATURA, ?

(a) ATUR (b) TURA
(c) RUTA (d) ARUT

13. Which one of the following diagrams represents the correct relationship among Lion, Fox and Carnivorous? **[SSC (10+2) 2014]**

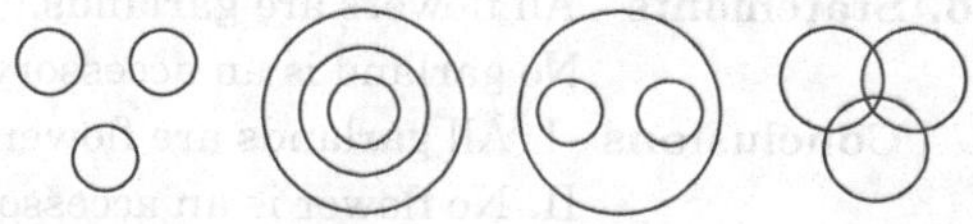

(a) (b) (c) (d)

Direction (Q. Nos. 14-18) *In the following questions, two/three statements followed by two conclusions I and II have been given. You have to take the given statements to be true even if they seem to be at variance from the commonly known facts and then decide which of the given conclusions logically follows from the given statements disregarding commonly known facts.*
[IBPS RRB (Office Assistant) 2015]

Give answer

(a) if neither Conclusion I nor II is true
(b) if both Conclusions I and II are true
(c) if either Conclusion I or II is true
(d) if only Conclusion II is true
(e) if only Conclusion I is true

14. Statements All roses are lotuses.
Some lotuses are orchids.
No orchid is a daisy.
Conclusions I. All roses are orchids.
II. No daisy is a lotus.

15. Statements Some huts are canopies.
Some canopies are tents.
Conclusions I. No tent is a hut.
II. At least some tents are huts.

16. Statements Some salads are vegetables.
All vegetables are fruits.
All fruits are juices.
Conclusions I. All vegetables are juices.
II. Some salads are definitely not fruits.

17. Statements No stem is a root.
Some roots are trunks.
All trunks are woods.

Conclusions I. All trunks can never be stems.
II. At least some roots are woods.

18. Statements All flowers are garlands.
No garland is an accessory.

Conclusions I. All garlands are flowers.
II. No flower is an accessory.

19. If in a certain code language 'ROPE' is written as '% 5 7 $', 'DOUBT' is written as '3 5 # 8 ★', and 'LIVE' is written as '@ 2 4 $', then how will 'TROUBLE' be written in that language?

(a) ★ % 5 $ 8 @ $
(b) ★ % # 58 @ $
(c) ★ % 5 # 8 @ 4
(d) None of the above

20. Group the given figures into three classes using each figure only once.

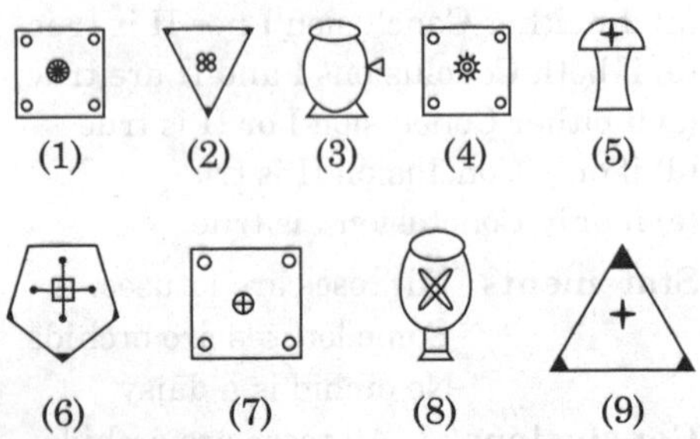

(a) 1, 4, 7
3, 6, 9
2, 5, 8
(b) 1, 4, 7
2, 6, 9
3, 5, 8
(c) 1, 6, 9
2, 4, 7
3, 5, 8
(d) 1, 5, 7
2, 6, 9
3, 4, 8

21. If 'lion' is called 'fish', 'fish' is called 'parrot', 'parrot' is called 'rat', 'rat' is called 'cat' and 'cat' is called 'tiger', then which of the following is a bird?

(a) Fish
(b) Parrot
(c) Rat
(d) Tiger

Direction (Q. Nos. 22-24) *Read the information given below and answer the questions that follow.*

I. Six friends Rahul, Kabeer, Anup, Raghu, Amit and Alok were engineering graduates. All six of them were placed in six different companies and were posted in six different locations namely Tisco-Jamshedpur, Telco-Pune, Wipro-Bengaluru, HCL-Noida, Mecon-Ranchi and Usha Martin- Kolkata. Each of them has their personal e-mail id's with different email providers i.e. gmail, Indiatimes, Rediffmail, Yahoo, Hotmail, Sancharnet though not necessarily in the same order.
II. The one having e-mail account with Sancharnet works in Noida and the one having an email account with Indiatimes works for Tisco.
III. Amit does not stay in Bengaluru and does not work for Mecon, the one who works for Mecon has an email id with gmail.
IV. Rahul has an email id with Rediffmail and works at Pune.
V. Alok does not work for Mecon and the one who works for Wipro does not have an e-mail account with Yahoo.
VI. Kabeer is posted in Kolkata and does not have an account with Hotmail.
VII. Neither Alok nor Raghu work in Noida.
VIII. The one who is posted in Ranchi has an e-mail id which is not an account of Rediffmail or Hotmail.
IX. Anup is posted in Jamshedpur.

22. The man who works in Wipro has an email account with

(a) Sancharnet (b) Yahoo
(c) Rediffmail (d) None of these

23. Which of the following email, place of posting and person combination is correct?

(a) Kabeer-Kolkata-Rediffmail
(b) Alok-Bengaluru-Indiatimes
(c) Amit-Noida-Yahoo
(d) Raghu-Ranchi-Gmail

24. Which of the following is true?

(a) Amit is posted at Ranchi
(b) Raghu is posted at Jamshedpur
(c) Kabeer has an email id with Yahoo
(d) Rahul has an email id with Indiatimes

25. Four friends A, B, C, D contribute money to a pool. A Contributes double the amount C contributes and B contributes half the amount A contributes. D contributes half the amount of B. Which two are contributing equal amount?

(a) B , D (b) A , D
(c) A , B (d) B , C

26. Find the digit at the face opposite to the face having digit 5 in the given dice

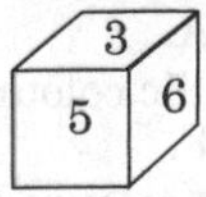

(a) 1 (b) 2
(c) 1/4 (d) 1/2/4

27. A Statement is given followed by three Conclusions I, II and III. You have to consider the statement to be true even if it seems to be at variance from commonly known facts. You have to decide which of the given conclusions, if any, follows from the given statement.

Statement Comic books contain pictures.

Conclusions

I. All books contain pictures.
II. Books may or may not contain pictures.
III. Books other than the comic books do not contain pictures.

(a) Only Conclusion I follows
(b) Only Conclusion II follows
(c) Only Conclusion III follows
(d) None of the conclusions follows

28. A clock strikes 12 taking 48 s. In order to strike 3 at the same rate, the time taken is

(a) 24 s
(b) 12 s
(c) $8\frac{8}{11}$ s
(d) $8\frac{2}{11}$ s

29. How many pairs of letters are there in these word which have as many letters between them as in the English alphabet?

CREDIBLE

(a) None
(b) One
(c) Two
(d) More than three

30. A train runs 120 km in West direction, 30 km in South direction and then 90 km in East direction before reaching the station. In which direction is the station from the train's starting point? **[MAT 2014]**

(a) South-West (b) North-West
(c) South-East (d) South

31. From the given answer figures, select the one in which the question figure is hidden/embedded.

Question Figure

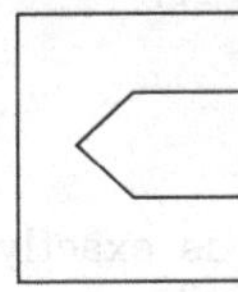

Answer Figures

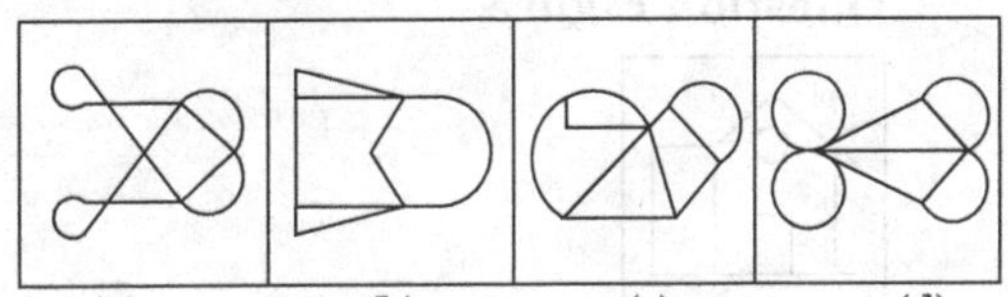

(a) (b) (c) (d)

32. If a mirror is placed on the line AB, then which of the answer figures is the right image of the given figure? **[SSC Multitasking 2014]**

Question Figure

Answer Figures

(a) (b) (c) (d)

33. Find the odd figure from the given alternatives.

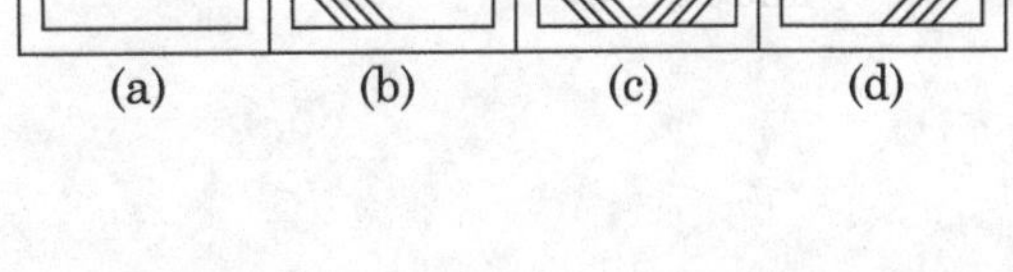

(a) (b) (c) (d)

34. In the given question, there are two statements labelled as Assertion (A) and Reason (R).

Assertion (A) The colour of light with the shortest wavelength is violet.

Reason (R) One can notice this colour of light on one end of the rainbow which has seven colours of different wavelengths.

(a) if both 'A' and 'R' is the correct explanation of 'A'
(b) if both 'A' and 'R' are true but 'R' is not the correct explanation of 'A'.
(c) if 'A' is true but 'R' is false
(d) if 'A' is false but 'R' is true
(e) if both 'A' and 'R' are false

35. Which of the answer figure is exactly the water image of the given figure?

Question Figure

Answer Figures

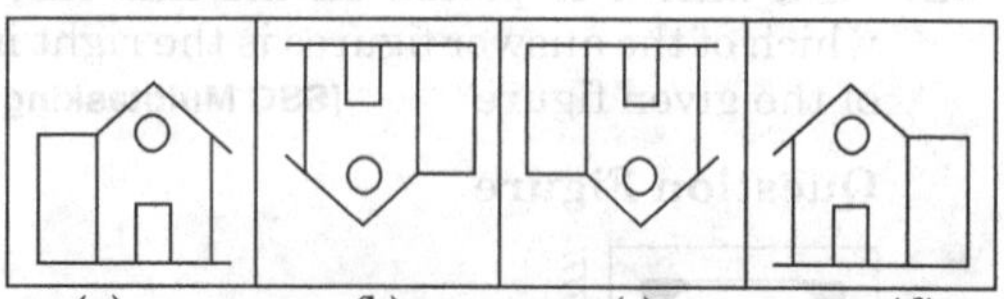

(a) (b) (c) (d)

36. A word is given, followed by four other words, one of which can be formed by using the letters of given word, then find the word.

MEASUREMENT

(a) ASSURE (b) MANTLE
(c) MASTER (d) SUMMIT

37. Nightingale : Warble : : Frog : ? **[UPPSC (RO) 2014]**

(a) Yell (b) Crackle
(c) Squeak (d) Croak

Direction (Q. Nos. 38-39) *Answer the following questions based on the statements given below.* **[CLAT 2013]**

I. There are 3 poles on each side of the road.
II. These six poles are labelled A, B, C, D, E and F.
III. The poles are different colours namely—Golden, Silver, Metallic, Black, Bronze and White.
IV. The poles are of different heights.
V. E, the tallest pole, is exactly opposite to the golden coloured pole.
VI. The shortest pole is exactly opposite to the metallic coloured pole.
VII. F, the black coloured pole, is located between A and D.
VIII. C, the bronze coloured pole, is exactly opposite to A.
IX. B, the metallic coloured pole, is exactly opposite to F.
X. A, the white coloured pole, is taller than C but shorter than D and B.

38. Which is the second tallest pole?

(a) A
(b) D
(c) B
(d) None of the above

39. Which is the colour of the tallest pole?

(a) Golden (b) Silver
(c) Bronze (d) None of these

Direction (Q. Nos. 40-42) *Study the following information carefully to answer the given questions*

I. Eight friends A, B, C, D, E, F, G and H are seated in a circle facing the centre.
II. D is between B and G and F is between A and H.
III. E is second to the right of A.

40. Which of the following is A's position?

(a) Left of F
(b) Right of F
(c) Between E and F
(d) Cannot be determined

41. Which of the following information is not required to ascertain the position of C?

(a) I
(b) Either II or III
(c) III
(d) All required

42. Which of the following is C's position?

(a) Between E ana F
(b) Between G and E
(c) Second to the left of B
(d) None of the above

43. Find the missing character from the given alternatives.

372	580	918
235	405	735
274	350	?

(a) 432 (b) 366
(c) 345 (d) 482

44. What day of week was it on 5th November 1987, if it was Monday on 4th April, 1988?
(a) Wednesday
(b) Friday
(c) Thursday
(d) Saturday

45. Which of the following interchange of signs or numbers would make the given equation correct?

$$(18 \div 9) + 3 \times 5 = 45$$

(a) $\times$ and $\div$ (b) + and $\div$
(c) 18 and 5 (d) 3 and 9

46. In a family of five persons, Dinesh is Jairam's son and Gopal's brother while Meeta is Gopal's mother and Jayanti's daughter. If there are no step brothers or half brothers in the family, then which of the following statements is true? **[IB (ACIO) 2012]**
(a) Jayanti is Dinesh's mother
(b) Meeta is Dinesh's mother
(c) Jayanti is Jairam's grandmother
(d) All of the above

47. It was Shriram's and Sreedevi's 12th wedding anniversary. Shriram said, 'when we got married, Sreedevi was 3/4th of my age, but now she is 5/6th of my age'. What actually are their present ages?
(a) Shriram 38 yr, Sreedevi 32 yr
(b) Shriram 36 yr, Sreedevi 30 yr
(c) Shriram 30 yr, Sreedevi 24 yr
(d) Shriram 40 yr, Sreedevi 34 yr

Direction (Q. Nos. 48-49) *In the following questions, the symbols δ, ★, %, @ and # are used with the following meaning as illustrated below.*

'A % B' means 'A is neither greater than nor equal to B'.

'A # B' means 'A is neither smaller than nor equal to B'.

'A δ B' means 'A is neither smaller than nor greater than B'.

'A ★ B' means 'A is not smaller than B'.

'A @ B' means 'A is not greater than B'.

Now in each of the following questions assuming the given statements to be true, find which of the three Conclusions I, II and III given them is/are definitely true and give your answer accordingly.

48. Statements M # R, R%P, P δ J
Conclusions I. M # P
II. J # R
III. J % M
(a) None is true (b) Only I is true
(c) Only II is true (d) Only III is true
(e) Only II and III are true

49. Statements P ★ D, D # Q, Q @ R
Conclusions I. Q % P
II. R # D
III. P # D
(a) None is true (b) Only I is true
(c) Only II is true (d) Only III is true
(e) None of the above

50. How many triangles are there in the following figure?

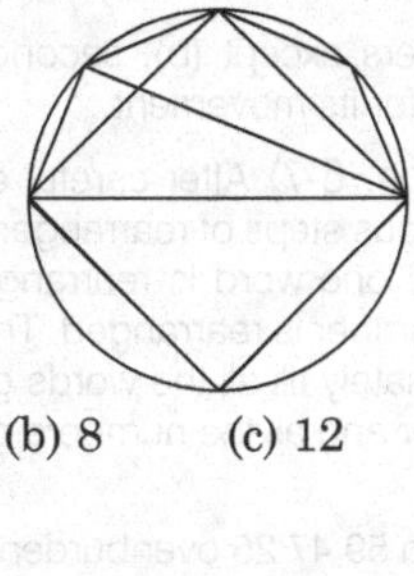

(a) 10 (b) 8 (c) 12 (d) 11

Hints and Solutions

1. (*a*) According to the question, the direction diagram is as follows

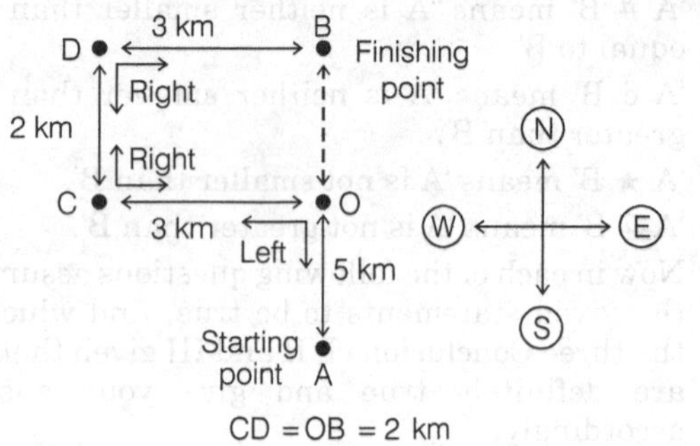

CD = OB = 2 km

OC = BD = 3 km

AO = 5 km

∴ Required distance, AB = AO + OB = 5 + 2 = 7 km

2. (*b*) Each set is made of the digits 2, 4, 6, 8.

3. (*d*) Days by Ayush, [13, [14, 15]] in January

Days by Mehar, [[14, 15], 16] in January

Clearly, 14th and 15th January are common in both the groups.

Hence, the correct answer is either 14th of 15 th January.

4. (*b*)

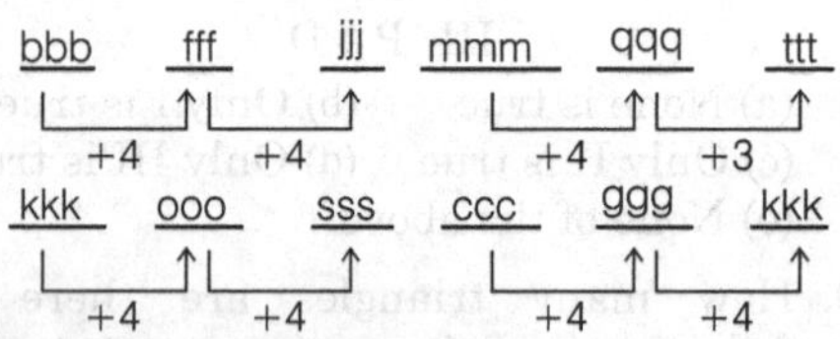

So, it is clear from above that option (b) is different.

5. (*b*) In all others except (b), second is the organ used by first for its movement.

Solution (Q. Nos. 6-7) After careful analysis of the given input and various steps of rearrangement, it is clear that in the first step one word is rearranged and in the second step one number is rearranged. These two steps are continued alternately till all the words get rearranged in alphabetical order and all the numbers get rearranged in ascending order.

6. (*b*) **Input** train 59 47 25 over burden 63 sky

***Step* I** burden train 59 47 25 over 63 sky

***Step* II** burden 25 train 59 47 over 63 sky

***Step* III** burden 25 over train 59 47 63 sky

***Step* IV** burden 25 over 47 train 59 63 sky

***Step* V** burden 25 over 47 sky train 59 63

***Step* VI** burden 25 over 47 sky 59 train 63

7. (*e*) **Input** service 46 58 96 over there desk 15

***Step* I** desk service 46 58 96 over there 15

***Step* II** desk 15 service 46 58 96 over there

***Step* III** desk 15 over service 46 58 96 there

***Step* IV** desk 15 over 46 service 58 96 there

***Step* V** desk 15 over 46 service 58 there 96

8. (*d*) It is given in the statement that cooperation between the proprietor and the employees is required for profit making reasons. It is therefore, required that both employees and proprietor should cooperate with each other.

9. (*d*) Arrangement of words according to the Dictionary.

(iv) Invariable

↓

(i) Inventory

↓

(v) Investigate

↓

(iii) Invisible

↓

(ii) Involuntary

10. (c) D → 00,14, 23, [32], 41

O → 01, 10, [24], 33, 42

W → 55, 69, 78, [87], 96

N → 56, 65, 79, [88], 97

DOWN → [32, 24, 87, 88]

11. (*d*) The first digits of the numbers form the series 1, 2, 3, 4, 5, the second digits form the series 2, 3, 4, 5, 6 and the third digits form the series 3, 4, 5, 6, 7 while the last digit in each of the numbers is 6.

Hence, number 5686 is wrong and must be replaced by 5676.

12. (a) Last and first letters get disappear alternately.

∴ = ATUR

13. (*c*)

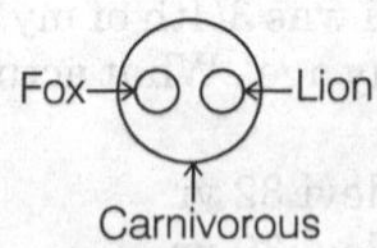

14. (*a*)

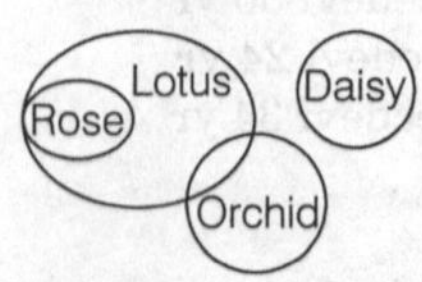

Conclusions

I. [✗] II. [✗]

So, neither Conclusion I nor II is true.

15. (*c*)

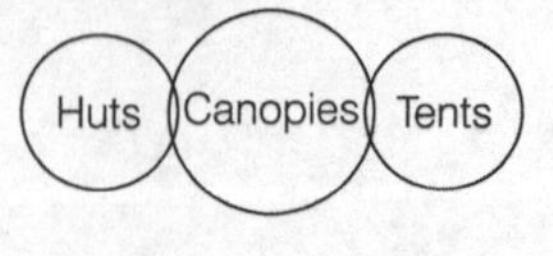

Conclusions

I. [✗]

II. [✗] Complementary pair.

So, either Conclusion I or II is true.

16. (*e*)

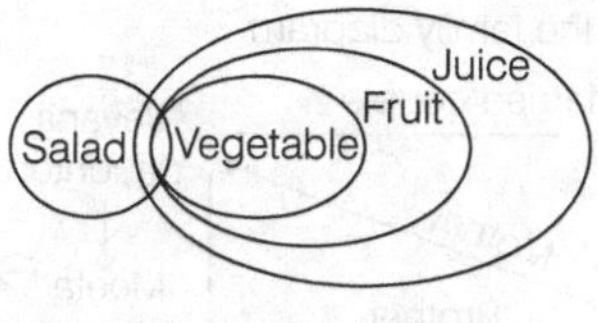

Conclusions I. [✔] II. [✗]

So, only Conclusion I is true.

17. (*b*)

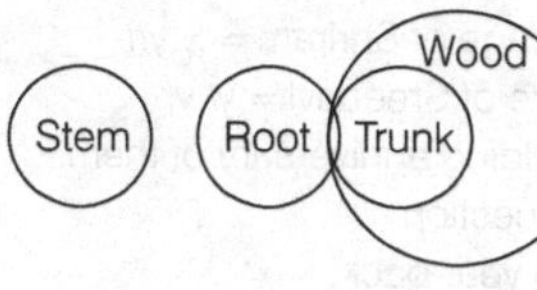

Conclusions I. [✔] II. [✔]

So, both Conclusions I and II are true.

18. (*d*)

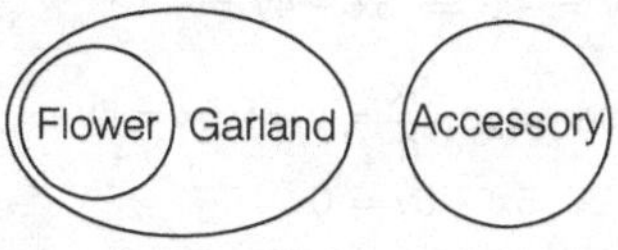

Conclusions I. [✗] II. [✔]

So, only Conclusion II is true.

19. (*d*) As,

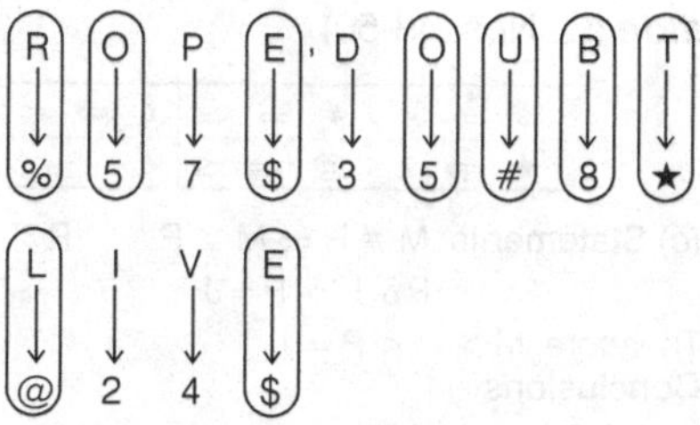

Similarly,

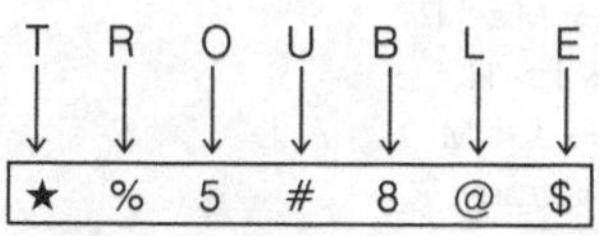

TROUBLE ⇒ ★ % 5 # 8 @ $

20. (*b*) Figures 1, 4 and 7; 2, 6 and 9; 3, 5 and 8 are similar.

21. (*c*) 'Parrot' is a bird but here 'parrot' is called 'rat'. Hence, in this case 'rat' is a bird.

Solution (Q. Nos. 22-24) Following table can be drawn from the given information

Name	Email provider	Company	City
Rahul	Rediffmail	Telco	Pune
Kabeer	Yahoo	Usha martin	Kolkata
Anup	Indiatimes	Tisco	Jamshedpur
Raghu	gmail	Mecon	Ranchi
Amit	Sancharnet	HCL	Noida
Alok	hotmail	Wipro	Bengaluru

22. (*d*) Alok works in Wipro and has id with hotmail.

23. (*d*) Raghu-Ranchi-gmail is the correct combination.

24. (c) Kabeer has an id with Yahoo.

25. (*d*) Let C contributes ₹ x

Therefore, A's contribution = ₹2x

B's contribution = ₹ $\frac{2x}{2}$ = ₹ x

D's contribution = ₹ $\frac{x}{2}$

Therefore, B and C are contribution equal amount.

26. (*b*) According to the question,

$$3+5=8 \Rightarrow 5+6=11 \Rightarrow 6+3=9$$

Clearly, it is a standard dice.

∴ Digit at the face opposite to 5 = 7 − 5 = 2

27. (*b*) Only Conclusion II follows. Comic books and some other books may contain pictures. Some books do not contain pictures.

28. (*c*) There are 11 intervals when the clock strikes 12.

Time taken for 11 intervals = 48 s

∴ Time taken for 1 intervals = $\left(\frac{48}{11}\right)$ s

In order to strike 3, there are 2 intervals, for which the time taken = $\left(\frac{48}{11}\times 2\right) = 8\frac{8}{11}$ s

29. (*d*)

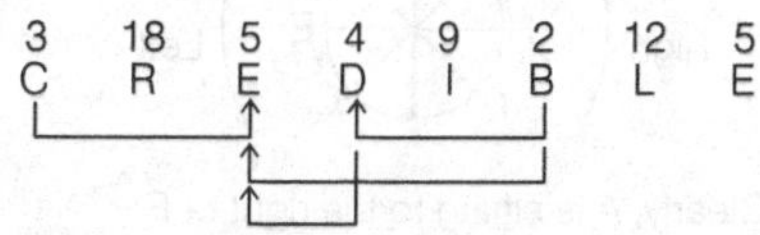

∴ Letter pairs = CE ,BD ,BE ,DE = Four

30. (*a*) According to the question, the direction diagram will be as follows

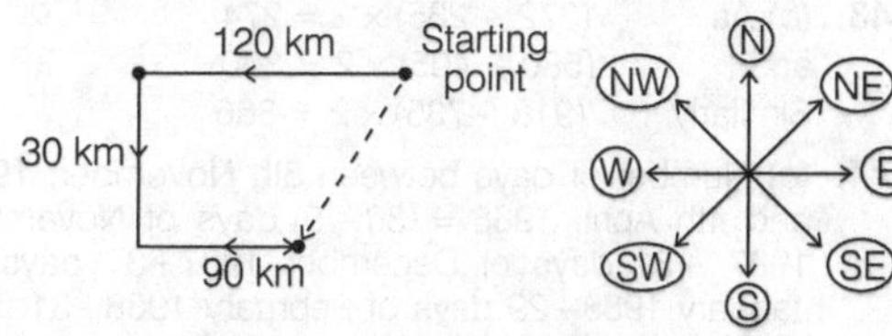

Clearly station is in South-West direction from the train's starting point.

31. (*a*) Clearly, question figure is embedded in answer figure (a) as shown below

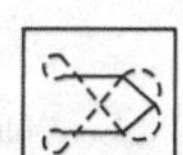

32. (*a*) The correct laterally inverted mirror image of the question figure is as follows

33. (*b*) In the given question, option (b) is different of all other three options because in every option lines are meeting in shape except figure (b).

34. (*b*) Both A and R are but R is not the correct explanation of A.

35. (*b*) The correct vertically inverted water image of the question figure is as follows

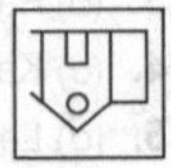

36. (*c*) By using the letters of the given word 'MEASUREMENT' we can form the word 'MASTER'.

37. (*d*) As sound of nightingale is warble, similarly croaking is sound of frog.

Solution (Q. Nos. 38-39) On the basis of given information the arrangement is as following:

E-Silver	B-Metalic	C-Bronze
⊡	⊡	⊡
Tallest	Shortest	
⊡	⊡	⊡
D-Golden	F-Black	A-White

Also, E>B, D>A>C>F

38. (*d*) It cannot be established that which of the two poles B/D is taller but it is sure that either of B or D is the second tallest.

39. (*b*) The colour of tallest pole is silver.

Solution (Q. Nos. 40-42) On the basis of the given information, the sitting arrangement of the eight persons is as follows

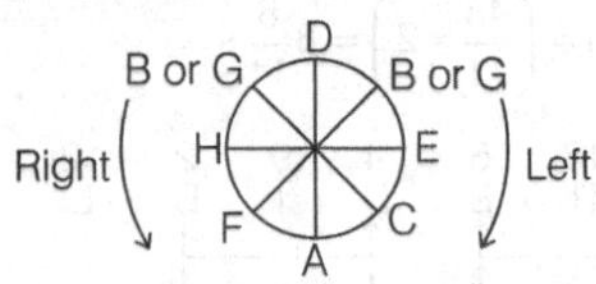

40. (*b*) Clearly, A is sitting to the right of F.

41. (*d*) Each piece of the given information is required to ascertain the position of C.

42. (*d*) C is sitting between A and E.

43. (*b*) As, $(372 - 235) \times 2 = 274$
and $(580 - 405) \times 2 = 350$
Similarly, $(918 - 735) \times 2 = 366$

44. (*c*) Number of days between 5th November, 1987 and 4th April, 1988 = (30 – 5) days of November 1987 +31 days of December 1987+31 days of January 1988+29 days of February 1988+31days of March 1988+4 days of April 1988 [since, 1988 is a leap year, so February has 29 days]
= 25 + 31 + 31 + 29 + 31 + 4
= 151days = 21weeks +4 days
∴ Number of odd days = 4
Thus, 5th November, 1987 will be 4 days before Monday.
So, the required day is Thursday.

45. (*b*) Given, $(18 \div 9) + 3 \times 5 = 45$
$\Rightarrow (18 + 9) \div 3 \times 5 = 45 \Rightarrow 27 \div 3 \times 5 = 45$
$\Rightarrow 9 \times 5 = 45 \Rightarrow 45 = 45$

46. (*b*) Let us draw the family diagram

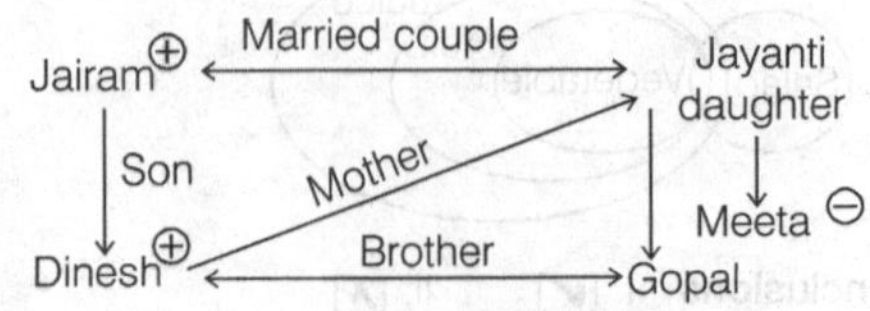

Now, it is clear that Meeta is Dinesh's mother.

47. (*b*) Let the present age of Shriram = x yr
and the present age of Sreedevi = y yr
It was the 12th wedding anniversary of them.
According to the question
Their age of twelve year back,

$$\frac{3}{4}(x - 12) = y - 12 \Rightarrow \frac{3x}{4} - 9 = y - 12$$

$$\Rightarrow \frac{3x}{4} - y = -3 \Rightarrow 3x - 4y = -12 \quad \ldots \text{(i)}$$

Now, their present age, $\frac{5x}{6} = y \Rightarrow 5x = 6y$

$$\Rightarrow 5x - 6y = 0 \quad \ldots \text{(ii)}$$

On solving Eqs. (i) and (ii), we get
x = 36 and y = 30
Hence, present age of Shriram = 36 yr
and present age of Sreedevi = 30 yr.

Solution (Q. Nos. 48-50)

% ⇒ <	# ⇒ >	δ ⇒ =
★ ⇒ ≥	@ ⇒ ≤	

48. (*c*) **Statements** M # R ⇒ M > R R % P ⇒ R < P
P δ J ⇒ P = J
Therefore, M > R < P = J
Conclusions
I. M # P ⇒ M > P (Not True)
II. J # R ⇒ J > R (True)
III. J % M ⇒ J < M (Not True)
So, only II is true.

49. (*b*) **Statements** P ★ D ⇒ P ≥ D D # Q ⇒ D > Q
Q @ R ⇒ Q ≤ R
Therefore, P ≥ D > Q ≤ R
Conclusions
I. Q % P ⇒ Q < P (True)
II. R # D ⇒ R > D (Not True)
III. P # D ⇒ P > R (Not True)
So, only I is true.

50. (*a*) The figure may be labelled as

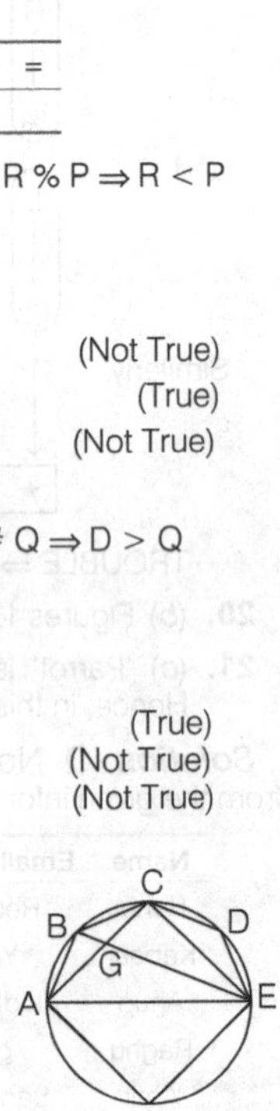

Total triangle are,
ΔABG, ΔBCE, ΔAGE, ΔCDE,
ΔACE, ΔABC, ΔBCG, ΔGCE,
ΔAFE and ΔABE = 10.

PRACTICE SET 15

1. Find the missing character from the given alternatives.

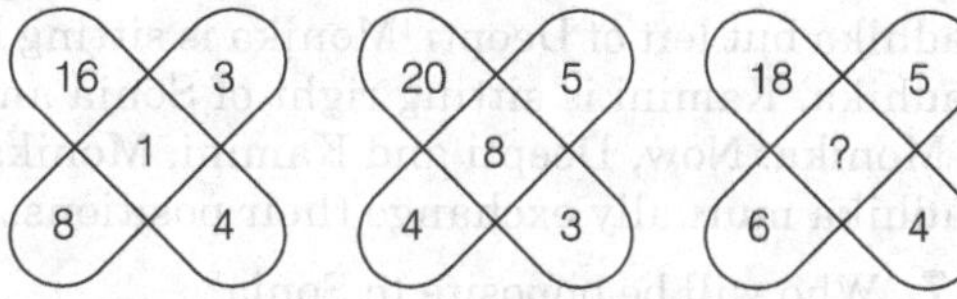

(a) 3 (b) 10 (c) 15 (d) 60

2. If A means '+', B means '–', C means '×' and D means '÷', then which of the following equations is correct?

(a) 8 A 8 B 8 C 8 = – 48
(b) 3 A 3 B 3 C 3 A 3 D 3 = 41
(c) 9 C 9 B 9 D A 9 = 17
(d) 8 B 6 D A 4 C 3 = 15

3. In a row of students, Anil is 7th from the left while jack is 18th from right. Both of them interchange the positions such that Anil becomes 21st from the left. How many people are there in the row?

(a) 38 (b) 39
(c) 40 (d) None of these

Direction (Q. Nos. 4-6) *In the following questions the symbols ×, @ , ©, $ and # are used with the following meaning.*

'A× B' means 'A is neither smaller than nor equal to B'.

'A @ B' means 'A is not greater than B'.

'A © B' means 'A is neither greater than nor smaller than B'.

'A $ B' means 'A is not smaller than B'.

'A # B' means 'A is neither greater than nor equal to B'.

Now, in each of the following questions assuming the given statements to be true, find out which of the two Conclusions I and II given below them is/are definitely true?

Give answer

(a) if only Conclusion I is true
(b) if only Conclusion II is true
(c) if either Conclusion I or II is true
(d) if neither Conclusion I nor II is true
(e) if both Conclusions I and II are true

4. Statements S $ T, T @ R, R # M

Conclusions I. M × T
II. M © T

5. Statements K × B, B @ D, D # K

Conclusions I. B @ K
II. B # K

6. Statements N © R, R @ M, M $ J

Conclusions I. N © M
II. N # M

7. A solid red coloured cube is painted yellow on all sides. The cube is cut into 125 equal cubes. How many cubes will have 3 sides yellow?

(a) 10 (b) 4 (c) 8 (d) 12

8. Group the given figures into different classes on the basis of their orientation, shape etc.

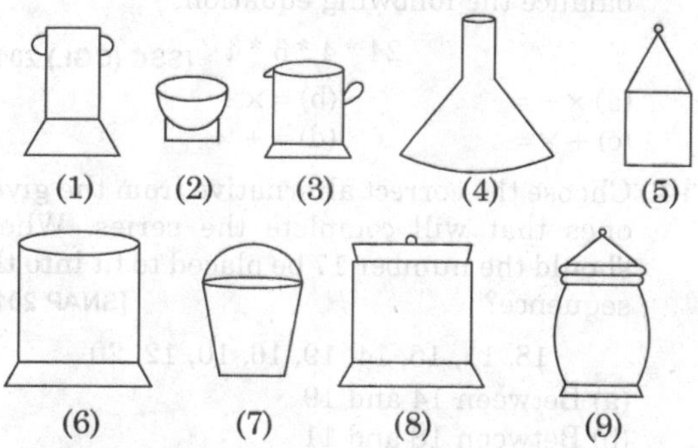

(a) 1, 4, 7
2, 5, 9
3, 8, 6

(b) 2, 6, 9
1, 4, 7
5, 8, 3

(c) 1, 4, 7
2, 3, 6
5, 8, 9

(d) 3, 5, 1
4, 7, 8
6, 2, 9

9. 'S× T' means that S is the mother of T, 'S+ T' means that S is the father of T, 'S– T' means that S is the sister of T. On the basis of this information, you have to select the option which shows that A is the grandfather of T? **[CMAT 2013]**

(a) A+ S+ B– T (b) A× B+ C– T
(c) A+ B– C× T (d) A– C+ B× T

10. The age of a man is three times the sum of the ages of his two sons. 5 yr, hence his age will be double of the sum of the ages of his sons. The father's present age is

(a) 40 yr (b) 45 yr
(c) 50 yr (d) 55 yr

11. Which one of the given responses would be a meaningful order of the following?

(i) Seed (ii) Flower
(iii) Soil (iv) Plant
(v) Fruit

(a) (iv), (ii), (v), (i), (iii)
(b) (ii), (v), (iv), (i), (iii)
(c) (iii), (ii), (i), (v), (iv)
(d) (iii), (i), (iv), (ii), (v)

12. Sashi is 2 yr elder than Sunita, Sunita is 3 yr elder than Bindu, Shekhar is 1 yr elder than Bindu. Who is the youngest in the group?

(a) Sashi (b) Shekhar
(c) Bindu (d) Sunita

13. Select the correct combination of mathematical signs to replace '*' signs and to balance the following equation.

24 * 4 * 5 * 4 **[SSC (CGL) 2012]**

(a) × + = (b) = × +
(c) + × = (d) = + ×

14. Choose the correct alternative from the given ones that will complete the series. Where should the number 17 be placed to fit into the sequence? **[SNAP 2013]**

18, 11, 15, 14, 19, 16, 10, 12, 20

(a) Between 14 and 19
(b) Between 18 and 11
(c) Between 19 and 16
(d) Between 12 and 20

15. There are some boys and dogs at a place. If total number of heads is 7 and total number of legs is 20, then how many boys and how many dogs are there?

(a) 2 boys and 5 dogs
(b) 3 boys and 4 dogs
(c) 4 boys and 3 dogs
(d) 5 boys and 2 dogs

16. Which one set of letters when sequentially placed at the gaps in the given letters series shall complete it?

pqr _ _ rs _ rs _ _ s _ q _

(a) spqpprr (b) pqrrppq
(c) sqppqpr (d) sqprrqr

Direction (Q. Nos. 17-19) *Read the following information carefully to answer the questions that follow.* **[CMAT 2014]**

Six girls are sitting in a circle. Sonia is sitting opposite to Radhika. Poonam is sitting right of Radhika but left of Deepti. Monika is sitting left of Radhika. Kamini is sitting right of Sonia and left of Monika. Now, Deepti and Kamini, Monika and Radhika mutually exchange their positions.

17. Who will be opposite to Sonia?

(a) Radhika (b) Monika
(c) Kamini (d) Sonia

18. Who will be sitting left of Kamini?

(a) Poonam (b) Deepti
(c) Radhika (d) Sonia

19. Who will be sitting left of Deepti?

(a) Sonia (b) Monika
(c) Radhika (d) Poonam

Direction (Q. Nos. 20-21) *Each of the following questions below consists of a question and three statements numbered* I, II *and* III *given below it. You have to decide whether the data provided in the statements are sufficient to answer the question.*

20. On which day Suresh went to Chennai, if week starts on Monday?

I. Suresh took leave on Wednesday.
II. Suresh went to Chennai the next day of the day his mother came to his house.
III. Suresh's mother came to his house neither on Monday nor Friday.

(a) II and III
(b) I and II
(c) I and III
(d) All are needed
(e) Even I, II and III together are not sufficient

21. How is Q related to T?

I. M and R are brothers.
II. S has two sons and one daughter, R being one of the sons.
III. S is the mother of T and married to Q.

(a) I and III (b) Only III
(c) I and II (d) II and III
(e) None of these

22. In this question, a statement is given followed by three courses of action numbered I, II and III. You have to assume everything in the statement to be true and on the basis of the information given in the statement, decide which of the suggested courses of action logically follows for pursuing.

Statement India's pre-eminent position in the world black pepper production and trade is in danger as some of the countries, which recently started production of the 'King of the spices' crop from Indian root stocks, are farming better by adopting modern cultivation practices.

Courses of Action

I. India should immediately stop supplying root stocks of black pepper to other countries.

II. India should adopt modern technology for cultivating black pepper to compete in the international market.

III. India should reduce the price of its black pepper to remain competitive in the world market.

(a) All follow (b) Only II follows
(c) Only I follows (d) Only III follows

23. A word is represented by only one set of numbers are given in anyone of the alternatives. The sets of numbers given in the alternatives are represented by two classes of alphabets as in the two given matrices. The columns and rows of Matrix I are numbered from 0 to 4 and those of Matrix II from 5 to 9. A letter from these matrices can be represented first by its row and then the column number e.g. 'M' can be represented by 58, 67 etc. O can be represented by 01,10 etc. Similarly you have to identify the correct set for the word given in each question.

Matrix I

	0	1	2	3	4
0	D	O	B	A	I
1	O	B	A	I	D
2	B	A	I	O	D
3	A	I	D	O	B
4	I	D	O	B	A

Matrix II

	5	6	7	8	9
5	W	N	R	M	L
6	N	R	M	L	W
7	R	M	L	W	N
8	M	L	W	N	R
9	L	W	N	R	M

BOND

(a) 43, 21, 97, 33 (b) 11, 33, 79, 41
(c) 34, 44, 66, 14 (d) 20, 30, 89, 23

Direction (Q. Nos. 24-25) *Study the following information to answer the given questions.*

A word and number arrangement machine when given an input line of words and numbers rearranges them following a particular rule. The following is an illustration of input and rearrangement.

(All numbers in these questions are two digit numbers)

Input 16 today 32 waiting 21 are 11 people 46 bus 66 long

***Step* I** 16 today 32 waiting 21 11 people 46 bus 66 long are

***Step* II** 16 today 32 waiting 21 people 46 bus 66 long 11 are

***Step* III** 16 today 32 waiting 21 people 46 66 long bus 11 are

***Step* IV** today 32 waiting 21 people 46 66 long 16 bus 11 are

***Step* V** today 32 waiting people 46 66 21 long 16 bus 11 are

***Step* VI** today 32 waiting 46 66 people 21 long 16 bus 11 are

***Step* VII** today waiting 46 66 32 people 21 long 16 bus 11 are

***Step* VIII** waiting 46 66 today 32 people 21 long 16 bus 11 are

***Step* IX** waiting 66 46 today 32 people 21 long 16 bus 11 are

***Step* X** 66 waiting 46 today 32 people 21 long 16 bus 11 are

Step X is the last Step of the arrangement of the above input as the intended arrangement is obtained.

Now, answer the questions based on the following input.

Input 23 you 13 wake 81 me 43 before 72 go 34 up

24. Which of these words/numbers would be fourth (from left side) in Step IV for the input?

(a) me (b) 43
(c) 81 (d) wake
(e) None of these

25. Which step number would be following rearrangement?

you wake 81 43 72 34 up me 23 go 13 before.

(a) IX (b) IV
(c) VI (d) V
(e) None of these

26. In making decisions about important questions, it is desirable to distinguish between a 'strong' argument and a 'weak' argument. A 'strong' argument must be both important and directly related to the question. A 'weak' argument may not be directly related to the question and may be of minor importance or may be related to the trivial aspect of the question. Each question below is followed by two arguments numbered I and II. You have to decide which of the arguments is 'strong' and which is 'weak'.

Statements Will the Cauveri river water dispute be settled down at last?

Arguments

I. Yes, the politicians of Karnataka and Tamil Nadu will come to some satisfactory political settlement.

II. No, both the states have their own interests, hence, the dispute will be prolonged.

(a) if only Argument I is strong
(b) if only Argument II is strong
(c) if either I or II is strong
(d) if neither I nor II is strong
(e) if both I and II are strong

27. 41537 is related to 4 in the same way as 421 is related to

(a) 50 (b) 137 (c) 2 (d) 49

28. Select the related words pair from the given alternatives.

Vertex : Pyramid : ? **[SNAP 2014]**

(a) Strand : Hair (b) Rung : Ladder
(c) Summit : Mountain (d) Frame : Picture

29. Find out the number of triangles in the given pattern. **[SSC (Multitasking) 2013]**

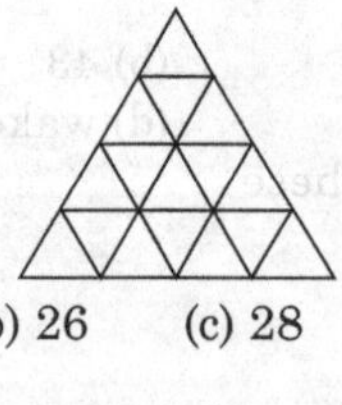

(a) 23 (b) 26 (c) 28 (d) 27

Direction (Q. Nos. 30-31) *In the following questions, find the odd word/number pair from the given alternatives.* **[SSC (CGL) 2014]**

30. (a) 9 – 72 (b) 8 – 56
(c) 11 – 15 (d) 10 – 90

31. (a) Guitar (b) Violin
(c) Flute (d) Veena

Direction (Q. Nos. 32-33) *In each of the questions below are given two statements followed by two Conclusions numbered I and II. You have to take the two given statements to be true even if they seem to be at variance from commonly known facts and decide which of the given conclusion(s) logically follow(s) from the two given statements, disregarding commonly known facts.*

Give answer

(a) if only Conclusion I follows
(b) if only Conclusion II follows
(c) if either Conclusion I or II follows
(d) if neither Conclusion I nor II follows
(e) if both Conclusions I and II follow

32. Statements Some trees are plants.
All bushes are plants.

Conclusions I. Atleast some trees are bushes.
II. Some trees are definitely not bushes.

33. Statements All bottles are glasses.
No cup is a glass.

Conclusions I. No bottle is a cup.
II. Atleast some glasses are bottles.

34. At what angle the hands of a clock are inclined at 15 min past 5?

(a) 58.5° (b) 64° (c) 67.5° (d) 72.5°

35. Identify the missing part of the figure and select it from the given alternatives.

Question Figure

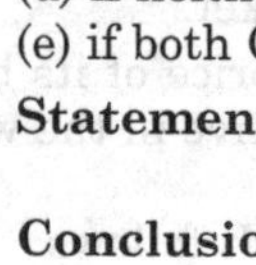

Answer Figures

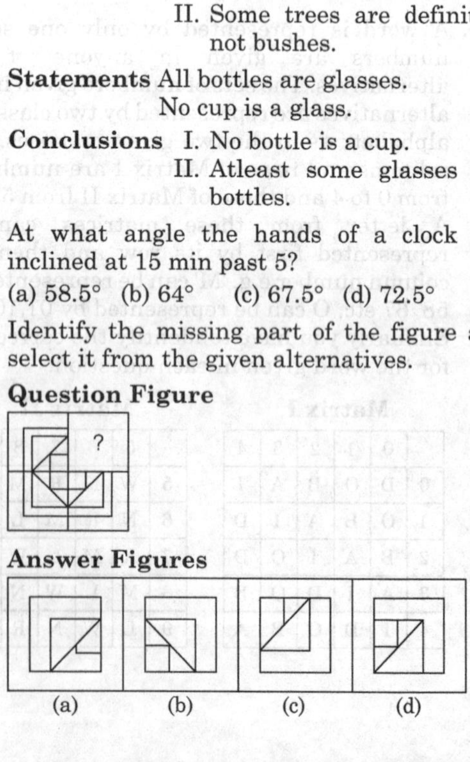

(a) (b) (c) (d)

36. Which figure is different from the rest of the three? **[SSC (10 + 2) 2013]**

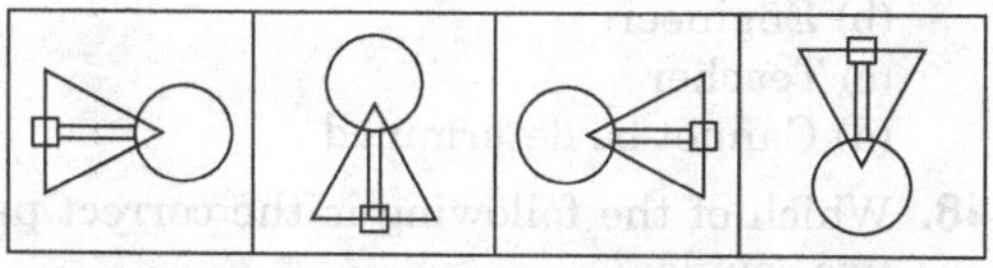

(a) (b) (c) (d)

37. The houses of A and B face each other on a road going North-South, A's being on the western side, A comes out of his house, turns left, travels left, travels 5 km, turns right, travels 5 km to the front of D's house. B does exactly the same and reaches the front of C's house. In this context, which one of the following statements is correct?

(a) C and D live on the same street
(b) C's house faces South
(c) The houses of C and D are less than 20 km apart
(d) None of the above

Direction (Q. Nos 38-40) *Read the following information carefully to answer the given questions.*

In a certain code language 461 means 'where are you', 169 means 'you are good' and 8652 means 'flowers are not bad'.

38. What is the code for 'not'?
(a) 6 (b) 8 (c) 2 (d) 8 or 5 or 2

39. What is the code for 'good'?
(a) 4 (b) 9 (c) 6 (d) 6 or 1

40. How will 'where not are good flowers' be written in coded language?
(a) 68954
(b) 46598
(c) 45698
(d) Data inadequate

41. Consider the following Venn diagram and answer the questions that follow.

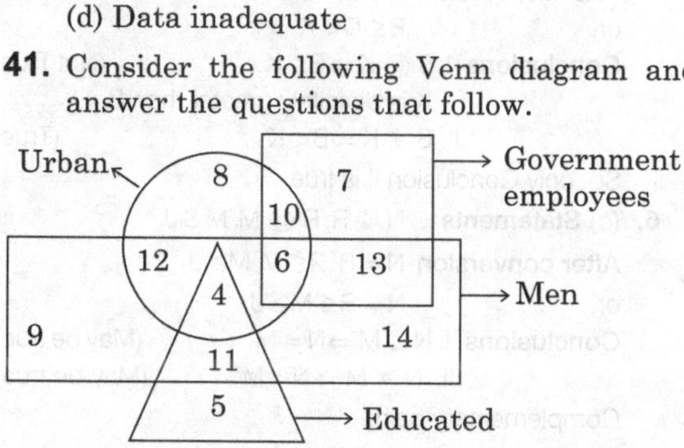

In the given diagram, which of the following represents the educated men but not urban?
(a) 9 (b) 5
(c) 4 (d) 11

42. A word is given followed by four other words, one of which cannot be formed by using the letters of the given word. Find that word.

CONSTITUTIONAL

(a) CONSULT (b) LOCATION
(c) TUTION (d) TALENT

43. Number of letters skipped in between adjacent letters in the series starting from behind decreases by one. Which of the following series observes this rule?
(a) DBPUY (b) DBUYP
(c) DBYPU (d) DBYUP

44. A word is represented by only one set of numbers as given in any one of the alternatives. The sets of numbers given in the alternatives are represented by two classes of alphabets as in two matrices given below. The columns and rows of Matrix I are numbered from 0 to 4 and that of Matrix II are numbered from 5 to 9. A letter from these matrices can be represented first by its row and next by its column, e.g. M can be represented by 01, 10 etc., and A can be represented by 56, 65 etc. Similarly, you have to identify the set for the word 'ROD'. **[SSC (10+2) 2015]**

Matrix I

	0	1	2	3	4
0	I	M	W	S	Q
1	M	W	S	Q	I
2	W	S	Q	I	M
3	S	Q	I	M	W
4	Q	I	M	W	S

Matrix II

	5	6	7	8	9
5	O	A	D	R	N
6	A	D	R	N	O
7	D	R	N	O	A
8	R	N	O	A	D
9	N	O	A	D	R

(a) 58, 66, 78 (b) 56, 66, 86
(c) 67, 96, 57 (d) 58, 69, 65

45. A girl is facing North. She turns 180° in the anti-clockwise direction and then 225° in the clockwise direction. Which direction is she facing now? **[CG PSC 2013]**
(a) West (b) North-East
(c) South-West (d) East
(e) North-West

Direction (Q. Nos. 46-50) *Read the following information carefully to answer these questions.* **[CLAT 2014]**

I. In a family of six persons, there are people from three generations. Each person has separate profession and also each one likes different colours. There are two couples in the family.

II. Charan is a CA and his wife neither is a doctor nor likes green colour.

III. Engineer likes red colour and his wife is a teacher.

IV. Vanita is mother-in-law of Namita and she likes orange colour.

V. Mohan is grandfather of Raman and Raman, who is a principal, likes black colour.

VI. Sarita is granddaughter of Vanita and she likes blue colour. Sarita's mother likes white colour.

46. Who is an engineer?
(a) Sarita (b) Vanita
(c) Namita (d) Mohan

47. What is the profession of Namita?
(a) Doctor
(b) Engineer
(c) Teacher
(d) Cannot be determined

48. Which of the following is the correct pair of two couples?
(a) Mohan—Vanita and Charan—Sarita
(b) Vanita—Mohan and Charan—Namita
(c) Charan—Namita and Raman—Sarita
(d) Cannot be determined

49. How many ladies are there in the family?
(a) Two
(b) Three
(c) Four
(d) None of the

50. Which colour is liked by CA?
(a) White
(b) Blue
(c) Black
(d) None of the above

Hints and Solutions

1. (*a*) As, 16 – (3 + 4 + 8) = 1
and 20 – (5 + 3 + 4) = 8
Similarly, 18 – (5 + 4 + 6) = 3

2. (*a*) Let us check all the options one by one.
From option (a).

8 A 8 B 8 C 8 = – 48
↓ ↓ ↓
\+ – ×

⇒ 8 + 8 – 8 × 8 = – 48
⇒ 8 + 8 – 64 = – 48 (using VBODMAS rule)
⇒ 16 – 64 = – 48 ⇒ – 48 = – 48
∴ LHS = RHS

So, option (a) is correct and there is no need to check remaining options.

3. (*a*) Anil's original position from left = 7 th
Jack's original position from right = 18th
Anil's position from left after interchange = 21st
Since, Anil exchanged his seat with Jack, it means Jack's original position is 21st from the left.
∴ Total number of people = (Initial/position of Jack from the right + Initial position of Jack from the left) – 1
= 18 + 21 – 1 = 38

Solution (Q. Nos. 4-6)

× ⇒ >	@ ⇒ ≤	© ⇒ =	$ ⇒ ≥	# ⇒ <

4. (*a*) **Statements** S $ T, T @ R, R # M
After conversion S ≥ T, T≤ R, R< M
or, S ≥ T≤ R< M
Conclusions I. M× T⇒M > T (True)
II. M © T⇒M= T (Not True)
So, only Conclusion I is true.

5. (*b*) **Statements** K× B, B @ D, D # K
After conversion K> B, B≤ D, D< K
or, B≤ D< K
Conclusions I. B @ K ⇒B≤ K (Not True)
K is definitely greater than B.
II. B # K⇒B< K (True)
So, only Conclusion II is true.

6. (*c*) **Statements** N © R, R @ M, M $ J
After conversion N= R, R≤ M, M≥ J
or, N= R≤ M≥ J
Conclusions I. N © M ⇒N= M (May be true)
II. N # M⇒N< M (May be true)
Complementary pairs.
So, either Conclusion I or II is true.

7. (*c*)

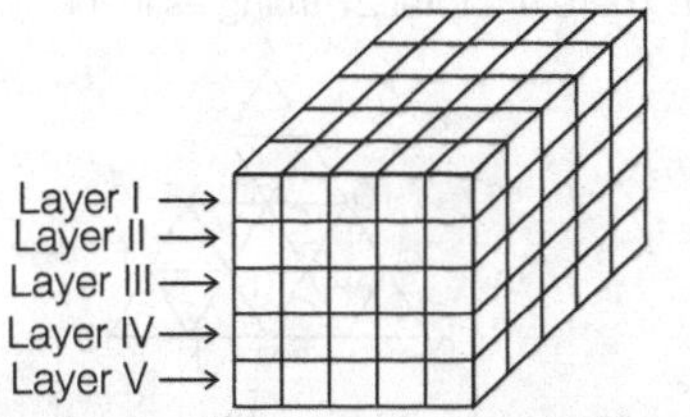

In layer I, the nine central cubes have only one face painted, four cubes at the corner have three faces painted and the remaining 12 cubes have two faces painted. In each of the layers II, III and IV, the nine central cubes have no face painted, the four cubes at the corner have two faces painted and the remaining 12 cubes have one face painted.

In layer V, the nine central cubes have only one face painted, the four cubes at the corner have three faces painted and the remaining 12 cubes have two faces painted.

Thus, the number of cubes having three faces painted

$$= 4 + 4 = 8$$

8. (*c*) Figures 1, 4, 7; 2, 3, 6 and 5, 8, 9 are similar.

9. (*a*) By using option (a) i.e. A+ S+ B− T

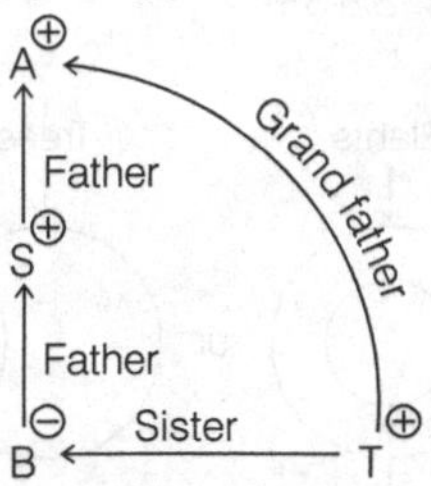

Now, from the diagram it is clear that A is grandfather of T.

10. (*b*) Let us assume, sum of ages of two sons = x yr

and age of their father = 3x yr

After 5 yr,

Father's age = (3x + 5) yr

Sum of his son's age = x + 5 + 5 = x + 10 yr

$\therefore \quad 3x + 5 = 2\,(x + 10)$

$\Rightarrow \quad 3x - 2x = 20 - 5$

$\therefore \quad x = 15$

and father's age = 3x = 3 × 15 = 45

Hence, father's age is 45 yr.

11. (*d*) Meaningful order of words

(iii) Soil
↓
(i) Seed
↓
(iv) Plant
↓
(ii) Flower
↓
(v) Fruit

12. (*c*) According to the question,

Sashi > Sunita (2 yr)

Sunita > Bindu (3 yr)

Shekhar > Bindu (1 yr)

∴ Sashi > Sunita > Shekhar > Bindu

So, youngest person in the group is Bindu.

13. (*b*) From option (b), $24 = 4 \times 5 + 4$

$\Rightarrow \quad 24 = 20 + 4$

$\Rightarrow \quad 24 = 24$

14. (*a*) We put 17 in between 14 and 19 and the following pattern is obtained

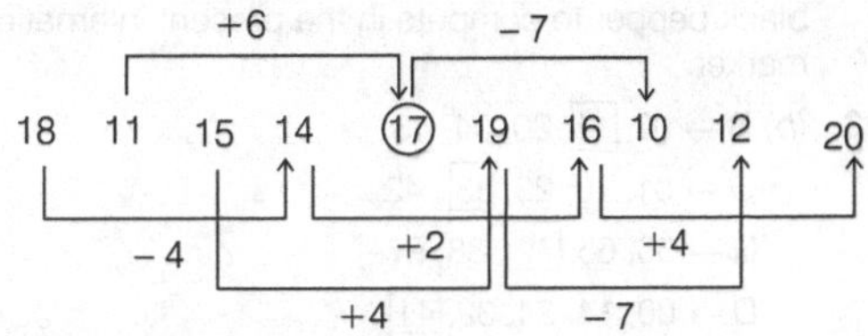

15. (*c*) Number of heads = B + D = 7 ...(i)

Number of legs = 2 B + 4 D = 20 ...(ii)

From Statements (i) and (ii)

B = 4and D = 3

16. (*c*) Series pattern p q r s̲ / q̲ r s p̲ / r s p q̲ / s p̲ q r̲

∴ Required answer = s q p p q p r

Solution (Q. Nos. 17-19) Arrangements according to the question are as follows

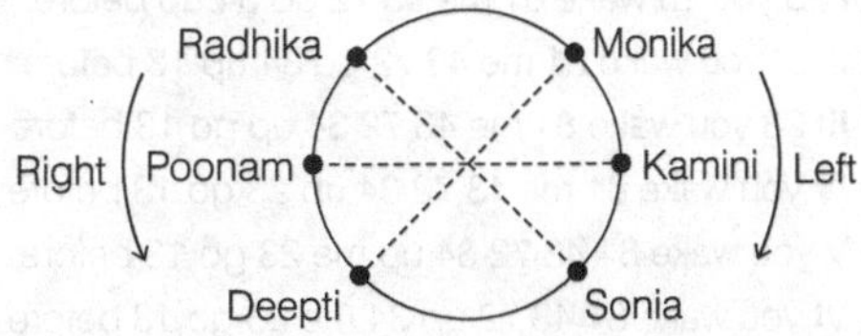

Original positions

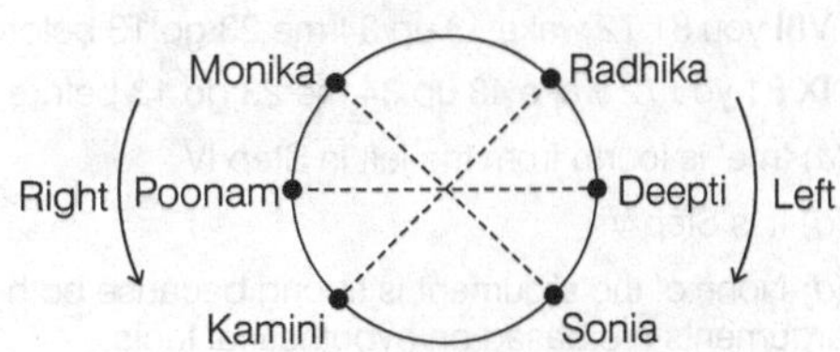

New arrangement

17. (*b*) Clearly, Monika will be opposite to Sonia.

18. (*a*) Clearly, Poonam will be sitting left of Kamini.

19. (*a*) Clearly, Sonia will be sitting left of Deepti.

20. (*e*) Statements I, II and III together are not sufficient as the required day can be anyone of Wednesday, Thursday, Friday and Sunday.

21. (*b*) From Statements I and II, it is not possible as no information is given about Q and T.

From Statement III, it is obvious that Q is the father of T (from Statements I and III) or (Statements II and III) is not possible as Statement III alone is sufficient.

As, Statement III alone is sufficient, (I + II + III) is also not possible.

So, only Statement III is sufficient to answer the question.

22. (*b*) Only better quality can put India back in the competitive field of black pepper production. So, India should go for modern technology for cultivating black pepper to compete in the present international market.

23. (*b*) B → 02, 11, 20, 34, 43

O → 01, 10, 23, 33, 42

N → 56, 65, 79, 88, 97

D → 00, 14, 24, 32, 41

BOND → 11, 33, 79, 41

Solution (Q. Nos. 24-26) After careful analysis of the given input and various steps of rearrangement it is evident that words and numbers are rearranged from right to left. In the first step one word is rearranged and in the second step one number is rearranged. The words are rearranged in alphabetical order and the numbers are arranged in ascending order from right to left.

Input 23 you 13 wake 81 me 43 before 72 go 34 up

***Step* I** 23 you 13 wake 81 me 43 72 go 34 up before

***Step* II** 23 you wake 81 me 43 72 go 34 up 13 before

***Step* III** 23 you wake 81 me 43 72 34 up go 13 before

***Step* IV** you wake 81 me 43 72 34 up 23 go 13 before

***Step* V** you wake 81 43 72 34 up me 23 go 13 before

***Step* VI** you wake 81 43 72 up 34 me 23 go 13 before

***Step* VII** you wake 81 72 43 up 34 me 23 go 13 before

***Step* VIII** you 81 72 wake 43 up 34 me 23 go 13 before

***Step* IX** 81 you 72 wake 43 up 34 me 23 go 13 before

24. (*a*) 'me' is fourth from the left in Step IV.

25. (*d*) It is Step V.

26. (*d*) None of the argument is strong because both the arguments are based on hypothetical facts.

27. (*d*) As, 41537 $\Rightarrow 4 + 1 + 5 + 3 + 7 = 20$

$\Rightarrow \quad 2 + 0 = 2 \quad \Rightarrow \quad (2)^2 = 4$

Similarly, 421 $\Rightarrow 4 + 2 + 1 = 7$

$\Rightarrow \quad (7)^2 = 49$

28. (*c*) Vertex is a highest point of pyramid. Similarly, summit is the highest point of mountain.

29. (*d*) There are total 27 triangles in the given figure.

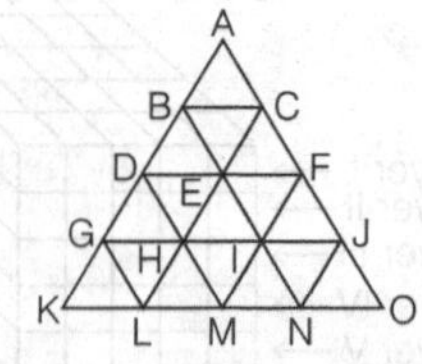

From this figure it is clear that,

Triangles formed by single units = ΔABC, ΔBDE, ΔBCE, ΔCEF, ΔDGH, ΔDHE, ΔHEI, ΔEIF, ΔFIJ, ΔGKL, ΔGLH, ΔLHM, ΔHMI, ΔMIN, ΔINJ and ΔNJO i.e. 16 triangles.

Triangles formed by combining four triangles are ΔADF, ΔBGI, ΔCHJ, ΔDKM, ΔLEN, ΔMFO and ΔDFM i.e. 7 triangles.

Triangle formed by combining 9 triangles are ΔAGJ, ΔBKN and ΔCLO i.e. 3 triangles. One triangle ΔAKO formed by complete figure.

So, total number of triangles = 16 + 7 + 3 + 1 = 27

30. (*c*) Except 11-15, in all others options right side number is a multiple of left number.

31. (*c*) Except 'Flute', all others are string instruments.

Solution (Q. Nos. 32-33)

32. (*c*)

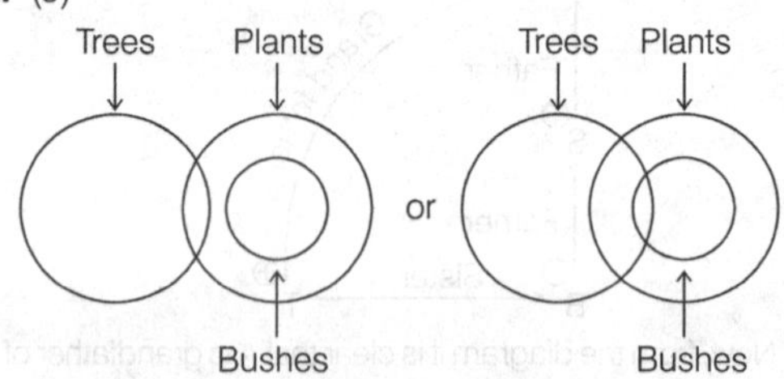

Conclusions

I. Atleast some trees are bushes. (May be true)

II. Some trees are definitely not bushes. (May be true)

Complementary pair (I-O)

So, either Conclusion I or II follows.

33. (*e*)

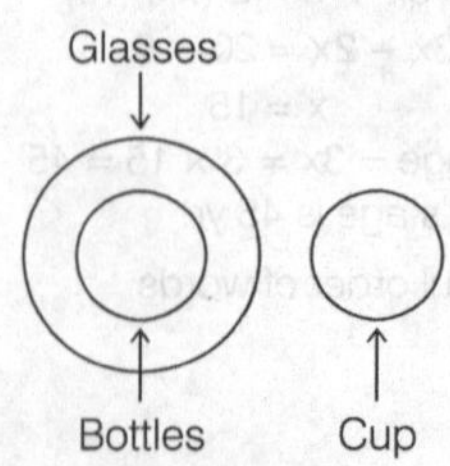

Conclusions I. No bottle is a cup. (✔)

II. Atleast some glasses are bottles. (✔)

So, both Conclusions I and II follow.

34. (*c*) Hands of a clock are inclined at 5h 15 min,

i.e. $5\frac{15}{60} = \frac{21}{4}$ h

$\therefore$ Total angle $= \frac{21}{4} \times 30° = 21 \times 7.5 = 157.5°$

Angle displaced by minute hand in 15 min

$= 15 \times 6° = 90°$

$\therefore$ Angle difference $= 157.5° - 90° = 67.5°$

35. (*b*) It is clear that answer figure (b) completes the original figure. Hence, alternative (b) is the correct answer.

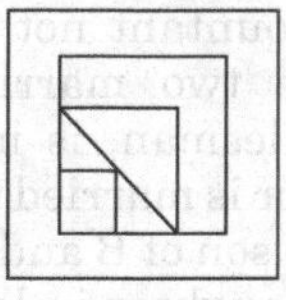

36. (*b*) Except in figure (b), the pipe is not in the square.

37. (*c*) According to the question, the direction diagram will be as follows

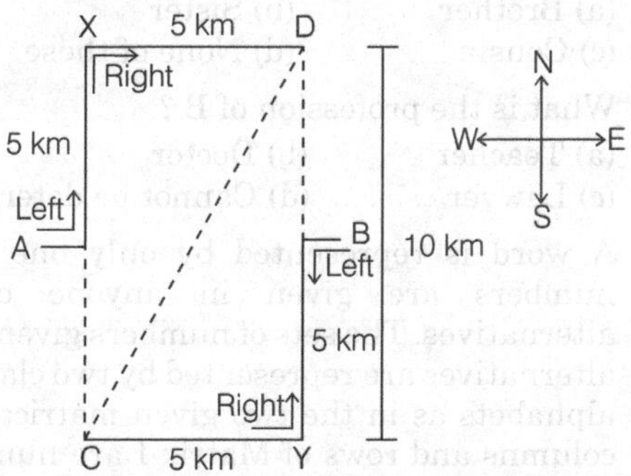

Now, AX = DB = BY = CA = 5 km, XD = CY = 5 km

XC = XA + AC = 5 + 5 = 10 km

$\therefore$ Distance between C and D, i.e.

$CD = \sqrt{(XD)^2 + (XC)^2}$ (by Pythagoras theorem)

$= \sqrt{5^2 + 10^2} = \sqrt{25 + 100}$

$= \sqrt{125} = 5\sqrt{5} = 5 \times 2.23 = 11.15$ km

So, it is clear from the figure that the houses of C and D are less than 20 km apart.

Solution (Q. Nos. 38-40)

where (are) [you] ⟶ 4 (6) [1] ...(i)

[you] (are) good ⟶ [1] (6) 9 ...(ii)

flowers (are) not bad ⟶ 8 (6) 5 2 ...(iii)

From Eqs. (i), (ii) and (iii), are ⇒ 6

From Eqs. (i) and (ii) you ⇒ 1

$\therefore$ where ⇒ 4

good ⇒ 9

From Eq (iii), flower ⇒ 8/5/2

not ⇒ 8/5/2

bad ⇒ 8/5/2

38. (*d*) According to the question,
Code for 'not' ⇒ 8 or 5 or 2

39. (*b*) According to the question,
Code for 'good' ⇒ 9

40. (*d*) Data inadequate to answer the question. as code for 'flowers' and 'not' cannot be determined.

41. (*d*) Educated men who are not urban are represented by the region which is common to both the triangle and the rectangle but not to the square and circle. So, the required region is 11.

42. (*d*) 'TALENT' word cannot be formed using the letters of the given word because letter E is not present in the given word.

43. (*d*) From the given question,

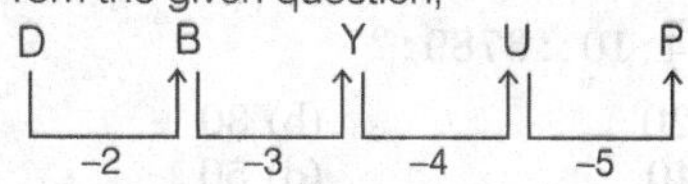

Now, it is clear that only DBYUP is a group of letters which follows the given rule.

44. (*c*) R → 58, [67], 76, 85, 99

O → 55, 69, 78, 87, [96]

D → [57], 66, 75, 89, 98

ROD ⇒ 67, 96, 57

45. (*b*) According to the question, the direction diagram will be as follows

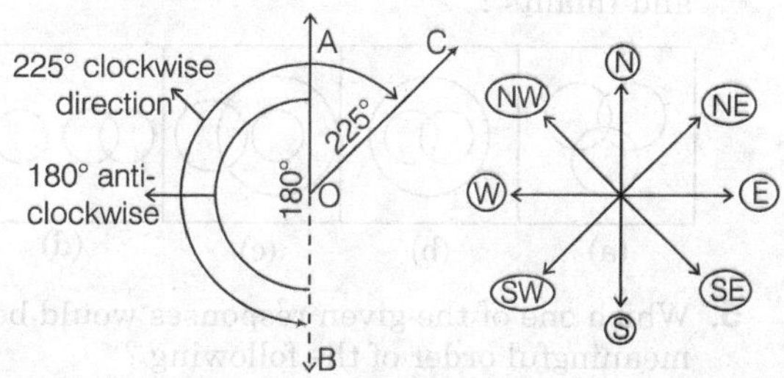

Clearly, the girl is facing North-East.

Solutions (Q. Nos. 46-50) According to given conditions, we can make the below table

Grandparents	Mohan (Engg) (Red)	Vanita (Teacher) (Orange)
Parents	Charan (CA)	Namita (White)
Children	Raman (Principal) (Black)	Sarita (Blue)

46. (*d*) Mohan is an Engineer.

47. (*d*) Namila's profession is not given.

48. (*b*) Pair of two couples are
Vanita—Mohan and Charan—Namita.

49. (*b*) There are three ladies in the family.

50. (*d*) Charan is a CA and colour liked by him is not given.

PRACTICE SET 16

Direction (Q. Nos. 1-3) *In the following questions, select the related word/ number pair from the given alternatives.*

1. Heart : Cardiologist : : Brain : ?
[SSC (10+2) 2015]

(a) Ophthalmologist
(b) Nephrologist
(c) Neurologist
(d) Gynaecologist

2. 1234 : 10 : : 6789 : ?

(a) 20 (b) 30
(c) 40 (d) 50

3. (223, 324, 425)
(a) (225, 326, 437)
(b) (451, 552, 636)
(c) (554, 655, 756)
(d) (623, 723, 823)

4. Which of the following diagrams best depicts the relationship between Professor, Author and Infants ?

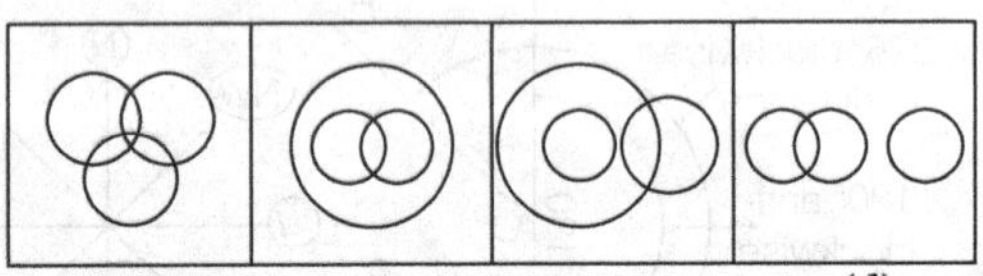

(a) (b) (c) (d)

5. Which one of the given responses would be a meaningful order of the following ?
(i) Adult (ii) Child
(iii) Infant (iv) Boy
(v) Adolescent
(a) (i), (iii), (iv), (v), (ii)
(b) (iii), (ii), (iv), (v), (i)
(c) (ii), (iii), (v), (iv), (i)
(d) (ii), (iii), (iv), (i), (v)

6. Loking at a woman sitting next to him, Amit said, "She is the sister of the husband of my wife." How is the woman related to Amit ?
[SSC (CGL) 2013]

(a) Niece
(b) Daughter
(c) Sister
(d) Wife

Direction (Q. Nos. 7-8) *Read the following information carefully to answer the questions that follow.*

There is a family of six members A, B, C, D, E and F. They are lawyer, doctor, teacher, salesman, engineer and accountant not necessarily in that order. There are two married couples in the family. D, the salesman, is married to the lady teacher. The doctor is married to the lawyer. F, the accountant, is the son of B and brother of E. C, the lawyer, is the daughter-in-law of A. E is the unmarried engineer. A is the grandmother of F.

7. How is E related to F ?
(a) Brother (b) Sister
(c) Cousin (d) None of these

8. What is the profession of B ?
(a) Teacher (b) Doctor
(c) Lawyer (d) Cannot be determined

9. A word is represented by only one set of numbers are given in anyone of the alternatives. The sets of numbers given in the alternatives are represented by two classes of alphabets as in the two given matrices. The columns and rows of Matrix I are numbered from 0 to 4 and those of Matrix II from 5 to 9. A letter from these matrices can be represented first by its row and then the column number e.g., 'M' can be represented by 58, 67, etc., O can be represented by 01, 10 etc. Similarly you have to identify the correct set for the word given in each question.

Matrix I

	0	1	2	3	4
0	D	O	B	A	I
1	O	B	A	I	D
2	B	A	I	D	O
3	A	I	D	O	B
4	I	D	O	B	A

Matrix II

	5	6	7	8	9
5	W	N	R	M	L
6	N	R	M	L	W
7	R	M	L	W	N
8	M	L	W	N	R
9	L	W	N	R	M

BOLD
(a) 11, 68, 42, 69
(b) 21, 95, 33, 97
(c) 34, 24, 59, 14
(d) 34, 86, 44, 78

Direction (Q. Nos. 10-11) *Study the following information carefully and answer the given questions.*

A word and number arrangement machine when given an input line of words and numbers rearranges them following a particular rule in each step. The following is an illustration of input and rearrangement.

Input 'sale data 18 23 for 95 then 38'
***Step* I** data sale 18 23 for 95 then 38
***Step* II** data 95 sale 18 23 for then 38
***Step* III** data 95 for sale 18 23 then 38
***Step* IV** data 95 for 38 sale 18 23 then
***Step* V** data 95 for 38 sale 23 18 then
***Step* VI** data 95 for 38 sale 23 then 18

and Step VI is the last step of the rearrangement of the above input .

As per the rules followed in the above steps, find out in each of the following questions the appropriate step for the given input.

10. **Input** 'year 39 stake 47 house full 94 55'

How many steps will be required to complete the rearrangement ?

(a) Five (b) Six (c) Four (d) Seven
(e) None of these

11. Step II of an input is 'car 83 lost ever 32 46 74 now'

How many more steps will be required to complete the rearrangement ?

(a) Three (b) Four (c) Five (d) Six
(e) None of these

12. Find the figure out of the answer choice figure that can be formed by joining the pieces given in the questions figure.

Question Figure

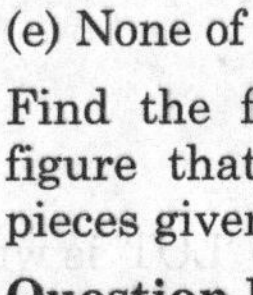

Answer Figures

(a) (b) (c) (d)

13. Identify the missing part of the question figure and select it from given answer figures.

Question Figure

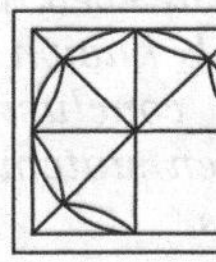

Answer Figures

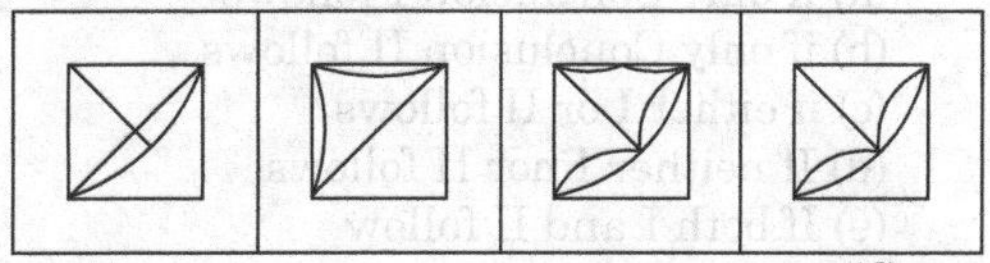

(a) (b) (c) (d)

14. A five member business delegation to Pakistan has to be chosen from five politicians Khansaab, Lalaji, Mohanlal, Nathumal and Omprakash and four prominent businessmen Popatlal, Quareshi, Ramprasad and Sorabseth. But there are some conditions. Khansaab and Sorabseth have to be together.

Mohanlal and Omprakash too cannot be separated. Nathumal and Quareshi cannot go together. Ramprasad had disputes with Popatlal and Lalaji, he will not go with any of these two. If Popatlal and at least two other businessmen are selected, then members of the delegation besides Popatlal are

(a) Quareshi, Sorabseth, Khansaab, Lalaji
(b) Quareshi, Sorabseth, Lalaji, Nathumal
(c) Ramprasad, Sorabseth, Khansaab, Nathumal
(d) Quareshi, Sorabseth, Mohanlal, Nathumal

Direction (Q. Nos. 15 -16) *In the following series, replace the question mark (?) with the suitable option.*

15. 51975, 9450, 2100, 600, 240, 160, ?

(a) 80 (b) 120
(c) 320 (d) 240

16. AYBZC, DWEXF, GUHVI, JSKTL,?

(a) MQORN
(b) QMONR
(c) MQNRO
(d) NQMOR

Direction (Q. Nos. 17-18) *In each of the questions below are given two statements followed by two conclusions numbered* I *and* II. *You have to take the two given statements to be true even if they seem to be at variance from commonly known facts and decide which of the given conclusion(s) logically follow(s) from the two given statements, disregarding commonly known facts.*

Give answer
(a) if only Conclusion I follows
(b) if only Conclusion II follows
(c) if either I or II follows
(d) If neither I nor II follows
(e) If both I and II follow

17. Statements All cars are balls.
All balls are tables.
Conclusions I. Some tables are balls.
II. Some tables are cars.

18. Statments Some rats are cats.
All cats are bats.
Conclusions I. No rats are cats.
II. Some rats are bats.

19. From the given three positions of a single dice, find the digit at the face opposite to the face having digit 3.

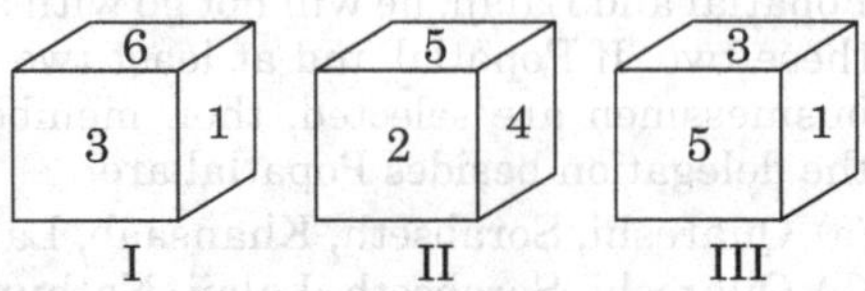

(a) 2 (b) 4
(c) 5 (d) 6

20. In a language, FIFTY is written as CACTY. CAR as POL, TAR as TOL. How can TARIFF be written in that language ? **[Assistant SI 2015]**
(a) TOEFDD
(b) TOEFEL
(c) TOLADD
(d) TOLACC

Direction (Q. Nos. 21-22) *In making decisions about important questions, it is desirable to distinguish between a 'strong' argument and a 'weak' argument. A 'strong' argument must be both important and directly related to the question. A 'weak' argument may not be directly related to the question and may be of minor importance or may be related to the trivial aspect of the question. Each question below is followed by two arguments numbered* I *and* II. *You have to decide which of the arguments is strong and which is weak.*

Give answer
(a) if only Argument I is strong
(b) if only Argument II is strong
(c) if either I or II is strong
(d) if neither I nor II is strong
(e) if both I and II are strong

21. Statement Should competitive examinations for selecting candidates for job consist through objective test only?
Arguments
I. Yes, the assessment of objective test is reliable.
II. No, the number of questions to be answered is always very large.

22. Statement Should strikes in the field of education be banned?
Arguments
I. Yes, it is against professional ethics.
II. Yes, it affects the students adversely.

Direction (Q. Nos. 23-24) *In the following questions, find the odd words/number pair from the given alternatives.*
[SSC (Multitasking) 2014]

23. (a) 5 – 2 (b) 19 – 16
(c) 27 – 23 (d) 31 – 28

24. (a) Chandragupta : Mauryan
(b) Babar : Mughal
(c) Kanishka : Kushan
(d) Mahavira : Jainism

25. If in a certain code language 'LOT' is written as '111314161921', 'SIP' is written as '18208101517', then how will 'GO' be written in that language ?
(a) 681416
(b) 864161
(c) 681476
(d) 681461

26. There are some flowers in a basket and at every next minute they get double. At the 30th minute the basket becomes full. Then, at exactly which minute the basket is half-filled?
(a) 15 min (b) 20 min
(c) 29 min (d) 12 min

Direction (Q. Nos. 27-28) *Each of the following questions below consists of a questions and two statements numbered* I *and* II *given below it. You have to decide whether the data provided in the statements are sufficient to answer questions.*

Give answer

(a) if the data in Statement I alone are sufficient to answer the question, while the data in Statement II alone are not sufficient to answer the question

(b) if the data in Statement II alone are sufficient to answer the question, while the data in Statement I alone are not sufficient to answer the question

(c) if the data either in Statement I alone or Statement II alone are sufficient to answer the question

(d) if the data in both the Statements I and II together are not sufficient to answer the question

(e) if the data in both the Statements I and II are together necessary to answer the question

27. On what day of the week does Arun's birthday fall?

I. Arun's brother correctly remembers that Arun's birthday comes after Wednesday but before Sunday.

II. Arun's sister correctly remembers that Arun's birthday is before Friday.

28. How many daughters does 'L' have?

I. R's father has three daughters.

II. T is R's sister and the daughter of L.

29. The age of X is $\frac{2}{3}$rd that of Y. After 6 yr X will be 46 yr old. The present age of Y is

(a) 40 yr (b) 56 yr
(c) 60 yr (d) 100 yr

30. If it is possible to make only one meaningful word from the 2nd, the 4th, the 6th and the 9th letters of the word 'PROACTIVE', using each letter only once, 2nd letter of that word is your answer. If more than one word can be formed your answer is 'M' and if no such word can be formed your answer is 'N'.

(a) A (b) E (c) T (d) M
(e) N

31. A word is given, followed by four other words, one of which can be formed by using the letters of given word, then find the word. **[SSC (Multitasking) 2012]**

MEASUREMENTED

(a) MASTERO
(b) RENT
(c) TENANT
(d) INSURANCE

Direction (Q. Nos. 32-33) *Read the following information carefully and answer the questions that follow.*

Point H is 6 m towards the East of point G, point R is 8 m North of point G. Point Q is exactly midway between point R and point G. Point K is 10 m to the South of point Q. Point L is 3 m towards the East of point Q. Point S is exactly midway between point G and point H.

32. If a persons walks 4 m towards the South from point L, takes a right turn and walks for another 3 m, then which of the following points would he reach ?

(a) Q (b) G
(c) K (d) H
(e) None of these

33. If a person walks 8 m towards North from point S, then which of the following points would he cross and how far will he be from point R ?

(a) G, 4 m (b) H, 3 m
(c) L, 6 m (d) L, 3m

Direction (Q. Nos. 34-36) *In the following questions, the symbols @, ©, $\underline{@}$, =, $\underline{©}$ are used with following meanings.*

P @ Q ⇒ P is greater than Q.
P © Q ⇒ P is smaller than Q.
P = Q ⇒ P is equal to Q.
P $\underline{@}$ Q ⇒ P is either greater than or equal to Q.
P $\underline{©}$ Q ⇒ P is either smaller than or equal to Q.

Give answer

(a) if only Conclusion I is true
(b) if only Conclusion II is true
(c) if either Conclusion I or II is true
(d) if neither Conclusion I nor II is true
(e) if both Conclusions I and II are true

34. **Statements** B @ V, K © C, C $\underline{\underline{©}}$ B

Conclusions I. V @ C

II. B @ K

35. **Statements** K @ T, S = K, T © R

Conclusions I. S @ T

II. T = R

36. **Statements** U = M, P $\underline{\underline{@}}$ U, M $\underline{\underline{@}}$ B

Conclusions I. P = B

II. P @ B

Direction (Q. Nos. 37-38) *Study the following information carefully to answer the given questions that follow.* **[IBPS (PO) 2012]**

Each of the six friends A ,B ,C ,D ,E and F scored different marks in an examinations. C scored more than only A and E. D scored less than only B. E did not score the least. The one who scores the third highest marks scored 81 marks. E scored 62 marks.

37. Which of the following could possibly by C's score?

(a) 70 (b) 94 (c) 86 (d) 61
(e) 81

38. Which of the following is true with respect to the given information?

(a) D's score was definitely less than 60
(b) F scored the maximum marks
(c) Only two people scored more than C
(d) There is a possibility that B scored 79 marks
(e) None of the above

Direction (Q. Nos. 39-43) *Study the given information carefully to answer the given questions.* **[IBPS RRB (PO) 2015]**

Eight people E, F, G, H, W, X, Y and Z are sitting in two parallel rows containing four people each. E, F,G and H are sitting in row 1 facing North and W, X, Y and Z are sitting in row 2 facing South (but not necessarily in the same order). Thus, each person sitting in row 1 faces another person sitting in row 2. Each of the two rows consists of one Doctor, one Engineer, one Pilot and one Scientist (but not necessarily in the same order).

- The Doctor of row 1 sits second to the right of H. X faces one of the immediate neighbours of H. Only one person sits between the X and the Scientist.
- The one who faces the Scientist of row 2 is an immediate neighbour of E. Only one person sits between E and the Pilot.
- W sits second to the right of Z. Y does not face to G. The Scientist of row 1 faces the Engineer of row 2.
- G faces one of the immediate neighbours of the Doctor of row 2. The Doctor of row 2 does not sit at any of the extreme ends of the line. Z is not a Doctor.

39. Which of the following represents the people sitting at extreme ends of both the lines?

(a) F, H and X, Y
(b) F, H and Z,W
(c) G, E and Z, X
(d) E, H and X, Z
(e) G, E and W, Y

40. Who amongst the following sits to the immediate left of pilot of row 1?

(a) H
(b) The Doctor of row 1
(c) The Engineer of row 1
(d) G
(e) F

41. Which of the following represent both the immediate neighbours of Y?

(a) Z and the Scientist of row 2
(b) X and the Engineer of row 2
(c) W and the Doctor of row 2
(d) X and the Pilot of row 2
(e) W and the Pilot of row 2

42. Which of the given statements is true with respect to the given arrangement?

(a) Y sits to the immediate right of X
(b) F and Z face each other
(c) G is a Scientist
(d) None of the given statements is true
(e) The Engineer of one row faces the Doctor of another row

43. If Y and X interchange their places, so do H and Z, then who amongst the following not face E?

(a) Y
(b) H
(c) F
(d) W
(e) Other than those given as options

44. Group the given figures into different classes on the basis of their orientation, shape etc.

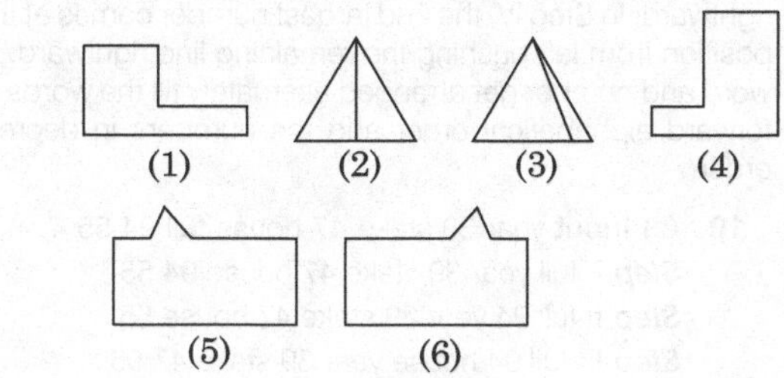

(a) 1, 4
2, 3
5, 6

(b) 1, 5
2, 6
4, 3

(c) 1, 6
2, 3
4, 5

(d) 1, 2
3, 6
4, 5

45. If '–' stands for division, '+' stands for subtraction, '÷' stands for multiplication and '×' stands for addition, then which one of the following equations is correct ? **[SSC (CGL) 2011]**

(a) $70 - 2 + 4 \div 5 \times 6 = 44$
(b) $70 - 2 + 4 \div 5 \times 6 = 21$
(c) $70 - 2 + 4 \div 5 \times 6 = 341$
(d) $70 - 2 + 4 \div 5 \times 6 = 36$

46. If a mirror is placed on line AB, then which of the answer figures is the right image of the given figure? **[SSC (10+2) 2011]**

Question Figure

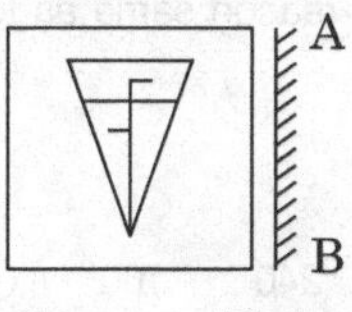

Answer Figures

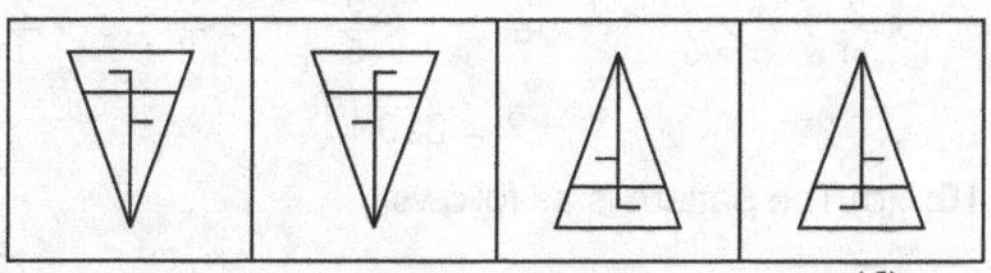

(a) (b) (c) (d)

47. Which answer figure is embedded in the question figure ?

Question Figure

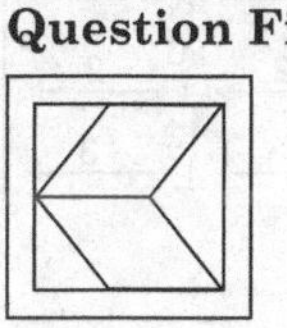

Answer Figures

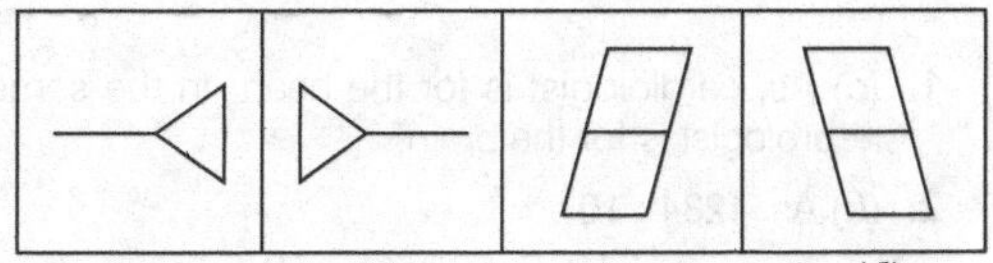

(a) (b) (c) (d)

48. At what time between 9 and 10 O'clock will the hands of a watch be together?

(a) 45 min past 9
(b) 50 min past 9
(c) $49\frac{1}{11}$ min past 9
(d) $48\frac{2}{11}$ min past 9

Direction (Q. Nos. 49-50) *In the following two statements are given followed by two conclusions* I *and* II. *You have to consider the two statements to be true even if they seem to be at variance from commonly known facts. You have to decide which of the given conclusions, if any follow from the given statements.*

(a) Only Conclusion I follow
(b) Only Conclusion II follow
(c) Both Conclusion I and II follow
(d) Either Conclusion I or II follow

49. Statements The increasing population of our nation will lead to depletion of many essential resources. **[SSC (CPO) 2013]**

Conclusions

I. Population of our nation can be controlled.

II. The nation will not be able to provide a decent living to its citezens.

50. Statements The government will review the present policy of the diesel price in view of further spurt in the international oil prices.

Conclusions **[CAT 2011]**

I. The government will increase the price of the diesel after the imminent spurt in the international oil prices.

II. The government will not increase the price of diesel to maintain the proper balance between expenditure and growth rate.

Hints and Solutions

1. (*c*) As, cardiologist is for the heart. In the same way, neurologist is for the brain.

2. (*b*) As, 1234 : 10

$1 + 2 + 3 + 4 = 10$

Similarly, 6789 : 30

$6 + 7 + 8 + 9 = 30$

3. (*c*) In each set, 2nd number = 1st number + 101

3rd number = 2nd number + 101

Let us see

As, $223 + 101 = 324$ and $324 + 101 = 425$

Similarly, $554 + 101 = 655$ and $655 + 101 = 756$

4. (*d*) Some professors can be authors and some authors can be professors but the class of infants is entirely different from these two.

5. (*b*) Meaningful order of words

(iii) Infant → (ii) Child → (iv) Boy → (v) Adolescent → (i) Adult

6. (*c*) As,

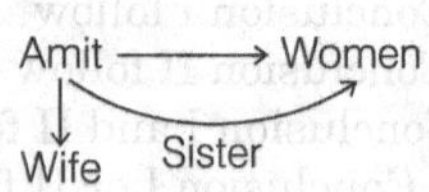

Husband of Amit's wife is Amit himself and his sister is the sister of Amit.

Solution (Q Nos. 7-8) Let us draw the family diagram

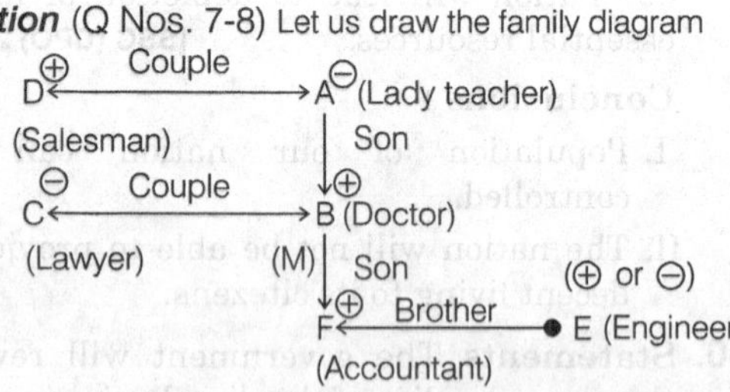

7. (*d*) As it is not clear that E is male or female, so we cannot conclude that E is brother or sister of F.

8. (*b*) B is a Doctor.

9. (*c*) B → 02, 11, 20, (34), 43, O → 01, 10, (24), 33, 42

L → (59), 68, 77, 86, 95, D → 00, (14), 23, 32, 41

BOLD → 34, 24, 59, 14

Solution (Q Nos. 10-11) In the Step I, the word coming first alphabetically comes at the 1st place from left pushing the remaining line rightward; in Step II largest number comes at the 2nd position from left pushing the remaining line rightward; in Step III, the word coming second alphabetically comes at the 3rd place from left pushing the remaining line rightward; in Step IV, the 2nd largest number comes at the 4th position from left pushing the remaining line rightward. Thus, word and number get arranged alternately till the words are in forward alphabetical order and the numbers in decreasing order.

10. (*b*) **Input** year 39 stake 47 house full 94 55

***Step* I** full year 39 stake 47 house 94 55

***Step* II** full 94 year 39 stake 47 house 55

***Step* III** full 94 house year 39 stake 47 55

***Step* IV** full 94 house 55 year 39 stake 47

***Step* V** full 94 house 55 stake year 39 47

***Step* VI** full 94 house 55 stake 47 year 39

∴ Required steps = Six

11. (*b*) ***Step* II** car 83 lost ever 32 46 74 now

***Step* III** car 83 ever lost 32 46 74 now

***Step* IV** car 83 ever 74 lost 32 46 now

***Step* V** car 83 ever 74 lost 46 32 now

***Step* VI** car 83 ever 74 lost 46 now 32

∴ Required more steps = Four

12. (*b*) Option (b) is correct answer figure.

13. (*d*) Option (d) will complete the given pattern as follows

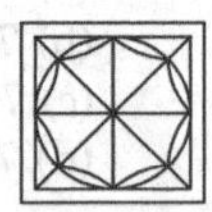

14. (*a*) Option (b) is eliminated on the ground that Quareshi and Nathumal cannot go together. Option (c) can be eliminated as Ramprasad has disputes with Popatlal, so they cannot go together.

Option (d) is also eliminated, reason same as for the option (b).

So, right option is (a).

15. (*c*) The pattern is as follows

51975 → 9450 → 2100 → 600 → 240 → 160 → (320)

$\times\frac{2}{11}$, $\times\frac{2}{9}$, $\times\frac{2}{7}$, $\times\frac{2}{5}$, $\times\frac{2}{3}$, $\times\frac{2}{1}$

∴ ? = 320

16. (*c*) The pattern is as follows

1st Letter	A (1)	+3 →	D (4)	+3 →	G (7)	+3 →	J (10)	+3 →	M (13)
2nd Letter	Y (25)	−2 →	W (23)	−2 →	U (21)	−2 →	S (19)	−2 →	Q (17)
3rd Letter	B (2)	+3 →	E (5)	+3 →	H (8)	+3 →	K (11)	+3 →	N (14)
4th Letter	Z (26)	−2 →	X (24)	−2 →	V (22)	−2 →	T (20)	−2 →	R (18)
5th Letter	C (3)	+3 →	F (6)	+3 →	I (9)	+3 →	L (12)	+3 →	O (15)

∴ ? = MQNRO

Solution (Q. Nos. 17-18)

17. (*e*)

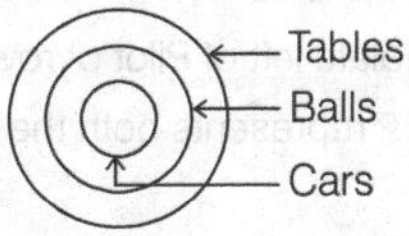

Conclusions I. (✔) II. (✔)

So, both Conclusion I and II follow.

18. (*d*)

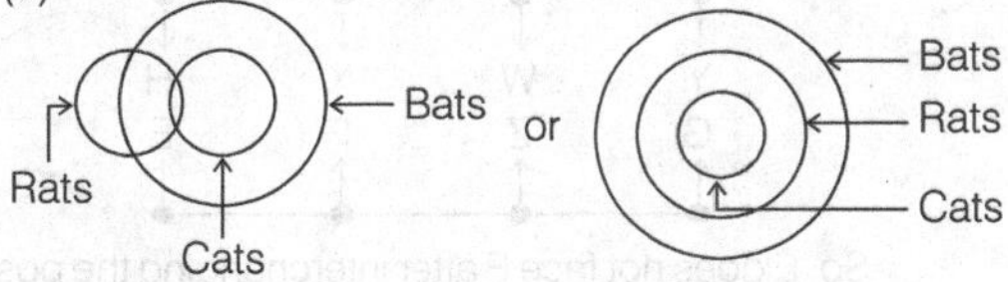

Conclusions I. (✗) II. (✗)

So, neither Conclusion I nor II follows.

19. (*b*) From positions II and III

Position II (clockwise) (5) (4) (2)

Position III (5) (3) (1)

Clearly, digit opposite to 3 = 4

20. (*d*) As, F I F T Y → C A C T Y

Also, C A R → P O L and T A R → T O L

By direct substitution method, we get T A R I F F → T O L A C C

21. (*a*) The second argument that the number of questions to be answered is always very large is very generalised. But the first argument that the assessment of objective test is reliable is a strong argument.

22. (*b*) Argument II is strong. Strike is against the professional ethics is weak argument, but it affects the students adversely, is strong one.

23. (*c*) 5 − 2 = 3, 19 − 16 = 3, 27 − 23 = 4, 31 − 28 = 3

Clearly, pair 27-23 is different from others.

24. (*d*) In all pairs except (d), first is the founder of second.

25. (*a*) Each letter is coded with its left and right letters positions.

As, L O T (12 15 20) → K M N P S U (11 13 14 16 19 21)

Also, S I P (19 9 16) → R T H J O Q (18 20 8 10 15 17)

Similarly, G O (7 15) → F H N P (6 8 14 16)

∴ GO ⇒ 681416

26. (*c*) At every next minute flowers in the basket get doubled. Therefore, it was half-filled in 29th min.

27. (*e*) According to Arun's brother, birthday = Thursday / Friday / Saturday

According to Arun's sister, birthday = Thursday

Clearly, required day of birthday = Thursday

So, both statements are required to answer the question.

28. (*e*) From Statement II, it is clear that T is R's sister and it is given in Statement I that R's father has three daughters it means that L is the father of R and T both. Hence, L has three daughters.

So, both statements are required to answer the question.

29. (*c*) $X = \frac{2}{3}Y \quad \therefore Y = \frac{3}{2}X$

Age of X after 6 years = 46 yr

∴ Present age of X = 46 − 6 = 40 yr

Now, present age of Y = $\frac{3}{2} \times 40 = 60$ yr

30. (*d*) P (R) O (A) C (T) I V (E)

(R) 2nd, (A) 4th, (T) 6th, (E) 9th

Meaningful words = TEAR, RATE

31. (*b*) By using the letters of given word, 'RENT' is the only word which can be formed.

Solution (Q. Nos. 32-33) According to the given information, the direction diagram is as follows

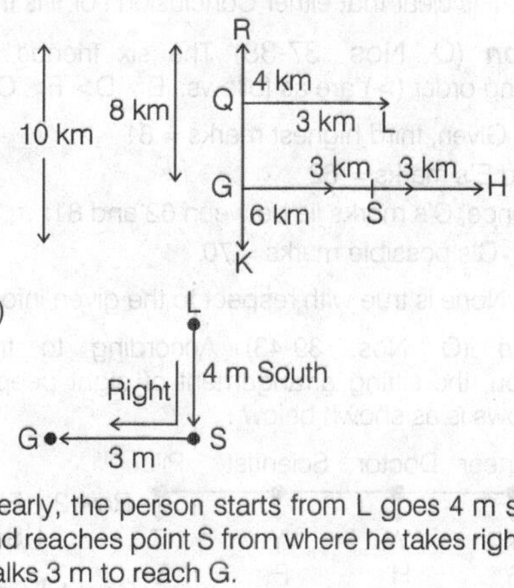

32. (*b*)

Clearly, the person starts from L goes 4 m southward and reaches point S from where he takes right turn and walks 3 m to reach G.

33. (*d*)

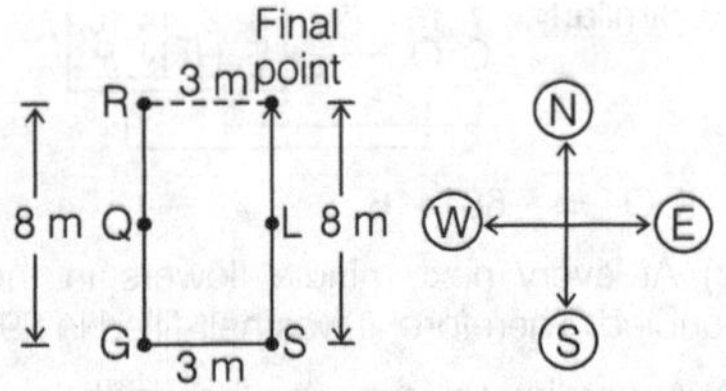

Clearly, man will cross L and at the final point, he will be at distance of 3 m from R.

Solution (Q. Nos 34-36) Given that,

@ ⇒ >	$\underline{@}$ ⇒ ≥	$\underline{©}$ ⇒ ≤	© ⇒ <	= ⇒ =

34. (*b*) According to the question, B @ V ⇒ B > V ...(i)
K © C ⇒ K < C ...(ii), C $\underline{©}$ B ⇒ C ≤ B ...(iii)
On combining Eqs. (i), (ii) and (iii), we get
K < C ≤ B > V
Conclusions I. V @ C ⇒ V > C (False)
II. B @ K ⇒ B > K (True)
So, it is clear that only Conclusion II is true.

35. (*a*) According to the question, K @ T ⇒ K > T ...(i)
S = K ⇒ S = K ...(ii), T © R ⇒ T < R ...(iii)
On combining Eqs. (i), (ii) and (iii), we get
S = K > T < R
Conclusions I. S @ T ⇒ S > T (True)
II. T = R ⇒ T = R (False)
So, it is clear that only Conclusion I is true.

36. (*c*) According to the question, U = M ⇒ U = M ...(i)
P $\underline{@}$ U ⇒ P ≥ U ...(ii), M $\underline{@}$ B ⇒ M ≥ B ...(iii)
On combining Eqs. (i), (ii) and (iii), we get P ≥ U = M ≥ B
Conclusions I. P = B ⇒ P = B (May be true)
II. P @ B ⇒ P > B (May be true)
So, it is clear that either Conclusion I or II is true.

Solution (Q. Nos. 37-38) The six friends marks in descending order (>) are as follows. B > D > F > C > E > A

37. (*a*) Given, third highest marks = 81
and E's marks = 62
Hence, C's possible marks lie between 62 and 81.
∴ C's possible marks = 70.

38. (*e*) None is true with respect to the given information.

Solution (Q. Nos. 39-43) According to the given information, the sitting arrangement of eight people in two parallel rows is as shown below :

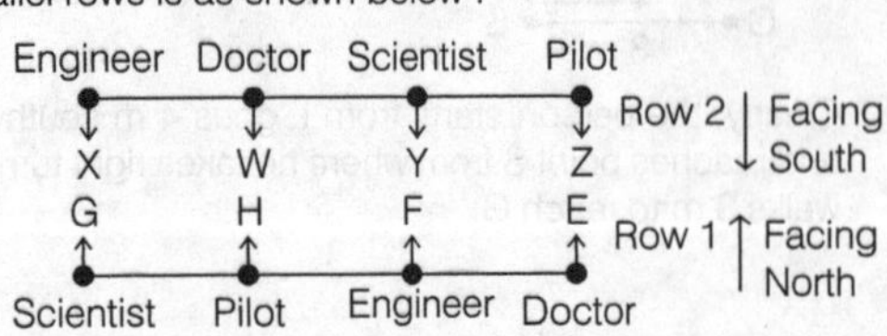

39. (*c*) G, E and Z, X represents the people sitting at extreme ends of both the lines.

40. (*d*) G sits to the immediate left of Pilot of row 1.

41. (*e*) W and Pilot of row 2 represents both the immediate neighbour of Y.

42. (*c*) G is a scientist

43. (*c*) If Y and X interchange their places, so do H and Z as shown below

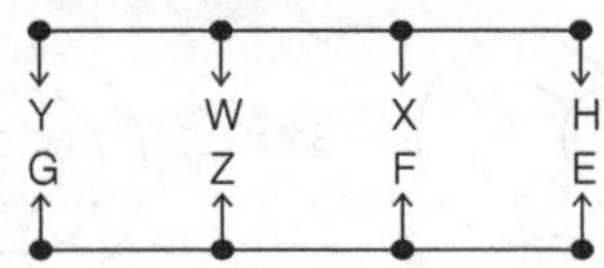

So, E does not face F after interchanging the positions.

44. (*a*) Figures 1 and 4 are similar.
Figures 2 and 3 are similar.
Figures 5 and 6 are similar.

45. (*b*)

− ⇒ ÷	+ ⇒ −
÷ ⇒ ×	× ⇒ +

From option (a), 70 − 2 + 4 ÷ 5 × 6 = 44
⇒ 70 ÷ 2 − 4 × 5 + 6 = 44 ⇒ 35 − 20 + 6 ≠ 44
From option (b), 70 − 2 + 4 ÷ 5 × 6 = 21
⇒ 70 ÷ 2 − 4 × 5 + 6 = 21
⇒ 35 − 20 + 6 = 21 ⇒ 41 − 20 = 21 ∴ 21 = 21

46. (*a*) The correct laterally inverted mirror image of the question figure is as follows

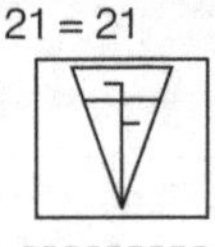

47. (*a*) Clearly, answer figure (a) is embedded in question figure and has been shown in the adjacent figure

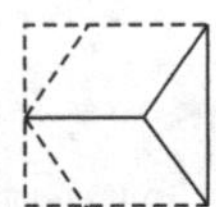

48. (*c*) Here, we have

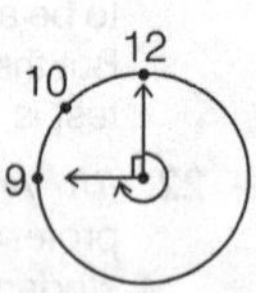

Total displacement = 270°
Relative displacement angle = 5.5°
Time taken to cover distance $= \frac{270}{5.5}$
$= \frac{270 \times 10}{55} = \frac{540}{11}$
$= 49\frac{1}{11}$ min
So, at $49\frac{1}{11}$ min past 9 the hands of the clock will be together.

49. (*b*) Only conclusion II follows because the nation will not be able to provide a decent living to its citizens cause of the increasing population of our nation.

50. (*a*) Only conclusion II is wrong which is not related to statement.

PRACTICE SET 17

1. There are four choices of words with their letters jumbled up. Three of them are alike but one is different. Find out the odd one.
(a) MDOANY (b) YFDRIA
(c) HIODALY (d) YADWESDEN

2. Point B is 12 m South of point A. Point C is 24 m East of point B. Point D is 8 m South of point C. Point D is 12 m East of point E and point F is 8 m North of point E. If a man has to travel to point E from point A (through these points by the shortest distance), then which of the following points will he pass through first?
(a) Point C (b) Point D
(c) Point F (d) Point B

3. Select the related word from the given alternatives.
Blind : Visual :: Deaf : ?
(a) Hearing (b) Listening
(c) Auditory (d) Sound

4. In the given diagram, find out the number of people who do not read any newspaper. **[SSC (10+2) 2012]**

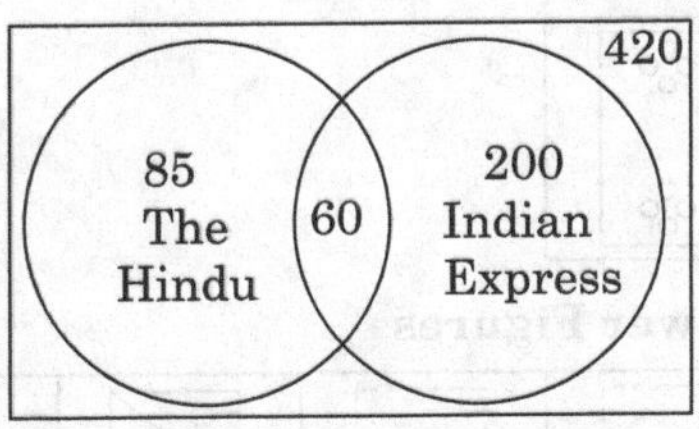

(a) 175 (b) 75 (c) 195 (d) 135

5. Select the related letters from the given alternative.
YTOJ : XSNI :: WRMH : ? **[SSC (CGL) 2014]**
(a) VQLG (b) TOJE
(c) RMHC (d) UPKF

Direction (Q. Nos. 6-8) *Read the following information carefully and answer the questions based on it.*

Ten students A, B, C, D, E, F, G, H, I and J are sitting in a row facing West.

I. B and F are not sitting on either of the edges.
II. G is sitting to the left of D and H is sitting to the right of J.
III. There are four persons between E and A.
IV. I is to the North of B and F is to the South of D.
V. J is in between A and D and G is in between E and F.
VI. There are two persons between H and C.

6. Who is sitting at the seventh place counting from left?
(a) H (b) C
(c) J (d) Either H or C

7. Who among the following is definitely sitting at one of the ends?
(a) C
(b) H
(c) E
(d) Cannot be determined

8. Who are immediate neighbours of I?
(a) BC (b) BH
(c) AH (d) Cannot be determined

Direction (Q. Nos. 9-10) *What will come in place of question mark (?) ?*

9. BEAG, DGCI, FIEK , ?
(a) HMIE (b) HKGM
(c) HGKJ (d) HKLJ

10. bc, cde, de, efg, fg, ?
(a) ghi (b) fgh (c) hij (d) ijk

11. Select the missing number from the given responses.

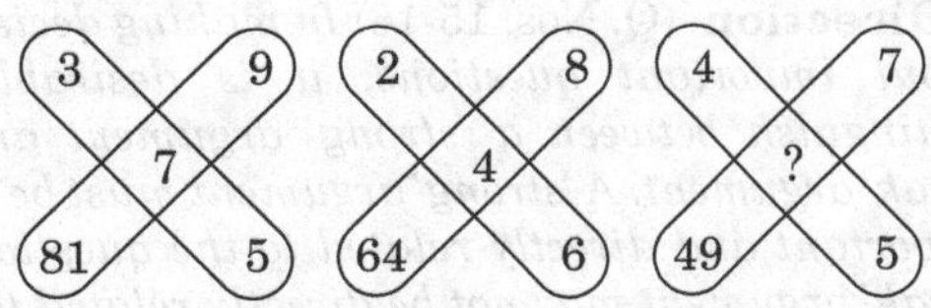

(a) 1 (b) 8 (c) 6 (d) 16

Direction (Q Nos. 12-13) *Each of the following questions below consists of a question and two statements numbered I and II given below it. You have to decide whether the data provided in the statements are sufficient to answer the question.*

Give answer

(a) if the data in Statement I alone are sufficient to answer the question, while the data in Statement II alone are not sufficient to answer the question
(b) if the data in Statement II alone are sufficient to answer the question, while the data in Statement I alone are not sufficient to answer the question
(c) if the data either in Statement I alone or Statement II alone are sufficient to answer the question
(d) if the data in both the Statements I and II together are not sufficient to answer the question
(e) if the data in both the Statements I and II are together necessary to answer the question

12. In a certain code language, '146' means 'adopt good habits'. What is the code of 'habit' in that language?

I. '473' means 'like good pictures'.
II. '826' means 'passion becomes habits'.

13. Point X is in which direction in respect of point Y? **[SBI (Clerk) 2011]**

I. Point Z is at equal distance from point X and point Y.
II. Point X is at a distance of 5 km from point Y.

14. From the given responses, find the odd figure out.

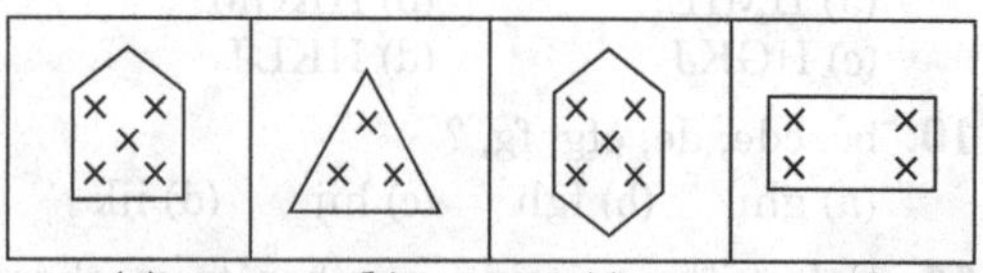

(a) (b) (c) (d)

Direction (Q. Nos. 15-16) *In making decisions about important questions, it is desirable to distinguish between a 'strong' argument and a 'weak' argument. A 'strong' argument must be both important and directly related to the question. A 'weak' argument may not be directly related to the question and may be of minor importance or may be related to the trivial aspect of the question. Each question below is followed by two arguments, numbered I and II. You have to decide which of the arguments is 'strong' and which is 'weak'.*

Give answer

(a) if only Argument I is strong
(b) if only Argument II is strong
(c) if either I or II is strong
(d) if neither I nor II is strong
(e) if both I and II are strong

15. Statement Do children adopted from poor families love their new rich parents like their own poor ones?

Arguments

I. Yes, because they are loved, cared for and provided with comforts of life.
II. No, because in the criminal world, they become selfish and hard boiled.

16. Statement Do Scientists believe in religion?

Arguments

I. Yes, because Science as a profession does not come in the way of faith.
II. No, because religion and faith donot go together.

17. A rectangular paper is folded in a particular manner and a punch is made. When unfolded, the paper appears as given below.

Find out the manner in which the paper is folded and punch is made from the responses given.

Question Figure

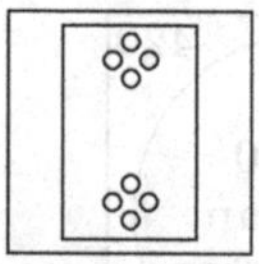

Answer Figures

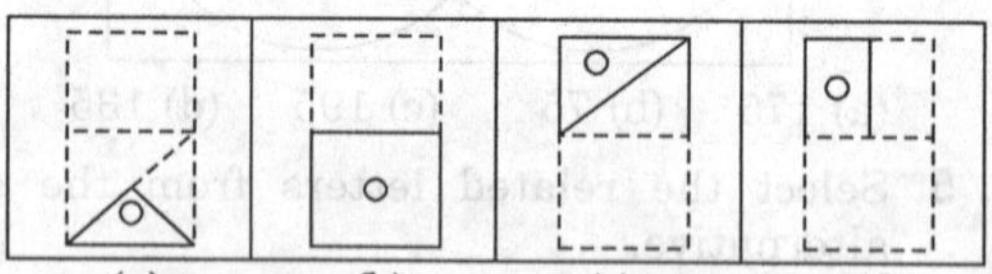

(a) (b) (c) (d)

Direction (Q. Nos.18-19) *Study the following information carefully and then answer the questions given below it.*

A word and number arrangement machine when given on input line of words and numbers rearranges them following a particular rule in each step. The following is an illustration of input and rearrangement.

Input 'past back 32 47 19 own fear 25'
***Step* I** 19 past back 32 47 own fear 25
***Step* II** 19 past 25 back 32 47 own fear
***Step* III** 19 past 25 own back 32 47 fear
***Step* IV** 19 past 25 own 32 back 47 fear
***Step* V** 19 past 25 own 32 fear back 47
***Step* VI** 19 past 25 own 32 fear 47 back
and Step VI is the last step.

As per rules followed in the above steps, find out in each of the following questions, the appropriate step for the given input.

18. Step II of an input is '21 win tyre 46 39 case file 51'

Which of the following will be Step VI?
(a) 21 win 39 tyre 46 file case 51
(b) 21 win 39 tyre 46 file 51 case
(c) 21 win 39 tyre file 46 51 case
(d) 21 win 39 tyre 46 case file 51
(e) There will be no such step

19. **Input** '83 42 bench lower 13 upper floor 37'. Which of the following will be Step III?
(a) 13 upper 37 83 42 bench lower floor
(b) 13 upper 37 lower 83 42 bench floor
(c) 13 83 42 bench lower upper floor 37
(d) 13 upper 83 42 bench lower floor 37
(e) None of the above

20. A word is represented by only one set of numbers are given in anyone of the alternatives. The sets of numbers given in the alternatives are represented by two classes of alphabets as in the two given matrices. The columns and rows of Matrix I are numbered from 0 to 4 and those of Matrix II from 5 to 9. A letter from these matrices can be represented first by its row and then the column number e.g. 'M' can be represented by 58, 67, etc., O can be represented by 01, 10 etc. Similarly you have to identify the correct set for the word given in each question.

Matrix I

	0	1	2	3	4
0	D	O	B	A	I
1	O	B	A	I	D
2	B	A	I	O	D
3	A	I	D	O	B
4	I	D	O	B	A

Matrix II

	5	6	7	8	9
5	W	N	R	M	L
6	N	R	M	L	W
7	R	M	L	W	N
8	M	L	W	N	R
9	L	W	N	R	M

RAIN
(a) 57, 12, 31, 56 (b) 57, 21, 23, 79
(c) 66, 44, 42, 96 (d) 75, 30, 31, 87

21. If a mirror is placed on line AB, then which of the answer figures is the right image of the given figure?

Question Figure

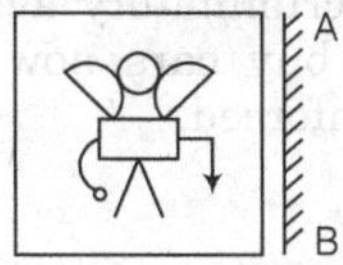

Answer Figures

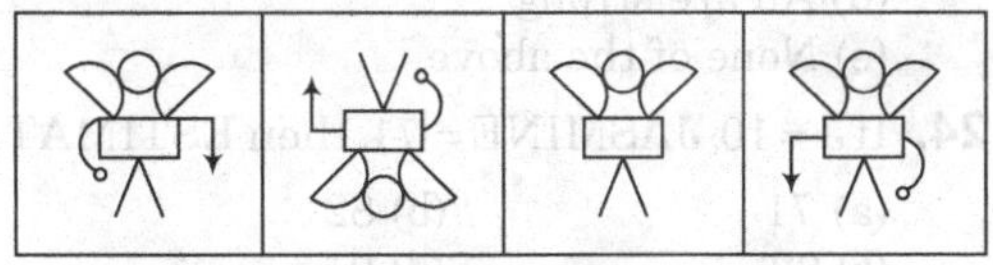

(a) (b) (c) (d)

22. Which answer figure will complete the pattern in the question figure?

Question Figure **[SSC (10+2) 2012]**

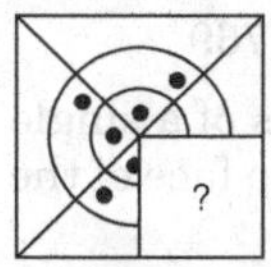

Answer Figures

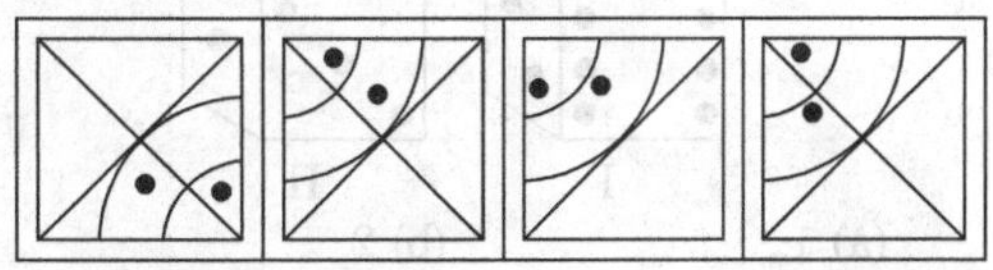

(a) (b) (c) (d)

23. In making decisions about important questions, it is desirable to distinguish between a 'strong' argument and a 'weak' argument. A 'strong' argument must be both important and directly related to the question. A 'weak' argument may not be directly related to the question and may be of minor importance or may be related to the trivial aspect of the question. Each question below is followed by three arguments numbered I, II and III. You have to decide which of the arguments is 'strong' and which is 'weak'.

Statements Should there be a complete ban on registration of new cars for a few months in the big cities in India?

Arguments

I. Yes, this will significantly reduce the number of cars on the already overcrowded roads of the big cities in India.

II. Yes, the existing car owners will be very happy as they will face less traffic snarls in peak hours.

III. No, this is highly discriminatory against those who decide to buy cars now and hence should not be enforced.

(a) Only I is strong
(b) I and II are strong
(c) Only III is strong
(d) All are strong
(e) None of the above

24. If J = 10, JASMINE = 71, then ESTIMATE = ?

(a) 71 (b) 82
(c) 92 (d) 91

25. If EXPANSION is written as 248537693, in a certain code how would PENSION be written in that code?

(a) 8236793 (b) 8237639
(c) 8237693 (d) 8233769

26. From the given two positions of a single dice, find the number of dots at top face of the dice, if its bottom face has 6 dots.

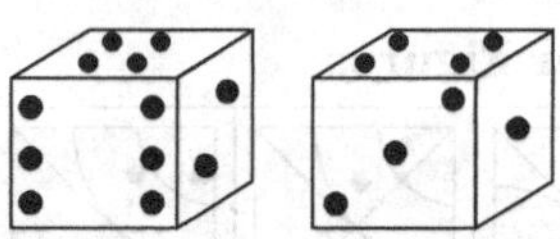

I II

(a) 1 (b) 2
(c) 4 (d) 5

Direction (Q. Nos. 27-29) *Study the following information carefully and answer the questions given below.* **[SBI (PO) 2013]**

Eight people E, F, G, H, J, K, L and M are sitting around a circular table facing the centre. Each of them is of a different profession Chartered Accountant, Columnist, Doctor, Engineer, Financial Analyst, Lawyer, Professor and Scientist but not necessarily in the same order. F is sitting second to the left of K. The Scientist is an immediate neighbour of K. There are only three people between the Scientist and E. Only one person sits between the Engineer and E. The Columnist is to the immediate right of the Engineer. M is second to the right of K, H is the Scientist. G and J are immediate neighbours of each other. Neither G nor J is an Engineer. The Financial Analyst is to the immediate left of F. The Lawyer is second to the right of the Columnist The Professor is an immediate neighbour of the Engineer. G is second to the right of the Chartered Accountant.

27. Who is sitting second to the right of E?

(a) Lawyer (b) G
(c) Engineer (d) F
(e) K

28. Who amongst the following is the professor?

(a) F (b) L
(c) M (d) K
(e) J

29. Four of the following five are alike in a certain way based on the given arrangement and hence form a group. Which of the following does not belong to that group?

(a) H-Chartered Accountant
(b) M-Doctor
(c) J-Engineer
(d) L-Financial Analyst
(e) K-Layer

30. How many quadrilaterals are there in the figure given below?

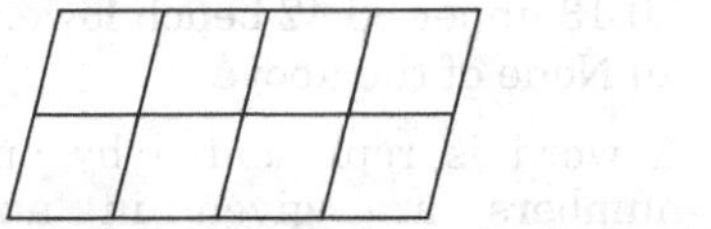

(a) 12 (b) 20 (c) 29 (d) 30

31. A group of ten students shake hands with one another among themselves. What is the total number of shaking of hands?

(a) 20 (b) 56 (c) 90 (d) 45

Direction (Q. Nos. 32-34) *In each of the questions below are given two statements followed by two conclusions numbered I and II. You have to take the two given statements to be true even if they seem to be at variance from commonly known facts and decide which of the given conclusion (s) logically follow (s) from the two given statements, disregarding commonly known facts.*

Give answer

(a) if only Conclusion I follows
(b) if only Conclusion II follows
(c) if either Conclusion I or II follows
(d) if neither Conclusion I nor II follows
(e) if both Conclusions I and II follow

32. Statements Some cities are towns
Some villages are cities.

Conclusions
I. Atleast some villages are towns.
II. No village is a town.

33. Statements Some pins are clips.
Some clips are pens.

Conclusions I. Some pins are pens.
II. Some pins are not pens.

34. Statements All Ds are As.
All As are Cs.

Conclusions I. All Ds are Cs.
II. Some Ds are As.

35. Sameer remembers that his brother's birthday is after fifteenth but before 18th of February whereas his sister Kanika remembers that her brother's birthday is after 16th but before 19th of February. On which day in February is Sameer's brother's birthday?
(a) 15th February (b) 18th February
(c) 17th February (d) None of these

36. From the given alternatives words, select the word which cannot be formed using the letters of the given word. **[SSC (10+2) 2011]**
EMBOSSMENT
(a) BOSS (b) TOMB
(c) STEM (d) MATS

37. Deepa starts walking Northwards and after a while, she turns to her right. After walking some distance, she turns to her left and walks a distance of 1 km. She then turns to her left again. In which direction is she moving now?
(a) North (b) West (c) East (d) South

38. Find the odd word from the given alternatives.
(a) Cement (b) Glue (c) Gum (d) Lock

39. The age of Mrs Anjali is five times the age of her son. After 12 yr, the age of Mrs Anjali will be only thrice the age of her son. Find the present age of Mrs Anjali's son.
(a) 4 yr (b) 16 yr (c) 12 yr (d) 18 yr

40. Arrange the following words as per order in the dictionary.
(i) Genuine (ii) Genesis
(iii) Gender (iv) Gentle
(v) General
(a) (iii), (v), (ii), (iv), (i)
(b) (ii), (v), (iii), (i), (iv)
(c) (iv), (v), (iii), (ii), (i)
(d) (i), (v), (iv), (iii), (ii)

41. In a row of girls, Veena is 12th from the start and 19th from the end. In another row of girls, Sunita is 14th from the start and 20th from the end. How many girls are there in both the rows together?
(a) 72 (b) 65
(c) 63 (d) 61

Direction (Q. Nos. 42-44) *In the following questions, the symbols @, ©, $, % and ★ are used with the following meaning as illustrated below :*
'P © Q' means 'P is not smaller than Q'.
'P ★ Q' means 'P is not greater than Q'.
'P @ Q' means 'P is neither greater than nor equal to Q'.
'P $ Q' means 'P is neither smaller than nor equal to Q'.
'P % Q' means 'P is neither greater than nor smaller than Q'.

42. Statements J $ K, K ★ T, T @ N, N © R
Conclusions
I. J $ T II. R ★ T
III. N $ K IV. R ★ K
(a) None is true (b) Only I is true
(c) Only II is true (d) Only III is true
(e) Only IV is true

43. Statements F % W, W © R, R @ M, M $ D
Conclusions
I. D @ R II. M $ F
III. R @ D IV. R ★ F
(a) None is true
(b) Only I is true
(c) Only II is true
(d) Only IV is true
(e) Only III is true

44. Statements H @ B, B ★ E, V©E, W $ V
Conclusions
I. W $ E II. H @ E
III. H @ V IV. W $ B
(a) I and II are true
(b) Only I, II and III are true
(c) Only II, III and IV are true
(d) All I, II, III and IVare true
(e) None of the above

Direction (Q. Nos. 45-46) *Select the missing number from the given responses.*

45. **[SSC (CPO) 2014]**

7	9	8
2	4	3
5	7	6
16	32	?

(a) 17 (b) 23 (c) 47 (d) 73

46. X, Q, K, F, ?

(a) E (b) B (c) C (d) Q

47. If A means '÷', B means '–' and C means '×', then find the value of following equation.

46 A 2 B 3 C 4 = ?

(a) 34 (b) 23
(c) 17 (d) 11

48. Tarun is the father of Rohit. Rohit is the brother of Kala. Kala is the wife of Dilip. How is Dilip related to Rohit? **[SSC (FCI) 2012]**

(a) Brother-in-law (b) Father-in-law
(c) Son (d) Uncle

49. Five birds Crow, Pigeon, Little Pigeon, Big Crow and Eagle fly one after other from a tree branch. Big Crow flew after Crow but is ahead of Eagle. Pigeon is between Crow and Big Crow. Little Pigeon is before Crow. Which bird is the last?

(a) Pigeon
(b) Big Crow
(c) Eagle
(d) None of the above

50. Which of the following diagrams represents the relationship among Apple, Banana and Mango?

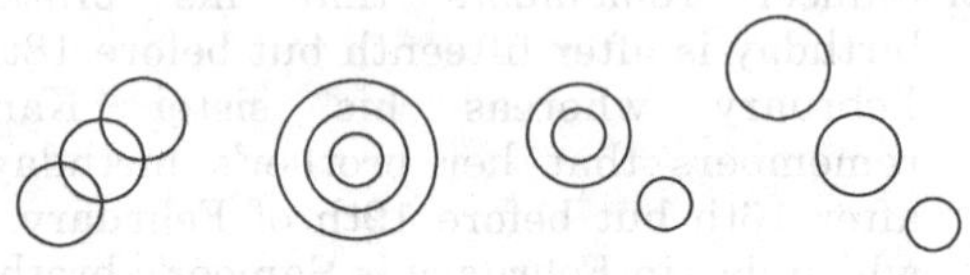

(a) (b) (c) (d)

Hints and Solutions

1. (*c*) Question is framed on jumbling of letters of words. By observing the options we can have following meaningful words.

From option (a) MDOANY, we have MONDAY
From option (b) YFDRIA, we have FRIDAY
From option (a) HIODALY, we have
HOLIDAY
and
From option (d) YADWESDEN, we have WEDNESDAY

Now, obviously we see Monday, Friday, Wednesday are week days and are alike entities while Holiday is odd one.

2. (*d*) From the given information following graph can be drawn

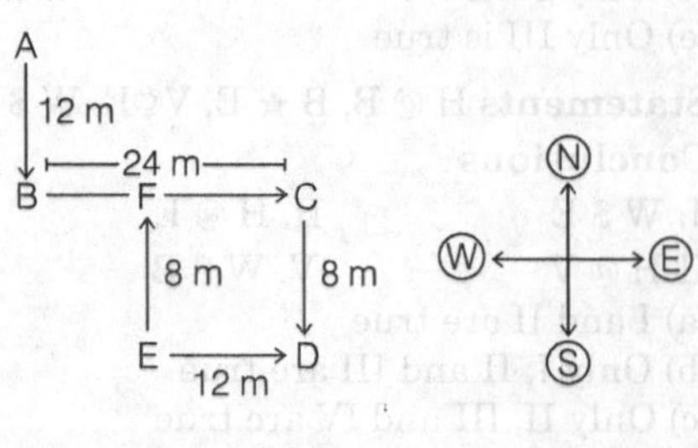

While travelling to point E from point A, he will pass through point B first.

3. (*c*) As, the visual defect is possessed by 'blind' person.

In the same way, 'Auditory' defect is possessed by 'Deaf' person.

4. (*c*) The number of people who do not read any newspaper

$= 420 - (200 + 85 - 60)$
$= 420 - 225$
$= 195$

5. (*a*) As,

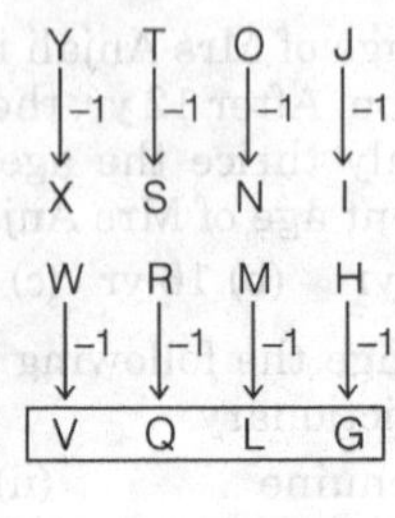

Similarly,

Solution (Q. Nos. 6-8) On the basis of the given information, exact positions of C and H cannot be determined. However, they will occupy the first and the fourth positions. Now, the arrangement is as follows

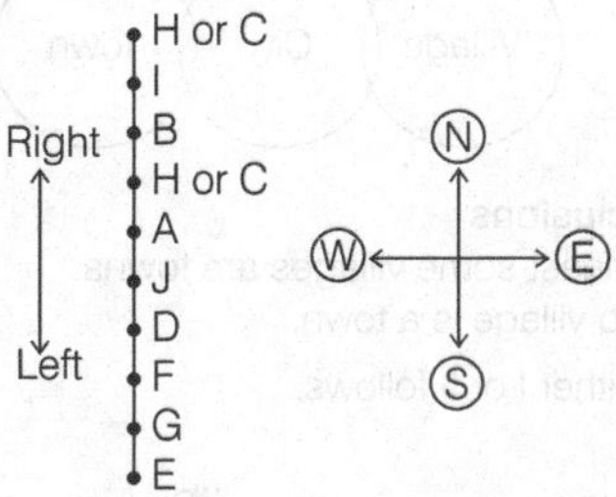

6. (*d*) Either H or C will occupy seventh position from the left.

7. (*c*) Clearly, E is definitely sitting at one of the ends.

8. (*d*) The immediate neighbours of I cannot be determined because the position of H and C are not fixed.

9. (*b*) We have following pattern,

B $\xrightarrow{+2}$ D $\xrightarrow{+2}$ F $\xrightarrow{+2}$ H
E $\xrightarrow{+2}$ G $\xrightarrow{+2}$ I $\xrightarrow{+2}$ K
A $\xrightarrow{+2}$ C $\xrightarrow{+2}$ E $\xrightarrow{+2}$ G
G $\xrightarrow{+2}$ I $\xrightarrow{+2}$ K $\xrightarrow{+2}$ M

From the above pattern, we notice that first letter of each group is promoted by two letters, second letter, third letter and fourth letter is also promoted by two letters.

Hence, answer will be HKGM.

10. (*a*) bc, cde, de, efg, fg, ghi

In this series, last letter of each alternate term (starting from first term) starts the new term and next two letters are included in the term.

11. (*c*) **Figure I** $[(7 + 5) - 3] \times 9 = 81$

Figure II $[(4 + 6) - 2] \times 8 = 64$

Likewise, in figure III $[(? + 5) - 4] \times 7 = 49$

$\Rightarrow \quad ? + 5 = 11 \Rightarrow ? = 6$

12. (*b*) Given that, 1 4 6 = adopt good habits ...(A)
From Statement I, 473 = like good pictures
From Statement II, 8 2 6 = passion becomes habits
From Statement II and (A), 6 = habits
So, Statement II alone is required to answer the question.

13. (*d*) Both statements are insufficient to answer the question as directions is not given in any of the statements or we can say that data is inadequate.

14. (*c*) Except figure (c), in all other figures there are as many cross signs as there are sides in the figure.

15. (*a*) If poor children are loved, cared for and provided with comforts of life, they will definitely respond strongly and positively in terms of respect to their parents. Argument II is not strong. So, only Argument I is strong.

16. (*a*) Argument I is strong because profession and religion are altogether different. Argument II is irrelevant.

17. (*a*) 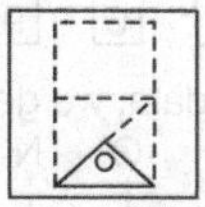

So, option (a) is correct Answer.

Solution (Q. Nos. 18-19) The given problem is based on arrangement in which numbers and words get arranged alternately. Numbers get arranged in ascending order while words get arranged in reverse alphabetical order.

18. (*e*) ***Step* II** 21 win tyre 46 39 case file 51
***Step* III** 21 win 39 tyre 46 case file 51
***Step* IV** 21 win 39 tyre 46 file case 51
***Step* V** 21 win 39 tyre 46 file 51 case
This is the last step. Hence, there will be no VI step.

19. (*a*) **Input** 83 42 bench lower 13 upper floor 37
***Step* I** 13 83 42 bench lower upper floor 37
***Step* II** 13 upper 83 42 bench lower floor 37
***Step* III** 13 upper 37 83 42 bench lower floor

20. (*a*) R → (57), 66, 75, 89, 98
A → 03, (12), 21, 30, 44
I → 04, 13, 22, (31), 40
N → (56), 65, 79, 88, 97
RAIN → 57, 12, 31, 56

21. (*d*) The correct laterally inverted mirror image of the question figure is as follows

22. (*b*) Clearly, option (b) figure will complete the pattern of the given figure

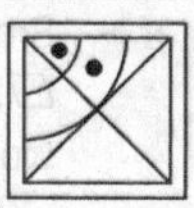

23. (*c*) Arguments I and II do not provide a strong enough reason for putting up a complete ban on registration of new cars because this is highly discriminatory against the new buyers. So, Argument III is strong argument because it opposes the statement with a strong reason.

24. (*c*) According to the question, we have position number as in English alphabetical series.

J A S M I N E
10 + 1 + 19 + 13 + 9 + 14 + 5 = 71

Similarly,

E S T I M A T E
5 + 19 + 20 + 9 + 13 + 1 + 20 + 5 = 92

25. (*c*) We have the following coding

E	X	P	A	N	S	I	O	N
↓	↓	↓	↓	↓	↓	↓	↓	↓
2	4	8	5	3	7	6	9	3

Similarly, using above coding data, we get

P	E	N	S	I	O	N
↓	↓	↓	↓	↓	↓	↓
8	2	3	7	6	9	3

26. (*d*) In both the positions, 4 dots are common at the same (top) face. So, face having 6 dots will be opposite to the face having 3 dots according to the clockwise direction.

Solution (Q. Nos. 27-29) According to the given information, we have the following arrangement

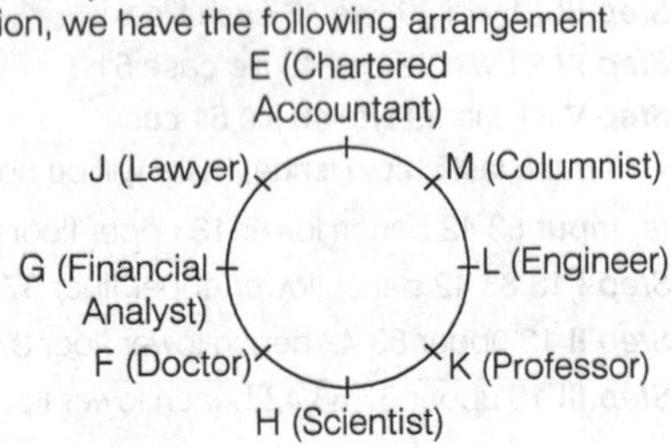

27. (*b*) G is sitting second to the right of E.

28. (*d*) K is the professor.

29. (*c*) Except J-Engineer, in all other options, there are three persons between first and second person.

30. (*d*)

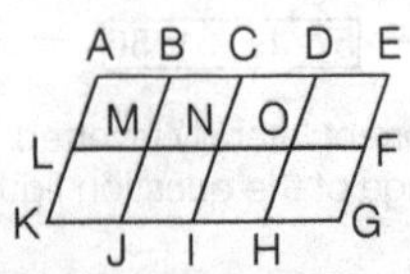

Smallest quadrilaterals = ▱ABML, ▱BCNM, ▱CDON, ▱DOFE, ▱LKJM, ▱MNIJ, ▱NIHO, ▱OFGH = 8

Quadrilaterals formed with two quadrilaterals
= ▱ABJK, ▱BCIJ, ▱CDHI, ▱DEGH, ▱ACNL, ▱CEFN, ▱LNIK, ▱NFGI, ▱BDOM, ▱MOHJ = 10

Quadrilaterals formed with three quadrilaterals
= ▱ADOL, ▱BEFM, ▱LOHK, ▱MFGJ = 4

Quadrilaterals formed with four quadrilaterals
= ▱ACIK, ▱CEGI, ▱BDHJ, ▱AEFL, ▱LFGK = 5

Quadrilaterals formed with six quadrilaterals
= ▱ADHK, ▱BEGJ = 2

Largest quadrilateral = ▱AEGK = 1

∴ Total number of quadrilaterals
$= 8 + 10 + 4 + 5 + 2 + 1 = 30$

Shortcut Method

Number of quadrilaterals $= (4 + 3 + 2 + 1) \times (2 + 1)$
$= 10 \times 3 = 30$

31. (*c*) Total number of handshakes $= 10 \times (10 - 1)$
$= 10 \times 9 = 90$

32. (*c*)

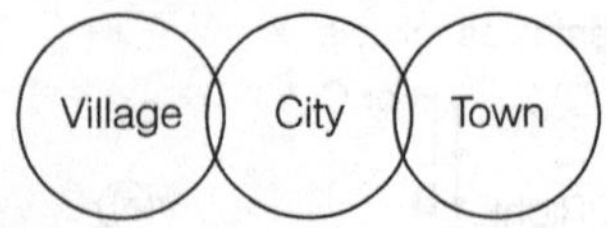

Conclusions
I. Atleast some villages are towns. (May be true)
II. No village is a town. (May be true)

So, either I or II follows.

33. (*c*)

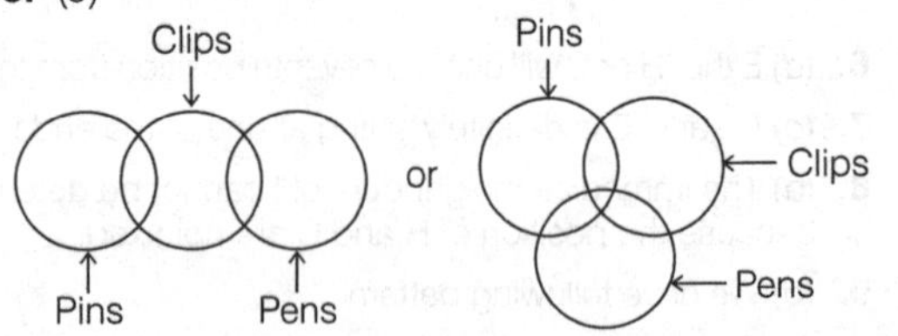

Conclusions I. Some pins are pens. (May be true)
II. Some pins are not pens. (May be true)

Complementary pair (I-O)

So, either I or II follows.

34. (*e*)

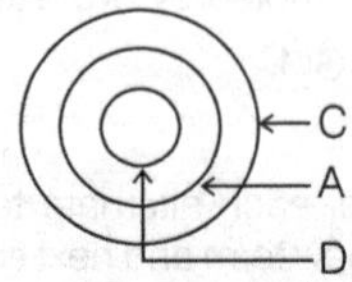

Conclusions I. All Ds are Cs. (True)
II. Some Ds are As (True)

So, both Conclusions I and II follow.

35. (*c*) Days by Sameer [16, 17] in February
Days by Kanika [17, 18] in February.
17th February is common in both the groups.
Clearly, the correct date is 17th February.

36. (*d*) Word MATS cannot be formed by using the letters of the given word because letter 'A' is not present in the given word.

37. (*b*) Route followed by Deepa

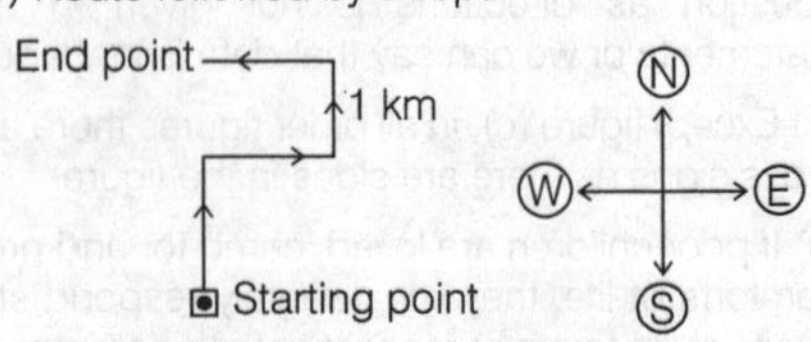

Now, she is moving towards West.

38. (*d*) Except lock, all others are used to stick something or paste something on the other thing.

39. (*c*) Let the age of Mrs Anjali's son be x yr.
Then, age of Mrs Anjali = 5x yr
Now, according to the question,
$\Rightarrow (5x+12) = 3(x+12) \Rightarrow 5x+12 = 3x+36$
$\Rightarrow \quad 2x = 24 \Rightarrow x = 12$ yr
So, present age of Mrs Anjali's son is 12 yr.

40. (*a*) Arrangement of words as per dictionary:
(iii) Gender
↓
(v) General
↓
(ii) Genesis
↓
(iv) Gentle
↓
(i). Genuine

41. (*c*) According to the question,
In first row, Veena is 12th from starting and 19th from end.
Then, total number of girls = (12 + 19 − 1) = 30
In second row, Sunita is 14th from starting and 20th from the end.
Then, total number of girls = (14 + 20 − 1) = 33
∴ Total number of girls = 30 + 33 = 63

Solution (Q. Nos. 42-44)

© ⇒ ≥	★ ⇒ ≤	@ ⇒ <	$ ⇒ >	% ⇒ =

42. (*d*) J $ K ⇒ J > K
K ★ T ⇒ K ≤ T
T @ N ⇒ T < N
N © R ⇒ N ≥ R
Therefore, J > K ≤ T < N ≥ R
Conclusions I. J $ T ⇒ J > T (Not true)
II. R ★ T ⇒ R ≤ T (Not true)
III. N $ K ⇒ N > K (True)
IV. R ★ K ⇒ R ≤ K (Not true)
So, only III is true.

43. (*d*) F % W ⇒ F = W
W © R ⇒ W ≥ R
R @ M ⇒ R < M
M $ D ⇒ M > D
Therefore, F = W ≥ R < M > D
Conclusions I. D @ R ⇒ D < R (Not true)
II. M $ F ⇒ M > F (Not True)
III. R @ D ⇒ R < D (Not True)
IV. R ★ F ⇒ R ≤ F (True)
So, only IV is true.

44. (*d*) H @ B ⇒ H < B
B ★ E ⇒ B ≤ E
V © E ⇒ V ≥ E
W $ V ⇒ W > V
Therefore, H < B ≤ E ≤ V < W
Conclusions I. W $ E ⇒ W > E (True)
II. H @ E ⇒ H < E (True)
III. H @ V ⇒ H < V (True)
IV. W $ B ⇒ W > B (True)
So, all are true.

45. (*b*) In each column,
Number of 4th cell = (Sum of numbers in 1st and 3rd cell) + (Square of number in 2 nd cell)
Column I $(7+5)+2^2 = 16$
Column II $(9+7)+4^2 = 32$
Likewise, in column III, we have
$(8+6)+3^2 = 23$

46. (*b*) We have following pattern,

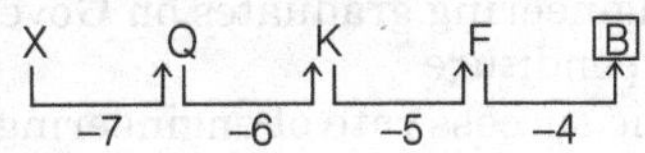

47. (*d*) According to the question,
? = 46 A 2 B 3 C 4
↓ ↓ ↓
÷ − ×
$\Rightarrow \quad ? = 46 \div 2 - 3 \times 4$
$= 23 - 3 \times 4 = 23 - 12 = 11$

48. (*a*) Following family diagram can be drawn from the given information

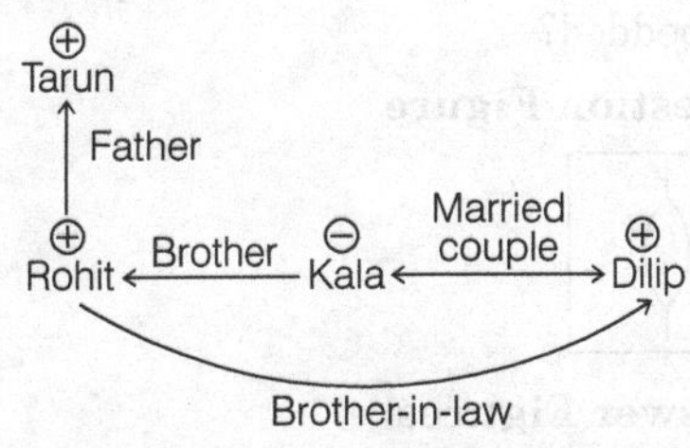

Now, it is clear that Dilip is the brother-in-law of Rohit.

49. (*c*) According to the question, we have following arrangement of bird flying,
Little pigeon—Crow—Pigeon—Big Crow—Eagle
Hence, Eagle is the last one.

50. (*d*) Apple, banana and mango all are fruits but they are entirely different from one another.

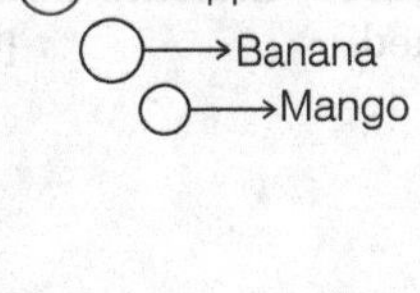

PRACTICE SET 18

1. Effect It has been reported in recent years that so many seats remain vacant in the engineering colleges of the country, at the end of admission session.

Which of the following can be possible cause for the effect mentioned above? **[IBPS (PO) 2011]**

(a) Because of the bad state of economy in the recent years, there has been dearth of jobs for engineering graduates
(b) Students have always given a priority to 3 yr engineering course instead of 4 yr
(c) Government has decided to give professional training to all qualified engineering graduates on Government expenditure
(d) The success rate of engineering graduates has always been very poor
(e) None of the above

2. The Independence day in 1988 was celebrated on a Wednesday. On what day was it celebrated in the year 1989?

(a) Monday (b) Tuesday
(c) Friday (d) Thursday

3. In which answer figure is the question figure embedded?

Question Figure

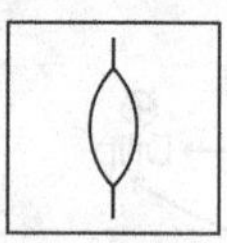

Answer Figures

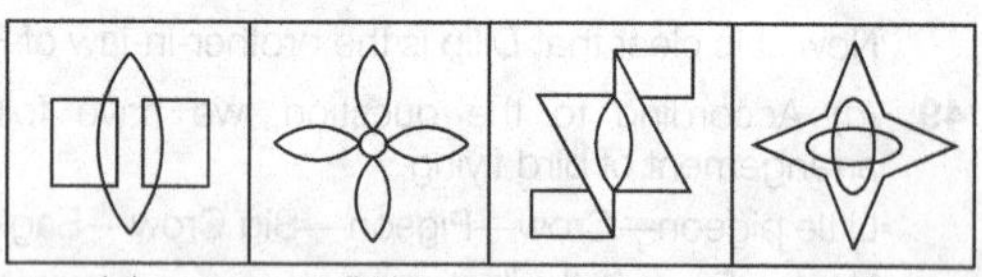

(a) (b) (c) (d)

4. A piece of paper is folded and cut as shown below in the question figures. From the given answer figures, indicate how it will appear when opened. **[SSC (10 + 2) 2012]**

Question Figures

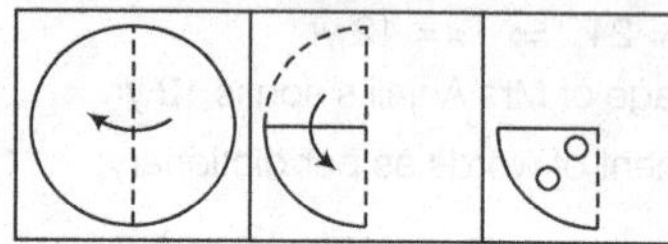

1 2 3

Answer Figures

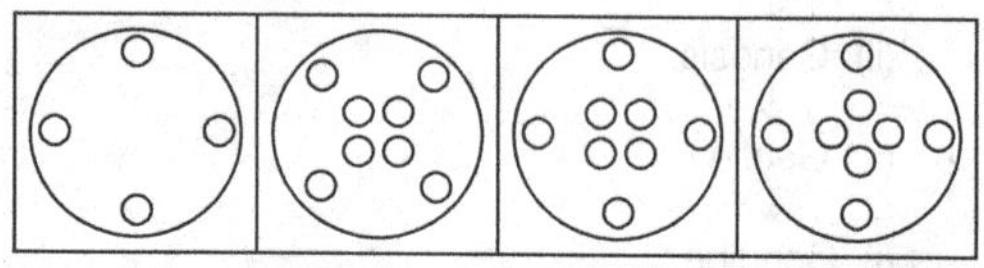

(a) (b) (c) (d)

5. Complete the given figure. **[SSC (10+2) 2012]**

Question Figure

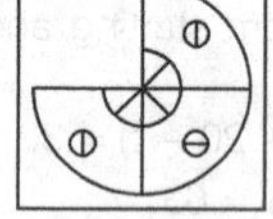

Answer Figures

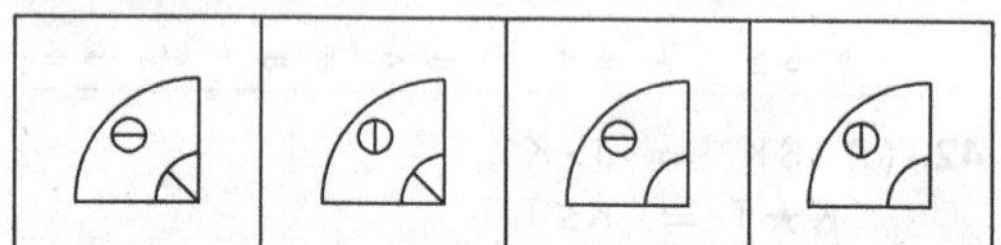

(a) (b) (c) (d)

6. If Ist half of the English alphabet is written in reverse order, then find the 15th letter from right. **[Canara Bank (Clerk) 2008]**

(a) A (b) B (c) C (d) D
(e) E

Direction (Q. Nos.7-9) *In the following questions, select the related letters/number pair from the given alternatives.*

7. STBP : 1920216 : : MNGO : ?

(a) 1314715 (b) 1413715
(c) 5173141 (d) 3114715

8. $\frac{G \times Q}{Q} : 20 :: \frac{B \times V}{V} : ?$

(a) 25 (b) 27 (c) 20 (d) 17

9. 225 : 256 : : 289 : ? **[SSC (CGL) 2014]**
(a) 234 (b) 361
(c) 324 (d) 432

10. A father's age is one more than 5 times of his son's age. After 3 yr, the father's age would be 2 less than four times the son's age. Find the present age of the father.
(a) 30 yr (b) 40 yr
(c) 31 yr (d) 29 yr

11. Pointing to a girl in a bus, a man tells his friend, "She is the daughter of the only son of my father's wife". How is the girl related to the man? **[SSC (DEO) 2011]**
(a) Cousin (b) Daughter
(c) Mother (d) Sister

12. Find the odd figure from the given alternatives. **[SSC (CGL) 2011]**

(a) (b) (c) (d)

Direction (Q. Nos 13-14) *In the following questions, find the odd words/pair from the given alternatives.*

13. (a) Cat : Mouse (b) Lion : Deer
(c) Cow : Hen (d) Hawk : Snake

14. (a) Rin (b) Hamam
(c) Pears (d) Cinthol

15. In a certain code language,
125 = go to school, 146 = Study in school
135 = Run to school
Which digit is used for 'run'?
(a) 6 (b) 2 (c) 3 (d) 1

16. How many meaningful English words can be made with letters TPSI, using each letter only once in each word?
(a) One (b) Two
(c) Three (d) Four

17. Find the digit at the face opposite to the face having digit 3 in the given dice.

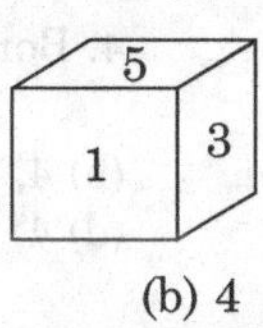

(a) 2 (b) 4
(c) 6 (d) 3

Direction (Q. Nos. 18-19) *Each of the following questions below consists of a question and two statements numbered* I *and* II *given below it. You have to decide whether the data provided in the statements are sufficient to answer the question.*

Give answer
(a) if the data in Statement I alone are sufficient to answer the question, while the data in Statement II alone are not sufficient to answer the question
(b) if the data in Statement II alone are sufficient to answer the question, while the data in Statement I alone are not sufficient to answer the question
(c) if the data either in Statement I alone or Statement II alone are sufficient to answer the question
(d) if the data in both the Statements I and II together are not sufficient to answer the question
(e) if the data in both the Statements I and II are together necessary to answer the question

18. In a code language, 'al ed hop' means 'we play chess'. What is the code of word 'chess'?
I. 'id nim hop' means 'we are honest'.
II. 'gob ots al' means 'they play cricket'.

19. On what day of the week does Aarti's birthday fall?
I. Sonu correctly remembers that Aarti's birthday comes after Wednesday but before Sunday.
II. Raj correctly remembers that Aarti's birthday comes before Friday but after Tuesday.

20. A word is given followed by four other words, one of which cannot be formed by using the letters of the given words, find that word.
COMMUNICATION
[SSC (Multitasking) 2014]
(a) ACTION (b) UNION
(c) NATION (d) UNISON

21. If in a code language letters, of the word 'CAMEL' are coded as '25106', the word 'LION' is coded as '6793' and the word 'TIRE' is coded as '4780'. How will the letters of the word 'ELITE' be coded in that language ?
(a) 06740 (b) 06470
(c) 60476 (d) 06704

Direction (Q. Nos. 22-23) *Study the following information to answer the given questions.*

A word arrangement machine, when given an input line of words, rearranges them following a particular rule in each step. The following is an illustration of input and the steps of rearrangement.

Input 'As if it on as zoo figure Of in at'
***Step* I** as As if it on zoo figure Of in at
***Step* II** as As at if it on zoo figure Of in
***Step* III** as As at figure if it on zoo Of in
***Step* IV** as As at figure if in it on zoo Of
***Step* V** as As at figure if in it Of on zoo

and Step V is the last step for this input.

As per the rules followed in the above steps, find out in the questions below, the appropriate steps for the given input.

22. **Input** 'you are at fault on this'.
Which of the following steps would be 'are at fault on you this' ?
(a) I (b) II
(c) III (d) IV
(e) V

23. Input 'am ace all if Is'
Which of the following will be the II step?
(a) all am ace if Is (b) ace all am Is if
(c) ace all am if Is (d) Is if am ace all
(e) None of these

24. Find out which of the answer figures (a) (b) (c) and (d) completes the figure matrix?

Question Figure

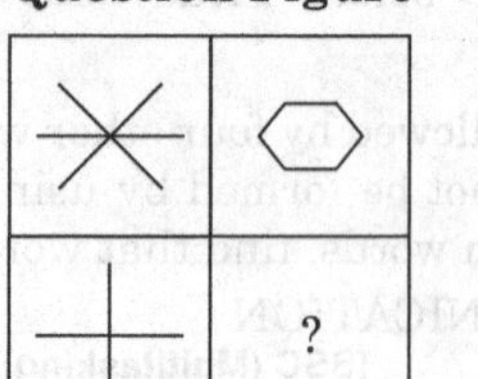

Answer Figures

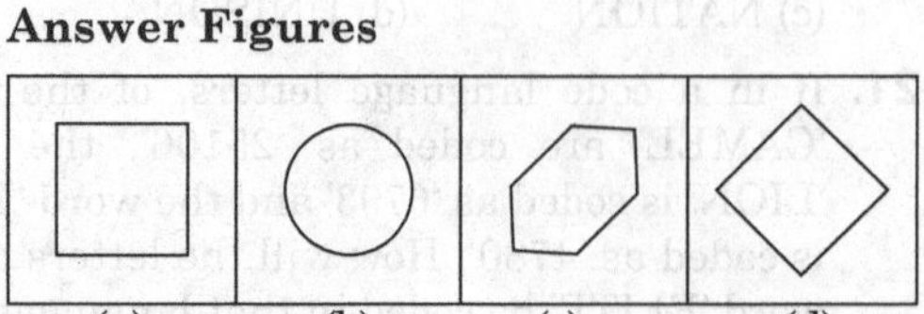

(a) (b) (c) (d)

25. Ram cycled 10 km Southward from his home, turned right and cycled 6 km, turned right cycled 10 km, turned left and cycled 15 km. How many kilometers will he have cycled to reach straight home? **[SSC (CGL) 2013]**
(a) 10 km (b) 21 km
(c) 16 km (d) 20 km

26. Complete the series given below
11, 23, 48, 99, 202, ? **[UPPSC (RO) 2014]**
(a) 268 (b) 407
(c) 368 (d) 409

27. Select the missing number from the given responses. **[SSC (10+2) 2013]**

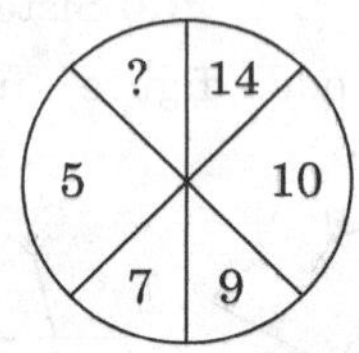

(a) 2 (b) 3 (c) 4 (d) 18

28. A, B, C, D are four friends. Average age of A and C is 35 yr and that of B and D is 40 yr. Average age of B, C and D is 40 yr. The sum of the ages of A and D is equal to that of B and C. Find out the ages (in yr) of A. B, C and D.
(a) 20, 30, 40, 50 (b) 20, 25, 30, 35
(c) 30, 35, 40, 45 (d) 30, 40, 50, 60

29. If 264 * 2 = 6, 870 * 3 = 11, then what should 735 * 5 be? **[SSC (CGL) 2013]**
(a) 05 (b) 12 (c) 16 (d) 03

30. Which of the following diagrams represents a relationship among India, Rajasthan and Jaipur ?

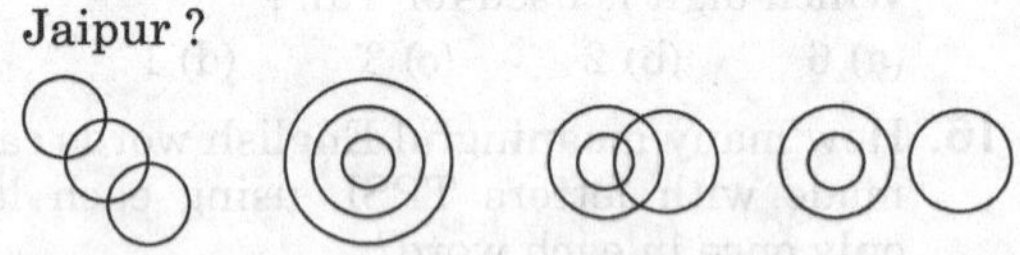

(a) (b) (c) (d)

31. Arrange the following words according to dictionary
1. Brush 2. Bread
3. Broad 4. Border
5. Butter
(a) 4, 1, 2, 3, 5 (b) 4, 2, 3, 1, 5
(c) 4, 2, 1, 3, 5 (d) 4, 3, 2, 1, 5

Direction (Q. Nos. 32-34) *Read the following information carefully and answer the following questions.*

Six friends Abhishek, Deepak, Mridul, Pritam, Ranjan and Salil married within a year in the months of February, April, July, September, November and December and in the cities of Ahmedabad, Bengaluru, Chennai, Delhi, Mumbai and Kolkata but not necessarily following the above order. The bride's names were Geetika, Jasmine, Hema, Brinda, Ipsita and Venna, once again not following any order. The following are some facts about their weddings.

I. Mridul's wedding took place in Chennai, however he was not married to Geetika or Veena.

II. Abhishek's wedding took place in Ahmedabad and Ranjan's in Delhi, however neither of them was married to Jasmine or Brinda.

III. The wedding in Kolkata took place in February.

IV. Hema's wedding took place in April but not in Ahmedabad.

V. Geetika and Ipsita got married in February and November and in Chennai and Kolkata but not following the above order.

VI. Pritam visited Bengaluru and Kolkata only after his marriage in December.

VII. Salil was married to Jasmine in September.

32. Hema's husband is
(a) Abhishek (b) Deepak
(c) Ranjan (d) Pritam

33. Deepak's wedding took place in
(a) Bengaluru (b) Mumbai
(c) Kolkata (d) Delhi

34. In Mumbai, the wedding of one of the friends took place in the month of
(a) April (b) September
(c) November (d) December

35. A word is represented by only one set of numbers are given in anyone of the alternatives. The sets of numbers given in the alternatives are represented by two classes of alphabets as in the two given matrices. The columns and rows of Matrix I are numbered from 0 to 4 and those of Matrix II from 5 to 9. A letter from these matrices can be represented first by its row and then the column number e.g. 'M' can be represented by 58, 67 etc. O can be represented by 01, 10 etc. Similarly you have to identify the correct set for the word given in each question.

Matrix I

	0	1	2	3	4
0	D	O	B	A	I
1	O	B	A	I	D
2	B	A	I	D	O
3	A	I	D	O	B
4	I	D	O	B	A

Matrix II

	5	6	7	8	9
5	W	N	R	M	L
6	N	R	M	L	W
7	R	M	L	W	N
8	M	L	W	N	R
9	L	W	N	R	M

LAND
(a) 68, 21, 79, 41 (b) 77, 44, 76, 33
(c) 86, 21, 67, 12 (d) 95, 30, 80, 20

36. Pratap correctly remembers that his mother's birthday is before 23rd April but after 19th April, whereas his sister correctly remembers that their mother's birthday is not on or after 22nd April. On which day in April is definitely their's mother's birthday?
(a) 20th
(b) 21th
(c) 20th or 21st
(d) Cannot be determined
(e) None of the above

37. In this question, one number is wrong in the series, find out the wrong number.
2, 8, 3, 27, 4, 64, 5, 225 **[IB (ACIO) 2011]**
(a) 27 (b) 8
(c) 225 (d) 64

38. While facing East you turn to your left and walk 10 yards. Then, turn to your left and walk 10 yards and now turn 45° to your right and go straight to cover 50 yards. Now, in what direction are you with respect to the starting point? **[SNAP 2013]**
(a) North-East (b) North
(c) South-East (d) North-West

39. Complete series given below
b_ac_cc_cb_ab_ac
(a) cbaba (b) abbbc
(c) bbaac (d) aabba

Direction (Q. Nos. 40-41) *In the following questions, the symbols @, ©, $, % and ★ are used with the following meaning as illustrated below*

'P © Q' means 'P is not greater than Q'

'P ★ Q' means 'P is not smaller than Q'

'P @ Q' means 'P neither greater than nor smaller than Q'

'P % Q' means 'P is neither greater than nor equal to Q'

'P $ Q' means 'P is neither smaller than nor equal to Q'

Now in each of the following questions assuming the given statements to be true find which of the three conclusions I, II and III given below them is / are definitely true and give your answer accordingly.

40. **Statements** M @ T, T ★ K, K % D
Conclusions I. D $ T
II. K @ M III. K % M
(a) None is true (b) Only I is true
(c) Only II is true (d) Only III is true
(e) Either II or III is true

41. **Statements** W % N, N © J, J ★ B
Conclusions I. W % J
II. B % N III. W % B
(a) Only I is true (b) Only II is true
(c) Only III is true (d) Only I and II are true
(e) None of these

42. 8 persons A, B, C, D, E, F, G and H are sitting around an octagonal dining table facing the centre. B is between G and D. H is third to the left of B and second to the right of A. C is between A and G. B and E are not in front of each other. Who is third to the left of D?
(a) H (b) G (c) F (d) E

43. Kavi ranked 9th from the top and 38th from the bottom in a class. How many students are there in the class?
(a) 45 (b) 42 (c) 46 (d) 44

44. Among Anil, Bibek, Charu, Debu and Eswar, Eswar is taller than Debu but not as fat as Debu. Charu is taller than Anil but shorter than Bibek. Anil is fatter than Debu but not as fat as Bibek. Eswar is thinner than charu who is thinner than Debu. Eswar is shorter than Anil. Who is the thinnest person?
(a) Bibek (b) Charu (c) Debu (d) Eswar

Direction (Q. Nos. 45-47) *Study the following information carefully to answer the questions that follow.*

Six couples have been invited to a dinner party. They are Niti, Geeta, Lata, Rakhi, Sita, Champa and Farookh, Hari, Amit Tilak, Ram, Ali. They are seated on a circular table, facing each other.

I. Geeta refuses to sit next to Ali.
II. Lata wants to be between Amit and Hari.
III. Champa refuses to sit next to Farookh.
IV. Niti is seated on Ali's right hand side.
V. Farookh and Tilak are seated exactly opposite to each other.
VI. Ram and Sita are seated to the left of Champa.
VII. Amit and Rakhi want to enjoy the company of Lata and Tilak respectively and are seated closest to them.
VIII. The seating arrangement is such that minimum one woman is always between two men.

45. Which of the following statements is correct?
(a) Lata is on Tilak's right
(b) Ali is on Champa's right
(c) Geeta is on Hari's right
(d) Geeta is on Farookh's left

46. If looked in an anti-clockwise manner, who are seated between Tilak and Farookh?
(a) Sita, Ram, Champa, Ali and Niti
(b) Sita, Ram, Rakhi, Amit and Lata
(c) Sita, Ram, Geeta, Hari and Lata
(d) Sita, Ram, Lata, Amit and Hari

47. Which of the following close neighbouring arrangements is correct?
(a) Ali, Champa and Ram
(b) Tilak, Ram and Ali
(c) Niti, Farookh and Lata
(d) Hari, Geeta and Amit

Direction (Q. Nos. 48-50) *In each of the questions below are given four statements followed by three Conclusions numbered I, II, and III. You have to take the given statements to be true even, if they seem to be at variance with commonly known facts. Read all the conclusion(s) and then decide which of the given conclusions logically follow(s) from the given statements disregarding commonly known facts.*

48. Statements Some fruits are flowers.
Some flowers are buds.
No bud is leaf.
All leaves are plants.

Conclusions I. No plant is bud.
II. Some plants are flowers.
III. Some buds are fruits.

(a) None follows
(b) Only I follows
(c) II and III follow
(d) Only III follows
(e) None of the above

49. Statements Some pearls are gems.
Some gems are diamonds.
All diamond are rings.
All rings are bangles.

Conclusions I. Some bangles are rings.
II. All rings are diamonds.
III. All rings are bangles

(a) Only I follows (b) I and II follow
(c) I and III follow (d) All follow
(e) None of the above

50. Statements All Chairs are tables.
All tables are telephones.
All telephones are cell phones.
No cell phone is computer.

Conclusions I. All cell phones are tables.
II. Some chairs are computers.
III. No chair is computer.

(a) Only I follows
(b) Only II follows
(c) Only III follows
(d) Either II or III follows
(e) None of the above

Hints and Solutions

1. (*a*) It is the obvious possible cause.

2. (*d*) The year 1989 was a normal year.
Days upto 15 August 1989 from August 15, 1988
$= 16 + 30 + 31 + 30 + 31 + 31 + 28 + 31 + 30 + 31 + 30 + 31 + 15 = 365 = 52$ weeks 1 day
Therefore, Wednesday $+1 =$ Thursday

3. (*c*) Clearly, question figure is embedded in answer figure (c) as shown below

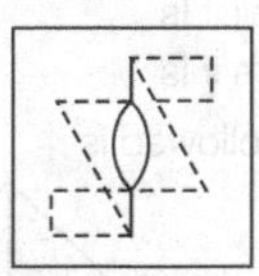

So, option (c) is correct answer.

4. (*b*)

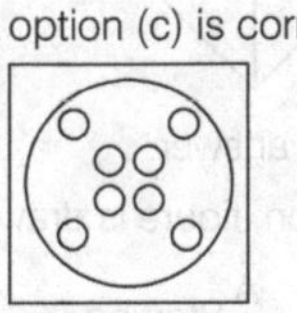

So, option (b) is correct answer.

5. (*a*) Option (a) will complete the given pattern as follows.

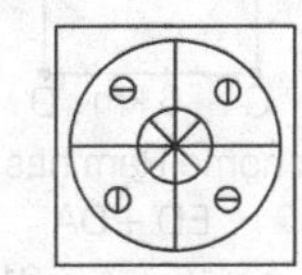

6. (*b*) According to the question,

15th 1st
From right
M - - - - - - C [B] A N O - - - - - - - Z
13 letters of 1st half get reversed
13 letters of 2nd half remain unchanged

∴ The required letter = B

7. (*a*) As, S T B P ⟶ 19 20 2 16 Positional values

Similarly, M N G O ⟶ 13 14 7 15

? = 13 14 7 15

8. (*a*) In backward order letter sequence,
Position of G = 20
Position of Q = 10

$$\therefore \frac{G \times Q}{Q} = \frac{20 \times 10}{10} = 20$$

Similarly, Position of B = 25
Position of V = 5

$$\therefore \frac{B \times V}{V} = \frac{25 \times 5}{5} = 25$$

9. (*c*) As, 225 : 256 → $(15)^2 : (15+1)^2$
Similarly, 289 : 324 → $(17)^2 : (17+1)^2$

10. (*c*) Let the present age of son be x yr
Then, the present age of father= $(5x + 1)$ yr
According to the question,
$$4(x+3) - 2 = (5x+1) + 3$$
$$\Rightarrow \quad 4x + 12 - 2 = 5x + 4$$
$$\Rightarrow \quad 12 - 2 - 4 = 5x - 4x \Rightarrow x = 6 \text{ yr}$$
∴ Present age of father = $5x + 1 = 5 \times 6 + 1 = 31$ yr

11. (*b*) Here, only son of man's father's wife is the man himself.
Now, it is clear that the girl is the daughter of that man.
Alternate Method

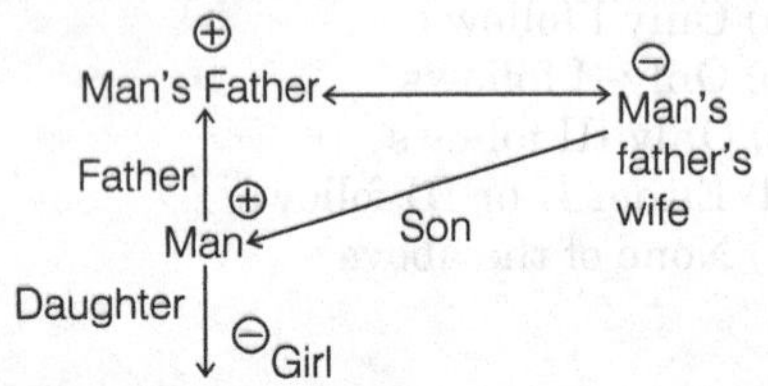

From the above family tree, it is clear that the girl is man's daughter.

12. (*c*) Figure (c) is different from the other three. The lower line segment is inverted in figure (c).

13. (*c*) In all other pairs, second one is the source of food for the first one.

14. (*a*) Except Rin, all others are bathing soap while Rin is a detergent soap.

15. (*c*) Given that,

(1) 2 [5] = Go [to] (School) ...(i)
(1) 4 6 = Study in (School) ...(ii)
(1) 3 [5] = Run [to] (School) ...(iii)

From Eqs. (i) and (iii), 3 is used for 'run'.

16. (*c*) Required words are TIPS, PITS, SPIT.

17. (*b*) According to the question, $5+1=6$
$1+3=4$
$3+5=8$
Clearly, it is a standard dice.
∴ Digit at the face opposite to $3 = 7 - 3 = 4$

18. (*e*) Given that,
(al) ed [hop] = [we] (play) chess. ...(A)
From Statement I, id nim [hop] = [we] are honest
From Statement II, gob ots (al) = they (play) cricket
From Statement I and (A), we = hop
From Statement II and (A), play = al
Clearly, chess = ed
So, both statements are required to answer the question.

19. (*e*) According to Sonu, birthday = Thursday/Friday/Saturday
According to Raj, birthday = Wednesday/ Thursday.
∴ Required day of birthday = [Thursday]
So, both statements are required.

20. (*d*) By using the letters of the given word, COMMUNICATION, 'UNISON' is the only word which cannot be formed due to the absence of letter '*S*'.

21. (*a*) As, C A M [E] [L] → 2 5 1 [0] [6], L [I] O N → 6 [7] 9 3

and [T] I R [E] → [4] 7 8 [0]

In these three words each letter is represented by a specific digit. Therefore,

E L I T E → [0 6 7 4 0]

Hence, ELITE is coded as 06740.

Solution (Q. Nos. 22-23) Here, each word of the input has been arranged in the alphabetical order giving preference to the word starting with the small letter.

22. (*d*) **Input** you are at fault on this
***Step* I** are you at fault on this
***Step* II** are at you fault on this
***Step* III** are at fault you on this
***Step* IV** are at fault on you this

23. (*c*) **Input** am ace all if Is
***Step* I** ace am all if Is
***Step* II** ace all am if Is

24. (*d*) The pattern followed is

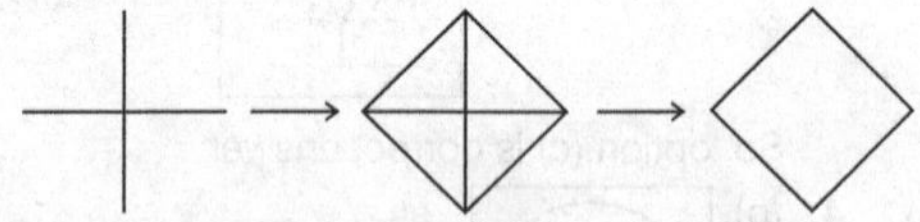

So, option (d) is the correct answer.

25. (*b*) According to the question, figure is drawn as

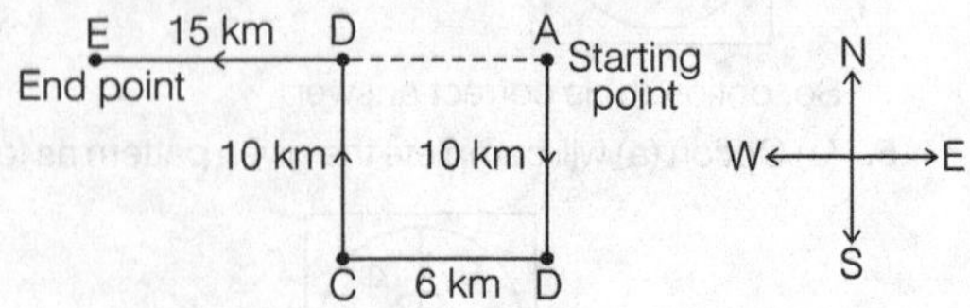

Now, to go back home Ram has to cycle
$$ED + DA$$
$$= 15 + 6 = 21 \text{ km}$$

26. (*d*) Given series, 11, 23, 48, 99, 202, ?
following pattern is visible in the above series
1st term = 11
2nd term = $(11 \times 2) + 1 = 22 + 1 = 23$
3rd term = $(23 \times 2) + 2 = 46 + 2 = 48$
4th term = $(48 \times 2) + 3 = 96 + 3 = 99$
5th term = $(99 \times 2) + 4 = 198 + 4 = 202$
Hence, asked 6th term = $(202 \times 2) + 5$
$= 404 + 5 = 409$

27. (*d*) As, $7 \times 2 = 14$
and $5 \times 2 = 10$
Similarly, $9 \times 2 = 18$
Hence, option (d) is correct.

28. (*c*) $A + C = 70$ yr
$B + D = 80$ yr
$B + C + D = 120$ yr
$\therefore C = 40$ years and $A = 30$ yr
$A + D = B + C$
$\Rightarrow 30 + D = B + 40$
or, $D - B = 10$
$\therefore B = 35$ yr and $D = 45$ yr
So, A = 30 yr, B = 35 yr, C = 40 yr and D = 45 yr.

29. (*b*) As, $\frac{264}{2} = 132$
$\Rightarrow 1 + 3 + 2 = 6$
$\Rightarrow \frac{870}{3} = 290$
$\Rightarrow 2 + 9 + 0 = 11$
Similarly, $\frac{735}{5} = 147$
$\Rightarrow 1 + 4 + 7 = 12$

30. (*b*) Rajasthan is a state (part) of India and Jaipur is a city (part) of Rajasthan. Hence, Jaipur is a city (part) of India.

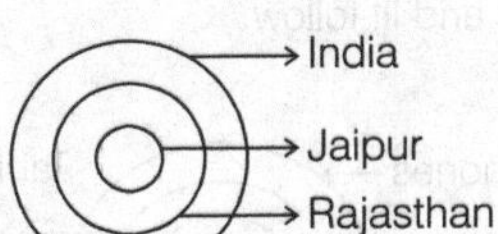

31. (*b*) Arrangement of words as per dictionary :
(4) Border
↓
(2) Bread
↓
(3) Broad
↓
(1) Brush
↓
(5) Butter

Solution (Q. Nos. 32-34) According to the given information, the arrangement is as following:

Months	Feb	April	July	Sep	Nov	Dec
Cities	Kolkata	Delhi	Ahmedabad	Bengaluru	Chennai	Mumbai
Friends	Deepak	Ranjan	Abhishek	Salil	Mridul	Pritam
Brides	Geetika	Hema	Veena	Jasmine	Ipsita	Brinda

32. (*c*) Hema's husband is Ranjan.

33. (*c*) Deepak's wedding took place in Kolkata.

34. (*d*) Pritam was married in Mumbai in the month of December.

35. (*a*)
L ⟶ 59, (68), 77, 86, 95
A ⟶ 03, 12, (21), 30, 44
N ⟶ 56, 65, (79), 88, 97
D ⟶ 00, 14, 23, 32, (41)
LAND ⟶ 68, 21, 79, 41
So, option (a) is correct answer.

36. (*c*) Days by Pratap – [20, 21 or 22] in April
Days by his sister: not on or after 22 April
Clearly, the answer is = [20 or 21] in April

37. (*c*) The pattern of the series is
$2^3 = 8,\ 3^3 = 27,\ 4^3 = 64,\ 5^3 = 125$
Hence, number 225 is wrong and should be replaced by 125.

38. (*d*) Let be the initial position of the man is A. He initially faced East and then turned his left in the direction of North and walked 10 yards.

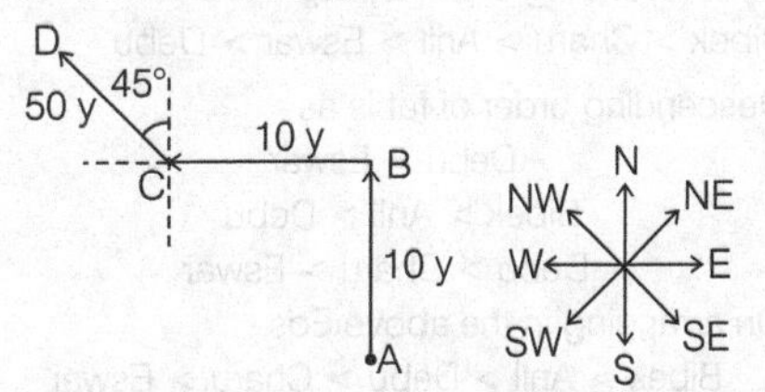

Then, turned his left in the direction of West and walked 10 yards. Now, he turned 45° to his right and walked 50 yards straight in the same direction. Now, the direction of the man with respect to his starting point is North - West.

39. (*d*) The pattern of the series is
b<u>a</u>ac/<u>a</u>cc<u>b</u>/cb<u>b</u>a/b<u>a</u>ac ⇒ aabba

Solution (Q. Nos. 40-41)

© ⇒ ≤	★ ⇒ ≥	@ ⇒ =
% ⇒ <	$ ⇒ >	

40. (*e*) M @ T ⇒ M = T
T ★ K ⇒ T ≥ K
K % D ⇒ K < D
Therefore, M = T ≥ K < D

Conclusions I. D $ T ⇒ D > T (Not True)
II. K @ M ⇒ K = M (May be True)
III. K % M ⇒ K < M (May be True)

So, either II or III is true.

41. (*a*) W % N ⇒ W < N
N © J ⇒ N ≤ J
J ★ B ⇒ J ≥ B
Therefore, W < N ≤ J ≥ B

Conclusions I. W % J ⇒ W < J (True)
II. B % N ⇒ B < N (Not True)
III. W % B ⇒ W < B (Not True)

So, only Conclusion I is true.

42. (*c*) Arrangement according to the question is as follows

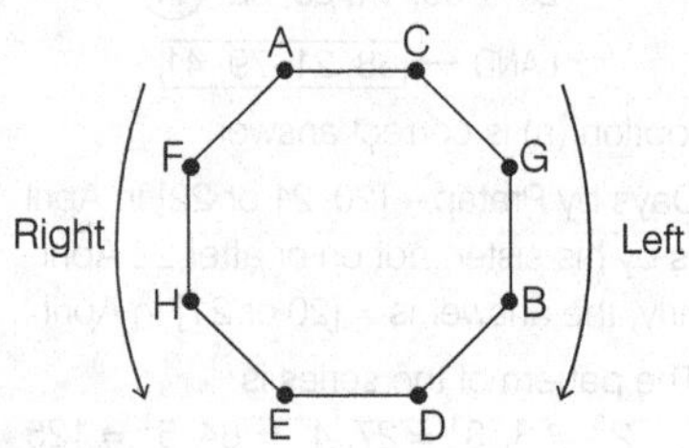

Clearly, F is third to the left of D.

43. (*c*) Required number = (38 + 9 − 1)
= 47 − 1 = 46

44. (*d*) Descending order of height is
Bibek > Charu > Anil > Eswar > Debu

Descending order of fat is as
Debu > Eswar ...(i)
Bibek > Anil > Debu ...(ii)
Debu > Charu > Eswar ...(iii)

On arranging in the above Eqs.
Bibek > Anil > Debu > Charu > Eswar

∴ Eswar is the thinnest person.

Solution (Q. Nos.45-47) Following sitting arrangement is formed from the given information

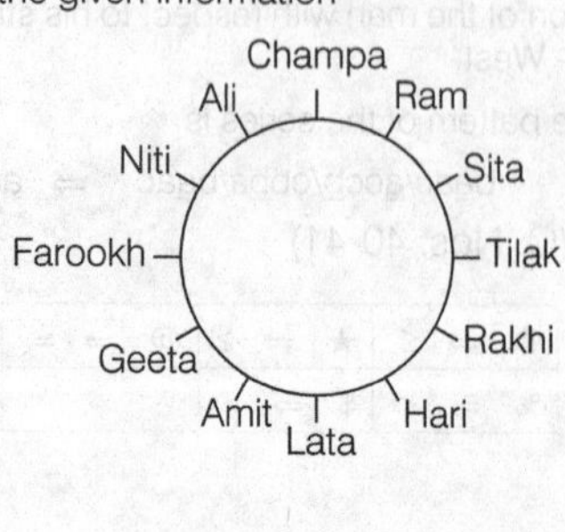

45. (*b*) Clearly, Ali is on Champa's right. So. statement (b) is correct.

46. (*a*) If looked in an anti-clockwise manner, Sita, Ram, Champa, Ali and Niti are seated between Tilak and Farookh.

47. (*a*) Clearly Ali, Champa and Ram are close neighbours.

48. (*a*)

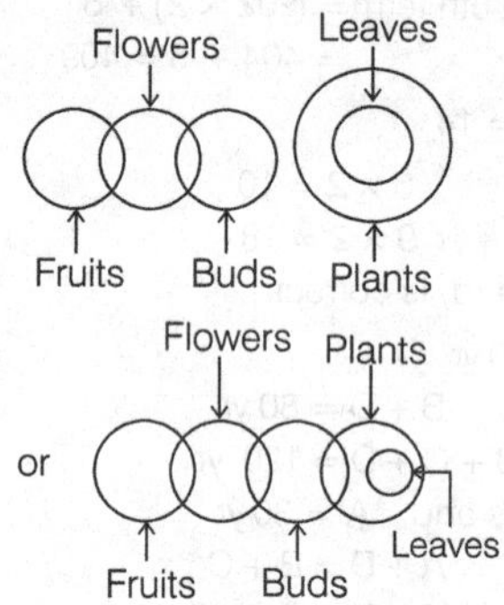

Conclusions I. No plant is bud. (✗)
II. Some plants are flowers. (✗)
III. Some buds are fruits. (✗)

So, none follows.

49. (*c*)

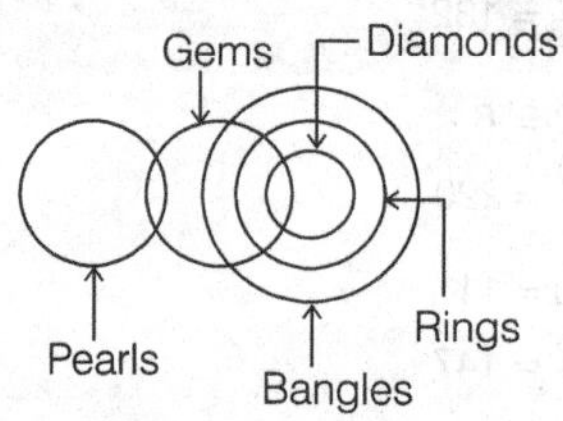

Conclusions I. Some bangles are rings. (✔)
II. All rings are diamonds. (✗)
III. All diamonds are bangles. (✔)

So, both I and III follow.

50. (*c*)

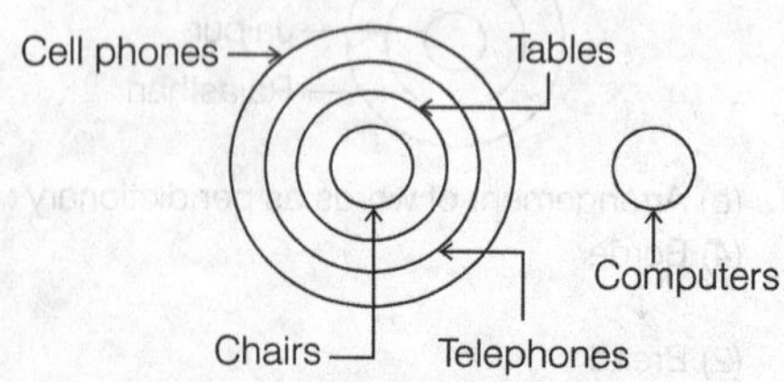

Conclusions I. All cell phones are tables. (✗)
II. Some chairs are computers. (✗)
III. No chair is computer. (✓)

So, only III follows.

PRACTICE SET 19

1. Select the one which is different from other three responses.
(a) 8-15 (b) 25-36 (c) 49-64 (d) 81-100

2. Raman is facing West. He turns 45° in the clockwise direction and then another 180° in the same direction and 270° in the anti-clockwise direction. Which direction is he facing now?
(a) West (b) North
(c) North-West (d) South-West

3. If A means, '+', B means '–', C means '×' and D means '÷', then 18 C 14 A 6 B 16 D 4 = ?
(a) 254 (b) 238 (c) 188 (d) 258
(e) None of these

4. Four kids P, Q, R and S are up on the ladder. P is further up the ladder than Q, Q is between P and R. If S is further up than P, then who is the third from the bottom? **[SSC (Assistant) 2012]**
(a) Q (b) R (c) P (d) S

5. Find the missing number in the matrix.

3	10	?
6	2	6
2	3	1
121	225	100

(a) 9 (b) 3 (c) 10 (d) 5

6. If the word LEADER is coded as 20-13-9-12-13-26, then how would you write LIGHT? **[SSC (CGL) 2013]**
(a) 20-16-17-15-27 (b) 20-15-16-18-23
(c) 20-17-15-16-28 (d) 20-16-15-17-22

7. A word is represented by only one set of numbers are given in anyone of the alternatives. The sets of numbers given in the alternatives are represented by two classes of alphabets as in the two given matrices. The colums and rows of Matrix I are numbered from 0 to 4 and those of Matrix II from 5 to 9. A letter from these matrices can be represented first by its row and then the column number e.g. S can be represented by 02, 33, etc. E can be represented by 01, 20 etc. Similarly you have to identify the correct set for the word given in each question.

Matrix I

	0	1	2	3	4
0	A	E	S	T	H
1	T	H	A	E	S
2	E	S	T	H	A
3	H	A	E	S	T
4	S	T	H	A	E

Matrix II

	5	6	7	8	9
5	P	O	R	K	L
6	K	L	P	O	R
7	O	R	K	L	P
8	L	P	O	R	K
9	R	K	L	P	O

TASTE
(a) 44, 32, 21, 03, 33
(b) 32, 31, 02, 04, 12
(c) 34, 00, 40, 22, 44
(d) 13, 12, 14, 10, 76

8. If each of the letters in the English alphabet is assigned an even numerical value by giving A = 2, B = 4 and so on, then what would be the total value of letters for the word LADY when similarly coded? **[SSC (CGL) 2013]**
(a) 74 (b) 72 (c) 84 (d) 82

9. Sheela is Ravi's sister-in-law. Ram is Ravi's brother. Ram's wife is Sheela. Deepa is Ravi's sister. Deepa's mother is Shanthi. How is Sheela related to Shanthi? **[SSC (10+2) 2012]**
(a) Mother-in-law (b) Daughter-in-law
(c) Granddaughter (d) Daughter

10. 3 yr earlier the father was 7 times as old as his son. 3 yr hence, the father's age would be four times that of his son. What is the present age of son?
(a) 7 yr (b) 8 yr (c) 9 yr (d) 10 yr

11. Which word will appear third in the dictionary? **[SSC Assistant Grade-III 2012]**
(a) Paralysis (b) Paralytic
(c) Paralyse (d) Parallelism

12. Which of the following diagrams represents a relationship between Animal and Cow?

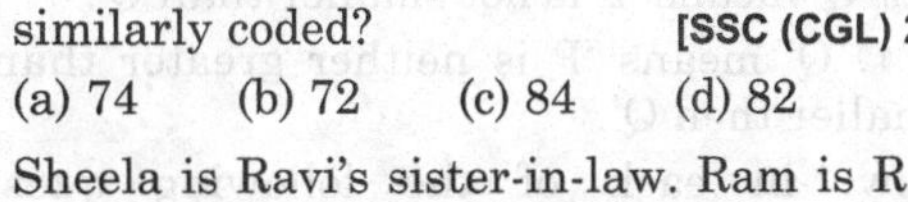

(a) (b) (c) (d)

Direction (Q. Nos. 13-14) *In the following questions, select the related word/number pair from the given alternatives.* **[SSC (CGL) 2015]**

13. 9 : 50 :: ?
(a) 20 : 105 (b) 22 : 110
(c) 18 : 190 (d) 15 : 225

14. Framework : House :: Skeleton : ?
(a) Ribs (b) Skull (c) Body (d) Grace

15. From the given four positions of a single dice, find the number of dots at the face opposite to the face having 3 dots.

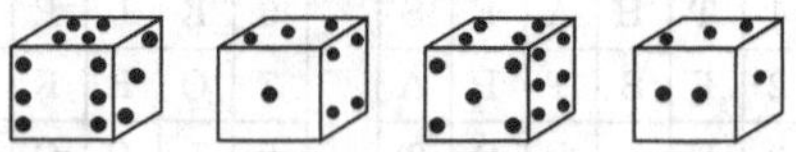

I II III IV

(a) 2 (b) 4 (c) 5 (d) 6

Direction (Q. Nos. 16-18) *In the following questions, the symbols @, ©, %, # and ★ are used with the following meaning as illustrated below.*

'P % Q' means 'P is neither greater than nor equal to Q'
'P ★ Q' means 'P is neither smaller than nor equal to Q.'
'P @ Q' means 'P is not greater than Q'.
'P # Q' means 'P is not smaller than Q'.
'P © Q' means 'P is neither greater than nor smaller then Q'.

Now, in each of the following questions assuming the given statements to be true, find which of the three Conclusions I, II and III given below them is/are definitely true and give your answer accordingly.

16. Statements D ★ K, K % N, N @ F
Conclusions I. D ★ N II. F ★ K
III. D @ N
(a) Only II is true
(b) Only either I or III and II are true
(c) Only either I or III is true
(d) Only I and II are true
(e) None of the above

17. Statements H # R, R @ M, M © N
Conclusions I. H ★ M II. N ★ R
III. N © R
(a) Only I is true
(b) Only either II or III and I are true
(c) Only either III or II is true
(d) Only III is true
(e) None of the above

18. Statements M @ R, R % T, T © N
Conclusions I. N ★ R
II. T ★ M
III. N # R
(a) Only I and II are true
(b) Only I and III are true
(c) Only II and III are true
(d) All I, II, and III are true
(e) None of the above

19. A bus leaves Delhi with half the number of women as men. At Meerut, ten men get down and five women get in. Now, there are equal number of men and women. How many passengers boarded the bus initially at Delhi?
(a) 36 (b) 45 (c) 15 (d) 30

20. From the following alternatives, select the word which can be formed using the letters of the given word. **[SSC (FCI) 2012]**

EXPERIENCE

(a) EXPIRE (b) PERCIEVE
(c) EMPIRE (d) EXPENSE

21. Select a figure from the four alternative, which when placed in the missing portion of the original figure as shown by figure (X) would complete the pattern.

Question Figure

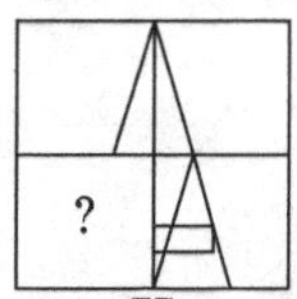

(X)

Answer Figures

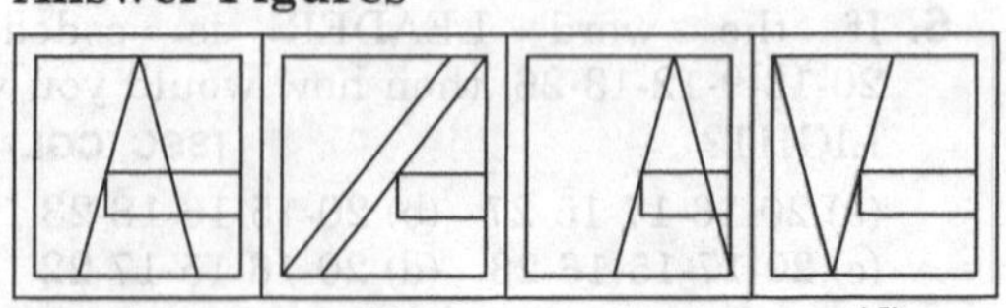

(a) (b) (c) (d)

Direction (Q. Nos. 22-23) *Read the following information carefully and then answer the questions based on that.*

From amongst five doctors A, B, C, D and E, four engineers G, H, K and L and six teachers M, N, O, P, Q and R, some teams are to be selected. Of these A, B,G,H,O,P and Q are females and the rest are males. The formation of teams is subject to the following conditions.

I. Whenever there is a male doctor, there will be no female teacher.

II. Whenever there is a male engineer, there will be no female doctor.

III. There shall not be more than two male teachers in any team.

22. If the team consists of two doctors, two female teachers and two engineers, all the following teams are possible except

(a) OPGHAB (b) ABGHPQ
(c) ABGHOQ (d) ABKLPQ

23. If the team consists of two doctors, three female teachers and two engineers, then the members of the team are

(a) CDOPQGH (b) ABOPQGH
(c) CDKLOPQ (d) DEGHOPQ

24. Rajat correctly remembers that his mother's birthday is not after 18th of June. His sister correctly remembers that their mother's birthday is before 20th June but after 17th June. On which day in June was definitely their mother's birthday?

(a) 17th (b) 19th (c) 18th (d) 17th or 18th

Direction (Q. Nos. 25-27) *Study the following arrangement carefully and answer the questions given below.*

F @ 3 9 H © A D I % 4 E ★ $ M K 2 U. R P 5 W δ 8 1 T J V 7

25. How many consonants are there in the given arrangement, which is preceded by a number and not followed by a letter?

(a) None (b) One
(c) Two (d) Three
(e) More than three

26. Four of the following five options are alike in a certain way, based on their positions, in the above arrangement and so form a group. Which is the one that does not belong to that group?

(a) D % © (b) 5 δ R
(c) T V 8 (d) A I H
(e) E % $

27. If all the symbols from the above arrangement are dropped, then which of the following will be the twelfth from the left end?

(a) 4 (b) K
(c) 2 (d) U
(e) None of these

28. Select the one which is different from other three responses. **[Assistant SI 2015]**

(a) Brass (b) Steel (c) Bronze (d) Tin

29. 'X' is in the East of 'Y' which is in the North of 'Z'. If 'P' is in the East of 'Z', then in which direction of 'X', is 'P' **[SSC (FCI) 2012]**

(a) South-West (b) South-East
(c) South (d) West

30. In this question, number of letters skipped in between adjacent letters in the series increased by one. Which of the following series observe the rule? **[SSC (CPO) 2014]**

(a) KORYBGJ (b) LMEYTPK
(c) KMPTYEL (d) KPTYELM

Direction (Q. Nos. 31-32) *What will come in place of question mark (?) ?.*

31. ABC, PQR, DEF, STU, ? **[SSC (CGL) 2014]**

(a) VWX (b) GHI (c) IJK (d) GKL

32. 0,7,26,63,? **[SSC (CGL) 2015]**

(a) 87 (b) 96
(c) 123 (d) 124

33. Select the one, which is different from the other there responses.

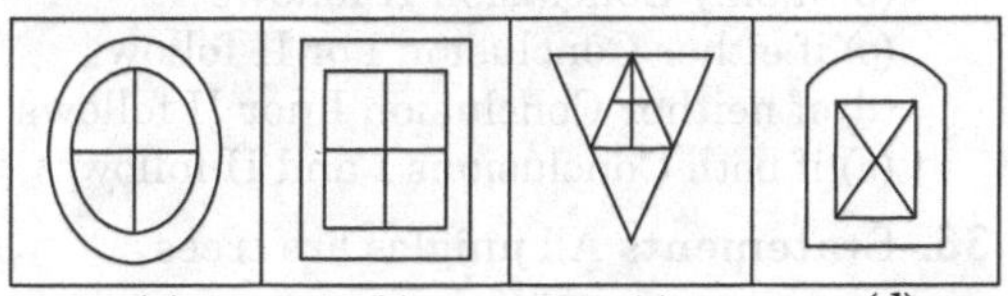

(a) (b) (c) (d)

34. Find the missing figure of the series from the given answer figures.

Question Figures

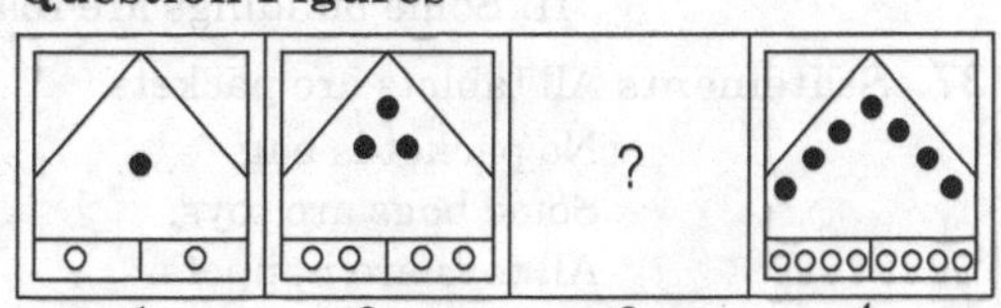

1 2 3 4

Answer Figures

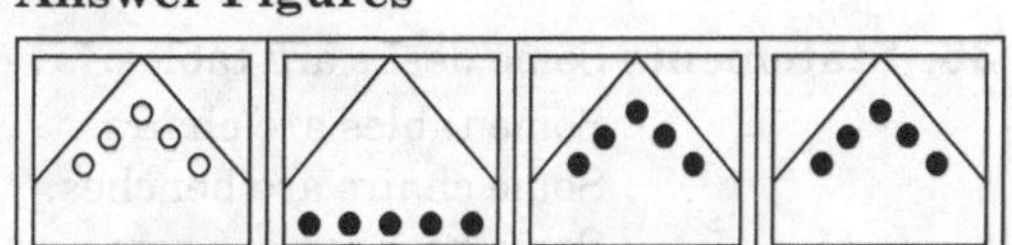

(a) (b) (c) (d)

35. Find the figure out of the answer choices figures that can be formed by joining the pieces given in the question figure.

Question Figure

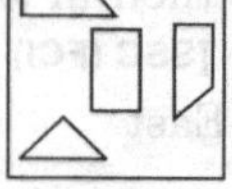

Answer Figures

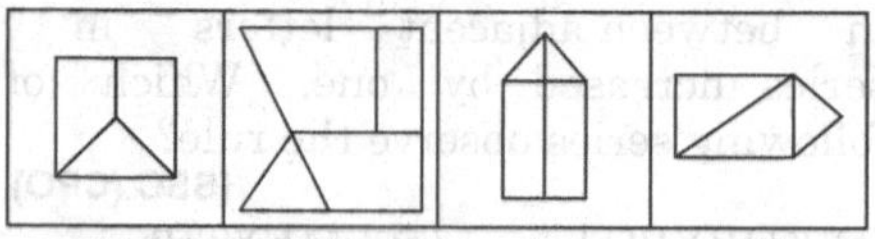

(a) (b) (c) (d)

Direction (Q. Nos. 36-38) *In each question below are four statements followed by two conclusions numbered I and II. You have to take the four given statements to be true even if they seem to be at variance with commonly known facts and then decide which of the given conclusions logically follows from the four statements disregarding commonly known facts.*

Give answer
(a) if only Conclusion I follows
(b) if only Conclusion II follows
(c) if either Conclusion I or II follows
(d) if neither Conclusion I nor II follows
(e) if both Conclusions I and II follow

36. Statements All jungles are trees.
All trees are roads.
All roads are houses.
All houses are buildings.
Conclusions I. All trees are houses.
II. Some buildings are roads.

37. Statements All tablets are packets.
No packet is bag.
Some bags are toys.
All toys are puppets.
Conclusions I. Some puppets are tablets.
II. Some puppets are bags.

38. Statements Some desks are tables.
Some tables are chairs.
Some chairs are benches.
Some benches are cots.
Conclusions I. Some chairs are desks.
II. Some cots are tables.

39. K is more beautiful than B. B is not as beautiful as Y. J is not as beautiful as B or Y. Whose beauty in the least degree?
(a) B (b) J **[SSC (10+2) 2012]**
(c) Y (d) K

40. If A means '×', B means '÷', C means '–' and D means '+', then
4 D 16 A 5 B 8 C 5 = ?
(a) 9 (b) 16
(c) 13 (d) 7.5
(e) None of these

Direction (Q. Nos. 41-43) *Study the following information carefully and answer the given questions.*

Given an input line, a coding machine rearranges the input following certain steps as explained below.

Input	47 desert go 56 there often 32 12
Step I	there 47 desert go 56 often 32 12
Step II	there 12 47 desert go 56 often 32
Step III	there 12 often 47 desert go 56 32
Step IV	there 12 often 32 47 desert go 56
Step V	there 12 often 32 go 47 desert 56

Arrangement in Step V is the final arrangement and Step V is the last step.

In each of the following questions the rearrangement is done following the same rules as explained in the above illustration.

41. If the fourth step of input is 'wonderful 22 seashore 36 48 fine 62 morning', then what was the first step ?
(a) fine 48 wonderful 22 seashore 36 62 morning
(b) fine 48 wonderful 22 36 seashore 62 morning
(c) fine 48 seashore wonderful 22 36 morning 62
(d) fine 48 seashore wonderful 36 22 morning 62
(e) Cannot be determined

42. What will be the third step for the following input ?
Input paper common 36 51 pencil 28 test 66
(a) test 28 paper pencil common 36 51 66
(b) test 28 pencil 66 paper common 36 51
(c) test 66 pencil paper 28 common 51 36
(d) test 28 pencil paper common 36 51 66
(e) None of the above

43. If Step II of an input is 'waive 14 available time 38 46 probation 85', then how many more steps will be required to complete the arrangement?

(a) Three (b) Four (c) Five (d) Two
(e) None of these

Direction (Q. Nos. 44-46) *Study the following information carefully to answer the given questions.*

Eight friends A, B, C, D, E, F, G and H are sitting around a circle facing the centre but not necessarily in the same order. G sits third to left of D. Only one person sits between D and F. B sits second to right of H. H is not an immediate neighbour of D. C is not an immediate neighbour of D. E is an immediate neighbour of H.

44. What is the position of E with respect to the position of C?

(a) Third to the left (b) Second to the left
(c) Immediate right (d) Third to the right
(e) Second to the right

45. Who amongst the following sits exactly between A and G?

(a) B (b) C (c) E (d) F (e) D

46. Four of the following five are alike in a certain way and thus form a group. Which is the one that does not belong to that group?

(a) CG(b) AE (c) HD (d) EC
(e) None of these

Direction (Q. Nos.47-48) *Each of the following questions below consists of a question and two statements numbered I and II given below it. You have to decide whether the data provided in the statements are sufficient to answer the question.*

Give answer

(a) If the data in Statement I alone are sufficient to answer the question, while the data in Statement II alone are not sufficient to answer the question
(b) If the data in Statement II alone are sufficient to answer the question, while the data in Statement I alone are not sufficient to answer the question
(c) If the data either in Statement I alone or Statement II alone are sufficient to answer the question
(d) If the data in both the Statements I and II together are not sufficient to answer the question
(e) If the data in both the Statements I and II are together necessary to answer the question

47. On which day of the same week is Ramesh's exam scheduled (Monday being the first day of the week)?

I. Ramesh correctly remembers that his exam is scheduled on a day after Tuesday but before Thursday of the same week.
II. Ramesh's friend correctly remembers that Ramesh's exam is scheduled on the third day of the week.

48. How is 'call' written in a code language?

I. 'call me back' is written as '531' in that code language.
II. 'you can call me any time' is written as '94163' in that code language.

49. Cause Two wings of a building complex in a residential area collapsed.

Which of the following is the possible effect of the cause mentioned above?

I. Most of the flats of such residential wings were vacant from long time.
II. A flat owner got done some major repairing works and in this process a main part got collapsed.
III. Residents of the other wings in the complex were said to vacate their flats immediately.

(a) Only I (b) Only II
(c) Only III (d) Both II and III
(e) None of these

50. Effect Cost of Petroleum products has been increased almost 20% in last two months. Which of the following may be the possible cause of the effect mentioned above?

(a) The cost of vegetables and other food items has been increased by more than 30%
(b) Union of truck owners has decided to increase carriage about 20% with immediate effect
(c) In last couple of weeks, the cost of crude oil in the international market has been increased immensely
(d) People have decided to protest against the inertia of government towards essential commodities
(e) None of the above

Hints and Solutions

1. (*a*) Given,

(a) 8—15 (b) 25 — 36
$\downarrow$ $\downarrow$
$(5)^2$ $(6)^2$

(c) 49 — 64 (d) 81 — 100
$\downarrow$ $\downarrow$ $\downarrow$ $\downarrow$
$(7)^2$ $(8)^2$ $(9)^2$ $(10)^2$

Except 8-15, in all other options, both of the numbers, are the square of any natural number. Thus, 8-15 is odd.

2. (*d*)

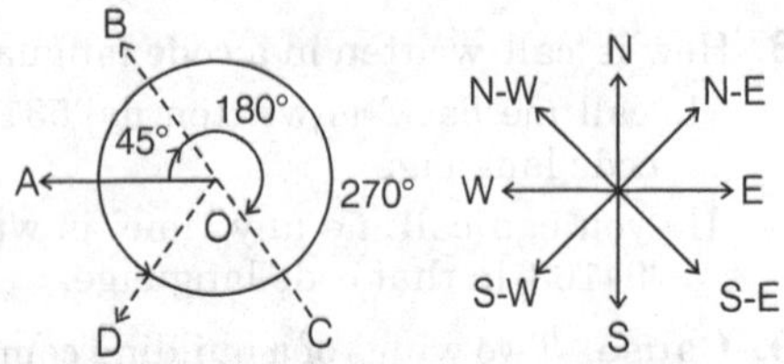

Clearly, Raman initially faces in the direction OA. On moving 45° clockwise, he faces the direction OB. On further moving 180° clockwise, he faces in the direction OC. Finally on moving 270° anti-clockwise, he faces in the direction OD, which is South-West.

3. (*a*) According to the question,

? = 18 C 14 A 6 B 16 D 4
C → ×, A → +, B → −, D → +

$= 18 \times 14 + 6 - 16 + 4$ (using VBODMAS rule)
$= 18 \times 14 + 6 - 4 = 252 + 6 - 4 = 258 - 4 = 254$

4. (*c*) According to the question, we have following ladder arrangement

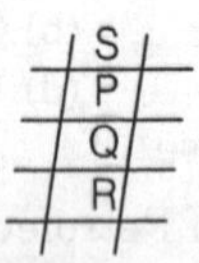

Thus, from above figure P is the 3rd from the bottom.

5. (*b*) $(3 + 6 + 2)^2 = 121$

$\Rightarrow (10 + 2 + 3)^2 = 225 \Rightarrow (? + 6 + 1)^2 = 100$

$\Rightarrow ? + 6 + 1 = 10 \quad \therefore ? = 10 - 7 = 3$

6. (*c*) We have following arranged position of alphabets

12	5	1	4	5	18
L	E	A	D	E	R
↓+8	↓+8	↓+8	↓+8	↓+8	↓+8
20	13	9	12	13	26

Similarly,

12	9	7	8	20
L	I	G	H	T
↓+8	↓+8	↓+8	↓+8	↓+8
20	17	15	16	28

$\therefore$ LIGHT can be coded as 20-17-15-16-28.

7. (*c*) We have the following pattern

T → 03, 10, 22, (34), 41
A → (00), 12, 24, 31, 43
S → 02, 14, 21, 33, (40)
T → 03, 10, (22), 34, 41
E → 01, 13, 20, 32, (44)
TASTE → 34, 00, 40, 22, 44

8. (*c*) According to the question, if we arrange the position of alphabets as A = 2, B = 4 and so on.

Then, the code for

LADY $= 2(12 + 1 + 4 + 25) = 2 \times 42 = 84$

9. (*b*) Following family diagram can be drawn from the given information,

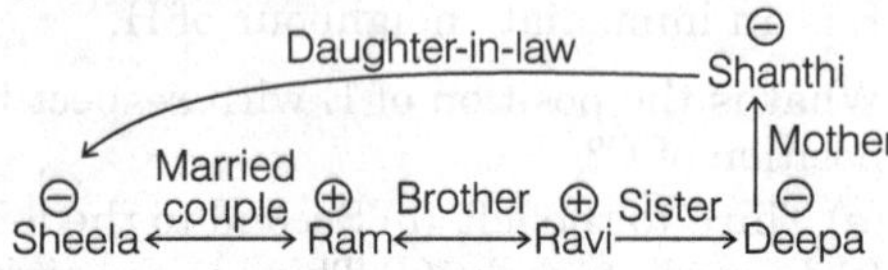

Now, it is clear that Sheela is the daughter-in-law of Shanthi.

10. (*c*) Let 3 yr ago, age of son be x yr.

The, age of father 3 yr son = 7x yr

Now, present age of son = (x + 3) yr

Present age of father = (7x + 3) yr

So, age of son after 3 yr = (x + 3 + 3)

$\Rightarrow$ (x + 6) yr

Age of father after 3 yr = (7x + 3 + 3)

$\Rightarrow$ (7x + 6) yr

Now, $(7x + 6) = 4(x + 6)$

$\Rightarrow 7x + 6 = 4x + 24$

$\Rightarrow 3x = 18$

$\Rightarrow x = 6$ yr

Hence, present age of son = (6 + 3) = 9 yr

11. (*a*) Arrangement of words as per dictionary.

(i) Parallelism → (ii) Paralyse → (iii) Paralysis → (iv) Paralytic

So, paralysis will appear third in the dictionary.

12. (*b*) Cow is an animal. This relationship can be represented by option (b).

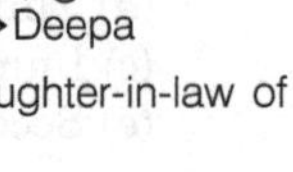

13. (*a*) As, $(9 \times 5) + 5 = 45 + 5 = 50$

Similarly, $(20 \times 5) + 5 = 100 + 5 = 105$

14. (*c*) Clearly, House rests on 'Framework' in the same way as 'Body' is built on 'Skeleton'.

15. (*c*) From positions I, II and IV,

Adjacent faces of the face having 3 dots = 1, 2, 4 and 6

So, face opposite to the face having 3 dots will be the face having 5 dots.

Solutions (Q. Nos. 16-18)

% ⇒ <	★ ⇒ >	@ ⇒ ≤	# ⇒ ≥	© ⇒ =

16. (*b*) D ★ K ⇒ D > K, K % N ⇒ K < N, N @ F ⇒ N ≤ F
Therefore, D > K < N ≤ F
Conclusions I. D ★ N ⇒ D > N (May be)
II. F ★ K ⇒ F > K (True)
III. D @ N ⇒ D ≤ N (May be)
D may be greater than or smaller than N or equal to N.
So, either I or III and II are true.

17. (c) H # R ⇒ H ≥ R, R @ M ⇒ R ≤ M, M © N ⇒ M = N
Therefore, H ≥ R ≤ M = N
Conclusions I. H ★ M ⇒ H > M (Not True)
II. N ★ R ⇒ N > R (May be)
III. N © R ⇒ N = R (May be)
So, either II or III is true.

18. (a) M @ R ⇒ M ≤ R, R % T ⇒ R < T, T © N ⇒ T = N
Therefore, M ≤ R < T = N
Conclusions I. N ★ R ⇒ N > R (True)
II. T ★ M ⇒ T > M (True)
III. N # R ⇒ N ≥ R (Not True)
So, only I and II are true.

19. (*b*) Suppose the number of women boarded the bus at Delhi is x.
Therefore, the number of men = 2x
According to question,
$$2x - 10 = x + 5$$
$$\Rightarrow \quad 2x - x = 10 + 5$$
$$\therefore \quad x = 15$$
Total number of passengers boarded the bus initially $= 3x = 3 \times 15 = 45$

20. (*a*) Word 'EXPIRE' can be formed from the letters of the given word.

21. (c) It is clear that alternative (c) completes the figure (x), when it is fitted into it. Figure (x) appears as such in the below figure when it gets completed.

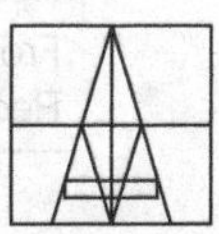

22. (*d*) Option (d), A B K L P Q violates Condition II because female doctors A, B cannot appear with male engineers K, L.

23. (*b*) Option (a), C D O P Q G H - violates condition I.
Option (b), A B O P Q G H - complies with all the conditions
Option (c), C D K L O P Q - violates condition I
Option (d), D E G H O P Q - violates condition I
Clearly, the required team = A, B, O, P, Q, G, H

24. (c) Days by Rajat, June 18th or earlier.
Days by his sister, June 18th or June 19th.
Clearly, June 18th is the required day.

25. (*c*) According to the question, in the given arrangement, 2 such consonants are there *viz.*
9 H © and 5 W δ which are preceded by a number and not followed by a letter.

26. (*e*) Here, in all the group except 'E % $', second element is two positions ahead of first element and the third element is two positions behind to the first element. Except 'E % $', all follow same rule/pattern.

27. (*c*) After droping all the symbols, the resultant arrangement will be
F 3 9 H A D I 4 E M K [2] U R P 5 W 8 1 T J V 7
|——————→ From left
So, twelfth from the left is 2.

28. (*d*) Except Tin, all other are solid metals.

29. (*c*) According to given data,

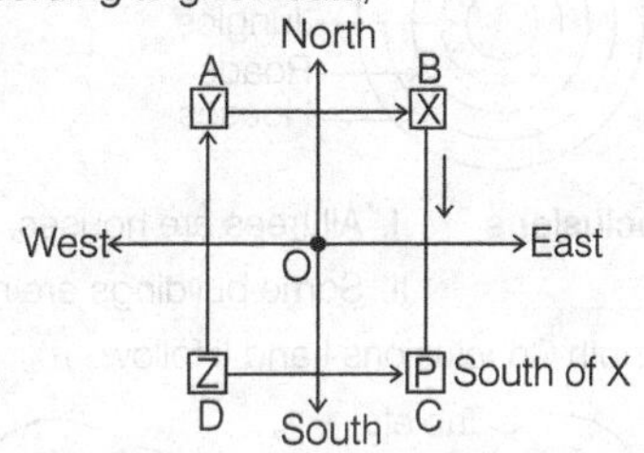

Let Y be at point A. Now, East of Y is located at X. So, X point is at B. Again, Y is North of Z. It means that Z is below Y or South of point A. So, we take a point at D. Further P is located East of Z. So, let it is at C. Therefore, complete figure is ABCD. Hence, P is located in South of X.

30. (*c*) Series given in option (c) follows this rule.
K M P T Y E L
+2 +3 +4 +5 +6 +7
Clearly, the number of letters skipped increases by 1 with each consecutive letter.

31. (b) We have the following pattern
+1 +1 +1 +1 +1 +1 +1 +1 +1 +1
A B C P Q R D E F S T U [G H I]
+1 +1 +1
Here, next sequence is GHI.

32. (*d*) The pattern of the series is
0, 7, 26, 63, 124
↓
$(1)^3 - 1 = 0$
$(2)^3 - 1 = 7$
$(3)^3 - 1 = 26$
$(4)^3 - 1 = 63$
$(5)^3 - 1 = 124$

33. (*d*) In all other figures, the outer and inner figures are similar and there is a plus (+) sign in each figure.

While there is a cross in figure (d) and the inner figure is not similar to outer figure.

34. (*c*) In each subsequent figure, two black circles are added in upper part and two white circles are added in lower part.

35. (*b*) Figure given in option (b) can be formed by joining the pieces given in the question figure as shown below

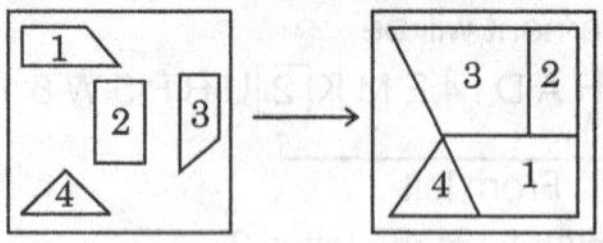

36. (*e*)

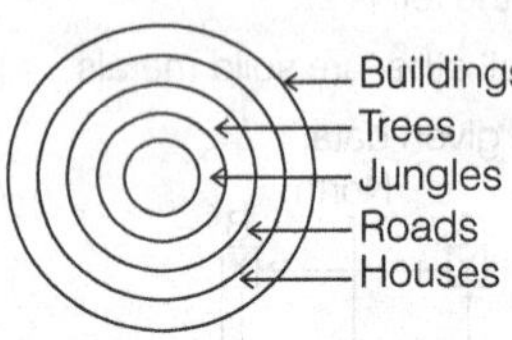

Conclusions I. All trees are houses. (✔)

II. Some buildings are roads. (✔)

So, both Conclusions I and II follow.

37. (*b*)

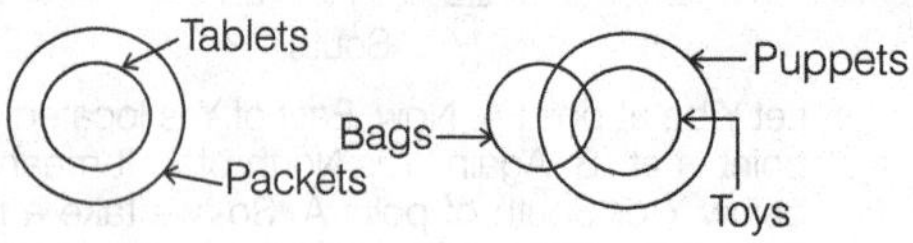

Conclusions I. Some puppets are tablets. (✘)

II. Some puppets are bags. (✔)

So, only Conclusion II follows.

38. (*d*)

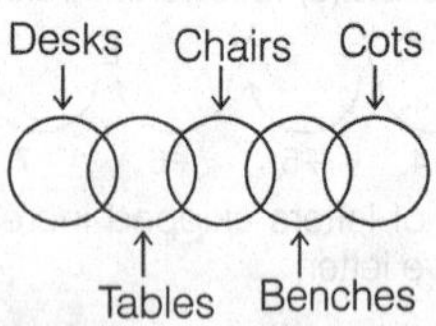

Conclusions I. Some chairs are desks. (✘)

II. Some cots are tables. (✘)

So, neither I nor II follows.

39. (*b*) Making equations from the given information,

$K > B$ ...(i)

$Y > B$ ...(ii)

$B, Y > J$ ...(iii)

After equating, (i), (ii) and (iii), we getK, $Y > B > J$

Thus, J's beauty is least.

40. (*a*) According to the question,

? = 4 D 16 A 5 B 8 C 5

D ↓ +, A ↓ ×, B ↓ ÷, C ↓ −

$= 4 + 16 \times 5 \div 8 - 5$ (using VBODMAS rule)

$= 4 + 16 \times 0.625 - 5 = 4 + 10 - 5 = 14 - 5 = 9$

Solution (Q. Nos. 41-43) After careful analysis of the given input and various steps of rearrangement we can conclude that in each step one word or a number is rearranged. The words are arranged in the reverse order of the English alphabets while the numbers are arranged in ascending order alternately.

41. (*e*) It is not possible to determine the previous step.

42. (*d*) **Input** paper common 36 51 pencil 28 test 66

***Step* I** test paper common 36 51 pencil 28 66

***Step* II** test 28 paper common 36 51 pencil 66

***Step* III** test 28 pencil paper common 36 51 66

43. (*b*) ***Step* II** waive 14 availabte time 38 46 probation 85

***Step* III** waive 14 time available 38 46 probation 85

***Step* IV** waive 14 time 38 available 46 probation 85

***Step* V** waive 14 time 38 probation available 46 85

***Step* VI** waive 14 time 38 probation 46 available 85

Therefore, four more steps will be required.

Solution (Q. Nos. 44-46) Arrangement according to the question is as follows

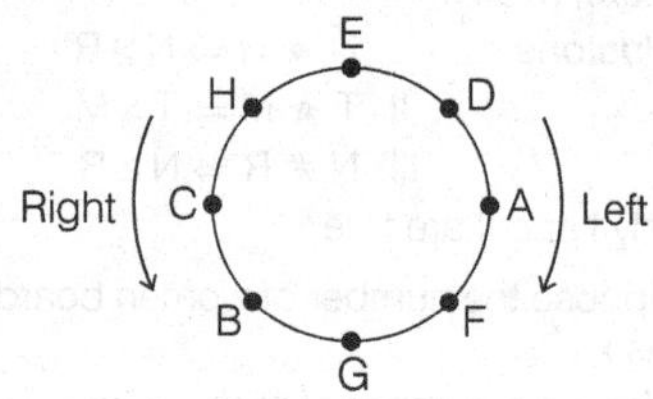

44. (*b*) Clearly, E is second to the left of C.

45. (*d*) Clearly, F sits between A and G.

46. (*c*) Except HD, in all other pairs, first member is present on the clockwise side of other.

47. (*c*) From Statement I,

Between Tuesday and Thursday

Required day = Wednesday

From Statement II,

Required day = Monday, Tuesday, Wednesday

3rd day of week

So, either Statement I or II alone is sufficient to answer the question.

48. (*d*) From Statements I and II,

call me back = 5 3 1

you can call me any time = 9 4 1 6 3

∴ call = 3/1

So, both the statements are not sufficient to answer the question.

49. (*c*) Because of the collapse of certain wings, the residents of other wings may be said to vacate their flats, so that the residents of other wings could be safe from possible danger.

50. (*c*) It is the obvious reason for the given effect.

PRACTICE SET 20

1. Which letter in the word WASHINGTON is the same number in the word (counting from the beginning) as it is in the alphabet?
(a) N (b) T **[UPPSC (RO) 2014]**
(c) O (d) G

2. If the following question, rearrange the scrambled letters to form the name of city, then find which letter will appear in the middle?

AIDMURA

(a) M (b) R (c) U (d) D

Direction (Q. Nos. 3-4) *In the following questions, select the related word/number from the given alternatives.*

3. Zephyr : Gale :: Trickle : ? **[UPPSC (RO) 2014]**
(a) Torrent (b) Gust
(c) Gusset (d) Decay

4. (12, 20, 28)
(a) (3, 15, 18) (b) (18, 27, 72)
(c) (18, 30, 42) (d) (7, 14, 28)

5. As, 'Bank' is related to 'Money', in the same way 'Transport' is related to
(a) Goods (b) Road (c) Movement (d) Traffic

6. If 2 & 6 % 7 = 33, 4 & 6 % 8 = 54, then what will be the value of 6 % 8 & 9?
(a) 95 (b) 77 (c) 99 (d) None of these

7. Select the one which is different from the other three responses.

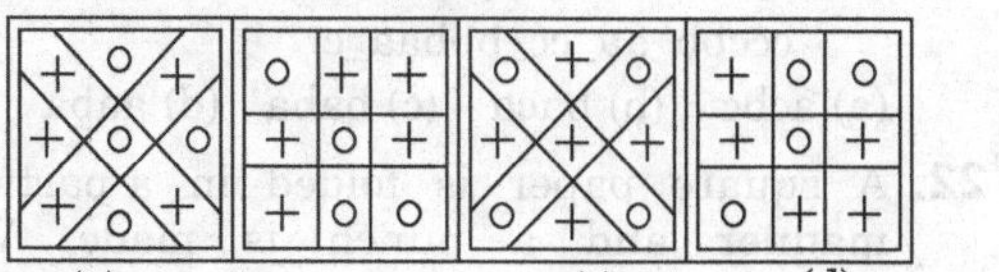

(a) (b) (c) (d)

Direction (Q. Nos. 8-9) *Read the following information carefully and answer the questions that follow.*

I. There is a group of five girls.
II. Kamini is second in height but younger than Rupa.
III. Pooja is taller than Monika but younger in age.
IV. Rupa and Monika are of the same age but Rupa is tallest between them.
V. Neelam is taller than Pooja and elder to Rupa.

8. If they are arranged in the ascending order of height, who will be in the third position?
(a) Monika (b) Monika or Rupa
(c) Rupa (d) None of these

9. If they are arranged in descending order of their ages, who will be in the fourth position?
(a) Monika or Rupa (b) Monika
(c) Kamini (d) None of these

10. Roshan, Vaibhav, Vinay and Sumit are playing cards. Roshan and Vaibhav are partners. Sumit faces towards North. If Roshan faces towards West, then who faces towards South? **[CLAT 2014]**
(a) Vinay (b) Vaibhav
(c) Sumit (d) Data inadequate

11. Insert the missing number.

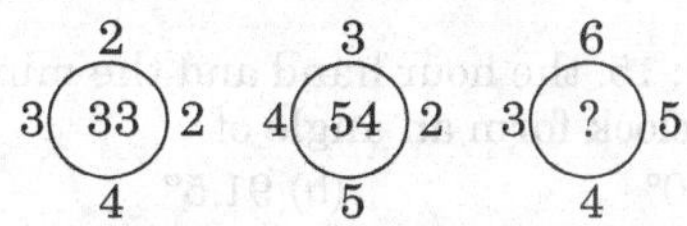

(a) 94 (b) 86
(c) 82 (d) 78

Direction (Q. Nos. 12-13) *In the following questions, find the odd term from the given alternatives.*

12. (a) Shovel : Mud (b) Screwdriver : Screw
(c) Hammer : Nail (d) Pen : Pencil

13. (a) Humming bird (b) Kingfisher
(c) Crane (d) Sparrow
[SSC (10+2) 2015]

Direction (Q. Nos. 14-16) *Study the following information to answer the given questions.*

Eight people S, T, U, V, W, X, Y and Z live on eight different floors of a building, but not necessarily in the same order. The lowermost floor of the building is numbered 1, the one above that is numbered 2 and so on till the topmost floor is numbered 8.

Y lives on an odd numbered floor. U lives on a floor that is immediately below Y's floor. Only four people live between W and S. S lives on one of the floors above W. Z lives on a floor which is immediately above S's floor. X lives on a floor which is immediately above 1's floor. T does not live on floor numbered 2. V does not live on an odd numbered floor.

14. Which of the following statements is true, according to the given arrangement?
(a) None of the given statements is true
(b) Only three people live between Y and W
(c) Z lives on floor numbered 6
(d) T lives on one of the floors below W's floor
(e) Only one person lives above V's floor

15. T lives on which of the following floor numbers?
(a) Floor number 4 (b) Floor number 1
(c) Floor number 5 (d) Floor number 3
(e) Floor number 6

16. Who amongst the following lives on floor number 8?
(a) U (b) V
(c) Z (d) S
(e) X

17. At 6 : 15, the hour hand and the minute hand of a clock form an angle of
(a) 90° (b) 91.5°
(c) 97.5° (d) 94.5°

18. Find the figure out of the answer figures that can be formed by joining the pieces given in the question figure.

Question Figure

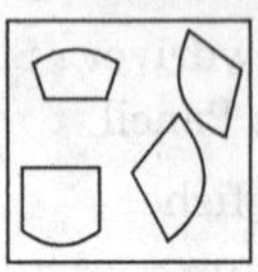

Answer Figures

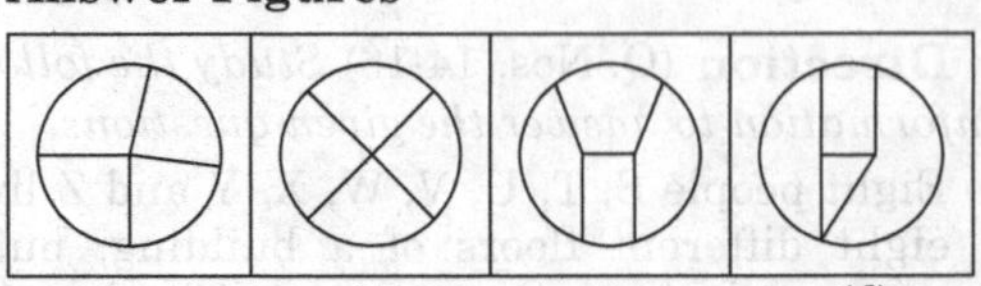

(a) (b) (c) (d)

19. Find a number in the following series which is wrongly placed into the series.

1, 5, 9, 15, 25, 37, 49 **[NIFT (UG) 2014]**

(a) 25 (b) 37
(c) 9 (d) 15

20. In this question, a word is represented by only one set of numbers are given in anyone of the alternatives. The sets of numbers given in the alternatives are represented by two classes of alphabets as in the two given matrices. The columns and rows of Matrix I are numbered from 0 to 4 and those of Matrix II from 5 to 9. A letter from these matrices can be represented first by its row and then the column number. e.g. S can be represented by 02, 33, etc., E can be represented by 01, 20 etc. Similarly you have to identify the correct set for the word given in each question.

Matrix I

	0	1	2	3	4
0	A	E	S	T	H
1	T	H	A	E	S
2	E	S	T	H	A
3	H	A	E	S	T
4	S	T	H	A	E

Matrix II

	5	6	7	8	9
5	P	O	R	K	L
6	K	L	P	O	R
7	O	R	K	L	P
8	L	P	O	R	K
9	R	K	L	P	O

HORSE
(a) 95, 75, 02, 32, 59
(b) 04, 75, 88, 21, 32
(c) 86, 67, 33, 44, 13
(d) 57, 87, 32, 33, 24

21. Which one set of letters when sequentially placed at the gaps in the given letters series shall complete it?

cccbb_aa_cc_bbbaa_c

(a) acbc (b) baca (c) baba (d) aaba

22. A square paper is folded in a particular manner and a punch is made. When unfolded, the paper appears as given below.

Question Figure

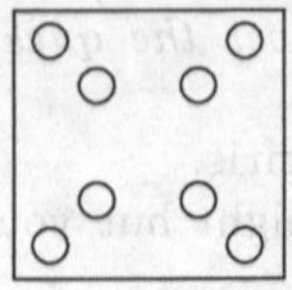

Find out the manner in which the paper is folded and punch is made from the responses given.

Answer Figures

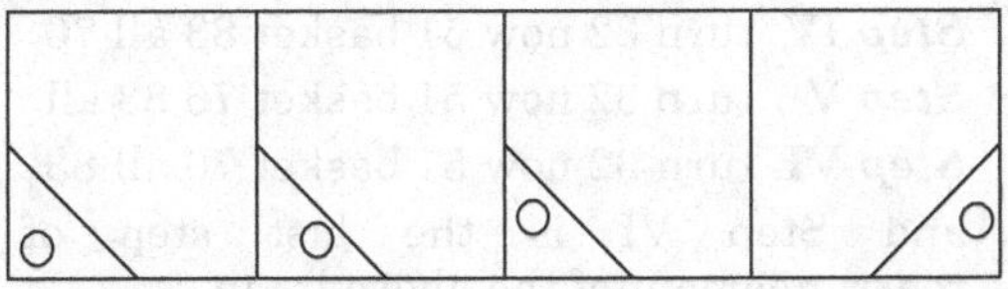

(a) (b) (c) (d)

23. A series is given with one term missing. Choose the correct alternative from the given ones that will complete the series.

Question Figures

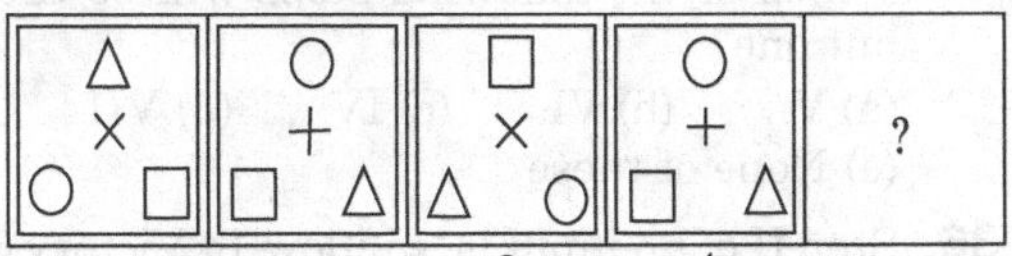

1 2 3 4

Answer Figures

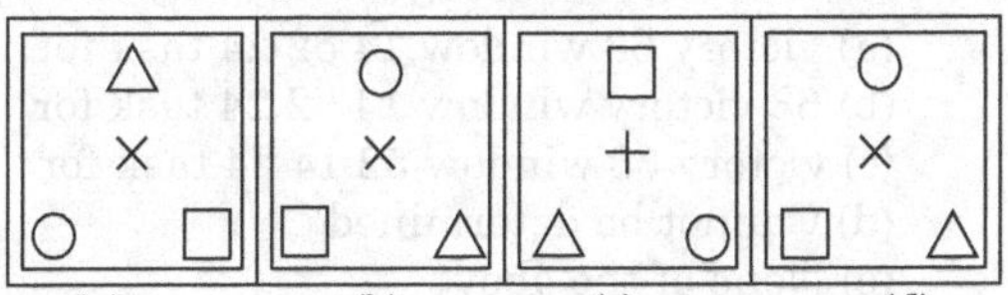

(a) (b) (c) (d)

24. The age of Shyam is $\frac{1}{3}$ rd that of his mother. He is 2 yr older than his sister. The age of his sister is 8 yr. What is the age of his mother?

(a) 25 yr (b) 60 yr
(c) 48 yr (d) 30 yr

25. Select the missing number from the given responses. **[SSC (10+2) 2011]**

14	22	37
04	06	03
05	03	05
61	135	?

(a) 120 (b) 112 (c) 116 (d) 555

26. Raju moved to his North-West side for 2 km. From there he turned 90° clockwise and moved 2 km. From there he turned 90° clockwise and travelled 2 km, then he would be in which direction from the original position?

(a) South-East Region
(b) North-East Region
(c) South-West Region
(d) Western Region

27. Starting from a point S, Mahesh walked 25 m towards South. He turned to his left and walked 50 m. He, then again turned to his left and walked 25 m. He again turned to his left and walked 60 m and reached a point T. How far Mahesh is from point S and in which direction?

(a) 10 m, West (b) 25 m, North
(c) 10 m, East (d) 25 m, West

Direction (Q. Nos. 28-30) *Study the following information carefully to answer the questions given below.*

Five persons are standing in a queue. One of the two persons at the extreme ends is a professor and the other is a businessman. An advocate is standing to the right of a student. An author is to the left of the businessman. The student is between the professor and the advocate.

28. Counting from the left, the author is at which place?

(a) First (b) Second
(c) Third (d) Fourth

29. Which of the following is in the middle of the queue?

(a) Professor (b) Advocate
(c) Student (d) Businessman

30. If advocate and the businessman exchange their positions, and also the author and the student, then who will be standing to the left of student?

(a) Author
(b) Businessman
(c) Professor
(d) Advocate

Direction (Q. Nos. 31-33) *In the following questions, the symbols @, ©, $, % and # are used with the following meaning as illustrated below.*

'A $ B' means 'A is not smaller than B'.

'A # B' means 'A is not greater than B'.

'A @ B' means 'A is neither smaller than nor equal to B'.

'A © B' means 'A is neither smaller than nor greater than B'.

'A % B' means 'A is neither greater than nor equal to B'.

Now, in each of the following questions assuming the given statements to be true, find which of the three conclusions I, II and III given below them is/are definitely true and give your answer accordingly.

31. Statements H % J, J © N, N @ R

Conclusions I. R% J

II. H @ J III. N @ J

(a) Only II is true
(b) I and III are true
(c) Only I is true
(d) Only III is true
(e) None is true

32. Statements M @ J, J $ T, T © N

Conclusions I. N # J

II. T%M III. M @ N

(a) I and II are true
(b) II and III are true
(c) I and III are true
(d) None is true
(e) All are true

33. Statements D © K, K # F, F @ P

Conclusions I. P @ D

II. K # P III. F $ D

(a) Only II is true
(b) I and II are true
(c) III is true
(d) II and III are true
(e) None is true

34. Which of the following diagram best depicts the relationship among Females, Mothers and Infants?

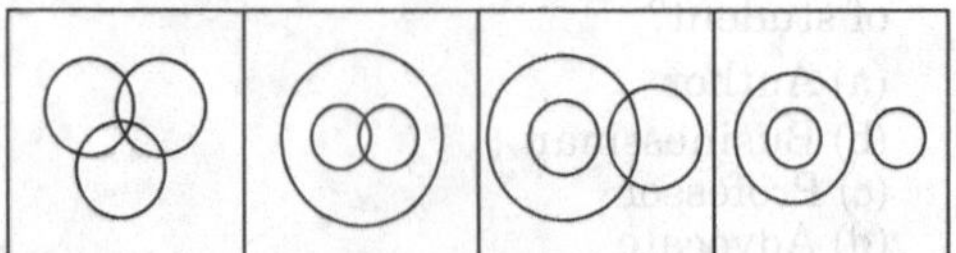

(a) (b) (c) (d)

Direction (Q. Nos. 35-37) *Study the following information carefully and answer the given questions.*

A word and number arrangement machine when given an input line of words and numbers rearranges them following a particular rule in each step. The following is an Illustration of input and rearrangement.

Input basket 83 32 all turn 76 51 now
***Step* I** turn basket 83 32 all 76 51 now
***Step* II** turn 32 basket 83 all 76 51 now
***Step* III** turn 32 now basket 83 all 76 51
***Step* IV** turn 32 now 51 basket 83 all 76
***Step* V** turn 32 now 51 basket 76 83 all
***Step* VI** turn 32 now 51 basket 76 all 83

and Step VI is the last step of the rearrangement of the above input.

As per the rules followed in the above steps, find out in each of the following questions the appropriate step for the given input.

35. Input 20 ask never 35 62 84 tall grass

Which of the following steps will be the last but one?

(a) V (b) VI (c) IV (d) VII
(e) None of these

36. Step II of an input is 'window 14 Victory 63 52 24 task for'.

Which of the following is definitely the input?

(a) victory 63 window 14 52 24 task for
(b) 63 victory window 14 52 24 task for
(c) victory 63 window 52 14 24 task for
(d) Cannot be determined
(e) None of the above

37. Step III of an input is 'yes 15 ultra 96 73 52 home rest'.

How many more step will be required to complete the rearrangement?

(a) Three (b) Five
(c) Four (d) Two
(e) None of these

Direction (Q. Nos. 38-40) *In each question below are given four statements followed by two conclusions numbered* I *and* II. *You have to take the four given statements to be true even if they seem to be at variance with commonly known facts and then decide which of the given conclusions logically follows from the four statements disregarding commonly known facts.*

Give answer

(a) if only Conclusion I follows
(b) if only Conclusion II follows
(c) if either Conclusion I or II follows
(d) if neither Conclusion I nor II follows
(e) if both Conclusions I and II follow

38. Statements Some computers are boards.
Some boards are chalks.
All chalks are bulbs.
No bulb is tubelight.

Conclusions I. Some bulbs are computers.
II. No chalk is a tubelight.

39. Statements All doors are floors.
Some floors are tiles.
All tiles are paints.
Some paints are stones.

Conclusions I. Some floors are paints.
II. Some doors are tiles.

40. Statements Some leaves are petals.
Some petals are flowers.
All flowers are fruits.
Some fruits are nuts.

Conclusions I. Some nuts are flowers.
II. No nut is flower.

41. A is the mother of D and sister of B. B has a daughter C, who is married to F. G is the husband of A. How is G related to D? **[SSC (10+2) 2012]**

(a) Uncle (b) Husband
(c) Son (d) Father

42. A person's present age is two-fifth of the age of his mother. After 8 yr, he will be one-half of the age of his mother. How old is the mother at present?

(a) 32 yr (b) 36 yr
(c) 40 yr (d) 48 yr

43. Arrange the following words as per order in the dictionary. **[SSC (CGL) 2012]**

(i) Detach (ii) Devise
(iii) Denote (iv) Digest
(v) Depict

(a) (v), (iv), (iii), (ii), (i)
(b) (iii), (v), (i), (ii), (iv)
(c) (iii), (ii), (i), (v), (iv)
(d) (v), (ii), (iv), (i), (iii)

44. If 'GERMANY' is written as '7, 5, 18, 13, 1, 14, 25', how can 'FRANCE' be written in that code? **[SSC (Steno) 2012]**

(a) 6, 18, 1, 14, 3, 5 (b) 6, 3, 18, 14, 1, 5
(c) 8, 2, 14, 5, 13, 6 (d) 8, 16, 14, 3, 1, 5

45. A solid cube of 4 inche has been painted red, green and black on pair of opposite faces. It has been cut into one inch cubes. How many cubes have only one face painted that too only red?

(a) 4 (b) 8
(c) 18 (d) 24

46. In a certain language, 'sun shines brightly' is written as 'ba lo sul', 'houses are brightly lit' as 'kado ula ari ba' and 'light comes from sun' as 'dopi kup lo mo'. What are the code words for 'sun' and 'brightly'?

(a) ba, sul (b) sul, lo
(c) lo, ba (d) ba, lo

Direction (Q. Nos. 47-48) *Each of the following questions below consists of a question and two statements numbered* I *and* II *given below it. You have to decide whether the data provided in the statements are sufficient to answer the questions*

Give answer

(a) if the data in Statement I alone are sufficient to answer the question, while the data in Statement II alone are not sufficient to answer the question
(b) if the data in Statement II alone are sufficient to answer the question, while the data in Statement I alone are not sufficient to answer the question
(c) if the data either in Statement I alone or Statement II alone are sufficient to answer the question
(d) if the data in both the Statements I and II together are not sufficient to answer the question
(e) if the data in both the Statements I and II are together necessary to answer the question

47. What is the code of 'fat' in a certain code language?

I. In that code language, 'she is fat' is written as 'he ra ca'.
II. In that code language, 'fat boy' is written as 'ra ka'.

48. How is M related to F?

I. F is the sister of N who is the mother of R.
II. M has two brothers, R is one of them.

Direction (Q. Nos. 49-50) *In making decisions about important questions, it is desirable to distinguish between a 'strong' argument and a 'weak' argument. A 'strong' argument must be both important and directly related to the question. A 'weak' argument may not be directly related to the question and may be of minor importance or may be related to the trivial aspect of the question. Each question below is followed by two arguments numbered* I *and* II. *You have to decide which of the arguments is 'strong' and which is 'weak'.*

Give answer

(a) if only Argument I is strong
(b) if only Argument II is strong
(c) if either I or II is strong
(d) if neither I nor II is strong
(e) if both I and II are strong

49. Statement Should the major part of school examinations be made objective type?

Arguments

I. No, objective type examination does not test the students ability to express.

II. Yes, this is the best method of assessing one's ability and knowledge.

50. Statement Should government service in rural areas atleast for two years after completion of graduation be made compulsory for the students of medicine?

Arguments

I. Yes, it is everyone's duty to serve the people in rural areas and contribute to their upliftment.

II. No, it cannot be applied only to the medicine students, since anyways they are contributing during their studies and particularly in the period of internship.

Hints and Solutions

1. (*d*) In given word, letter G is at 7th place and it comes in alphabet in 7th place too.

2. (*c*) The city name is 'MAD(U)RAI' and letter U exists exactly in the middle.

3. (*a*) Zephyr is kind of gentle wind while as strong wind is known as gale. Similarly, torrent is strong stream as compared to trickle.

4. (*c*) In (12, 20, 28), every next number is obtained by adding 8 with the previous number and similarly, in (18, 30, 42), every next number is obtained by adding 12 with the previous number.

5. (*a*) A 'Bank' deals with transaction of 'Money'. Likewise 'Transport' deals with the movement of 'Goods'.

6. (*a*) Here, sign '&' does not convey any meaning and sign '%' signifies '+'

$$26 + 7 = 33,\ 46 + 8 = 54$$

Therefore, $6 + 89 = 95$

7. (*c*) Except figure (c), in all other figures, two crosses and two circles are given together. In figure (c), cross and circle are placed alternately.

Solution (Q. Nos. 8-9) Descending order of heights and ages is as given below

Height Rupa > Kamini > Neelam > Pooja > Monika
Age Neelam > Rupa = Monika > Pooja > Kamimi
or Neelam > Rupa = Monika > Kamini > Pooja

8. (*d*) Neelam will be in the third position when the persons are arranged in ascending order of height.

9. (*d*) Fourth position cannot be determined, if they are arranged in descending order of their ages.

10. (*a*) According to the question, we have the following direction.

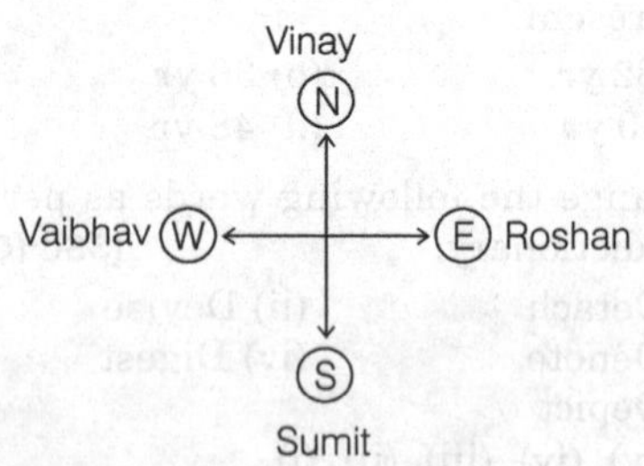

It is clear that Vinay faces towards South.

11. (*b*) The sum of squares of the outer numbers is equal to central number.

$(3)^2 + (2)^2 + (2)^2 + (4)^2 = 9 + 4 + 4 + 16 = 33$
$(3)^2 + (2)^2 + (5)^2 + (4)^2 = 9 + 4 + 25 + 16 = 54$
Similarly, $(6)^2 + (5)^2 + (4)^2 + (3)^2$
$= 36 + 25 + 16 + 9 = 86$

12. (*d*) In all pairs except (d), first is a tool which works on second.

13. (*c*) Humming bird, Kingfisher and Sparrow are small in size and can fly but Crane is large in size and cannot fly high. So, crane is odd one.

Solution (Q. Nos. 14-16) According to the given information, the arrangement is as follows

Floor	People
8	V
7	Z
6	S
5	Y
4	U
3	T
2	X
1	W

14. (*b*) Only three people live between Y and W.

15. (*d*) T lives on the floor number 3.

16. (*b*) V lives on floor number 8.

17. (*c*) Angle traced by hour hand in 12 h = 360°

Angle traced by hour hand in $\frac{25}{4}$ h $= \left(\frac{360}{12} \times \frac{25}{4}\right)^\circ$

= 187.5°

Angle traced by minute hand in 60 min = 360°

Angle traced by it in 15 min $= \left(\frac{360}{60} \times 15\right)^\circ = 90^\circ$

∴ Required angle = (187.5° − 90°) = 97.5°

18. (*c*) Figure given in option (c) can be formed by joining the pieces given in the question figure as shown below

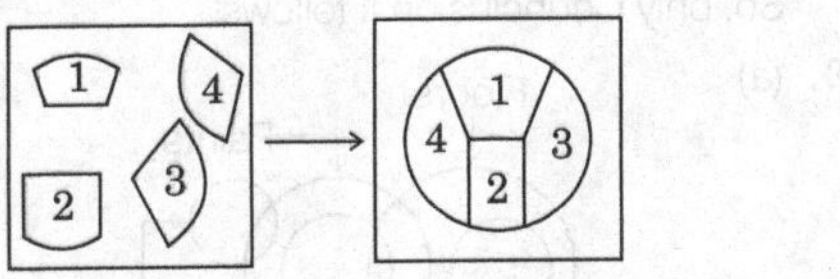

19. (*d*) The pattern is as follows

1	5	9	17 (15)	25	37	49
↓	↓	↓	↓	↓	↓	↓
1^2	(2^2+1)	3^2	(4^2+1)	5^2	(6^2+1)	7^2

Hence, number 15 is wrong and should be replaced by 17.

20. (*b*) According to the matrices,

H ⟶ (04), 11, 23, 30, 42
O ⟶ 56, 68, (75), 87, 99
R ⟶ 57, 69, 76, (88), 95
S ⟶ 02, 14, (21), 33, 40
E ⟶ 01, 13, 20, (32), 44

HORSE ⟶ 04, 75, 88, 21, 32

21. (*b*) Series pattern cccbb<u>b</u>aa<u>a</u>/cc<u>c</u>bbbaa<u>a</u>/c
∴ Required answer = baca.

22. (*a*)

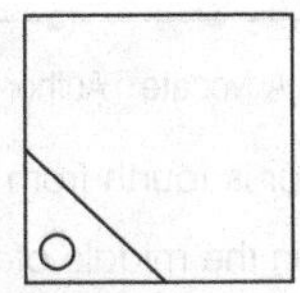

So, option (a) is correct answer.

23. (*a*) In the question figures, the design in centre moves through 45° and other design moves in clockwise direction. But from figures (3) and (4), we get that each are moving two steps ahead. Thus, the blank space will be filled by figure (a).

24. (*d*) Age of Shyam's sister = 8 yr
Age of Shyam = 2 + 8 = 10 yr
Let the age of Shyam's mother = x yr

According to the question, $\frac{x}{3} = 10$

∴ $x = 3 \times 10 = 30$ yr

25. (*c*) Ist column $14 \times 4 + 5 = 56 + 5 = 61$
IInd column $22 \times 6 + 3 = 132 + 3 = 135$
Similarly,
IIIrd column $37 \times 3 + 5 = 111 + 5 = 116$

26. (*b*) Route followed by Raju is given below

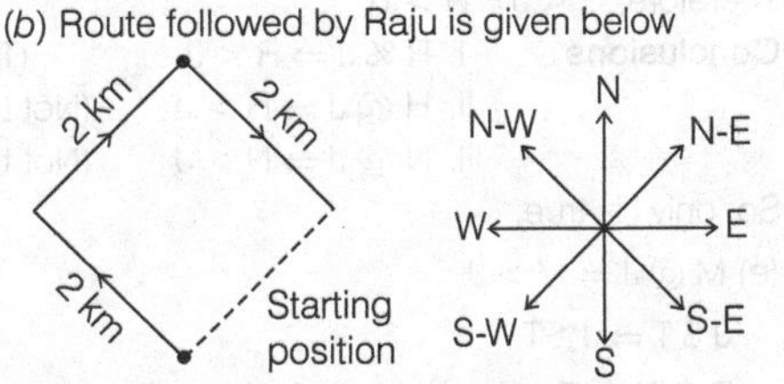

Raju will be in North-East direction from the original position.

27. (*a*) According to the question, the direction diagram is as follows

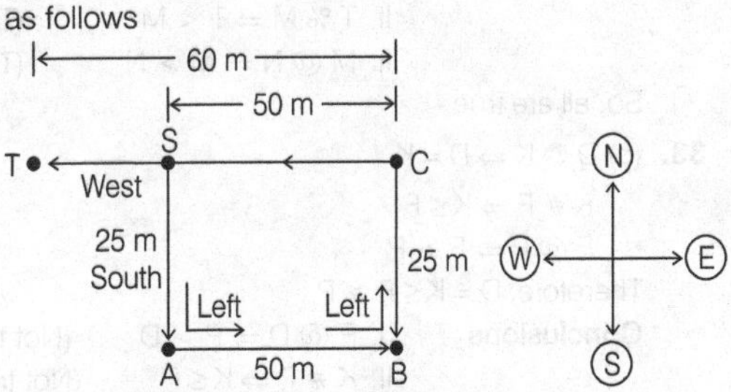

S = Starting point, T = Finishing point
AS = BC = 25 m
AB = SC = 50 m
CT = 60 m
∴ Required distance, ST = CT − SC = 60 − 50 = 10 m
Clearly, at point T, Mahesh is 10 m West from S.

Solution (Q. Nos. 28-30) Arrangement according to the question is as follows

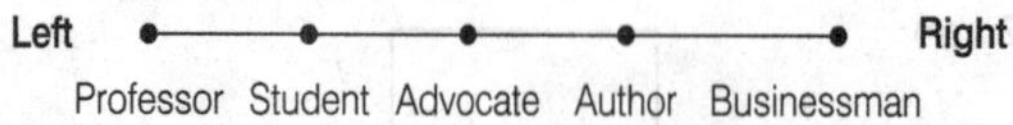

28. (*d*) Clearly, author is fourth from the left

29. (*b*) Advocate is in the middle of the queue.

30. (*b*) New arrangement, according to the question is as follows

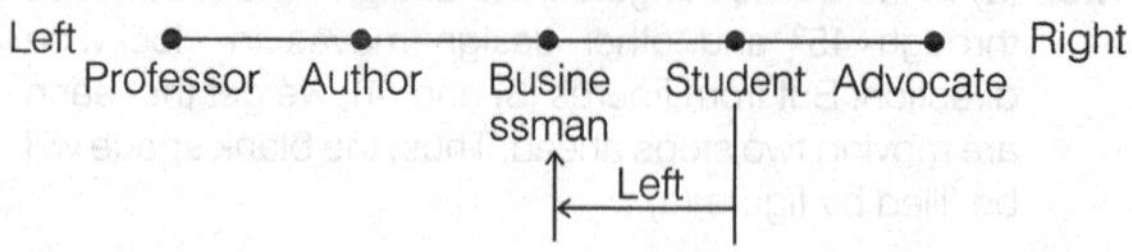

Clearly, businessman is standing to the left of student.

Solution (Q. Nos. 31-33)

$	#	@	©	%
≥	≤	>	=	<

31. (*c*) H % J $\Rightarrow$ H < J
J © N $\Rightarrow$ J = N
N @ R $\Rightarrow$ N > R
Therefore, H < J = N > R
Conclusions I. R % J $\Rightarrow$ R < J (True)
II. H @ J $\Rightarrow$ H > J (Not true)
III. N @ J $\Rightarrow$ N > J (Not true)
So, only I is true.

32. (*e*) M @ J $\Rightarrow$ M > J
J $ T $\Rightarrow$ J ≥ T
T © N $\Rightarrow$ T = N
Therefore, M > J ≥ T = N
Conclusions I. N # J $\Rightarrow$ N ≤ J (True)
II. T % M $\Rightarrow$ T < M (True)
III. M @ N $\Rightarrow$ M > N (True)
So, all are true.

33. (*c*) D © K $\Rightarrow$ D = K
K # F $\Rightarrow$ K ≤ F
F @ P $\Rightarrow$ F > P
Therefore, D = K ≤ F > P
Conclusions I. P @ D $\Rightarrow$ P > D (Not true)
II. K # P $\Rightarrow$ K ≤ P (Not true)
III. F $ D $\Rightarrow$ F ≥ D (True)
So, only III is true.

34. (c) All mothers and females. Also, some infants are females but infants cannot be mothers. This can be expressed as given in option (c).

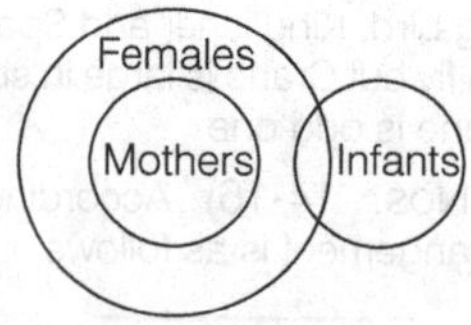

35. (*c*) **Input** 20 ask never 35 62 84 tall grass
***Step* I** tall 20 ask never 35 62 84 grass
***Step* II** tall 20 never ask 35 62 84 grass
***Step* III** tall 20 never 35 ask 62 84 grass
***Step* IV** tall 20 never 35 grass ask 62 84
***Step* V** tall 20 never 35 grass 62 ask 84.

36. (*d*) From the given step the input cannot be determined.

37. (c) ***Step* III** yes 15 ultra 96 73 52 home rest
***Step* IV** yes 15 ultra 52 96 73 home rest
***Step* V** yes 15 ultra 52 rest 96 73 home
***Step* VI** yes 15 ultra 52 rest 73 96 home
***Step* VII** yes 15 ultra 52 rest 73 home 96
Hence, four more steps are required to complete the rearrangement.

38. (*b*)

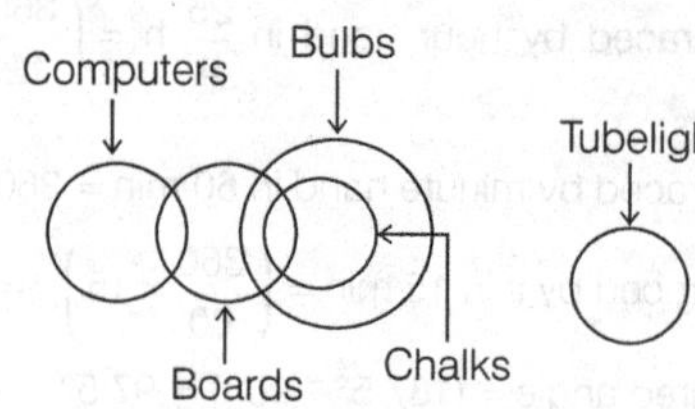

Conclusions I.Some bulbs are computers. (✘)
II. No chalk is tubelight. (✔)
So, only Cconclusion II follows.

39. (*a*)

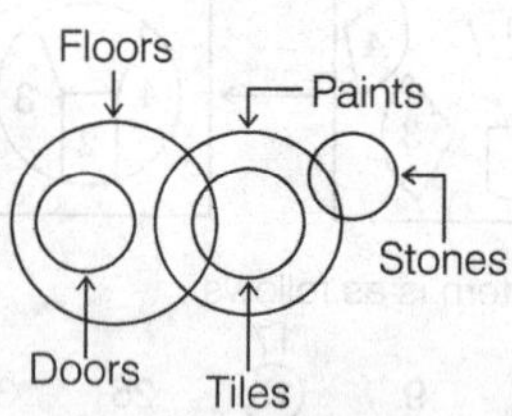

Conclusions I. Some floors are paints. (✔)
II. Some doors are tiles. (✘)
So, only Conclusion I follows.

40. (*c*)

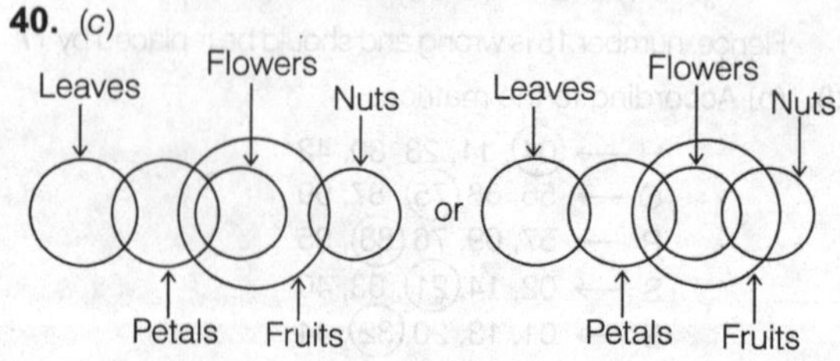

Conclusions

I. Some nuts are flowers. (May be true)

II. No nut is flower. (May be true)

Complementary pair (I-E)

So, either Conclusion I or II follows.

41. (*d*) Following family diagram can be drawn from the given information.

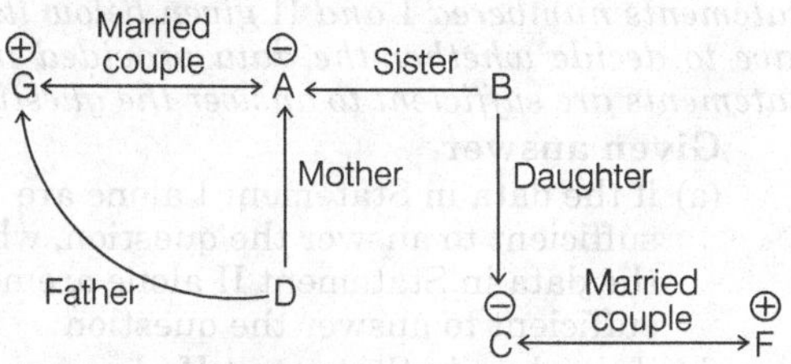

Now, it is clear that G is the father of D.

42. (*c*) Let person's mother present age = x yr

∴ Person's present age = $\frac{2}{5}$x yr

According to the question,

After 8 yr, $\frac{1}{2}(x+8) = \left(\frac{2x}{5} + 8\right)$

$\Rightarrow \frac{x+8}{2} = \frac{2x+40}{5}$

$\Rightarrow 5x + 40 = 4x + 80$

$\Rightarrow x = 40$ yr

∴ Present age of person's mother = 40 yr

43. (*b*) Arrangement of words as per dictionary

(iii) Denote
↓
(v) Depict
↓
(i) Detach
↓
(ii) Devise
↓
(iv) Digest

44. (*a*) Letters are coded with their corresponding positions.

As,

G	E	R	M	A	N	Y
↓	↓	↓	↓	↓	↓	↓
7	5	18	13	1	14	25

Similarly,

F	R	A	N	C	E
↓	↓	↓	↓	↓	↓
6	18	1	14	3	5

∴ FRANCE ⇒ 6, 18, 1, 14, 3, 5

45. (*b*)

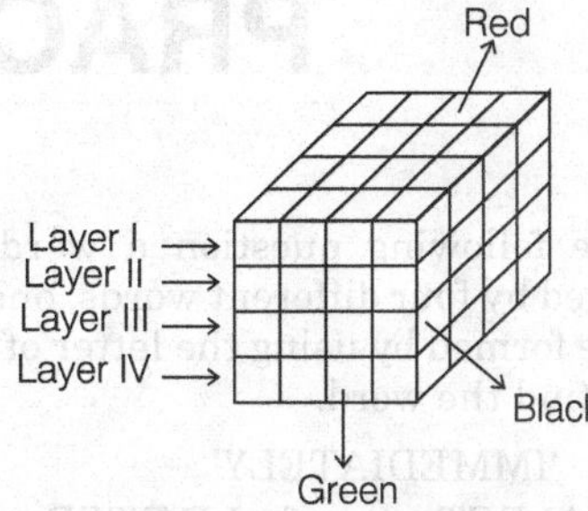

There are four cubes in Layer I and four cubes in Layer IV which have only one face painted red and all other faces not painted at all. Thus there are eight such cubes.

46. (*c*) Given that, ☐ shines ⬭ → ◯ ☐ sul ...(i)

houses are ⬭ lit → kado ula ari ...(ii)

light comes from ☐ → dopi kup ☐ mo ...(iii)

From Eqs. (i) and (ii), brightly → ba

From Eqs. (i) and (iii), sun → lo

Hence, sun → lo and brightly → ba

47. (*e*) From Statement I, she is <u>fat</u> = he <u>ra</u> ca

From Statement II, <u>fat</u> boy = <u>ra</u> ka

Clearly, fat = ra

So, both statements are required to answer the question.

48. (*d*) Since, M is not available in Statement I while F is not available in Statement II.

So, none of the statements alone is sufficient. From Statements I and II, the final diagram is as under

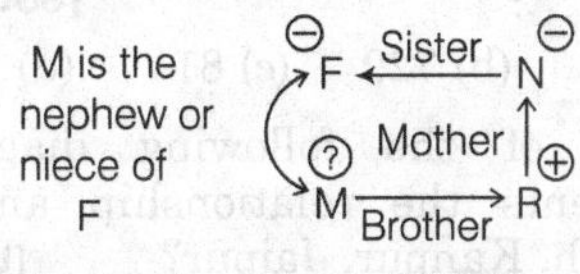

Clearly, M is nephew/niece of F but as gender of M is not known, hence definite relation of M in respect of F cannot be determined.

So, both the statements are not sufficient to answer the question.

49. (*a*) Argument I is strong as the ability to express gives groundness to one's education. Argument II is weak because to call a method 'the best' without giving any reason is a simplistic assertion.

50. (*d*) Argument I is weak because it is not true. You cannot sweep 'everyone' with the same brush. Argument II is ambiguous. It first says, 'it cannot be applied only to the medicine students'. But remaining part of the argument has got nothing to do with this only.

PRACTICE SET 21

1. In the following question a word is given followed by four different words, one of which can be formed by using the letter of the given word find the word.

'IMMEDIATELY'

(a) DIALECT (b) LIMITED
(c) DIAMETER (d) DICTATE

2. In the given number series, how many 9's are there which are immediately followed by 1 but not immediately preceded by 8?

18 91 35 79 13 91 57 98 69 14 20 86 49 12

(a) 3 (b) 6 (c) 4 (d) None of these

Direction (Q. Nos. 3-5) *In the following questions, select the related words/letters/numbers from the given alternatives.*

3. A : Ocean :: Stone : B

(a) A. Glacier, B. Granite
(b) A. River, B. Pebble
(c) A. Lake, B. Rock
(d) A. Continent, B. Mountain

4. GREAT : 25 :: NUMBER : ?

(a) 36 (b) 38 (c) 27 (d) 24

5. 64 : 4 :: ? : 9 **[SSC (10+2) 2014]**

(a) 18 (b) 729 (c) 81 (d) 144

6. Which of the following diagrams best represents the relationship among Uttar Pradesh, Kanpur, Jaipur? **[UP B Ed 2011]**

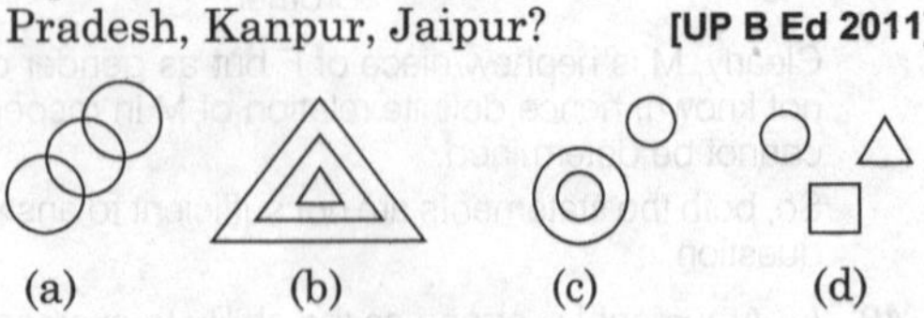

Direction (Q. Nos. 7-8) *In the following questions, find the odd word/number pair from the given alternatives.*

7. (a) Apple : Jam
(b) Lemon : Citrus
(c) Orange : Squash
(d) Tomato : Pury

8. (a) (42, 14) (b) (69, 23) **[SSC (CGL) 2015]**
(c) (108, 36) (d) (56, 19)

Direction (Q. Nos. 9-10) *Each of the following questions below consists of a question and two statements numbered* I *and* II *given below it. You have to decide whether the data provided in the statements are sufficient to answer the questions.*

Given answer

(a) if the data in Statement I alone are sufficient to answer the question, while the data in Statement II alone are not sufficient to answer the question
(b) if the data in Statement II alone are sufficient to answer the question, while the data in Statement I alone are not sufficient to answer the question
(c) if the data either in Statement I alone or Statement II alone are sufficient to answer the question
(d) if the data in both the Statements I and II together are not sufficient to answer the question
(e) if the data in both the Statements I and II are together necessary to answer the question

9. What does '$' mean in a certain code language?

I. '5 $ # 3' means 'flowers are really good'.
II. '7 # 3 5' mean 'good flowers are available'.

10. On which date is Amit's birthday in September 2010?

I. Last year his birthday was on the last Thursday of the month in September 2009.
II. This year his birthday will be on the last Friday of the month in September 2010.

11. If in a certain code 'CHARACTER' is written as '241612376' and 'CHILDREN' is written as '24859670', then how can 'HIRALAL' be written in the same code? **[SSC (CGL) 2014]**

(a) 4861551 (b) 4861515
(c) 4685151 (d) 4685511

12. If 'orange' is called 'butter', 'butter' is called 'soap', 'soap' is called 'ink', 'ink' is called 'honey' and 'honey' is called 'orange', then which of the following will be used for washing clothes?

(a) Honey (b) Butter
(c) Orange (d) ink

13. If it is possible to make only one meaningful word with the 1st, 2nd, 6th and 10th letters of the word 'DISCLAIMER', which of the following will be the 3rd letter from left? If no such word can be made give 'X' as your answer and if more than one such word can be made give 'Y' as your answer.

(a) I (b) R (c) D (d) X
(e) Y

Direction (Q. Nos. 14-15) *Read the following information carefully and answer the questions given below.*

Four security guards P, Q, R and S have been posted at the four corners of a huge cashew plantations farm as show in the adjacent figure.

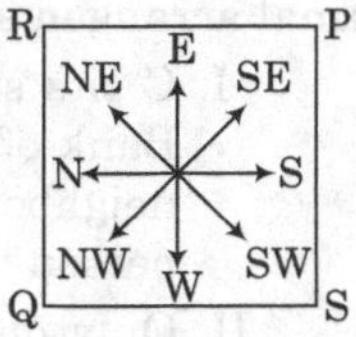

14. Given the condition that none of the corners should be unmanned and both P and R start moving towards diagonally opposite corners, in which direction should S start moving, so that he occupies a corner by travelling the minimum possible distance?

(a) Clockwise
(b) Anti-clockwise
(c) Either clockwise or anti-clockwise
(d) None of the above

15. From the original position, P and Q move one arm length clockwise and then cross over to the corner diagonally opposite, R and S move one arm length anti-clockwise and cross over to the corner diagonally opposite. The original setting PSQR has now changed to

(a) RSPQ (b) SRPQ
(c) RQSP (d) None of these

16. Which one of the given responses would be a meaningful descending order of the following?

(i) Major (ii) Captain
(iii) Colonel (iv) Brigadier
(v) Lt. General

(a) (v), (iv), (iii), (i), (ii)
(b) (v), (i), (iv), (ii), (iii)
(c) (iv), (v), (i), (iii), (ii)
(d) (iii), (iv), (ii), (v), (i)

17. N is more intelligent than M. M is not as intelligent as Y. X is more intelligent than Y but not as good as N. Who is the most intelligent of all? **[SSC (CGL) 2013]**

(a) N (b) M (c) X (d) Y

18. In a class of 45 students, a boy is ranked 20th. When two boys joined, his rank was dropped by one. What is his new rank from the end? **[UPSC (CSAT) 2013]**

(a) 25th (b) 26th
(c) 27th (d) 28th

Direction (Q. Nos. 19-20) *In each of the questions below is given a statement followed by three courses of action numbered I, II and III. A course of action is a step or administrative decision to be taken for improvement, follow-up or further action in regard to the problem, policy, etc. On the basis of information given in the statement, you have to assume everything in the statement to be true and then decide which of the three given suggested courses of action logically follows worth pursuing. Then, decide which of the alternatives* (a), (b), (c) *or* (d) *is correct.*

19. Statement In the Teacher's Day function, Shri Sharma, a State Awardee and a retired Principal, had questioned the celebration of Teacher's Day in today's materialistic world.

Courses of Action

I. The expenditure of Teacher's Day celebration should be reduced.
II. More funds should be allocated for the celebration of Teacher's Day.
III. The role and responsibilities of teachers should be seen in today's perspective.

(a) All follow
(b) None follows
(c) Either I or II follows
(d) Only III follows

20. Statement The members belonging to two local clubs occasionally fight with each other on the main road and block traffic movement.

Courses of Action

I. The local police station should immediately deploy police personel round the clock on the main road.
II. Those involved in fighting should be identified and put behind bars.
III. The local administration should disband the management of the two clubs with immediate effect.

(a) Both I and II follow
(b) Both II and III follow
(c) Both I and III follow
(d) All follow

Direction (Q. Nos. 21-23) *Study the given information and answer the questions.* **[SBI (PO) Pre 2015]**

When a word and number arrangement machine is given an input line of words and numbers, it arranges them following a particular rule. The following is an illustration of input and rearrangement:

(All the numbers are two digit numbers)

Input initiators 32 67 of 40 the company 21 are 18 96 humble

***Step* I** 21 initiators 32 67 of 40 the company are 96 humble 18

***Step* II** company 21 initiators 32 67 of 40 the 96 humble 18 are

***Step* III** 40 company 21 initiators 67 of the 96 humble 18 are 32

***Step* IV** initiators 40 company 21 67 of the 96 18 are 32 humble

***Step* V** 96 initiators 40 company 21 of the 18 are 32 humble 67

***Step* VI** the 96 initiators 40 company 21 18 are 32 humble 67 of

Step VI is the last step of above arrangement as the intended arrangement is obtained.

As per the rules followed in the given steps, find out the appropriate steps for the given input.

Input parenting 16 36 and raising 44 children 21 is 89 very 95 demanding 72 job 65

21. In which step are the elements '95 job 16 and' found in the same order?
(a) Not found in any step
(b) Fifth (c) Fourth (d) Second (e) Third

22. What is the position of the '72' from the right end in the fourth step?
(a) Fifth (b) Eight (c) Ninth (d) Seventh
(e) Sixth

23. Which element is fifth to the left of the element which is tenth from the left end of the third step?
(a) raising (b) parenting (c) is (d) 72
(e) job

Direction (Q. Nos. 24-28) *Study the following information carefully and answer the given questions.* **[IBPS (PO) 2011]**

Eight persons from different banks *viz.* UCO Bank, Syndicate Bank, Canara Bank, PNB, Dena Bank, Oriental Bank of Commerce, Indian Bank and Bank of Maharashtra are sitting in two parallel rows containing four people each, in such a way that there is an equal distance between adjacent persons.

In row 1, A, B, C and D are seated and all of them are facing South. In row 2, P, Q, R and S are seated and all of them are facing North. Therefore, in the given sitting arrangement each member seated in row faces another member of the other row. (All the information given above does not necessarily represent the order of seating as in the final arrangement.)

I. C sits second to right of the person from Bank of Maharashtra. R is an immediate neighbour of the person who faces the person from Bank of Maharashtra.

II. Only one person sits between R and the person from PNB. The immediate neighbour of the person from PNB faces the person from Canara Bank.

III. The person from UCO Bank faces the person from Oriental Bank of Commerce. R is not from Oriental Bank of Commerce. P is not from PNB. P does not face the person from Bank of Maharashtra.

IV. Q faces the person from Dena Bank. The one who faces S sits to the immediate left of A.

V. B does not sit at any of the extreme ends of the line. The person from Bank of Maharashtra does not face the person from Syndicate Bank.

24. Which of the following is true regarding A?
(a) The person from UCO Bank faces A
(b) The person from Bank of Maharashtra is an immediate neighbour of A
(c) A faces the person who sits second to the right of R
(d) A is from Oriental Bank of Commerce
(e) A sits at one of the extreme ends of the line

25. Who is seated between R and the person from PNB?
(a) The person from Oriental Bank of Commerce
(b) P
(c) Q
(d) The person from Syndicate Bank
(e) S

26. Who amongst the following sit at extreme ends of the rows?
(a) D and the person from PNB
(b) The persons from Indian Bank of UCO Bank
(c) The persons from Dena Bank and P
(d) The persons from Syndicate Bank and D
(e) C, Q

27. Who amongst the following faces the person from Bank of Maharashtra?
(a) The person from Indian Bank
(b) P
(c) R
(d) The person from Syndicate Bank
(e) The person from Canara Bank

28. P is related to Dena Bank in the same way as B is related to PNB based on the given arrangement. Who amongst the following is D related to, following the same pattern?
(a) Syndicate Bank
(b) Canara Bank
(c) Bank of Maharashtra
(d) Indian Bank
(e) Oriental Bank of Commerce

29. In the following question, which one set of letters when sequentially placed at the gaps in the given letters series shall complete it?

PBA, QDC, RFE, ?

(a) SHG (b) OAB (c) TJI (d) ULK

Direction (Q. Nos. 30-31) *In the following questions, a series is given, with one term missing. Choose the correct alternative from the given ones that will complete the series.*

30. 4,2.5, 3.5, 6.5, 15.5, 41.25, 126.75
(a) 2.5 (b) 3.5 (c) 6.5 (d) 15.5
(e) 41.25

31. 71 XW 13, 67 UT 17, ?, 59 ON 25, 55 LK 29 **[MAT 2014]**
(a) 65 RQ 18 (b) 63 RQ 21
(c) 61 RQ 19 (d) 60 RQ 126

32. Six persons are playing a card game. Suresh is facing Raghubir who is to the left of Ajay and to the right of Pramod. Ajay is to the left of Dhiraj. Yogendra is to the left of Pramod. If Dhiraj exchanges his seat with Yogendra and Pramod exchanges with Raghubir, who will be sitting to the left of Dhiraj?
(a) Yogendra (b) Raghubir
(c) Suresh (d) Ajay

Direction (Q. Nos. 33-34) *Read the following information carefully and then answer the questions given below.*

Seven boys A, B, C, D, E, F and G are standing in a line.

I. G is between A and E.
II. F and A have one boy between them.
III. E and C have two boys between them.
IV. D is to the immediate right of F.
V. C and B have three boys between them.

33. Who is second from left?
(a) C (b) G (c) E (d) A

34. C is standing between
(a) A and F (b) D and G
(c) A and D (d) F and G

35. A square paper is folded in a particular manner and a punch is made. When unfolded the paper appears as given below. Find out the manner in which the paper is folded and punch is made from the responses given.

Question Figure

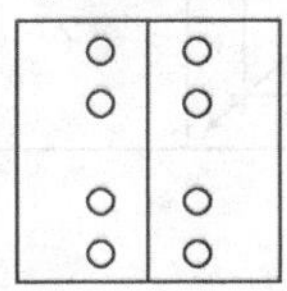

Answer Figures

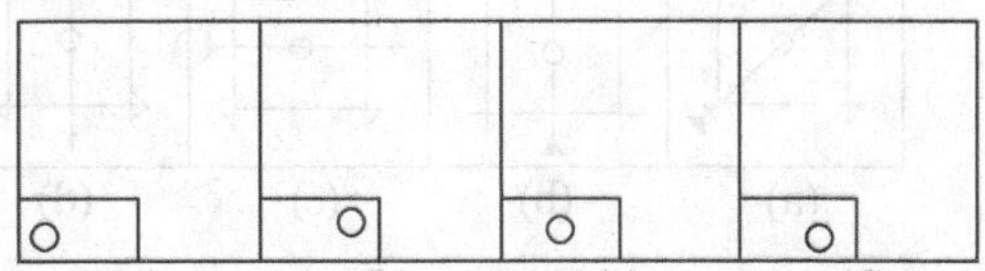

(a) (b) (c) (d)

36. Find the missing number from the given responses.

8	7	10	12
13	12	15	17
10	9	?	14

(a) 12 (b) 10
(c) 21 (d) 25

37. An accurate clock shows the time as 3:00 after hour hand has moved 135°, the time would be
(a) 7:30 (b) 6:30
(c) 8:00 (d) 9:30

38. Find the digit at the face opposite to the face having digit 1 in the given dice.

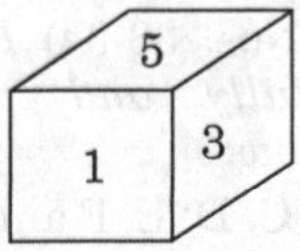

(a) 2 (b) 4 (c) 6 (d) 3

39. What is the number of straight lines in the following figure?

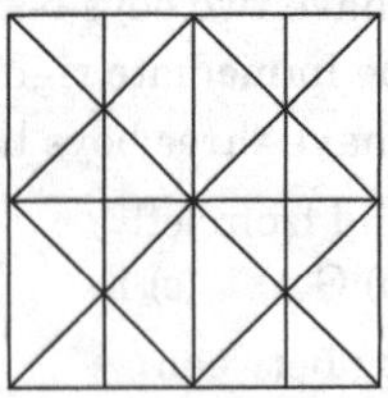

(a) 11 (b) 14
(c) 16 (d) 17

40. A series is given with one term missing. Choose the correct alternative from the given ones that will complete the series.

Question Figures

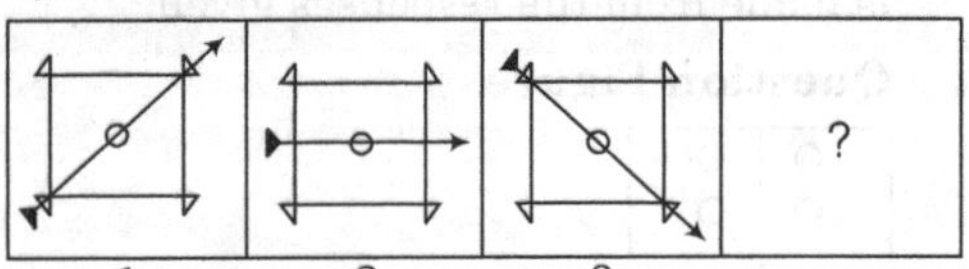

1 2 3

Answer Figures

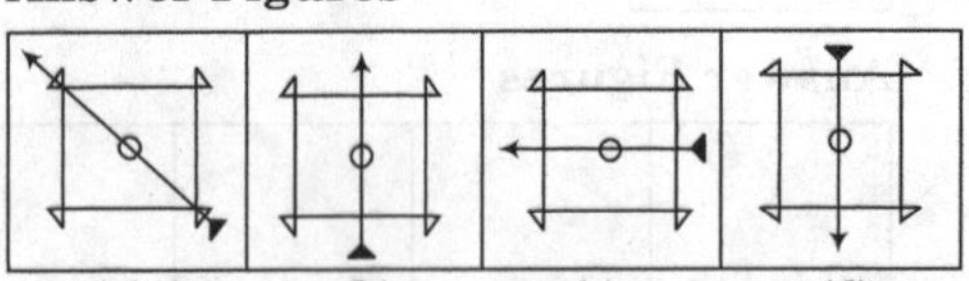

(a) (b) (c) (d)

Direction (Q. Nos. 41-43) *In each questions below are four statements followed by two conclusions numbered I and II. You have to take the four given statements to be true even if they seem to be at variance with commonly known facts and then decide which of the given conclusions logically follows from the four statements disregarding commonly known facts.*

Give answer

(a) if only Conclusion I follows
(b) if only Conclusion II follows
(c) if either Conclusion I or II follows
(d) if neither Conclusion I nor II follows
(e) if both Conclusions I and II follow

41. Statements All pictures are paintings.
All paintings are photographs.
Some photographs are designs.
Some designs are movies.

Conclusions
I. Some paintings are designs.
II. Some photographs are movies.

42. Statements Some tablets are capsules.
All capsules are syrups.
Some syrups are medicines.
All medicines are powders.

Conclusions I. Some syrups are powders.
II. Some syrups are tablets.

43. Statements All bangles are rings.
All rings are bracelets.
Some bracelets are jewels.
Some jewels are stones.

Conclusions I. Some stones are bangles.
II. Some jewels are rings.

44. Choose the right water image of the question figure from the given answer figures.

Question Figure

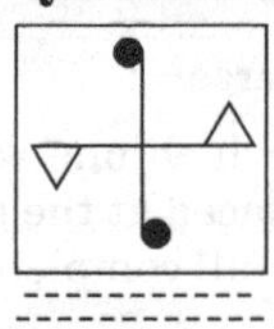

Answer Figures

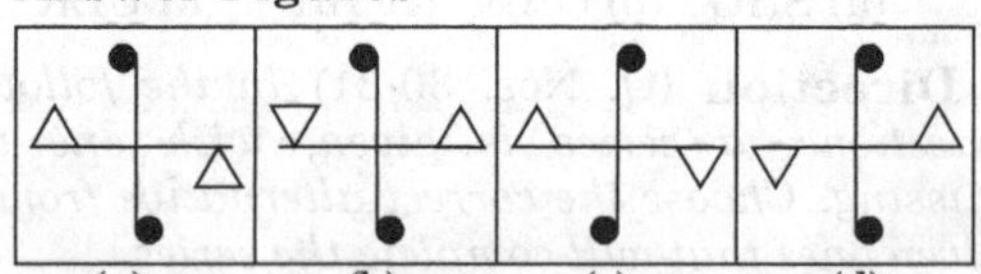

(a) (b) (c) (d)

45. From the given answer figures, select the one in which the question figure is hidden/embedded.

Question Figure

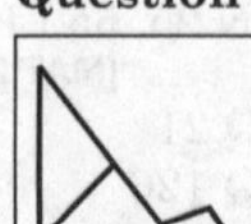

Answer Figures

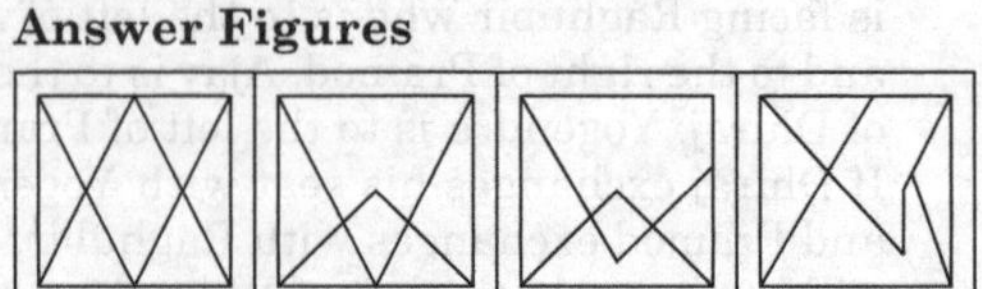

(a) (b) (c) (d)

46. A is B's brother. C is A's father. D is C's sister and E is D's mother. How is E related to B?
(a) Grandmother (b) Great granddaughter
(c) Grandaunt (d) Daughter

47. Devendra is older by 4 yr to Rajendra. After 16 yr, Devendra will be thrice his present age and Rajendra will be five times, of his present age. How old would Rajendra be after 16 yr?
(a) 30 yr (b) 25 yr (c) 24 yr (d) 20 yr

Direction (Q. Nos. 48-50) *In the following questions, the symbols @, ©, #, $ and ★ are used with the following meanings illustrated.*

'P © Q' means 'P is not smaller than Q'

'P ★ Q' means 'P is neither greater than nor smaller than Q'

'P @ Q' means 'P is neither greater than nor equal to Q'

'P $ Q' means 'P is not greater than Q'

'P # Q' means 'P is neither smaller than nor equal to Q'

48. Statements M @ T, T $ R, R © J
Conclusions I. J # M
II. R # M III. J ★ T
(a) Only I is true
(b) Only II is true
(c) Only III is true
(d) Only I and II are true
(e) None of the above

49. Statements D © B, B # H, H ★ F
Conclusions I. F @ B
II. F @ D
III. H @ D
(a) Only I is true
(b) Only II is true
(c) Only III is true
(d) Only I and II are true
(e) All are true

50. Statements H ★ M, M @ T, T $ K
Conclusions I. K # M
II. T # H
III. H @ K
(a) Only I is true
(b) Only I and II are true
(c) Only II and III are true
(d) Only I and III are true
(e) All are true

Hints and Solutions

1. (*b*) 'LIMITED' is the only word which can be formed by using the letters of given word.

2. (*c*) Given that,

1 8 (9) 1 3 5 7 (9) 13 (9) 1 5 7 (9) 8 6 (9) 14 20 86 4 (9) 12

(first and last-but-two circled 9 in the first group: ×; the two middle ones: ✓; both circled 9s in the second group: ✓)

✓ = Condition fulfilled
× = Condition not fulfilled

∴ Required number of 9 = 4 times

3. (*c*) Second is an enlarged form of the first.

4. (*a*) As, 'GREAT' has 5 letters, it is represented by square of 5 i.e. 25. Similarly, 'NUMBER' has 6 letters it is represented by square of 6 i.e. 36.

5. (*b*) As, $(4)^3 \rightarrow 64$
Same as, $(9)^3 \rightarrow 729$

6. (*c*) Kanpur is a city in the state of Uttar Pradesh while Jaipur is entirely different as it is a city in Rajasthan. This can be expressed as given in option (c).

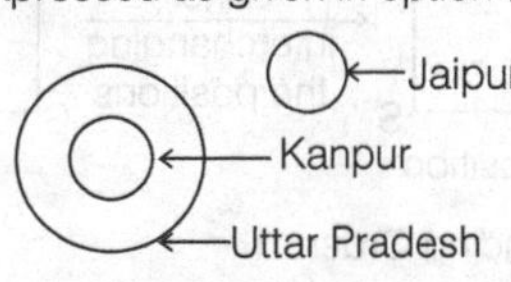

7. (*b*) In all pairs except (b), second in made by first.

8. (*d*) The pattern is as follows
$(42, 14) \rightarrow 14 \times 3 = 42$
$(69, 23) \rightarrow 23 \times 3 = 69$
$(108, 36) \rightarrow 36 \times 3 = 108$
But $(56, 19) \rightarrow 19 \times 3 = 57 \neq 56$
So, option (d) is odd one.

9. (*e*) From Statement I and II,

(5) $ (#) (3) = (flowers) (are) really (good)

7 (#) (3) (5) = (good) (flowers) (are) available

∴ $ = really

So, both statement are required to answer the question.

10. (*c*) The calendar method is helpful in either case.

So, either Statement I or II alone are sufficient to answer the question.

11. (*b*) Given,

C H A R A C T E R
↓ ↓ ↓ ↓ ↓ ↓ ↓ ↓ ↓
2 4 1 6 1 2 3 7 6

and

C H I L D R E N
↓ ↓ ↓ ↓ ↓ ↓ ↓ ↓
2 4 8 5 9 6 7 0

So, code for,

H I R A L A L
↓ ↓ ↓ ↓ ↓ ↓ ↓
4 8 6 1 5 1 5

12. (*d*) 'Soap' is used for washing 'clothes' as here 'soap' is called 'ink'.

13. (*e*) Ⓓ Ⓘ S C L Ⓐ I M E Ⓡ

1st 2nd 6th 10th

Words formed = ARID, RAID

14. (*b*) When P and R move towards diagonally opposite corners the two top positions become vacant. Hence, in order S should travel minimum distance, he should move anti-clockwise to occupy P's position.

15. (*c*) Original setting of PSQR change to RQSP, as shown below

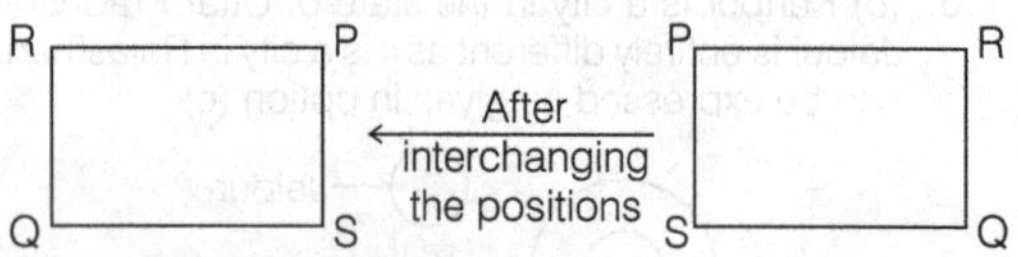

16. (*a*) Descending Order

(v) Lt General, → (iv) Brigadier, → (iii) Colonel → (i) Major, → (ii) Captain

17. (*a*) According to the question,

$N > M$

$Y > M$

$N > X > Y$

On arranging the above data, we get

$\because \quad N > X > Y > M$

So, N is the most intelligent among them.

18. (*c*) Total number of boys after 2 new boys joined = 47

Since, the rank of the boy dropped by 1, it became 21st from 20th.

$\therefore$ His new rank from the end = 47 − 21 + 1 = 27th

19. (*d*) In the statement, celebration of Teacher's Day in today's materialistic world is in question which means that the role and responsibilities of teachers should be seen in today's perspective. Hence, course of action III is the right course of action.

20. (*c*) A proper course of action would be serving notices to these clubs to behave themselves. Even police personnel may be deployed but only during the sensitive hours.

Solution (Q. Nos. 21-23)

Input Parenting 16 36 and raising 44 children 21 is 89 very 95 demanding 72 job 65

***Setp* I** 21 parenting 36 and raising 44 children is 89 very 95 demanding 72 job 65 16

***Step* II** Children 21 parenting 36 raising 44 is 89 very 95 demanding 72 job 65 16 and

***Step* III** 44 children 21 parenting raising is 89 very 95 demanding 72 job 65 16 and 36

***Step* IV** is 44 children 21 parenting raising 89 very 95 72 job 65 16 and 36 demanding

***Step* V** 72 is 44 children 21 parenting raising 89 very 95 job 16 and 36 demanding 65

***Step* VI** parenting 72 is 44 children 21 raising 89 very 95 16 and 36 demanding 65 job

***Step* VII** 95 parenting 72 is 44 children 21 raising very 16 and 36 demanding 65 job 89

***Step* VIII** very 95 parenting 72 is 44 children 21 16 and 36 demanding 65 job 89 raising

21. (*b*) In fifth step the elements '95 job 16 and' found in same order.

22. (*d*) '72' is seventh from the right end in the fourth step.

23. (*a*) 'raising' element is fifth to the left of the element which is tenth from the left end of the third step.

Solution (Q. Nos. 24-28) Following sitting arrangement is formed from the given information.

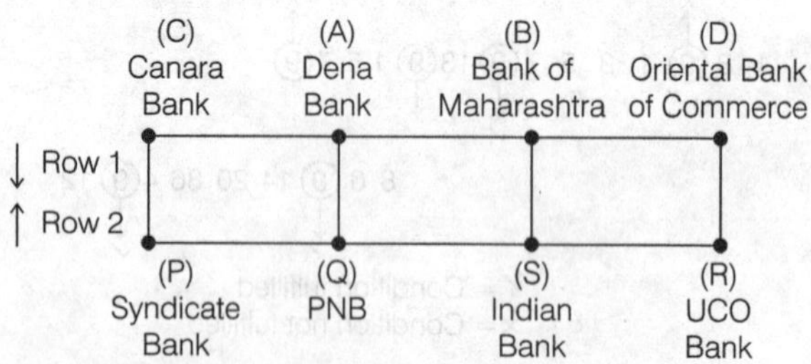

24. (*b*) The person from Bank of Maharashtra is an immediate neighbour of A.

25. (*e*) S is the person between R and the person from PNB.

26. (*d*) The person from Syndicate Bank i.e. P and D are sitting at the extreme ends of the rows.

27. (*a*) The person from Indian Bank i.e. S faces the person from Bank of Maharashtra.

28. (*d*) D is related to Indian bank in the same manner.

29. (*a*) The pattern is as follows

1st Letter $\overset{16}{P} \xrightarrow{+1} \overset{17}{Q} \xrightarrow{+1} \overset{18}{R} \xrightarrow{+1} \boxed{\overset{19}{S}}$

2nd Letter $\overset{2}{B} \xrightarrow{+2} \overset{4}{D} \xrightarrow{+2} \overset{6}{F} \xrightarrow{+2} \boxed{\overset{8}{H}}$

3rd Letter $\overset{1}{A} \xrightarrow{+2} \overset{3}{C} \xrightarrow{+2} \overset{5}{E} \xrightarrow{+2} \boxed{\overset{7}{G}}$

30. (*c*) The pattern is as follows

4 → 2.5 → 3.5 → (6.5) [6.75] → 15.5 → 41.25 → 126.75

$\times\frac{1}{2}+\frac{1}{2}$, $\times 1 + 1$, $\times\frac{3}{2}+\frac{3}{2}$, $\times 2 + 2$, $\times\frac{5}{2}+\frac{5}{2}$, $\times 3 + 3$

Hence, number 6.5 is wrong and should be replaced by 6.75.

31. (*b*) Pattern of given alpha-numeric series is as follows

$-71 \xrightarrow{-4} 67 \xrightarrow{-4} \boxed{63} \xrightarrow{-4} 59 \xrightarrow{-4} 55$

$X \xrightarrow{-3} U \xrightarrow{-3} \boxed{R} \xrightarrow{-3} O \xrightarrow{-3} L$

$W \xrightarrow{-3} T \xrightarrow{-3} \boxed{Q} \xrightarrow{-3} N \xrightarrow{-3} K$

$13 \xrightarrow{+4} 17 \xrightarrow{+4} \boxed{21} \xrightarrow{+4} 25 \xrightarrow{+4} 29$

∴ Missing term 63 RQ 19

32. (*c*) Arrangements according to the question is as follows

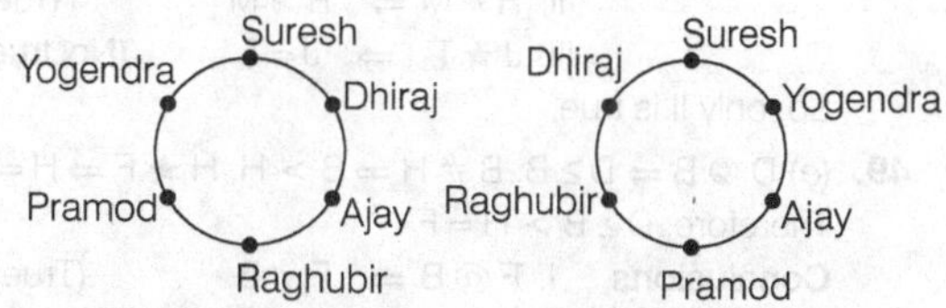

Original arrangement **New arrangement**

Clearly, Suresh is sitting to the left of Dhiraj.

Solution (Q. Nos. 33-34) Arrangement according to the question is as follows

Left • B E G A C F D • Right

33. (*c*) Clearly, E is second from left.

34. (*a*) Clearly, C is standing between A and F.

35. (*d*)

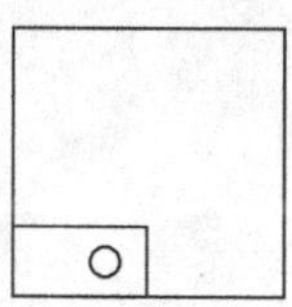

36. (*a*) As,

8	7	10	12
+ 5 ↓	+ 5 ↓	+ 5 ↓	+ 5 ↓
13	12	15	17
− 3 ↓	− 3 ↓	− 3 ↓	− 3 ↓
10	9	**12**	14

So, ? = 12

37. (*a*) Angle of 360° is covered by hour hand in 12h.

So, angle of 135° is covered by hour hand in

$$\frac{12}{360°} \times 135° = 4.5\,h$$

Thus, required time = (3 + 4.5) h = 7.5 h = 7:30

38. (*c*) According to the question,

$5 + 1 = 6$

$1 + 3 = 4$

$3 + 5 = 8$

Clearly, it is a standard dice.

∴ Digit at the face opposite to 1 = 7 − 1 = 6

39. (*b*) The figure has been labelled as shown in the following figure

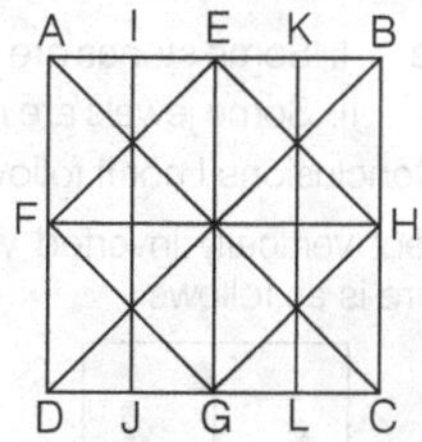

It is clear from the figure that the straight lines in the figure are as follow

(i) Straight lines from the outer square = AB, BC, CD, AD = 4

(ii) Straight lines in the diagonals = AC, BD = 2

(iii) Other straight lines inside the square = EG, FH, EF, FG, GH, EH, IJ, KL = 8

Therefore, total number of straight lines is 14.

40. (*d*) From first figure to second figure and from second figure to third figure, the shaded arrow moves through 45° in clockwise direction. Then, the same procedure is followed.

41. (*d*)

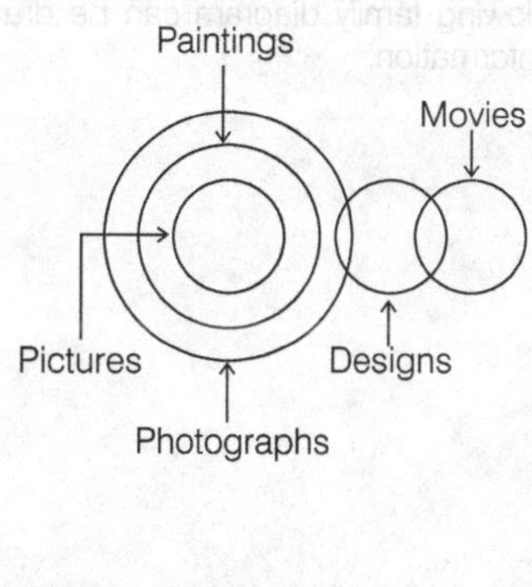

Conclusions I. Some paintings are designs. (✗)
II. Some photographs are movies. (✗)

So, neither I nor II follows.

42. (*e*)

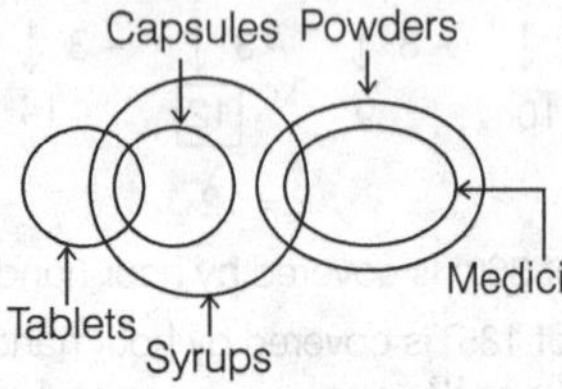

Conclusions I. Some syrups are powders. (✔)
II. Some syrups are tablets. (✔)

So, both Conclusions I and II follow.

43. (*d*)

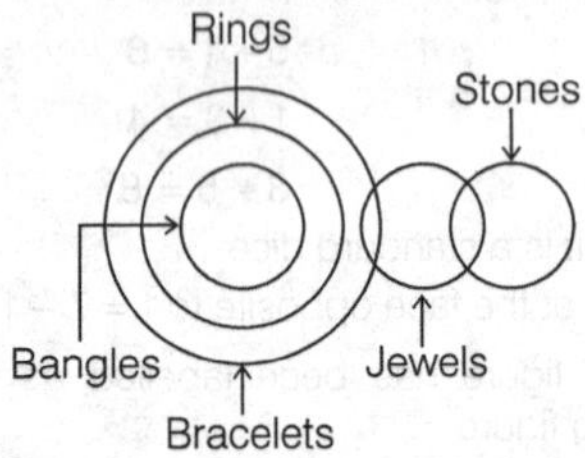

Conclusions I. Some stones are bangles. (✗)
II. Some jewels are rings. (✗)

So, neither Conclusions I nor II follow.

44. (c) The correct vertically inverted water image of the question figure is as follows

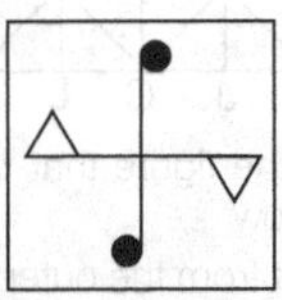

45. (c) Clearly, question figure is embedded in answer figure (c) as shown below

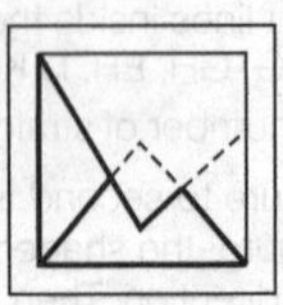

46. (*a*) Following family diagram can be drawn from the given information,

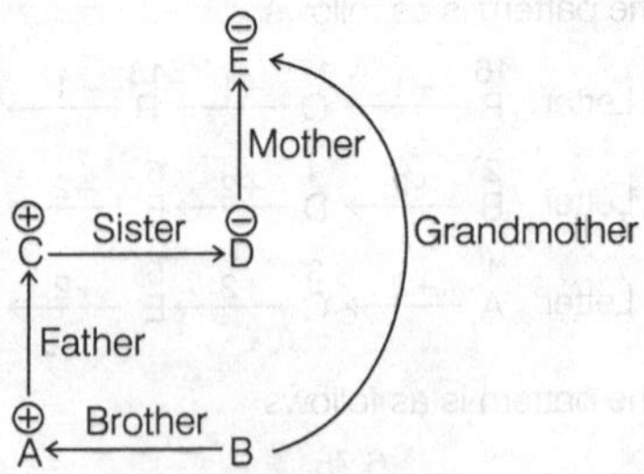

So, E is grandmother of B.

47. (*d*) Suppose Rajendra's age = x yr
and Devendra's age = (x + 4) yr
Then, according to the question,

$$(x + 4) + 16 = 3(x + 4)$$
$$\Rightarrow \quad x + 20 = 3x + 12$$
$$\Rightarrow \quad 2x = 8 \Rightarrow x = 4 \text{ yr}$$

∴ Rajendra's age after 16 yr = x + 16 = 4 + 16 = 20 yr
or Rajendra's age after 16 yr = 5x = 5 × 4 = 20 yr

Solution (Q. Nos. 48-50)

©	★	@	$	#
≥	=	<	≤	>

48. (*b*) M @ T ⇒ M < T, T $ R ⇒ T ≤ R, R © T ⇒ R ≥ J
Therefore, M < T ≤ R ≥ J

Conclusions I. J # M ⇒ J < M (Not true)
II. R # M ⇒ R > M (True)
III. J ★ T ⇒ J = T (Not true)

So, only II is true.

49. (*e*) D © B ⇒ D ≥ B, B # H ⇒ B > H, H ★ F ⇒ H = F,
Therefore, D ≥ B > H = F

Conclusions I. F @ B ⇒ F < B (True)
II. F @ D ⇒ F < D (True)
III. H @ D ⇒ H < D (True)

So, all are true.

50. (*e*) H ★ M ⇒ H = M, M @ T ⇒ M < T, T $ K ⇒ T ≤ K,
Therefore, H = M < T ≤ K

Conclusions I. K # M ⇒ K > M (True)
II. T # H ⇒ T > H (True)
III. H @ K ⇒ H < K (True)

So, all are true.

PRACTICE SET 22

1. In a certain code, LUTE is written as 'MUTE' and GATE is written as 'HATE', then how BLUE will be written in that code? **[SSC (CGL) 2015]**

(a) CLUE (b) GLUE (c) FLUD (d) FLUE

2. How many triangles are there in the given figure?

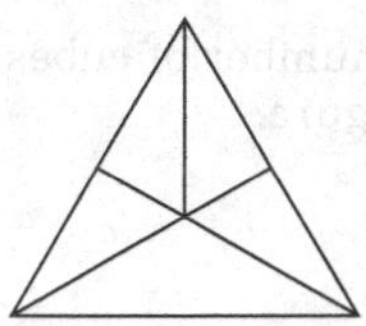

(a) 11 (b) 16 (c) 14 (d) 12

3. Select the related number from the given alternatives.

12 : 140 :: 156 : ? **[SSC (10+2) 2014]**

(a) 1820 (b) 1500 (c) 1250 (d) 1121

4. Raghu jogged 2 km Southwards, then he turned right and walked 5 km. He again turned right and walked and jogged 8 km. In which direction was he seen moving last? **[SSC (10+2) 2015]**

(a) West (b) South (c) East (d) North

Direction (Q. Nos. 5-6) *In each of the following questions, two statements are given followed by two Conclusion I and II. You have to consider the two statements to be true even if they seem to be at variance from commonly known facts. You have to decide which of the given conclusions, if any follow from the given statements.*

5. Statements

I. Best performance in Olympics fetches a gold medal.

II. Player X got gold medal but later was found to be using a prohibited drug.

Conclusions

I. X should be allowed to keep the gold medal.

II. Gold medal should be withdrawn and given to the next person.

(a) Only Conclusion II follows
(b) Neither Conclusion I nor II follows
(c) Both Conclusions I and II follow
(d) Only Conclusion I follows

6. Statements

I. There are monks among those who are felicitated for remarkable social service.

II. Jitananda and Vidyananda are among those felicitated.

Conclusions

(a) Jitananda and Vidyananda did remarkable social service
(b) All monks do social service
(c) Jitananda and Vidyananda are not monks
(d) All monks are felicitated

Direction (Q. Nos. 7-9) *In the following questions, the symbols @, ©, $, % and δ are used with the following meaning a illustrated below*

'P © Q' means 'P is either greater than or equal to Q'.

'P % Q' means 'P is either smaller than or equal to Q'

'P @ Q' means 'P is neither smaller than nor greater than Q.'

'P $ Q' means 'P is smaller than Q'.

'P δ Q' means 'P is greater than Q.'

Now, in each of the following questions assuming the given statement to be true, find which of the two conclusions I and II given below them is/are definitely true?

Give answer

(a) if only Conclusion I is true
(b) if only Conclusion II is true
(c) if either Conclusion I or II is true
(d) if neither Conclusion I nor II is true
(e) if both Conclusions I and II are true

7. Statements H © T, T % M, M δ F

Conclusions I. F $ T

II. H δ M

8. Statements B @ N, N © T, T $ K

Conclusions I. T @ B

II. T $ B

9. Statements R $ J, J δ F, F % H

Conclusions I. H δ J

II. R $ F

Direction (Q. Nos. 10-12) *In the following questions, select the related word/letters/number/pair from the given alternatives.*

10. World War II : United Nations : : World war I : ?
(a) Treaty of Versailles
(b) International Commission of Jurists
(c) League of Nations
(d) International Court of Justice

11. acme : mace : : face : ? **[SSC (Steno) 2013]**
(a) cefa (b) cfae (c) cfea (d) afce

12. 9 : 24 :: ? : 6 **[Assistant SI 2015]**
(a) 1 (b) 2 (c) 5 (d) 3

13. Given below are two matrices of 25 cells each containing two classes of letters. The columns and rows of Matrix I are numbered from 0 to 4 and those of Matrix II from 5 to 9. A letter from these matrices can be represented first by its row number and next by its column number e.g. 'B' can be represented as 00, 14 etc. Similarly, M can be represented by 55, 67, etc. In the following question identify one set of number pair out of A, B, C and D which represents the given word.

Matrix I

	0	1	2	3	4
0	B	D	E	T	O
1	D	E	T	O	B
2	E	B	O	D	T
3	T	O	B	E	D
4	O	T	D	B	E

Matrix II

	5	6	7	8	9
5	M	U	I	L	R
6	U	L	M	R	I
7	I	M	R	U	L
8	L	R	U	I	M
9	R	I	L	M	U

RUDE
(a) 56, 65, 10, 33 (b) 59, 95, 34, 11
(c) 77, 56, 02, 01 (d) 95, 87, 42, 11

Direction (Q. Nos. 14-15) *Study the following arrangement carefully and answer the questions given below.*

F 4 © T 2 E % M P 5 W 9 @ L Q R 6 U H 3 Z 7 ★ A T B 8 V # G $ Y D

14. What should come in place of question mark (?) in the following series based on the above arrangement?

TEM, 59L, RU3, ?

(a) 7AB (b) 7AT
(c) ★78 (d) ABV
(e) None of these

15. How many such consonants are there in the arrangement, each of which is immediately preceded by a number but not immediately followed by a number?
(a) None (b) One (c) Two (d) Three
(e) None of the above

16. Madhuri travels 14 km Westwards and then turns left and travels 6 km and further turns left and travels 26 km. How far is Madhuri now from the starting point? **[NIFT (UG) 2013]**
(a) $\sqrt{180}$ km (b) $\sqrt{80}$ km
(c) $\sqrt{100}$ km (d) None of these

17. Count the number of cubes in the given figure.

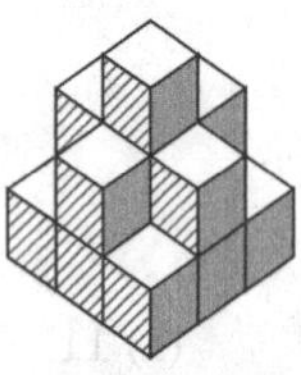

(a) 8
(b) 9
(c) 12
(d) 15

Direction (Q. Nos. 18-19) *In the following questions, find the odd letters/number pair from the given alternatives.*

18. (a) 3-4-14 (b) 56-57-67
(c) 102-103-113 (d) 22-23-13

19. (a) LORU (b) WZCF **[SSC (10+2) 2015]**
(c) ADGJ (d) IMQU

Direction (Q. Nos. 20-22) *Study the information given below carefully and then answer the questions that follow.*

Eight people A, B, C, D, E, F, G and H work in three different companies X, Y and Z. Out of these, two are females who work in different companies and have different specialisations. Two of them are specialists in Finance, two in HR, two in marketing and one each is an engineer and a computer specialist.

D, working in a company X has specialised in HR and her friend G, a finance specialist is working in company Z. H, an HR specialist, is working with B, a marketing specialist and does not work in company Y. C is not a computer specialist. No two people with the same specialisation work together. F is a specialist in marketing working in company Y and his friend, A is specialist in finance and is working in company X with only another specialist. Not more than three of them work in any company. No female is an engineer or computer specialist.

20. In which two companies do the HR specialist work?

(a) X and Y (b) Y and Z
(c) X and Z (d) Data inadequate

21. Who is the computer specialist?

(a) C (b) E
(c) H (d) Data inadequate

22. Which of the following represents the two females?

(a) DB (b) DH
(c) DG (d) Either (a), (b) or (c)

23. A was born 5 yr before B, B is 4 yr older than C and 3 yr younger to D. If A is now 17 yr old, how old is D?

(a) 19 yr (b) 15 yr
(c) 12 yr (d) 8 yr

24. In question below is given a statement followed by two assumptions numbered I and II. An assumption is something supposed or taken for granted. You have to consider the statement and the following assumptions and decide which of the assumption(s) is/are implicit in the statement.

Statements It is surprising that India beat Australia even after follow on. It happens 2nd time in the history of test cricket.

Assumptions

I. Winning after follow on is possible.
II. India cannot repeat such victory again.

Give answer

(a) if only Assumption I is implicit
(b) if only Assumption II is implicit
(c) if either Assumption I or II is implicit
(d) if neither Assumption I nor II is implicit
(e) if both Assumption I and II are implicit

Direction (Q. Nos. 25-26) *Each of the following questions below consists of a question and two statements numbered* I *and* II *given below it. You have to decide whether the data provided in the statements are sufficient to answer the question.*

Give answer

(a) if the data in Statement I alone are sufficient to answer the question, while the data in Statement II alone are not sufficient to answer the question
(b) if the data in Statement II alone are sufficient to answer the question, while the data in Statement I alone are not sufficient to answer the question
(c) if the data either in Statement I alone or Statement II alone are sufficient to answer the question
(d) if the data in both the Statements I and II together are not sufficient to answer the question
(e) if the data in both the Statements I and II are together necessary to answer the question

25. Kumud is facing which direction?

I. Nikhil is facing North and if he turns to his left he faces opposite direction as that of Kumud.
II. Saroj who is facing East is to the right of Kumud.

26. Among five people—A, B, C, D and E sitting around a circular table facing the centre, who is sitting second to the left of D?

I. C is second to the left of A, B and D are immediate neighbours of each other.
II. D is to the immediate left of B. E is not an immediate neighbour of D and B.

27. Choose the right water image of the question figure from the given answer figures.

Question Figure **Answer Figures**

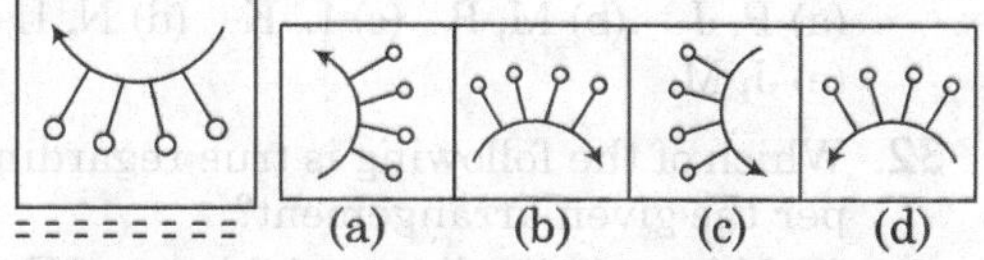

28. Samant remembers that his brother's birthday is after 16th but before 20th of January, while his sister remembers that her brother's birthday is after 17th but before 19th of February. On which date of January, is Samart's brother's birthday?

(a) 16th (b) 18th
(c) 19th (d) 17th

29. In a row of children facing North, Ritesh is 12th from the left end. Sudhir, who is 22nd from the right end is 4th to the right of Ritesh. How many total children are there in the row?

(a) 35 (b) 36
(c) 37 (d) 34
(e) None of these

Direction (Q. Nos. 30-32) *Study the information carefully and answer the given questions.*

Eight friends J, K, L, M, N, O, P and Q are sitting around a circular table but not necessarily in the same order. Some of them are facing the centre and some of them are facing outside. (i.e. in a direction opposite to the centre.)

- Only one person sits between K and O. Q sits third to the right of O.
- M sits to the immediate right of Q. Q faces outside.
- L sits second to the left of P. P is not an immediate neighbour of O.
- L faces a direction opposite to that of O. Immediate neighbours of L face opposite directions.
- J sits third to the left of N. J is not an immediate neighbour of P nor K.
- M and J face a direction same as that of N.

30. Four of the following five are alike in a certain way based on the directions they are forming and so form a group. Which is the one that does not belong to the group?
(a) KL (b) QM (c) PQ (d) NP
(e) OL

31. Who among the following sit exactly between Q and O when counted from the right of Q?
(a) P, J (b) M, P (c) L, K (d) N, L
(e) J, M

32. Which of the following is true regarding K as per the given arrangement?
(a) N is an immediate neighbour of K
(b) None of the given options is true
(c) Only three people sit between K and M
(d) L sits to the immediate left of K
(e) K faces outside

33. In a solid cube made up of 27 small cubes, two opposite sides are painted red, two opposite sides yellow and two other sides white. How many small cubes have the colours yellow and white along in them?
(a) 4 (b) 8 (c) 12 (d) 16

Direction (Q. Nos. 34-36) *Study the following information carefully and answer the given questions.*

A word and number arrangement machine when given an input line of words and numbers rearranges them following a particular rule in each step. The following is an illustration of input and rearrangement.

Input 'put over there 39 56 now 28 84'
***Step* I** there put over 39 56 now 28 84
***Step* II** there 28 put over 39 56 now 84
***Step* III** there 28 put 39 over 56 now 84

and Step III is the last step of the above input.
As per the rules followed in the above steps, find out in each of the following questions the appropriate step for the given input.

34. **Input** bag cover 43 32 tyre 51 ship 25
Which of the following will be Step V of the above input?
(a) tyre 25 ship 32 bag cover 43 51
(b) tyre 25 ship 32 cover 43 bag 51
(c) tyre 25 ship 32 cover bag 43 51
(d) There will be no such step
(e) None of the above

35. Step II of an input is 'party 23 81 68 53 call all invite'
Which of the following is definitely the input?
(a) 81 23 party 68 53 call all invite
(b) 81 68 53 call all invite 23 party
(c) 81 68 53 call all 23 invite party
(d) Cannot be determined
(e) None of the above

36. Step III of an input is 'mine 17 lamp 86 51 34 how day'
Which of the following steps will be the last but one?
(a) VII (b) VIII (c) IX (d) VI
(e) None of these

37. Selected the related figure from the given alternatives.

Question Figures

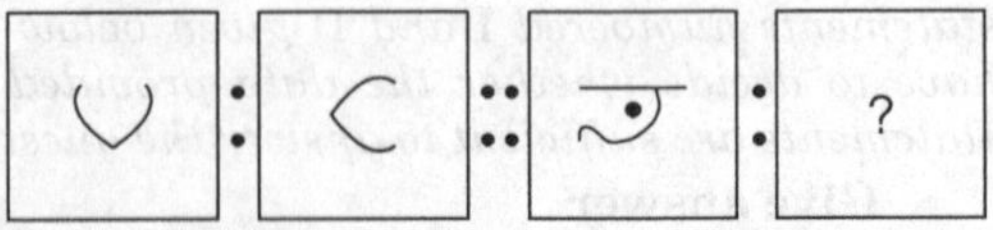

Answer Figures

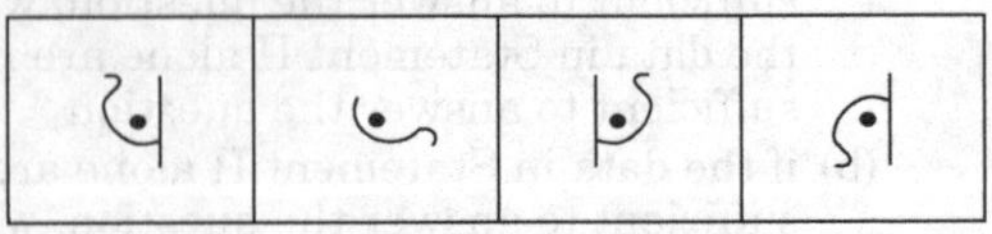

(a) (b) (c) (d)

38. A square paper is folded in a particular manner and punches are made. When unfolded the paper appears as given below. Find out the manner in which the paper was folded and punches were made.

Question Figure

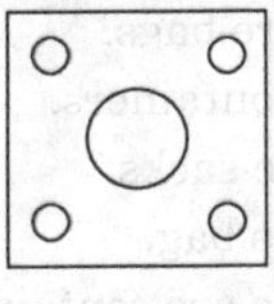

Answer Figures

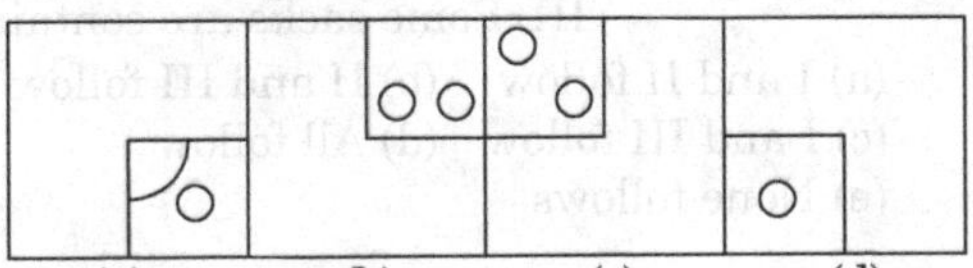

(a) (b) (c) (d)

39. Find the missing number from the given responses.

2	7	4
5	2	3
1	?	6
10	42	72

(a) 2 (b) 4 (c) 5 (d) 3

40. Choose the correct alternative from the given ones that will complete the series.

Q1F, S2E, U6D, W24C, ?

(a) Y120B (b) Y44B (c) Z88B (d) Y66B

41. Find the wrong term in the given series.

2, 10, 18, 54, 162, 486, 1458

(a) 18 (b) 54 (c) 162 (d) 10
(e) 486

42. If '–' stands for division, '÷' stands for multiplication, '+' stands for subtraction and '×' for addition, then which of the following equation is correct?

(a) $20 + 8 - 7 \div 6 \times 4 = 25$
(b) $20 - 5 \div 4 + 6 \times 5 = 15$
(c) $20 \times 5 - 6 \div 7 + 4 = 28$
(d) $20 \div 4 - 8 \times 10 + 6 = 36$

43. The diagram given below represents owner, broker and worker. Identify the region which represents all the three i.e. owner, broker and worker.

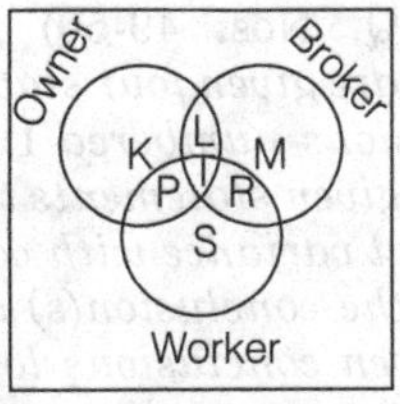

(a) L (b) T (c) P (d) R

44. Find the missing number from the given responses.

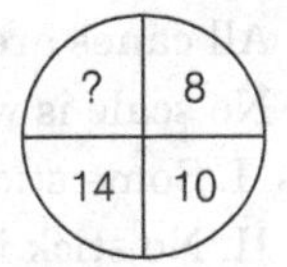

(a) 20 (b) 16 (c) 12 (d) 18

45. Which one set of letters when sequentially placed at the gaps in the given letters series shall complete it?

XYZ, ABC, UVW, DEF, RST, GHI,?

(a) UVW (b) JKL (c) OPQ (d) NOP

46. Which one of the given responses would be a meaningful order of the following words in ascending order? **[FCI Assistant Grade III 2012]**

(i) Grandfather (ii) Brother
(iii) Father (iv) Son
(v) Grandson

(a) (iv), (v), (ii), (i), (iii)
(b) (v), (i), (iii), (ii), (iv)
(c) (v), (iv), (i), (iii), (ii)
(d) (v), (iv), (ii), (iii), (i)

Direction (Q. Nos. 47-48) *Read the following information carefully to answer the questions.*

Mr and Mrs Sharma has two children Asha and Shashi. Shashi has married to Radha who is daughter of Mr Mahajan who is married to Reeta, Sonu and Rocky are the children of Suresh and Reeta. Uma and Sudha are daughters of Shashi and Radha.

47. What is the surname of Sonu?

(a) Mahajan (b) Sharma
(c) Shashi (d) None of these

48. What is the relation of Suresh to Sudha?

(a) Brother
(b) Uncle
(c) Maternal grandfather
(d) Niece

Direction (Q. Nos. 49-50) *In each of the questions below are given four statements followed by three conclusions numbered I, II and III. You have to take the given statements to be true even, if they seem to be at variance with commonly known facts. Read all the conclusion(s) and then decide which of the given conclusions logically follow(s) from the given statements disregarding commonly known facts.*

49. Statements Some pens are sticks.
Some sticks are canes.
All canes are scales.
No scale is weight.

Conclusions I. Some sticks are scales.
II. No stick is scale.
III. No cane is weight.

(a) Either I or II follows
(b) I and III follow
(c) Either I or II and III follow
(d) All I, II and III follow
(e) None of the above

50. Statements Some folders are boxes.
Some boxes are bags.
All bags are containers.
Some bags are sacks.

Conclusions I. No folder is bag.
II. Some boxes are containers.
III. Some sacks are containers.

(a) I and II follow (b) II and III follow
(c) I and III follow (d) All follow
(e) None follows

Hints and Solutions

1. (*a*) As,
L U T E
+1 ↓ ↓ ↓ ↓
M U T E

and
G A T E
+1 ↓ ↓ ↓ ↓
H A T E

Similarly,
B L U E
+1 ↓ ↓ ↓ ↓
C L U E

2. (*d*) Smallest triangles = ΔAOD, ΔAOE, ΔCOE, ΔBOD, ΔBOC = 5

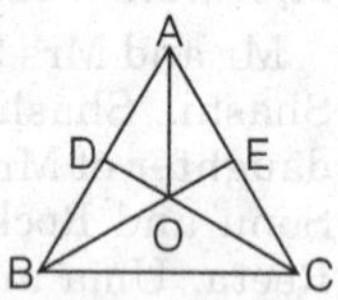

Triangles formed with two triangles
= ΔAOC (ΔAOE + ΔCOE),
ΔAOB (ΔAOD + ΔBOD),
ΔBCD (ΔBOD + ΔBOC),
ΔBCE (ΔBOC + ΔCOE)= 4

Triangles formed with three triangles
= ΔACD(ΔAOD + ΔAOE + ΔCOE),
ΔABE(ΔBOD + ΔAOD + ΔAOE) = 2

Largest triangle = ΔABC = 1

∴ Total triangles = 5 + 4 + 2 + 1 = 12

3. (*a*) As, 12 × 13 = 156
Same as, 140 × 13 = 1820

4. (*d*) The direction movements of Raghu is as follows

It is clearly shown that, Raghu is moving last in North direction.

5. (*a*) If a player is found guilty of doping, his medal is confiscated. Therefore, only Conclusion II follows.

6. (*a*) From both the statements it is clear that Conclusion I is true.

Solution (Q. Nos. 7-9)

© ⇒ ≥	% ⇒ ≤	@ ⇒ =	$ ⇒ <	δ ⇒ >

7. (*d*) H © T ⇒ H ≥ T, T % M ⇒ T ≤ M
M δ F ⇒ M > F
Therefore, H ≥ T ≤ M > F

Conclusions I. F $ T ⇒ F < T (Not true)
II. H δ M ⇒ H > M (Not true)

So, neither Conclusion I nor II is true.

8. (*c*) B @ N ⇒ B = N, N © T ⇒ N ≥ T
T $ K ⇒ T < K
Therefore, B = N ≥ T < K

Conclusions I. T @ B ⇒ T = B (May be)
II. T $ B ⇒ T < B (May be)

So, either I and II is true.

9. (*d*) R $ J ⇒ R < J, J δ F ⇒ J > F
F % H ⇒ F ≤ H
Therefore, R < J > F ≤ H

Conclusions I. H δ J ⇒ H > J (Not true)
II. R $ F ⇒ R < F (Not true)

So, neither I nor II is true.

10. (*c*) United Nations was created after World War II and League of Nations was created after World war I.

11. (*b*) As, a c m e → m a c e

1 2 3 4   3 1 2 4

Similarly, f a c e → c f a e

1 2 3 4   3 1 2 4

12. (*d*) As, $9 \times 3 - 3 = 27 - 3 = 24$

Same as, $? \times 3 - 3 = 6$

$\Rightarrow \quad ? \times 3 = 6 + 3 = 9$

$\Rightarrow \quad ? = \frac{9}{3} = 3 \Rightarrow ? = 3$

13. (*d*) Here, R → 59, 68, 77, 86, ◯

U → 56, 65, 78, ◯, 99

D → 01, 10, 23, 34, ◯

E → 02, ◯, 20, 33, 44

So, the word RUDE can be denoted by the number group 95, 87, 42, 11.

14. (*a*)

F 4 © T 2 E % M P 5W 9@L Q R 6 U H 3 |2 7 ★ A T| B 8 V # G $ Y D

So, following the sequence will be 7 AB.

15. (*b*)

F 4 © (T) 2E % (M) P5 (W)9@L (Q) R6U (H) 3 (Z)7 ★ A(T)(B)8(V)

#(G) $ (Y)(D)

✔ = Condition fulfilled, ✗ = Condition not fulfilled

Clearly, V is the required consonant.

16. (*a*) According to the question, the direction diagram will be as follows

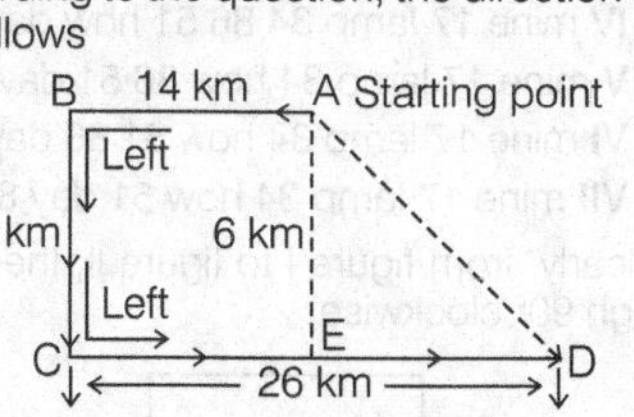

Now, AB = CE = 14km

BC = AE = 6km

CD = 26km

ED = CD − CE = 26 − 14 = 12 km

∴ Required distance, $AD = \sqrt{(AE)^2 + (ED)^2}$

(by Pythagoras theorem)

$= \sqrt{6^2 + 12^2}$

$= \sqrt{16 + 144}$

$= \sqrt{180}$ km

17. (*d*) From the given question figure, it is clear that

4 columns containing 1 cube each

1 column containing 3 cubes

4 columns containing 2 cubes each

∴ Total cubes

$= (4 \times 1) + (1 \times 3) + (4 \times 2)$

$= 4 + 3 + 8 = 15$

18. (*d*) In all other options except (d), second number is obtained by the addition of 1 in first number and third number is obtained by the addition of 10 in second number.

19. (*d*) As, $L \xrightarrow{+3} O \xrightarrow{+3} R \xrightarrow{+3} U$

$W \xrightarrow{+3} Z \xrightarrow{+3} C \xrightarrow{+3} F$

and $A \xrightarrow{+3} D \xrightarrow{+3} G \xrightarrow{+3} J$

But $I \xrightarrow{+4} M \xrightarrow{+4} Q \xrightarrow{+4} U$

Hence, IMQU is odd letters group.

Solution (Q. Nos. 20-22) The given information can be represented as in the table given below

Person	Company	Gender	Occupation
A	X	Male	Finance
B	Z	Male/Female	Marketing
C	Y	Male	Engineer
D	X	Female	HR
E	Y	Male	Computer
F	Y	Male	Marketing
G	Z	Male/Female	Finance
H	Z	Male/Female	HR

20. (*c*) HR specialist works in companies X and Z.

21. (*b*) E is the computer specialist.

22. (*d*) D and B/G/H

23. (*b*) A = 17 yr

B = 17 − 5 = 12 yr

C = 12 − 4 = 8 yr

D = 12 + 3 = 15 yr

24. (*a*) Assumption I is implicit as if it had not been possible India would not have won after follow on. Further, the word 'suprising' tells that winning after follow on is very difficult and this is the reason it happens only 2nd time. But if it is possible. We cannot say that India will not repeat such victory again. Hence, Assumption II is invalid.

25. (*a*) From Statement I,

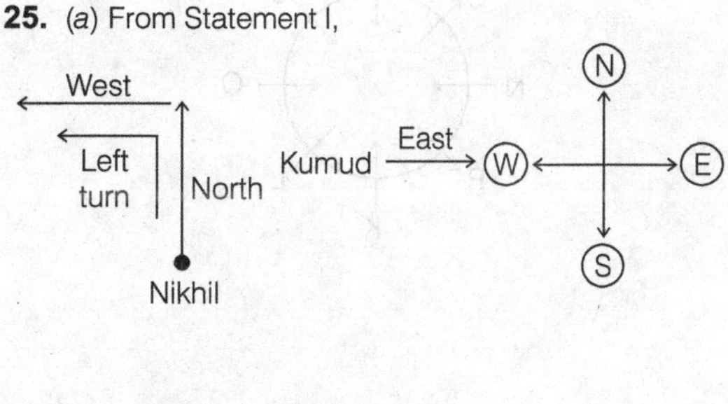

Clearly, after left turn Nikhil will face West. Here, Kumud will face the direction opposite to what Nikhil will face after the left turn. Hence, Kumud will face East which is opposite to West what Nikhil is facing.

Hence, Statement I along is sufficient to answer the question.

From Statement II, it is not clear that Kumud is facing which direction. Hence, only Statement I alone is sufficient to answer the question.

26. (*b*) From Statement II,

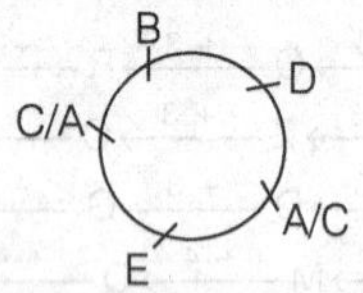

So, E is sitting second to the left of D.

Hence, data in Statement II alone is sufficient to answer the question.

27. (*d*) The correct vertically inverted mirror image of the question figure is as follows

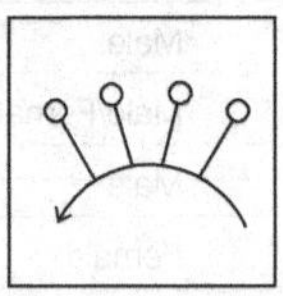

28. (*b*)

According to	Possibility of Date
Samant	17, (18), 19
Sister	(18)

Here, 18th is common to both. Hence, the correct date is 18th January.

29. (*c*) Sudhir's position from left = (12 + 4) = 16 th from left

Sudhir's position from right = 22nd

Total number of children

$$= (16 + 22 - 1)$$
$$= 38 - 1$$
$$= 37$$

Solution (Q. Nos. 30-32) According to the given information, the sitting arrangement of eight friends around a circular table is as follows.

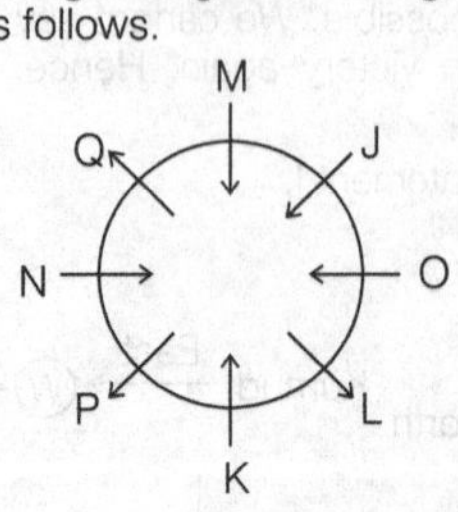

30. (*c*) PQ does not belong to the group because all other pair have opposite faces.

31. (*e*) J, M sit exactly between Q and O when counted from the right of Q.

32. (*c*) Only three people sit between K and M.

33. (*a*)

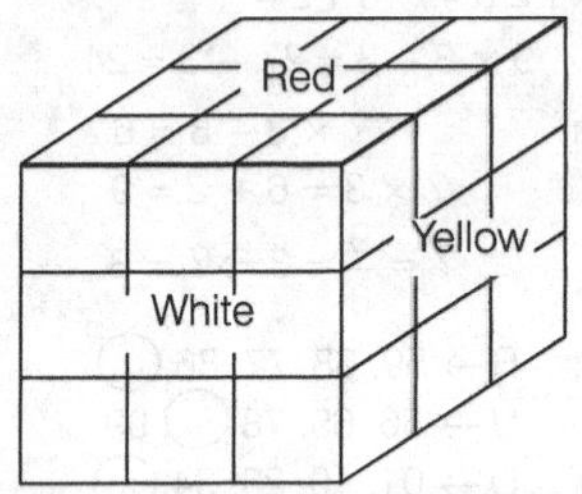

The cubes of middle row will have no red colour ⇒ 9 cubes

The central cube will have no colour.

Now, out of 8 cubes, 4 cubes have both yellow and white colour.

Solution (Q. Nos. 34-36) After analysing the various steps of arrangement it is evident that words are arranged in the reverse alphabetical order while the numbers are arranged in ascending order

34. (*c*) **Input** bag cover 43 32 tyre 51 ship 25
***Step* I** tyre bag cover 43 32 51 ship 25
***Step* II** tyre 25 bag cover 43 32 51 ship
***Step* III** tyre 25 ship bag cover 43 32 51
***Step* IV** tyre 25 ship 32 bag cover 43 51
***Step* V** tyre 25 ship 32 cover bag 43 51

35. (*d*) From the given step it is not possible to determine the input.

36. (*a*) ***Step* III** mine 17 lamp 86 51 34 how day
***Step* IV** mine 17 lamp 34 86 51 how day
***Step* V** mine 17 lamp 34 how 86 51 day
***Step* VI** mine 17 lamp 34 how 51 86 day
***Step* VII** mine 17 lamp 34 how 51 day 86

37. (*a*) Clearly, from figure I to figure II, the design rotates through 90° clockwise.

38. (*a*)

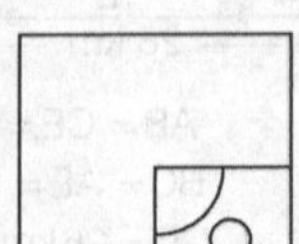

So, option (a) is correct answer.

39. (*d*) The product of the first three numbers is the lowest number in each column.

1st column $2 \times 5 \times 1 = 10$

2nd column $7 \times 2 \times ? = 42$

$$\therefore \quad ? = \frac{42}{14} = 3$$

40. (*a*) Pattern of given alpha-numeric series is as follows

$\overset{17}{Q} \xrightarrow{+2} \overset{19}{S} \xrightarrow{+2} \overset{21}{U} \xrightarrow{+2} \overset{23}{W} \xrightarrow{+2} \overset{25}{Y}$

$1 \xrightarrow{\times 2} 2 \xrightarrow{\times 3} 6 \xrightarrow{\times 4} 24 \xrightarrow{\times 5} 120$

$\overset{6}{F} \xrightarrow{-1} \overset{5}{E} \xrightarrow{-1} \overset{4}{D} \xrightarrow{-1} \overset{3}{C} \xrightarrow{-1} \overset{2}{B}$

$\therefore$? = Y 120B

41. (*d*) The pattern is as follows

2   (10) [6]   18   54   162   486   1458

×3   ×3   ×3   ×3   ×3   ×3

Hence, number 10 is wrong and should be replaced by 6.

42. (*b*) According to the question, we can arrange the given mathematical symbols as

$- \Rightarrow \div, \div \Rightarrow \times$

$+ \Rightarrow -, \times \Rightarrow +$

Option (b)

$\Rightarrow \quad 20 - 5 \div 4 + 6 \times 5 = 15$

$\Rightarrow \quad 20 \div 5 \times 4 - 6 + 5 = 15$

$\Rightarrow \quad 4 \times 4 - 6 + 5 = 15$

$\Rightarrow \quad 16 - 6 + 5 = 15$

$\Rightarrow \quad 15 = 15$

So, option (b) is correct equation.

43. (*b*) The region common to all the three circles is represented by T.

44. (*a*) As, $8 + 2 = 10, 10 + 4 = 14 \Rightarrow 14 + 6 = 20$

45. (c) Considering odd places elements first.

1st Letter $\overset{24}{X} \xrightarrow{-3} \overset{21}{U} \xrightarrow{-3} \overset{18}{R} \xrightarrow{-3} \overset{15}{O}$

2nd Letter $\overset{25}{Y} \xrightarrow{-3} \overset{22}{V} \xrightarrow{-3} \overset{19}{S} \xrightarrow{-3} \overset{16}{P}$

1st Letter $\overset{26}{Z} \xrightarrow{-3} \overset{23}{W} \xrightarrow{-3} \overset{20}{T} \xrightarrow{-3} \overset{17}{Q}$

Considering even place elements secondly.

1st Letter $\overset{1}{A} \xrightarrow{+3} \overset{4}{D} \xrightarrow{+3} \overset{7}{G}$

2nd Letter $\overset{2}{B} \xrightarrow{+3} \overset{5}{E} \xrightarrow{+3} \overset{8}{H}$

1st Letter $\overset{3}{C} \xrightarrow{+3} \overset{6}{F} \xrightarrow{+3} \overset{9}{I}$

$\therefore$?= OPQ

46. (*d*) Meaningful order of words in ascending order
(v) Grandson, → (iv) Son, → (ii) Brother
→ (iii) Father, → (i) Grandfather

Solution (Q. Nos. 47-48) Let us make the family diagram

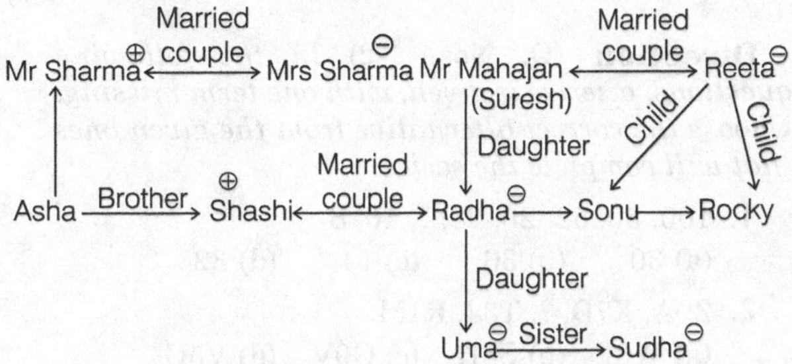

47. (*a*) It is clear from the above graph that the surname of Sonu is Mahajan.

48. (*c*) It is clear from the above graph that Suresh is maternal grandfather of Sudha.

49. (*b*)

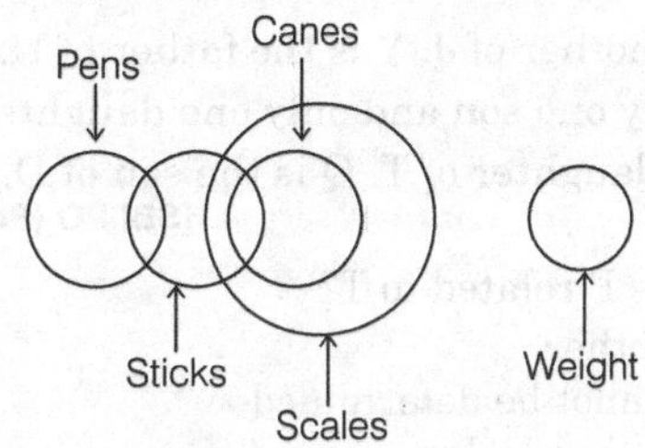

Conclusions I. Some sticks are scales. (✔)
II. No stick is scale. (✗)
III. No cane is weight. (✔)

So, only Conclusions I and III follow.

50. (*b*)

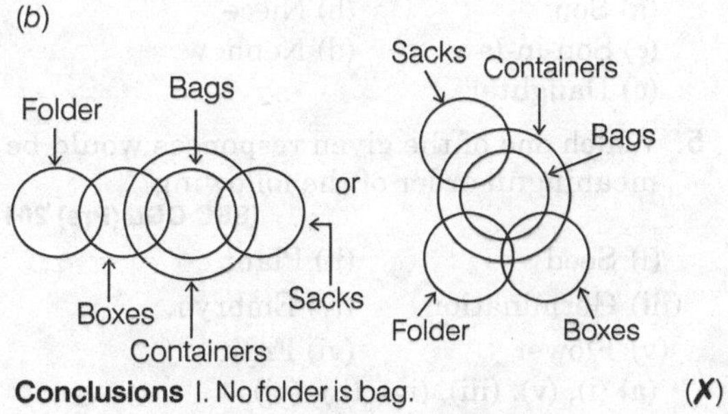

Conclusions I. No folder is bag. (✗)
II. Some boxes are containers. (✔)
III. Some sacks are containers. (✔)

So, only Conclusion II and III follow.

PRACTICE SET 23

Direction (Q. Nos. 1-2) *In the following questions, a series is given, with one term missing. Choose the correct alternative from the given ones that will complete the series.*

1. 100, 50, 52, 26, 28, ?, 16, 8
(a) 30 (b) 36 (c) 14 (d) 32

2. Z9A, X7D, ?, T3J, R1M
(a) W6F (b) S3H (c) G9V (d) V5G

Direction (Q. Nos. 3-4) *Study the following information and answer the given questions.*

T is the sister of D.D is married to P. P is the son of M.

T is the mother of J. Y is the father of U.

Y has only one son and only one daughter.

U is the daughter of T. Q is the son of D.

[SBI PO (Pre) 2015]

3. How is P related to T?
(a) Brother
(b) Cannot be determined
(c) Brother-in-law
(d) Cousin brother
(e) Uncle

4. How is J related to D?
(a) Son (b) Niece
(c) Son-in-law (d) Nephew
(e) Daughter

5. Which one of the given responses would be a meaningful order of the following?

[SSC CGL (Pre) 2014]

(i) Seed (ii) Plant
(iii) Germination (iv) Embryo
(v) Flower (vi) Fruit
(a) (i), (v), (iii), (iv), (ii), (vi)
(b) (i), (iv), (iii), (ii), (v), (vi)
(c) (vi), (v), (iv), (iii), (i), (ii)
(d) (i), (v), (vi), (iv), (ii), (iii)

Direction (Q Nos. 6-7) *In the following questions, find the odd numbers/letters from the given alternatives.*

6. (a) 11, 17, 23 (b) 12, 14, 16
(c) 8, 10, 12 (d) 18, 36, 72

7. (a) CEH (b) KMP (c) XZC (d) NPT

8. In the question below, three Statements I, II and III are given. You are required to find out which of the given statements is/are sufficient to answer the question.

What is the code of 'rope' in the code language?

I. In that code 'use the rope' is written as 'nik ta re'.
II. In that code language 'rope is straight' is written as 'pe da ta'.
III. In that code language 'always use rope' is written as 'ma re ta'.

(a) I and II or II and III
(b) I and III
(c) II and III
(d) I, II and III

Direction (Q. Nos. 9-11) *Study the following information carefully to answer the given questions.*

A word and number arrangement machine when given an input line of words and numbers rearranges them following a particular rule in each step. The following is an illustration of input and rearrangement.

Input	go now 52 38 17 for again 65
Step I	65 go now 52 38 17 for again
Step II	65 again go now 52 38 17 for
Step III	65 again 52 go now 38 17 for
Step IV	65 again 52 for go now 38 17
Step V	65 again 52 for 38 go now 17
Step VI	65 again 52 for 38 go 17 now

As per the rule followed in the above steps, find out in each of the following questions the appropriate step for the given input.

9. **Input** home turf 39 24 86 44 roll over

Which of the following steps will be the last?
(a) X (b) IX (c) VIII (d) VII
(e) None of these

10. Step II of an input is '94 car 86 window shut 52 31 house'

Which of the following is definitely the input?

(a) 94 car window 86 shut 52 31 house
(b) 86 window 94 car shut 52 31 house
(c) car shut window 86 52 31 house 94
(d) Cannot be determined
(e) None of the above

11. Step IV of an input is '58 box 47 dew 15 21 town pot'
Which of the following steps will be the last?
(a) VII (b) VI (c) VIII (d) IX
(e) None of these

12. The positions of how many digits in the number 351462987 will remain unchanged after the digits are rearranged in ascending order within the number?
(a) None (b) One
(c) Two (d) Three

13. If 'Hindi' is called'ENGLISH'; 'ENGLISH' is called 'URDU' ; 'URDU' is called 'HISTORY'; 'HISTORY' is called 'ECONOMICS' and 'ECONOMICS' is called 'BIOLOGY', then in which subject we read the story of Mughal King Shahjahan?
(a) History (b) English
(c) Urdu (d) Economics

14. Shiv goes 4 km straight from his school. He turns to his right and walks 3 km. He again moves 2 km after turning right to reach his house. If his house is located in South-East from his school, then in which direction Shiv started moving initially from his school ?
(a) North-East (b) West
(c) East (d) North

15. Which one of the following figures represents the relationship among brinjal, meat, vegetables?

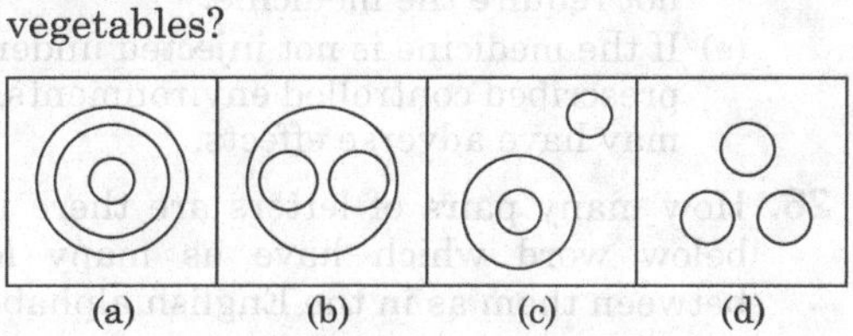

16. This question is based on the given four-digit numbers: **[IBPS RRB (Office Assistant) 2015]**
2413 9406 8492 6736 4940
Which of the following will be the sum of the fourth digit of the number which is third from the left and the second digit of the number which is first from the right?
(a) Other than those given as options
(b) 5 (c) 12
(d) 9 (e) 11

Direction (Q. Nos.17-18) *In the following questions, the symbols @, ©, $,% and δ are used with the following meaning as illustrated below.*

'P © Q' means 'P is either greater than or equal to Q'.
'P % Q' means 'P is either smaller than or equal to Q'.
'P @ Q' means 'P is neither smaller than nor greater than Q'.
'P $ Q' means 'P is smaller than Q'.
'P δ Q' means 'P is greater than Q'.

Now, in each of the following questions assuming the given statements to be true, find which of the two Conclusions I and II given below them is/are definitely true?

Give answer
(a) if only Conclusion I is true
(b) if only Conclusion II is true
(c) if either Conclusion I or II is true
(d) if neither Conclusion I nor II is true
(e) if both Conclusions I and II are true

17. Statements W % V, V @ Z, Z © D
Conclusions I. D % V
II. W % Z

18. Statements M % R, R $ T, T © K
Conclusions I. T δ M
II. R $ K

Direction (Q. Nos. 19-21) *Study the following information and answer the questions.*

Seven friends, namely M, N, O, P, Q, R and S have an essay competition on seven different days of the same week namely, Monday, Tuesday, Wednesday, Thursday, Friday, Saturday and Sunday. Each friend also studies in a different standard namely First, Second, Third, Fourth, Fifth, Sixth and Seventh but not necessarily in the same order.

The one who studies in First standard has a competition on Saturday. S studies in Second standard and has a competition on Wednesday. N has a competition immediately before Q. N does not have a competition on any of the days after S. The one who studies in Seventh standard does not have a competition on any of the days on or before Friday. The one who studies in Third standard has a competition immediately after O. Q does not study in Fifth standard. The one who studies in Sixth standard does not have a competition immediately before or after S. R does not have a competition on Sunday and does not study in Third standard. P does not have competition on any of the days before M.

[NICL Assistant Class III Cadre 2015]

19. Which of the following standards does R study in?

(a) Seventh (b) Fifth
(c) First (d) Second
(e) Fourth

20. Four of the following five form a group as per the given arrangement. Which of the following does not belong to that group?

(a) O - Tuesday
(b) M - Wednesday
(c) P - Saturday
(d) S - Monday
(e) R - Thursday

21. Based on the given arrangement, which of the following statements is true?

(a) M has a competition on Saturday
(b) Q studies in the Sixth standard
(c) All the given statements are true
(d) Only two people have their competition between S and P
(e) R has a competition immediately after M

22. A bus left with some definite number of passengers. At the first stop, half the passengers left the bus and 35 boarded the bus. At the second stop $\frac{1}{5}$th of the passengers left and 40 boarded the bus. Then, the bus moved with 80 passengers towards its destination without stopping anywhere. How many passengers were there originally?

(a) 25 (b) 30 (c) 40 (d) 50

23. Group the given figures into different classes on the basis of their orientation, shape etc.

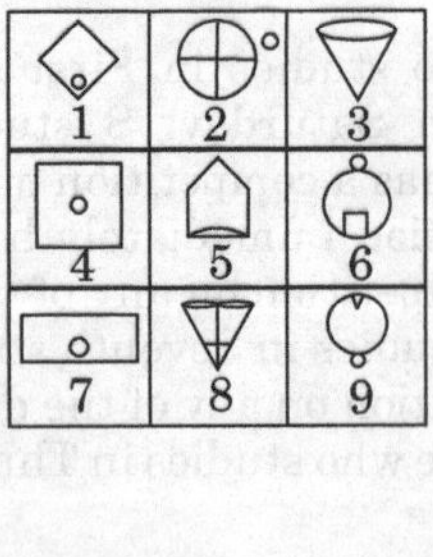

(a) (1,2,4), (3,5,6), (8,7,9)
(b) (9,7,6), (5,3,1), (4,8,2)
(c) (2,3,4), (7,6,5), (9,8,1)
(d) (1,4,7), (2,6,9), (3,5,8)

24. The age of Arvind's father is 4 times his son's age. If 5 yr ago, father's age was 7 times of the age of his son at that time, then what is Arvind's father's present age?

(a) 84 yr (b) 70 yr
(c) 40 yr (d) 35 yr

25. *Study the given information carefully to answer the question.*

A fatal disease has spread across the 'Spatter' village of State X. Even though the prescribed medicine is abundantly available in one of the cities near 'Spatter' which can cause the disease, the Medical Association of the State has decided not to allow the medicine to be transported to 'Spatter' and is calling the infected people to the city to be injected with the medicine. **[IBPS RRB (Officers) 2015]**

Which of the following can be a reason behind the decision of the Medical Association?

(a) The Association may not be able to earn high profits from selling the medicine to 'Spatter'.
(b) Many of the villagers may not be able to afford the medicine as it is highly priced.
(c) The disease has started to spread in other villages also, making it challenging for the association to provide the medicine everywhere.
(d) Reportedly, many of the villagers are trying home remedies to reduce the effect of the disease and hence they may not require the medicine.
(e) If the medicine is not injected under the prescribed controlled environments, it may have adverse effects.

26. How many pairs of letters are there in the below word which have as many letters between them as in the English alphabet?

PENCIL

(a) Nil (b) One
(c) Two (d) Three

27. If it is possible to make only one meaningful word from the 3rd, the 6th, the 9th and the 10th letters of the word 'PARENTHESIS', using each letter only once, last letter of the word is your answer. If no such word can be formed your answer is 'X' and if more than one such word can be formed your answer is 'Y'.

(a) R (b) T (c) S (d) X
(e) Y

28. How many triangles are there in the figure given below ?

(a) 20 (b) 27 (c) 18 (d) 29

29. Find the mirror image of the figure given from amongst the four alternatives.

Question Figure

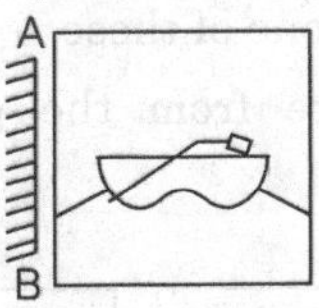

Answer Figures

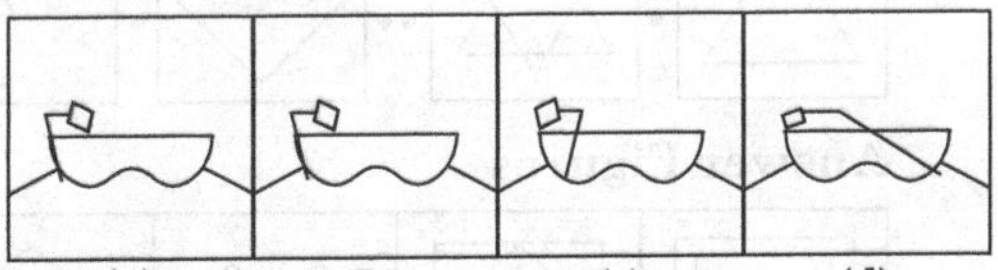

(a) (b) (c) (d)

30. The time on the watch is 9 : 15 and the hour hand points towards West. The direction of the minute hand is

(a) North (b) South (c) East (d) West

31. If in a certain code language 'STAR' is written as '5 $ ★ 2', 'TORE' is written as '$ 3 2 @', then how will 'OATS' be written in that language?

(a) 3 ★ 5 $ (b) 3 ★ $ 5
(c) 3 $ ★ 5 (d) 3 5 ★ $
(e) None of the above

32. If × stands for '+' and ÷ stands for '–', then find the value of the following equation.

$$39 \times 23 \div 21 \times 5$$

(a) 46 (b) 36 (c) 62 (d) 89

Direction (Q. Nos. 33-34) *In the following questions, select the related word/number pair from the given alternatives.*

33. 64 : 513 : : 144 : ? **[UPPSC (RO) 2014]**

(a) 1727 (b) 1729
(c) 1728 (d) 1730

34. Adult : Baby :: Flower : ?

(a) Seed (b) Bud
(c) Fruit (d) Butterfly

35. In this series, some letters are missing. Select the correct alternative. **[WBBSC (Pre) 2014]**

a_c b_ _b c _ c a b c b _

(a) a a c c b (b) b a a c a
(c) b c a b c (d) a a a a b

36. Mukesh is taller than Suresh but shorter than Rakesh. Rakesh is taller than Harish but shorter than Amar. Who among them is the shortest ?

(a) Mukesh (b) Suresh
(c) Harish (d) Cannot be determined

37. Find the missing number from the given responses.

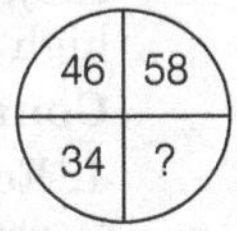

(a) 92 (b) 72
(c) 22 (d) 68

38. In making decisions about important questions, it is desirable to distinguish between a 'strong' argument and a 'weak' argument. A 'strong' argument must be both important and directly related to the question. A 'weak' argument may not be directly related to the question and may be of minor importance or may be related to the trivial aspect of the question. Each question below is followed by two arguments numbered I and II. You have to decide which of the arguments in 'strong' and and which is 'weak.'

Statement Should private sector be permitted to operate telephone services?

Arguments

I. Yes, they are operating in advanced western countries.

II. No, it is risky to put them in private hands.

(a) if only Argument I is strong
(b) if only Argument II is strong
(c) if either Argument I or II is strong
(d) if neither Argument I nor II is strong
(e) if both Argument I and II are strong

39. Select the one, which is different from the other three responses.

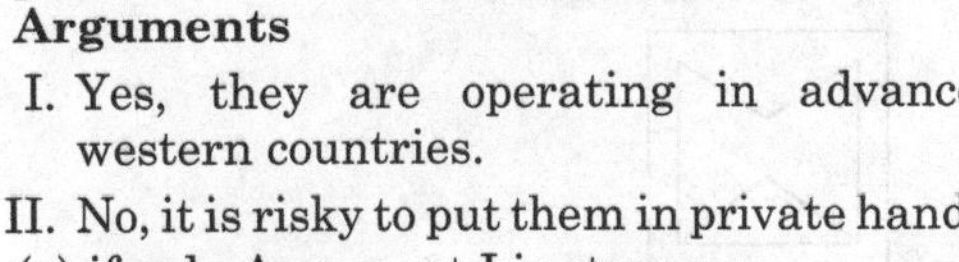

(a) (b) (c) (d)

40. In each of the question below is given a statement followed by three courses of action numbered I, II and III. A course of action is a step or administrative decision to be taken for improvement, follow-up or further action in regard to the problem, policy, etc. On the basis of information given in the statement, you have to assume everything in the statement to be true and then decide which of the three given suggested courses of action logically follows worth pursuing. Then, decide which of the alternatives (a), (b), (c), (d) or (e) is correct.

Statement Many students at school and degree level are not able to master the subjects even if they have passed out with high scores.

Courses of Action

I. Education boards should examine and revise the examination system to tap the real talent.

II. Examination system at all levels should be so designed as to discourage rote learning.

III. Difficulty level of the examination papers should be significantly increased.

(a) Only I follows
(b) Only II follows
(c) Both I and II follow
(d) Either I or II follows
(e) None of the above

41. In which answer figure is the question figure embedded ?

Question Figure

Answer Figures

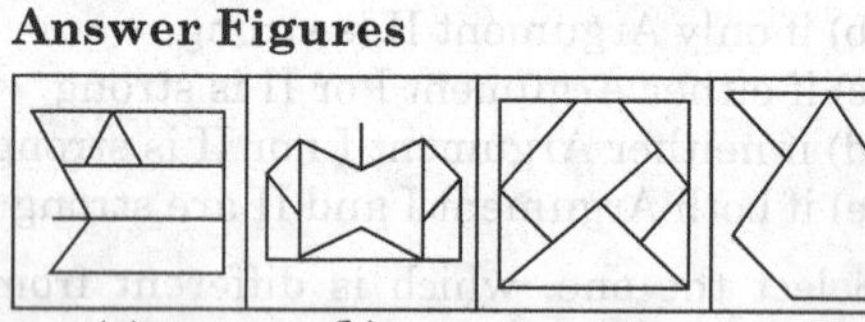

(a) (b) (c) (d)

Direction (Q. Nos. 42-44) *Study the following information to answer the given questions.* **[GIC 2012]**

Eight friends, A, B, C, D, E, F, G and H are sitting in a circle facing the centre, not necessarily in the same order. D sits third to the left of A. E sits to the immediate right of A, B is third to the left of D. G is second to the right of B. C is an immediate neighbour of B. C is third to the left of H.

42. Who amongst the following is sitting exactly between F and D?

(a) C (b) E (c) H (d) A

43. Three of the following four are alike in a certain way based on the information given above and so form a group. Which is the one that does not belong to that group?

(a) DC (b) AH
(c) EF (d) CB

44. Who amongst the following is sitting second to the left of H?

(a) E (b) B
(c) A (d) None of these

45. Select the related figure from the given alternatives.

Question Figures

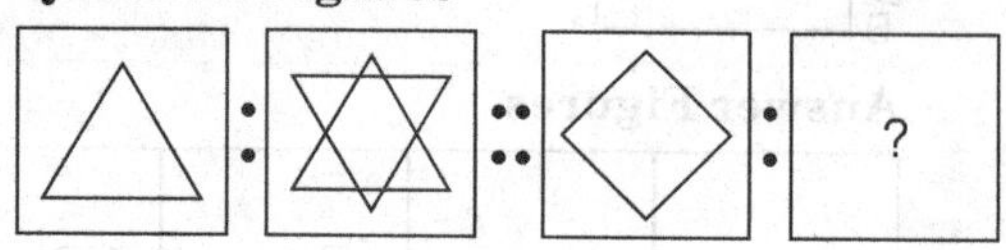

Answer Figures

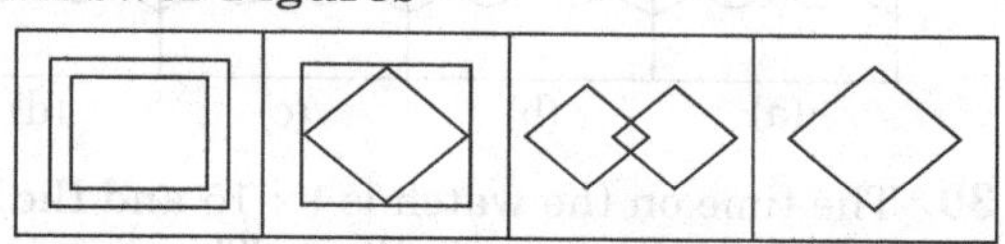

(a) (b) (c) (d)

46. In the given question, two positions of a single dice are given. Find the digit at the face opposite to the face having digit 1.

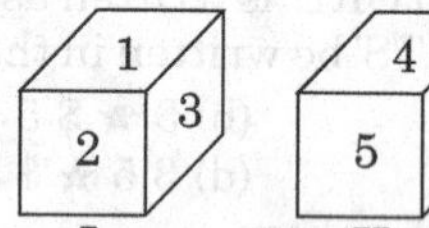

I II

(a) 4 (b) 5
(c) 6 (d) 4/5/6

Direction (Q.Nos. 47-49) *In each of the questions below are given four statements followed by three conclusions numbered I, II, and III. You have to take the given statements to be true even, if they seem to be at variance with commonly known facts. Read all the conclusion(s) and then decide which of the given conclusions logically follow(s) from the given statements disregarding commonly known facts.*

47. Statements Some caps are umbrellas.
Some umbrellas are raincoats.
All raincoats are trousers.
All trousers are jackets.

Conclusions I. Some raincoats are caps.
II. Some trousers are umbrellas.
III. All raincoats are jackets.

(a) None follows (b) I and II follow
(c) II and III follow (d) I and III follow
(e) None of these

48. Statements Some fans are coolers.
Some coolers are machines.
Some machines are computers.
All computers are televisions.

Conclusions I. Some televisions are machines.
II. Some machines are fans.
III. No machine is a fan.

(a) None follows
(b) Only I follows
(c) Either II or III follows
(d) Only I and either II or III follow
(e) All follow

49. Statements All keys are staplers.
All staplers are blades.
Some blades are erasers.
Some erasers are sharpeners.

Conclusions I. Some sharpeners are keys.
II. All keys are blades.
III. Some erasers are keys.

(a) I and II follow (b) Only I follows
(c) Only II follows (d) All follow
(e) None of the above

50. Given below are two matrices of 25 cells each containing two classes of letters. The columns and rows of Matrix I are numbered from 0 to 4 and those of Matrix II from 5 to 9. A letter from these matrices can be represented first by its row number and next by its column number e.g. 'B' can be represented as 00, 14 etc. Similarly, M can be represented by 55, 67 etc. In the following question, identify one set of number pair out of (a), (b), (c) and (d) which represents the given word.

Matrix I

	0	1	2	3	4
0	B	D	E	T	O
1	D	E	T	O	B
2	E	B	O	D	T
3	T	O	B	E	D
4	O	T	D	B	E

Matrix II

	5	6	7	8	9
5	M	U	I	L	R
6	U	L	M	R	I
7	I	M	R	U	L
8	L	R	U	I	M
9	R	I	L	M	U

TRUE

(a) 24, 77, 56, 03 (b) 41, 86, 99, 23
(c) 30, 95, 87, 20 (d) 03, 58, 78, 11

Hints and Solutions

1. (*c*) The pattern is as follows

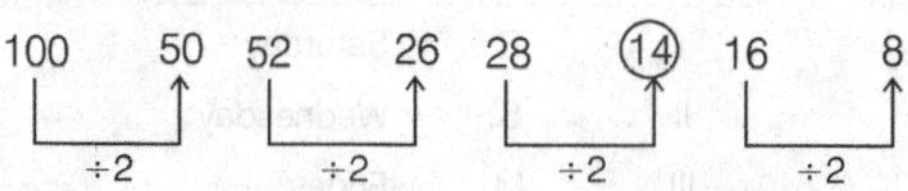

∴ Missing number $= \frac{28}{2} = 14$

2. (*d*) Pattern of given alpha-numeric series is as follows

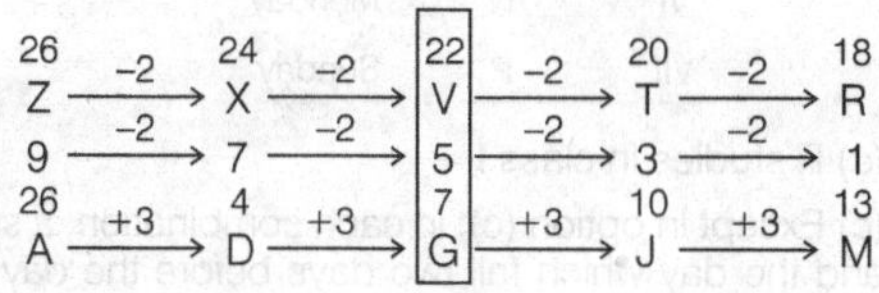

∴ ? = V5G

Solution (Q. Nos. 3-4) According to the information given in the question, the relation chart is given below

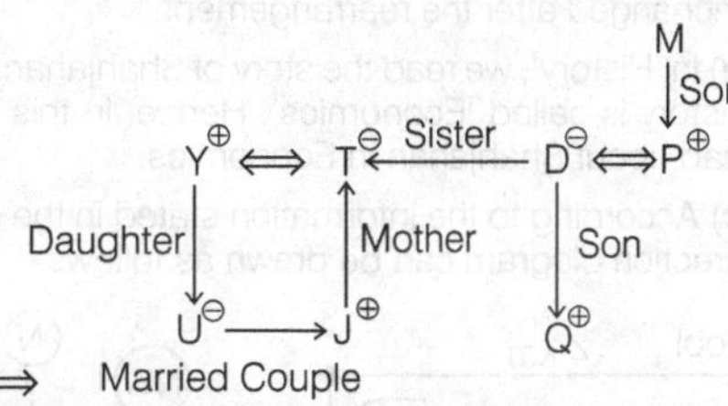

3. (*c*) P is the husband of T's sister, i.e. brother-in-law of T.

4. (*d*) J is the son of D's sister, therefore J is the nephew of D.

5. (*b*) The meaningful order of the given words is as follows

Seed → Embryo → Germination → Plant → Flower → Fruit i.e. (i), (iv), (iii), (ii), (v), (vi).

6. (*a*) Except (a) in all the other options, numbers are even numbers but in option (a) all numbers are prime numbers.

7. (*d*) In all other groups, there is a gap of one letter between first and second letters and gap of two letters between second and third letters.

8. (*a*) From Statements I and II, use the rope = nik ta tre

∴ rope in straight = pe da ta

From Statements II and III, rope is straight = pe da ta

always use rope = ma re ta

rope = ta

From Statements I and III, use the rope = nik ta re

always use rope = ma re ta

rope = ta/re

Hence, Statements I and II or II and III are sufficient to find answer.

Solution (Q. Nos. 9-11) After careful analysis of input and various steps of rearrangement it is evident that in each step one number or word is rearranged.

The numbers are arranged in descending order and the words are arranged in alphabetical order.

9. (*e*) **Input** home turf 39 24 86 44 roll over
Step **I** 86 home turf 39 24 44 roll over
Step **II** 86 home 44 turf 39 24 roll over
Step **III** 86 home 44 over turf 39 24 roll
Step **IV** 86 home 44 over 39 turf 24 roll
Step **V** 86 home 44 over 39 roll turf 24
Step **VI** 86 home 44 over 39 roll 24 turf

10. (*d*) From the given step input cannot be determined.

11. (*b*) ***Step*** **IV** 58 box 47 dew 15 21 town pot
Step **V** 58 box 47 dew 21 15 town pot
Step **VI** 58 box 47 dew 21 pot 15 town

12. (c) Given number 3 5 1 [4] 6 2 9 [8] 7
After rearrangement 1 2 3 [4] 5 6 7 [8] 9
Hence, there are two numbers, 4 and 8 remain unchanged after the rearrangement.

13. (*d*) In 'History', we read the story of Shahjahan; but here History is called 'Economics'. Hence, in this case, we read about Shahjahan in Economics.

14. (*c*) According to the information stated in the question, direction diagram can be drawn as follows

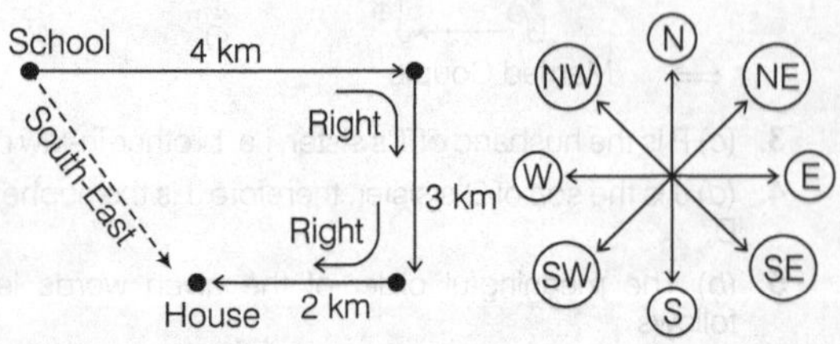

Clearly, he started moving towards East initially.

15. (*c*) Brinjal is a vegetable but meat is not a vegetable.

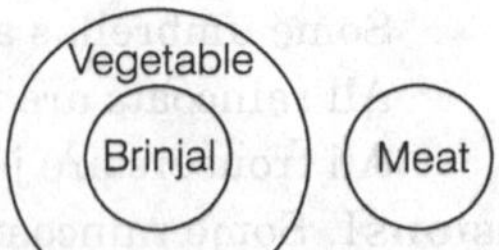

16. (*e*) The number which is third from the left = 8492
The fourth digit of 8492 is 2.
The number which is first from the right = 4940
The second digit of 4940 is 9.
Therefore, the sum is 9 + 2 = 11

Solution (Q. Nos. 17-18)

$P © Q \rightarrow P \geq Q$
$P \% Q \rightarrow P \leq Q$
$P @ Q \rightarrow P = Q$
$P \$ Q \rightarrow P < Q$
$P \delta Q \rightarrow P > Q$

17. (*e*) $W \% V \Rightarrow W \leq V$
$V @ Z \Rightarrow V = Z$
$Z © D \Rightarrow Z \geq D$
Therefore, $W \leq V = Z \geq D$
Conclusions I. $D \% V \Rightarrow D \leq V$ (True)
II. $W \% Z \Rightarrow W \leq Z$ (True)
So, both Conclusions I and II are true.

18. (*a*) $M \% R \Rightarrow M \leq R$
$R \$ T \Rightarrow R < T$
$T © K \Rightarrow T \geq K$
Therefore, $M \leq R < T \geq K$
Conclusions I. $T \delta M \Rightarrow T > M$ (True)
II. $R \$ K \Rightarrow R < K$ (Not True)
So, only I is true.

Solution (Q. Nos. 19-21) The given information can be arranged as below

Class	Friend	Day
I	R	Saturday
II	S	Wednesday
III	M	Friday
IV	Q	Tuesday
V	O	Thursday
VI	N	Monday
VII	P	Sunday

19. (*c*) R studies in class I.

20. (*c*) Except in option (c), in each combination, a student and the day which fall two days before the day of his competition are given.

21. (*e*) R has a competition (on Saturday) immediately after M (M has his competition on Friday)

22. (*b*) Suppose there were *x* passengers initially

Number of passengers after first stop $= \frac{x}{2} + 35$

Number of passengers after second stop

$$= \frac{4}{5}\left(\frac{x}{2} + 35\right) + 40 = 80$$

$$\Rightarrow \quad \frac{x}{2} + 35 = \frac{(80-40)}{4} \times 5$$

$$\Rightarrow \quad \frac{x}{2} = 50 - 35 = 15$$

$$\therefore \quad x = 30$$

23. (*d*) Clearly, 1,4 and 7 comprise of a quadrilateral in which a circle is enclosed. 2, 6 and 9 contain one smaller circle attached to a larger circle. 3,5 and 8 contain figure in which atleast one curve is present. Thus, the given nine figures may be divided into three groups as (1,4,7),(2,6,9) and (3,5,8).

24. (c) Let the age of Arvind be *x* yr.

Then, age of Arvind's father = 4*x* yr

Now, age of Arvind 5 yr ago = (*x* – 5) yr

Age of Arvind's father 5 yr ago = (4*x* – 5) yr

Now, $(4x - 5) = 7(x - 5)$

$\Rightarrow \quad 4x - 5 = 7x - 35$

$\Rightarrow \quad 3x = 30 \Rightarrow x = 10$ yr

Hence, Arvind's father's present age = 4 × 10 = 40 yr

25. (c) According to the information, the disease has started to spread in other villages also, making it challenging for the association to provide the medicine everywhere is the best reason behind the decision of the medical association.

26. (c) As,

16 5 14 3 9 12
P E N C I L

∴ Letter pairs = CE, NP ⇒ Two

27. (*a*) As,

P A (R) E N (T) H E (S) (I) S

3rd 6th 9th 10th

Meaningful word = STIR

∴ Required letter = R

28. (*a*) According to the question,

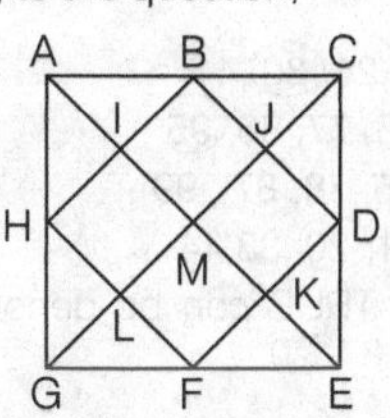

Smallest triangles are ABI, BCJ, CDJ, DEK, EFK, FGL, GHL, HAI = 8

Small triangles formed with two triangles

BCD, DEF, FGH, HAB = 4

Large triangles formed with two triangles

ACM, CEM, EGM, GAM = 4

Largest triangles ACE, AGE, GAC, GEC = 4

∴ Total triangles = 8 + 4 + 4 + 4 = 20

29. (*d*) Here, the mirror is placed vetically at AB on the LHS of the question figure. Hence, only the figure given in answer figure (d) would be obtained as the correct mirror image.

30. (c) According to the question, the direction diagram will be as follows

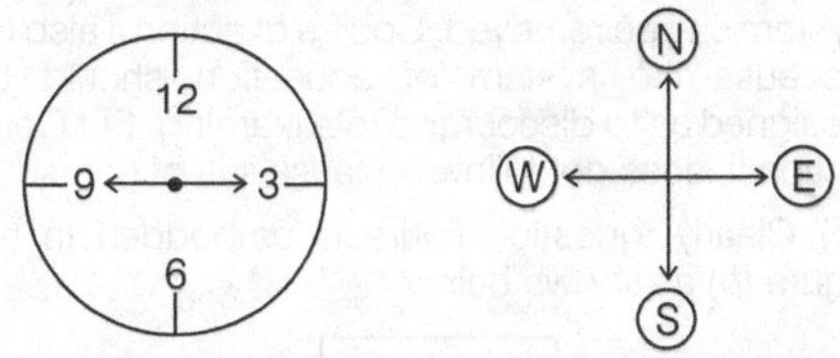

So, when hour hand is pointing towards West, then the minute hand will be pointing towards East at 9 : 15.

31. (*b*) As,

S T A R → 5 $ ★ 2 and T O R E → $ 3 2 @

Similarly, O A T S → 3 ★ $ 5

∴ OATS ⇒ 3 ★ $ 5

32. (*a*) Clearly, we have following arrangement of mathematical symbols.

× ⇒ +	÷ ⇒ –

$$? = 39 \times 23 \div 21 \times 5$$

$$\Rightarrow \quad ? = 39 + 23 - 21 + 5$$

$$\Rightarrow \quad ? = 67 - 21 = 46$$

33. (*b*) Given, 64 : 513 : : 144 : ?

Observe first pair

$$(8)^2 = 64, (8)^3 + 1 = 512 + 1 = 513$$

Similarly, $(12)^2 = 144$ and $? = (12)^3 + 1$

$$= 1728 + 1 = 1729$$

34. (*b*) Former is the grown up state of latter.

35. (c) a b c b c/ a b c b c/ a b c b c ⇒ b c a b c

a b c b c is repeating.

36. (*d*) According to the question,

Rakesh > Mukesh > Suresh

Amar > Rakesh > Harish

The relation between Harish and Suresh cannot be established from the given information.

So, it is not possible to find out the shortest person.

37. (c) Subtract 12 from the preceding number and proceed anti-clockwise.

$58 - 12 = 46$; $46 - 12 = 34$

$34 - 12 = 22$

38. (*d*) None of the arguments is strong. Argument I is weak because if it is operating successtully in westem countries, it may not necessarily succeed in India i.e. based on example. Argument II is irrelevant.

39. (*b*) In all other figure two different designs partially intersect each other. Where in figure (b) both rectangles are bisecting each other.

40. (c) Course of action I follows because on examining the examination system, the defects of the education system can be removed. Course of action II also follows because the system of education should be so designed as to discourage rote learning. But Course of action III does not follow because it is of no use.

41. (*b*) Clearly, question figure is embedded in answer figure (*b*) as shown below

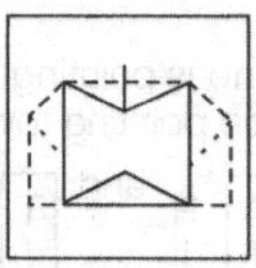

Solution (Q. Nos. 42-44) Arrangement according to the question is as follows

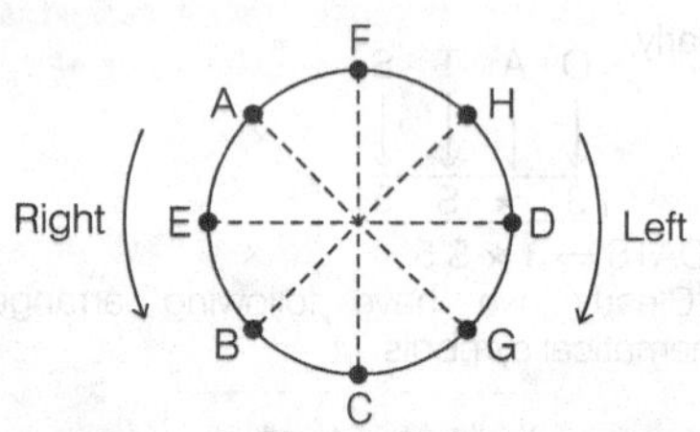

42. (c) Clearly, H is sitting exactly between F and D.

43. (*d*) D G C A F H E A F C None B

↑ Skipped ↑ Skipped ↑ Skipped ↑ No Number is skipped in between

So, CB does not belong to the group.

44. (*d*) Clearly, *G* is sitting second to the left of H.

45. (*d*) Clearly, from figure I to figure II, an inverted figure is also added.

46. (*d*) As, in figure I, 1 is at the top and 2 and 3 are the adjacent faces of 1. Hence, 1 may have any one of digits given in figure II at its opposite face. It means 1 may have 4 or 5 or 6 at it opposite face.

47. (c)

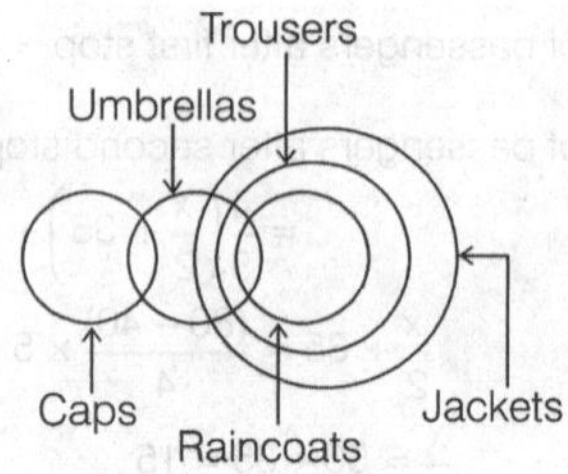

Conclusions I. Some raincoats are caps. (✗)

II. Some trousers are umbrellas. (✔)

III. All raincoats are jackets. (✔)

So, II and III follow.

48. (*d*)

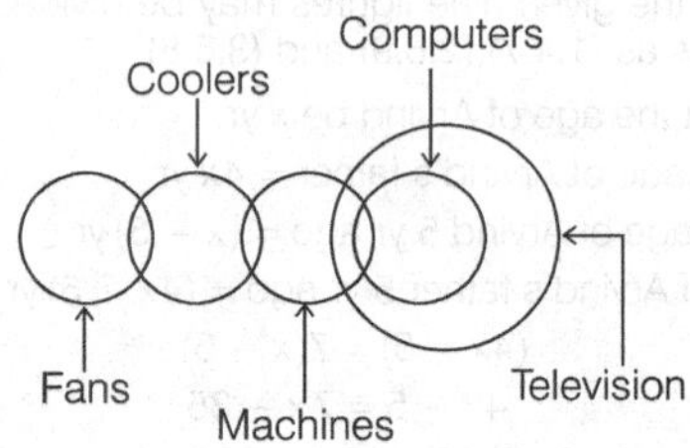

Conclusions I. Some televisions are machines. (✔)

II. Some machines are fans. (May be true)

III. No machine is fan. (May be true)

Complementary pair (I-E)

So, only I and either II or III follow.

49. (*c*)

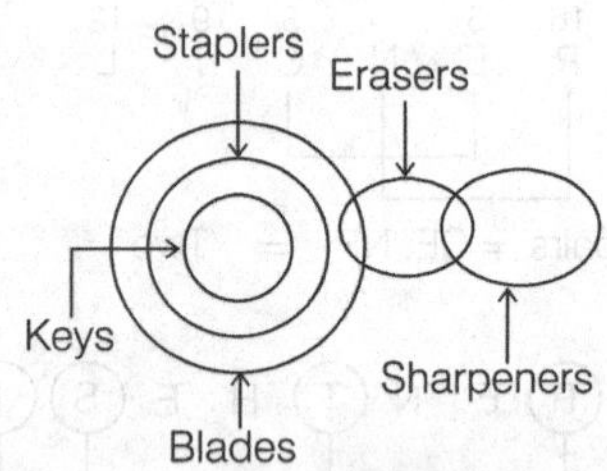

Conclusions I. Some sharpeners are keys. (✗)

II. All keys are blades. (✔)

III. Some erasers are keys. (✗)

So, only II follows.

50. (c) Here,

T → 03,12,24,(30),41

R → 59, 68, 77, 86,(95)

U → 56, 65, 78,(87), 99

E → 02,11,(20),33,44

So, the word TRUE can be denoted by the number group 30, 95, 87, 20.

PRACTICE SET 24

Direction (Q. Nos. 1-2) *In the following questions, find the odd word/number pair from the given alternatives.* **[SSC (10+2) 2015]**

1. (a) 57-75 (b) 34-43
(c) 15-41 (d) 12-21

2. (a) Apple (b) Orange
(c) Potato (d) Guava

3. Find the missing number from the given responses.

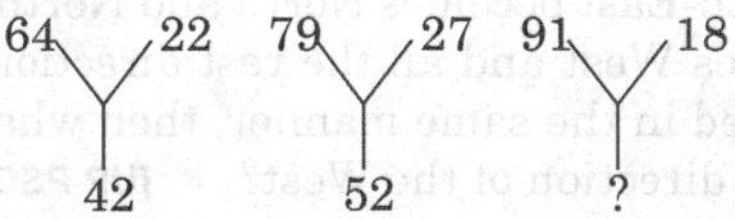

(a) 62 (b) 37
(c) 73 (d) 19

4. Pankaj travels 10 m in North direction, he turns right and travels 20 m. Again he turns towards right and travels 25 m. Then, he turns towards left and travels 15 m. In which direction and how far is Pankaj from his original position?
(a) 35 m, East (b) 10 m, West
(c) 25 m, East (d) None of these

5. Which one of the given responses would be a meaningful order of the following? **[SSC CPO (SI, ASI and IO Exam 2015]**
(i) Birth (ii) Death
(iii) Childhood (iv) Infancy
(v) Adolescence (vi) Adulthood
(vii) Old age
(a) (ii), (vi), (vii), (v), (iv), (iii), (i)
(b) (i), (iv), (iii), (v), (vi), (vii), (ii)
(c) (i), (iv), (iii), (vi), (v), (vii), (ii)
(d) (ii), (vii), (vi), (iv), (v), (iii), (i)

Direction (Q. Nos. 6-8) *Study the following information carefully and answer the given questions.*

A word and number arrangement machine when given an input line of words and numbers rearranges them following a particular rule in each step. The following is an illustration of input and rearrangement.

Input shop 17 table 20 53 over desk 39
***Step* I** 17 shop table 20 53 over desk 39
***Step* II** 17 table shop 20 53 over desk 39
***Step* III** 17 table 20 shop 53 over desk 39
***Step* IV** 17 table 20 shop 39 53 over desk
***Step* V** 17 table 20 shop 39 over 53 desk

And Step V is the last step of the rearrangement.

As per the rules followed in the above steps, find out in each of the following questions the appropriate step for the given input.

6. Step II of an input is '15 yes 62 51 48 talk now gone'.
Which of the following will be Step VI ?
(a) 15 yes 48 talk 51 now gone 62
(b) 15 yes 48 talk 51 62 now gone
(c) 15 yes 48 talk 51 now 62 gone
(d) There will be no such step
(e) None of the above

7. Step III of an input is '21 victory 30 joint 64 47 all gone'.
How many more steps will be required to complete the rearrangement ?
(a) Three (b) Four
(c) Five (d) Six
(e) None of these

8. **Input** '89 bind 32 goal house 61 12 joy'
How many steps will be required to complete the arrangement ?
(a) Four (b) Five (c) Six (d) Seven
(e) None of these

Direction (Q. Nos. 9-11) *In the following questions, select the related word/letters/number pair from the given alternatives.*

9. STAR : RATS :: WARD : ? **[Assistant SI 2015]**
(a) DRAW (b) FAME
(c) SHINE (d) MICE

10. Action : Reaction ?
(a) Stimulus : Response
(b) Book : Cover
(c) Firing : Running
(d) Birth : Death

11. 7544 : 5322 :: 4673 : ?
(a) 2367 (b) 2451
(c) 2531 (d) 4472

12. For the Assertion (A) and Reason (R) below, choose the correct alternative from the given option.

Assertion (A) Rajiv Gandhi was Prime Minister of India for many years.

Reason (R) Rajiv Gandhi was the grandson of Pandit Nehru. **[MAT 2014]**

(a) if both A and R are true and R is the correct explanation of A
(b) if both A and R are true but R is not the correct explanation of A
(c) if A is true but R is false
(d) if A is false but R is true

13. If you are eleventh in a queue starting from either end. How many persons are there in the queue ?
(a) Eleven (b) Twenty
(c) Twenty one (d) Twenty two

Direction (Q. Nos.14-16) *Study the following information carefully to answer the given questions.*

I. J, K, L, M, N and O are six family members having different professions.
II. There are two married couples in the family.
III. M is a doctor and his wife is an engineer.
IV. J is the granddaughter of O and sister of L, who is a typist.
V. K is the grandfather of L and is married to a teacher.
VI. J's mother, who is an engineer, is the daughter-in-law of a lawyer.

14. What is the profession of J?
(a) Teacher
(b) Lawyer
(c) Engineer
(d) Cannot be determined

15. Which of the following is one of the married couples?
(a) KN (b) MO
(c) NM (d) Cannot be determined

16. Who is the wife of M?
(a) N (b) O
(c) J (d) Cannot be determined

17. If 879 = 8, 625 = 1 and 586 = 9 then 785 = ?
(a) 6 (b) 7
(c) 8 (d) 9

18. Meena correctly remembers that her father's birthday is after 18th May but before 22nd May. Her brother correctly remembers that their father's birthday is before 24th May but after 20th May. On which date in May was definitely their father's birthday?
(a) 20th
(b) 19th
(c) 18th
(d) Cannot be determined
(e) None of the above

19. If South-East becomes North and North-East becomes West and all the rest directions are changed in the same manner, then what will be the direction of the West? **[UP PSC 2012]**
(a) North-East (b) South
(c) South-East (d) South-West

20. Find the missing number.

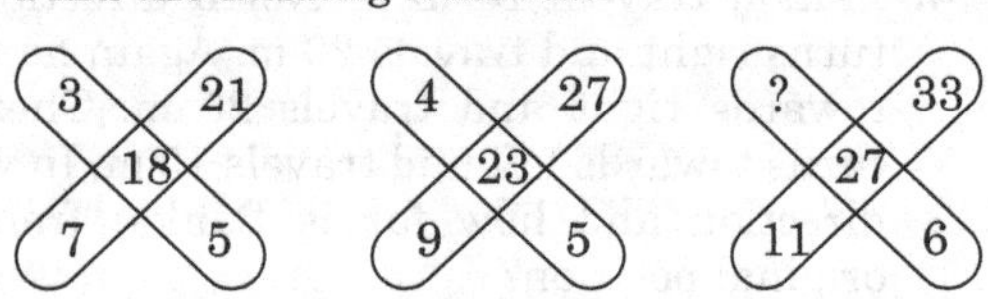

(a) 7 (b) 6 (c) 5 (d) 4

Direction (Q. Nos. 21-22) *In each of the questions below are given four statements followed by three conclusions numbered I, II, and III. You have to take the given statements to be true even, if they seem to be at variance with commonly known facts. Read all the conclusion (s) and then decide which of the given conclusions logically follow(s) from the given statements disregarding commonly known facts.*

21. Statements Some shoes are socks.
All socks are towels.
All towels are bed sheets.
No bedsheet is blanket.

Conclusions I. No towel is blanket.
II. Some shoes are towels.
III. Some shoes are bedsheets.

(a) I and II follow (b) II and III follow
(c) I and III follow (d) All follow
(e) None of these

22. Statements Some rocks are hills.
All hills are mountains.
All mountains are rivers.
No river is canal.

Conclusions I. All rocks are rivers.
II. Some hills are canals.
III. Some rivers are canals.

(a) Only I follows (b) II and III follow
(c) I and III follow (d) Only II follows
(e) None follows

23. Find out which of the answer figures (a), (b), (c) and (d) completes the figure matrix?

Question Figure

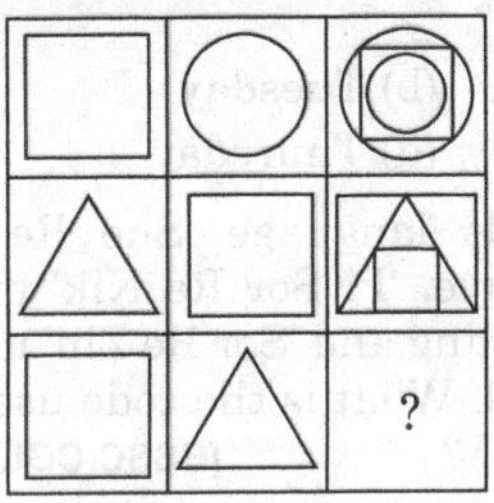

Answer Figures

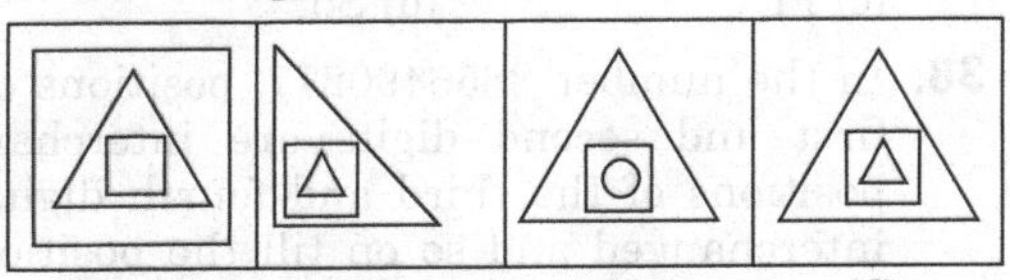

(a) (b) (c) (d)

24. How many triangles are there in the following square? **[SI (DI & CAPFs) and ASI (CISF) 2015]**

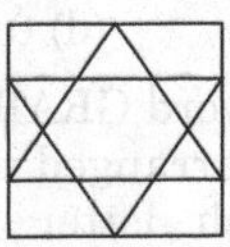

(a) 6 (b) 14 (c) 9 (d) 7

25. A bus for Delhi leaves every 30 min from a bus stand. An enquiry clerk told a passenger that the bus had already left 10 min ago and next but will leave at 9 : 35 am. At what time did the enquiry clerk give this information to the passenger?

(a) 9 : 10 am (b) 8 : 55 am
(c) 9 : 08 am (d) 9 : 15 am

26. Given below are two matrices of 25 cells each containing two classes of letters. The columns and rows of Matrix I are numbered from 0 to 4 and those of Matrix II from 5 to 9. A letter from these matrices can be represented first by its row number and next by its column number. e.g. B can be represented as 00, 14 etc. Similarly, M can be represented by 55, 67 etc. In the following question, identify one set of number pair out of (a), (b), (c) and (d) which represents the given word.

Matrix I

	0	1	2	3	4
0	B	D	E	T	O
1	D	E	T	O	B
2	E	B	O	D	T
3	T	O	B	E	D
4	O	T	D	B	E

Matrix II

	5	6	7	8	9
5	M	U	I	L	R
6	U	L	M	R	I
7	I	M	R	U	L
8	L	R	U	I	M
9	R	I	L	M	U

LIME

(a) 58, 69, 76, 03 (b) 79, 88, 98, 10
(c) 97, 75, 56, 33 (d) 66, 96, 89, 02

Direction (Q. Nos. 27-29) *Read the following information carefully to answer the questions that follow.*

Six persons are sitting in a circle. A is facing B. B is to the right of E and left of C. C is to the left of D. F is to the right of A. Now, D exchanges his seat with F and E with B.

27. Who will be sitting to the left of D?
(a) B (b) D (c) E (d) A

28. Who will be sitting to the left of C?
(a) E (b) F (c) A (d) B

29. Who will be sitting opposite of A?
(a) E (b) F (c) D (d) B

30. Choose the correct alternatives from the given ones that will complete the series.
0, 4, 18, 48, ?, 180
(a) 58 (b) 68 (c) 84 (d) 100

31. In making decisions about important questions, it is desirable to distinguish between a 'strong' argument and a 'weak' argument. A 'strong' argument must be both important and directly related to the question. A 'weak' argument may not be directly related to the question and may be of minor importance or may be related to the trivial aspect of the question. Each question below is followed by three arguments numbered I, II and III. You have to decide which of the arguments is 'strong' and which is 'weak'.

Statement Should there be a complete ban on genetically modified imported seeds?

Arguments

I. Yes, this will boost the demand of domestically developed seeds.

II. No, this is the only way to increase production substantially.

III. Yes, genetically modified products will adversely affect the health of those who consume these products.

(a) I and II are strong
(b) Only II is strong
(c) II and III are strong
(d) I and III are strong
(e) All are strong

32. Which one set of letters, when sequentially placed at the gaps in the given letters series shall complete it?

_aa_ba_bb_ab_aab

(a) aaabb (b) babab
(c) bbaab (d) None of these

33. Find the odd figure from the given alternatives.

K	F	N	W
(a)	(b)	(c)	(d)

Direction (Q. Nos. 34-35) *Each of the questions below consists of a question and three statements numbered I, II and III given below it. You have to decide the data provided in which of the statements are sufficient to answer the question, and choose your answer accordingly.*

34. How is Raju related to Manohar?

I. Pramila is the mother-in-law of Rashmi, the wife of Raju.

II. Pramila's brother is Raju's maternal uncle.

III. Pramila's husband is the only son of Manohar.

(a) Only I and II
(b) I and III
(c) Only I and either II or III
(d) Any two of the three
(e) Question cannot be answered even with the information in all three statements

35. Who amongst Subodh, Neeraj, Tara, Meena and Anil is the first to take the lecture ?

I. Subodh takes lecture before Meena and Neeraj but not before Anil.

II. Tara is not the first to take the lecture.

III. Meena is not the last to take the lecture.

(a) Only I
(b) Only I and II
(c) I and either II or III
(d) All I, II and III are necessary
(e) Question cannot be answered even with the information in all three statements.

36. If the 23rd of a month is a Sunday, then what day it would have been two weeks and four more days earlier?

(a) Monday (b) Tuesday
(c) Wednesday (d) Thursday

37. In a certain code language 'Sue Re Nik' means She is brave, 'Pi Sor Re Nik' means She is always smiling and 'Sor Re Zhi' means is always cheerful. What is the code used for the word 'smiling' ? **[BSSC CGL 2015]**

(a) Nik (b) Re
(c) Pi (d) Sor

38. In the number 3856490271, positions of the first and second digits are interchanged, positions of the third and fourth digits are interchanged and so on till the positions of ninth and tenth digits are interchanged, then which digit will be fifth from the left end?

(a) 6 (b) 4
(c) 9 (d) 0

39. How will the word GRAPES be written, if all its letters are arranged in alphabetical order and then each letter is replaced by its immediately next letter in the English alphabetical series? **[IBPS RRB (Office Assistant) 2015]**

(a) CGIPRS (b) BEIQSR
(c) BFHQST (d) CEUPTS
(e) BFHQUW

40. In which answer figure is the question figure embedded?

Question Figure

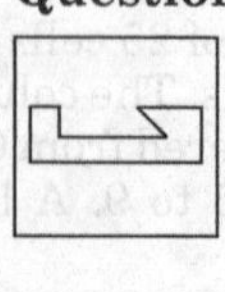

Answer Figures

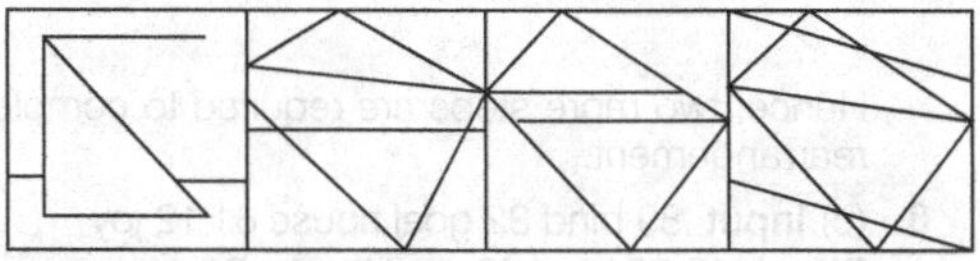

(a) (b) (c) (d)

41. In a certain code language, BLUNT is coded as 'AKSOU' and COINS is coded as 'BNGOT'. In the same code language, how will TRUST be coded ? **[IBPS Clerk (Pre) 2015]**

(a) SSTUV (b) SQTRS
(c) RQSRS (d) SQSTU
(e) RSSQN

42. From the given alternative words, select the word which can be formed using the letters of the given word. **[SSC CGL (Pre) 2014]**

DEMOCRACY

(a) SECRECY (b) MICRO
(c) MARCY (d) DEMON

Direction (Q. Nos. 43-44) *Read the following information carefully to answer the question that follow.*

'A + B' means 'A is the son of B'.
'A − B' means 'A is the wife of B'.
'A × B' means 'A is the brother of B'.
'A ÷ B' means 'A is the mother of B'.
'A = B' means 'A is the sister of B'.

43. What does 'P × R ÷ Q' mean?

(a) P is the nephew of Q
(b) P is the uncle of Q
(c) P is the brother of Q
(d) P is the father of Q

44. What does 'P = R ÷ Q' mean?

(a) P is the aunt of Q
(b) Q is the daughter of P
(c) P is the sister of Q
(d) Q is the niece of P

45. Which number is on the face opposite to 6 in the dice whose four views are given below? **[FCI Assistant Grade III 2015]**

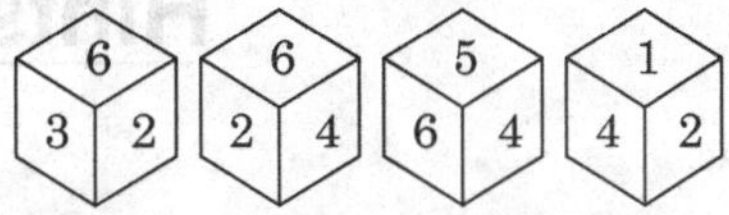

(I) (II) (III) (IV)

(a) 2 (b) 4
(c) 3 (d) None of these

46. How many cubes are there in this diagram ? **[SSC (10+2) 2012]**

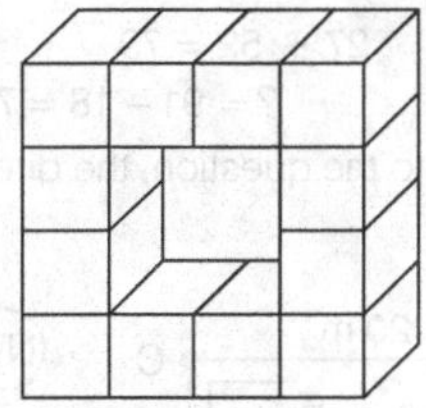

(a) 16 (b) 12 (c) 10 (d) 8

47. As per the below diagram, which diagram represents the relationship given in the following statements? **[NIFT UG 2015]**

Soccer players, Chess players, Athletes.

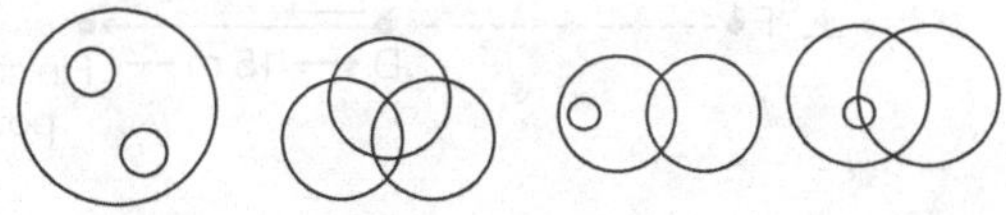

(a) (b) (c) (d)

Direction (Q. Nos. 48-50) *In these questions, relationship between different elements is shown in the statements. The statements are followed by two conclusions.*

Give answer

(a) if only Conclusion I is true
(b) if only Conclusion II is true
(c) if either Conclusion I or II is true
(d) if neither Conclusion I nor II is true
(e) if both Conclusions I and II are true

48. Statements $F \geq G = H$; $G > J \geq K$

Conclusions I. $F \geq K$ II. $K < H$

49. Statements $P < Q = R \geq S \geq T$

Conclusions I. $T \leq Q$ II. $R > P$

50. Statements $A \leq B < C$; $A \geq D$; $C \leq F$

Conclusions I. $D < C$ II. $F \geq D$

Hints and Solutions

1. (*c*) As,

57 $\xrightarrow{\text{Reverse}}$ 75, 34 $\xrightarrow{\text{Reverse}}$ 43

12 $\xrightarrow{\text{Reverse}}$ 21 But 15 $\xrightarrow{\text{Not Reverse}}$ 41

2. (*c*) Except potato, all others are fruits.

3. (*c*) As, 22 + 42 = 64

and 27 + 52 = 79

Similarly, ? = 91 − 18 = 73

4. (*d*) According to the question, the direction diagram will be as follows

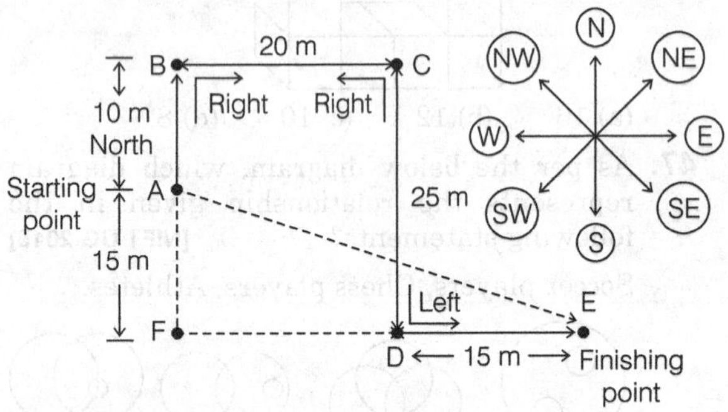

A = Starting point, E = Finishing point

DE = 15 m, BC = FD = 20 m

FE = FD + DE = 20 + 15 = 35 m

AF = BF − AB = 25 − 10 = 15 m

$\therefore$ Required distance, $AE = \sqrt{(AF)^2 + (FE)^2}$

$= \sqrt{(15)^2 + (35)^2}$

$= \sqrt{225 + 1225}$

$= \sqrt{1450}$

and direction is South-East.

5. (*b*) Meaningful order

(i) Birth → (iv) Infancy → (iii) Childhood → (v) Adolescence → (vi) Adulthood → (vii) Old age → (ii) Death

6. (*c*) ***Step*** **II** 15 yes 62 51 48 talk now gone

Step **III** 15 yes 48 62 51 talk now gone

Step **IV** 15 yes 48 talk 62 51 now gone

Step **V** 15 yes 48 talk 51 62 now gone

Step **VI** 15 yes 48 talk 51 now 62 gone

Hence, two more steps are required to complete (c) the rearrangement.

7. (*e*) ***Step*** **III** 21 victory 30 joint 64 47 all gone

Step **IV** 21 victory 30 joint 47 64 all gone

Step **V** 21 victory 30 joint 47 gone 64 all

Hence, two more steps are required to complete the rearrangement.

8. (*c*) **Input** 89 bind 32 goal house 61 12 joy

Step **I** 12 89 bind 32 goal house 61 joy

Step **II** 12 joy 89 bind 32 goal house 61

Step **III** 12 joy 32 89 bind goal house 61

Step **IV** 12 joy 32 house 89 bind goal 61

Step **V** 12 joy 32 house 61 89 bind goal

Step **VI** 12 joy 32 house 61 goal 89 bind

9. (*a*) As, STAR $\xrightarrow{\text{Reverse}}$ RATS

Same as, WARD $\xrightarrow{\text{Reverse}}$ DRAW

Note Here, the letters are written in reverse order.

10. (*d*) 'Reaction' is opposite to 'Action'. In the same way, 'Death' is opposite to 'Birth'.

11. (*b*) As,

7544 : 5322 (−2222) Similarly, 4673 : 2451 (−2222)

$\therefore$? = 2451

12. (*b*) It is true that Rajiv Gandhi was Prime Minister of India for many years and he was the grandson of Pandit Nehru.

So, both (A) and (R) are true, but (R) is not the correct explanation of A.

13. (*c*) According to the question,

→ 11th

←

Total number of persons in the queue

= (11 + 11) − 1 = 21

Solution (Q. Nos. 14-16) Let us draw the family diagram

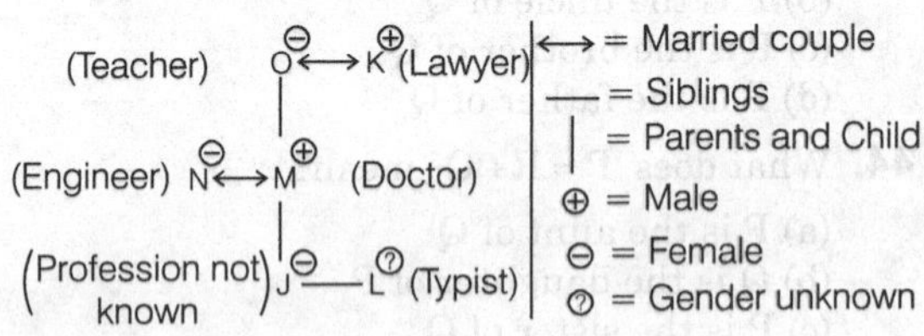

14. (*d*) J's profession cannot be determined.

15. (*c*) NM and OK are the two married couples in the family. NM is one out of them.

16. (*a*) N is M's wife.

17. (*a*) As, 879 = (7 + 9) − 8 = 8

625 = (2 + 5) − 6 = 1

and 586 = (8 + 6) − 5 = 9

Similarly, 785 = (8 + 5) − 7 = 6

18. (*e*) Days by Meena, 19th, 20th or 21st May.

Days by her brother, 21st 22nd or 23rd May.

Clearly, 21st may is common in both the groups and hence it is the required day.

19. (*c*) According to the question, the direction diagram will be as follows

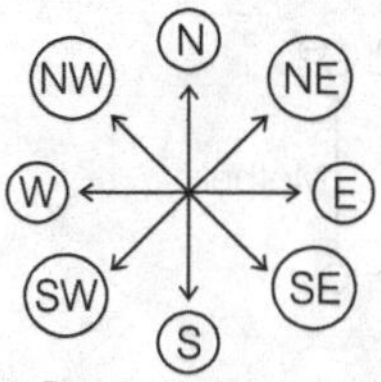

Original direction

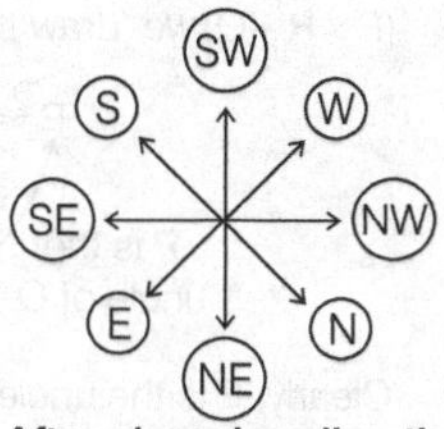

After changing direction

Now, from the above diagrams it is clear that South-East will be the direction for West.

20. (*b*) As, $3 + 18 = 21$

and $4 + 23 = 27$

Similarly, $? + 27 = 33$

$\therefore$ $? = 33 - 27 = 6$

21. (*d*)

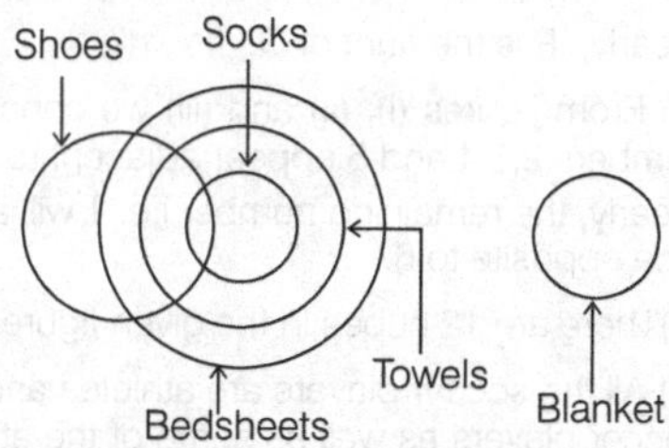

Conclusions I. No towel is blanket. (✔)

II. Some shoes are towels. (✔)

III. Some shoes are bed sheets. (✔)

So, all follow.

22. (*e*)

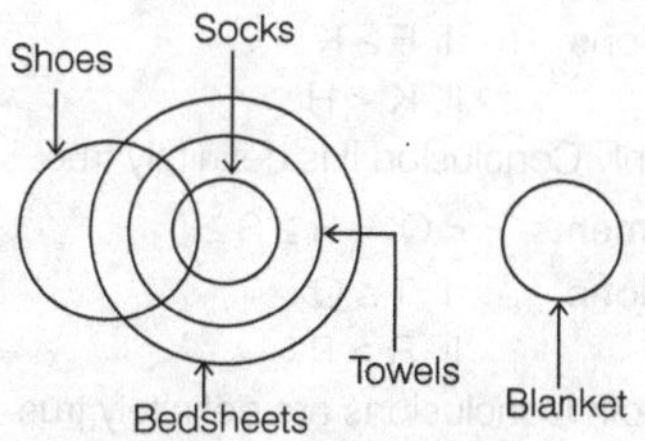

Conclusions I. All rocks are rivers. (✗)

II. Some hills are canals. (✗)

III. Some rivers are canals. (✗)

So, none follows.

23. (*d*) Clearly, in each row, the second figure forms the innermost which is also at the outermost position and first figure at middle position.

24. (*b*)

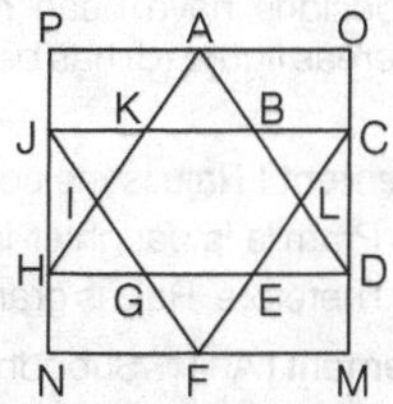

$\therefore$ Number of triangles = ABK, BCL, CLD, LDE, EFG, GHI, HIJ, IJK, AHD, JCF, CFM, JNF, PAH, AOD = 14

Hence, there are 14 triangles in the given figure.

25. (*d*) Next but will leave at 9 : 35 am.

So, last but left at (9 : 35 – 0 : 30) = 9 : 00 am

So, enquiry clerk gave the information to the passenger = (9 : 05 + 0 ; : 10) = 9 : 15 am

26. (*d*) Here, L → 58, (66), 79, 85, 97

I → 57, 69, 75, 88, (96)

M → 55, 67, 76, (89), 98

E → (02), 11, 20, 33, 44

So, the word LIME can be denoted by the number group 66, 96, 89, 02.

Solution (Q. Nos. 27-29) Arrangements according to the question are as follows

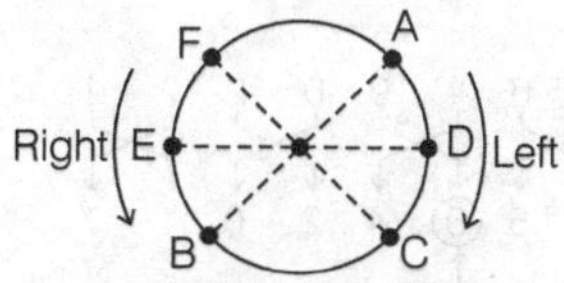

Original Position

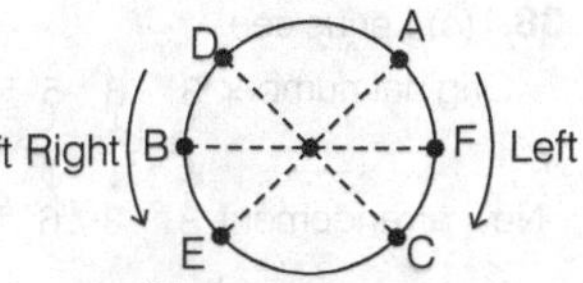

New arrangement

27. (*d*) Clearly, A is sitting to the left of D.

28. (*a*) Clearly, E is sitting to the left of C.

29. (*a*) Clearly E is sitting opposite to A.

30. (*d*) The pattern is as follows

0	4	18	48	(100)	180
↑	↑	↑	↑	↑	↑
$1^2 \times 0$	$2^2 \times 1$	$3^2 \times 2$	$4^2 \times 3$	$5^2 \times 4$	$6^2 \times 5$

$\therefore$ $? = 5^2 \times 4 = 25 \times 4 = 100$

31. (*d*) If there is a complete ban on genetically modified seeds, it will boost the demand of domestically developed seeds, so Argument I is strong. Argument II is not strong due to the word 'only'. Argument III is strong because genetically modified products will adversely affect the health of those who consume these products.

32. (*c*) The series is as follows baab/baab/baab/baab

$\therefore$ Required answer = bbaab

33. (*d*) All other designs have been made of three line segments, whereas figure (d) has been made up of four line segments.

34. (*b*) From **Statement I** Raju is the son of Pramila.
Statement III Pramila is daughter-in-law of Manohar.
Therefore, Raju is grandson of Manohar.

35. (*b*) From **Statement I** Anil > Subodh > Meena, Neeraj
Statement II Tara is somewhere after Anil.
Therefore, Anil is the first to take the lecture.

36. (*c*) Two weeks earlier than 23rd was also Sunday.

$23 - 7 = 16$

$16 - 7 = 9$

4 days earlier than 9 means 5th

9th ⇒ Sunday
8th ⇒ Saturday
7th ⇒ Friday
6th ⇒ Thursday
5th ⇒ Wednesday

37. (*c*) Sue (Re) Nik ⟶ She (is) brave ...(i)
Pi [Sor] (Re) Nik ⟶ She (is) [always] smiling ...(ii)
[Sor] (Re) Zhi ⟶ (is) [always] cheerful ...(iii)
From Eq. (ii), we get
Smiling ⟶ 'Pi'

38. (*c*) Let us see

Original number 3 8 5 6 4 9 0 2 7 1

New arrangement 8 3 6 5 (9) 4 2 0 1 7

From left ⟶ 5th

So, the required digit is 9.

39. (*c*) Given word → G R A P E S

After rearranged in alphabetical order → A E G P R S
+1 +1 +1 +1 +1 +1
Next letter → B F H Q S T

40. (*a*) Clearly, question figure is embedded in answer figure (a).

41. (*d*) As, B L U N T
−1 −1 −2 +1 +1
A K S O U

and, C O I N S
−1 −1 −2 +1 +1
B N G O T

Similarly, T R U S T
−1 −1 −2 +1 +1
S Q S T U

42. (*c*) 'MARCY' can be formed using the letters of the given word.

43. (*b*) By applying the given decoding method for $(P \times R \div Q)$ we draw the following family diagram

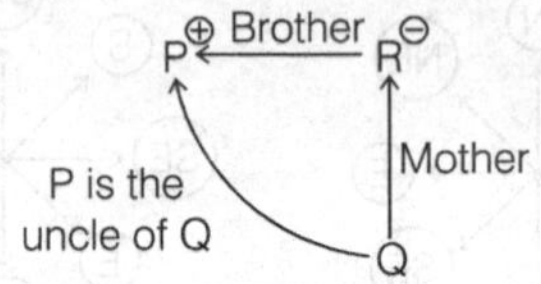

Clearly, P is the uncle of Q.

44. (*a*) By applying the given decoding method for $(P = R \div Q)$ we draw the following family diagram

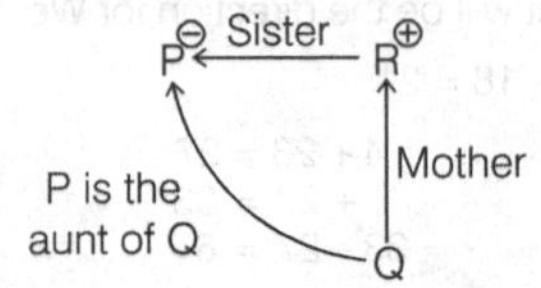

Clearly, P is the aunt of Q.

45. (*d*) From figures (i), (ii) and (iii) we conclude that the numbers 2,3,4 and 5 appear adjacent to 6.
Clearly, the remaining number i.e. 1 will appear on the face opposite to 6.

46. (*b*) There are 12 cubes in the given figure.

47. (*d*) All the soccer players are athletes and some of the soccer players as well as some of the athletes can be chess players.

48. (*b*) **Statements** $F \geq G = H; G > J \geq K$
On combining both the statement, we get

$$F \geq G = H > J \geq K$$

Conclusions I. $F \geq K$ (False)
II. $K < H$ (True)

Hence, only Conclusion II is definitely true.

49. (*e*) **Statements** $P < Q = R \geq S \geq T$

Conclusions I. $T \leq Q$ (True)
II. $R > P$ (True)

Hence, both Conclusions are definitely true.

50. (*a*) **Statements** $A \leq B < C; A \geq D; C \leq F$
On combining these statements, we get
$D \leq A \leq B < C \leq F$

Conclusions I. $D < C$ (True)
II. $F \geq D$ (False)

Hence, only Conclusion I is definitely true.

PRACTICE SET 25

1. Find out the incorrect term in the series.
2, 5, 10, 3, 6, 18, 4, 7, 30 **[SSC (10+2) 2015]**
(a) 10 (b) 30
(c) 6 (d) 7

2. How many meaningful English words can be made with the letters DREO, using each letter only once in each word? **[UBI (PO) 2010]**
(a) None (b) One
(c) Two (d) Three
(e) More than three

3. In the following question, from the given alternative words, select the word which cannot be formed using the letters of the given word.
INTERVENTION **[SSC (10+2) 2013]**
(a) ENTER (b) INTENTION
(c) INVENTION (d) ENTERTAIN

4. Examine the following statements: **[UPSC CSAT 2015]**

I. Ladyfinger is tastier than cabbage.
II. Cauliflower is tastier than ladyfinger.
III. Cabbage is not tastier than peas.

The conclusion that can be drawn from these statements is that
(a) Peas are as tasty as ladyfinger.
(b) Peas are as tasty as cauliflowers and ladyfinger.
(c) Cabbage is the least tasty of the four vegetables.
(d) Cauliflower is tastier than cabbage.

Direction (Q. Nos. 5-6) *In the following questions, find the odd word/word pair from the given alternatives.*

5. (a) Bengaluru (b) Patna
(c) Bhagalpur (d) Ranchi

6. (a) Horse : Neigh (b) Lion : Grunt
(c) Owl : Hoot (d) Sheep : Bleat

7. In a queue, Sohan is 10th from left and 28th from right. How many people in the queue?
(a) 38 (b) 35
(c) 37 (d) 42

Direction (Q. Nos. 8-9) *Read the following information carefully and answer the questions that follow.*

I. Six flats on a floor in two rows facing North and South are allotted to P, Q, R, S, T and U.
II. Q gets a North facing flat and is not next to S.
III. S and U get diagonally opposite flats.
IV. R next to U, gets a South facing flat and T gets a North facing flat.

8. Whose flat is between Q and S?
(a) T (b) U (c) R (d) P

9. The flats of which of the pair, other than SU, are diagonally opposite to each other?
(a) PT (b) QP
(c) QR (d) TS

Direction (Q. Nos. 10-12) *Study the given information carefully to answer the given questions.* **[IBPS RRB (Office Assistant)2015]**

In a certain code language,
'Keep your eyes open' is written as 'nx co kh wd'
'eyes on school bus' is written as 'vy co rs te'
'keep bag in bus' is written as 'rs ef bn kh'
'open your school bag' is written as 'wd ef nx vy'
(All codes are two-letter codes only)

10. What is the code for 'bus' in the given code language?
(a) rs (b) vy
(c) bn (d) ef
(e) Other than those given as option

11. In the given code language, what does the code 'nx' stand for?
(a) in
(b) Either 'your' or 'open'
(c) eyes
(d) school
(e) Either 'bag' or 'keep'

12. What may be the possible code for 'garbage bag' in the given code language?
(a) av bn (b) ef av
(c) kh bn (d) ef kh
(e) nx rs

13. Which number is present only in one geometrical figure?

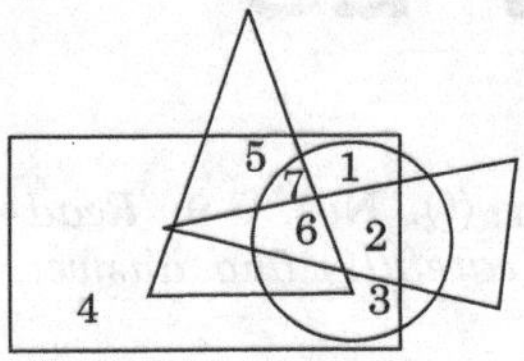

(a) 3 (b) 2 (c) 5 (d) 4

Direction (Q. Nos. 14-15) *In the following questions, the symbols $, %, @, © and ★ are used with the following meaning as illustrated below:*

'P % Q' means 'P is not smaller than Q'.

'P $ Q' means 'P is not greater than Q'.

'P ★ Q' means 'P is neither greater than nor equal to Q'.

'P © Q' means 'P is neither smaller than nor equal to Q'.

'P @ Q' means 'P is neither greater than nor smaller than Q'.

14. Statements R @ K, K $ F, F ★ N

Conclusions I. N © R
II. F @ R III. F © R

(a) Only I is true
(b) Either II or III is true
(c) Only I and either II or III are true
(d) Only III is true
(e) None of the above

15. Statements J © M, M ★ K, K % D

Conclusions I. J © D
II. D ★ M III. K © D

(a) None is true (b) Only I is true
(c) Only II is true (d) Only III is true
(e) I and II are true

16. How many even numbers are there in the following series of numbers, each of which is preceded by an odd number, but not followed by an even number?

5 3 4 8 9 7 1 6 5 3 2 9 8 7 3 5

(a) 0 (b) 1 (c) 2 (d) 3

17. Find the missing number in the following figure.

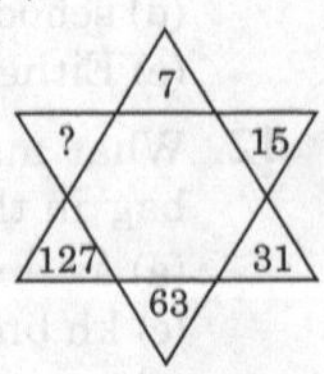

(a) 190 (b) 255
(c) 221 (d) 236

Direction (Q. Nos. 18-20) *Study the following information carefully and answer the given questions.*

A word and number arrangement machine when given an input line of words and numbers rearranges them following a particular rule in each step. The following is an illustration of input and rearrangement.

Input base 35 or gone 62 49 87 ahead
Step I 87 base 35 or gone 62 49 ahead
Step II 87 ahead base 35 or gone 62 49
Step III 87 ahead 62 base 35 or gone 49
Step IV 87 ahead 62 base 49 35 or gone
Step V 87 ahead 62 base 49 gone 35 or

and Step V is the last step of the rearrangement.

As per the rules followed in the above steps, find out in each of the following questions the appropriate step for the given input.

18. Input how was your stay 56 25 36 64

Which of the following will be Step VI?

(a) 64 how 56 was your stay 25 36
(b) 64 how 56 stay 36 was 25 your
(c) 64 how 56 stay 36 was your 25
(d) There will be no such step
(e) None of the above

19. Input power fail now 52 24 75 gate 34

Which of the following steps will be the last but one?

(a) IV (b) V (c) VI (d) VII
(e) None of these

20. Step III of an input is '91 car 85 14 27 few new house'

Which of the following is definitely the input?

(a) 85 14 91 car few new house
(b) car 91 85 14 27 few new house
(c) car 85 14 27 few new house 91
(d) Cannot be determined
(e) None of the above

21. In the following questions, find the figure out of the answer choices figures that can be formed by joining the pieces given in the question figure.

Question Figure

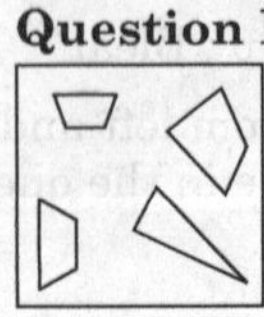

Answer Figures

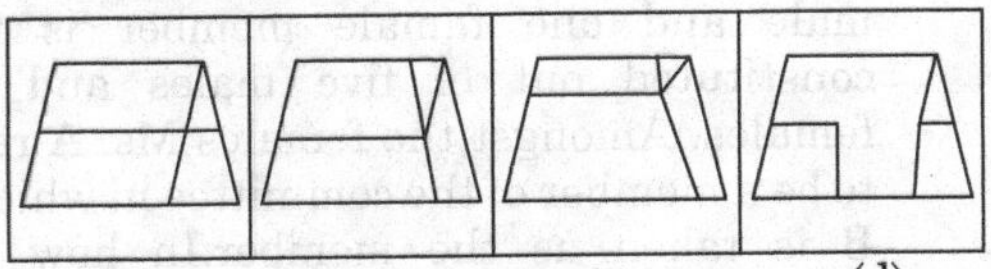

(a) (b) (c) (d)

22. C is wife of B, E is the son of C. A is the brother of B and father of D. What is the relationship of E to D?

(a) Mother (b) Sister
(c) Brother (d) Cousin

23. Find the missing figure in the series from the given answer figure.

Question Figures

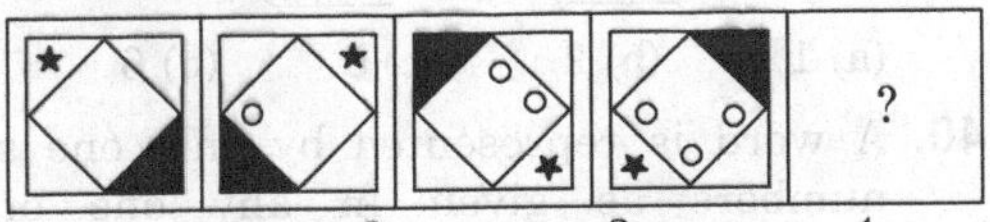

1 2 3 4

Answer Figures

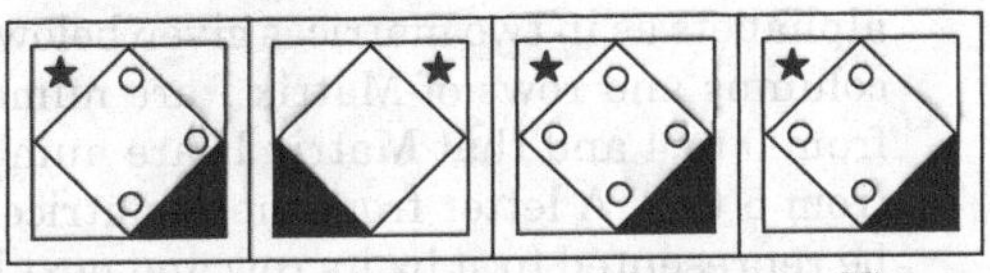

(a) (b) (c) (d)

Direction (Q. Nos. 24-26) *Read the following information to answer the questions given below.*

From a group of six boys M, N, O, P, Q and R and five girls G, H, I, J and K a team of six is to be selected. Some of the criteria of selection are as follows

I. M and J go together.
II. O cannot be placed with N.
III. I cannot go with J.
IV. N goes with H.
V. P and Q have to be together.
VI. K and R go together.
VII. Unless otherwise stated these criteria are applicable to all the following questions.

24. If the team consists of two girls and I is one of them, the other members are

(a) GMRPQ (b) KOPQR
(c) HNOPQ (d) KRMNP

25. If the team has four boys including O and R, the members of the team other than O and R are

(a) HIPQ (b) GJPQ
(c) GKPQ (d) GJMP

26. If four members are boys, which of the following cannot constitute the team?

(a) GJMOPQ (b) JKMNOR
(c) HJMNPQ (d) JKMPQR

27. Identify the missing part of the question figure and select it from given anwer figures.

Question Figure **[SSC (10+2)2012]**

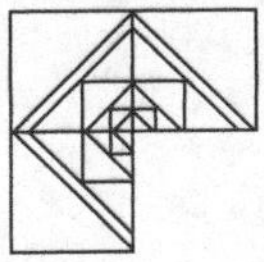

Answer Figures

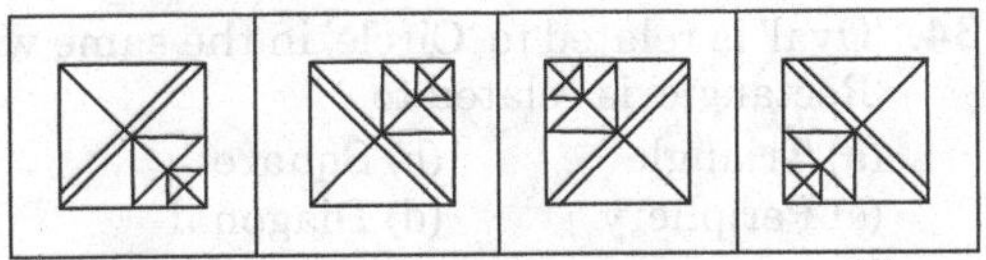

(a) (b) (c) (d)

28. In the following question, there are two statements labelled as Assertion (A) and Reason (R).

Assertion (A) Autism is a development disability.

Reason (R) Heredity and lower development of brain are the causes of the Autism.

(a) 'A' is false and 'R' is true
(b) Both 'A' and 'R' are false
(c) Both 'A' and 'R' are true
(d) 'A' is true and 'R' is false

29. Which one set of letters when sequentially placed at the gaps in the given letter series shall complete it? **[SSC (CGL) 2014]**

ipi _ upog _ pig _ pogi _ _ g

(a) iupgg (b) upgii
(c) puigp (d) giupi

30. How many triangles are there in the following figure?

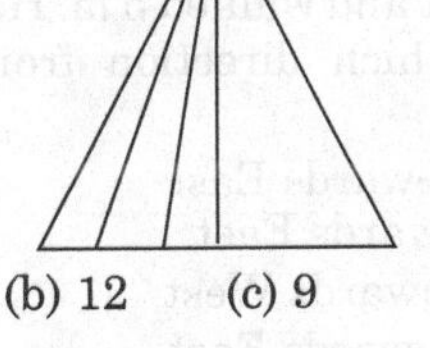

(a) 5 (b) 12 (c) 9 (d) 10

31. Some equations are solved on the basis of a certain system. Find out the correct answer for the unsolved equation on that basis. If $3 \div 5 = 5, 4 \div 7 = 8, 8 \div 7 = 6$, then what should $9 \div 6$ be? **[SSC FCI 2012]**

(a) 4 (b) 9 (c) 5 (d) 6

Direction (Q. Nos. 32-34) *In the following questions, select the related words/letters/number from the given alternatives.*

32. HCM : FAK : : SGD : ?

(a) QEB (b) QIB
(c) ESQ (d) GES

33. 4 : 9 : : 8 : ?

(a) 2 (b) 13
(c) 31 (d) 10

34. 'Oval' is related to 'Circle' in the same way as 'Rectangle' is related to

(a) Triangle (b) Square
(c) Periphery (d) Diagonal

35. Select the related figure from the given alternatives.

Question Figures

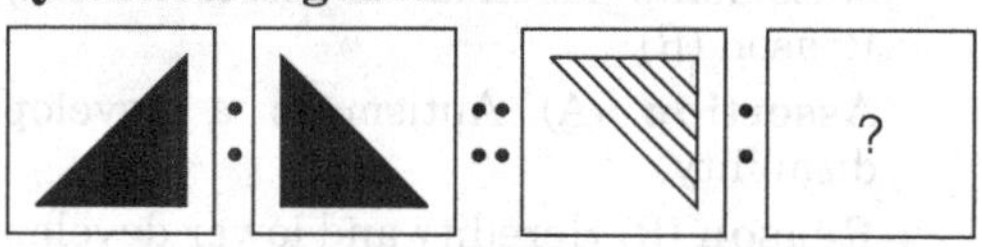

Answer Figures

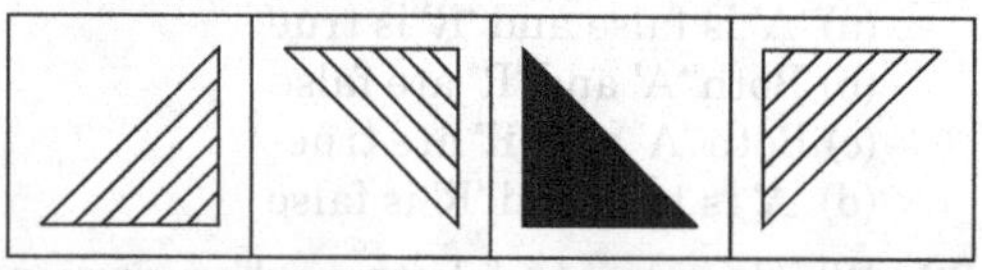

(a) (b) (c) (d)

36. A father is twice as old as his son. 20 yr ago, the age of the father was 12 times the age of the son. The present age of the son is

(a) 20 yr (b) 21 yr
(c) 22 yr (d) 23 yr

37. Starting from a point, Raju walked 12 m North, he turned right and walked 10 m, he again turned right and walked 12 m, then the turned left and walked 5 m. How far is he now and in which direction from the starting point?

(a) 27 m towards East
(b) 5 m towards East
(c) 10 m towards West
(d) 15 m towards East

38. A two member committee comprising of one male and one famale member is to be constituted out of five males and three females. Amongst the females Ms. A refuses to be a member of the committee in which Mr. B is taken as the member.In how many different ways can the committee be constiuted?

(a) 11 (b) 12 (c) 13 (d) 14

39. In the following question, two positions of a single dice are given. Find the dots at the face opposite to the face having 3 dots.

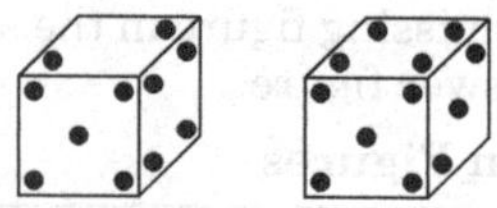

(a) 1 (b) 2 (c) 5 (d) 6

40. A word is represented by only one set of numbers as given in any one of the alternatives. The set of numbers given in the alternatives are represented by two classes of alphabets as in two matrices given below. The columns and rows of Matrix I are numbered from 0 to 4 and that Matrix II are numbered from 5 to 9. A letter from these matrices can be represented first by its row and next by its column, e.g., 'M' can be represented by 42, 31, etc and 'P' can be represented by 95 88, etc. Similarly, you have to identify the set for the word given 'ROST'. **[BSSC (CGL) 2015]**

Matrix I

	0	1	2	3	4
4	K	L	M	N	O
3	L	M	K	O	N
2	N	O	L	M	K
1	M	N	O	K	L
0	O	K	N	L	M

Matrix II

	5	6	7	8	9
9	P	Q	R	S	T
8	T	S	Q	P	R
7	R	T	S	Q	P
6	S	P	T	R	Q
5	Q	R	P	T	S

(a) 56, 44, 67, 40 (b) 97, 21, 66, 29
(c) 75, 00, 10, 92 (d) 68, 33, 65, 58

41. Find the missing number from the given responses.

9	3	7
12	2	9
13	5	?
1404	30	504

(a) 5 (b) 8 (c) 15 (d) 56

42. Which one of the given responses would be a meaningful order of the following?

(i) Book (ii) Pulp
(iii) Timber (iv) Jungle
(v) Paper

(a) (iii), (ii), (v), (i), (iv)
(b) (ii), (v), (i), (iv), (iii)
(c) (iv), (iii), (ii), (v), (i)
(d) (v), (iv), (iii), (i), (ii)

Direction (Q. Nos. 43-45) *In each of the questions below are given four statements followed by four conclusions numbered* I, II, III *and* IV. *You have to take the given statement to be true even if they seem to be at variance with commonly known facts. Read all the conclusions and then decide which of the given conclusion (s) logically follow (s) from the given statements disregarding commonly known facts.*

43. Statements Some shirts are pants.
All pants are caps.
All caps are ties.
No tie is socks.

Conclusions I. No cap is socks.
II. Some pants are shirts.
III. All caps are pants.

(a) I and II follow (b) Only II follows
(c) Only III follows (d) None follows
(e) All follow

44. Statements All boxes are foxes.
All foxes are schools.
No school is college.
All colleges are markets.

Conclusions I. No fox is college.
II. No college is school.
III. No box is fox.

(a) Only I follows (b) Only III follows
(c) I and II follow (d) None follows
(e) All follow

45. Statement Some leaves are flowers.
No flower is fruit.
Some fruit are branches.
Some branches are stems.

Conclusions I. Some leaves are stems.
II. All leaves are either stems or fruits.
III. All stems areeither branches or fruits.

(a) Only I follows (b) II and III follow
(c) Only III follows (d) All follow
(e) None follows

46. If a mirror is place on the line MN, then which of the answer figures is the right image of the question figure? **[SSC (CGL) 2014]**

Question Figure

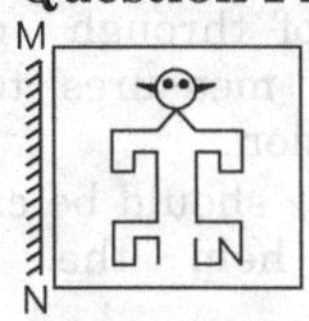

Answer Figures

(a) (b) (c) (d)

Direction (Q. Nos. 47-48) *In each of the question below is given a statement followed by three courses of action numbered* I, II *and* III. *A course of action is a step or administrative decision to be taken for improvement, follow-up or further action in regard to the problem, policy, etc. On the basis of information given in the statement, you have to assume everything in the statement to be true and then decide which of the three given suggested courses of action logically follows worth pursuing. Then, decide which of the alternatives (a), (b), (c), (d) or (e) is correct.*

47. Statement Many student of the local school fell ill for the fourth time in a row in the last six months after consuming food prepared by the school canteen.

Courses of Action

I. The school management should immediately terminate the contract of the canteen and aks for compensation.
II. The school management should advise all the students not a eat food articles from the canteen.
III. The owner of the canteen should immediately be arrested for negligence.

(a) None follows (b) Only II follows
(c) Only III follows (d) Both I and II follow
(e) Both II and III follow

48. Statement Cholera broke out recently in most of the cities killing a large number of people and affecting hundreds of households.

Courses of Action

I. An enquiry should be initiated to identify the cause of the catastrophe.

II. The civic administration should make the general public aware of through mass media, the preventive measures to be adopted in such a situation.

III. The para-military forces should be called into the cities to help the civic administration.

(a) None follows
(b) Only II follows
(c) Both I and II follow
(d) All follow

Direction (Q. Nos. 49-50) *Each of the questions below consists of a question and three statements numbered* I, II *and* III *given below it. You have to decide the data provided in which of the statements are sufficient to answer the question, and choose your answer accordingly.*

49. What is the code for 'rope' in a code language?

I. 'use the rope' is written as 'nik ta re' in the code language.

II. 'rope is straight' is written as 'pe da ta'.

III. 'always use rope' is written as 'ma re ta'.

(a) Either I and II or II and III
(b) I and III
(c) II and III
(d) All I, II and III are necessary
(e) Question cannot be answered even with the information in all three statements

50. P is in which direction with respect to Q?

I. M is to the North to R who is to the West of Q.

II. P is to the East of M.

III. P is to the North-East of R.

(a) I and II
(b) Only III
(c) Any two of the three
(d) All I, II and III are necessary
(e) Question cannot be answered even with the information in all three statements.

Hints and Solutions

1. (*b*) The pattern of the series is

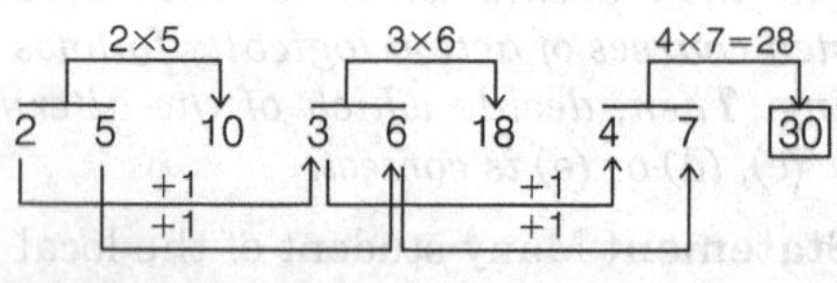

So, 30 should be replace by 28.

2. (*b*) Required word = RODE

3. (*d*) From the given word, 'ENTERTAIN' is the only word which cannot be formed due to the absence of letter A.

4. (*c*) Ladyfinger > Cabbage ...(i)

Cauliflower > Ladyfinger ...(ii)

Peas > Cabbage ...(iii)

From the above three equations, we can conclude that cabbage is the least tasty of the four vegetables.

5. (*c*) All others are capital cities of Indian states.

6. (*b*) All except 'Lion-Grunt' are correct match of animals and their sounds.

7. (*c*) Total persons in the queue = (Sum of position of Sohan from both ends) − 1

= (10 + 28) − 1 = 38 − 1 = 37

Solution (Q. Nos. 8-9) Arrangement according to the question is as follows

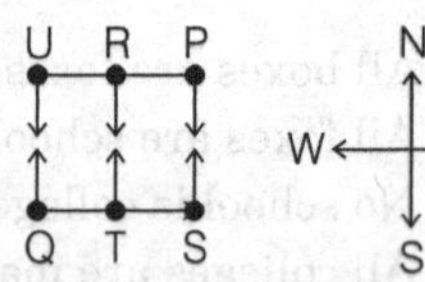

8. (*a*) Clearly, T's flat is between Q and S.

9. (*b*) Flats of Q and P are diagonally opposite to each other.

Solution (Q. Nos. 10-12) According to the given information

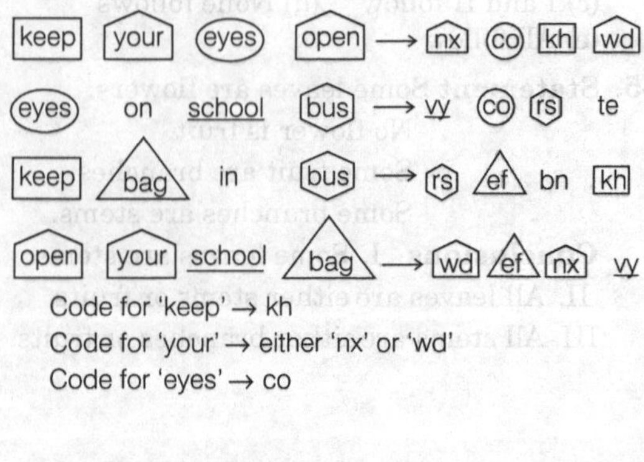

Code for 'keep' → kh

Code for 'your' → either 'nx' or 'wd'

Code for 'eyes' → co

Code for 'open' → either 'nx' or 'wd'
Code for 'school' → vy
Code for 'bus' → rs
Code for 'bag' → ef
Code for 'on' → te
Code for 'in' → bn

10. (*a*) The code for 'bus' in the code language is 'rs'.

11. (*b*) The code 'nx' stands for either 'your' or 'open'.

12. (*b*) The possible code for 'garbage bag' in the given code language is 'ef av'.

13. (*d*) The number '4' is present only in rectangle.

Solution Q.Nos. (14-15)

% ⇒ ≥	$ ⇒ ≤	★ ⇒ <	© ⇒ >	@ ⇒ =

14. (c) R @ K ⇒ R = K
K $ F ⇒ K ≤ F
F ★ N ⇒ F < N
Therefore, R = K ≤ F < N
Conclusions I. N © R ⇒ N > R (True)
II. F @ R ⇒ F = R (May be True)
III. F © R ⇒ F > R (May be True)
F is either greater than or equal to R.
So, only I and either II or III are true.

15. (*a*) J © M ⇒ J > M
M ★ K ⇒ M < K
K % D ⇒ K ≥ D
Therefore, J > M < K ≥ D
I. J © D ⇒ J > D (False)
II. D ★ M ⇒ D < M (False)
III. K © D ⇒ K > D (False)
So, none is true.

16. (*d*) 5 3 4 8 9 7 1 [6] 5 3 [2] 9 [8] 7 3 5
There are three such even numbers 6, 2 and 8 each of which is preceded by an odd number and not followed by an even number.

17. (*b*) Proceed clockwise starting with the lowest number in the following manner

$7 \times 2 + 1 = 15$
$15 \times 2 + 1 = 31$
$31 \times 2 + 1 = 63$
$63 \times 2 + 1 = 127$
$127 \times 2 + 1 = 255$

18. (*d*) From the analysis of given input and various steps of rearrangement, it is evident that alternately one number and one word are arranged. The numbers get arranged in descending order and the words get arranged as per dictionory.

Input	how	was	your	stay
	56	25	36	64
***Step* I**	64	how	was	your
	stay	56	25	36
***Step* II**	64	how	56	was
	your	stay	25	36
***Step* III**	64	how	56	stay
	was	your	25	36
***Step* IV**	64	how	56	stay
	36	was	your	25
***Step* V**	64	how	56	stay
	36	was	25	your

Step V is the last step.

19. (*c*)

Input	power	fail	now	52
	24	75	gate	34
***Step* I**	75	power	fail	now
	52	24	gate	34
***Step* II**	75	fail	power	now
	52	24	gate	34
***Step* III**	75	fail	52	power
	now	24	gate	34
***Step* IV**	75	fail	52	gate
	power	now	24	34
***Step* V**	75	fail	52	gate
	34	power	now	24
***Step* VI**	75	fail	52	gate
	34	now	power	24
***Step* VII**	75	fail	52	gate
	34	now	24	power

20. (*d*) From the given step it is not possible to determine the input.

21. (*b*) Figure given in option (b) can be formed by joining the pieces given in the question figure.

22. (*d*) Following family diagram can be drawn from the given information

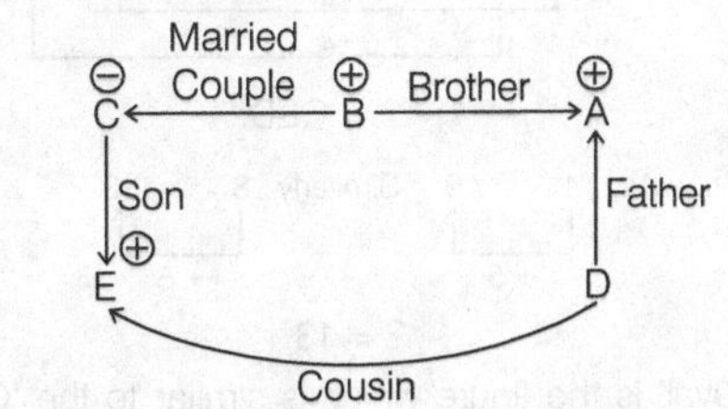

Now, it is clear that E is the cousin of D.

23. (c) In the given question figures, the star is moving one step in clockwise direction, shaded triangle shifts one step in clockwise direction and one circle is added in each subsequent figure.

24. (*b*) With M, J is necessary i.e. (a) is not possible. Either N or O is selected. Hence, (c) is not possible. With N, H is necessary. Hence, (d) is not possible. Only option (b) complies with all the conditions.

25. (c) With R, K is necessary. Hence (a), (b) and (d) are not possible.

26. (*b*) O cannot be with N. Hence, (b) is not possible.

27. (*c*) Option (c) will complete the given pattern.

28. (*c*) Both A and R are true.

29. (*d*) ip/ i g/up/og/ip/ig/up/og/ i p /ig ⇒ giupi

30. (*d*)

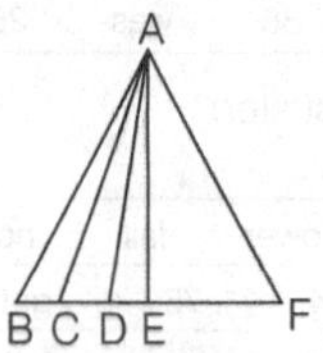

Smallest triangles = ΔABC, ΔACD, ΔADE = 3

Triangles formed with two triangles
= ΔABD, ΔACE, ΔADF = 3

Triangles formed with three triangle
= ΔABE, ΔACF = 2

Largest triangles = ΔAEF, ΔABF = 2

∴ Total triangles = 3 + 3 + 2 + 2 = 10

31. (*a*) According to the questions, we have

$3 \div 5 \Rightarrow 3 \times 5 = 1\boxed{5}$

$4 \div 7 \Rightarrow 4 \times 7 = 2\boxed{8}$

$8 \div 7 \Rightarrow 8 \times 7 = 5\boxed{6}$

Similarly, $9 \div 6 \Rightarrow 9 \times 6 = 5\boxed{4}$

32. (*a*) As, H(8) C(3) M(13) ⟶ F(6) A(1) K(11)

H → F: −2, C → A: −2, M → K: −2

Similarly, S(19) G(7) D(4) ⟶ Q(17) E(5) B(2)

S → Q: −2, G → E: −2, D → B: −2

∴ ? = QEB

33. (*b*) As, As, 4 : 9 (+5) Similarly, 8 : 13 (+5)

∴ ? = 13

34. (*b*) 'Oval' is the figure which is similar to the 'Circle'. Likewise 'Rectangle' is the figure which is similar to 'Square', as both of them have four corners.

35. (*d*) Clearly, figure II is mirror image of figure I.

36. (*c*) Let the age of son be x yr.

Then, age of father = $2x$ yr

Now, age of son 20 yr ago = $(x - 20)$ yr

Age of father 20 yr ago = $(2x - 20)$ yr

Now, $(2x - 20) = 12(x - 20)$

$\Rightarrow 2x - 20 = 12x - 240$

$\Rightarrow 10x = 220$

$\Rightarrow x = 22$ yr

Hence, the age of son = 22 yr

37. (*d*) According to the question, the direction diagram is as follows

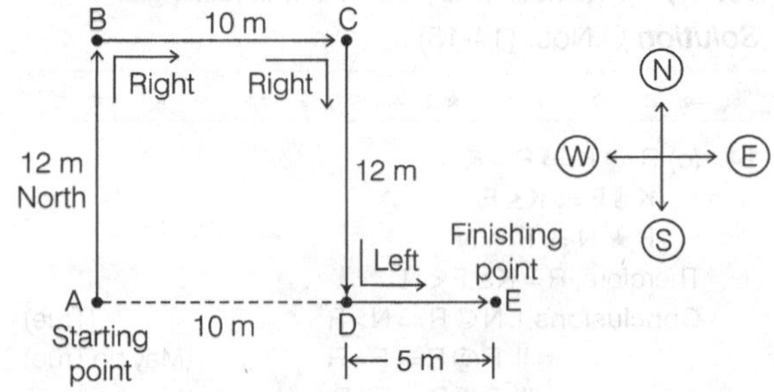

AB = CD = 12 m

BC = AD = 10 m

DE = 5m

∴ Required distance, AE = AD + DE = 10 + 5 = 15 m

Hence, at finishing point E, Raju is 15 m East form starting point A.

38. (*d*) Total number of ways in which the committee can be formed

$= 5 \times 3 = 15$

But Ms A refuses to be a member of the committee in which Mr. B is taken as a member.

Therefore, the required anwer

$= 15 - 1 = 14$

39. (*b*) Common dots in positions I and II

= 4 and 5

∴ Face opposite to the face having 3 dots

= Face having 2 dots

40. (*d*) Here, R = 97, 89, 75, (68), 56

O = 44, (33), 21, 12, 00

S = 98, 86, 77, (65), 59

T = 99, 85, 76, 67, (58)

∴ ROST = 68, 33, 65, 58.

41. (*b*) The product of the first three numbers in each column is equal to the lowermost number.

1st column $9 \times 12 \times 13 = 1404$

2nd column $3 \times 2 \times 5 = 30$

3rd column $7 \times 9 \times ? = 504$

$$\therefore \quad ? = \frac{504}{7 \times 9} = 8$$

42. (*c*) The meaningful order would be
(iv) Jungle
↓
(iii) Timber
↓
(ii) Pulp
↓
(v) Paper
↓
(i) Book

43. (*a*)

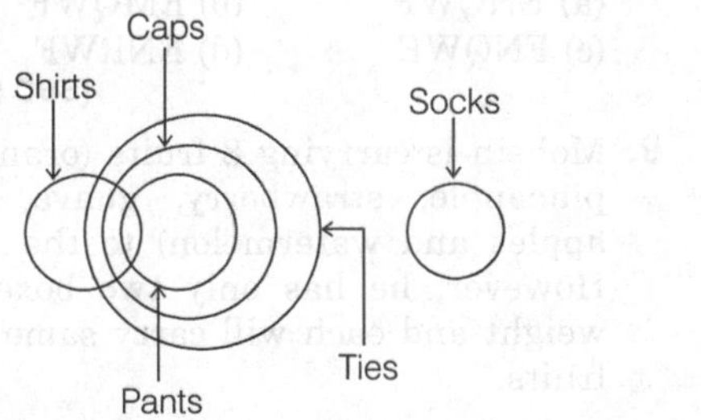

Conclusions I. No cap is socks. (✔)
II. Some pants are shirts. (✔)
III. All caps are pants. (✗)

Clearly, I and II follow.

44. (*c*)

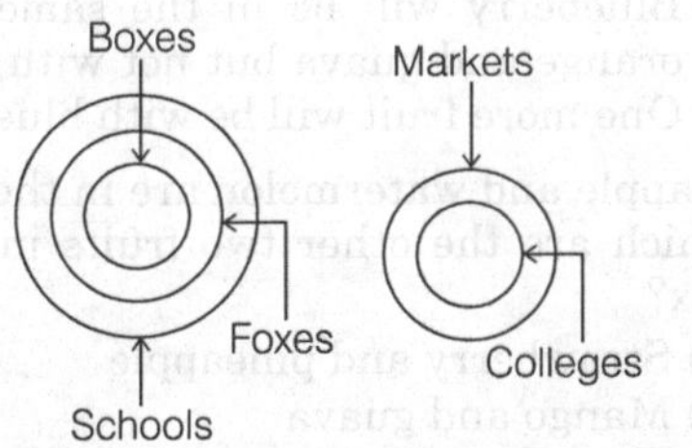

Conclusions I. No fox is college. (✔)
II. No college is school. (✔)
III. No box is fox. (✗)

Clearly, I and II follow.

45. (*e*)

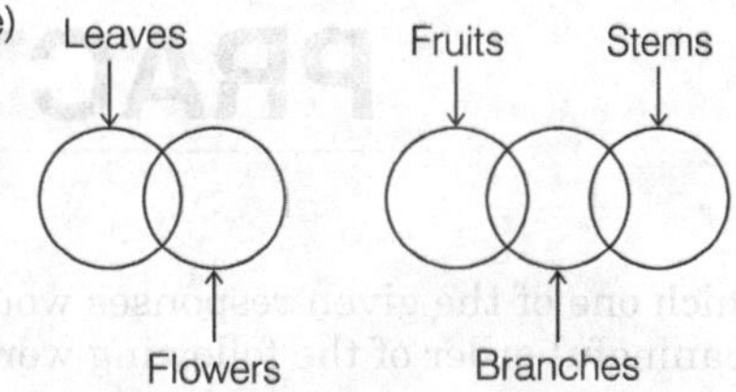

Conclusions I. Some leaves are stones. (✗)
II. All leaves are either stems or fruits. (✗)
III. All stems are either branches or fruits. (✗)
∴ None follows.

46. (*b*) Answer figure (b) is correct mirror image.

47. (*a*) Courses of action I and II would be too harsh; II is absurd. Efforts should be made to supervise the quality of the food prepared by the canteen.

48. (*d*) All the courses of action provide the feasible and effective steps for the problem discussed in the statement. Hence, all the courses of action are correct.

49. (*a*) I. use the [rope] ⊖ nik [ta] re ...(i)
II. [rope] is straight ⊖ pe [da] ta ...(ii)
III. always use [rope] ⊖ ma re [ta] ...(iii)

Hence, the data given in both statements I and II or II and III together are sufficient to answer the question.

50. (*e*) From Statement I,

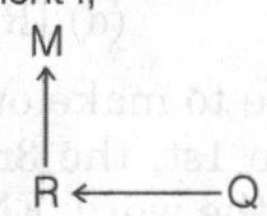

From Statement II,

From Statements I and II, we get

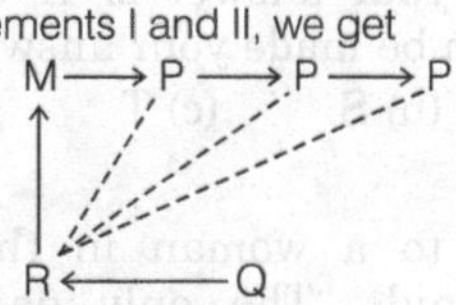

Hence, question cannot be answered.

PRACTICE SET 26

1. Which one of the given responses would be a meaningful order of the following words ?

(i) Honey (ii) Flower
(iii) Bee (iv) Wax

(a) (ii), (i), (iv), (iii) (b) (ii), (iii), (i), (iv)
(c) (iv), (iii), (ii), (i) (d) (i), (iii), (iv), (ii)

Direction (Q. Nos. 2-3) *In the following questions, find the odd word/letters from the given alternatives.*

2. (a) M K H B D (b) G F K H C
(c) B D F A T (d) X V R P I

[SSC (10+2) 2014]

3. (a) Bus (b) Scooter
(c) Cycle (d) Boat **[SSC (CGL) 2011]**

4. From the given alternatives, select the word which cannot be formed using the letters of the given word 'IRREGULARITRIES'

(a) REGULAR (b) TIRED
(c) TRAILER (d) IRRIGATE

5. If it is possible to make only one meaningful word from the 1st, the 3rd, the 5th and the 8th letters of the word 'ENTERPRISE' using each letter only once, 1st letter of the word is your answer. If more than one such word can be made your answer is 'X' and if no such words can be made your answer is 'Y'.

(a) P (b) S (c) T (d) X
(e) Y

6. Pointing to a woman in the photograph, Rajesh said, "The only daughter of her grandfather is my wife". How is Rajesh related to that woman ?

(a) Uncle (b) Father
(c) Maternal Uncle (d) Brother

7. A man leaves for his office from his house. He walks towards South. After walking a distance of 300 m, he turns towards West and walks 200 m. Then, he walks 100 m towards North and further 100 m towards West. He then turns towards North and walks 200 m. What is the straight distance in metres between his initial and final positions ?

[FCI Assistant Grade III 2015]

(a) 300 m (b) 200 m
(c) 250 m (d) 400 m

8. In a certain code RAIN is written as 'TCKP'. How is CLOUD written in that code ?

(a) ENQWF (b) EMQWF
(c) FNQWE (d) ENRWF

[SSC (Steno) 2011]

9. Mohsin is carrying 8 fruits (orange, mango, pineapple, strawberry, guava, blueberry, apples and watermelon) to the farmhouse. However, he has only two boxes of equal weight and each will carry same number of fruits. **[CMAT 2015]**

Therefore, he has to ensure

I. Orange and pineapple will be together, but not with watermelon.
II. Mango and strawberry cannot be with pineapple.
III. Blueberry will be in the same box with orange and guava but not with the apple. One more fruit will be with blueberry.

If apple and watermelon are in the same box which are the other two fruits in the same box?

(a) Strawberry and pineapple
(b) Mango and guava
(c) Mango and strawberry
(d) Indeterminant

10. In a survey, 70% of those surveyed owned a car and 75% of those surveyed owned a TV. If 55% owned both a car and a TV, then what percent of those surveyed did not own either a car or a TV?

(a) 25% (b) 20%
(c) 10% (d) 5%

Direction (Q. Nos. 11-12) *Select the related words/number pair from the given alternatives.*

11. 20 : 11 : : 102 : ?

(a) 49 (b) 52 (c) 61 (d) 98

12. Cinema : Audience : : Church : ?

(a) Prayer (b) Meditation
(c) Loneliness (d) Congregation

Direction (Q. Nos. 13-15) *Read the following information to answer the given questions.*

Five frinds A, B, C, D and E are sitting on a beanch and wearing different colours shirt, i.e. blue, red, yellow, white and green (not necessarily in this order).

I. A is sitting next to B and wearing red shirt.
II. C is sitting next to D and not wearing either blue or green shirt.
III. D is not sitting with E and E is wearing blue shirt.
IV. E is on the left end of the bench.
V. C is on the second position from the right.
VI. A is on the right of B and E.
VII. B is wearing green shirt.
VIII. A and C sitting together.
IX. D is not wearing white shirt.

13. Where is A sitting ?
(a) Between B and D (b) Between D and C
(c) Between E and D (d) Between B and C

14. What is the colour of C's shirt?
(a) Blue (b) Red (c) White (d) Yellow

15. Who is sitting in the centre?
(a) A (b) B (c) C (d) D

Direction (Q. Nos. 16-17) *Study the following information carefully and answer the given questions.*

A word and number arrangement machine when given an input line of words and numbers rearranges them following a particular rule in each step. The following is an illustration of input and rearrangement.

Input joy far 35 27 16 96 height star
***Step* I** 96 joy far 35 27 16 height star
***Step* II** 96 far joy 35 27 16 height star
***Step* III** 96 far 35 joy 27 16 height star
***Step* IV** 96 far 35 height joy 27 16 star
***Step* V** 96 far 35 height 27 joy 16 star

and Step V is the last step of the rearrangement.

As per the rules followed in the above steps, find out in each of the following questions the appropriate step for the given input.

16. Input organise 19 12 stable room 35 72 house
How many steps will be required to complete the arrangement ?
(a) Five (b) Six (c) Seven (d) Four
(e) None of these

17. Input bake never store 51 26 33 age 49
Which of the following will be Step V ?
(a) 51 age 49 bake 33 never 26 store
(b) 51 age 49 bake never store 26 33
(c) 51 age bake never store 26 33 49
(d) 51 bake never store 26 33 age 49
(e) There will be no such Step

18. In a row of boys, if A who is 10th from the left and B whose is 9th from the right interchange their positions, A becomes 15th from left. How many boys are there in the row?
(a) 23 (b) 27 (c) 28 (d) 31

19. Choose the correct alternatives from the given ones that will complete the series.
3.5, 7, 10.5, 14, ? **[SSC Multitasking 2013]**
(a) 15.5 (b) 16.5
(c) 18.5 (d) 17.5

20. Which of the following figures are similar?

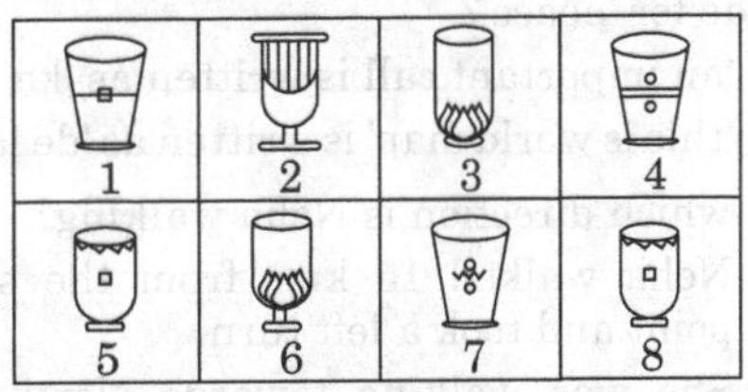

(a) 1-5 (b) 3-6
(c) 5-8 (d) 4-7

21. One evening before sunset, two friends Raman and Arjun were talking to each other face to face. If Raman's shadow was exactly to his left side, then which direction was Arjun facing ? **[SSC (Steno) 2013]**
(a) West (b) East (c) North (d) South

22. Which one set of letters when sequentially placed at the gaps in the given letters series shall complete it ?
a_bc_c_abb_bca_
(a) abbba (b) accba
(c) cccbc (d) cbbac

23. If 'a' means '+', 'b' means '×', 'c' means '÷' and 'd' means '–', then 20a 10b 45c 5d 12 = ? **[SSC (10+2) 2015]**
(a) 68 (b) 88 (c) 74 (d) 98

Direction (Q. Nos. 24-25) *Each of the questions below consists of a question and two statements numbered I and II given below it. You have to decide whether the data provided in the statements are sufficient to answer the question.*

Given answer

(a) if the data in Statement I alone are sufficient to answer the question, while the data in Statement II alone are not sufficient to answer the question.

(b) if the data in Statement II alone are sufficient to answer the question, while data in Statement I alone are not sufficient to answer the question.

(c) if the data in Statement I alone or in the Statement II alone are sufficient to answer the question.

(d) if the data in both the Statements I and II are not sufficient to answer the question.

(e) if the data in the Statements I and II together are necessary to answer the question.

24. If 'world peace is important' is written as 'ni pe la so' in a code language, then what is the code for 'peace'?

I. 'an important call is written as 'ka so ba'.

II. 'this is world map' is written as 'de la ni ru'.

25. In which direction is Neha walking?

I. Neha walked 15 kms from the starting point and took a left turn.

II. She was walking towards North before taking a left turn.

26. A word is represented by only one set of numbers as given in anyone of the alternatives. The set of numbers given in the alternatives are represented by two classes of alphabets as in two matrices given below. The columns and rows of Matrix I are numbered from 0 to 4 and that of Matrix II are numbered from 5 to 9. A letter from these matrices can be represented first by its row and next by its column, e.g. 'A' can be represented by 55, 67, 86 etc., and R can be represented by 04, 23, 30 etc. Identify the set for the word 'DOOR'.

Matrix I

	0	1	2	3	4
0	F	O	M	S	R
1	S	R	F	O	M
2	O	M	S	R	F
3	R	F	O	M	S
4	M	S	R	F	O

Matrix II

	5	6	7	8	9
5	A	T	D	I	P
6	I	P	A	T	D
7	T	D	I	P	A
8	P	A	T	D	I
9	D	I	P	A	T

(a) 69, 44, 20, 43 (b) 76, 01, 44, 24
(c) 95, 20, 44, 12 (d) 57, 13, 32, 23

27. Little wooden cubes each with a side of one inch are put together to form a solid cube with a side of three inches. This big cube is then painted red all over on the outside. When the big cube is broken up into the original little ones, how many cubes will have paint on two sides?

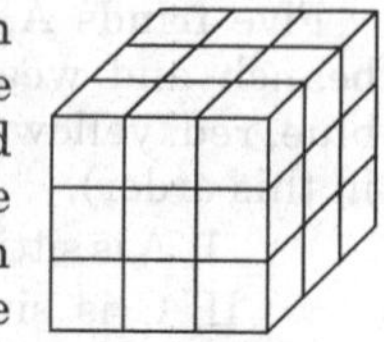

(a) 4 (b) 8 (c) 12 (d) 0

Direction (Q. Nos. 28-30) *Study the following information carefully and answer the given questions.*

Eight friends Q, R, S, T, U, V, W and X are sitting around a square table in such a way that four of them sit at four corners of the square while four sit in the middle of each of the four sides. The ones those who sit in the middle of the sides face the centre while those who sit at the four corners face outside (i.e. opposite to the centre). R sits to immediate left of T.

T sits at one of the corners of the table. Only two people sit between R and W. X sits second to right of S. S faces the same direction as W (i.e. if W faces the centre, then S also faces the centre and *vice-versa*). U is neither an immediate neighbour of X nor T. V is not an immediate neighbour of W.

[IBPS RRB (Office Assistant) 2015]

28. Four of the following five are alike in a certain way and so form a group. Which is the one that does not belong to that group?

(a) X (b) Q (c) V (d) R
(e) U

29. Who sit exactly between R and W when counted from the left of W?

(a) Q, T (b) S, V
(c) S, U (d) V, X
(e) U, X

30. Who sits second to the right of U?

(a) X (b) R (c) W (d) T
(e) Q

31. A clock is started at 6 O'clock in the morning. Through how many degrees will the hour hand rotate when the clock shows 11 O'clock in the morning?

(a) 140° (b) 180°
(c) 150° (d) 160°

32. In a certain code, 'DOWN' is written as '5@9#' and 'NAME' is written as '#6%3'. How would 'MODE' be written in that code ?

(a) % 653 (b) %@63

(c) %5@3 (d) %@53

(e) None of these

33. At present, the ratio between the ages of Arun and Deepak is 4 : 3. After 6 yr, Arun's age will be 26 yr. What is the age of Deepak at present?

(a) 12 yr (b) 15 yr (c) $19\frac{1}{2}$ yr (d) 25 yr

34. Sushma has a dentist appointment at 7 : 20 in the evening. While entering the dentist's office, she saw reflection of the wall clock. The hands of clock read 4 : 40. She knew that this being the reflection of the clock, the time she read is not the correct time. She is not on appointed time. **[UPPSC (RO) 2014]**

(a) She is 20 min late

(b) She is 20 min before time

(c) She is on time

(d) None of the above

Direction (Q. Nos. 35-37) *In each of the questions below are given four statements followed by four conclusions numbered* I, II, III *and* IV. *You have to take the given statements to be true even if they seem to be at variance with commonly known facts. Read all the conclusions and then decide which of the given conclusion (s) logically follow (s) from the given statements disregarding commonly known facts.*

35. Statements Some trains are cars.
All cars are branches.
All branches are nets.
Some nets are dresses.

Conclusions I. Some dresses are cars.
II. Some nets are trains.
III. Some branches are trains.
IV. Some dresses are trains.

(a) I and III follow (b) II and III follow

(c) I and IV follow (d) II, III and IV follow

(e) None of these

36. Statements Some pencils are kites.
Some kites are desks.
All desks are jungles.
All jungles are mountains.

Conclusions I. Some mountains are pencils.
II. Some jungles are pencils.
III. Some mountains are desks.
IV. Some jungles are kites.

(a) I and III follow (b) I, II and III follow

(c) III and IV follow (d) II, III and IV follow

(e) None of the above

37. Statements All papers are clips
Some clips are boards.
Some boards are lanes.
All lanes are roads.

Conclusions I. Some roads are boards
II. Some lanes are clips.
III. Some boards are papers.
IV. Some roads are clips.

(a) I and II follow

(b) I and III follow

(c) I, II and III follow

(d) II, III and IV follow

(e) None of the above

38. Consider the statement and the following conclusions. Decide which of the conclusions follows from the statement. **[MAT 2014]**

Statement Many engineering and medical graduates are taking up jobs in administrative services and banks and thus wasting the application of knowledge earned during these courses.

Conclusions

I. All the professionals should be advised to refrain from taking up such jobs.

II. The government should appoint a committee to find out the reasons for these professionals taking up such jobs and to suggest the remedial measures.

(a) if Conclusion I follows

(b) if Conclusion II follows

(c) if neither Conclusion I nor II follows

(d) if both Conclusions I and II follow

39. How many straight lines are there in the following figure ?

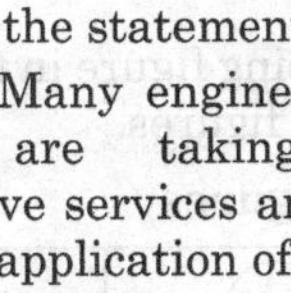

(a) 5 (b) 10 (c) 9 (d) 8

40. In which answer figure is the question figure embedded ?

Question Figure

Answer Figures

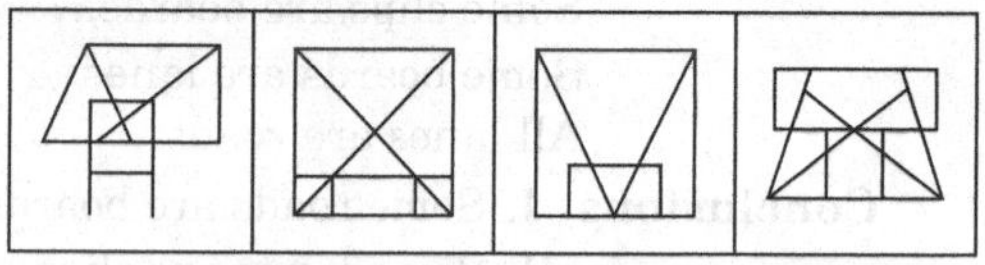

(a) (b) (c) (d)

41. Identify the diagram that best represents the relationship among the classes given below

Soda water, Mineral water, Liquid. **[SSC CGL (Pre) 2015]**

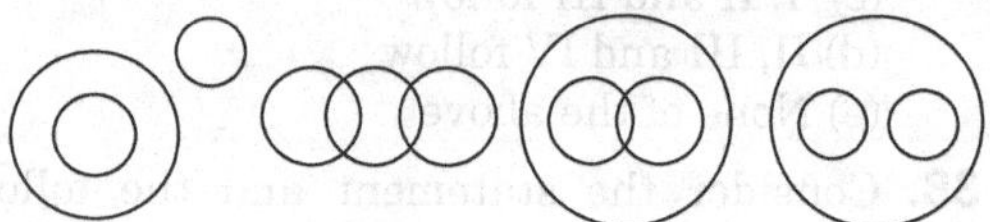

(a) (b) (c) (d)

42. Find the missing figure in the series from the given answer figures.

Question Figures

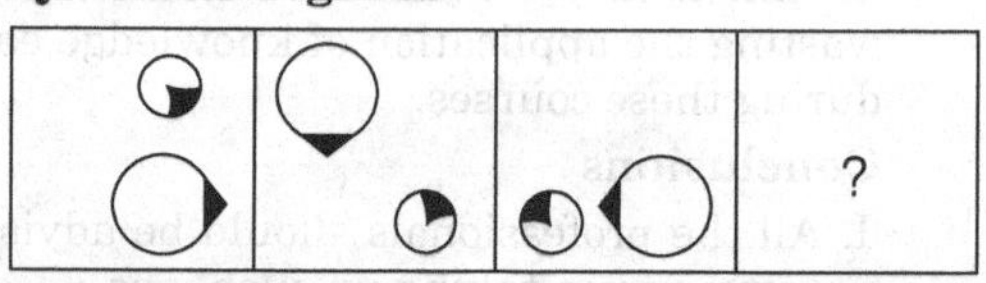

1 2 3 4

Answer Figures

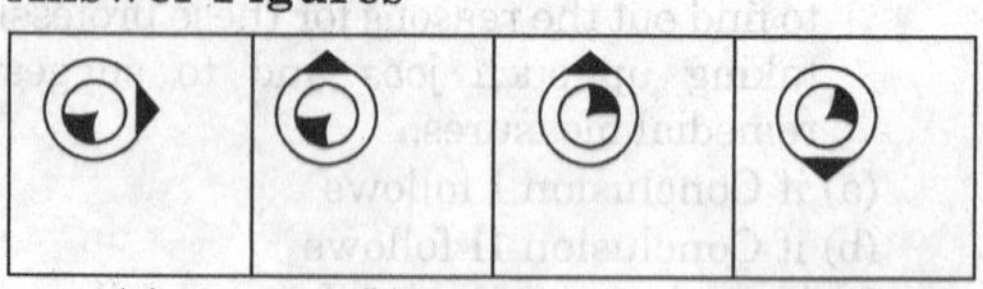

(a) (b) (c) (d)

43. Select the missing number from the given responses.

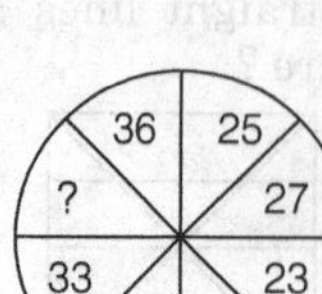

(a) 35 (b) 32 (c) 22 (d) 19

44. Find out which of the answer figures (a), (b), (c) and (d) completes the figure matrix?

Question Figure

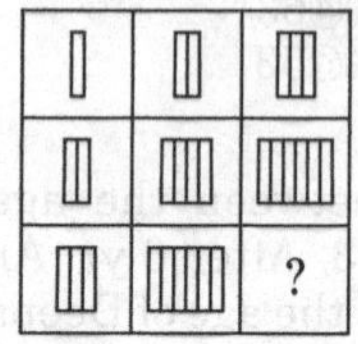

Answer Figures

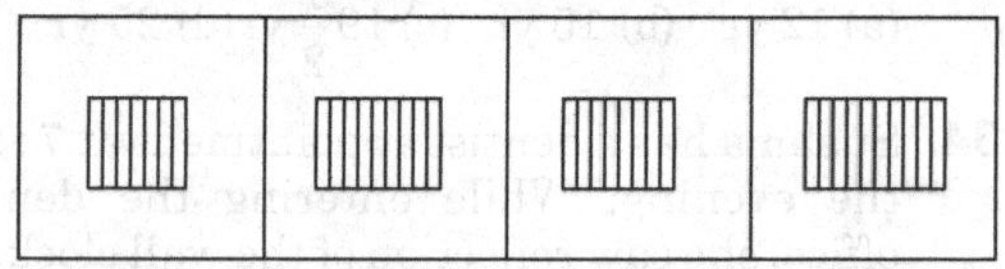

(a) (b) (c) (d)

45. Choose the right water image of the question figure from the given answer figures.

Question Figure

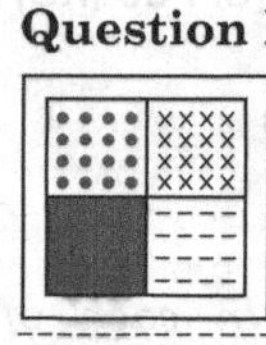

Answer Figures

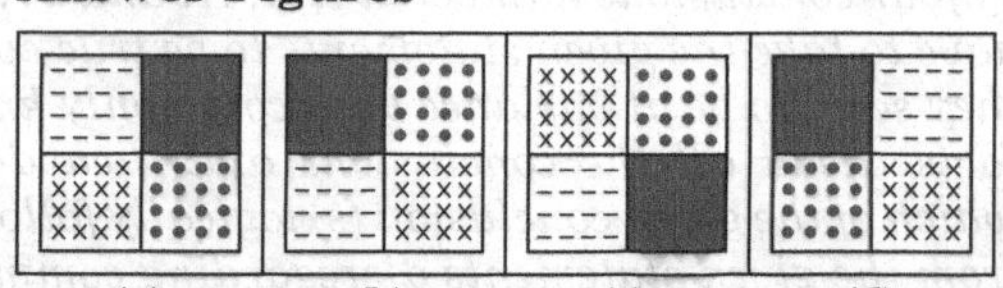

(a) (b) (c) (d)

46. Radha, Sheela, Mahima and Seeta are sitting along a rectangular table. Radha is to the right of Sheela. Mahima is to the left of Seeta. Which of the persons given in the options are sitting opposite to each other?

(a) Sheela-Seeta (b) Radha-Seeta

(c) Radha-Sheela (d) Mahima-Radha

47. In making decisions about important questions, it is desirable to distinguish between a 'strong' argument and a 'weak' argument. A 'strong' argument must be both important and directly related to the question. A 'weak' argument may not be directly related to the question and may be of minor importance or may be related to the trivial aspect of the question. Each question below is followed by two arguments numbered I and II. You have to decide which of the arguments is 'strong' and which is 'weak'.

Statement Should the practice of rewarding high scores be stopped to handle frustration among the moderate scorers ?

Arguments

I. No, it is necessary to motivate the high scorers and reward is one of the best ways of motivating.

II. Yes, too much appreciation for high scores affects the moderate students adversely at times leading to extreme situations.

(a) if only Argument I is strong
(b) if only Argument II is strong
(c) if either I or II is strong
(d) if neither I nor II is strong
(e) if both I and II are strong

Direction (Q. Nos. 48-50) *In the following questions, the symbols, ©, %, $ and @ are used with the following meaning illustrated below.*

'P © Q' means 'P is either smaller than or equal to Q'.

'P ★ Q' means 'P is either greater than or equal to Q'.

'P $ Q' means 'P is greater than Q'.

'P % Q' means 'P is smaller than to Q'.

'P @ Q' means 'P is equal to Q'.

Now, in each of the following questions, assuming the given statements to be true, find which of the two Conclusions I and II given below them is/are definitely true ?

Give answer

(a) if only Conclusion I is true
(b) if only Conclusion II is true
(c) if either Conclusion I or II is true
(d) if neither Conclusion I nor II is true
(e) if both Conclusions I and II are true

48. Statements M % T, T $ K, K © D
Conclusions I. T $ D
II. D $ M

49. Statements F@ B, B % N, N $ H
Conclusions I. N $ F
II. H $ F

50. Statements R ★ M, M @ K, K © J
Conclusions I. J $ M
II. J @ M

Hints and Solutions

1. (*b*) Meaningful order of words
(ii) Flower, → (iii) Bee, → (i) Honey, → (iv) Wax

2. (*d*) Except XVRPI, in all other terms letters are increasing and decreasing but in XVRPI letters are decreasing only.

3. (*d*) Except Boat, all others are road vehicles.

4. (*b*) Word 'TIRED' cannot be formed by using the letters of the given word because letter 'D' is not present in the given word.

5. (*d*) As,

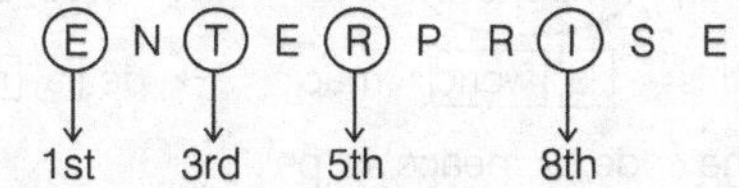

Meaningful words = TIRE, TIER, RITE

6. (*b*)

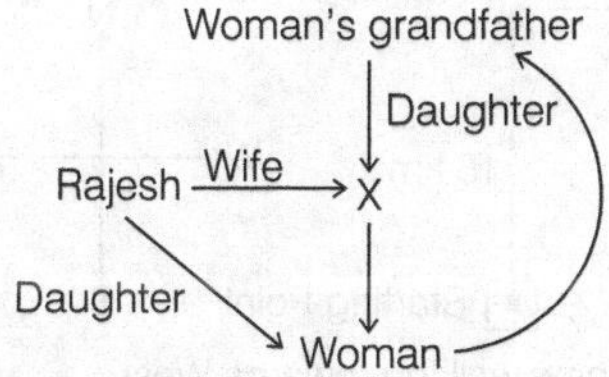

So, Rajesh is father of that woman.

7. (*a*) The walking diagram of a man is as shown below.

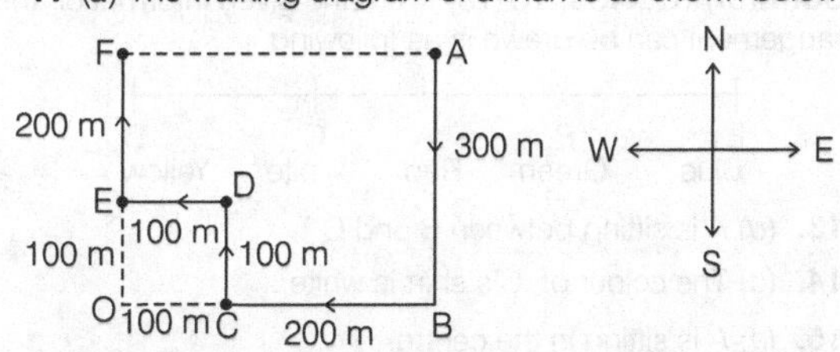

Let A is the starting point of man and F is the ending point of man.

Here, AB = 300 m, BC = 200 m, CD = ED = 100 m
EF = 200 m, EO = OC = 100 m

Now, straight distance between initial and final position
= AF = BO = BC + OC
= 200 + 100 = 300 m

8. (*a*) According to the given coding data

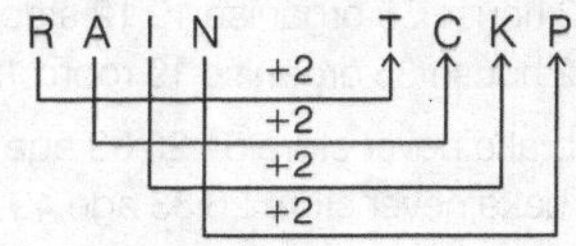

Similarly, we can write

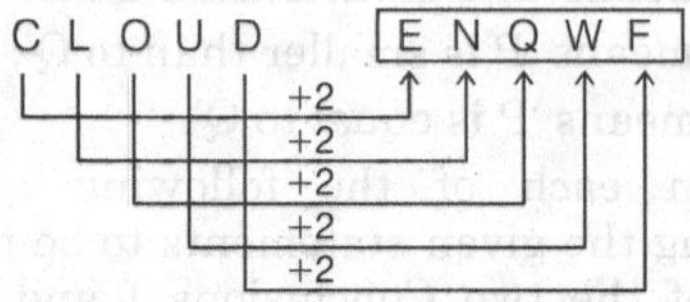

9. (*d*)

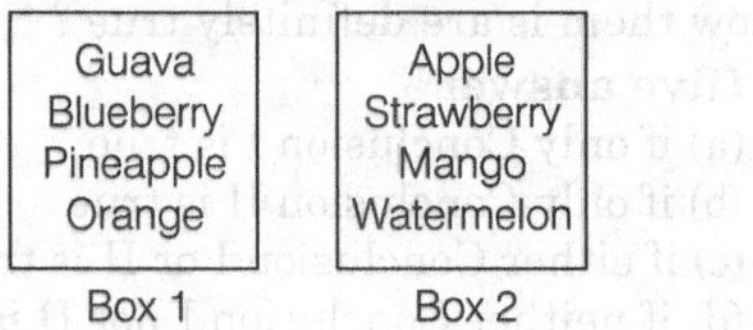

∴ Mango and strawberry are in the same box.

10. (*c*)

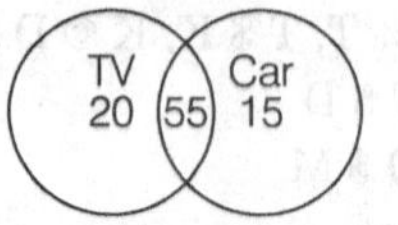

Percent of those surveyed who did not own either a car or a TV

= 100 − (20 + 55 + 15)
= 100 − 90 = 10%

11. (*b*) As, 20 → 11 (÷2 +1) Similarly, 102 → 52 (÷2 +1)

∴ ? = 52

12. (*d*) As, Audience gathers to see Cinema. In the same way, 'Congregation' prays in Church.

Solution (Q. Nos. 13-15) From the given information the arrangement can be drawn is as following

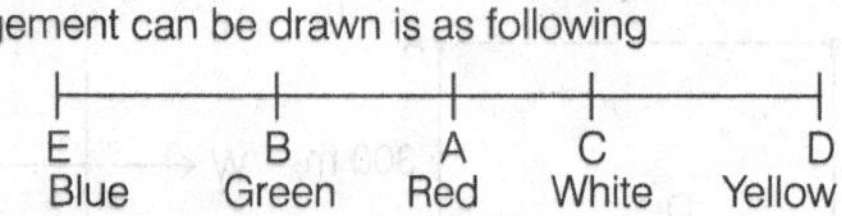

13. (*d*) A is sitting between B and C.

14. (*c*) The colour of C's shirt is white.

15. (*a*) A is sitting in the centre.

Solution (Q. Nos. 16-17) After careful analysis of the input and various steps of rearrangement it is evident that in each step one number or word is rearranged. The numbers are rearranged in descending order while the words are rearranged according to dictionary.

16. (*d*) **Input** organise 19 12 stable room 35 72 house
***Step* I** 72 organise 19 12 stable room 35 house
***Step* II** 72 house organise 19 12 stable room 35
***Step* III** 72 house 35 organise 19 12 stable room
***Step* IV** 72 house 35 organise 19 room 12 stable

17. (a) **Input** brake never store 51 26 33 age 49
***Step* I** 51 bake never store 26 33 age 49
***Step* II** 51 age bake never store 26 33 49
***Step* III** 51 age 49 bake never store 26 33
***Step* IV** 51 age 49 bake 33 never store 26
***Step* V** 51 age 49 bake 33 never 26 store

18. (*a*) Clearly, B is 9th from the right end and 15th from the left end.
∴ Total numbers of boys in the row = 9 + 15 − 1 = 23

19. (*d*) The pattern is as follow

3.5 → 7 → 10.5 → 14 → (17.5)
(+3.5, +3.5, +3.5, +3.5)

? = 17.5

20. (*c*) Clearly, figures 5 and 8 are similar. So, correct option is (c).

21. (c) According to the question,

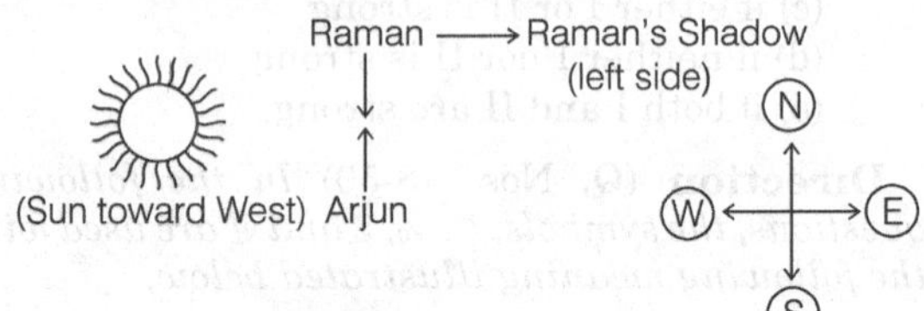

So, Arjun was facing North.

22. (*b*) The series is as follows aabcc/ccabb/bbcaa
∴ Required answer = accba

23. (*d*) Given that, 20a10b45c5d12 = ?
After putting given sign, we get
⇒ 20 + 10 × 45 ÷ 5 − 12 = ?
⇒ 20 + 10 × 9 − 12 = ?
⇒ 20 + 90 − 12 = ?
⇒ 110 − 12 = ?
⇒ 98 = ?
So, 98 is correct answer.

24. (*e*) From both the statements.

world peace is (important) → ni pe la (so)
an (important) call → ka (so) ba
this is world map → de la ni ru

The code for 'peace' is 'pe'.

25. (*b*) From statement II

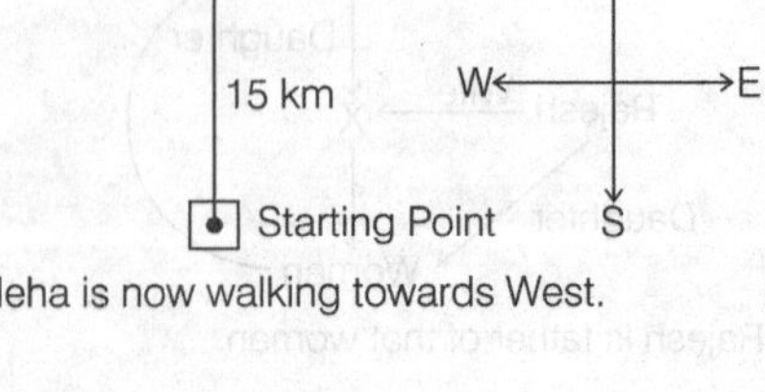

Neha is now walking towards West.

26. (*d*) According to the matrices,
D – (57), 69, 76, 88, 95
O – 01, (13), 20, (32), 44
R – 04, 11, (23), 30, 42
DOOR ⇒ 57, 13, 32, 23

27. (*c*) A smaller cube with two sides painted is present on each of the 12 edges of the cube.
Therefore, total number of cubes having paint on two sides = 12

Solution (Q. Nos. 28-30) According to the information, the seating arrangement around a square table is as follows:

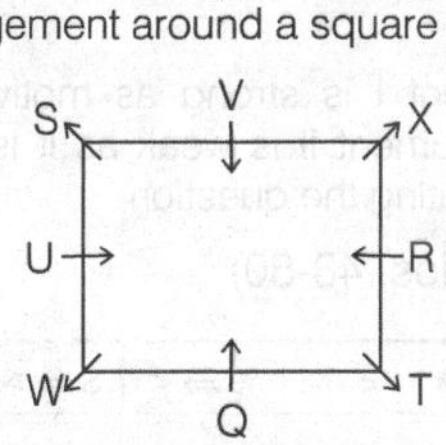

28. (*a*) Except X, all others are facing the centre.

29. (*a*) Q and T sit exactly between R and W when counted from the left of W.

30. (*e*) Q sits second to the right of U.

31. (*c*) Angle traced by hour hand in 12 h = 360°
Angle traced by hour hand in 5 h = $\left(\frac{360}{12} \times 5\right)^\circ = 150^\circ$

32. (*d*) As,
D ⟶ 5 and N ⟶ #
O ⟶ @ A ⟶ 6
W ⟶ 9 M ⟶ %
N ⟶ # E ⟶ 3

Similarly,
M ⟶ %
O ⟶ @
D ⟶ 5
E ⟶ 3

MODE ⇒ % @ 5 3

33. (*b*) Let the present ages of Arun and Deepak be $4x$ yr and $3x$ yr, respectively.
Then, $4x + 6 = 26$
⇒ $4x = 20$
∴ $x = 5$
Hence, Deepak's present age = $3x = 3 \times 5 = 15$ yr

34. (*c*) What Sushma could see is the mirror image of clock and time seen is 4 : 40. It will resemble to time 7 : 20 hence, Sushma is on time.

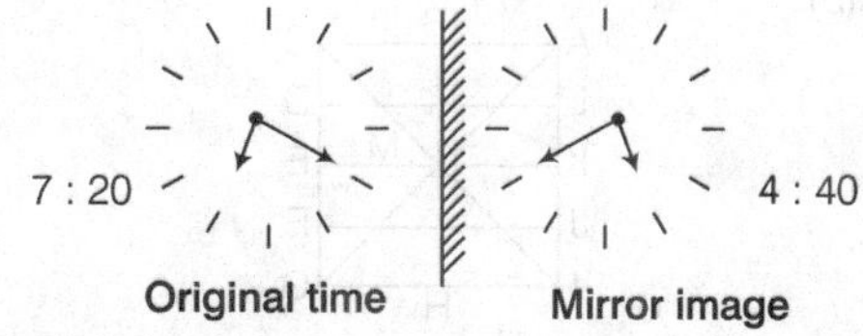

Solution (Q. Nos. 35-37)

35. (*b*)

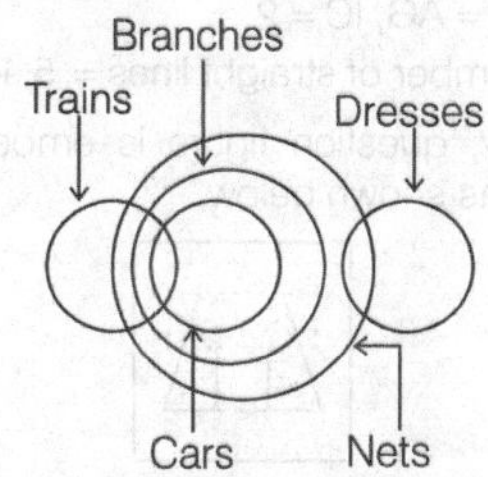

Conclusions I. Some dresses are cars. (✗)
II. Some nets are trains. (✓)
III. Some branches are trains. (✓)
IV. Some dresses are trains. (✗)

So, II and III follow.

36. (*c*)

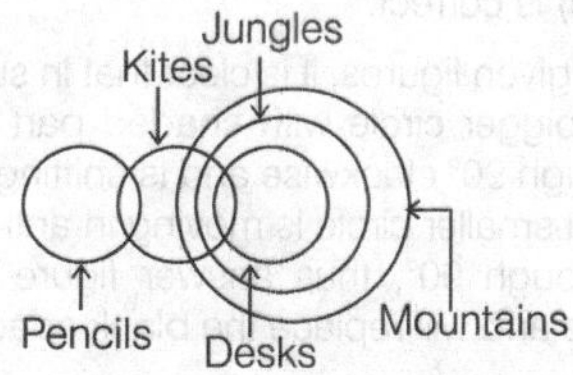

Conclusions I. Some mountains are pencils. (✗)
II. Some jungles are pencils. (✗)
III. Some mountains are desks. (✓)
IV. Some jungles are kites. (✓)

So, III and IV follow.

37. (*e*)

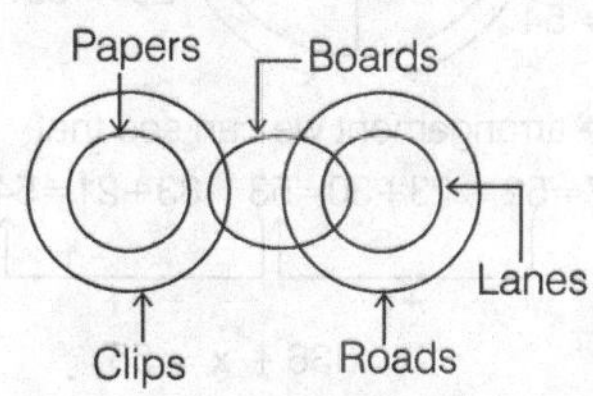

Conclusions I. Some roads are boards. (✓)
II. Some lanes are clips. (✗)
III. Some boards are papers (✗)
IV. Some roads are clips. (✗)

So, only Conclusion I follows.

38. (*b*) I. It is not possible to convince people not to take up such jobs.
II. This will help to find out the exact reason for such attitude of graduates.

39. (*b*)

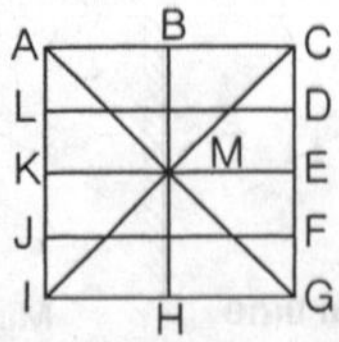

Horizontal lines = AC, LD, KE, JF, IG = 5
Vertical lines = AI, BH, CG = 3
Slant lines = AG, IC = 2
∴ Total number of straight lines = 5 + 3 + 2 = 10

40. (*d*) Clearly, question figure is embedded in answer figure (d) as shown below.

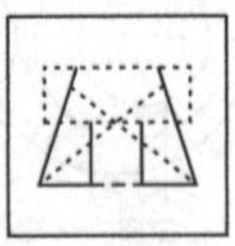

41. (*d*)

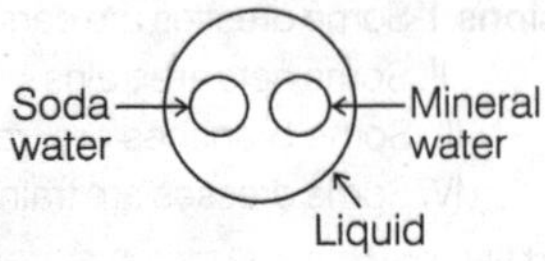

So, option (b) is correct.

42. (*b*) From the given figures, it is clear that in subsequent figures, the bigger circle with shaded part outside is moving through 90° clockwise and is shifting along the diagonal and smaller circle is moving in anti-clockwise direction through 90°, thus answer figure (b) is the correct figure and will replace the blank space.

43. (*d*)

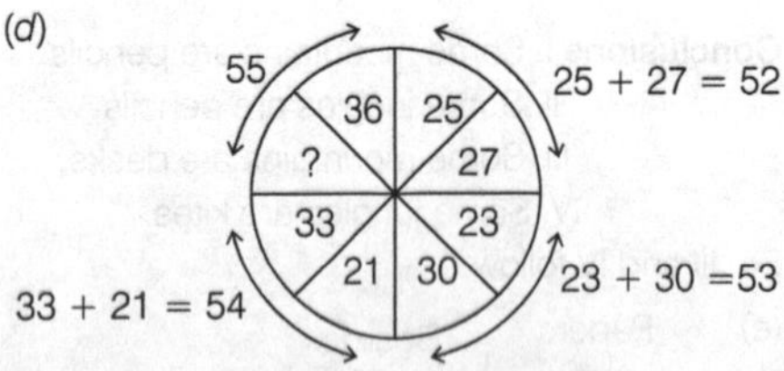

from above arrangement we can see that

25+27=52 23+30=53 33+21=54
+1 +1

Similarly, 36 + x = 55

⇒ x = 55 − 36 = 19

44. (*b*) The matrix is as follows

1	1+1=2	2+1=3
2	2+2=4	4+2=6
3	3+3=6	6+3=9

45. (*d*) The correct vertically inverted water image of the question figure is as follows

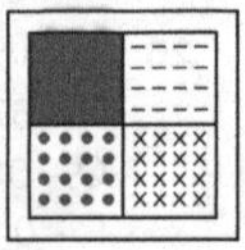

46. (*b*) Arrangement according to the question is as follows

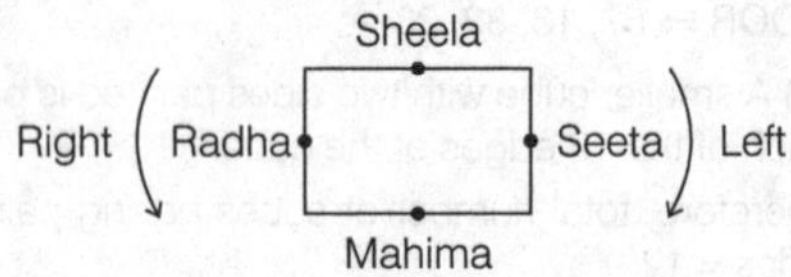

Clearly, Radha and Seeta are sitting opposite to each other.

47. (*a*) Argument I is strong as motivation is desirable action. Argument II is weak as it is superfluous. It is simply restating the question.

Solution (Q. Nos. 48-50)

© ⇒ ≤	★ ⇒ ≥	% ⇒ <	$ ⇒ >	@ ⇒ =

48. (*d*) According to the question,

M % T ⇒ M < T ...(i)
T $ K ⇒ T > K ...(ii)
K © D ⇒ K ≤ D ...(iii)

On combining the statements (i), (ii) and (iii), we get

M < T > K ≤ D

Conclusions I. T $ D ⇒ T > D (False)
II. D $ M ⇒ D > M (False)

So, it is clear that neither Conclusion I nor II is true.

49. (*a*) According to the question,

F @ B ⇒ F = B ...(i)
B % N ⇒ B < N ...(ii)
N $ H ⇒ N > H ...(iii)

On combining the statements (i), (ii) and (iii), we get

F = B < N > H

Conclusions I. N $ F ⇒ N > F (True)
II. H $ F ⇒ H > F (False)

So, it is clear that only Conclusion I is true.

50. (*c*) According to the question,

R ★ M ⇒ R ≥ M ...(i)
M @ K ⇒ M = K ...(ii)
K © J ⇒ K ≤ J ...(iii)

On combining the statements (i), (ii) and (iii), we get

R ≥ M = K ≤ J

Conclusions I. J $ M ⇒ J > M (may be true)
II. J @ M ⇒ J = M (may be true)

So, it is clear that either Conclusion I or II is true.

PRACTICE SET 27

1. If Q denotes addition; J denotes multiplication; T denotes subtraction and K denotes division, then **[BSSC CGL 2015]**

30 K 2Q 3J 6T5 = ?

(a) 18 (b) 28 (c) 31 (d) 6

Direction (Q. Nos. 2-3) *In the following questions, select the related words/letters from the given alternatives.*

2. Good : Bad : : Virtue : ?

(a) Blame (b) Sin
(c) Despair (d) Vice

3. BCFE : HILK : : NORQ : ?

(a) TXWU (b) TXUW
(c) TUXW (d) TVWX

Direction (Q. Nos. 4-6) *Study the following information carefully and answer the given questions.*

A word and number arrangement machine when given an input line of words and numbers rearranges them following a particular rule in each step. The following is an illustration of input and rearrangement.

Input cup for hot 34 69 72 tea 27
***Step* I** 27 cup for hot 34 69 72 tea
***Step* II** 27 tea cup for hot 34 69 72
***Step* III** 27 tea 34 cup for hot 69 72
***Step* IV** 27 tea 34 hot cup for 69 72
***Step* V** 27 tea 34 hot 69 cup for 72
***Step* VI** 27 tea 34 hot 69 for cup 72
***Step* VII** 27 tea 34 hot 69 for 72 cup

and Step VII is the last step of the rearrangement.

As per the rules followed in the above steps, find out in each of the following questions the appropriate step for the given input.

4. Input kind 12 96 heart water 59 42 yes

How many steps will be required to complete the rearrangement ?

(a) Three (b) Four
(c) Five (d) Six
(e) None of these

5. Input jungle 43 mode 25 basket 39 target 19

Which of the following steps will be the last but one ?

(a) VII (b) VIII (c) IX (d) VI
(e) None of these

6. Step III of an input is '12 world 31 ask cart ball 87 75'

Which of the following will definitely be the input ?

(a) 31 ask cart ball 87 75 world 12
(b) 31 ask cart ball 87 75 12 world
(c) 31 ask 12 world cart ball 87 75
(d) Cannot be determined
(e) None of the above

7. If in certain code, PATTERN is written as NRETTAP, then how MENTION can be written in that code ? **[SSC CISF 2011]**

(a) NOITMEN (b) NMOEINT
(c) NOITNEM (d) NOTIMEN

8. Find the number that replaces the question mark.

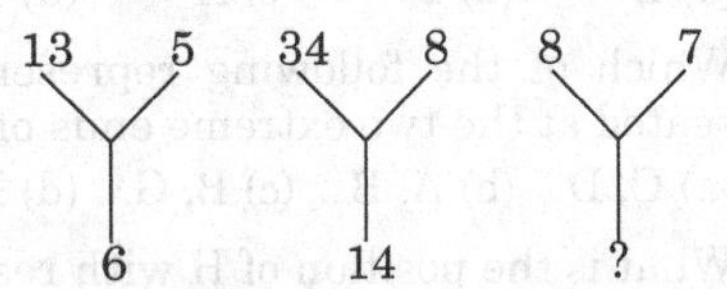

(a) 2 (b) 4 (c) 5 (d) 11

9. Among the four answer figures, which figure can be formed from the cut-pieces given below in the question figure ? **[SSC (10+2) 2014]**

Question Figure **Answer Figures**

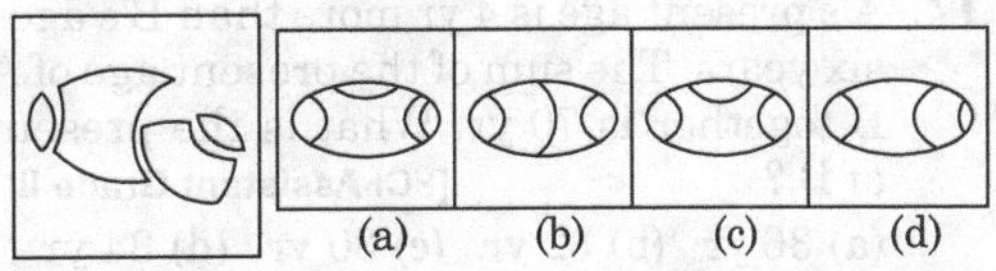

10. Which one set of letters when sequentially placed at the gaps in the given letters series shall complete it ?

l_n_mllm_n_l

(a) mnmn (b) mnnm
(c) mnmm (d) nmmm

11. If it is possible to make only one meaningful word with the 3rd, 7th, 8th and 10th letters of the word 'COMPATIBILITY', which of the following would be the last letter of that word? If no such word can be made, give 'X' as your answer and if more than one such word can be formed, give your answer as 'Y'.

(a) I (b) B (c) L (d) X
(e) Y

Direction (Q. Nos. 12-16) *Study the following information carefully to answer the given questions.* **[GIC 2012]**

A, B, C, D, E, F, G and H are seated in straight line facing North. C sits fourth to left of G. D sits second to right of G. Only two people sit between D and A. B and F are immediate neighbours of each other. B is not an immediate neighbour of A. H is not an immediate neighbour of D.

12. Who amongst the following sits exactly in the middle of the persons who sit fifth from the left and the person who sits sixth from the right?

(a) C (b) H (c) E (d) F

13. Who amongst the following sits third to the right of C?

(a) B (b) F (c) A (d) E

14. Which of the following represents persons seated at the two extreme ends of the line?

(a) C, D (b) A, B (c) B, G (d) D, H

15. What is the position of H with respect to F?

(a) Third to the left (b) Immediate right
(c) Second to the right (d) Fourth to the left

16. How many persons are seated between A and E?

(a) One (b) Two (c) Three (d) Four

17. A's present age is 4 yr more than B's age after six years. The sum of the present age of A and B together is 70 yr. What is the present age of B? **[FCI Assistant Grade III 2015]**

(a) 36 yr (b) 32 yr (c) 30 yr (d) 34 yr

Direction (Q. Nos. 18-19) *Find the missing letter / number.*

18. CIG, FLJ, IOM, ? **[SSC (FCI) 2012]**

(a) LRP (b) JLG
(c) PSU (d) QUB

19. 101, 100, ? , 87, 71, 46

(a) 92 (b) 88 (c) 89 (d) 96

20. A man drives his car 50 km towards Eastward direction. He turned right went for 30 km, then he turned West and drive for 10 km. How far is he from the starting point?

(a) 50 km (b) 60 km
(c) 100 km (d) 20 km

Direction (Q. Nos. 21-23) *Read the information carefully and then answer the questions given below.*

Shalu, Charu, Lata, Tom and Sandy help themselves to take some sweets from bowl. Four of them each take a gulab jamun. Charu and Tom do not take a burfy as all the others do. Infact, Charu takes only one sweet, which is a laddu. Laddu is not taken by others apart from Charu, only Shalu and Sandy do not take peda.

21. Who only had a peda and a gulab jamun?

(a) Charu (b) Sandy
(c) Shalu (d) Tom

22. Who takes three sweets?

(a) Charu (b) Sandy
(c) Shalu (d) Lata

23. Who are the two people taking the same number and same type of sweets?

(a) Shalu and Lata (b) Sandy and Lata
(c) Shalu and Sandy (d) Tom and Sandy

24. Out of 100 families in the neighbourhood, 50 have radios, 75 have TVs and 25 have VCRs. Only 10 families have all three and each VCR owner also has a TV. If some families have radio only. How many have only TV?

(a) 30 (b) 35 (c) 40 (d) 45

25. Find the missing term.

CE, GI, KM, OQ ? **[SSC (10+2) 2014]**

(a) TW (b) TV (c) SU (d) RT

Direction (Q. Nos. 26-27) *Find the missing character from the given alternatives.*

26.

5	9	15
16	29	?
49	89	147

[FCI Assistant Grade III 2015]

(a) 48 (b) 45 (c) 42 (d) 49

27. If 'football' is called 'hockey', 'hockey' is called 'badminton', 'badminton' is called 'cricket', cricket is called 'tennis', 'tennis' is called 'squash' and 'squash' is called 'chess', then which game Sachin Tendulkar associated with ?

(a) Squash (b) Cricket
(c) Badminton (d) Tennis

28. A is older than B but younger than C. D is younger than E but older than A. If C is younger than D, then who is the oldest of all ?

(a) A (b) C (c) D (d) E

29. Mohan has to revise 8 chapters (A, B, C, D, E, F, G, H) two days before the board exams. Considering the complexity of different chapters, he has decided **[CMAT 2015]**

I. cannot revise A and G on the same day.
II. E must be revised after B on the same day.
III. G must be revised after C on the same day.
IV. cannot revised D and F on the same day.
V. cannot revised C and H on the same day.
VI. D is revised on the 1st day .
VII. D and E cannot be revised on the same day.
VIII. C is not revised on 1st day .
IX. more chapters are revised on the 2nd day compared to 1st day.
X. no chapters will be revised twiced.

Which are the chapters revised on the 2nd day?

(a) A, B, E, F, C, G
(b) B, E, A, C, G
(c) B, E, F, C, G
(d) Cannot be determined

Direction (Q. Nos. 30-31) *Each of the questions below consists of a question and two statements numbered* I *and* II *given below it. You have to decide whether the data provided in the statements are sufficient to answer the question.*

Give answer

(a) if the data in Statement I alone are sufficient to answer the question, while the data in Statement II alone are not sufficient to answer the question.
(b) if the data in Statement II alone are sufficient to answer the question, while data in Statement I alone are not sufficient to answer the question.
(c) if the data in Statement I alone or in the Statement II alone are sufficient to answer the question.
(d) if the data in both the Statements I and II are not sufficient to answer the question.
(e) if the data in the Statements I and II together are necessary to answer the question.

30. How many marbles does Sanjay have?

I. Sanjay has 3 times more marbles than Ahmed.
II. Ahmed has one third the number of marbles which Suresh has who has as many marbles as Sanjay.

31. How is Ramesh related to Lata?

I. Yogendra is Lata's father.
II. The only sibling of Ramesh's maternal aunt is married to Yogendra.

32. Select the related numbers from the given alternatives. **[SSC (10+2) 2015]**

235 : 587 : : 435 : ?

(a) 789 (b) 788 (c) 989 (d) 988

33. On the basis of the given two positions of single dice, find the letter at the face opposite to the face having letter A.

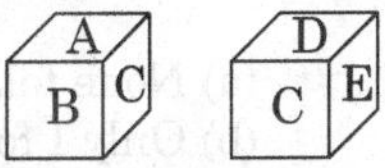

I II

(a) B (b) C (c) E (d) D

Direction (Q. Nos. 34-36) *In each of the questions below are given four statements followed by four conclusions numbered* I, II, Ill *and* IV. *You have to take the given statements to be true even if they seem to be at variance with commonly known facts. Read all the conclusions and then decide which of the given conclusion (s) logically follow (s) from the given statements disregarding commonly known facts.*

34. Statements All birds are horses.
All horses are tigers.
Some tigers are lions.
Some lions are monkeys.

Conclusions I. Some tigers are horses.
II. Some monkeys are birds.
III. Some tigers are birds.
IV. Some monkeys are horses.

(a) I and III follow
(b) I, II and III follow
(c) II, III and IV follow
(d) All follow
(e) None of the above

35. Statements Some benches are walls.
All walls are houses.
Some houses are jungles.
All jungles are roads.

Conclusions I. Some roads are benches.
II. Some jungles are walls.
III. Some houses are benches.
IV. Some roads are houses.

(a) I and II follow
(b) I and III follow
(c) III and IV follow
(d) II, III and IV follow
(e) None of the above

36. Statements Some sticks are lamps.
Some flowers are lamps.
Some lamps are dresses.
All dresses are shirts.

Conclusions I. Some shirts are sticks.
II. Some shirts are flowers.
III. Some flowers are sticks.
IV. Some dresses are sticks.

(a) None follows
(b) Only I follows
(c) Only II follows
(d) Only III follows
(e) Only IV follows

37. A word is represented by only one set of numbers as given in anyone of the alternatives. The sets of numbers given in the alternatives are represented by two classes of alphabets as in two matrices given below. The columns and rows of Matrix I are numbered from 0 to 4 and that of Matrix II are numbered from 5 to 9. A letter from these matrices can be represented first by its row and next by its column, e.g. 'A' can be represented by 01, 12, 33 etc., and 'K' can be represented by 57, 68, 85 etc. Identify the set for the word 'EAST'. **[SSC (FCI) 2012]**

Matrix I

	0	1	2	3	4
0	E	A	R	W	P
1	W	P	A	E	R
2	A	W	P	R	E
3	P	R	E	A	W
4	R	E	W	P	A

Matrix II

	5	6	7	8	9
5	S	B	K	T	C
6	B	C	T	K	S
7	T	S	C	B	K
8	K	T	S	C	B
9	C	K	B	S	T

(a) 00, 12, 76, 58 (b) 32, 34, 76, 68
(c) 41, 20, 77, 59 (d) 24, 02, 55, 76

Direction (Q. Nos. 38-39) *In each of the questions below is given a statement followed by three courses of action numbered* I, II *and* III. *A course of action is a step or administrative decision to be taken for improvement, follow-up or further action in regard to the problem, policy, etc. On the basis of information given in the statement, you have to assume everything in the statement to be true and then decide which of the three given suggested course of action logically follows worth pursuing. Then, decide which of the alternatives* (a), (b), (c), (d) *or* (e) *is correct.*

38. Statement A blast was triggered off injuring many, when the night shift workers at an ordinance factory were handling 'fox signalling explosive'.

Courses of Action

I. The factory management should train its staff as regards to the safety aspects of handling such explosive materials.
II. The service of the supervisor incharge of the night shift should be terminated immediately.
III. The factory should immediately stop carrying out such exercises at night.

(a) None follows
(b) All follow
(c) Only I follows
(d) Both I and II follow
(e) None of these

39. Statement A major railway accident involving a mail train was averted due to the presence of mind of one signal man at a wayside cabin.

Courses of Action

I. The railway track for atleast 50 km should be cleared off any traffic ahead of all the mail trains.
II. The railway signalling systems should immediately be made automatic.
III. The signal man should be rewarded so as to encourage others.

(a) All follow
(b) None follows
(c) Both I and II follow
(d) Both II and III follow
(e) None of the above

40. Count the number of triangles in the following figure ?

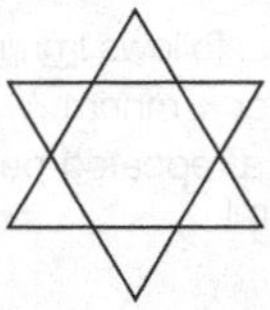

(a) 6 (b) 7 (c) 8 (d) 9

41. In which answer figure is the question figure embedded ?

Question Figure

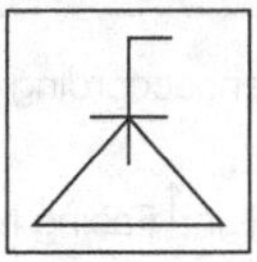

Answer Figures

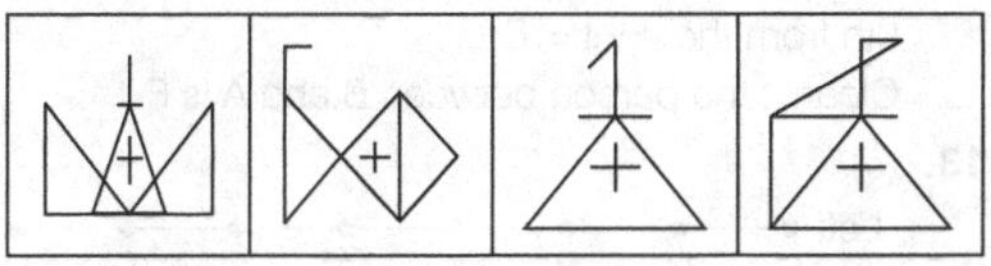

(a) (b) (c) (d)

42. If 9th of the month falls on the day preceding Sunday, then on what day will 1st of the month fall ?

(a) Friday (b) Saturday
(c) Sunday (d) Monday

43. A is the brother of B, B is the daughter of C and D is the father of A. Then, how is C related to D ? **[SSC CGL 2014]**

(a) Husband (b) Wife
(c) Granddaughter (d) Grandfather

44. Which answer figures will complete the pattern in the questions figure ?

Question Figure

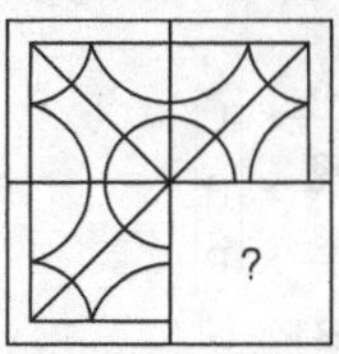

Answer Figures

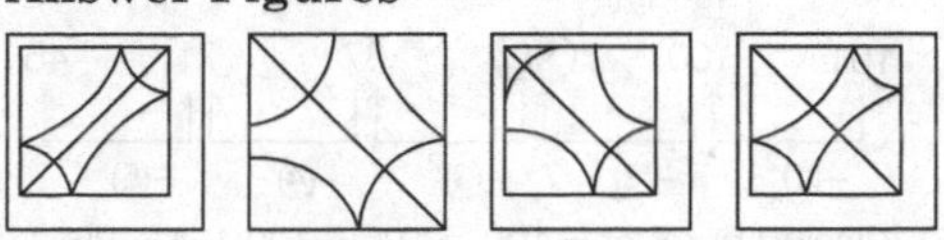

(a) (b) (c) (d)

Direction (Q. Nos. 45-47) *In the following questions, the symbols, ©, ★, %, $ and @ are used with the following meaning, illustrated below.*

'P © Q' means 'P is either smaller than or equal to Q'.

'P ★ Q' means 'P is either greater than or equal to Q'.

'P % Q' means 'P is smaller than Q'.

'P $ Q' means 'P is greater than Q'.

'P @ Q' means 'P is equal to Q'.

Now, in each of the following questions, assuming the given statements to be true, find which of the two Conclusions I and II given below is/are definitely true?

Give answer

(a) if only Conclusion I is true
(b) if only Conclusion II is true
(c) if either Conclusion I or II is true
(d) if neither Conclusion I nor II is true
(e) if both Conclusions I and II are true

45. Statements B $ N, N ★ R, R @ K
Conclusions I. K © N II. B $ K

46. Statements J © K, K $ N, N ★ D
Conclusions I. J % N II. D % K

47. Statements R @ D, D © M, M $ T
Conclusions I. T % D II. M ★ R

48. If 5×4 = 15, 7×8 = 49 and 6×5 = 24, then 8×4 is equal to

(a) 24 (b) 26 (c) 28 (d) 30

49. Which one of the given responses would be a meaningful order of the following words ?

(i) Plant (ii) Food (iii) Seed
(iv) Leaf (v) Flower

(a) (i), (iii), (iv), (v), (ii)
(b) (iii), (ii), (iv), (v), (i)
(c) (iii), (i), (iv), (v), (ii)
(d) (v), (iv), (iii), (ii), (i)

50. Which are the numbers that make their presence felt in only one of the geometric figures?

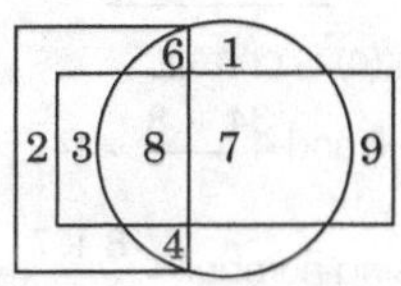

(a) 4, 6, 7 (b) 1, 2, 9
(c) 3, 7, 9 (d) 2, 3, 8

Hints and Solutions

1. (*b*) 30 K2 Q 3 J 6 T5 = ?

After interchanging symbols,

$\Rightarrow$ $30 \div 2 + 3 \times 6 - 5 = ?$

$\Rightarrow$ $15 + 18 - 5 = ?$

$\Rightarrow$ $33 - 5 = ?$

$\Rightarrow$ $28 = ?$

2. (*d*) Both the words are opposite in meaning to each other.

3. (*c*) As,

B(2) +6 → H(8), C(3) +6 → I(9), F(6) +6 → L(12), E(5) +6 → K(11)

Similarly, N(14) +6 → T(20), O(15) +6 → U(21), R(18) +6 → X(24), Q(17) +6 → W(23)

$\therefore$? = TUXW

Solution (Q. Nos. 4-6) After careful analysis of the input and various steps of rearrangement, it is clear that in the first step one number is rearranged and in the second step one word is rearranged. These two steps are continued till all the numbers get arranged in ascending order and all the words get arranged in reverse order of alphabets.

4. (*c*) **Input** kind 12 96 heart water 59 42 yes

Step **I** 12 kind 96 heart water 59 42 yes

Step **II** 12 yes kind 96 heart water 59 42

Step **III** 12 yes 42 kind 96 heart water 59

Step **IV** 12 yes 42 water kind 96 heart 59

Step **V** 12 yes 42 water 59 kind 96 heart.

5. (*e*) **Input** jungle 43 mode 25 basket 39 target 19

Step **I** 19 jungle 43 mode 25 basket 39 target

Step **II** 19 target jungle 43 mode 25 basket 39

Step **III** 19 target 25 jungle 43 mode basket 39

Step **IV** 19 target 25 mode jungle 43 basket 39

Step **V** 19 target 25 mode 39 jungle 43 basket

7. (*c*) We have the following pattern,

P A T T E R N —Reverse Order→ N R E T T A P

Similarly, we can write

M E N T I O N —Reverse Order→ N O I T N E M

Hence, option (c) is correct.

8. (*c*) $\frac{13+5}{3} = 6$ and $\frac{34+8}{3} = 14$

Similarly, missing number $= \frac{8+7}{3} = \boxed{5}$

9. (*d*) Option figure (d) is correct.

10. (*b*) The series is as follows lmn/nml/lmn/nml

$\therefore$ Required answer = mnnm

The sequence is a repeated pattern of two alternative blocks lmn and nml.

11. (*b*) Given that,

C O (M) P A T (I) (B) I (L) I T Y

M → 3rd, I → 7th, B → 8th, L → 10th

The only word formed = L I M B

$\therefore$ Last letter = B

Solution (Q. Nos. 12 -16) Arrangement according to the question is as follows

Left H C B F A G E D Right (Facing North)

12. (*d*) 5th from left = A

6th from the right = B

Clearly, the person between B and A is F.

13. (*c*)

Left H C B F (A) G E D Right

(3rd to the right of C)

Clearly, A sits third to the right of C.

14. (*d*) Clearly, D and H are at the extreme ends.

15. (*a*) Clearly, H is third to the left of F.

16. (*a*) Only one person i.e. G is sitting between A and E.

17. (*c*) Let A's present age be x yr and B's present age be y yr

Given, $x + y = 70$ ...(i)

and $x = (y + 6) + 4$

$\Rightarrow$ $x = y + 10$

$\Rightarrow$ $x - y = 10$ ...(ii)

Now, solving Eqs. (i) and (ii), we get $x = 40$ and $y = 30$

$\therefore$ B's present age $= y = 30$ yr

18. (*a*) The pattern is as follows

C —+3→ F —+3→ I —+3→ L

I —+3→ L —+3→ O —+3→ R

G —+3→ J —+3→ M —+3→ P

? = L R P

19. (*d*) The pattern is as follows

101 —$(1)^2$→ 100 —$(2)^2$→ (96) —$(3)^2$→ 87 —$(4)^2$→ 71 —$(5)^2$→ 46

Missing number $= 100 - (2)^2 = 100 - 4 = 96$

20. (*a*) Route followed by man

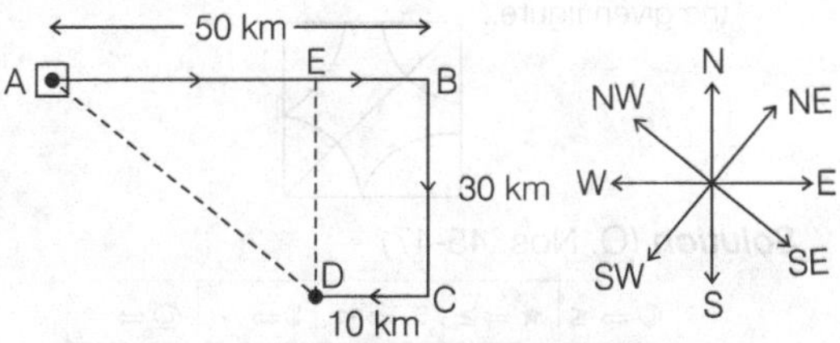

Required distance, $AD = \sqrt{(AE)^2 + (DE)^2}$

$= \sqrt{(40)^2 + (30)^2}$

$= \sqrt{1600 + 900} = \sqrt{2500}$

$= 50 km$

Solution (Q. Nos. 21-23) Following table can be drawn from the given information

Name	GulabJamun	Burfy	Laddu	Peda
Shalu	✔	✔	✗	✗
Charu	✗	✗	✔	✗
Lata	✔	✔	✗	✔
Tom	✔	✗	✗	✔
Sandy	✔	✔	✗	✗

21. (*d*) Tom took a peda and gulab jamun.

22. (*d*) Lata took gulab jamun, burfy and peda .

23. (c) Shalu and Sandy took gulab jamun and burfy.

24. (c) 25 have VCRs and each VCR owner also has a TV. Therefore, the TV owners who have not VCRs $75 - 25 = 50$. Now, 10 have all the three. Therefore, $50 - 10 = 40$ have only TV.

25. (c) The pattern is as follows

$C \xrightarrow{+4} G \xrightarrow{+4} K \xrightarrow{+4} O \xrightarrow{+4} \boxed{S}$

$E \xrightarrow{+4} I \xrightarrow{+4} M \xrightarrow{+4} Q \xrightarrow{+4} \boxed{U}$

$\therefore \quad ? = SU$

26. (*a*) As, $5 \times 3 = 15$ and $49 \times 3 = 147$

Same as, $16 \times 3 = 48$

27. (*d*) Sachin Tendulkar is a cricketer but here cricket is called tennis. Hence, in this case Sachin Tendulkar is associated with tennis.

28. (*d*) According to the question,

$C > A > B$ ...(i)

$E > D > A$ ...(ii)

$D > C$ ...(iii)

From all three equations $E > D > C > A > B$

Clearly, E is the oldest among them.

29. (*c*) On the basis of given information, the arrangement is as follows.

1st Day	2nd Day
D	F
A	B
H	E
	C
	G

∴ Chapters revised on the 2nd day are F, B, E, C, and G, considering all the given conditions.

30. (*d*) No answer can be found even using the data given in both the statements.

31. (*d*) From both the statements. The sibling of Ramesh's maternal aunt is wife of Yogendra.

Therefore, Ramesh is sibling of Lata.

The gender of Ramesh is not known.

32. (*a*) As, 235 : 587

$2 + 3 + 5 : 5 + 8 + 7$

$10 : 20$

Here, second is the double of first by adding the digits.

Similarly, 435 : 789

$4 + 3 + 5 : 7 + 8 + 9$

$12 : 24$

33. (c) Common letter = C (on different face)

	Common	Opposite	Opposite
From Position I	C	B	A
From Position II	C	D	E

Clearly, E is opposite to A.

34. (*a*)

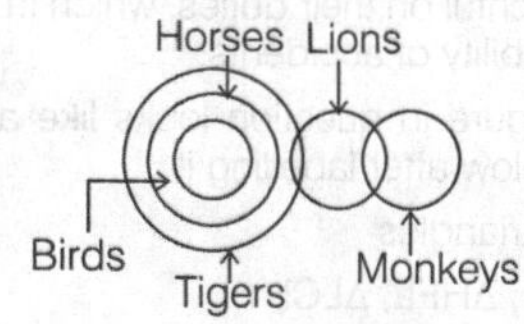

Conclusions I. Some tigers are horses. (✔)

II. Some monkeys are birds. (✗)

III. Some tigers are birds. (✔)

IV. Some monkeys are horses. (✗)

So, I and III follow.

35. (*c*)

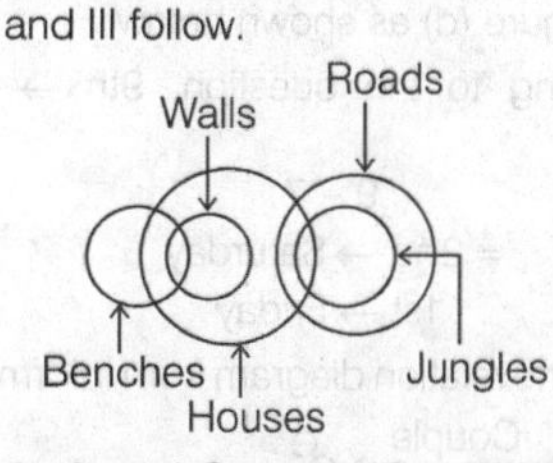

Conclusions I. Some roads are benches. (✗)

II. Some jungles are walls. (✗)

III. Some houses are benches. (✔)

IV. Some roads are houses. (✔)

So, III and IV follow.

36. (*a*)

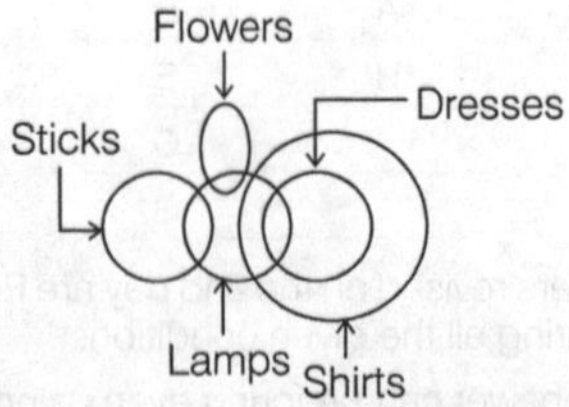

Conclusions I. Some shirts are sticks. (✗)
II. Some shirts are flowers. (✗)
III. Some flowers are sticks. (✗)
IV. Some dresses are sticks. (✗)

So, none follows.

37. (a) According to the matrices,

E — (00), 13, 24, 32 , 41
A — 01, (12), 20, 33, 44
S — 55, 69, (76), 87, 98
T — (58), 67, 75, 86, 99

∴ EAST ⇒ 00, 12, 76, 58.

38. (*d*) Course of action I is the right course of action because training to the staff as to the safety aspects of handling explosive material will reduce the chances of such accidents in future. Course of action II is also a right course as it will work as deterrent to check any negligence, in such work.

39. (*a*) Courses of action I and II will directly improve the working condition of railways. Course of action III though not directly related with improving railway traffic conditions but will encourage other signal men to be more watchful on their duties, which in turn, will reduce the probability of accidents.

40. (c) The figure in question looks like as shown below after labelling it.

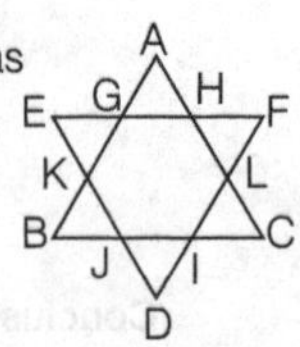

Smallest triangles
= ΔGAH, ΔHFL, ΔLCI,
ΔIDJ, ΔJBK, ΔKEG = 6

Largest triangles = ΔABC, ΔEFD = 2

∴ Total triangles = 6 + 2 = 8

41. (*d*) Clearly, question figure is embedded in answer figure (d) as shown below

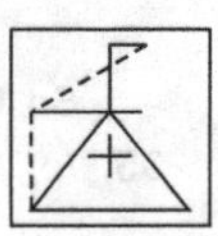

42. (*a*) According to the question, 9th → Saturday

Therefore, 9 − 7
= 2nd → Saturday
∴ 1st → Friday

43. (*b*) Making the relation diagram from information given,

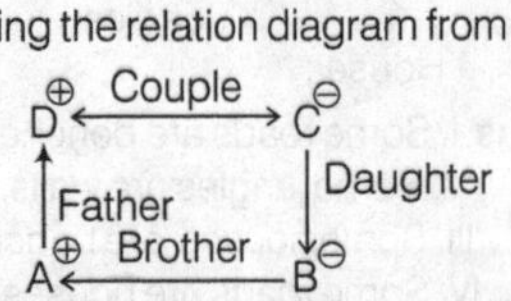

Hence, it is clear from diagram that C is wife of D.

44. (*b*) Clearly, option (b) figure will complete the pattern of the given figure.

Solution (Q. Nos. 45-47)

© ⇒ ≤	★ ⇒ ≥	% ⇒ <	$ ⇒ >	@ ⇒ =

45. (*e*) According to the question,

B$N ⇒ B > N ...(i)
N★R ⇒ N ≥ R ...(ii)
R@K ⇒ R = K ...(iii)

On combining the statements (i), (ii) and (iii), we get

B > N ≥ R = K

Conclusions I. K © N ⇒ K ≤ N (True)
II. B$K ⇒ B > K (True)

So, it is clear that both the Conclusions I and II are true.

46. (*b*) According to the question,

J©K ⇒ J ≤ K ...(i)
K$N ⇒ K > N ...(ii)
N★D ⇒ N ≥ D ...(iii)

On combining the statements (i), (ii) and (iii), we get
J ≤ K > N ≥ D

Conclusions I. J % N ⇒ J < N (False)
II. D % K ⇒ D < K (True)

So, it is clear that only Conclusions II is true.

47. (*b*) According to the question,

R@D ⇒ R = D ...(i)
D©M ⇒ D ≤ M ...(ii)
M$T ⇒ M > T ...(iii)

On combining the statements (i), (ii) and (iii), we get

R = D ≤ M > T

Conclusions I. T % D ⇒ T < D (False)
II. M ★ R ⇒ M ≥ R (True)

So, it is clear that only Conclusion II is true.

48. (*a*) As, $5 \times 4 = 5 \times (4-1) = 5 \times 3 = 15$

$7 \times 8 = 7 \times (8-1) = 7 \times 7 = 49$

and $6 \times 5 = 6 \times (5-1) = 6 \times 4 = 24$

Similarly, $8 \times 4 = 8 \times (4-1)$

$= 8 \times 3 = 24$

49. (*c*) Meaningful order of words.

(iii) Seed, → (i) Plant, → (iv) Leaf, → (v) Flower, → (ii) Food

50. (*b*) The number 1 is present in circle only.

The number 9 is present in bigger rectangle, only.

The number 2 is present in smaller rectangle, only.

PRACTICE SET 28

1. Which one set of letters when sequentially placed at the gaps in the letter series shall complete it?

m_ommn_m_nommn_m

(a) onmo (b) nomo
(c) monm (d) nnmo

2. Which one number is wrong in the series? **[SSC (10+2) 2014]**

A	B	C	D	E
225	256	121	289	324

(a) 225 (b) 256 (c) 121 (d) 324

3. Choose the correct alternative from the given ones that will complete the series

3, 4, 7, 11, 18, 29, ?

(a) 31 (b) 39
(c) 43 (d) 47

4. A solid cube has been formed with 64 smaller cubes. How many smaller cubes are completely invisible? **[SSC (10+2) 2010]**

(a) 2 (b) 4
(c) 6 (d) 8

Direction (Q. Nos. 5-6) *In the following questions, find the odd words/numbers from the given alternatives.*

5. (a) Clerk : File
(b) Lawyer : Client
(c) Doctor : Patient
(d) Shopkeeper : Customer

6. (a) 13 (b) 17 (c) 19 (d) 27

7. A word is represented by only one set of numbers as given in anyone of the alternatives. The set of numbers given in the alternatives are represented by two classes of alphabets as in two matrices, given below. The columns and rows of Matrix I are numbered from 0 to 3 and that of Matrix II are numbered from 4 to 7. A letter from these matrices can be represented first by its row and next by its column. e.g. 'A' can be represented by 00, 76 and 'S' can be represented by 11, 66. Identify the set for the word 'PUSH'. **[SSC (10+2) 2011]**

Matrix I

	0	1	2	3
0	A	D	G	H
1	P	S	V	Z
2	C	F	I	M
3	T	L	E	Q

Matrix II

	4	5	6	7
4	R	U	B	O
5	N	W	J	X
6	T	K	S	G
7	I	H	A	F

(a) 10, 66, 45, 03
(b) 30, 11, 54, 10
(c) 10, 45, 66, 75
(d) 01, 54, 66, 57

Direction (Q. Nos. 8-9) *Each of the questions below consists of a question and two statements numbered* I *and* II *given below it. You have to decide whether the data provided in the statements are sufficient to answer the question.*

Give answer

(a) if the data in Statement I alone are sufficient to answer the question, while the data in Statement II alone are not sufficient to answer the question.
(b) if the data in Statement II alone are sufficient to answer the question, while the data in Statement I alone are not sufficient to answer the question.
(c) if the data either in Statement I alone or in Statement II alone are sufficient to answer the question.
(d) if the data given in both the Statements I and II together are not sufficient to answer the question.
(e) if the data in both the Statements I and II together are necessary to answer the question.

8. Who among A, B, C, D and E is the tallest?

I. Each of A, B, C, D and E has a different height.

II. D is shorter than only A.

9. How is 'walk' written in a code language?

I. 'morning walk is good' is written as 'na pa ta sa' in that code language.

II. 'wish you good morning' is written as 'la na sa da' in that code language.

Direction (Q. Nos. 10-12) *In the following questions, select the related words/letters/numbers pair from the given alternatives.*

10. ACEG : DFHJ : : QSUW : ? **[IB (ACIO) 2013]**
(a) TVNZ (b) TVZX
(c) TVXZ (d) XVTZ

11. 25 : 625 : : 35 : ?
(a) 1575 (b) 1205
(c) 875 (d) 635

12. PIGEON : PEACE : : ?
(a) CROWN : HEAD
(b) WHITE FLAG : SURRENDER
(c) LAURELS : VICTORY
(d) WAR : LIBERTY

13. Pointing to a lady in a photograph, Meera said, "Her father's only son's wife is my mother-in-law". How is Meera's husband related to that lady in the photo?
(a) Nephew (b) Uncle
(c) Son (d) Father

14. In the year 1996, the Republic day was celebrated on Friday. On which day was the Independence day celebrated in the year 2000?
(a) Tuesday (b) Monday
(c) Friday (d) Saturday

15. If 'goat' is called 'cow', 'cow' is called 'lion', 'lion' is called 'ass', 'ass' is called 'rat', 'rat' is called 'cat' and 'cat' is called 'dog', then which of the following is a Rodent?
(a) Lion (b) Ass
(c) Rat (d) Cat

16. Find the missing character from the given responses.

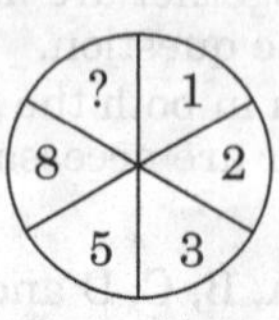

(a) 10 (b) 15 (c) 13 (d) 12
(e) None of these

17. Which one of the given responses would be a meaningful order of the following? **[SSC (CGL) 2015]**
(i) Frog (ii) Eagle
(iii) Grasshopper (iv) Snake
(v) Grass
(a) (iii), (iv), (ii), (v), (i)
(b) (i), (iii), (v), (ii), (iv)
(c) (v), (iii), (i), (iv), (ii)
(d) (v), (iii), (iv), (ii), (i)

Direction (Q. Nos. 18-20) *Study the following information carefully to answer the questions based on that.*

I. There is a family of six persons representing three generations.
II. There are two married couples and both the wives are housewives.
III. Pratap, the lawyer, is father of Prashant and has one grandchild.
IV. Pooja, the doctor, is the sister of the teacher.
V. Madhu's daughter-in-law Sumati is married to a teacher.
VI. Bindu, granddaughter of one of the housewives is studying in 9th standard.

18. What is the profession of Prashant?
(a) Student
(b) Teacher
(c) Lawyer
(d) Cannot be determined

19. Who among the following is one of the married couples?
(a) Pratap-Bindu
(b) Madhu-Pratap
(c) Prashant-Bindu
(d) Cannot be determined

20. Who are the children of Madhu?
(a) Pooja and Prashant
(b) Sumati and Pooja
(c) Prashant and Sumati
(d) Cannot be determined

21. In this question has an Assertion (A) and a Reason (R).

Assertion (A) Salt is added to cook food at higher altitudes.

Reason (R) Temperature is lower at higher altitudes.

(a) if both 'A' and 'B' are true and 'R' is the correct explanation of 'A'
(b) if both 'A' and 'R' are true but 'R' is not the correct explanation of 'A'
(c) if 'A' is true but 'R' is false
(d) if 'A' false but 'R' is true

22. There are three baskets of fruits. First basket has twice the number of fruits in the 2nd basket. Third basket has $\frac{3}{4}$ th of the fruits in the first. The average of the fruits in all the baskets is 30. What is the number of fruits in the first basket?

(a) 20 (b) 30
(c) 35 (d) 40

23. Out of four figures which figure will best represent the relationship amongst the classes

Sparrow, Birds and Mice

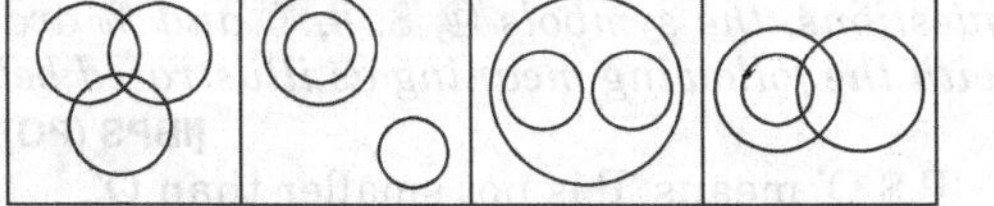

(a) (b) (c) (d)

24. Find the missing character from the given responses.

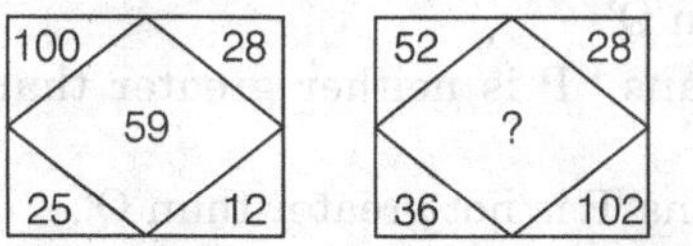

[SSC (Steno) 2014]

(a) 50 (b) 90 (c) 218 (d) 64

25. If 'PARK' is coded as '5394', 'SHIRT' is coded as '17698' and 'PANDIT' is coded as '532068', then how would you code 'NISHAR' in that code language?

(a) 266734 (b) 231954
(c) 201739 (d) 261739

26. Find the water image of the given number from the given alternatives.

13101989

(a) I3I0I689 (b) I3I0I68ɘ
(c) 1310I689 (d) 13101989

27. Which answer figure will complete the question figure.

Question Figure

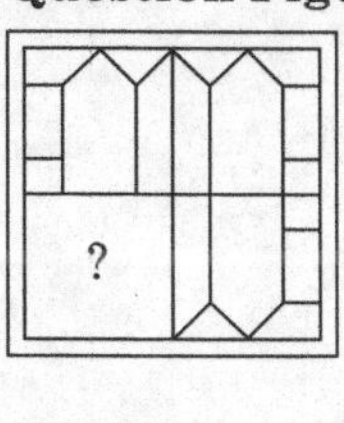

Answer Figures

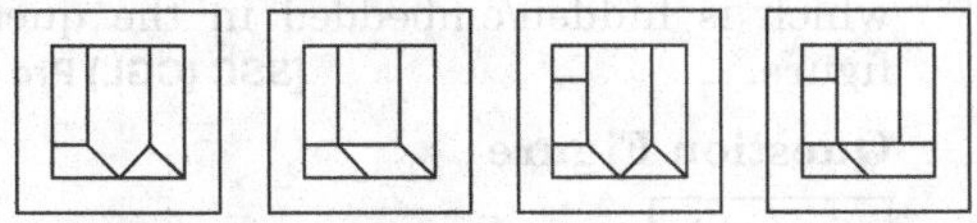

(a) (b) (c) (d)

28. How many pairs of letters are there in these words which have as many letters between them as in the English alphabet.

TRIBUNAL

(a) One (b) Two
(c) Three (d) More than three

29. If it is possible to make only one meaningful word with the 3rd, 4th, 8th and 9th letters of the words 'CENTURIES' which would be the 2nd letter of the word from left? If more than one such word can be formed, give 'A' as the answer. If no such word can be formed, give 'Z' as your answer.

(a) A (b) N (c) T (d) E
(e) Z

Direction (Q. Nos. 30-31) *Study the following information carefully and answer the given questions.*

A word and number arrangement machine when given an input line of words and numbers rearranges them following a particular rule in each step. The following is an illustration of input and rearrangement.

Input rose petal 29 32 86 goal 41 toll
Step I 29 rose petal 32 86 goal 41 toll
Step II 29 toll rose petal 32 86 goal 41
Step III 29 toll 32 rose petal 86 goal 41
Step IV 29 toll 32 rose 41 petal 86 goal

30. **Input** man 79 over 63 like 43 joy 15

How many steps will be required to complete the rearrangement?

(a) Six (b) Seven
(c) Eight (d) Nine
(e) None of these

31. Step II of an input is '27 world go 57 48 stem 35 kite'.

How many more steps will be required to complete the rearrangement?

(a) Five (b) Four
(c) Three (d) Six
(e) None of these

32. From the given answer figures, select the one which is hidden/embedded in the question figure. **[SSC (CGL) Pre 2015]**

Question Figure

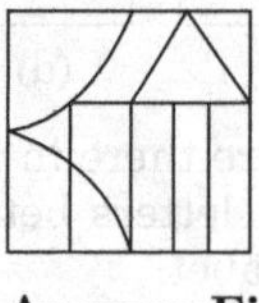

Answer Figures

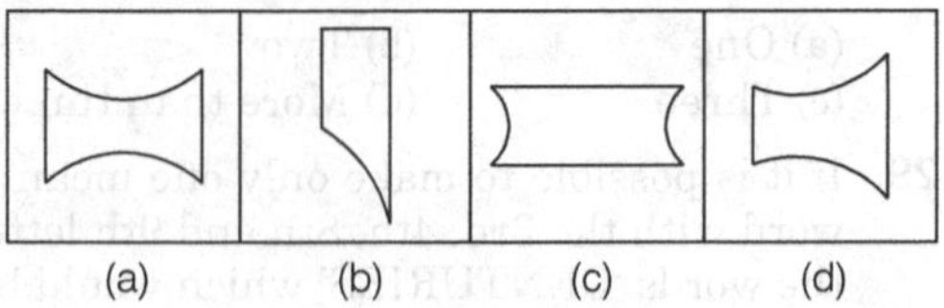

Direction (Q.Nos. 33-34) *Read the following information carefully and answer the questions given below.*

'P × Q' means 'P is sister of Q'.
'P + Q' means 'P is mother of Q'.
'P − Q' means 'P is father of Q'.
'P ÷ Q' means 'P is brother of Q'.

33. Which of the following represents 'M is the nephew of R'?
(a) M ÷ T − R
(b) R ÷ T − M
(c) R × T + M × J
(d) R ÷ T − M ÷ J
(e) None of these

34. Which of the following represents 'W is grandfather of H'?
(a) W + T − H (b) W ÷ T − H
(c) W × T + H (d) W ÷ T + H
(e) None of these

35. Kishankant walks 10 km towards North. From there he walks 6 km towards South. Then, he walks 3 km towards East. How far and in which direction is he from his starting point? **[UPPSC (RO) 2014]**
(a) 5 km, North-East
(b) 7 km, East
(c) 5 km, East
(d) 7 Km, West

36. Identify the missing part of the question figure and select it from given answer figures.

Question Figure

Answer Figures

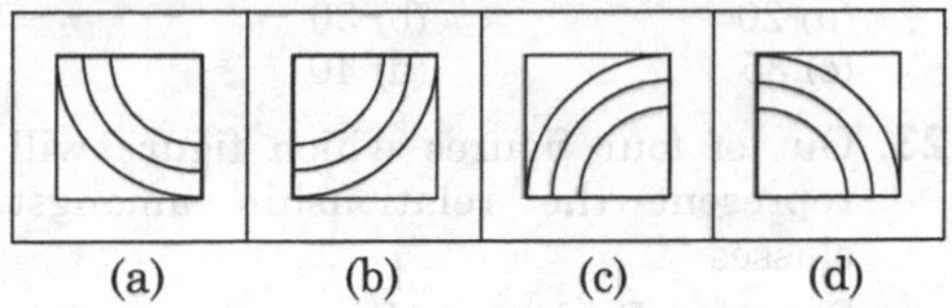

Direction (Q. Nos. 37-38) *In the following questions, the symbols @, $, #, © and % are used with the following meaning as illustrated below.* **[IBPS (PO) 2012]**

'P $ Q' means 'P is not smaller than Q'.
'P # Q' means 'P is neither smaller than nor equal to Q'.
'P @ Q' means 'P is neither greater than nor smaller than Q'.
'P © Q' means 'P is neither greater than nor equal to Q'.
'P % Q' means 'P is not greater than Q'.

Now, in each of the following questions, assuming the given statements to be true, find which of the four Conclusions I, II, III and IV given below them is/are definitely true and give your answer accordingly.

37. Statements R # J, J $ D, D @ K, K % T
Conclusions I. T # D II. T @ D
III. R # K IV. J $ T
(a) Either I or II is true
(b) Only III is true
(c) III and IV are true
(d) Either I or II and III are true
(e) None of the above

38. Statements T % R, R $ M, M @ D, D © H
Conclusions I. D % R II. H # R
III. T © M IV. T % D
(a) Only I is true
(b) I and IV are true
(c) I and II are true
(d) II and IV are true
(e) None of the above

39. Group the given figures into three classes using each figure only once.

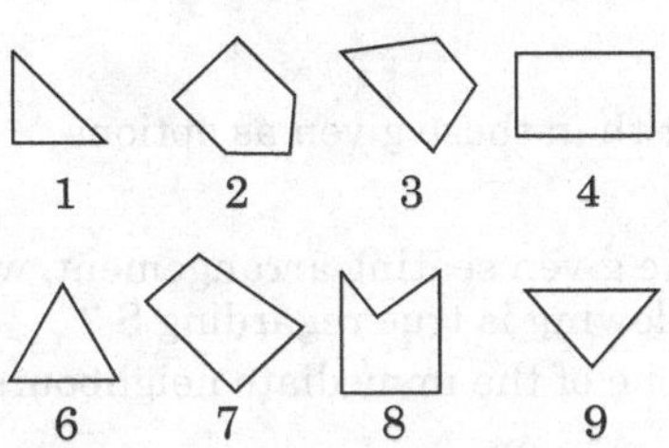

(a) (7, 8, 9) (2, 4, 3) (1, 5, 6)
(b) (1, 3, 2) (4, 5, 7) (6, 8, 9)
(c) (1, 6, 8) (3, 4, 7) (2, 5, 9)
(d) (1, 6, 9) (3, 4, 7) (2, 5, 8)

40. On the centenary celebrations of the public school, principal wants to have a gala festival 'fest foe', for which an organising committee is to be formed from class X and class XII students. Class X students are Arya, Boman, Chiki and the class XII students are the Rajni, Sonam, Tapu and Umeed. Total 4 students are selected of which at least two must be from class X. Boman will not work with Rajni and Arya will not work with Tapu. Based on the given information which option(s) is/are correct?

I. If Arya is choosen, then Umeed must also be choosen.
II. If Arya is rejected, then Sonam must be choosen.
III. If Arya is rejected, then Chiki must be choosen. **[CMAT 2015]**

(a) I and III (b) I and II
(c) Only II (d) Only III

Direction (Q. Nos. 41-42) *Two statements are given below followed by two Conclusions* I *and* II. *You have to consider the two statements to be true even if they seem to be at variance with commonly known facts. You have to decide which of the conclusions, if any, follow from the given statements.*

(a) if only Conclusion I follows
(b) if only Conclusion II follows
(c) if either Conclusion I or II follows
(d) if neither Conclusion I nor II follows
(e) if both Conclusions I and II follow

41. Statements Some books are magazines.
Some magazines are novels.

Conclusions I. Some books are novels.
II. Some novels are magazines.

42. Statements All good hockey players are in the Indian hockey team.
'X' is not a good hockey player. **[CLAT 2014]**

Conclusions
I. 'X' is not in the Indian Hockey team.
II. 'X' wants to be in the Indian Hockey team.

43. How many rectangles are there in the figure given below ?

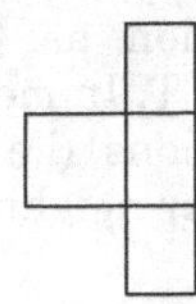

(a) 16 (b) 10 (c) 8 (d) 11

44. State which of the expression is true, if → stands for +, ← stands for –, ↓ stands for ×, ↑ stands for ÷, ↖ stands for = and ↘ stands for >. **[SSC (10+2) 2015]**

(a) 5 ↓ 6 → 6 ← 12 ↑ 4 ↖ 30
(b) 3 ↓ 4 → 15 ↑ 3 ← 7 ↖ 10
(c) 10 ← 8 → 5 ↓ 4 ← 3 ↑ 1 ↘ 20
(d) 6 → 7 → 82 ↓ 16 ↑ 8 ↖ 15

45. In a row of girls, Kamla is tenth from the left and Vimla is twelth from the right. When they exchange their places, Kamla is sixteenth from the left. What is the new position of Vimla from the right?

(a) 18th (b) 22nd
(c) 26th (d) 28th

46. In the question, two statements are given. You have to answer considering the statements to be true, even if they seem to be at variance from commonly known facts. **[SSC (10+2) 2015]**

Statements
I. Plants grow from seeds.
II. Seeds are produced by flowers.

Conclusions
(a) Flowers and seeds are produced by plants.
(b) Seeds are produced by plants.
(c) Plants grow from flowers.
(d) Flowers are produced by plants.

Direction (Q. Nos. 47-50) *Study the information carefully and answer the questions.*

N, O, P, Q, R, S, T and U are sitting around a circular area at equal distances between each other, but not necessarily in the same order. Some of the people are facing the centre while some face outside (i.e. in a direction opposite to the centre).

R sits second to the right of T.T face the centre. O sits third to the left of R. R and O face opposite directions. Immediate neighbours of O face the centre. P sits second to the right of O. U sits to the immediate left of P. N sits second to the left of Q. Q faces the same direction as O. Q is not an immediate neighbour of T. Immediate neighbours of R face opposite directions, (i.e. if one neighbour faces the centre the other neighbour faces outside and *vice-versa*.)

47. Four of the following five are alike in a certain way based on the given seating arrangement and so form a group. Which is the one that does not belong to that group?
(a) U (b) S (c) P (d) N
(e) Q

48. Who sits second to the left of U?
(a) T
(b) O
(c) S
(d) Other than those given as options
(e) Q

49. As per the given seating arrangement, which of the following is true regarding S ?
(a) U is one of the immediate neighbours of S.
(b) S sits third to the right of R.
(c) S faces the centre.
(d) Only two people sit between S and T.
(e) Only one person sits between S and N.

50. What is P's position with respect to N?
(a) Second to the left
(b) Second to the right
(c) Third to the right
(d) Third to the left
(e) Fourth to the left

Hints and Solutions

1. (*b*) The letter series will be
m n o m / m n o m / m n o m / m n o m ⇒ nomo

2. (c)

A	B	C	D	E
225	256	121	289	324
↓	↓	↓	↓	↓
$(15)^2$	$(16)^2$	$(11)^2$	$(17)^2$	$(18)^2$

+1 +1 +1

From the above observation, we see that the given series is square of consecutive numbers from 15 to 18. But 121 is square of 11. So, 121 is wrong number in given series.

3. (*d*) Every third element is the sum of its previous two elements.

$$3 + 4 = 7$$
$$4 + 7 = 11$$
$$7 + 11 = 18$$
$$11 + 18 = 29$$
$$18 + 29 = 47$$
$$\therefore \quad ? = 47$$

4. (*d*)

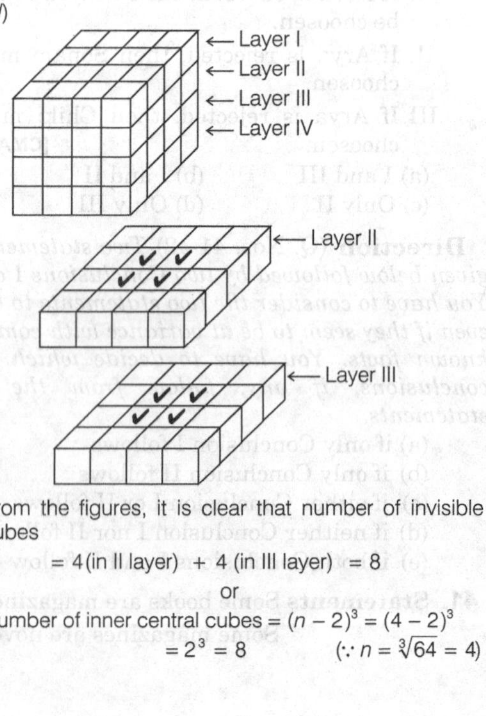

From the figures, it is clear that number of invisible cubes

= 4(in II layer) + 4 (in III layer) = 8

or

Number of inner central cubes = $(n-2)^3 = (4-2)^3$
$= 2^3 = 8$ $\quad (\because n = \sqrt[3]{64} = 4)$

5. (*a*) In all others, second is the person for whom the first works to earn money.

6. (*d*) Except (d), all others are prime numbers.

7. (*c*) According to the matrices,

P — (10)
U — (45)
S — 11, (66)
H — 03, (75)

$\therefore$ PUSH $\Rightarrow$ 10, 45, 66, 75.

8. (*b*) From Statement II,
D is shorter than only A.
Therefore, A is the tallest.

9. (*d*) From both the statements,

[morning] walk is [good] → [na] pa ta [sa]

wish you [good morning] → la [na sa] da

The code for 'walk' is either 'pa' or 'ta'.

10. (*c*) As,

A, C, E, G each +3 → D, F, H, J

Similarly, Q, S, U, W each +3 → [T V X Z]

11. (*d*) As, 25 : 625 → 25 is common in both and 6 is added before it.

12. (*b*) As, Pigeon is a symbol of peace. In the same way, 'White' flag is a symbol of surrender. Hence, option (b) is correct.

13. (*a*) Here, the wife of brother of lady in photograph is the mother-in-law of Meera. Also, Meera is the daughter-in-law of that lady's brother. Now, it is clear that the husband of Meera is the nephew of tha lady.

14. (*a*) The year 1996 was a Leap Year.

Number of days remaining in the 1996.

$= 366 - 26 = 340$ days

$= 48$ weeks 4 odd days.

There 1 odd day in each of the years 1997, 1998 and 1999.

2000 was a Leap Year.

Days upto 15th August 2000

$31 + 29 + 31 + 30 + 31 + 30 + 31 + 15 = 228$ days

$\frac{228}{7} = 32$ weeks 4 odd days

Now, total number of odd days $= 4 + 3 + 4 = 11$

$\frac{11}{7} = 1$ week 4 odd days

15th August 2000 was 4 days beyond Friday, i.e. Tuesday.

15. (*d*) Rat is a rodent but here rat is called cat. Hence, in this case cat is a rodent.

16. (*c*) The pattern in clockwise direction is

$1 + 2 = 3, \quad 2 + 3 = 5$

$3 + 5 = 8, \quad 5 + 8 = 13$

$\therefore \quad ? = 13$

17. (*c*) The meaningful order is

Grass → Grasshopper → Frog → Snake → Eagle
(v) (iii) (i) (iv) (ii)

Solution (Q. Nos. 18-20) Let us draw the family diagram

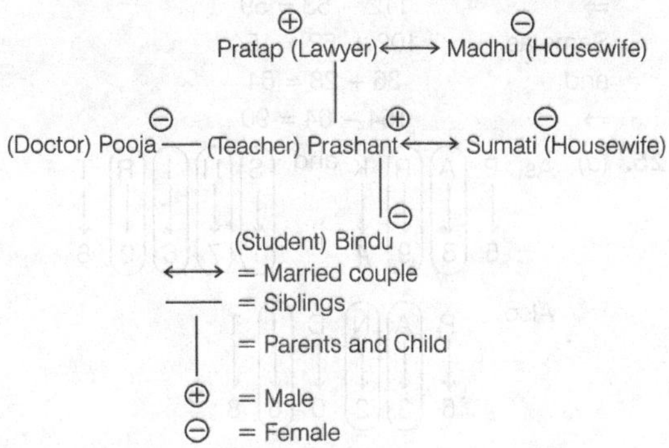

18. (*b*) Prashant is a teacher.

19. (*b*) Pratap-Madhu and Prashant-Sumati are the two married couples in the family and Pratap-Madhu is one of them.

20. (*a*) Pooja and Prashant are the children of Madhu.

21. (*b*) As pressure decreases at higher altitudes, water boils much below 100°C, so that the food does not get sufficient heat for being cooked. Salt increases the boiling point of water.

22. (*d*)

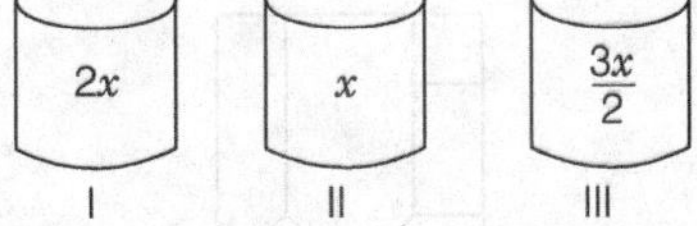

Suppose the number of fruits in the second basket $= x$

Number of fruits in the first basket $= 2x$

Number of fruits in the third basket $= 2x \times \frac{3}{4} = \frac{3x}{2}$

Now, $2x + x + \frac{3x}{2} = 30 \times 3$

$= \frac{4x + 2x + 3x}{2} = 30 \times 3$

$= 9x = 30 \times 3 \times 2$

$\therefore \quad x = \frac{30 \times 3 \times 2}{9} = 20$

Number of fruits in the first basket $= 2x = 2 \times 20 = 40$

23. (*b*) Sparrow cames under the class birds. But mice is different from birds.

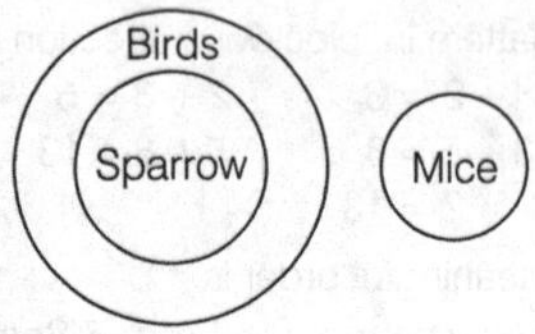

24. (*b*) As, 100 + 12 = 112
and, 28 + 25 = 53
⇒ 112 − 53 = 59
Same as, 102 + 52 = 154
and 36 + 28 = 64
⇒ 154 − 64 = 90

25. (*d*) As,

P	A	R	K	and	S	H	I	R	T
5	3	9	4		1	7	6	9	8

Also,

P	A	N	D	I	T
5	3	2	0	6	8

Similarly,

N	I	S	H	A	R
2	6	1	7	3	9

∴ NISHAR ⇒ 261739

26. (*b*) Reflection of the given number would be seen in the water as

13101989
13101989 (reflected)

27. (*c*) Clearly, option (c) figure will complete the pattern of the given figure

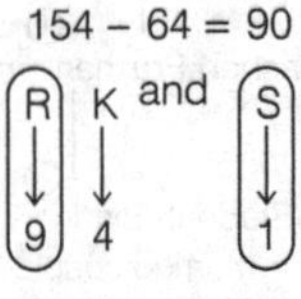

28. (*d*) As,

20	18	9	2	21	14	1	12
T	R	I	B	U	N	A	L

∴ Letter pairs = RU, NR, LN, LR ⇒ Four

29. (*a*) As, C E (N) (T) U R I (E) (S)

N → 3rd, T → 4th, E → 8th, S → 9th

∴ Words formed = NEST, NETS, SENT, TENS

30. (*e*) **Input** man 79 over 63 like 43 joy 15
***Step* I** 15 man 79 over 63 like 43 joy
***Step* II** 15 over man 79 63 like 43 joy
***Step* III** 15 over 43 man 79 63 like joy
Step IV 15 over 43 man 63 79 like joy
***Step* V** 15 over 43 man 63 like 79 joy

31. (*a*) ***Step* II** 27 world go 57 48 stem 35 kite
***Step* III** 27 world 35 go 57 48 stem kite
***Step* IV** 27 world 35 stem go 57 48 kite
***Step* V** 27 world 35 stem 48 go 57 kite
***Step* VI** 27 world 35 stem 48 kite go 57
***Step* VII** 27 world 35 stem 48 kite 57 go
Hence, five more steps will be required to complete the rearrangement.

32. (*b*) Answer figure (b) is embedded in the question figure.

Solution (Q. Nos. 33-34) By decoding given information with symbols of family diagram, we get

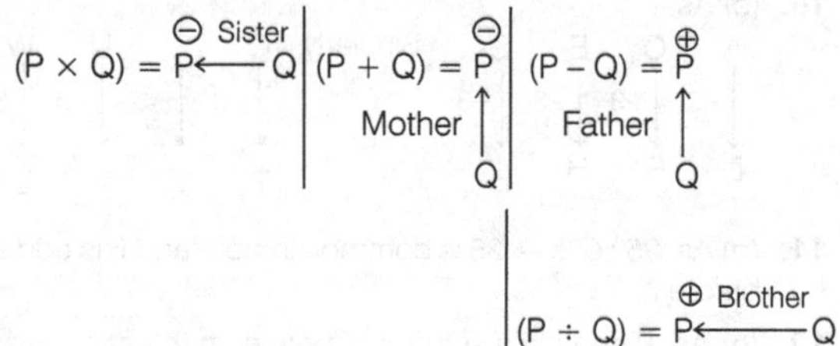

33. (*d*) By applying above decoding method, we can check all the options for the required relationship.

(a) (M ÷ T − R) = Rejected

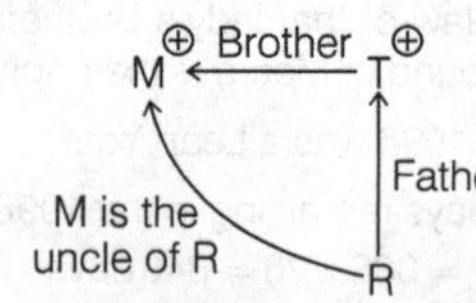

(b) (R ÷ T − M) = Rejected

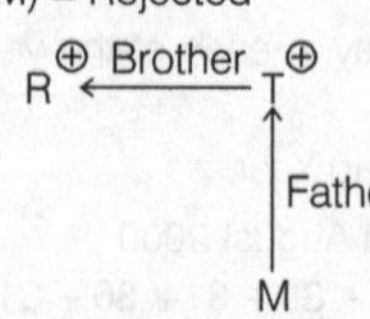

Here, gender of M is not known. So, M is either niece or nephew of R.

(c) (R × T + M × J) = Rejected

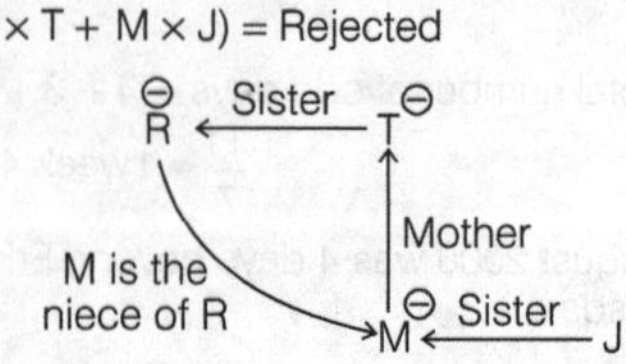

(d) (R ÷ T − M ÷ J) = Selected

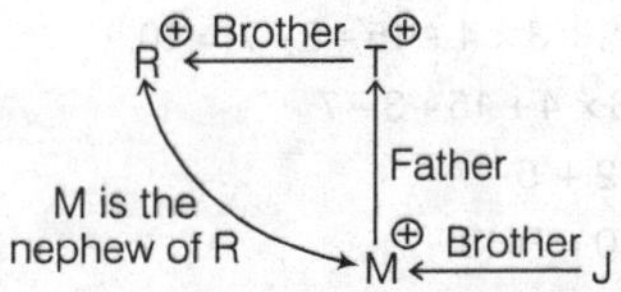

Hence, only option (d) satisfies the given relation between M and R.

34. (*e*) By applying above decoding method, we can check all the options for the required relationship.

(a) (W + T − H) = Rejected

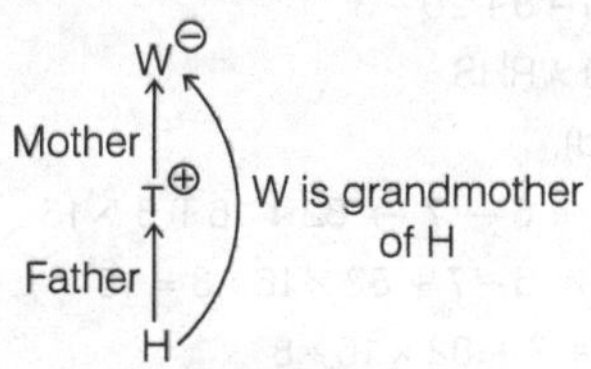

(b) (W ÷ T − H) = Rejected

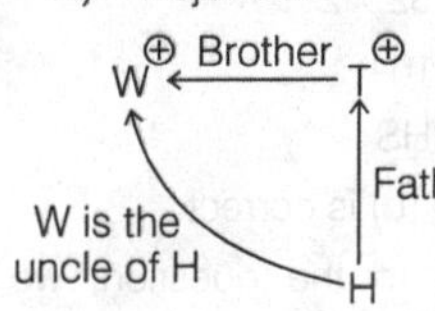

(c) (W × T + H) = Rejected

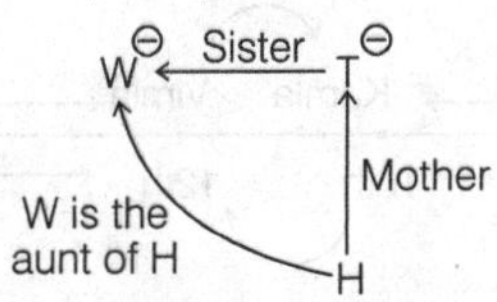

(d) (W ÷ T + H) = Rejected

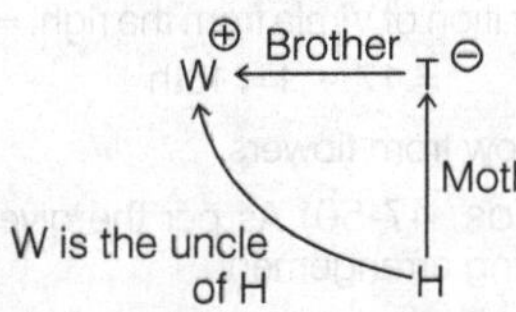

There is no option which satisfies the required relationship between W and H. So, option (e) is correct to answer.

35. (*a*) Let A be the starting point

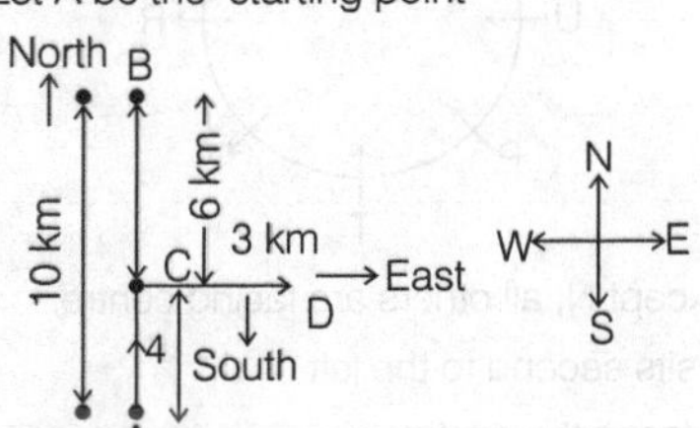

Kishankant goes 10 km North from A to point 'B' (Let) then he travers back in South that is the opposite direction upto 6 km, i.e. point C, hence

AC = 4km [AB − BC]

Now, from point C he goes last ward for a distance of 3 km to point D (Let).

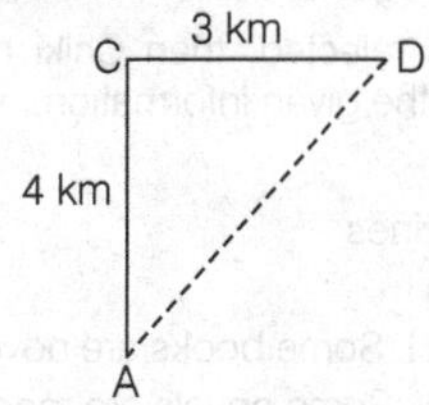

By Pythagoras theorem

$$AD = \sqrt{CD^2 + AC^2}$$
$$= \sqrt{(3)^2 + (4)^2}$$
$$= \sqrt{9 + 16} = \sqrt{25}$$
$$AD = 5 \text{ km}$$

and point D lies in North-East.

36. (*c*) Option (c) will complete the given pattern as follows

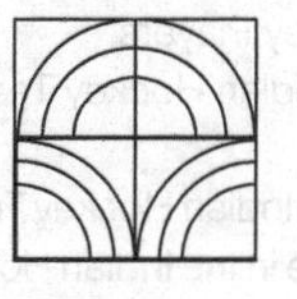

Solution (Q. Nos. 37-38)

$ ⇒ ≥	© ⇒ <	# ⇒ >	% ⇒ ≤	@ ⇒ =

37. (*d*) According to the question,

R # J ⇒ R > J ...(i)

J $ D ⇒ J ≥ D ...(ii)

D @ K ⇒ D = K ...(iii)

K % T ⇒ K ≤ T ...(iv)

On combining the statements (i), (ii), (iii) and (iv), we get

R > J ≥ D = K ≤ T

Conclusions I. T # D ⇒ T > D

II. T @ D ⇒ T = D (Either I or II is true)

III. R # K ⇒ R > K (True)

IV. J $ T ⇒ J ≥ T (False)

So, it is clear that either Conclusions I or II and III are true.

38. (*a*) According to the question,

T % R ⇒ T ≤ R ...(i)

R $ M ⇒ R ≥ M ...(ii)

M @ D ⇒ M = D ...(iii)

D © H ⇒ D < H ...(iv)

On combining the statements (i), (ii), (iii) and (iv), we get

T ≤ R ≥ M = D < H

Conclusions I. D % R ⇒ D ≤ R (True)

II. H # R ⇒ H > R (False)

III. T © M ⇒ T < M (False)

IV. T % D ⇒ T ≤ D (False)

So, it is clear that only Conclusion I is true.

39. (*d*) Figures (1), (6) and (9) are all triangles.
Figures (3), (4) and (7) are all quadrilaterals.
Figures (2), (5) and (8) are all pentagons.

40. (*d*) If Arya is rejected, then Chiki must be choosen according to the given information.

41. (*b*) B : Books
M : Magazines
N : Novels

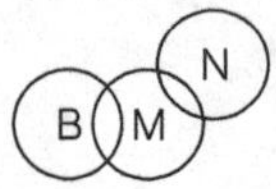

Conclusions I. Some books are novels. (✗)
II. Some novels are magazines. (✓)

42. (*d*) Neither of the two conclusions follows 'X' may or may not be inside the outer circle (representing people in the Indian Hockey Team)

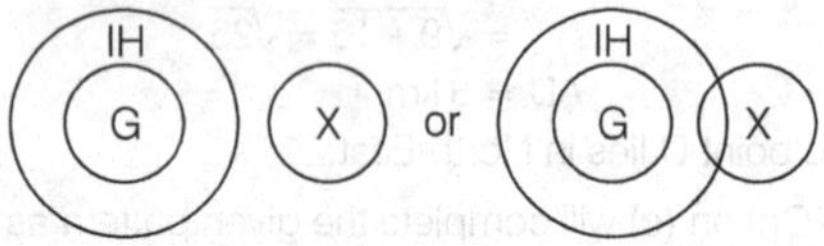

G : Good Hockey Players
IH : People in Indian Hockey Team

Conclusions
I. 'X' is not in the Indian Hockey Team. (✗)
II. 'X' wants to be in the Indian Hockey Team. (✗)

43. (*d*)

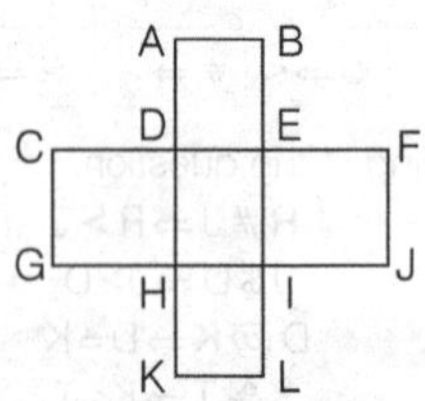

Smallest rectangles
= ☐ABED, ☐EFJI, ☐ILKH, ☐HGCD, ☐DEIH = 5
Rectangles formed with two rectangles
= ☐ ABIH, ☐ DELK, ☐ CEIG, ☐ DFJH = 4
Rectangles formed with three rectangles
= ☐ ABLK, ☐ CFJG = 2
∴ Total number of rectangles = 4 + 2 + 5 = 11

44. (*b*) Evaluating each of the given options one by one, we get

Option (a),

$$5 \downarrow 6 \rightarrow 6 \leftarrow 12 \uparrow 4 \nwarrow 30$$

$$5 \times 6 + 6 - 12 \div 4 = 30$$

$$\text{LHS} = 5 \times 6 + 6 - 12 \div 4$$
$$= 30 + 6 - 3$$
$$= 33 \neq \text{RHS}$$

Option (b),

$$3 \downarrow 4 \rightarrow 15 \uparrow 3 \leftarrow 7 \nwarrow 10$$

$$\Rightarrow \quad 3 \times 4 + 15 \div 3 - 7 = 10$$

$$\text{LHS} = 3 \times 4 + 15 \div 3 - 7$$
$$= 12 + 5 - 7$$
$$= 10 = \text{RHS}$$

Option (c),

$$10 \leftarrow 8 \rightarrow 5 \downarrow 4 \leftarrow 3 \uparrow 1 \searrow 20$$

$$\Rightarrow \quad 10 - 8 + 5 \times 4 - 3 \div 1 > 20$$

$$\text{LHS} = 10 - 8 + 5 \times 4 - 3 \div 1$$
$$= 10 - 8 + 20 - 3$$
$$= 19 \ngtr \text{RHS}$$

Option (d),

$$6 \rightarrow 7 \rightarrow 82 \downarrow 16 \uparrow 8 \nwarrow 15$$

$$\Rightarrow \quad 6 + 7 + 82 \times 16 \div 8 = 15$$

$$\text{LHS} = 6 + 7 + 82 \times 16 \div 8$$
$$= 6 + 7 + 82 \times 2$$
$$= 6 + 7 + 164$$
$$= 177 \neq \text{RHS}$$

Hence, option (b) is correct.

45. (*a*) According to the question, we have following seating arrangement.

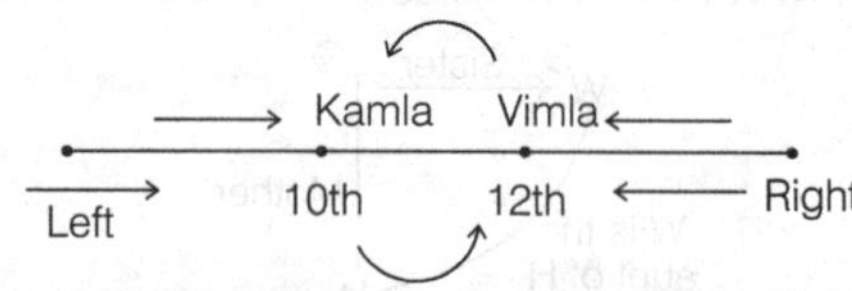

Total number of persons in the row = 16 + 12 − 1 = 27
Now, the ppsition of Vimla from the right = 27 − 10 + 1
= 17 + 1 = 18th

46. (c) Plants grow from flowers.

Solution (Q. Nos. 47-50) As per the given information, we draw the following arrangement.

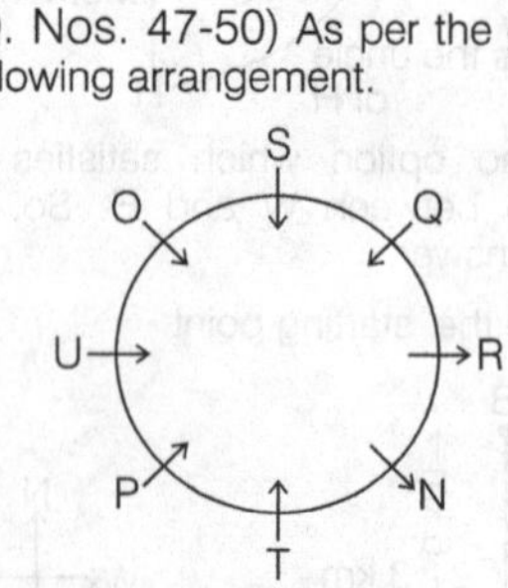

47. (*d*) Except N, all others are facing centre.

48. (*c*) S sits second to the left of U.

49. (*c*) S faces the centre.

50. (*b*) P is second to the right of N.

PRACTICE SET 29

1. If GOODNESS is coded as HNPCODTR, then how GREATNESS can be written in that code? **[SSC (CPO) 2015]**

(a) HQZSMFRT (b) HQFZUFRTM
(c) HQFZUODTR (d) HQFZUMFRT

2. If '+' stands for division, '÷' stands for multiplication, '×' stands for subtraction and '–' stands for addition which one of the following is correct?

(a) $18 \div 6 - 7 + 5 \times 2 = 20$
(b) $18 + 6 \div 7 \times 5 - 2 = 18$
(c) $18 \times 6 + 7 \div 5 - 2 = 16$
(d) $18 \div 6 \times 7 + 5 - 2 = 22$

3. This question consists of a statement and two conclusions numbered I and II given below it. A conclusion is something which can be directly deducted from the given information in light of all the given facts. You have to decide which of the given conclusions logically-follows from the given statements and select the appropriate answer.

Statement At present 10% of our villages receive 24 h electricity. In the next two years, the State government would strive to add 16% more villages to this list.

Conclusions **[SBI (PO) 2014]**

I. At present 60% villages in the State have no access to electricity at all.

II. Even after a couple of years, more than that of the villages may lack access to 24 h electricity.

(a) Only II can he concluded from the given information.
(b) Only I can be concluded from the given information I.
(c) Neither I nor II can be concluded from the given information.
(d) Both I and II can be concluded from the given information.
(e) Either I or II can be concluded from the given information.

4. *Read the following information carefully and answer the question which follows.* **[SBI (PO) 2014]**

Most students from State X prefer to move base to other States for higher education. The government of the State is concerned about this problem as these students might not come back even after completing their education.

Which of the following statements may be a **course of action** to deal with this problem?

(a) The government should set-up well equipped State of the art universities which will provide quality education.
(b) The government should not give much importance to this problem as there is high density of population per square km in the State.
(c) Scholarships should be declared for those students who perform well in tenth and twelfth standard examinations.
(d) All the colleges and universities should be asked to emphasise the importance of higher education and benefits of studying in their institute should also be highlighted.
(e) The government should make education free for all people of the State.

5. How many triangles are there in the figure given below? **[SSC (CGL) 2013]**

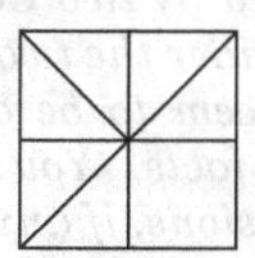

(a) 8 (b) 10
(c) 12 (d) 11

6. Select the related word from the given alternatives.

Carrot : Root :: Apple : ?

(a) Plant (b) Fruit
(c) Flower (d) Seed

7. In making decisions about important questions, it is desirable to distinguish between a 'strong' argument and a 'weak' argument A 'strong' argument must be both important and directly related to the question. A 'weak' argument may not be directly related to the question and may be of minor importance or may be related to the trivial aspect of the question. Each question below is followed by three arguments numbered I, II and III. You have to decide which of the arguments is 'strong' and which is 'weak'.

Statement Should there be a complete ban on Indian professionals seeking jobs elsewhere after getting their education in India?

Arguments

I. Yes, this is the only way to sustain present rate of technological development in India.

II. No, the Indians settled abroad send huge amount of foreign exchange and this constitutes a significant part of foreign exchange reserve.

III. No, the practical knowledge gained by Indians by working in other countries help India to develop its economy.

(a) None is strong
(b) All are strong
(c) I and II are strong
(d) Only III is strong
(e) II and III are strong

Direction (Q. Nos. 8-9) *Two statements are given below followed by two Conclusions I and II. You have to consider the two statements to be true even if they seem to be at variance with commonly known facts. You have to decide which of the conclusions, if any, follow from the given statements.*

Give answer

(a) Only I follows
(b) Only II follows
(c) Both I and II follow
(d) Neither I nor II follows

8. Statements Some scales are pencils.
Some erasers are pencils.

[SSC (Multitasking) 2014]

Conclusions I. Some pencils are erasers.
II. Some pencils are scales.

9. Statements Some chairs are made up of wood.
Some tables are made up of wood.

Conclusions I. All wooden things are either chairs or tables.
II. Some chairs are tables.

10. Identify which one of the given alternatives will be another member of the group of that class.
Lucknow, Patna, Bhopal, Jaipur?

[SSC (CGL) 2015]

(a) Shimla (b) Mysore
(c) Pune (d) Indore

11. In the following questions, find the odd numbers from the given alternatives.

(a) 26 (b) 34 (c) 72 (d) 46
(e) 38

Direction (Q. Nos. 12-13) *Each of the questions below consists of a question and two statements numbered I and II given below it. You have in decide whether the data provided in the statements are sufficient to answer the question.*

Give answer

(a) if the data in Statement I alone are sufficient to answer the question, while the data in Statement II alone are not sufficient to answer the question.
(b) if the data in Statement II alone are sufficient to answer the question, while the data in Statement I alone are not sufficient to answer the question.
(c) if the data either in Statement I alone or in Statement II alone are sufficient to answer the question.
(d) if the data given in both the Statements I and II together are not sufficient to answer the question.
(e) if the data in both the Statements I and II together are necessary to answer the question.

12. On which day of the week is Arun's birthday ?

I. Arun's brother correctly remembers that Arun's birthday is after Wednesday but before Sunday.

II. Arun's sister correctly remembers that Arun's birthday is before Friday.

13. How many daughters does Q have?

I. M and T are brothers of R.

II. R's mother T is wife of Q.

14. A piece of paper is folded and punched as shown below in the question figures. From the given answer figures, indicate how it will appear when opened. **[SSC (10+2) 2015]**

Question Figures

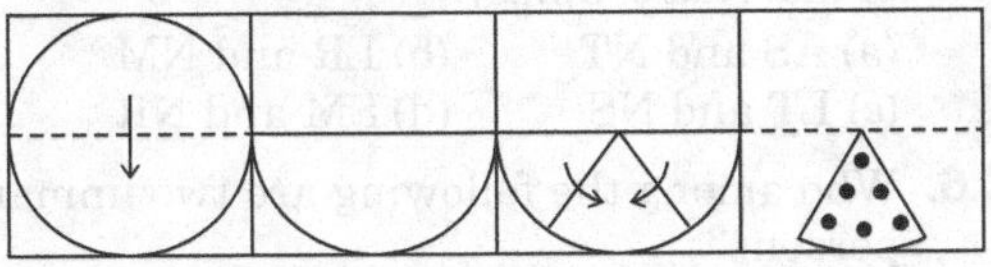

Answer Figures

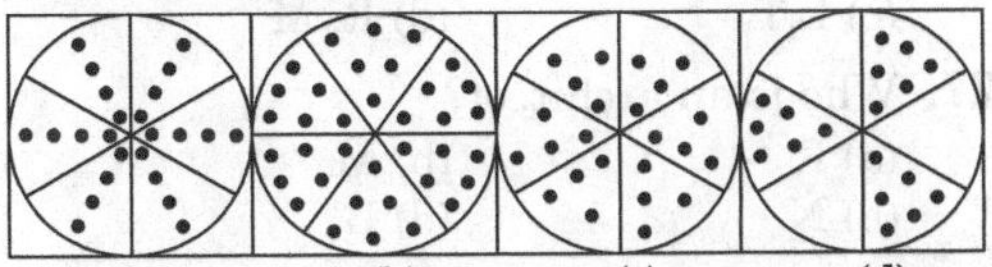

(a) (b) (c) (d)

15. A word is represented by only one set of numbers as given in anyone of the alternatives. The set of numbers given in the alternatives are represented by two classes of alphabets as in two matrices given below. The columns and rows of Matrix I are numbered from 0 to 4 and that of Matrix II are numbered from 5 to 9. A letter from these matrices can be represented first by its row and next by its column. e.g. 'A' can be represented by 02, 14, 33, etc., and K can be represented by 57, 69,88 etc. Identify the set for the word 'SOAP'. **[SSC (Steno) 2012]**

Matrix I

	0	1	2	3	4
0	R	S	A	C	N
1	C	N	R	S	A
2	S	A	C	N	R
3	N	R	S	A	C
4	A	C	N	R	S

Matrix II

	5	6	7	8	9
5	O	B	K	E	P
6	E	P	O	B	K
7	B	K	E	P	O
8	P	O	B	K	E
9	K	E	P	O	B

(a) 13, 55, 21, 66 (b) 01, 56, 21, 64
(c) 32, 56, 20, 66 (d) 20, 56, 21, 66

16. How many meaningful English word can be made with the letters ESLA, using each letter only once in each word?

(a) None (b) One
(c) Two (d) Three

17. In the number 76534218, each digit is replaced by the next digit, i.e. '1' is replaced by '2', '2' is replaced by '3' and so on and then the digits are arranged in ascending order from left to right, which digit will be 5th from the left end?

(a) 6 (b) 5 (c) 7 (d) 4

Direction (Q. Nos. 18-19) *A word and number arrangement machine when given an input line of words and numbers rearranges them following a particular rule in each step. The following is an illustration of an input and rearrangement.*

Input 17 put show on 39 27 85 gold
Step I show 17 put on 39 27 85 gold
Step II show 85 17 put on 39 27 gold
Step III show 85 put 17 on 39 27 gold
Step IV show 85 put 39 17 on 27 gold
Step V show 85 put 39 on 17 27 gold
Step VI show 85 put 39 on 27 17 gold
Step VII show 85 put 39 on 27 gold 17

and Step VII is the last step of the rearrangement of the above input.

As per the rules followed in the above steps, find out in each of the following questions the appropriate step for the given input.

18. **Input** glass full 15 37water now 85 67

Which of the following will be Step VI of the above input?

(a) water 85 now 67 full glass 15 37
(b) water 85 now 67 glass full 15 37
(c) water 85 now 67 glass 37 full 15
(d) There will be no such step
(e) None of the above

19. **Step II** of an input is 'ultra 73 12 16 mail sort 39 kite'

Which of the following steps will be the last but one?

(a) VIII (b) IX
(c) VII (d) VI
(e) None of these

20. Which one set of letters sequentially placed at the gaps in the given letters series shall complete it?

_PSRQ_SRQP_RQPS_

(a) PRQS (b) PQRS
(c) QPSR (d) SRQP

21. Find out the false date of birth given in the series. **[SSC (10 + 2) 2014]**

1. 15-02-1969 2. 16-03-1969
3. 18-04-1969 4. 30-01-1969
5. 31-02-1970 6. 31-12-1969

(a) 4 (b) 6 (c) 3 (d) 5

22. Choose the correct alternatives from the given ones that will complete the series.

1CV, 5FU, 9IT, ? 17OR

(a) 11LS (b) 14JS
(c) 15JS (d) 13LS

23. Where is the invisible number in the two positions of the same cube?

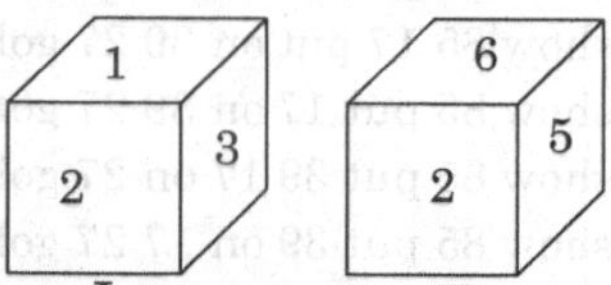

I II

(a) Opposite of 2 (b) Opposite of 3
(c) Opposite of 4 (d) Opposite of 6

24. Select the suitable alternative to satisfy the relationship in the following question.
[FCI Assistant Grade III 2015]

Question Figures

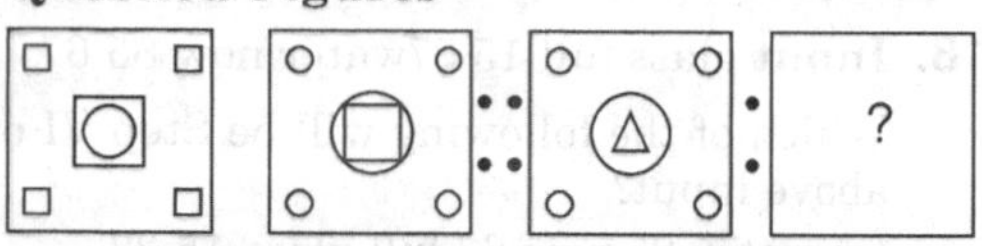

Answer Figures

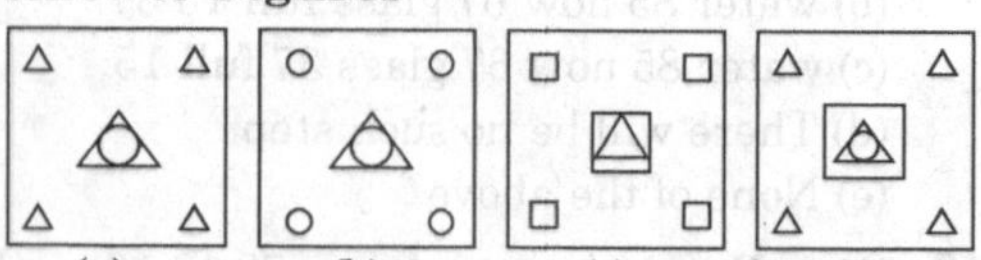

(a) (b) (c) (d)

Direction (Q. Nos. 25-27) *Read the following information carefully and answer the questions based on it.*

In a family of six members, there are three men L, M and N and three women R, S and T. The six persons are architect, lawyer, CA, professor, doctor and engineer by profession but not in the same order.

I. There are two married couples and two unmarried persons.
II. N is not R's husband.
III. The doctor is married to a lawyer. R's grandfather is a professor.
IV. M is neither L's son nor he is an architect or a professor.
V. The lawyer is T's daughter-in-law.
VI. N is T's son and the engineer's father.
VII. L is married to the CA.

25. Which among the following is the correct pair of married couples?

(a) AS and NT (b) LR and NM
(c) LT and NS (d) SM and NR

26. Who among the following are two unmarried persons?

(a) L, S (b) L, M
(c) L,T (d) R, M

27. Who is an architect?

(a) R (b) M
(b) N (d) L

28. A clock strikes 5 taking 8 s. In order to strike 9 at the same rate, the time taken is

(a) 16 s (b) 12 s
(c) 14 s (d) 18 s

29. In a group of equal number of cows and herdsmen the number of legs was 28 less than four times the number of heads. The number of herdsmen was

(a) 7 (b) 28
(c) 21 (d) 14

30. Mani is double the age of Prabhu. Ramona is half the age of Prabhu. If Mani is sixty, then find out the age of Ramona.
[SSC (10+2) 2014]

(a) 20 (b) 15
(c) 10 (d) 24

Direction (Q. Nos. 31-33) *Study the following information carefully and answer the questions given below.*

A, B, C, D, E, F, G, H and K are sitting around a circle facing the centre. B is fourth to the left of G who is second to the right of C. F is fourth to the right of C and second to the left of K. A is fourth to the right of K. D is not immediate neighbour of either K or B. H is third to the right of E.

31. Who is fourth to the right of D?

(a) K (b) H
(c) E (d) B
(e) None of these

32. In which of the following combinations is the third person sitting in between the first and second persons?

(a) EKB (b) CHB
(c) AGC (d) FGD
(e) None of these

33. Who is third to the right of H?

(a) A (b) D
(c) G (d) F
(e) None of these

34. In which answer figure is the question figure embedded?

Question Figure

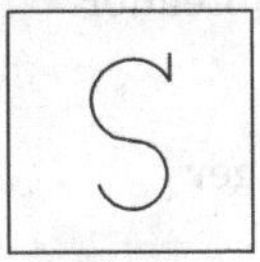

Answer Figures

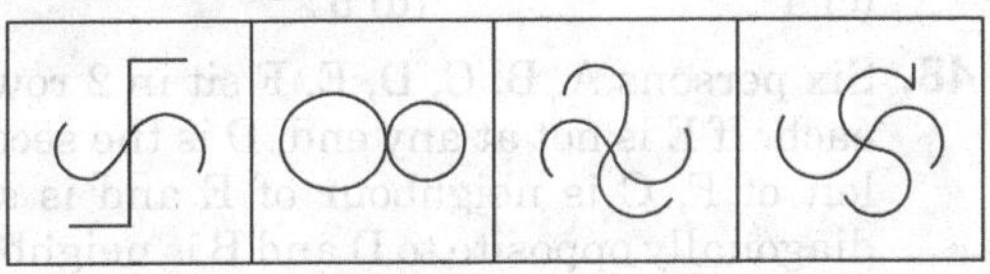

(a) (b) (c) (d)

35. A watch reads 4:30. If the minute hand points East, then in what direction will the hour hand point? **[NIFT (UG) 2015]**

(a) North (b) North-West
(c) South-East (d) North-East
(e) None of these

36. Select related number from the given alternatives.

COME : 36 : : PRANK : ?

(a) 50 (b) 60 (c) 30 (d) 35

37. Which of the following diagrams best represents a relationship among Criminal, Thief and Pick pocket?

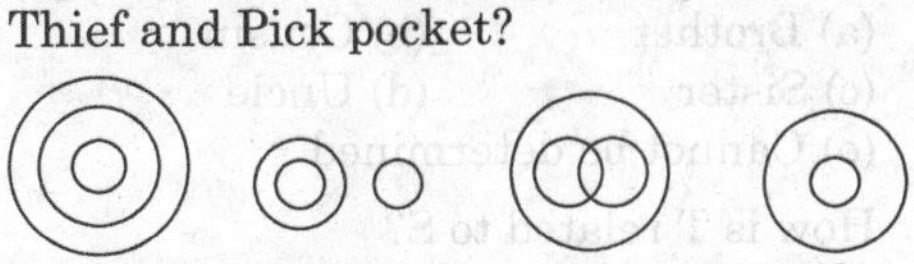

(a) (b) (c) (d)

38. Ranjana correctly remembers that Kiran's birthday was after Tuesday but before Friday. Rajan correctly remembers that Kiran's birthday was after Wednesday but before Sunday. On which day of the week does Kiran's birthday definitely fall?

(a) Monday
(b) Thursday
(c) Saturday
(d) Cannot be determined

39. In a class of 45 students rank of Ayush is 15 from top, then rank of Ayush from bottom is

(a) 30 (b) 32
(c) 31 (d) 35

40. If C = 3, CEP = 24, then what will be the value of HUX? **[SSC (10+2) 2008]**

(a) 47 (b) 49
(c) 51 (d) 53

41. Find the missing number. **[FCI Assistant Grade III 2015]**

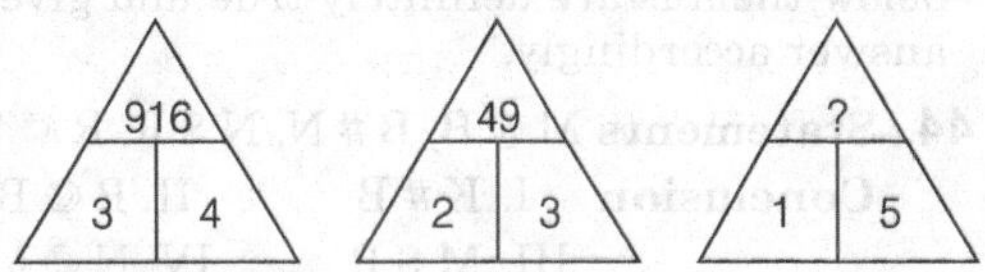

(a) 512 (b) 125
(c) 256 (d) 315

42. If a mirror is placed on the line AB, then which of the answer figures is the right image of the question figure?

Question Figure

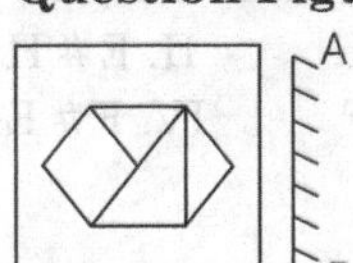

Answer Figures

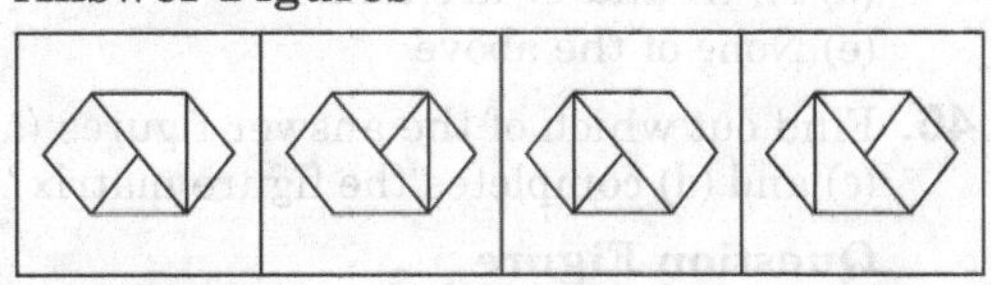

(a) (b) (c) (d)

43. Which one of the given responses would be meaningful order of the following? **[SSC (CGL) 2015]**

(i) Crop
(ii) Root
(iii) Stem
(iv) Seed
(v) Flower

(a) (ii), (iii), (iv), (i), (v)
(b) (ii), (iv), (v), (i), (iii)
(c) (iv), (ii), (iii), (v), (i)
(d) (ii), (iii), (v), (i), (iv)

Direction (Q. Nos. 44-45) *In the following question, the symbols @, $, #, © and % are used with the following meaning as illustrated below.* **[IBPS (PO) 2012]**

'P $ Q' means 'P is not smaller than Q'.

'P # Q' means 'P is neither smaller than nor equal to Q'.

'P @ Q' means 'P is neither greater than nor smaller than Q'.

'P © Q' means 'P is neither greater than nor equal to Q'.

'P % Q' means 'P is not greater than Q'.

Now, in each of the following question, assuming the given statements to be true, find of the four Conclusions I, II, III and IV given below them is/are definitely true and give your answer accordingly.

44. **Statements** M @ B, B # N, N $ R, R © K

Conclusion I. K # B II. R © B III. M $ R IV. N © M

(a) I and III are true
(b) I and II are true
(c) II and IV are true
(d) II, III and IV are true
(e) None of the above

45. **Statements** F # H, H @ M, M © E, E $ J

Conclusions I. J © M II. E # H III. M © F IV. F # E

(a) I and II are true
(b) II and III are true
(c) I, II and III are true
(d) II, III and IV are true
(e) None of the above

46. Find out which of the answer figures (a), (b), (c) and (d) completes the figure matrix?

Question Figure

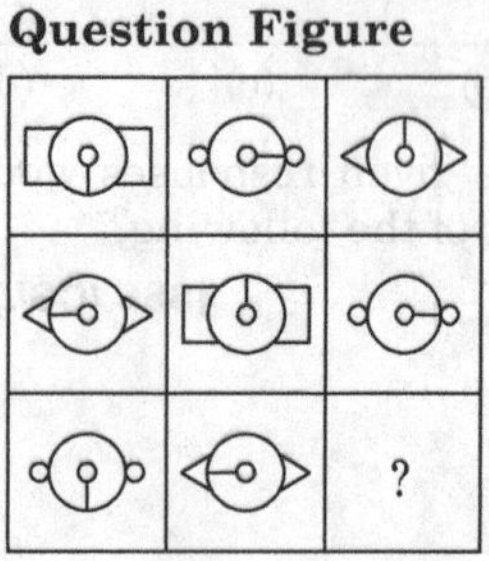

Answer Figures

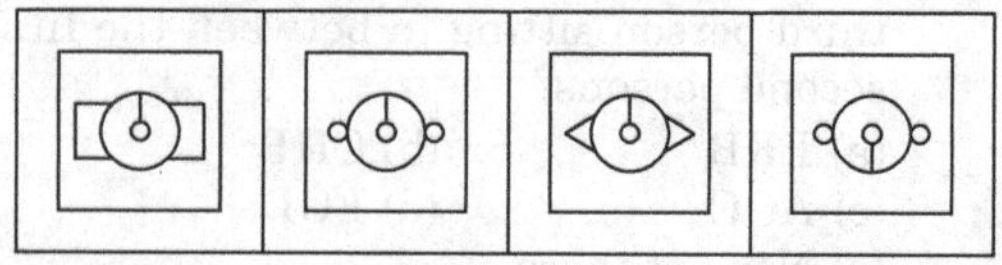

(a) (b) (c) (d)

47. In the given figure numbers indicate Indian, Leader and Singer. Study the figure carefully. Which region among them denotes Indian leaders who are not singers, indicate that numbers. **[BSSC (CGL) 2015]**

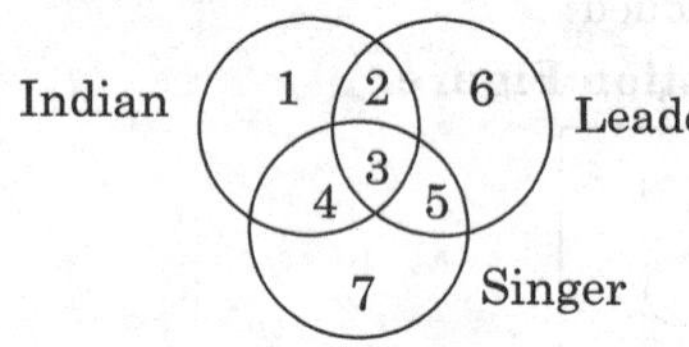

(a) 2 (b) 3
(c) 4 (d) 5

48. Six persons A, B, C, D, E, F sit in 2 row, 3 in each. If E is not at any end, D is the second to left of F, C is neighbour of E and is sitting diagonally opposite to D and B is neighbour of F, who will be opposite of B?

(a) A (b) E
(c) C (d) D

Direction (Q. Nos. 49-50) *Study the following information and answer the given questions.* **[IBPS RRB (PO) 2015]**

S is the sister of B. K is the brother of B.

K is the son of L. L is married to Y. Y is the daughter of J.

Y has only one daughter. J is married to C.

K is the brother of D. D is married to T.

49. If P is the brother of C, then how is J related to P?

(a) Brother (b) Cousin
(c) Sister (d) Uncle
(e) Cannot be determined

50. How is T related to S?

(a) Brother-in-law (b) Cousin
(c) Sister-in-law (d) Sister
(e) Brother

Hints and Solutions

1. (*d*) As,

G	O	O	D	N	E	S	S
+1↓	−1↓	+1↓	−1↓	+1↓	−1↓	+1↓	−1↓
H	N	P	C	O	D	T	R

Similarly,

G	R	E	A	T	N	E	S	S
+1↓	−1↓	+1↓	−1↓	+1↓	−1↓	+1↓	−1↓	+1↓
H	Q	F	Z	U	M	F	R	T

2. (*b*) According to the question, we can arrange the mathematical symbols as $+ = \div, \div = \times$

$\times = -, - = +$

option (b), $18 + 6 \div 7 \times 5 - 2 = 18$

$\Rightarrow \quad 18 \div 6 \times 7 - 5 + 2 = 18 \Rightarrow 21 - 5 + 2 = 18$

3. (*d*) Nothing is given in the statement about the villages which have no access to electricity at all. So, conclusion I does not follow. It is clear from the statement that even after a couple of years, more than that of the villages may lack access to 24h electricity.

4. (*d*) Course of action (d) is correct answer.

5. (*b*) Smallest triangles = ΔBOC, ΔCOD, ΔFOG, ΔGOH, ΔHOA, ΔAOB = 6

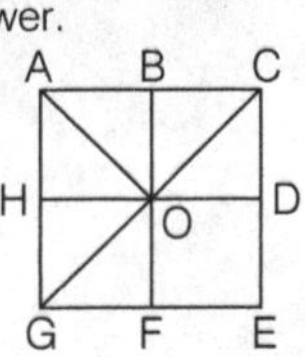

Triangles formed with two small triangles

= ΔAOG, ΔAOC = 2

Largest triangles = ΔACG, ΔEGC = 2

∴ Total triangles = 6 + 2 + 2 = 10

6. (*b*) Carrot is a modified 'Root'. In the same way, Apple is a 'Fruit'.

7. (*a*) None of the given arguments is strong.

8. (*c*)

Conclusions I. Some pencils are erasers. (✔)

II. Some pencils are scales. (✔)

So, both I and II follow.

9. (*d*)

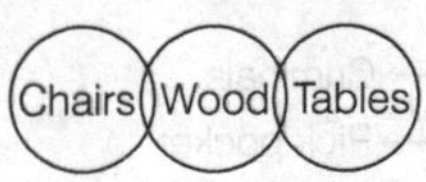

Conclusions I. All wooden things are either chairs or tables. (✗)

II. Some chairs are tables. (✗)

So, neither I nor II follows.

10. (*a*) We known that Capital of Uttar Pardesh is Lucknow. Capital of Bihar is Patna. Capital of Madhya Pradesh is Bhopal and Capital of Rajasthan is jaipur.

From the options we choose Shimla as it is capital of Himachal Pradesh.

11. (*c*) All others have only two factors with prime numbers.

$26 = 2 \times 13,\ 34 = 2 \times 17,\ 72 = 2 \times 2 \times 2 \times 3 \times 3$

$46 = 2 \times 23,\ 38 = 2 \times 19$

12. (*e*) From both the statements, Arun's birthday is on Thursday.

13. (*d*) Both the statements are not sufficient to answer the question.

14. (*b*) Option figure (b) is correct answer.

15. (*a*) According to the matrices,

S — 01, 13, 20, 32, 44

O — 55, 67, 79, 86, 98

A — 02, 14, 21, 33, 40

P — 59, 66, 78, 85, 97

SOAP ⟹ 13, 55, 21, 66

16. (*c*) Required words = SEAL, SALE

17. (*a*) Let us see

Original number	7	6	5	3	4	2	1	8
Step I Arrangement	8	7	6	4	5	3	2	9
Step II Arrangement	2	3	4	5	6	7	8	9

From left → 5th

Hence, the required digit is 6.

Solution (Q. Nos. 18-19) After careful analysis of the given input and various steps of rearrangement it is evident that in the first step one word is rearranged and in the second step one number is rearranged. These two steps are repeated alternately until all the words are arranged alphabetically in the reverse order and all the numbers are arranged in descending order.

18. (*d*) **Input** glass full 15 37 water now 85 67

***Step* I** water glass full 15 37 now 85 67

***Step* II** water 85 glass full 15 37 now 67

***Step* III** water 85 now glass full 15 37 67

***Step* IV** water 85 now 67 glass full 15 37

***Step* V** water 85 now 67 glass 37 full 15

Step V is the last step

19. (*d*) ***Step* II** ultra 73 12 16 mail sort 39 kite

***Step* III** ultra 73 sort 12 16 mail 39 kite

***Step* IV** ultra 73 son 39 12 16 mail kite

***Step* V** ultra 73 sort 39 mail 12 16 kite

***Step* VI** ultra 73 son 39 mail 16 12 kite

***Step* VII** ultra 73 sort 39 mail 16 kite 12

20. (*c*) The letter series will be

Q P S R / Q P S R / Q P S R / Q P S R ⟹ QPSR

21. (*d*) We know that, in the case of February in an ordinary year, there are 28 days and in a leap year there are 29 days. So, 31-02-1970 is the false date of birth given in the series.

22. (*d*) Pattern of given alpha-numeric series is as follows

$1 \xrightarrow{+4} 5 \xrightarrow{+4} 9 \xrightarrow{+4} \boxed{13} \xrightarrow{+4} 17$

$\overset{1}{C} \xrightarrow{+3} \overset{6}{F} \xrightarrow{+3} \overset{9}{I} \xrightarrow{+3} \boxed{\overset{12}{L}} \xrightarrow{+3} \overset{15}{O}$

$\overset{22}{V} \xrightarrow{-1} \overset{21}{U} \xrightarrow{-1} \overset{20}{T} \xrightarrow{-1} \boxed{\overset{19}{S}} \xrightarrow{-1} \overset{18}{R}$

∴ ? = 13 LS

23. (*a*) The invisible number is 4 and it is opposite to number 2.

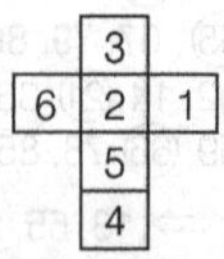

24. (*a*) Answer figure (a) is the suitable alternative to satisfy the relationship in the question figure.

Solution (Q. Nos. 25-27) Let us draw the family diagram

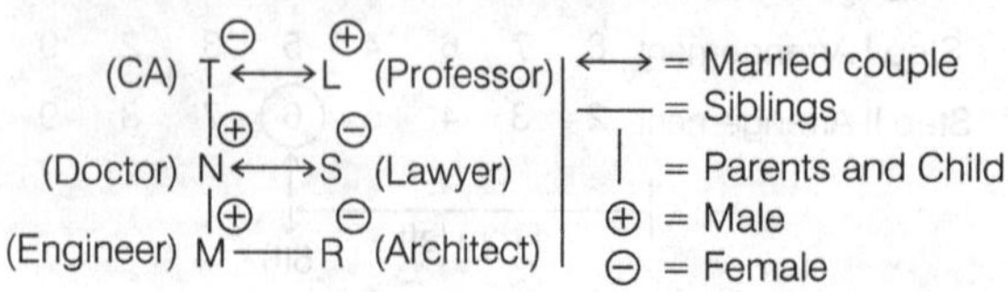

25. (c) LT and NS are the married couples in the family.

26. (*d*) M and R are two unmarried persons.

27. (*a*) R in an architect.

28. (*a*) There are 4 intervals when the clock strikes 5. Time taken for 4 intervals = 8 s

∴ Time taken for 1 interval = 2 s

In order to strike 9, there are 8 intervals, for which the time taken is $(8 \times 2) = 16$ s.

29. (*d*) Suppose the number of cows = x

Therefore, the number of herdsmen = x

According to question,

$$4 \times 2x - 28 = x \times 2 + x \times 4$$

$$\Rightarrow \quad 8x - 28 = 2x + 4x \Rightarrow 8x - 6x = 28$$

$$\therefore \quad x = \frac{28}{2} = 14$$

30. (*b*) According to the question,

Age of Mani = 2 × Age of Prabhu and

Age of Ramona = $\frac{1}{2}$ × Age of Prabhu

Now, Age of Mani = 60 yr

∴ 60 = 2 × Age of Prabhu ⇒ Age of Prabhu = 30 yr

∴ Age of Ramona = $\frac{1}{2} \times 30$ = 15 yr

Solution (Q. Nos. 31-33) According to given information, the final arrangement is as following

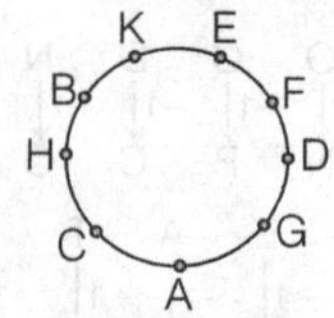

31. (*d*) B is fourth to the right of D.

32. (*d*) D is sitting between F and G.

33. (*c*) G is the third to the right of H.

34. (*d*) Clearly, question figure is embedded in answer figure (d) as shown below

35. (*d*)

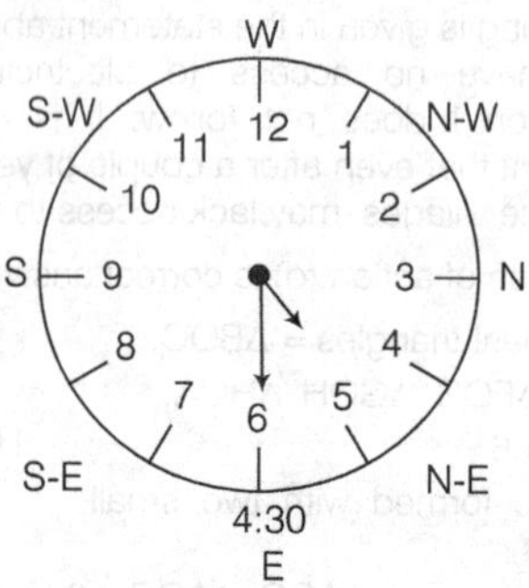

If the minute hand points East direction, then hour hand point is in North-East.

36. (*b*) As, C O M E → Positional values 3 15 13 5

∴ 3 + 15 + 13 + 5 = 36

Similarly, P R A N K → Positional values 16 18 1 14 11

∴ 16 + 18 + 1 + 14 + 11 = 60

37. (*c*) Some thieves are pick pockets and they both under the category of criminals. This can be expressed as given in option (c).

38. (*b*)

According to	Possibility of Date
Ranjana	Wednesday, Thursday
Rajan	Thursday, Friday, Saturday

Clearly, Thursday is common to both. Hence, the correct day is Thursday.

39. (c)

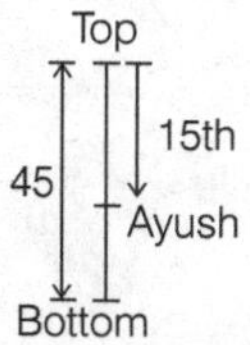

Ayush's rank from the bottom = Total number of students − Rank of Ayush from top +1 = 45 − 15 + 1 = 31

40. (d) According to the question, we have the C = 3

⇒ Position number in the English alphabet

C E P
↓ ↓ ↓
3 + 5 + 16 = 24

Similarly, H U X
↓ ↓ ↓
8 + 21 + 24 = 53

41. (b) As, 3 4
↓ ↓
$(3)^2$ $(4)^2$
↓ ↓
9 16 → 916

and 2 3
↓ ↓
$(2)^2$ $(3)^2$
↓ ↓
4 9 → 49

Same as, 1 5
↓ ↓
$(1)^2$ $(5)^2$
↓ ↓
1 25 → 125

42. (d) The correct laterally inverted mirror image of the question figure is as follows

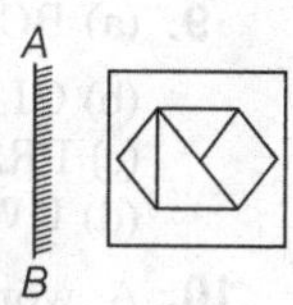

43. (c) The meaningful order is
(iv) Seed → (ii) Root → (iii) Stem → (v) Flower → (i) Crop

Solution (Q. Nos 44-45) Given that,

\$ ⇒ ≥	© ⇒ <	# ⇒ >	% ⇒ ≤	@ ⇒ =

44. (c) According to the question,

M @ B ⇒ M = B ...(i)
B # N ⇒ B > N ...(ii)
N \$ R ⇒ N ≥ R ...(iii)
R © K ⇒ R < K ...(iv)

On combining the statements (i), (ii), (iii) and (iv), we get

M = B > N ≥ R < K

Conclusions I. K # B ⇒ K > B (False)
II. R © B ⇒ R < B (True)
III. M \$ R ⇒ M ≥ R (False)
IV. N © M ⇒ N < M (True)

So, it is clear that both Conclusions II and IV are true.

45. (b) According to the question,

F # H ⇒ F > H ...(i)
H @ M ⇒ H = M ...(ii)
M © E ⇒ M < E ...(iii)
E \$ J ⇒ E ≥ J ...(iv)

On combining the statements (i), (ii), (iii) and (iv), we get

F > H = M < E ≥ J

Conclusions I. J © M ⇒ J < M (False)
II. E # H ⇒ E > H (True)
III. M © F ⇒ M < F (True)
IV. F # E ⇒ F > E (False)

So, it is clear that both Conclusions II and III are true.

46. (a) In each row, the central part of the first figure rotates either 90° clockwise or 90° anti-clockwise to form the central part of the second figure and the central part of the first figure rotates 180° to form the central part of the third figure. Also, in each row, there are three types of geometrical figures are there — rectangles, circles and triangles.

47. (a) Region '2' denotes Indian leaders who are not singers.

48. (b) According to the given condition in the question, the sitting arrangement of six person will be as shown below:

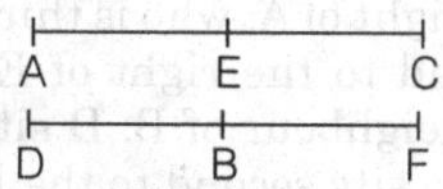

So, E is opposite to B.

Solution (Q. Nos. 49-50) According to the information, the blood relation can be represented as shown below:

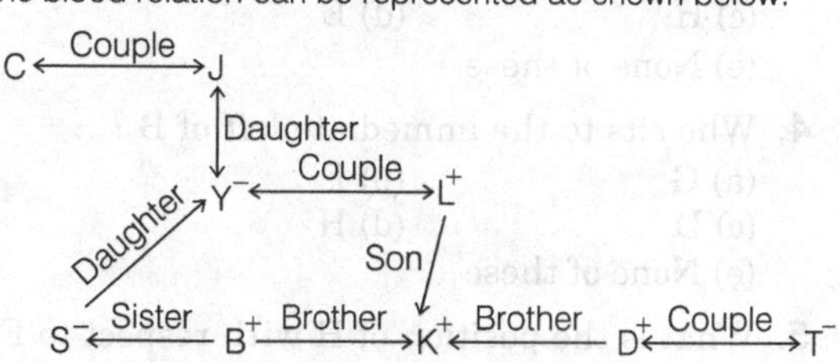

49. (e) If P is the brother of C,

P^+ ←Brother→ C ←Couple→ J

Then, we cannot determined how J is related to P, because the gender of J is not mentioned. So, J either male or female.

50. (c) T is sister-in-law of S.

PRACTICE SET 30

1. From the given alternative words, select the word which can be formed using the letters of the given word ESTABLISHMENT **[SSC (CGL) 2014]**

(a) ESTEEMED (b) ESTIMATE
(c) TABULAR (d) ASTONISH

2. Six faces of a block have been painted with green, yellow, red, black, pink and white. Two positions of this block are given below. If the pink colour be at the top, then which colour will be at the bottom?

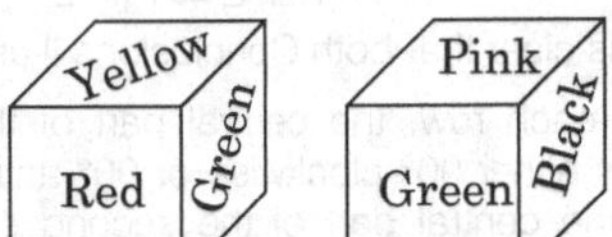

I II

(a) Blue (b) Green
(c) Yellow (d) Red

Direction (Q. Nos 3-5) *Study the following information carefully to answer these questions.*

Eight friends A, B, C, D, E, F, G and H are sitting around a circle facing the centre. B is third to the right of A, who is third to the right of C. F is second to the right of E who is not an immediate neighbour of B. D sits second to the left of H, who sits second to the left of G.

3. Who sits second of the left of A ?
(a) G (b) D
(c) H (d) E
(e) None of these

4. Who sits to the immediate left of B ?
(a) G (b) F
(c) D (d) H
(e) None of these

5. What is the position of H with respect to F ?
(a) To the immediate right
(b) Third to the left
(c) Second to the left
(d) Second to the right
(e) Third to the right

6. Find out which of the answer figures (a), (b), (c) and (d) completes the figure matrix ?

Question Figure

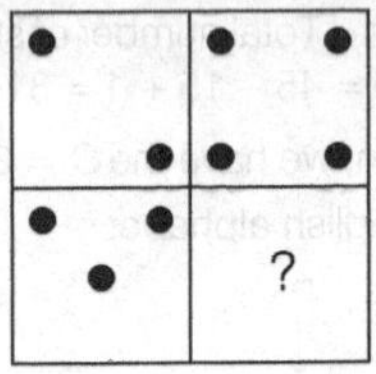

Answer Figures

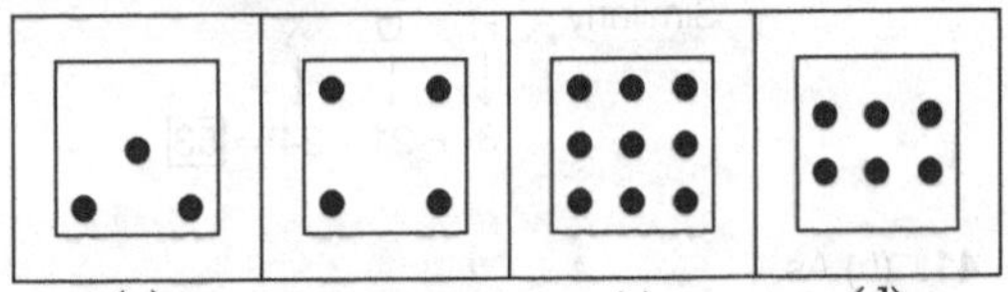

(a) (b) (c) (d)

7. Anil reached a place on Friday. He came to know that he was three days earlier than the scheduled day. If he had reached there on the following Sunday, then how many days late/ early he would have been?
(a) One day earlier (b) One day late
(c) Two days late (d) Two days earlier

Direction (Q. Nos. 8-9) *In the following questions, find the odd letters/ words from the given alternatives.*

8. (a) Rose (b) Lily
(c) Lotus (d) Grapes

9. (a) BCDG **[SSC (10+2) 2014]**
(b) GIJL
(c) PRSU
(d) UWXZ

10. A word is represented by only one set of numbers as given in any one of the alternatives. The set of numbers given in the alternatives are represented by two classes of alphabets as in two matrices given below. The coloumns and rows of Matrix I are numbered from 0 to 4 and that of Matrix II are numbered from 5 to 9 . A letter from these matrices can be represented first by its row and next by its column. e.g. T can be represented by 00, 13, 30 and R can be represented by 56, 79, 87 etc. Identify the set for the word 'DEAL' .

Matrix I

	0	1	2	3	4
0	T	C	K	K	G
1	F	B	R	T	O
2	M	D	I	O	Q
3	T	A	U	A	N
4	Y	K	P	R	Y

Matrix II

	5	6	7	8	9
5	C	R	I	G	E
6	P	M	S	L	T
7	E	Y	N	B	R
8	A	U	R	O	A
9	O	T	A	Q	K

(a) 11, 23, 76, 68 (b) 21, 75, 97, 68
(c) 21, 32, 86, 89 (d) 43, 75, 89, 69

11. Find the missing number.

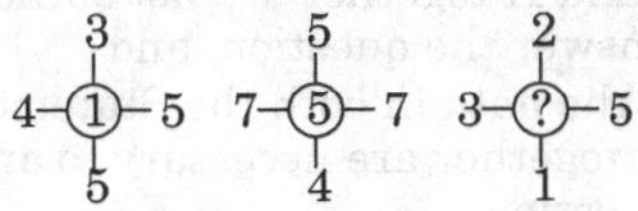

(a) 11 (b) 3 (c) 1 (d) 5

12. In a certain code language, BAKED is coded as 'YZPVW' and PRINT is coded as 'KIRMG'. How will SHRED be coded in the same code language?

(a) HSIVW (b) HSITH
(c) GRJVW (d) GRJJV
(e) Cannot be determined

13. How many straight lines are there in the following figure?

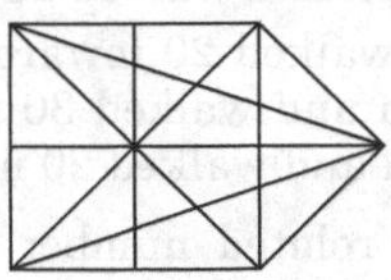

(a) 10 (b) 12
(c) 13 (d) 17

Direction (Q. Nos. 14 - 18) *Read the following information carefully to answer the questions that follow.* **[Hotal Mgmt 2011]**

I. A, B, C, D, E and F are the members of a family.
II. These members are engineer, doctor, designer, lawyer, manager and professor but not in the same order.
III. There are two married couples in the family.
IV. C is the designer and is married to lawyer.
V. B is either father or mother of F and E.
VI. A is married to manager D.
VII. F is professor who is the grandson or granddaughter of doctor.
VIII. B is female while doctor is a male member.

14. Which of the following is one of the pairs of couples in the family ?

(a) AD (b) AC
(c) AB (d) Cannot be determined

15. What is the profession of A?

(a) Doctor (b) Lawyer
(c) Designer (d) Manager

16. What is the profession of E?

(a) Professor (b) Manager
(c) Designer (d) None of these

17. How many females are there in the family?

(a) 1 (b) 3
(c) 4 (d) Cannot be determined

18. How is A related to E?

(a) Grandfather (b) Father
(c) Uncle (d) Brother

Direction (Q. Nos. 19-20) *Study the following information carefully and answer the given questions.*

A word and number arrangement machine when given an input line of words and numbers rearranges them following a particular rule in each step. The following is an illustration of input and rearrangement.

Input gone 93 over 46 84 now for 31
***Step* I** 31 gone 93 over 46 84 now for
***Step* II** 31 over gone 93 46 84 now for
***Step* III** 31 over 46 gone 93 84 now for
***Step* IV** 31 over 46 now gone 93 84 for
***Step* V** 31 over 46 now 84 gone 93 for

and Step V is the last step of the rearrangement of the above input.

As per the rules followed in the above steps, find out in each of the following questions the appropriate step for the given input.

19. Step III of an Input '15 window 29 93 86 sail tower buy'

Which of the following will be Step VI?

(a) 15 window 29 tower 86 sail 93 buy
(b) 15 window 29 tower 86 93 sail buy
(c) 15 window 29 tower 93 86 sail buy
(d) There will be no such step.
(e) None of the above

20. **Input** station hurry 39 67 all men 86 59
How many steps will be required to complete the rearrangement ?
(a) Four (b) Five (c) Six (d) Three
(e) None of these

21. A is the son of B, while B and C are sisters to one another. E is the mother of C. If D is the son of E, then which of the following statements is correct?
(a) D is the maternal uncle of A
(b) E is the brother of B
(c) D is the cousin of A
(d) B and D are brothers

22. Select the related number from the given alternatives. **[SSC (CGL) 2014]**

720 : 840 : : 60 : ?

(a) 76 (b) 80 (c) 70 (d) 74

23. 'Good' is related to 'Bad' in the same way as 'Roof' is related to
(a) Wall (b) Pillar
(c) Terrace (d) Floor

24. Select the related letters from the given alternatives. BJNT : CIOS : : DHPV : ?
(a) EGQU (b) ELQW
(c) ELPV (d) EIOU

25. Which of the answer figures is exactly the mirror image of the given figure, when the mirror is held on the line MN? **[SSC DEO 2011]**

Question Figure

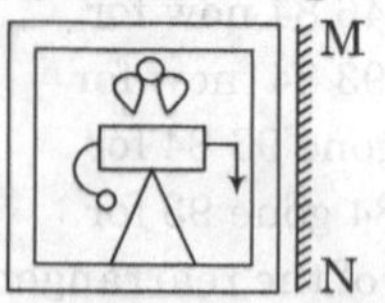

Answer Figures

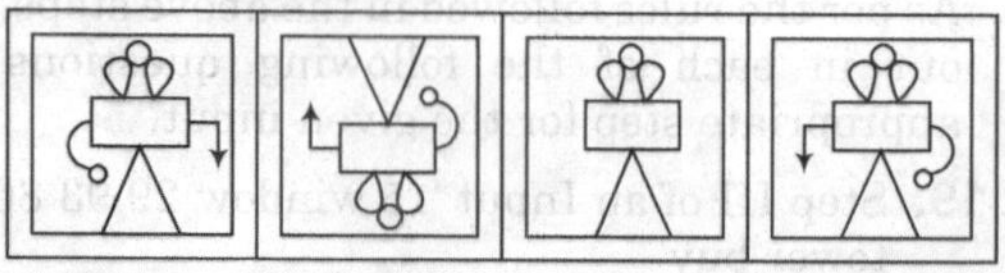

Direction (Q. Nos. 26-27) *Each of the questions below consists of a question and two statements numbered I and II given below it. You have to decide whether the data provided in the statements are sufficient to answer the questions.*

Give answer
(a) if the data in Statement I alone are sufficient to answer the question, while the data in Statement II alone are not sufficient to answer the question.
(b) if the data in Statement II alone are sufficient to answer the question, while the data in Statement I alone are not sufficient to answer the question.
(c) if the data either in Statement I alone in statement II alone or in Statement II alone are sufficient to answer the question.
(d) if the data given in both the Statements I and II together are not sufficient to answer the question, and
(e) if the data in both the Statements I and II together are necessary to answer the question.

26. How is 'sure' written in a code language ?
I. 'he is sure' is written as 'ja ha ma' in that code language
II. 'is she sure' is written as 'ka ja ma' in that code language

27. How far did Mohan walk from the starting point ?
I. Mohan walked 20 m towards West, took a right turn and walked 30 m, again took a right turn and walked 20 m
II. Mohan walked 20 towards South, took a left turn and walked 30 m, again took a left turn and walked 20 m

28. Select the related number from the given alternatives. **[SSC (Steno) 2014]**

7 : 47 : : 9 : ?

(a) 79 (b) 94 (c) 50 (d) 81

29. Which one of letters when sequentially placed at the gaps in the given letter series shall complete it ?

ac _ ga _ eg _ ce_

(a) dbag (b) ecag
(c) deag (d) ebdg

30. Choose the correct alternative from the given ones that will complete the series.

C4X, F9U, I16R, ?

(a) L25P (b) K25P
(c) L27P (d) L25O

31. If the following equation has to be balance, then the signs of which of the following options will be used? 24 6 12 16 = 0
(a) ÷, + and − (b) −, ÷ and +
(c) −, − and − (d) ÷, + and ÷

Direction (Q. Nos. 32 - 33) *Two statements are given below followed by two Conclusions I and II. You have to consider the two statements to be true even if they seem to be at variance with commonly known facts. You have to decide which of the conclusions, if any, follow from the given statements.*

Give answer
(a) Only I follows
(b) Only II follows
(c) Both I and II follow
(d) Neither I nor II follows

32. Statements All good athletes win.
All good athletes eat well. **[MAT 2014]**
Conclusions I. All those who eat well are good athletes.
II. All those who win eat well.

33. Statements Some scooters are trucks.
All trucks are trains.
Conclusions I. Some scooters are trains.
II. No truck is a scooter.

34. A bus leaves the city A with half the number of women as men. At the next city B, 10 men get down and 5 women get in. Now, there are equal number of men and women. How many passengers boarded the bus initially?
(a) 36 (b) 45 (c) 15 (d) 30

35. Select missing figure from the given responses. **[UPSC CSAT 2015]**

Question Figures

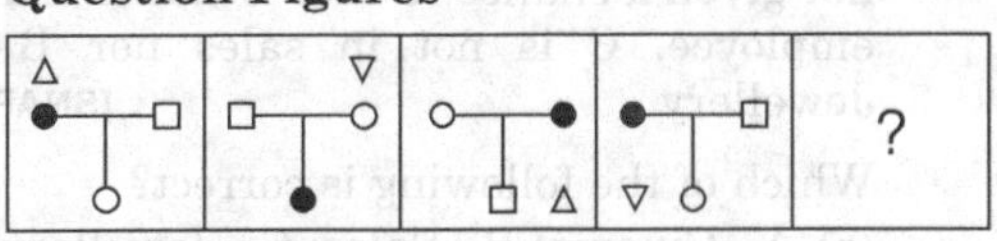

Answer Figures

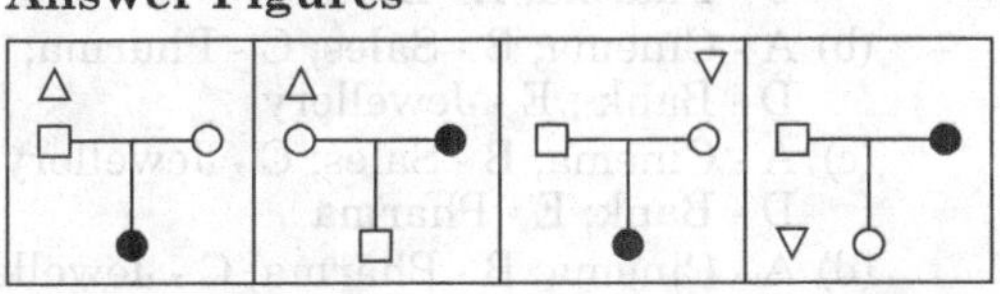

(a) (b) (c) (d)

Direction (Q. Nos. 36-38) *In the following questions, the symbols $, %, @, © and ★ are used with the following meaning as illustrated below.*

'P % Q' means 'P is neither greater than nor smaller than Q'
'P $ Q' means 'P is neither smaller than nor equal to Q'
'P © Q' means 'P is neither greater than nor equal to Q'
'P ★ Q' means 'P is not greater than Q'
'P @ Q' means 'P is not smaller than Q'

Now, in each of the following questions assuming the given statements to be true, find which of the three Conclusions I, II and III given below them is/are **definitely true** and give your answer accordingly.

36. Statements V © K, K @ B, B $ M
Conclusions I. V © B II. M © K
III. M © V
(a) None is true (b) Only I is true
(c) Only II is true (d) Only III is true
(e) II and III are true

37. Statements D ★ R, R % F, F $ T
Conclusion I. F % D II. F $ D
III. T © R
(a) Only I is true (b) Only II is true
(c) Only III is true (d) Either I or II is true
(e) Either I or II and III are true

38. Statements N @ D, D ★ K, K $ A
Conclusions I. K @ N II. A © D
III. N $ A
(a) None is true (b) Only I is true
(c) Only II is true (d) Only III is true
(e) Only II and III are true

39. Pointing to a lady a man said, "The son of her only brother is the brother of my wife." How is the lady related to the man?
(a) Mother's sister (b) Grandmother
(c) Mother-in-law (d) Sister of father-in law

40. In a class among the passed students Neeta is 22nd from the top and Kalyan, who is 5 ranks below Neeta is 34th from the bottom. All the students from the class appeared for an examination. If the ratio of the students who passed in the examination to those who failed

is 4 : 1 for the class, then how many students were there in the class ?
(a) 90 (b) 60
(c) 75 (d) Data inadequate

41. Seema correctly remembers that she took leave after 21st October and before 27th October. Her colleague Rita took leave on 23rd October but Seema was present on that day. If 24th October was a public holiday and 26th October was Sunday, then on which day in October did Seema take leave ?
(a) 22nd October
(b) 25th October
(c) 22nd or 25th October
(d) Data inadequate

42. The positions of the first and the sixth digit in the number 5109238674 are interchanged. Similarly, the positions of the second and the seventh digit are interchanged and so on. Which of the following will be the third digit from the right end after the rearrangement?
(a) 9 (b) 0 (c) 6 (d) 3

43. Which will appear 3rd in the dictionary ?
(a) Colloquy (b) Collinear
(c) Collegiate (d) Collision
[SSC Level Data Entry Operator & LDC Exam 2012]

44. If GECA means 8642, then HFBD means **[IBPS RRB (Office Assistant) 2015]**
(a) 9735 (b) 7953
(c) 7935 (d) 5379

45. Find the missing number.

7	21	15
49	441	225
98	882	450
140	1302	?

(a) 6750 (b) 690
(c) 1380 (d) 660

46. If each vowel in the word 'GLADIOLUS' is substituted with the next letter of the English alphabetical series and each consonant is substituted with the letter preceding it. How many vowels are present in the new arrangement?
(a) None (b) One
(c) Two (d) Three
(e) None of these

47. Which one of the following diagrams represents insects, flies and dogs ?

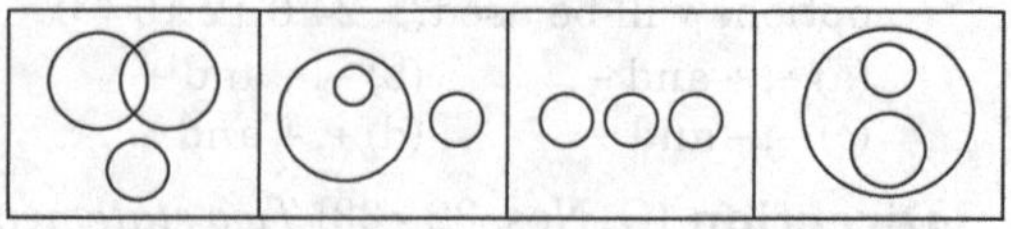
(a) (b) (c) (d)

48. Find the figure out of the answer choice figures that can be formed by joining the pieces given in the question figure?

Question Figure

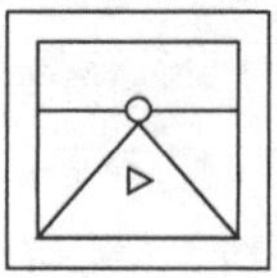

Answer Figures

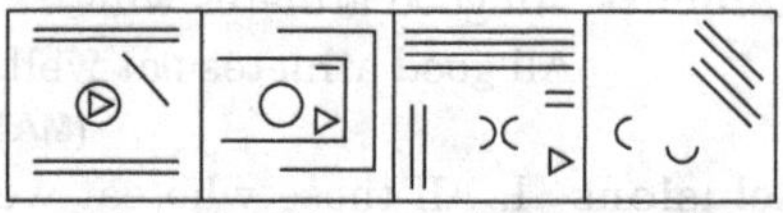
(a) (b) (c) (d)

49. A house faces North. A man coming out of his house walked straight for 10 m, turned left and walked 25 m. He then turned right and walked 5 m and again turned right and walked 25 m . How far is he from his house ? **[SSC (FCI) 2012]**
(a) 15 m (b) 55 m (c) 60 m (d) 65 m

50. Five friends A, B, C, D and E have different jobs. They work with either Bank or Cinema or Pharma or Sales or Jewellery. Pick the right job in which they are employed, if B is neither concerned with Bank nor with Sales. E has nothing to do with Cinema or Jewellary. C is not in Bank or Cinema. D has nothing to do in sales or Pharma. Cinema has not given a chance to B or D nor E is a bank employee. C is not in sales nor B is in Jewellery. **[SNAP 2014]**

Which of the following is correct?
(a) A - Cinema; B - Sales; C - Jewellery; D - Pharma; E - Bank
(b) A - Cinema; B - Sales; C - Pharma; D - Bank ; E - Jewellery
(c) A - Cinema; B - Sales; C - Jewellery; D - Bank; E - Pharma
(d) A - Cinema; B - Pharma; C - Jewellery; D - Bank; E - Sales

Hints and Solutions

1. (*b*) Only the word 'ESTIMATE' can be formed from the given word as all the letters used in 'ESTIMATE' are contained in the given word.

2. (*d*) From both the positions I and II,
Common colour = green (at different faces)

From position I,	Green	Red	Yellow
From position II,	Green	Pink	Black

Clearly, red is opposite to pink. It means red is at the bottom, if pink is at the top.

Solution (Q. Nos. 3 - 5) According to the given information, the final arrangement is as following

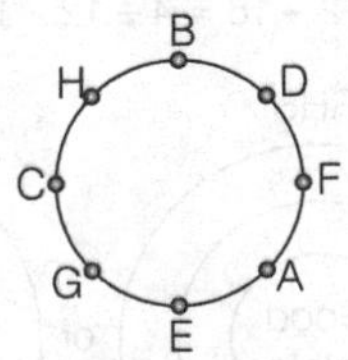

3. (*a*) G sits second to the left of A.

4. (*c*) D sits to the immediate left of B.

5. (*e*) H is third to the right of F.

6. (*d*) Clearly, in the upper row, the number of dots in the second figure is twice the number of dots in the first figure. Similarly, in the lower row, the number of dots in the second figure must be twice the number of dots in the lower first figure.
So, number of dots in missing segment is $= 2 \times 3 = 6$

7. (*a*) Anil reached the place on Friday and he was three days earlier than the scheduled day.
Therefore, the scheduled day
= Friday + 3 days = Monday
If he had reached on Sunday, then he would have earlier than one day.

8. (*d*), Except (d), all others are flowers.

9. (*a*) As,

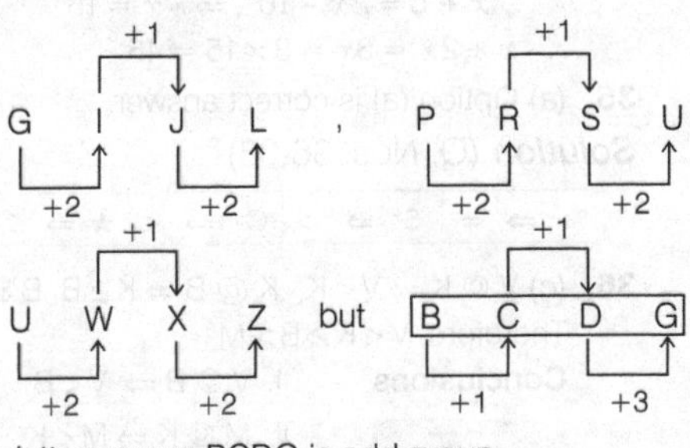

Clearly, letters group BCDG is odd group.

10. (*b*) According to the matrices,
D — (21)
E — 59, (75)
A — 31, 33, 85, 89, (97)
L — (68)

$\therefore$ DEAL $\Rightarrow$ 21, 75, 97, 68

11. (*d*) As, $(4+5)-(3+5)=1 \Rightarrow 9-8=1$
and $(7+7)-(5+4)=5 \Rightarrow 14-9=5$
Same as, $(3+5)-(2+1)=?$
$\Rightarrow \quad ?=8-3 \Rightarrow \quad ?=5$

12. (*a*) As, B A K E D $\xrightarrow{\text{Opposite}}$ Y Z P V W
and P R I N T $\xrightarrow{\text{Opposite}}$ K I R M G
So, S H R E D $\xrightarrow{\text{Opposite}}$ H S I V W

13. (*b*) Horizontal = AB, GO, CD = 3
Vertical lines = AC, EF, BD = 3
Slant lines = BO, DO, AO, CO, AD, BC = 6
$\therefore$ Total number of lines
$= 3 + 3 + 6 = 12$

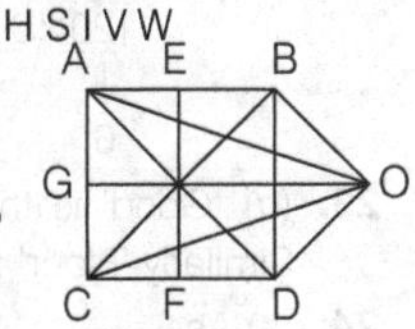

Solution (Q. Nos. 14 - 18) Let us draw the family diagram

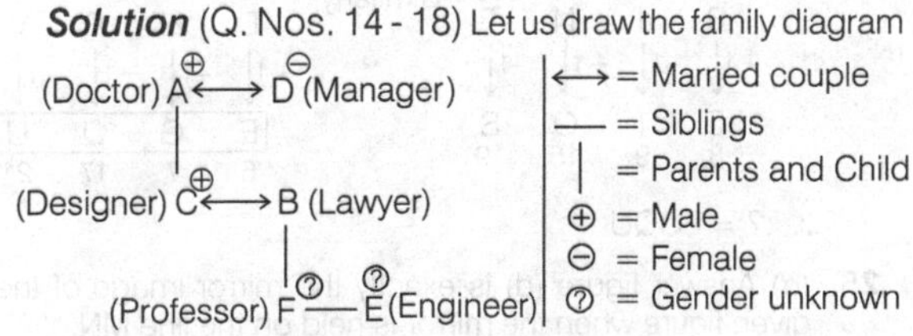

14. (*a*) AD and BC are the two couples and AD is one of them which is given in the options.

15. (*a*) A is a doctor.

16. (*d*) E is an engineer.

17. (*d*) Gender of F and E is not known. So, total number of females in the family cannot be determined.

18. (*a*) A is the grandfather of E.

Solution (Q. Nos. 19-20) After careful analysis of the given input and various steps of rearrangement it becomes clear that in the first step one number is rearranged and in the second step one word is rearranged. These two steps are continued alternately till all the numbers get rearranged in ascending order and all the words get rearranged in reverse alphabetical order.

19. (*a*) **Step III** 15 window 29 93 86 sail tower buy
Step IV 15 window 29 tower 93 86 sail buy
Step V 15 window 29 tower 86 93 sail buy
Step VI 15 window 29 tower 86 sail 93 buy
Eventually, Step VI is the last step.

20. (*b*) **Input** Station hurry 39 67 all men 86 59
Step I 39 station hurry 67 all men 86 59
Step II 39 station 59 hurry 67 all men 86
Step III 39 station 59 men hurry 67 all 86
Step IV 39 station 59 men 67 hurry all 86
Step V 39 station 59 men 67 hurry 86 all

21. (*a*) Following family diagram can be drawn from the given information,

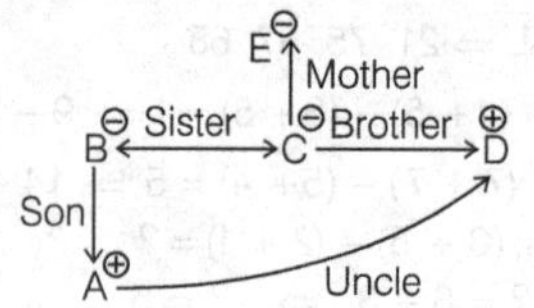

Now, it is clear that D is the maternal uncle of A.

22. (*c*) As, 720 : 840 → 120×6 : 120×7 → 6 : 7
Same as, 60 : 70 → 10×6 : 10×7 → 6 : 7

23. (*d*) 'Good' is the word opposite in meaning to 'Bad'. Similarly 'Floor' is the antonym of 'Roof'.

24. (*a*) As,
B(2) J(10) N(14) T(20) → +1, −1, +1, −1 → C(3) I(9) O(15) S(19)
Similarly, D(4) H(8) P(16) V(22) → +1, −1, +1, −1 → E(5) G(7) Q(17) U(21)

$\therefore$? = EGQU

25. (*d*) Answer figure (d) is exactly the mirror image of the given figure when the mirror is held on the line MN.

26. (*d*) From both the statements

he [is sure] ⟶ [ja] ha [ma]

[is] she [sure] ⟶ ka [ja ma]

The code for 'sure' is either 'ja' or 'ma'.
Hence, both the statement are not sufficient to answer the question.

27. (*c*) From Statement I,

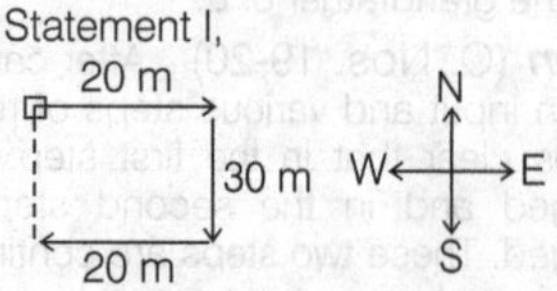

Mohan is 30 m away from the starting point.
From Statement II,

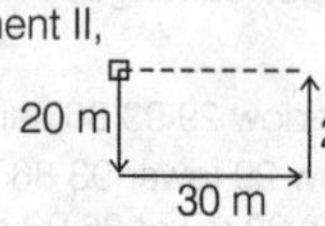

Mohan is 30 m away from the starting point.
Hence, either statement I or Statement II is sufficient to answer the question.

28. (*a*) As, $(7)^2 - 2 = 49 - 2 = 47$
Same as, $(9)^2 - 2 = 81 - 2 = 79$

29. (*b*) The complete letter series will be
a c e g/a c e g/a c e g ⇒ ecag

30. (*d*) Pattern of given alpha - numeric series is as follows:

C(3) —+3→ F(6) —+3→ I(9) —+3→ L(12)
4 —+5→ 9 —+7→ 16 —+9→ 25
X(24) —−3→ U(21) —−3→ R(18) —−3→ O(15)

$\therefore$? = L25O

31. (*a*) From option (a), $24 \div 6 + 12 - 16 = 0$

$$\text{LHS} = \frac{24}{6} + 12 - 16 = 4 + 12 - 16 = 16 - 16 = 0$$

$\therefore$ LHS = RHS

32. (*d*)

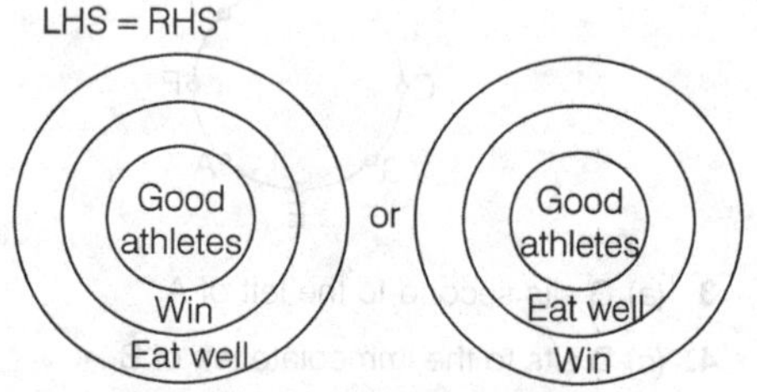

Conclusions
I. All those who eat well are good athletes. (✗)
II. All those who win eat well. (✗)

33. (*a*)

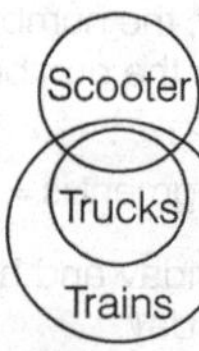

Conclusions I. Some scooters are trains. (✔)
II. No truck is a scooter. (✗)

34. (*b*) Suppose, the number of women was x initially.
Therefore, number of men = $2x$
According to the question,

$$x + 5 = 2x - 10 \Rightarrow x = 15$$

$$\therefore x + 2x = 3x = 3 \times 15 = 45$$

35. (*a*) Option (a) is correct answer.

Solution (Q. Nos. 36-38)

% ⇒ =	\$ ⇒ >	© ⇒ <	★ ⇒ ≤	@ ⇒ ≥

36. (*c*) V © K ⇒ V < K, K @ B ⇒ K ≥ B, B \$ M ⇒ B > M
Therefore, V < K ≥ B > M

Conclusions
I. V © B ⇒ V < B (False)
II. M © K ⇒ M < K (True)
III. M © V ⇒ M < V (False)

So, only II is true.

37. (*e*) D ★ R ⇒ D ≤ R, R % F ⇒ R = F, F $ T ⇒ F > T

Therefore, D ≤ R = F > T

Conclusions I. F % D ⇒ F = D (May be true)

II. F $ D ⇒ F > D (May be true)

Either I or II is true.

III. T © R ⇒ T < R (True)

So, either I or II and III are true.

38. (*a*) N @ D ⇒ N ≥ D, D ★ K ⇒ D ≤ K, K $ A ⇒ K > A

Therefore, N ≥ D ≤ K > A

Conclusions I. K @ N ⇒ K ≥ N (False)

II. A © D ⇒ A < D (False)

III. N $ A ⇒ N > A (False)

So, none is true.

39. (*d*) Let us draw the family diagram from the given information as follows

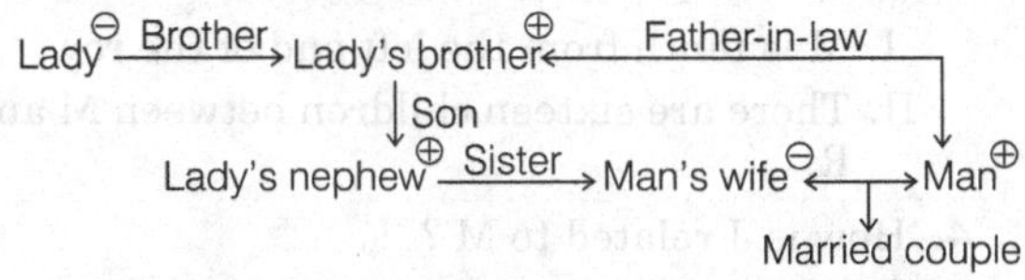

Now, it is clear that the lady is the sister of man's father-in-law.

40. (c) From among those who passed Neeta is 22nd from the top and Kalyan is 22 + 5 = 27th from the top and 34th from the bottom. Therefore, total number of students who passed the examination

= 27 + 34 − 1 = 60.

Therefore, total number of students in the class

$= \frac{60}{4} \times 5 = 75$

41. (*c*)

According to	Leave Date
Seema	22, 23, 24, 25, 26

But Seema was present on 23rd. Also, it was holiday on 24th and 26th October was Sunday. Hence, possible date may be either 22nd or 25th October.

42. (*d*) Given number = 5109238674

After interchanging the digits,

new number = 3867451092

Hence, third digit from the right end = 0

43. (*d*) Arrangement of words as per dictionary:

(iii) Collegiate → (ii) Collinear → (iv) Collision → (i) Colloquy

44. (*a*) Clearly, by using the position of alphabets

G → 8 → 7 + 1, E → 6 → 5 + 1

C → 4 → 3 + 1, A → 2 → 1 + 1

1 is added in all alphabets. Similarly, we can write.

H ⟶ 8 + 1 = 9
F ⟶ 6 + 1 = 7
B ⟶ 2 + 1 = 3
D ⟶ 4 + 1 = 5

45. (*d*) Subtract the upper number from the sum of the second and the third number to get the lowest number in each column

49 + 98 − 7 = 147 − 7 = 140

441 + 882 − 21 ⇒ 1323 − 21 = 1302

⇒ 225 + 450 − 15 = 675 − 15 = 660

46. (*a*) According to the question,

Given word	G	L	A	D	I	O	L	U	S
	↓	↓	↓	↓	↓	↓	↓	↓	↓
New word	F	K	B	C	J	P	K	V	R

So, no such vowel is present in the new arrangement.

47. (*b*) Dog is different from insects. Flies come under the class insects.

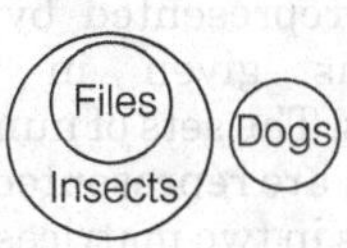

48. (*c*) Here, the question figure can be formed by joining the pieces given in option (c) as shown below

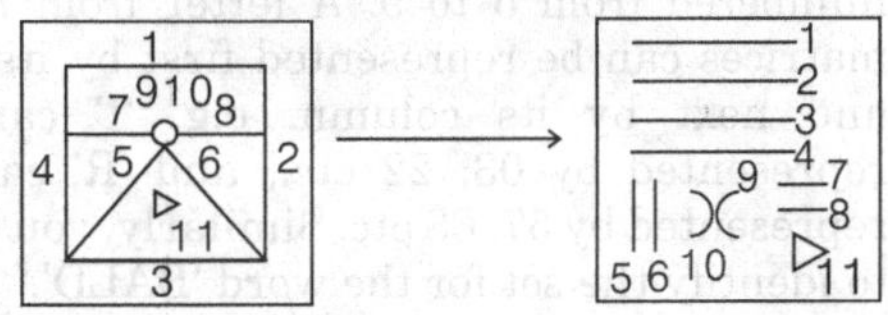

49. (*a*) Route followed by man.

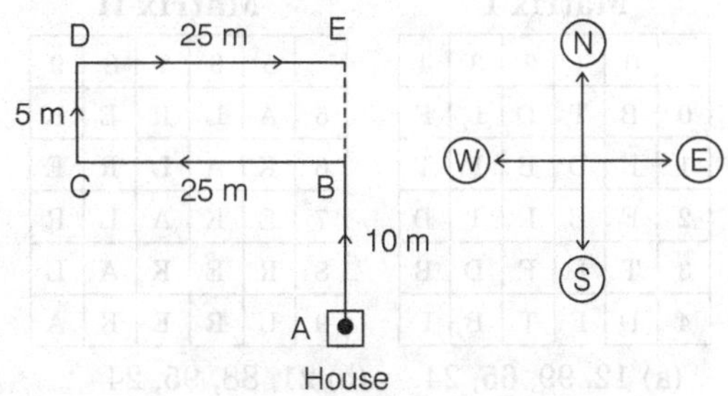

Required distance, = AE = AB + BE = (10 + 5) m = 15 m

50. (*d*) The given information can be summarised as :

	A	B	C	D	E
Bank	✗	✗	✗	✔	✗
Cinema	✔	✗	✗	✗	✗
Pharma	✗	✔	✗	✗	✗
Sales	✗	✗	✗	✗	✔
Jewellery	✗	✗	✔	✗	✗

So, A - Cinema, B - Pharma, C- Jewellery D- Bank and E - Sales is correct.

PRACTICE SET 31

1. Q's mother is the sister of P and daughter of M. S is the daughter of P and sister of T. How is M related to T?

(a) Grandmother
(b) Father
(c) Grandfather
(d) Grandfather or Grandmother

2. A word is represented by only one set of numbers as given in anyone of the alternatives. The sets of numbers given in the alternatives are represented by two classes of alphabets as in two matrices given below. The columns and rows of Matrix I are numbered from 0 to 4 and that of Matrix II are numbered from 5 to 9. A letter from these matrices can be represented first by its row and next by its column. e.g. 'T' can be represented by 03, 22 etc., and 'R' can be represented by 57, 68 etc. Similarly, you have to identify the set for the word 'BALD'.

[SSC (Multitasking) 2013]

Matrix I

	0	1	2	3	4
0	B	T	D	I	F
1	I	D	B	F	T
2	F	B	I	T	D
3	T	I	F	D	B
4	D	F	T	B	I

Matrix II

	5	6	7	8	9
5	A	L	R	E	K
6	K	A	L	R	E
7	E	K	A	L	R
8	R	E	K	A	L
9	L	R	E	K	A

(a) 12, 99, 65, 24 (b) 21, 88, 95, 24
(c) 43, 55, 67, 04 (d) 34, 77, 76, 42

Direction (Q. Nos. 3-4) *Each of the questions below consists of a question and two statements numbered I and II given below it. You have to decide whether the data provided in the statements are sufficient to answer the question.*

Give answer

(a) if the data in Statement I alone are sufficient to answer the question, while the data in Statement II alone are not sufficient to answer the question.
(b) if the data in Statement II alone are sufficient to answer the question, while the data in Statement I alone are not sufficient to answer the question.
(c) if the data either in Statement I alone or in Statement II alone are sufficient to answer the question.
(d) if the data given in both the Statements I and II together are not sufficient to answer the question.
(e) if the data in both the Statements I and II together are necessary to answer the question.

3. What is the R's position from the left end in a row?

I. M is tenth from the left end of the row.
II. There are sixteen children between M and R.

4. How is J related to M ?

I. M has only one brother and two sisters.
II. J is daughter of T who is wife of M.

Direction (Q. Nos. 5-6) *In the following questions, select the related word/letters/number from the given alternatives.*

5. Maharashtra : India : : Texas : ?

[SSC (10+2) 2014]

(a) Canada (b) Mexico
(c) Brazil (d) USA

6. ACB : 06 : : ?

(a) PNB : 09 (b) GEF : 18
(c) MNO : 11 (d) TUV : 07

7. How many circles are there in the figure given below?

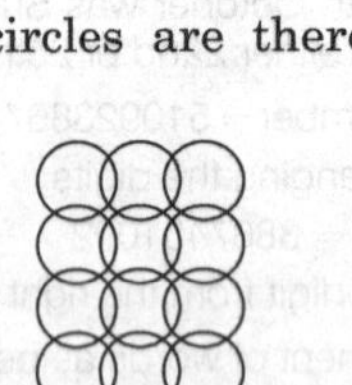

(a) 10 (b) 14 (c) 12 (d) 18

8. From the given three positions of a single dice, find the digit at the face opposite to the face having digit 4.

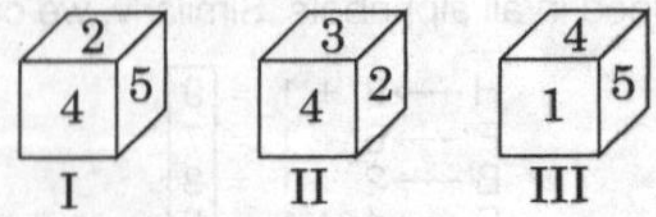

I II III

(a) 1 (b) 3 (c) 5 (d) 6

Direction (Q. Nos. 9-11) *Read the following information carefully and answer the questions given below.*

I. A, B, C, D, E, F, G and H are standing in a row facing North.
II. B is not neighbour of G.
III. F is to the immediate right of G and neighbour of E.
IV. G is not at the extreme end.
V. A is sixth to the left of E.
VI. H is sixth to the right of C.

9. Who among the following are neighbours?
(a) AB (b) CG
(c) FH (d) CA
(e) None of these

10. Which one among the following defines the position of D?
(a) Fourth to the right of H
(b) Third to the right of A
(c) Neighbour of B and F
(d) To the immediate left of B
(e) None of the above

11. Which of the following is true?
(a) C is to the immediate left of A
(b) D is neighbour of B and F
(c) G is to the immediate right of D
(d) A and E are at the extreme ends
(e) None of the above

12. Find the missing character. **[SSC (10+2) 2015]**

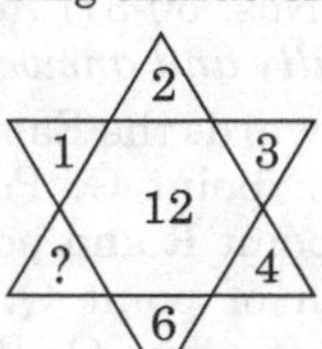

(a) 6 (b) 8 (c) 1 (d) 12

13. Identify the answer figure that completes the pattern in the question figure.

Question Figure **[SSC (10+2) 2011]**

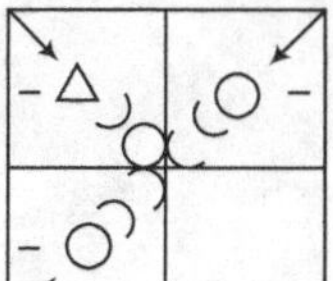

Answer Figures

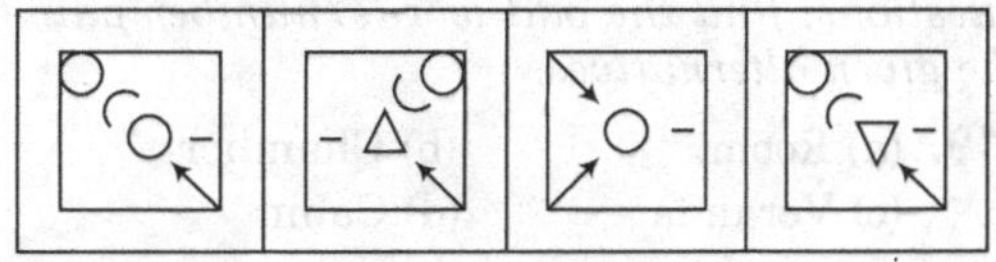

(a) (b) (c) (d)

14. In which answer figure is the question figure embedded?

Question Figure

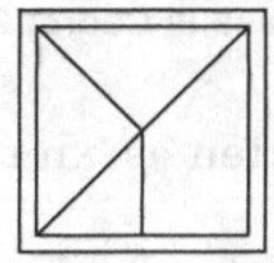

Answer Figures

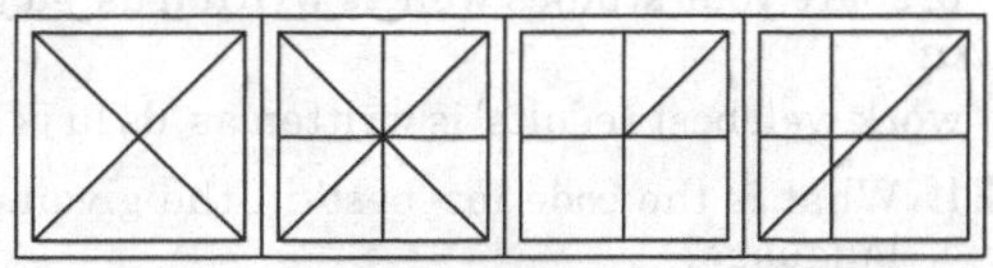

(a) (b) (c) (d)

15. Mr. Mani's age is 47 yr and John's age is 13 yr. In how many years will Mr. Mani's age be double of John's age? **[SSC (CGL) 2014]**
(a) 20 yr (b) 21 yr
(c) 10 yr (d) 15 yr

Direction (Q. Nos. 16-17) *In the following questions, a series is given with one term missing. Choose the correct alternative from the given ones that will complete the series.*

16. K, A, M, A, L, L, A, M, A, ?
(a) L (b) M
(c) K (d) J

17. 1331, 729, 343, 125, ?
(a) 27 (b) 64
(c) 216 (d) 512

18. Which one of the given responses would be a meaningful order of the following?
(i) Police (ii) Punishment
(iii) Crime (iv) Judge
(iv) Judgement
(a) (iii), (i), (iv), (v), (ii)
(b) (iii), (i), (ii), (iv), (v)
(c) (i), (ii), (iv), (iii), (v)
(d) (v), (iv), (iii), (ii), (i)

Direction (Q. Nos. 19-20) *In the following questions, find the odd words/number pair from the given alternatives.*

19. (a) Room (b) Chamber
(c) Veranda (d) Cabin

20. (a) (324, – 18) (b) (441, 21)
(c) (169, 13) (d) (186, 14)

Direction (Q. Nos. 21-23) *Study the information and answer the given questions.*

[NICL Assistant (Class III Cadre) 2015]

In a certain code language
'prepare for your exams' is written as 'xn nt oz wl'
'hard work for prepare' is written as 'nt ml oz tk'
'prepare your studies well' is written as 'sd jk nt xn'
'work well best results' is written as 'ds lu jk ml'

21. What is the code for 'best' in the given code language?
(a) lu (b) ml
(c) sd (d) ds
(e) Either (a) or (d)

22. In the given code language, 'nt' is the code of which word?
(a) prepare (b) your
(c) hard (d) work
(e) Either (a) or (b)

23. What may be the code for 'exams are hard' in the given code language?
(a) wl ml tk (b) zr tk ko
(c) wl xn tk (d) tk zr wl
(e) ko wl xn

24. Select the one, which is different from the other three responses.

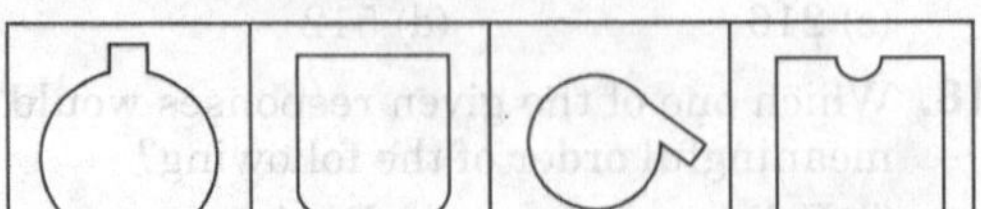

(a) (b) (c) (d)

Direction (Q. Nos. 25-27) *In the given questions, assuming the given statements to be true. Find which one of the given two Conclusions I and II stands definitely true and give your answer accordingly.*

Give answer
(a) if only Conclusion II is true
(b) if either Conclusion I or II is true
(c) if only Conclusion I is true
(d) if both Conclusions I and II are true
(e) if neither Conclusion I nor II is true

[IBPS RRB (Officers) 2015]

25. Statements
$F = A < L \leq C > Q \geq N; Y > L; Q > C$
Conclusions I. $Y \geq N$
II. $Q > F$

26. Statements $R = E < Q \geq B; S \geq Q$
Conclusions I. $S < E$
II. $B \leq S$

27. Statements $J > K \geq L; A \geq K < P$
Conclusions I. $L \leq A$
II. $P > J$

28. How many meaningful English words can be formed with the letters LEGU, using each letter only once in each word?
(a) None (b) One
(c) Two (d) Three
(e) More than three

29. Which number has come maximum time in the following number series?
5 4 3 3 5 4 8 8 3 2 5 3 6 5 5
(a) 5 (b) 4 (c) 3 (d) 2

Direction (Q. Nos. 30-31) *Read the following information carefully and answer the questions.*

Point H is 6 m towards the East of point G. Point R is 8 m North of point G. Point Q is exactly midway between point R and point G. Point K is 10 m to the South of point Q. Point L is 3 m towards the East of point Q. Point S is exactly midway between point G and point H.

[NIACL (AO) 2014]

30. If a person walks 4 m towards the south from point L, takes right turn and walks for another 3 m, then which of the following points would be reach?
(a) Q
(b) G
(c) K
(d) H
(e) Cannot be determined

31. If a person walks 8 m towards North from point S, then which of the following points would he crossed and how far will he be from point R?
(a) G, 4 m (b) H, 3 m
(c) L, 6 m (d) L, 3 m
(e) G, 8 m

Direction (Q. Nos. 32-34) *Study the following information carefully and answer the given questions.*

A word and number arrangement machine when given an input line of words and numbers rearranges them following a particular rule in each step. The following is an illustration of input and rearrangement.

Input nine poll 19 34 12 69 hour call
***Step* I** call nine poll 19 34 12 69 hour
***Step* II** call 12 nine poll 19 34 69 hour
***Step* III** call 12 hour nine poll 19 34 69
***Step* IV** call 12 hour 19 nine poll 34 69
***Step* V** call 12 hour 19 nine 34 poll 69

and Step V is the last step of the rearrangement of the above input.

As per the rules followed in the above steps, find out in each of the following questions the appropriate step for the given input.

32. Step II of input is 'bend 15 will care 46 53 29 then'
How many more steps will be required to complete the rearrangement?
(a) Five (b) Three
(c) Four (d) Six
(e) None of these

33. **Input** land 62 clear over 41 37 again 56
Which of the following steps will be the last but one?
(a) VIII (b) IX (c) VII (d) VI
(e) None of these

34. Step II of an input is 'desk 12 year victory 86 71 store 65'
Which of the following will be Step VII?
(a) desk 12 store 65 year 71 victory 86
(b) desk 12 store 65 71 year victory 86
(c) desk 12 store 65 year victory 86 71
(d) There will be no such step
(e) None of the above

35. In this question, four alternatives are given, which follow the word number marked as question. You have to select one alternative, which exactly matches with the mirror image of the word/number in the question.

OBSTINATE

(a) ƎTAИITƧBO (b) ETANITSBO
(c) BOSTINATE (d) SOBNIATE

36. Which figure best represents the relationship between Editor, Newspaper and Journalist?
[SI (Delhi Police & CAPFs) & Assistant SI (CISF) 2015]

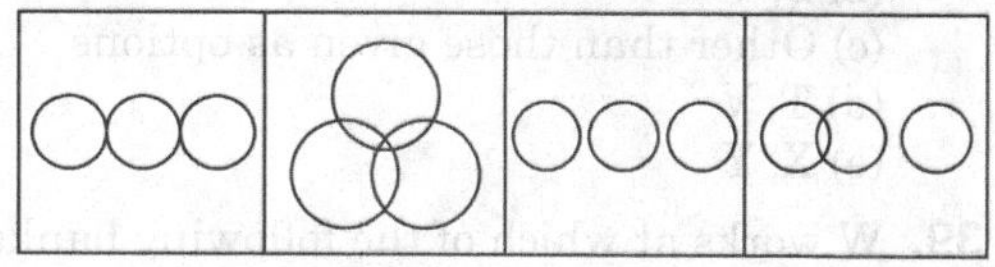

(a) (b) (c) (d)

Direction (Q. Nos. 37-39) *Study the following information and answer the questions.*

S, T, U, V, W, X, Y and Z live on eight different floors of a building but not necessarily in the same order. The lowermost floor of the building is numbered one, the one above that is numbered two and so on till the topmost floor is numbered eight. Each of them also works at a different bank namely, IDBI, SBI, HDFC, BOI, PNB, TJSB, Axis bank and SVC, but not necessarily in the same order.

- Z lives on an even numbered floor. Only three people live between Z and the one who works at BOI.
- W lives immediately below the one who works at BOI.
- Only three people live between W and the one who works at Axis bank.
- V lives immediately above T. V lives on an odd numbered floor. T does not work at BOI.
- Only two people live between T and the one who works at SBI. The one who works at SBI does not live on the lowermost floor.
- The one who works at SVC lives immediately above the one who works at PNB. The one who works at SVC lives on an even numbered floor but not on floor numbered two.
- Only one person lives between the one who works at SVC and the one who works at IDBI.

- X lives immediately above S. X lives on an even numbered floor. X does not work at TJSB.
- U does not work at PNB and does not live on floor numbered four.

37. V works at which of the following banks?
(a) Axis bank (b) SVC
(c) IDBI (d) SBI
(e) Other than those given as options

38. Which of the following pair represent those who live immediately above and immediately below Z?
(a) S, T
(b) S, V
(c) Other than those given as options
(d) T, V
(e) X, Y

39. W works at which of the following banks?
(a) Other than those given as options
(b) PNB (c) Axis bank
(d) BOI (e) SBI

40. A 25 ft 6 inch long piece of wood is cut to make three piece of equal length. The length of one piece is
(a) 8 ft 1 inch (b) 8 ft 6 inch
(c) 8 ft 3 inch (d) 8 ft 4 inch

41. Which of the following pair is odd one out.
(a) Broad : Wide (b) Light : Heavy
(c) Tiny : Small (d) Big : Large

42. If the seventh day of month is three days earlier than Friday, then what day will be on the nineteenth day of the month?
(a) Sunday (b) Monday
(c) Wednesday (d) Friday

43. Each of J, K, L, M and N have different heights. M is only shorter than J only. K is not as tall as N and N is shorter than L. Who is the shortest of them?
(a) J (b) N (c) K (d) L
(e) None of these

44. Find the missing number.

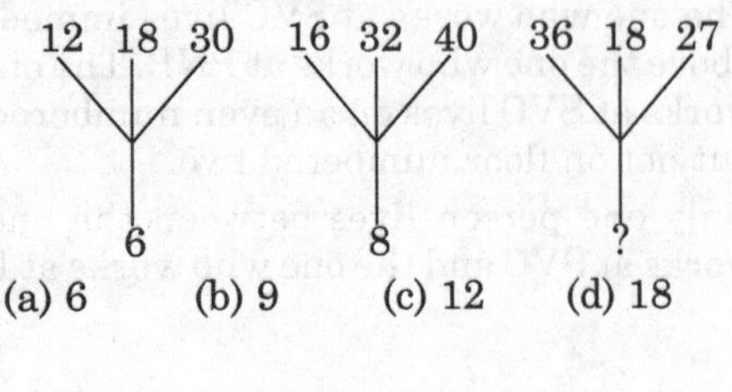

(a) 6 (b) 9 (c) 12 (d) 18

Direction (Q. Nos. 45-47) *In each question/set of questions below are two/three statements followed by two conclusions numbered* I *and* II. *You have to take the two/three given statements to be true even if they seem to be at variance from commonly known facts and then decide which of the given conclusions logically follows from the given statements disregarding commonly known facts*

Give answer
(a) if only Conclusion I follows
(b) if only Conclusion II follows
(c) if either Conclusion I or II follows
(d) if neither Conclusion I nor II follows
(e) if both Conclusions I and II follow

45. Statements Some doctors are fools.
Joshi is a doctor.
Conclusions I. Joshi is a fool.
II. Some fools are doctors.

46. Statements Some balls are points.
All points are pens.
All pens are gels.
Conclusions I. All balls are pens.
II. All pens are balls.
[MHA-CET 2011]

47. Statements No space is air.
All distances are spaces.
Conclusions I. No air is a distance.
II. All spaces are distances.
[Bihar Keshtriya (GBO) 2012]

48. Cause The Government has recently increased its taxes on Petrol and diesel by about 10%.
Which of the following can be a possible effect of the above cause?
(a) The petroleum companies will reduce the prices of petrol and diesel by about 10%.
(b) The petroleum companies will increase the price of petrol and diesel by about 10%.
(c) The petroleum companies will increase the prices of petrol and diesel by about 5%.
(d) The petrol pumps will stop selling petrol and diesel till the taxes are rolled back by the Government.
(e) None of the above

49. **Effect** Majority of the employees of the ailing organisation opted for voluntary retirement scheme and left the organisation with all their retirement benefits whithin a fortnight of launching the scheme.

Which of the following can be a probable cause of the above effect?

(a) The company has been making huge losses for the past 5 yr and is unable to pay salary to its employees in time.

(b) The management of the company made huge person a gains through unlawful activities.

(c) One of the competitons of the company went bankrupt last year.

(d) The company owns large tracts of land in the state which will fetch huge sum of its owners.

(e) None of the above

50. If '–' means '+', '+' means '–', '×' means '÷' and '÷' means '×', then which of the following equation is correct?

(a) $30 - 5 + 4 \div 10 \times 5 = 62$

(b) $30 + 5 \div 4 - 10 \times 5 = 22$

(c) $30 + 5 - 4 \div 10 \times 5 = 28$

(d) $30 \times 5 - 4 \div 10 + 5 = 41$

Hints and Solutions

1. (*d*) We can summarise the informations in a family tree.

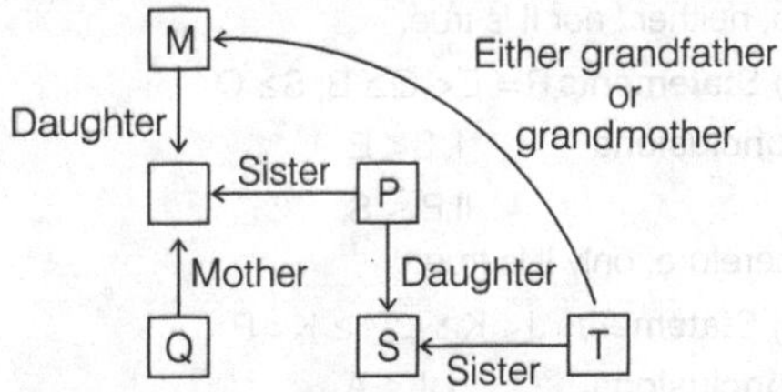

Hence, M is either the Grandfather or Grandmother of T.

2. (*b*) According to the matrices,

B — 00, 12, (21), 34, 43

A — 55, 66, 77, (88), 99

L — 56, 67, 78, 89, (95)

D — 02, 11, (24), 33, 40

∴ BALD ⇒ 21 , 88, 95, 24

3. (*e*) From both the statements,

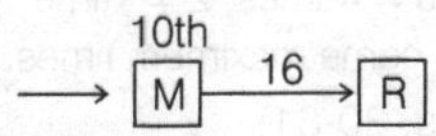

R's position from the left

= 10 + 16 + 1 = 27th

4. (*b*) From Statement II,

M is the husband of T.

So, J is daughter of M and T.

5. (*d*) As, Maharashtra is one of the states in India. In the same way, Texas is one of the states in the USA.

6. (*b*) As, A C B → 1 + 3 + 2 = 06; Similarly, G E F → 7 + 5 + 6 = 18

∴ Required answer = GEF : 18

7. (*c*) In the given question figure, we start counting of circles and mark them as 1, 2 and so on and finally we end on getting 12 number of circles as shown in the following figure.

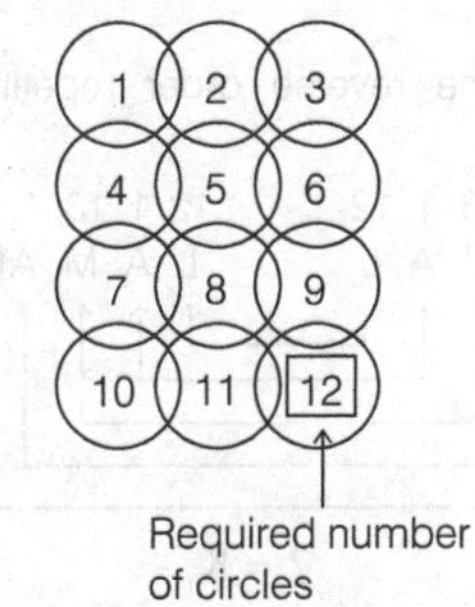

8. (*d*) From all the three positions of the dice, adjacent faces of 4 = 1, 2, 3 and 5.

It is clear that, the digit opposite to 4 = 6

Solution (Q. Nos. 9-11) According to the given information, the final arrangement is as following

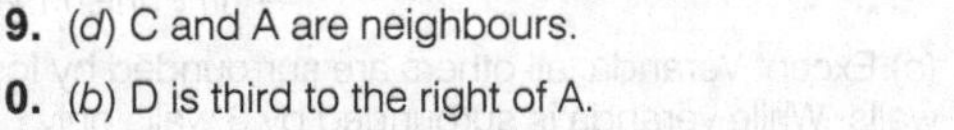

9. (*d*) C and A are neighbours.

10. (*b*) D is third to the right of A.

11. (*c*) G is to the immediate right of D.

12. (*d*) As, $6 \times 2 = 12$

$3 \times 4 = 12$

Similarly, $1 \times 12 = 12$

13. (*d*) Option (d) will complete the given pattern as follows

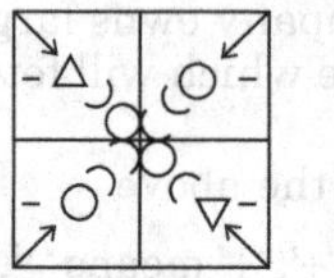

14. (*b*) Clearly, question figure is embedded in answer figure (b) as shown below

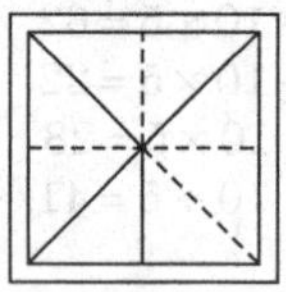

15. (*b*) Given, Mr. Mani's present age

$= 47$ yr

and John's present age $= 13$ yr

Let in x years Mr. Mani's age be double of John's age. According to the question,

$$47 + x = 2\,(13 + x)$$

$$\Rightarrow \quad 47 + x = 26 + 2x$$

$$\Rightarrow \quad 2x - x = 47 - 26 \Rightarrow x = 21 \text{ yr}$$

Hence, after 21 yr Mr. Mani's age be double of John's age.

16. (*c*) Here, the reverse order repetition pattern is followed

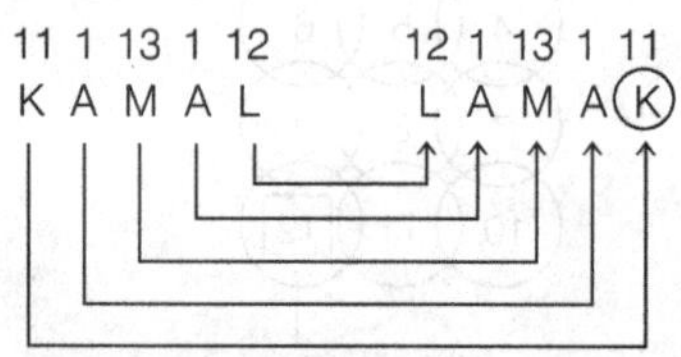

$\therefore$? = K

17. (*a*) The series follows the following pattern

1331 → 11^3, 729 → 9^3, 343 → 7^3, 125 → 5^3, [27] → 3^3

18. (*a*) Meaningful order of the words
(iii) Crime → (i) Police → (iv) Judge → (v) Judgement → (ii) Punishment

19. (*c*) Except Veranda, all others are surrounded by four walls. While veranda is surounded by 3 walls only.

20. (*d*) $(-18)^2 = 324, (21)^2 = 441, (13)^2 = 169$

But $(14)^2 = 196$. Hence, option (d) is odd one.

Solution (Q. Nos. 21-23)

[prepare] for [your] exams → [xn] [nt] oz wl
hard (work) for preprare → (nt) (ml) oz tk
[prepare] [your] studies (well) → sd (jk) [nt] [xn]
(work) (well) best results → ds lu (jk) (ml)

21. (*e*) The code for 'best' either 'ds' or 'lu'.

22. (*e*) 'nt' stands for either prepare or your.

23. (*d*) The code for 'exams are hard' is 'tk zr wl'.

24. (*b*) All other figures have small mouth but figure (b) has big mouth.

Solution (Q. Nos. 25-27) According to the given information,

25. (*e*) **Statements** F = A < L ≤ C > Q ≥ N; Y > L; Q > C
Therefore, F = A < L ≤ C > Q ≥ N, L < Y, Q > C
Conclusions I. Y ≥ N (✗)
II. Q > F (✗)
So, neither I nor II is true.

26. (*a*) **Statements** R = E < Q ≥ B; S ≥ Q
Conclusions I. S < E (✗)
II. B ≤ S (✔)
Therefore, only II is true.

27. (*d*) **Statements** J < K ≥ L; A ≥ K < P
Conclusions I. L ≤ A (✔)
II. P > J (✔)
Therefore, both Conclusions I and II are true.

28. (*b*) Required word is GLUE.

29. (*a*)

(5) [4] △3 △3 (5) [4] 8 8 △3 2 (5) △3 6 (5) (5)

8 = 2 times, 6 = 1 time
5 = 5 times, 4 = 2 times
3 = 4 times, 2 = 1 time

Clearly, 5 has come maximum times.

Solution (Q. Nos. 30-31)

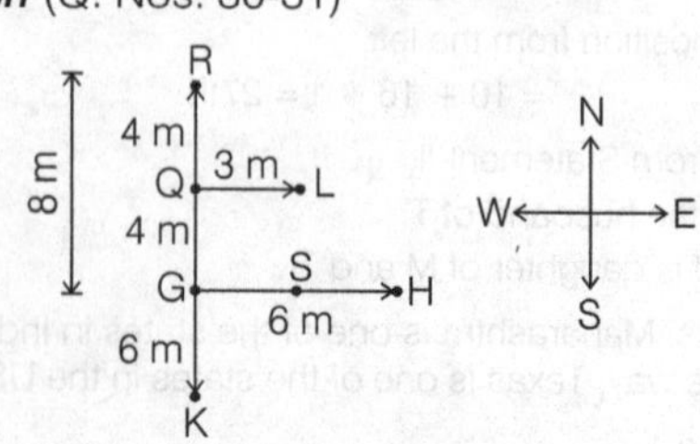

30. (*b*) He would be reach at point G.

31. (*d*) He crossed point L and he will be 4m from point R.

Solution (Q. Nos. 32-34) After careful analysis of the Input and various steps of rearrangement it is evident that in each step one number or word is rearranged. These two steps are continued alternately till all the words get rearranged in alphabetical order and all the numbers get rearranged in ascendig order.

32. (c) ***Step* II** bend 15 will care 46 53 29 then
***Step* III** bend 15 care will 46 53 29 then
***Step* IV** bend 15 care 29 will 46 53 then
***Step* V** bend 15 care 29 then will 46 53
***Step* VI** bend 15 care 29 then 46 will 53
Hence, four more steps are required to complete the rearrangement.

33. (e) **Input** land 62 clear over 41 37 again 56
***Step* I** again land 62 clear over 41 37 56
***Step* II** again 37 land 62 clear over 41 56
***Step* III** again 37 clear land 62 over 41 56
***Step* IV** again 37 clear 41 land 62 over 56
***Step* V** again 37 clear 41 land 56 62 over
***Step* VI** again 37 clear 41 land 56 over 62
Step V is the last but one step.

34. (d) ***Step* II** desk 12 year victory 86 71 store 65
***Step* III** desk 12 store year victory 86 71 65
***Step* IV** desk 12 store 65 year victory 86 71
***Step* V** desk 12 store 65 victory year 86 71
***Step* VI** desk 12 store 65 victory 71 year 86

35. (a) Option (a) is correct answer.

36. (d)

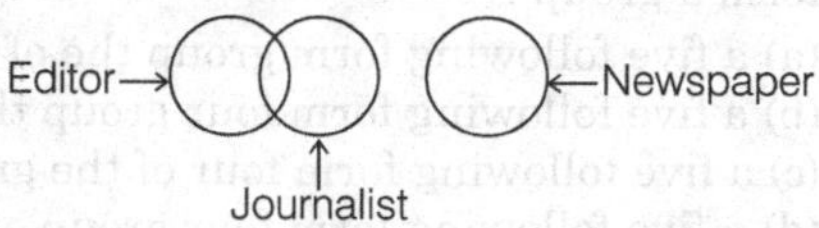

Solution (Q. Nos. 37-39) According to the given information,

Floor	Person	Bank
8	X	HDFC
7	S	SBI
6	Z	IDBI
5	V	Axis bank
4	T	SVC
3	Y	PNB
2	U	BOI
1	W	TJSB

37. (a) V works in Axis bank.

38. (b) S and V are immediate neighbours of Z.

39. (a) W works in TJSB bank.

40. (b) 25 ft 6 inch = $25 \times 12 + 6 = 300 + 6 = 306$ inch

$$\frac{306}{3} = 102 \text{ inch}$$

102 inch = 8 ft 6 inch

41. (b) Light is antonym of heavy. But in other pairs words are synonyms.

42. (a) Three days earlier than Friday means Tuesday.
So, 7th day of month will be Tuesday.
14th day of month will be Tuesday.
19th day of month will be Sunday.

43. (c) According to the question,

$$J > M$$
$$L > N > K$$
$$\therefore \quad J > M > L > N > \text{(K)}$$

So, shortest is K.

44. (b) The upper numbers are multiples of the lower number.

Hence, the answer is 9.

Solution (Q. Nos. 45-47)

45. (b)

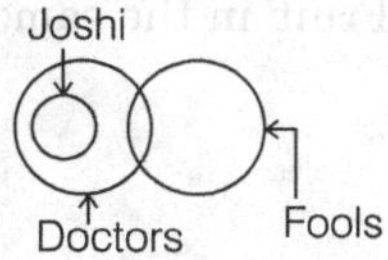

Conclusions I. Joshi is a fool. (✗)
II. Some fools are doctors. (✔)
So, only Conclusion II follows.

46. (d)

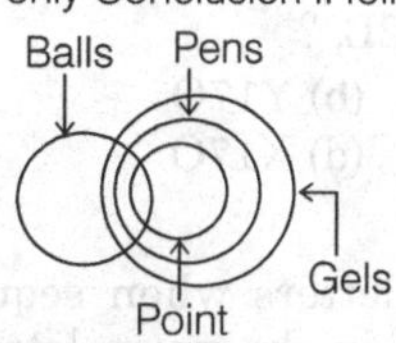

Conclusions I. All balls are pens. (✗)
II. All pens are balls. (✗)
So, neither conclusion I nor II follows.

47. (a)

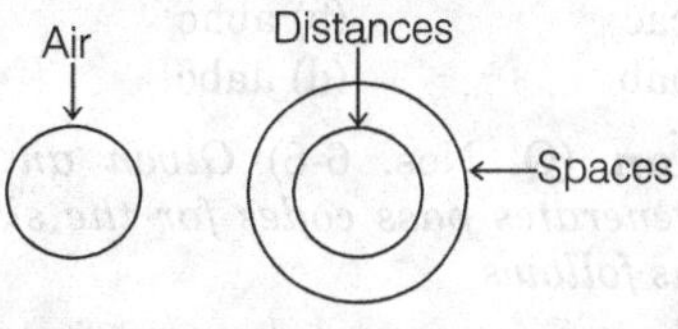

Conclusions I. No air is a distance (✔)
II. All spaces are distance (✗)
So, Conclusion I follows.

48. (e) Companies may hike the price to cover the loss because of the increased tax. But increase in price is totally the matter of company, we cannot make any guesses about it.

49. (a) It should be the obvious cause for the given effect.

50. (d) From option (d), $30 \times 5 - 4 + 10 + 5 = 41$

$\Rightarrow \quad 30 \div 5 + 4 \times 10 - 5 = 41$

$\Rightarrow \quad 6 + 4 \times 10 - 5 = 41 \Rightarrow 6 + 40 - 5 = 41$

$\Rightarrow \quad 46 - 5 = 41 \Rightarrow 41 = 41$

PRACTICE SET 32

1. A cube has to be painted in such a way that there is no similar colour on adjacent faces. How many colours are needed for this?

(a) 3 (b) 4 (c) 6 (d) 2

2. Select the related letters group from the given alternatives.

AFKP : BGLQ : : CHMR : ?

[BSSC (CGL) 2015]

(a) DINS (b) DNIS
(c) DFKP (d) DJOT

3. 'Seed' is related to 'Fruit' in the same way as 'Fruit' is related to

(a) Tree
(b) Branch
(c) Flower
(d) Petal

4. Find the missing term.

P3C, R5F, T8I, V12L, ?

(a) X16O (b) Y17O
(c) X17M (d) X17O
(e) None of these

5. Which one set of letters when sequentially placed at the gaps in the given letter series shall complete it?

cc_ccbc_accbcc_c_b

(a) acac (b) abac
(c) abab (d) aabc

Direction (Q. Nos. 6-8) *Given an input, a machine generates pass codes for the six batches each day as follows*

Input these icons were taken out from the sea

Pass Codes

Batch I from sea the out taken were icons these

Batch II from icons these were taken out the sea

Batch III from icons out sea the taken were these

Batch IV from icons out sea these were taken the, and so on

First batch starts at 10:00 am and each batch is for one hour. There is a rest period of one hour after the end of the fourth batch.

6. The pass code for the first batch on a day was 'he so used to sell the surplus items'.

What was the input on that day?

(a) he items surplus the sell to used so
(b) so used to sell the surplus items he
(c) items surplus the sell to used so he
(d) Cannot be determined
(e) None of the above

7. If the pass code for the batch at 1:00 pm on a day was 'back go here people who settle want to'.

What was the pass code for batch at 3:00 pm on that day?

(a) back go here people to want settle who
(b) back go here people settle who want to
(c) back go here people settle to want who
(d) Cannot be determined
(e) None of the above

8. What will be the pass code for the batch at 3:00 pm, if input is 'four of the following five form a group'?

(a) a five following form group the of four
(b) a five following form four group the of
(c) a five following form four of the group
(d) a five following form four group of the
(e) None of the above

9. Consider the figure given below and find the least number of colours to be used to fill the figure, if not two adjacent area can have the same colour?

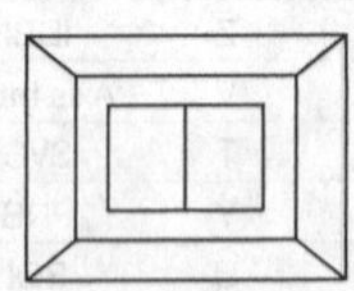

(a) 2 (b) 4
(c) 3 (d) 6

Direction (Q. Nos. 10-11) *In the following questions, find the odd word/letters/from the given alternatives.*

10. (a) BDGK (b) PRUY
(c) FGJK (d) KMPT

11. (a) Hindi (b) Tamil
(c) Punjabi (d) Urdu

12. A word is represented by only one set of numbers as given in anyone of the alternatives. The set of numbers given in the alternatives are represented by two classes of alphabets as in two matrices given below. The columns and rows of Matrix I are numbered from 0 to 4 and that of Matrix II are numbered from 5 to 9. A letter from these matrices can be represented first by its row and next by its column. e.g. 'A' can be represented by 00, 12, 23 etc., and 'P' can be represented by 58, 69, 75 etc. Similarly, you have to identify the set for the word given in each question.

Matrix I

	0	1	2	3	4
0	A	R	S	N	C
1	N	C	A	R	S
2	S	N	C	A	R
3	R	S	N	C	A
4	C	A	R	S	N

Matrix II

	5	6	7	8	9
5	O	E	L	P	T
6	T	O	E	L	P
7	P	T	O	E	L
8	L	P	T	O	E
9	E	L	P	T	O

PAST
(a) 75, 21, 14, 65
(b) 86, 12, 31, 76
(c) 58, 41, 12, 67
(d) 88, 77, 41, 67

Direction (Q. Nos. 13-14) *Each of the questions below consists of a question and two statements numbered* I *and* II *are given below it. You have to decide whether the data provided in the statements are sufficient to answer the question.* **[NICL (AO) 2014]**

Give answer
(a) if the data in Statement I alone are sufficient to answer the question, while the data in Statement II alone are not sufficient to answer the question
(b) if the data in Statement II alone are sufficient to answer the question, while the data in Statement I alone are not sufficient to answer the question
(c) if the data either in Statement I alone or in Statement II alone are sufficient to answer the question
(d) if the data in both Statements I and II together are not sufficient to answer the questions
(e) if the data in both Statements I and II together are necessary to answer the question.

13. How far is point D from point S?
I. Point R is 5 m to the South of point S. Point J is 5 m to the North of point S. Point L is 2 m to the West of point J. Point K is to the North of point L. The distance between points D and K is 2 m.
II. Point J is 5 m to the South of point D. Point M is 2 m to the East of point J. Point V is to the South of point M. The distance between points V and M is equal to the distance between points D and J. Point S is 2 m to the West of point V.

14. Among students P, Q, R, S and T, each having a different height, who is the third tallest?
I. T is shorter than only one person. R is taller than both P and S.
II. P is taller than only one person. R is shorter than both T and Q.

15. Which of the following figures shown below, when folded along the dotted lines, will from a pyramid shaped box with a rectangular base?

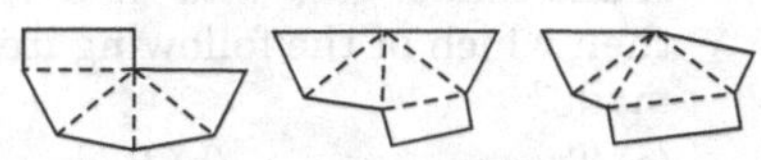

(a) (b) (c) (d)

Direction (Q. Nos. 16-18) *Read the following information carefully and answer the questions which follows.*

Six friends P, Q, R, S, T and V are sitting around a circular table facing either centre or outside. P sits third to the left of R. R faces the centre. V sits second to left of P. Q sits second to right of V. T sits to immediate right of Q. Immediate neighbours of P face direction opposite to that of P. T sits second to left of R.

16. Who amongst the following sits second to right of R?
(a) T (b) S (c) V (d) P
(e) None of these

17. Which of the following is true with regard to the given information?

(a) Four of the five friends are facing the centre
(b) R and S are immediate neighbours of each other
(c) V sits to the immediate right of both S and R
(d) P faces outside
(e) Three people sit between Q and S

18. Four of the following five are alike in a certain way based upon the given seating arrangement and so form a group. Which is the one that does not belong to that group?

(a) P (b) T (c) S (d) V
(e) Q

19. In a certain code language, WORLD is coded as 'XNQKE', similarly TERMS is coded as 'UDQLT'. How will GIVEN be coded in the same code? **[LIC (ADO) 2015]**

(a) HJUDO (b) FHUDO
(c) HHUDO (d) UHHDO
(e) None of these

20. In an accurate clock, in a period of 2 h 20 min, the minute hand will move over **[UPSC (Civil Services) 1996]**

(a) 520° (b) 320° (c) 840° (d) 140°

21. If 'flower' is called 'tree', 'tree' is called 'red', red is called 'gold' and 'gold' is called 'white', then which of the following items, jwellery is made? **[IBPS (PO) 2011]**

(a) Tree (b) Red
(c) White (d) Flower
(e) None of these

Direction (Q. Nos. 22-24) *In the following questions, three statements followed by two conclusions numbered I and II have been given. You have to take the given statements to be true even if they seem to be at variance from the commonly known facts and then decide which of the given conclusion logically follows from the given statements disregarding commonly known facts.* **[NICL (AO) 2014]**

Give answer

(a) if either Conclusion I or II is true
(b) if neither Conclusion I nor II is true
(c) if both Conclusions I and II are true
(d) if only Conclusion I is true
(e) if only Conclusion II is true

22. Statements All alphabets are letters.
All letters are digits.
No digit is a number.

Conclusions I. No alphabet is a digit.
II. All alphabets are digits.

23. Statements All fruits are flowers.
No flower is sweet.
Some sweets are desserts.

Conclusions I. Some desserts are flowers.
II. No dessert is flower.

24. Statements Some planes are ships.
No ship is a radar.
All cars are radars.

Conclusions I. No car is a ship.
II. All radars being planes is a possibility.

25. Which of the answer figures is exactly the mirror image of the given figure, when the mirror is held on the line MN? **[SSC (FCI) 2012]**

Question Figure

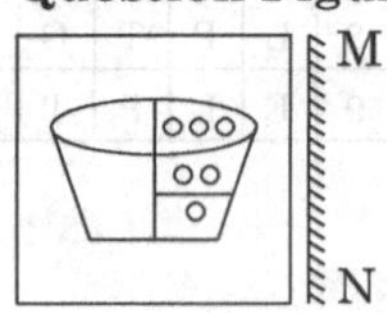

Answer Figures

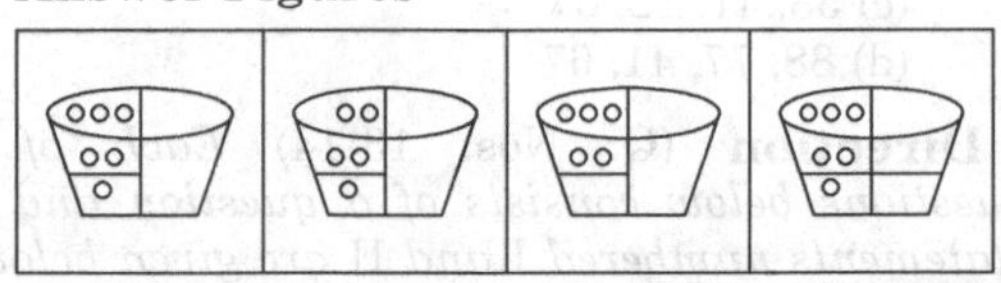

(a) (b) (c) (d)

26. If it is possible to make a meaningful word with the 2nd, the 6th, the 9th and the 12th letters of the word 'CONTRIBUTION', which of the following will be the last letter of that word? If more than one such word can be formed, give 'M' as the answer and if no such word is there, give 'X' as the answer.

(a) T (b) O (c) N (d) M

27. How many N's are there in the following series which are immediately preceded by M and also immediately followed by M?

M M N M N M E N M N F P N M N M N M N M

(a) 3 (b) 5 (c) 2 (d) None of these

Direction (Q. Nos. 28-29) *In the following questions, one or more statements are given followed by four conclusions (a), (b), (c) and (d). You have to consider the statements to be true even if they seem to be at variance from commonly known facts. You have to decide which of the given conclusions, if any, follow from the given statements.*

28. Statements I. Ravi has five pens.
II. No one else in the class has five pens. **[SSC (CGL) 2013]**

Conclusions

(a) All students in the class have pens
(b) All students in the class have five pens each
(c) Some of the students have more than five pens
(d) Only one student in the class has exactly five pens

29. Statements To pass the examination one must work hard. **[CMAT 2013]**

Conclusions

(a) Examination is related with hard work
(b) All those who work hard pass
(c) Examination causes some anxiety and those who work hard overcome it
(d) Without hard work, one does not pass

Direction (Q. Nos. 30-32) *Read the following information and answer the questions given below it.*

I. Mr Akhil Thakur has five sons Ajay, Madan, Ramesh, Nagesh and Shashi and three daughters, Tia, Kanta and Jaya.
II. Shashi is the eldest child and Jaya the youngest.
III. Kanta, the eldest daughter, plays chess.
IV. Tia and Ramesh study at St. Xavier's.
V. The children who are at St. Michael's have been born in succession.
VI. Only St. Michael's offers cricket while only St. Thomas' offers chess. Besides, these schools offer no other games.
VII. Madan and Nagesh are cricketers while Ajay plays football.
VIII. Three of the children are at St. Thomas' and three at St. Xavier's.
IX. Mrs. Thakur first gave birth to three sons and then to two daughters.
X. Ramesh, who was born just before Jaya, plays hockey.

30. Ajay is the .... child of Mr. Thakur.
(a) 2nd (b) 3rd (c) 6th (d) 5th
(e) 4th

31. Shashi is a student of which school?
(a) St. Thoma's
(b) St. Xavier's
(c) St. Michael's
(d) Cannot be determined
(e) He does not go to school

32. What game does Tia Play?
(a) Cricket
(b) Football
(c) Hockey
(d) Cannot be determined
(e) She does not play

33. If 879 = 8, 625 = 1 and 586 = 9, then 785 = ?
(a) 6 (b) 7 (c) 8 (d) 9

34. Choose the figures which form a pair of identical figures.

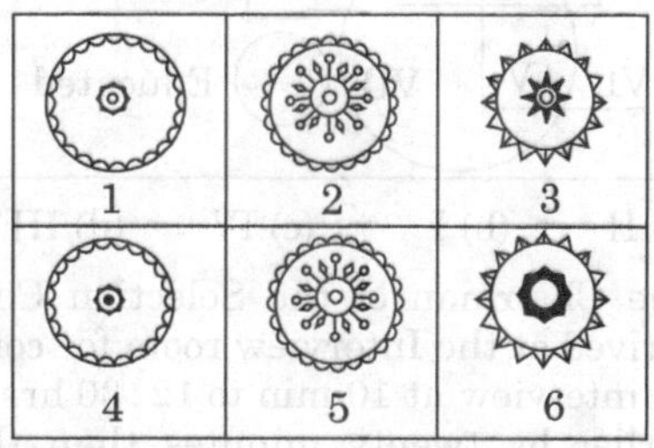

(a) (3, 6) (b) (1,4)
(c) (2,4) (d) (2,5)

35. If the uncle of the father of Rani is the grandson of the father of Anup and Anup is the only son of his father, then how Anup is related to Rani? **[BSSC (CGL) 2015]**
(a) Grandfather (b) Uncle
(c) Maternal Uncle (d) Great grandfather

36. If '×' means '–', '÷' means '+' and '+' means '×', then 18 × 5 ÷ 5 + 6 is equal to
(a) 58 (b) 49 (c) 43 (d) 37

37. In which answer figure is the question figure embedded?

Question Figure

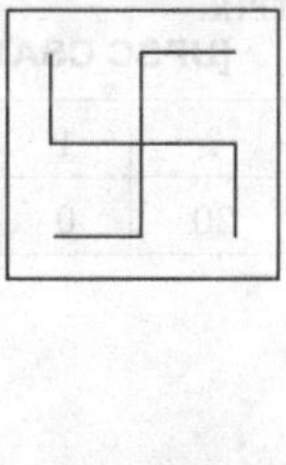

Answer Figures

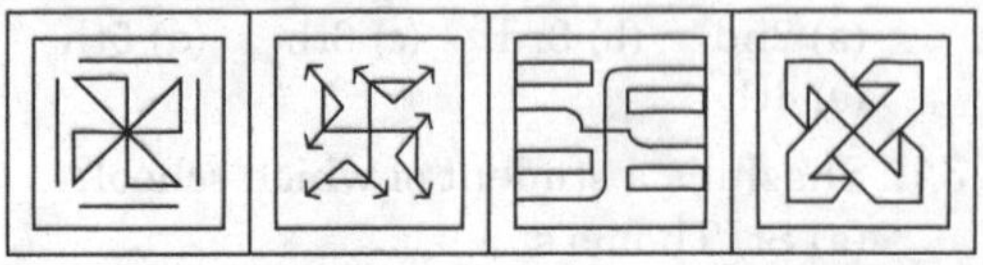

(a) (b) (c) (d)

38. If the present ages of Nandu and Shobhit are 20 yr and 24 yr respectively, then find the ratio between the age of Nandu (before 4 yr) and Shobhit (after 4 yr).

(a) 5 : 6 (b) 4 : 7
(c) 2 : 3 (d) 5 : 6

39. Which one of the areas marked I-VII represents the urban educated who are not hardworking? **[SSC (CGL) 2015]**

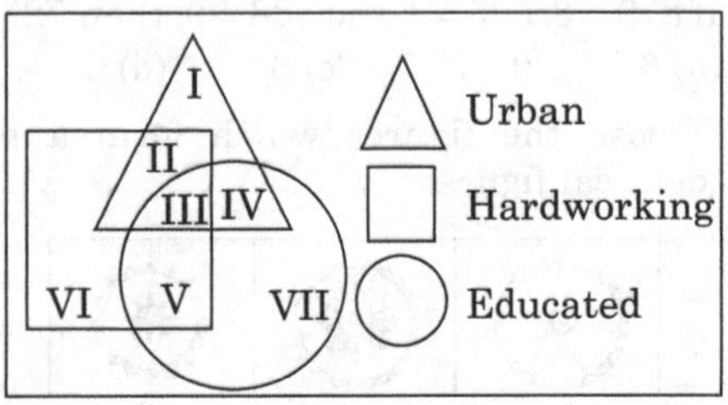

(a) II (b) I (c) IV (d) III

40. The Chairman of the Selection Committee arrived at the Interview room for conducting an interview at 10 min to 12 : 30 hrs. He was earlier by twenty minutes than the other members of the board, who arrived late by 30 min. At what time were the interview scheduled?

(a) 12 : 10 (b) 12 : 20
(c) 12 : 30 (d) 12 : 40

41. Which one of the given responses would be a meaningful order of the following?

(i) Feedback (ii) Teach
(iii) Reteach (iv) Plan
(v) Replan

(a) (iv), (ii), (i), (v), (iii)
(b) (i), (iv), (ii), (v), (iii)
(c) (iii), (v), (ii), (iv), (i)
(d) (ii), (iv), (i), (v), (iii)

42. Consider the following matrix. **[UPSC CSAT 2015]**

3	8	10	2	?	1
6	56	90	2	20	0

What is the missing number at '?' in the matrix?

(a) 5 (b) 0 (c) 7 (d) 3

43. A child is looking for his father. He went 90 m in the East before turning to his right. He went 20 m before turning to his right again to look for his father at his uncle's place 30 m from this point. His father was not there. From here he went 100 m to his North before meeting his father in a street. How far did the son meet his father from the starting point?

(a) 80 m (b) 100 m
(c) 260 m (d) 140 m

Direction (Q. Nos. 44-46) *In the following questions, the symbols $, %, @, © and ★ are used with the following meaning as illustrated below.*

'P % Q' means 'P is neither greater than nor smaller than Q'.

'P $ Q' means 'P is neither smaller than nor equal to Q'.

'P © Q' means 'P is neither greater than nor equal to Q'.

'P ★ Q' means 'P is not greater than Q'.

'P @ Q' means 'P is not smaller than Q'.

Now, in each of the following questions assuming the given statements to be true, find which of the three Conclusions I, II and III given below them is/are definitely true and give your answer accordingly.

44. Statements K @ T, T $ N, N © R

Conclusions I. R $ K
II. N ★ K III. K $ N

(a) None is true (b) Only I is true
(c) Only II is true (d) Only III is true
(e) II and III are true

45. Statements W % K, K © F, D $ F

Conclusions I. D $ K
II. D $ W III. F @ W

(a) I and II (b) I and II
(c) II and III (d) I, II and III
(e) None of these

46. Statements B ★ K, K © F, F % R

Conclusions I. R $ K
II. R $ B III. F $ B

(a) I and II (b) I and III
(c) II and III (d) I, II and III
(e) None of these

47. A clock is so placed that at 12 noon its minute hand points towards North-East. In which direction does its hour hand point at 1:30 pm?
(a) North (b) South **[NIFT (UG) 2014]**
(c) East (d) West

48. Find the missing character.

3	4	2
2	3	1
1	2	?
6	24	0

(a) 3 (b) 4
(c) 0 (d) 5

49. Find the figure out of the answer choice figures that can be formed by joining the pieces given in the question figure.

Question Figure

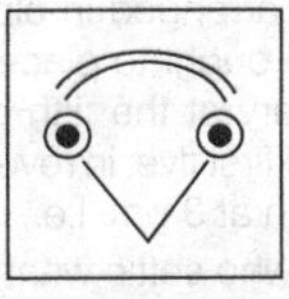

Answer Figures

(a) (b) (c) (d)

50. B is twice as old as A but twice younger than F. C is half the age of A but is twice older than D. Who is the second oldest? **[SSC (CGL) 2011]**
(a) B (b) F
(c) D (d) C

Hints and Solutions

1. (*a*) Clearly, when opposite faces are painted with different colours, then colours on adjacent faces will be different.

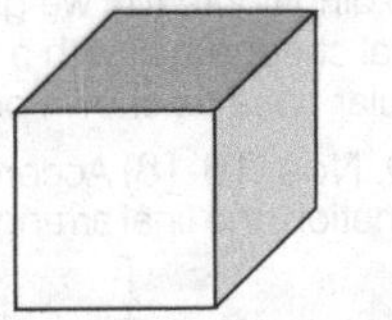

As we know that,
Number of pairs of opposite faces = 3
∴ Required number of colours = 3

2. (*a*) As,

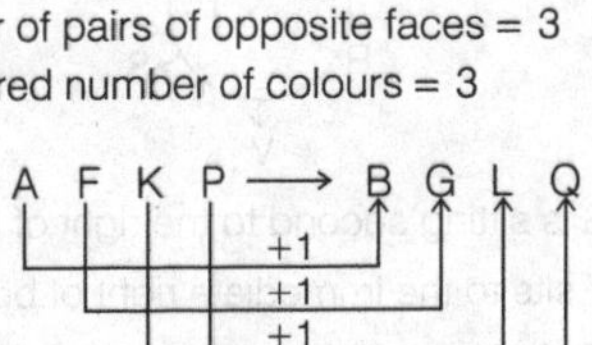

Similarly,

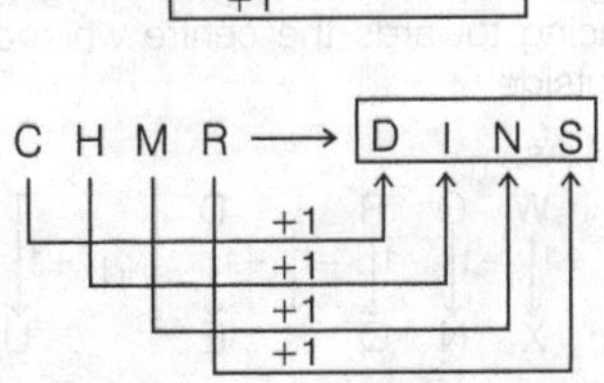

3. (*a*) Seed is the part of 'Fruit' in the same way 'Fruit' is part of 'Tree'

4. (*d*) Pattern of given alpha-numberic series is as follows

P $\xrightarrow{+2}$ R $\xrightarrow{+2}$ T $\xrightarrow{+2}$ V $\xrightarrow{+2}$ X

3 $\xrightarrow{+2}$ 5 $\xrightarrow{+3}$ 8 $\xrightarrow{+4}$ 12 $\xrightarrow{+5}$ 17

C $\xrightarrow{+3}$ F $\xrightarrow{+3}$ I $\xrightarrow{+3}$ L $\xrightarrow{+3}$ O

∴ ? = X 17 O

5. (*a*) The complete letter series will be
c c <u>a</u> c c b / c <u>c</u> a c c b / c c <u>a</u> c c b
⇒ acac

Solution (Q. Nos. 6-8) The pattern followed is as under:
In the first step, the word which comes first in the dictionary is placed at the first place and the remaining words are written in a reverse order.
In the second step, the word which comes second in the dictionary is placed at the second place and all words except the first and the second are written in a reverse order. The process continues in the same manner to give the pass codes for the subsequent batches.

6. (*d*) The input may be obtained by writing all words except 'he' in the given pass code in the reverse order and then placing 'he' at any of the eight positions. So, there are eight possible inputs. Thus, it is not possible to determine the exact input.

7. (*c*) Clearly, Batch IV starts at 1 pm. Thus, in the pass code for batch IV, first four words are arranged in alphabetical order. So, as per the pattern, we ought to place the word which comes fifth in the dictionary at the fifth place and then write all the words except the first five, in reverse order, to get the pass code for the batch at 3 pm. i.e., Batch V.

Batch IV : Back go here people who settle want to

Batch V : Back go here people settle to want who.

8. (*b*) Input : four of the following five form a group

Batch I (10 to 11 am): a group form five following the of four.

Batch II (11 to 12 noon): a five four of the following form group

Batch III (12 to 1 pm): a five following group form the of four

Batch IV (1 to 2 pm): a five following form four of the group

Rest Hour (2 to 3 pm)

Batch V (3 to 4 pm): a five following form four group the of.

9. (*c*)

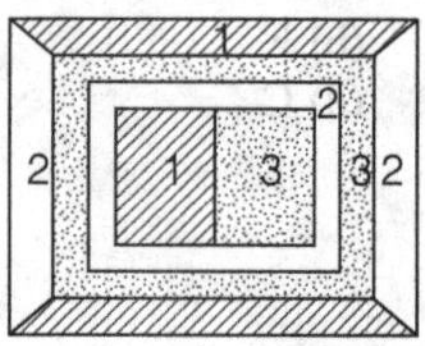

So, there are only 3 colours needed to fill the figure

10. (*c*) As,

B $\xrightarrow{+2}$ D $\xrightarrow{+3}$ G $\xrightarrow{+4}$ K

P $\xrightarrow{+2}$ R $\xrightarrow{+3}$ U $\xrightarrow{+4}$ Y

F $\xrightarrow{+1}$ G $\xrightarrow{+3}$ J $\xrightarrow{+1}$ K

K $\xrightarrow{+2}$ M $\xrightarrow{+3}$ P $\xrightarrow{+4}$ T

Except options (c), all others follows pattern(+2, + 3, + 4)

11. (*d*) Except Urdu, all others are indigenous languages. Urdu was developed from Persian (a foreign language).

12. (*b*) According to the matrices,

P—58, 69, 75, (86), 97

A—00, (12), 23, 34, 41

S—02, 14, 20, (31), 43

T—59, 65, (76), 87, 98

∴ PAST ⇒ 86, 12, 31, 76

13. (*b*) From Statement I,

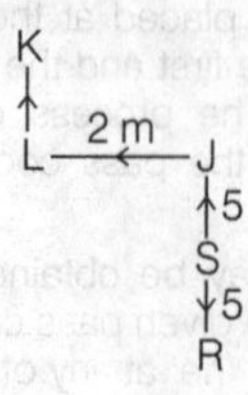

There is no information about the direction of D. So, it is not sufficient to answer the question.

From Statement II,

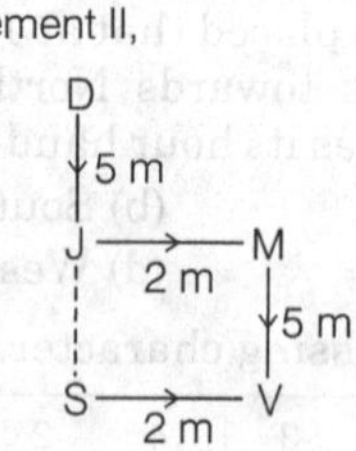

Here, JS = MV, MV = 5 m, JS = 5 m

So, JS + JD = 5 + 5 = 10 m

So, point D is 10 m from point S.

Therefore, the data in Statement II alone are sufficient to answer the question, while the data in Statement I alone are not sufficient to answer the question.

14. (*e*) From Statement I. _<_<_< T <_

R > P and S

From Statement II. _>_>_>_P > _

R < T / Q

By combining both the statements, we get

Q > T > R > P > S

Therefore, R is the third tallest.

So, both the Statements I and II together are necessary to answer the question.

15. (*d*) By folding figure (d), we get a pyramidal shaped box with a rectangular base as shown below

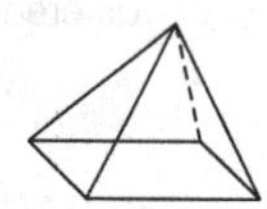

Solution (Q. Nos. 16-18) According to the given information, the final arrangement is as following

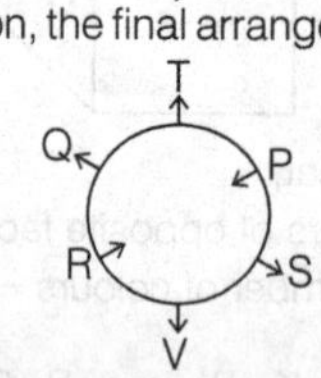

16. (*b*) S is sitting second to the right of R.

17. (*c*) V sits to the immediate right of both S and R.

18. (*a*) P does not belong to this group because P is facing towards the centre while others are facing outside.

19. (*c*) As,

W $\xrightarrow{+1}$ X, O $\xrightarrow{-1}$ N, R $\xrightarrow{-1}$ Q, L $\xrightarrow{-1}$ K, D $\xrightarrow{+1}$ E

and

T $\xrightarrow{+1}$ U, E $\xrightarrow{-1}$ D, R $\xrightarrow{-1}$ Q, M $\xrightarrow{-1}$ L, S $\xrightarrow{+1}$ T

Similarly,

G $\xrightarrow{+1}$ H, I $\xrightarrow{-1}$ H, V $\xrightarrow{-1}$ U, E $\xrightarrow{-1}$ D, N $\xrightarrow{+1}$ O

HHUDO

20. (*c*) 2 h 20 min = 140 min

In every hour the minute hand move over 360°.

So, in every minute it will move = $\frac{360°}{60°} = 6°$

So, in 140 min the minute hand will move over

$= 6 \times 140° = 840°$

21. (*c*) 'Jewellery' is made up of 'gold' but here 'gold' is called 'white'. Hence, in this case jewellery is made up of white.

22. (*e*)

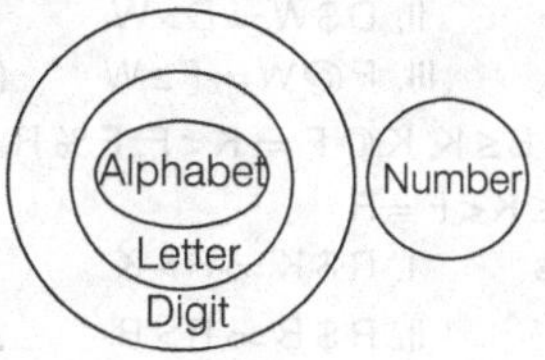

Conclusions I. (✗) II. (✔)

From diagram, it is clear that only Conclusion II is true.

23. (*a*)

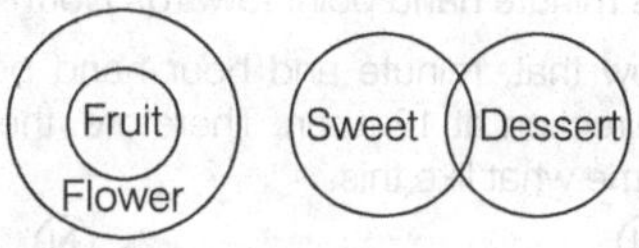

Conclusions I. (May be true) II. (May be true)

From diagram, it is clear that either conclusion I or II is true.

24. (*d*)

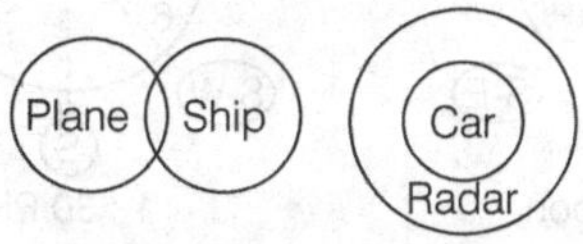

Conclusions I. (✔) II. (✗)

From diagram, it is clear that only Conclusion I is true.

25. (*a*) The mirror image of the given figure is

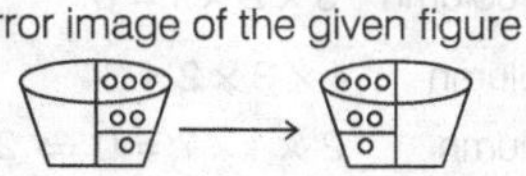

26. (*b*) From letters O, I, T, N, only one meaningful word 'INTO' can be formed and last letter of this word is O.

27. (*b*)

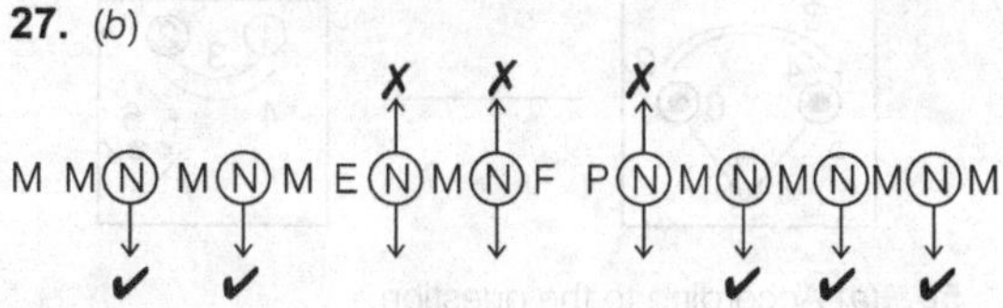

✔ = Condition fulfilled

✗ = Condition not fulfilled

∴ Required number of N = 5

28. (*d*) From both the statements it is clear that, only Ravi has five pens in the class. Therefore, only Conclusion (d) follows.

29. (*d*) Without hard work, one does not pass can be concluded.

Solution (Q. Nos. 30-32) From Statements I, II, III, IV, VII and X we get the following table.

Children	Ajay	Madan	Ramesh	Nagesh	Shashi	Tia	Kanta	Jaya
Age order			7		1	5	4	8
School			St. Xavier's			St. Xavier's		
Game	Football	Cricket	Hockey	Cricket			Chess	

Now, from VI, Madan and Nagesh are at St. Michael's while Kanta is at St. Thomas'.

Ajay is at St. Xavier's

From V, Madan and Nagesh have been born in Ruccession. So, they have been born at 2-3 position.

Now, the final table will be as following

Child	Ajay	Madan	Ramesh	Nagesh	Shashi	Tia	Kanta	Jaya
Age order	6	2 or 3	7	3 or 2	1	5	4	8
School	St. Xavier's	St. Michael's	St. Xavier's	St. Michael's	St. Thomas'	St. Xavier's	St. Thomas'	St. Thomas'
Game	Football	Cricket	Hockey	Cricket	Chess		Chess	Chess

30. (*c*) Ajay is the 6th child of Mr. Thakur.

31. (*a*) Shashi is the student of St. Thomas'.

32. (*d*) The game which Tia played is not determined

33. (*a*) As, $879 = (7 + 9) - 8 = 8$

$625 = (2 + 5) - 6 = 1$ and $586 = (8 + 6) - 5 = 9$

Similarly, $785 = (8 + 5) - 7 = 6$

34. (*d*) 2 and 5 form a pair of identical figures.

35. (*d*) From the given information,

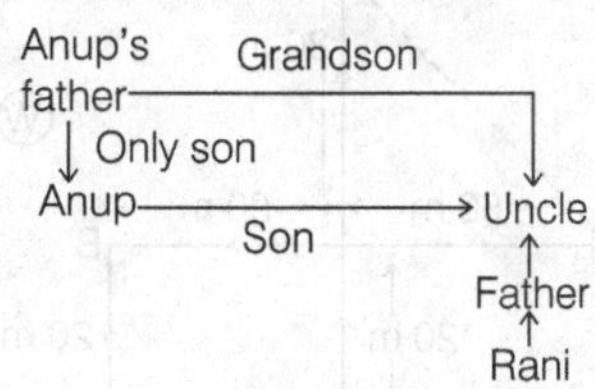

So, Anup is great grandfather of Rani.

36. (*c*) Change of symbols according to the question,

$? = 18 \times 5 \div 5 + 6$

$\downarrow \quad \downarrow \quad \downarrow$

$- \quad + \quad \times$

$= 18 - 5 + 5 \times 6$ (Using VBODMAS Rule)

$= 18 - 5 + 30 = (18 + 30) - 5 = 43$

37. (*b*) Clearly question figure is embedded in answer figure (b) as shown below

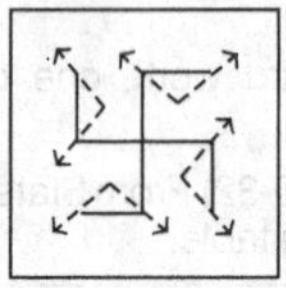

38. (*b*) $\frac{\text{Age of Nandu (before 4 yr)}}{\text{Age of Shobhit (after 4 yr)}} = \frac{\text{Age of Nandu} - 4}{\text{Age of Shobhit} + 4}$

$= \frac{20-4}{24+4} = \frac{16}{28} = 4:7$

39. (*c*) Area IV represents the urban educated who are not hard working.

40. (*a*) The Chairman of the Selection Committee arrived at 12:20 hrs. Other members arrived at 12:40 hrs

Scheduled time of Interview = 12:10 hrs

41. (*a*) Meaningful order of the words

(iv) Plan → (ii) Teach → (i) Feedback → (v) Replan → (iii) Reteach

42. (*a*) As,

3	8	10	2	?	1
6	56	90	2	20	0

In each column, let the number at the top be *x*, and the one at the bottom be *y*, then

$y = x(x-1)$

In column I, $6 = 3(3-1)$

$6 = 6$

Similarly, in column V $20 = ?(? - 1)$

So, $? = 5$

43. (*b*) Route followed by the child

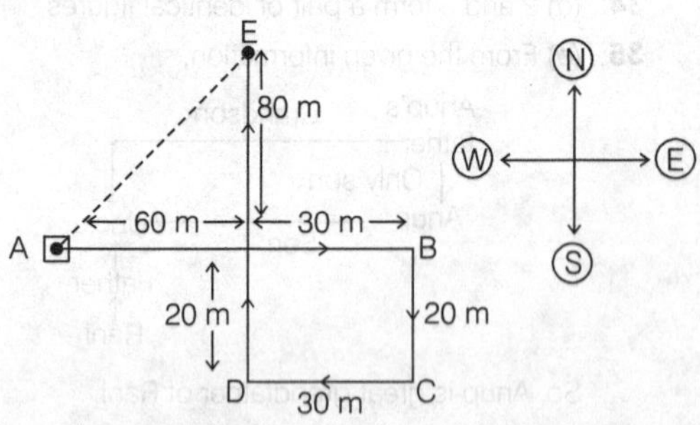

Required distance = AE

$= \sqrt{(80)^2 + (60)^2} = \sqrt{6400 + 3600} = \sqrt{10000} = 100$ m

Solution (Q. Nos. 44-46)

% ⇒ =	$ ⇒ >	© ⇒ <	★ ⇒ ≤	@ ⇒ ≥

44. (*d*) K @ T ⇒ K ≥ T, T $ N ⇒ T > N, N © R ⇒ N < R

Therefore, K ≥ T > N < R

Conclusions I. R $ K ⇒ R > K (Not True)

II. N ★ K ⇒ N ≤ K (Not True)

III. K $ N ⇒ K > N (True)

45. (*b*) W % K ⇒ W = K, K © F ⇒ K < F, D $ F ⇒ D > F

Therefore, W = K < F < D

Conclusions I. D $ K ⇒ D > K (True)

II. D $ W ⇒ D > W (True)

III. F @ W ⇒ F ≥ W (Not True)

46. (*d*) B ★ K ⇒ B ≤ K, K © F ⇒ K < F, F % R ⇒ F = R

Therefore B ≤ K < F = R

Conclusions I. R $ K ⇒ R > K (True)

II. R $ B ⇒ R > B (True)

III. F $ B ⇒ F > B (True)

47. (*c*) In this question, the clock is placed, so that at 12 noon its minute hand point towards North-East.

We know that, minute and hour hand point in the same direction at 12 noon. Therefore, the clock will look some what like this.

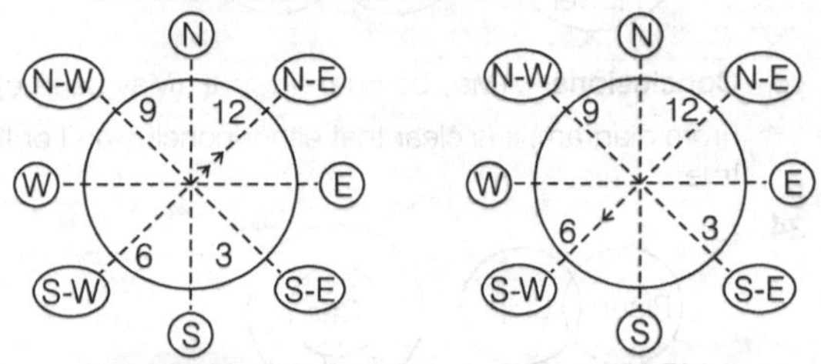

12 : 00 Noon 1 : 30 PM

At 1:30 pm, the hour hand will point in the East direction.

48. (*c*) 1st column 3 × 2 × 1 = 6

2nd column 4 × 3 × 2 = 24

3rd column 2 × 1 × ? = 0 ⇒ 2 × 1 × 0 = 0

49. (*c*)Here, the question figure can be formed by joining the pieces given in option (c) as shown below

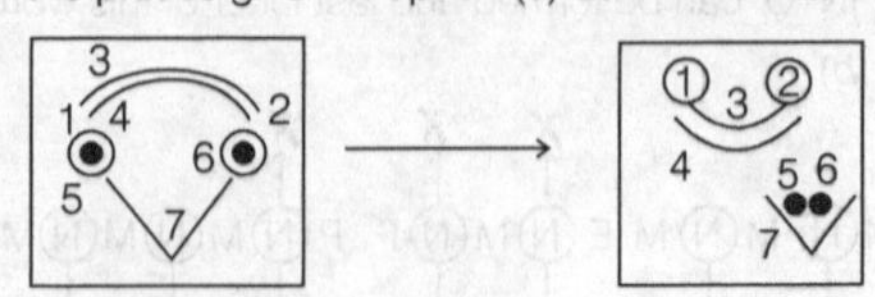

50. (*a*) According to the question,

B = 2A ...(i), F = 2B ...(ii)

A = 2C ...(iii), C = 2D ...(iv)

After equating Eqs. (i), (ii), (iii) and (iv), we get

F > B > A > C > D

∴ B is the second oldest.

PRACTICE SET 33

1. Let J = 1, K = 2, L = 5, M = 7, N = 11, O = 13 and P = 17. Find the letter to be inserted in the box in the relation given
$(N \times \square + M) \div K = 31$ **[SSC (10+2) 2014]**
(a) L (b) P
(c) J (d) O

Direction (Q. Nos. 2-3) *In the following questions, find the odd numbers/words from the given alternatives.*

2. (a) Violin (b) Sitar
(c) Veena (d) Flute

3. (a) 3-4-14 (b) 56-57-67
(c) 102-103-113 (d) 22-23-13

Direction (Q. Nos. 4-5) *In making decisions about important questions, it is desirable to distinguish between a 'strong' argument and a 'weak' argument. A 'strong' argument must be both important and directly related to the question. A 'weak' argument may not be directly related to the question and may be of minor importance or may be related to the trivial to the trivial aspect of the question. Each question below is followed by two arguments numbered I and II. You have to decide which of the arguments is 'strong' and which is 'weak'.*

Give answer
(a) if only Argument I is strong
(b) if only Argument II is strong
(c) if either I or II is strong
(d) if neither I nor II is strong
(e) if both I and II are strong

4. Statement Should there be a total ban on use of plastic bags?

Arguments
I. No, instead the thickness of plastic bags, which can be used without much damage to the environment, should be specified.
II. Yes, use of plastic bags causes various problems like water pollution and water logging and hence, it is necessary to ban it.

5. Statement Should there be a complete ban on sale of soft drinks within the premises of all the schools in India?

Arguments
I. Yes, this will considerably decrease the consumption of such drinks by the school children as these contain harmful chemicals.
II. No, the authorities do not have right to impose such restriction in a democratic country.

6. The average age of a cricket team is 27 yr. Two players with 24 and 27 yr of age are replaced of 23yr and 28 yr of age. What is the average age of the team now?
(a) 27 yr (b) 26 yr
(c) 24 yr (d) 28 yr

7. Find the missing number from the given responses.

11	6	8
17	12	?
25	34	19
19	28	11

(a) 13 (b) 15
(c) 16 (d) 9

8. Find the missing figure in the series from the given answer figures.

Question Figures

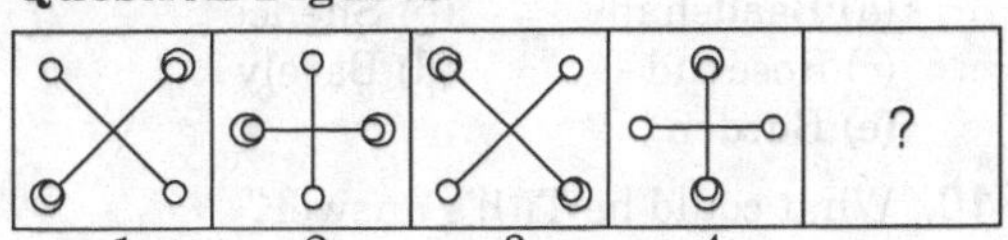

1 2 3 4

Answer Figures

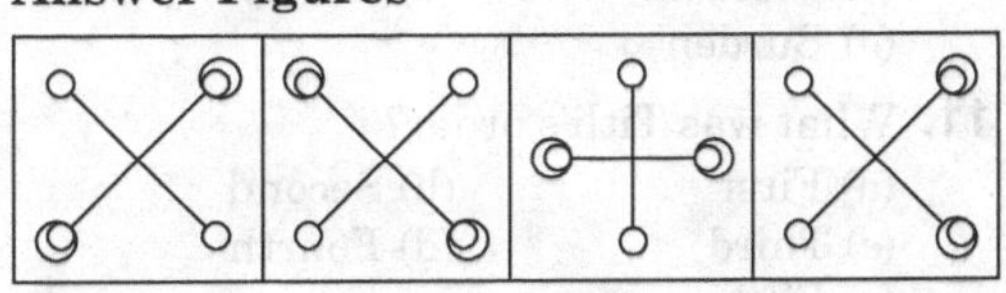

(a) (b) (c) (d)

Direction (Q. Nos. 9 -11) *These questions are based on a set of conditions. In answering some of the questions, it may be useful to draw rough diagram. Choose the response that most accurately and completely answers each question.*

Five colleagues pooled their efforts during the office lunch - hour to solve the crossword in the daily paper. Colleagues Mr. Bineet, Mr. Easwar. Ms. Elsie, Ms. Sheela and Mr. Titli.

Answers Burden, Barely, Baadshah, Rosebud, Silence.

Numbers 4 down, 8 across, 15 across, 15 down, 21 across.

Order First, second, third, fourth, fifth.

(i) Titli produced the answer to 8 across, which had the same number of letters as the previous answer to be inserted and one more than the subsequent answer which was produced by one of the men.

(ii) It was not Bineet who solved the clue to 'Burden' and Easwar did not solve 4 down.

(iii) The answers to 15 across and 15 down did not have the same number of letters.

(iv) 'Silence' which was not the third word to be inserted was the answer to an across clue.

(v) 'Barely' was the first word to be entered in the grid but 'Baadshah' was not the second answer to be found.

(vi) Elsie's word was longer than Bineet's Sheela was neither the first nor the last to come up with an answer.

(vii) Fifth one to be worked out was an answer to an across clue.

9. What was Sheela's word?
(a) Baadshah (b) Silence
(c) Rosebud (d) Barely
(e) Burden

10. What could be Titli's answer?
(a) Baadshah (b) Silence
(c) Rosebud (d) Barely
(e) Burden

11. What was Titli's order?
(a) First (b) Second
(c) Third (d) Fourth
(e) Fifth

12. If 15th June falls 3 days after tomorrow, that is Friday, then on what day will the last of the month fall?
(a) Monday (b) Tuesday
(c) Wednesday (d) Thursday

13. In this questions, there are two statements labelled as Assertion (A) and Reason (R).

Assertion (A) Inside the Earth metals are present in molten state.

Reason (R) Earth absorbs the Sun's rays.

(a) if both 'A' and 'R' are true and 'R' is the correct explanation of 'A'
(b) if both 'A' and 'R' are true but 'R' is not the correct explanation of 'A'
(c) if 'A' is true but 'R' is false
(d) if 'A' is false but 'R' is true
(e) if both 'A' and 'R' are false

14. Which one of the given responses would be a meaningful order of the following ?
(i) Infancy (ii) Childhood
(iii) Adulthood (iv) Babyhood
(v) Adolescence
(a) (i), (iv), (ii), (v), (iii)
(b) (i), (iii), (v), (ii), (iv)
(c) (i), (ii), (iii), (iv), (v)
(d) (i), (iv), (v), (ii), (iii)

Direction (Q. Nos. 15-16) *In the following questions, select the related word/number from the given alternatives.* **[SSC (10+2) 2014]**

15. Qualm : Nausea : : Burn : ?
(a) Fresh
(b) Sear
(c) Sensible
(d) Wet

16. 583 : 488 : : 293 : ?
(a) 581 (b) 291
(c) 378 (d) 487

17. Find out which of the answer figures (a), (b), (c) and (d) completes the figure matrix?

Question Figure

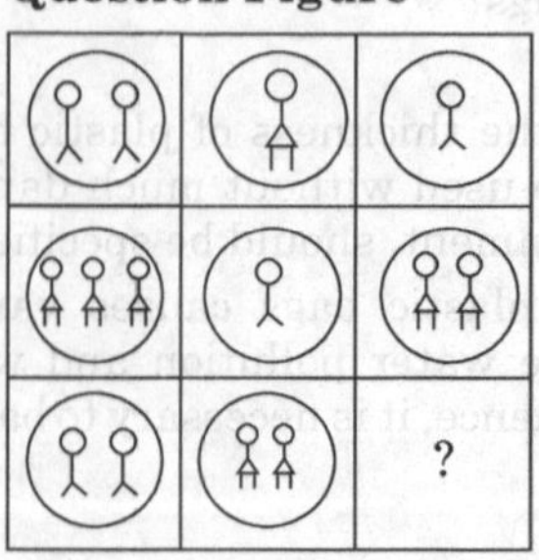

Answer Figures

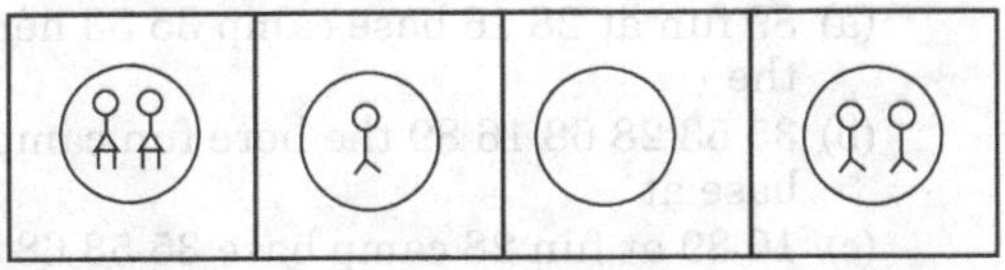

(a) (b) (c) (d)

18. If the digits in the number 86435192 are arranged in ascending order, then what will be the difference between the digits which are second from the right and fourth from the left in the new arrangement ?
(a) One (b) Two
(c) Three (d) Four
(e) None of these

19. If PALE is coded as '2134', EARTH is coded as '41590', then how is PEARL coded as ? **[SSC (10+2) 2014]**
(a) 29530 (b) 24153
(c) 25413 (d) 25430

20. Rahul put his timepiece on the table in such a way that at 6 pm hour hand points to North. In which direction the minute hand will point at 9:15 pm ?
(a) South-East (b) South
(c) North (d) West

21. Which one of the following diagrams represents the correct relationship among Lion , Fox and Carnivorous **[SSC (10+2) 2014]**

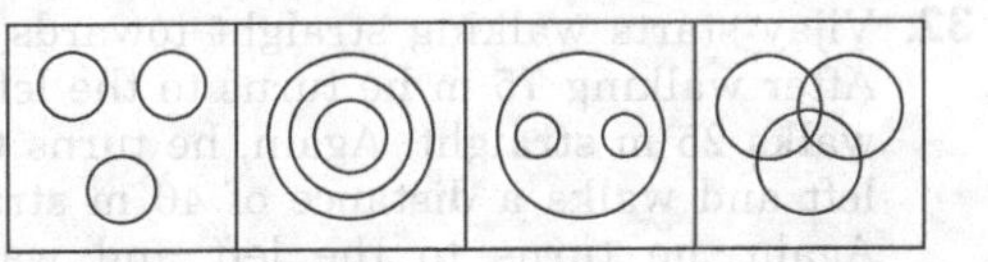

(a) (b) (c) (d)

22. A word is represented by only one set of numbers as given in anyone of the alternatives. The set of numbers given in the alternatives are represented by two classes of alphabets as in two matrices given below. The columns and rows of Matrix I are numbered from 0 to 4 and that of Matrix II are numbered from 5 to 9. A letter from these matrices can be represented first by its row and next by its column, e.g. 'A' can be represented by 00, 12, 23 etc., and 'P' can be represented by 58,69,75 etc. Similarly, you have to identify the set for the word given in each questions.

Matrix I

	0	1	2	3	4
0	A	R	S	N	C
1	N	C	A	R	S
2	S	N	C	A	R
3	R	S	N	C	A
4	C	A	R	S	N

Matrix II

	5	6	7	8	9
5	O	E	L	P	T
6	T	O	E	L	P
7	P	T	O	E	L
8	L	P	T	O	E
9	E	L	P	T	O

RATE
(a) 13,12,98,67
(b) 42,23,56,76
(c) 30,14,95,89
(d) 24,43,89,95

Direction (Q. Nos. 23-24) *Read the following information carefully and answer the questions given below.*
(i) There are five friends.
(ii) They are standing in a row facing South.
(iii) Jayesh is to the immediate right of Alok.
(iv) Pramod is between Bhagat and Subodh.
(v) Subodh is between Jayesh and Pramod.

23. Who is at the extreme left end?
(a) Alok (b) Bhagat
(c) Subodh (d) Data inadequate

24. Who is in the middle?
(a) Bhagat (b) Jayesh
(c) Pramod (d) Subodh

25. Find the figure out of the answer choice figure that can be formed by joining the pieces given in the question figure.

Question Figure

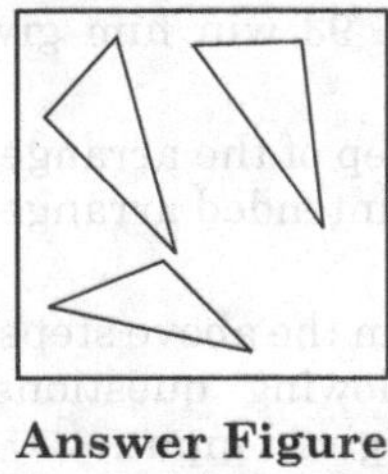

Answer Figures

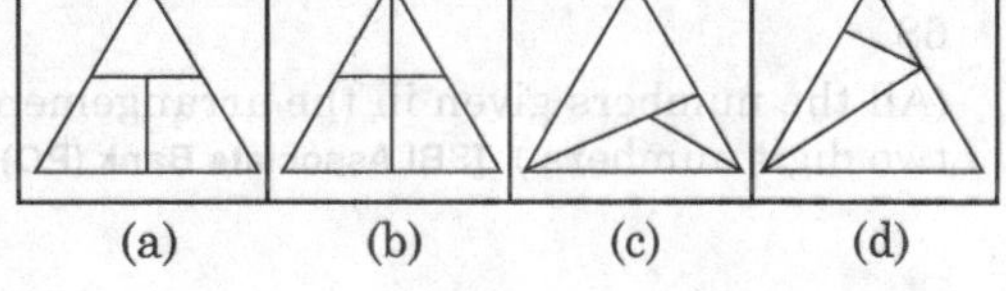

(a) (b) (c) (d)

26. How many such pairs of letters are there in the word LAYOUTS each of which has as many letters between them (both forward and backward directions) as they have between in the English alphabetical series ? **[LIC (ADO) 2015]**

(a) Three (b) None
(c) More than three (d) One
(e) Two

27. If D= 4 and READ is coded as 7, then how is HEAR coded as

(a) 32 (b) 33
(c) 7 (d) 8

Direction (Q. Nos. 28 -30) *Study the following information to answer the given questions.*

A word and number arrangement machine when given an input line of words and numbers rearranges them following a particular rule in each step. The following is an illustration of input and rearrangement. (All the numbers are two digits numbers and are arranged as per some logic based on the value of the number.)

Input win 56 32 93 bat for 46 him 28 11 give chance

***Step* I** 93 56 32 bat for 46 him 28 11 give chance win

***Step* II** 11 93 56 32 bat for 46 28 give chance win him

***Step* III** 56 11 93 32 bat for 46 28 chance win him give

***Step* IV** 28 56 11 93 32 bat 46 chance win him give for

***Step* V** 46 28 56 11 93 32 bat win him give for chance

***Step* VI** 32 46 28 56 11 93 win him give for chance bat

and Step VI is the last Step of the arrangement of the above input as the intended arrangement is obtained.

As per the rules followed in the above steps, find out in each of the following questions the appropriate steps for the given input.

Input fun 89 at the 28 16 base camp 35 53 here 68

(All the numbers given in the arrangement are two digit numbers.) **[SBI Associate Bank (PO) 2011]**

28. Which of the following would be the Step II ?

(a) 89 fun at 28 16 base camp 35 53 here 68 the
(b) 35 53 28 68 16 89 the here fun camp base at
(c) 16 89 at fun 28 camp base 35 53 68 the here
(d) 53 28 68 16 89 35 the here fun camp base at
(e) None of the above

29. Which word/number would be at 7th position from the left in Step IV?

(a) base (b) at (c) 35 (d) the
(e) 53

30. Which step number would be the following output ?

53 28 68 16 89 at 35 the here fun camp base

(a) There will be no such step
(b) III (c) II
(d) V (e) IV

31. How many rectangles are there in the following figure ?

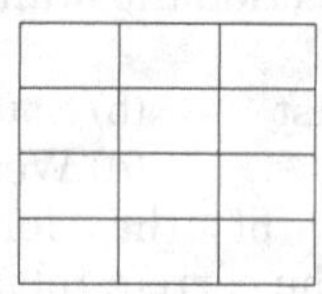

(a) 48 (b) 60 (c) 61 (d) 56

32. Vijay starts walking straight towards East. After walking 75 m he turns to the left and walks 25 m straight. Again, he turns to the left and walks a distance of 40 m straight. Again, he turns to the left and walks a distance of 25 m. How far is he from the starting point ? **[SSC (10+2) 2013]**

(a) 125 (b) 50 (c) 115 (d) 35

33. Mohan correctly remenbers that his father's birthday is before 20th January but after 16th January where as his sister correctly remembers that their father's birhtday is after 18th January but before 23rd January. On which date in January is definitely their father's birthday?

(a) 18th (b) 19th
(c) 20 th (d) Data inadequate
(e) None of these

Direction (Q. Nos. 34 -36) *In each of the questions below are given four statements followed by four conclusions numbered I, II, III and IV. You have to take the given statements to be true even if they seem to be at variance with commonly known facts. Read all the conclusions and then decide which of the given conclusion (s) logically follow (s) from the given statements disregarding commonly known facts.*

34. Statements Some baskets are glasses.
All glasses are pots.
Some pots are plates.
All plates are cups.

Conclusions I. No glasses are pots.
II. All glasses are baskets.
III. Atleast some pots are baskets.
IV. Some plates being glasses is a possibility.

(a) III and IV follow (b) Only IV follows
(c) I and II follow (d) None follows
(e) All follow

35. Statements All potatos are onions.
All onions are grapes.
Some grapes are mangoes.
All mangoes are brinjals.

Conclusions I. Potatos are grapes.
II. Some brinjals being potatos is a possibility.
III. Each potato is grape.
IV. Some potatos are definitely onions.

(a) All follow
(b) None follows
(c) Only IV follows
(d) Follow II, III and IV
(e) Only I follows

36. Statements All bats are cats.
No cat is rat.
All rats are tigers.
Some tigers are fighters.

Conclusions I. Some tigers are cats.
II. Atleast some fighters being rats is a possibility.
III. Atleast some cats are definitely bats.
IV. None of the fighters is rat.

(a) All follow (b) None follows
(c) Only III follows (d) I, II and IV follow
(e) II and III follow

37. Select one alternative, which exactly matches with the mirror image of the word in the question.

FIXING

(a) ƏИIXIF (b) ꟻIXIИƏ
(c) ƏИIXIF (d) ƏИIXIꟻ

38. Lakshmi is elder than Meenu. Leela is elder than Meenu but younger than Lakshmi. Latha is younger than both Meenu and Hari but Hari is younger than Meenu. Who is the youngest ? **[NICL Assistant (Class III Cadre) 2015]**

(a) Lakshmi (b) Meenu
(c) Leela (d) Latha
(e) Hari

39. Select the missing number from the given alternatives. **[BSSC (CGL) 2015]**

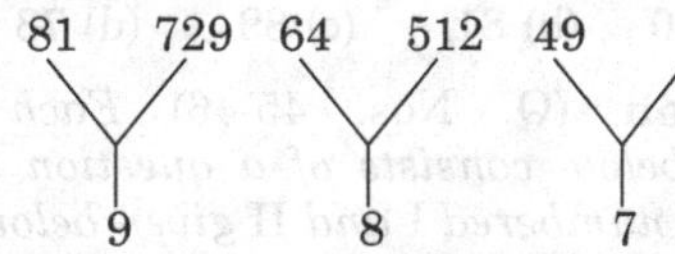

(a) 444 (b) 515
(c) 343 (d) 373

40. Four positions of a dice are given below. Which letter will be opposite to D ? **[SSC (CGL) 2013]**

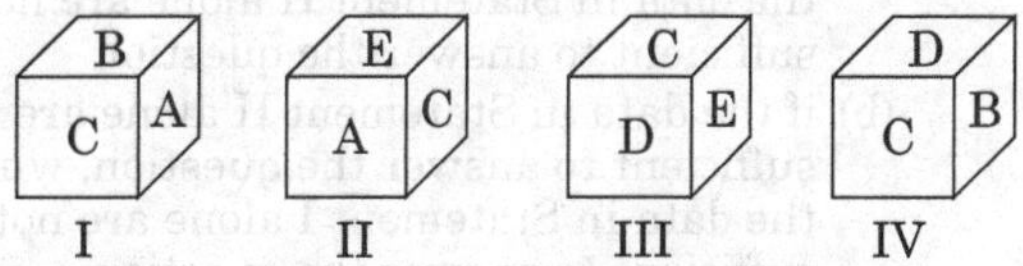

(a) D (b) A (c) B (d) C

41. If 'A ₹ B' means 'A is the father of B',
'A @ B' means 'A is the mother of B' and
'A ! B' means 'A is the wife of B',
then which of the following means and 'T is the grandmother of U' ?
[FCI Assistant (Grade III) 2015]

(a) T @ R ₹ Y ! U (b) T @ S ₹ U ! Y
(c) T @ R ! S ! U (d) None of these

42. A square paper is folded in a particular manner and a punch is made. When unfolded the paper appears as given below. Find the manner in which the paper is folded and punch is made.

Question Figure

Answer Figures

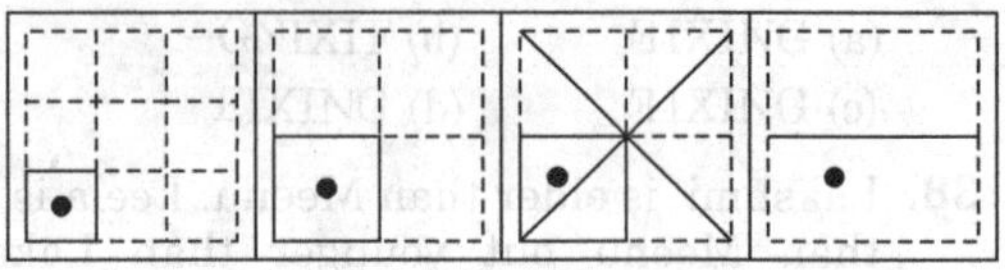

(a) (b) (c) (d)

Direction (Q. Nos. 43-44) *Find the missing term.*

43. Y, ?, ?, M, I, E

(a) Z, X (b) P, R
(c) Q, T (d) U, Q

44. 11, 29, 55, ?, 131 **[SSC (CPO) 2013]**

(a) 110 (b) 81 (c) 89 (d) 78

Direction (Q. Nos. 45-46) *Each of the questions below consists of a question and two statements numbered* I *and* II *given below it. You have to decide whether the data provided in the statements are sufficient to answer the question.*

Give answer

(a) if the data in Statement I alone are sufficient to answer the question, while the data in Statement II alone are not sufficient to answer the question
(b) if the data in Statement II alone are sufficient to answer the question, while the data in Statement I alone are not sufficient to answer the question
(c) if the data either in Statement I alone or in Statement II alone are sufficient to answer the question
(d) if the data given in both the Statements I and II together are not sufficient to answer the question
(e) if the data in both the Statements I and II together are necessary to answer the question

45. Town P is towards which direction of town T ?

I. Town T is towards South of town K which is towards West of town P.
II. Town R is towards South of town V and towards East of town T.

46. Among P,Q,R,S and T each having different age, who is the youngest among them ?

I. Q is younger than only P.
II. S is older than only R.

47. Pointing to a man in a photograph, a woman said, "His brother's father is the only son of my grandfather". How is the woman related to the man in the photograph ?

(a) Mother (b) Aunt
(c) Sister (d) Daughter

Direction (Q. Nos. 48 -50) *In the following questions symbols δ, ★, %, @ and © are used with the following meaning as illustrated below :*

'P ★ Q' means 'P is not greater than Q'.

'P @ Q' means 'P is neither greater than nor equal to Q'.

'P © Q' means 'P is not smaller than Q'.

'P % Q' means 'P is neither smaller than nor greater than Q'.

'P δ Q' means 'P is neither smaller than nor equal to Q'.

Now, in each of the following questions assuming the given statements to be true, find which of the three Conclusions I, II and III given below them is/are definitely true and give your answer accordingly.

48. Statements R© K, K δ M, M ★ J

Conclusions I. J δ K
II. M @ R III. M % R

(a) None is true (b) Only I is true
(c) Only II is true (d) Only III is true
(e) Either II or III is true

49. Statements D @ K, K % F, F © B

Conclusions I. F δ D
II. B @ K III. B % K

(a) Only I is true (b) Only II is true
(c) Only III is true (d) Either II or III is true
(e) Either II or III and I are true

50. Statements H ★ W, W @ N, N % R

Conclusions I. R δ W
II. N δ W III. H @ R

(a) I and II are true
(b) II and III are true
(c) I and III are true
(d) All I, II and III are true
(e) None of the above

Hints and Solutions

1. (*a*) By putting 'L', we get
$(N \times L + M) \div K = 31$
$(11 \times 5 + 7) \div 2 = 31 \Rightarrow (55 + 7) \div 2 = 31$
$62 \div 2 = 31 \Rightarrow 31 = 31$

2. (*d*) Except flute, all others are string instruments.

3. (*d*) In the other options except (d), second number is obtained by the addition of 1 in first number and third number is obtained by the addition of 10 in second number.

4. (*e*) Argument I is strong as it takes a wise, reconciliatory approach to the problem. Argument II is also strong as water pollution, etc. may severally harm mankind.

5. (*a*) Argument I is strong because soft drinks contain some harmful chemicals which are harmful to school children. But Argument II is not strong i.e. we cannot ban wrong things in a democracy.

6. (*a*) The total age of the two players which were replaced is the same as that of the total age of two players which replaced them.

Therefore, the new average will remain unchanged.

7. (*c*) As, $25 + 11 - 17 = 19 \Rightarrow 34 + 6 - 12 = 28$
$19 + 8 - ? = 11 \quad \therefore \; ? = 27 - 11 = 16$

8. (*a*) All the three designs inside the square move through 45° in clockwise direction. Hence, option (a) is correct.

Solution (Q. Nos. 9-11) On the basis of given information, we get the following information

Order	First	Second	Third	Fourth	Fifth
Numbers	4 down	across	8 across	15 down	across
Colleagues	Mr. Bineet	Ms. Sheela	Mr. Titli	Mr. Easwar	Ms. Elsie
Answers	Barely	Silence	Rosebud	Burden	Baadshah

9. (*b*) Sheela's word was Silence.

10. (*c*) Titli's answer is Rosebud.

11. (*c*) Titli's order was Third.

12. (*b*) Tomorrow $\Rightarrow$ Friday
Friday + 3 = Monday
Monday = 15 th
Other Monday $\Rightarrow$ 22, 29
Therefore, 30th June = Tuesday

13. (*c*) Inside the Earth, the high temperature and pressure keep the metals in molten state. The Earth does not absorb the Sun's rays but reflects them.

14. (*a*) Meaningful order of the words
(i) Infancy → (iv) Babyhood → (ii) Childhood
→ (v) Adolescence → (iii) Adulthood

15. (*b*) As, Nausea is one of the synonyms of Qualm. In the same way, Sear is one of the synonyms of Burn.

16. (*c*) Taking option (c),
As, sum of digits of 583 = 5 + 8 + 3 = 16
and sum of digits of 488 = 4 + 8 + 8 = 20
Similarly, sum of digits of 293 = 2 + 9 + 3 = 14
and sum of digits of 378 = 3 + 7 + 8 = 18
Here, difference of both are (20 − 16) = (18 − 14) = 4
$\therefore$? = 378

17. (*c*) Clearly, in each row, the number of elements in the third figure is equal to the difference between the number of elements in the first and second figures.

Also, the third figure has the same types of elements as that of first figure.

18. (*d*)

Original number 8 6 4 3 5 1 9 2
Ascending order 1 2 3 (4) 5 6 (8) 9

From left 4th; From right 2nd

$\therefore$ Required difference = 8 − 4 = 4

19. (*b*) As,

P	A	L	E	and	E	A	R	T	H
↓	↓	↓	↓		↓	↓	↓	↓	↓
2	1	3	4		4	1	5	9	0

So, by direct substitution method, we get

P	E	A	R	L
↓	↓	↓	↓	↓
2	4	1	5	3

20. (*d*)

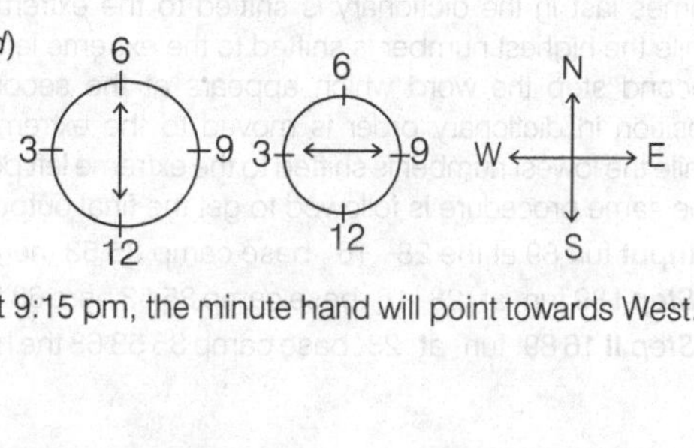

At 9:15 pm, the minute hand will point towards West.

21. (*c*) Lion and fox both are carnivorous but both are different.

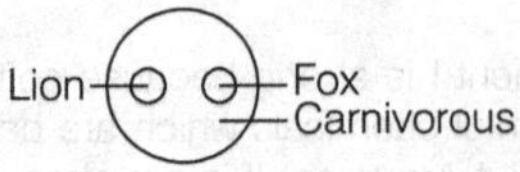

22. (*a*) According to the matrices,

R—01, (13), 24, 30, 42 A—00, (12), 23, 34, 41
T—59, 65, 76, 87, (98) E—56, (67), 78, 89, 95

∴ RATE ⇒ 13, 12, 98, 67

Solution (Q. Nos. 23-24) According to the given information, the final arrangement is as following

Bhagat — Pramod — Subodh — Jayesh — Alok ↓ Facing South

23. (*a*) Alok is at the extreme left end.

24. (*d*) Subodh is in the middle.

25. (*c*) Option (*c*) is correct answer.

26. (*c*)

12 1 25 15 21 20 19
L A Y O U T S

Hence, option (*c*) is correct.

27. (*d*) According to the question, we have

R E A D
↓ ↓ ↓ ↓
$18 + 5 + 1 + 4 = 28$

After dividing the value of READ by 4, we get,

$$\frac{28}{4} = 7$$

Similarly, we can write

H E A R
↓ ↓ ↓ ↓
$8 + 5 + 1 + 18 = 32$

After dividing the value of HEAR by 4, we get

$$\frac{32}{4} = \boxed{8}$$

Hence, option (*d*) is correct.

Solution (Q. Nos. 28 -30) After careful analysis of the given input and various steps of rearrangement it is evident that one word and one number are arranged in each step. The numbers are arranged from the left and the words are arranged from the right. In the first step the word which comes last in the dictionary is shifted to the extreme right while the highest number is shifted to the extreme left. In the second step the word which appears at the second last position in dictionary order is moved to the extreme right while the lowest number is shifted to the extreme left position. The same procedure is followed to get the final output.

Input fun 89 at the 28 16 base camp 35 53 here 68
***Step* I** 89 fun at 28 16 base camp 35 53 here 68 the
***Step* II** 16 89 fun at 28 base camp 35 53 68 the here
***Step* III** 68 16 89 at 28 base camp 35 53 the here fun
***Step* IV** 28 68 16 89 at base 35 53 the here fun camp
***Step* V** 53 28 68 16 89 at 35 the here fun camp base
***Step* VI** 35 53 28 68 16 89 the here fun camp base at

28. (*e*) None of the above

29. (*c*) 35 would be at 7th position from the left in Step IV.

30. (*d*) This is Step V.

31. (*b*) Total number of rectangles

$$= (4 + 3 + 2 + 1) \times (3 + 2 + 1)$$
(here, R = 4 and C = 3)
$$= 10 \times 6 = 60$$

32. (*d*) According to the question, the direction diagram is as shown below

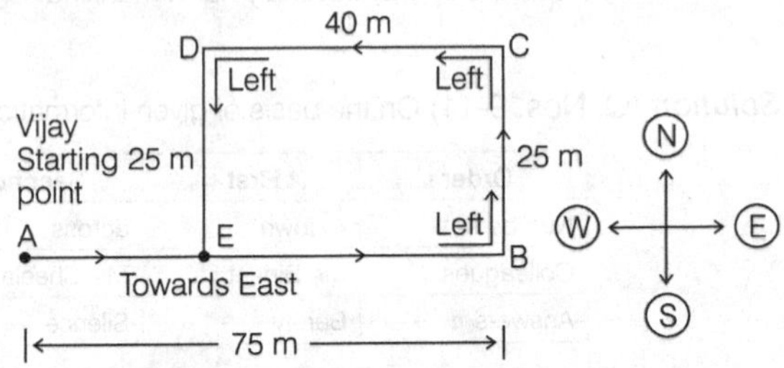

∴ Distance between starting and ending point.

AE = AB − EB = 75 − 40 = 35 m (∵ EB = DC)

33. (*b*) Days by Mohan, [17th, 18th or (19th)] January.

Days by sister, [(19th), 20th, 21st or 22nd] January.

Required day is 19th January as it is common in both the groups.

34. (*a*)

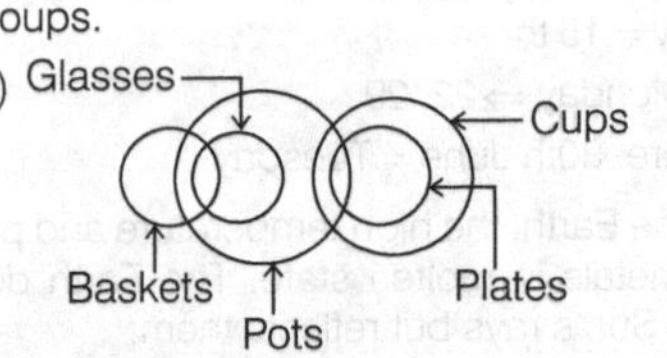

Conclusions

I. No glasses are pots. (✗)
II. All glasses are baskets. (✗)
III. At least some pots are baskets. (✔)
IV. Some plates being glasses is a possibility. (✔)

35. (*a*)

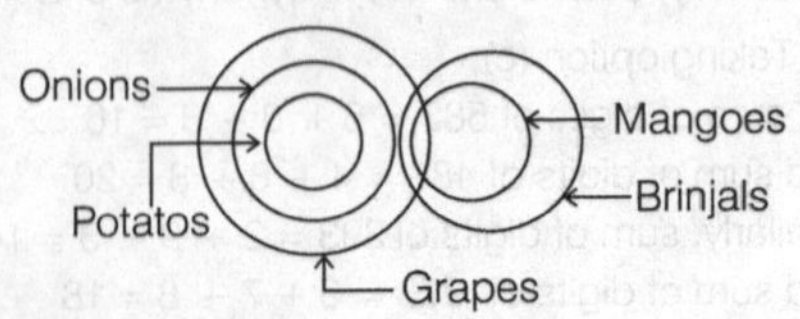

Conclusions

I. Potatos are grapes. (✔)
II. Some brinjals being potatos is a possibility. (✔)
III. Each potato is grape. (✔)
IV. Some potatos are definitely onions. (✔)

36. (*e*)

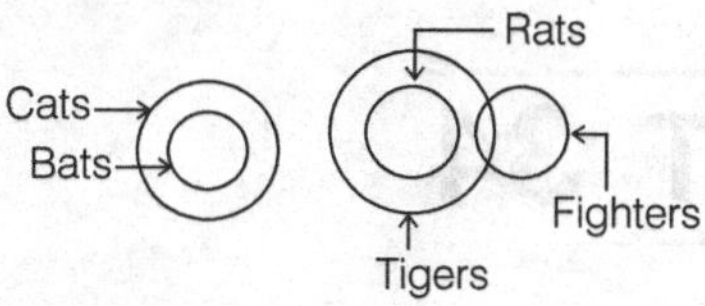

Conclusions

I. Some tigers are cats. (✗)
II. Atleast some fighters being rats is a possibility. (✔)
III. At least some cats are definitely bats. (✔)
IV. None of the fighters is rat. (✗)

37. (*d*) Option (d) is correct answer.

38. (*d*) According to the question,

Lakshmi > Meenu ...(i)
Lakshmi > Leela > Meenu ...(ii)
Meenu > Hari > Latha ...(iii)

On combining all the equations, we get

⇒ Lakshmi > Leela > Meenu > Hari > Latha

So, Latha is the youngest.

39. (*c*) As, in first figure, $9 \rightarrow 9^2 \rightarrow 81 \quad 9^3 \rightarrow 729$

and, in second figure, $8 \rightarrow 8^2 \rightarrow 64, \; 8^3 \rightarrow 512$

Similarly, in third figure, $7 \rightarrow 7^2 \rightarrow 49 \quad 7^3 \rightarrow 343$

40. (*b*) Dice can be shown as

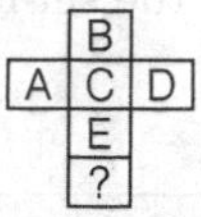

So, from the unfolded dice, it is clear that the letter opposite to D is A.

41. (*b*) From option (b) T @ S ₹ U ! Y

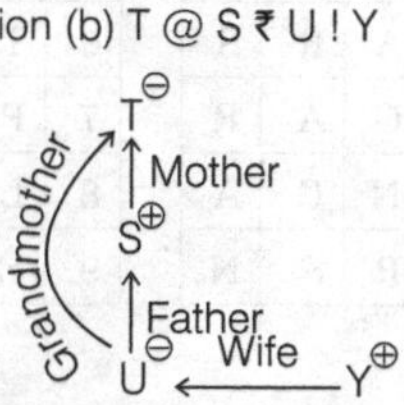

42. (*a*)

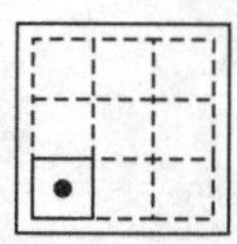

So, option (a) is correct.

43. (*d*) The pattern is as follows

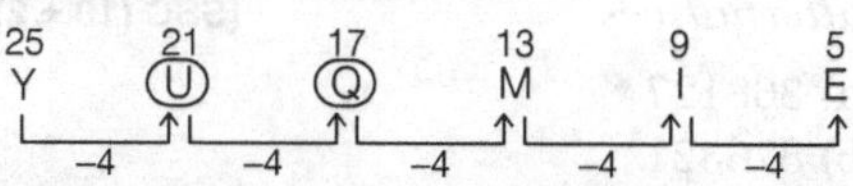

First (?) = U and second (?) = Q

∴ Required answer = U, Q

44. (*c*) The pattern is as follows

$$3^2 + 2 = 11 \Rightarrow 5^2 + 4 = 29$$
$$7^2 + 6 = 55 \Rightarrow 9^2 + 8 = \textcircled{89}$$
$$11^2 + 10 = 131 \Rightarrow ? = 89$$

45. (*a*) From Statement I

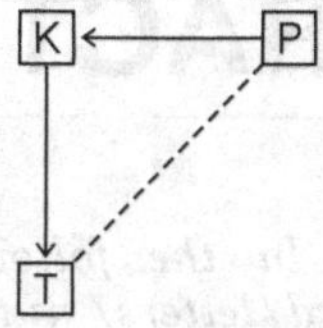

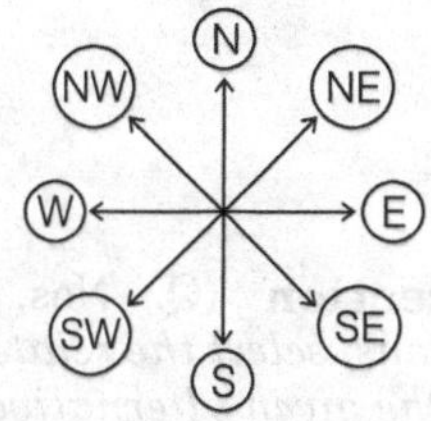

From the diagram it is clear that town P is towards North-East of town T.

From Statement II,

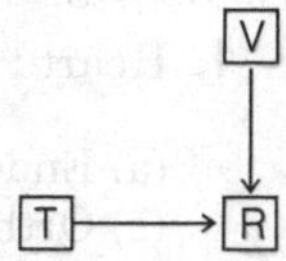

So, only I statement alone is sufficient.

46. (e) From both the statements

P > Q > T > S > R

So, R is youngest among them.

47. (*c*) We can summarise the informations in a family tree as shown below

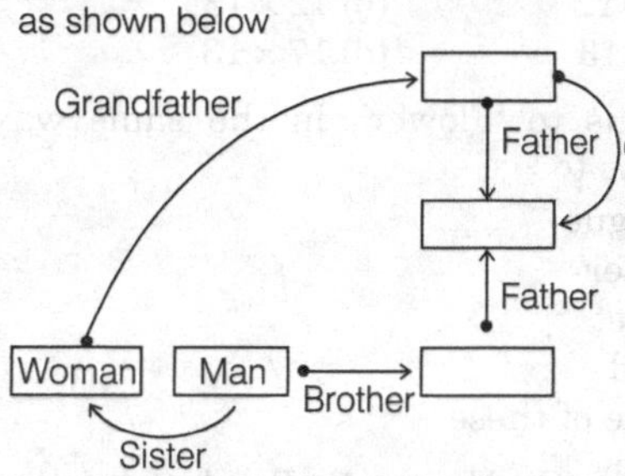

Hence, woman is sister of that man.

Solution (Q. Nos. 48 - 50)

★ ⇒ ≤	@ ⇒ <	© ⇒ ≥
% ⇒ =	δ ⇒ >	

48. (*c*) R © K ⇒ R ≥ K, K δ M ⇒ K > M, M ★ J ⇒ M ≤ J

Therefore, R ≥ K > M ≤ J

Conclusions I. J δ K ⇒ J > K (Not True)
II. M @ R ⇒ M < R (True)
III. M % R ⇒ M = R (Not True)

So, only II is true.

49. (*e*) D @ K ⇒ D < K, K % F ⇒ K = F, F © B ⇒ F ≥ B

Therefore, D < K = F ≥ B

Conclusions I. F δ D ⇒ F > D (True)
II. B @ K ⇒ B < K (May be true)
III. B % K ⇒ B = K (May be true)

B is either smaller than or equal to K. Therefore, either II or III is true.

So, either II or III and I are true.

50. (*d*) H ★ W ⇒ H ≤ W, W @ N ⇒ W < N, N % R ⇒ N = R

Therefore, H ≤ W < N = R

Conclusions I. R δ W ⇒ R > W (True)
II. N δ W ⇒ N > W (True)
III. H @ R ⇒ H < R (True)

So, I, II and III are true.

PRACTICE SET 34

Direction (Q. Nos. 1-2) *In the following questions, select the related word/letters/ number from the given alternatives.*

1. Heart : Cardiologist :: Kidney : ? **[SSC (10+2) 2014]**

(a) Endocrinologist
(b) Orthodontist
(c) Nephrologist
(d) Neurologist

2. P × Q : 16 × 17 : : L × M : ?

(a) 13 × 12 (b) 12 × 13
(c) 16 × 13 (d) 17 × 13

3. 'Smell' is to 'Flower', in the same way as 'Taste' is to

(a) Tongue
(b) Water
(c) Sweet
(d) Food
(e) None of these

Direction (Q. Nos. 4-5) *Read the following information carefully and answer the given questions.*

B is the father of W and T. R is the son of W. R is the only brother of C. M is the mother of C. M is the daughter-in-law of Z. Z has only one daughter and only one son. **[LIC (AAO) 2014]**

4. Which of the following is definitely true based upon the given relationships?

(a) None of the given options is definitely true
(b) W is the son-in-law of Z
(c) W has only one daughter
(d) T is the aunt of C
(e) T is married to M

5. Which of the following is/are required to establish that C is the daughter of M ?

(a) No extra information is required as the relation can be established from the given information
(b) T is unmarried
(c) Z is the mother of T
(d) M has only one son
(e) R is the grandson of B

6. If the day before yesterday was Sunday, then what day will it be three days after the day after tomorrow?

(a) Sunday (b) Monday
(c) Wednesday (d) Saturday

7. A word is represented by only one set of numbers as given in anyone of the alternatives. The set of numbers given in the alternatives are represented by two classes of alphabets as in two matrices given below. The columns and rows of Matrix I are numbered from 0 to 4 and that of Matrix II are numbered from 5 to 9. A letter from these matrices can be represented first by its row and next by its column. e.g. 'A' can be represented by 00, 12, 23 etc. and 'P' can be represented by 58,69,75 etc. Similarly, you have to identify the set for the word given in each question.

Matrix I

	0	1	2	3	4
0	A	R	S	N	C
1	N	C	A	R	S
2	S	N	C	A	R
3	R	S	N	C	A
4	C	A	R	S	N

Matrix II

	5	6	7	8	9
5	O	E	L	P	T
6	T	O	E	L	P
7	P	T	O	E	L
8	L	P	T	O	E
9	E	L	P	T	O

PEST

(a) 97, 89, 34, 59
(b) 58, 67, 43, 98
(c) 57, 59, 31, 98
(d) 68, 95, 31, 76

Direction (Q. Nos. 8-9) *In the following questions, find the odd numbers/ letters from the given alternatives.* **[SSC (10 + 2) 2014]**

8. (a) 368127
(b) 876321
(c) 742956
(d) 564327

9. (a) HJM (b) OQT
(c) BDG (d) VXZ

Direction (Q. Nos. 10-12) *Each of the questions below consists of a question and two statements numbered I and II given below it. You have to decide whether the data provided in the statements are sufficient to answer the question.*

Give answer

(a) if the data in Statement I alone is sufficient to answer the question, while the data in Statement II alone is not sufficient to answer the question

(b) if the data in Statement II alone is sufficient to answer the question, while the data in Statement I alone is not sufficient to answer the question

(c) if the data either in Statement I alone or in Statement II alone is sufficient to answer the question

(d) if the data in both the Statements I and II together are not sufficient to answer the question

(e) if the data in both the Statements I and II together are necessary to answer the question

10. What is the total number of students in the school ?

I. The respective ratio of girls and boys is 2 : 3.

II. The number of students has grown by 5% this year as compared to 4% last year from the number 2000 which it was year before last.

11. Who among the six of them is the tallest, if Geeta is taller than Shilpa and Deepa is taller than Meeta?

(Sunita and Sadhana are the other two).

I. Sadhana is taller than Sunita.

II. Sadhana is taller than Shilpa and Meeta as well as Deepa.

12. On which date is Amit's birthday in September 2010 ?

I. Last year his birthday was on the last Thursday of the month in September 2009.

II. This year his birthday will be on the last Friday of the month in September 2010.

13. From the given three positions of a single dice, find the letter at the face opposite to the face having letter 'a'.

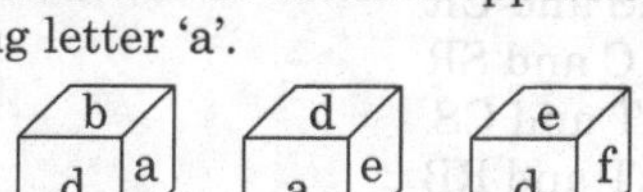

I II III

(a) b (b) d
(c) e (d) f

14. Find the missing number from the given responses.

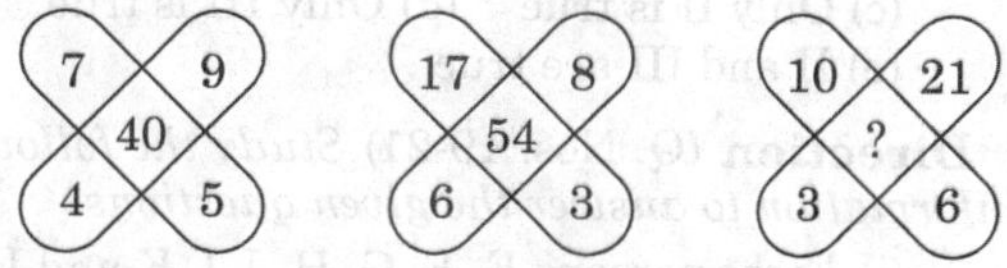

(a) 60 (b) 62
(c) 64 (d) 66

15. If SCHOOL is written as 'TBINPK', then how TEACHER can be written in that code ? **[SSC (Steno) 2014]**

(a) UDBBIDS (b) DUBBIDS
(c) NDBBISD (d) SEIDIFDS

Direction (Q. Nos. 16-18) *In the following questions, the symbols @, ©, %, \$ and ★ are used with the following meanings as illustrated below :*

'P © Q' means 'P is not greater than Q'.

'P ★ Q' means 'P is not smaller than Q'.

'P % Q' means 'P is neither greater than nor equal to Q'.

'P \$ Q' means 'P is neither smaller than nor equal to Q'.

'P @ Q' means 'P is neither greater than nor smaller than Q'.

In each of the following questions assuming the given statements to be true, find out which of the three Conclusions I, II and III given below them is/are definitely true?

16. Statements J \$ D, D © K, K % R

Conclusions I. R \$ J
II. R \$ D III. K \$ J

(a) None is true
(b) Only I is true
(c) Only II is true
(d) Only III is true
(e) Only II and III are true

17. Statements M ★ K, K @ R, R%N

Conclusions I. R % M
II. R @ M III. N \$ K

(a) Only I is true
(b) Only II is true
(c) Only III is true
(d) Either I or II is true
(e) Either I or II and III are true

18. Statements B % H, H $ J, J ★ M

Conclusions I. B % J

II. M % B III. H $ M

(a) None is true (b) Only I is true

(c) Only II is true (d) Only III is true

(e) II and III are true

Direction (Q. Nos. 19-21) *Study the following information to answer the given questions.*

(i) Eight persons E, F, G, H, I,J, K and L are seated around a square table-two on each side.

(ii) There are three lady members and they are not seated next to each other.

(iii) J is between L and F.

(iv) G is between I and F.

(v) H, a lady member is second to the left of J.

(vi) F, a male member is seated opposite to E, a lady member.

(vii) There is a lady member between F and I.

19. Who among the following are the three lady members?

(a) E, H and J

(b) E, G and J

(c) G, H and J

(d) Cannot be determined

(e) None of the above

20. Which of the following is true about J?

(a) J is a male member

(b) J is a female member

(c) Sex of J cannot be determined

(d) Position of J cannot be determined

(e) None of the above

21. Who among the following is seated between E and H?

(a) I

(b) J

(c) F

(d) Cannot be determined

(e) None of the above

22. At a ticket counter there are 17 persons in a queue. If every second person in the queue is a female and also in the starting and at the end there is a female, then the total number of males in the queue is

(a) 7 (b) 10

(c) 8 (d) 9

23. Some equations are solved on the basis of a certain system. Find the correct answer for the unsolved equation on that basis. **[SSC (CGL) 2014]**

5 * 3 = 125; 4 * 3 = 64; 8 * 2 = ?

(a) 28 (b) 16

(c) 32 (d) 64

24. If in a certain code language, 'O' is written as 'E', 'A' as 'C', 'M' as 'I', 'S' as 'O', 'N' as 'P', 'E' as 'M', 'I' as 'A', 'P' as 'N' and 'C' as 'S', then how will 'COMPANIES' be written in that code language ?

(a) SEIACPAMO

(b) SMINCPAMO

(c) SEINCPAMO

(d) SEINCPMIO

(e) None of the above

25. Arrange the following in chronological order.

(i) S. Radhakrishnan

(ii) Rajendra Prasad

(iii) Giani Zail Singh

(iv) V.V. Giri

(v) A P J Abdul Kalam **[SSC (CGL) 2012]**

(a) (i), (iii), (ii), (v), (iv)

(b) (ii), (iv), (i), (v), (iii)

(c) (ii), (i), (iv), (iii), (v)

(d) (iii), (ii), (iv), (i), (v)

26. *Answer the question based on the details given in the paragraph.*

In a family of six, there are three men A, B and C and three women R, S and T.

The six persons are Architect, Lawyer, CA, Professor, Doctor and Engineer by profession, but not in the same order. There are two married couples and two unmarried persons. C is not R's husband. The Doctor is married to a Lawyer. R's grandfather is a Professor. B is neither A's son, nor he is an Architect or a Professor. The Lawyer is T's daughter-in-law. C is T's son and the Engineer's father. A is married to the CA. **[SNAP 2014]**

Which among the following is the correct pair of married couples?

(a) AS and CR

(b) AC and SR

(c) AT and CS

(d) AT and RB

27. Find out which of the diagrams given in the alternatives correctly represents the relationship stated in the question.

Sharks, whales, turtles.

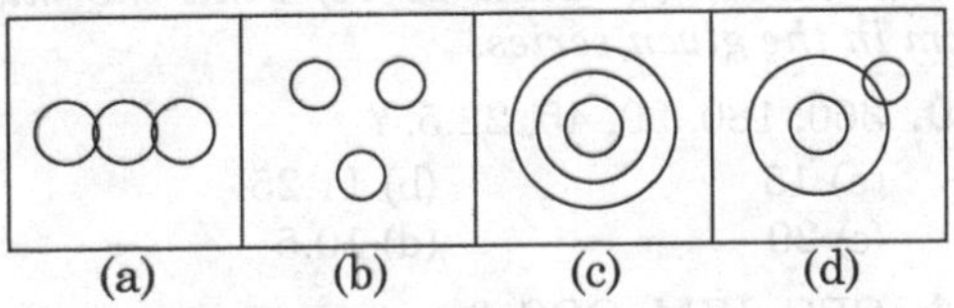

28. How many 7's immediately preceded by 6 but not immediately followed by 4 are there in the following series ?

7427643675357843767240674 3

(a) One (b) Two (c) Four (d) Six

29. From the given alternatives, select the word which can be formed using the letters of the given word. **[SSC (FCI) 2012]**

CORRESPONDING

(a) CORRECT (b) DISCERN
(c) REPENT (d) RESPONSE

Direction (Q. Nos. 30 -31) *In each of the questions below are given four statements followed by four conclusions numbered I, II, III and IV. You have to take the given statements to be true even if they seem to be at variance with commonly known facts. Read all the conclusions and then decide which of the given conclusion (s) logically follow (s) from the given statements disregarding commonly known facts.*

30. Statements Some books are journals.
All journals are papers.
Some papers are cards.
All cards are boards.

Conclusions
I. Some papers are books.
II. Some papers are boards.
III. Some boards are journals.
IV. Some boards are books.
(a) I and II follow
(b) Only I follows
(c) I, II and III follow
(d) All follow
(e) None of the above

31. Statements Some grapes are apples.
Some apples are bananas.
All bananas are guavas.
No guava is pomegranate.

Conclusions
I. No grapes are pomegranates.
II. Some guavas are grapes.
III. Some guavas are apples.
IV. No bananas are pomegranates.
(a) None follows
(b) II and III follow
(c) Either I or III follows
(d) Both III and IV follow
(e) None of the above

Direction (Q. Nos. 32-34) *Read the following information carefully and then answer the questions based on them.*

Gurgaon is an important part of the National Capital Region (NCR Delhi) and is a very progressive town of Haryana State. Of late, it has come to be known as town of malls and high rise buildings. Now, it can easily be compared to Dubai. The malls in Gurgaon have become very popular and daily footfall is around 1 lakh which goes up to 1.5 lakh during first week of the month. A survey conducted on five prominent malls as to the four vital items on which the sale amounts to more than 60% of total revenue, revealed the following information. Mall A earns from ladies garments, artificial jewellery, cosmetics and electronics. Mall B earns mostly from furniture, cosmetics, sports and footwear. Mall C's greatest earnings are from electronics, sports, artificial jewellery and ladies garments. Mall D's main revenues are from furniture, footwear, ladies garments and cosmetics. Mall E's main earning departments are electronics, artificial jewellery, ladies garments and sports.

32. Which pair of malls earns mostly from electronic items and artificial jewellery but not from furniture and footwear?
(a) A and B (b) C and D
(c) A and C (d) B and E

33. Which of the following malls earns most from sports and electronics but not from cosmetics and furniture?
(a) A (b) B
(c) D (d) E

34. Which mall does not earn much from ladies garments and artificial jewellery but gets maximum from footwear and furniture?
(a) A (b) B
(c) C (d) E

Direction (Q. Nos. 35-36) *In making decisions about important questions, it is desirable to distinguish between a 'strong' argument and a 'weak' argument. A 'strong' argument must be both important and directly related to the question. A 'weak' argument may not be directly related to the question and may be of minor importance or may be related to the trivial aspect of the question. Each question below is followed by two arguments numbered* I *and* II. *You have to decide which of the arguments is 'strong' and which is 'weak'.*

Give answer

(a) if only Argument I is strong
(b) if only Argument II is strong
(c) if either I or II is strong
(d) if neither I nor II is strong
(e) if both I and II are strong

35. Statement Should so much of money be spent on games and sports?

Arguments

I. Yes, we are a rich nation and can easily spare any amount of money for games and sports.

II. No, our teams are unable to put up a good show in international competitions.

36. Statement Are educational institutions responsible for unrest among the youth?

Arguments

I. Yes, there is no discipline in educational institutions.

II. No, there is no disciplinary problem in educational institutions.

37. The priest told the devotee, 'The temple bell rings at regular intervals of 45 min. The last bell rang 5 min ago. The next bell is due to be rung at 7 : 45 am'. At what time did the priest give this information to the devotee?

(a) 7 : 00 am (b) 7 : 05 am
(c) 7 : 40 am (d) 6 : 55 am

38. A and B starts walking from the same point. A goes North and covers 3 km, then turns right and covers 4 km. B goes West and covers 5 km, then turns right and covers 3 km. How far apart are they from each other ?

[SSC (FCI) 2012]

(a) 10 km (b) 9 km (c) 8 km (d) 5 km

39. Which one set of letters when sequentially placed at the gaps in the given letter series shall complete it ?

ZYX_W_YZZ_XWWXY_

(a) WXYZ (b) WYXZ
(c) WXZY (d) XYZW

Direction (Q. Nos. 40-41) *Find the missing term in the given series.*

40. 360, 180, 90, 45, 22.5, ?

(a) 15 (b) 11.25
(c) 20 (d) 10.5

41. CEG, IKM, OQS, ?

(a) VXZ (b) TVX
(c) TUV (d) UWY

Direction (Q. Nos. 42 - 43) *Study the following information carefully and answer the questions which follow :*

A word and number rearrangement machine when given an input line of words and numbers rearranges them following a particular rule. Following is an illustration of input and the rearrangement.

Input flight 37 delay an 53 87 hour 19 by 46
***Step* I** 87 flight 37 delay 53 hour 19 by 46 an
***Step* II** 87 53 flight 37 delay hour 19 46 by an
***Step* III** 87 53 46 flight 37 hour 19 delay by an
***Step* IV** 87 53 46 37 hour 19 flight delay by an
***Step* V** 87 53 46 37 19 hour flight delay by an

Step V is the last step of the arrangement of the above input as the intended rearrangement is obtained.

As per the rules followed in the above steps, answer the following questions based upon the input

'24 cross 82 road 93 safe 13 jam halt 46'.

42. Which of the following would be the second step after the rearrangement ?

(a) 93 82 46 24 13 safe road jam halt cross
(b) 93 82 46 24 road safe 13 jam halt cross
(c) 93 82 24 road safe 13 jam 46 halt cross
(d) 93 24 82 road safe 13 jam halt 46 cross
(e) None of the above

43. Which of the following would be the final arrangement ?

(a) 93 82 46 24 13 safe road jam halt cross
(b) 93 82 46 13 24 safe road jam halt cross
(c) 13 24 46 82 93 safe road jam halt cross
(d) 93 82 46 24 13 cross halt jam road safe
(e) safe road jam halt cross 93 82 46 24 13

44. Examine the following statements. **[UPSC (CSAT) 2012]**

I. Rama scored more than Rani.
II. Rani scored less than Ratna.
III. Ratna scored more than Rama.
IV. Padma scored more than Rama but less than Ratna.

Who scored the highest ?

(a) Rama (b) Padma
(c) Rani (d) Ratna

45. If the following pattern is drawn in a rectangular transparent sheet and folded along the dotted lines, then how does it appear ?

Question Figure

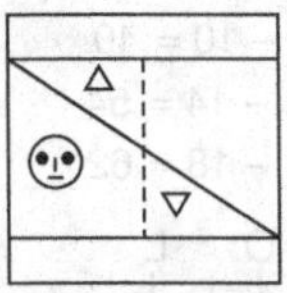

Answer Figures

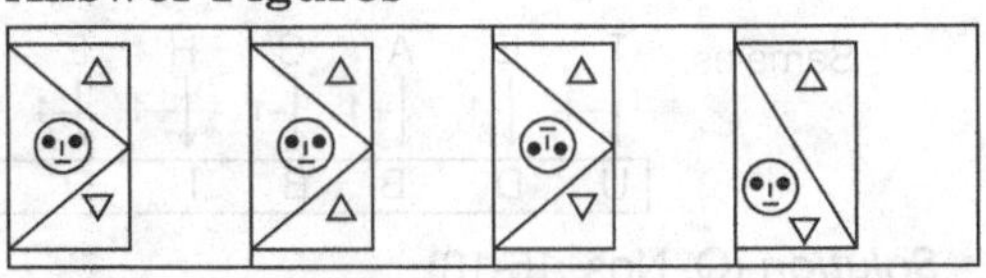

(a) (b) (c) (d)

46. If a mirror is placed on the line MN, then which of the answer figures is the right image of the given figure ? **[SSC (CGL) 2014]**

Question Figure

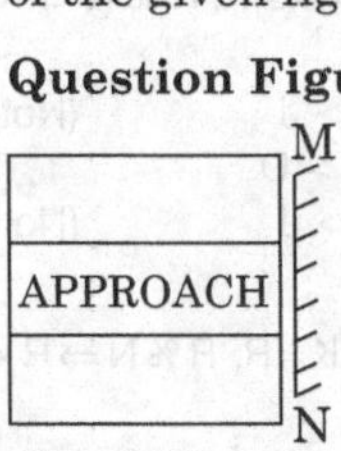

Answer Figures

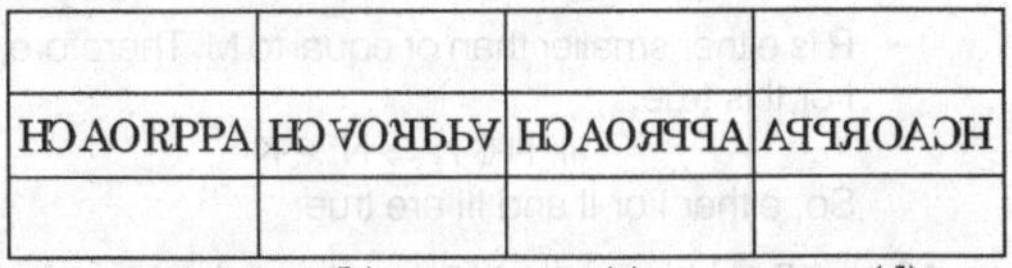

(a) (b) (c) (d)

47. A, B, C, D and E belong to five different cities P, Q, R, S and T (not necessarily in that order). Each one of them comes from a different city. Further it is given that

I. B and C do not belong to Q.
II. B and E do not belong to P and R.
III. A and C do not belong to R, S and T.
IV. D and E do not belong to Q and T.

Which one of the following is not correct?

(a) C belong to P **[UPSC (CSAT) 2013]**
(b) D belongs to R
(c) A belongs to Q
(d) B belongs to S

48. How many rectangles are there in the figure given below ?

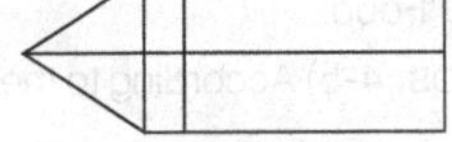

(a) 7 (b) 8
(c) 9 (d) 12

49. Which of the following answer figure can complete the given series ?

Question Figure

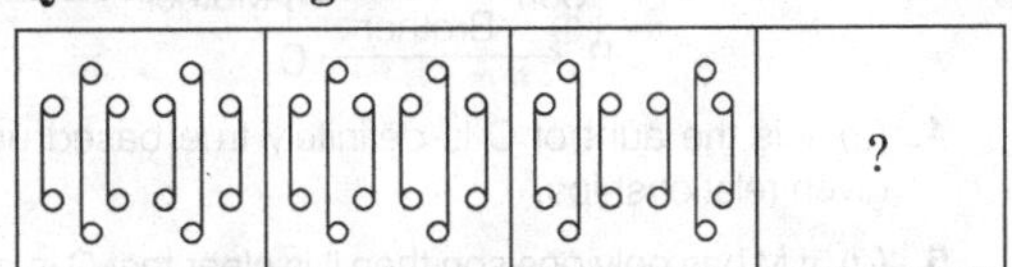

1 2 3

Answer Figures

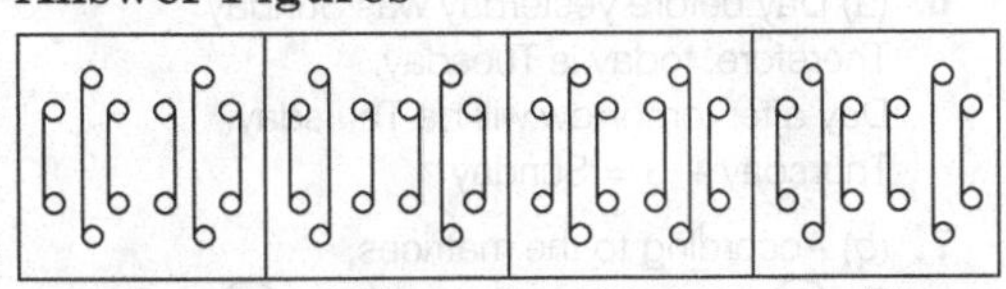

(a) (b) (c) (d)

50. In which answer figure is the given figure embedded ?

Question Figure

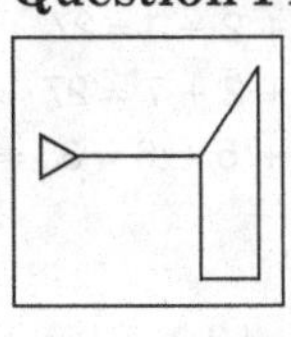

Answer Figures

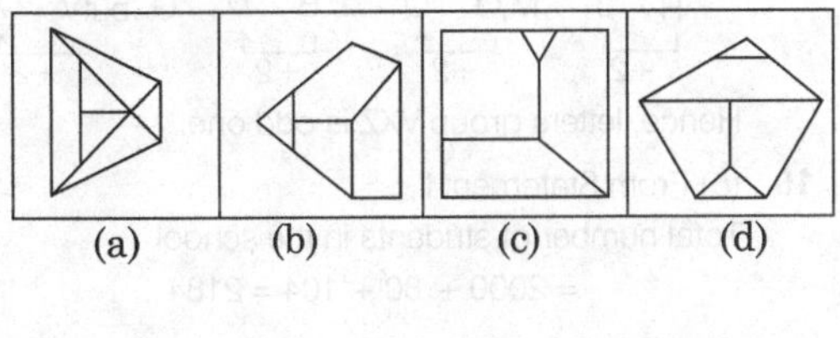

(a) (b) (c) (d)

Hints and Solutions

1. (*c*) As heart disease is checked by Cardiologist. In the same way, kidney disease is checked by Nephrologist.

2. (*b*) In forward order letter sequence,
Position of P = 16, Position of Q = 17
$\therefore \quad P \times Q = 16 \times 17$
Similarly, Position of L = 12, Position of M = 13
$\therefore \quad L \times M = 12 \times 13$
$\therefore \quad ? = 12 \times 13$

3. (*d*) 'Smell' comes from 'flower' in the same way 'Taste' comes from 'Food'.

Solution (Q. Nos. 4-5) According to the given information,

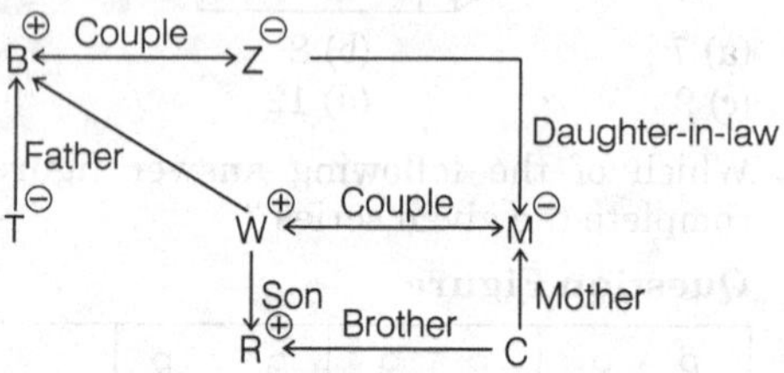

4. (*d*) T is the aunt of C is definitely true based upon the given relationships.

5. (*d*) If M has only one son then it is clear that C is a female and a daughter of M.

6. (a) Day before yesterday was Sunday.
Therefore, today is Tuesday.
Day after tomorrow will be Thursday.
Thursday + 3 = Sunday

7. (*b*) According to the matrices,
P – (58), 69, 75, 86, 97 E – 56, (67), 78, 89, 95
S – 02, 14, 20, 31, (43) T – 59, 65, 76, 87, (98)
$\therefore$ PEST ⇒ 58, 67, 43, 98

8. (*c*) As, 368127 ⇒ 3 + 6 + 8 + 1 + 2 + 7 = 27
876321 ⇒ 8 + 7 + 6 + 3 + 2 + 1 = 27
and 564327 ⇒ 5 + 6 + 4 + 3 + 2 + 7 = 27
But, 742956 ⇒ 7 + 4 + 2 + 9 + 5 + 6 = 33 ≠ 27
Therefore, 742956 is odd one.
Hence, option (c) is answer.

9. (*d*)

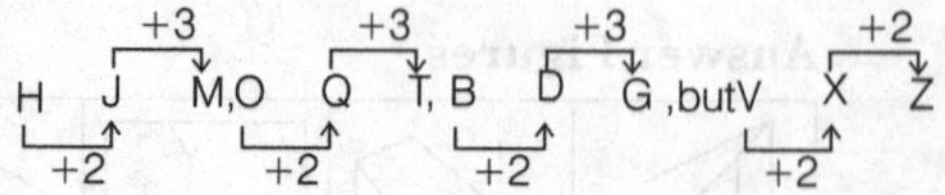

Hence, letters group VXZ is odd one.

10. (*b*) From Statement II,
Total number of students in the school
= 2000 + 80 + 104 = 2184

11. (*d*) From both the statements,
Geeta > Shilpa, Deepa > Meeta, Sadhana > Sunita
Sadhana > Shilpa, Meeta, Deepa
It is not clear whether Sadhana or Geetha is the tallest.

12. (*c*) From Statement I,
Amit's birthday is on 24th September.
From Statement II,
Last Friday in September 2010 ⇒ 24th

13. (*d*) From positions II and III,
Common letters = d and e
Clearly, f is opposite to a.

14. (*b*) As, $(7 + 9 + 5 + 4) \times 2 - 10 = 40$
and, $(17 + 8 + 3 + 6) \times 2 - 14 = 54$
Similarly, $(10 + 21 + 6 + 3) \times 2 - 18 = 62$

15. (*a*) As,

S	C	H	O	O	L
↓+1	↓–1	↓+1	↓–1	↓+1	↓–1
T	B	I	N	P	K

Same as,

T	E	A	C	H	E	R
↓+1	↓–1	↓+1	↓–1	↓+1	↓–1	↓+1
U	D	B	B	I	D	S

Solution (Q. Nos. 16-18)

© ⇒ ≤	★ ⇒ ≥	% ⇒ <
$ ⇒ >	@ ⇒ =	

16. (*c*) J $ D ⇒ J > D, D © K ⇒ D ≤ K, K % R ⇒ K < R
Therefore, J > D ≤ K < R
Conclusions I. R $ J ⇒ R > J (Not true)
II. R $ D ⇒ R > D (True)
III. K $ J ⇒ K > J (Not true)
So, only II is true.

17. (*e*) M ★ K ⇒ M ≥ K, K @ R ⇒ K = R, R % N ⇒ R < N
Therefore, M ≥ K = R < N
Conclusions I. R % M ⇒ R < M (May be true)
II. R © M ⇒ R = M (May be true)
R is either smaller than or equal to M. Therefore, either I or II is true.
III. N $ K ⇒ N > K (True)
So, either I or II and III are true.

18. (*d*) B % H ⇒ B < H, H $ J ⇒ H > J, J ★ M ⇒ J ≥ M
Therefore, B < H > J ≥ M
Conclusions I. B % J ⇒ B < J (Not true)
II. M % B ⇒ M < B (Not true)
III. H $ M ⇒ H > M (True)
So, only III is true.

Solution (Q. Nos. 19-21) According to given information, the final arrangement is as following

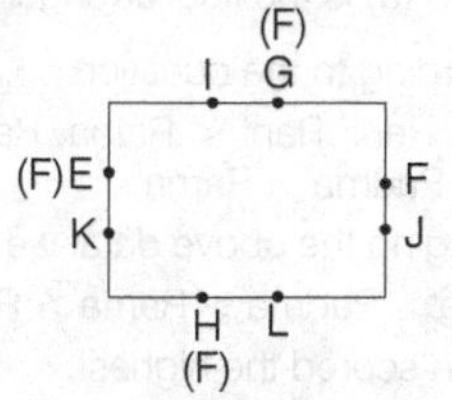

19. (*e*) E, H and G are lady members.

20. (*a*) J is a male member.

21. (*e*) K is sitting between E and H.

22. (*c*) Queue of the 17 persons can be shown as

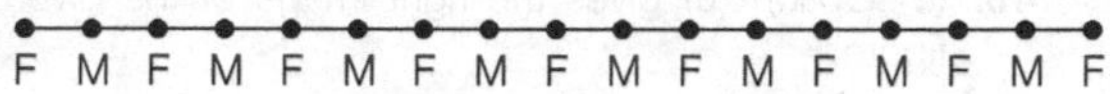

Total number of males = 8

23. (*d*) As, 5 * 3 = 125 ⇒ $(5)^3 = 125$

and 4 * 3 = 64 ⇒ $(4)^3 = 64$

Same as, 8 * 2 = ? ⇒ $(8)^2 = 64$

∴ ? = 64

24. (*c*) C O M P A N I E S

↓ ↓ ↓ ↓ ↓ ↓ ↓ ↓ ↓

S	E	I	N	C	P	A	M	O

COMPANIES ⇒ SEINCPAMO

25. (*c*) Chronological order of Presidents of India :

(ii) Rajendra Prasad (1950-1962)

↓

(i) S Radhakrishnan (1962-1967)

↓

(iv) V V Giri (1969-1974)

↓

(iii) Giani Zail Singh (1982-1987)

↓

(v) APJ Abdul Kalam (2002-2007)

26. (*c*) According to the given information,

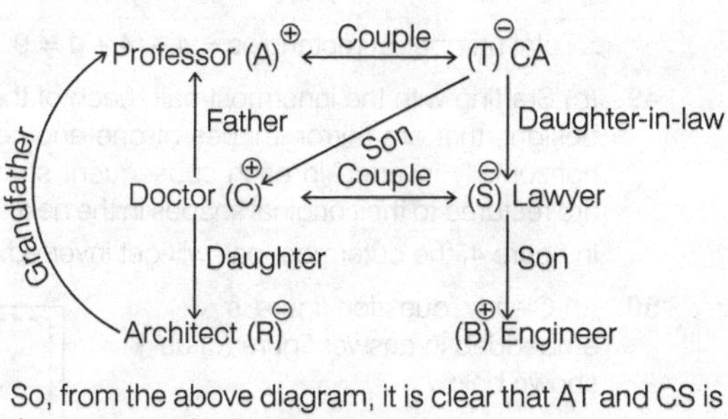

So, from the above diagram, it is clear that AT and CS is the correct pair of married couples.

27. (*b*) Sharks belong to the class pisces. Whale is a mammal and turtle belongs to the class reptile.

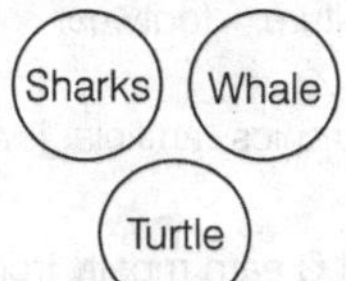

28. (*b*) Let us see

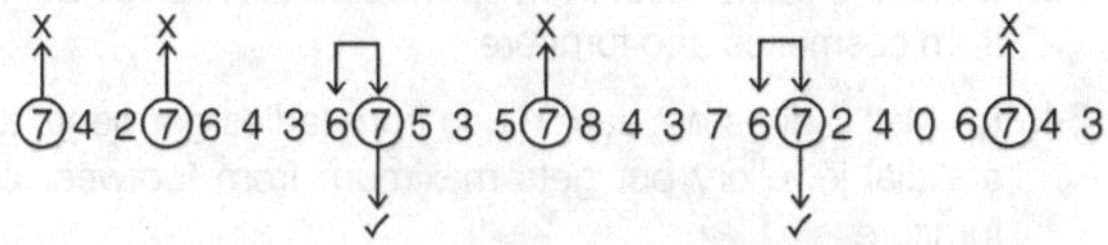

✔ = Condition fulfilled

✗ = Condition not fulfilled

Clearly, there are two such 7's.

29. (*b*) Word DISCERN can be formed from the letters in the given word.

30. (*a*)

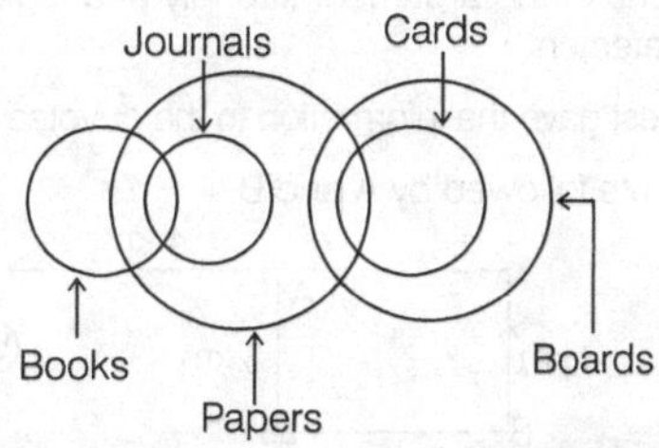

Conclusions I. Some papers are books. (✔)

II. Some papers are boards. (✔)

III. Some boards are journals. (✗)

IV. Some boards are books. (✗)

Hence, only Conclusion I and II follow.

31. (*d*)

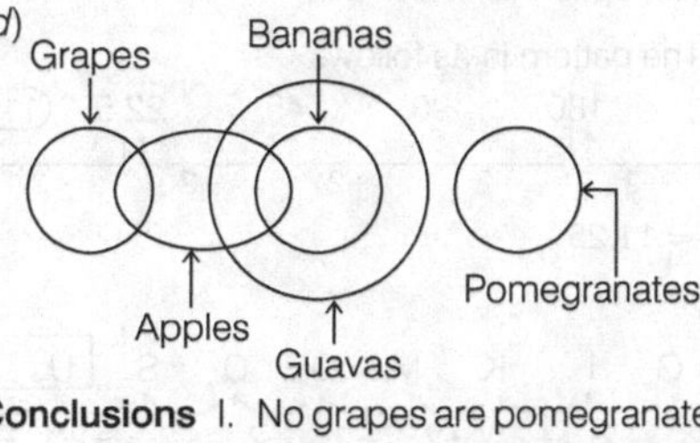

Conclusions I. No grapes are pomegranates. (✗)

II. Some guavas are grapes. (✗)

III. Some guavas are apples. (✔)

IV. No bananas are pomegranates. (✔)

Hence, only Conclusion III and IV follow.

Solution (Q. Nos. 32-34) Data is arranged as follows

Mall A Ladies garments, artificial jewellery, cosmetics and electronics.

Mall B Furniture, cosmetics, sports and footwear.

Mall C Electronics, sports, artificial jewellery and ladies garments.

Mall D Furniture, footwear, ladies garments and cosmetics.

Mall E Electronics, artificial jewellery, ladies garments and sports.

32. (*c*) Malls A and C earn mostly from electronics items and artificial jewellery but not from furniture and footwear.

33. (*d*) Mall E earns most from sports and electronics but not from cosmetics and furniture.

34. (*b*) Mall B does not earn much from ladies garments and artificial jewellery but gets maximum from footwear and furniture.

35. (*d*) None of the arguments is strong. Spending money just because of being rich is not a valid reason. Argument II is weak because it is absolutely illogical that just because of poor performance in international competitions, we should not finance games and sports.

36. (*d*) None of the argument strongly and logically supports the statement.

37. (*b*) Priest gave the information to the devotee at 7 : 05 am.

38. (*b*) Route followed by A and B

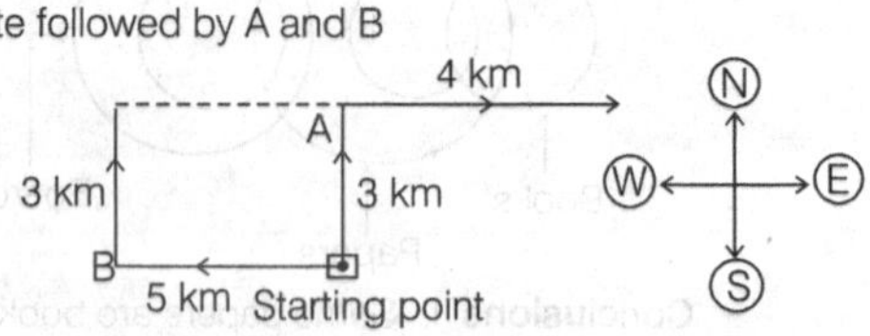

Distance between A and B = 5 + 4 = 9 km

39. (*a*) The complete letter series will be

ZYXW / WXYZ / ZYXW / WXYZ ⇒ WXYZ

Hence, option (a) is correct.

40. (*b*) The pattern is as follows

360 → 180 → 90 → 45 → 22.5 → (11.25)

÷2 ÷2 ÷2 ÷2 ÷2

∴ ? = 11.25

41. (*d*)

C E G I K M O Q S U W Y

+2 +2 +2 +2 +2 +2 +2 +2 +2 +2 +2

Solution (Q. Nos. 42-43)

In each step one number and one word are rearranged. The numbers are arranged from the left in descending order and the words are arranged from the right in alphabetical order.

Input 24 cross 82 road 93 safe 13 jam halt 46

***Step* I** 93 24 82 road safe 13 jam halt 46 cross

***Step* II** 93 82 24 road safe 13 jam 46 halt cross

***Step* III** 93 82 46 24 road safe 13 jam halt cross

***Step* IV** 93 82 46 24 13 safe road jam halt cross

42. (*c*) Step II 93 82 24 road safe 13 jam 46 halt cross

43. (*a*) Option (a) is the final arrangement.

44. (*d*) According to the question,

Rama > Rani, Rani < Ratna, Ratna > Rama and Ratna > Padma > Rama

On arranging the above data, we get

∴ (Ratna) > Padma > Rama > Rani

So, Ratna scored the highest.

45. (*a*)

So, option (a) is correct.

46. (*c*) Option (c) gives the right image of the given figure.

47. (*d*) From the given information, following table can be drawn.

Cities	**P**	**Q**	**R**	**S**	**T**
A	✗	✔	✗	✗	✗
B	✗	✗	✗	✗	✔
C	✔	✗	✗	✗	✗
D	✗	✗	✔	✗	✗
E	✗	✗	✗	✔	✗

Now, it is clear from the above table that B does not belong to S. So, statement (d) is incorrect.

48. (*c*)

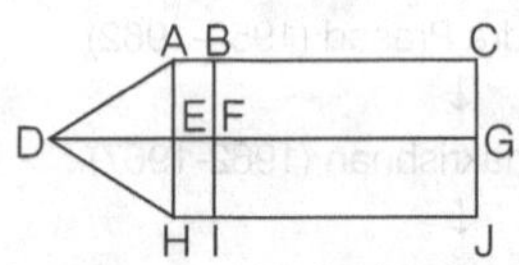

Smallest and single rectangles

= ABFE, EFIH, BCGF, FGJI = 4

Rectangles formed with two rectangles.

= ABIH, AEGC, EGJH, BCJI = 4

Largest rectangle = ACJH

∴ Total number of rectangles = 4 + 4 + 1 = 9

49. (*c*) Starting with the innermost pair, each of the two designs that are mirror images of one another get horizontally inverted in each subsequent step and are restored to their original shapes in the next step. In figure 4, the outermost pair will get inverted.

50. (*c*) Clearly, question figure is embedded in answer figure (c) as shown below

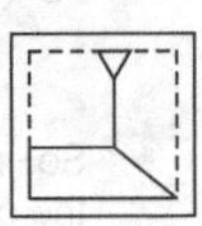

PRACTICE SET 35

Direction (Q. Nos. 1-3) *In the following questions, select the related word/letters/number pair from the given alternatives.*

1. Rat : Cat :: Worm : ?
(a) Silk (b) Bird
(c) Earth (d) Fishing

2. 6 : 35 : : 7 : ?
(a) 48 (b) 42 (c) 34 (d) 13

3. BFG : EIJ : : RVW : ? **[SSC (Multitasking) 2014]**
(a) UWY (b) UYZ (c) SWX (d) QUV

Direction (Q. Nos. 4-5) *In the following questions, find the odd term from the given alternatives.*

4. (a) Foal (b) Hen **[BSSC (CGL) 2015]**
(c) Lamb (d) Leveret

5. (a) Seldom : Often
(b) Good : Nice
(c) Honest : Cheat
(d) Extravagant : Thifty

6. If 'PALE' is coded as '2134', 'EARTH' is coded as '41590', then how is 'PEARL' coded as ? **[SSC (10+2) 2014]**
(a) 29530 (b) 24153
(c) 25413 (d) 25430

7. In the given diagram, square represents doctors, triangle represents ladies and circle represents surgeons. Which of the following letters represents those ladies who are doctors and surgeon both ?

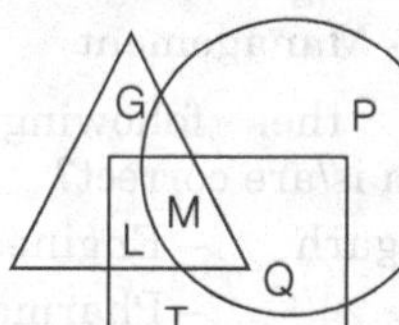

(a) M (b) G (c) Q (d) P

8. By looking in a mirror it appears that it is 6 : 30 in the clock. What is the real time ?
(a) 6 : 30 (b) 5 : 30
(c) 6 : 00 (d) 5 : 00

9. How many meaningful English words can be made from the letters EOPR, using each letter only once ?
(a) None (b) One (c) Two (d) Three
(e) More than three

10. The positions of how many digits will remain same if the digits in the number 49276381 are arranged in the ascending order within the number from left to right? **[SBI SO (IT) 2016]**
(a) None (b) Three (c) Two (d) One
(e) More than three

11. Mahima goes 10 km North, then goes 6 km South, again she moves on 3 km East. At what distance is she now from original position and in which direction? **[SBI SO (IT) 2016]**
(a) 5 km; North-East
(b) 5 km; South-East
(c) 8 km; North-East
(d) 10 km; South-East
(e) 10 km; North

12. Ramya has 52 marbles. If Janani had 9 more than what she now has, she would have half as many as Ramya. How many marbles are there with Janani now?
(a) 17 (b) 15 (c) 26 (d) 35

13. In a small organisation, Saurav and Kartik plays tennis and basketball very well. Manpreet and Lokesh are very good in athletics, tennis and swimming. Kartik and Nikhil are good in athletics and badminton. Ganesh and Lokesh are good in badminton and hockey. Prakash and Rohit are good in hockey and basketball. Ganesh, Prakash and Saurav are good in swimming. Manpreet and Nikhil also play hockey well. If an inter-organisational event is arranged and only one person can be selected from one organisation, who will be selected from this organisation if tennis, swimming and badminton has to be played in the competition? **[CMAT 2015]**
(a) Saurav (b) Kartik
(c) Manpreet (d) Lokesh

Direction (Q. Nos. 14-16) *Study the given information carefully to answer the given questions.*

C, D, E, F, P, Q, R and S are sitting around a circular table facing the centre with equal distance between each other (but not necessarily in the same order). Each one of them is also related to D in some way or the other. P sits third to the right of E. D sits to the immediate left of E. Only one person sits between P and D's son. R sits to the immediate right of D's son. Only three people sit between D's husband and R. Only one person sits between D's husband and C. F sits to the immediate right of Q. D's father sits second to the right of F. Only three people sit between D's father and D's brother. D's daughter sits second to the right of S. D's sister sits third to the right of D's mother. **[IBPS (PO/MT) Pre 2015**

14. Which of the following statements is TRUE with respect to the given information?
(a) S is the brother of R.
(b) Only three people sit between Q and S.
(c) E sits third to the right of D's daughter.
(d) All the given options are true.
(e) R is an immediate neighbour of D.

15. Who amongst the following is the brother of D ?
(a) Q (b) E (c) F (d) C
(e) R

16. As per the given seating arrangement, Q : P in the same way as R : E. Then, following the same pattern D : ?
(a) R (b) S (c) Q (d) C
(e) F

17. If the day after tomorrow is Tuesday, then what day will two days after the day after tomorrow be?
(a) Monday (b) Wednesday
(c) Saturday (d) Thursday

18. In question below is given a statement followed by two assumptions numbered I and II. An assumption is something supposed or taken for granted. You have to consider the statement and the following assumptions and decide which of the assumption (s) is / are implicit in the statement.

Statement "We must appoint more subordinate officers on our office staff", the manager said to the chairman.

Assumptions
I. Subordinate officers are available.
II. The present offiice staff is inefficient.
(a) if only Assumption I is implicit
(b) if only Assumption II is implicit
(c) if either Assumption I or II is implicit
(d) if neither Assumption I nor II is implicit
(e) if both Assumptions I and II are implicit

Direction (Q. Nos. 19-21) *Read the following information carefully and give answer of the questions based on this.* **[CG PSC 2013]**

Seven friends Anu, Beena, Kanika, Mohini, Samina, Easther and Rani study different disciplines such as Arts, Commerce, Science, Engineering, Architecture, Management and Pharmacy, not necessarily in the same order. Each of them belongs to a different state *viz.* Andhra Pradesh, Uttar Pradesh, Maharashtra, Karnataka, Kerala, Chhattisgarh and Punjab but not necessarily in the same order.

Kanika studies Engineering and does not belong to either Uttar Pradesh or Punjab. The one who belongs to Chhattisgarh does not study Architecture or Pharmacy. Anu belongs to Maharashtra. Samina belongs to Kerala and studies Science. The one who belongs to Andhra Pradesh studies Commerce. Mohini studies Management and Rani studies Arts. Beena belongs to Karnataka and does not study Architecture. The one who studies Arts does not belong to Punjab.

19. Which of the following student and subject combination is correct?
(a) Anu - Architecture
(b) Easther - Pharmacy
(c) Beena - Commerce
(d) Mohini - Engineering
(e) Samina - Management

20. Which of the following state-subject combination is/are correct?
I. Chhattisgarh – Engineering
II. Punjab – Pharmacy
III. Andhra Pradesh – Commerce
IV. Andhra Pradesh – Architecture
(a) I and II
(b) II and III
(c) I and IV
(d) I and III
(e) III and IV

21. Which of the following student-state combination is/are correct?

I. Kanika – Chhattisgarh
II. Samina – Andhra Pradesh
III. Easther – Karnataka
IV. Mohini – Punjab

(a) I and II (b) I and III
(c) I and IV (d) II and III
(e) II and IV

22. Sneha correctly remembers that her father's birthday is before 16th June but after 11th June whereas, her younger brother correctly remembers that their father's birthday is after 13th June but before 18th June and her elder brother correctly remembers that their father's birthday is on an even date. On what date in June, is definitely their father's birthday?

(a) Sixteenth (b) Twelfth
(c) Fourteenth (d) Data inadequate
(e) None of these

23. Lalit is elder than Prakash and Kishore, Mukesh is elder than Rakesh but not as old as Lalit, Prakash is younger than Rakesh but is not the youngest. Who is the eldest? **[SSC (FCI)2012]**

(a) Lalit (b) Mukesh
(c) Rakesh (d) Kishore

Direction (Q. Nos. 24-25) *Find the missing term in the given series.*

24. 6, 9, 12, 15, 18, ? **[SSC (Multitasking) 2013]**

(a) 21 (b) 20
(c) 19 (d) 22

25. BFG, HLM, NRS, ? **[SSC (FCI)2012]**

(a) TWX (b) RVW
(c) TYZ (d) TXY

26. *Read the following information carefully and answer the questions given below.*

A word is represented by only one set of numbers as given in anyone of the alternatives. The set of numbers given in the alternatives are represented by two classes of alphabets as in two matrices given below. The columns and rows of Matrix I are numbered from 0 to 4 and that of Matrix II are numbered from 5 to 9. A letter from these matrices can represented first by its row and next by its column. e.g 'A' can be represented by 00, 12, 23 etc. and 'P' can be represented by 58,69,75 etc. Similarly, you have to identify the set for the word given in each question.

Matrix I

	0	1	2	3	4
0	A	R	S	N	C
1	N	C	A	R	S
2	S	N	C	A	R
3	R	S	N	C	A
4	C	A	R	S	N

Matrix II

	5	6	7	8	9
5	O	E	L	P	T
6	T	O	E	L	P
7	P	T	O	E	L
8	L	P	T	O	E
9	E	A	P	T	O

NEST

(a) 32, 56, 20, 89
(b) 10, 65, 41, 76
(c) 32, 76, 34, 98
(d) 21, 67, 14, 59

Direction (Q. Nos. 27-28) *Each of the questions below consists of a question and two statements numbered I and II given below it. You have to decide whether the data provided in the statements are sufficient to answer the question.*

Give answer

(a) if the data in Statement I alone is sufficient to answer the question, while the data in Statement II alone is not sufficient to answer the question
(b) if the data in Statement II alone is sufficient to answer the question, while the data in Statement I alone is not sufficient to answer the question
(c) if the data either in Statement I alone or in Statement II alone is sufficient to answer the question
(d) if the data in both the Statements I and II together are not sufficient to answer the question
(e) if the data in both the Statements I and II together are necessary to answer the question

27. On which day was Yasir born?

(His date of birth is February 29)

I. He was born between year 2005 and 2011.
II. He will complete 4 yr on February 29, 2012.

28. Out of 64 students, 38 play both chess and cricket. How many students play only chess?

I. Out of 64 students, 22 students do not play any game. 4 students play only cricket.

II. Out of 64 students, 20 are girls and 10 of them do not play any game.

29. All the faces of a cube are painted blue and then it is divided into 27 smaller cubes. How many smaller cubes have only one face painted ? **[UP BEd 2012]**

(a) 0 (b) 6
(c) 8 (d) 18

30. A father is 7 yr older than the mother and the mother's age now is 3 times the age of the daughter. The daughter is 10 yr old now. What was the father's age when the daughter was born ? **[BSSC (CGL) 2015]**

(a) 27 yr (b) 37 yr
(c) 15 yr (d) 40 yr

31. Pointing towards a person, a man said to a woman, " His mother is the only daughter of your father". How is the woman related to that person ?

(a) Daughter (b) Sister
(c) Mother (d) Wife
(e) None of the above

32. If in a certain code language 'how can you go' is written as 'ja da ka pa', 'you come here' is written as 'na ka sa' and 'come and go' is written as 'ra pa sa', then how will 'here' be written in that language ?

(a) ja (b) na
(c) pa (d) Data inadequate

33. Which of the following expressions will be true if the expression $R > O = A > S < T$ is definitely true ?

(a) $O > T$ (b) $S < R$
(c) $T > A$ (d) $S = O$
(e) $T < R$

34. Which of the following symbols should replace the question mark (?) in the given expression in order to make the expressions '$P < A$' as well as '$T \le L$' definitely true ?

$$P > L \ ? \ A \ge N = T$$

(a) $\le$ (b) $>$
(c) $<$ (d) $\ge$
(e) Either $\le$ or $<$

35. Find the water image of the given figure.

Question Figure

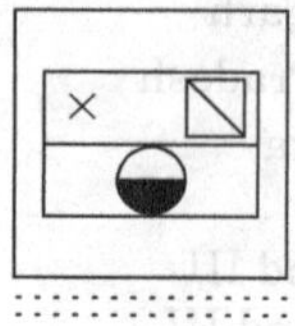

(A)

Answer Figures

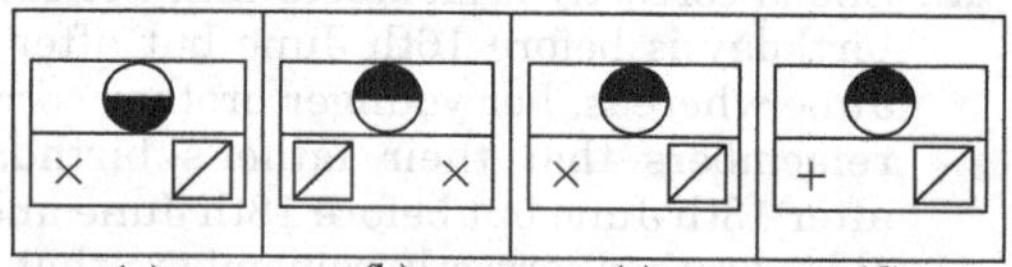

(a) (b) (c) (d)

36. Find the missing number from the given responses.

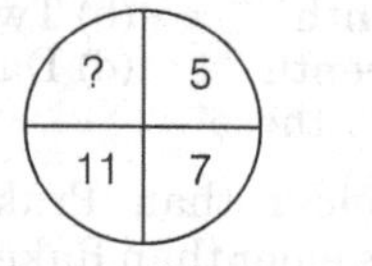

(a) 1 (b) 9 (c) 12 (d) 17

37. If '>' stands for 'division', '∨' stands for 'multiplication', '–' stands for 'greater than', '×' stands for 'less than', '<' stands for 'addition', '∧' stands for 'subtraction', '+' stands for 'equal to', then which of the following equations is correct ? **[SSC (CGL) 2014]**

(a) $10 \wedge 3 < 5 < 4 + 16$
(b) $4 \wedge 6 < 4 < 4 + 16$
(c) $12 \wedge 3 < 5 < 4 + 12$
(d) $11 \wedge 12 < 5 < 4 + 12$

38. Which of the following words appear first in a dictionary ? **[SSC (CGL) 2012]**

(a) Improve
(b) Impress
(c) Imprint
(d) Impugn

39. If 'blue' is called 'green', 'green' is called 'orange', orange' is called 'yellow', 'yellow' is called 'black', 'black' is called 'red' and 'red' is called 'white', then what is the colour of turmeric ?

(a) Orange (b) Green
(c) White (d) Black
(e) None of these

Direction (Q. Nos. 40-42) *Study the following information to answer the given questions.*

A word and number arrangement machine when given an input line of words and numbers rearranges them following a particular rule. The following is an illustration of input and rearrangement.

Input mix 12 in form 35 are 20 with 47 given

***Step* I** are form mix 12 in 35 20 with 47 given

***Step* II** are form given in mix 12 35 20 with 47

***Step* III** are form given in mix with 12 35 20 47

***Step* IV** are form given in mix with 47 35 12 20

***Step* V** are form given in mix with 47 35 20 12

and Step V is the last step of the arrangement of the above input as the intended arrangement is obtained.

As per the rules followed in the above steps, find out in each of the following questions the appropriate steps for the given input.

Input 'When 11 given fine 37 provide zero 90 over 45 is 29 team 89'

40. Which of the following would be the Step I ?

(a) Fine given when 11 37 provide zero 90 over 45 is 29 team 89
(b) Fine when 11 given 37 provide zero 90 over 45 is 29 team 89
(c) Zero when 11 given fine 37 provide 90 over 45 is 29 team 89
(d) Fine given when 90 89 11 37 provide zero over 45 is 29 team
(e) None of the above

41. Which word/number would be on 4th position (from left) in Step II ?

(a) Given
(b) is
(c) when
(d) 11
(e) None of these

42. How many steps would be needed to complete the arrangement ?

(a) V
(b) VI
(c) VII
(d) VIII
(e) None of these

Direction (Q. Nos. 43-45) *In each question/set of questions below are two/three statements followed by two conclusions numbered* I *and* II. *You have to take the two/three given statements to be true even if they seem to be at variance from commonly known facts and then decide which of the given conclusions logically follows from the given statements disregarding commonly known facts.*

Give answer

(a) if only Conclusion I follows
(b) if only Conclusion II follows
(c) if either Conclusion I or II follows
(d) if neither Conclusion I nor II follows
(e) if both Conclusions I and II follow

43. Statements All kings are queens.
Some queens are rulers.
[Bihar Keshtriya Grameen bank(GBO) 2012]

Conclusions
I. No ruler is a king.
II. All rulers being king is a possibility.

44. Statements Some lights are rays.
All rays are optics.
[Bihar Keshtriya Grameen bank (GBO) 2012]

Conclusions
I. Some lights are definitely not optics.
II. Some rays are definitely not lights.

45. Statements All vacancies are jobs.
Some jobs are occupations.

Conclusions **[IBPS (PO) 2012]**
I. All vacancies are occupations.
II. All occupations being vacancies is a possibility.

46. Effect The prices of food grains and vegetables have increased by about 30% in the past three months.

Which of the following can be a probable cause of the above effect ? **[CG PSC 2013]**

(a) The farmers have decided to change their farming style
(b) The prices of other products have increased more than 30%
(c) The number of farmers has reduced
(d) Occupation of farming has not been viewed as a reputed work
(e) None of the above

47. Examine the following statements.

I. None but students are members of the club.

II. Some members of the club are married persons.

III. All married persons are invited for dance.

Which one of the following conclusions can be drawn from the above statements ?

(a) All students are invited for dance

(b) All married students of the club, are invited for dance

(c) All members of the club are married persons

(d) None of the above

48. How many triangles are there in the figure given below ?

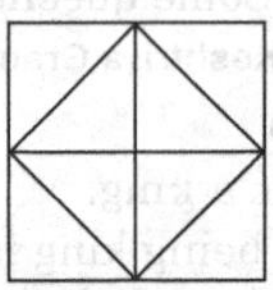

(a) 4 (b) 12 (c) 16 (d) 10

49. A square transparent sheet with a pattern is given figure out from amongst the four alternatives as to how the pattern appear when folded along the marked line?

Question Figure

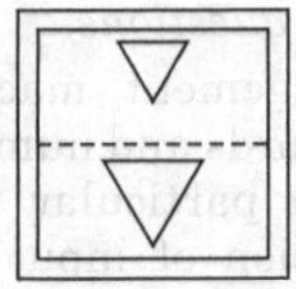

Answer Figures

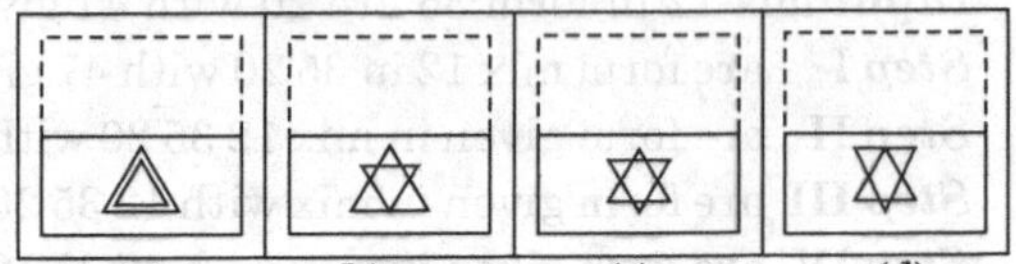

(a) (b) (c) (d)

50. Group the given figures into three classes using each figure only once.

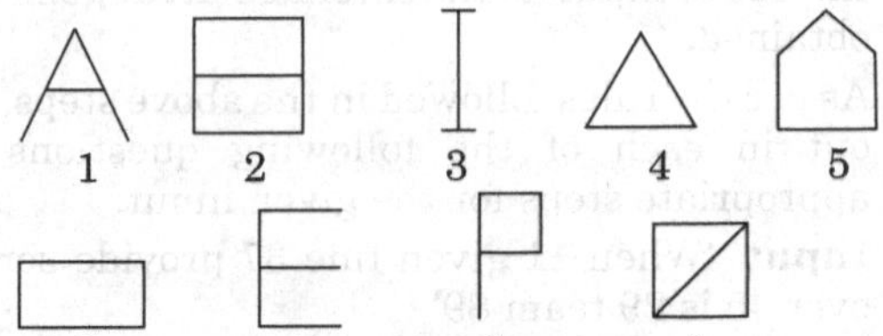

(a) 1, 3, 4; 2, 5, 9; 6, 7, 8

(b) 1, 2, 3; 4, 5, 6; 7, 8, 9

(c) 1, 5, 9; 2, 4, 7; 3, 6, 8

(d) 3, 7, 8; 1, 6, 5; 4, 2, 9

Hints and Solutions

1. (*b*) As, 'rat' is eaten by 'cat'. In the same way, 'Worms' are eaten by 'Bird'. Hence, option (b) is correct.

2. (*a*) As,

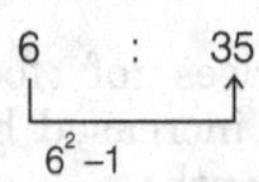

Similarly,

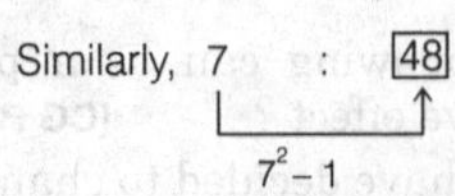

3. (*b*) As,

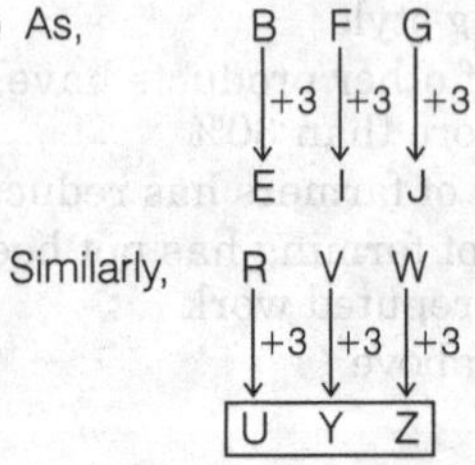

4. (*b*) Hen is odd from the given alternatives.

5. (*b*) Except (b), all others are antonyms.

6. (*b*) As,

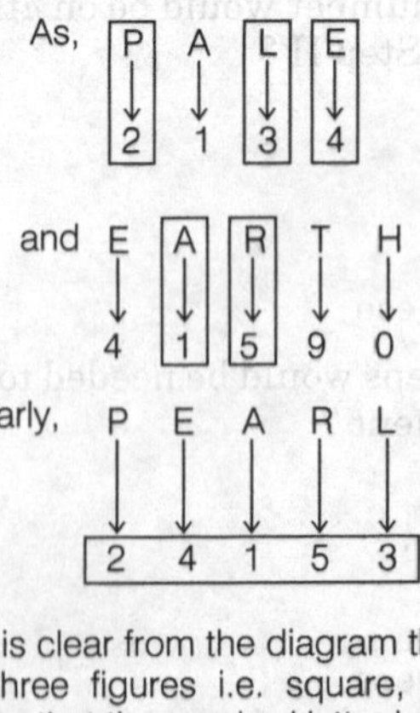

7. (*a*) It is clear from the diagram that M is common in all the three figures i.e. square, triangle and circle. It means that the required letter is M.

8. (*b*) When it appears 6 : 30 in mirror, the real time would be (12:00 – 6:30) = 5 : 30.

9. (*c*) Required words = PORE, ROPE

10. (*c*) Let us see

The given number	4	9	2	7	6	3	8	1
Ascending order arrangement	1	2	3	4	6	7	8	9

So, two digits are unchanged after rearranged in ascending order within the number.

11. (*a*) According to the question,

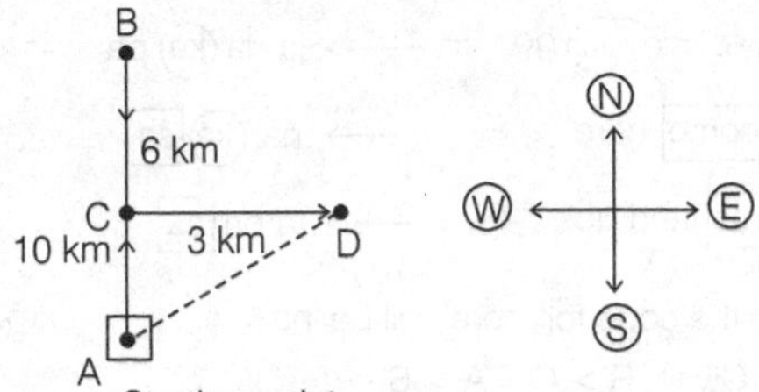

Starting point

$$AD = \sqrt{(CD)^2 + (AC)^2} \quad \left[\because AC = AB - BC = 10 - 6 = 4\right]$$

$$= \sqrt{(3)^2 + (4)^2}$$

$$= \sqrt{9 + 16}$$

$$= \sqrt{25}$$

$$= 5 \text{ km}$$

Clearly, Mahima is in North-East direction from original position and 5 km far.

12. (*a*) According to question,

$$\frac{52}{2} - 9 = \text{Number of marbles with Janani.}$$

$$= 17$$

13. (*d*) According to the given information,

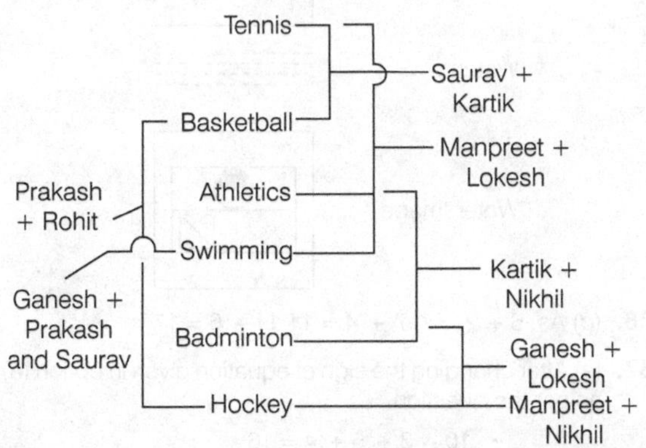

From the above diagram we can say that, Saurav does not play badminton. So, option (a) is eliminated. Kartik does not swim, so option (b) eliminated. Manpreet does not play tennis, so option (c) is eliminated. Lokesh only play all the three games. So, right option is (d).

Solution (Q. Nos. 14-16)

According to the question,

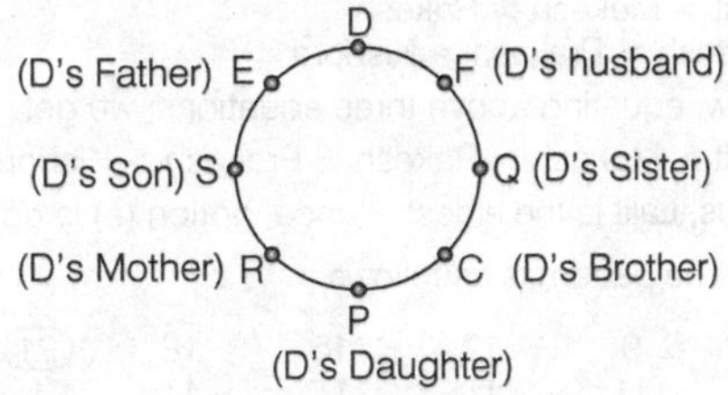

14. (*b*) Only three people sit between Q and S.

15. (*d*) C is D's brother.

16. (*c*) D : Q

17. (*d*) Two days after Tuesday will be Thursday.

18. (*a*) Here, the manager stresses the need to appoint more subordinate officers. It does mean that present staff is not efficient. In fact he wants to say that work is much more than the working capacity of present staff strength. Hence, Assumption II is invalid. But Assumption I is implicit because without assuming the availability of subordinate officers, the manager would not have said so.

Solution (Q. Nos. 19-21) Following table can be drawn from the given instructions.

Friends	Discipline							States						
	Arts	Commerce	Science	Engineering	Architecture	Management	Pharmacy	AP	UP	Maharashtra	Karnataka	Kerala	Chattisgarh	Punjab
Anu	✗	✗	✗	✗	✓	✗	✗	✗	✗	✓	✗	✗	✗	✗
Beena	✗	✗	✗	✗	✗	✗	✓	✗	✗	✗	✓	✗	✗	✗
Kanika	✗	✗	✗	✓	✗	✗	✗	✗	✗	✗	✗	✗	✓	✗
Mohini	✗	✗	✗	✗	✗	✓	✗	✗	✗	✗	✗	✗	✗	✓
Samina	✗	✗	✓	✗	✗	✗	✗	✗	✗	✗	✗	✓	✗	✗
Easther	✗	✓	✗	✗	✗	✗	✗	✓	✗	✗	✗	✗	✗	✗
Rani	✓	✗	✗	✗	✗	✗	✗	✗	✓	✗	✗	✗	✗	✗

19. (a) Anu - Architecture is the correct combination.

20. (d) Both I and III combinations are correct.

21. (c) Both I and IV combinations are correct.

22. (c)

According to	Possibility of Date
Sneha	12, 13, (14), 15
Younger Brother	(14), 15, 16, 17
Elder Brother	..., (14), 16 ...

Here, 14 is common to all the groups. Hence, the correct date is fourteenth..

23. (*a*) Making equations from the given information,
Lalit > Prakash, Kishore ...(i)
Lalit > Mukesh > Rakesh ...(ii)
Rakesh > Prakash > Kishore ...(iii)
Now, equating above three equations, we get
Lalit > Mukesh > Rakesh > Prakash > Kishore
Thus, Lalit is the eldest. Hence, option (a) is correct.

24. (*a*) The pattern is as follows

6 →(+3)→ 9 →(+3)→ 12 →(+3)→ 15 →(+3)→ 18 →(+3)→ (21)

∴ ? = 21

25. (*d*) The pattern is as follows

B →(+6)→ H →(+6)→ N →(+6)→ T
F →(+6)→ L →(+6)→ R →(+6)→ X
G →(+6)→ M →(+6)→ S →(+6)→ Y

∴ ? = TXY

26. (*d*) According to the matrices,
N— 03, 10, (21), 32, 44
E— 56, (67), 78, 89, 95
S— 02, (14), 20, 31, 43
T— (59), 65, 76, 87, 98
∴ NEST ⇒ 21, 67, 14, 59

27. (*c*) The date of birth of Yasir is February 29. It means he was born in a Leap Year.
From Statement I Leap year between 2005 and 2011 was 2008.
From Statement II 2012 − 4 = 2008 and 2008 was a Leap year.

28. (a) **From Statement I** Out of 42 students, 38 play both chess and cricket and the remaining four play only cricket. Therefore, no student plays only chess.

29. (*b*) As we know that, when all the faces of a cube are painted with a single colour, then central cubes have only one face painted.
∴ Required number of central cubes

$$= 6(n-2)^2$$
$$= 6(3-2)^2 \quad (\because n = \sqrt[3]{27} = 3)$$
$$= 6$$

30. (*a*) Here,
Daughter's age = 10 yr
then mother's age = 3 × 10 = 30 yr.
Father's age = 30 + 7 = 37 yr.
Age of father when daughter was born = 37 − 10 = 27 yr.

31. (*c*) According to the given information,

Father
↑
Mother (Woman)
↑
Person

So, woman is the mother of that person.

32. (*b*) Given that,

how can (you) go ⟶ ja da (ka) pa ...(i)
(you) [come] here ⟶ na (ka) [sa] ...(ii)
[come] and go ⟶ ra pa [sa] ...(iii)

So, the code for 'here' will be 'na'

33. (*b*) Given, R > O = A > S < T

O > T (Not True)
T > A (Not True)
S = O (Not True) as O > S
T < R (Not True)
But, S < R (True)

34. (*d*) P > L [≥] A ≥ N = T
P > A (True)
T = N ≤ A ≤ L
Therefore, T ≤ L

35. (*c*) The figure in option (c) represents the correct water image of figure (A) as shown below

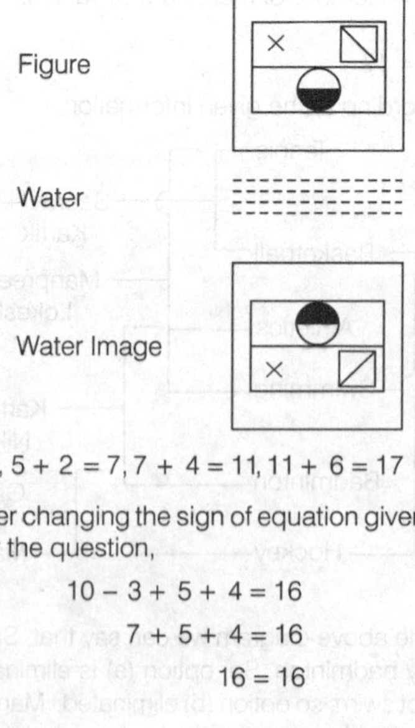

36. (*d*) As, 5 + 2 = 7, 7 + 4 = 11, 11 + 6 = 17

37. (*a*) After changing the sign of equation given in option (a) as per the question,
10 − 3 + 5 + 4 = 16
⇒ 7 + 5 + 4 = 16
⇒ 16 = 16

38. (*b*) Arrangement of words as per dictionary.

(b) Impress
↓
(c) Imprint
↓
(a) Improve
↓
(d) Impugn

39. (*d*) The colour of Turmeric is 'yellow' but here, 'yellow' is called 'black'. Hence, in this case colour of turmeric is 'black'.

Solution (Q. Nos. 40-42) First of all, the words get rearranged in alphabetical order and two words are rearranged in each step. Then, the numbers are rearranged in descending order.

Input when 11 given fine 37 provide zero 90 over 45 is 29 team 89

***Step* I** fine given when 11 37 provide zero 90 over 45 is 29 team 89

***Step* II** fine given is over when 11 37 provide zero 90 45 29 team 89

***Step* III** fine given is over provide team when 11 37 zero 90 45 29 89

***Step* IV** fine given is over provide team when zero 11 37 90 45 29 89

***Step* V** fine given is over provide team when zero 90 89 11 37 45 29

***Step* VI** fine given is over provide team when zero 90 89 45 37 11 29

***Step* VII** fine given is over provide team when zero 90 89 45 37 29 11

40. (*a*) **Step I** fine given when 11 37 provide zero 90 over 45 is 29 team 89.

41. (*e*) 'over' is 4th from left in step II.

42. (*c*) VII steps would be needed to complete the arrangement.

43. (*b*)

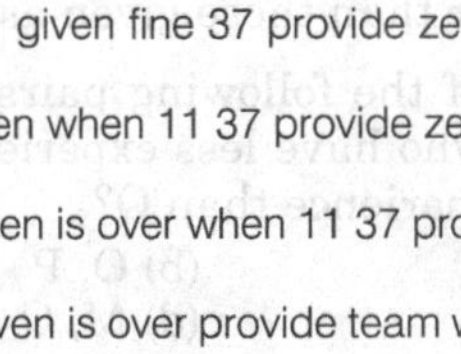

Conclusions

I. No ruler is a king. (✗)
II. All rulers being king is a possibility. (✔)

44. (*d*)

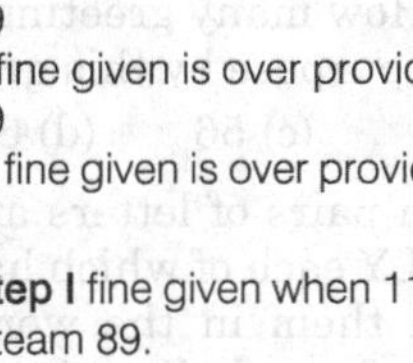

Conclusions

I. Some lights are definitely not optics. (✗)
II. Some rays are definitely not lights (✗)

45. (*b*)

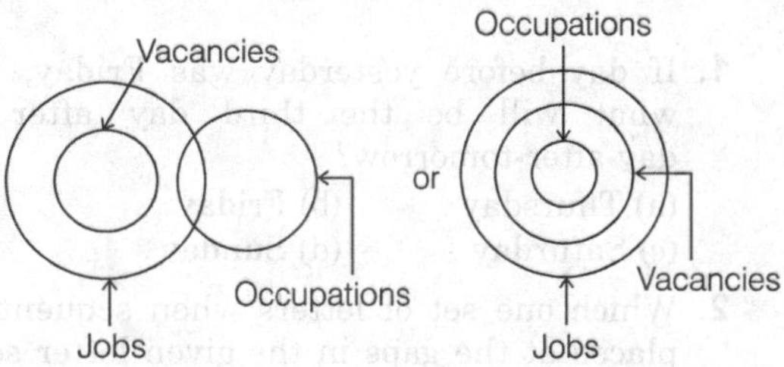

Conclusion

I. All vacancies are occupations. (✗)
II. All occupations being vacancies is a possibility. (✔)

46. (*b*) The prices of foodgrains and vegetables have increased by about 30% due to increase of more than 30% in the price of other products, because farmers will need 30% more funding for purchasing other products.

47. (*b*) It is given that all married persons are invited for the dance and some members of the club are married persons. So, all married students of the club are invited for the dance.

48. (*b*)

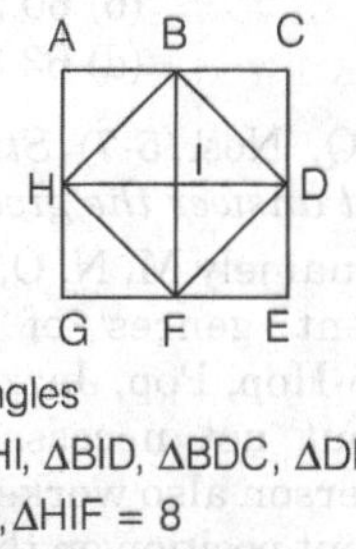

Smallest triangles
= ΔABH, ΔBHI, ΔBID, ΔBDC, ΔDIF, ΔDEF, ΔFGH, ΔHIF = 8

Triangles formed with two triangles
= ΔFHB, ΔFBD, ΔBDH, ΔDFH = 4

∴ Total number of triangles = 8 + 4 = 12

49. (*d*)

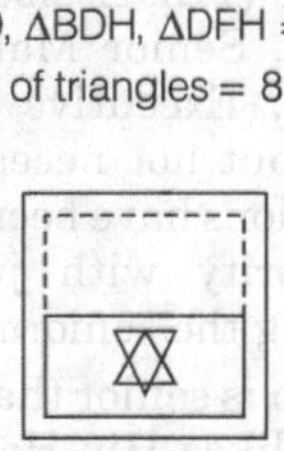

So, option (d) is correct.

50. (*a*) Grouping the figures on the basis of sides, we get

Figures made by three lines = 1, 3, 4

Figures made by four lines = 6, 7, 8

Figures made by five lines = 2, 5, 9

PRACTICE SET 36

1. If day before yesterday was Friday, then what will be the third day after the day-after-tomorrow?

(a) Thursday (b) Friday
(c) Saturday (d) Sunday

2. Which one set of letters when sequentially placed at the gaps in the given letter series shall complete it?

a_ba_bb_ab_a

(a) aabb (b) baaa (c) abab (d) baab

3. In the following series, how many KGN occur in such a way that 'G' is in the middle and 'K' and 'N' are adjacent to it on both sides?

A K G L M N D Q K G C S N G K T G K G N D Z P U X G K E **[SSC (CGL) 2014]**

(a) 3 (b) 5 (c) 1 (d) 2

4. Find the missing term.

980, 392, 156.8, ?, 25.088, 10.0352

(a) 65.04 (b) 60.28
(c) 62.72 (d) 63.85

Direction (Q. Nos. 5-7) *Study the following information and answer the given questions.*

Seven people namely M, N, O, P, Q, R and S like seven different genres of music namely—Classical, Hip-Hop, Pop, Jazz, Opera, Rock and Electronica but not necessarily in the same order. Each person also works in the same office but at a different position on the basis of seniority namely Trainee (TE), Assistant Manager (AM), Manager (MG), Senior Manager (SM), Chief Manager (CM), Executive Director (ED) and Director (DR) but not necessarily in the same order. The positions have been given in increasing order of seniority with juniormost position (whilst DR being the seniormost position.)

Only one person is senior than O. The one who is senior than O likes Hip-Hop. Only two people are junior than R. M is junior than R and likes Electronica. M is not the junior most. Q is junior than the CM but senior than the one who likes Opera. The one who likes Opera is not the senior most. Q likes Classical. The one who likes pop is senior than Q but not the ED. S does not like Pop. **[RBI (Officers) 2015]**

5. As per the given arrangement, R is related to Opera and Q is related to classical in a certain way. To which of the following is P related to in the same way?

(a) Pop (b) Jazz
(c) Rock (d) Electronica
(e) Hip-Hop

6. Who amongst the following works as a MG?

(a) Q (b) R (c) S (d) P
(e) Other than those given as options

7. Which of the following pairs represents the people who have less experience than R and more experience than Q?

(a) M, S (b) O, P
(c) N, P (d) M, O
(e) Q, O

8. There are 8 members in a friends group who greet each other on the Deepawali day be sending cards. How many greeting cards will be used for this purpose by this group?

(a) 50 (b) 64 (c) 56 (d) 60

9. How many such pairs of letters are there in the word TIMELY each of which has as many letters between them in the word (in both forward and backward directions) as they have between them in the English alphabetical series? **[IBPS (Clerk) Pre 2015]**

(a) Two (b) None
(c) Three (d) One
(e) More than three

Direction (Q.Nos. 10-11) *Read the following information carefully and answer the questions.*

'A ★ B' means 'A is the son of B'.

'A + B' means 'A is the father of B'.

'A > B' means 'A is the daughter of B'.

'A < B' means 'A is the wife of B'. **[NICL (AO) 2015]**

10. Which of the following pairs of people represents first cousins with regard to the relations given in the expressions, if it is provided that A is the sister of J : 'L > V < J + P' and 'S ★ A < D + F < E + K'.

(a) LP (b) SP (c) SK (d) SF
(e) Cannot be determined

11. What will come in the place of question mark (?), if it is provided that M is the grandmother of F in the expression 'F ★ R < S ? M'

(a) > (b) < (c) + (d) ★
(e) Cannot be determined

Direction (Q. Nos. 12-14) *In the following questions, select the related word/letters/number from the given alternatives.* **[SSC (CPO) 2015]**

12. DCBA : WXYZ :: IJKL : ?
(a) SRQP (b) QPON (c) RQPO (d) PONM

13. Goldsmith : Gold : : ?
(a) Carpenter : Wood (b) Cobbler : Shoes
(c) Jeweller : Jewellery (d) Barber : Shave

14. 14 : 70
(a) 75 : 375 (b) 15 : 90 (c) 80 : 480 (d) 19 : 57

Direction (Q.Nos. 15-17) *Each of the questions below consists of a question and two statements numbered I and II are given below it. You have to decide whether the data provided in the statements are sufficient to answer the question. Read both statements and give answer.* **[NICL (AO) 2014]**

(a) If the data in Statement I alone are sufficient to answer the question, while the data in Statement II alone are not sufficient to answer the question
(b) If the data in Statement II alone are sufficient to answer the question, while the data in Statement I alone are not sufficient to answer the question
(c) If the data either in Statement I alone or in Statement II alone are sufficient to answer the question
(d) If the data in both Statements I and II together are not sufficient to answer the question
(e) If the data in both Statements I and II together are necessary to answer the question

15. How is 'time' coded in the given code language? (All the codes are two-letter codes only)

I. In the given code language, 'take your own time' is coded as 'sa nv jr pt' and in the same code language, 'fix your study time' is coded as 'dq sa pt bz'.

II. In the given code language, 'come by dinner time' is coded as 'od es rg sa' and in the same code language, 'come home some time' is coded as 'sa gk es co'.

16. What is the position of B from the right end in a straight line of eight people? (All are facing North.)

I. A sits second from the left end of the line. Only three people sit between A and U.B sits third to the right of X. Neither B nor X is an immediate neighbour of U.

II. Z sits at the extreme right end of the line. E sits third to the left of Z. B sits exactly between E and R. U sits second to the right of B.

17. How is B related to F?

I. A is the son of Z. F is married to Z. F is the mother of B.

II. F is the wife of W. K and B are the children of W. A is the son of B.

18. Which one of the following is the sequential order of colours in Rainbow? **[SSC (CGL) 2012]**

(i) Red (ii) Green
(iii) Violet (iv) Yellow
(v) Orange

(a) (iii), (ii), (iv), (v), (i)
(b) (iv), (iii), (ii), (v), (i)
(c) (iii), (iv), (ii), (i), (v)
(d) (ii), (v), (iv), (i), (iii)

19. In a certain code, PARTICLE is written as USBQFMDJ and GENERATE is written as FOFHFUBS. How is DOCUMENT written in that code? **[IBPS (PO/MT) Mains 2015]**

(a) VDEPUONF (b) VDPENFUQ
(c) VDPEUOFN (d) VDPENFOU
(e) None of these

20. In a class of 35, first year students, Karuna is placed 7th from the bottom where as Surinder is placed 9th from the top. Mohan is placed exactly between the two. What is Karuna's position from Mohan? **[SSC (CGL) 2014]**

(a) 9th (b) 10th (c) 12th (d) 13th

21. How many educated people are employed? **[SSC (10+2) 2012]**

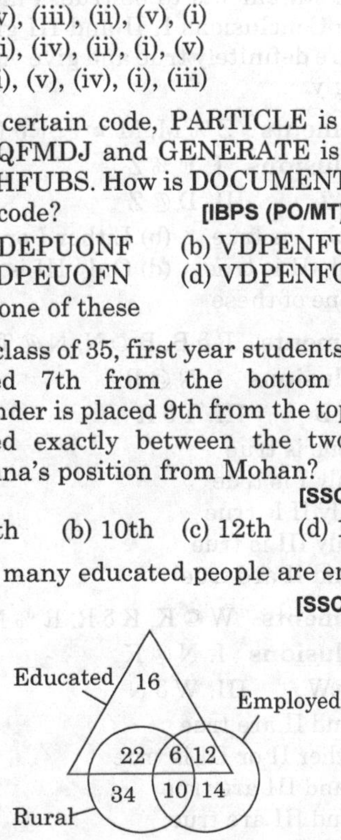

(a) 24 (b) 16 (c) 18 (d) 26

22. From the given three positions of a single dice, find the number of dots at the face opposite to the face having 3 dots.

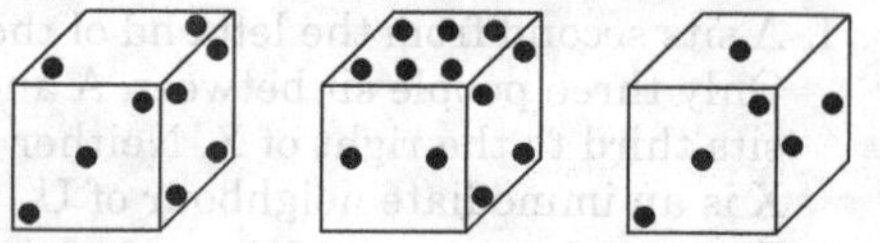

I II III

(a) 2 (b) 4 (c) 5 (d) 6

Direction (Q. Nos. 23-25) *In the following questions, the symbols δ, ★, %, @ and © are used with the following meaning as illustrated below.*

'P ★ Q' means 'P is not greater than Q'.

'P @ Q' means 'P is neither greater than nor equal to Q'.

'P © Q' means 'P is not smaller than Q'.

'P % Q' means 'P is neither smaller than nor greater than Q'.

'P δ Q' means 'P is neither smaller than nor equal to Q'.

Now in each of the following questions assuming the given statements to be true. Find which of the three Conclusions I, II and III given below them is/are definitely true and give your answer accordingly.

23. Statements Z % M, M ★ F, F δ D

Conclusions I. F % Z

II. F δ Z III. D @ Z

(a) Only I is true (b) Either I or II is true
(c) Only II is true (d) Only III is true
(e) None of these

24. Statements R δ B, B © N, N @ T

Conclusions I. N @ R

II. T δ B III. T δ R

(a) None is true
(b) Only I is true
(c) Only II is true
(d) Only III is true
(e) I and II are true

25. Statements W © K, K δ R, R % N

Conclusions I. N @ K

II. R @W III. W δ N

(a) I and II are true
(b) Either II or III is true
(c) II and III are true
(d) I and III are true
(e) All I, II and III are true

Direction (Q. Nos. 26-27) *Find the odd one out from the given alternatives.*

[FCI Assistant Grade III 2015]

26. (a) ACE (b) FHJ
(c) KLM (d) SUW

27. (a) Tomato (b) Potato
(c) Carrot (d) Onion

28. Statement The ministry of Aviation has ordered to procure 35 new aircrafts to be added to the existing fleet this year.

Which of the following most appropriately proves that the decision taken by the Aviation Minister is unrealistic and not based on scientific projections?

[IBPS (PO/MT) Mains 2015]

(a) A recent survey showed that the existing aircrafts in the fleet fail to match the international standards and quality norms.
(b) These new aircrafts have better technology and greater number of seats as compared to ones already existing in the fleet.
(c) The neighbouring country which also procured aircrafts lacked enough number of trained pilots.
(d) As the number of passengers has declined significantly this year, the existing fleet is not being used to its full potential.
(e) As many as 12 pilots are not on flying duties for two straight weeks due to lack of sufficient aircrafts to ply on the routes.

29. Find the missing number from the given responses. **[SSC (10+2) 2014]**

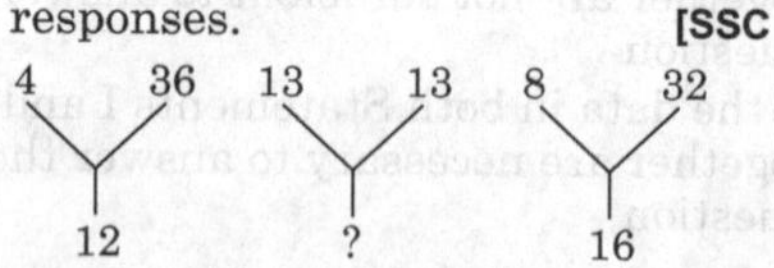

(a) 8 (b) 13 (c) 4 (d) 12

30. If M = 13 and MAD = 52 , then MOOD = ?

(a) 11700 (b)10181 (c) 12500 (d) 95000

Direction (Q. Nos. 31-33) *Read the following information carefully and answer the questions given below.*

Six girls A, B, K, D, E and P are standing in a row. B is between D and P. A does not stand next to either P or D. K does not stand next to D. E stands between A and K.

31. P stands between
(a) B and K (b) E and A
(c) D and B (d) A and K
(e) Cannot be determined

32. Who occupy the extreme ends of the row?
(a) D and E (b) D and A
(c) A and P (d) B and E
(e) None of these

33. K stands between
(a) P and B (b) P and D
(c) P and E (d) E and A
(e) None of these

34. Which of the following best depicts the relationship between doctors, human beings and cats?

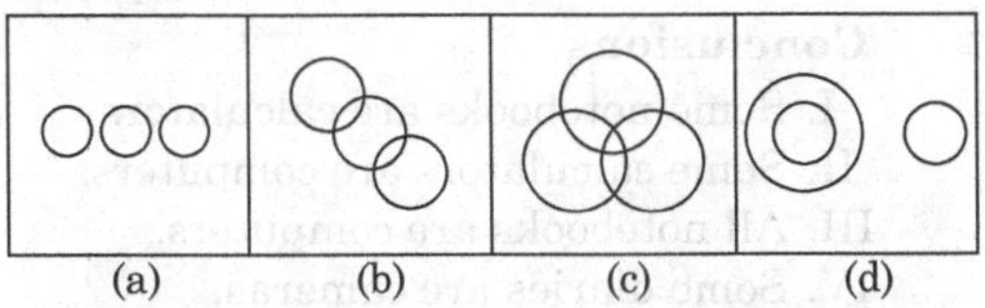

35. In the following questions, select the related figure from the given alternatives.

Question Figures

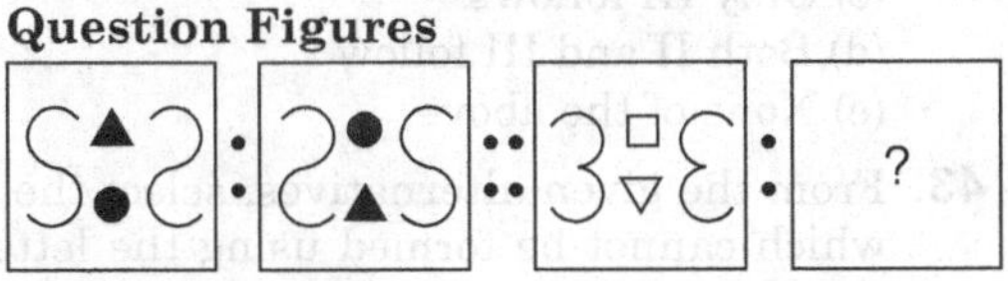

Answer Figures

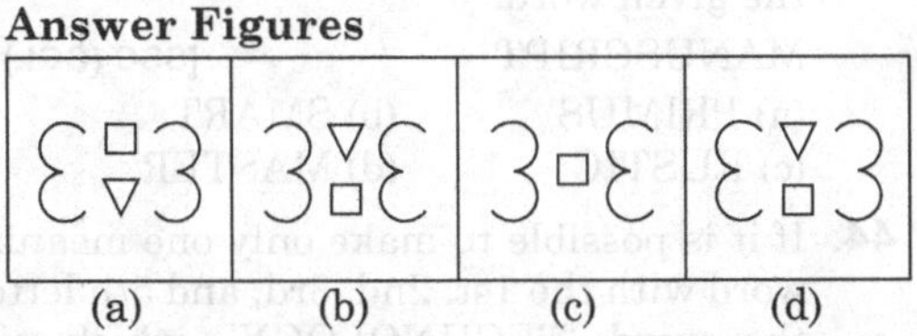

Direction (Q. Nos. 36-37) *Study the following information carefully to answer the given questions.*

A word and number arrangement machine when given an input line of words and numbers rearranges them following a particular rule. The following is an illustration of input and rearrangement, steps—

Input why is 25 bigger than 14 but smaller than 32

Step I than 14 why is 25 bigger but smaller than 32

Step II than 14 is 25 why bigger but smaller than 32

Step III than 14 is 25 than 32 why bigger but smaller

Step IV than 14 is 25 than 32 why smaller bigger but

Step V than 14 is 25 than 32 why smaller but bigger

and Step V is the last step of the rearrangement of the above input as the intended rearrangement is obtained.

As per the rules followed in the above steps, indicate the answer in each of the following questions with respect to the appropriate step for the given input.

Input 'any number less than 30 and more than 20 does not equal 40'

36. Which step number would be the following output?
than 20 any number less than 30 and more does not equal 40.
(a) III (b) IV (c) V (d) VI
(e) None of these

37. How many steps would be needed to complete the arrangement?
(a) X (b) VIII (c) IX (d) VII
(e) None of these

38. In the question below is given a statement followed by three courses of action numbered I, II and III.

A course of action is a step or administrative decision to be taken for improvement, follow-up or further action in regard to the problem, policy, etc. On the basis of information given in the statement, you have to assume everything in the statement to be true and then decide which of the three given suggested courses of action logically follows worth pursuing. Then, decide which of the alternatives (a), (b), (c), (d) or (e) is correct.

Statement A large number tribal inhabitants are found to have been suffering from various diseases due to exposure to radioactive waste near the uranium mine.

Course of Action

I. The Government should immediately close down the mine.

II. The Government should immediately take steps to save local people from exposure to radioactive waste.

III. The tribals should be rehabilitated at a safer place.
(a) Both II and III follow
(b) Both I and II follow
(c) Both I and III follow
(d) Only III follows

39. In the question below is given a statement followed by two assumptions numbered I, II and III. An assumption is something supposed or taken for granted. You have to consider the statement and the following assumptions and decide which of the assumption(s) is/are implicit in the statement.

Statement "Do not lean out of the moving train", a warning in the railway compartment.

Assumptions

I. Such warning will have some effect.
II. Leaving out of a moving train is dangerous.
III. It is the duty of railway authorities to take care of passenger's safety.

(a) I and II are implicit
(b) II and III are implicit
(c) Only II is implicit
(d) I and III are implicit
(e) All are implicit

40. Seven army recruits Laxman, Mahender, Narender, Omprakash, Preetam, Qutab and Raman are standing in a column for physical inspection in order of height, shorter first. Omprakash is standing between Laxman and Qutab. Narender is taller than Laxman. Raman is shorter than Narender. Mahender and Preetam are not the two tallest. Preetam is two places ahead of Qutab. Which of the following is true?
(a) Narender is the tallest
(b) Qutab is taller than Laxman
(c) Raman is ahead of Omprakash
(d) Mahender is the shortest

Direction (Q. Nos. 41-42) *In each of the questions below are given four statements followed by four conclusions numbered I, II, III and IV. You have to take the given statements to be true even if they seem to be at variance with commonly known facts. Read all the conclusions and then decide which of the given conclusion (s) logically follow (s) from the given statements disregarding commonly known facts.*

41. Statements All snakes are eagles.
Some eagles are rabbits.
All rabbits are birds.
Some birds are animals.

Conclusions I. Some animals are snakes.
II. Some birds are snakes.
III. Some birds are eagles.
IV. All birds are rabbits.

(a) None follows (b) Only II follows
(c) Only III follows (d) Both II and III follow
(e) None of these

42. Statements Some cameras are calculators.
Some calculators are diaries.
All notebooks are diaries.
All diaries are computers.

Conclusions

I. Some notebooks are calculators.
II. Some calculators are computers.
III. All notebooks are computers.
IV. Some diaries are cameras.

(a) None follows
(b) Only II follows
(c) Only III follows
(d) Both II and III follow
(e) None of the above

43. From the given alternatives, select the word which cannot be formed using the letters of the given word.
MANUSCRIPT **[SSC (CGL) 2013]**
(a) PRIMUS (b) SMART
(c) RUSTIC (d) MASTER

44. If it is possible to make only one meaningful word with the 1st, 2nd, 3rd, and 5th letters of the word 'TECHNOLOGY', which of the following would be the 3rd letter of that word? If no such word can be made, give 'X' as your answer and if more than one such word can be formed, give your answer as 'Y'.
(a) C (b) T (c) N (d) X
(e) Y

45. Find the missing number. **[SSC (10+2) 2014]**

5	7	9
4	8	2
8	6	?
160	336	108

(a) 4 (b) 7 (c) 6 (d) 8

46. If the word PRINCIPAL is written as LAPICNIRP, then how ADOLESCENCE can be written in that code? **[SSC (10+2) 2014]**
(a) ECNCESELODA (b) ECNECSLEODA
(c) ECNSCEELODA (d) ECNECSELODA

47. Ram and Sam start walking towards North and cover 20 m. Ram turns to his left and Sam to his right. After sometime, Ram walks 10 m in the same direction in which he turned. On the other hand, Sam walks only 7m. Later, Ram turns towards his left and Sam to his right. Both walk 25m forward. How far is Ram from Sam now? **[SSC (CGL) 2013]**
(a) 10 m (b) 20 m (c) 17 m (d) 5 m

48. How many parallelograms are there in the following figure?

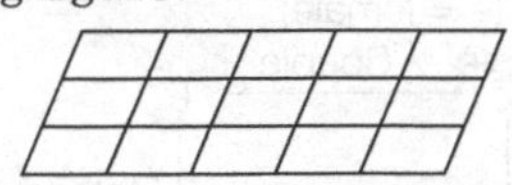

(a) 90 (b) 85
(c) 60 (d) 70

49. In the following questions, find out which of the answer figures (a), (b), (c) and (d) completes the figure matrix?

Question Figure

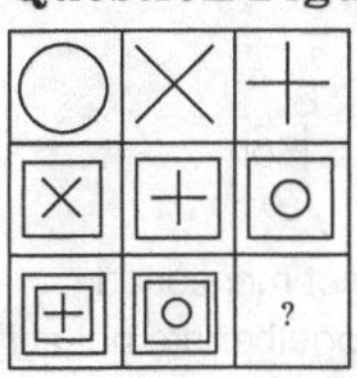

Answer Figures

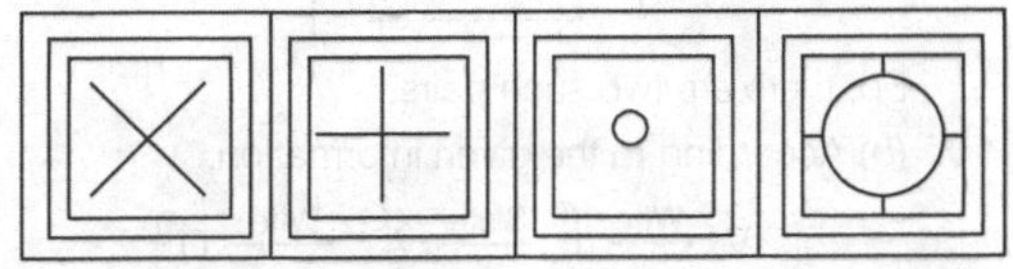

(a) (b) (c) (d)

50. A word is represented by only one set of numbers as given in anyone of the alternatives. The set of numbers given in the alternatives are represented by two classes of alphabets as in two matrices given below. The columns and rows of Matrix I are numbered from 0 to 4 and that of Matrix II are numbered from 5 to 9. A letter from these matrices can be represented first by its row and next by its column. e.g. 'A' can be represented by 00, 12, 23 etc. and 'P' can be represented by 58, 69, 75 etc. Similarly, you have to identify the set for the word given in each question.

Matrix I

	0	1	2	3	4
0	A	R	S	N	C
1	N	C	A	R	S
2	S	N	C	A	R
3	R	S	N	C	A
4	C	A	R	S	N

Matrix II

	5	6	7	8	9
5	O	E	L	P	T
6	T	O	E	L	P
7	P	T	O	E	L
8	L	P	T	O	E
9	E	L	P	T	O

POET
(a) 69, 88, 67, 65 (b) 75, 56, 65, 67
(c) 77, 88, 98, 78 (d) 75, 66, 76, 78

Hints and Solutions

1. (*b*) The day before yesterday was Friday.
Therefore, today is Sunday.
The day-after-tomorrow will be Tuesday.
Tuesday + 3 = Friday

2. (*d*) The complete letter series will be
$a\underline{b}ba/\underline{a}bb\underline{a}/ab\underline{b}a \Rightarrow$ baab
Hence, option (d) is correct.

3. (*d*) A K G L M N D Q K G C S $\underline{NGK}$ T G $\underline{KGN}$ D Z P U X G K E
Only two such series occur.

4. (*c*) The pattern is as follows

$$980 \xrightarrow[\times\frac{2}{5}]{} 392 \xrightarrow[\times\frac{2}{5}]{} 156.8 \xrightarrow[\times\frac{2}{5}]{} \boxed{62.72} \xrightarrow[\times\frac{2}{5}]{} 25.088 \xrightarrow[\times\frac{2}{5}]{} 10.0352$$

$\therefore$? = 62.72

Solution (Q, Nos. 5-7) According to the given information, the arrangement is as follows:

Position	People	Music
Trainee	S	Rock
Assistant Manager	M	Electronica
Manager	R	Opera
Senior Manager	Q	Classical
Chief Manager	N	Pop
Executive Director	O	Jazz
Director	P	Hip-Hop

5. (*e*) **6.** (*b*) **7.** (*d*)

8. (c) Number of greeting cards used = 8 × 7 = 56

9. (*a*)

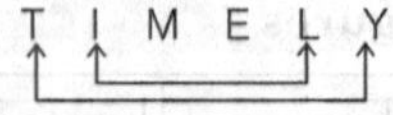

So, there are two such pairs.

10. (*b*) According to the given information,

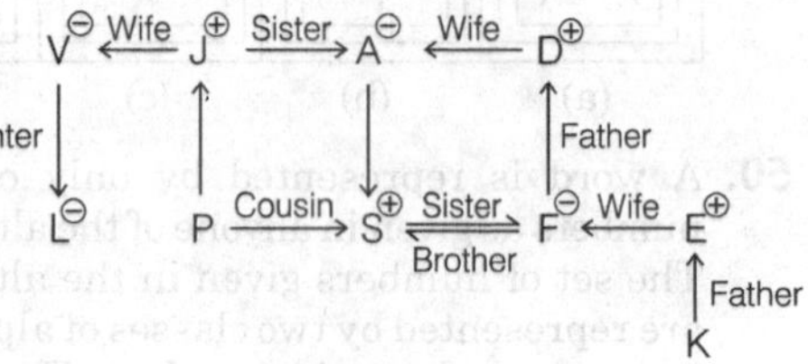

So, SP are the first cousins.

11. (*d*) According to the given information,

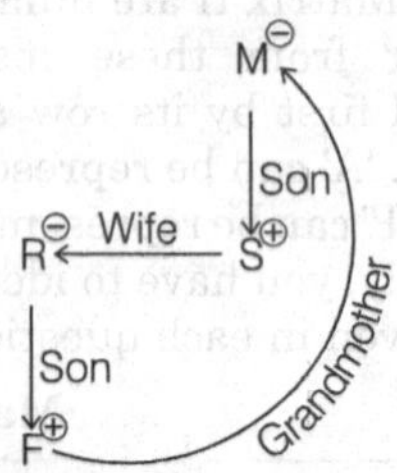

12. (c) As,

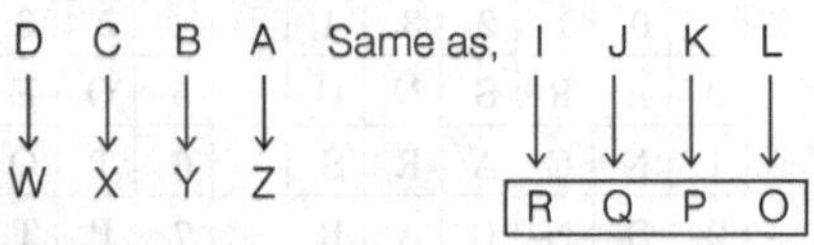

Note Here, every letter has its opposite letter.

13. (*a*) Goldsmith works on 'Gold'. Similarly, Carpenter works on 'Wood'.

Hence, option (a) is correct.

14. (*a*) First number is multiplied by 5 to get second number.

As, $14 \times 5 = 70$

Similarly, $75 \times 5 = 375$

15. (*e*) From Statement I,

take your own time ⟶ sa nv jr pt

fix your study time ⟶ dq sa pt bz

The code for 'time' is either 'sa' or 'pt'.

From Statement II,

come by dinner time ⟶ od es rg sa

come home some time ⟶ sa gk es co

The code for 'time' is either 'es' or 'sa'.

By combining both Statements I and II, we get

take your own time ⟶ sa nv jr pt

fix your study time ⟶ dq sa pt bz

come by dinner time ⟶ od es rg sa

come home some time ⟶ sa gk es co

From above, it is clear that the code for 'time' is 'sa'.

So, both the Statements I and II together are necessary to answer the question.

16. (*e*) From Statement I,

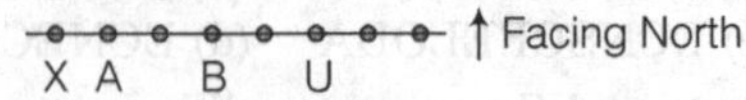

From Statement II,

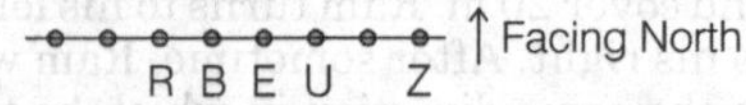

Now, by combining both the Statements, we get

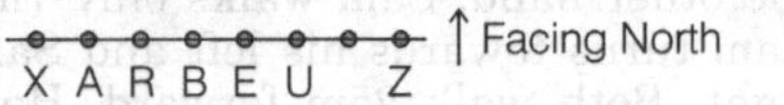

So, B is at fifth position from the right end.

Hence, both the Statements I and II together are necessary to answer the question.

17. (*d*) From Statement I,

(+ = Male) (– = female)

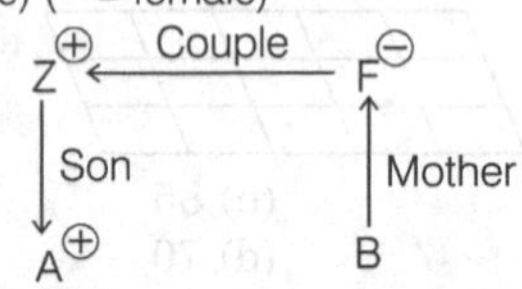

We cannot determined the relation of B to F because the gender of B is not mentioned.

From Statement II,

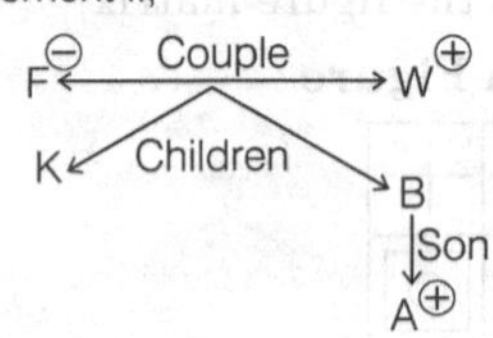

Here, also the gender of B is not mentioned.

So, both Statements I and II together are not sufficient to answer the question.

18. (*a*) The sequential order of colours in Rainbow is Violet, Indigo, Blue, Green, Yellow, Orange, and Red.

(iii) Violet → (ii) Green → (iv) Yellow → (v) Orange → (i) Red

As,

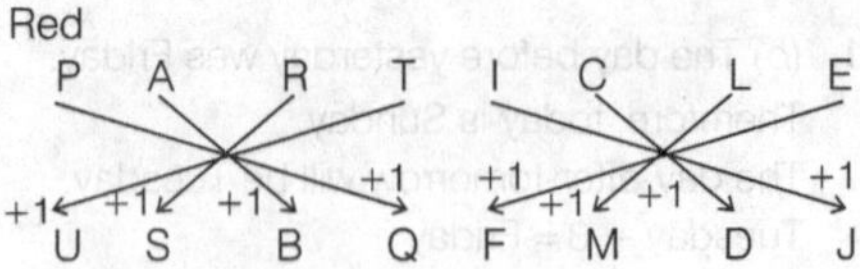

and

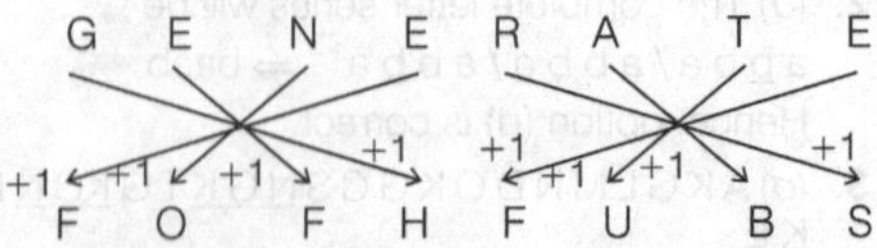

Similarly,

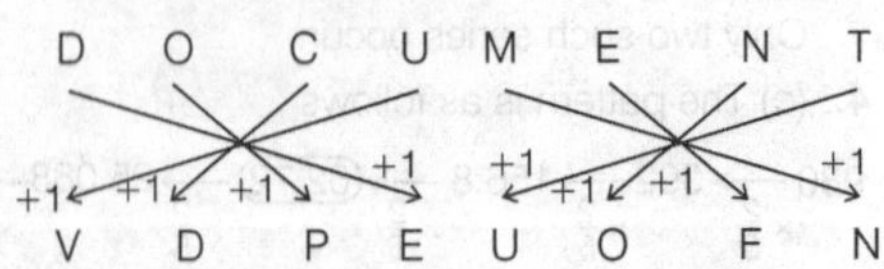

20. (*b*)

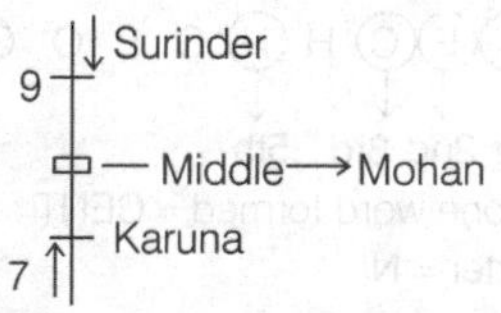

Number of students between the Surinder and Mohan $= 35 - (9 + 7) = 19$ students. Mohan is at middle 5, therefore, position of Karuna from Mohan

$$= \frac{19+1}{2} = 10\text{th}$$

Hence, option (b) is correct.

21. (*c*) 12 + 6 = 18 educated people are employed.

22. (*d*) From positions I and II, common dots = 2 and 4 (at the common right face)

So, the face opposite to face having 3 dots will be the face having 6 dots.

23. (*b*)

★ ≤	@ <	© ≥	% =	δ >

$Z \% M \Rightarrow Z = M$, $M ★ F \Rightarrow M \le F$, $F \delta D \Rightarrow F > D$

Therefore, $Z = M \le F > D$

Conclusions I. $F \% Z \Rightarrow F = Z$ (May be true)

II. $F \delta Z \Rightarrow F > Z$ (May be true)

F is either greater than or equal to Z. Therefore, I or II is true.

III. $D @ Z \Rightarrow D < Z$ (Not true)

24. (*b*) $R \delta B \Rightarrow R > B$, $B © N \Rightarrow B \ge N$, $N @ T \Rightarrow N < T$

Therefore, $R > B \ge N < T$

Conclusions I. $N @ R \Rightarrow N < R$ (True)

II. $T \delta B \Rightarrow T > B$ (Not True)

III. $T \delta R \Rightarrow T > R$ (Not True)

25. (*e*) $W © K \Rightarrow W \ge K$, $K \delta R \Rightarrow K > R$, $R \% N \Rightarrow R = N$

Therefore, $W \ge K > R = N$

Conclusions I. $N @ K \Rightarrow N < K$ (True)

II. $R @ W \Rightarrow R < W$ (True)

III. $W \delta N \Rightarrow W > N$ (True)

26. (*c*) As, A →(+2)→ C →(+2)→ E, F →(+2)→ H →(+2)→ J

K →(+1)→ L →(+1)→ M, S →(+2)→ U →(+2)→ W

Hence, KLM is different from others.

27. (*a*) Except tomato, all others grow under soil.

28. (*d*) As the number of passengers has declined significantly this year, the existing fleet is not being used to its full potential.

29. (*b*) As, $\frac{36}{4} = 9 = (3)^2$

$\Rightarrow$ $3 \times 4 = 12$

and $\frac{32}{8} = 4 = (2)^2$

$\Rightarrow$ $2 \times 8 = 16$

Similarly, $\frac{13}{13} = 1 = (1)^2$

$\Rightarrow$ $1 \times 13 = 13$

30. (*a*) As, M = 13

and M(13) A(1) D(4) ⟶ $13 \times 1 \times 4 = 52$

Similarly M(13) O(15) O(15) D(4) ⟶ $13 \times 15 \times 15 \times 4 = \boxed{11700}$

$\therefore$ MOOD $\Rightarrow$ 11700

Solution (Q. Nos. 31-33) B is between D and P. So, DBP or PBD.

E stands between A and K. So, AEK or KEA.

A does not stand next to either P or D and K does not stand to next D. So, the final arrangement will be as following

D — B — P — K — E — A

31. (*a*) P stands between B and K.

32. (*b*) D and A occupy the extreme ends of the row.

33. (*c*) K stands between P and E.

34. (*d*) All doctors come under the group of human beings but all human beings do not come under the group of doctors and cats are entirely different from doctors and human beings. This relation can be expressed by the diagram as given in option (d).

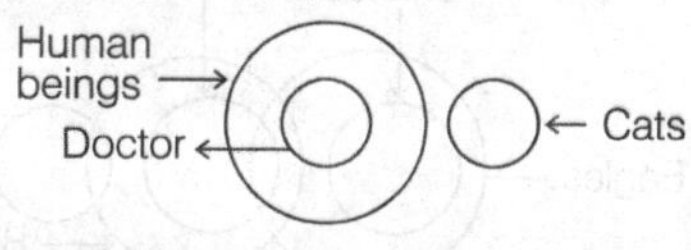

35. (*d*) Both the corner shapes are laterally inverted and remain at their original place. The middle two shapes interchange their positions.

Solution (Q. Nos. 36-37) First of all the numbers and their preceding letters are arranged. The numbers are arranged in ascending order.

Then, the words are arranged in alphabetical but in reverse order.

Input any number less than 30 and more than 20 does not equal 40

***Step* I** than 20 any number less than 30 and more does not equal 40

***Step* II** than 20 than 30 any number less and more does not equal 40

***Step* III** than 20 than 30 equal 40 any number less and more does not

***Step* IV** than 20 than 30 equal 40 number any less and more does not

***Step* V** than 20 than 30 equal 40 number not any less and more does

***Step* VI** than 20 than 30 equal 40 number not more any less and does

***Step* VII** than 20 than 30 equal 40 number not more less any and does

***Step* VIII** than 20 than 30 equal 40 number not more less does any and

Step VIII is the last step.

36. (*e*) It is step I.

37. (*b*) Eight steps would be required to complete the arrangement.

38. (*a*) Course of action I is not practical one, hence does not follow. Courses of action II and III are right courses and deal with the problem positively and effectively.

39. (*e*) The warning against leaving out of moving train is made to need against the dangers involved. So, both I and II assumptions are implicit. Since, the warning has been put up in the railway compartment, So, III is also implicit.

40. (*a*) According to the given information,

Preetam
Raman/Mahender
Qutab
Omprakash
Laxman
Raman/Mahender
Narender

So, from the above places, we conclude that Narender is the tallest.

41. (*c*)

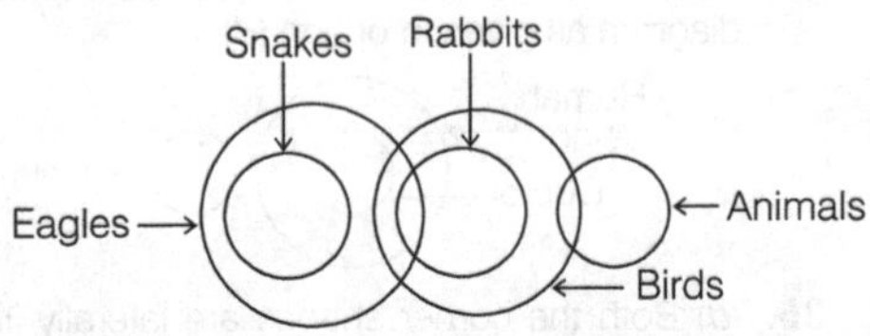

Conclusions
I. Some animals are snakes. (✗)
II. Some birds are snakes. (✗)
III. Some birds are eagles. (✔)
IV. All birds are rabbits. (✗)

42. (*d*)

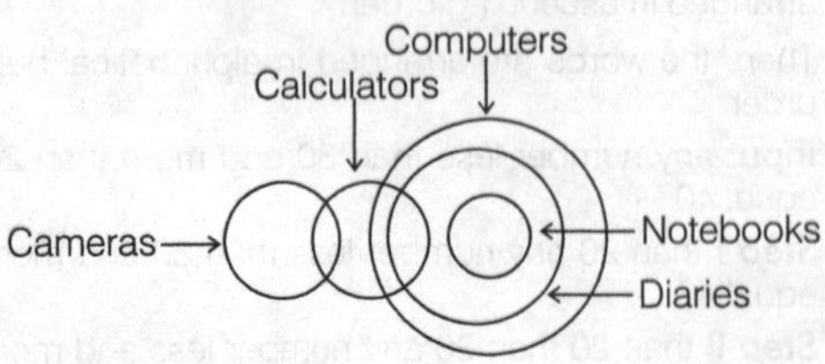

Conclusions
I. Some notebooks are calculators. (✗)
II. Some calculators are computers. (✔)
III. All notebooks are computers. (✔)
IV. Some diaries are cameras. (✗)

43. (*d*) The word 'MASTER' cannot be formed by using the letters of the given word because in the given word 'E' is not present. Hence, option (d) is correct.

44. (*c*)

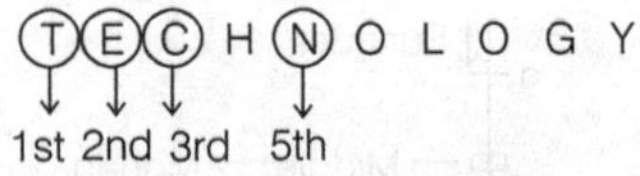

The only one word formed = CENT

∴ Third letter = N

45. (c) The pattern is as follows

In column I, $5 \times 4 \times 8 = 160$

and in column II, $7 \times 8 \times 6 = 336$

Similarly, in column III,

$$9 \times 2 \times ? = 108 \Rightarrow ? = \frac{108}{18}$$

$$\therefore \quad ? = 6$$

46. (*d*) Here, given word is written in reverse order.

PRINCIPAL → LAPICNIRP

Similarly, ADOLESCENCE → ECNECSELODA

47. (*c*)

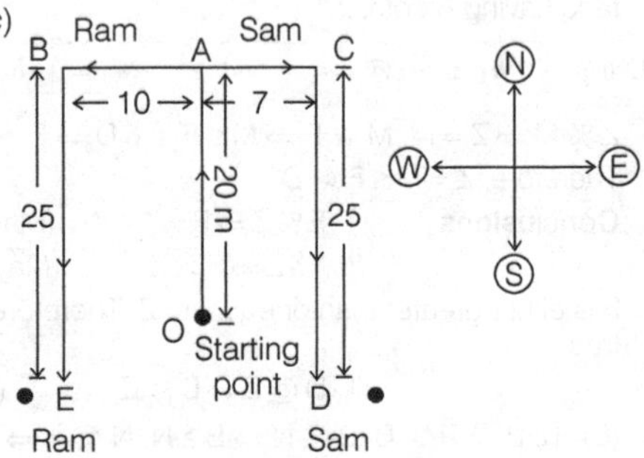

According to given data, Ram and Sam moves from starting point 'O' towards North, cover 20 m. While Ram turns left and travels 10 m. But Sam turns right and travels 7 m. Further, Ram turns towards his left and travels 25 m. Sam turn toward he right and travels 25 m. Therefore, from figure

ED = BC, BE = CD

Distance between Ram and Sam at final point (E and D)

= ED = BC (from figure)
= AB + AC = 10 m + 7 m
= 17 m

48. (*a*) Total number of parallelograms

$= (3 + 2 + 1) \times (5 + 4 + 3 + 2 + 1)$

$= 6 \times 15 = 90$ (here, R = 3 and C = 5)

49. (*a*) Each column has one '+', one 'o' and one '×'. First figure of each column is without boundary and second one is in the square. Third figure is in two squares. As, there are '+' and 'o' in third column.

So, figure '×' will be surrounded by two squares.

50. (*a*) According to the matrices,

P — 58, (69) 75, 86, 97 , O — 55, 66, 77, (88) 99

E — 56, (67), 78, 89, 95 , T — 59, (65) 76, 87, 98

∴ POET ⇒ 69, 88, 67, 65

PRACTICE SET 37

Direction (Q. Nos.1-2) *In the following questions, select the related letters/number pair from the given alternatives.*

1. $\frac{1}{9}:\frac{1}{81}::\frac{1}{13}:?$ **[SSC (CGL) April 2014]**

(a) $\frac{1}{127}$ (b) $\frac{1}{169}$

(c) $\frac{1}{125}$ (d) $\frac{1}{120}$

2. MN : OP : : ?

(a) AD : HF (b) AB : PQ

(c) QR : ST (d) RS : TV

3. Among five friends A is shorter than B but taller than E,C is slightly taller than B but D is slightly shorter than B and slightly taller than A. Who is the shortest ?

(a) A (b) E (c) C (d) D

4. If 'PENCIL' is coded as ? @ , = ; 7 and 'PAPER' is coded as ? 9 ? @ 5, then how will you code 'CLIP' ?

(a) @ 7 ; ? (b) @ ? : ?

(c) = 7 ? ; (d) = 7 ; ?

5. A clock gains five minutes every hour. What will be the angle traversed by the second hand in one minute ?

(a) 360° (b) 360.5°

(c) 390° (d) 380°

Direction (Q. Nos. 6-7) *Each question given below consists of five or six statements followed by options consisting of three statements put together in a specific order. Choose the option which indicates a valid argument containing logically related statements that is, where the third statement is a conclusion drawn from the preceding two statements.* **[CMAT 2014]**

6. A : All synopses are poets.

B : Some synopses are mentors.

C : Some X are not mentors.

D : All X are poets.

E : All synopses are mentors.

F : All synopses are X.

(a) ACB (b) AEC (c) FEC (d) DFA

7. A : All heroines are pretty.

B : Some heroines are popular.

C : Sweta is pretty.

D : Sweta is a popular heroine.

E : Some popular girls are pretty.

(a) ABE (b) ACD

(c) DCA (d) EDC

8. There are three statements followed by three conclusions. You have to determine which of these conclusion follow.

Statements All kids like to play.

Some kids like ice-cream.

Some kids look like their mothers.

Conclusions **[SNAP 2013]**

I. All kids who like ice-cream look like their mothers.

II. Kids who like ice-cream also like to play.

III. Kids who like to play do not look like their mothers.

(a) Only I

(b) Only II

(c) II and III

(d) None can be follow

Direction (Q. Nos. 9-10) *In the following questions, find the odd numbers/word from the given alternatives.*

9. (a) Deck (b) Quay

(c) Stern (d) Bow

(e) Mast

10. (a) 1876 (b) 1984

(c) 2024 (d) 2014

[SSC (10+2) 2014]

Direction (Q. Nos. 11-12) *Below in each question are given two Statements I and II. These statements may be either independent causes or may be effects of independent causes or of a common cause. One of these statements may be the effect of the other statement. Read both the statements and decide which of the following answer choices correctly depicts the relationship between these two statements.*

Give answer
(a) if Statement I is the cause and Statement II is its effect
(b) if Statement II is the cause and Statement I is its effect
(c) if both statements are independent causes
(d) if both statements are effects of independent causes
(e) if both statements are effects of some common cause

11. I. Ravi died while on the way to the hospital.
II. A car dashed into the motorcycle Ravi was driving.

12. I. The average day temperature of the city has increased by about 2 degrees in the current year over the average of past ten years.
II. More people living in rural areas of the state have started migrating to the urban areas in comparison with the earlier year.
[SBI (PO) 2010]

13. A word is represented by only one set of numbers as given in anyone of the alternatives. The sets of numbers given in the alternatives represented by two classes of alphabets as in two matrices given below. The columns and rows of Matrix I are numbered from 0 to 4 and that of Matrix II are numbered from 5 to 9. A letter from these matrices can be represented first by its row and next by its column ,e.g. 'H' can be represented by 02, 20, 43 etc. and 'V' can be represented by 58, 79, 95 etc. Similarly, you have to identify the set for the word given SOFT. **[SSC (Multitasking) 2014]**

Matrix I

	0	1	2	3	4
0	F	G	H	O	M
1	O	M	F	G	H
2	H	O	M	F	G
3	G	H	O	M	F
4	M	F	G	H	O

Matrix II

	5	6	7	8	9
5	S	T	U	V	W
6	U	V	W	S	T
7	W	S	T	U	V
8	T	U	V	W	S
9	V	W	S	T	U

(a) 55, 03, 22, 77 (b) 89, 32, 12, 97
(c) 68, 11, 12, 97 (d) 89, 03, 12, 98

14. If B = 2, MAT = 34, then JOGLEX = ?
(a) 70 (b) 71 (c) 72 (d) 73

15. In a row of children facing North, Neeta is fifteenth from the left end of the row. If she is shifted towards the right end of the row by four places, she becomes eighth from the right end. How many children are there in the row? **[IBPS (PO/MT) Mains 2015]**
(a) 24 (b) 28
(c) Other than those given as options
(d) 27 (e) 26

16. A large sheet of paper is cut into two halves. The two halves are put together i.e. one above the other and again cut into halves. How many pieces will there be for ten such cuttings?
(a) 20 (b) 512
(c) 1024 (d) 2048

17. Pointing to a man, a lady said "His mother is the only daughter of my mother". How is the lady related to the man ? **[SSC (CPO) 2014]**
(a) Mother (b) Daughter
(c) Sister (d) Aunt

18. Some letters have been coded but no specific code is indicated. Use your judgement to pick the coded word which represents the given word the best. **[FCI Assistant (Grade III) 2015]**

TENTANT

(a) 1 4 2 1 3 2 1 (b) 7 5 8 1 8 7 1
(c) 2 2 2 5 5 5 2 (d) 1 1 9 7 2 8 1

19. Which number comes least in the given series ?
8 4 6 7 3 4 3 7 8 3 4 4 5 6 3 4 6 4 3 4 8
(a) 8 (b) 7 (c) 5 (d) 4

Direction (Q. Nos. 20-22) *In the following questions, a series is given, with one term missing. Choose the correct alternatives from the given ones that will complete the series.*

20. 0, 6, 24, 60, 120, 210 ? **[CLAT 2014]**
(a) 290 (b) 240 (c) 336 (d) 504

21. C, E, I, K, O, Q ? **[BOI (Clerk) 2011]**
(a) R (b) S (c) T (d) U
(e) None of these

22. Which one set of letters when sequentially placed at the gaps in the given letter series shall complete it ?

_bbm_amb_m_a_bb

(a) mbabm (b) abmab
(c) mabam (d) ambbm

Direction (Q. Nos. 23-25) *In these questions, relationship between different elements is shown in the statements. The statements are followed by conclusions. Study the conclusions based on the given statement and select the appropriate answer.*

Give answer **[SBI SO (IT) 2016]**

(a) if both conclusions I and II are true
(b) if neither conclusions I nor II is true
(c) if either conclusions I or II is true
(d) if only conclusion I is true
(e) if only conclusion II is true

23. **Statements** $Z \leq H = N \leq C \geq M > S; G = K \geq C$
Conclusions I. $K > H$ II. $H = K$

24. **Statements** $Z \leq H = N \leq C \geq M > S; G = K \geq C$
Conclusions I. $Z \leq C$ II. $G > S$

25. **Statements** $B < L \leq A = M \geq E;$
$Q \geq M < O; D \leq L$
Conclusions I. $Q \geq D$ II. $E < O$

26. How many circles are there in the figure given below ?

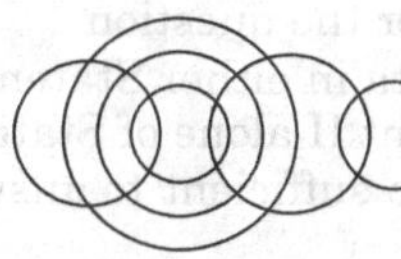

(a) 6 (b) 7
(c) 10 (d) 8

27. If + means '÷', – means '×', × means '+', and ÷ means '–', then give the value for
$45 + 9 - 3 \times 15 \div 2$ **[BSSC (CGL) 2015]**

(a) 40 (b) 36
(c) 56 (d) 28

28. Find the missing number from the given responses.

3	4	5
4	5	3
4	3	?
48	60	105

(a) 2 (b) 6
(c) 7 (d) 9

29. Which figure represents the relation among lawyers, teachers and educated ?

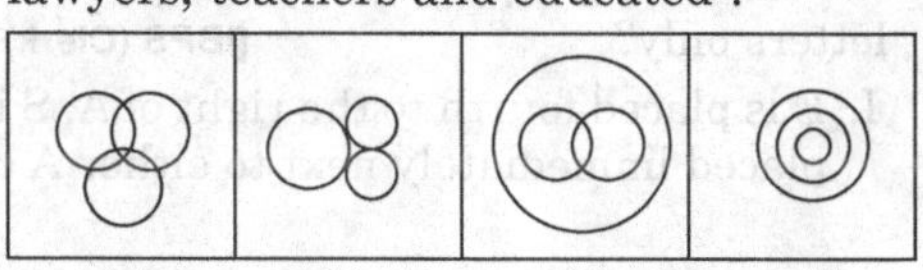

(a) (b) (c) (d)

30. A man starts from his house and walked straight for 10 m towards North and turned left and walked 25 m. He then turned right and walked 5 m and again turned right and walked 25 m. Which direction is he facing now ? **[SSC (FCI) 2012]**

(a) North (b) East
(c) South (d) West

31. If two days before yesterday was Friday, then what day will be day after tomorrow?

(a) Monday (b) Sunday
(c) Saturday (d) Wednesday

32. Which one of the given responses would be a meaningful order of the given words ?

(i) Pulp (ii) Print
(iii) Paper (iv) Purchase
(v) Publish

(a) (i), (iii), (ii), (v), (iv)
(b) (i), (iv), (v), (ii), (iii)
(c) (i), (ii), (iii), (v), (iv)
(d) (i), (v), (iv), (ii), (iii)

33. All the faces of a cube having side 5 cm are painted green and then it is divided into smaller cubes of 1 cm side. How many smaller cubes have three faces painted with green ?

(a) 4 (b) 8
(c) 12 (d) 24

Direction (Q. Nos. 34- 36) *Study the following information carefully and answer the given questions.*

A word and number arrangement machine when given an input line of words and numbers rearranges them following a particular rule in each step. The following is an illustration of input and rearrangement.

Input sale data 18 23 for 95 then 38
***Step* I** data sale 18 23 for 95 then 38
***Step* II** data 95 sale 18 23 for then 38
***Step* III** data 95 for sale 18 23 then 38
***Step* IV** data 95 for 38 sale 23 18 then
***Step* V** data 95 for 38 sale 23 then 18
***Step* VI** data 95 for 38 sale 23 then 18

and step VI is the last step of the rearrangement of the above input.

As per the rules followed in the above steps, find out in each of the following questions the appropriate step for the given input.

34. **Input** year 39 stake 47 house full 94 55
How many steps will be required to complete the rearrangement ?
(a) Five (b) Six
(c) Four (d) Seven
(e) None of these

35. Step II of an input is 'car 83 lost ever 32 46 74 now'.
How many more steps will be required to complete the rearrangement ?
(a) Three (b) Four
(c) Five (d) Six
(e) None of these

36. Step III of an input is 'and code 27 18 new goal 34'.
Which of the following will definitely be the input ?
(a) code and 79 27 18 new goal 34
(b) code 27 18 new goal 34 and 79
(c) code 27 and 18 79 new goal 34
(d) Cannot be determined
(e) None of the above

37. In this question, there are two statements labelled as Assertion (A) and Reason (R).
Assertion (A) The British sovereignty continued to exist in India.
Reason (R) The British sovereign appointed the last Governor-General of free India.
(a) if both 'A' and 'R' are true and 'R' is the correct explanation of 'A'
(b) if both 'A' and 'R' are true but 'R' is not the correct explanation of 'A'
(c) if 'A' is true but 'R' is false
(d) if 'A' is false but 'R' is true
(e) if both 'A' and 'R' are false

38. Which of the following figures (a),(b),(c) and (d) when folded along the lines will produce the question figure ?

Question Figure

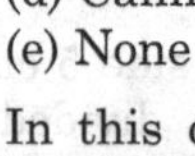

Answer Figures

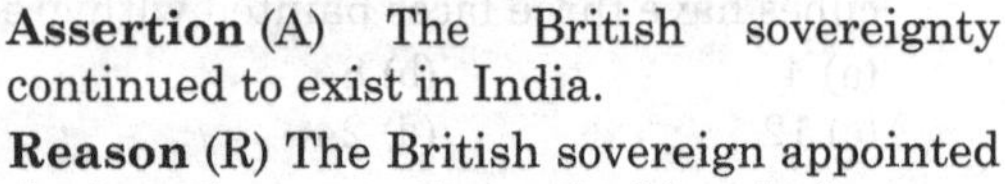

(a) (b) (c) (d)

39. What comes in place of question mark (?) in the following series?
Z9A, X7D, ?, T3J, R1M
(a) W6F (b) S3H
(c) G9V (d) V5G

Direction (Q. Nos.40-41) *Each of the questions below consists of a question and three statements numbered I, II and III given below it. You have to decide whether the data provided in the statements are sufficient to answer the question.*

Give answer **[IBPS (PO/MT) 2012]**
(a) if the data in Statements I and II are sufficient to answer the question, while the data in Statement III are not required to answer the question
(b) if the data in Statements I and III are sufficient to answer the question, while the data in Statement II are not required to answer the question
(c) if the data in Statements II and III are sufficient to answer the question, while the data in Statement I are not required to answer the question
(d) if the data in either Statement I alone or Statement II alone of Statement III alone are sufficient to answer the question
(e) if the data in all the Statements I, II and III together are necessary to answer the question

40. Point D is in which direction with respect to Point B ?
I. Point A is to the West of Point B. Point C is to the North of Point B. Point D is to the South of Point C.
II. Point G is to the South of point D. Point G is 4 m from point B. Point D is 9m from point B.
III. Point A is to the West of point B. Point B is exactly midway between points A and E. Point F is to the South of point E. Point D is to the West of point F.

41. There are six letters W, A, R, S, N and E. Is 'ANSWER' the word formed after performing the following operations using these six letters only? **[IBPS (Clerk) 2011]**
I. E is placed fourth to the right of A. S is not placed immediately next to either A or E.

II. R is placed immediately next (either left of right) to E. W is placed immediately next (either left or right) To S.

III. Both N and W are placed immediately next to S. The word does not begin with R. A is not placed immediately next to W.

Direction (Q. Nos. 42-44) *Study the information carefully to answer these questions.*

Five female friends namely Tulsi, Sunanda, Nalini, Arushi and Prerna and five male friends namely Atul, Karan, Pran, Sudarshan and Tarun sat together on the two sides of a rectangular table for a quiz competition. Females sat alternatingly with and opposite to male members. Sudarshan sat in a central position. Arushi sat opposite to Atul. Sunanda sat next to the right of Sudarshan and at fourth place from Atul. Prerna sat to the left of Arushi at the extreme end. Nalini sat two places from Sunanda to her left and Pran sat opposite to Sunanda. Karan was seated three places from Prerna to her right. **[MAT Feb 2012]**

42. Who sat opposite to Sundarshan ?
(a) Sunanda (b) Tulsi
(c) Nalini (d) Prerna

43. Who sat opposite to Tarun ?
(a) Nalini (b) Arushi
(c) Tulsi (d) Prerna

44. Which pair is occupying diagonally opposite ends ?
(a) Tarun and Arushi
(b) Tarun and Prerna
(c) Tulsi and Atul
(d) Arushi and Prerna

45. In which answer figure is the question figure embedded ?

Question Figure

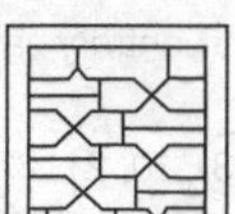

Answer Figures

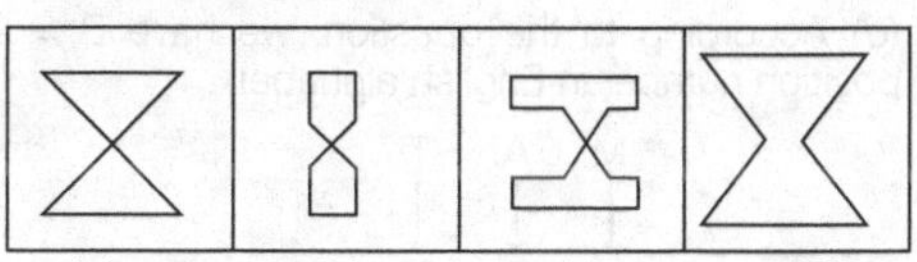

(a) (b) (c) (d)

Direction (Q. Nos. 46-48) *On the basis of the information given below, select the correct alternative as answer for the questions which follow the information.*

Six plays A, B, C, D E and F are to be staged. One on each day from Monday to Saturday. The schedule of the plays is to be in accordance with the following information.

(i) A must be staged a day before E.
(ii) C must not be staged on Tuesday.
(iii) B must be staged on the day following the day on which F is staged.
(iv) D must be staged on Friday only and should not be immediately preceded by B.
(v) E must not be staged on the last day of the schedule.

46. Which of the following plays is staged immediately after E ?
(a) B (b) D (c) E (d) F
(e) None of these

47. Which of the following plays is played on Monday ?
(a) E (b) F (c) C (d) B
(e) A

48. Play D is between which of the following pair of plays ?
(a) B and E (b) E and F
(c) A and E (d) C and E
(e) None of the above

49. How many meaningful English words can be formed from the letters ADRW, using each letter only once in each word ?
(a) None (b) One (c) Two (d) Three

50. Find the figure out of the answer choice figure that can be formed by joining the pieces given in the question figure.

Question Figure

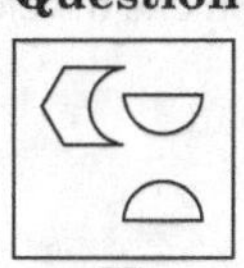

(X)

Answer Figures

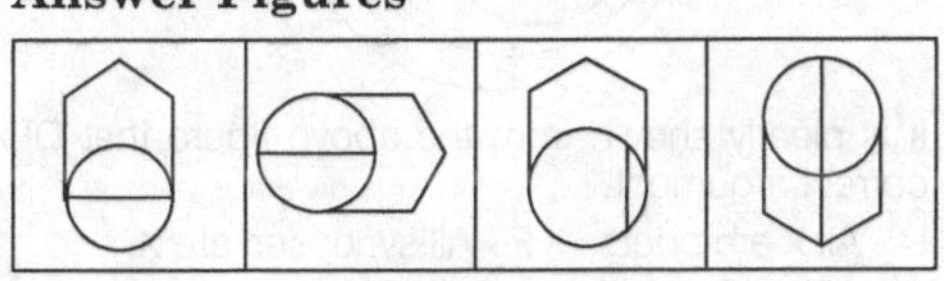

(a) (b) (c) (d)

Hints and Solutions

1. (*b*) As, $\left(\frac{1}{9}\right)^2 = \frac{1}{81}$

   Similarly, $\left(\frac{1}{13}\right)^2 = \frac{1}{169}$

2. (*c*) The letters in both the groups in a pair are consecutive letters in the order.

   $M \xrightarrow[+1]{} N \xrightarrow[+1]{} O \xrightarrow[+1]{} P$

   Similarly, $Q \xrightarrow[+1]{} R \xrightarrow[+1]{} S \xrightarrow[+1]{} T$

3. (*b*) According to the question,

   $B > A > E$ ...(i)

   $C > B$ ...(ii)

   $B > D > A$ ...(iii)

   From Eqs. (i), (ii) and (iii), we get

   $\therefore \quad C > B > D > A > E$

   Thus, 'E' is the shortest.

4. (*d*) According to the question, we have

   P E N C I L
   ↓ ↓ ↓ ↓ ↓ ↓
   ? @ , = ; 7

   and

   P A P E R
   ↓ ↓ ↓ ↓ ↓
   ? 9 ? @ 5

   Using above given coding data

   C L I P
   ↓ ↓ ↓ ↓
   = 7 ; ?

   Hence, option (d) is correct.

5. (*b*) Each second space equals 1°.

   A clock gains five minutes every hour.

   It means the clock gains $\frac{5}{60}$ minutes in one minute.

   $\frac{5}{60} \times 360 = 30$

   The second hand will traverse 360.5° in one minute.

6. (*d*)

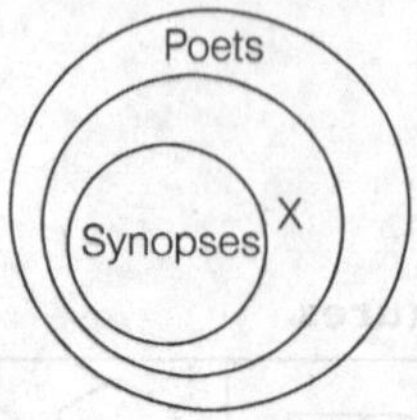

   It is clearly shown from the above figure that DFA is correct argument.

   D - All X are poets.   F - All synopses are X.

   A - All synopses are poets.

7. (*a*)

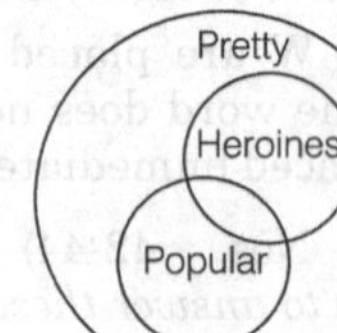

   It is clear from the above figure that ABE is valid argument.

   A - All heroines are pretty.

   B - Some heroines are popular.

   E - Some popular girls are pretty.

8. (*b*)

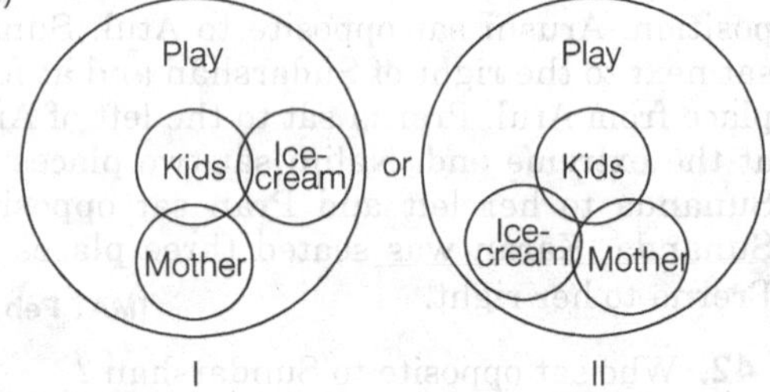

   Statement I

   'All kids who like ice-cream look like their mothers'. (✗)

   Statement II

   'Kids who like ice-cream also like to play'. (✔)

   Statement III

   'Kids who like to play do not look like their mothers'. (✗)

9. (*b*) All except quay are parts of a ship.

10. (*d*) Except 2014, all others are leap years.

    Note A year will be a leap year, if it is divisible by 4.

    i.e. $\frac{1876}{4} = 469 \qquad \frac{1984}{4} = 496$

    $\frac{2024}{4} = 506 \qquad \frac{2014}{4} = 503.5$

    So, 2014 is not divisible by 4. Thus, 2014 is not leap year.

11. (*b*) Ravi died because of the accident.

12. (*d*) The two statements seems to have contrary causes.

13. (*d*) According to the matrices,

    S - 55, 68, 76, (89), 97 ,   O - (03), 10, 21, 32, 44

    F - 00, (12), 23, 34, 41,   T - 56, 69, 77, 85, (98)

    $\therefore$ SOFT ⇒ 89, 03, 12, 98

14. (*d*) According to the question, we have B = 2 (the position number in English alphabet)

    M A T
    ↓ ↓ ↓
    13 + 1 + 20 = 34

Similarly, J O G L E X

$10 + 15 + 7 + 12 + 5 + 24 = \boxed{73}$

Hence, option (d) is correct.

15. (*e*)

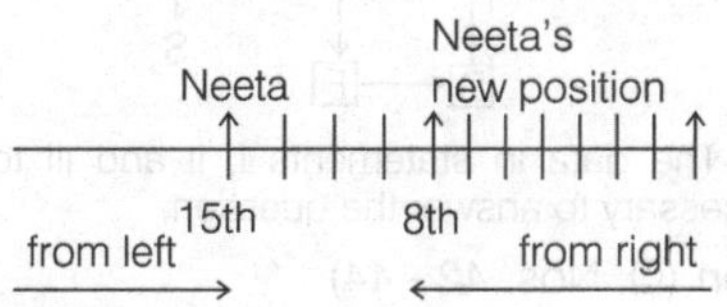

∴ Number of children in row

$= 15 + 8 + 3 = 26$

So, there are 26 children in the row.

16. (*a*) Required number of cuttings = AR^{n-1}

Here, $A = 2, R = 2$ and $n = 10$

$2 \times 2^{10-1} = 2 \times 2^9 = 1024$

17. (*a*) Only daughter of the lady's mother is the lady herself. So, the lady is the man's mother.

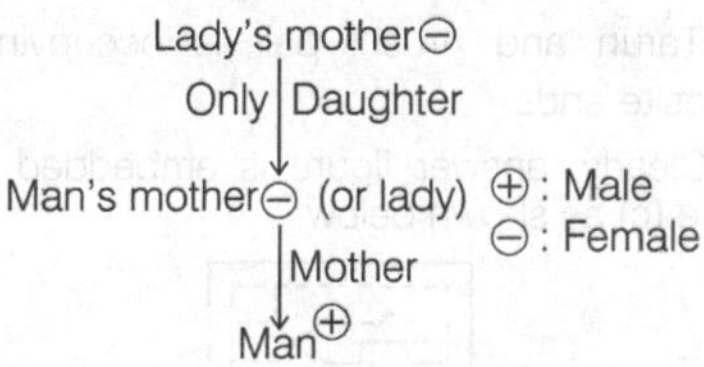

18. (*a*) Here, sequence of given letters and code are same for option (a).

So, code for given word TENTANT is 1421321.

19. (*c*)

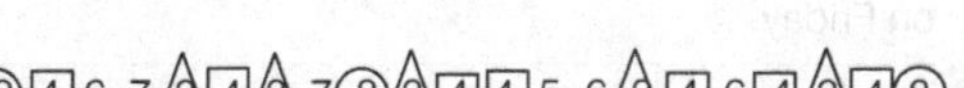

8 = 3 times, 7 = 2 times , 6 = 3 times , 5 = 1 times

4 = 7 times, 3 = 5 times

Clearly, 5 is minimum.

20. (*c*) The pattern is as follows

$0^3 - 0 = 0 \quad 2^3 - 2 = 6$

$3^3 - 3 = 24 \quad 4^3 - 4 = 60$

$5^3 - 5 = 120 \quad 6^3 - 6 = 210$

$7^3 - 7 = 336$

∴ ? = 336

21. (*d*) The pattern is as follows

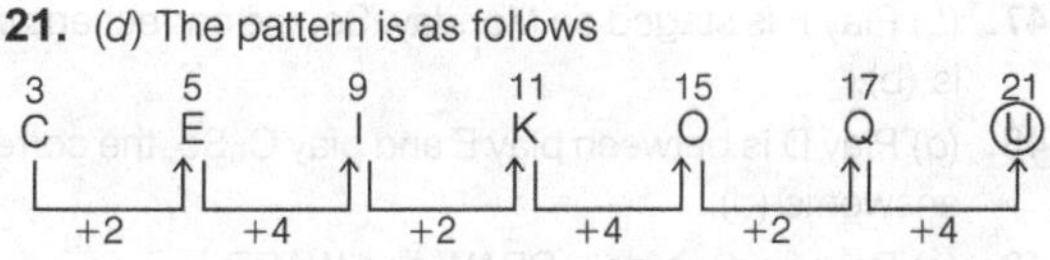

∴ ? = U

22. (*c*) The complete letter series will be

<u>m</u> bb/ m <u>a</u> a/ m b <u>b</u> / m <u>a</u> a / <u>m</u> b b ⇒ mabam

Hence, option (c) is correct.

23. (*c*) According to the statement,

G
||
K
IV
$Z \le H = N \le C \ge M > S$

Conclusions

I. $K > H$ (✗)
II. $H = K$ (✗) — Complementary pair

Hence, either Conclusion I or II is true.

24. (*a*) According to the statement,

G
||
K
IV
$Z \le H = N \le C \ge M > S$

Conclusions I. $Z \le C$ (✔)
II. $G > S$ (✔)

Hence, both Conclusions I and II are true.

25. (*a*) According to the statement,

D Q
IV IV
$B < L \le A = L \ge E$
^
O

Conclusions I. $Q \ge D$ (✔)
II. $E < O$ (✔)

Hence, both Conclusions I and II are true.

26. (*a*)

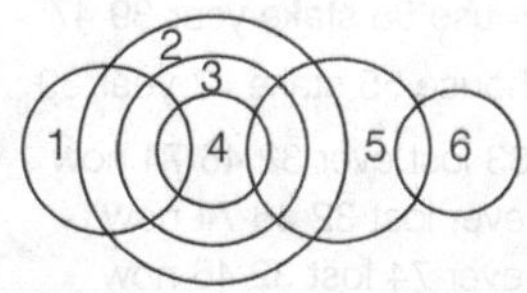

Clearly shown that, total number of circles = 6

27. (*d*) By putting signs,

$\Rightarrow 45 \div 9 \times 3 + 15 - 2$

$\Rightarrow 5 \times 3 + 15 - 2$

$\Rightarrow 15 + 15 - 2$

$\Rightarrow 30 - 2 \Rightarrow 28$

28. (*c*) The product of three numbers in each column is equal to lowermost number.

As, $3 \times 4 \times 4 = 48$

and, $4 \times 5 \times 3 = 60$

Similarly, $5 \times 3 \times ? = 105$

$\Rightarrow ? = \frac{105}{15} = 7$

29. (*c*) All lawyers are educated. All teachers are educated. Some lawyers may be teachers and *vice-versa*.

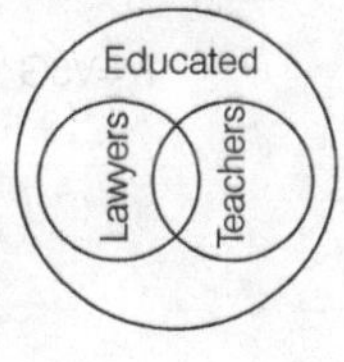

30. (*b*) Route followed by man,

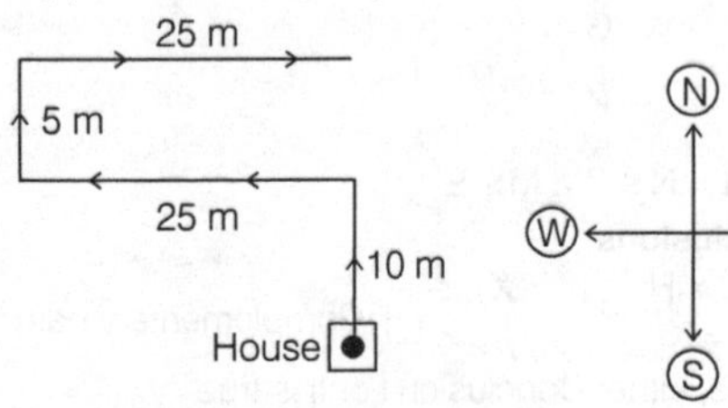

He is facing East direction.

31. (*d*) Three days before today was Friday.
Today is Monday.
Therefore, day after tomorrow will be Wednesday.

32. (*a*) Meaningful order
(i) Pulp → (iii) Paper → (ii) Print → (v) Publish → (iv) Purchase

33. (*b*) Number of cubes having three faces painted = Number of corner (vertex)cubes = 8 (always)

34. (*b*) **Input** year 39 stake 47 house full 94 55
***Step* I** full year 39 stake 47 house 94 55
***Step* II** full 94 year 39 stake 47 house 55
***Step* III** full 94 house year 39 stake 47 55
***Step* IV** full 94 house 55 year 39 stake 47
***Step* V** full 94 house 55 stake year 39 47
***Step* VI** full 94 house 55 stake 47 year 39

35. (*b*) ***Step* II** car 83 lost ever 32 46 74 now
***Step* III** car 83 ever lost 32 46 74 now
***Step* IV** car 83 ever 74 lost 32 46 now
***Step* V** car 83 ever 74 lost 46 32 now
***Step* VI** car 83 ever 74 lost 46 now 32
Hence, four steps are required to complete the rearrangement.

36. (*d*) **Input** cannot be determined

37. (*d*) India draffted its own constitution and formed its own goverment after gaining independence. Hence, A is false but R is true.

38. (*c*) Option (c) is correct answer.

39. (*d*) Pattern of given alpha-numeric series is as follows

$\overset{26}{Z} \xrightarrow{-2} \overset{24}{X} \xrightarrow{-2} \boxed{\overset{22}{V}} \xrightarrow{-2} \overset{20}{T} \xrightarrow{-2} \overset{18}{R}$

$9 \xrightarrow{-2} 7 \xrightarrow{-2} \boxed{5} \xrightarrow{-2} 3 \xrightarrow{-2} 1$

$\overset{1}{A} \xrightarrow{+3} \overset{4}{D} \xrightarrow{+3} \boxed{\overset{7}{G}} \xrightarrow{+3} \overset{10}{J} \xrightarrow{+3} \overset{13}{M}$

∴ ? =V5G

40. (*b*) From Statements I and III

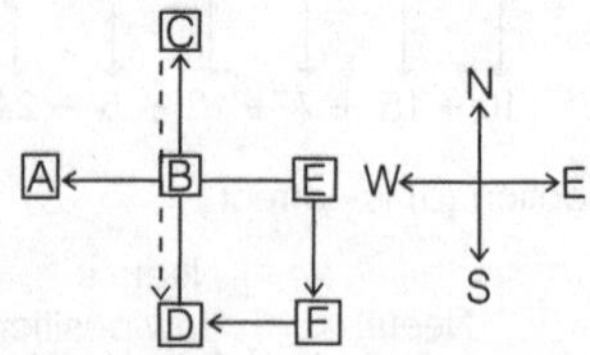

41. (e) The data in statements I, II and III together are necessary to answer the question.

Solution (Q. Nos. 42 - 44)

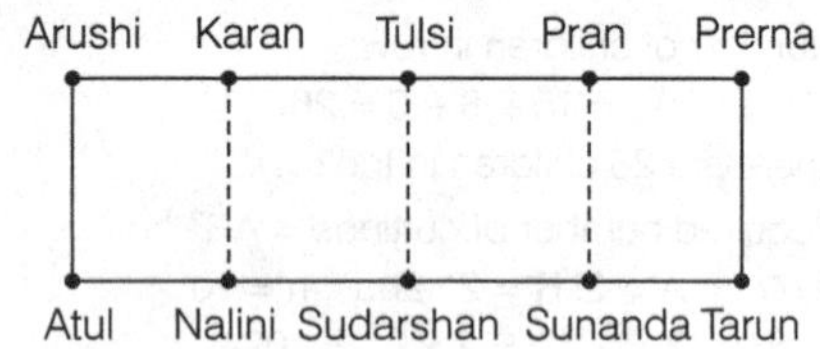

42. (*b*) Tulsi opposite to Sudarshan.

43. (*d*) Prerna sat opposite to Tarun.

44. (*a*) Tarun and Arushi pair is occupying diagonal opposite ends.

45. (*c*) Clearly, answer figure is embedded in question figure (c) as shown below

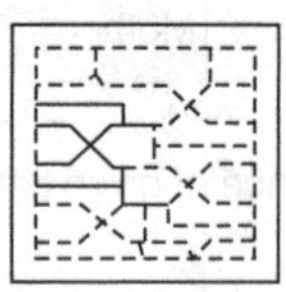

Solution (Q.Nos.46- 48) From (iv), play D will be staged on Friday.

Day	**Monday**	**Tuesday**	**Wednesday**	**Thursday**	**Friday**	**Saturday**
Play	F	B	A	E	D	C

From (i) and (iii), play E will follow play A and play B will follow play F. For these two pairs of plays two consecutive days available are Monday, Tuesday and Wednesday. Friday Again from (iv), play B cannot be immediately before play D. So, plays F and B will be staged on Monday and Tuesday respectively and plays A and E will be staged on Wednesday and Thursday.

46. (*b*) Play D is staged immediately after play E. So, the correct answer is (b).

47. (*b*) Play F is staged on Monday. So, the correct answer is (b).

48. (*d*) Play D is between play E and play C. So, the correct answer is (d).

49. (*c*) Required words = DRAW and WARD

50. (*b*) Option (b) is correct answer.

PRACTICE SET 38

1. If the letters in PRABA are coded as '27595' and THILAK are coded '368451', then how can BHARATHI be coded? **[SSC (Multitasking) 2011]**

(a) 96575368 (b) 57686535
(c) 96855368 (d) 37536689

2. In a certain code, STYLE is written as 'UVZJC' and 'BLUNT' is coded as 'DNVLR'. How is MOULD coded in that code? **[SBI SO (IT) 2016]**

(a) KMVNF (b) OQSNF
(c) OMSUB (d) KMTNF
(e) OQVJB

Direction (Q. Nos. 3-5) *Study the following information carefully and answer the given questions.*

S, T, U, V, W, X, Y and Z are sitting around a circular table facing the centre but not necessarily in the same order. S sits third to the right of T. Only three people sit between U and Y. U is neither an immediate neighbour of S nor T. Only three people sit between T and W. Z sits to the immediate right of W. V sits third to the left of W. **[IBPS Clerk (Pre) 2015]**

3. How many people are seated between S and Z, when counted from the right of S?

(a) None (b) Two
(c) Four (d) Three
(e) One

4. Who among the following sits second to the left of Y?

(a) T (b) X (c) W (d) Z
(e) S

5. Four of the following five are alike in a certain way based on their positions in the given arrangement and so form a group. Which is the one that does not belong to the group?

(a) UYV (b) TVY
(c) SWU (d) XSZ
(e) VXW

6. How many times does the number 8 occur between the numbers 1 and 99?

(a) 10 (b) 9
(c) 20 (d) 19

7. Which term will replace the question mark (?) in the series

ABD, DGK, HMS, MTB, SBL, ?

(a) ZKU (b) ZKW
(c) ZAB (d) XKW

8. Find the missing term in the given series. **[SSC (10+2) 2014]**

3, 15, 4, 16, 5, 17, 6, ? ,7

(a) 12 (b) 13 (c) 15 (d) 18

9. Which one set of letters when sequentially placed at the gaps in the given letter series shall complete it?

a_n_b_ _ ncb _ _ ncb

(a) bcabab (b) bacbab
(c) abcbcb (d) abbbcc

10. Which number will appear on the face opposite to 1? **[SSC (10 + 2) 2012]**

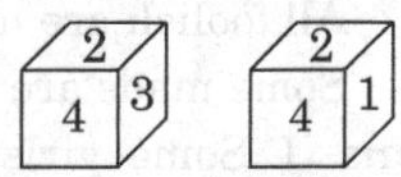

I II

(a) 6 (b) 5 (c) 4 (d) 3

11. In a family, a couple has a son and daughter. The age of the father is three times that of his daughter and age of the son is half, of his mother. The wife is 9 yr younger to her husband and the brother is 7 yr older than his sister. What is the age of the mother?

(a) 40 yr (b) 45 yr (c) 50 yr (d) 60 yr

Direction (Q. Nos. 12-14) *In these questions, select the related letter/word/number pair from the given alternatives.*

12. Poem : Poet : : Book : ? **[SSC (Steno) 2014]**

(a) Editor (b) Author
(c) Writer (d) Publisher

13. EGIK : LJHF : : SUWY : ? **[SSC (10+2) 2011]**

(a) ZXVT (b) TVXZ
(c) LNPR (d) MOQS

14. 2 : 8 : : 3 : ?

(a) 20 (b) 21
(c) 24 (d) 27

Direction (Q. Nos. 15-16) *In each of the questions below are given four statements followed by four conclusions numbered I, II, III and IV. You have to take the given statements to be true even if they seem to be at variance with commonly known facts. Read all the conclusions and then decide which of the given conclusion (s) logically follow (s) from the given statements disregarding commonly known facts.*

15. Statements Some doors are walls.
All walls are floors.
All floors are rooms.
Some rooms are windows.

Conclusions I. All walls are rooms.
II. Some rooms are doors.
III. Some rooms are walls.
IV. Some floor are doors.

(a) None follows (b) I and II follow
(c) II and III follow (d) II, III and IV follow
(e) All follow

16. Statements Some men are girls.
Some girls are foolish.
All foolish are mads.
Some mads are bads.

Conclusions I. Some girls are definitely mads.
II. Most of the mads are foolish.
III. At least some girls are men.
IV. All foolish except few are girls.

(a) None follows (b) Only I follows
(c) Only II follows (d) All follow
(e) II and III follow

17. A word is represented by only one set of numbers as given in anyone of the alternatives. The sets of numbers given in the alternatives are represented by two classes of alphabets as in two matrices given below. The columns and rows of Matrix I are numbered from 0 to 4 and that of Matrix II are numbered from 5 to 9. A letter from these matrices can be represented first by its row and next by its column, e.g. 'A' can be represented by 01, 13 etc., and 'E' can be represented by 56, 67, etc. Similarly, you have to identify the set for the word 'BOTH'.

Matrix I

	0	1	2	3	4
0	F	A	N	O	I
1	I	O	F	A	N
2	A	N	O	I	F
3	O	F	I	N	A
4	N	I	A	F	O

Matrix II

	5	6	7	8	9
5	S	E	H	B	T
6	H	S	E	T	B
7	B	T	S	E	H
8	E	H	T	B	S
9	T	S	E	H	B

(a) 88, 30, 85, 86 **[SSC (Steno) 2013]**
(b) 58, 02, 68, 65
(c) 69, 67, 68, 59
(d) 75, 22, 76, 79

Direction (Q. Nos. 18-19) *Find the odd numbers/ letters from the given alternatives.* **[SSC (CGL) 2013]**

18. (a) MORV (b) CEHL
(c) CENT (d) JLOS

19. (a) 272 (b) 210
(c) 240 (d) 304

Direction (Q. Nos. 20-21) *Study the following information and answer the given questions.*

D is the father of A. D is married to P. P is the mother of J. P has only one daughter. J is married to U. U is the son of L. **[IBPS PO/MT (Pre) 2015]**

20. How is J related to L.
(a) Daughter
(b) Granddaughter
(c) Cannot be determined
(d) Niece
(e) Daughter-in-law

21. How is A related to U?
(a) Cannot be determined
(b) Brother-in-law
(c) Brother
(d) Sister
(e) Sister-in-law

Direction (Q. Nos. 22-23) *In these questions, relationship between different elements is shown in the statements. These statements are followed by two conclusions.* **[RBI (Assistant) 2012]**

(a) if Conclusion I is true
(b) if Conclusion II is true
(c) if either Conclusion I or II is true
(d) if neither Conclusion I nor II is true
(e) if both Conclusions I and II are true

22. **Statements** $D > E \leq F, J < F$

Conclusions I. $D > J$ II. $E < J$

23. **Statements** $P < Q > T, R \geq Q$

Conclusions I. $R > P$ II. $T < R$

24. From the given alternatives, select the word which can be formed using the letters given in the word.

INTERNATIONAL

(a) ANNUAL (b) LAMINATION
(c) TERMINATE (d) INTERNAL

25. How many pairs of letters are there in these words which have as many letters between them as in the English alphabet?

JOURNEY

(a) None (b) One (c) Two (d) Three
(e) None of these

26. Select the set of symbols which can be fitted correctly in the equation.

5 _ 3 _ 8 _ 4 _ 2 = 21 **[SSC (10+2) 2015]**

(a) −, ×, +, ÷ (b) +, ×, −, ÷
(c) ×, +, −, ÷ (d) +, ×, +, ÷

Direction (Q. Nos. 27-28) *Find the missing number from the given responses.*

27.

12	6	8
3	2	?
9	10	5
13	13	13

(a) 1 (b) 0 (c) 10 (d) 11

28.

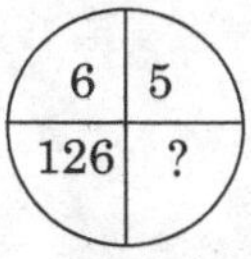

(a) 127 (b) 31 (c) 217 (d) 328

Direction (Q. Nos. 29-30) *In each of the questions below is given a statement followed by two courses of action numbered* I *and* II. *A course of action is a step or an administrative decision to be taken for improvement, follow-up or further action in regard to the problem, policy etc. On the basis of the information given in the statement, you have to assume everything in the statement to be true, then decide which of the suggested courses of action logically follow (s) worth pursuing.*

Give answer
(a) if only I follows
(b) if only II follows
(c) if either I or II follows
(d) if neither I nor II follows
(e) if both I and II follow

29. **Statement** While laying pipelines by one of the utility companies a huge fire broke out due to damage done to the pipeline.

Courses of Action

I. All the licences of the utility company should immediately be suspended pending enquiry into the incident.

II. People residing in the area should be advised to stay indoors to avoid burn injuries.

30. **Statement** There has been large number of internet hacking in the recent months creating panic among the internet users.

Courses of Action

I. The Government machinery should make an all out effort to check those who are responsible and put them behind bars.

II. The internet users should be advised to stay away from using internet till the culprits are caught.

Direction (Q. Nos. 31-32) *Each of the questions below consists of a question and two statements numbered* I *and* II *given below it. You have to decide whether the data provided in the statements are sufficient to answer the question.*

Give answer
(a) if the data in Statement I alone is sufficient to answer the question, while the data in Statement II alone is not sufficient to answer the question
(b) if the data in Statement II alone is sufficient to answer the question, while the data in Statement I alone is not sufficient to answer the question
(c) if the data either in Statement I alone or in Statement II alone is sufficient to answer the question
(d) if the data in both the Statements I and II together are not sufficient to answer the question
(e) if the data in both the Statements I and II together are necessary to answer the question

31. How many sisters does Priya have?

I. Rohan, Priya's brother has only two siblings.

II. Priya's grandparents have two children and two granddaughters.

32. On which day of the week was Shahid born?

I. Shahid's mother correctly mentions that he was born before Friday and after Tuesday.

II. Shahid's father correctly remembers that Shahid was not born on a Wednesday.

33. Which one of the given responses would be a meaningful order of the following words in ascending order?

(i) Cure (ii) Doctor
(iii) Disease (iv) Diagnosis
(v) Medicine **[FCI Assistant Grade II 2012]**

(a) (ii), (iv), (iii), (v), (i)
(b) (iii), (ii), (iv), (v), (i)
(c) (iv), (ii), (iii), (v), (i)
(d) (iv), (iii), (ii), (v), (i)

34. If it is possible to make only one meaningful English word with the second, third, sixth and ninth letters of the word REGULATOR (using each letter only once in the words) which would be the second letter of the word from right? If more than one such word can be formed give 'Y' as the answer. If no such word can be formed give 'Z' as your answer. **[SBI SO (IT) 2016]**

(a) 0 km (b) 10 km (c) 20 km (d) 30 km

35. The day before yesterday was Sunday. What will be the day after tomorrow?

(a) Monday (b) Thursday
(c) Friday (d) Saturday

Direction (Q. Nos. 36-38) *Read the following information carefully and answer the given questions.*

Six friends Abhishek, Deepak, Mridul, Pritam, Ranjan and Salil married within a year in the months of February, April, July, September, November and December and in the cities of Ahmedabad, Bengaluru, Chennai, Delhi, Mumbai and Kolkata, but not necessarily following the above order. The brides' names were Geetika, Jasmine, Hema, Brinda, Ipsita and Veena, once again not following any order. The following are some facts about their weddings.

- Mridul's wedding took place in Chennai, however he was not married to Geetika or Veena.
- Abhishek's wedding took place in Ahmedabad and Ranjan's in Delhi; however neither of them was married to Jasmine or Brinda.
- The wedding in Kolkata took place in February.
- Hema's wedding took place in April, but not in Ahmedabad.
- Geetika and Ipsita got married in February and November and in Chennai and Kolkata but not following the above order.
- Pritam visited Bengaluru and Kolkata only after his marriage in December.
- Salil was married to Jasmine in September.

36. Hema's husband is

(a) Abhishek (b) Deepak
(c) Ranjan (d) Pritam

37. Deepak's wedding took place in

(a) Bengaluru (b) Mumbai
(c) Kolkata (d) Delhi

38. In Mumbai, the wedding of one of the friends took place in the months of

(a) April (b) September
(c) November (d) December

39. Find out the answer figure which completes the question figure matrix.

Question Figure

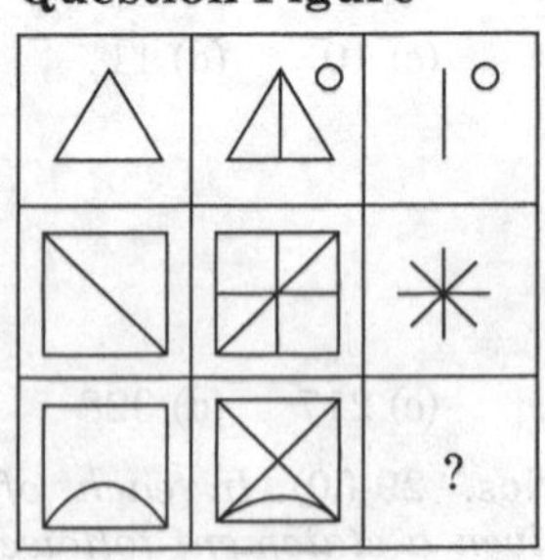

Answer Figures

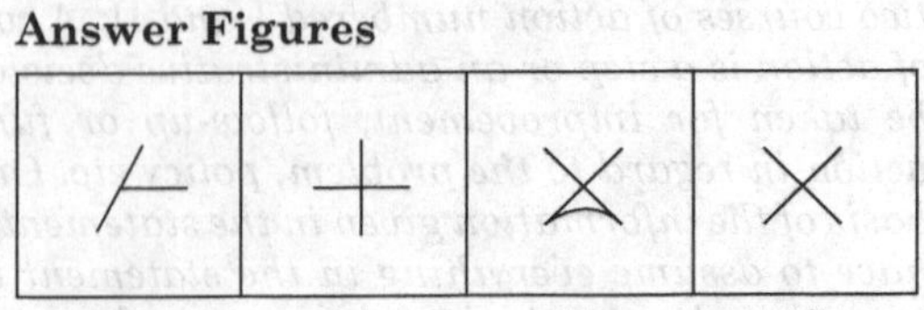

(a) (b) (c) (d)

40. Find the figure out of the answer choices figures that can be formed by joining the pieces given in the question figure.

Question Figure

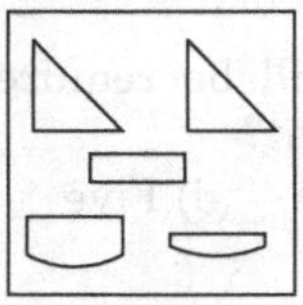

(X)

Answer Figures

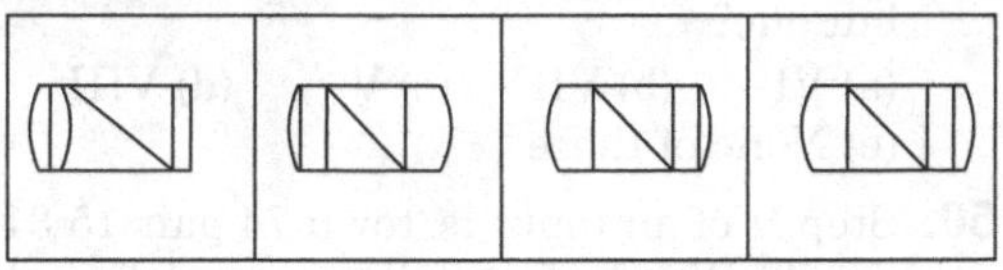

(a) (b) (c) (d)

41. Which number represents the women doctors who are not employed? **[SSC (10+2) 2011]**

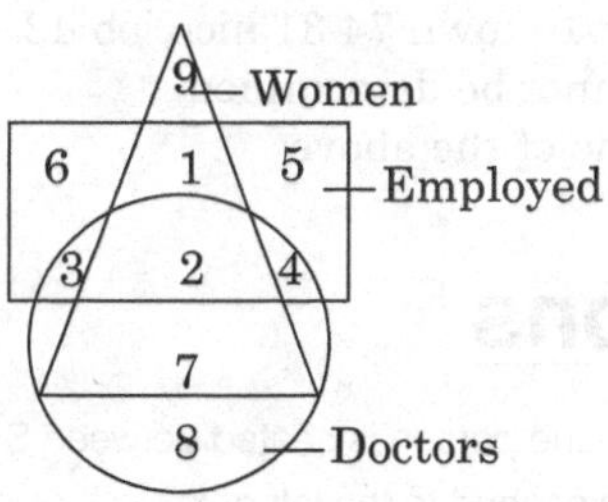

(a) 7 (b) 3 (c) 1 (d) 8

42. How many squares are there in the following figure?

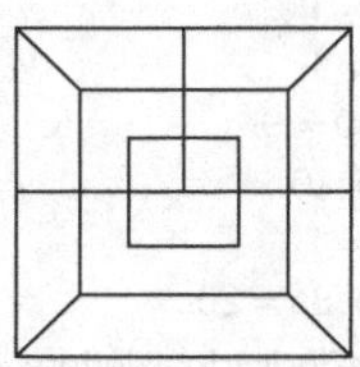

(a) 5 (b) 9 (c) 7 (d) 8

Direction (Q. Nos. 43-44) *Study the information carefully and answer the given questions.*

L, M, N, O and P are five different poles, each of different length. O is not the third shortest pole. N is bigger than only P. L is shorter than only one pole. The size of the shortest pole is 7ft and that of the second tallest pole is 13ft.

[IBPS (PO/MT) Mains 2015]

43. Which of the following poles is the third tallest?

(a) M (b) Cannot be determined
(c) N (d) P
(e) L

44. According to the given arrangement, which of the following combinations of pole and length is correct?

(a) N–14 ft (b) P–5 ft
(c) O–12 ft (d) L–13 ft
(e) Other than those given as options

45. In this question, there are two statements labelled as Assertion (A) and Reason (R).

Assertion (A) Increase in carbon dioxide would melt polar ice.

Reason (R) Global temperature would rise.

(a) if both 'A' and 'R' are true and 'R' is the correct explanation of 'A'
(b) if both 'A' and 'R' are true but 'R' is not the correct explanation of 'A'
(c) if 'A' is true but 'R' is false
(d) if 'A' is false but 'R' is true
(e) if both 'A' and 'R' are false

46. Find out which of the answer figures (a), (b), (c) and (d) completes the figure matrix?

Question Figure

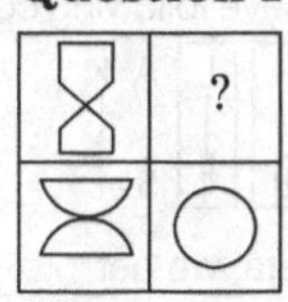

Answer Figures

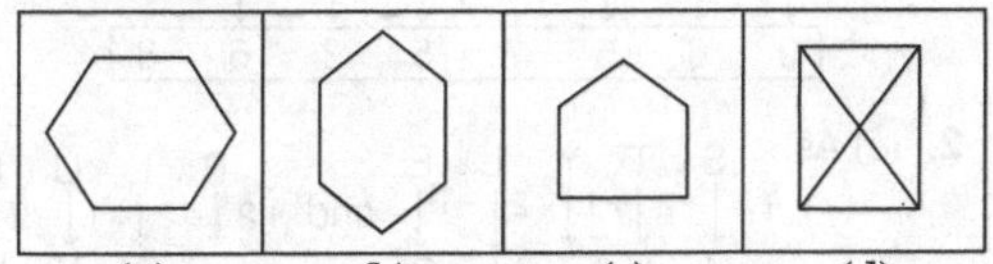

(a) (b) (c) (d)

47. Identify the missing part of the question figure and select it from given answer figures.

Question Figure **[SSC (10+2) 2011]**

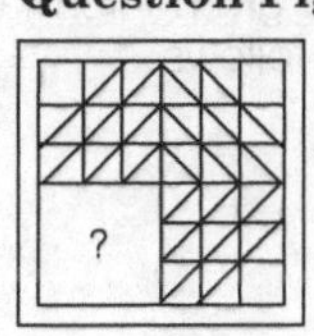

Answer Figures

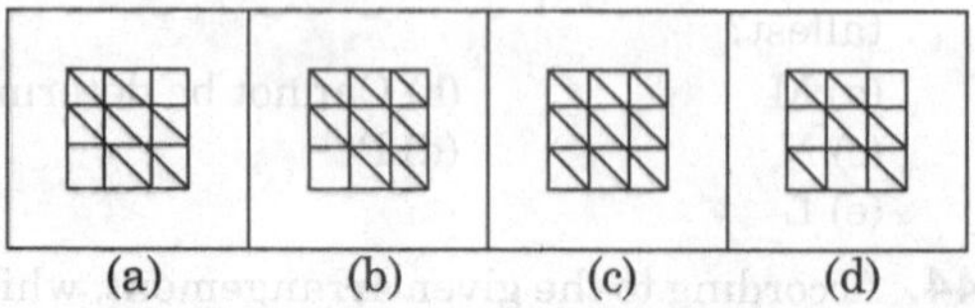

Direction (Q. Nos. 48-50) *Study the following information carefully and answer the given questions.*

A word and number arrangement machine when given an input line of words and numbers rearrange them following a particular rule in each step. The following is an illustration of input and rearrangement.

Input but 32 71 glory fair south 65 84
***Step* I** south but 32 71 glory fair 65 84
***Step* II** south 84 but 32 71 glory fair 65
***Step* III** south 84 glory but 32 71 fair 65
***Step* IV** south 84 glory 71 but 32 fair 65
***Step* V** south 84 glory 71 fair but 32 65
***Step* VI** south 84 glory 71 fair 65 but 32

and Step VII is the last step of the rearrangement.

As per the rules of followed in the above steps, find out in each of the following questions the appropriate step for the given input.

48. Step III of an input is 'year 92 ultra 15 23 strive house 39'.

How many more steps will be required to complete the rearrangement?

(a) Three (b) Four (c) Two (d) Five
(e) None of these

49. Input 'any how 49 24 for wide 34 69'.

Which of the following steps will be the last but one?

(a) VI (b) VII (c) V (d) VIII
(e) None of these

50. Step II of an input is 'town 74 pair 15 31 nice job 42'. Which of the following is definitely the input?

(a) pair 15 31 town nice job 42 74
(b) pair 15 town 31 74 nice job 42
(c) pair 15 town 74 31 nice job 42
(d) Cannot be determined
(e) None of the above

Hints and Solutions

1. (*a*) According to the question, we have following coding

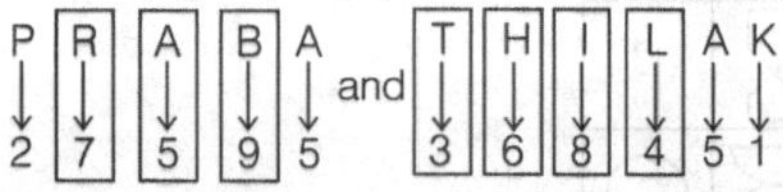

After using above given coding data, we get

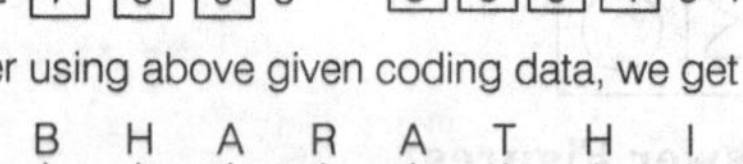

2. (*e*) As,

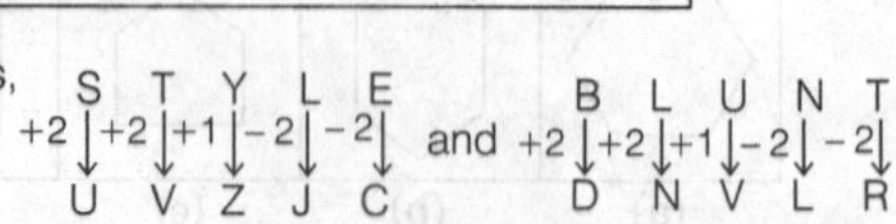

Similarly,

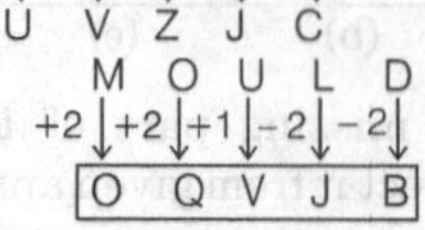

Solution (Q. Nos. 3-6) From the given information, the seating arrangement will be as follows

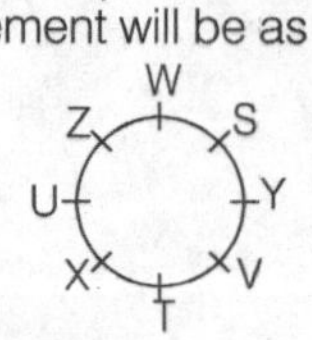

3. (*e*) Only one person is seated between S and Z.

4. (*a*) T sits second to the left of Y.

5. (*b*) Only T, V and Y are seated together.

6. (*c*) From 1 to 10 = 1
From 11 to 20 = 1
From 21 to 30 = 1
i.e. From 1 to 80 = 9
From 81 to 90 = 10
From 91 to 99 = 1
Total number of 8s = 20

7. (*b*) Clearly, the individual letters of the terms of the given series follow the pattern shown below

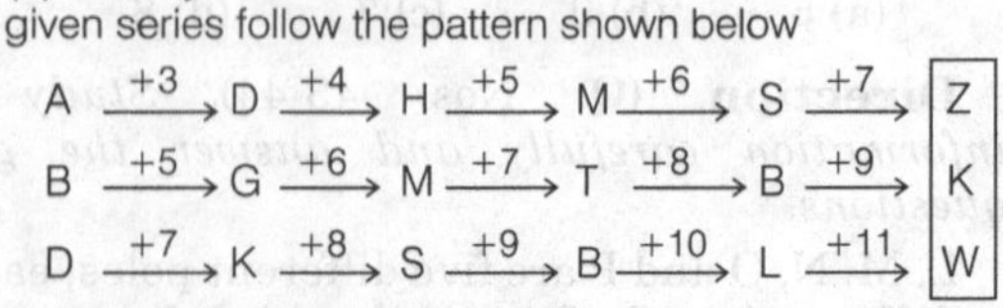

Thus, the missing term is ZKW.

8. (*d*) From the given series,

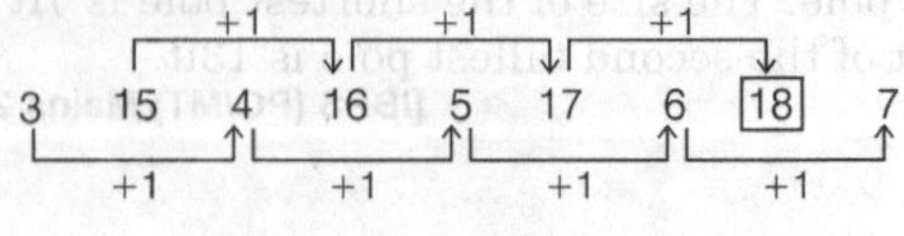

9. (*a*) The complete letter series will be

a b̲ n c̲ b / a̲ b̲ n c b / a̲ b̲ n c b ⇒ bcabab

10. (*d*) Dice I → 234
Dice II → 214

So, opposite side of 1 is 3.

11. (*d*) Let the mother's age be *x* yr.

∴ The age of father = $(x + 9)$ yr

The age of son = $\frac{x}{2}$ yr

The age of daughter = $\left(\frac{x}{2} - 7\right)$ yr

Now, according to the questions,

$$x + 9 = 3\left(\frac{x}{2} - 7\right) \Rightarrow x + 9 = \frac{3x - 42}{2}$$

$$\Rightarrow 2x + 18 = 3x - 42 \Rightarrow x = 60$$

Hence, mother's age will be 60 yr.

12. (*b*) As, poet writers the poem, in the same way, Author writes the book.

13. (*a*) As,

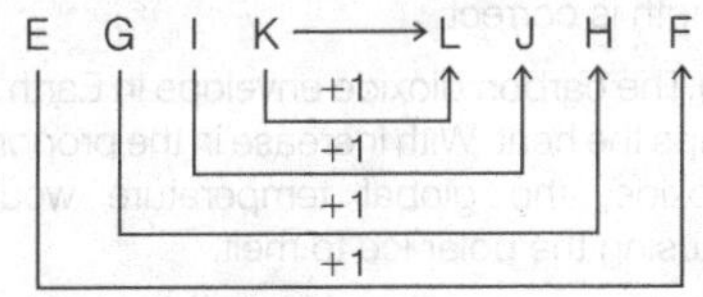

Similarly,

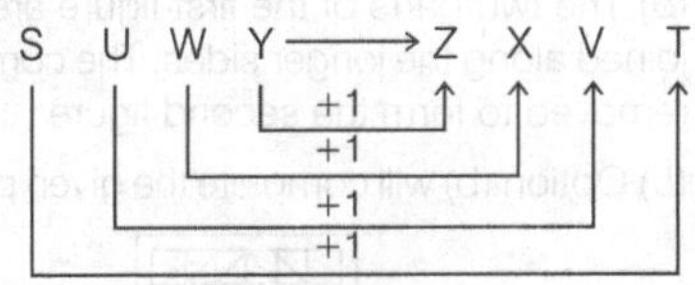

∴ ? = ZXVT

14. (*d*) Second number is the cube of first number. Hence, 3 : 27, As 27 is the cube of 3.

15. (*e*)

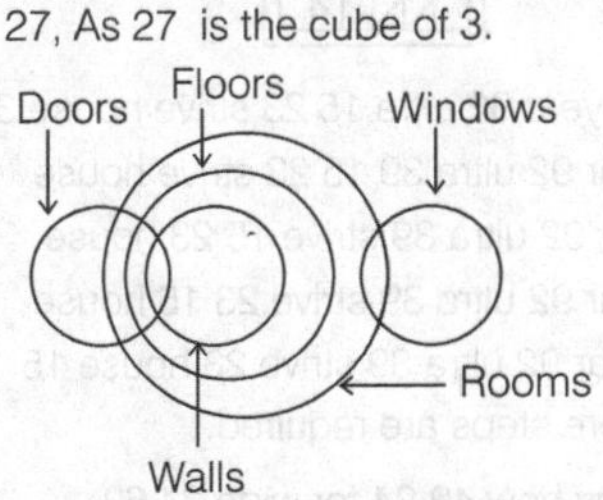

Conclusions I. All walls are rooms. (✔)
II. Some rooms are doors. (✔)
III. Some rooms are walls. (✔)
IV. Some floors are doors. (✔)

16. (d)

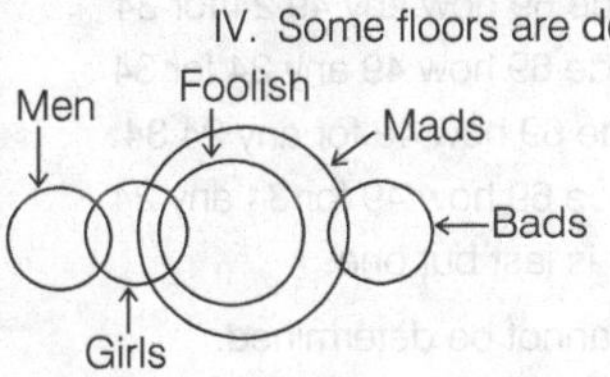

Conclusions I. Some girls are definitely mads. (✔)
II. Most of the mads are foolish. (✔)
III. Atleast some girls are men. (✔)
IV. All foolish except few are girls. (✔)

17. (*d*) According to the matrices,

B — 58, 69, (75), 88, 99 O — 03, 11, (22), 30, 44

T — 59, 68, (76), 87, 95 H — 57, 65, (79), 86, 98

∴ BOTH ⇒ 75, 22, 76, 79

18. (*c*) In the given options (a), (b) and (d) the 2nd letters is obtained by adding '2' in 1st letter. 3rd letter is obtained by adding '3' in 2nd letter and 4th letter is obtained by adding '4' in the 3rd letter. But option (c) is not following the sequence. Hence, it is 'odd' from other options.

19. (*c*) As, $272 = 2 + 7 + 2 = 11 \Rightarrow 210 = 2 + 1 + 0 = 3$
$240 = 2 + 4 + 0 = 6 \Rightarrow 304 = 3 + 0 + 4 = 7$

The sum of digits of all number except 240 is a prime number, whereas sum of number 240 digit is a non-prime. Hence, it is different from all other options.

Solution (Q. Nos. 20-21) According to the question,

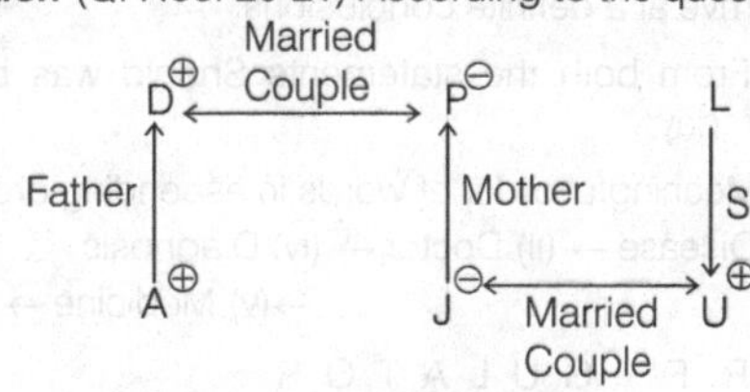

20. (*e*) J is the daughter-in-law of L.

21. (b) A is the brother-in-law of U.

22. (*d*) Given that, D > E ≤ F ... (i)
and J < F ... (ii)

On combining the Statements (i) and (ii), we get

D > E ≤ F > J

Conclusions I. D > J (False)
II. E < J (False)

So, neither Conclusion I nor II is true.

23. (*e*) Given that, P < Q > T ... (i)
and R ≥ Q ... (ii)

On combining the Statements (i) and (ii), we get

P < Q ≤ R and R ≥ Q > T

Conclusions I. R > P (True)
II. T < R (True)

So, it is clear that both Conclusions I and II are true.

24. (*d*) Word INTERNAL can be formed by using the letters of the given word.

25. (*d*)

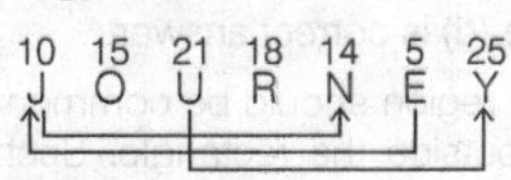

∴ Such pairs = JN, UY, EJ ⇒ Three

26. (*c*) From option (c)

$$5 \times 3 + 8 - 4 \div 2 = 21 \Rightarrow 5 \times 3 + 8 - 2 = 21$$

$$\Rightarrow 15 + 8 - 2 = 21$$

$$\Rightarrow 23 - 2 = 21$$

$$\Rightarrow 21 = 21$$

27. (*a*) As, $\frac{12}{3} = 4$ and $4 + 9 = 13$

$\frac{6}{2} = 3$ and $3 + 10 = 13$

Similarly, $\frac{8}{1} = 8$ and $8 + 5 = 13$

28. (*c*) $(5)^3 + 1 = 125 + 1 = 126$

$(6)^3 + 1 = 216 + 1 = 217$

29. (*b*) It is an accident and hence suspending licence of other utilities for this happening is not a right course of action. However, instructions should be given to the people to remain inside their houses.

30. (*a*) Only Course of action I is appropriate.

31. (*d*) The data given in both statements are not sufficient to arrive at a definite conclusions.

32. (*e*) From both the statements Shahid was born on Thursday.

33. (*b*) Meaningful order of words in ascending order :

(iii) Disease → (ii) Doctor → (iv) Diagnosis →(v) Medicine → (i) Cure

34. (*d*) R E G U L A T O R

E ↓ 2nd, G ↓ 3rd, A ↓ 6th, R ↓ 9th

Meaningfull word = GEAR, RAGE, GARE, AGER

35. (*d*) Today is Tuesday. Therefore, the day after tomorrow would be Thursday.

Solution (Q. Nos. 36-38) On the basis of given information, we get the following table.

Months	February	April	July	September	November	December
Cities	Kolkata	Delhi	Ahmedabad	Bengaluru	Chennai	Mumbai
Friends	Deepak	Ranjan	Abhishek	Salil	Mridul	Pritam
Brides	Geetika	Hema	Veena	Jasmine	Ipsita	Brinda

36. (*c*) Hema's husband is Ranjan.

37. (*c*) Deepak's wedding took place in Kolkata.

38. (*d*) In Mumbai, the wedding of Pritam took place in December.

39. (*d*) The third figure in each row comprises of parts which are not common to the first two figures.

40. (*d*) Option figure (d) is correct answer.

41. (*a*) The required region should be common to triangle and circle but outside the rectangle. Such region is marked as 7.

42. (*b*) The figure in question has been marked as shown in the following figure

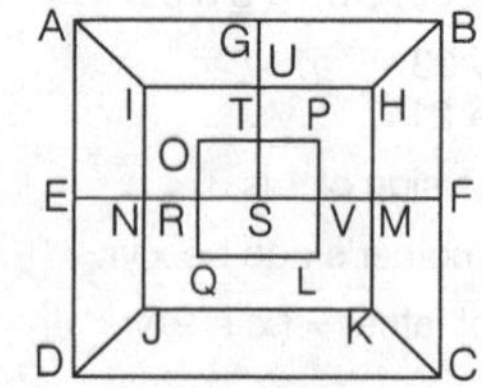

Clearly, there are total nine squares in the figure namely; □ABCD, □AGSE, □GBFS, □IUSN, □UHMS, □OTSR, □TPVS, □IHKJ and □OPLQ.

∴ Total number of squares = 9

Solution (Q. Nos. 43-44) According to the given information, the arrangement of five different poles is as below.

O > L > M > N > P

13ft 7ft

43. (*a*) M is the third tallest.

44. (*d*) L–13 ft is the following combinations of pole and length is correct.

45. (*a*) The carbon dioxide envelope in Earth's atmosphere traps the heat. With increase in the proportion of carbon dioxide, the global temperature would rise, thus causing the polar ice to melt.

46. (*b*) The two parts of the first figure are rearranged and joined along the longer sides. The common side is then removed to form the second figure.

47. (*b*) Option (b) will complete the given pattern as follows.

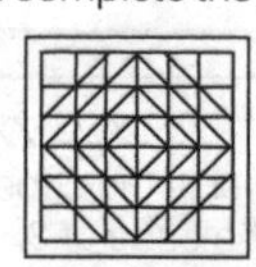

48. (*b*) ***Step*** **III** year 92 ultra 15 23 strive house 39

Step **IV** year 92 ultra 39 15 23 strive house

Step **V** year 92 ultra 39 strive 15 23 house

Step **VI** year 92 ultra 39 strive 23 15 house

Step **VII** year 92 ultra 39 strive 23 house 15

So, four more steps are required.

49. (*c*) **Input** any how 49 24 for wide 34 69

Step **I** wide any how 49 24 for 34 69

Step **II** wide 69 any how 49 24 for 34

Step **III** wide 69 how any 49 24 for 34

Step **IV** wide 69 how 49 any 24 for 34

Step **V** wide 69 how 49 for any 24 34

Step **VI** wide 69 how 49 for 34 any 24

So, Step V is last but one.

50. (*d*) Input cannot be determined.

PRACTICE SET 39

Direction (Q. Nos. 1-2) *In the following questions, select the related letters/number pair from the given alternatives.*

1. 08 : 28 : : 15 : ? **[SSC (Constable) 2012]**
(a) 63 (b) 65 (c) 126 (d) 124

2. MUMBAI : LTLAZH : : DELHI : ?
(a) CDKGG (b) IHLED
(c) CDKGH (d) BCKGH

Direction (Q. Nos. 3-4) *In the following questions, find the odd word/letters from the given alternatives.*

3. (a) ONRQ (b) HIKL **[SBI SO (IT) 2016]**
(c) UTXW (d) BAED
(e) KJNM

4. (a) Play — Actor
(b) Building — Architect
(c) Craft — Artisan
(d) Cloth — Skirt

5. If in a certain code MOTHER is coded as NPUIFS, then ZENITH will be coded as **[BSSC (CGL) 2015]**
(a) AFOGHJ (b) BGPKVJ
(c) AFOJUI (d) AFOGHI

6. In a certain code language, 'avoid going out' is coded as '319'. Similarly 'going for party' is coded as '612' and 'out' for party is coded as '362'. What will be the code for 'party' in the given code language? **[IBPS Clerk (Pre) 2015]**
(a) 3 (b) 1
(c) 9 (d) Either 3 or 1
(e) Either 2 or 6

7. If it is possible to make only one meaningful word from the 1st, the 3rd, the 6th and the 8th letters of the word 'EXAMINATION', using each letter only once, 1st letter of that word is your answer. If more than one such word can be formed your answer is 'X' and if no such word can be formed your answer is 'Y'.
(a) A (b) T
(c) N (d) X
(e) Y

8. From the given alternative words, select the word which cannot be formed using the letters of the given word. **[SSC (10+2) 2011]**
COLLABORATION
(a) ACTION (b) BILL
(c) BORN (d) CRITERION

9. An accurate clock shows 8 O' clock in the morning through how many degrees will the hour hand rotate when the clock shows 2 O' clock in the afternoon?
(a) 150° (b) 144°
(c) 168° (d) 180°

10. Kartik start moving from a point, facing in East direction. After walking 10 m, he turned to his left and walked 20 m, before turning to his right. Then, he walked a distance of 15 m, then turned to his right and stop after walking further a distance of 20m. Find how far Kartik is from his starting point. **[CMAT 2015]**
(a) 20 m (b) 30 m
(c) 15 m (d) 25 m

Direction (Q. Nos. 11-13) *Study the following information to answer the given questions.*

S, T, U, V, W, X, Y and Z are seated in a straight line but not necessarily in the same order. Some of them are facing South while some are facing North. S sits fourth to left of X. X sits at one of the extreme ends of the line.

Both the immediate neighbours of S face North. T sits second to left of Z. Z is not an immediately neighbour of S. Neither Z nor U sits at the extreme end of the line. Both the immediate neighbours of U face North. W sits to immediate left of Y.

Immediate neighbours of V face opposite directions (i.e. if one neighbour of V faces North then the other faces South and *vice-versa*). Immediate neighbours of T face opposite directions (i.e. if one neighbours of T faces North then the other faces South and *vice-versa*). People sitting at the extreme ends face the opposite directions (i.e. if one person faces North, then the other faces South and *vice-versa*).

[IBPS (PO/MT) Mains 2015]

11. Which of the following pairs represents immediate neighbours of the persons seated at the two extreme ends of the line?
(a) Y, X (b) T, Y
(c) W, Z (d) U, Z
(e) S, T

12. How many persons are seated between T and X?
(a) Four (b) More than four
(c) One (d) Three
(e) Two

13. If each of the persons is made to sit in alphabetical order from right to left the positions of how many will remain unchanged as compared to the original seating arrangement?
(a) One (b) Two
(c) Four (d) None
(e) Three

14. 1/2 of a number is greater than 1/3 of that number by 17. What is the number?
(a) 54 (b) 84
(c) 102 (d) 112

Direction (Q. Nos. 15-17) *Study the following information to answer the given questions.*

(i) In a family of 6 persons, there are two couples.
(ii) The Lawyer is the head of the family and has only two sons Mukesh and Rakesh both Teachers.
(iii) Mrs. Reena and her mother-in-law both are Lawyers.
(iv) Mukesh's wife is a Doctor and they have a son, Ajay.

15. Which of the following is definitely a couple?
(a) Lawyer-Teacher
(b) Doctor-Lawyer
(c) Teacher-Teacher
(d) Cannot be determined
(e) None of the above

16. What is the profession of Rakesh's wife?
(a) Teacher
(b) Doctor
(c) Lawyer
(d) Cannot be determined
(e) None of the above

17. How many male members are there in the family?
(a) Two
(b) Three
(c) Four
(d) Cannot be determined
(e) None of the above

18. In this questions, there are two statements labelled as Assertion (A) and Reason (R).
Assertion (A) Aurangzeb failed in his Deccan policy.
Reason (R) He could not follow the policy of appeasement.
(a) if both 'A' and 'R' are true and 'R' is the correct explanation of 'A'
(b) if both 'A' and 'R' are true but 'R' is not the correct explanation of 'A'
(c) if 'A' is true but 'R' is false
(d) if 'A' is false but 'R' is true
(e) if both 'A' and 'R' are false

19. Find the figure out of the answer choice figure that can be formed by joining the pieces given in the question figure.

Question Figure

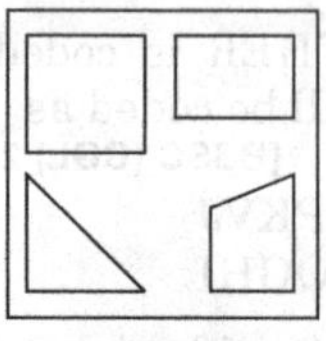

Answer Figures

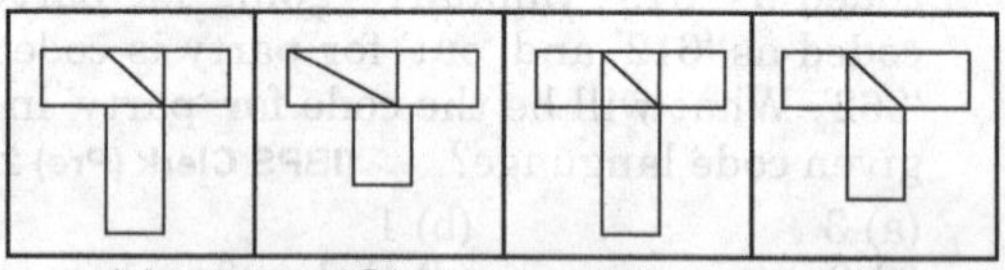

(a) (b) (c) (d)

20. Vinay remembers that his brother Anupam's birthday is after 20th of August but before 28th of August, while Rita remembers that Anupam's birthday is before 22nd of August but after 12th of August. On which date does Anupam's birthday fall?
(a) 20th August
(b) 21th August
(c) 22nd August
(d) Cannot be determined
(e) None of the above

21. Find out the answer figure which completes the question figure matrix.

Question Figure

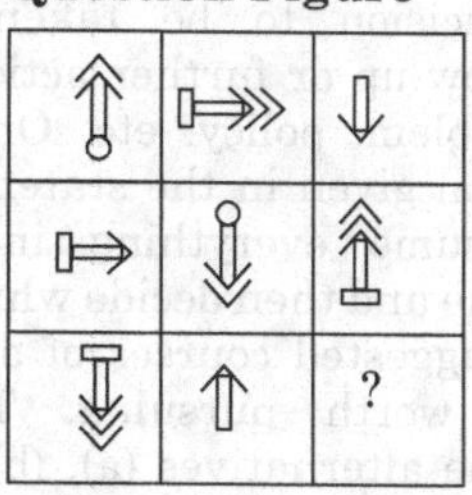

Answer Figures

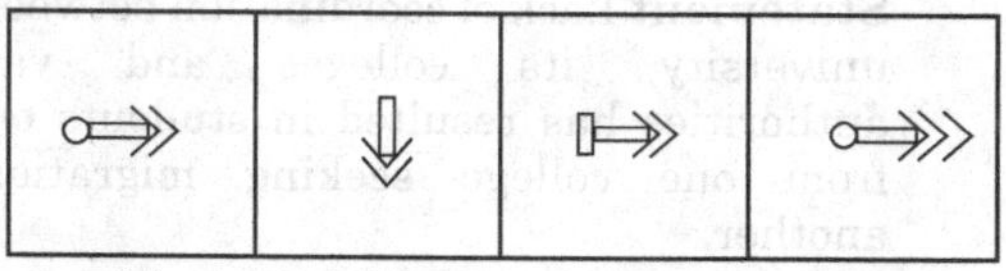

(a) (b) (c) (d)

Direction (Q. Nos. 22-23) *In the following questions, a series is given with one term missing. Choose the correct alternatives from the given ones that will complete the series.*

22. 230, 246, 271, 307, ?

(a) 412 (b) 356
(c) 518 (d) 612

23. C-3, E-5, G-7, I-9, ?, ? **[SSC (CGL) 2013]**

(a) X-24, M-21 (b) K-11, M-13
(c) O-15, X-24 (d) M-18, K-14

24. Which one set of letters when sequentially placed at the gaps in the given letters series shall complete it?

ba_b_aab_a_b

(a) abaa (b) abba
(c) baab (d) babb

Direction (Q. Nos. 25-28) *Study the following information carefully and answer the given questions.* **[IBPS Clerk 2011]**

When an input line of words and numbers is given to a word and number arrangement machine, it rearranges them following a particular rule in each step. The following is an illustration of input and rearrangement. (All the numbers are two-digit numbers).

Input pink for 25 72 white jar 12 96
***Step* I** 96 pink for 25 72 white jar 12
***Step* II** 96 for pink 25 72 white jar 12
***Step* III** 96 for 72 pink 25 white jar 12
***Step* IV** 96 for 72 jar pink 25 white 12
***Step* V** 96 for 72 jar 25 pink white 12
***Step* VI** 96 for 72 jar 25 pink 12 white

Step VI is the last step of the rearrangement as the desired arrangement is reached.

As per the rules followed in the above steps, find out in each of the following questions the appropriate step for the given input. (All the numbers are two-digit numbers).

25. Input '16 power failure 61 53 new cost 27'

How many steps will be required to complete the rearrangement?

(a) Six (b) Seven
(c) Five (d) Four
(e) None of these

26. Step II of an input is '84 ask quit these 39 12 old 51'.

Which of the following will definitely be the input?

(a) quit these 39 12 old 84 ask 51
(b) quit these 39 12 old 51 84 ask
(c) quit 84 these ask 39 12 old 51
(d) Cannot be determined
(e) None of the above

27. Step III of an input is '63 bed 58 never go home 46 28'.

How many more steps will be required to complete the rearrangement?

(a) Four (b) Three
(c) Five (d) Six
(e) None of these

28. Input 'rows 25 columns 39 46 fear star 72'.

Which of the following will be the last step?

(a) V (b) VI
(c) VII (d) VIII
(e) None of these

29. A painted cube having 25 cm side is divided into smaller cubes of 5 cm side. How many smaller cube have atleast two faces painted?

(a) 40 (b) 44
(c) 48 (d) 50

Direction (Q. Nos. 30-31) *Each of the questions below consists of a question and three statements numbered I, II and III given below it. You have to decide whether the data provided in the statements are sufficient to answer the questions.*

[IBPS Bank PO/MT 2012]

Give answer

(a) if the data in Statements I and II are sufficient to answer the question, while the data in Statement III are not required to answer the question
(b) if the data in Statement I and III are sufficient to answer the question, while the data in Statement II are not required to answer the question
(c) if the data in Statements II and III are sufficient to answer the question, while the data in Statement I are not required to answer the question
(d) if the data in either Statement I alone or Statement II alone or Statement III alone are sufficient to answer the question
(e) if the data in all the Statement I, II and III together are necessary to answer the question

30. Among six people P, Q, R, S, T and V each lives on a different floor of a six storey building having six floors numbered one to six (the ground floor is numbered 1, the floor above it, number 2 and so on and the topmost floor is numbered 6). Who lives on the topmost floor?

I. There is only one floor between the floors on which R and Q live. P lives on an even numbered floor.
II. T does not live on an even numbered floor. Q lives on an even numbered floor. Q does not live on the topmost floor.
III. S lives on an odd numbered floor. There are two floors between the floors on which S and P live. T lives on a floor immediately above R's floor.

31. There are six letters W, A, R, S, N and E. Is 'ANSWER' the word formed after performing the following operations using these six letters only?

I. E is placed fourth to the right of A. S is not placed immediately next to either A or E.
II. R is placed immediately next (either left or right) to E. W is placed immediately next (either left or right) to S.
III. Both N and W are placed immediately next to S. The word does not begin with R. A is not placed immediately next to W.

32. In the question below is given a statement followed by three courses of action numbered I, II and III. A course of action is a step or administrative decision to be taken for improvement, follow-up or further action in regard to the problem, policy, etc. On the basis of information given in the statement, you have to assume everything in the statement to be true and then decide which of the three given suggested courses of action logically follows worth pursuing. Then, decide which of the alternatives (a), (b), (c), (d) or (e) is correct.

Statement Lack of coordination between the university, its colleges and various authorities has resulted in students ousted from one college seeking migration to another.

Course of Action

I. If a student is ousted from a college, the information should be sent to all the other colleges of university.
II. The admissions to all the colleges of the universities should be handled by the university directly.
III. A separate section should be made for taking strict action against students indulging in anti-social activities.

(a) Only I (b) Only II
(c) Only III (d) All follow
(e) None follows

Direction (Q. Nos. 33-34) *In the following questions, a statement is given followed by three Assumptions* I, II *and* III. *In the context of the questions an assumption is something to be taken for granted. You have to consider the statement and the assumptions and decide which of the assumptions is implicit in the statement, then decide which one of the answer is correct.* **[JMET 2011]**

33. A word is represented by only one set of numbers given in anyone of the alternatives. The sets of numbers given in the alternatives are represented by two classes of alphabets as in two matrices given below. The columns and rows of Matrix I are numbered from 0 to 4 and that of Matrix II are numbered from 5 to 9. A letter from these matrices can be represented first by its row and next by its column, e.g., 'M' can be represented by 42, 31, etc. Similarly, you have to identify the set for the word given 'ROST'. **[SSC (CGL) 2014]**

Matrix I

	0	1	2	3	4
4	K	L	M	N	O
3	L	M	K	O	N
2	N	O	L	M	K
1	M	N	O	K	L
0	O	K	N	L	M

Matrix II

	5	6	7	8	9
9	P	Q	R	S	T
8	T	S	Q	P	R
7	R	T	S	Q	P
6	S	P	T	R	Q
5	Q	R	P	T	S

(a) 68, 33, 65, 58 (b) 56, 44, 67, 40
(c) 97, 21, 66,29 (d) 75, 00, 10, 92

34. Statement Prakash decided to get his railway reservation done in the month of May for the journey he wants to undertaken in July to Mumbai.

Assumptions

I. The railways open reservation two months in advance.
II. There is more than one train to Mumbai.
III. There will be a vacancy in the desired class.

(a) Both II and III (b) Only I
(c) Both I and II (d) Only III

35. Statement In a recently held all-India conference, the session on Brand Management in India surprisingly attracted a large number of participants and also received excellent media coverage in the leading newspapers.

Assumptions

I. Nobody expected such an encouraging response to Brand Management.
II. Brands are not managed properly in India.
III. The Media is always very positive towards Brands.

(a) Only I (b) Both I and II
(c) Both I and III (d) I, II and III

Direction (Q. Nos. 36-37) *Read the following information carefully and answer the questions given below.*

Ravi is son of Aman's father's sister. Sahil is son of Divya, who is the mother of Gaurav and grandmother of Aman. Ashok is the father of Tanya and grandfather of Ravi. Divya is wife of Ashok.

36. How is Ravi related to Divya?
(a) Nephew (b) Grandson
(c) Son (d) Data inadequate

37. How is Gaurav's wife related to Tanya?
(a) Niece
(b) Sister
(c) Sister-in-law
(d) Data inadequate

Direction (Q. Nos. 38-39) *Each question comprises two statements (numbered as I and II). You have to take the statements as true even if they seem to be at variance with commonly known facts. Read all the conclusions and then decide which of the given conclusions logically follow from the given statements, disregarding commonly known facts.* **[CLAT 2014]**

38. Statements

I. All contracts are agreements.
II. All agreements are accepted offers.

Which of the following derivations is correct?
(a) All accepted offers are contracts
(b) All agreements are contracts
(c) All contracts are accepted offers
(d) None of the above

39. Statements

I. Some beautiful women are actresses.
II. All actresses are good dancers.

Which of the following derivations is correct?
(a) Some beautiful women are good dancers
(b) All good dancers are actresses
(c) Both (a) and (b)
(d) None of the above

Direction (Q. Nos. 40-41) *In the following questions, the symbols @, ©, %, $ and ★ are used with the following meanings as illustrated below.*

'P © Q' means 'P is not greater than Q'.

'P ★ Q' means 'P is not smaller than Q'.

'P % Q' means 'P is neither greater than nor equal to Q'.

'P $ Q' means 'P is neither smaller than nor equal to Q'.

'P @ Q' means 'P is neither greater than nor smaller than Q'.

In each of the following questions assuming the given statements to be true, find out which of the three Conclusions I, II and III given below them is/are definitely true?

40. Statements Z © K, K % E, E @ R
Conclusions I. R $ K
II. Z % E III. R $ Z
(a) Only I is true
(b) I and II are true
(c) I and III are true
(d) II and III are true
(e) I, II and III are true

41. Statements W @ M, M © R, R $ F
Conclusions I. F % M
II. R ★ W III. W % F
(a) None is true (b) Only I is true
(c) Only III is true (d) I and II are true
(e) Only II is true

Direction (Q. Nos. 42-43) *Find the missing number from the given responses.* **[SSC (CGL) 2015]**

42.

18	21	24
3	9	3
6	4	8
21	26	?

(a) 22 (b) 24 (c) 27 (d) 29

43.

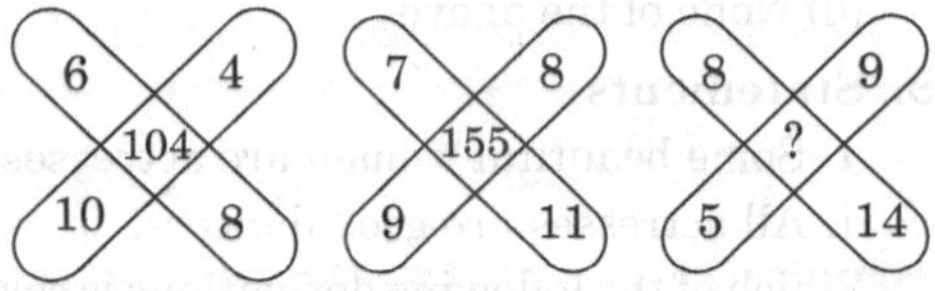

(a) 152 (b) 164
(c) 140 (d) 142

44. Identify the correct response from the given premises stated according to following symbols.
If $> = \div$, $< = +$, $\wedge = -$, $\times = <$, $- = >$, $+ = =$ and $\vee = \times$
(a) $6 > 3 < 2 \wedge 4 \vee 8 - 13$
(b) $6 \wedge 3 < 2 > 4 \vee 8 + 13$
(c) $6 \vee 3 \wedge 2 > 4 < 8 \times 13$
(d) $6 \vee 3 > 2 < 4 \wedge 8 \times 13$

45. Which of the following words will appear fourth in the dictionary?
(a) Sanctity (b) Sanatorium
(c) Sanskrit (d) Sanction
[FCI Assistance Grade III 2012]

46. Find out which of the diagrams as given in the alternatives correctly represents the relationship among Earth, Forest and Mountains.

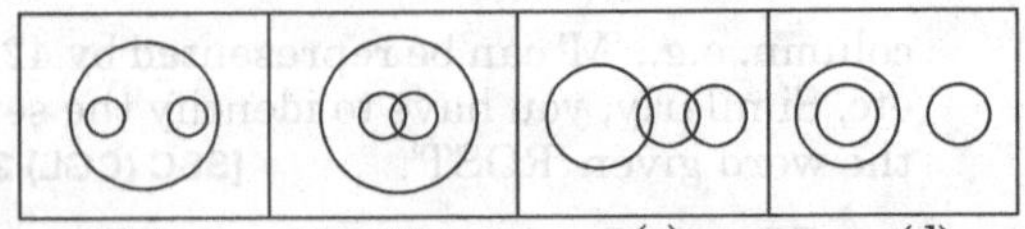

(a) (b) (c) (d)

47. Different designs can be made by placing nine safety matches. Which of the following designs cannot be made, at all by, nine safety matches?

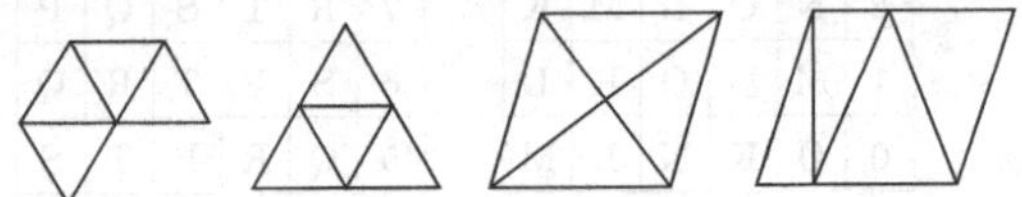

(a) (b) (c) (d)

48. Consider the figure given below and answer the item that follows.

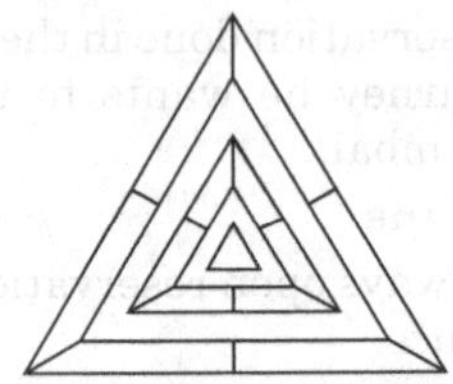

Find the least number of colours to be used to fill the figure, if not two adjacent areas can have the same colour.
(a) 3 (b) 4 (c) 5 (d) 6

49. In which of the following expressions does the expression 'Q ≥ Z' definitely true? **[RBI (Officers) 2015]**
(a) $E \geq Z \geq R \geq B = C \geq Q$
(b) $N \geq Q \geq A = C \leq I \geq Z$
(c) $Q \geq R \geq M = P \leq A \geq Z$
(d) $Z \leq S = B \leq L < O \leq Q$
(e) $Z = T \leq D \leq Y = X \leq Q$

50. Which answer figure is embedded in the question figure?

Question Figure

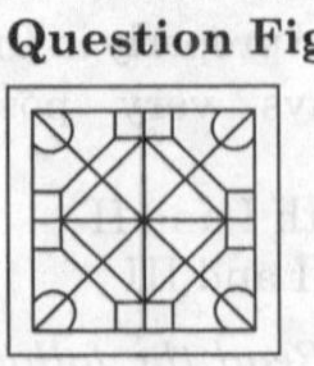

Answer Figures

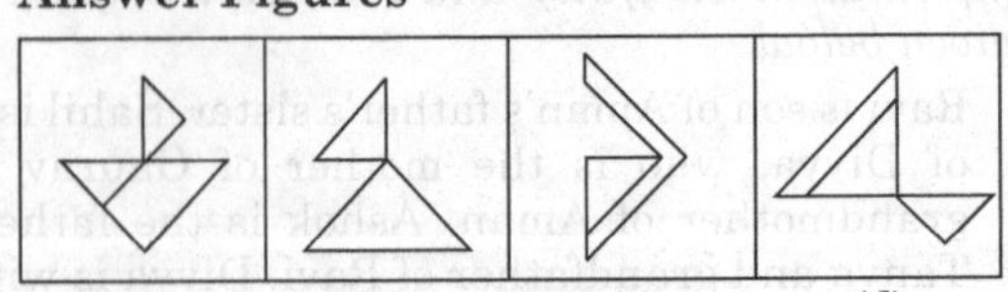

(a) (b) (c) (d)

Hints and Solutions

1. (*b*) As, $08 \times 02 = 16$ and $16 = 2 \times 8 = 28$

Similarly, $15 \times 02 = 30$ and $30 = 6 \times 5 = 65$

$\therefore$? = 65

2. (*c*) Each letter of the first group is moved one step backward to obtain the corresponding letter of the second group.

So, DELHI → CDKGH

3. (*b*)

O (−1) N, R (−1) Q, H (+1) I, K (+1) L

U (−1) T, X (−1) W, B (−1) A, E (−1) D

K (−1) J, N (−1) M

Clearly, letters group HIKL is odd one out.

4. (*d*) Except Cloth—Skirt, in all others work and worker relationship has been shown.

5. (*c*) As,

M O T H E R
+1 +1 +1 +1 +1 +1
N P U I F S

Similarly,

Z E N I T H
+1 +1 +1 +1 +1 +1
A F O J U I

6. (*e*) Avoid going out ⇔ 319 …(i)

Going for party ⇔ 612 …(ii)

Out for party ⇔ 362 …(iii)

From Eqs. (i) and (ii),

Going ⇒ 1

From Eqs. (i) and (ii)

for party ⇒ 62

So, 'party' will be coded as either 2 or 6.

7. (*d*) (E) X (A) M I (N) A (T) I O N

1st, 3rd, 6th, 8th

Since, 1st, 3rd, 6th and 8th letters are E, A, N and T, respectively. Hence, three meaningful words NEAT, ANTE and ATEN can be formed.

8. (*d*) Word CRITERION cannot be formed by using the letters of the given word because letter 'E' is not present in the given word.

9. (*d*) Since, in a clock hour hand completes an angle of 360° in 12 h and there is a gap of 6 h between 8 am and 2 pm. So, in 6 h, hour hand completes an angle of 180°.

10. (*d*) The direction map of Kartik's walk can be drawn as

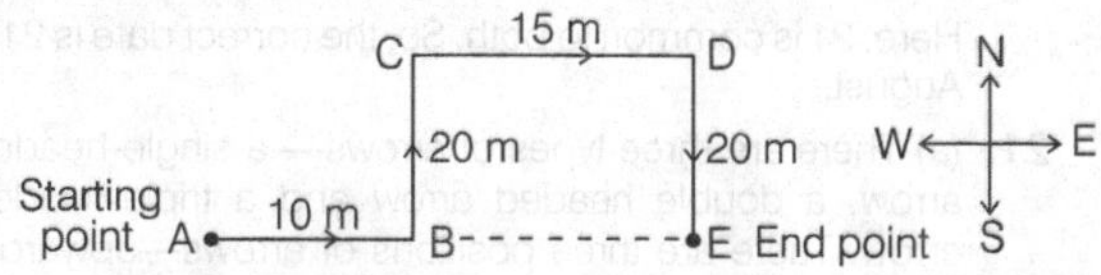

$\therefore$ The distance between the starting point and end point is AB + BE = 10 + 15 = 25 m

Solution (Q. Nos. 11-13) According to the given information, the sitting arrangement is as follows

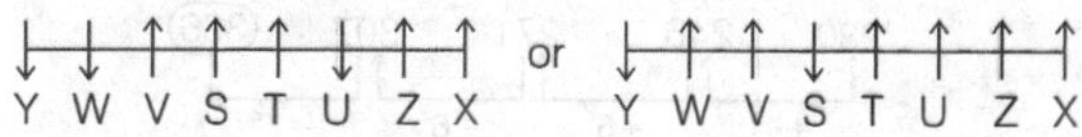

11. (*a*) W, Z pairs represents the immediate neighbours of the persons seated at the two extreme ends of the line.

12. (*e*) Two

13. (*a*) Original position ⟶ Y W V S T U Z X

Alphabetical order from right to left ⟶ Z Y X W V U T S

So, it is clearly shown that only U remain unchanged as compared to the original seating arrangement.

14. (*c*) Suppose number be x.

$$\frac{1}{2}x - \frac{1}{3}x = 17$$

or, $$\frac{3x - 2x}{6} = 17$$

$$\therefore \quad x = 6 \times 17 = 102$$

Solution (Q. Nos. 15-17) From the given information, we can draw the following figure.

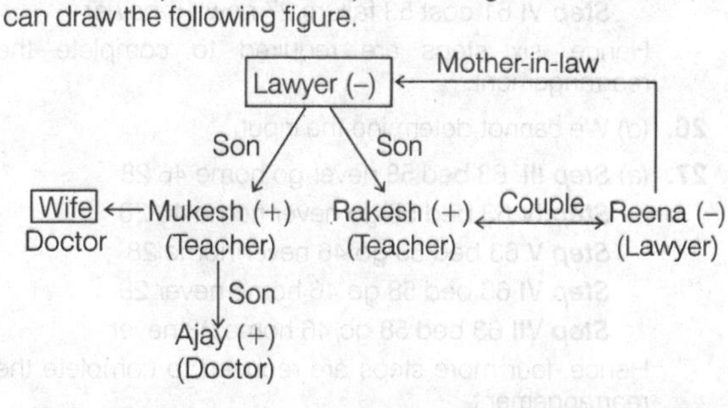

15. (*a*) Reena and Rakesh are couple and their professions are Lawyer and Teacher, respectively.

16. (*c*) Rakesh's wife is Mrs. Reena and she is a lawyer.

17. (*b*) There are three male members- Mukesh, Rakesh and Ajay.

18. (*b*) R explains A as Aurangzeb failed in his Deccan policy mainly due to political and religions intolerance.

19. (*d*) Option figure (d) is correct.

20. (*b*)

According to	Possibility of Date
Vinay	(21), 22, 23, 24, 25, 26, 27
Rita	13, 14, 15, 16, 17, 18, 19, 20, (21)

Here, 21 is common to both. So, the correct date is 21st August.

21. (*a*) There are three types of arrows— a single-headed arrow, a double headed arrow and a triple-headed arrow. There are three positions of arrows—upwards, downwards and towards right. The arrows have 3 types of bases-plane, rectangular and circular. Each of these features is used once in each row.

22. (*b*) The pattern is as follows

230 → 246 → 271 → 307 → (356)

$+4^2$ $+5^2$ $+6^2$ $+7^2$

∴ ? = 356

23. (*b*) In this series, every letter is given its alphabetical position number and one letter is skipped in between each term.

C $\xrightarrow{+2}$ E $\xrightarrow{+2}$ G $\xrightarrow{+2}$ I $\xrightarrow{+2}$ K $\xrightarrow{+2}$ M

3 $\xrightarrow{+2}$ 5 $\xrightarrow{+2}$ 7 $\xrightarrow{+2}$ 9 $\xrightarrow{+2}$ 11 $\xrightarrow{+2}$ 13

Hence, the missing terms are K-11 and M-13.

24. (*b*) Series pattern baab/baab/baab

∴ Required answer = abba

25. (*a*) **Input** 16 power failure 61 53 new cost 27

***Step* I** 61 16 power failure 53 new cost 27

***Step* II** 61 cost 16 power failure 53 new 27

***Step* III** 61 cost 53 16 power failure new 27

***Step* IV** 61 cost 53 failure 16 power new 27

***Step* V** 61 cost 53 failure 27 16 power new

***Step* VI** 61 cost 53 failure 27 new 16 power

Hence, six steps are required to complete the rearrangement.

26. (*d*) We cannot determine the input.

27. (*a*) ***Step* III** 63 bed 58 never go home 46 28

***Step* IV** 63 bed 58 go never home 46 28

***Step* V** 63 bed 58 go 46 never home 28

***Step* VI** 63 bed 58 go 46 home never 28

***Step* VII** 63 bed 58 go 46 home 28 never

Hence, four more steps are required to complete the rearrangement.

28. (*a*) **Input** rows 25 columns 39 46 fear star 72

***Step* I** 72 rows 25 columns 39 46 fear star

***Step* II** 72 columns rows 25 39 46 fear star

***Step* III** 72 columns 46 rows 25 39 fear star

***Step* IV** 72 columns 46 fear rows 25 39 star

***Step* V** 72 columns 46 fear 39 rows 25 star

Hence, Step V is the last step.

29. (*b*) Number of smaller cubes having atleast two faces painted

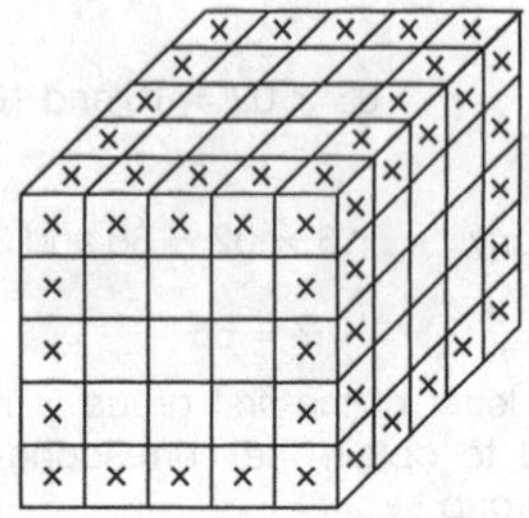

= (Number of smaller cubes having 2 faces painted) + (Number of smaller cubes having 3 faces painted)

= (Number of middle cubes) + (Number of corner cubes)

∴ Number of middle cubes = $12(n-2) = 12(5-2)$

$= 12 \times 3 = 36$ (here, $n = 5$)

Number of corner (vertex) cubes = 8

∴ Required number of cubes = 36 + 8 = 44

30. (*e*) From Statements I, II and III

Floor number	Person
6	P
5	T
4	R
3	S
2	Q
1	V

31. (*b*) From Statements I and III.

1 2 3 4 5 6

A S E

A N S W E R

32. (*a*) Only Course of action I is the right course of action which says that, if a student is ousted from a college, the information should be sent to all the other colleges of university. This is the way by which coordination between the university and the colleges can be maintained.

33. (*a*) According to the matrices,

R — 97, 89, 75, (68), 56

O — 44, (33), 21,12, 00

S — 98, 86, 77, (65), 59

T — 99, 85, 76, 67, (58)

∴ ROST ⇒ 68, 33, 65, 58

34. (*b*) Only Assumption I is implicit.

35. (*a*) Only Assumption I is implicit.

36. (*b*)

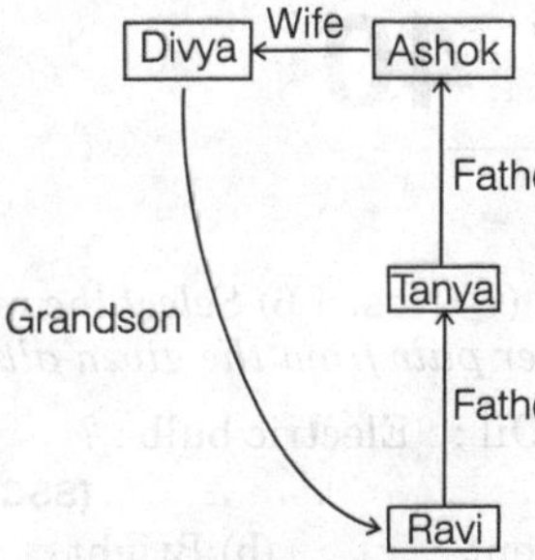

Hence, Ravi is the grandson of Divya.

37. (*c*)

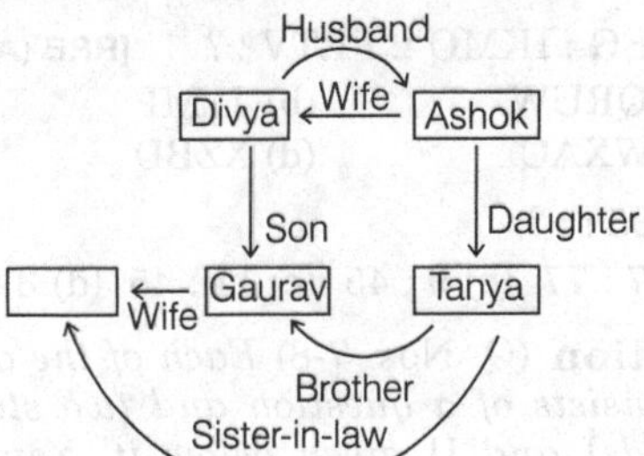

Hence, Gaurav's wife is Tanya's sister-in-law.

38. (*c*)

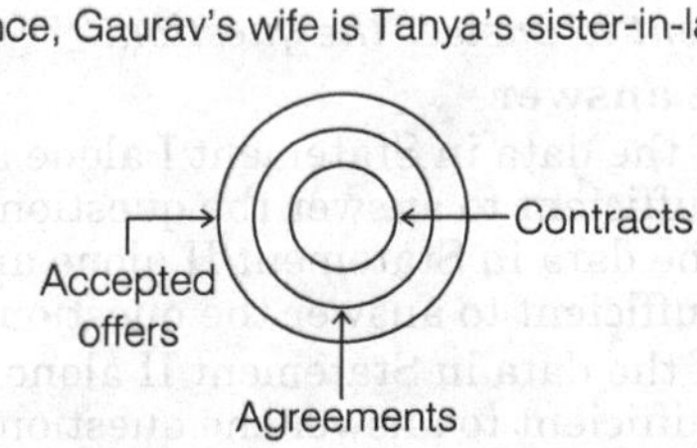

So, all contracts are accepted offers is the correct.

39. (*a*)

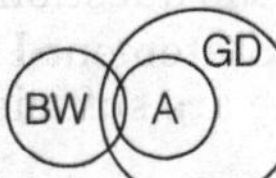

BW : Beautiful Women

A : Actresses

GD : Good Dancers

Some beautiful women are good dancers but there are some good dancers who are not actresses.

40. (*e*)

© ⇒ ≤	★ ⇒ ≥	% ⇒ <	$ ⇒ >	@ ⇒ =

Z © K ⇒ Z ≤ K

K % E ⇒ K < E

E @ R ⇒ E = R

Therefore, Z ≤ K < E = R

Conclusions I. R $ K ⇒ R > K (True)

II. Z % E ⇒ Z < E (True)

III. R $ Z ⇒ R > Z (True)

41. (*e*) W @ M ⇒ W = M

M © R ⇒ M ≤ R

R $ F ⇒ R > F

Therefore, W = M ≤ R > F

Conclusions I. F % M ⇒ F < M (Not true)

II. R ★ W ⇒ R ≥ W (True)

III. W % F ⇒ W < F (Not true)

42. (*d*) As, $6 - 3 = 3 + 18 = 21$

and, $9 - 4 = 5 + 21 = 26$

Similarly, $8 - 3 = 5 + 24 = \boxed{29}$

43. (*d*) As, $(6 \times 4) + (10 \times 8) = 24 + 80 = 104$

and $(7 \times 8) + (9 \times 11) = 56 + 99 = 155$

Similarly, $(8 \times 9) + (5 \times 14) = 72 + 70 = \boxed{142}$

44. (*d*) $6 \vee 3 > 2 < 4 \wedge 8 \times 13$

$\Rightarrow \quad 6 \times 3 \div 2 + 4 - 8 < 13$

$\Rightarrow \quad \dfrac{6 \times 3}{2} + 4 - 8 < 13$

$\Rightarrow \quad 9 + 4 - 8 < 13$

$\Rightarrow \quad 5 < 13$

45. (c) (b) Sanatorium → (d) Sanction → (a) Sanctity → (c) Sanskrit

46. (*a*) Forests are different from mountains but both are part of Earth.

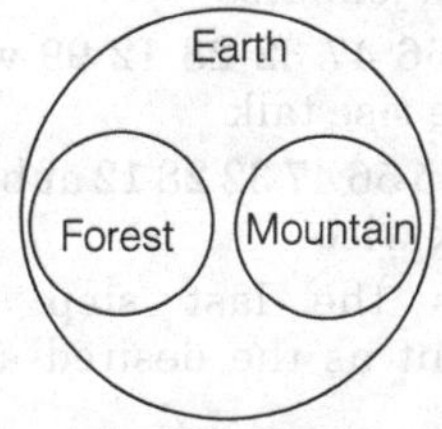

47. (c) Option (c) is correct answer.

48. (*a*)

So, there are only three colours needed to fill the figure.

49. (*e*) In expression, Z = T ≤ D ≤ Y = X ≤ Q, Q ≥ Z is definitely true.

50. (*a*) Clearly, answer figure (a) is embedded in question figure as shown below

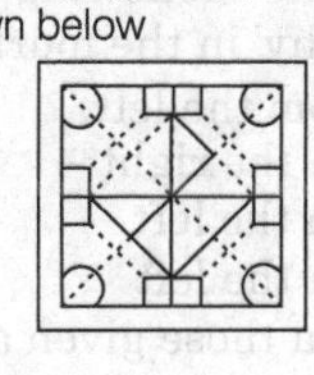

PRACTICE SET 40

Direction (Q. Nos. 1-3) *A word and number arrangement machine when given an input line of words and numbers rearranges them following a particular rule in each step. The following is an illustration of input and rearrangement. (All the numbers are two digit numbers)* **[IBPS (PO/MT) Mains 2015]**

Input talk 47 12 rise at 99 75. 32 wise joke high 28 56 be

***Step* I** 12 talk 47 rise 99 75 32 wise joke high 28 56 be at

***Step* II** 28 12 talk 47 rise 99 75 32 wise joke high 56 at be

***Step* III** 32 28 12 talk 47 rise 99 75 wise joke 56 at be high

***Step* IV** 47 32 28 12 talk rise 99 75 wise 56 at be high joke

***Step* V** 56 47 32 28 12 talk 99 75 wise at be high joke rise

***Step* VI** 75 56 47 32 28 12 99 wise at be high joke rise talk

***Step* VII** 99 75 56 47 32 28 12 at be high joke rise talk wise

Step VII is the last step of the above rearrangement as the desired arrangement is obtained.

Input 83 why sat 14 32 no be ink feet 50 27 vain 67 92

1. Which word/number would be at fifth position from the right in step V?

(a) 14 (b) 92 (c) feet (d) be
(e) sat

2. How many elements (words or numbers) are there between 'feet' and '32' as they appear in the last step of the output?

(a) One (b) Three (c) Four (d) Five
(e) Two

3. Which of the following represents the position of 'why' in the fourth step?

(a) Eighth from the left
(b) Fifth from the right
(c) Sixth from the left
(d) Fifth from the left
(e) Other than those given as options

Direction (Q. Nos. 4-6) *Select the related letters /word/number pair from the given alternatives.*

4. Lamp : Oil : : Electric bulb : ? **[SSC (Steno) 2014]**

(a) Current (b) Bright
(c) Holder (d) Switch

5. ACEG : IKMO :: PRTV : ? **[RRB (ASM) 2010]**

(a) QRUW (b) JLMP
(c) WXAC (d) XZBD

6. 5 : 35 : : ?

(a) 7 : 77 (b) 9 : 45 (c) 11 : 45 (d) 3 : 28

Direction (Q. Nos. 7-8) *Each of the questions below consists of a question and two statements numbered I and II given below it. You have to decide whether the data provided in the statements are sufficient to answer the question.*

Give answer

(a) if the data in Statement I alone are sufficient to answer the question, while the data in Statement II alone are not sufficient to answer the question
(b) if the data in Statement II alone are sufficient to answer the question, while the data in Statement I alone are not sufficient to answer the question
(c) if the data either in Statement I alone or in Statement II alone are sufficient to answer the question
(d) if the data given in both the Statements I and II together are not sufficient to answer the question
(e) if the data in both the Statements I and II together are necessary to answer the question

7. Who is the heaviest amongst P, Q, R, S and T?

I. R is heavier than Q but not as heavy as T.
II. P is heavier only than S.

8. How is B related to S? **[RBI (Officers) 2015]**

I. N is married to T. B is the sister of N. T has only one daughter K. K is the grand-daughter of S.
II. N is the daughter of S. N is married to T. T is the only child of Z. B is the sister-in-law of T.

9. In 1930, a person's age was 8 times that of his son. In 1938, the father's age become 10 times that of his son's age in 1930. The ages of the son and father in 1940 were, respectively

(a) 16 yr, 58 yr (b) 15 yr, 50 yr
(c) 14 yr, 42 yr (d) 13 yr, 34 yr

Direction (Q. Nos. 10-12) *Study the following information carefully to answer the given questions.* **[SBI (PO) 2013]**

In a certain code language,
'economics is not money' is written as 'ka la ho ga'
'demand and supply economies' is written as 'mo ta pa ka'
'money makes only part' is written as 'zi la ne ki'
'demand makes supply economics' is written as 'zi mo ka ta'

10. What is the code for 'money' is the given code language?

(a) ga (b) mo (c) pa (d) ta
(e) la

11. What is the code for 'supply' in the given code language?

(a) Only ta (b) Only mo
(c) Either pa or mo (d) Only pa
(e) Either mo or ta

12. What may be the possible code for 'demand only more' in the given code language?

(a) xi ne mo (b) mo zi ne
(c) ki ne mo (d) mo zi ki
(e) xi ka ta

Direction (Q. Nos. 13-14) *In each of the following questions, there are two statements labelled as Assertion* (A) *and Reason* (R).

Give answer

(a) if both 'A' and 'R' are true and 'R' is the correct explanation of 'A'
(b) if both 'A' and 'R' are true but 'R' is not the correct explanation of 'A'
(c) if 'A' is true but 'R' is false
(d) if 'A' is false but 'R' is true
(e) if both 'A' and 'R' are false

13. Assertion (A) Silver is not used to make wires.
Reason (R) Silver is a bad conductor.

14. Assertion (A) In India, people elect their own representatives.
Reason (R) India is a democratic country.

15. A word is represented by only one set of numbers as given in anyone of the alternatives. The sets of numbers given in the alternatives are represented by two classes of alphabets as in the two matrices given below. The columns and rows of Matrix I are numbered from 0 to 4 and that of Matrix II are numbered from 5 to 9. A letter from these matrices can be represented first by its row and next by its column, e.g. 'E' can be represented by 00, 13, 32 etc. and 'S' can be represented by 55, 76, 87, etc. Similarly, you have to identify the set for the word given CART. **[SSC (Multitasking) 2014]**

Matrix I

	0	1	2	3	4
0	E	A	R	W	P
1	W	P	A	E	R
2	A	W	P	R	E
3	P	R	E	A	W
4	R	E	W	P	A

Matrix II

	5	6	7	8	9
5	S	B	K	T	C
6	B	C	T	K	S
7	T	S	C	B	K
8	K	T	S	C	B
9	C	K	B	S	T

(a) 65, 33, 40, 86 (b) 66, 12, 40, 58
(c) 88, 44, 31, 89 (d) 59, 20, 32, 89

16. A sheet of paper is folded in a particular manner, punched once and then unfolded. The punched, unfolded paper appears as in the given figure. Find out the manner in which the paper was folded and punched by choosing the correct answer. **[SSC (10+2) 2012]**

Question Figure

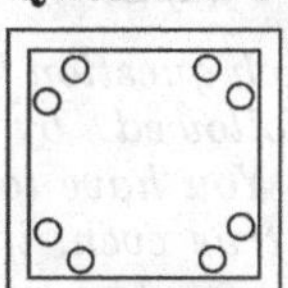

Answer Figures

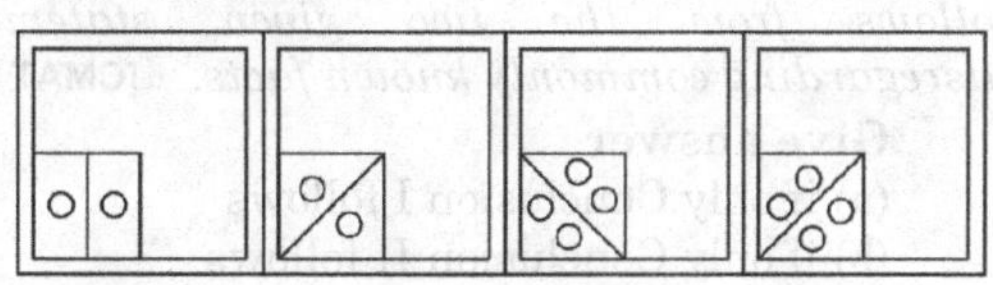

(a) (b) (c) (d)

Direction (Q. Nos. 17-18) *In the following questions, find the odd word/number pair from the given alternatives.*

17. (a) 547-563 (b) 71-55 **[SSC (CGL) 2013]**
(c) 517-523 (d) 248-231

18. (a) Pear (b) Apple
(c) Litchi (d) Guava
(e) Orange

19. Fill the correct number at the sign of interrogation. **[FCI (Assistant) Grade III 2015]**

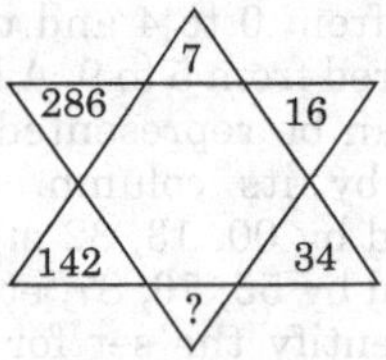

(a) 70 (b) 68 (c) 56 (d) 92

20. A stands for 'addition', B for subtraction', C for division', D for multiplication', E for 'less than', F for 'greater than' and G for 'equal to'.
Out of the alternatives only one expression is correct according to the letter symbols. Identify that
(a) 18 C 2 A 4 B 6 G 9
(b) 6 D 4 B 12 A 4 C 2 F 18
(c) 10 C 2 D 4 B 6 E 12
(d) 9 A 7 B 4 C 2 G 14

21. How many triangles are there in the following figure?

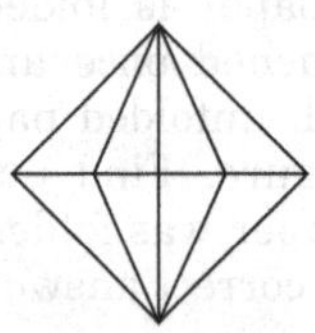

(a) 10 (b) 24 (c) 22 (d) 20

Direction (Q. Nos. 22-23) *Each question below are given two statements followed by two conclusions numbered* I *and* II. *You have to take the two given statements to be true even, if they seem to be at variance from commonly known facts and decide which of the given conclusions logically follows from the two given statements, disregarding commonly known facts.* **[CMAT 2014]**

Give answer
(a) if only Conclusion I follows
(b) if only Conclusion II follows
(c) if either I or II follows
(d) if neither I nor II follows

22. Statements Some books are papers.
No copies are papers.
Conclusions I. Some books are not copies.
II. No books are copies.

23. Statements Some cups are plates.
Some plates are jugs.
Conclusions I. Some cups are jugs.
II. All cups are jugs.

24. How many meaningful four letter English words can be formed with the letters KEAB, using each letter only once in each word?
(a) One (b) Two
(c) Three (d) Four

25. If all the numbers in 42731658 are arranged in ascending order from left to right, the position (s) of the how many number(s) will remain unchanged? **[IBPS (Clerk) Pre 2015]**
(a) Three (b) More than three
(c) None (d) Two
(e) One

26. Identify the missing part of the question figure and select it from given answer figures.

Question Figure **[SSC (10+2) 2011]**

Answer Figures

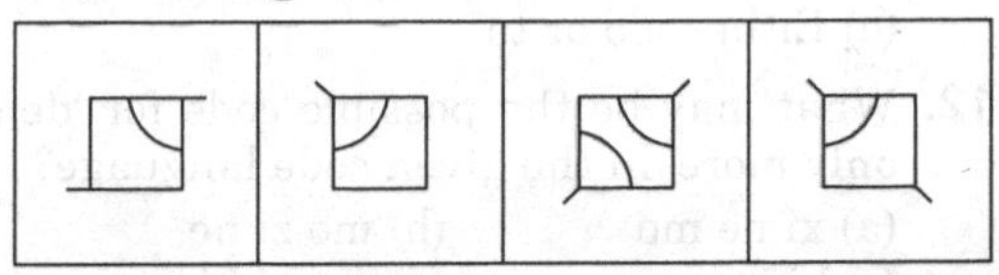

(a) (b) (c) (d)

27. How many numbers are there between 1 and 100 which can be exactly divided by 3 and have 4 as a digit?
(a) 6 (b) 9 (c) 4 (d) 7

28. A person walks towards his house at 8 : 00 am and observes his shadow to his right. In which direction he is walking?
(a) North (b) South **[SSC (CPO) 2014]**
(c) East (d) West

Direction (Q. Nos. 29-30) *Read the following information carefully and answer the questions, which follow.*

'A – B' means 'A is father of B'.
'A + B' means 'A is daughter of B'.
'A ÷ B' means 'A is son of B'.
'A × B' means 'A is wife of B'.

29. In the expression 'P + Q × T', how is T related to P?
(a) Mother (b) Father
(c) Son (d) Brother
(e) None of these

30. Which of the following means T is wife of P?
(a) P × S ÷ T (b) P ÷ S × T
(c) P − S ÷ T (d) P + T ÷ S
(e) None of these

Direction (Q. Nos. 31-33) *Study the following information carefully and answer the questions given below.*

P, Q, R, S, T, V, W, Y and Z are sitting around a circle facing the centre. V is second to the left of P who is third to the left of Y. S is fourth to the left of P. T is third to the right of Q who is the immediate right of V. W is fourth to the right of Z.

31. Who is third to the left of S?
(a) Y (b) W
(c) T (d) Data inadequate
(e) None of these

32. In which of the following pairs is the first person sitting to the immediate right of the second person?
(a) VQ (b) ZV
(c) SZ (d) RS
(e) YT

33. In which of the following combinations is the first person sitting in between the second and the third persons?
(a) RSZ (b) YTW (c) WPQ (d) VZQ
(e) PQV

34. At what time between 1 and 2 O' clock are the hands of a clock together?
(a) $5\frac{5}{11}$ min past 1 (b) $5\frac{2}{11}$ min past 1
(c) $5\frac{1}{11}$ min past 1 (d) $5\frac{9}{11}$ min past 1
(e) Data inadequate

35. From the given blocks when 10 is at the bottom, which number will be at the top? **[SSC (CGL) 2013]**

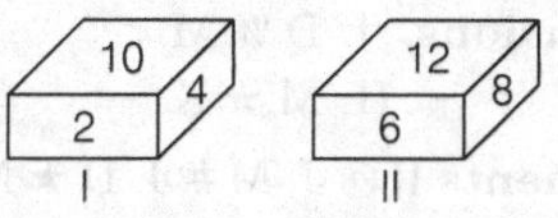

(a) 8 (b) 12
(c) 6 (d) 4

36. Select the one, which is different from the other three responses.

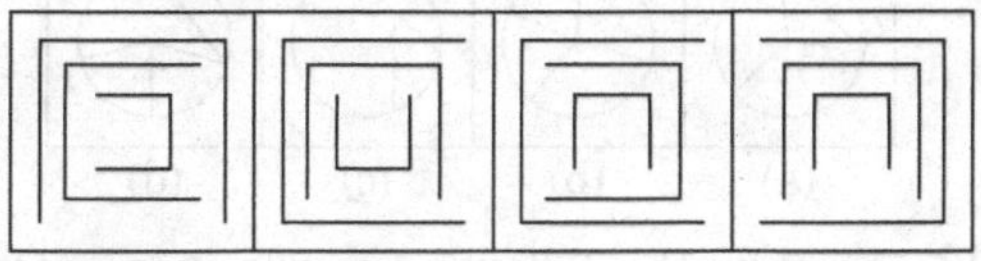

Direction (Q. Nos. 37-39) *Study the following information carefully and answer the questions given below.*

P, Q, R, S, T and M are six students of a school, one each studies in Class I-VI. Each of them has a favourite colour from red, black, blue, yellow, pink and green, not necessarily in the same order.

Q likes black and does not study in Class IV or V. The one who studies in Class IV does not like green. P studies in Class II. M likes blue and does not study in Class IV. The one who likes yellow, studies in Class VI. S likes pink and studies in Class I. R does not study in Class VI.

37. In which class does R study?
(a) V (b) III
(c) IV (d) Data inadequate
(e) None of these

38. Which colour does R like?
(a) Black (b) Yellow
(c) Green (d) Blue
(e) None of these

39. Which colour does P like?
(a) Green (b) Yellow
(c) Red (d) Data inadequate
(e) None of these

40. If two days after day after tomorrow is Sunday, then what day was the day before yesterday?
(a) Wednesday (b) Tuesday
(c) Monday (d) Sunday

41. Find the figure out of the answer choice figures that can be formed by joining the pieces given in the question figure.

Question Figure

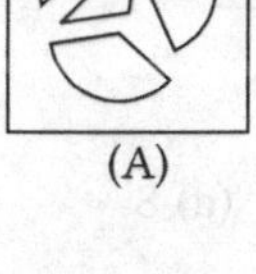

(A)

Answer Figures

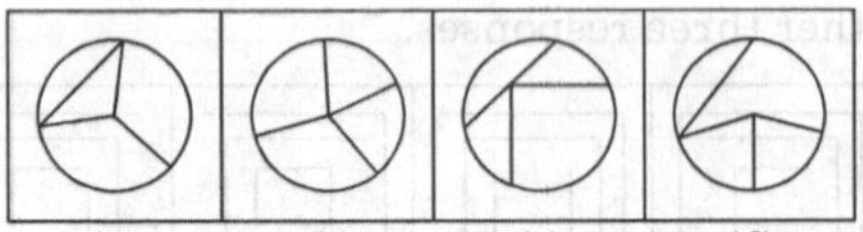

(a) (b) (c) (d)

42. Arrange the following words in a meaningful order.

(i) House (ii) Road
(iii) Room (iv) Hamlet
(v) District

(a) (iii), (ii), (i), (iv), (v)
(b) (iii), (i), (iv), (ii), (v)
(c) (iii), (i), (ii), (iv), (v)
(d) (iii), (i), (ii), (v), (iv)

43. Suresh is 7 ranks ahead of Ashok in the class of 39 students. If Ashok's rank is 17th from the last, then what is Suresh's rank from the start?

(a) 16th (b) 23th (c) 24th (d) 15th

44. Find out the answer figure which completes the problem figure matrix.

Question Figure

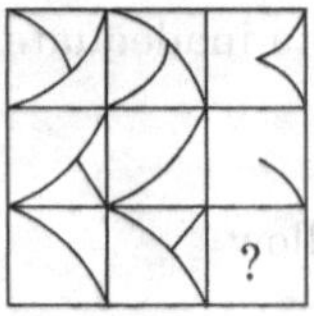

(X)

Answer Figures

(a) (b) (c) (d) (e)

45. In the given figure in garden, square represents the area where jackfruit trees are grown; circle represents mango trees and triangle represents coconut trees. Which number represents the common area in which all types of trees are grown?

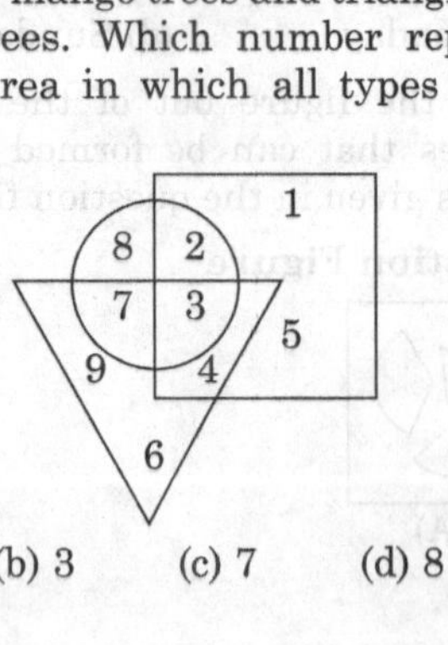

(a) 4 (b) 3 (c) 7 (d) 8

46. Which one set of letters when sequentially placed at the gaps in the given letter series shall complete it?

_ aa_ba_bb_ab_aab

(a) babab
(b) aaabb
(c) bbaab
(d) bbbaa

Direction (Q. Nos. 47-48) *In the following questions, a series is given, with one term missing. Choose the correct alternative from the given ones that will complete the series.*

47. AFI, JOR, MRU, ?

(a) GJN (b) HMP
(c) PMO (d) RJL

48. 5, 10, 8, 12, 11, 14, ?, 16 **[NIFT (UG) 2014]**

(a) 17 (b) 13
(c) 20 (d) 14

Direction (Q. Nos. 49-50) *In the following questions, the symbols @, %, $, # and ★ are used with the following meaning as illustrated below:*

'P $ Q' means 'P is not smaller than Q.'

'P @ Q' means 'P is not greater than Q.'

'P ★ Q' means 'P is neither smaller than nor equal to Q.'

'P # Q' means 'P is neither greater than nor smaller than Q.'

'P % Q' means 'P is neither greater than nor equal to Q.'

Now in each of the following questions assuming the given statements to be true, find which of the two Conclusions I and II given below them is/are definitely true?

Give answer

(a) If only Conclusion I is true
(b) If only Conclusion II is true
(c) If either Conclusion I or II is true
(d) If neither Conclusion I nor II is true
(e) If both Conclusions I and II are true

49. Statements M ★ T, T $ K, K # D

Conclusions I. D % M
II. M ★ K

50. Statements R @ J, M # J, D ★ M

Conclusions I. D ★ J
II. R # M

Hints and Solutions

Solution (Q. Nos. 1-3) Patterns of the arrangement of steps of given input are as follows

Input 83 why sat 14 32 no be ink feet 50 27 vain 67 92
Step I 14 83 why sat 32 no ink feet 50 27 vain 67 92 be
Step II 27 14 83 why sat 32 no ink 50 vain 67 92 be feet
Step III 32 27 14 83 why sat no 50 vain 67 92 be feet ink
Step IV 50 32 27 14 83 why sat vain 67 92 be feet ink no
Step V 67 50 32 27 14 83 why vain 92 be feet ink no sat
Step VI 83 67 50 32 27 14 why 92 be feet ink no sat vain
Step VII 92 83 67 50 32 27 14 be feet ink no sat vain why

1. (*d*) 'be' would be at fifth position from the right in step V.

2. (*b*) Three elements are there between 'feet' and '32' as they appear in the last step of the output.

3. (*c*) 'why' is sixth from the left in the fourth step.

4. (*a*) As, we can get the light from lamp by filling oil in it. In the same manner, we can get the light from bulb by flowing current in it.

5. (*d*) As,

1	3	5	7			16	18	20	22
A	C	E	G		Similarly,	P	R	T	V
+8↓	+8↓	+8↓	+8↓			+8↓	+8↓	+8↓	+8↓
I	K	M	O			X	Z	B	D
9	11	13	15			24	26	2	4

∴ ? = XZBD

6. (*a*) The first number is multiplied by the next prime number to obtain the second number.

So, $7 \times 11 = 77$

7. (*e*) From both the statements, T is the heaviest.

$$T > R > Q > P > S$$

T, R and Q are heavier than P and S.

8. (*b*) From Statement II,

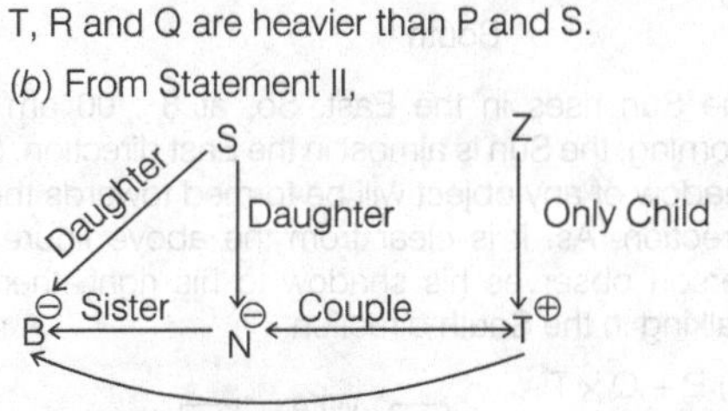

So, B is daughter to S. Therefore, statement II alone sufficient to answer the question.

9. (*c*) Let son's age in 1930 be x yr, then father's age in 1930 be 8x yr.

In 1938, father's age = (8x + 8) yr

As per the question, $8x + 8 = 10x \Rightarrow 2x = 8 \Rightarrow x = 4$

Hence, son's age in 1930 = 4 yr

∴ Age of son in 1940 = 4 + 10 = 14 yr

and age of father in 1940 = $8 \times 4 + 10 = 32 + 10 = 42$ yr

Therefore, the ages of son and father in 1940 will be 14 yr and 42 yr, respectively.

Solution (Q. Nos. 10-12) On the basis of given information,

economics is not money → ka la hoga -(i)

demand and supply economics → mo ta pa ka -(ii)

money makes only part → zi la ne ki -(iii)

demand makes supply economics → zi mo ka ta -(iv)

From Eqs. (i), (ii) and (iv), economics ⇒ ka
From Eqs. (i) and (iii), money ⇒ la
From Eqs. (iii) and (iv), makes ⇒ zi
From Eqs. (ii) and (iv), demand ⇒ mo/ta
supply ⇒ mo/ta
From Eq. (i), is ⇒ ho/ga
not ⇒ ho/ga
From Eq. (ii) and ⇒ pa
From Eq. (iii), only ⇒ ne/ki
part ⇒ ne/ki

10. (*e*) It is clear that money ⇒ la

11. (*e*) According to the question,
code for supply ⇒ 'mo' or 'ta'

12. (*a*) According to the question,
demand ⇒ mo/ta, only ⇒ ne/ki
So, according to option (a), code for 'more' will be xi.
Hence, demand only more ⇒ xi ne mo

13. (*c*) Silver is not used to make wires, hence Assertion is true but silver is not a bad conductor, it is a good conductor. Hence, Reason is false.

14. (*a*) India is a democratic country and people here elect their own representatives. Therefore, both the Assertion and Reason are correct. Since, India is a democratic country, hence people elect their own representatives. Therefore, Reason (R) is the correct explanation of the Assertion.

15. (*b*) According to the matrices,

C—59, (66), 77, 88, 95   A—01, (12), 20, 33, 44

R—02, 14, 23, 31, (40)   T—(58), 67, 75, 86, 99

$\therefore$ CART $\Rightarrow$ 66, 12, 40, 58

16. (*b*)

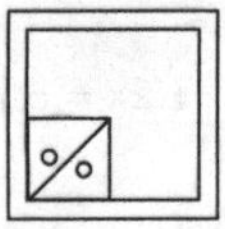

So, option (b) is correct answer.

17. (*d*) As, $547 - 563 \Rightarrow (563) - (547) = \frac{16}{2} = 8$

$71 - 55 \Rightarrow (71) - (55) = \frac{16}{2} = 8$

$517 - 523 \Rightarrow (523) - (517) = \frac{6}{2} = 3$

But, 248 – 231

$\Rightarrow (248) - (231) = \frac{17}{2}$ (non-divisible by 2)

Except option (d) difference of all other numbers is divisible by 2.

Hence, option (d) is different from others.

18. (*e*) Out of given fruits orange is citrus fruit. So, it is different from others.

19. (*a*) The pattern is as follows:

$7 \times 2 + 2 = 16$, $16 \times 2 + 2 = 34$,

$34 \times 2 + 2 = \boxed{70}$

$70 \times 2 + 2 = 142$

$142 \times 2 + 2 = 286$

20. (*d*) According to the question, we can arrange the given mathematical symbols as

$A \to +, B \to -, C \to \div, D \to \times,$

$E \to <, F \to >, G \to =$

Option (d), 9 A 7 B 4 C 2 G 14

$\Rightarrow 9 + 7 - 4 \div 2 = 14 \Rightarrow 9 + 7 - 2 = 14$

$\Rightarrow 16 - 2 = 14 \Rightarrow 14 = 14$

21. (*b*) Given figure can be labelled as follows

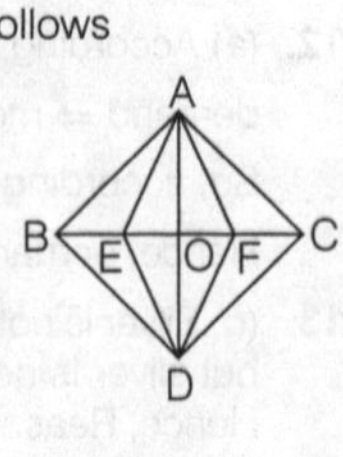

In the above figure, triangles formed by single units are ΔABE, ΔAEO, ΔAOF, ΔAFC, ΔDEB, ΔDOE, ΔDFO and ΔDCF i.e. 8 triangles.

Triangles formed by combining 2 units are ΔABO, ΔAEF, ΔAOC, ΔBOD, ΔDEF, ΔDOC, ΔAED and ΔADF i.e. 8 triangles.

Triangles formed by combining 3 units are ΔABF, ΔAEC, ΔBDF and ΔEDC i.e. 4 triangles.

Triangles formed by combining 4 units are ΔABC, ΔBCD, ΔABD and ΔACD i.e. 4 triangles.

So, total number of triangles = 8 + 8 + 4 + 4 = 24

22. (*a*)

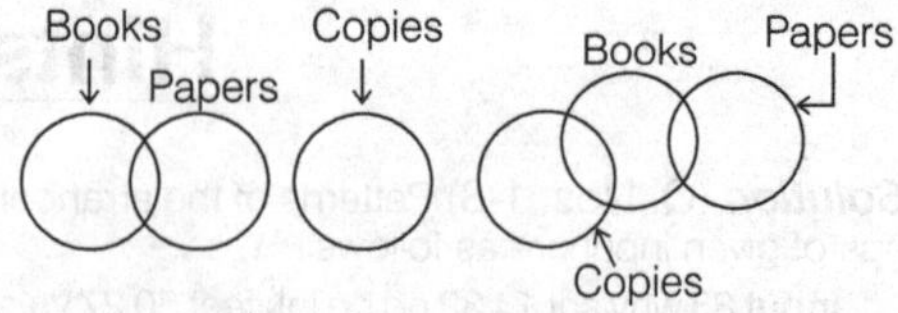

Conclusions I. Some books are not copies. (✔)

II. No books are copies. (✗)

23. (*d*)

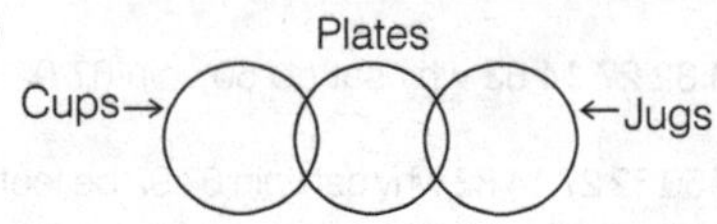

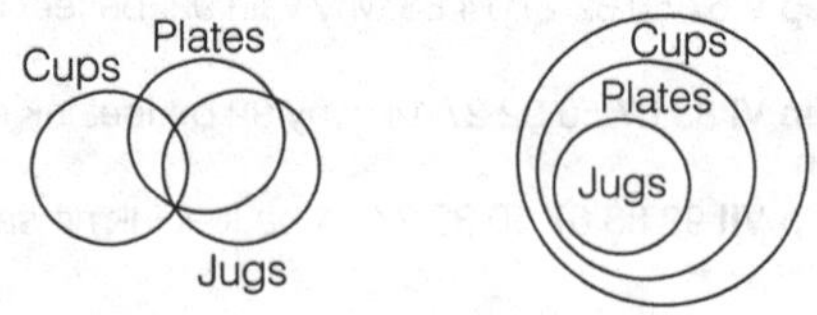

Conclusions I. Some cups are jugs. (✗)

II. All cups are jugs. (✗)

24. (*b*) Required words = BEAK, BAKE

25. (*a*)

Given numbers → 4 [2] 7 3 1 [6] 5 [8]

Ascending order arrangement → 1 [2] 3 4 5 [6] 7 [8]

From above it is clear that three numbers will remain unchanged.

26. (*b*) Option (b) will complete the given pattern as follows

27. (*a*) Such numbers are : 24, 42, 45, 48, 54 and 84.

28. (*b*)

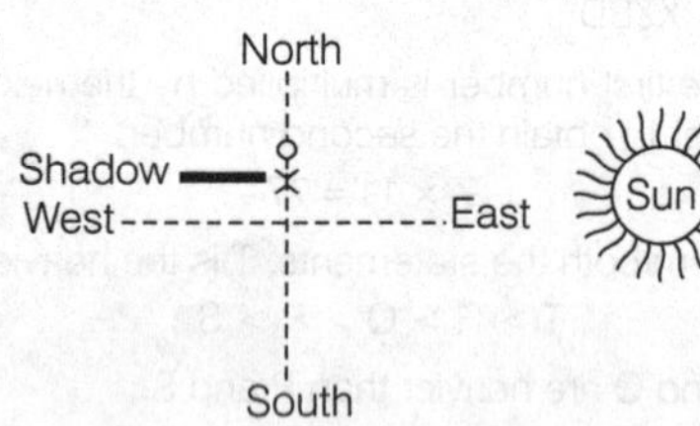

The Sun rises in the East. So, at 8 : 00 am in the morning, the Sun is almost in the East direction. So, the shadow of any object will be formed towards the West direction. As, it is clear from the above figure, if the person observes his shadow to his right, then he is walking in the South direction.

29. (*b*) P + Q × T

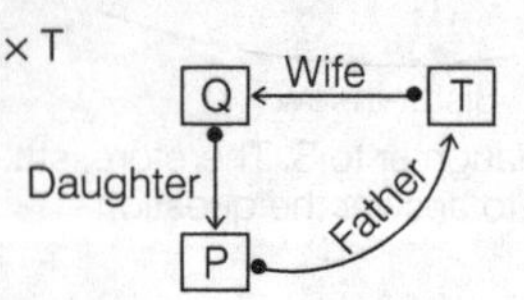

Hence, T is father of P.

30. (*e*) As, T is wife of P. So, T should be female. In options (a) and (c), gender of T cannot be determined.

Options (b) and (d) show T is male. Hence, these options are superfluous.

Solution (Q. Nos. 31-33) According to the given information, the final arrangement is as following

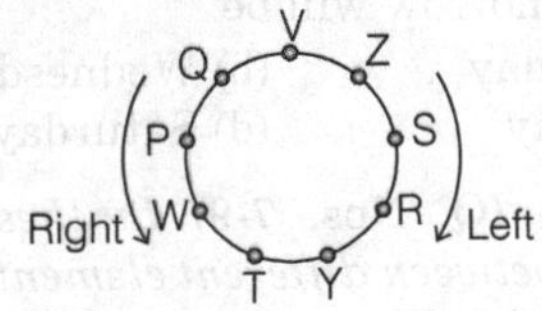

31. (*c*) T is third to the left of S.

32. (*e*) Y is sitting to the immediate right of T.

33. (*d*) V is sitting between Z and Q.

34. (*a*) At 1 O' clock the hour hand is at 1 and the minute hand is at 12.

Thus, they are 5 min spaces apart.

To be together, the minute hand must gain 5 min over the hour hand.

55 min are gained by minute hand in 60 min.

5 min will be gained by it in $= \left(\frac{60}{55} \times 5\right) = \frac{60}{11} = 5\frac{5}{11}$ min

Hence, the hands will coincide at $5\frac{5}{11}$ min past 1.

35. (*b*) From the two views of blocks it is clear that when 10 is at the bottom, number 12 will be at the top.

36. (*d*) In all other figures, all the three designs face different directions, but in figure (d), two of the three designs face the same directions.

Solution (Q. Nos. 37-39) On the basis of given information, we get the following table.

Student	P	Q	R	S	T	M
Class	II	III	IV	I	VI	V
Favourite colour	Green	Black	Red	Pink	Yellow	Blue

37. (c) R studies in IV class.

38. (*e*) R likes red colour.

39. (*a*) P likes green colour.

40. (*c*) The day after tomorrow would be Friday.

Today is Wednesday.

The day before yesterday was Monday.

41. (*a*) Option figure (a) is correct.

42. (*c*) Meaningful order :

(iii) Room → (i) House → (ii) Road → (iv) Hamlet → (v) District

43. (*a*) According to the question, we have following sitting arrangement

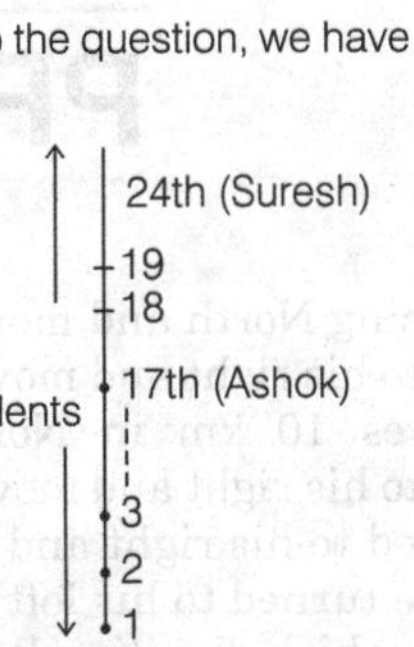

Thus, the Suresh's rank from the start

$= (39 - 24) + 1 = 15 + 1 = 16$

44. (*b*) The contents of the third figure in each row (and column) are determined by the contents of the first two figures. Lines are carried forward from the first two figures to the third one, except where two lines appear in the same position, in which they are cancelled out.

45. (*b*) Number 3 is present in all the three figures.

46. (*c*) The complete letter series will be

<u>b</u> a a <u>b</u>/b a <u>a</u> b/b <u>a</u> a b/<u>b</u> a a b ⇒ bbaab

47. (*b*) We have following pattern,

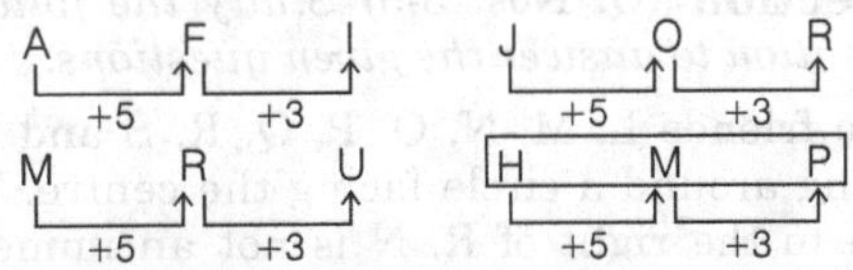

∴ By hit and trial we see that 'HMP' is also following the same order. Hence, option (b) is correct.

48. (*d*) There are two alternate series

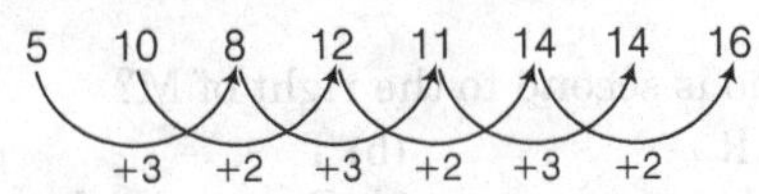

∴ ? = 14

Solution (Q. Nos. 49-50)

\$ ⇒ ≥	★ ⇒ >	@ ⇒ ≤	# ⇒ =	% ⇒ <

49. (*e*) **Statements** M ★ T ⇒ M > T

T \$ K ⇒ T ≥ K

K # D ⇒ K = D

Therefore, M > T ≥ K = D

Conclusions I. D % M ⇒ D < M (True)

II. M ★ K ⇒ M > K (True)

50. (*a*) **Statements** R @ J ⇒ R ≤ J

M # J ⇒ M = J

D★M ⇒ D>M

Therefore, R ≤ J = M < D

Conclusions I. D ★ J ⇒ D > J (True)

II. R # M ⇒ R = M (Not true)

PRACTICE SET 41

1. Raju facing North and moves 20 km, then he turned to his right and moves 20 km and then he moves 10 km in North-East, then he turned to his right and moves 20 km and then he turned to his right and moves 20 km, and again he turned to his left and moves 20 km. Now, in which direction Raju is facing?

(a) South-East (b) North-East
(c) South-West (d) North-West

2. Rohit drives a car from Bengaluru to Mysore. After 80 km he turns right and goes 50 km. After that he again turns to his right and moves on 70 km. Finally, he turns to his right and stops after moving a distance of 50 km. At what distance is Rohit now from Bengaluru? **[MAT 2011]**

(a) 10 km (b) 40 km
(c) 20 km (d) 30 km

Direction (Q. Nos. 3-5) *Study the following information to answer the given questions.*

Nine friends L, M, N, O, P, Q, R, S and T are sitting around a circle facing the centre. T sits fifth to the right of R. N is not an immediate neighbour of either R or T. M sits between S and P. N sits fourth to left of the P. O sits second to the right of Q. S is not an immediate neighbour of T.

3. Who is second to the right of M?

(a) R (b) T
(c) L (d) Cannot be determined
(e) None of these

4. If all the nine friends are made to sit alphabetically in the clockwise direction starting from L, positions of how many will remain unchanged (excluding L)?

(a) None (b) One
(c) Two (d) Three
(e) Four

5. Four of the following five are alike in a certain way based on their seating positions in the above arrangement and so form a group. Which is the one that does not belong to the group?

(a) LP (b) SP (c) TS (d) LN
(e) QO

6. If day before yesterday was Tuesday, the day after tomorrow will be

(a) Monday (b) Wednesday
(c) Friday (d) Saturday

Direction (Q. Nos. 7-9) *In these questions, relationship between different elements is shown is the statement(s). The statements are followed by conclusions. Study the conclusions based on the given statements and select the appropriate answer.* **[IBPS (PO/MT) Pre 2015]**

Give answer

(a) if only Conclusion I follows
(b) if only Conclusion II follows
(c) if either Conclusion I or II follows
(d) if neither Conclusion I nor II follows
(e) if both Conclusion I and II follow

7. Statements $P < L \leq A = N \geq E \geq D$;
$Q \geq N < O$

Conclusions I. $L \leq E$
II. $P < Q$

8. Statements $P \leq U = N \leq C \geq H > S; K \geq C$

Conclusions I. $P \leq C$
II. $U > H$

9. Statements $P \leq U = N \leq C \geq H > S; K \geq C$

Conclusions I. $K > U$
II. $U = K$

Direction (Q. Nos. 10-11) *In the following questions, select the related word/letter/number from the given alternatives.*

10. 17 : 24 : : 153 : ? **[BSSC (CGL) 2015]**

(a) 213 (b) 216
(c) 144 (d) 198

11. Taste : Tongue : Walk : ?

(a) Pavement
(b) Crutch
(c) Legs
(d) Walking stick

12. 'Hare' is related to 'Burrow', in the same way 'Owl' is related to ......

(a) Hole (b) Hive
(c) Nest (d) Barn

Direction (Q. Nos. 13-14) *In each of the following questions, find the missing number from the given responses.*

13.

8	9	10
5	4	3
28	?	16
12	25	14

(a) 28 (b) 11
(c) 32 (d) 18

14. 341 (16) 521
613 (25) 816
452 (?) 326
(a) 27 (b) 22
(c) 30 (d) 41

15. While going to his office Tejveer meets Rakesh who is related to Tejveer because is Deepak's father who is married to Garima. Garima is the daughter of Rakesh. Garima has a daughter named Disha. How is Tejveer related to Disha? **[SBI SO (IT) 2016]**
(a) Uncle (b) Father-in-law
(c) Grandfather (d) Brother-in-law
(e) Niece

16. Which one of the given responses would be a meaningful order of the following words?
(i) Wall (ii) Clay
(iii) House (iv) Room
(v) Bricks
(a) (v), (ii), (i), (iv), (iii)
(b) (ii), (v), (iv), (i), (iii)
(c) (ii), (v), (i), (iv), (iii)
(d) (i), (ii), (iii), (iv), (v)

17. In a class of 40 children, Sunetra's rank is eighth from the top. Sujit is five ranks below Sunetra. What is Sujit's rank from the bottom? **[IBPS (PO/MT) Mains 2015]**
(a) 17 (b) 28 (c) 29 (d) 26
(e) Other than those given as options

Direction (Q Nos. 18-21) *Read the following information and answer the questions.*

Seven people namely A, B, C, D, E, F and G have a seminar on seven different days of the same week namely Monday, Tuesday, Wednesday, Thursday, Friday, Saturday and Sunday, but not necessarily in the same order. Each person also likes seven different colours namely, Green, Grey, White, Black, Orange, Pink and Blue, but not necessarily in the same order. C like Orange and has a seminar on Friday. Only one person has a seminar between C and the one who likes White. E has a seminar immediately before the one who likes White. Only three people have a seminar between E and D. B does not have a seminar on Wednesday. The one who likes Blue has a seminar immediately after B. Only three people have their seminars between the one who likes Blue and the one who likes Pink. The one who likes Black has a seminar immediately after the one who likes Grey. Neither G nor F likes Grey. F has a seminar on one of the days after G. **[NIACL (AO) 2014]**

18. Which of the following combinations is definitely correct?
(a) Monday-B-Black
(b) Monday-A-Grey
(c) Tuesday-B-Green
(d) Wednesday-A-Grey
(e) Tuesday-D-Green

19. Which of the following represents the day on which G has his seminar?
(a) Saturday
(b) Wednesday
(c) Monday
(d) Sunday
(e) Thursday

20. Based on the given arrangement, which of the following statements is true?
(a) A has a seminar on Monday
(b) D likes Green colour
(c) Only three people have a seminar between C and D
(d) None of the given statements is true
(e) The one who likes Pink colour has a seminar on Saturday

21. Which of the following colours does F like?
(a) Blue (b) Green
(c) Black (d) Pink
(e) White

Direction (Q. Nos. 22-23) *In the following questions find the odd words/letters from the given alternatives.*

22. (a) DI (b) KQ
(c) OU (d) AG

23. (a) Wolf (b) Cat
(c) Dog (d) Fox

Direction (Q. Nos. 24-26) *Study the following information to answer the given questions.*

A word and number arrangement machine when given an input line of words and numbers rearranges them following a particular rule. The following is an illustration of input and rearrangement.

Input 52 peak 91 snow freeze 46 cold 15 high 31 73 trek

***Step* I** 15 52 peak snow freeze 46 cold high 31 73 trek 91

***Step* II** 15 31 52 peak snow freeze 46 cold high trek 73 91

***Step* III** 15 31 46 peak snow freeze cold high trek 52 73 91

***Step* IV** 15 31 46 cold peak snow freeze high trek 52 73 91

***Step* V** 15 31 46 cold freeze peak snow high trek 52 73 91

***Step* VI** 15 31 46 cold freeze high peak snow trek 52 73 91

Step VI is the last step of the rearrangement. As per the rules followed in the above steps, find out in each of the following questions the appropriate steps for the given input.

Input 67 hot sun 19 best 83 ice 49 ace 77 cut 37

24. How many steps would be needed to complete the arrangement?

(a) X (b) VIII
(c) IX (d) VII
(e) None of these

25. Which step number would be the following output?

19 37 49 ace best hot sun ice cut 67 77 83

(a) II
(b) VI
(c) V
(d) IV
(e) None of the above

26. Which of the following would be the Step I ?

(a) 19 37 49 hot sun best ice ace cut 67 77 83
(b) 83 67 hot sun best ice 49 ace 77 cut 37 19
(c) 19 67 ace best hot sun ice 49 77 cut 37 83
(d) 19 67hot sun best ice 49 ace 77 cut 37 83
(e) None of the above

27. How many triangles are there in the following figure?

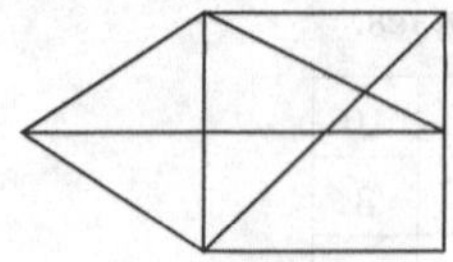

(a) 12 (b) 14
(c) 15 (d) 13

28. From the given alternative words, select the word which cannot be formed using the letters of the given word.

MISFORTUNE

(a) FORT (b) TURN
(c) SOFT (d) ROAM

29. In the following question a word is given. How many pairs of letters are there in these words which have as many letters between them as in the English alphabet?

PREAMBLE

(a) Nil (b) One
(c) Two (d) Three
(e) More than three

30. In the question given below an unfolded dice is given in the left side while in the right side, four answer choices are given in the form of complete dice. You are required to select the correct answer choice(s) which is/are formed by folding the unfolded dice.

Unfolded Dice

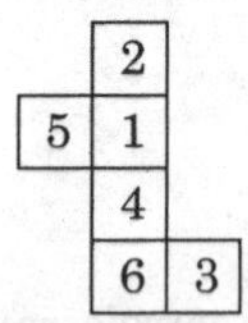

Answer Figures

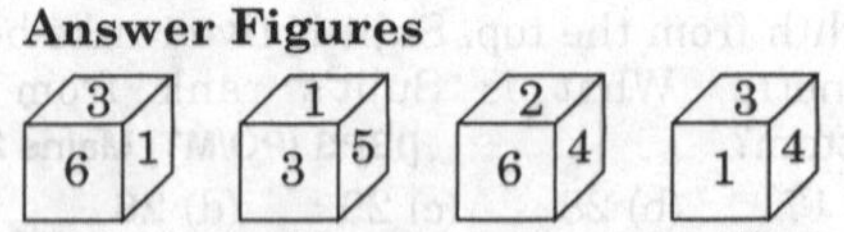

(a) (b) (c) (d)

Direction (Q. Nos. 31-32) *In each question below, the three Statements I, II and III are given. You are required to find out which of the given statement(s) is/are sufficient to answer the question. Mark your answer accordingly.*

31. In which year was Tarun born?

I. Tarun is 6 yr older than Rabin.

II. Rabin's brother was born in 1982.

III. Tarun's brother is 2 yr younger than Rabin's brother who was 8 yr younger than him.

(a) I and III
(b) II and III
(c) All I, II and III
(d) I and II

32. Who among P, Q, R, S and T is in the middle while standing in a line?

I. Q is to the right of T.

II. S is between P and T.

III. Q is between T and R.

(a) I and II (b) II and III
(c) I and III (d) All of the above

33. Five boy A, B, C, D and E are standing in row. D is on the right of E. B is on the left of E, but on the right of A. D is on the left of C, who is standing on the extreme right. Who is standing in the middle? **[SSC (10+2) 2013]**

(a) B (b) C
(c) D (d) E

34. If the day after tomorrow is Sunday, then what day was tomorrow's day before yesterday?

(a) Friday (b) Thursday
(c) Monday (d) Tuesday

35. In below question, which one set of letters when sequentially placed at the gaps in the given letter series shall complete it?

_ _ a a b _ a _ a _ b a

(a) bbaab (b) aaabb
(c) ababa (d) babab

Direction (Q. Nos 36-37) *In the following questions, a series is given, with one term missing. Choose the correct alternatives from the given ones that will complete the series.*

36. 68, 81, 96, ?, 132 **[SSC (10+2) 2014]**

(a) 105 (b) 110
(c) 113 (d) 130

37. DF, GJ, KM, NQ, RT, ? **[MAT 2013]**

(a) UX (b) UW
(c) YZ (d) XZ

Direction (Q. Nos. 38-40) *In each of the questions below are given some statements followed by some conclusions. You have to take the given statements to be true even if they seem to be at variance with commonly known facts. Read all the conclusions and then decide which of the given conclusions logically follows from the given statements disregarding commonly known facts.*

38. Statements Some pencils are windows.
All windows are roads.
Some roads are cups.
All cups are chains.

Conclusions I. Some chains are pencils.
II. Some cups are pencils.
III. Some chains are windows
IV. Some roads are pencils.

(a) None follows
(b) Only II follows
(c) Only IV follows
(d) III and IV follow
(e) Only III follows

39. Statements Some beds are mirrors.
Some mirrors are dolls.
Some dolls are cheques.
Some cheques are pins.

Conclusions I. Some pins are dolls.
II. Some cheques are beds.
III. Some cheques are mirrors.
IV. Some dolls are beds.

(a) None follows (b) Only I follows
(c) Only II follows (d) Only III follows
(e) Only IV follows

40. Statements All chocolates are holders.
No holder is a lamp.
Some lamps are desks.
All desks are pens.

Conclusions I. Some pens are holders.
II. Some desks are lamps.
III. No pen is a holder.
IV. Some pens are chocolates.

(a) Only I follows
(b) Only II follows
(c) Only III follows
(d) Either I or III follows
(e) Either I or III and II follow

41. Choose the correct figure that represents the given relation Blue eyed, Females, Doctors.

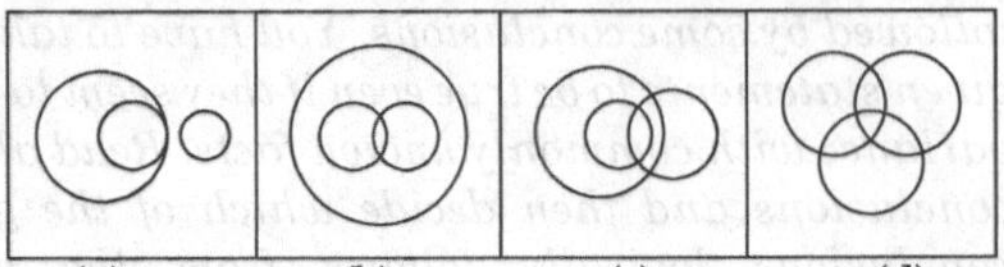

(a) (b) (c) (d)

42. Cause It has been reported by some important newspapers that current year monsoon can be lower than desired level as in so many part of the country it is not raining as it is required.

Which of the following can be a possible effect of above mentioned situation? **[UBI (PO) 2011]**

(a) People from less rain affected area can be displaced towards urban area
(b) Government can help the farmers of these areas with money package
(c) Government can declare these areas as drought regions
(d) People can blame government for this situation and they can protest for not getting sufficient water for agriculture
(e) None of the above

43. In a class of 42 students, Mahesh's rank is 16th from the bottom. What is his rank from the top?

(a) 125th (b) 126 th (c) 24th (d) 27 th

Direction (Q. Nos. 44-45) *Read the following information carefully and answer the questions which follow.* **[RBI (Officers) 2015]**

If 'P ★ Q' means 'P is the mother of Q'.
If 'P × Q' means 'P is the father of Q'.
If 'P + Q' means 'P is the sister of Q'.
If 'P – Q' means 'P is the brother of Q'.
If 'P > Q' means 'P is the son of Q'.
If 'P < Q' means 'P is the daughter of Q'

44. In the expression '$A \times B + R > S$', how is S related to A?

(a) Daughter-in-law
(b) Daughter
(c) Wife
(d) Sister
(e) Cannot be determined

45. In the expression '$P + Q > A - B$', how is P related to B?

(a) Daughter (b) Son
(c) Niece (d) Nephew
(e) Cannot be determined

46. If the word PRINCIPAL is written as LAPICNIRP, then how ADOLESCENCE can be written in that code? **[SSC (10+2) 2014]**

(a) ECNCESELODA
(b) ECNECSLEODA
(c) ECNSCEELODA
(d) ECNECSELODA

47. If in a certain code language 'SSC' is written as '19193', then how will 'BBC' be written in that language? **[SSC (CPO) 2012]**

(a) 113 (b) 221
(c) 223 (d) 213

48. If in a certain code language 'nik ka pa' means 'who are you', 'ka na ta da' means 'you may come here' and 'ho ta sa' means 'come and go', then what does 'nik' mean in that language? **[IBPS (Clerk) 2011]**

(a) who (b) are
(c) 'who' or 'are' (d) Data inadequate
(e) None of these

49. Identify the missing part of the question figure and select it from given answer figures.

Question Figure **[SSC (10+2) 2011]**

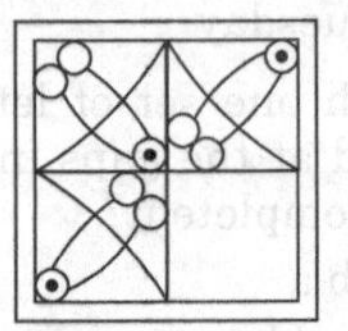

Answer Figures

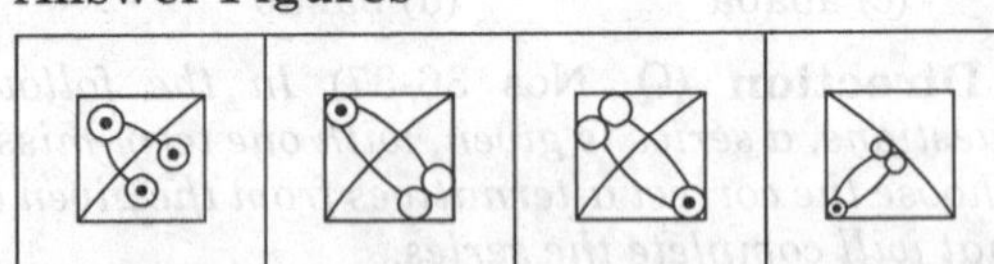

(a) (b) (c) (d)

50. If 4 ★ 2 @ 3 = 6, 18 ★ 6 @ 4 = 12, then what will be the value of 24 ★ 3 @ 7 ?

(a) 21 (b) 27
(c) 72 (d) 156

Hints and Solutions

1. (*a*) Direction followed by Raju

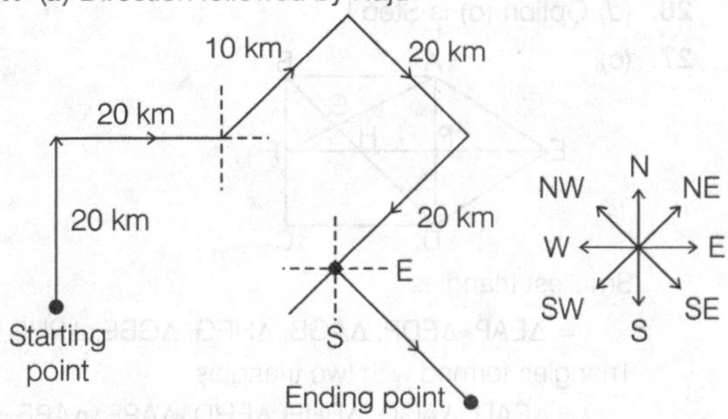

From the above figure, we see that Raju is facing in 'South-East' direction.

2. (*a*) According to the question, the direction diagram is as follows

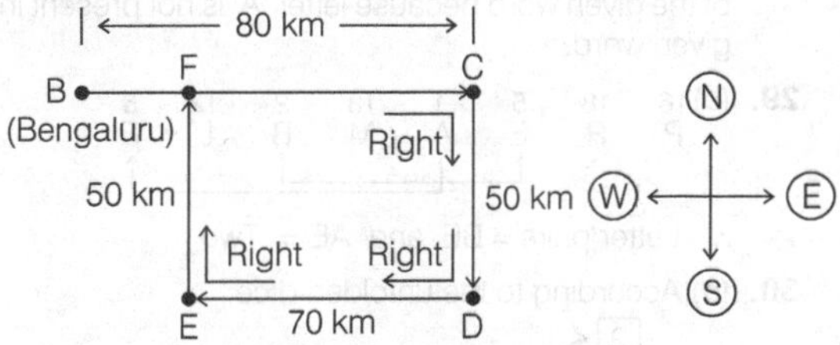

BC = 80 km, CD = FE = 50

DE = FC = 70 km

∴ Required distance, BF = BC − FC = 80 − 70 = 10 km

Solution (Q. Nos. 3-5) According to the given information, the sitting arrangement is as following

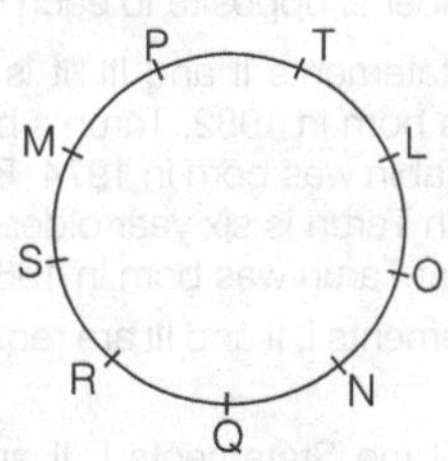

3. (*a*) R is second to the right of M.

4. (*c*) According to the question, the arrangement will be as following

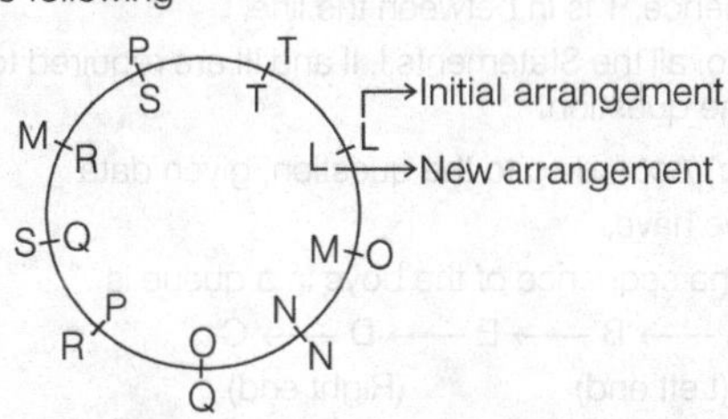

So, the positions of N and T will not changed.

5. (*c*) TS does not belong to this group because two persons are sitting between T and S while in others, one person is sitting between them.

6. (*d*) The day before yesterday was Tuesday.

Today, it is Tuesday + 2 = Thursday.

Tomorrow ⇒ Friday

The day after tomorrow ⇒ Saturday

7. (*b*) **Statements** $P < L \le A = N \ge E \ge D$; $Q \ge N < Q$

Therefore, $P < L \le A = N \ge E \ge D$ (with Q ≥ N above and N < Q below)

Conclusions I. $L \le E$ (✗)

II. $P < Q$ (✔)

So, only Conclusion II follows.

8. (*a*) **Statements** $P \le U = N \le C > H > S$; $K \ge C$

Therefore, $P \le U = N \le C \ge H > S$ (with K ≥ C below)

Conclusions I. $P \le C$ (✔)

II. $U > H$ (✗)

So, only Conclusion I follows.

9. (*c*) **Statements** $P \le U = N \le C > H > S$; $K \ge C$

Therefore, $P \le U = N \le C \ge H > S$ (with K ≥ C below)

Conclusions I. $K > U$ ⎤ Complementary pair

II. $U = K$ ⎦

So, either Conclusion I or II follows.

10. (*b*) As, $17 \times 9 \Rightarrow 153$

Similarly, $24 \times 9 \Rightarrow 216$

11. (*c*) Tongue is used to 'Taste' something. In the same way, 'Leg' is used to 'Walk'.

12. (*d*) 'Burrow' is the dwelling place of 'Hare'. Similarly, 'Barn' is the dwelling place of 'Owl'.

13. (*b*) As, $8 \times 5 - 28 = 40 - 28 = 12$

and $10 \times 3 - 16 = 30 - 16 = 14$

Similarly, $9 \times 4 - ? = 25$

⇒ $36 - ? = 25$

∴ $? = 36 - 25 = 11$

14. (*b*) As, $(3 + 4 + 1) + (5 + 2 + 1) = 8 + 8 = 16$

and $(6 + 1 + 3) + (8 + 1 + 6) = 10 + 15 = 25$

Similarly, $(4 + 5 + 2) + (3 + 2 + 6) = 11 + 11 = \boxed{22}$

15. (*c*) According to the question,

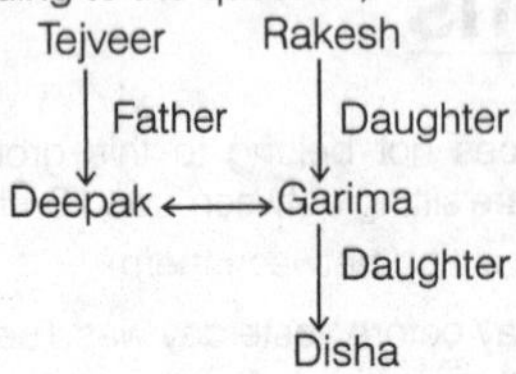

Clearly, Tezveer is Disha's grandfather.

16. (*c*) Meaningful order of words
(ii) Clay → (v) Bricks → (i) Wall → (iv) Room → (iii) House

17. (*a*) According to the information,

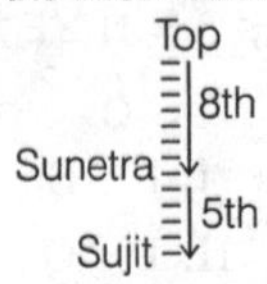

So, $8+5=13$ $\therefore$ $40-13=27$
Sujit is 27th from the bottom.

Solution (Q. Nos. 18-21) According to the question,

Person	Day	Colour
G	Thursday	Green
C	Friday	Orange
E	Sunday	Pink
F	Saturday	White
A	Monday	Grey
B	Tuesday	Black
D	Wednesday	Blue

18. (*b*) Monday-A-Grey combination is definitely correct.

19. (*e*) G has his seminar on Thursday.

20. (*a*) A has a seminar on Monday is true.

21. (*e*) F likes White colour.

22. (*a*) D $\xrightarrow{+5}$ I, K $\xrightarrow{+6}$ Q, O $\xrightarrow{+6}$ U and A $\xrightarrow{+6}$ G
Thus, 'DI' is different from all others, because the difference between 'D' and 'I' is of '5' places, while others have difference of '6' places.

23. (*b*) Except Cat, all others belong to Dog family. The members of cat family are cat, lions, tiger, leopard etc.

Solution (Q. Nos. 24-26)

Input 67 hot sun 19 best 83 ice 49 ace 77 cut 37
***Step* I** 19 67 hot sun best ice 49 ace 77 cut 37 83
***Step* II** 19 37 67 hot sun best ice 49 ace cut 77 83
***Step* III** 19 37 49 hot sun best ice ace cut 67 77 83
***Step* IV** 19 37 49 ace hot sun best ice cut 67 77 83
***Step* V** 19 37 49 ace best hot sun ice cut 67 77 83
***Step* VI** 19 37 49 ace best cut hot sun ice 67 77 83
***Step* VII** 19 37 49 ace best cut hot ice sun 67 77 83

24. (*d*) Seven steps are needed to complete the arrangement.

25. (*c*) It is Step V.

26. (*d*) Option (d) is Step I.

27. (*c*)

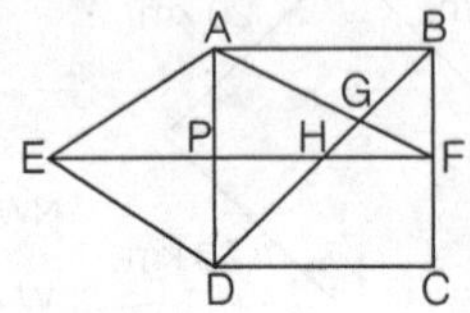

Smallest triangles
$= \Delta EAP, \Delta EDP, \Delta AGB, \Delta HFG, \Delta GBF, \Delta PHD = 6$
Triangles formed with two triangles
$= \Delta EAD, \Delta AGD, \Delta BHF, \Delta EHD, \Delta APF, \Delta ABF = 6$
Largest triangles $= \Delta BDC, \Delta AEF, \Delta ABD = 3$
$\therefore$ Total triangles $= 6+6+3=15$

28. (*d*) Word ROAM cannot be formed by using the letters of the given word because letter 'A' is not present in the given word.

29. (*c*)

16	18	5	1	13	2	12	5
P	R	E	A	M	B	L	E

$\therefore$ Letter pairs = BE and AE ⇒ Two

30. (*d*) According to the unfolded dice,

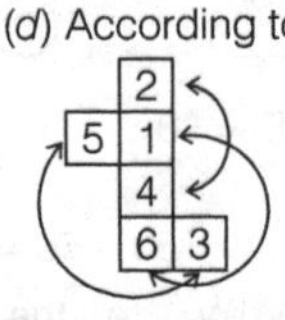

So, 1 is opposite to 6
2 is opposite to 4
and 3 is opposite to 5

Hence, only option (d) is the correct answer because in this no number is opposite to each other.

31. (*c*) From Statements II and III, it is clear that Rabin's brother was born in 1982, Tarun's brother was born in 1984 and Rabin was born in 1974. From Statement I, it is given than Tarun is six year older than Rabin, hence we know that Tarun was born in 1968.
So, all Statements I, II and III are required to answer the question.

32. (*d*) From all the Statements I, II and III, the order of ranking of P, Q, R, S and T in a line is as

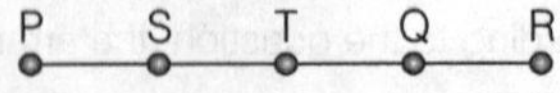

Hence, T is in between the line.
So, all the Statements I, II and III are required to answer the question.

33. (*d*) According to the question, given data we have,
The sequence of the boys in a queue is
A ⟶ B ⟶ E ⟶ D ⟶ C
(Left end) (Right end)
So, E is in the middle.

34. (*b*) The day after tomorrow is Sunday.
Therefore, today is Friday.
The day on tomorrow's day before yesterday
= Friday −1 = Thursday

35. (*c*) The complete series will be
a <u>b</u> a / a b <u>a</u> / a <u>b</u> a / <u>a</u> b a ⇒ ababa

36. (*c*) From the given series,

68 →(+13)→ 81 →(+15)→ 96 →(+17)→ (113) →(+19)→ 132
(+2, +2, +2)

37. (*a*) The pattern is as follows

D →(+3)→ G →(+4)→ K →(+3)→ N →(+4)→ R →(+3)→ U
F →(+4)→ J →(+3)→ M →(+4)→ Q →(+3)→ T →(+4)→ X

∴ ? = UX

38. (*c*)

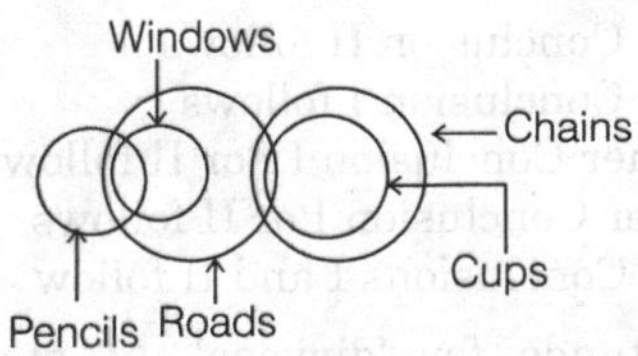

Conclusions I. Some chains are pencils. (✗)
II. Some cups are pencils. (✗)
III. Some chains are windows (✗)
IV. Some roads are pencils. (✔)

39. (a)

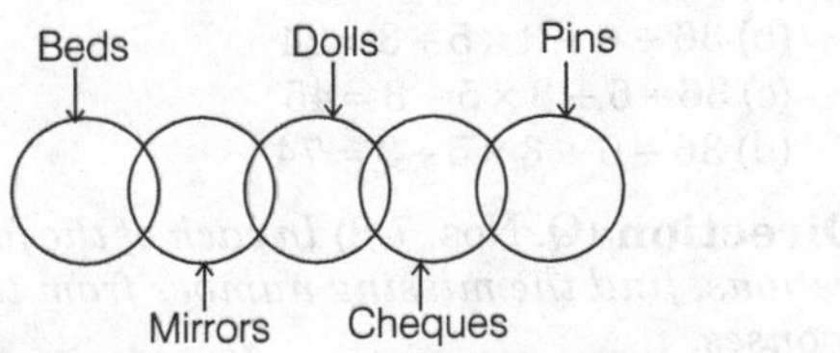

Conclusions I. Some pins are dolls. (✗)
II. Some cheques are beds. (✗)
III. Some cheques are mirrors. (✗)
IV. Some dolls are beds. (✗)

40. (*e*)

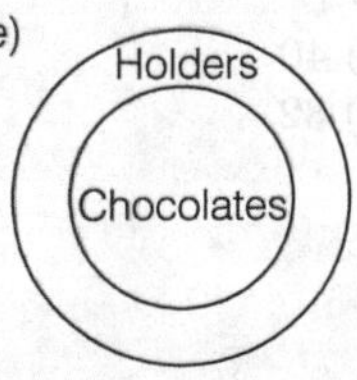

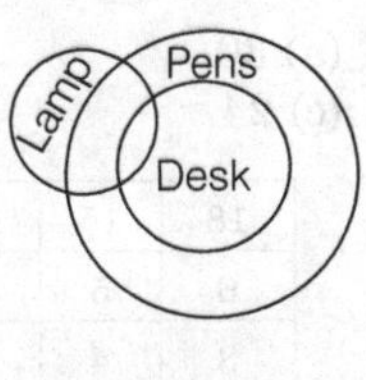

Conclusions I. Some pens are holders. (✗)
II. Some desks are lamps. (✔)
III. No pen is a holder. (✔)
IV. Some pens are chocolates. (✗)

41. (*d*) Some blue eyed may be females and vice-versa.
Some females may be doctors and vice-versa.
Some blue eyed may be doctors and vice-versa.
Some blue eyed females may be doctors.

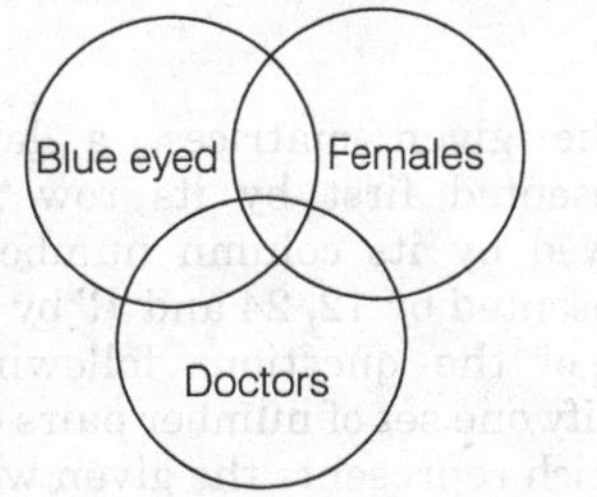

42. (*c*) Option (b) is also possible, but its possibility can only be after declaring the area as drought regions.

43. (*d*) Mahesh's rank from the top = 42 − 16 + 1 = 27

44. (*c*) A × B + R > S → S is the wife of A.

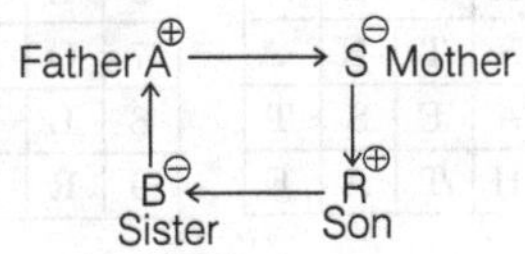

45. (*c*) P + Q > A − B → P is the niece of B.

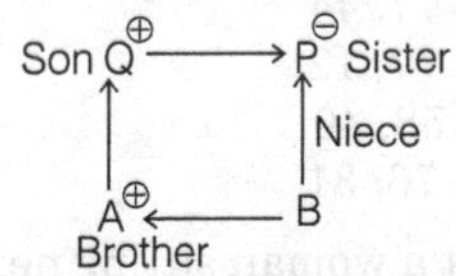

46. (*d*) As, PRINCIPAL → LAPICNIRP
Here, given word is written in reverse order.
Same as, ADOLESCENCE →(Reverse)→ ECNECSELODA

47. (*c*) As, S S C → 19 19 3 ← Positional Values
Similarly, B B C → 2 2 3
∴ BBC ⇒ 223

48. (c) As, nik (ka) pa → who are (you) ...(i)
(ka) na ta da → (you) may come here ...(ii)
ho ta sa → come and go ...(iii)

From Eqs. (i) and (ii), ka ⇒ you
nik ⇒ 'who' or 'are'

49. (*b*) Option (b) will complete the given pattern.

50. (c) Here ★ → ÷, @ → X

∴ 4 ÷ 2 × 3 = 6
18 ÷ 6 × 4 = 12

Therefore, 24 ÷ 3 × 7 = 56

PRACTICE SET 42

1. In the given matrices, a letter can be represented first by its row number and followed by its column number. e.g. 'A' is represented by 12, 24 and 'R' by 57, 76 etc. In each of the questions following matrices, identify one set of number pairs out of (a, b, c, d) which represents the given word.

Matrix I

	0	1	2	3	4
0	A	E	S	T	H
1	T	H	A	E	S
2	E	S	T	H	A
3	H	A	E	S	T
4	S	H	T	A	E

Matrix II

	5	6	7	8	9
5	P	O	R	K	L
6	K	L	P	O	R
7	O	R	K	L	P
8	L	P	O	R	K
9	R	K	L	P	O

LAKE

(a) 85, 31, 77, 44
(b) 97, 00, 77, 12
(c) 66, 12, 58, 40
(d) 77, 43, 76, 31

2. Looking at a woman sitting next to him, Amit said, "She is the sister of the husband of my wife". How is the woman related to Amit? **[SSC (CGL) 2014]**

(a) Daughter
(b) Sister
(c) Wife
(d) Niece

Direction (Q. Nos. 3-5) *In these questions, relationship between different elements is shown in the statement. The statement is followed by two conclusions. Study the conclusions based on the given statement and select the appropriate answer.* **[IBPS (Clerk) 2013]**

3. Statement $B > A > S < I > C > L > Y$

Conclusions I. $B > L$

II. $A > Y$

(a) Only Conclusion I follows
(b) Only Conclusion II follows
(c) Either Conclusion I or II follows
(d) Neither Conclusion I nor II follows
(e) Both Conclusions I and II follow

4. Statement $K \geq L > M \geq N$

Conclusions I. $N \leq K$

II. $N < K$

(a) Both Conclusions I and II follow
(b) Neither Conclusion I nor II follows
(c) Either Conclusion I or II follows
(d) Only Conclusion I follows
(e) Only Conclusion II follows

5. Statement $Z \geq Y = W \leq X$

Conclusions I. $W < Z$

II. $W = Z$

(a) Only Conclusion II follows
(b) Only Conclusion I follows
(c) Neither Conclusion I nor II follows
(d) Either Conclusion I or II follows
(e) Both Conclusions I and II follow

6. If '+' stands for 'division', '×' stands for 'addition', '–' stands for 'multiplication' and '÷' stands for 'subtraction', then which of the following equations is correct?

(a) $36 \times 6 + 7 \div 2 - 6 = 20$
(b) $36 + 6 - 3 \times 5 \div 3 = 24$
(c) $36 \div 6 + 3 \times 5 - 3 = 45$
(d) $36 - 6 + 3 \times 5 \div 3 = 74$

Direction (Q. Nos. 7-8) *In each of the following questions, find the missing number from the given responses.*

7.

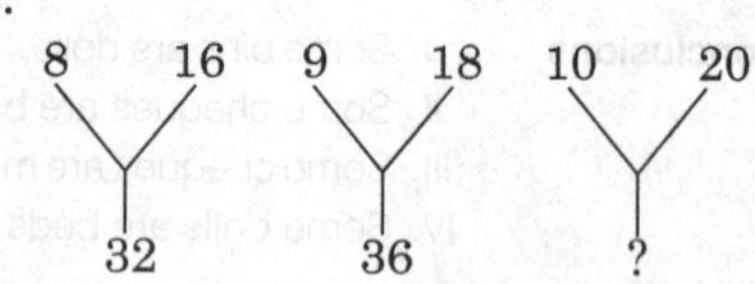

(a) 30 (b) 40
(c) 24 (d) 32

8.

18	15	11
6	5	8
3	4	?
324	300	528

(a) 7 (b) 5
(c) 6 (d) 4

9. Arrange the following words as per order in the dictionary. **[SSC (CGL) 2011]**

(i) Noble (ii) Nobilitary
(iii) Noblesse (iv) Nobility
(v) Nobble

(a) (i), (iv), (iii), (ii), (v)
(b) (iii), (iv), (i), (ii), (v)
(c) (v), (ii), (iv), (i), (iii)
(d) (ii), (iv), (iii), (v), (i)

10. In the following figure, the triangle represents teachers, the circle represents students and the rectangle represents actors. Which number represents teachers who are also students and actors? **[SSC (Constable) 2012]**

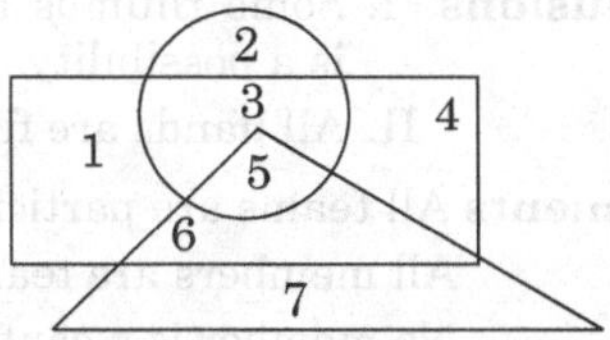

(a) 3 (b) 6 (c) 5 (d) 2

Direction (Q. Nos. 11-13) *Study the following information carefully and answer the questions which follow:*

A word and number arrangement machine when given an input line of words and numbers rearranges them following a particular rule. Following is an illustration of input and the rearrangement.

(Single digit numbers are preceded by a zero. All other numbers are two-digit numbers.)

Input when 19 will you 07 be 40 coming 62 home 100 89
***Step* I** be when 19 will you 07 40 coming 62 home 100 89
***Step* II** be 07 when 19 will you 40 coming 62 home 100 89
***Step* III** be 07 coming when 19 will you 40 62 home 100 89
***Step* IV** be 07 coming 19 when will you 40 62 home 100 89
***Step* V** be 07 coming 19 home when will you 40 62 100 89
***Step* VI** be 07 coming 19 home 40 when will you 62 100 89
***Step* VII** be 07 coming 19 home 40 when 62 will you 100 89
***Step* VIII** be 07 coming 19 home 40 when 62 will 89 you 100

Step VIII is the last step of the arrangement of the above input as the intended arrangement is obtained.

As per the rules followed in the above steps. Find out in each of the following questions the appropriate steps for the given input.

Input next 57 problem 82 14 trend 02 purchase growth 41

11. How many steps would be needed to complete the arrangement?
(a) V (b) VI (c) VIII (d) VII
(e) Cannot be determined

12. Which of the following would be the final arrangement?
(a) growth 02 next 14 problem 41 purchase 57 82 trend
(b) growth next problem purchase trend 02 14 41 57 82
(c) growth 02 next 14 problem 41 purchase 57 trend 82
(d) growth 82 next 57 purchase 41 problem 14 next 02
(e) None of the above

13. Which of the following would be Step I ?
(a) 41 purchase 02 trend 14 82 problem 57 next growth
(b) growth 02 next 57 problem 82 14 trend purchase 41
(c) 41 growth next 57 problem 82 14 trend 02 purchase
(d) growth next 57 problem 82 14 trend 02 purchase 41
(e) growth next 57 purchase 82 14 trend 02 problem 41.

Direction (Q. Nos. 14-15) *Each of the questions below consists of a question and two statements numbered* I *and* II *given below it. You have to decide whether the data provided in the statements are sufficient to answer the question.*

Give answer **[RBI (Officers) 2015]**
(a) if the data in Statement I alone is sufficient to answer the question, while the data in statement II alone is not sufficient to answer the question
(b) if the data in Statement II alone is sufficient to answer the question, while the data in Statement I alone is not sufficient to answer the question

(c) if the data either in Statement I alone or in Statement II alone is sufficient to answer the question
(d) if the data in both the Statements I and II together are not sufficient to answer the question
(e) if the data in both the Statements I and II together are necessary to answer the question

14. How many people are standing between H and U in a straight line of 15 people (All are standing in a straight line facing North)?
I. M stands fifth from the left end of the line. H and K are immediate neighbours of M. Only two people stand between M and U.
II. B stands third from the right end of the line. Only six people stand between K and B. Only one person stands between H and K. K stands exactly between H and U.

15. Among people A, B, C, D, E and F, each having a different weight, who is the second highest?
I. C is heavier than only two people. A is heavier than F but lighter than B. D is not the lightest.
II. F is lighter than only two people. C is lighter than F but heavier than D. A is lighter than only B.

16. Present ages of Anupam and Raju are in the ratio of 5 : 4, respectively. Three years hence, the ratio of their ages will become 11 : 9, respectively. What is Raju's present age?
(a) 24 yr (b) 27 yr
(c) 40 yr (d) Data inadequate

17. After 9 O' clock at what time between 9 pm and 10 pm will the hour and minute hands of a clock point in opposite direction? **[SSC (CGL) 2011]**
(a) 15 min past 9 (b) 16 min past 9
(c) $16\frac{4}{11}$ min past 9 (d) $17\frac{1}{11}$ min past 9

Direction (Q.Nos. 18-20) *In each of the questions below are given three statements followed by two conclusions numbered I and II. You have to take the given statements to be true even if they seem to be at variance from commonly known facts and decide which of the given conclusion(s) logically follow(s) from the three given statements.* **[IBPS (PO/MT) Mains 2015]**

Give answer
(a) if only Conclusion I follows
(b) if only Conclusion II follows
(c) if either Conclusion I or II follows
(d) if neither Conclusion I nor II follows
(e) if both Conclusions I and II follow

18. Statements No metting is an argument.
All debates are arguments.
Some debates are fights.
Conclusions I. No fight is a meeting.
II. Some fight are meetings.

19. Statements All hands are limbs.
All limbs are fingers.
Some fingers are thumbs.
Conclusions I. Some thumbs being limbs is a possibility.
II. All hands are fingers.

20. Statements All teams are participants.
All members are teams.
No member is a captain.
Conclusions I. At least some participants are members.
II. All teams being captains is a possibility.

21. Examine the following statements.
I. Only those who have a pair of binoculars become the members of the birdwatcher's club.
II. Some members of the birdwatcher's club have participate cameras.
III. Those members who have cameras cannot photo-contests.

Which of the following conclusions can be drawn from the above statements?
(a) All those who have a pair of binoculars are members of the birdwatcher's club
(b) All members of the birdwatcher's club have a pair of binoculars
(c) All those who take part in photo-contests are members of the birdwatcher's club
(d) No conclusion can be drawn

22. In making decisions about important questions, it is desirable to distinguish between a 'strong' argument and a 'weak' argument. A 'strong' argument must be both important and directly related to the question. A 'weak' argument may not be directly related to the question and may be of minor importance or may be related to the trivial aspect of the question. Each question below is followed by three arguments numbered I, II and III. You have to decide which of the arguments is 'strong' and which is 'weak'.

Statement Should the government impose restrictions on access to sensitive information to the journalists to avoid the media hype?

Arguments

I. Yes, the media creates hype and publishes distorted information at times.

II. No, journalists should have an access to all the information as media is the best source to expose the malfunction sin the society.

III. Yes, at times it leads to harassment of those who are affected and alleged to be involved in the crisis.

(a) All I, II and III are strong
(b) I and II are strong
(c) II and III are strong
(d) Only II is strong
(e) None is strong

Direction (Q. Nos. 23-24) *In the following questions, select the related word/letters from the given alternatives.*

23. EIGK : EACY : : RVTY : ? **[SSC (CGL) 2014]**

(a) RVSQ (b) RNPM
(c) RWUY (d) RMPL

24. House : Rent : : Capital : ?

(a) Interest (b) Investment
(c) Country (d) Money

25. Choose that set of numbers from the four alternative sets, that is similar to the given set.

Given set : (32, 24, 8)

(a) (26, 32, 42) (b) (34, 24, 14)
(c) (24, 16, 0) (d) (42, 34, 16)

Direction (Q.Nos. 26-27) *In the following questions, find the odd numbers/letters/number pair from the given alternatives.*

26. (a) Garden — Gardener
(b) Song — Singer
(c) Art — Artist
(d) Dance — Dancer

27. (a) 392–21 (b) 483 – 15
(c) 602 – 42 (d) 917 – 35

28. In a certain code language, 'nik ka pa' means 'who are you' ; 'ka na ta da' means 'you may come here' and 'ho ta sa' means 'come and go'; what does 'nik' mean in that code language? **[NICL (Assistant) Grade III 2015]**

(a) Who
(b) Are
(c) Who or are
(d) Data inadequate
(e) None of these

29. A man is engaged for planting tress for 10 h. He plants 10 trees in an hour. He takes rest for 30 min after every hour.

How many trees does he plant in 10 h?

(a) 100 (b) 50 (c) 70 (d) 45

30. In a code TIGER is written as SHFDQ, how shall HORSE be written in that code?

(a) GNRQD (b) GNQRD
(c) GRNQD (d) GMQRD

31. How many meaningful three letters English words can be formed with the letters WNO using each letter only once in each word?

(a) None (b) One
(c) Two (d) Three
(e) Four

32. A dice is thrown four times and its different positions are shown below. What number is opposite to face showing 2 ? **[SSC (CPO) 2013]**

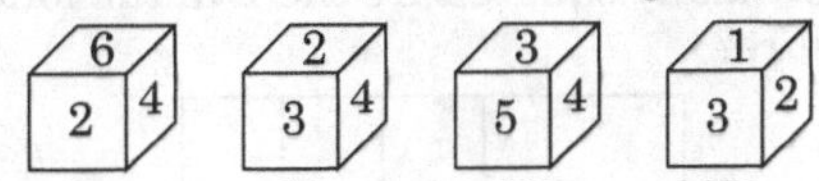

I II III IV

(a) 2 (b) 3
(c) 4 (d) 5

33. Babu is Rahim's neighbour and his house is 200 m away in the North-West direction. Joseph is Rahim's neighbour and his house is located 200 m away in the South-West direction. Gopal is Joseph's neighbour and he stays 200 m away in the South-East direction. Roy is Gopal's neighbour and his house is located 200 m away in the North-East direction. Then, where is the position of Roy's house in relation to Babu's?

(a) South-East (b) South-West
(c) North (d) North-East

34. In a clock, the angle between the hour hand and minute hand at 5 h 10 min, is

(a) 60° (b) 95°
(c) 120° (d) 90°

Direction (Q.Nos. 35-37) *Study the following arrangement carefully and answer the questions.*

5 8 3 1 7 9 2 5 1 2 8 3 4 5 2 8 5 4 2 3 7 3 9 6 2 4 2 9 5 3 6 4 6 1 2 **[SBI SO (IT) 2016]**

35. How many such 3s are there in the given arrangement each of which is immediately preceded as well as immediately followed by an even digit?

(a) More than three
(b) One
(c) Three
(d) Two
(e) None

36. How many such 2s are there in the given arrangement each of which is immediately followed by a perfect square?
(**Note** 1 is also a perfect square)

(a) One (b) More than three
(c) Two (d) Three
(e) None

37. Which of the following is fifth to the left of the sixteenth digit from the left end of the given arrangement?

(a) 5 (b) 7 (c) 2 (d) 8
(e) 3

38. How many squares are there in the following figure?

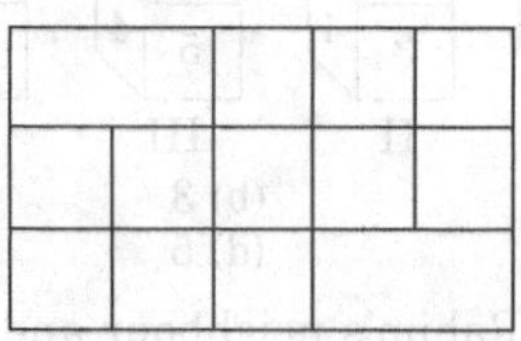

(a) 10 (b) 16 (c) 14 (d) 19

Direction (Q.Nos. 39-41) *Read the following passage and answer the questions based on it.*

There are four persons A, B, C and D. One of them is Lecturer and plays Football and Cricket. A and B are Accountants. A plays Badminton. Both the Accountants are Swimmers. D is Bank Clerk. One Accountant also plays Tennis. The Bank Clerk plays Carrom and is a Swimmer. All the four persons play two games each and follow one profession.

39. Who is the Lecturer?

(a) A (b) B
(c) C (d) D
(e) None of these

40. Who cannot swim?

(a) A
(b) B
(c) C
(d) D
(e) Cannot be determined

41. Who plays Tennis?

(a) A (b) B
(c) C (d) D
(e) None of these

42. Find out the answer figure which completes the question figure matrix.

Question Figure

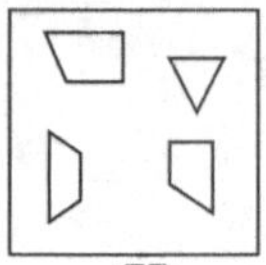

(X)

Answer Figures

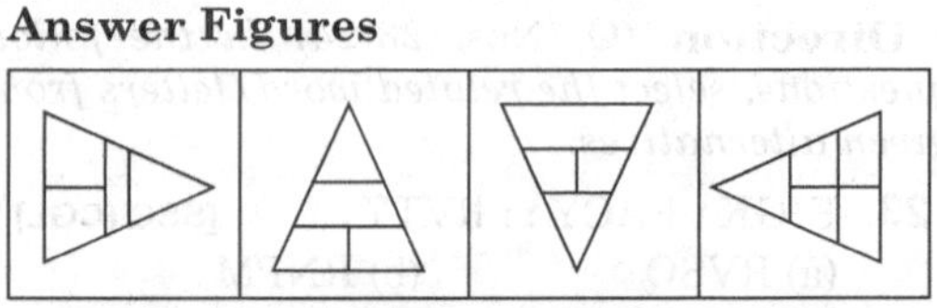

(a) (b) (c) (d)

43. In a straight line of twelve people (facing North), P sits fifth from the left end of the line. Only three people sit between J and P. S sits second to the right of J. O sits third to the right of S. How many people sit between O and P ? **[IBPS (Clerk) Pre 2015]**

(a) None
(b) Cannot be determined
(c) Three
(d) One
(e) Two

44. In an examination, Rahul got the 11th rank and he was 47th from the bottom among those who passed. 3 students could not appear for the exam. 1 student failed. What is the total number of students?

(a) 60 (b) 62 **[SSC (Steno) 2011]**
(c) 59 (d) 61

Direction (Q. Nos. 45-46) *In the following questions, a series is given, with one term missing. Choose the correct alternative from the given ones that will complete the series.*

45. 121, 253, 374, 495, ? **[SSC (10+2) 2014]**

(a) 565 (b) 523
(c) 5116 (d) 5102

46. PBA, QDC, RFE, ? **[UP BEd 2011]**

(a) SHG (b) OAB
(c) TJI (d) ULK

47. Which one set of letters when sequentially placed at the gaps in the given letter series shall complete it?

_ n m m n _ m m n n _ m n n m _

(a) n n m m (b) n m n m
(c) m n n m (d) n m m n

48. Mr Biswas is planning for 2 weeks holiday with his family to UK, Germany, France, Switzerland, Belgium, Italy, Norway and Austria. However, his family has imposed certain conditions for travel. **[CMAT 2015]**

I. Will travel to Austria and Switzerland in different weeks.
II. Germany must be visited after Belgium in the same week.
III. Switzerland must be visited after France in the same week.
IV. Will travel to Germany and Norway in different weeks.
V. Will travel to UK and France in different weeks.
VI. Will travel to Austria and Belgium in the same weeks.
VII. Italy must be visited in the 2nd week.
VIII. Equal numbers of places must be visited in weeks 1 and 2.

Which places are visited in week 2, if all places are visited only once?

(a) Italy, UK, Switzerland, Norway
(b) Italy, France, Germany, Norway
(c) Italy, UK, Austria, Switzerland
(d) Italy, France, Switzerland, Norway

49. Which one of the answer figures is hidden in the following question figure?

Question Figure

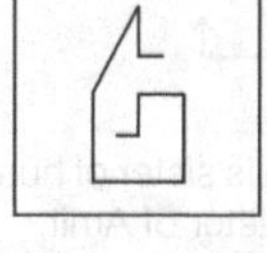

Answer Figures

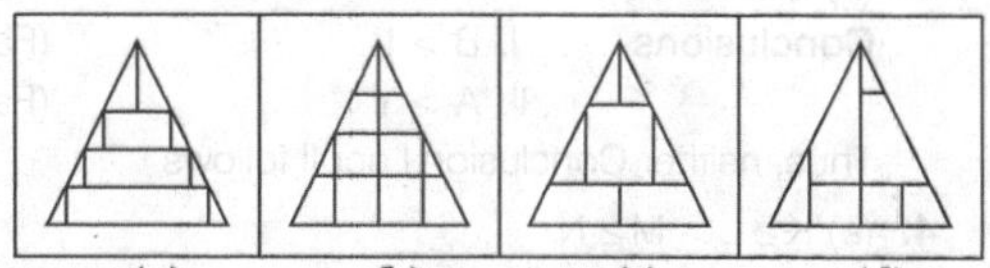

(a) (b) (c) (d)

50. In the following question, a series is given with one term missing. Choose the correct alternative from the given ones that will complete the series.

Question Figures

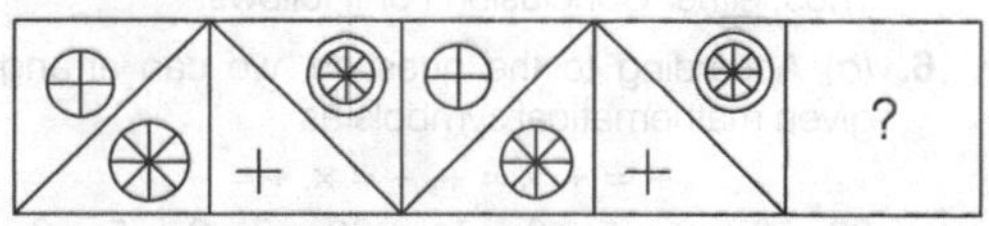

Answer Figures

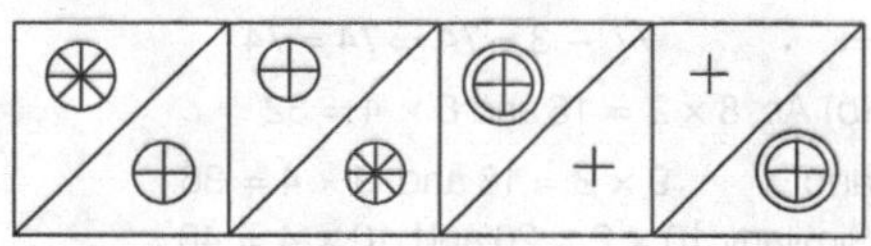

(a) (b) (c) (d)

Hints and Solutions

1. (*a*) According to the matrices,

L — 59, 66, 78, (85), 97 A — 00, 12, 24, (31), 43
K — 58, 65, (77), 89, 96 E — 01, 13, 20, 32, (44)

∴ LAKE ⇒ 85, 31, 77, 44

2. (*b*) According to the given information,

Amit is referring to himself while he said, "husband of my wife."

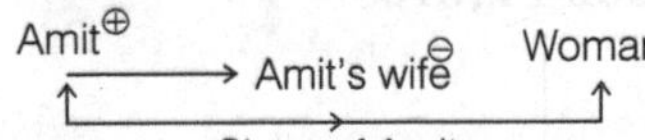

So, Amit is husband and a woman is sister of husband of my wife. Therefore, woman is sister of Amit.

3. (*d*) $B > A > S < I > C > L > Y$

Conclusions I. $B > L$ (False)
II. $A > Y$ (False)

Thus, neither Conclusion I nor II follows.

4. (*e*) $K \geq L > M \geq N$

Conclusions I. $N \leq K$ (False)
II. $N < K$ (True)

Thus, only Conclusion II follows.

5. (*d*) $Z \geq Y = W \leq X$

Conclusions I. $W < Z$ (May be true)
or II. $W = Z$ (May be true)

Thus, either Conclusion I or II follows.

6. (*d*) According to the question, we can arrange the given mathematical symbols as

$+ = \div, \times = +, - = \times, \div = -$

$36 - 6 + 3 \times 5 \div 3 = 74 \Rightarrow 36 \times 6 \div 3 + 5 - 3 = 74$

$\Rightarrow 36 \times 2 + 5 - 3 = 74 \Rightarrow 72 + 5 - 3 = 74$

$\Rightarrow 77 - 3 = 74 \Rightarrow 74 = 74$

7. (*b*) As, $8 \times 2 = 16$ and $8 \times 4 = 32$

and $9 \times 2 = 18$ and $9 \times 4 = 36$

Similarly, $10 \times 2 = 20$ and $10 \times 4 = 40$

8. (*c*) As, $18 \times 6 \times 3 = 324$ and $15 \times 5 \times 4 = 300$

Similarly, $? = \frac{528}{11 \times 8} = 6$

9. (*c*) Arrangement of words as per dictionary:

(v) Nobble → (ii) Nobilitary → (iv) Nobility → (i) Noble → (iii) Noblesse

10. (*c*) The required region should be common in all the three figures. Such region is represented by '5'.

Solution (Q. Nos. 11-13) After careful analysis of the given input and various steps of rearrangement it is evident that words and numbers are rearranged alternately. Words are arranged in alphabetical order and the numbers are arranged in ascending order.

Input next 57 problem 82 14 trend 02 purchase growth 41
***Step* I** growth next 57 problem 82 14 trend 02 purchase 41
***Step* II** growth 02 next 57 problem 82 14 trend purchase 41
***Step* III** growth 02 next 14 57 problem 82 trend purchase 41
***Step* IV** growth 02 next 14 problem 57 82 trend purchase 41
***Step* V** growth 02 next 14 problem 41 57 82 trend purchase
***Step* VI** growth 02 next 14 problem 41 purchase 57 82 trend
***Step* VII** growth 02 next 14 problem 41 purchase 57 trend 82

Step VII is the last step of arrangement.

11. (*d*) Seven steps would be needed to complete the arrangement.

12. (*c*) Option (c) is the final arrangement.

13. (*d*) Option (d) is the Step I.

14. (*b*) From Statement II,

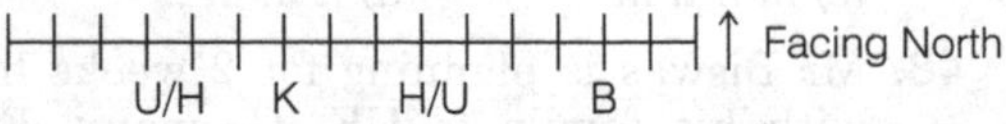

So, it is clearly shown that, there are three people standing between H and U in straight line of 15 people. Therefore, Statement II alone sufficient to answer the question.

15. (*e*) From Statement I, C>_>_ ...(i)
B >A>F ...(ii)
From Statement II, _>_>F ...(iii)
F>C>D ...(iv)
B > A ...(v)

By combining both the statements, we get

$B > A > F > C > D > E$

So, A is the second highest.

Therefore, both statements together are necessary to answer the question.

15. (*e*) From both the statements,

Jyoti > Sadhana/Pinki > Meera

16. (*a*) Let the present ages of Anupam and Raju be 5x yr and 4x yr, respectively.

After 3 yr, Age of Anupam = $(5x + 3)$ yr

After 3 yr, Age of Raju = $(4x + 3)$ yr

According to the question, $\frac{5x + 3}{4x + 3} = \frac{11}{9}$

$\Rightarrow 45x + 27 = 44x + 33$

$\Rightarrow x = 33 - 27 = 6$ yr

∴ Present age of Raju = $4 \times 6 = 24$ yr

17. (*c*) At 9 O'clock, the minute hand is $9 \times 5 = 45$ min spaces behind the hour hand. Therefore, the minute hand will have to gain $45 - 30 = 10$ min spaces over the hour hand.

∵ Gain of 55 min spaces equals 60 min.

$\therefore$ Gain of 15 min spaces $= \frac{60}{55} \times 15 = \frac{180}{11} = 16\frac{4}{11}$

Therefore, hour and minute hands of a clock point in opposite direction after 9 O'clock at $16\frac{4}{11}$ min past 9.

18. (*c*)

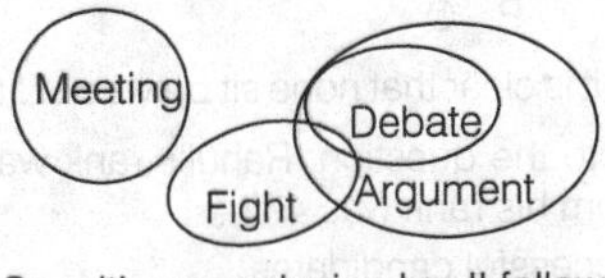

Conclusions

I. ⌉ Complementary
II. ⌋ pairs

So, either conclusion I or II follows.

19. (*e*)

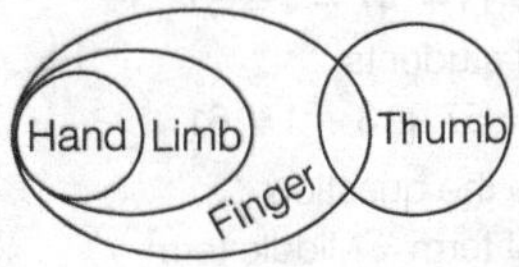

Conclusions

I. (✔)
II. (✔)

So, both conclusions I and II follow.

20. (*a*)

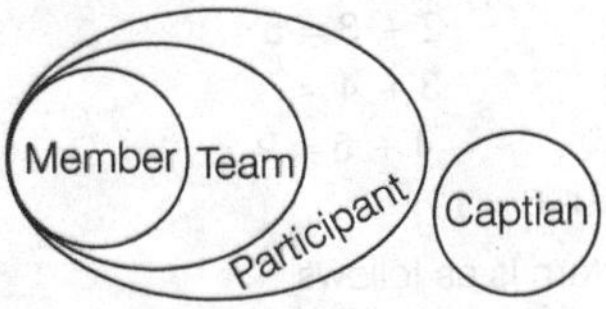

Conclusions

I. (✔)
II. (✗)

So, only Conclusion I follows.

21. (*b*) Only those who have binoculars can be a part of birdwatcher's club, hence all the members of birdwatcher's club will have binoculars for sure. But all those who have binoculars may not be part of birdwatcher's club.

22. (*a*) Argument I is strong because at times media can be responsible for creating hype of a distorted information. Also, journalists play an important role in exposing the malfunctioning of the society, so Argument II is also strong. Argument III is strong because it some times leads to harassment of affected person. So, all three statements are strong.

23. (*b*) As,

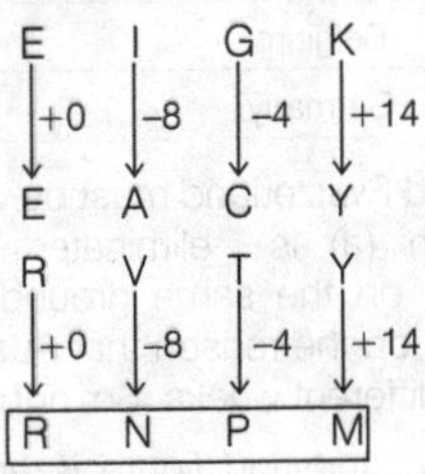

Similarly,

24. (*a*) House is lent on 'Rent'. In the same way, 'Capital' is lent on 'Interest'.

25. (*c*) As,

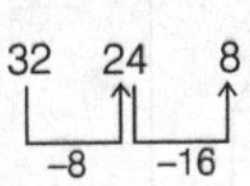

Similarly,

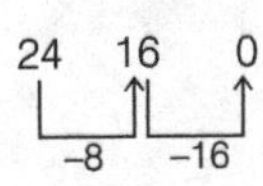

26. (*a*) One who works in garden is called gardener. All others are Art forms.

27. (*b*) In the number pair 483-15, both the numbers are multiples of 3.

$$\frac{483}{3} = 161, \frac{15}{3} = 5$$

But, all other pair numbers are not multiples of 3.

28. (*c*) As,

nik (ka) pa ⟶ who are (you) ...(i)

(ka) na [ta] da ⟶ (you) may [come] here ...(ii)

ho [ta] sa ⟶ [come] and go ...(iii)

It is clear from Eq. (i) that meaning for 'nik' is either 'who' or 'are'.

29. (*c*) The man plants 10 trees in 1 : 30 hours.
In 9 h he would plant 60 trees.
In the last 10th hour he would plant 10 trees.
Therefore, in 10 h he would plant 70 trees.

30. (*b*) As,

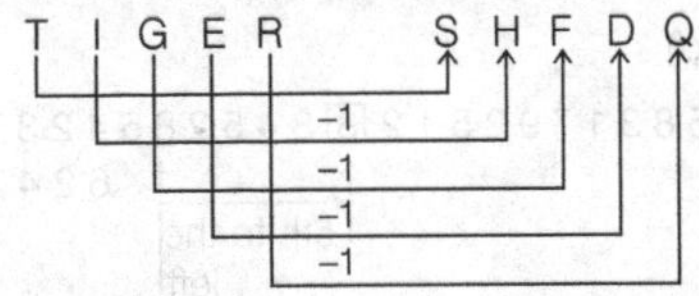

Similarly,

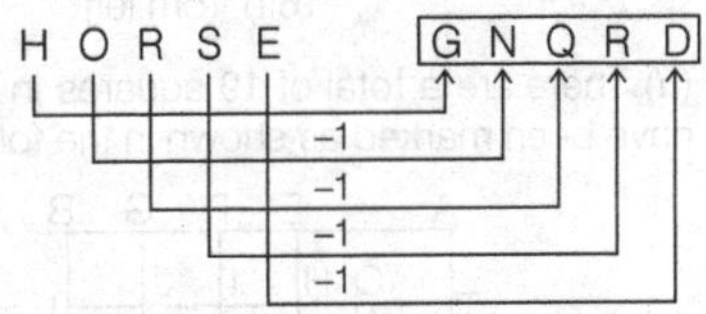

31. (*d*) Required words are NOW, WON and OWN.

32. (*d*) It is quite clear from the positions I, II and IV that except 5, all numbers (6, 4, 3 and 1) are on adjacent faces of 2. Hence, 5 and 2 are opposite to each other.

33. (*a*) According to given data,

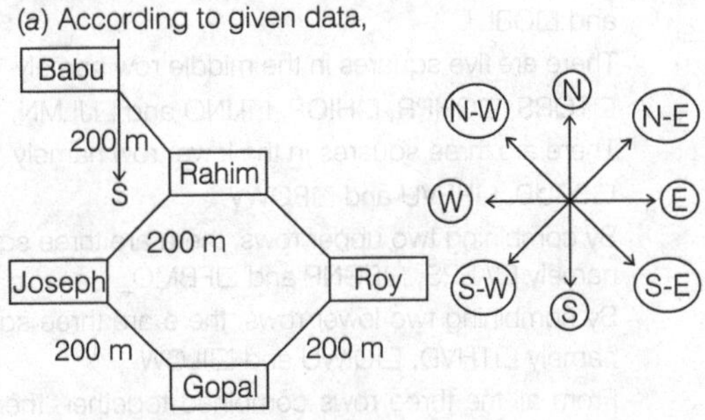

When we notice position of Roy's house with respect to Babu's, then the position of Roy with respect to Babu is South-East.

34. (*b*) The angle between hour hand and minute hand at 5 O'clock

$$= 5 \times 30° = 150°$$

Minute hand moves in 10 min $= 2 \times 30° = 60°$

Hour hand moves in 10 min $= \frac{30°}{6} = 5°$

$\therefore$ Angle between hour and minute hands at 5 h 10 min

$$= 150° - 60° + 5° = 95°$$

Alternate Method

Based on concept of angles between hands of a clock

$= \left[30\left(T-\frac{n}{5}\right)+\frac{n}{2}\right]^\circ$

$= \left[30\left(5-\frac{10}{5}\right)+\frac{10}{2}\right]^\circ$ [here, $T = 5$ and $n = 10$]

$= 30 \times 3 + 5 = 95^\circ$

Solution (Q. Nos. 35-37)

35. (*b*) 5 8 3 1 7 9 2 5 1 2 8 [3] 4 5 2 8 5 4 2 3 7 3 9 6 2 4 2 9 5 3 6 4 6 1 2

Hence, there is one such 3's.

36. (*b*) 5 8 3 1 7 9 2 5 1 2 8 3 4 5 2 8 5 4 2 3 7 3 9 6 [2] 4 [2] 9 5 3 6 4 6 1 2

Hence, there are two such 2's

37. (*d*)

5 8 3 1 7 9 2 5 1 2 [8] 3 4 5 2 8 5 4 2 3 7 3 9 6 2 4 2 9 5 3 6 4 6 1 2

5th to the left

16th from left

38. (*d*) There are a total of 19 squares in the figure, which have been marked as shown in the following figure.

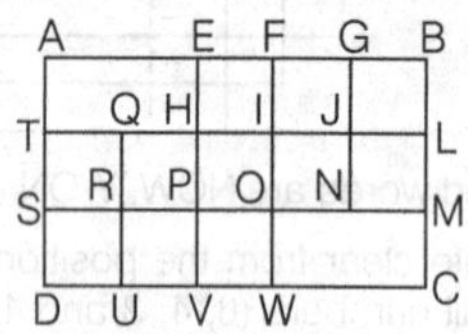

There are three squares in the upper row □EFIH, □FGJI and □GBLJ.

There are five squares in the middle row namely □TQRS, □QHPR, □HIOP, □IJNO and □JLMN.

There are three squares in the lower row namely □SRUD, □RPVU and □POWV.

By combining two upper rows, there are three squares namely □AEPS, □EGNP and □FBMO.

By combining two lower rows, there are three squares namely □THVD, □QIWU and □ILCW.

From all the three rows combined together, there are two squares namely □AFWD and □EBCV.

∴ Total number of squares

$= 3 + 5 + 3 + 3 + 3 + 2 = 19$

Solution (Q. Nos. 39-41) From the given information, we can get the following table.

Person	A	B	C	D
Profession	Accountant	Accountant	Lecturer	Clerk
Game	Swimming, Badminton	Swimming, Tennis	Football, Cricket	Swimming, Carrom

39. (*c*) C is the Lecturer.

40. (*c*) C cannot swim.

41. (*b*) B plays Tennis.

42. (*b*) option (b) is correct answer.

43. (*a*) • J • • S • • • P • O • • • • • • • • (↑)

From diagram it is clear that none sit between O and P.

44. (*d*) According to the question, Rahul's rank was 11th and from bottom his rank was 47th.

Number of successful candidates

$= 11 + 47 - 1 = 57$

Total number of students

$= 57 + 3 + 1 = 61$

45. (*c*) According to the question

First term + Last term = Middle term

$\Rightarrow \quad 1 + 1 = 2$

$\Rightarrow \quad 2 + 3 = 5$

$\Rightarrow \quad 3 + 4 = 7$

$\Rightarrow \quad 4 + 5 = 9$

Similarly, $5 + 6 = 11$

46. (*a*) The pattern is as follows

1st Letter $\overset{16}{P} \xrightarrow{+1} \overset{17}{Q} \xrightarrow{+1} \overset{18}{R} \xrightarrow{+1} \overset{19}{S}$

2nd Letter $\overset{2}{B} \xrightarrow{+2} \overset{4}{D} \xrightarrow{+2} \overset{6}{F} \xrightarrow{+2} \overset{8}{H}$

3rd Letter $\overset{1}{A} \xrightarrow{+2} \overset{3}{C} \xrightarrow{+2} \overset{5}{E} \xrightarrow{+2} \overset{7}{G}$

47. (*a*) The complete letter series will be

n nmm/nnmm/nnmm/nnmm ⇒ nnmm

48. (*d*)

1st Week Visiting	2nd Week Visiting
UK	France
Austria	Switzerland
Belgium	Italy
Germany	Norway

France and Switzerland must be visited in same week. So, option (a) is eliminated, option (b) is also eliminated on the same ground. Option (c) is also eliminated on the reason that Austria and Switzerland visited in different weeks. So, right option is (d).

49. (*b*) Clearly, question figure is embedded in answer figure (b) as shown below

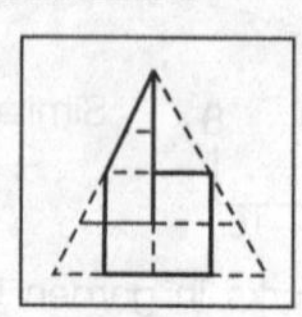

50. (*b*) In given figure series, alternative figures are similar, Hence, option (b) will be the correct choice.

PRACTICE SET 43

Direction (Q. Nos. 1-3) *Study the following information carefully and answer the given questions.*

A word and number arrangement machine, when given an input line of words and numbers, it rearranges them following a particular rule. The following is an illustration of input and rearrangement.

Input 25 93 as hill stamp bolt 45 34 63 total 13 alter rise

***Step* I** alter 25 93 as hill stamp bolt 45 34 63 total rise 13

***Step* II** alter as 93 hill stamp bolt 45 34 63 total rise 25 13

***Step* III** alter as bolt 93 hill stamp 45 63 total rise 34 25 13

***Step* IV** alter as bolt hill 93 stamp 63 total rise 45 34 25 13

***Step* V** alter as bolt hill rise 93 stamp total 63 45 34 25 13

***Step* VI** alter as bolt hill rise stamp total 93 63 45 34 25 13

Step VI is the last step of the above arrangement as the intended arrangement is obtained.

As per the rules followed in the above steps, find out in each of the following questions the appropriate steps for the given input.

Input ropes 12 33 strong 35 19 in blue ample kite 47 77 57

1. What is the position of '47' in Step III ?
(a) Fifth from the left end
(b) Seventh from the left end
(c) Sixth from the left end
(d) Sixth from the right end
(e) Seventh from the right end

2. Which of the following is fifth from the left end of Step V in the above arrangement ?
(a) kite (b) ropes (c) strong (d) 35
(e) None of these

3. What is the position of 'in' in Step IV?
(a) Fourth from the left end
(b) Third from the right end
(c) Second from the left end
(d) Third from the left end
(e) Fifth from the left end

4. The age of father is thrice of his son. If the sum of their ages is 48 yr, then what is the age of father?
(a) 30 yr (b) 32 yr
(c) 36 yr (d) 40 yr

Direction (Q. Nos 5-6) *In the following questions, select the related word/letters from the given alternatives.*

5. FLOWER : REWOLF : : FRUITS : ?
[BSSC (CGL) 2015]
(a) STUIRF (b) STUIFR
(c) STIURF (d) STRUIF

6. 'Konkani' is related to 'Goa', in the same way as 'Dogri' is related to ....
(a) Madhya Predesh
(b) Odisha
(c) Jammu and Kashmir
(d) Gujarat

7. What is the product of all the numbers in the dial of a telephone?
(a) 1,59,480 (b) 0
(c) 1,59 450 (d) 1,58,480

Direction (Q. Nos. 8-9) *Each of the questions below consists of a question and two statements numbered* I *and* II *given below it. You have to decide whether the data provided in the statements are sufficient to answer the question.*

Give answer
(a) if the data in Statement I alone is sufficient to answer the question, while the data in Statement II alone is not sufficient to answer the question
(b) if the data in statement II alone is sufficient to answer the question, while the data in Statement I alone is not sufficient to answer the question
(c) if the data either in Statement I alone or in Statement II alone is sufficient to answer the question
(d) if the data in both the Statements I and II together are not sufficient to answer the question
(e) if the data in both the Statements I and II together are necessary to answer the question

8. In which month of the year did the construction of the building begin?

I. The construction engineer correctly remembers that the construction began before September but after May and that particular month did not have 31 days.

II. The builder correctly remembers that the construction began after February but before October and the fact that, that particular month did not have 31 days.

9. Is Jay a sibling (brother or sister) of Rishi?

I. Jay's mother Shalini is the only child of Rishi's grandfather.

II. Rishi's father has a daughter Smita, of whom Jay is a brother.

10. In the question below is given a statement followed by three courses of action numbers I, II and III. A course of action is a step or administrative decision to be taken for improvement, follow up or further action in regard to the problem, policy, etc. On the basis of information given in the statement, you have to assume everything in the statement to be true and then decide which of the three given suggested courses of action logically follows worth pursuing. Then, decide which of the alternatives (a), (b), (c), (d) or (e) is correct.

Statement Any further increase in pollution level in the city, by way of industrial effluent and automobile exhaustion, would pose a severe threat to the inhabitants.

Course of Action

I. All the factories in the city should be immediately closed down.

II. The automobiles should not be allowed to on the road for more than four hours per day.

III. The Government should restrict the issue of fresh licenses to factories and automobiles.

(a) Only III
(b) All follow
(c) Only II
(d) None follows
(e) Only course of action III is the right course of action because other courses are not feasible

11. *Read the given information and answer the question.*

Company S has recently rented many apartments in building Y for providing office quarters to its employees. However, although many employees had requested the company to provide accommodation around six months ago, since the announcement of quarters last month, hardly any employee has signed up for the new facility. **[RBI (Officers) 2015]**

Which of the following may not be a reasom for the emoloyees' unwillingness to live in the apartments?

(a) All the employees of company S were informed just two months ago that the company had decided to triple the house rent allowance (HRA) shortly
(b) The area where the company has rented the apartments does not have a school, college of hospital in its 3 km radius
(c) The maintenance amount for the apartments, which have been rented by the company is very high and the company has announced that employees would have to pay the amount on their own
(d) There have been talks about the company changing its current office location and the new office location is every far from the area in which the apartments have been rented
(e) Apartments which have been rented by the company are located at an area, which does not have adequate public transport facilities

Direction (Q. Nos. 12-13) *Find the odd word/ number pair from the given alternatives.*

12. (a) Wheat (b) Rice (c) Jowar (d) Beans

13. (a) 3-9 (b) 5-25 (c) 7-49 (d) 8-64

14. Select the figure which represents the relationship between athletes, football players and cricket players.

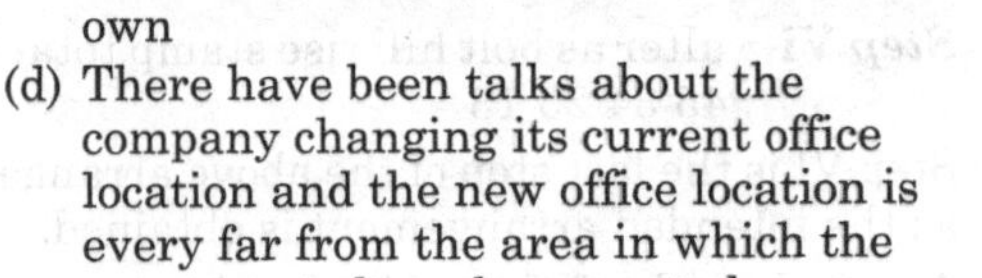

(a) (b) (c) (d)

15. All the letters of the word HALFTIME arranged in alphabetical order from left to right. Then, all the vowels are replaced with the next alphabet (as per the English alphabetical order), then which of the following will be the second letter from the left end? **[IBPS (Clerk) Pre 2015]**

(a) H (b) F (c) M (d) L
(e) E

16. If in a certain code, ONE is coded as 231, FIVE is coded as 9641, then how will be NINE coded? **[SSC (10+2) 2015]**

(a) 3316 (b) 3361
(c) 3613 (d) 3631

17. If three days after today will be Tuesday, then what day was four days before yesterday?

(a) Tuesday (b) Sunday
(c) Monday (d) Wednesday

18. Arrange the following words according to dictionary arrangement.

(i) Wound (ii) Writer
(iii) Whiter (iv) Worst
(v) Worked

(a) (v), (iii), (ii), (i), (iv)
(b) (i), (iv), (iii), (v), (ii)
(c) (iii), (v), (iv), (i), (ii)
(d) (ii), (i), (iii), (iv), (v)

19. Given below are the different positions of a dice. What shall come in the place of 'X'?

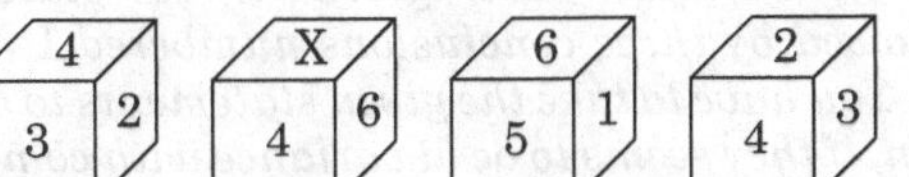

I II III IV

(a) 3 (b) 5 (c) 2 (d) 1

Direction (Q. Nos. 20 -22) *Study the following information carefully and answer the questions given below.*

Seven friends A, B, C, D, E ,F and G studied in colleges X, Y and Z are currently in different professions, namely medicines, fashion designing, engineering, business, acting, teaching and architecture (not necessarily in the same order). At least two and not more than three friends had studied in the same college. C is an architect and studied in college Y. E is not a businessman. Only G amongst the seven friends studied in college Y. B is an actor and did not study in the same college as F. A did not study in college Z. Those who studied in college X are neither fashion designers nor teachers. None of those who studied in college Y is a teacher. **[SBI SO (IT) 2016]**

20. Who amongst the following have studied in college Z?

(a) B, A (b) C, F (c) B, D, F (d) A, D
(e) D,F

21. Which of the following groups represents the students of college Y?

(a) C, E, G (b) A, C, D
(c) A, B, C (d) D, B, C
(e) None of these

22. What is the profession of F?

(a) Engineering (b) Business
(c) Medicines (d) Acting
(e) None of these

23. In the question below is given a statements followed by two assumptions numbered I and II. An assumption is something supposed or taken for granted. You have to consider the statement and the following assumptions and decide which of the assumption(s) is/are implicit in the statement.

Give answer

(a) if only Assumption I is implicit
(b) if only Assumption II is implicit
(c) if either Assumption I or II is implicit
(d) if neither Assumption I nor II is implicit
(e) if both Assumptions I and II are implicit

Statement Even after retirement from international cricket, the 'Rawalpindi express' is in the controversy again. This time he targeted Sachin Tendulkar through his book 'Controversially Yours', a news about Shoaib Akhtar.

Assumptions

I. Shoaib Akhtar does not play test cricket now.

II. One can target anybody through one's write up.

24. Find the water image from the given alternatives.

Question Figure

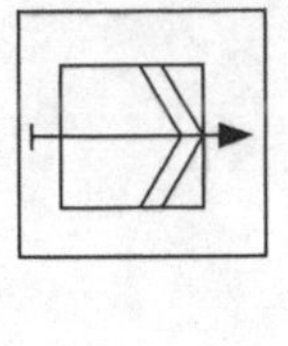

Answer Figures

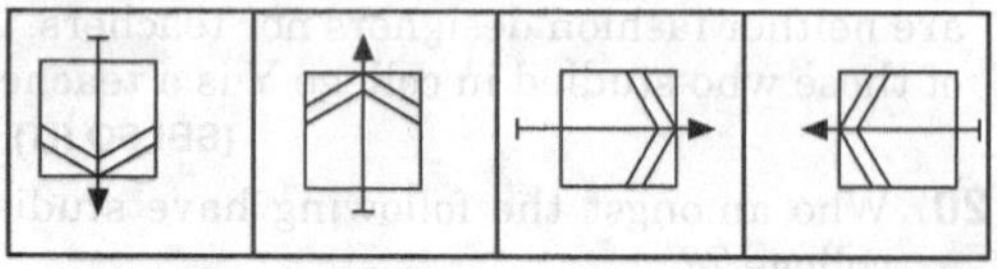

(a) (b) (c) (d)

25. Select the word which can be formed using the letters given in the word.

INFORMATION

(a) FARMER (b) MOTION
(c) FIREMAN (d) NAME

26. How many such pair of digits are there in the number 536142 each of which has as many digits between them in the number as when the digits are arranged in the ascending order within the number?

(a) None (b) One
(c) Two (d) Three

27. In each of the following questions, group the given figures into three classes using each figure only once.

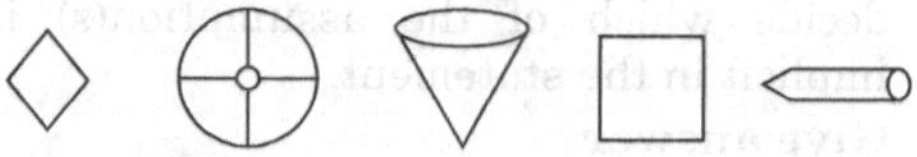

1 2 3 4 5

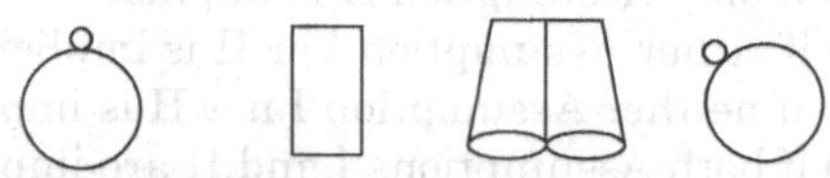

6 7 8 9

(a) 1, 2, 4 / 3, 5, 6 / 8, 7, 9
(b) 9, 7, 6 / 5, 3, 1 / 9, 8, 1
(c) 2, 3, 4 / 7, 6, 5 / 9, 8, 1
(d) 1, 4, 7 / 2, 6, 9 / 3, 5, 8

28. Which one of the given responses would be a meaningful order of the following?

(i) Leaves (ii) Branch
(iii) Flower (iv) Tree
(v) Fruit

(a) (iv), (iii), (i), (ii), (v)
(b) (iv), (ii), (v), (i), (iii)
(c) (iv), (iii), (ii), (i), (v)
(d) (iv), (ii), (i), (iii), (v)

Direction (Q. Nos. 29-30) *Find the missing number from the given responses.*

29.

25	49	81
5	7	?
15	13	11
20	20	20

(a) 9 (b) 3 (c) 61 (d) 31

30. 836 (316) 112
213 (?) 420

(a) 368 (b) 420 (c) 211 (d) 468

Direction (Q. Nos. 31-33) *Read the following information to answer the given questions.*

Seven children A, B. C, D, E, F and G are standing in a line. G is to the right of D and to the left of B, A is on the right of C. A and D have one child between them. E and B have two children between them. D and F have two children between them.

31. Who is on the extreme right?

(a) B (b) E (c) F (d) G

32. Who is exactly in the middle?

(a) A (b) C (c) D (d) E

33. Who is on the extreme left?

(a) A (b) B (c) C (d) D

Direction (Q. Nos. 34-36) *In each of the questions below are given three statements followed by three conclusions numbered* I, II *and* III. *You have to take the given statements to be true even, if they seems to be at variance with commonly known facts. Read all the conclusions and then decide which of the given conclusions logically follows from the given statements disregarding commonly known facts.*

34. Statements Some carrots are brinjals.
Some brinjals are apples.
All apples are bananas.

Conclusions I. Some apples are carrots.
II. Some bananas are brinjals.
III. Some bananas are carrots.

(a) Only I follows
(b) Only II follows
(c) Only III follows
(d) Either II or III follows
(e) None of the above

35. Statements All keys are locks.
All locks are bangles.
All bangles are cars.
Conclusions I. Some cars are locks.
II. Some bangles are keys.
III. Some cars are keys.
(a) Only I follows (b) I and II follow
(c) I and III follow (d) II and III follow
(e) All I, II and III follow

36. Statements All fruits are leaves.
Some leaves are trees.
No tree is house.
Conclusions I. Some houses are fruits.
II. Some trees are fruits.
III. No house is a fruit.
(a) Only I follows
(b) Only II follows
(c) Only III follows
(d) Either I or III follows
(e) None follows

37. A is B's sister and C is B's mother. D is C's father. E is D's mother. How is A related to D?
(a) Grandfather **[SSC (CGL) 2014]**
(b) Daughter
(c) Grandmother
(d) Granddaughter

Direction (Q. Nos. 38-40) *In the following questions, the symbols @, %, $, # and ★ are used with the following meaning as illustrated below.*
'P $ Q' means 'P is not smaller than Q'.
'P ★ Q' means 'P is neither smaller than nor equal to Q'.
'P @ Q' means 'P is not greater than Q'.
'P # Q' means 'P is neither greater than nor smaller than Q'.
'P % Q' means 'P is neither greater than nor equal to Q'.
Now in each of the following questions assuming the given statements to be true, find which of the two Conclusions I and II given below them is/ are definitely true?
Give answer
(a) if only Conclusion I is true
(b) if only Conclusion II is true
(c) if either Conclusion I or II is true
(d) if neither Conclusion I nor II is true
(e) if both Conclusions I and II are true

38. Statements F $ M, N @ M, N % W
Conclusions I. F # N II. N % F

39. Statements B # J, J @ D, F $ D
Conclusions I. B # F II. F ★ B

40. Statements Z%T, T ★ N, H $ N
Conclusions I. H ★ Z II. T ★ H

41. How many circles are there in the following figure?

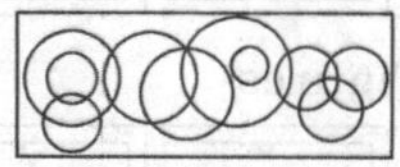

(a) 12 (b) 14 (c) 13 (d) 10

42. Six teachers from different departments of same institute went to Paris for a faculty development programe on enhancing teaching skills. The various departments are Maths, Science, English, Physics, Chemistry and Biology. During the session, they all were sitting on the round table facing the centre. Maths teacher was sitting in front of Physics teacher. English teacher was sitting between the Maths and Science teacher, to the right of the Maths teacher. Biology teacher who was good friend of Maths teacher sitting between Chemistry and Maths teacher. From the above information, find out who is sitting to the immediate right of Science teacher?
(a) Biology teacher (b) Physics teacher
(c) English teacher (d) Maths teacher

43. In the given matrices, a letter can be represented first by its row number and followed by its column number. e.g.'A' is represented by 12, 24 and 'R' by 57, 76 etc. In each of the questions following matrices, identify one set of number pairs out of (a, b, c, d) which represents the given word.

Matrix I

	0	1	2	3	4
0	A	E	S	T	H
1	T	H	A	E	S
2	E	S	T	H	A
3	H	A	E	S	T
4	S	T	H	A	E

Matrix II

	5	6	7	8	9
5	P	O	R	K	L
6	K	L	P	O	R
7	O	R	K	L	P
8	L	P	O	R	K
9	R	K	L	P	O

ROSE
(a) 86,67,33 44 (b) 88, 76,31 32
(c) 95, 75,02,32 (d) 57,87,32,33

44. A piece of paper is folded and punched cut as shown below in the question figures. From the given answer figures, indicate how it will appear when opened? **[SSC (CPO) 2011]**

Question Figures

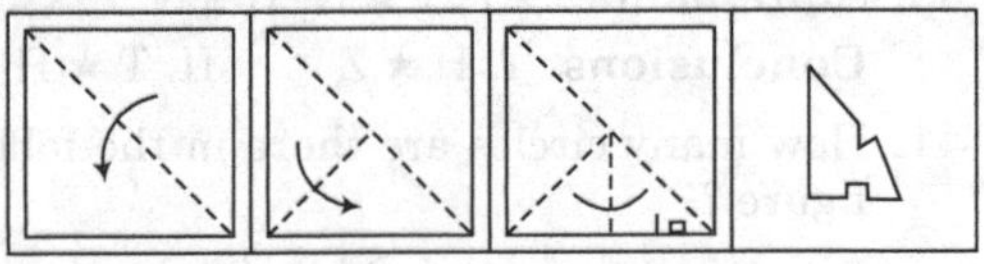

Answer Figures

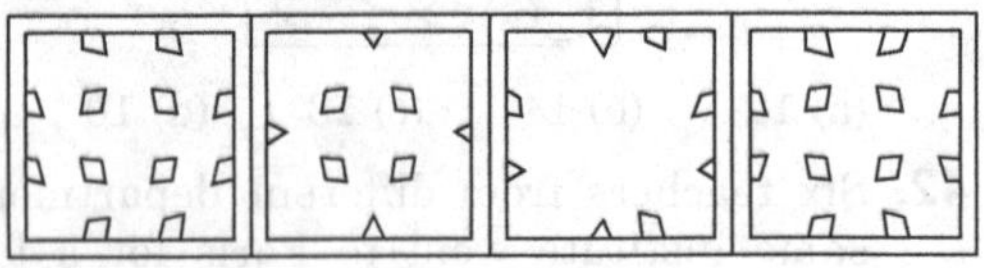

(a) (b) (c) (d)

45. Which one set of letters when sequentially placed at the gaps in the given letter series shall complete it ?

ab _ _ b a a _ _ a b _

(a) b a a b b
(b) a a b a b
(c) a a b a a
(d) a a a a a

Direction (Q. Nos. 46-47) *In the following questions, a series is given with one term missing. Choose the correct alternatives from the given ones that will complete the series.*

46. 3F, 6G, 11I, 18 L, ?
(a) 27 P (b) 25 N (c) 27 Q (d) 21 O

47. 7, 9, 13, 21, 37, ?
(a) 58 (b) 63 (c) 69 (d) 72

48. A is richer than B, C is richer than A. D is richer than C and E is the richest of all. If they are made to sit in the above degree of richness, then who will be in the middle position (central position)?
(a) A (b) B (c) C (d) D

Direction (Q. Nos. 49-50) *Study the given information carefully and answer the given questions.*

Point A is 11 m North of point B.
Point C is 11 m East of point B.
Point D is 6 m North of point C.
Point E is 7 m West of point D.
Point F is 8 m North of point E.
Point G is 4 m West of point F.

49. How far is F from point A ?
(a) 43 m (b) 4 m (c) 3 m (d) 7 m
(e) 5 m

50. How far and in which direction is point G from point A ?
(a) 3 m North (b) 5 m North
(c) 4 m North (d) 4 m South
(e) 3 m South

Hints and Solutions

Solution (Q. Nos. 1-3)

Input ropes 12 33 strong 35 19 in blue ample kite 47 77 57
***Step* I** ample ropes 33 strong 35 19 in blue kite 47 77 57 12
***Step* II** ample blue ropes 33 strong 35 in kite 47 77 57 19 12
***Step* III** ample blue in ropes strong 35 kite 47 77 57 33 19 12
***Step* IV** ample blue in kite ropes strong 47 77 57 35 33 19 12
***Step* V** ample blue in kite ropes strong 77 57 47 35 33 19 12

1. (*d*) 47 is sixth from the right end in Step III.

2. (*b*) The word 'ropes' is fifth from the left end in Step V.

3. (*d*) The word 'in' is third from the left end in Step IV.

4. (c) Let the age of son be x yr.
Then, the age of father = 3x yr
Now, $3x + x = 48$ yr
$\Rightarrow$ $4x = 48$ yr $\Rightarrow x = 12$ yr
Hence, the age of father = $3 \times 12 = 36$ yr

5. (c)

As,

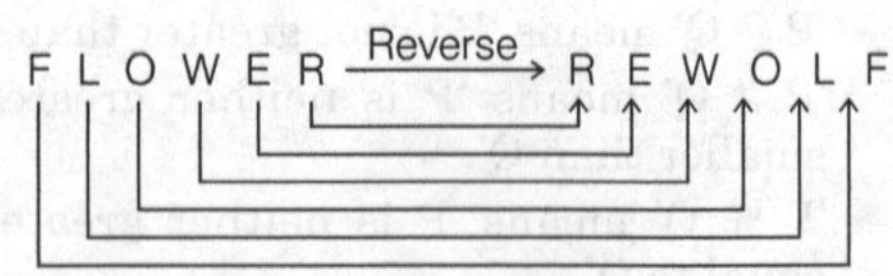

Similarly,

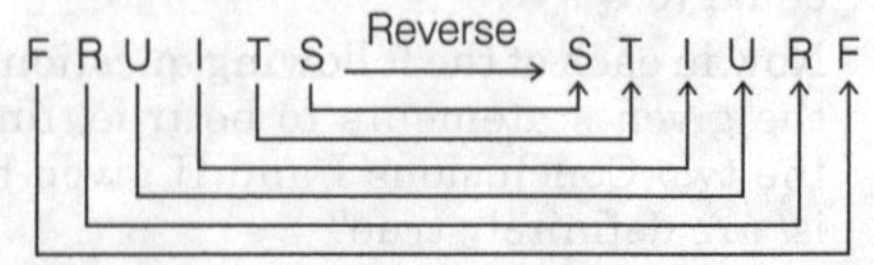

6. (c) 'Konkani' is the language of 'Goa'. Similarly, 'Dogri' is the language of 'Jammu and Kashmir'.

7. (*b*) We know that any number multiplied by zero is always zero.

8. (a) From Statement I,
Construction of the building begins in June.
From Statement II,
Construction begins in April or June or September.
Hence, the data in Statement I alone is sufficient to answer the question.

9. (c) From Statement I, Jay is sibling of Rishi.
From Statement II, Jay is brother of Rishi.
Hence, the data either in Statement I alone or in Statement II alone is sufficient to answer the question.

10. (a) Only Course of action III is the right course of action because other courses are not feasible.

11. (a) All the other statements expect (a) provide strong reasons for not to opt the facility.

12. (*d*) Except Beans, all others are grains (Cereals and coarse cereals).

13. (*d*) Except 8-64 , all others groups contain odd numbers while 8 is an even number and 64 its square is also an even number.

14. (*b*) Some athletes may be football players and *vice - versa*.
Some athletes may be cricket players and *vice-versa*.
Some athletes may be both cricket players and football players.
Some cricket players may be football players and *vice-versa*.

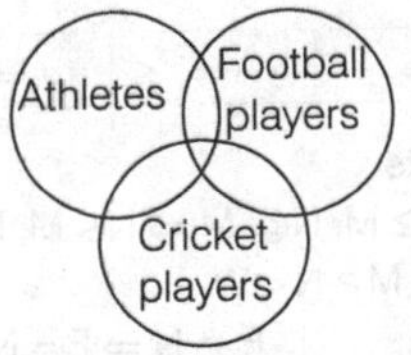

15. (*b*) Given, HALFTIME
Alphabetical arrangement = A E F H I L M T
New arrangement = B F F H J L M T
∴ Second from left = F

16. (*d*) As, O N E → 2 3 1 and F I V E → 9 6 4 1
Similarly, N I N E → 3 6 3 1
(By direct substitution method)

17. (c) Today + 3 = Tuesday
∴ Today = Tuesday − 3 = Saturday
Yesterday = Saturday − 1 = Friday
Friday − 4 = Monday

18. (c) Dictionary arrangement of words is as shown below
(iii) Whiter → (v) Worked → (iv) Worst → (i) Wound → (ii) Writer

19. (*a*) Expanded form of the dice is

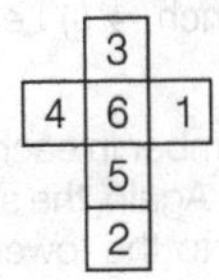

Thus, X = 3

Solution (Q. Nos. 20-22) Following table can be drawn from the given information

Friend	College	Profession
A	Y	Fashion
B	Y	Acting
C	Y	Architecture
D	Z	Teaching
E	X	Medicine
F	Z	Engineering
G	X	Business

20. (*e*) D and F studied in college Z.

21. (c) A, B and C studied in college Y.

22. (*a*) F is an engineer.

23. (*e*) 'Retirement from international cricket' means Shoaib does not play test cricket now as test cricket is a part of international cricket. Hence, Assumption I is implicit. Assumption II is also implicit because it is clearly said that Shoaib targeted Sachin Tendulkar through his book and a book is a write up.

24. (*c*) The figure in option (c) represents the correct water image of question figure as shown below

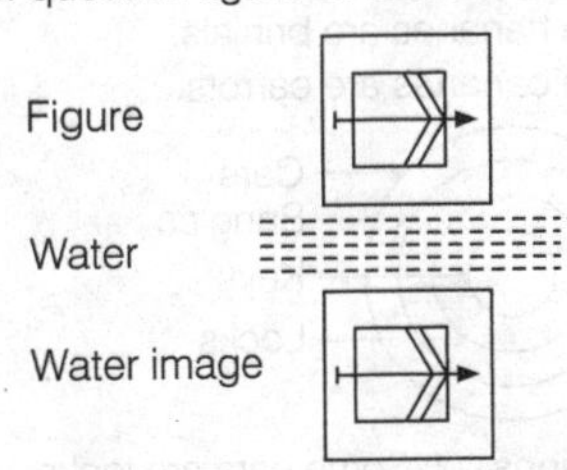

25. (*b*) Word MOTION can be formed by using the letters of the given word.

26. (*c*) Let us see

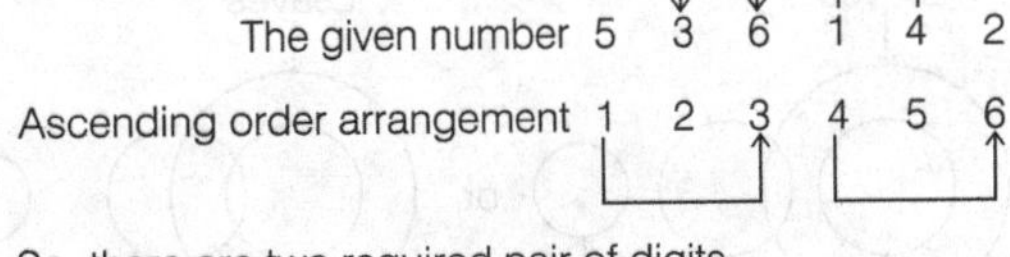

So, there are two required pair of digits.

27. (*d*) Figures of four sides = 1, 4, 7
Figures of one big and small circle = 2, 6, 9
Figures 3, 5 and 8 are wide and narrow from other sides.

28. (*d*) Meaningful order of words is
(iv) Tree → (ii) Branch → (i) Leaves → (iii) Flower → (v) Fruit

29. (*a*) The second number in each column is square root of the first number. Again, the sum of second and third numbers is equal to the lowermost number in each column.

$$\sqrt{81} = 9 \text{ or } 20 - 11 = 9$$

30. (*c*) As, $836 + 112 = 948$

$$\frac{948}{3} = 316$$

Similarly, $213 + 420 = 633$

$$\frac{633}{3} = 211$$

Solution (Q. Nos. 31-33) According to the given information, the final arrangement is as following

C	A	E	D	G	B	F

31. (*c*) F is on the extreme right.

32. (*c*) D is exactly in the middle.

33. (*c*) C is on the extreme left.

34. (*b*)

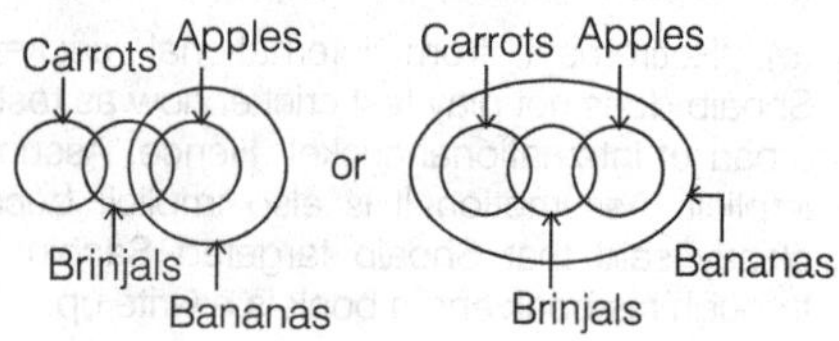

Conclusions
I. Some apples are carrots. (✗)
II. Some bananas are brinjals. (✔)
III. Some bananas are carrots. (✗)

35. (*e*)

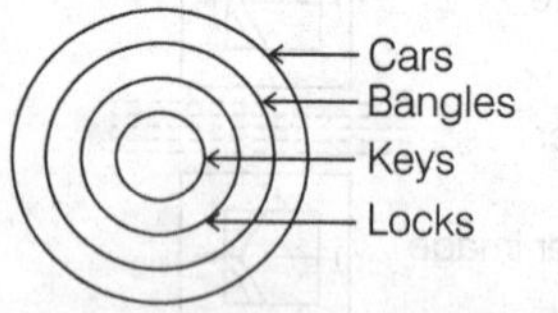

Conclusions I. Some cars are locks. (✔)
II. Some bangles are keys. (✔)
III. Some cars are keys. (✔)

36. (*d*)

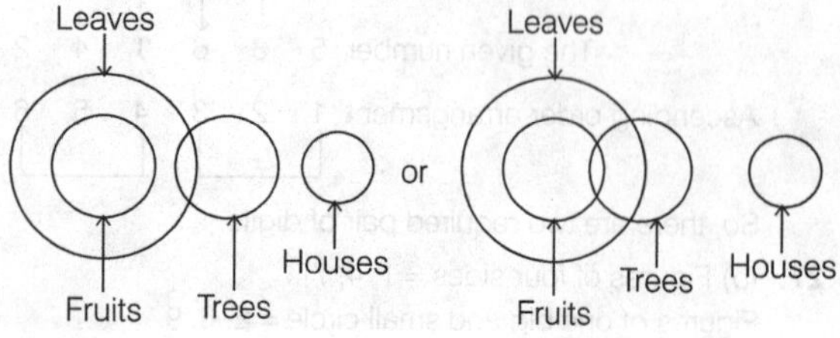

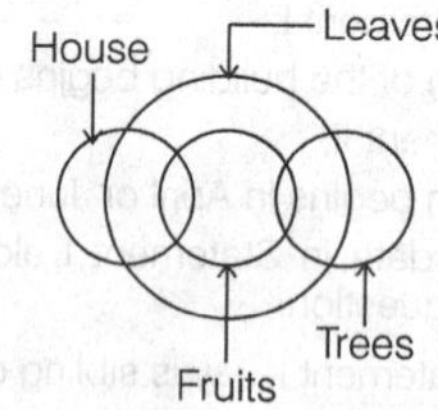

Conclusions I. Some houses are fruits. (✗)
II. Some trees are fruits. (✗)
III. No house is a fruit. (✗)

These are complementary pairs.

37. (*d*)

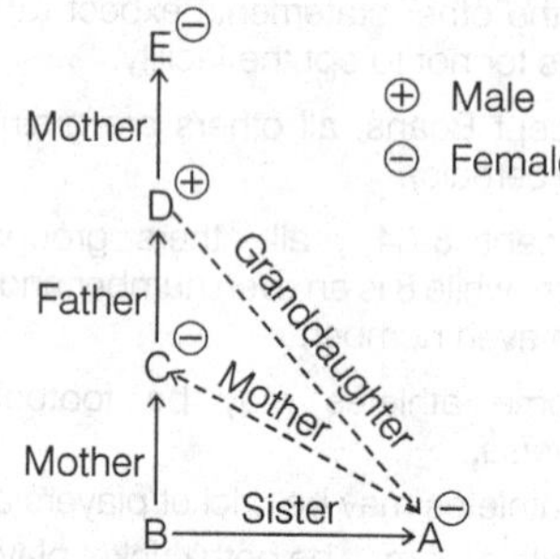

As, this can be seen from the above figure that A is the granddaughter of D.

Solution (Q. Nos. 38-40)

$ ⇒ ≥	★ ⇒ >	@ ⇒ ≤	# ⇒ =	% ⇒ <

38. (*c*) **Statements**

F $ M ⇒ F ≥ M, N @ M ⇒ N ≤ M, N % W ⇒ N < W

Therefore, F ≥ M ≥ N < W

Conclusions I. F # N ⇒ F = N (May be true)
II. N % F ⇒ N < F (May be true)

These are complementary pairs.
Hence, N is either smaller than or equal to F.

39. (*c*) **Statements**

B # J ⇒ B = J, J @ D ⇒ J ≤ D, F $ D ⇒ F ≥ D

Therefore, B = J ≤ D ≤ F

Conclusions I. B # F ⇒ B = F (May be true)
II. F ★ B ⇒ F > B (May be true)

These are complementary pairs.
Hence, B is either smaller than or equal to F.

40. (*d*) **Statements**

Z % T ⇒ Z < T
T ★ N ⇒ T > N
H $ N ⇒ H ≥ N
Therefore, Z < T > N ≤ H

Conclusions I. H ★ Z ⇒ H > Z (Not true)
II. T ★ H ⇒ T > H (Not true)

41. (*d*)

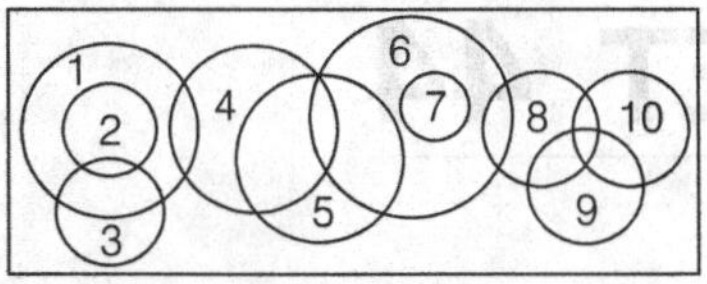

Clearly, shown that total number of circles = 10

42. (*b*) According to the given information,

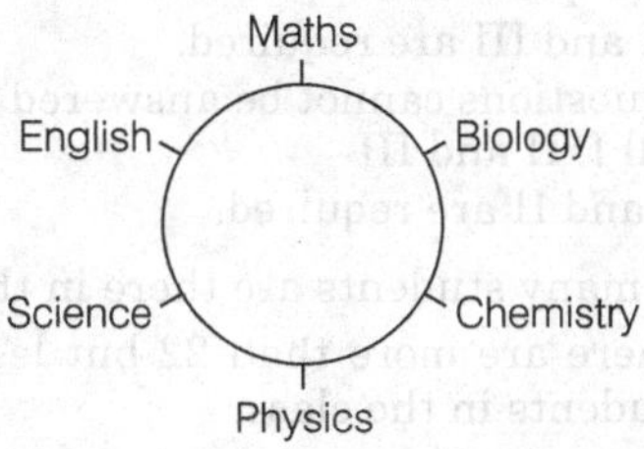

From the given figure, it is clear that Physics teacher is sitting to the immediate right of Science teacher.

43. (c) According to the matrices,

R — 57, 69, 76, 88, (95)

O — 56, 68, (75), 87, 99

S — (02), 14, 21, 33, 40

E — 01, 13, 20, (32), 44

∴ ROSE ⇒ 95, 75, 02, 32

44. (*d*)

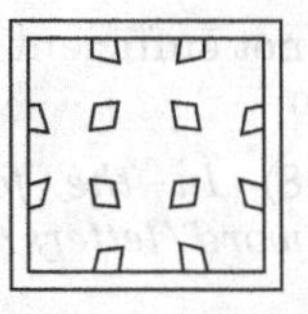

So, option (d) is correct.

45. (c) The complete letter series will be

a b <u>a</u> / <u>a</u> b a / a <u>b</u> <u>a</u> / a b <u>a</u>

∴ Required letters = aabaa

46. (a) The pattern of given alpha-numeric series is as follows

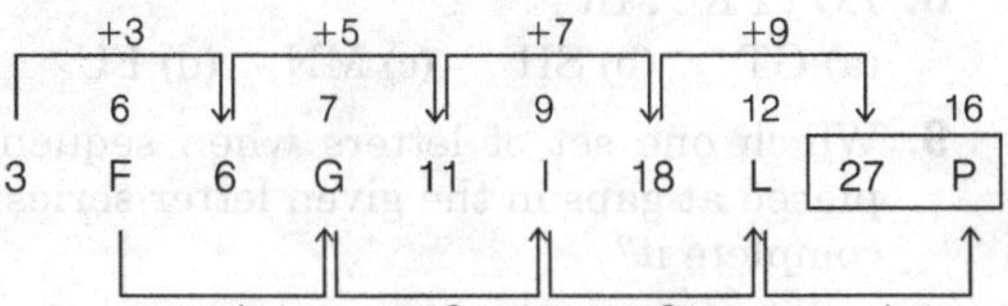

∴ ? = 27 P

47. (*c*) The pattern is as follows

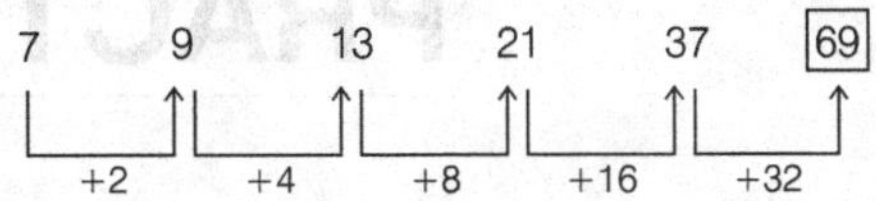

? = 69

48. (*c*) It is given that,

A > B ...(i)

C > A ...(ii)

From Eqs. (i) and (ii), we get

C > A > B

D > C and E is the richest.

∴ E > D > C > A > B

Clearly, C is at the middle position.

Solution (Q. Nos. 49-50)

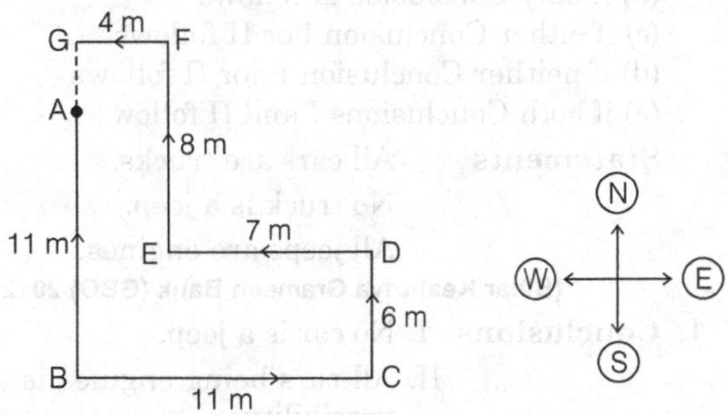

49. (*e*) AG = BG − AB

= (CD + EF) − (AB)

= (6 + 8) − 11 = 3 m

and GF = 4 m

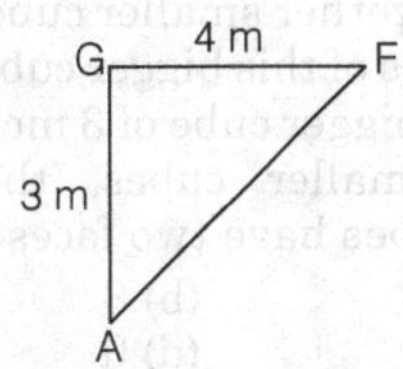

$\therefore \quad AF = \sqrt{(AG)^2 + (FG)^2}$

$= \sqrt{9 + 16} = \sqrt{25} = 5$ m

50. (*a*) Point G is in the 'North' direction from point A and AG = 3 m (from above solution)

PRACTICE SET 44

Direction (Q. Nos. 1-2) *In each question/set of questions below are two/three statements followed by two conclusions numbered* I *and* II. *You have to take the two/three given statements to be true even if they seem to be at variance from commonly known facts and then decide which of the given conclusions logically follows from the given statements disregarding commonly known facts.*

Give answer

(a) if only Conclusion I follows
(b) if only Conclusion II follows
(c) if either Conclusion I or II follows
(d) if neither Conclusion I nor II follows
(e) if both Conclusions I and II follow

Statements All cars are trucks.
No truck is a jeep.
All jeeps are engines.

[Bihar Keshtriya Grameen Bank (GBO) 2012]

1. Conclusions I. No car is a jeep.
II. All cars being engines is a possibility.

2. Conclusions I. No engine is a car.
II. No truck is an engine.

3. A bigger cube of 3 inch side is formed by keeping together smaller cubes of 1 inch side. All the faces of this bigger cube is painted red. When the bigger cube of 3 inch is divided into original smaller cubes, then how many smaller cubes have two faces painted?

(a) 4 (b) 8
(c) 12 (d) 0

Direction (Q. Nos. 4-5) *Each of the questions below consists of a question and three statements numbered* I, II *and* III *given below it. You have to decide whether the data provided in the statements are sufficient to answer the question*

4. Who is the daughter-in-law of B?

I. I is the brother of D. S is the wife of J's nephew.
II. R is the brother of N. T is the son of N. S is the mother of T.
III. B is the wife of D. D is the father of N. D has two children.

(a) I and III are required.
(b) All I, II and III are required to answer the question
(c) II and III are required.
(d) Questions cannot be answered even with all I, II and III
(e) I and II are required.

5. How many students are there in the class?

I. There are more than 22 but less than 36 students in the class.
II. If students of the class are divided into groups each group has exactly 11 students.
III. There are more than 29 but less than 45 students in the class. **[IBPS (PO/MT) 2014]**

(a) I and II are required.
(b) II and either I or III are required to answer the question
(c) II and III are required.
(d) All I, II and III are required to answer the question
(e) All I, II and III are not sufficient to answer the question

Direction (Q. Nos. 6-8) *In the following questions, select the related word/letters/number from the given alternatives.*

6. 20 : 11 : : 102 : ?
(a) 49 (b) 52 (c) 61 (d) 98

7. Optimist : Cheerful : : Pessimist : ? **[SSC (CGL) 2014]**
(a) Petty (b) Selfish (c) Gloomy (d) Mean

8. LO : PK : : IR : ?
(a) GT (b) SH (c) MN (d) FU

9. Which one set of letters when sequentially placed at gaps in the given letter series shall complete it?

m _ p l _ p p l m p_l m p p_

(a) p m p l (b) l m p l (c) p m m l (d) l m m l

10. Raman is a student of 10th class. In his class, his position is 16th from the top and 49th from the bottom. What is the total number of the students in the class?
(a) 64 (b) 65 (c) 66 (d) 63

Direction (Q. Nos. 11-12) *In each question below is given a statement followed by two assumptions numbered I and II. An assumption is something supposed or taken for granted. You have to consider the statement and the following assumptions and decide which of the assumption(s) is/are implicit in the statement.*

Give answer

(a) if only Assumption I is implicit
(b) if only Assumption II is implicit
(c) if either Assumption I or II is implicit
(d) if neither Assumption I nor II is implicit
(e) if both Assumptions I and II are implicit

11. **Statement** Imprisonment for 27 yr made Nelson Mandela the President.

Assumptions

I. Only who will be imprisoned for 27 yr will become the President.

II. To become the President, imprisonment is a qualification.

12. **Statement** There has been a remarkable increase in the air traffic in India during the past few years.

Assumptions

I. Travelling by air has become a status symbol now.

II. Large number of people are able to afford air travel now.

13. The sum of the ages of 5 children born at the intervals of 3 yr each is 50 yr. What is the age of the youngest child?

(a) 4 yr (b) 8 yr (c) 10 yr (d) None of these

Direction (Q. Nos. 14-15) *In the following questions, find the odd terms from the given alternatives.*

14. (a) Mustard (b) Onion
(c) Corn (d) Olive
(e) Seasame

15. (a) 21 : 24 (b) 28 : 32 (c) 14 : 16 (d) 70 : 80
(d) 54 : 62

16. If in the word EQUALITY, the positions of first and the fifth letters are interchanged; similarly the positions of the second and the sixth letters are interchanged and so on. Which letter will be third from the right end? **[IBPS (PO/MT) Mains 2015]**

(s) I (b) U (c) Q (d) T
(e) None of these

17. If 'Tree' means 'Mountain'; 'Mountain' means 'Water'; 'Water' means 'Jungle'; Jungle' means 'Bus'; 'Bus' means 'Truck' and 'Truck' means 'House'; then where do the fish live? **[NICL (AO) 2015]**

(a) Water (b) Jungle
(c) Bus (d) Truck
(e) Mountain

18. Five persons A, B, C, D and E are sitting in a row facing you such that D is on the left of C and B is on the right of E. A is on the right of C and B is one the left of D. If E occupies a corner position, then who is sitting in the middle? **[SSC (FCI) 2012]**

(a) A (b) B
(c) C (d) D

19. If Friday falls on 15th of September 2000, then what will be the day of 15th of September 2001?

(a) Friday (b) Saturday
(c) Thursday (d) Sunday

20. A word is represented by only one set of numbers as given in anyone of the alternatives. The set of numbers given in the alternatives are represented by two classes of alphabets as in the two matrices given below. The columns and rows of Matrix I are numbered from 0 to 4 and that of Matrix II from 5 to 9. A letter can be represented first by its row and next by its column number, e.g. 'N' can be represented by 02, 14, etc. 'O' can be represented by 65, 96, etc. Similarly, you have to identify the correct set for the word given in question.

Matrix I

	0	1	2	3	4
0	P	W	N	I	S
1	I	S	P	W	N
2	W	N	I	S	P
3	S	P	W	N	I
4	N	I	S	P	W

Matrix II

	5	6	7	8	9
5	A	E	R	O	H
6	O	H	A	E	R
7	E	R	O	H	A
8	H	A	E	R	O
9	R	O	H	A	E

PENS

(a) 12, 67, 21, 30
(b) 43, 56, 13, 23
(c) 43, 56, 21, 42
(d) 31, 57, 21, 42

Direction (Q. Nos. 21-23) *Read the following information carefully and answer the questions given below.* **[MAT 2013]**

Rajneesh, Kavita, Suresh, Gambhir and Mahesh are friends and good players. Rajneesh and Kavita are good in hockey and volleyball. Suresh and Rajneesh are good in hockey and tennis. Gambhir and Kavita are good in cricket and volleyball. Suresh, Gambhir and Mahesh are good in football and tennis.

21. Who is good in hockey, volleyball and cricket?
(a) Rajneesh (b) Suresh
(c) Kavita (d) Gambhir

22. Who is good in tennis, cricket, volleyball and football?
(a) Suresh (b) Kavita
(c) Rajneesh (d) Gambhir

23. Who is good in tennis, volleyball and hockey?
(a) Gambhir (b) Kavita
(c) Suresh (d) Rejneesh

24. Select the related figure from the given alternatives.

Question Figures

F	:	E	::	I	:	?

Answer Figures

(a)	(b)	(c)	(d)
T	L	J	K

25. If it is possible to make only one meaningful English word from the second, fifth, seventh and eighth letters of the word PHYSICAL using each letter only once, second letter of that word is your answer. If more than one such words can be formed, your answer is M. If no such word can be formed, your answer is N. **[NICL (AO) 2015]**
(a) I (b) A
(c) L (d)M
(e) N

26. How many times will you write even numerals if you write all the numbers from 291 to 300?
(a) 11 (b) 13
(c) 15 (d) 17

27. In a certain code language, DEALT is coded as FDCKV and HOPES is coded as JNRDU. In the same code language how will CHALK be coded as? **[IBPS (Clerk) Pre 2015]**
(a) EFGJM (b) EGCKM
(c) BFCKU (d) EGCJL
(e) BFCJM

28. Find out which of the answers figures (a), (b), (c) and (d) completes the figure matrix?

Question Figure

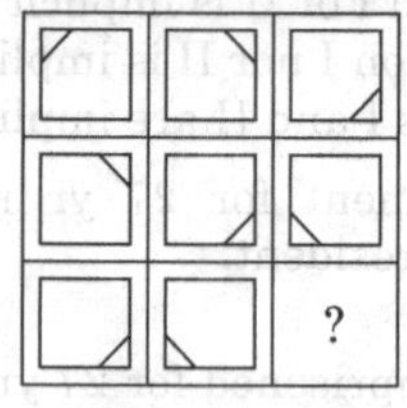

Answer Figures

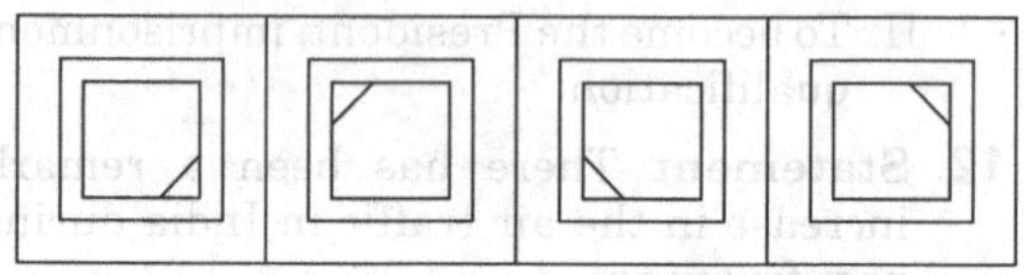

(a) (b) (c) (d)

Direction (Q. Nos. 29-31) *Read the following information to answer these questions.*

Six boys namely Manish, Banku, Kanu, Dheeraj, Nanu and Raj are standing in a row in an award giving ceremony, not necessarily in the same order, and are facing North. Manish and Banku standing adjacent to each other. Kanu, who is not standing at either ends, is not adjacent to Raj. Nanu is to the left of Banku. Dheeraj is standing between Kanu and Manish, Banku is standing at one of the ends. **[MAT 2014]**

29. If it is known that Raj and Nanu are standing adjacent to each other, then who is standing to the immediate left of Kanu?
(a) Deeraj (b) Banku (c) Raj (d) Nanu

30. If Kanu, Dheeraj and Manish are standing in the same order (from West to East), then who is standing at the extreme East?
(a) Nanu (b) Banku (c) Raj (d) Manish

31. If Dheeraj were to stand at the West end, then Raj would stand between
(a) Dheeraj and Manish
(b) Dheeraj and Kanu
(c) Dheeraj and Nanu
(d) Cannot be determined

32. If D is the daughter of A and D is the sister of M and A's brother is C, then how are C and M related? **[SSC (Multitasking) 2014]**
(a) Mother and Daughter
(b) Uncle and Niece
(c) Father and Daughter
(d) Aunt and Niece

33. If A = 1; AND = 19, then BAT = ?
(a) 22 (b) 23 (c) 21 (d) 20

Direction (Q. Nos. 34-35) *Study the following information to answer the given questions.*

Amongst five friends P, Q, R, S and T, each scored different marks in an examination out of a total of 100 marks. S scored more then only T. R scored less than P. Only one person scored more than Q. The one who scored second highest marks scored 87 marks. **[RBI (Officers) 2015]**

34. Who scored the third least marks in the examination ?
(a) P (b) Q (c) R (d) S
(e) T

35. If S scored 23 marks less than the marks scored by Q, which of the following could possibly be R's score?
(a) 64 (b) 93 (c) 61 (d) 89
(e) 78

Direction (Q. Nos. 36-37) *In the following questions the symbols +, ×, ?, @ and $ are used with the following meaning.*

'A + B' means 'A is neither smaller nor greater than B'.

'A × B' means 'A is neither equal to nor smaller than B'.

'A ? B' means 'A is neither greater nor equal to B'.

'A @ B' means 'A is either greater or equal to B'.

'A $ B' means 'A is not equal to B'.

Now, in each of the following questions assuming the given statements to be true, find out which of the Conclusions I and II given below them is/are definitely true?

Give answer
(a) if only Conclusion I is true
(b) if only Conclusion II is true
(c) if either I or II is true
(d) if neither I nor II is true
(e) If both I and II are true

36. Statements C + D, D $ M, M ? C
Conclusions I. M $ C
II. D + M

37. Statements K $ M, M × B, K + B
Conclusions I. M × K
II. K ? M

38. Rohit drives his car from Bengaluru towards Mysore. At a distance of 80 km, he turns right and proceeds for 50 km. Again, he turns right and travels for 70 km. Finally, he turns again towards right and travels for 50 km and stops there. How far is Rohit from Bengaluru?
(a) 10 km (b) 40 km (c) 20 km (d) 30 km

39. If 'P' denotes '+', 'Q' denotes '–', 'R' denotes '÷' and 'S' denotes '×', then 18 S 36 R 12 Q 6 P 7 =?
(a) 115 (b) 25 (c) 55 (d) $\frac{648}{13}$

40. A piece of paper is folded and cut as shown below in the question figures. From the given answer figures, indicate how it will appear when opened? **[SSC (10+2) 2012]**

Question Figures

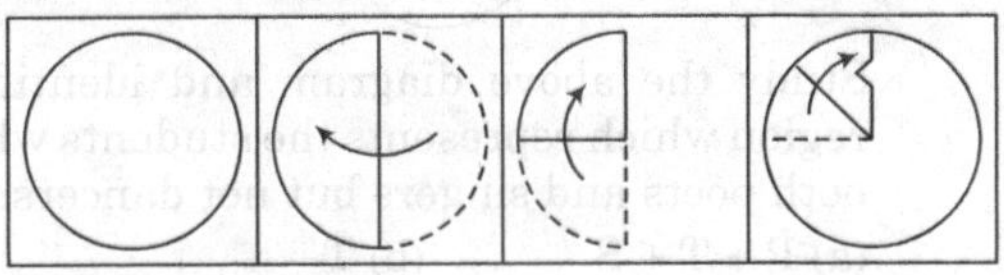

Answer Figures

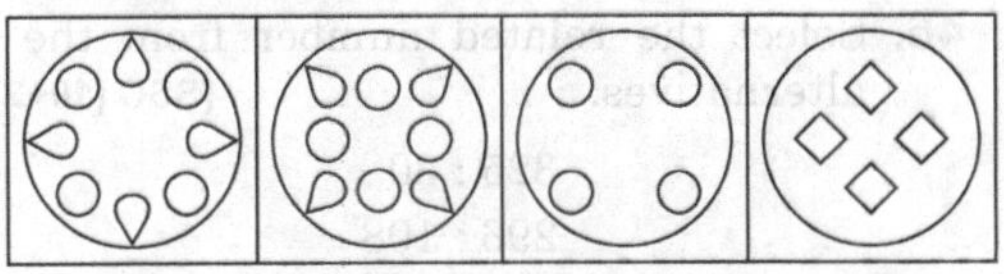

(a) (b) (c) (d)

41. Find the missing number? **[SSC (10+2) 2014]**

18	11	6	12
9 38 6	19 32 9	26 44 3	9 ? 20
17	11	15	8

(a) 9 (b) 40 (c) 7 (d) 36

Direction (Q. Nos. 42-43) *In the following questions, a series is given, with one term missing. Choose the correct alternative from the given ones that will complete the series.*

42. 2B, 4C, 8E, 14H, ?
(a) 22 L (b) 16 K
(c) 20 L (d) 22 L

43. W, U, S, P, M, I, ?

(a) E (b) A
(c) H (d) F
(e) None of these

44. If in the given figure, no two adjacent areas can have the same colour, then find the least number of colour to be needed to fill the figure/areas.

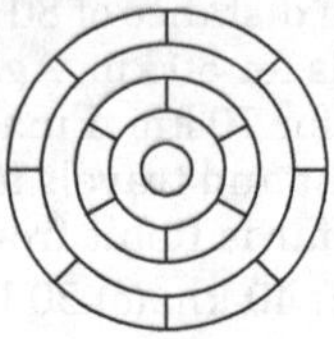

(a) 3 (b) 4
(c) 5 (d) 6

45. The diagram represents the students who are singers, dancers and poets.

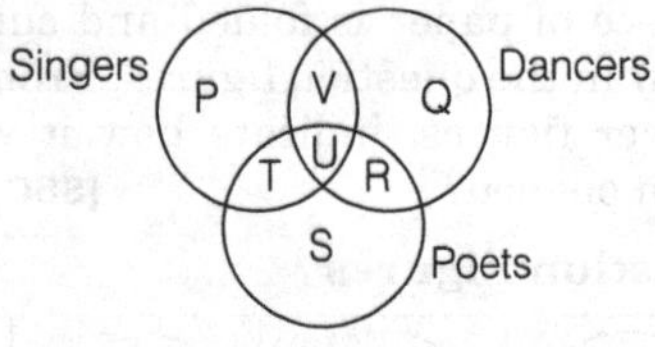

Study the above diagram and identify the region which represents the students who are both poets and singers but not dancers.

(a) P + T + S (b) T
(c) T + U + R + S (d) P + T + U + S

46. Select the related number from the given alternatives. **[SSC (10+2) 2014]**

325 : 30
296 : 108
628 : ?

(a) 306 (b) 96
(c) 314 (d) 36

47. In which answer figure is the question figure embedded?

Question Figure

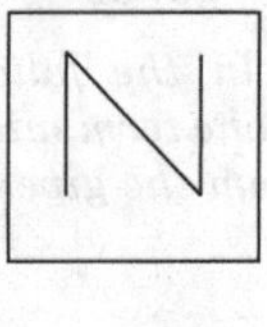

Answer Figures

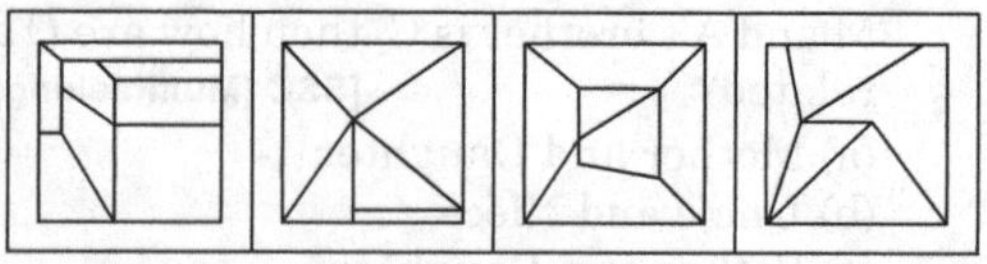

(a) (b) (c) (d)

48. Arrange the following words according to the dictionary.

(i) Sound (ii) Socks
(iii) Shock (iv) Sharp
(v) Snooker

(a) (v), (iv), (iii), (i), (ii)
(b) (iv), (iii), (v), (ii), (i)
(c) (iii), (iv), (v), (i), (ii)
(d) (iv), (iii), (ii), (v), (i)

Direction (Q. Nos. 49-50) *Given an input line, the machine rearranges them step by step as per the illustration given below.*

Input	show must 73 85 go 69 on 32
***Step* I**	32 show must 73 85 go 69 on
***Step* II**	32 go show must 73 85 69 on
***Step* III**	32 go 69 show must 73 85 on
***Step* IV**	32 go 69 must show 73 85 on
***Step* V**	32 go 69 must 73 show 85 on
***Step* VI**	32 go 69 must 73 on show 85
***Step* VII**	32 go 69 must 73 on 85 show

Step VII is the last step in the arrangement.

As per the rules followed in the following questions the appropriate step for the given input.

49. Step III of an input is '14 but 26 not just 63 fundamental 47'.

Which of the following is definitely the input?

(a) 26 14 but not just 63 fundamental 47
(b) 26 but 14 not just 63 fundamental 47
(c) fundamental 26 14 but not just 63 47
(d) Cannot be determined
(e) None of the above

50. Step I of an input is '34 fire dress well 63 43 prime 52'.

Which of the following steps will be the last but one?

(a) IV (b) III (c) VI (d) VII
(e) V

Hints and Solutions

Solution (Q. Nos. 1-2)

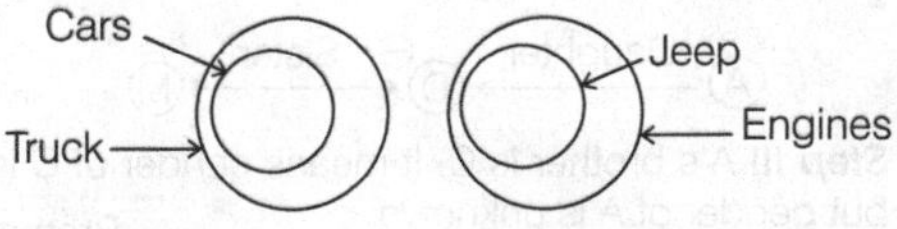

1. (*e*) **Conclusions** I. No car is a jeep. (✔)
II. All cars being engines is a possibility. (✔)

2. (*d*) **Conclusions** I. No engine is a car. (✗)
II. No truck is an engine. (✗)

3. (*c*) As we know that, when all the faces of a cube are painted with a single colour, then smaller cubes with only two faces painted are the middle cubes present at the edges.
$\therefore$ Number of middle cubes $= 12(n-2) = 12(3-2)$
$= 12 \times 1 = 12$ (here, $n = 3$)

4. (*c*) From Statements II and III, it is clear that S is the daughter - in-law of B.
B is the mother of N and R.
T is the son of N and S is the mother of T.
So, S is the wife of N.
Hence, S is the daughter-in-law of B.

5. (*a*) From Statements I and II, there are 33 students in the class.
From Statements II and III, there may be 33 or 44 students in the class.
Hence, only I and II are required.

6. (*b*) As, 20 → 11 ($\div 2 + 1$) Similarly, 102 → [52] ($\div 2 + 1$)

7. (*c*) As, Optimist is always Cheerful, in the same way Pessimist is always Gloomy.

8. (*c*) As, LO : PK : (-4, $+4$) Similarly, IR : [MN] (-4, $+4$)

9. (*a*) The complete letter series will be
m p̲ p l / m̲ p p l / m p p̲ l / m p p l̲
$\therefore$ Required letters = pmpl

10. (*a*) According to the question, the position of the, Raman from top is 16th and from bottom is 49th.
Then, total number of students $= 16 + 49 - 1 = 64$

11. (*d*) The given statement does not mean imprisonment is necessary. Nelson Mandela's dedicated service to the nation and his struggle for freedom, despite so many hardships won him the desired public appeal to be elected the President. Hence, neither I nor II is implicit.

12. (*b*) The given statement hints that in recent years, the number of people travelling by air has increased. This implies that large number of travellers can now afford air travel. Hence, only II is a valid assumption.

13. (*a*) Let the ages of the children be x, $(x+3)$, $(x+6)$, $(x+9)$ and $(x+12)$ yr, respectively.
Then, $x + (x+3) + (x+6) + (x+9) + (x+12) = 50$
$\Rightarrow 5x + 30 = 50$
$\Rightarrow 5x = 20$
$\Rightarrow x = 4$ yr
Hence, age of the youngest child is 4 yr.

14. (*b*) All except onion are used for extracting oil.

15. (*e*) Here, $\frac{21}{24} = \frac{7}{8}; \frac{28}{32} = \frac{7}{8}; \frac{14}{16} = \frac{7}{8}; \frac{70}{80} = \frac{7}{8}$
But $\frac{54}{62} = \frac{27}{31}$

16. (*c*) Given,

1	2	3	4	5	6	7	8
E	Q	U	A	L	I	T	Y

After interchanging the position,

8	7	6	5	4	3	2	1
L	I	T	Y	E	[Q]	U	A

Q ← Third from the right end

17. (*b*) Since, fish live in water and in question, water is called jungle. So, fish live in the jungle.

18. (*d*) According the given data, we have
From above row, D is in the middle.

19. (*b*) Number of days from 15 September, 2000 to 15 September 2001
= 365 day
= 1 odd day
$\therefore$ 15 September, 2001 = Saturday

20. (*c*) According to the matrices,
P — 00, 12, 24, 31, (43)
E — (56), 68, 75, 87, 99
N — 02, 14, (21), 33, 40
S — 04, 11, 23, 30, (42)
$\therefore$ PENS $\Rightarrow$ 43, 56, 21, 42

Solution (Q. Nos. 21-23) Following table can be drawn from the given information.

	Hockey	Volleyball	Tennis	Cricket	Football
Rajneesh	✔	✔	✔	✗	✗
Kavita	✔	✔	✗	✔	✗
Suresh	✔	✗	✔	✗	✔
Gambhir	✗	✔	✔	✔	✔
Mahesh	✗	✗	✔	✗	✔

21. (*c*) Kavita is good in hockey, volleyball and cricket.

22. (*d*) Gambhir is good in tennis, cricket, volleyball and football.

23. (*d*) Rajneesh is good in tennis, volleyball and hockey.

24. (*b*) Clearly, from figure I to figure II, one line segment is added to the bottom of the design.

25. (*b*) The second, fifth, seventh and eighth letters of given word are H, I, A and L, respectively. There is only one such word can be made from these letters, i.e. HAIL.

26. (*b*) Even numerals from 291 to 300

= 10 times 2, once each 4, 6, 8

Hence, the total times are 13.

27. (*b*)

As, D E A L T → (+2, −1, +2, −1, +2) → F D C K V and H O P E S → (+2, −1, +2, −1, +2) → J N R D U

Similarly, C H A L K → (+2, −1, +2, −1, +2) → E G C K M

28. (*b*) Figures in each row are rotating clockwise 90°.

Solution (Q. Nos. 29-31) According to given information the standing pattern of six boys will be like this

Raj Nanu Kanu Dheeraj Manish Banku

29. (*d*) Nanu is standing immediate left of Kanu.

30. (*b*) Banku is standing at the extreme East.

31. (*c*) If Dheeraj were to stand at the West end, then the pattern would be like this.

Dheeraj, Raj, Nanu, Kanu, Manish, Banku.

Form the above pattern.

Raj would stand between Dheeraj and Nanu.

32. (*b*) Here we draw a tree diagram

According to the given data,

***Step* I** D is the daughter of A, it means that D is female, but gender of A is unknown.

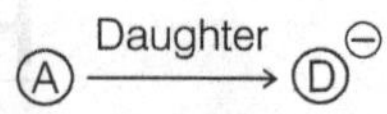

***Step* II** D is the sister of M, it means that D is female but gender of M is not known.

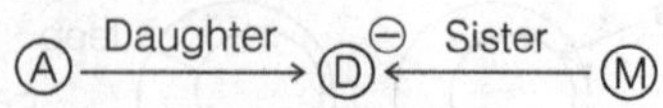

***Step* III** A's brother is C. It means gender of C is male but gender of A is unknown.

Therefore, final tree diagram is

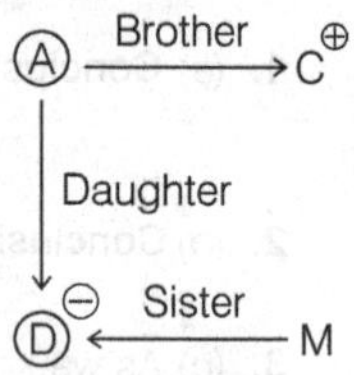

Now, we find relation between C and M. But, here gender of M is still unknown.

Therefore, M may be male or female. But we know the gender of C is male. Hence, the relation between C and M can be that of an uncle and niece or uncle and nephew.

Uncle and niece is one of the given options. So, relation between C and M = Uncle and Niece.

33. (*b*) According to the question, A = 1 (the position number in English alphabet)

A N D → 1 + 14 + 4 = 19

Similarly, B A T → 2 + 1 + 20 = 23

Solution (Q. Nos. 34-35) According to the given information,

Five friends scored marks are as follows:

$$P > Q > R > S > T$$

34. (*c*) R scored the third least marks in the examination.

35. (*e*) Given, Q's Marks = 87

∴ S's Marks = 87 − 23 = 64

∴ R scored between 87 and 64.

From the given options it is clear that R scored 78 marks.

Solution (Q. Nos. 36-37)

+ ⇒ =	× ⇒ >	? ⇒ <	@ ⇒ ≥	$ ⇒ ≠

36. (*d*) **Statements** C + D, D $ M, M ? C

After conversion C = D, D > M or D < M, M < C

Either (i) C = D > M < C or (ii) C = D < M < C

Conclusions

I. M $ C = M > C or M < C

It is clear that M is smaller than C.

II. D + M ⇒ D = M

It is clear that D is either greater or smaller than M.

37. (*e*) **Statements** K $ M, M × B, K + B

After conversion K > M or K < M, M > B, K = B

or, M > B = K

Conclusions I. $M \times K \Rightarrow M > K$

K is equal to B and M is greater than B. Therefore, M is definitely greater than K.

II. $K ? M \Rightarrow K < M$

It is clear that K is smaller than M.

38. (*a*) ∴ Route followed by Rohit

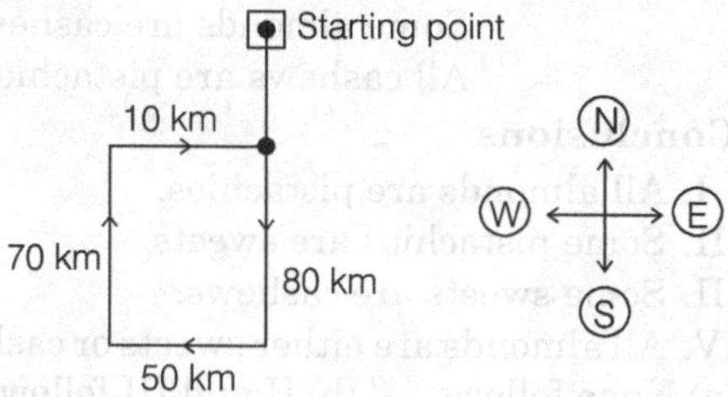

Now, Rohit is away (80 − 70) = 10 km from Bengaluru.

39. (*c*) According to the question, we can arrange the mathematical symbols as

P = +, Q = − R = ÷, S = ×

18 S 36 R 12 Q 6 P 7 = ?

$\Rightarrow$? = 18 × 36 ÷ 12 − 6 + 7
= 18 × 3 − 6 + 7
= 54 − 6 + 7 = 61 − 6 = 55

40. (*d*)

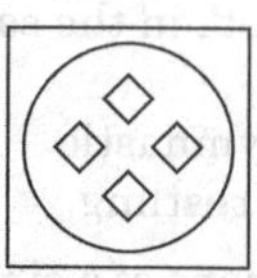

So, option (d) is correct.

41. (*a*) As, (18 + 9 + 17) − 6 ⇒ 44 − 6 = 38
and (11 + 19 + 11) − 9 ⇒ 41 − 9 = 32
and (6 + 26 + 15) − 3 ⇒ 47 − 3 = 44
Similarly, (12 + 9 + 8) − 20 ⇒ 29 − 20 = 9

42. (*a*) Pattern of given alpha-numeric series is as follows

+1 +2 +3 +4
2 B 4 C 8 E 14 H 22 L
+2 +4 +6 +8

∴ ? = 22 L

43. (*a*) The pattern is as follows

23 21 19 16 13 9 5
W U S P M I E
−2 −2 −3 3 −4 −4

∴ ? = E

44. (*a*) We shall label the various regions in the given figure as shown.

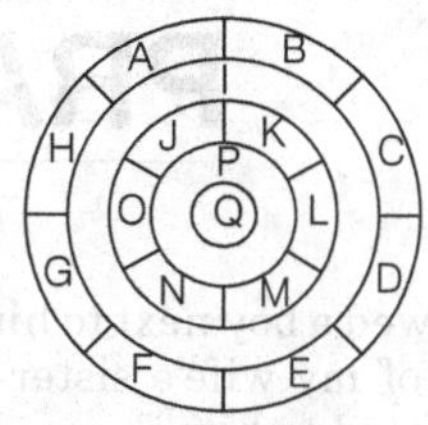

The regions A, C, E and G can have the same colour say colour 1.

The regions B, D, F and H can have the same colour (but different from colour 1) say colour 2.

The region I lies adjacent to each one of the regions A, B, C, D, E, F, G and H and therefore it should have a different colour say colour 3.

The regions J, L and N can have the same colour (different from colour 3) say colour 1.

The regions K, M and O can have the same colour (different from the colours 1 and 3). Thus, these regions will have colour 2.

The region P cannot have any of the colours 1 and 2 as it lies adjacent to each one of the regions J, K, L, M, N and O and so it will have colour 3.

The region Q can have any of the colours 1 or 2.

So, minimum number of colours required is 3.

45. (*b*) Region T is common to the both singers and poets but not dancers.

46. (*b*) The pattern is as follows :

352 : 30 ⇒ 3 × 5 × 2 = 30
and 296 : 108 ⇒ 2 × 9 × 6 = 108
Similarly, 628 : ? ⇒ 6 × 2 × 8 = 96

47. (*a*) Clearly, question figure is embedded in answer figure (a) as shown below

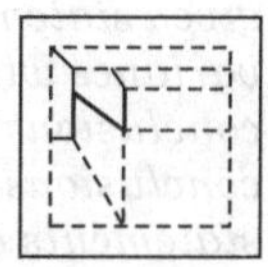

48. (*b*) Arrangement of words as per dictionary.

(iv) Sharp → (iii) Shock → (v) Snooker → (ii) Socks → (i) Sound

49. (*d*) Cannot be determined.

50. (*e*) ***Step* I** 34 fire dress well 63 43 prime 52
***Step* II** 34 dress fire well 63 43 prime 52
***Step* III** 34 dress 43 fire well 63 prime 52
***Step* IV** 34 dress 43 fire 52 well 63 prime
***Step* V** 34 dress 43 fire 52 prime well 63
***Step* VI** 34 dress 43 fire 52 prime 63 well
So, the step last but one is Step V.

PRACTICE SET 45

1. A man showed a boy next to him and said, "He is the son of my wife's sister-in-law. How is my son related to him?" **[SSC (CGL) 2013]**
(a) Cousin (b) Brother
(c) Uncle (d) Nephew

Direction (Q. Nos. 2-3) *In these questions, relationship between different elements is shown in the statement. The statement is followed by two conclusions. Study the conclusions based on the given statement and appropriate answer.* **[IBPS (Clerk) 2013]**
(a) Neither Conclusion I nor II follows
(b) Both Conclusions I and II follow
(c) Only Conclusion II follows
(d) Either Conclusion I or II follows
(e) Only Conclusion I follows

2. Statements $K > I \geq T \geq E; O < R < K$
Conclusions I. $R < E$
II. $O < T$

3. Statement $C < L < O = U = D \geq S > Y$
Conclusions I. $O > Y$ II. $C < D$

Direction (Q. Nos. 4-5) *In each of the questions below are given some statements followed by some conclusions. You have to take the given statements to be true even if they seem to be at variance with commonly known facts. Read all the conclusions and then decide which of the given conclusions logically follows from the given statements disregarding commonly known facts.*

4. Statements All glasses are rooms.
Some rooms are planes.
All planes are ducks.
Some ducks are lanterns.
Conclusions I. Some lanterns are planes.
II. Some ducks are rooms.
III. Some rooms are glasses.
IV. Some ducks are glasses.
(a) I and II follow
(b) II and III follow
(c) I, II and II follow
(d) All I, II, III and IV follow
(e) None of the above

5. Statements Some sweets are almonds.
Some almonds are cashews.
All cashews are pistachios.
Conclusions
I. All almonds are pistachios.
II. Some pistachios are sweets.
III. Some sweets are cashews.
IV. All almonds are either sweets or cashews.
(a) None follows (b) II and III follow
(c) Only IV follows (d) Either I or IV follows
(e) None of these

Direction (Q. Nos. 6-7) *In the following questions, select the related word/letters/number from the given alternatives.* **[BSSC (CGL) 2015]**

6. 23 : 13 : : 54 : ?
(a) 40 (b) 41 (c) 44 (d) 39

7. 'Pitch' is related to 'Cricket', in the same way 'Arena' is related to ......
(a) Tennis (b) Gymnastic
(c) Badminton (d) Wrestling

8. From the given four positions of a single dice, find the number of dots at the face opposite to the face having 1 dot.

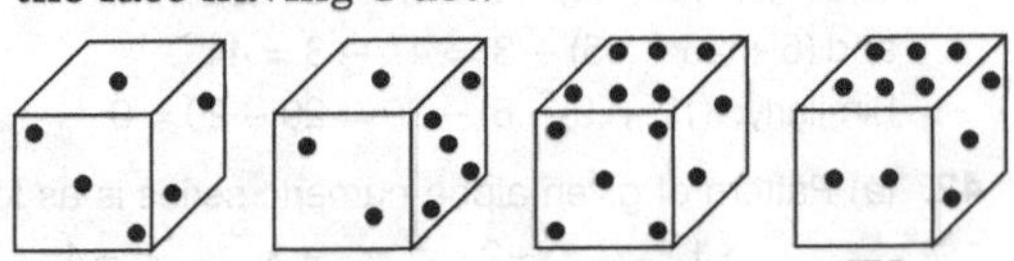

I II III IV

(a) 3 (b) 4 (c) 5 (d) 6

Direction (Q. Nos. 9-10) *Each of the questions below consists of a question and two statements numbered I and II given below it. You have to decide whether the data provided in the statements are sufficient to answer the question.*
Give answer
(a) if the data in Statement I alone is sufficient to answer the question, while the data in Statement II alone is not sufficient to answer the question
(b) if the data in Statement II alone is sufficient to answer the question, while the data in Statement I alone is not sufficient to answer the question

(c) if the data either in Statement I alone or in Statement II alone is sufficient to answer the question
(d) if the data in both the Statements I and II together are not sufficient to answer the question
(e) if the data in both the Statements I and II together are necessary to answer the question

9. How many runs did Team X make?
I. The umpire of the match correctly mentions that had the batsman from team X scored two more runs, the team would have won the match by 28 runs.
II. The coach correctly mentions that the batsman from Team X missed his century by two runs.

10. Who among P, Q, R and S is the shortest?
I. S is not as tall as R, but is taller than Q.
II. R is not the tallest.

11. In the following question, two statements are given followed by three conclusions. You have to consider the statements to be true even if they seem to be at variance from commonly known facts. You have to decide which of the given conclusions if any follows from the given statements. **[SSC (CGL) 2013]**

Statements Water has shape, has volume. The knowledge is like water, flowed from one side to other.

Conclusions
I. The knowledge is interdisciplinary.
II. The knowledge is bound within a specific area.
III. The knowledge influences the core of mental activity directly.
(a) Only Conclusion I follows
(b) Only Conclusion II follows
(c) Both Conclusions I and II follow
(d) Both Conclusions I and III follow

12. In the question below is given a statement followed by three courses of action numbered I, II and III. A course of action is a step or administrative decision to be taken for improvement, follow-up or further action in regard to the problem, policy, etc. On the basis of information given in the statement, you have to assume everything in the statement to be true and then decide which of the three given suggested courses of action logically follows worth pursuing. Then decide which of the alternatives (a), (b), (c), (d) or (e) is correct.

Statement A large private bank has decided to retrench one-third of its employees in view of the huge losses incurred by it during the past three quarters.

Courses of Action
I. The Government should issue a notification to general public to immediately stop all transactions with the bank.
II. The Government should direct the bank to refrain from retrenching its employees.
III. The Government should ask the Central Bank of the country to initiate an enquiry into the bank's activities and submit its report.
(a) None follows (b) Only I follows
(c) Only II follows (d) Only III follows
(e) Both I and II follow

Direction (Q. Nos. 13-14) *In the following questions, find the odd numbers/words pair from the given alternatives.*

13. (a) 11, 17, 23 (b) 12, 14, 16
(c) 8, 10, 12 (d) 18, 36, 72

14. (a) Cockroach : Anternae
(b) Lizard : Flagella
(c) Hydra : Tentacles
(d) Plasmodium: Cilia

15. Find a number which when multiplied by any number of the digits, the digits in the product gives the number when these are added.
(a) 8 (b) 7 (c) 6 (d) 9

Direction (Q. Nos. 16-18) *Examine carefully the following statements and answer the three items that follow.* **[UPSC 2013]**

Out of four friends A, B, C and D
I. A and B play football and cricket.
II. B and C play cricket and hockey.
III. C and D play basketball and football.
IV. C and D play hockey and basketball.

16. Who does not play hockey?
(a) D (b) C (c) B (d) A

17. Who plays football, basketball and hockey?
(a) D (b) C (c) B (d) A

18. Which game do B, C and D play?
(a) Basketball (b) Hockey
(c) Cricket (d) Football

19. Mrs. Susheela celebrated her wedding anniversary on Tuesday, 30th September, 1997. When will she celebrate her next wedding anniversary on the same day?
(a) 30th September, 2003 **[SSC (CGL) 2011]**
(b) 30th September, 2004
(c) 30th September, 2002
(d) 30th October, 2003

20. A word is represented by only one set of numbers as given in anyone of the alternatives. The set of numbers given in the alternatives are represented by two classes of alphabets as in the two matrices given below. The columns and rows of Matrix I are numbered from 0 to 4 and that of Matrix II from 5 to 9. A letter can be represented first by its row and next by its column number. e.g., 'N' can be represented by 02, 21, etc. 'O' can be represented by 65,96 etc. Similarly, you have to identify the correct set for the word given in question.

Matrix I

	0	1	2	3	4
0	P	W	N	I	S
1	I	S	P	W	N
2	W	N	I	S	P
3	S	P	W	N	I
4	N	I	S	P	W

Matrix II

	5	6	7	8	9
5	A	E	R	O	H
6	O	H	A	E	R
7	E	R	O	H	A
8	H	A	E	R	O
9	R	O	H	A	E

HIPS
(a) 85, 41, 24, 11 (b) 66, 21, 24, 11
(c) 67, 41, 24, 42 (d) 78, 34, 23, 04

Direction (Q. Nos 21-23) *In the following questions, a series is given, with one term missing. Choose the correct alternatives from the given ones that will complete the series.*

21. ACE, BDF, CEG,? **[SSC (CGL) 2014]**
(a) DFE (b) DEF (c) DFH (d) DEH

22. 8, 18, 32, 50, 72, ?
(a) 76 (b) 98 (c) 80 (d) 70

23. C5, F4, E7, H6, ?
(a) 8 G (b) G9 (c) F9 (d) D7

24. Which one of the following figures represents the relationship among dog, animal, pets?

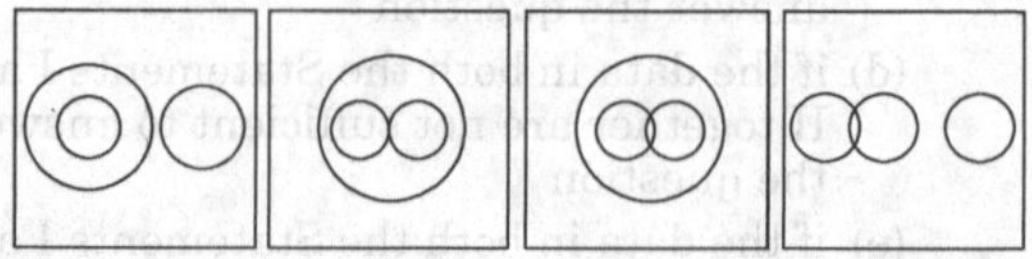

(a) (b) (c) (d)

25. Select the one, which is different from the other three responses.

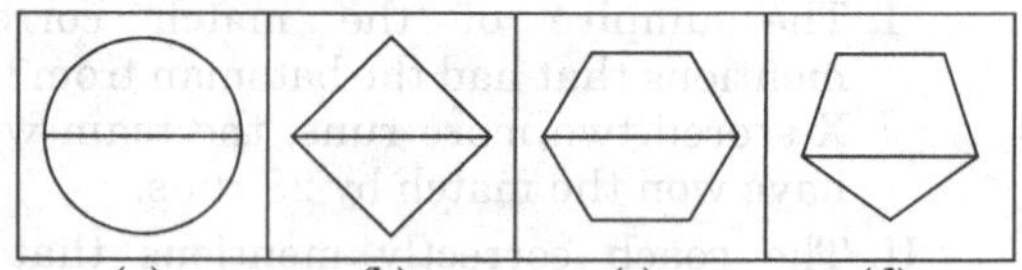

(a) (b) (c) (d)

26. P, Q, R and T answered an examination. In the results Q was immediately followed by 'P' but no one was thereafter 'P'. 'R' was ahead of 'Q' but could not score as much as 'T'. Who scored the second highest?
(a) P (b) Q (c) R (d) T

Direction (Q. Nos. 27-29) *The following questions are based on five three-digit number given below.* **[IBPS (clerk) Pre 2015]**

415 764 327 542 256

27. What will be the resultant if second digit of the lowest number and third digit of the highest number are multiplied?
(a) 30 (b) 14
(c) 8 (d) 20
(e) 36

28. If '1' is added to the first digit of every odd number and '2' is subtracted from the second digit of every even number, in how many numbers will a digit appear twice?
(a) Two (b) Three
(c) Four (d) None
(e) One

29. The positions of the first and the second digits of each of the numbers are interchanged. What will be the resultant if third digit of highest number thus formed is divided by the second digit of the lowest number thus formed?
(a) 3 (b) 4
(c) 2.5 (d) 1.5
(e) 1

Direction (Q. Nos. 30-31) *Study the following information carefully and answer the given questions.* **[IBPS (PO) 2012]**

A word and number arrangement machine when given an input line of words and numbers rearranges them following a particular rule in each step. The following is an illustration of input and rearrangement. (All the numbers given in the arrangement are two-digit numbers).

Input gone over 35 69 test 72 park 27

***Step* I** 27 gone over 35 69 test 72 park

***Step* II** 27 test gone over 35 69 72 park

***Step* III** 27 test 35 gone over 69 72 park

***Step* IV** 27 test 35 park gone over 69 72

***Step* V** 27 test 35 park 69 gone over 72

***Step* VI** 27 test 35 park 69 over gone 72

***Step* VII** 27 test 35 park 69 over 72 gone

and Step VII is the last step of the rearrangement of the above input as the desired arrangement is obtained. As per the rules followed in the above steps, find out the appropriate step for the given input in each of the following questions.

30. **Input** '86 open shut door 31 49 always 45'. How many steps will be required to complete the rearrangement?
(a) Five (b) Six (c) Seven (d) Four
(e) None of these

31. Step II of an input is '18 win 71 34 now if victory 61'.
How many more steps will be required to complete the rearrangement?
(a) Three (b) Four (c) Five (d) Six
(e) More than six

32. How many triangles are there in the following figure?

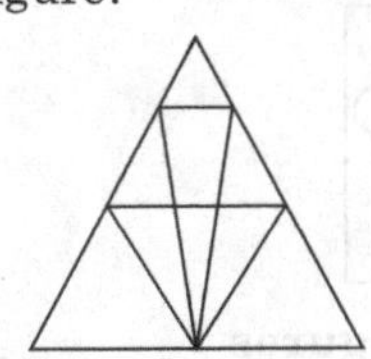

(a) 18 (b) 16
(c) 22 (d) 26

33. Which one set of letters when sequentially placed at the gaps in the given letter series shall complete it?

ab _ aa _ aaa _ a _ ab _ a
(a) a b b a b (b) a b a a a
(c) a a b b a (d) a b b a a

34. The symbols for addition (+), subtraction (–), multiplication (×) and division (÷) will have to be inserted in the blank squares in order to get answer 3 as shown in the equation
20□5□8□2□17 = 3
Find out which set below is correct.
(a) – + + × (b) + – × ÷
(c) × – ÷ + (d) ÷ + × –

35. Five friends are sitting in a row facing South. Here, Mohan is between Balu and Raju and Raju is to the immediate right of Praveen and Amit is to the right of Balu. Who is in extreme right end? **[SSC (10+2) 2012]**
(a) Amit (b) Balu
(c) Praveen (d) Mohan

36. If EDITION is written as IDETNOI, then how is MEDICAL written in that code? **[SSC (Multitasking) 2011]**
(a) DEMILAC (b) LACIMED
(c) DIEMCAL (d) CADILEM

37. Which single letter can be prefixed to the following words in order to obtain entirely new words? (Same letter has to be prefixed in all five words of each) **[SSC (CGL) Pre 2015]**
EAT OUR IS AS AT
(a) S (b) H (c) C (d) B

38. In the following question a word is given. How many pairs of letters are there in these words which have as many letters between them as in the English alphabet?

ADJUSTING

(a) None (b) One
(c) Two (d) Three

39. If a mirror is placed on the line AB, then which of the answer figures is the right image of the question figure?

Question Figure

Answer Figures

(a) 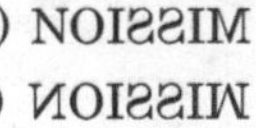 (b) 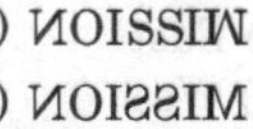
(c) (d)

40. Select the missing number from the given responses. **[SSC (10+2) 2014]**

6	7	4
5	3	5
7	?	6
3	3	6

(a) 7 (b) 3 (c) 8 (d) 5

Direction (Q. Nos. 41-44) *Read the following information carefully and answer the questions given below.*

A, B, C, D, E, F, G, H and J are sitting around a circle facing a centre. C is third to the left of A. E is fourth to the right of A. D is fourth to the left of J, who is second to the right of A. F is third to the right of B. G is not an immediate neighbour of A. **[NICL (AO) 2015]**

41. What is H's position with respect to E?
(a) Third to the left (b) Fourth to the left
(c) Fifth to the right (d) Fifth to the left
(e) Sixth to the left

42. Who is third to the right of G?
(a) B (b) D
(c) A (d) Data inadequate
(e) None of these

43. Who is fifth to the right of E?
(a) F (b) C (c) H (d) A
(e) None of these

44. Who is second to the left of H?
(a) A (b) F
(c) D (d) Data inadequate
(e) None of these

45. Arrange the following words as per dictionary.
(i) Live (ii) Litter
(iii) Little (iv) Literacy
(v) Living
(a) (iv), (iii), (v), (ii), (i)
(b) (iv), (ii), (iii), (i), (v)
(c) (iii), (iv), (ii), (i), (v)
(d) (iii), (ii), (iv), (v), (i)

46. A man goes 5 km East, then he turns right and goes 4 km, then he turns left and goes 5 km. Which direction is he facing now? **[SSC (CGL) 2012]**
(a) North
(b) South
(c) East
(d) West

47. In the question, there are two statements, labelled as Assertion (A) and Reason (R). Choose the correct alternatives from the given option.
Assertion (A) We prefer to wear white clothes in winter.
Reason (R) White clothes are good reflectors of heat.
(a) if both 'A' and 'R' are true and 'R' is the correct explanation of 'A'
(b) if both 'A' and 'R' are true but 'R' is not the correct explanation of 'A'
(c) if 'A' is true but 'R' is false
(d) if 'A' is false but 'R' is true
(e) if both 'A' and 'R' are false

48. Complete the missing segment by selecting from the given alternatives (a), (b), (c) and (d).

Question Figure

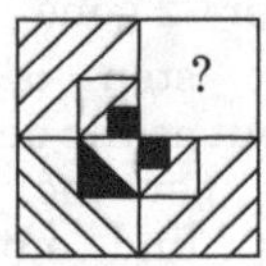

Answer Figures

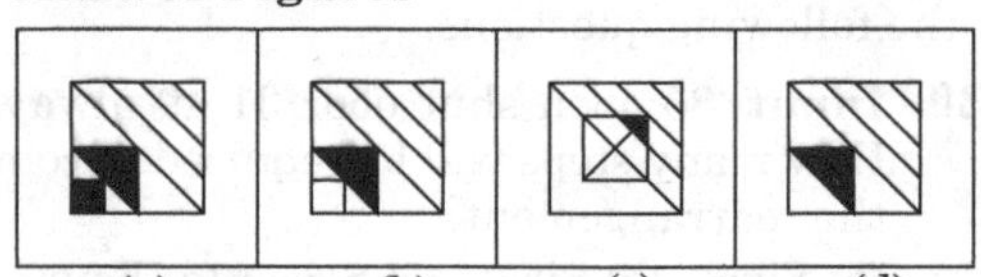

(a) (b) (c) (d)

49. When the time in the wall clock is 3:25 pm, the acute angle between the hour hand and minute hand is
(a) 60° (b) 52.5° (c) 47.5° (d) 42°

50. Identify the answer figure from which the pieces given in the questions figure have been cut. **[SSC (CGL) 2015]**

Question Figure

Answer Figures

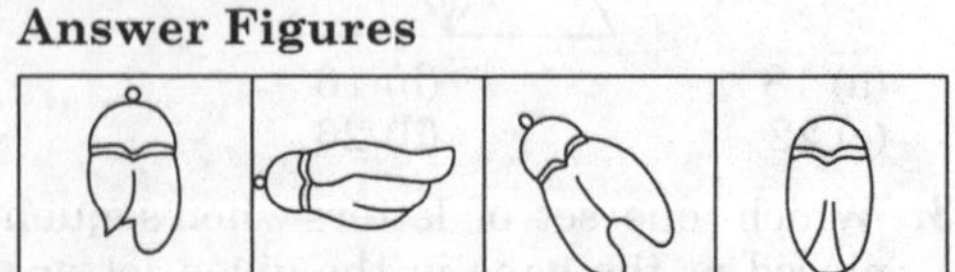

(a) (b) (c) (d)

Hints and Solutions

1. (*a*) Following family diagram can be drawn from the given information,

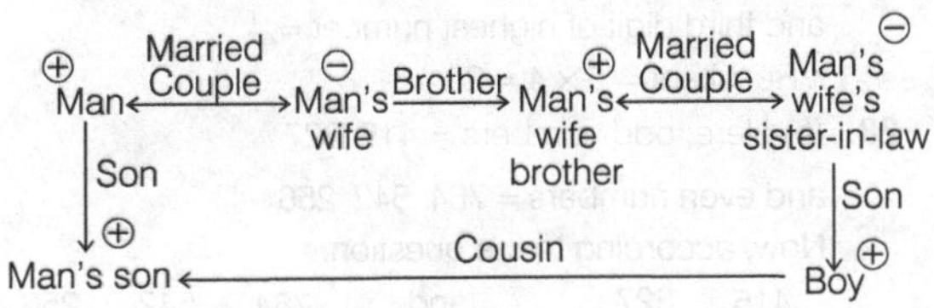

Now, it is clear that man's son is the cousin of that boy.

2. (*a*) $K > I \geq T \geq E$; $O < R < K$

On combining both the statements, we get

$O < R < K > I \geq T \geq E$

Conclusions I. $R < E$ (False)

II. $O < T$ (False)

Thus, neither Conclusion I nor II follows.

3. (*b*) $C < L < O = U = D \geq S > Y$

Here, statements are already combined.

Conclusions I. $O > Y$ (True)

II. $C < D$ (True)

Thus, both Conclusions I and II follow.

4. (*b*)

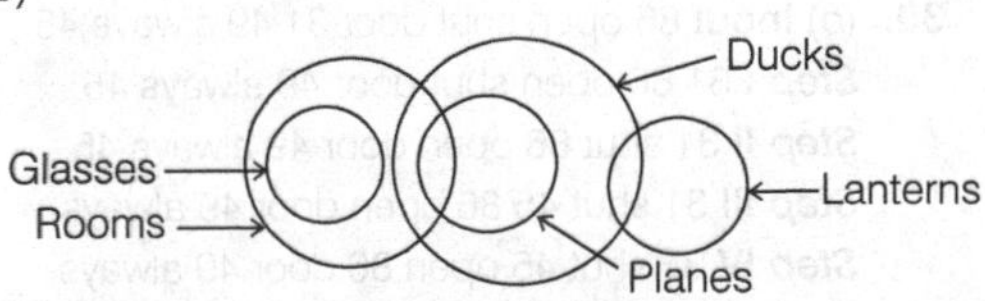

Conclusions I. Some lanterns are planes. (✗)

II. Some ducks are rooms. (✔)

III. Some rooms are glasses. (✔)

IV. Some ducks are glasses. (✗)

5. (*a*)

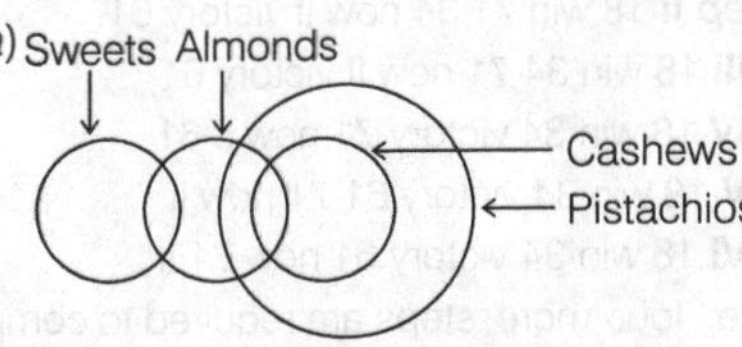

Conclusions I. All almonds are pistachios. (✗)

II. Some pistachios are sweets. (✗)

III. Some sweets are cashews. (✗)

IV. All almonds are either sweets or cashews. (✗)

6. (*c*) As, $23 - 13 = 10$

Similarly, $54 - 44 = 10$

7. (*d*) 'Cricket' is played on 'Pitch'. Similalry, 'Wrestling' is done in 'Arena'.

8. (*d*) From positions I and III

Common points = 2 [at the common (right) face]

So, face opposite to the face having 1 dot will be the face having 6 dots.

9. (*d*) From Statement I,

No answer

From Statement II,

One batsman of Team X makes 98 runs.

10. (*e*) From both the statements, $P > R > S > Q$

11. (*a*) From the given statements it is clear that knowledge is interdisciplinary. Thus, Conclusion I follows.

12. (*d*) Course of action I would be an extreme step. Course of action II is not within the Government's preview. Course of action III is advisable when there is retrenchment on such a large scale.

13. (*a*) Except (a) in all the other options, numbers are even numbers but in option (a) all numbers are prime numbers.

14. (*b*) In all others except (b), second is the organ used by first for its movement.

15. (*d*) As, $9 \times 1 = 9$

$9 \times 2 = 18 \Rightarrow 1 + 8 = 9$

$9 \times 3 = 27 \Rightarrow 2 + 7 = 9$

$9 \times 4 = 36 \Rightarrow 3 + 6 = 9$

$9 \times 5 = 45 \Rightarrow 4 + 5 = 9$

$9 \times 6 = 54 \Rightarrow 5 + 4 = 9$

$9 \times 7 = 63 \Rightarrow 6 + 3 = 9$

$9 \times 8 = 72 \Rightarrow 7 + 2 = 9$

$9 \times 9 = 81 \Rightarrow 8 + 1 = 9$

$9 \times 10 = 90 \Rightarrow 9 + 0 = 9$

$9 \times 27 = 243 \Rightarrow 2 + 4 + 3 = 9$

$9 \times 697 = 6273 \Rightarrow 6 + 2 + 7 + 3 = 18 \Rightarrow 1 + 8 = 9$

Solution (Q. Nos 16-18) Following table can be drawn with the help of given information.

	Football	Cricket	Hockey	Basketball
A	✔	✔	✗	✗
B	✔	✔	✔	✗
C	✔	✔	✔	✔
D	✔	✗	✔	✔

16. (*d*) From the above table, it is clear that A does not play hockey.

17. (*a*) It is clear from the above table that D plays football, basketball and hockey.

18. (*b*) From the above table, it is clear that B, C and D play hockey.

19. (*a*) 30th September, 1998 ⇒ Wednesday
30th September, 1999 ⇒ Thursday
30th September, 2000 ⇒ Saturday
Because 2000 is a leap year and there is one extra day in the month of February.
30th September, 2001 ⇒ Sunday
30th September, 2002 ⇒ Monday
30th September, 2003 ⇒ Tuesday
An ordinary year has one odd day.

20. (*a*) According to the matrices,
H — 59, 66, 78, (85), 97
I — 03, 10, 22, 34, (41)
P — 00, 12, (24), 31, 43
S — 04, (11), 23, 30, 42
∴ HIPS ⇒ 85, 41, 24, 11

21. (*c*) The pattern is as follows
A $\xrightarrow{+1}$ B $\xrightarrow{+1}$ C $\xrightarrow{+1}$ D
C $\xrightarrow{+1}$ D $\xrightarrow{+1}$ E $\xrightarrow{+1}$ F
E $\xrightarrow{+1}$ F $\xrightarrow{+1}$ G $\xrightarrow{+1}$ H
∴ ? = DFH

22. (*b*) Here, the sequence of given series is as follows
8 18 32 50 72 (98)
+10 +14 +18 +22 +26
+4 +4 +4 +4

23. (*b*) Pattern of given alpha-numeric series is as follows
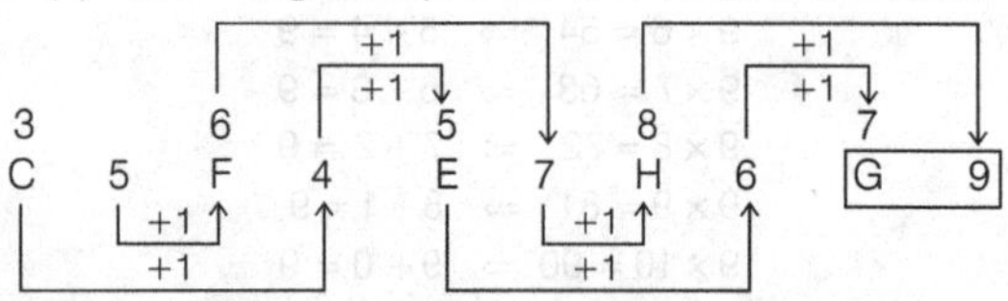

24. (*c*) Dogs come under the class animal.
Some dogs are pets.
Some animals other than dogs are also pets but all pets are animals.
Therefore, the correct diagram would be
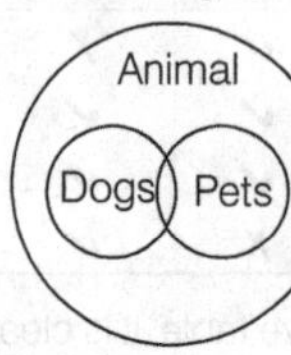

25. (*d*) Except figure (d), all others are divided into two equal parts.

26. (*c*) As, Q > P … (i)
T > R > Q … (ii)
On combining Eqs. (i) and (ii) we get
T > R > Q > P
Thus, R scored the second highest.

27. (*d*) Here, lowest number = 256
and highest number = 764
Now, second digit of lowest number = 5
and third digit of highest number = 4
∴ Resultant = 5 × 4 = 20

28. (*b*) Here, odd numbers = 415, 327
and even numbers = 764, 542, 256
Now, according to the question,
415 (+1) → [515]; 327 (+1) → 427
and
764 (−2) → [744]; 542 (−2) → [522]; 256 (−2) → 236
Hence, there are three numbers such that a digit appear twice.

29. (*e*) Given numbers
4 1 5 → 1 [4] 5; 7 6 4 → 6 7 [4]; 3 2 7 → 2 3 7; 5 4 2 → 4 5 2; 2 5 6 → 5 2 6

$$\text{Resultant} = \frac{\text{Third of highest number}}{\text{Second digit of the lowest number}} = \frac{4}{4} = 1$$

30. (*b*) **Input** 86 open shut door 31 49 always 45
***Step* I** 31 86 open shut door 49 always 45
***Step* II** 31 shut 86 open door 49 always 45
***Step* III** 31 shut 45 86 open door 49 always
***Step* IV** 31 shut 45 open 86 door 49 always
***Step* V** 31 shut 45 open 49 86 door always
***Step* VI** 31 shut 45 open 49 door 86 always
Hence, six steps are required to complete the rearrangement.

31. (*b*) ***Step* II** 18 win 71 34 now if victory 61.
***Step* III** 18 win 34 71 now if victory 61
***Step* IV** 18 win 34 victory 71 now if 61
***Step* V** 18 win 34 victory 61 71 now if
***Step* VI** 18 win 34 victory 61 now 71 if
Hence, four more steps are required to complete the rearrangement.

32. (*a*) The figure in question may be labelled as shown in the following figure
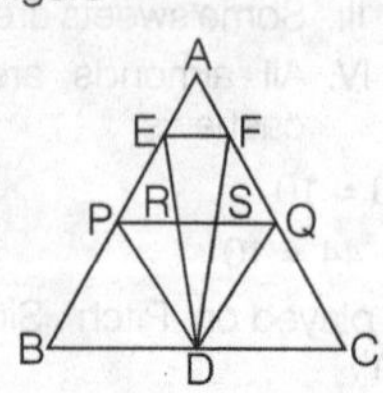

Smallest triangles = ΔAEF, ΔEPR, ΔFSQ, ΔPRD, ΔRSD, ΔSQD = 6

Single triangles = ΔPBD, ΔQDC, ΔEFD = 3

Triangles formed with two trinagles = ΔPSD, ΔRQD, ΔFDQ, ΔEDP = 4

Triangles formed with three or four triangles = ΔAPQ, ΔFDC, ΔBDE, ΔPQD = 4

Largest triangle = ΔABC = 1

∴ Total triangles = 6 + 3 + 4 + 4 + 1 = 18

33. (*d*) The complete letter series will be

a b a a/a b a a/a b a a / a b a a ⇒ abbaa

34. (*d*) According to the given option (d) symbols, we can apply as

$20 \div 5 + 8 \times 2 - 17 = 3$

$\Rightarrow 4 + 16 - 17 = 3$

$\Rightarrow 20 - 17 = 3$

$\Rightarrow 3 = 3$

35. (*a*) According to the question, all five friends are sitting in a row facing South. So, sitting arrangement will be

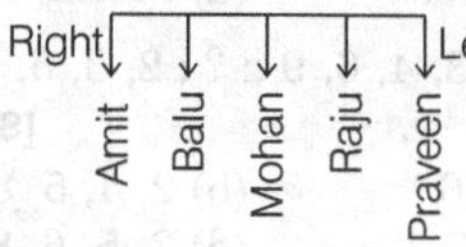

Thus, Amit is at extreme right end.

36. (*a*) According to the question, we have following data

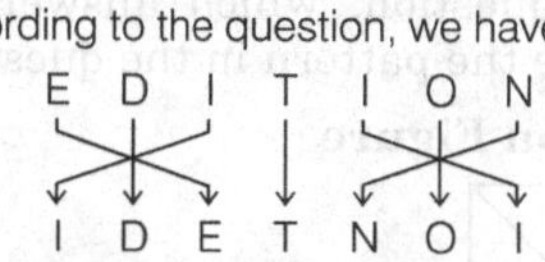

Similarly, we can write

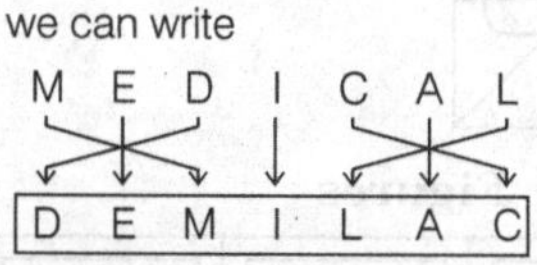

37. (*b*) H is prefixed to the following words

H + EAT → HEAT, H + OUR → HOUR

H + IS → HIS H + AS → HAS

H + AT → HAT

38. (*d*) 1 4 10 21 19 20 9 14 7

A D J U S T I N G

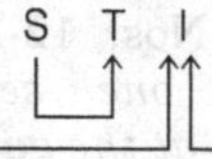

Letters' pairs = DI, GI, ST ⇒ Three

39. (*d*) The correct laterally inverted image of the question figure is as follows.

ИOISSIM

40. (*c*) The pattern is as follows

In Column I, 6 + 5 + 7 + 3 = 21

In Column III, 4 + 5 + 6 + 6 = 21

Similarly, in Column II,

$7 + 3 + ? + 3 = 21$

$\Rightarrow ? + 13 = 21$

$\Rightarrow ? = 21 - 13$

$\Rightarrow ? = 8$

Solution (Q. Nos. 41-44) According to the given information the sitting arrangement is as following:

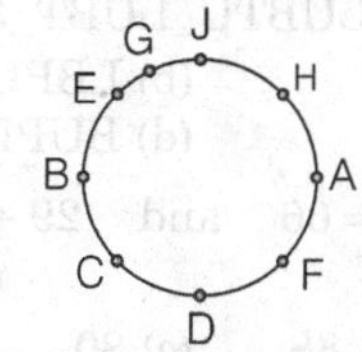

41. (*a*) H's position with respect to E is third to the left.

42. (*e*) C is third to the right of G.

43. (*d*) A is fifth to the right of E.

44. (*b*) F is second to the left of H.

45. (*b*) Arrangement of words as per dictionary

(iv) Literacy → (ii) Litter → (iii) Little → (i) Live → (v) Living

46. (*c*) According to the question, the direction diagram will be as follows

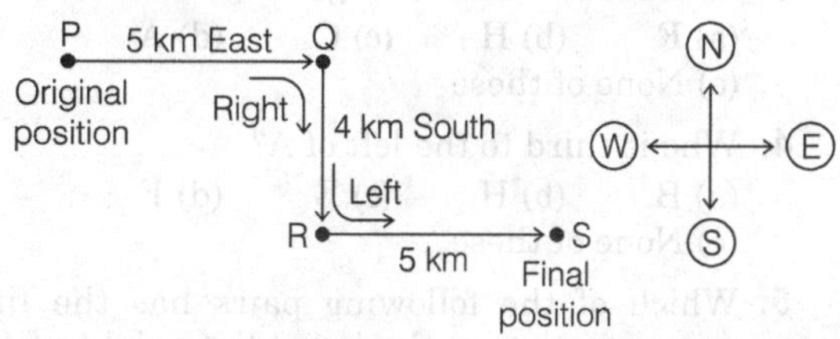

Clearly, man is facing East.

47. (*d*) We prefer to wear dark clothes in winter as they absorb the heat and keep the body warm. However, white clothes are good reflectors of heat and are worn in summer.

48. (*d*) If figure, as shown in the alternative (d), is placed in the missing portion of the original figure, it gets completed figure.

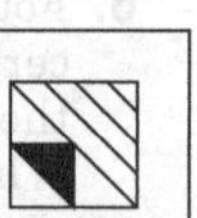

Hence, option (d) is the correct.

49. (*c*) Since, angle between two numbers is 360° ÷ 12 = 30°. When the time is 3:25 pm, the minute hand will be at 5 and will have moved 60° from 3 and hour hand would be between 3 and 4 it will move 30° in 60 min and so in 25 min it would have moved $\frac{30 \times 25}{60} = 12.5°$

So, angle between two hands = 60 − 12.5 = 47.5°

50. (*b*) Answer figure (b) is correct answer.

PRACTICE SET 46

1. Which one set of letters when sequentially placed at the gaps in the given letters series shall complete it?

LU_TUPLUBTU_LUBT_P_UBTUP

(a) BPUL (b) LBPU
(c) PBUL (d) BUPL

2. If $38+15=66$ and $29+36=99$, then $82+44=?$ **[BSSC (CGL) 2015]**

(a) 77 (b) 88 (c) 80 (d) 94

Direction (Q. Nos. 3-6) *Study the following information carefully to answer these questions.*

Eight friends A, B, C, D, E, F, G and H are sitting around a circle facing the centre. H is to the immediate left of E who is third to the right of B. C is second to the right of D and is not a neighbour of B. F is second to the right of G and is not a neighbour of C. **[NICL (Assistant) Cadre III 2015]**

3. Who is second to the right of E?

(a) F (b) H (c) C (d) A
(e) None of these

4. Who is third to the left of A?

(a) B (b) H (c) E (d) F
(e) None of these

5. Which of the following pairs has the first person sitting to the immediate right of the second person?

(a) DA (b) AC (c) GC (d) BF
(e) None of these

6. Four of the following, five are alike in a certain way and based on their positions in the above arrangement and so form a group. Which is the one that does not belong to the group?

(a) EC (b) AB (c) FD (d) HA
(e) CH

7. In a class of thirty students, Mahesh is 14th from the left and Ramesh is 20th from the right end. How many students are there between Ramesh and Mahesh?

(a) 3 (b) 2
(c) 4 (d) Data inadequate

8. Nitin correctly remembers that Nidhi's birthday is before Friday but after Tuesday. Deepak correctly remembers that Nidhi's birthday is after Wednesday but before Saturday. On which of the following days does Nidhi's birthday definitely fall?

(a) Monday (b) Tuesday
(c) Wednesday (d) Thursday

Direction (Q. Nos. 9-10) *In the following questions, select the related word/letters/numbers from the given alternatives.*

9. Piety : Pilgrim :: Curiosity : ? **[SNAP 2014]**

(a) Explorer (b) Pinchpenny
(c) Gamester (d) Monk

10. 1, 2, 4, 7 : 3, 4, 6, 9 :: ? : 2, 3, 5, 8 **[SSC (10+2) 2012]**

(a) 0, 1, 3, 6 (b) 2, 4, 5, 8
(c) 1, 3, 4, 7 (d) 3, 5, 6, 8

11. In the question, which answer figure will complete the pattern in the question figure?

Question Figure

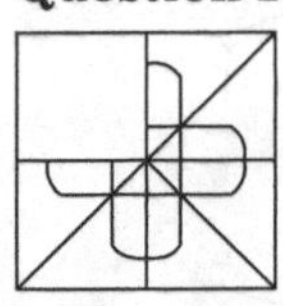

Answer Figures

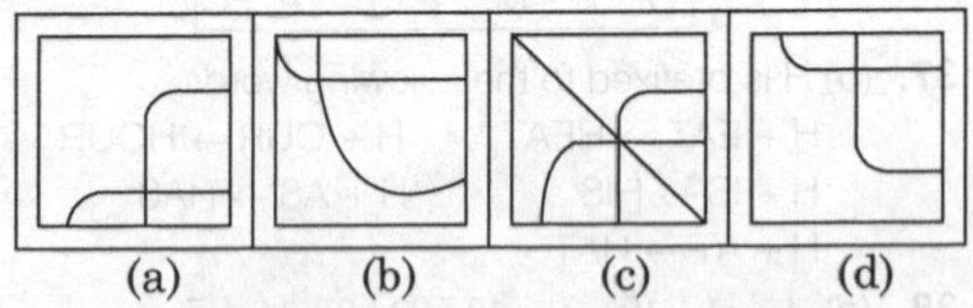

Direction (Q. Nos. 12-14) *In the following questions, which one set of letters when sequentially placed at the gaps in the given letters series shall complete it?* **[SSC (CPO) 2013]**

12. YW, US, ?, MK

(a) RP (b) BD (c) FH (d) QO

13. 27, 32, 30, 35, 33, ?

(a) 28 (b) 31 (c) 36 (d) 38

14. C-3, E-5, G-7, I-9, ?, ? **[SSC (CGL) 2013]**

(a) X-24, M-21 (b) K-11, M-13

(c) O-15, X-24 (d) M-18, K-14

15. Find the digit at the face opposite to the face having digit 4 in the given dice. **[UP BEd 2012]**

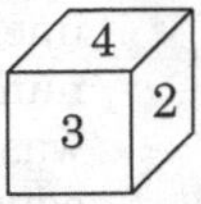

(a) 1 (b) 5

(c) 6 (d) 1/5/6

Direction (Q. Nos. 16-18) *Read the following information carefully and answer the questions given below.*

Six persons A, B, C, D, E and F are expert in six different fields P, Q, R, S, T and U (not respectively), won different prizes-Kalinga Award, Gandhi Peace Prize, Vyas Samman, Kabir Samman, Iqbal Samman and Saraswati Samman though not respectively, for the year 2000.

C and F have not won Gandhi Peace and Iqbal Samman. The winner of Kabir Samman is expert in the field S but he is certainly not E and B. D and A have won Kalinga Award and Kabir Samman though not, respectively. The experts of the field Q and E have won Gandhi Peace Prize and Iqbal Samman though not, respectively. A is expert in field P, and winner of Iqbal Samman is expert in the field T.

16. Who has won the Vyas Samman?

(a) B (b) C

(c) F (d) Either C or F

(e) None of these

17. The winner of the Saraswati Samman is an expert in the field

(a) R (b) U

(c) Either R or U (d) Data inadequate

(e) None of these

18. D has expertise in which of the following fields?

(a) S (b) Q

(c) T (d) Cannot be determined

(e) None of these

19. Chosse the correct mirror image from the given alternatives.

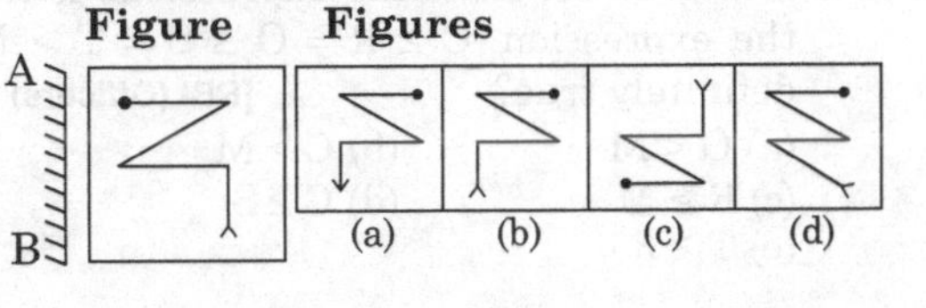

20. If the day that will come two days after tomorrow is Thursday, then what day of the week was three days before yesterday?

(a) Monday

(b) Tuesday

(c) Wednesday

(d) Thursday

Direction (Q. Nos. 21-22) *Each of the questions below consists of a question and two statements numbered I and II given below it. You have to decide whether the data provided in the statements are sufficient to answer the question.*

Give answer **[IBPS (PO/MT) Mains 2015]**

(a) if the data in Statement I alone is sufficient to answer the question, while the data in Statement II alone is not sufficient to answer the question

(b) if the data in Statement II alone is sufficient to answer the question, while the data in Statement I alone is not sufficient to answer the question

(c) if the data either in Statement I alone or in Statement II alone is sufficient to answer the question

(d) if the data in both the Statements I and II together are not sufficient to answer the question

(e) if the data in both the Statements I and II together are necessary to answer the question

21. P, Q, R, S and T are sitting around a circle facing towards the centre of the circle. Who is to the immediate right of T?

I. R, Q and S are in the same respective sequence to the immediate left of T.

II. P is between S and T.

22. How many dresses does 'P' have?

I. P has two dresses less than what T has.

II. M has seven dresses, which are thirty per cent less than what T has.

23. Group the given figures into three classes using each figure only once.

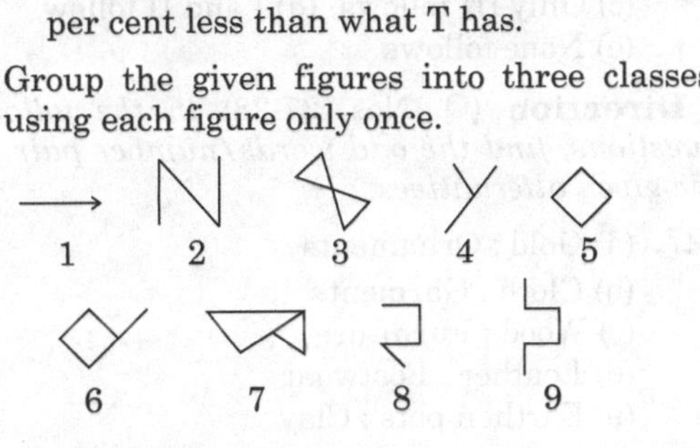

(a) 1, 5, 6 2, 3, 4 7, 8, 9	(b) 1, 2, 4 3, 5, 8 6, 7, 9
(c) 5, 6, 7 1, 2, 4 3, 8, 9	(d) 1, 2, 4 3, 5, 7 6, 8, 9

24. The ages of Ram and Mohan differs by 16 yr. 6 yr ago, Mohan's age was thrice as that of Ram's age. Find the sum of their ages.
(a) 30 yr (b) 27 yr
(c) 44 yr (d) 25 yr

Direction (Q. Nos. 25-26) *In each of the questions below are given some statements followed by some conclusions. You have to take the given statements to be true even if they seem to be at variance with commonly known facts. Read all the conclusions and then decide which of the given conclusions logically follows from the given statements disregarding commonly known facts.*

25. Statements Some animals are fighters.
All fighters are tigers.
No tiger is lighter.

Conclusions
I. None of the lighters is tiger.
II. Some tigers are definitely not lighters.
III. Most of the fighters are animals.
(a) None follows (b) Only I follows
(c) Only II follows (d) Only III follows
(e) All follow

26. Statements Some onions are pumpkins.
All pumpkins are gingers.
Some gingers are apples.

Conclusions
I. Atleast some onions are definitely gingers.
II. Apples are gingers.
III. All apples except a few are gingers.
(a) Only I follows (b) I and III follow
(c) Only III follows (d) I and II follow
(e) None follows

Direction (Q. Nos. 27-28) *In the following questions, find the odd words/number pair from the given alternatives.*

27. (a) Gold : Ornaments
(b) Cloth : Garments
(c) Wood : Furniture
(d) Leather : Footwear
(e) Earthen pots : Clay

28. (a) 33-5 (b) 72-9
(c) 40-4 (d) 23-5

29. A research study recorded that the number of unemployed educated youth was equal to the number of unemployed uneducated youth. It was concluded by the researchers that being educated does not enhance the probability of being employed.

Which of the following information would be required to validate the above conclusion? **[IIFT 2013]**

(a) The number of unemployed educated and uneducated people in other age groups
(b) The number of organisations employing youth
(c) The percentage of unemployment in uneducated
(d) The percentage increase in number of educated youth versus last year

30. In the question below is given a statement followed by two assumptions numbered I, II and III. An assumption is something supposed or taken for granted. You have to consider the statement and the following assumptions and decide which of the assumption(s) is/are implicit in the statement.

Statement Training must be given to all the employees for increasing productivity and profitability.

Assumptions
I. Training is an essential component of productivity.
II. Employees cannot function effectively without proper training.
III. Profitability and productivity are supplementary to each other.
(a) None is implicit
(b) All are implicit
(c) Only III is implicit
(d) I and II are implicit
(e) I and III are implicit

31. Which of the following expressions is true if the expression '$C \geq R = O \leq S = T > M$' is definitely true? **[RBI (Officers) 2015]**
(a) $O < M$ (b) $C > M$
(c) $R > M$ (d) $C \geq S$
(e) $T \geq R$

Direction (Q. Nos. 32-34) *Study the following information carefully answer the given questions.*

In a certain code **[IBPS (Clerk) 2013]**

'very large risk associated' is written as 'nu ta ro gi'
'risk is very low' is written as 'gi se nu mi'
'is that also associated' is written as 'ta mi po fu'
'inherent risk also damaging' is written as 'fu, nu di yu'
(All the codes are two letter codes only)

32. Which of the following represents 'risk also large'?
(a) nu fu po (b) nu gi ro
(c) ro po ta (d) fu nu ro
(e) ro yu fu

33. What is the code for 'very'?
(a) ta (b) fu (c) ro (d) nu
(e) gi

34. What is the code for 'associated'?
(a) mi (b) ta (c) ro (d) gi
(e) nu

Direction (Q. Nos. 35-37) *In these questions, relationship between different elements is shown in the statements. The statements are followed by conclusions. Study the conclusions based on the given statement and select the appropriate answer.* **[SBI (PO) 2014]**

35. Statement $B \geq L > A \geq N < K$
Conclusions I. $L > N$ II. $L = N$
(a) Only Conclusion I is true
(b) Only Conclusion II is true
(c) Neither Conclusion I nor II is true
(d) Either Conclusion I or II is true
(e) Both Conclusions I and II are true

36. Statement $A > B > C \leq D = E \leq F$
Conclusions I. $C < F$ II. $C = F$
(a) Only Conclusion I is true
(b) Only Conclusion II is true
(c) Neither Conclusion I nor II is true
(d) Either Conclusion I or II is true
(e) Both Conclusions I and II are true

37. Statement $A > B \leq C > D = E \leq F$
Conclusions I. $A > D$ II. $B \leq E$
(a) Only Conclusion I is true
(b) Only Conclusion II is true
(c) Neither Conclusion I nor II is true
(d) Either Conclusion I or II is true
(e) Both Conclusions I and II are true

38. Find the missing number from the given responses.

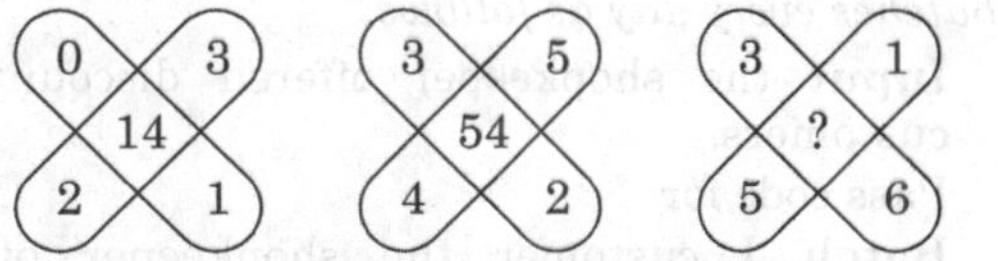

(a) 35 (b) 72 (c) 94 (d) 71

39. How many pairs of letters are there in these words which have as many letters between them as in the English alphabet?
PERFORATE
(a) None (b) One
(c) Two (d) Three
(e) More than three

40. If it is possible to make only one meaningful English word with the 4th, the 6th, the 9th and the 11th letters of the word 'QUALIFICATION', which of the following will be the 3rd letter of that word? If more than one such word can be formed give M as the answer and if no such word can be formed give N as the answer.
(a) A (b) I (c) L (d) M
(e) N

41. If all the numbers in 86312749 are arranged in ascending order from left to right, the positions of how many numbers will remain unchanged? **[IBPS (Clerk) Pre 2015]**
(a) Three (b) One
(c) Two (d) More than three
(e) None

42. Arrange the following words in a logical order.
(i) Butterfly (ii) Cocoon
(iii) Egg (iv) Worm
(a) (i), (iv), (iii), (ii)
(b) (i), (iii), (iv), (ii)
(c) (ii), (iv), (i), (iii)
(d) (iii), (iv), (ii), (i)

43. Which one of the following diagrams represents the relationship between cows, animals and goats?

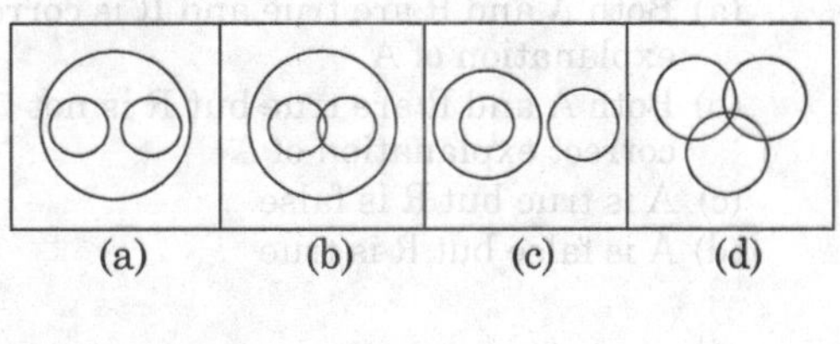

(a) (b) (c) (d)

Direction (Q. Nos. 44-45) *Given an input, coding machine generates pass-codes for six batches every day as follows.*

Input the shopkeeper offered discount to customers.

Pass code for

Batch I customer the shopkeeper offered discount to

Batch II customer discount the shopkeeper offerd to

Batch III customer discount offered the shopkeeper to and so on until the arrangement is completed. After the arrangement is completed the next batch gets the same code as that for batch I.

Duration of each batch is 1 h. There is a break of one hour after the fourth batch. Sixth batch is the last batch. Now, answer the following questions.

44. If the pass-code for the second batch is, 'do lean window out of not', then what will be the pass-code for the fourth batch?
(a) do lean of not out window
(b) do lean of out not window
(c) do lean not out window of
(d) do lean not of window out
(e) None of the above

45. If the input is, 'please do not delay the matter', then what will be the pass-code for third batch?
(a) do please not delay the matter
(b) delay do matter please not the
(c) delay do matter not please the
(d) delay do matter not the please
(e) None of the above

46. For the Assertion (A) and Reason (R) below, choose the correct alternatives from the given option.

Assertion (A) The President is a part of Parliament.

Reason (R) A bill passed by two Houses of Parliament cannot become law without the assent of the President.
(a) Both A and R are true and R is correct explanation of A
(b) Both A and R are true but R is not correct explanation of A
(c) A is true but R is false
(d) A is false but R is true

47. A word is represented by only one set of numbers as given in anyone of the alternatives. The set of numbers given in the alternatives are represented by two classes of alphabets as in the two matrices given below. The columns and rows of Matrix I are numbered from 0 to 4 and that of Matrix II from 5 to 9. A letter can be represented first by its row and next by its column number. e.g, 'N' can be represented by 02, 21, etc. 'O' can be represented by 65, 96 etc. Similarly, you have to identify the correct set for the word given in question.

Matrix I

	0	1	2	3	4
0	P	W	N	I	S
1	I	S	P	W	N
2	W	N	I	S	P
3	S	P	W	N	I
4	N	I	S	P	W

Matrix II

	5	6	7	8	9
5	A	E	R	O	H
6	O	H	A	E	R
7	E	R	O	H	A
8	H	A	E	R	O
9	R	O	H	A	E

SORROW
(a) 23, 86, 69, 88, 65, 33
(b) 23, 43, 14, 33, 65, 78
(c) 11, 66, 69, 65, 59, 97
(d) 42, 65, 95, 88, 77,44

48. B is the father of Q. B has only two children. Q is the brother of R. R is the daughter of P. A is the granddaughter of P. S is the father of A. How is S related to Q? **[IDBI (PO) 2011]**
(a) Son (b) Son-in-law
(c) Brother (d) Brother-in-law
(e) None of these

49. After starting from a point, a man walks 4 km towards West, then turning to his right he moves 4 km. After this he again turns right and moves 4 km. Which choice given below indicates the correct direction in which he is from his starting point? **[WBSSC (CGL) 2015]**
(a) North (b) East (c) South (d) West

50. My friend and I started simultaneously towards each other from two places 100 m apart. After walking 30 m, my friend turns left and goes 10 m, then he turns right and goes 20 m, and then turns right again and comes back to the road on which he had started walking. If we walk with the same speed, then what is the distance between us at this point of time? **[SSC (CPO) 2010]**
(a) 50 m (b) 20 m (c) 30 m (d) 40 m

Hints and Solutions

1. (*a*) LUB/TUP/LUB/TUP/LUB/TUP/LUB/TUP
Hence, correct option is (a) i.e., BPUL.

2. (*c*) As, $(3 + 8) \times (1 + 5)$
$\Rightarrow \quad 11 \times 6 = 66$
and $\quad (2 + 9) \times (3 + 6)$
$\Rightarrow \quad 11 \times 9 = 99$
Similarly, $\quad (8 + 2) \times (4 + 4)$
$\Rightarrow \quad 10 \times 8 = 80$

Solution (Q. Nos. 3-6) According to the given information, the seating arrangement is as following

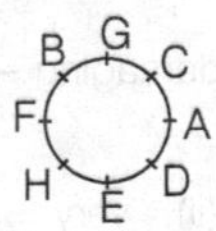

3. (*d*) A is second to the right of E.

4. (*b*) H is third to the left of A.

5. (*c*) GC is the pairs which has the first person sitting to the immediate right of the second person.

6. (*e*) CH does not belong to the group because all others having gap of two persons in between them while CH having three persons of gap in between them.

7. (*b*)

Left ⊢———— 20th (Ramesh) ———— 14th (Mahesh) ————⊣ Right

Ramesh's position from left
$= 30 - 20 + 1$
$= 10 + 1 = 11\text{th}$

Mahesh's position from left = 14 th
Clearly, there are 2 students in between Ramesh and Mahesh.

8. (*d*)

According to	Nitin's Birhtday
Nitin	Wednesday, Thursday
Deepak	Thursday, Friday

Here, Thursday is a common to both. Hence, correct day is Thursday.

9. (*a*) Option (a) is correct answer.

10. (*a*)

As, 1 2 4 7 → (+2 +2 +2 +2) → 3 4 6 9

Similarly, 0 1 3 6 → (+2 +2 +2 +2) → 2 3 5 8

11. (*c*) Clearly, option (c) figure will complete the pattern of the figure

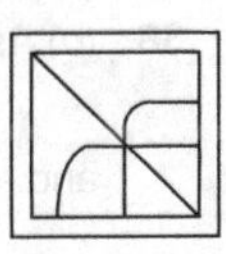

12. (*d*) The pattern is as follows

25 Y, 23 W, 21 U, 19 S, 17 Q, 15 O, 13 M, 11 K
(−2 each step)

$\therefore \quad ? = \text{QO}$

13. (*d*) The pattern is as follows

27 →(+5)→ 32 →(−2)→ 30 →(+5)→ 35 →(−2)→ 33 →(+5)→ 38

$\therefore \quad ? = 38$

14. (*b*) In this series, every letter is given its alphabetical position number and one letter is skipped in between each term. Hence, the missing terms are K-11 and M-13.

15. (*d*) According to the question,
$4 + 3 = 7$
$4 + 2 = 6$
$3 + 2 = 5$
Clearly, it is not a standard dice.
$\therefore$ Digit opposite 4 = 1 or 5 or 6

Solution (Q. Nos. 16-18) On the basis of given information, we get the following table

Person	Expertise	Awards
A	P	Kalinga Award
B	Q	Gandhi Peace Prize
C	R/U	Vyas Samman / Saraswati Samman
D	S	Kabir Samman
E	T	Iqbal Samman
F	U/R	Saraswati Samman / Vyas Samman

16. (*d*) Vyas Samman has been won by either C or F.

17. (c) Winner of Saraswati Samman is an expert in the field of either R or U.

18. (*a*) D has expert in the field of S.

19. (*b*) Option (b) is correct answer.

20. (*d*) Today is Monday
Yesterday was Sunday.
Sunday − 3 = Thursday

21. (*a*) From Statement I,
It is clearly shown that, data in Statement I alone are sufficient to answer the question.

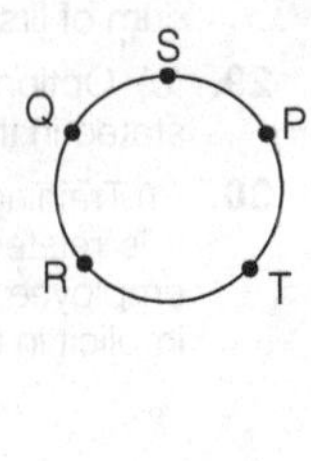

22. (*e*) From statement II, M = 7
So, T has 10 dresses.
From Statement I, P = 8 dresses
So, data in both the statements together are necessary to answer the question.

23. (*b*) Figures 1, 2 and 4 are made of three lines. Figures 3, 5 and 8 are made of four lines. Figures 6, 7 and 9 are made of five lines.

24. (*c*) Let the ages of Ram and Mohan be x yr and (16 + x) yr, respectively,

Now, $(16 + x - 6) = 3(x - 6)$
$\Rightarrow x + 10 = 3x - 18$
$\Rightarrow 2x = 28$
$\Rightarrow x = 14$ yr

Now, required sum = 14 + (16 + 14)
= 14 + 30 = 44 yr

Solution (Q. Nos. 25-26)

25. (*e*)

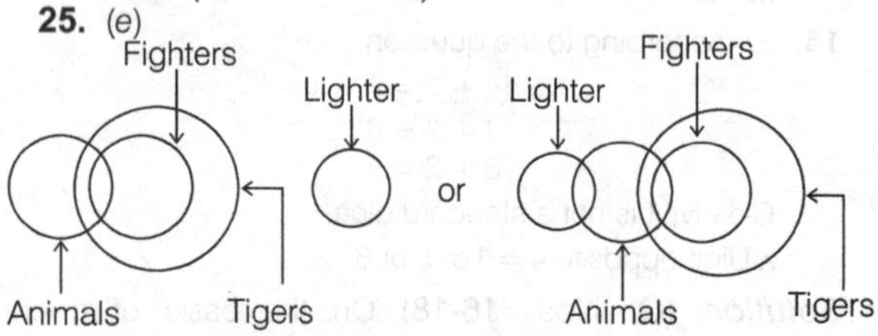

Conclusions I. None of the lighters is tiger. (✔)
II. Some tigers are definitely not lighters. (✔)
III. Most of the fighters are animals. (✔)

So, Conclusions I, II and III are follow.

26. (*b*)

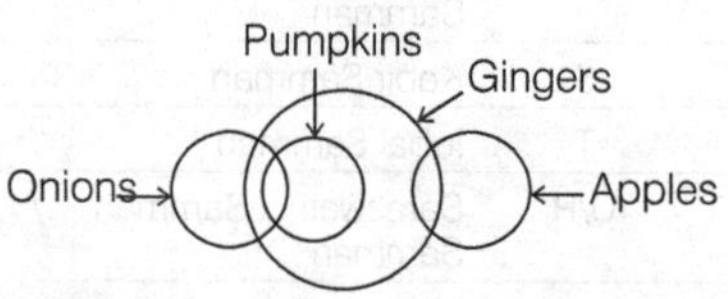

Conclusions
I. Atleast some onions are definitely gingers. (✔)
II. Apples are gingers. (✗)
III. All apples except a few are gingers. (✔)

So, Conclusion I and III are follow.

27. (*e*) Except pair (e), in all other pairs, the first is the raw material used to make the second.

28. (*a*) Except option (a), in all options second number is sum of first two numbers.

29. (*c*) Option (c) is required to validate the conclusion stated in the given passage.

30. (*d*) Training has been necessitated in the statement, i.e. it is related to the efficiency and effectiveness of an employee. Therefore, both the Assumptions I and II are implicit in the statement.

31. (*e*) Given expression C ≥ R = O ≤ S = T > M
Now, according to the above given expression, T ≥ R is definitely true.

Solution (Q. Nos. 32-34) On the basis of given information.

very large risk associated → nu ta ro gi ...(i)
risk is very low → gi se nu mi ...(ii)
is that also associated → ta mi po fu ...(iii)
inherent risk also damaging → fu nu di yu ...(iv)

From Eqs. (i) and (ii), very ⇒ gi
From Eqs. (i), (ii) and (iv), risk ⇒ nu
From Eqs. (i) and (iii), associated ⇒ ta
From Eqs. (iii) and (iv), also ⇒ fu
From Eqs.(i) large ⇒ ro
From Eqs. (ii) low ⇒ se
From Eqs (ii) and (iii), is ⇒ mi
From Eqs. (iii) that ⇒ po
From Eq. (iv) inherent ⇒ di/yu
damaging ⇒ di/yu

32. (*d*) risk also large → nu fu ro
33. (*e*) very → gi
34. (*b*) associated → ta

Solution (Q. Nos.35-37)

35. (*a*) **Statement**
B ≥ L > A ≥ N < K
Conclusions I. L > N (True)
II. L = N (False)
So, only Conclusions I is true.

36. (*d*) **Statement** A > B > C ≤ D = E ≤ F
Conclusions I. C < F (May be true)
II. C = F (May be true)
So, either Conclusion I or II is true.

37. (*c*) **Statement** A > B > C ≤ D = E ≤ F
Conclusions I. A > D (False)
II. B ≤ E (False)
So, neither Conclusion I nor II is true.

38. (*d*) As, $(0)^2 + (3)^2 + (1)^2 + (2)^2$
$= 0 + 9 + 1 + 4 = 14$
and $(3)^2 + (5)^2 + (2)^2 + (4)^2$
$= 9 + 25 + 4 + 16 = 54$

Similarly, $(3)^2 + (1)^2 + (6)^2 + (5)^2$

$= 9 + 1 + 36 + 25 = 71$

39. (*c*)

16 5 18 6 15 18 1 20 5
P E R F O R A T E

∴ Letter pairs = PR, RT ⇒ Two

40. (*b*)

Q U A (L) (F) C (A) T (I) O N

(L) → 4th, (F) → 6th, (A) → 9th, (I) → 11th

Word formed = FAIL

Required letter = I

41. (*a*) Given, 8 6 [3] 1 2 [7] 4 [9]

After arrangement 1 2 [3] 4 6 [7] 8 [9]

Clearly, three numbers remain unchanged.

42. (*d*) Logical order of the given words

(iii) Egg → (iv) Worm → (ii) Cocoon → (i) Butterfly

43. (*a*) Cow and goat are different from each other but both are animals.

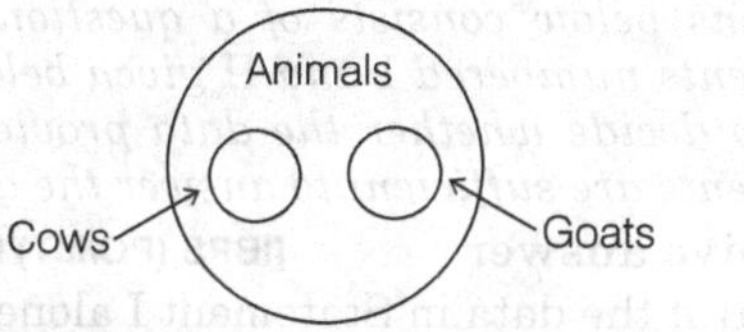

44. (*d*) **Batch II** do lean window out of not

Batch III do lean not window out of

Batch IV do lean not of window out

45. (*b*) **Input** please do not delay the matter

Batch I delay please do not the matter

Batch II delay do please not the matter

Batch III delay do matter please not the

46. (*a*) It is true that the President is a part of Parliament and when a bill passed by two houses of Parliament cannot become law without the assent of the President.

47. (*d*) According to the matrices,

S —04, 11,23, 30, (42)

O— 58, (65), (77), 89, 96

R —57, 69, 76, (88), (95)

W —01, 13, 20, 32, (44)

∴ SORROW ⇒ 42, 65, 95, 88, 77, 44

48. (*d*)

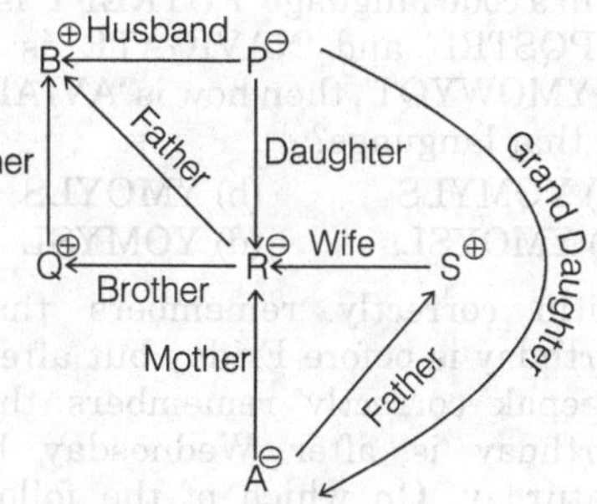

Hence, S is the brother-in-law of Q.

49. (*a*) The walking diagram of a man is as given below

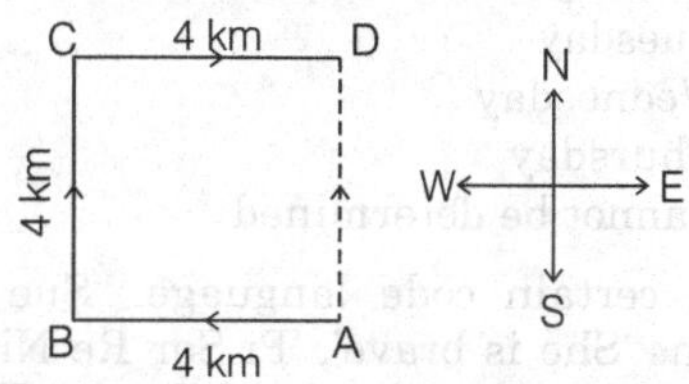

Let A is the starting and D is the ending point of man. It is clear from diagram that he is in North direction from his starting point.

50. (*b*) Route followed by me and my friend.

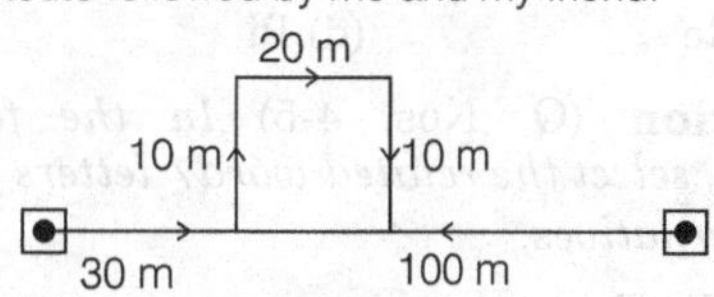

Friend cover a total distance of

$= (30 + 10 + 20 + 10) = 70$ m

Distance between them $= 70 - 50 = 20$ m

PRACTICE SET 47

1. If in a code language 'PUTREFY' is written as 'XPQSTRL' and 'NAVIGATE' is written as 'GYMOWYQT', then how is 'AVIARY' written in that language?
(a) YOMYLS (b) YMOYLS
(c) YMOYSL (d) YOMYSL

2. Nitin correctly remembers that Nidhi's birthday is before Friday but after Tuesday. Deepak correctly remembers that Nidhi's birthday is after Wednesday but before Saturday. On which of the following days does Nidhi's birthday definitely fall?
(a) Monday
(b) Tuesday
(c) Wednesday
(d) Thursday
(e) Cannot be determined

3. In a certain code language, 'Sue Re Nik' means 'She is brave', 'Pi Sor Re Nik' means 'She is always smiling' and 'Sor Re Zhi' means 'is always cheerful'. What is the code used for the word 'smiling'? **[SSC (CGL) 2014]**
(a) Sor (b) Nik
(c) Re (d) Pi

Direction (Q. Nos. 4-5) *In the following questions, select the related word/ letters from the given alternatives.*

4. Cloth : Texture **[MAT 2014]**
(a) Body : Weight (b) Silk : Cloth
(c) Wood : Grains (d) Ornaments : Gold

5. QTU : ILM :: BEF : ?
(a) PSZ (b) CFH
(c) WZA (d) UXB

6. From the given four positions of a single dice, find the digit at the face opposite to the face having digit 3.

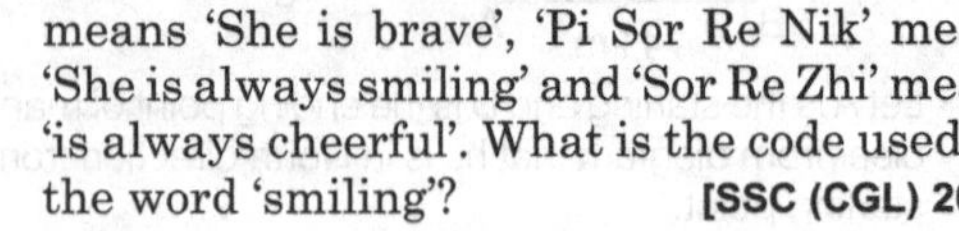

I II III IV

(a) 1 (b) 2
(c) 4 (d) 5

Direction (Q. Nos. 7-9) *In each of the following questions, find the missing term in the given series.*

7. 71, 59, 48, 38, 29, ?
(a) 18 (b) 21
(c) 20 (d) 12

8. XYZ, XZY, YZX, ?, ZXY **[MAT 2013]**
(a) XZZ (b) YXZ
(c) YZW (d) ZYX

9. KM5, IP8, GS11, EV14, ?
(a) BY17 (b) CZ17
(c) BX17 (d) CY17

Direction (Q. Nos. 10-11) *Each of the questions below consists of a question and two statements numbered* I *and* II *given below it. You have to decide whether the data provided in the statements are sufficient to answer the question.*

Give answer **[IBPS (PO/MT) Mains 2015]**
(a) if the data in Statement I alone are sufficient to answer the question, while the data in Statement II alone are not sufficient to answer the question
(b) if the data in Statement II alone are sufficient to answer the question, while the data in Statement I alone are not sufficient to answer the question
(c) if the data either in Statements I alone or in Statement II alone are sufficient to answer the question
(d) if the data in both the Statements I and II are not sufficient to answer the question
(e) if the data in both the Statements I and II together are necessary to answer the question

10. How is 'smoking' written in a code language?
I. 'thanks for not smoking' is written as 'be je we no' in that code language.
II. 'no smoking area' is written as 'no se do' in that code language.

11. Who is the youngest among A, B, C, D and E?
I. B is younger than C and D.
II. A is younger than C but older than E.

12. Which of the answer figures is embedded in the question figure? **[SSC (CPO) 2014]**

Question Figure

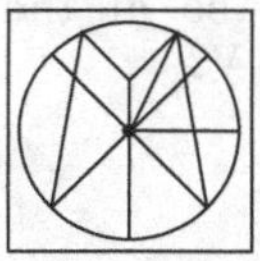

Answer Figures

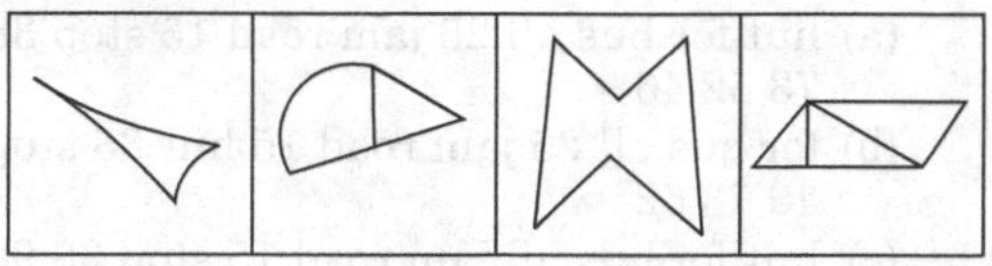

(a) (b) (c) (d)

13. If $16-2=2, 9-3=0, 81-1=8$, then what is $64-4=?$ **[BSSC (CGL) Pre 2015]**

(a) 4 (b) 2
(c) 6 (d) 8

14. 5th of a month falls two days after Monday. What day of the month will precede 19th of it?

(a) Wednesday (b) Thursday
(c) Tuesday (d) Monday

15. If $=3$ and $=24$, then what is FAULT?

(a) 60 (b) 57
(c) 64 (d) 72

16. If in a row, Rohan is 10th from left and Mukesh is 13th from right and there are four persons in between Rohan and Mukesh, then find the maximum and minimum number of persons in the row.

(a) 27, 18 (b) 27, 17
(c) 30, 15 (d) 30, 19

Direction (Q. Nos. 17-21) *Read the given information carefully and answer the given questions.* **[SBI (PO) 2014]**

Ten people are sitting in two parallel rows, containing five people each in such a way that there is equal distance between adjacent persons. In row 1, J, K, L, M and N are seated and all of them are facing North and in row 2, P, Q, R, S and T are seated and are facing South (but not necessarily in the same order). Each person also likes a different cartoon character namely, Batman, Ban 10, Dexter, Donald Duck, Tom, Jerry, Noddy, Oswald, Superman and Spiderman (not necessarily in the same order).

N sits exactly in the centre of the row and faces the one who likes Tom. Only one person sits between S and the one who likes Tom. S faces one of the immediate neighbours of the one who likes Jerry. Only two people sit between K and the one who like Jerry. K faces the one who likes Oswald. P faces one of the immediate neighbours of L. P does not like Oswald. M is an immediate neighbour of L.

The one who likes Donald Duck is not an immediate neighbour of L. T is not an immediate neighbour of P and faces the one who likes Ben 10. R faces the one who likes Superman. The one who likes Spiderman faces North.

P does not face the one who likes Spiderman. The one who likes Batman sits to the immediate right of the person who likes Noddy. S does not like Batman.

17. Which of the following pairs represent the people sitting at the extreme end of the two rows?

(a) S, M (b) Q, L (c) P, N (d) Q, J
(e) R, L

18. Who amongst the following likes Donald Duck?

(a) S (b) P (c) T (d) R
(e) Q

19. Who amongst the following is an immediate neighbour of the one who likes Spiderman?

(a) The one who likes Jerry
(b) The one who likes Noddy
(c) K
(d) The one who likes Ben 10
(e) T

20. Which of the following cartoon character does T like?

(a) Batman (b) Tom
(c) Jerry (d) Noddy
(e) Oswald

21. Which of the following is definitely true as per the given arrangement?

(a) L faces R
(b) Q likes Oswald
(c) Q is an immediate neighbour of P
(d) The one who like Superman is an immediate neighbour of P
(e) The one who likes Dexter faces N

Direction (Q. Nos. 22-23) *In each question below are three statements followed by two conclusions numbered* I *and* II. *You have to take the statements to be true even if they seem to be at variance from commonly known facts and then decide which of the given conclusions logically follows from the given statements.*

Give answer

(a) if only I follows
(b) if only II follows
(c) if either I or II follows
(d) if neither I nor II follows
(e) if both I and II follow

Statements No shoe is glove.
All gloves are caps.
All caps are jackets.

22. Conclusions I. Atleast some shoes are caps.
II. Atleast some jackets are gloves.

23. Conclusions I. No shoe is a jacket.
II. All gloves are jackets.

Direction (Q. Nos. 24-25) *Study the following information to answer the given questions.*

A word and number arrangement machine when given an input line of words and numbers rearranges them following a particular rule. The following is an illustration of input and rearrangement. (All the numbers are two-digit numbers.)

Input sine 88 71 cos theta 14 56 gamma delta 26

***Step* I** cos sine 71 theta 14 56 gamma delta 26 88

***Step* II** delta cos sine theta 14 56 gamma 26 88 71

***Step* III** gamma delta cos sine theta 14 26 88 71 56

***Step* IV** sine gamma delta cos theta 14 88 71 56 26

***Step* V** theta sine gamma delta cos 88 71 56 26 14

and Step V is the last step of the arrangement of the above input as the intended arrangement is obtained. As per the rules followed in the above steps, find out in each of the following questions the appropriate steps for the given input.

Input for 52 all 96 25 jam road 15 hut 73 bus stop 38 46 (All the numbers given in the arrangement are two-digit numbers).

24. Which word/number would be at the 6th position from the left in Step V?
(a) 25 (b) stop
(c) jam (d) all
(e) road

25. Which of the following would be the Step III?
(a) hut for bus all 25 jam road 15 stop 38 96 73 52 46
(b) for bus all 25 jam road 15 hut 38 stop 96 46 73 52
(c) hut for bus all jam road 15 stop 38 96 73 52 46 25
(d) for bus all 25 jam road 15 hut stop 38 46 96 73 52
(e) None of the above

26. Find the number of triangles in the following diagram. **[UPPSC 2013]**

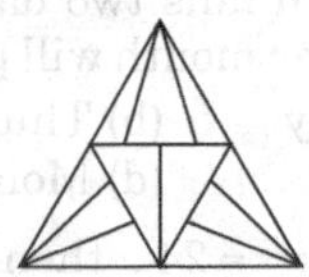

(a) 22 (b) 23 (c) 19 (d) 20

27. A man said to woman, "The only son of your brother is the brother of my wife". How is that woman related to the wife of that man?
(a) Aunt (b) Sister
(c) Mother (d) Grandmother
(e) None of these

28. Which one set of letters when sequentially placed at the gaps in the given letters series shall complete it?

B_CCABB_CABBC_AB_CCA
(a) BBBC (b) BBCC
(c) BCCB (d) BCBC

Direction (Q. Nos. 29-30) *In the following questions, find the odd number/words from the given alternatives.*

29. (a) 125 (b) 216
(c) 729 (d) 525
(e) 343

30. (a) Gallon (b) Ton
(c) Quintal (d) Kilogram

31. In making decisions about important questions, it is desirable to distinguish between a 'strong' argument and a 'weak' argument. A 'strong' argument must be both important and directly related to the question. A 'weak' argument may not be directly related to the question and may be of minor importance or may be related to the trivial aspect of the question. Each question below is followed by three arguments numbered I, II and III. You have to decide which of the arguments is 'strong' and which is 'weak'.

Statement Should the Government introduce a system of obtaining bond from students for working in India before sanctioning education loan for higher studies?

Arguments

I. No, this is not a workable solution and will obstruct the development of young talent in the country.

II. Yes, this is the only way to ensure use of the talent of our country for the development of the country and not only an individual.

III. No, this step will be too harsh.

(a) Only I is strong
(b) Only II is strong
(c) Both I and II are strong
(d) None is strong
(e) None of the above

32. Consider the following three statements.

I. Only students can participate in the race.
II. Some participants in the race are girls.
III. All girl participants in the race are invited for coaching.

Which one of the following conclusions can be drawn from the above statements?

(a) All participants in the race are invited for coaching
(b) All students are invited for coaching
(c) All participants in the race are students
(d) None of the above

33. Some equations are solved on the basis of a certain system. On the same basis, find out the correct answer for the unsolved equation.

$2 \times 3 \times 4 = 432$, $5 \times 6 \times 7 = 765$, $7 \times 8 \times 9 = 987$ and $2 \times 5 \times 7 = ?$

(a) 572 (b) 752 (c) 725 (d) 257

34. A watch reads 4:30. If the minute hand points East, then in which direction will the hour hand point? **[SSC (10+2)2015]**

(a) South (b) South-West
(c) North-East (d) North

35. A number of friends decided to go on a picnic and planned to spend ₹ 96 on eatables. Four of them, however, did not turn up. As a consequence, the remaining ones had to contribute ₹ 4 each extra. The number of those who attended the picnic was

(a) 8 (b) 12
(c) 16 (d) 24

36. A word is represented by only one set of numbers as given in anyone of the alternatives. The set of numbers given in the alternatives are represented by two classes of alphabets as in the two matrices given below. The columns and rows of Matrix I are numbered from 0 to 4 and that of Matrix II from 5 to 9. A letter can be represented first by its row and next by its column number. e.g. 'N' can be represented by 02, 21, etc. 'O' can be represented by 65, 96 etc. Similarly, you have to identify the correct set for the word given in question.

Matrix I

	0	1	2	3	4
0	P	W	N	I	S
1	I	S	P	W	N
2	W	N	I	S	P
3	S	P	W	N	I
4	N	I	S	P	W

Matrix II

	5	6	7	8	9
5	A	E	R	O	H
6	O	H	A	E	R
7	E	R	O	H	A
8	H	A	E	R	O
9	R	O	H	A	E

WEAR

(a) 44, 68, 67, 87
(b) 44, 87, 98, 69
(c) 20, 86, 67, 87
(d) 32, 87, 78, 95

37. Which one of the given responses would be a meaningful order of the following words?

(i) Book (ii) Words
(iii) Letters (iv) Sentences
(v) Chapters (vi) Pages

(a) (iii), (ii), (vi), (v), (iv), (i)
(b) (iii), (ii), (v), (iv), (vi), (i)
(c) (iii), (ii), (iv), (v), (vi), (i)
(d) (iii), (ii), (iv), (vi), (v), (i)

Direction (Q. Nos. 38-40) *Study the following information and answer the given questions.*

Eight friends namely P, Q, R, S, T, U, V and W live on eight different floors of a building but not necessarily in the same order. The ground floor is numbered 1 and the one above that is numbered 2 and so on till the topmost floor is numbered 8.

S lives on an even numbered floor. Only three people live between S and T. Only one person lives between T and V. V lives on one of the floors below. T Only two persons live between V and U. W lives on a floor that is immediately below U. Only two persons live between T and Q.P does not live on the lowermost floor. **[SBI SO (IT) 2016]**

38. Who amongst the following lives immediately above Q's floor?

(a) V (b) S
(c) U (d) P
(e) W

39. Who amongst the following lives on the topmost floor?

(a) Q (b) T
(c) V (d) W
(e) R

40. On which of the following floors does P live?

(a) 1 (b) 3
(c) 7 (d) 5
(e) 4

41. In a class, there are 80 students who study both Computer Science and Electronics while 100 students study Computer Science, 120 students study Electronics. How many of them study Computer Science only?

(a) 100 (b) 40
(c) 180 (d) 20

42. How many such pairs of digits are there in the number 5234816 each of which has as many digits between them in the number as when the digits are arranged in descending order within the number?

(a) None (b) One
(c) Two (d) More than three

43. Which word cannot be formed from the letters of the word "CARDIOGRAM"?

(a) AEROGRAM
(b) RADIO
(c) DIAGRAM
(d) CARGO

44. Showing the lady in the park, Vineet said, "She is the daughter of my grandfather's only son." How is Vineet related to that lady?

(a) Brother (b) Cousin
(c) Father (d) Uncle
(e) None of these

45. Find the missing number from the given responses.

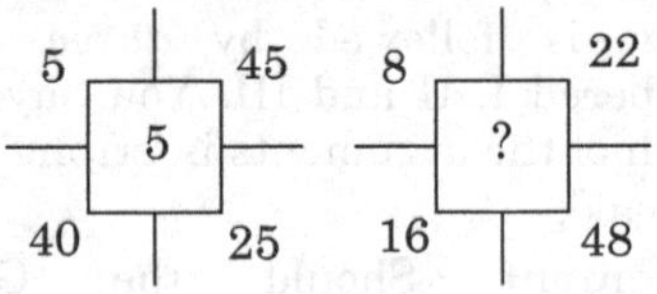

(a) 5 (b) 6
(c) 12 (d) 9

Direction (Q. Nos. 46-48) *In these questions, relationship between different elements is shown in the statements. The statements are followed by conclusions. Study the conclusions based on the given statement and select the appropriate answer.*
[NICL (Assistant) Cadre III 2015]

46. Statement $C \geq O = M < U \leq N < D$

Conclusions I. $O < D$

II. $C > N$

(a) Both Conclusions I and II are true
(b) Only Conclusion I is true
(c) Neither Conclusion I nor II is true
(d) Either Conclusion I or II is true
(e) Only Conclusion II is true

47. Statement $P > L = A \geq C = E$

Conclusions I. $E \leq L$

II. $P > C$

(a) Either Conclusion I or II is true
(b) Only Conclusion II is true
(c) Both Conclusions I and II are true
(d) Only Conclusion I is true
(e) Neither Conclusion I nor II is true

48. Statements $S > T \leq A = I$; $L \geq A$

Conclusions I. $L \geq T$

II. $A > S$

(a) Only Conclusion II is true
(b) Neither Conclusion I nor II is true
(c) Only Conclusion I is true
(d) Either Conclusion I or II is true
(e) Both Conclusions I and II are true

49. Select the related figure from the given alternatives.

Question Figures

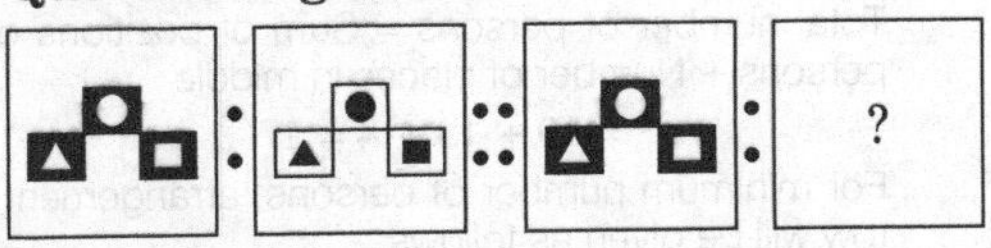

Answer Figures

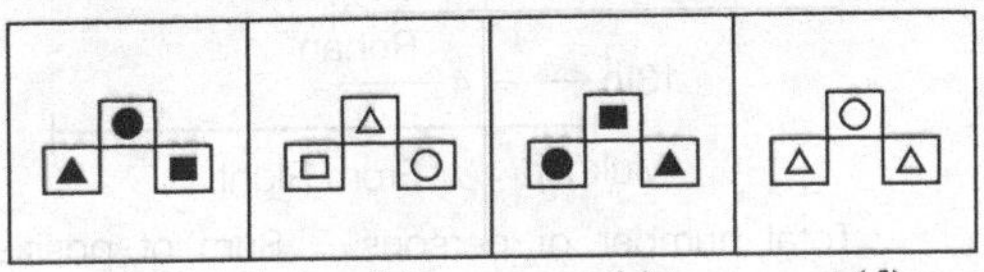

(a) (b) (c) (d)

50. If a mirror is placed on the line MN, then which of the answer figures is the right image of the given figure? **[SSC (10+2) 2014]**

Question Figure

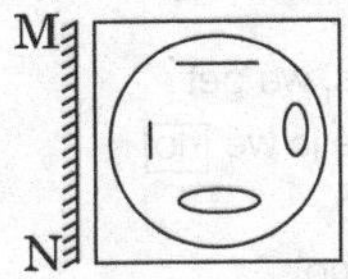

Answer Figures

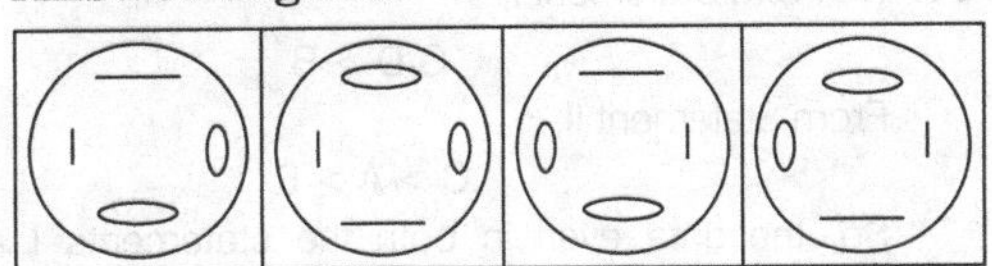

(a) (b) (c) (d)

Hints and Solutions

1. (c) According to the question, we have following coding data

P → X, U → P, T → Q, R → S, E → T, F → R, Y → L

and

N → G, A → Y, V → M, I → O, G → W, A → Y, T → Q, E → T

Similarly, code for AVIARY is

A → Y, V → M, I → O, A → Y, R → S, Y → L

Y M O Y S L

Hence, option (c) is correct.

2. (*d*)

According to	Nidhi's Birthday
Nitin	Wednesday, Thursday
Deepak	Thursday, Friday

Here, Thursday is common to both. Hence, correct day is Thursday.

3. (*d*) Sue Re Nik ⟶ She is brave

Pi Sor Re Nik ⟶ She is always smiling

Sor Re zhi ⟶ is always cheerful

So, from the above coded language, the code for smiling is 'Pi'.

4. (c) As, quality of cloth is identified by its texture and that of wood by its a grains.

5. (c) The pattern is as follows

17 20 21 : 9 12 13 : 2 5 6 : 23 26 1

Q T U : I L M : B E F : W Z A

+3 +1 : +3 +1 : +3 +1 : +3 +1

∴ ? = WZA

6. (c) From positions II and IV,

Common digit 6 is at the same (side) face in both the positions.

∴ Digit opposite to 3 = 4

7. (*b*) The pattern is as follows

71 →(−12) 59 →(−11) 48 →(−10) 38 →(−9) 29 →(−8) 21

∴ ? = 21

8. (*b*) The pattern is as follows

1 2 3 : 1 3 2 : 1 2 3 : 1 3 2

X Y Z : X Z Y : Y Z X : Y X Z : Z X Y

∴ ? = YXZ

9. (*d*) Pattern of given alpha-numeric series is as follows

11 K →(−2) 9 I →(−2) 7 G →(−2) 5 E →(−2) 3 C

13 M →(+3) 16 P →(+3) 19 S →(+3) 22 V →(+3) 25 Y

5 →(+3) 8 →(+3) 11 →(+3) 14 →(+3) 17

∴ ? = CY17

Solution (Q. Nos.10-11)

10. (*e*) From Statement I,

Thank for not smoking → be je we no

From Statement II,

No Smoking Area → no se do

By combining both statements, we get

Thanks for not [smoking] → be je we [no]

No [Smoking] Area → [no] se do

So, the code for 'smoking' is 'no'.

11. (*d*) From Statement I,

$C/D > B$

From Statement II,

$C > A > E$

So, the data even in both the statements I and II together are not sufficient to answer the question.

12. (*c*) The question figure is hidden in answer figure (c).

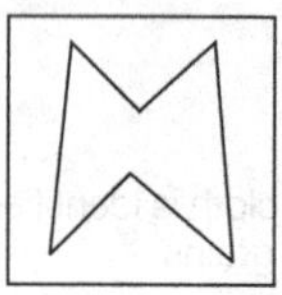

13. (*a*) As, $16 - 2 = 2$

$4^2 - 2 \Rightarrow 4 - 2 \Rightarrow 2$

$9 - 3 = 0$

$3^2 - 3 \Rightarrow 3 - 3 = 0$

and $81 - 1 = 8$

$9^2 - 1 = 8 \Rightarrow 9 - 1 \Rightarrow 8$

Similarly, $64 - 4 = ?$

$8^2 - 4 \Rightarrow 8 - 4 = 4$

14. (*c*) Two days after Monday means Wednesday.

5 → Wednesday

5 + 7 = 12 → Wednesday

12 + 7 = 19 → Wednesday

Therefore, Tuesday will precede 19th that month.

15. (*a*) According to the question, we have C = 3 (Position number in English) alphabet

C A T → 3 + 1 + 20 = [24]

Similarly,

F A U L T → 6 + 1 + 21 + 12 + 20 = [60]

Hence, option (a) is correct.

16. (*b*) For maximum number of persons, arrangement in the row will be as follows

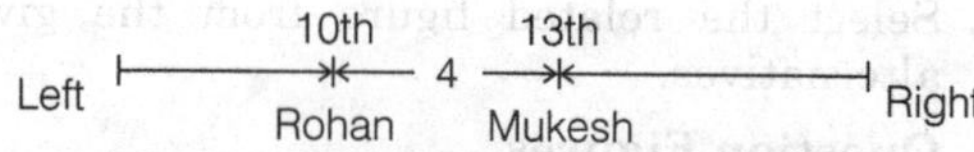

Total number of persons = Sum of positions of both persons + Number of places in middle

= 10 + 13 + 4 = 27

For minimum number of persons, arrangement in the row will be given as follows

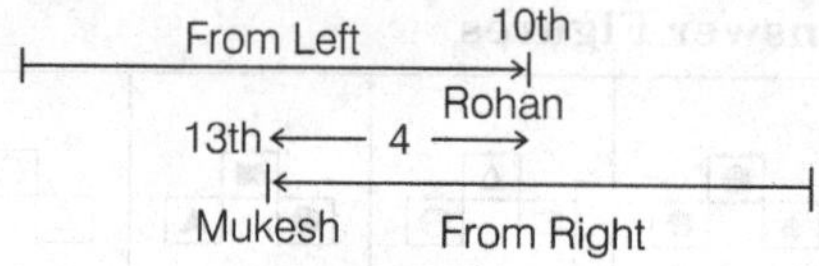

∴ Total number of persons = Sum of positions of both places − Number of places in middle − 2 = (10 + 13) − 4 − 2 = 17

Hence, option (b) is the correct answer.

Solution (Q. Nos. 17-21) On the basis of given information, the arrangement is as following:

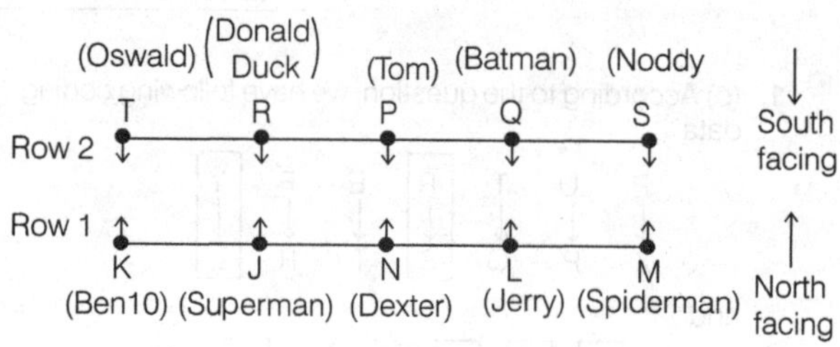

17. (*a*) S, M pairs represents the people sitting at the extreme end of the two rows.

18. (*d*) R likes Donald Duck.

19. (*a*) The one who likes Jerry.

20. (*e*) T likes Oswald cartoon character.

21. (*c*) Q is an immediate neighbour of P.

Solution (Q. Nos. 22-23)

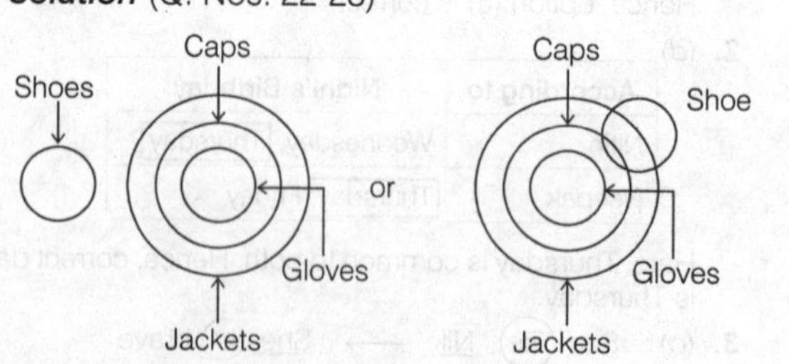

22. (*b*) **Conclusions**

I. Atleast some shoes are caps. (✗)

II. Atleast some jackets are gloves. (✔)

23. (*b*) **Conclusions** I. No shoe is a jacket. (✗)

II. All gloves are jacket. (✔)

Solution (Q. Nos. 24-25) The word and number arrangement stepwise.

Input for 52 all 96 25 jam road 15 hut 73 bus stop 38 46

***Step* I** all for 52 25 jam road 15 hut 73 bus stop 38 46 96

***Step* II** bus all for 52 25 jam road 15 hut stop 38 46 96 73

***Step* III** for bus all 25 jam road 15 hut stop 38 46 96 73 52

***Step* IV** hut for bus all 25 jam road 15 stop 38 96 73 52 46

***Step* V** jam hut for bus all 25 road 15 stop 96 73 52 46 38

***Step* VI** road jam hut for bus all 15 stop 96 73 52 46 38 25

***Step* VII** stop road jam hut for bus all 96 73 52 46 38 25 15

24. (*a*) 25 would be at the 6th position from the left in Step V.

25. (*d*) for bus all 25 jam road 15 hut stop 38 46 96 73 52 would be the Step III.

26. (*a*) In the given diagram, there are 22 triangles which can be better understood with the help of following diagram.

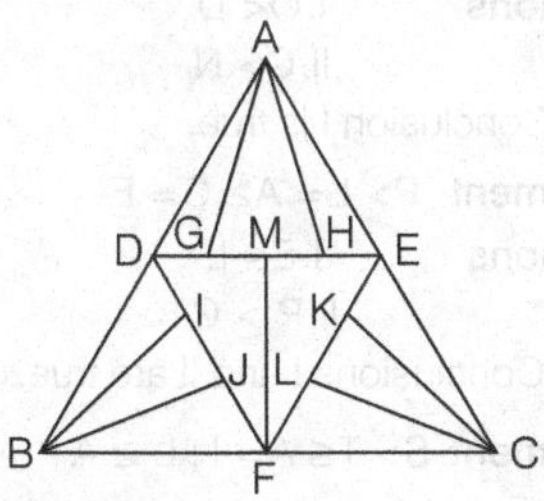

In the above figures,

Triangles consisting of 1 unit are ΔADG, ΔAGH, ΔAHE, ΔDMF, ΔFME, ΔDIB, ΔIBJ, ΔJBF, ΔCFL, ΔCLK and ΔCKE, i.e. 11 triangles.

Triangles consisting of 2 units are ΔADH, ΔAGE, ΔDFE, ΔDBJ, ΔIBF, ΔECL and ΔCKF, i.e. 7 triangles.

Triangles consisting of 3 units are ΔADE, ΔBDF and ΔCFE, i.e. 3 triangles.

Triangle consisting of whole figure is ΔABC, i.e. 1 triangle.

So, total number of triangles = 11 + 7 + 3 + 1 = 22

27. (*a*)

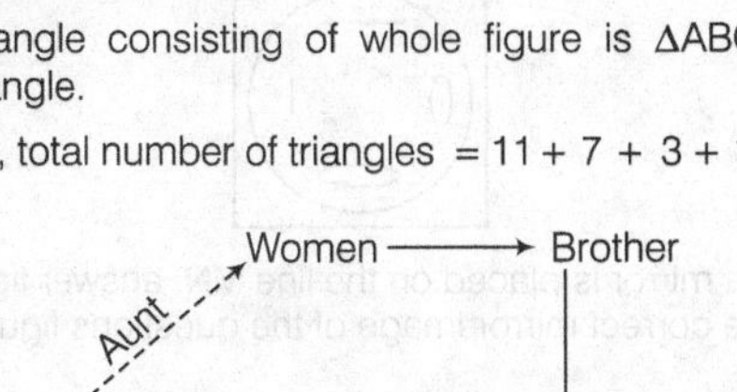

So, woman is aunt to the wife of that man.

28. (*c*) BBCCA/BBCCA/BBCCA/BB CCA

Hence, correct option is (c), i.e. BCCB.

29. (*d*) Except 525, all other numbers are cubes of natural numbers.

30. (*a*) Only 'Gallon' is different because this is use for liquid measurement.

31. (*a*) Only Argument I holds strong because this is definitely not the solution. Arguments II and III are weak arguments.

32. (*c*) From Statement I, it can be concluded that 'All participants in the race are students'. Since, it is given in Statement III that 'All girl participants in the race are invited for coaching'. So, options (a) and (b) cannot be concluded. Hence, answer is option (c).

33. (*b*) As, $2 \times 3 \times 4 = 432$

and $5 \times 6 \times 7 = 765$

and $7 \times 8 \times 9 = 987$

Here, we see that in all equations numbers are written in reverse order.

So, $2 \times 5 \times 7 = 752$

34. (*c*)

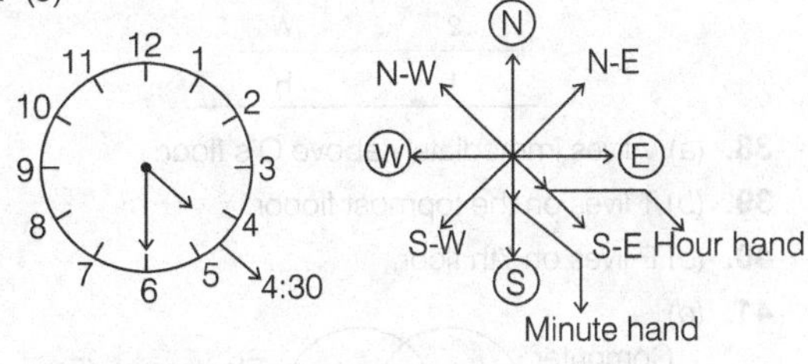

If the minute hand points East, then the hour hand point in North-East direction as shown below.

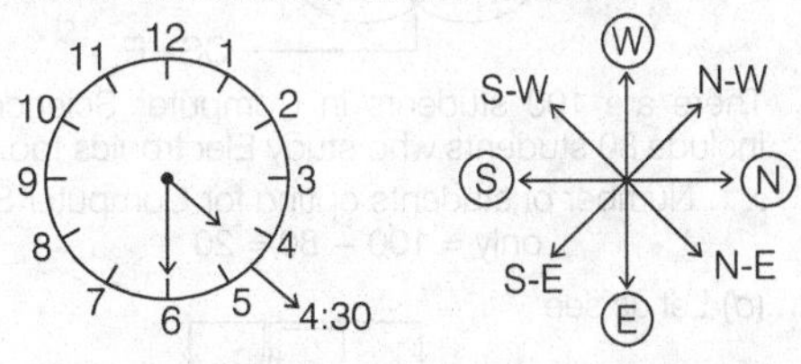

35. (*d*) Let the number of persons be x. Then,

$$\Rightarrow \quad \frac{96}{x-4} - \frac{96}{x} = 4$$

$$\Rightarrow \quad \frac{1}{x-4} - \frac{1}{x} = \frac{4}{96}$$

$$\Rightarrow \quad \frac{x-(x-4)}{x(x-4)} = \frac{1}{24}$$

$$\Rightarrow \quad x^2 - 4x - 96 = 0$$

$$\Rightarrow \quad (x-12)(x+8) = 0$$

$$\Rightarrow \quad x = 12$$

So, required number $= x - 4 \Rightarrow 12 - 4 = 8$

36. (*b*) According to the matrices,

W — 01, 13, 20, 32, (44)

E — 56, 68, 75, (87), 99

A — 55, 67, 79, 86, (98)

R — 57, (69), 76, 88, 95

∴ WEAR ⇒ 44, 87, 98, 69

37. (*d*) Meaningful order

(iii) Letters → (ii) Words → (iv) Sentences → (vi) Pages → (v) Chapters → (i) Book

Solution (Q. Nos. 38-40) According to the given information, the arrangement is as following

Floor	People
8	T
7	P
6	V
5	Q
4	S
3	U
2	W
1	R

38. (*a*) V lives immediately above Q's floor.

39. (*b*) T lives on the topmost flooor.

40. (*c*) P lives on 7th floor.

41. (*d*)

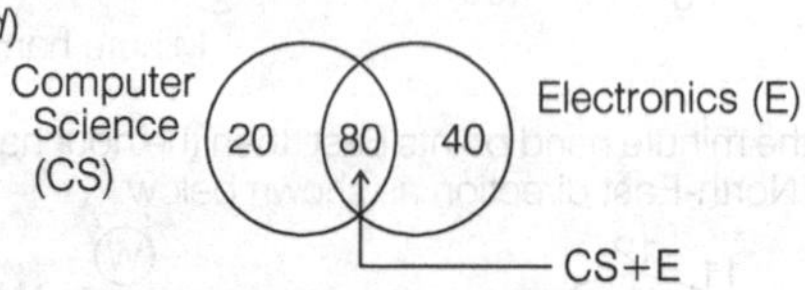

There are 100 students in Computer Science which include 80 students who study Electronics too.

∴ Number of students opting for Computer Science only = 100 − 80 = 20

42. (*d*) Let us see

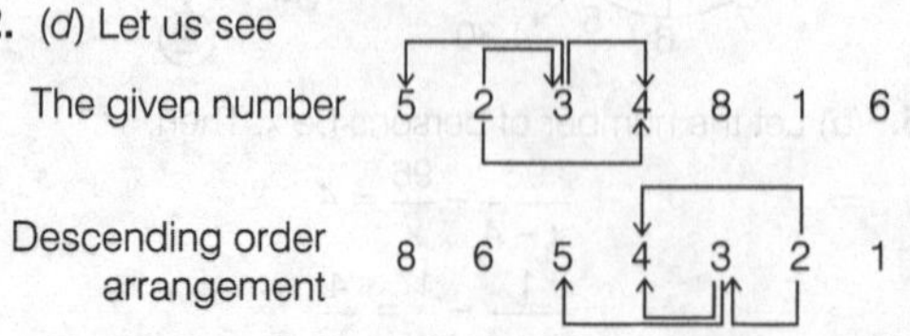

∴ Required pairs = (53), (23), (34) and (24)

43. (*a*) Word AEROGRAM cannot be formed by using the letters of the given word because letter 'E' is not present in the given word.

44. (*a*)

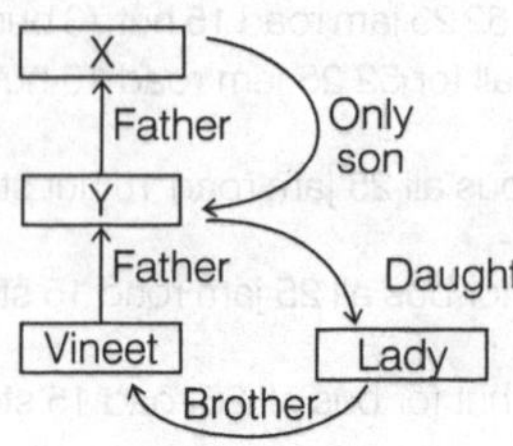

Hence, Vineet is the brother of that lady.

45. (*b*) Here, in first figure,

$$\frac{25}{5} = 45 - 40 = 5$$

$$5 = 5 = 5$$

Similarly, in second figure,

$$\frac{48}{8} = 22 - 16 = ?$$

So, $6 = 6 = \boxed{6}$

46. (*b*) **Statement** C≥ O= M< U≤ N< D

Conclusions I. O< D (True)

II. C> N (False)

So, only Conclusion I is true.

47. (*c*) **Statement** P> L= A≥ C= E

Conclusions I. E≤ L (True)

II. P > C (True)

So, both Conclusions I and II are true.

48. (*c*) **Statement** S> T≤ A= I ; L ≥ A

Therefore, S > T ≤ A = I or S > T≤ A ≤ L

Conclusions I. L≥ T (True)

II. A> S (False)

So, only Conclusion I is true.

49. (*a*) Clearly, from figure I to figure II the shaded parts becomes unshaded and *vice-versa*.

50. (*c*)

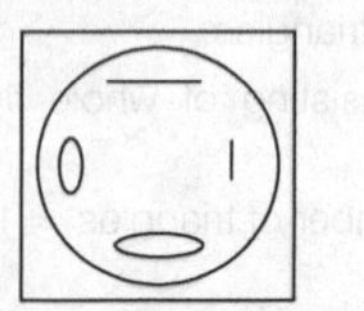

If a mirror is placed on the line MN, answer figure (c) is the correct mirror image of the questions figure.

PRACTICE SET 48

1. Which among the options below comes at third place in the English dictionary? **[BSSC (CGL) 2015]**
(a) Monarchy (b) Monastic
(c) Monetary (d) Moneyed

Direction (Q. Nos. 2-3) *In the following questions, find the odd numbers/words pair from the given alternatives.*

2. (a) Stamp : Letter (b) Ticket : Train
(c) Ink : pen (d) Car : Engine

3. (a) 77, 70, 49, 56 (b) 56, 64, 96, 48
(c) 66, 44, 23, 60 (d) 21, 27, 63, 84

Direction (Q. Nos. 4-5) *Read the following information carefully to answer the questions that follow.*

I. Anita, Mahima, Rajan, Lata and Deepti are five cousins.
II. Anita is twice as old as Mahima.
III. Rajan is half the age of Mahima.
IV. Anita is half the age of Deepti.
V. Rajan is twice the age of Lata.

4. Who is the youngest?
(a) Deepti (b) Rajan
(c) Lata (d) Anita

5. Who is the eldest?
(a) Deepti (b) Lata
(c) Anita (d) Rajan

Direction (Q. Nos. 6-8) *Read the following information carefully and answer the following questions.*

Eight executives A, B, C, D, E, F, G and H are sitting for a meeting around a circular table. F is third to the right of C who is third to the right of G. A is second to the left of B and neither A nor B is an immediate neighbour of G. D is not an immediate neighbour of F. H is third to the right of B.

6. Which of the following is the correct position of E with respect to D?
(a) Third to the right (b) Fourth to the right
(c) Fourth to the left (d) Third to the left
(e) Both (b) and (c)

7. Who sits between A and B?
(a) E (b) C (c) D (d) H
(e) None of these

8. Who sits between G and F?
(a) H (b) E (c) D (d) C
(e) None of these

9. A pineapple costs ₹7 each. A watermelon costs ₹5 each. X spends ₹38 on these fruits. The number of pineapples purchased is
(a) 2 (b) 3
(c) 4 (d) Data inadequate

10. An accurate clock shows 8 O'clock in the morning. Through how many degrees will the hour hand rotate when the clock shows 2 O'clock in the afternoon?
(a) 144° (b) 150° (c) 168° (d) 180°

11. In the English alphabet, 'BDG' is to 'CFJ' in the same way as 'EGJ' is to?
(a) FIL (b) FJM (c) FIM (d) FIN
(e) None of these

Direction (Q. Nos. 12-13) *In the following questions, select the related word /number pair from the given alternatives.*

12. Malaria : Disease :: Spear : ?
(a) Wound (b) Sword (c) Weapon (d) Death

13. 14 : 9 :: 26 : ? **[SSC (FCI) 2012]**
(a) 12 (b) 13 (c) 15 (d) 31

14. How many such pairs of letters are there in the word FASTER each of which has as many letters between them in the word (in both forward and backward directions) as they have between them in the English alphabetical series? **[IBPS (Clerk) Pre 2015]**
(a) More than three (b) None
(c) Two (d) One
(e) Three

15. Two positions of a cube are given. Based on them find out which number is found opposite number 4 in a given cube?

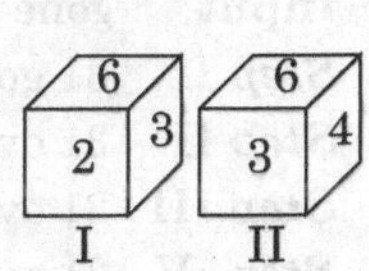

(a) 1 (b) 2 (c) 3 (d) 4

16. Identify the alternative which resembles the mirror image of the given word.

ENDURANCE

(a) ƎƆИAЯUᗡИƎ (b) ƎCИAЯUᗡИƎ
(c) ƎƆИAЯꓵᗡИƎ (d) ƎƆИAЯUᗡИƎ

17. Which of the given statements will be definitely true if the expression '$V < E > B = H \geq N \geq P$' is definitely true? **IBPS (Clerk) Pre 2015**

(a) $P \leq B$ (b) $H < V$ (c) $N \geq V$ (d) $E \geq N$
(e) $E \geq P$

18. A word is represented by only one set of numbers as given in anyone of the alternatives. The set of numbers given in the alternatives are represented by two classes of alphabets as in the 2 matrices given below. The columns and rows of Matrix I are from 0 to 4 and that of Matrix II from 5 to 9. A letter can be represented first by its row and next by its column number. e.g. C can be represented by 02, 21, etc. T can be represented by 65, 96 etc. Similarly, you have to identify the correct set for the word given in each question.

Matrix I

	0	1	2	3	4
0	D	V	C	P	M
1	P	M	D	V	C
2	V	C	P	M	D
3	M	D	V	C	P
4	C	P	M	D	V

Matrix II

	5	6	7	8	9
5	S	A	U	T	J
6	T	J	S	A	U
7	A	U	T	J	S
8	J	S	A	U	T
9	U	T	J	S	A

DUST

(a) 00, 76, 86, 59 (b) 13, 76, 98, 59
(c) 21, 69, 55, 65 (d) 12, 57, 67, 58

Direction (Q. Nos. 19-20) *Study the following information carefully and answer the given questions.*

A word and number arrangement machine, when given an input line of words and numbers rearranges them following a particular rule in each step. The following is an illustration of input and rearrangement.

Input	gone 93 over 46 84 now for 31
***Step* I**	31 gone 93 over 46 84 now for
***Step* II**	31 over gone 93 46 84 now for
***Step* III**	31 over 46 gone 93 84 now for
***Step* IV**	31 over 46 now gone 93 84 for
***Step* V**	31 over 46 now 84 gone 93 for

and Step V is the last step of the rearrangement of the above input. As per the rules followed in the above steps, find out in each of the following questions the appropriates step for the given input.

19. Step III of an input is '15 window 29 93 86 sail tower buy'.
Which of the following will be Step VI?
(a) 15 window 29 tower 86 sail 93 buy
(b) 15 window 29 tower 86 93 sail buy
(c) 15 window 29 tower 93 86 sail buy
(d) There will be no such step
(e) None of the above

20. **Input** station hurry 39 67 all men 86 59.
How many steps will be required to complete the rearrangement?
(a) Four (b) Five (c) Six (d) Three
(e) None of these

Direction (Q. Nos. 21-23) *In the following questions, the symbols ★, δ, %, @ and © used with the following meaning as illustrated below:*

'P % Q' means 'P is not smaller than Q'.
'P © Q' means 'P is neither smaller than nor equal to Q'.
'P ★ Q' means 'P is neither greater than nor equal to Q'.
'P δ Q' means 'P is not greater than Q'.
'P @ Q' means 'P is neither greater than nor smaller than Q'.

Now, in each of the following questions assuming the given statements to be true, find which of the three Conclusions I, II and III given below them is/are definitely true and given your answer accordingly.

21. **Statements** R δ K, K ★ M, M @ J
Conclusions I. J © K
II. M © R III. R ★ J
(a) I and II are true
(b) II and III are true
(c) I and III are true
(d) All I, II and III are true
(e) None of the above

22. **Statements** Z @ M, M © K, K ★ F
Conclusions I. F © Z
II. K ★ Z III. F © M
(a) None is true (b) Only I is true
(c) Only II is true (d) Only III is true
(e) II and III are true

23. Statements B ★ J, J % W, W © M

Conclusions I. M ★ J
II. W ★ B III. B © M

(a) None is true
(b) Only I is true
(c) Only II is true
(d) Only III is true
(e) Only I and III are true

24. How many triangles are there in the following figure?

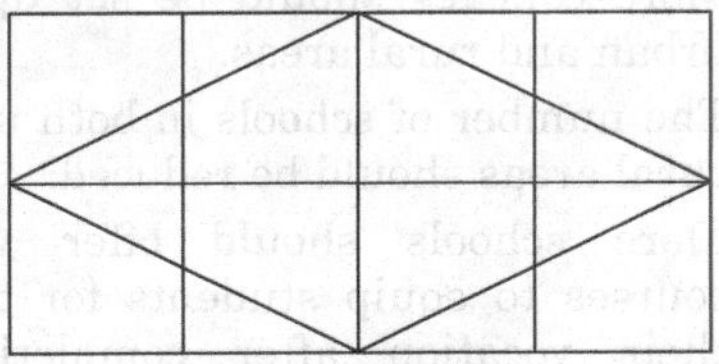

(a) 22 (b) 18
(c) 20 (d) 24

25. In making decisions about important questions, it is desirable to distinguish between a 'strong' argument and a 'weak' argument. A 'strong' argument must be both important and directly related to the question. A 'weak' argument may not be directly related to the question and may be of minor importance or may be related to the trivial aspect of the question. Each question below is followed by three arguments numbered I, II and III. You have to decide which of the arguments is 'strong' and which is 'weak'.

Statement Should there be only few banks in place of numerous smaller banks in India?

Arguments

I. Yes, this will help to secure the investor's money as these big banks will be able to withstand intermittent market related shocks.

II. No, a large number of people will lose their jobs as after the merger many employees will be redundant.

III. Yes, this will help consolidate the entire banking industry and will lead to healthy competition. **[SBI (PO) 2012]**

(a) None is strong
(b) I and II are strong
(c) II and III are strong
(d) I and III are strong
(e) All are strong

Direction (Q. Nos. 26-28) *In these questions two statements followed by two conclusions numbered I and II have been given. You have to take the two given statements to be true even if they seem to be at variance from commonly known facts and then decide which of the given conclusions logically follows from the given statements disregarding commonly known facts.*

Give answer

(a) Both Conclusions I and II are true
(b) Neither Conclusion I nor II is true
(c) Only Conclusion I is true
(d) Only Conclusion II is true
(e) Either Conclusion I or II is true

26. Statements No win is a loss. All losses are victories.

Conclusions I. No victory is a win.
II. Some victories are wins.

27. Statements All sides are lengths.
No length is breadth.

Conclusions I. All lengths are sides.
II. No breadth is a side.

28. Statements No remark is a wish.
Some wishes are hopes.

Conclusions I. At least some remarks are hopes.
II. All hopes are wishes.

Direction (Q. Nos. 29-30) *Each of the following questions below consists of a question and two statements numbered I and II. You have to decide whether the data provided in the statements are sufficient to answer the question.* **[NIACL (AO) 2014]**

Give answer

(a) if the data in Statement I alone are sufficient to answer the question, while the data in Statement II alone are not sufficient to answer the question
(b) if the data in Statement II alone are sufficient to answer the question, while the data in Statement I alone are not sufficient to answer the question
(c) if the data either in Statement I alone or in Statement II alone are sufficient to answer the question.
(d) if the data in both Statements I and II together are necessary to answer the question.
(e) if the data in both the Statements I and II together are not sufficient to answer the question.

29. Who amongst L, M, N, O and P is the shortest?

I. O is shorter than P but taller than N.

II. M is not as tall as L.

30. Point A is towards which direction from point B?

I. If a person walks 4 m towards the North from point A and takes two consecutive right turns, each after walking 4 m, he would reach point C, which is 8 m away from point B.

II. Point D is 2 m towards the East of point A and 4 m towards the West of point B.

Direction (Q. Nos. 31-32) *In the following questions select the missing character from the given responses.*

31.

5	8	13
6	9	15
4	12	?
60	432	1560

(a) 16 (b) 32 (c) 29 (d) 120

32.

(a) Z (b) X (c) I (d) D

33. Identify the diagram that represents the best relationship among classes given below.

Women, Sisters and Wives **[SSC (10+2) 2014]**

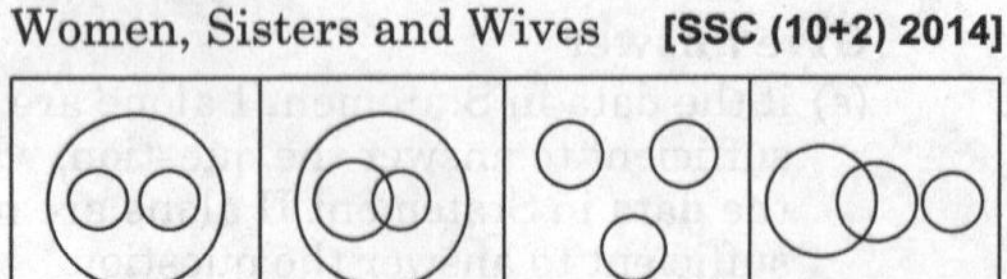

(a) (b) (c) (d)

34. In the question below is given a statement followed by three courses of action numbered I, II and III. A course of action is a step or administrative decision to be taken for improvement follow-up or further action in regard to the problem, policy, etc. On the basis of information given in the statement, you have to assume everything in the statement to be true and then decide which of the three given suggested courses of action logically follows worth pursuing. Then, decide which of the alternatives (a), (b), (c), (d) or (e) is correct.

Statement Every year thousands of eligible students do not get admission in colleges, both in urban and rural areas, after passing their school leaving certificate examination.

Courses of Action

I. More colleges should be set up in both urban and rural areas.

II. The number of schools in both urban and rural areas should be reduced.

III. More schools should offer vocational courses to equip students for taking up their vocation after completing their school education.

(a) I follows
(b) Both II and III follow
(c) All follow
(d) Both I and III follow

35. Ten new TV shows started in January, 5 sitcoms, 3 drama and 2 news magazines. By April only seven of the new shows were still on, five of them being sitcoms.

Based on the above information, four conclusions, as given below, have been made. Which one of these logically follows from the information given above?

(a) Only one news magazine show is still on
(b) Only one of the drama show is still on
(c) At least one discontinued show was a drama
(d) Viewers prefer sitcoms over drama

Direction (Q. Nos. 36-37) *Read the following informations carefully and answer the questions which follow.*

'P × Q' means 'P is brother of Q'.
'P − Q' means 'P is mother of Q'.
'P + Q' means 'P is father of Q'.
'P ÷ Q' means 'P is sister of Q'.

36. Which of the following means 'M is niece of N'?

(a) M × R − N b) N ÷ J + M ÷ D
(c) N ÷ J + M (d) N × J − M
(e) None of the above

37. Which of the following means 'B is the grandfather of F'?
(a) B + J − F (b) B − J + F
(c) B × T − F (d) B ÷ T + F
(e) None of the above

38. There are two statements labelled as Assertion (A) and Reason (R). Choose the correct alternatives from the given options.
Assertion (A) Leakages in household gas cylinders can be detected.
Reason (R) LPG has a strong smell.
(a) if both A and R are true and R is the correct explanation of A
(b) if both A and R are true but R is not the correct explanation of A
(c) if A is true but R is false
(d) if A is false but R is true
(e) if both A and R are false

Direction (Q. Nos. 39-41) *In the following questions, a series is given, with one term missing. Choose the correct alternatives from the given ones that will complete the series.* **[BSSC (CGL) 2015]**

39. D E 2, E F 4, G G 8, J H 16, ? ? ?
(a) K I 18 (b) L I 20 (c) N I 30 (d) N I 32

40. 198, 202, 211, 227, ?
(a) 236 (b) 252 (c) 275 (d) 245

41. AN, BO, CP, DQ, ?
(a) EG (b) ER (c) EH (d) EF

Direction (Q. Nos. 42-44) *Read the following information carefully to answer these questions.*

Three friends Surinder, Varinder and Joginder wore shirts of black, blue and orange colours (not necessarily in that order) and pants of green, yellow and orange colours (not necessarily in that order). No person wore pant and shirt of the same colour. Further, it is given that

- Surinder did not wear shirt of black colour.
- Joginder did not wear shirt of orange colour.
- Varinder wore pant of orange colour.
- Varinder did not wear shirt of blue colour.
- Surinder did not wear pant of green colour.

42. What were the colours of pant and shirt wore by Joginder, respectively?
(a) Orange and black (b) Yellow and black
(c) Green and blue (d) Yellow and blue

43. What was the colour of the shirt wore by Varinder?
(a) Blue (b) Orange (c) Black (d) Green

44. What was the colour of the pant wore by Surinder?
(a) Orange (b) Green
(c) Yellow (d) blue

45. If PNLJ : 2468, then QOKL : ? **[SSC (10+2) 2015]**
(a) 1276 (b) 1367 (c) 1376 (d) 3591

46. In a certain, code 'nee tim see' means 'who is it', 'ble nee see' means 'where is it', 'ble see tee' means 'where is what'. What is the code for 'who is where'? **[CMAT 2015]**
(a) tim ble see (b) tim nee see
(c) tim ble nee (d) nee ble see

47. A is 3 yr older to B and 3 yr younger to C, while B and D are twins. How many years older is C to D?
(a) 2 (b) 3 (c) 6 (d) 12

48. A and B start walking in opposite directions. A covers 3 km and B covers 4 km. Then, A turns right and walks 4 km while B turns left and walks 3 km. How far is each from the starting point? **[SSC (Steno) 2013]**
(a) 10 km (b) 8 km (c) 5 km (d) 4 km

49. From the given alternatives, select the word which cannot be formed using the letters of the given word.
HISTORICAL
(a) RICHES (b) CHARIOT
(c) CHART (d) CHAOS

50. Group the given figures into different classes on the basis of their orientation, shape etc.

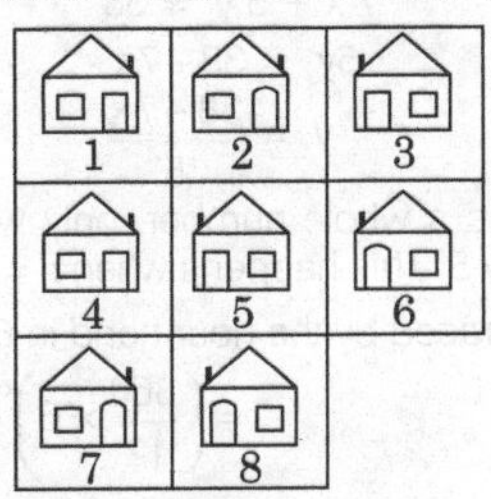

(a) (1, 7), (2, 4), (3, 5), (6, 8)
(b) (1, 4), (2, 7), (3, 5), (6, 8)
(c) (1, 3), (2, 7), (6, 8), (4, 5)
(d) (1, 4), (3, 6), (3, 5), (7, 8)

Hints and Solutions

1. (*c*) Monetary comes at third place in the English dictionary.

2. (*d*) In all others first is required for second to use.

3. (*d*) Except option (c), in all the other options, all numbers are divisible by a particular number as option (a) by 7, option (b) by 8 and option (d) by 7.

Solution (Q. Nos. 4-5)

Let age of Mahima = x

Then, age of Anita = 2x

$$\text{Age of Rajan} = \frac{x}{2}$$

Age of Deepti = 4x

$$\text{Age of Lata} = \frac{x}{4}$$

Now, we have the following arrangement in descending order.

Deepti > Anita > Mahima > Rajan > Lata

4. (*c*) Lata is youngest.

5. (*a*) Deepti is eldest.

Solution (Q. Nos. 6-8) According to the given information, the final arrangement is as following.

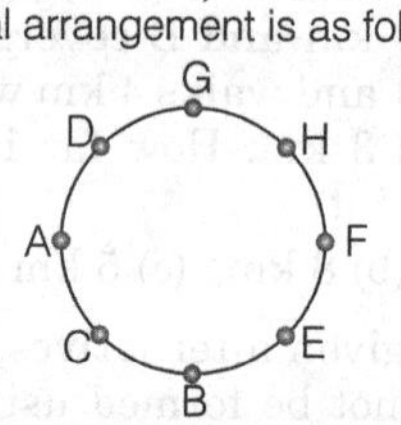

6. (*e*) E is fourth to the right of D and he is also fourth to the left of D.

7. (*b*) C sits between A and B.

8. (*a*) H sits between G and F.

9. (*c*) Let the number of pineapples and watermelons be x and y, respectively.

Then, $7x + 5y = 38$

$\Rightarrow \quad 5y = 38 - 7x$

$\Rightarrow \quad y = \dfrac{38 - 7x}{5}$

Clearly, y is a whole number, only when (38 − 7x) is divisible by 5. This happens when x = 4.

10. (*d*) Angle traced by the hour hand in 6h

$$= \left(\frac{360}{12} \times 6\right)^\circ = 180^\circ$$

11. (*c*) Given,

B → (+1) → C, D → (+2) → F, G → (+3) → J

Similarly,

E → (+1) → F, G → (+2) → I, J → (+3) → M

F I M

12. (*c*) As, 'Malaria' is a kind of 'Disease'. Similarly, 'Spear' is a kind of 'Weapon'.

13. (*c*) As, (9 × 2) = 18 − 4 = 14

Similarly, (15 × 2) = 30 − 4 = 26

∴ ? = 15

14. (*c*)

F A S T E R

Hence, there are two pairs ST and RT in the given word.

15. (*b*) In the given two dices two numbers are common i.e. 3 and 6. So, remaining two numbers are opposite to each other.

Hence, number 2 is opposite to the number 4.

16. (*d*) The mirror image of the given word is as follows.

ENDURANCE | ƎƆNAЯUDNƎ

17. (*a*) As, V<E>B=H≥N≥P

P≤ B, will be definitely true from the given expression.

18. (*d*) According to the matrices,

D — 00, (12), 24, 31, 43

U — (57), 69, 76, 88, 95

S — 55, (67), 79, 86, 98

T — (58), 65, 77, 89, 96

∴ DUST ⇒ 12, 57, 67, 58

Solution (Q. Nos. 19-20)

19. (*a*) ***Step* III** 15 window 29 93 86 sail tower buy

***Step* IV** 15 window 29 tower 93 86 sail buy

***Step* V** 15 window 29 tower 86 93 sail buy

***Step* VI** 15 window 29 tower 86 sail 93 buy

Input Station hurry 39 67 all men 86 59

20. (*b*) ***Step* I** 39 station hurry 67 all men 86 59

***Step* II** 39 station 59 hurry 67 all men 86

***Step* III** 39 station 59 men hurry 67 all 86

***Step* IV** 39 station 59 men 67 hurry all 86

***Step* V** 39 station 59 men 67 hurry 86 all

Solution (Q. Nos. 21-23)

% ⇒ ≥	© ⇒ >	★ ⇒ <	δ ⇒ ≤	@ ⇒ =

21. (*d*) R δ K ⇒ R ≤ K

K ★ M ⇒ K < M

M @ J ⇒ M = J

Therefore, R ≤ K < M = J

Conclusions I. J © K ⇒ J > K (True)
II. M © R ⇒ M > R (True)
III. R ★ J ⇒ R < J (True)

22. (*c*) Z @ M ⇒ Z = M, M © K ⇒ M > K, K ★ F ⇒ K < F
Therefore, Z = M > K < F

Conclusions I. F © Z ⇒ F > Z (Not True)
II. K ★ Z ⇒ K < Z (True)
III. F © M ⇒ F > M (Not True)

23. (*b*) B ★ J ⇒ B < J, J % W ⇒ J ≥ W, W © M ⇒ W > M
Therefore, B < J ≥ W > M

Conclusions I. M ★ J ⇒ M < J (True)
II. W ★ B ⇒ W < B (Not True)
III. B © M ⇒ B > M (Not True)

24. (*a*)

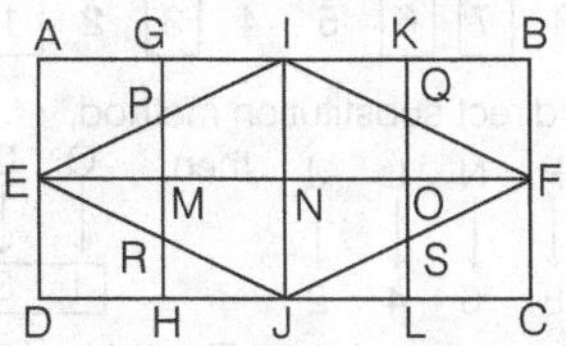

From the figure, it is clear that there are 9 triangles in the upper half of the figure ABFE, namely ΔPEM, ΔPGI, ΔAEI, ΔEIN, ΔIKQ, ΔQOF, ΔIBF, ΔINF, and ΔIEF.

Likewise, there are 9 triangles in the lower half EFCD of the main figure.

There are 4 more triangles ΔEPR, ΔEIJ, IFJ and ΔQFS.

Hence, there are a total of 22 triangles in the figure.

25. (*a*) All arguments stated do not strongly support the statement because if there are few banks in place of several small banks, then security for investor cannot be ensured. Also, it cannot help to consolidate the entire banking industry.

26. (*e*)

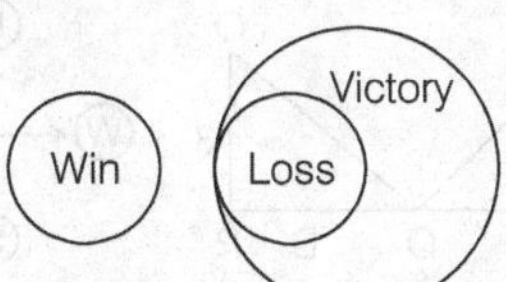

Conclusions I. No victory is a win. (May be)
II. Some victories are wins . (May be)

Complementry pairs.

So, either Conclusion I or II is true.

27. (*d*)

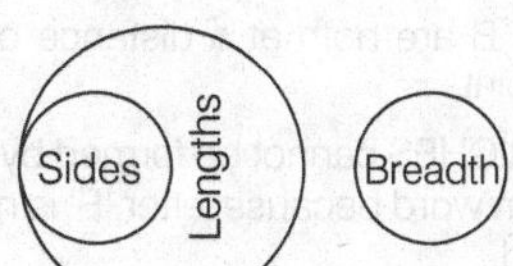

Conclusions I. All lengths are sides. (✗)
II. No breadth is a side. (✔)

So, only Conclusion II is true.

28. (*b*)

or

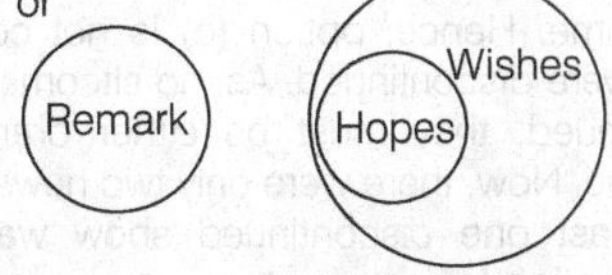

Conclusions I. At least some remarks are hopes. (✗)
II. All hopes are wishes. (✗)

So, neither Conclusion I nor II is true.

29. (*e*) From both statements

$$P > O > N \quad \ldots(i)$$

$$L > M \quad \ldots(ii)$$

No relation is given between these two equations.

30. (*b*) From Statement II,

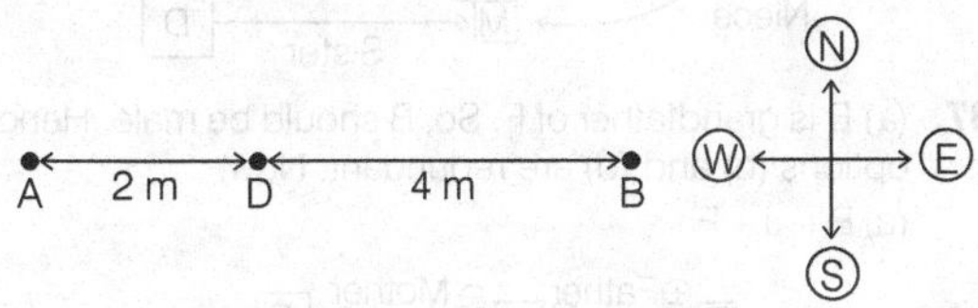

Now, it is clear from diagram that point A is in West direction from point B.

31. (*a*) From the given arrangement we can see that, in each column.

Lowest number $= \frac{1}{2}$ (multiplication of upper three numbers).

i.e. $60 = \frac{1}{2}(5 \times 6 \times 4) = \frac{1}{2} \times 120 = 60$

$432 = \frac{1}{2}(8 \times 9 \times 12)$

Similarly, $1560 = \frac{1}{2}(13 \times 15 \times ?)$

$\Rightarrow \quad ? = \frac{2 \times 1560}{13 \times 15} = 16$

The blank space can be filled by '16'.

32. (*a*) Moving clockwise, we have

$$B \xrightarrow{+1} C \xrightarrow{+2} E \xrightarrow{+3} H \xrightarrow{+4}$$

$$L \xrightarrow{+5} Q \xrightarrow{+6} W \xrightarrow{+7} \boxed{D}$$

$\therefore \quad ? = D$

33. (*a*) All women can be sisters and wives.

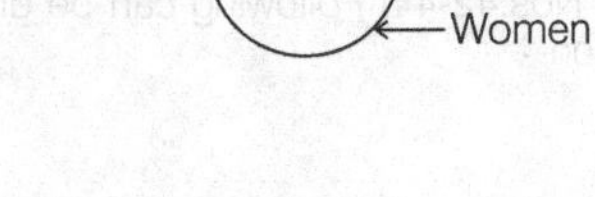

34. (*d*) The statement describes the problem of admission in colleges faced by students. Both the courses of action I and III are the right steps towards providing solution of this problem.

35. (*c*) No reason is provided for discontinuation of any programme. Hence, option (d) is not correct. Three shows were discontinued. As, no sitcoms shows were discontinued, they must be either drama or news magazine. Now, there were only two news magazines. So, atleast one discontinued show was a drama. Hence, option (c) is correct.

36. (*b*) M is niece of N. So, M is female. Here, option (a) is redundant. Also, gender of M cannot be determined using options (c) and (d). Now,

N ÷ J + M ÷ D

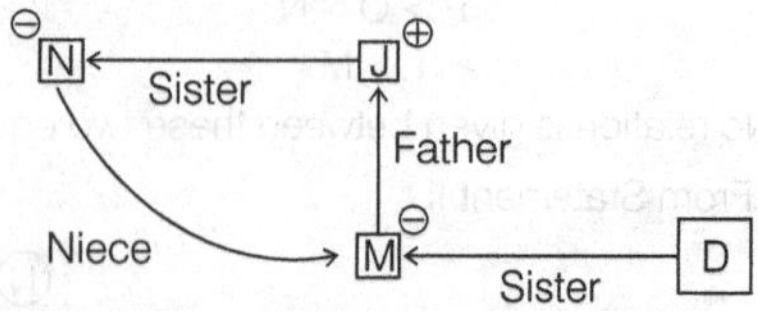

37. (*a*) B is grandfather of F. So, B should be male. Hence, options (b) and (d) are redundant. Now,

(a) B+ J− F

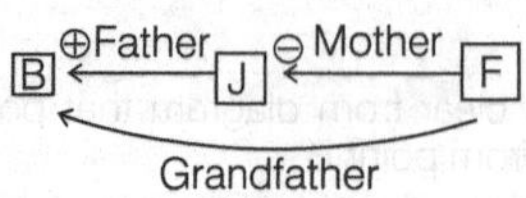

Hence, option (a) is true.

38. (*a*) LPG contains ethyl merceptan which has strong smell. Because of this, smell leakages in household gas cylinders can be detected.

39. (*d*)The pattern is as follows

D $\xrightarrow{+1}$ E $\xrightarrow{+2}$ G $\xrightarrow{+3}$ J $\xrightarrow{+4}$ N

E $\xrightarrow{+1}$ F $\xrightarrow{+1}$ G $\xrightarrow{+1}$ H $\xrightarrow{+1}$ I

2 $\xrightarrow{\times 2}$ 4 $\xrightarrow{\times 2}$ 8 $\xrightarrow{\times 2}$ 16 $\xrightarrow{\times 2}$ 32

∴ ? = N I 32

40. (*b*)The pattern of the series is

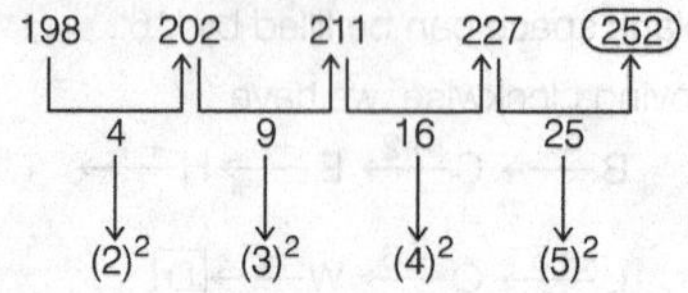

41. (*b*) The pattern of the series is

A $\xrightarrow{+1}$ B $\xrightarrow{+1}$ C $\xrightarrow{+1}$ D $\xrightarrow{+1}$ E

N $\xrightarrow{+1}$ O $\xrightarrow{+1}$ P $\xrightarrow{+1}$ Q $\xrightarrow{+1}$ R

Solution (Q. Nos.42-44) Following can be drawn from the given information

	Shirts			Pants		
	Black	Blue	Orange	Green	Yellow	Orange
Surinder	✗	✗	✔	✗	✔	✗
Varinder	✔	✗	✗	✗	✗	✔
Joginder	✗	✔	✗	✔	✗	✗

42. (*c*) Joginder wore pant and shirt of green and blue colour, respectively.

43. (*c*) Varinder wore shirt of black colour.

44. (*c*) Surinder wore pant of yellow colour.

45. (*c*) The alphabets in increasing order and the numbers in decreasing order from J to Q as shown below

J	K	L	M	N	O	P	Q
↓	↓	↓	↓	↓	↓	↓	↓
8	7	6	5	4	3	2	1

Now, by direct substitution method,

P	N	L	J	then,	Q	O	K	L
↓	↓	↓	↓		↓	↓	↓	↓
8	6	4	2		1	3	7	6

46. (*a*) nee tim see → who is it

ble nee see → where is it

ble see tee → where is what

So, the code for 'who is where' would be 'tim ble see'.

47. (*c*) Since, B and D are twins, so B = D.

Now, A = B + 3 and A = C − 3

Thus, B + 3 = C − 3 D + 3 = C − 3

C − D = 6

48. (*c*) Let A and B started from point O.

A towards West and B towards East and atlast they reached N and Q, respectively.

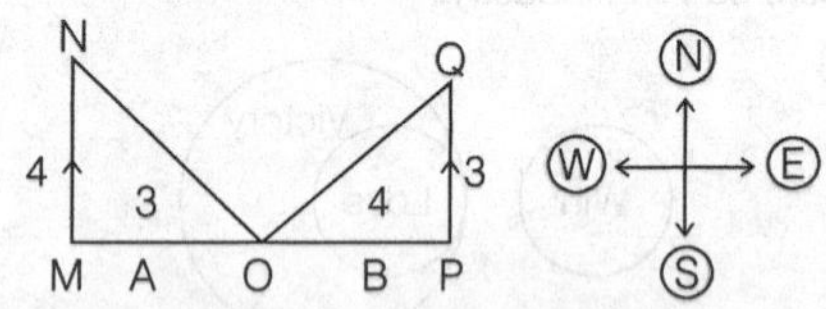

Distance of A from O,

$$ON = \sqrt{(OM)^2 + (MN)^2} = \sqrt{3^2 + 4^2} = 5 \text{ km}$$

Distance of B from O,

$$OQ = \sqrt{(OP)^2 + (PQ)^2} = \sqrt{4^2 + 3^2} = 5 \text{ km}$$

So, A and B are both at a distance of 5 km from the starting point.

49. (*a*) Word RICHES cannot be formed by using the letters of the given word because letter 'E' is not present in the given word.

50. (*b*) (1, 4), (2, 7), (3, 5) and (6, 8) are groups of identical figures.

PRACTICE SET 49

1. In the given figure, which letter represents those actors who are also dancers, singers as well as violinists? **[SSC (CGL) 2014]**

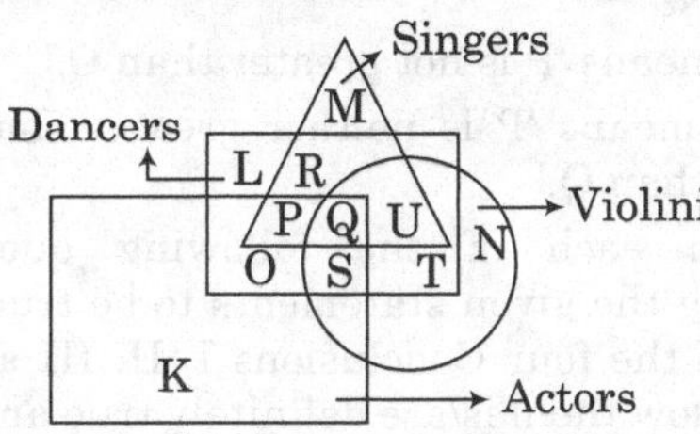

(a) S (b) Q (c) P (d) U

2. Arrange the following words in a sequence as would be found in the English dictionary. **[BSSC (CGL) 2015]**

(i) Banquet (ii) Bangle
(iii) Bandage (iv) Bantam
(v) Bangalore

(a) (iii), (ii), (iv), (v), (i)
(b) (iii), (v), (ii), (i), (iv)
(c) (iii), (ii), (i), (v), (iv)
(d) (iii), (ii), (v), (i), (iv)

Direction (Q. Nos. 3-4) *These questions consists of a question and two statements numbered I and II given below it. You have to decide whether the data provided in the statements are sufficient to answer the questions.*

Give answer **[NICL (AO) 2015]**

(a) if the data in both the Statements I and II together are necessary to answer the question
(b) if the data neither in Statement I nor in Statement II are sufficient to answer the question
(c) if the data either in Statement I alone or in Statement II alone are sufficient to answer the question
(d) if the data in Statement II alone are sufficient to answer the question, while the data in Statement I alone are not sufficient to answer the question
(e) if the data in Statement I alone are sufficient to answer the question, while the data in Statement II alone are not sufficient to answer the question

3. How is 'cost' written in the given code language?

I. In the code language, 'tell me the cost' is coded as '@ 0 # 9' and 'cost was very high' is coded as '& 6 # 1'.

II. In the code language, 'some cost was discount' is coded as '1 8 7 #' and 'some people like discount' is coded as '8 7 5 %'.

4. Is D the mother of S?

I. L is the husband of D. L has only three children.

II. N is the brother of S and P. P is the daughter of L.

Direction (Q. Nos. 5-6) *Study the following information carefully and answer the given questions.*

A word and number arrangement machine, when given an input line of words and numbers rearranges them following a particular rule in each step. The following is an illustration of an input and rearrangement.

Input 17 put show on 39 27 85 gold
***Step* I** show 17 put on 39 27 85 gold
***Step* II** show 85 17 put on 39 27 gold
***Step* III** show 85 put 17 on 39 27 gold
***Step* IV** show 85 put 39 17 on 27 gold
***Step* V** show 85 put 39 on 17 27 gold
***Step* VI** show 85 put 39 on 27 17 gold
***Step* VII** show 85 put 39 on 27 gold 17

and Step VII is the last step of the rearrangement of the above input.

As per the rules followed in the above steps, find out in each of the following questions the appropriate step for the given input.

5. **Input** glass full 15 37 water now 85 67

Which of the following will be Step VI of the above input?

(a) water 85 now 67 full glass 15 37
(b) water 85 now 67 glass full 15 37
(c) water 85 now 67 glass 37 full 15
(d) There will be no such step
(e) None of the above

6. Step II of an input is 'ultra 73 12 16 mail sort 39 kite'.

Which of the following steps will be the last but one?

(a) VIII (b) IX (c) VII (d) VI
(e) None of these

7. The ratio of the age of a father to that of his son is 5 : 2. If the product of their ages is 1000, then the father's age after 10 yr will be

(a) 50 yr (b) 60 yr (c) 80 yr (d) 100 yr

8. In the question below is given a statement followed by two assumptions numbered I and II. An assumption is something supposed or taken for granted. You have to consider the statement and the following assumptions and decide which of the assumption(s) is/are implicit in the statement.

Statement 'Our bank provides all your banking requirements in one location', an advertisement of a bank.

Assumptions

I. Customers prefer to carry out all banking transactions at one place.
II. People may get attracted by the advertisement and carry out their transactions with the bank.

(a) if only Assumption I is implicit
(b) if only Assumption II is implicit
(c) if either Assumption I or II is implicit
(d) if neither Assumption I nor II is implicit
(e) if both Assumptions I and II are implicit.

9. A statement/group of statements is given followed by two conclusions. Choose the conclusion which logically follows from the given statements.

Statements

The constitution assures the fundamental rights.

Parliament has right to amend the constitution. **[SSC (CGL) 2013]**

Conclusions

I. Parliament included fundamental rights in the constitution.
II. Parliament did not assure the fundamental rights.

(a) Only Conclusion I follows
(b) Only Conclusion II follows
(c) Both Conclusion I and II follow
(d) None of the above

Direction (Q. Nos. 10-12) *In the following questions, the symbols @, $, #, © and % are used with the following meaning as illustrated below :*

'P $ Q' means 'P is not smaller than Q.'

'P © Q' means 'P is neither greater than nor equal to Q.'

'P # Q' means 'P is neither smaller than nor equal to Q.'

'P % Q' means 'P is not greater than Q.'

'P @ Q' means 'P is neither greater than nor smaller than Q.'

Now, in each of the following questions assuming the given statements to be true, find which of the four Conclusions I, II, III and IV given below them is/are definitely true and give your answer accordingly. **[IBPS (SO) 2012]**

10. Statements R # J, J $ D, D @ K, K % T

Conclusions I. T # D
II. T @ D
III. R # K
IV. J $ T

(a) Either I or II is true
(b) Only III is true
(c) III and IV are true
(d) Either I or II and III are true
(e) None of the above

11. Statement T % R, R $ M, M @ D, D © H

Conclusions I. D % R
II. H # R
III. T ©M
IV. T % D

(a) Only I is true
(b) I and IV are true
(c) I and II are true
(d) II and IV are true
(e) None of the above

12. Statements M @ B, B # N, N $ R, R © K

Conclusions I. K # B
II. R © B
III. M $ R
IV. N © M

(a) I and III are true
(b) I and II are true
(c) II and IV are true
(d) II, III and IV are true
(e) None of the above

Direction (Q. Nos. 13-14) *In each question below are two or three statements followed by two conclusions numbered* I *and* II. *You have to take the two given statements to be true even if they seem to be at variance from commonly known facts and then decide which of the given conclusions logically follows from the given statements disregarding commonly known facts.*

Give answer **[LIC (ADO) 2015]**

(a) if only Conclusion I follows
(b) if only Conclusion II follows
(c) if either Conclusion I or II follows
(d) if neither Conclusion I nor II follows
(e) if both Conclusions I and II follow

13. Statements All kites are balls.
Some balls are toys.
Some toys are pebbles.

Conclusions I. No pebble is a kite.
II. All toys being kites is a possibility.

14. Statements Some clocks are watches.
All watches are lights.
No light is a fan.

Conclusions I. All watches are fans.
II. Some fans are clocks.

15. If ROAD = 152 and MAP = 90, then RAIL = ? **[FCI (Assistant) Grade III 2015]**

(a) 120 (b) 140 (c) 160 (d) 180

16. There are two statements labelled as Assertion (A) and Reason (R). Choose the correct alternative from the given options.

Assertion (A) Indian President is the head of the state.

Reason (R) Indian Parliament consists of the President, Lok Sabha and Rajya Sabha.

(a) if both A and R are true and R is the correct explanation of A
(b) if both A and R are true but R is not the correct explanation of A
(c) if A is true but R is false
(d) if A is false but R is true
(e) if both A and R are false

17. Cause There has been incessant rain during the last 48 h.

Which of the following can be a possible effect for the cause mentioned above?

I. Transport system of the city has completely failed from last 48 h.
II. There is flood like situation in most down town areas of the city.
III. So many slum dwellers have been shifted to municipal schools.

(a) Both I and II (b) Both II and III
(c) Both I and III (d) All I, II and III

18. If in a certain code 'DICKINSON' is written as '357950210' and 'DIPP' is written as 3566, then how can 'PICNIC' be written in the same code? **[BSSC (CGL) 2015]**

(a) 650757 (b) 657057
(c) 657507 (d) 560757

Direction (Q. Nos. 19-20) *Following questions are based on the five three-digit numbers given below.*

528 739 846 492 375

19. Which of the following represents the sum of the first two-digits of the highest number?

(a) 7 (b) 10
(c) 12 (d) 13
(e) None of these

20. If the positions of the first and the second digits of each number are interchanged, then which of the following will be third digit of the second lowest number?

(a) 8 (b) 9 (c) 6 (d) 2
(e) 5

21. A solid cube is divided into 27 smaller cubes of equal volume. If two opposite faces of this bigger cube are painted with different colours and remaining faces are left unpainted, then how many smaller cubes are obtained which have no faces painted?

(a) 1 (b) 9 (c) 27 (d) 36

Direction (Q. Nos. 22-24) *Study the given information carefully and answer the questions.*

Each of the six people A, B, C, D, E and F buys different number of shirts. C buys more shirts than only F and D. A buys more number of shirts than F but less than E. E does not buy the maximum number of shirts. D does not buy the least number of shirts. The one who have the maximum number of shirts buys 15 shirts. The one who buys the second least number of shirts buys 4 shirts. A buys five more shirts than D. **[SBI (SO) IT 2016]**

22. Which of the following may represent the number of shirts bought by C?
(a) 7 (b) 3 (c) 9 (d) 11
(e) 13

23. If the number of shirts bought by E is a number which is divisible by 3, then how many shirts does E buy?
(a) 3 (b) 9
(c) 6 (d) 15
(e) 12

24. Who amongst the following buys the second highest number of shirts?
(a) A (b) E
(c) C (d) D
(e) B

Direction (Q. Nos. 25-26) *In the following questions, find the odd letters/number pair from the given alternatives.*

25. (a) C9F (b) H20L
(c) N31Q (d) E29Y

26. (a) 21 : 24 (b) 28 : 32
(c) 14 : 16 (d) 54 : 62

27. A piece of paper is folded and cut as shown below in the question figures. From the given answer figures, indicates how will appear when opened?

Question Figures

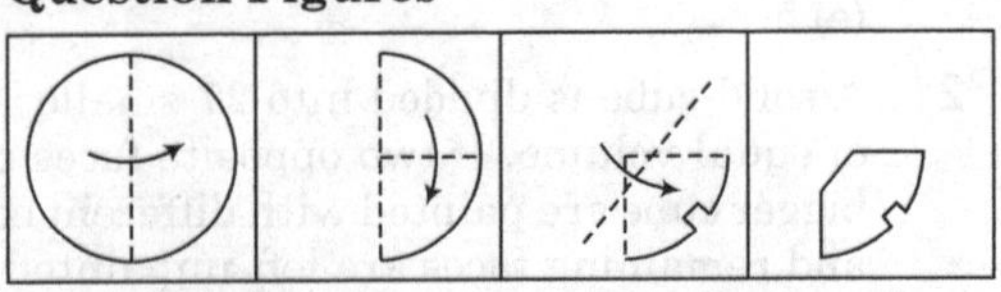

Answer Figures

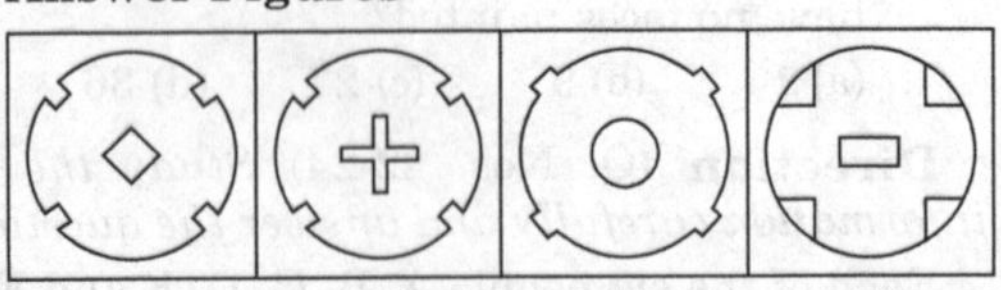

(a) (b) (c) (d)

28. Which of the following figure can be made with given broken figures below?

Question Figure **[SSC (CGL) 2012]**

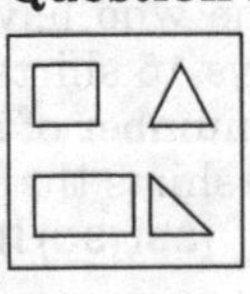

Answer Figures

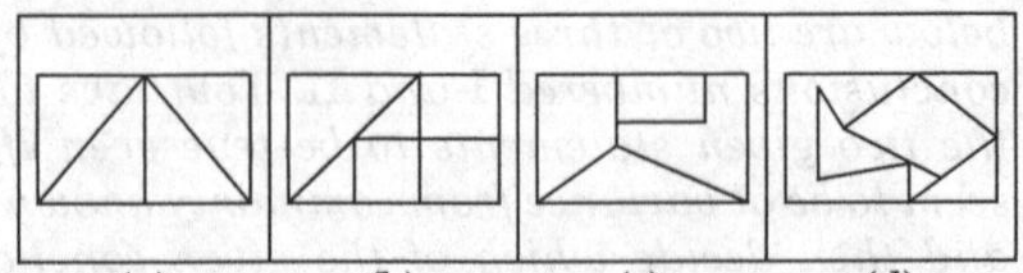

(a) (b) (c) (d)

29. If 'lily' is called 'Lotus', 'Lotus' is called 'Rose', 'Rose' is called 'Sunflower' and 'Sunflower' is called 'Marigold' the which will be the national flower of India?
(a) Lily (b) Lotus
(c) Rose (d) Sunflower

Direction (Q. Nos. 30-32) *Study the following information to answer the given questions.*

P, Q, R, S, T, V, X and Y are seated in a straight line facing North. P sits fourth to the left of V. V sits either sixth from the left end of the line or fourth from the right end of the line. S sits second to right of R. R is not an immediate neighbour of V. T and Q are immediate neighbours of each other but neither T nor Q sits at extreme ends of the line. Only one person sits between T and X. X does not sit at the extreme end of the line.

30. What is the position of Q with respect to P?
(a) Fifth to the right
(b) Immediate neighbour
(c) Second to right
(d) Third to left
(e) None of the above

31. Which of the following represents persons seated at the two extreme ends of the line?
(a) P, V (b) Y, S (c) R, V (d) Y, P
(e) R, Y

32. How many persons are seated between R and T?
(a) One (b) Two (c) Three (d) Four
(e) None of these

33. A clock is started at noon. By 10 min past 5, the hour hand has turned through.
(a) 145° (b) 150° (c) 155° (d) 160°

34. In a garden, there are 10 rows and 12 columns of mango trees. The distance between the two trees is 2 m and a distance of 1m is left from all sides of the boundary of the garden. The length of the garden is
(a) 20 m (b) 22 m (c) 24 m (d) 26 m

35. X and Y are brothers. R is the father of Y. S is the brother of T and maternal uncle of X. What is T to R?

(a) Mother (b) Wife
(c) Sister (d) Brother

36. How many squares are there in the figure given below? **[CMAT 2014]**

(a) 4 (b) 5 (c) 6 (d) 7

37. If three days before yesterday was Wednesday, then what will be two days after tomorrow?

(a) Wednesday (b) Monday
(c) Friday (d) Tuesday

38. Sharada started to move in the direction of South. After moving 15 m, she turned to her left twice and moved 15 m each time. Now, how far is she and in which direction from her starting point? **[SSC (CGL) 2014]**

(a) 20 m, West (b) 15 m, East
(c) 15 m, South (d) 30 m, East

39. Select the missing number from the given responses.

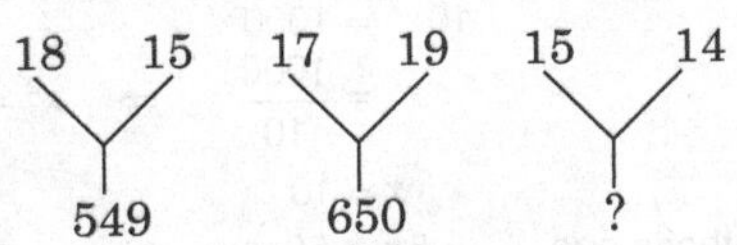

(a) 210 (b) 225
(c) 196 (d) 421

40. If + means 'minus', – means 'multiplied by', ÷ means 'plus' and × means 'divided by', then

$$10 \times 5 \div 3 - 2 + 3 = ?$$

(a) 5 (b) 21
(c) $\frac{53}{3}$ (d) 18

41. Kamal remembers that his brother Dinu's birthday falls after 20th May but before 28th May, while Garima remembers that Dinu's birthday falls before 22nd May but after 12th May. On what date Dinu's birthday falls?

(a) 22nd May
(b) 21st May
(c) Cannot be determined
(d) None of the above

42. In a row of boys, Jeevan is 7th from the start and 11th from the end. In another row of boys, Vikas is 10th from the start and 12th from the end. How many boys are there in both the rows together?

(a) 38
(b) 40
(c) 32
(d) Cannot be determined
(e) None of the above

43. Which one set of letters when sequentially placed at the gaps in the given letters series shall complete it?

nc_dcn_cddc_n_ddcnn_d

(a) cdndc (b) dnncc
(c) dcndd (d) nccdn

Direction (Q. Nos. 44-46) *In the following questions, a series is given with one term missing. Choose the correct alternative from the given ones that will complete the series.* **[SSC (10+2) 2015]**

44. 1, 16, 81, 256, 625, ?

(a) 1225 (b) 4163
(c) 2225 (d) 1296

45. 1, 5, 13, 25, 41, 61, ?

(a) 85 (b) 81
(c) 77 (d) 91

46. EZ, FY, XG ?

(a) WH (b) GW (c) WG (d) HW

47. Find out which of the answer figures (a), (b), (c) and (d) completes the figure matrix?

Question Figure

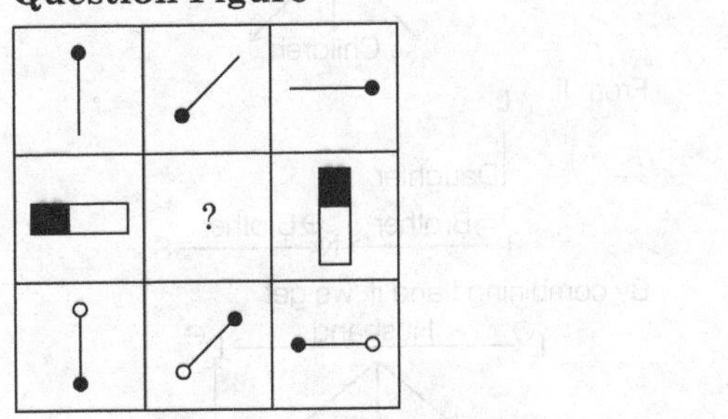

Answer Figures

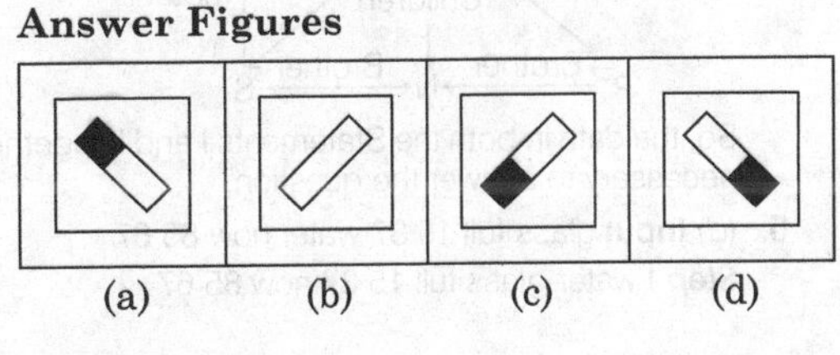

(a) (b) (c) (d)

Direction (Q. Nos. 48-50) *In the following questions, select the related word/letters/number pair from the given alternatives.*

48. Given set (8, 3, 2)
(a) (10, 6, 5)
(b) (63, 8, 3)
(c) (95, 24, 5)
(d) (168, 15, 4)

49. ACEG : ZXVT :: HJLM : ?
(a) QOMK (b) SRPO
(c) RPNL (d) SQON
(e) None of these

50. Fodder : Cattle :: ?
(a) Pen : Ink (b) Ball : Stick
(c) Fruit : Juice (d) Grass : Horse

Hints and Solutions

1. (*b*) From figure, rectangle, small rectangle, triangle and circle represent actors, dancers, singers and violinists, respectively. It is evident that only Q falls in all the above four figures.

2. (*b*) (iii) Bandage → (v) Bangalore → (ii) Bangle → (i) Banquet → (iv) Bantam
So, (iii), (v), (ii), (i) and (iv) would be found in the English dictionary.

3. (*e*) From I,
tell me the cost → @ 0 # 9
cost was very high → & 6 # 1
So, the code for cost is #.
From II,
Some cost was discount → 1 8 7 #
Some people like discount → 8 7 5 %
So, here the code for cost either 1 or #.
So, only data in Statement I alone are sufficient to answer the question.

4. (*a*) From I,

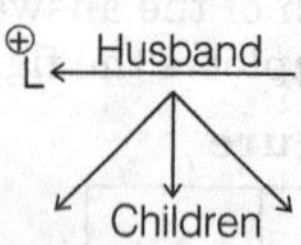

From II,

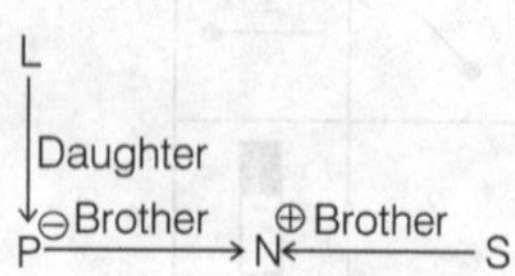

By combining I and II, we get

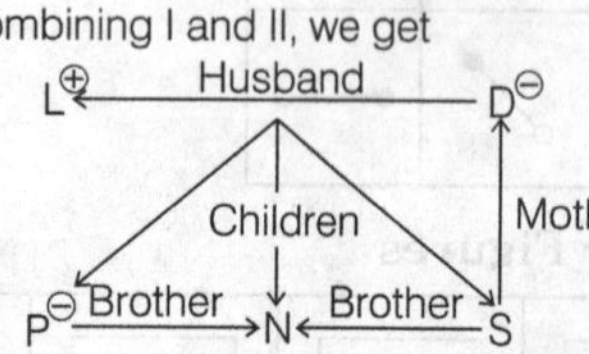

So, the data in both the Statements I and II together are necessary to answer the question.

5. (*d*) **Input** glass full 15 37 water now 85 67
***Step* I** water glass full 15 37 now 85 67
***Step* II** water 85 glass full 15 37 now 67
***Step* III** water 85 now glass full 15 37 67
***Step* IV** water 85 now 67 glass full 15 37
***Step* V** water 85 now 67 glass 37 full 15
Step V is the last step and Step VI is not possible.

6. (*d*) ***Step* II** ultra 73 12 16 mail sort 39 kite
***Step* III** ultra 73 sort 12 16 mail 39 kite
***Step* IV** ultra 73 sort 39 12 16 mail kite
***Step* V** ultra 73 sort 39 mail 12 16 kite
***Step* VI** ultra 73 sort 39 mail 16 12 kite
***Step* VII** ultra 73 sort 39 mail 16 kite 12
So, last step is Step VII and last but one step is Step VI.

7. (*b*) Let the father's age be $5x$ yr and his son's age be $2x$ yr.
∴ Product of their age $= 5x \times 2x = 1000$
$\Rightarrow \quad 10x^2 = 1000$
$x^2 = \frac{1000}{10} \quad \Rightarrow \quad x^2 = 100$
$\Rightarrow \quad x = 10$
∴ Father's age $= 5x = 50$ yr
and son's age $= 2x = 20$ yr
After 10 yr, father's age = 50 + 10 = 60 yr.

8. (*e*) Both the assumptions are implicit in the statement. The point which is highlighted in any advertisement is liked by people.

9. (*d*) From the given two statements, it is not clear whether the parliament can assure the fundamental rights or not.

Solution (Q. Nos. 10-12)

$ ⇒ ≥	© ⇒ <	# ⇒ >	% ⇒ ≤	@ ⇒ =

10. (*d*) R # J ⇒ R > J
J $ D ⇒ J ≥ D
D @ K ⇒ D = K
K % T ⇒ K ≤ T
Therefore, R > J ≥ D = K ≤ T

Conclusions I. T # D ⇒ T > D (May be)
II. T @ D ⇒ T = D (May be)
III. R # K ⇒ R > K (True)
IV. J $ T ⇒ J ≥ T (Not true)

Conclusions I and II form complementary pair.
So, either Conclusion I or II and Conclusion III are true.

11. (*a*) T % R ⇒ T ≤ R, R $ M ⇒ R ≥ M
M @ D ⇒ M = D, D © H ⇒ D < H

Therefore, T ≤ R ≥ M = D < H

Conclusions I. D % R ⇒ D ≤ R (True)
II. H # R ⇒ H > R (Not true)
III. T © M ⇒ T < M (Not true)
IV. T % D ⇒ T ≤ D (Not true)

So, Conclusion I is true.

12. (*c*) M @ B ⇒ M = B, B # N ⇒ B > N
N $ R ⇒ N ≥ R, R © K ⇒ R < K

Therefore, M = B > N ≥ R < K

Conclusions I. K # B ⇒ K > B (Not true)
II. R © B ⇒ R < B (True)
III. M $ R ⇒ M ≥ R (Not true)
IV. N © M ⇒ N < M (true)

So, Conclusion II and IV are true.

13. (*b*)

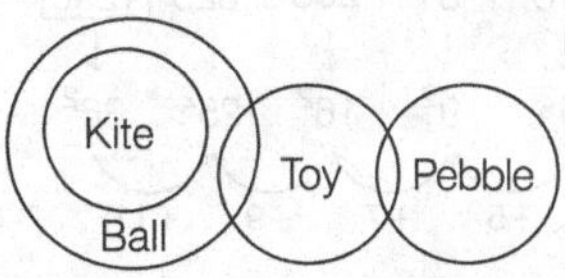

Conclusions I. No pebble is a kite. (✗)
II. All toys being kites is a possibility. (✔)

Therefore, only Conclusion II follows.

14. (*d*)

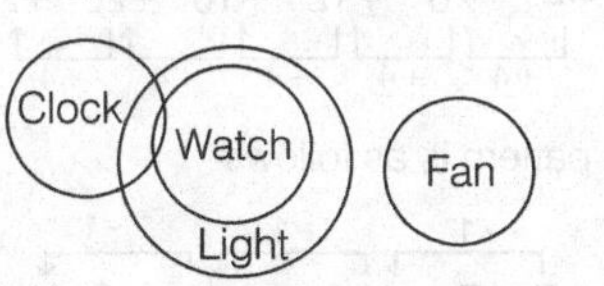

Conclusions I. All watches are fans. (✗)
II. Some fans are clocks. (✗)

Therefore, neither Conclusion I nor II follows.

15. (*c*) As, ROAD → 18 + 15 + 1 + 4 = 38
38 → 38 × 4 = 152
because four letters are there in word ROAD.
and MAP → 13 + 1 + 16 = 30
30 → 30 × 3 = 90
because three letters are there in word MAP.
Same as, RAIL → 18 + 1 + 9 + 12 = 40
40 → 40 × 4 = 160
because four letters are there in word RAIL.

16. (*b*) Both A and R are true. Indian President is the constitutional or titular head of the executive, the real power being vested in the Council of Ministers.

17. (*d*) I, II and III all the three can be the possible effects.

18. (*b*) As,

D I C K I N S O N
↓ ↓ ↓ ↓ ↓ ↓ ↓ ↓ ↓
3 5 7 9 5 0 2 1 0

and

D I P P
↓ ↓ ↓ ↓
3 5 6 6

By direct substitution method, we get

P I C N I C
↓ ↓ ↓ ↓ ↓ ↓
6 5 7 0 5 7

19. (*c*) Highest number = 846
∴ Sum of the first two digits of
846 = 8 + 4 = 12

20. (*b*) According to the question,

Original number 5 2 8 7 3 9 8 4 6 4 9 2 3 7 5

Rearrangement 2 5 8 3 7 ⑨ 4 8 6 9 4 2 7 3 5

↑ 2nd lowest

∴ Third digit of 3 7 ⑨ = 9.

21. (*b*) Total number of smaller cubes = 27
Clearly, cubes in middle layer are unpainted.
∴ Smaller cubes in middle layer $= \frac{27}{3} = 9$

Solution (Q. Nos. 22-24) According to the given information

B > E > A > C > D > F
15 9 4

22. (*a*) C buys more than 4 shirts and less than 9 shirts. So, from the given alternatives, C buys 7 shirts.

23. (*e*) E buys 12 shirts.

24. (*b*) E buys the second highest number of shirts.

25. (*d*) In all other group of words, numeric component in between the first and second letters is the sum of positions of first and last letters in the alphabet.

26. (*d*) The ratio among the number is 7 : 8.

27. (*a*) After cut the paper will appear as figure (a).

28. (*b*) Option figure (b) can be made with given broken figures.

29. (*e*) We know that, national flower of India is Lotus and here, Lotus is called Rose.

Solution (Q. Nos. 30-32) According to the given information, the final arrangement is as following.

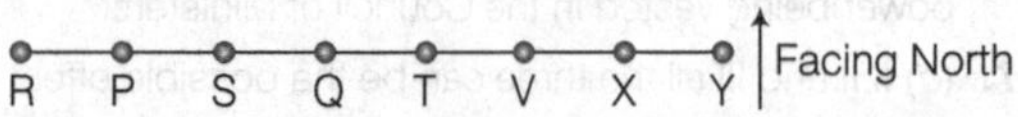

30. (*c*) Q is second to the right of P.

31. (*e*) R and Y are sitting on the extreme ends of line.

32. (*c*) Three persons P, S and Q are seated between R and T.

33. (*c*) Angle traced by hour hand in 12 h = 360°.

Angle traced by hour hand in 5 h 10 min, i.e. $\frac{31}{6}$ h

$$= \left(\frac{360}{12} \times \frac{31}{6}\right)^{\circ} = 155°$$

34. (*c*) Each row contains 12 plants.

There are 11 gapes between the two corners trees (11×2) m and 1 m on each side is left.

Therefore, length = (22 + 2) m $\Rightarrow$ 24 m.

35. (*b*) Following family diagram can be drawn from the given information,

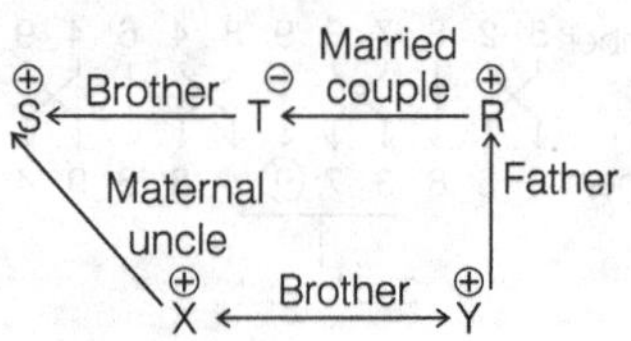

Now, it is clear that T is the wife of R.

36. (*d*) It is clear from the figure that there are 7 squares in the figure.

☐ EPOQ, ☐ FPOS, ☐ QORG, ☐ ORHS, ☐ ABCD, ☐ PQRS and ☐ EGHF.

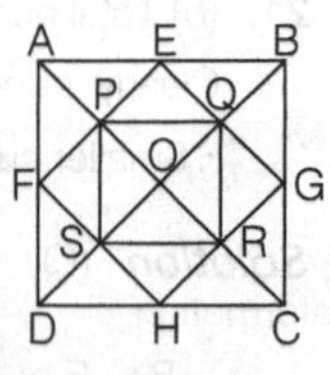

37. (*a*) Today is Wednesday + 4 = Sunday

Two days after tomorrow = Sunday + 3 = Wednesday

38. (*b*) Let Sharada starts from point A and passing through paints B and C and she reaches at point D.

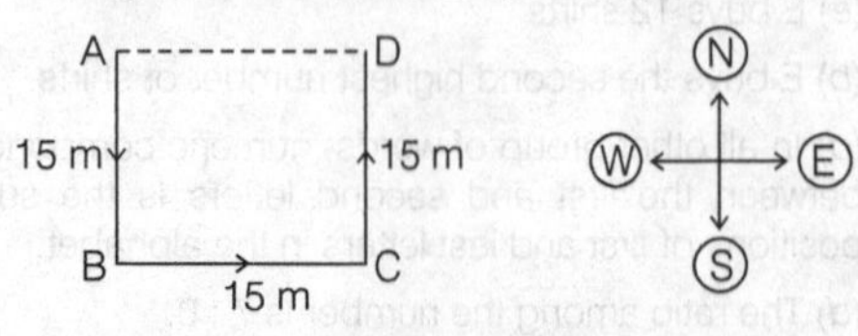

Clearly, she is in East and at a distance of 15 m from her original position.

39. (*d*) As, $(18)^2 + (15)^2 = 324 + 225 = 549$

and $(17)^2 + (19)^2 = 289 + 361 = 650$

Similarly, $(15)^2 + (14)^2 = 225 + 196 = 421$

40. (*a*) According to the question, we can arrange the given mathematical symbols as

$$+ = -,\ - = \times \qquad \div = +,\ \times = \div$$

$\Rightarrow$ $10 \times 5 \div 3 - 2 + 3 = ?$

$\Rightarrow$ $? = 10 \div 5 + 3 \times 2 - 3$

$\Rightarrow$ $? = 2 + 6 - 3 = 5$

41. (*b*) According to Kamal, Dinu's birthday falls on one of the days – 21st, 22nd, 23rd, 24th, 25th, 26th or 27th May.

According to Garima, Dinu's birthday falls on one of the days 13th, 14th, 15th, 16th, 17th, 18th, 19th, 20th or 21st May.

Clearly, Dinu's birthday falls on 21st May.

42. (*a*) Total number of boys

= (Number of boys in Jeevan's row) + (Number of boys in Vikas's row)

$= (6 + 1 + 10) + (9 + 1 + 11) = (17 + 21) = 38$

43. (*b*) The complete letter series will be

n c d d c n/ n c d d c n/ n c d d c n/ n c d

$\Rightarrow$ dnncc

44. (*d*) The pattern is as follows

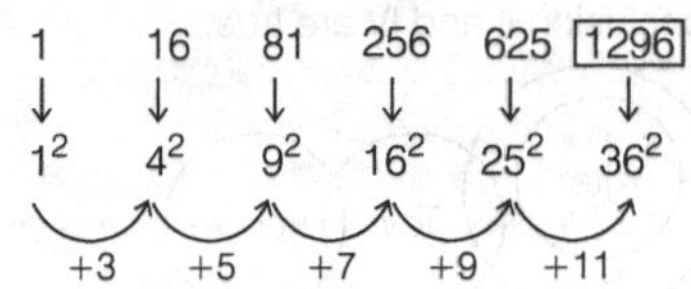

45. (*a*) The pattern is as follows

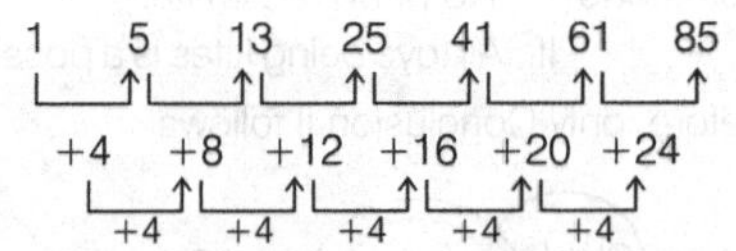

46. (*a*) The pattern is as follows

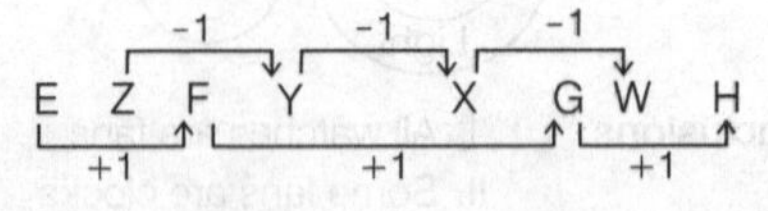

47. (*d*) In each row, the second figure is obtained by rotating the first figure 135° anti-clockwise.

48. (*b*) Here,

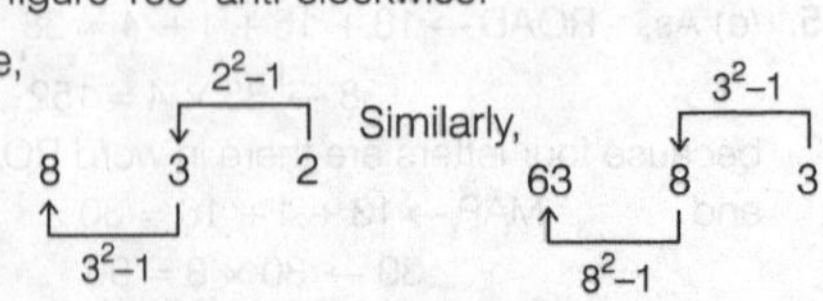

49. (*d*) Here, opposite letter is english alphabetical order is given of each letter.

50. (*d*) 'Fodder' is food for 'Cattle' in the same way 'Grass' is food for 'Horse'.

PRACTICE SET 50

Direction (Q. Nos. 1-3) *In the following questions, a series is given with one term missing. Choose the correct alternative from the given ones that will complete the series.* **[SSC (10+2) 2014]**

1. 25, 35, 55, ?, 125
(a) 65 (b) 75 (c) 85 (d) 95

2. 7, 8, 18, 57, ?, 1165
(a) 174 (b) 232
(c) 224 (d) 228

3. CE, GI, KM, OQ, ?
(a) TW (b) TV (c) SU (d) RT

4. A and B are brother and sister, respectively. C is A's father, D is C's sister and E is D's mother. How is B related to E?
(a) Granddaughter
(b) Great granddaughter
(c) Aunt
(d) Daughter

5. Find out which of the answer figures will complete the pattern in the question figure? **[SSC (CGL) 2014]**

Question Figure **Answer Figures**

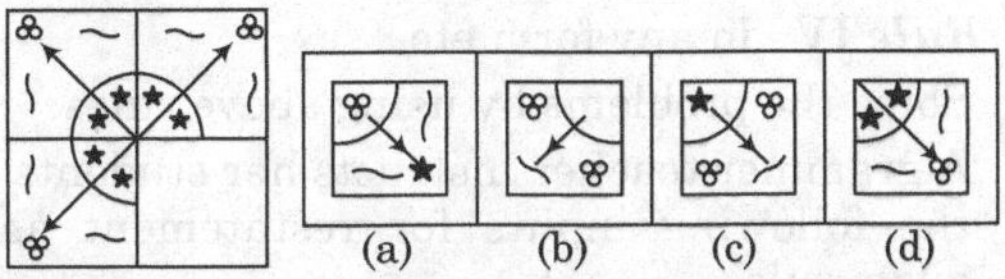

Direction (Q. Nos. 6-7) *Study the following information to answer the given questions.*

Twelve people are sitting in two parallel rows containing six people each, in such a way that there is an equal distance between adjacent persons. In row 1, P, Q, R, S, T and V are seated and all of them are facing South. In row 2, A, B, C, D, E and F are seated and all of them are facing North. Therefore, in the given seating arrangement each member seated in a row faces another member of the other row.

A sits third to right of D. Neither A nor D sits at extreme ends. T faces D. V does not face A and V does not sit at any of the extreme ends. V is not an immediate neighbour of T. B sits at one of the extreme ends. Only two people sit between B and E. E does not face V. Two persons sit between R and Q. R is not an immediate neighbour of T. C does not face V. P is not an immediate neighbour of R.

6. Who amongst the following sit at extreme ends of the rows?
(a) B, E (b) S, T (c) P, R (d) B, F
(e) None of these

7. Who amongst the following faces A?
(a) R (b) T (c) P (d) Q
(e) S

8. A tailor had a number of shirt piece to cut from a roll of fabric. He cut each roll of equal length into 10 pieces. He cut at the rate of 45 cuts a minute. How many rolls would be cut in 24 min?
(a) 32 rolls (b) 54 rolls
(c) 108 rolls (d) 120 rolls

Direction (Q. Nos. 9-10) *In the following questions, the symbols @, #, %, $ and © are used with the following meaning as illustrated below:*

'P # Q' means 'P is neither greater than nor equal to Q'.

'P © Q' means 'P is neither equal to nor smaller than Q'.

'P % Q' means 'P is neither smaller than nor greater than Q'.

'P $ Q' means 'P is not smaller than Q'.

'P @ Q' means 'P is not greater than Q'.

Now, in each of the following questions assuming the given statements to be true, find which of the three Conclusions I, II and III given below them is/are definitely true and give your answer accordingly.

9. Statements R @ D, D © W, B $ W
Conclusions I. W# R
II. B © D III. W $ R
(a) None is true
(b) Only Conclusion I is true
(c) Only Conclusion III is true
(d) Either Conclusion I or III is true
(e) All are true

10. **Statements** H $ V, V % M, K © M
Conclusion I. K © V
II. M @ H III. H © K
(a) Conclusions I and III are true
(b) Conclusions II and III are true
(c) Conclusions I and II are true
(d) All are true
(e) None of the above

11. If L denotes ×, M denotes ÷, P denotes + and Q denotes –, then find the value of
16 P 24 M 8 Q 6 M 2 L 3 = ?
[SSC (FCI) 2012]
(a) 6 (b) 8 (c) 10 (d) 12

12. During the last summer vacation, Ankit went to a summer camp where he took part in hiking, swimming and boating. This summer, he is looking forward to a music camp where he hopes to sing, dance and learn to play the guitar.
Based on the above information, four conclusions, as given below, have been made. Which one of these logically follows from the information given above?
(a) Ankit's parents want him to play the guitar
(b) Ankit prefers music to outdoor activities
(c) Ankit goes to some type of camp every summer
(d) Ankit likes to sing and dance

Direction (Q. Nos. 13-14) *In the following questions, select the related word/letters from the given alternatives.* **[SSC (10+2) 2015]**

13. Car : Garrage : : ? : Hangar
(a) Truck (b) Bus
(c) Train (d) Aeroplane

14. HIJK : GFED : : NOPQ : ?
(a) FDEC (b) MLKJ
(c) EFGH (d) BCDE

15. From the given answer figures, select the one in which question figure is hidden/embedded.
[SSC (CGL) 2014]

Question Figure **Answer Figures**

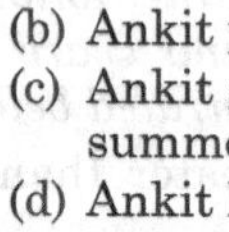

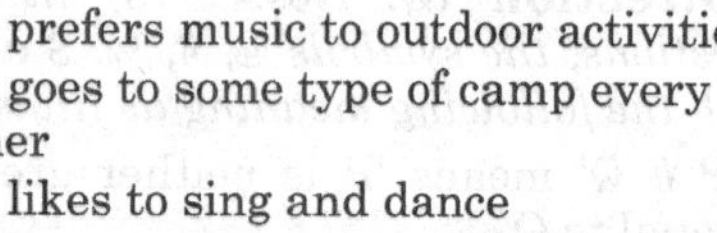

(a) (b) (c) (d)

16. Which one set of letters when sequentially placed at the gaps in the given letter series shall complete it?
r_se_os_ro_er_se
(a) o r e s o (b) r o r e s
(c) o e s r s (d) r o e s o

17. Arrange the following words as per order in the dictionary. **[SSC (10+2) 2015]**
(i) Plate (ii) Plane
(iii) Plaster (iv) Plasma
(v) Plastic
(a) (ii), (v), (iii), (iv), (i)
(b) (ii), (i), (v), (iii), (iv)
(c) (i), (ii), (iii), (iv), (v)
(d) (ii), (iv), (iii), (v), (i)

18. Which one of the following diagrams best depicts the relationship among tigers, lions and animals? **[SSC (FCI) 2012]**

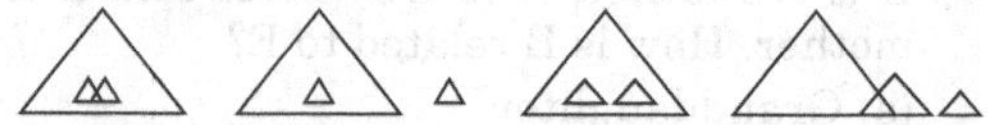

(a) (b) (c) (d)

Direction (Q. Nos. 19-20) *The following questions are based on grammatical rules.*

Input cigarette smoking is injurious to health
***Rule* I** follows smoking of rule
***Rule* II** cigarette when smoked
***Rule* III** due to
***Rule* IV** in any form etc.

Solve the problems by using above rules.
A grammer teacher instructs her students with the following inputs for restatement as per given rules.

Input cigarette smoking is injurious to health.
***Rule* I** smoking of cigarette is injurious to health
***Rule* II** cigarette when smoked injurious health
***Rule* III** health is injured due to smoking
***Rule* IV** smoking in any form is injurious to health.

As per rules dictated by the teacher, find out (as a student), the relevant step or the input, as asked in the given problems.

19. **Input** tobacco chewing is injurious for teeth. Which of the following rules is chewing of tobacco is injurious for teeth?
(a) II (b) III (c) I (d) IV
(e) None of these

20. Rule IV of an input is 'coachings in any form are beneficial for the students', what would be Rule I for the input?
(a) taking of coachings is beneficial to the students
(b) coachings when taken, benefit the student
(c) students are benefited due to coachings
(d) Data inadequate
(e) None of the above

21. Among the four answer figures, which figure can be formed from the cut-pieces given below in the question figure? **[SSC (CGL) 2014]**

Question Figure **Answer Figures**

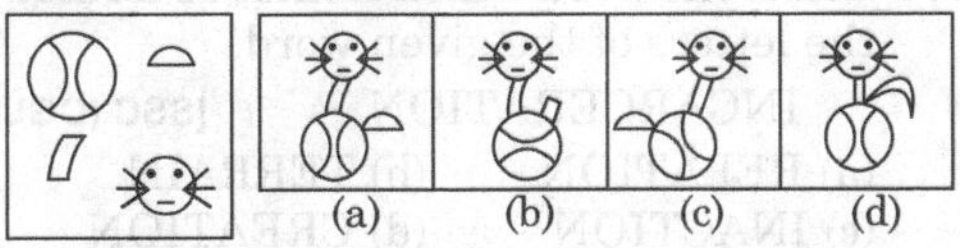

Direction (Q. Nos. 22-24) *Select the one which is different from other three alternatives.* **[SSC (CGL) 2014]**

22. (a) Rival (b) Opponent (c) Foe (d) Ally

23. (a) 27 (b) 35 (c) 18 (d) 9

24. (a) TUVX (b) OPRS (c) BCDF (d) HIJL

25. Raju ranks 10th from the top and Ravi ranks 21st from the bottom. If there are 3 students between them, then how many maximum students are there in the class?
(a) 34 (b) 33 (c) 31 (d) 32

26. How many triangles are there in the figure given below?

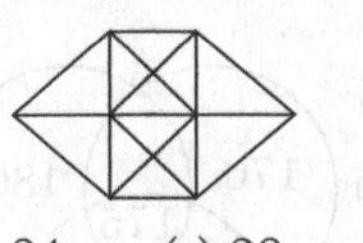

(a) 20 (b) 24 (c) 28 (d) 32

27. From the given four positions of a single dice, find the digit at the face opposite to the face having digit 6.

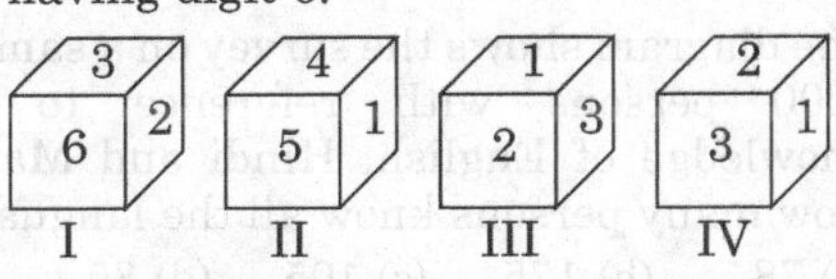

(a) 1 (b) 3 (c) 4 (d) 5

Direction (Q. Nos. 28-29) *Each of the questions below consists of a question and three statements numbered I, II and III given below it. You have to decide whether the data provided in the statements are sufficient to answer the question.*

28. How many daughters does P have?
I. B and D are sisters of M.
II. M's father T is husband of P.
III. Out of the three children which T has, only one is a boy.
(a) I and III
(b) All I, II and III are required
(c) II and III
(d) None is sufficient
(e) I and II

29. Who among A, B, C, D, E and F each having a different height, is the tallest?
I. B is taller than A but shorter than E.
II. Only two of them are shorter than C.
III. D is taller than only F.
(a) I and II
(b) I and III
(c) II and III
(d) All I, II and III are required
(e) None is sufficient

30. If 'LIBERALIZATION' is coded as 34256134918470, then 'AERATION' can be coded as
(a) 15168470 (b) 15186471
(c) 15618470 (d) 51618471

31. If the 1st of November falls on Monday, then what day will the 25th of November be?
(a) Tuesday (b) Thursday
(c) Wednesday (d) Friday

32. There are two statements labelled as Assertion (A) and Reason (R). Choose the correct alternative from the given options.
Assertion (A) Land breeze blows during night.
Reason (R) Land gets heated up quickly.
(a) if both A and R are true and R is the correct explanation of A
(b) if both A and R are true but R is not the correct explanation of A
(c) if A is true but R is false
(d) if A is false but R is true
(e) if both Aand R are false

33. If a mirror is placed on the line MN, then which of the answer figures is the right image of the given figure? **[BSSC (CGL) 2015]**

Question Figure **Answer Figures**

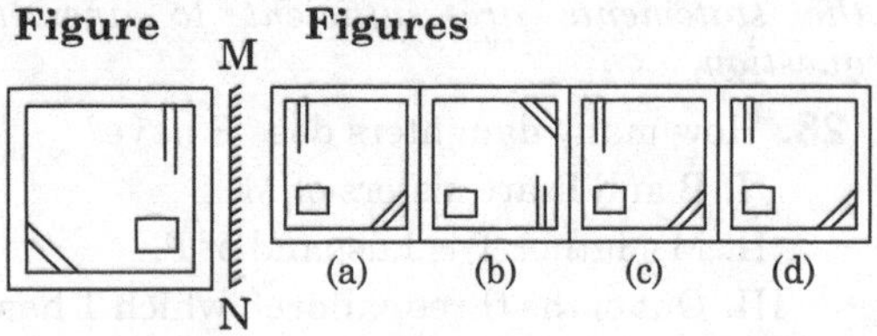

Direction (Q. Nos. 34-35) *In each of the question sets below are two/three statements followed by two conclusions numbered I and II. You have to take the given statements to be true even, if they seem to be at variance from commonly known facts and then decide which of the given conclusions logically follows from the given statements disregarding commonly known facts.*

Give answer

(a) if only Conclusion I follows
(b) if only Conclusion II follows
(c) if either Conclusion I or II follows
(d) if neither Conclusion I nor II follows
(e) if both Conclusions I and II follow

34. Statements Some symbols are figures.
All symbols are graphics.
No graphic is a picture. **[IBPS (PO) 2012]**

Conclusions I. Some graphics are figures.
II. No symbol is a picture.

35. Statements Some mobiles are telephones.
All telephones are pagers.
No pager is a camera.

Conclusions I. Some mobiles are definitely pagers.
II. No mobile is a camera.

36. A word is represented by only one set of numbers as given in anyone of the alternatives. The set of numbers given in the alternatives are represented by two classes of alphabets as in the two matrices given below. The columns and rows of Matrix I are from 0 to 4 and that of Matrix II from 5 to 9. A letter can be represented first by its row and next by its column number. e.g. C can be represented by 02, 21, etc. T can be represented by 65, 96 etc. Similarly, you have to identify the correct set for the word given in question.

Matrix I

	0	1	2	3	4
0	D	V	C	P	M
1	P	M	D	V	C
2	V	C	P	M	D
3	M	D	V	C	P
4	C	P	M	D	V

Matrix II

	5	6	7	8	9
5	S	A	U	T	J
6	T	J	S	A	U
7	A	U	T	J	S
8	J	S	A	U	T
9	U	T	J	S	A

PUMP

(a) 03, 69, 03, 54 (b) 41, 88, 23,02
(c) 10, 57, 23, 34 (d) 22, 95, 43,41

37. Select the word which cannot be formed using the letters of the given word.

INCARCERATION **[SSC (CGL) 2014]**

(a) RELATION (b) TERRAIN
(c) INACTION (d) CREATION

38. Select the word which can be formed using the letters of the given word.

ULTRANATIONALISM **[SSC (CPO) 2014]**

(a) ULTRAMONTANE
(b) ULTRAMODERN
(c) ULTRAIST
(d) ULULATE

39. Age of Nareen is equal to Naveen as they are twins. Nakul is younger than Nareen, Priyanka is younger than Balaji but elder than Naveen. Who is the eldest of all? **[SSC (10+2) 2012]**

(a) Nareen (b)Balaji
(c) Nakul (d) Naveen

Direction (Q. Nos.40-41) *Study the following diagram carefully and answer the questions based on it.* **[SSC (CGL) 2012]**

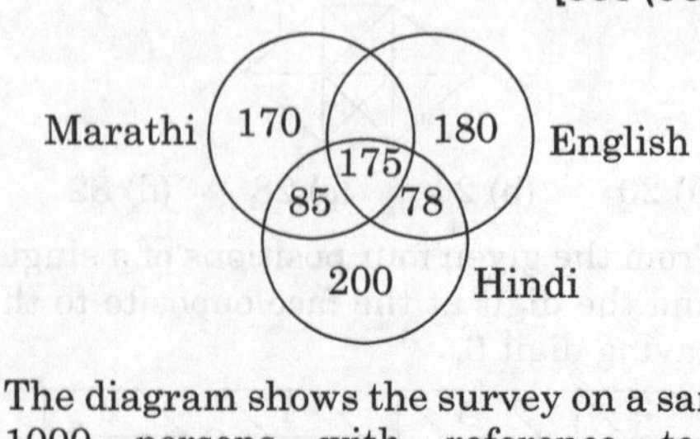

40. The diagram shows the survey on a sample of 1000 persons with reference to their knowledge of English, Hindi and Marathi. How many persons know all the languages ?

(a) 78 (b) 175 (c) 105 (d) 85

41. The diagram shows the survey on a sample of 1000 persons with reference to their knowledge of English, Hindi and Marathi. 78 people know...languages.

(a) Marathi, Hindi
(b) English, Hindi
(c) Marathi, English
(d) Hindi, Marathi, English

Direction (Q. Nos. 42-43) *Study the following information carefully to answer the given questions.*

Point P is 9 m towards the East of point Q. Point R is 5 m towards the South of point P. Point S is 3 m towards the West of point R. Point T is 5 m towards the North of point S. Point V is 7 m towards the South of point S.

42. If a person walks in a straight line for 8 m towards West from point R, then which of the following points would he cross the first?

(a) V (b) Q (c) T (d) S
(e) Cannot be determined

43. Which of the following points are in a straight line?

(a) P, R, V (b) S, T, Q (c) P, T, V (d) V, T, R
(e) S, V, T

Direction (Q. Nos. 44-45) *In the following questions, find the missing number from the given responses.*

44.

2	9	11	7
8	5	13	−3
7	?	10	−4
6	4	10	?

(a) 3 and (−2) (b) (−3) and (− 2)
(c) 3 and 2 (d) (− 3) and 2

45.

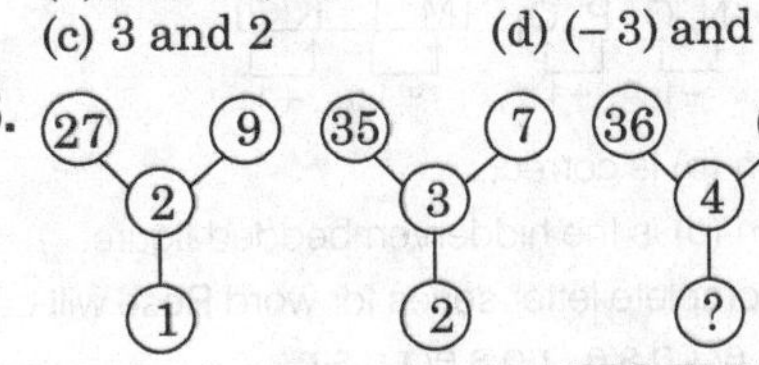

[SSC (Multitasking) 2013]

(a) 3 (b) 4 (c) 5 (d) 6

46. Vijay says, "Anand's mother is the only daughter of my mother". How is Anand related to Vijay?

(a) Brother (b) Father
(c) Nephew (d) Grandfather

Direction (Q. Nos. 47-49) *Study the following information and answer the given questions.*

A group of Management students visited the HR departments of five different orgnisations on five different days during a field study session. The first visit was on a Monday and the last visit was on the last day of the same week that is Sunday. Each visit was coordinated by a different student Pervez, Rajeev, Amit, Manish and Richa not necessarily in the same order.

The visit that was organised on Sunday was coordinated by Rajeev. The visit of Blue Dart was on Tuesday. The visit to the NGO- Tarang was coordinated by Manish and it was not on Saturday. The visit to Hotel Taj was neither on Friday nor Saturday and it was coordinated by Pervez. Amit coordinated the visit that was on Thursday. There was a holiday the day after the visit to Blue Dart. The visit to Aashirwad Plastics was before the visit to Group Pharmaceuticals.

47. Which of the following statements is true according to the given information?

(a) Richa organised the visit on Sunday
(b) There were two visits between the visit to Aashirwad Plastics and the visit to Group Pharmaceuticals
(c) There was one visit organised between the visit coordinated by Richa and the visit coordinated by Amit
(d) None is true

48. Visit to which of the following organisations was coordinated by Richa?

(a) Aashirwad Plastics
(b) Blue Dart
(c) Group Pharmaceuticals
(d) Cannot be determined

49. On which of the following days was the visit to Hotel Taj?

(a) Monday (b) Friday
(c) Saturday (d) Wednesday

50. Group the given figures into different classes on the basis of their orientation, shape etc.

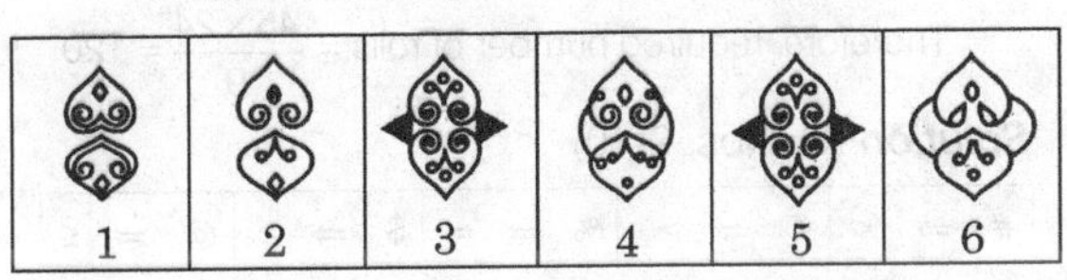

(a) (1, 3) (b) (3, 4) (c) (3, 5) (d) (4, 6)

Hints and Solutions

1. (c) In the given series, pattern is as follows:

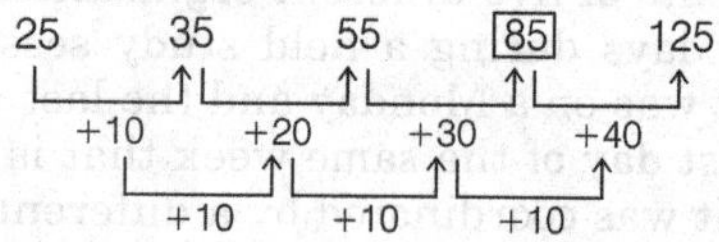

2. (b) The sequence of given series is as follows

$7 \times 1 + 1 = 8$

$\Rightarrow 8 \times 2 + 2 = 18$

$18 \times 3 + 3 = 57$

$\Rightarrow 57 \times 4 + 4 = \boxed{232}$

$232 \times 5 + 5 = 1165$

Hence, in the series, 232 will come in the place of question mark.

3. (c) According to the question,

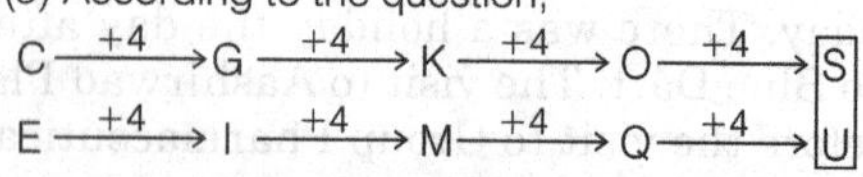

4. (a) Following family diagram can be drawn from the given information.

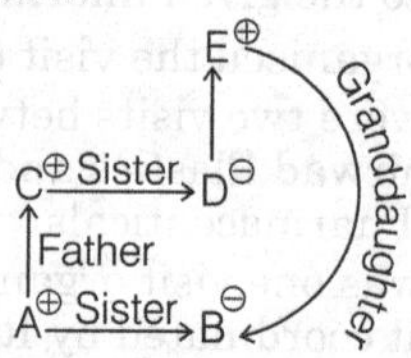

Now, it is clear that B is the granddaughter of E.

5. (d) Option (d) complete the pattern in the question figure.

Solution (Q. Nos. 6-8) According to the given information, the seating arrangement is as follows

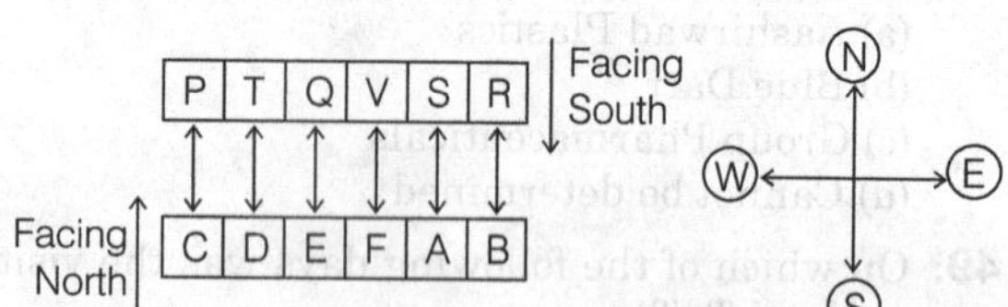

6. (c) P, R sit extreme ends of rows, who are facing Southward.

7. (e) S is facing A.

8. (d) Number of cuts made to cut a roll into 10 pieces = 9

Therefore, required number of rolls $= \frac{45 \times 24}{9} = 120$

Solution (Q. Nos. 9-10)

# ⇒ <	© ⇒ >	% ⇒ =	$ ⇒ ≥	@ ⇒ ≤

9. (d) R @ D ⇒ R ≤ D, D © W ⇒ D > W, B $ W ⇒ B ≥ W

Therefore, R ≤ D > W ≤ B

Conclusions I. W # R ⇒ W < R (May be)

II. B © D ⇒ B > D (Not true)

III. W $ R ⇒ W ≥ R (May be)

W is either smaller or greater than or equal to R.

10. (c) H $ V ⇒ H ≥ V, V % M ⇒ V = M, K © M ⇒ K > M

H ≥ V = M < K

Conclusions I. K © V ⇒ K > V (True)

II. M @ H ⇒ M ≤ H (True)

III. H © K ⇒ H > K (Not true)

So, Conclusions I and II are true.

11. (c) If we select option (c), then we get

L = ×, M = ÷, P = +, Q = −

Now, 16 P 24 M 8 Q 6 M 2 L 3 = ?

⇒ ? = 16 + 24 ÷ 8 − 6 ÷ 2 × 3

⇒ ? = 16 + 3 − 3 × 3 ⇒ ? = 16 + 3 − 9 = 10

12. (c) No reasons are specified in the question for going to different camps. As, Ankit has been going to different camps since the past two year, so it can be said that he goes to some type of camp every summer.

13. (d) First is temporarily parked in the second. Car is parked in Garrage, same as Aeroplane is parked in Hangar.

So, option (d) is correct.

14. (b) As,

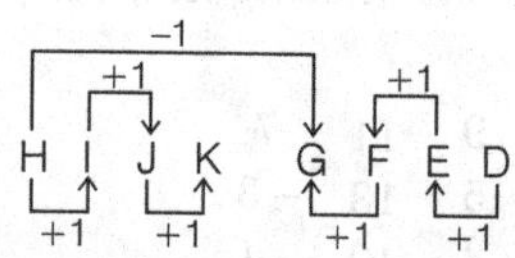

Similarly,

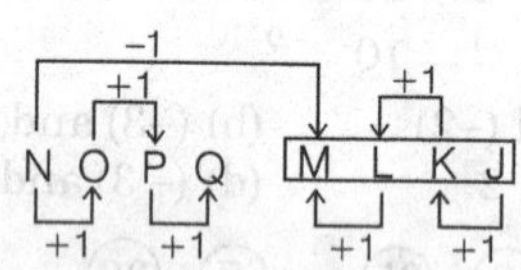

So, option (b) is correct.

15. (d) Option (d) is the hidden/embedded figure.

16. (a) The complete letter series for word Rose will be

r<u>o</u>s<u>e</u>/<u>r</u>o<u>s</u>e/r<u>o</u>s<u>e</u>/r<u>o</u>se

Hence, option (a) is correct.

17. (d) (ii) Plane → (iv) Plasma → (iii) Plaster → (v) Plastic → (i) Plate

So, (ii), (iv), (iii), (v) and (i) would be found in the English dictionary.

18. (*c*) A tiger is different from a lion. But both are animals.

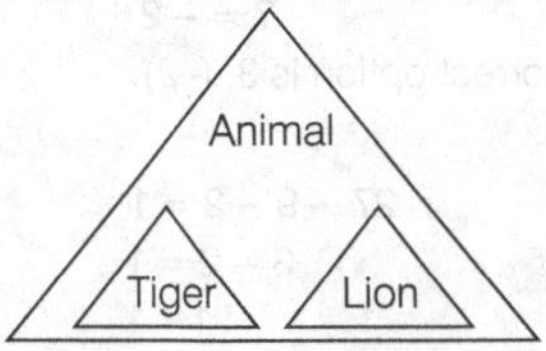

19. (*c*) **Input** tobacco chewing is injurious for teeth. Chewing of tobacco is injurious for teeth. So, rule I follows.

20. (*a*) **Rule IV** coachings in any form are beneficial for the students

Rule I taking of coachings is beneficial to the students

21. (*a*) Option (a) can be formed from the cut-pieces given in the question figure.

22. (*d*) Except Ally, all other are harmful for us.

23. (*b*) Except 35, all other are multiples of 9.

24. (*b*) Except OPRS, all other are increasing by + 1, + 1, + 2.

25. (*a*) According to the question, Raju ranks 10th from the top and Ravi ranks 21st from the bottom. and there are 3 students between them.

Then, total number of students in the class

= 10 + 3 + 21

= 34

26. (*c*)

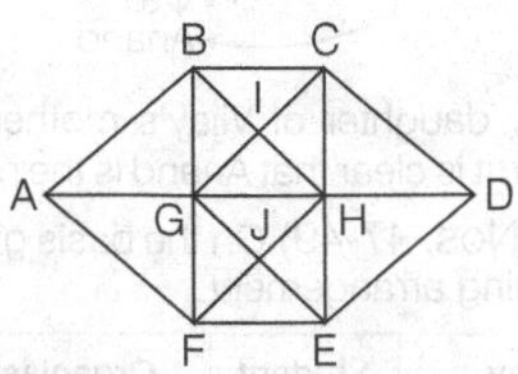

Total 28 triangles are as follow

ΔABG, ΔAFG, ΔCHD, ΔHDE, ΔBGI, ΔBCI, ΔHCI, ΔHGI, ΔGHJ, ΔHEJ, ΔEFJ, ΔGFJ, ΔABF, ΔCDE, ΔBCG, ΔBCH, ΔHCG, ΔBHG, ΔGHE, ΔHEF, ΔGFE, ΔGHF, ΔABH, ΔAFG, ΔCDG, ΔGDE, ΔBHF and ΔCGE.

27. (*a*) From positions I and III,

Common digits = 2 and 3

∴ Digit opposite to 6 = 1

28. (*b*) All I, II and III are required to answer the question.

P is the mother of B, D and M.

B and D are daughters of P.

29. (*d*) From Statement I,

E > B > A

From Statement II,

__ > __ > __ > C > __ > __

From Statement III,

__ > __ > __ > __ > D > F

From all the three statements

E > B > A > C > D > F

Hence, E is the tallest.

30. (*c*) We have given coding

L	I	B	E	R	A	L	I	Z	A	T	I	O	N
↓	↓	↓	↓	↓	↓	↓	↓	↓	↓	↓	↓	↓	↓
3	4	2	5	6	1	3	4	9	1	8	4	7	0

Similarly, we can write

A	E	R	A	T	I	O	N
↓	↓	↓	↓	↓	↓	↓	↓
1	5	6	1	8	4	7	0

Hence, option (c) is correct.

31. (*b*) Mondays ⇒ 1st, 8th, 15th 22nd and 29th

23rd → Tuesday

24th → Wednesday

25th → Thursday

32. (*b*) Land gets heated up quickly and also cools quicker than sea at right so that cool wind called the land breeze blows from land to sea.

33. (*a*) Option (a) is the right image of the given figure.

34. (*e*)

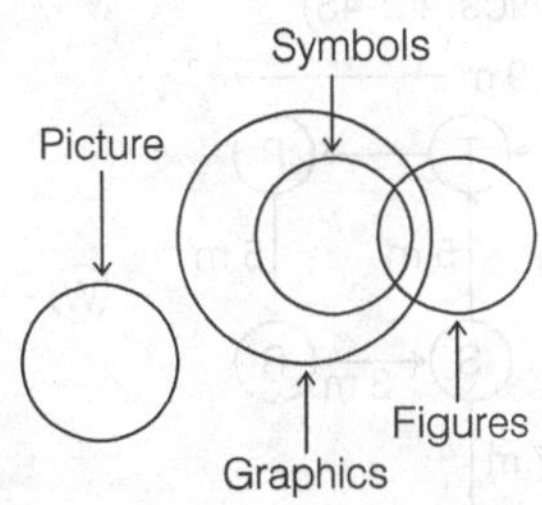

Conclusions I. Some graphics are figures. (✔)

II. No symbol is a picture. (✔)

So, both Conclusions I and II follow.

35. (*a*)

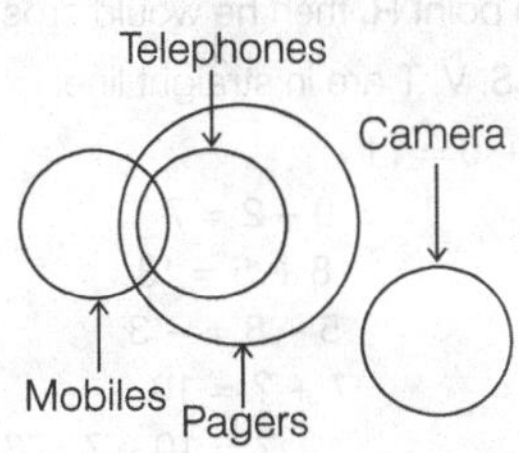

Conclusions

I. Some mobiles are definitely pagers. (✔)

II. No mobile is a camera. (✗)

So, only Conclusion I follows.

36. (*c*) According to the matrices,

P— 03, (10), 22, 34, 41
U— (57), 69, 76, 88, 95
M— 04, 11, (23), 30, 42
P— 03, 10, 22, (34), 41
∴ PUMP ⇒10, 57, 23, 34

37. (*a*) We cannot make "RELATION", as L is not there in the given word.

38. (*c*) 'E', is not there is the given word, so ULTRAMONTAN<u>E</u>, ULTRAMOD<u>E</u>RN and ULULAT<u>E</u> cannot be formed from the given word. Only 'ULTRAIST' can be formed as all the letters in this word are contained in the given word.

39. (*b*) Making equations from the given information,

Nareen = Naveen > Nakul ... (i)
Balaji > Priyanka > Naveen ... (ii)

After equating Eqs. (i) and (ii), we get

Balaji > Priyanka > Naveen = Nareen > Nakul

∴ Balaji is the eldest.

40. (*b*) The region which represents persons who know all the languages is 175. It is the common region of persons who know all the three languages.

41. (*b*) 78 people know English and Hindi because 78 represents common region of persons who know English and Hindi languages.

Solution (Q.Nos. 42-43)

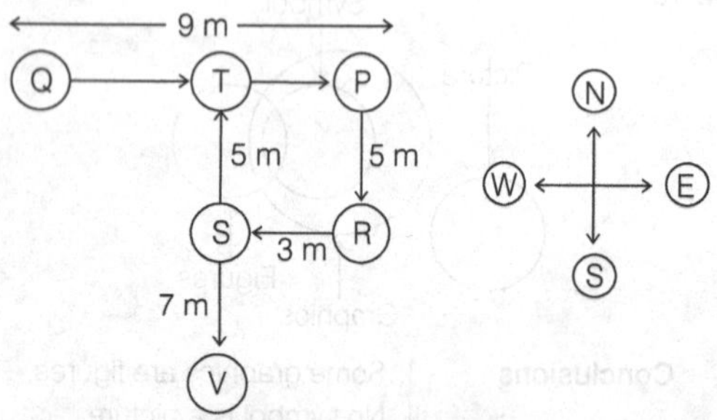

42. (*d*) If a person walks in a straight line for 8 m towards West from point R, then he would cross S.

43. (*e*) Points S, V, T are in straight line.

44. (*a*) As, $2 + 9 = 11$

$9 - 2 = 7$

and, $8 + 5 = 13$

$5 - 8 = -3$

Similarly, $7 + ? = 10$

$? = 10 - 7 = 3$

and, $4 - 6 = ?$

$? = -2$

So, the correct option is 3, (–2).

45. (*c*) As,

⇒ $27 \div 9 - 2 = 1$
⇒ $3 - 2 = 1$
⇒ $1 = 1$

and,

⇒ $35 \div 7 - 3 = 2$
⇒ $5 - 3 = 2$
⇒ $2 = 2$

Similarly,

⇒ $36 \div 4 - 4 = ?$
⇒ $9 - 4 = ?$
⇒ $? = 5$

∴ Hence, correct option is (c).

46. (*c*) Following family diagram can be drawn from the given information,

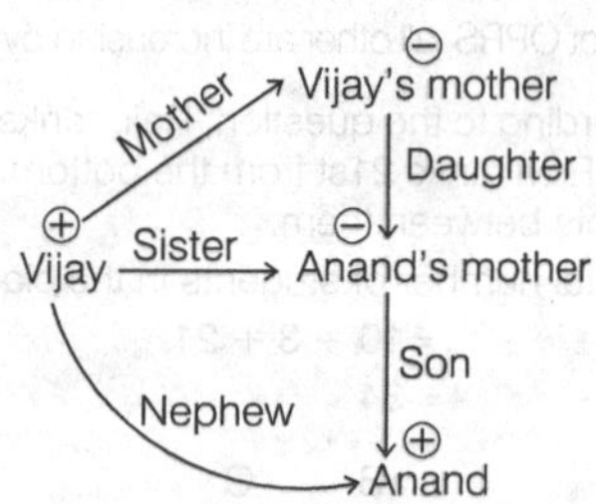

Here, only daughter of Vijay's mother is the sister of Vijay. Now, it is clear that Anand is the nephew of Vijay.

Solution (Q. Nos. 47-49) On the basis given information, we get the following arrangement.

Day	Student	Organisation
Monday	Pervez	Hotel Taj
Tuesday	Richa	Blue Dart
Wednesday	**Holiday**	
Thursday	Amit	Ashirwad Plastics
Friday	Manish	NGO-Tarang
Saturday	**Holiday**	
Sunday	Rajeev	Pharmaceuticals

47. (*d*) None of the given statements is true.

48. (*b*) The visit to the Blue Dart was coordinated by Richa.

49. (*a*) The unit to the Hotel Taj was on Monday.

50. (*c*) 3 and 5 form a pair of identical figures.